Contemporary Authors®

Explore your options!

Gale databases are offered in a variety of formats

GALE

The information in this Gale publication is also available in some or all of the formats described here. Your Gale Representative will be happy to fill you in. Call toll-free 1-800-877-GALE.

GaleNet ^{SM} your information community

GaleNet
A number of Gale databases are now available on GaleNet, our new online information resource accessible through the Internet. GaleNet features an easy-to-use end-user interface, the powerful search capabilities of BRS/SEARCH retrieval software and ease of access through the World Wide Web.

Diskette/Magnetic Tape

Many Gale databases are available on diskette or magnetic tape, allowing systemwide access to your most-used information sources through existing computer systems. Data can be delivered on a variety of mediums (DOS-formatted diskettes, 9-track tape, 8mm data tape) and in industry-standard formats (comma-delimited, tagged, fixed-field).

CD-ROM

A variety of Gale titles are available on CD-ROM, offering maximum flexibility and powerful search software.

Online

For your convenience, many Gale databases are available through popular online services, including DIALOG, NEXIS, DataStar, ORBIT, OCLC, Thomson Financial Network's I/Plus Direct, HRIN, Prodigy, Sandpoint's HOOVER, the Library Corporation's NLightN and Telebase Systems.

ISSN 0275-7176

Contemporary Authors®

**A Bio-Bibliographical Guide to
Current Writers in Fiction, General Nonfiction,
Poetry, Journalism, Drama, Motion Pictures,
Television, and Other Fields**

SCOT PEACOCK
Editor

volume 157

GALE

DETROIT · NEW YORK · TORONTO · LONDON

STAFF

Scot Peacock, *Editor, Original Volumes*

Kathleen J. Edgar, *Contributing Senior Editor*

David M. Galens, Jennifer Gariepy, *Contributing Editors*

Christine M. Bichler, *Associate Editor*

Elizabeth A. Cranston, Joshua Kondek, Patti Tippett, Pam Zuber, *Assistant Editors*

Carol A. Brennan, Richard Cohen, Eileen Daily, Laurie Di Mauro, Nancy Edgar, Marie Ellavich, Mary Gillis,
Nancy Godinez, Terry Kosdrosky, Jeanne M. Lesinski, Kevin O'Sullivan, Paula Pyzik Scott,
Pamela Shelton, Ken Shepherd, Les Stone, Michaela A. Swart,
Arlene True, Elizabeth Wenning, *Sketchwriters*

Pamela Willwerth Aue, *Managing Editor*

Victoria Cariappa, *Research Manager*

Andrew Guy Malonis, Michele LaMeau, Gary J. Oudersluys,
Research Specialists

Julia C. Daniel, Tamara C. Nott, Tracie A. Richardson
Norma Sawaya, Cheryl L. Warnock, *Research Associates*

Jeffrey D. Daniels, Talitha Dutton, Sara L. Turner, *Research Assistants*

This book is printed on acid-free paper that meets the minimum requirements
of American National Standard for Information Sciences-
Permanence Paper for Printed Library Materials, ANSI Z39.48-1984.

Library of Congress Catalog Card Number 62-52046
ISBN 0-7876-1183-2
ISSN 0010-7468

Printed in the United States of America

10 9 8 7 6 5 4 3 2 1

Contents

Indexing note: All *Contemporary Authors* entries are indexed in
the *Contemporary Authors* cumulative index, which is published
separately and distributed with even-numbered *Contemporary
Authors* original volumes and odd-numbered *Contemporary Authors
New Revision Series* volumes.

**As always, the most recent *Contemporary Authors* cumulative
index continues to be the user's guide to the location of an
individual author's listing.**

Preface

Contemporary Authors (*CA*) provides information on approximately 100,000 writers in a wide range of media, including:

- Current writers of fiction, nonfiction, poetry, and drama whose works have been issued by commercial publishers, risk publishers, or university presses (authors whose books have been published only by known vanity or author-subsidized firms are ordinarily not included)

- Prominent print and broadcast journalists, editors, photojournalists, syndicated cartoonists, graphic novelists, screenwriters, television scriptwriters, and other media people

- Authors who write in languages other than English, provided their works have been published in the United States or translated into English

- Literary greats of the early twentieth century whose works are popular in today's high school and college curriculums and continue to elicit critical attention

A *CA* listing entails no charge or obligation. Authors are included on the basis of the above criteria and their interest to *CA* users. Sources of potential listees include trade periodicals, publishers' catalogs, librarians, and other users.

How to Get the Most out of *CA:* Use the Index

The key to locating an author's most recent entry is the *CA* cumulative index, which is published separately and distributed with even-numbered original volumes and odd-numbered revision volumes. It provides access to *all* entries in *CA* and *Contemporary Authors New Revision Series* (*CANR*). Always consult the latest index to find an author's most recent entry.

For the convenience of users, the *CA* cumulative index also includes references to all entries in these Gale literary series: *Authors and Artists for Young Adults, Authors in the News, Bestsellers, Black Literature Criticism, Black Writers, Children's Literature Review, Concise Dictionary of American Literary Biography, Concise Dictionary of British Literary Biography, Contemporary Authors Autobiography Series, Contemporary Authors Bibliographical Series, Contemporary Literary Criticism, Dictionary of Literary Biography, Dictionary of Literary Biography Documentary Series, Dictionary of Literary Biography Yearbook, DISCovering Authors, DISCovering Authors: British, DISCovering Authors: Canadian, DISCovering Authors: Modules* (including modules for Dramatists, Most-Studied Authors, Multicultural Authors, Novelists, Poets, and Popular/Genre Authors), *Drama Criticism, Hispanic Literature Criticism, Hispanic Writers, Junior DISCovering Authors, Major Authors and Illustrators for Children and Young Adults, Major 20th-Century Writers, Native North American Literature, Poetry Criticism, Short Story Criticism, Something about the Author, Something about the Author Autobiography Series, Twentieth-Century Literary Criticism, World Literature Criticism,* and *Yesterday's Authors of Books for Children.*

A Sample Index Entry:

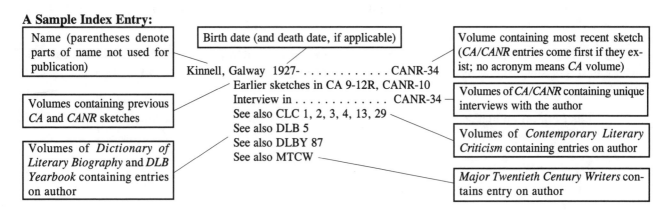

How Are Entries Compiled?

The editors make every effort to secure new information directly from the authors; listees' responses to our question-naires and query letters provide most of the information featured in *CA*. For deceased writers, or those who fail to reply to requests for data, we consult other reliable biographical sources, such as those indexed in Gale's *Biography and Genealogy Master Index,* and bibliographical sources, including *National Union Catalog, LC MARC,* and *British National Bibliography.* Further details come from published interviews, feature stories, and book reviews, as well as information supplied by the authors' publishers and agents.

An asterisk (*) at the end of a sketch indicates that the listing has been compiled from secondary sources believed to be reliable but has not been personally verified for this edition by the author sketched.

What Kinds of Information Does an Entry Provide?

Sketches in *CA* contain the following biographical and bibliographical information:

- **Entry heading:** the most complete form of author's name, plus any pseudonyms or name variations used for writing

- **Personal information:** author's date and place of birth, family data, ethnicity, educational background, politi-cal and religious affiliations, and hobbies and leisure interests

- **Addresses:** author's home, office, or agent's addresses, plus e-mail and fax numbers, as available

- **Career summary:** name of employer, position, and dates held for each career post; resume of other vocational achievements; military service

- **Membership information:** professional, civic, and other association memberships and any official posts held

- **Awards and honors:** military and civic citations, major prizes and nominations, fellowships, grants, and honorary degrees

- **Writings:** a comprehensive, chronological list of titles, publishers, dates of original publication and revised editions, and production information for plays, television scripts, and screenplays

- **Adaptations:** a list of films, plays, and other media which have been adapted from the author's work

- **Work in progress:** current or planned projects, with dates of completion and/or publication, and expected publisher, when known

- **Sidelights:** a biographical portrait of the author's development; information about the critical reception of the author's works; revealing comments, often by the author, on personal interests, aspirations, motivations, and thoughts on writing

- **Biographical and critical sources:** a list of books and periodicals in which additional information on an author's life and/or writings appears

Obituary Notices in *CA* provide date and place of birth as well as death information about authors whose full-length sketches appeared in the series before their deaths. These entries also summarize the authors' careers and writings and list other sources of biographical and death information.

Related Titles in the *CA* Series

Contemporary Authors Autobiography Series complements *CA* original and revised volumes with specially commissioned autobiographical essays by important current authors, illustrated with personal photographs they provide. Common topics include their motivations for writing, the people and experiences that shaped their careers, the rewards they derive from their work, and their impressions of the current literary scene.

Contemporary Authors Bibliographical Series surveys writings by and about important American authors since World War II. Each volume concentrates on a specific genre and features approximately ten writers; entries list works written by and about the author and contain a bibliographical essay discussing the merits and deficiencies of major critical and scholarly studies in detail.

Available in Electronic Formats

CD-ROM. Full-text bio-bibliographic entries from the entire *CA* series, covering approximately 100,000 writers, are available on CD-ROM through lease and purchase plans. The disc combines entries from the *CA, CANR,* and *Contemporary Authors Permanent Series* (*CAP*) print series to provide the most recent author listing. It can be searched by name, title, subject/genre, nationality/ethnicity, personal data, and as well as advanced searching using boolean logic. The disc is updated every six months. For more information, call 1-800-877-GALE.

Online. The *Contemporary Authors* database is made available online to libraries and their patrons through online public access catalog (OPAC) vendors. Currently, *CA* is offered through Ameritech Library Services' Vista Online (formerly Dynix), and is expected to become available through CARL Systems and The Library Corporation. More OPAC vendor offerings will soon follow.

GaleNet. *CA* is available on a subscription basis through GaleNet, a new online information resource that features an easy-to-use end-user interface, the powerful search capabilities of the BRS/Search retrieval software, and ease of access through the World Wide Web. For more information, call 1-800-877-GALE.

Magnetic Tape. *CA* is available for licensing on magnetic tape in a fielded format. Either the complete database or a custom selection of entries may be ordered. The database is available for internal data processing and nonpublishing purposes only. For more information, call 1-800-877-GALE.

Suggestions Are Welcome

The editors welcome comments and suggestions from users on any aspects of the *CA* series. If readers would like to recommend authors for inclusion in future volumes of the series, they are cordially invited to write: The Editors, *Contemporary Authors,* 835 Penobscot Bldg., 645 Griswold St., Detroit, MI 48226-4094; call toll-free at 1-800-347-GALE; or fax at 1-313-961-6599.

CA Numbering System and Volume Update Chart

Occasionally questions arise about the *CA* numbering system and which volumes, if any, can be discarded. Despite numbers like "29-32R," "97-100" and "157," the entire *CA* print series consists of only 142 physical volumes with the publication of *CA* Volume 157. The following charts note changes in the numbering system and cover design, and indicate which volumes are essential for the most complete, up-to-date coverage.

CA **First Revision**	• 1-4R through 41-44R (11 books) *Cover:* Brown with black and gold trim. There will be no further First Revision volumes because revised entries are now being handled exclusively through the more efficient *New Revision Series* mentioned below.
CA **Original Volumes**	• 45-48 through 97-100 (14 books) *Cover:* Brown with black and gold trim. • 101 through 157 (57 books) *Cover:* Blue and black with orange bands. The same as previous *CA* original volumes but with a new, simplified numbering system and new cover design.
CA **Permanent Series**	• *CAP*-1 and *CAP*-2 (2 books) *Cover:* Brown with red and gold trim. There will be no further *Permanent Series* volumes because revised entries are now being handled exclusively through the more efficient *New Revision Series* mentioned below.
CA **New Revision Series**	• *CANR*-1 through *CANR*-58 (58 books) *Cover:* Blue and black with green bands. Includes only sketches requiring significant changes; **sketches are taken from any previously published *CA*, *CAP*, or *CANR* volume.**

If You Have:	**You May Discard:**
CA First Revision Volumes 1-4R through 41-44R **and** *CA Permanent Series* Volumes 1 and 2	*CA* Original Volumes 1, 2, 3, 4 Volumes 5-6 through 41-44
CA Original Volumes 45-48 through 97-100 **and** 101 through 157	**NONE:** These volumes will not be superseded by corresponding revised volumes. Individual entries from these and all other volumes appearing in the left column of this chart may be revised and included in the various volumes of the *New Revision Series*.
CA New Revision Series Volumes *CANR*-1 through *CANR*-58	**NONE:** The *New Revision Series* does not replace any single volume of *CA*. Instead, volumes of *CANR* include entries from many previous *CA* series volumes. All *New Revision Series* volumes must be retained for full coverage.

A Sampling of Authors and Media People
Featured in This Volume

Nikolai Berdyaev
A Russian philosopher and political exile, Berdyaev is considered an apocalyptic writer. His first major work, *Subjectivism and Individualism in Social Philosophy,* discusses Marxist doctrine in relation to Christian ethics.

Lucian Blaga
Nobel Prize-wining poet, dramatist, and philosopher Blaga helped establish a literary picture of Romanian culture and character, but was prevented in his later years from publishing by Soviet authorities occupying his country.

Budd Boetticher
A Hollywood director and screenwriter, Boetticher earned an Oscar nomination for the script to *The Bullfighter and the Lady.* His memoir, *When In Disgrace,* describes how an interest in bullfighting led to a career in movies.

Charles Grodin
Grodin—an actor, director, and writer—has appeared in numerous films, including *Rosemary's Baby* and *The Great Muppet Caper.* He is the author of several plays as well as two volumes of memoirs.

Sadakichi Hartmann
Known as "The King of Bohemia," Hartmann consorted with such turn-of-the-century intellectuals as poet Walt Whitman and photographer Alfred Steiglitz. His published works include *The History of American Art* and *Conversations with Walt Whitman.*

Declan Kiberd
Kiberd delves into the psyche of Ireland with critical and sometimes controversial works like *Inventing Ireland* and *Men and Feminism in Modern Literature*; he has also written a classical analysis of Irish playwright J. M. Synge.

Henry Kuttner
A prolific writer in genres ranging from westerns to supernatural horror, Kuttner is best remembered for his contribution of tales to the Golden Age of Science Fiction, many of which were collaborations with his wife, C. L. Moore.

Wyndham Lewis
Lewis's work with Erza Pound on the literary review *Blast* confirmed him as a "feted figure on the intellectual scene." His iconoclastic style, as evidenced in the *roman a clef* novel *The Apes of God,* earned him many enemies.

Dusan Makavejev
A "talented trouble-maker," filmmaker Makavejev pushes his audiences to their emotional limits with provocative works like *Sweet Movie,* banned in England and Canada, and the dialectical *Man is Not a Bird.*

Anne Michaels
Six-time winner of awards for poetry, including the Epstein and Trillium awards, Michaels's *The Weight Of Oranges* exemplifies her superb use of language and insight into the mortality of love, loss, and human struggle.

Arthur Morrison
A prominent realistic novelist and short story writer during the 1890s and early 1900s, Morrison is the author of the story collection *Tales of Mean Streets* and the novels *A Child of the Jago* and *The Hole in the Wall.*

Kristine Kathryn Rusch
A Hugo and World Fantasy Award-winning editor, Rusch is also known as co-founder of Pulphouse Publishing and the author of such fantasy novels as *The Gallery of His Dreams, The White Mists of Power,* and *The Fey: The Sacrifice.*

Andrei Sakharov
Nobel Peace Prize recipient Sakharov was a Russian nuclear physicist who became one of the world's foremost human rights activists. His influential writings include *Progress, Peaceful Coexistence, and Intellectual Freedom.*

Peggy Reeves Sanday
Anthropologist Sanday has written several works exploring the evolution and effects of gender roles. Her books include *Female Power and Male Dominance: On the Origins of Sexual Inequality* and *Fraternity Gang Rape: Sex, Brotherhood, and Privilege on Campus.*

Botho Strauss
Strauss is a highly regarded German playwright whose works explore the inability of human beings to find connection in the modern world. In addition to numerous plays, he is the author of the novel *Die Widmung (Devotion).*

Joseph K. S. Yick
Hong Kong-born Yick is an expert on China's communist revolution. Now a naturalized citizen of the United States, he is the author of *Making Urban Revolution in China: The CCP-GMD Struggle for Beiping-Tianjin, 1945-1949.*

A-B

ADAIR, Gilbert

PERSONAL: Born in Scotland.

ADDRESSES: Agent—c/o HarperCollins, 10 East 53rd St., New York, NY 10022-5299.

CAREER: Freelance author, novelist, critic, and journalist.

WRITINGS:

NOVELS

The Holy Innocents: A Romance, Heinemann (London), 1988, E.P. Dutton (New York City), 1989.
Love and Death on Long Island, Heinemann, 1990.
The Death of the Author, Heinemann, 1992.

FOR CHILDREN

Alice through the Needle's Eye (sequel to Lewis Carroll's *Alice in Wonderland* and *Through the Looking Glass*), illustrations by Jenny Thorne, E.P. Dutton (New York City), 1984.
(Adaptor) *Alice: And Her Friends from Wonderland,* illustrations by Thorne, Macmillan (London), 1986.
Peter Pan and the Only Children (sequel to J. M. Barrie's *Peter Pan*), illustrations by Thorne, E.P. Dutton, c. 1987.
(Editor with Marina Warner) *Wonder Tales: Six French Stories of Enchantment,* illustrations by Sophie Herxheimer, Chatto and Windus (London), 1994, Farrar, Straus and Giroux (New York City), 1996.

OTHER

Hollywood's Vietnam: From "The Green Berets" to "Apocalypse Now," Proteus/Scribners (New York City), 1981, reprinted as *Hollywood's Vietnam,* Heinemann, 1989.
(With Nick Roddick) *A Night at the Pictures: Ten Decades of British Film,* Columbus Books (London), 1985.
Myths and Memories: A Dazzling Dissection of British Life and Culture, Fontana Paperbacks (London), 1986.
(Translator) Francois Truffaut, *Letters,* edited by Gilles Jacob and Claude de Givray, foreword by Jean-Luc Godard, Faber and Faber (London), 1989, published in United States as *Francois Truffaut: Correspondence, 1945-84,* Farrar, Straus and Giroux, 1990.
The Postmodernist Always Rings Twice: Reflections on Culture in the Nineties (essays), Fourth Estate (London), 1992.
Flickers: An Illustrated Celebration of One Hundred Years of Cinema, Faber and Faber, 1995.
(Translator) Georges Perec, *A Void* (novel), Harvill Press (London), 1995, HarperCollins (New York City), 1995.

Contributor to periodicals, including *Film Comment* and *Sight and Sound.*

SIDELIGHTS: Gilbert Adair is a versatile writer who has published novels, children's books, criticism, and translations. He is known for the intelligence and playfulness with which he invests his works, regardless of genre, and for the multiplicity of allusions that are likewise an inevitable aspect of his varied writings. Adair's affinity for allusions is evident in his first novel, *The Holy Innocents: A Romance,* which evokes Jean Cocteau's film *Les Enfants Terrible,* but also includes references to French New Wave masters such as Jean-Luc Godard and Jacques Rivette. This novel concerns the increasingly sordid pastimes enjoyed by a pair of movie-loving twins and their American friend. *Listener* reviewer Gavin Millar noted that the three protagonists' relationship degenerates "from sensuality to perverse eroticism and ends in violent nightmare."

Love and Death on Long Island, Adair's next novel, constitutes another excursion into degradation. Here an aging writer, who long ago rejected much of contemporary culture, finds himself obsessed with a teen idol, whereupon he becomes immersed in homosexual pornography as a means of vicariously gratifying his rampant desires. This novel, which has been perceived as a spoof of Thomas Mann's *Death in Venice,* was decried by *New Statesman and Society* reviewer Zoe Heller as "mean and demeaning."

Adair's third novel, *The Death of the Author,* derives from a controversy that ensued after the death of admired critic and educator Paul de Man, who was posthumously revealed to be the author of anti-Semitic works from the Nazi era. Leopold Sfax, the hero of Adair's novel, attempts to obscure his past through the unlikely imposition of his own ambiguous theories on the offensive texts in question. But Sfax's efforts at deception result in further complications that, in turn, continue to jeopardize his eminent standing. *Spectator* reviewer John Spurling noted that "the subject and setting are inescapably Nabokovesque," and he called Adair's novel "a highly polished piece of postmodernist marquetry."

Among Adair's other works of fiction are *Alice through the Needle's Eye,* which serves as a sequel to the noted children's books by Lewis Carroll. In Adair's first book for children, Carroll's famous heroine meets a particularly helpful kangaroo and enters a world where it actually rains cats and dogs. John Fuller, writing in the *New York Times Book Review,* contended that *Alice through the Needle's Eye* sometimes lacks "the peculiar tension that exists between the original Alice and the characters she meets." Fuller conceded, however, that the book proves Adair "strong on lexical play and well able to keep the narrative proceeding at a brisk pace."

In *Peter Pan and the Only Children* Adair continues the adventures of J. M. Barrie's beloved character. In Adair's update on this childhood classic, a child hurls

herself from a ship and discovers an undersea world in which Pan and his band once again do battle with the evil Captain Hook. Humphrey Carter proclaimed in the *Times Literary Supplement* that Adair "has caught the Barrie manner triumphantly."

Although Adair is perhaps best known for his various works of fiction, he has also gained recognition for several volumes of criticism. In the early 1980s he completed *Hollywood's Vietnam: From "The Green Berets" to "Apocalypse Now",* in which he decries many Hollywood films—including *The Green Berets, The Deer Hunter,* and *Apocalypse Now*—as distortions of the actual Vietnam conflict. *American Film* reviewer Jonathan Rosenbaum praised *Hollywood's Vietnam: From "The Green Berets" to "Apocalypse Now"* for "the gracefulness of its prose style," and he added that "Adair is deft in charting the surface of a moral dilemma—America's involvement in Vietnam—that Hollywood has tended either to ignore . . . or distort."

Adair produced additional film criticism in *Flickers: An Illustrated Celebration of One Hundred Years of Cinema,* in which he surveys the history of cinema by concentrating on a specific film for each year. The book includes commentaries on both vaunted classics such as *Battleship Potemkin* and *Citizen Kane* as well as the cult classic *Shock Corridor, Imitation of Life,* and Jerry Lewis's screwball comedy *The Nutty Professor.* Peter Matthews described *Flickers: An Illustrated Celebration of One Hundred Years of Cinema* in his *New Statesman and Society* critique as "witty and impassioned."

In Adair's other critical volumes, *Myths and Memories: A Dazzling Dissection of British Life and Culture* and *The Postmodernist Always Rings Twice: Reflections on Culture in the Nineties,* he surveys various aspects of contemporary culture and discusses film, television, fashion, even acknowledging the self-reflexive nature of his enterprise. *Listener* reviewer Colin McCabe deemed *Myths and Memories* "absolutely required reading for anybody who has to endure the dominant representations of our cultural life."

In appraising the essays collected in *The Postmodernist Always Rings Twice: Reflections on Culture in the Nineties,* wherein Adair concentrates on the nature of parody, Robert Hutchison wrote in the *Times Educational Supplement* that Adair is "good on—among other things—the genius of Brecht, the reasons why the concentration camp should never be fictionalized in film, and the need for 'a sense of passionate partisanship' in literary criticism."

In 1990 Adair served as the translator of *Francois Truffaut: Correspondence, 1945-1984,* a volume of letters written by the late French filmmaker. Dennis Potter wrote in the *New York Times Book Review,* "The sweet perils of self-invention are almost as tenderly on display in this hefty, well-annotated collection . . . as they are in the shining ironies of [Truffaut's] much-loved films." Potter added that the book is "capably translated" by Adair.

Adair also provided the translation of Georges Perec's novel *A Void,* which does not contain any words featuring the letter "e." Sarah A. Smith noted in *New Statesman and Society* that "Adair's translation is markedly similar to that of his own, rather knowing fiction" and lauded the translation as an achievement as "equally extraordinary" as Perec's French-language original.

BIOGRAPHICAL/CRITICAL SOURCES:

PERIODICALS

American Film, April 1982, pp. 71-72.
Contemporary Review, January, 1993, pp. 48-50.
Economist, August 15, 1981, p. 73.
Listener, October 2, 1986, pp. 24-25; November 19, 1987, pp. 39-40; October 13, 1988, p. 31.
London Review of Books, September 13, 1990, pp. 18-19; September 10, 1992, p. 22.
New Statesman and Society, July 6, 1990, p. 40; June 2, 1992, pp. 42-43; October 14, 1994, pp. 46-47.
New Yorker, May 13, 1985, p. 147.
New York Review of Books, October 11, 1990, pp. 14-16.
New York Times Book Review, May 5, 1985, p. 42; May 27, 1990, pp. 1, 25; March 12, 1995, p. 3.
Observer, September 13, 1992, p. 55.
Publishers Weekly, December 19, 1994, p. 45.
Spectator, December 10, 1988, p. 26; August 29, 1992, p. 30.
Times Educational Supplement, September 18, 1992, p. 9.
Times Literary Supplement, December 4, 1981, p. 1422; January 4, 1985, p. 18; November 20, 1987, p. 1282; September 9, 1988; August 21, 1992, p. 18; December 4, 1992, p. 13; December 18, 1992, pp. 3-4.
Washington Post Book World, August 20, 1995, p. 12.*

AHLGREN, Gillian T. W. 1964-

PERSONAL: Born March 30, 1964, in Washington, DC; daughter of James David and Barbara (Donne) Ahlgren; married Scott Campbell; children: Matthew Romero. *Education:* Oberlin College, B.A. (with high honors), 1985; Divinity School, University of Chicago, M.A., 1986, Ph.D., 1991. *Religion:* Roman Catholic. *Avocational interests:* Travel.

ADDRESSES: Office—Department of Theology, Xavier University, 3800 Victory Parkway, Cincinnati, OH 45207-4442.

CAREER: Xavier University, Cincinnati, OH, associate professor of theology, 1990—.

MEMBER: American Society of Church History, Society for Spanish and Portuguese Historical Studies.

AWARDS, HONORS: Grant from American Academy of Religion, 1994-95, and Spanish Ministry of Culture, 1995.

WRITINGS:

(Contributor) *Dear Sister: The Letters of Medieval Women,* edited by Karen Cherewatuk and Ulrike Wiethaus, University of Pennsylvania Press (Philadelphia, PA), 1993.
Teresa of Avila and the Politics of Sanctity, Cornell University Press (Ithaca, NY), 1996.

Contributor of articles and reviews to periodicals, including *Mystics Quarterly* and *Church History.*

WORK IN PROGRESS: Christian Theology in Context, Volume II: *Human Person and Church,* and Volume IV: *Sacraments and Spirituality,* for Orbis Books (Maryknoll, NY); "Francisca de los Apostoles: A Visionary Voice for Reform in Sixteenth-Century Toledo," to be included in *Daughters of the Inquisition,* edited by Mary E. Giles, publication by Johns Hopkins University Press (Baltimore, MD) expected in 1998.

SIDELIGHTS: Gillian T. W. Ahlgren told *CA:* "My work centers on women's expressions of religious experience in counter-Reformation Spain. I am also interested in documenting, through a series of studies of individual women, the influence of the Spanish Inquisition on religious life and theology. This work responds to larger questions I have about the nature and effects of the mystical life upon the church and the role of mystical experience—particularly that of women—in Christian theology.

"I study mysticism because I see it as an inherently creative and transformative force. Reading mystical texts allows me to see the many levels of transformation experienced by individuals who then become agents of change and reform in their church and their worlds. Mystical/visionary texts and their reception also give us a unique perspective on significant theological and historical questions. Current scholarly energy now being used to understand and define Christian mysticism will certainly generate new avenues for theological advancement in the deepest and richest ways.

"I am currently preparing a book-length study of Francisca de los Apostoles, a sixteenth-century visionary and reformer in Toledo, tried by the Inquisition between 1574 and 1578. I will also attempt a gender-sensitive definition of *alumbradismo* taken from inquisitional documents.

"I hope to prepare a collection of essays on hagiographical models for women in Golden Age Spain which will provide a clearer sense of how significant aspects of the medieval Christian tradition were 'translated' into sixteenth-century Spain."

* * *

ALLAN, Sidney
See HARTMANN, Sadakichi

* * *

ALLAN, Sydney
See HARTMANN, Sadakichi

* * *

ALLEN, Sidney H.
See HARTMANN, Sadakichi

* * *

ARVEY, Verna 1910-

PERSONAL: Born February 16, 1910, in Los Angeles, CA; daughter of David and Bessie (Tark) Arvey; married William Grant Still (a composer), February 8, 1939; children: Duncan Allan, Judith Anne. *Education:*

Graduated from Manual Arts High School in Los Angeles, CA, 1926; studied music privately with Margeurite d'Aleria, Rose Cooper Vinetz, Alexander Koslof, and Ann Eachus.

ADDRESSES: Home—1262 Victoria Ave., Los Angeles, CA 90019. *Office*—American Society of Composers, Authors, and Publishers, 575 Madison Ave., New York, NY 10022.

CAREER: Professional pianist; gave concerts in the U.S. and Latin America; performed with orchestras and on radio programs; journalist and writer.

MEMBER: American Society of Composers, Authors, and Publishers.

WRITINGS:

Choreographic Music, Dutton (New York, NY), 1941.
(With others) *William Grant Still and the Fusion of Cultures in American Music,* Black Sparrow Press (Los Angeles, CA), 1972.
In One Lifetime (biography), University of Arkansas Press (Fayetteville, AR), 1984.

Also author of a monograph about William Grant Still; writer of lyrics and texts for many of Still's musical compositions.

SIDELIGHTS: Verna Arvey is an accomplished pianist, who performed with symphonies and in concerts throughout the United States and Latin America. After marrying composer William Grant Still, she penned the lyrics and texts for many of her husband's musical compositions. A journalist as well as a musician, Arvey is also responsible for much of the available published material about Still's life and work. Her monograph on her husband saw print in 1939; in 1984 she went into more detail about Still's life experience with *In One Lifetime.* Arvey is also the author of her own book on compositions for dance, 1941's *Choreographic Music.*

Born in 1910, in Los Angeles, California, Arvey studied music privately with instructors such as Margeurite d'Aleria, Rose Cooper Vinetz, Alexander Koslof, and Ann Eachus. In addition to her concert appearances, Arvey also performed solo piano with Raymond Paige's orchestra when it played over the Columbia Broadcasting System (CBS) radio network in 1939. After she and her husband had a son and daughter, Arvey switched her focus from her own performing to advancing the public's appreciation of her husband's work.

William Grant Still was the first major African-American composer in the classical mode. He faced prejudice not only as an African-American in a genre usually associated with whites, but also because he was in an interracial marriage during a time when such marriages were extremely rare. In fact, the couple had to travel to Mexico to have their wedding ceremony performed, because interracial marriage was illegal in Arvey's native California at that time. Yet Still had many triumphs. As William Ratliff noted in the *Los Angeles Times Calendar,* "he was the first black to conduct a major American symphony orchestra—the Los Angeles Philharmonic in 1936." He was also, according to Ratliff, "the first black composer to have a symphony performed by major orchestras around the world." Still's better-known works include the "Afro-American Symphony"; operas such as "Troubled Island," "A Bayou Legend," and "A Southern Interlude"; and a composition commissioned by CBS entitled "Lenox Avenue." Arvey writes about many of the obstacles and triumphs of Still's career in *In One Lifetime.* Penned several years after Still's death, *In One Lifetime* discusses the couple's somewhat conservative approaches to music and culture. Speaking of many of the avant-garde changes which began to take place during the 1950s, Arvey states in *In One Lifetime:* "It did appear to us that we were living in an incredible era . . . when it became nasty to speak of loving one's country and when humility before God became something naive. Adherence to beauty in art made one a 'square,' and if one were not addicted to sick comedy, subversion, musicless music, dirty literature and meaningless daubs which purported to be art, he was out of the stream of life."

D.-R. de Lerma, reviewing *In One Lifetime* in *Choice,* asserted that Arvey's "account is as objective as one might expect possible"; the critic went on to praise the author's "literary lucidity." Ratliff hailed the volume as "a loving recollection of a life packed with dreams and premonitions, with friends and foes, with joys, perceived persecutions and frustrations."

BIOGRAPHICAL/CRITICAL SOURCES:

BOOKS

Arvey, Verna, *In One Lifetime,* University of Arkansas Press, 1984.

PERIODICALS

Choice, May, 1985, p. 1342.
Los Angeles Times, November 24, 1985, p. 58.*

AWDRY, Wilbert Vere 1911-1997

OBITUARY NOTICE—See index for *CA* sketch: Born in June, 1911, at Ampfield, near Romsey, England; died March 21, 1997, in Stroud, Gloucestershire, England. Priest of the Church of England and children's author. Awdry's *Thomas the Tank Engine* stories took shape in the 1940s when the Anglican priest had to write down the tales he regularly told to his son, otherwise the lad would point out the discrepancies from one telling to another. His wife noticed the stories and drawings that accompanied them and sent them to a literary agent. In time, Awdry entertained generations of children with twenty-six *Thomas the Tank Engine* stories that included several different characters. The stories, set in the imaginary island of Sodor, center on Thomas, an ambitious steam engine, and often teach morals that relate particularly to children. The *Thomas the Tank Engine* series didn't become popular in the United States until 1989, when PBS created an animated television series on Awdry's work. Several *Thomas* characters were also licensed for merchandise. The series won an Emmy Award and was one of PBS's most popular children's shows. Awdry's son, Christopher (for whom the stories were originally written), took over much of the work in 1972. The last book was *Thomas' Christmas Party* in 1984. Awdry was honored with the Order of the British Empire in 1996.

OBITUARIES AND OTHER SOURCES:

BOOKS

The Writers Directory: 1996-1998, St. James Press (Detroit, MI), 1995.

PERIODICALS

Chicago Tribune, March 24, 1997, sec. 4, p. 7.
Los Angeles Times, March 23, 1997, p. B3.
New York Times, March 23, 1997, p. 46.
Washington Post, March 23, 1997, p. B6.

* * *

BAKER, Samm Sinclair 1909-1997

OBITUARY NOTICE—See index for *CA* sketch: Born July 29, 1909, in Paterson, NJ; died following a stroke, March 5, 1997, in Port Chester, NY. Author and lecturer. Baker, a former advertising agency executive, turned to writing self-help and diet books in the 1960s. He received a bachelor's degree in economics from the University of Pennsylvania in 1929 and began his advertising career at the bottom—as a copywriter in Manhattan. But he became president of the Kiesewetter, Baker, Hagedorn and Smith agency and in 1955 became a vice president at Donahue and Coe. He began writing books in 1955 and his first self-help book was 1959's *Casebook of Successful Ideas for Advertising and Selling.*

Baker became an author full time in 1963, though he still worked as a freelance business consultant. Teaming up with experts in the fields of medicine and diet, Baker co-wrote several self-improvement books in the 1960s and 1970s including *The Doctor's Quick Weight Loss Diet* (with Doctor Irwin Stillman in 1967), *The Complete Scarsdale Medical Diet* (with Doctor Herman Tarnower in 1979) and *The Doctor's Quick Teen-Age Diet* (with Stillman in 1971). He also wrote several advice books on gardening and in 1984 penned *Erotic Focus: The New Way to Enhance Your Sexual Pleasure.* Baker's short essays were published in *McCalls, Popular Science* and *Suburbia Today.*

OBITUARIES AND OTHER SOURCES:

BOOKS

Who's Who in Writers, Editors, and Poets, 1992-1993, December Press, 1992.

PERIODICALS

Los Angeles Times, March 25, 1997, p. A22.
New York Times, March 23, 1997, p. 46.
Washington Post, March 24, 1997, p. D6.

*   *   *

BALAKRISHNAN, N. 1956-

PERSONAL: Born May 2, 1956, in Tamilnadu, India; Canadian citizen; son of R. Narayanaswamy (an accountant) and N. (a homemaker; maiden name, Lakshmi) Balakrishnan; married Colleen D. Cutler (a university teacher), December 15, 1985; children: Sarah Malathy, Julia Lakshmi. *Ethnicity:* "East Indian." *Education:* University of Madras, B.Sc., 1976, M.Sc., 1978; Indian Institute of Technology, Ph.D. (statistics), 1982. *Religion:* Hindu. *Avocational interests:* Classical Indian music, stamp collecting.

ADDRESSES: Home—59 Holbrook Cres., Cambridge, Ontario, Canada N1T 1V7. *Office*—Department of Mathematics and Statistics, McMaster University, Hamilton, Ontario, Canada L8S 4K1; fax 905-522-1676. *E-mail*—bala@mcmail.cis.mcmaster.ca.

CAREER: University of Guelph, Guelph, Ontario, Canada, visiting faculty member, 1984-85; McMaster University, Hamilton, Ontario, Canada, research fellow, 1985-86, assistant professor, 1986-89, associate professor, 1989-95, professor of mathematics and statistics, 1995—. Statpro Consulting, sole proprietor.

MEMBER: Statistical Society of Canada, Institute of Mathematical Statistics, American Statistical Association (fellow), American Society for Quality Control, Royal Statistical Society (fellow).

WRITINGS:

(With Barry C. Arnold) *Relations, Bounds, and Approximations for Order Statistics,* Springer-Verlag (New York City), 1989.
(With A. Clifford Cohen) *Order Statistics and Inference: Estimation Methods,* Academic Press (Boston, MA), 1991.
(Editor) *Handbook of the Logistic Distribution,* Dekker (New York City), 1992.
(With Barry C. Arnold and H. N. Nagaraja) *A First Course in Order Statistics,* Wiley (New York City), 1992.
(With Norman L. Johnson and Samuel Kotz) *Continuous Univariate Distributions,* Wiley, Volume 1, 1994, Volume 2, 1995.
(Editor) *Recent Advances in Life-Testing and Reliability,* CRC Press (Boca Raton, FL), 1995.
(Editor) *CRC Handbook of Applied Industrial Statistics,* CRC Press, 1996.
(Editor) *The Exponential Distribution: Theory, Methods and Applications,* Gordon and Breach (Langhorne, PA), 1996.
(With H. Leon Harter) *The CRC Handbook of Tables for the Use of Order Statistics in Estimation,* CRC Press, 1996.
The CRC Tables for the Use of Order Statistics in Tests of Hypotheses, CRC Press, 1997.
(With Harter) *The CRC Handbook of Tables for the Use of Range,* CRC Press, 1997.
(With Johnson and Kotz) *Discrete Multivariate Distributions,* Wiley, 1997.
(Editor with Norman L. Johnson) *Advances in the Theory and Practice of Statistics,* Wiley, 1997.
(Editor) *Advances in Combinatorial Methods and Applications to Probability and Statistics,* Birk-

heauser (Boston, MA), 1997.

(With William W.S. Chen) *CRC Handbook of Tables for Order Statistics from Inverse Gaussian Distributions with Applications,* CRC Press, 1997.

WORK IN PROGRESS: Research on order statistics, outliers, multivariate distribution theory, reliability, and quality control.

SIDELIGHTS: N. Balakrishnan told *CA:* "My primary motivation for writing is a desire to collect and synthesize all published results in a specific area. I choose a topic of current interest that does not have a consolidated volume. First I do an exhaustive search of the literature. Then I present the results in a coherent and logically organized form. I enjoy writing. I enjoy taking up such a task and facing the challenge that it poses."

*   *   *

BARBIER, Patrick   1956-

PERSONAL: Born February 28, 1956, in Nantes, France; married Marie-Liesse Bouchaud, June 28, 1980; children: Pierre-Emmanuel, Coralie. *Education:* Attended University of Nantes, University of Rennes, and University of Paris; earned doctorate in Italian. *Religion:* Roman Catholic.

ADDRESSES: Home—24 rue d'Epinal, 44300 Nantes, France. *Office*—Universite Catholique de l'Oust, BP 808, 49008 Angers, Cedex 1, France.

CAREER: Universite Catholique de l'Oust, Angers, France, professor of music history.

MEMBER: Academie de Bretagne et des Pays de la Loire, Dante Alighieri Association (vice president).

AWARDS, HONORS: Guest of Salon du Livre Francophone, Toronto, Ontario, 1995.

WRITINGS:

Histoire de Castrats, Grasset (Paris, France), 1989, translation published as *The World of the Castrati,* Souvenir Press (London, England), 1996.
Graslin, Nantes et l'Opera, Giffard (Nantes), 1993.
Farinelli, le castrat des Lumiers, Grasset (Paris), 1994.
Opera in Paris, 1800-1850, Amadeus Press (Portland, OR), 1995.

Author of theatrical monologues on the composers Mozart, Beethoven, and Schubert, for young adults.

WORK IN PROGRESS: La Maison des Italiens: Las castrats a la cour de Versailles.

*   *   *

BARCLAY, Florence L(ouisa Charlesworth) 1862-1921
(Brandon Roy, a pseudonym)

PERSONAL: Born December 2, 1862, in Limpsfield, Surrey, England; died March 10, 1921; daughter of a clergyman; married Charles W. Barclay (a clergyman), 1881; children: two sons, six daughters. *Religion:* Protestant. *Avocational interests:* Ran village Bible readings and cricket clubs.

CAREER: British romance novelist and lecturer; toured U.S. as public speaker.

WRITINGS:

NOVELS

(As Brandon Roy) *Guy Mervyn,* Blackett (London), 1891; revised by one of her daughters, Putnam (New York and London), 1932.
A Notable Prisoner, Marshall (London), 1905.
The Wheels of Time, Crowell (New York), 1908, Putnam (London), 1910.
The Rosary, Putnam (New York and London), 1909.
The Mistress of Shenstone, Putnam, 1910.
The Following of the Star, Putnam, 1911.
Through the Postern Gate, Putnam, 1912.
The Upas Tree, Putnam, 1912.
The Broken Halo, Putnam, 1913.
The Wall of Partition, Putnam, 1914.
My Heart's Right There, Putnam, 1914.
The White Ladies of Worcester, Putnam, 1917.
Returned Empty, Putnam, 1920.

NONFICTION

The Golden Censer, Hodder and Stoughton (London) and Doran (New York), 1914.
In Hoc + Vince: The Story of a Red Cross Flag, Putnam, 1915.

SIDELIGHTS: One of the most popular romance novelists of her day, Florence L. Barclay was the author of *The Rosary,* a phenomenal bestseller of the 1910s which, according to one report, was "read and wept over by three quarters of the housemaids in Great Britain." A woman of deep religious feeling, Barclay was both the daughter of a clergyman and the wife of a clergyman. As a child she sang at revival meetings and visited the poor; as an adult she lectured on her belief that she discovered Jacob's Well while on her honeymoon in the Holy Land. Happily married, she bore and raised eight children and also found time to write.

Barclay's first novel, the pseudonymous *Guy Mervyn,* was published in 1891, but the publisher went bankrupt and few copies were sold. On the novel's republication in 1932, in an edition somewhat revised by one of Barclay's daughters, the *New York Times Book Review* wrote, "*Guy Mervyn* is written with the sympathy, sentiment and strongly religious feeling found in all the writer's books, and with considerable insight into character and motive, despite the romantic approach." The reviewer also praised Barclay's daughter for having left the novel's 1890s atmosphere unchanged.

Barclay's second novel, *A Notable Prisoner,* did not appear until 1905, and her third, *The Wheels of Time,* until 1908. Her fame was secured in 1909, when *The Rosary* appeared. The novel is, in the words of the *Feminist Companion to Literature in English,* a "well-turned masochistic love story" in which the heroine, a plain young woman named Jane Champion, refuses to marry a young artist who loves beauty above all things, because she feels her face is unworthy of his love. The young man does love her faithfully, however, and they are united in marriage after he goes blind—a denouement that is regretted, in an abstract in *Book Review Digest,* as "too great a concession to a homely face and not enough of a justification for the illuminating beauty of the soul." Of all Barclay's novels, asserts Rachel Anderson in *Twentieth-Century Romance and Historical Writers, The Rosary* may have "the silliest plot," for it depends upon "the "masquerade device,'" in which the heroine disguises herself in order to be near her beloved.

Critics both then and now have often found Barclay's plots far-fetched and her sentiments overwrought; however, there is no doubt about the appreciation shown by her readers. *The Rosary* sold 150,000 copies in its first year and sold more than a million by 1921. Several critics, in addition, while not treating Baclay's novels as serious literature, applauded the skill and sincerity with which she crafted her work within its genre boundaries. A contemporaneous novelist, quoted by Anderson, said, "*The Rosary* will

probably live, because its power is very uncommon—as uncommon, on its lower plane, as the power of *Wuthering Heights* . . . Mrs. Barclay . . . was undoubtedly a great writer on her plane—Shakespeare of the servants' hall. Her power is terrific—at any rate in *The Rosary*. I had infinitely rather have written *The Rosary* than [John Galsworthy's] *The Forsyte Saga*."

Barclay's later novels were almost as commercially successful as *The Rosary,* and set forth Barclay's recurring themes: love as the fruit of a conversion to Christianity, and, sometimes, the love between a young man and an older woman. An example of the latter theme is found in *The Broken Halo* (1913), in which the young man, a doctor, falls in love with the sixty-year-old woman whose weak heart he has been treating. Their love cannot be consummated, for the lady dies of heart failure on the night appointed for that event. Responding to the book, the *Boston Transcript* called it "certainly her best work," but other reviewers found it difficult to believe in and excessively sentimental.

The Upas Tree (1912) "stand[s] second among the author's successes" in the view of an *Atlantic* reviewer; it is about a young novelist who travels to Africa in search of material, is psychologically poisoned by contact with a upas tree, and returns to England with a determination to improve his life. A *New York Times Book Review* contributor raised the usual objections to the novel's sentimentality, but concluded, "it must be said for Mrs. Barclay that she does this sort of modern fairy tale very well indeed. She writes well because she writes simply, she frequently shows glimpses of real penetration into character and motive, and she possesses an active imagination that is always lively, tender, and glowing." A *Spectator* critic called *The Upas Tree* "an unusually saisfactory specimen of Mrs. Barclay's art." The year 1912 was also the year of publication for *Through the Postern Gate,* a romance in which the hero is twenty-six and the heroine thirty-six. First serialized in the *Ladies' Home Journal, Through the Postern Gate* "is not profound," according to an *Independent* reviewer, "and never leaves one in much doubt as to the final outcome, yet it has about it a charm as irresistible as that of its "Little boy blue' [i.e., its male protagonist]." The *Spectator* critic observed, "In the art of effusion she has no rival among living novelists."

Mrs. Barclay adopted modern technology to romantic purposes in her 1914 novel, *The Wall of Partition:* the novel consists largely of telephone conversations between two would-be lovers who, believing themselves to have parted forever, do not realize that they are living in adjacent apartments. The novel also contains numerous references to a novel-within-the-novel, written by the leading man about his frustrated romance. A *Boston Transcript* critic called this tale an "entertaining story with a very evident ethical import. *The Wall of Partition* is a success in what Mrs. Barclay set out to achieve. It would not be fair to attempt to judge it by some other perhaps equally arbitrary standard of our own."

At the beginning of World War I Barclay produced a novella entitled *My Heart's Right There,* in which she made vivid for her mass audience the courage of British soldiers. A *New York Times Book Review* critic termed it "very tender and sweet in its sentiment and told with all its author's instinct for arousing the emotions of her reader." Barclay's output slowed during and after the war; her next novel, *The White Ladies of Worcester,* appeared in 1917. It was a medieval yarn, and a *Times Literary Supplement* contributor called it "[a] pleasing, sentimental romance," although commenting that the novel's ideas and feelings came more from the twentieth century than from the twelfth. Words of high praise came from the *Springfield Republican:* "The story has an excellent plot, and is told with commendable restraint, and without the cloying sentimentality and wearisome artificialities characterizing so many of the author's stories heretofore."

Barclay had a longstanding interest in mystical phenomena; a woman of reputed personal magnetism, she "showed many instances of psychic powers" during her life, according to the *Feminist Companion to Literature in English.* It was perhaps not surprising, then, that her final novel, the 1920 *Returned Empty,* was about reincarnation. The hero, a lonely foundling, grows up to be a lonely man; searching for something undefined in the windows of strangers' houses, he comes upon a widow who reveals to him that he is the reincarnation of her husband. They are unable to remain together for long in his new life, but they are enriched by their meeting. Reviewer Cornelia Van Pelt in *Publishers Weekly* believed that Barclay, in this novel, had "gotten away with" the risks of writing a novel of the occult—that she had created "a most appealing story which will interest readers who do not usually number Mrs. Barclay among their favorite authors." The book's attraction for the audience of the postwar years, Van Pelt felt, was "first and foremost to women mourning a promising young life cut off by sudden death in the prime of manhood. . . . In this book they will find a certain

comfort, and a kindly lesson." Barclay is credited with expanding her readership through her last novel and bringing, Anderson asserts, "genuine spiritual comfort to many" through "the mystical euphoria of her novels." The author is also noted for donating the proceeds of her major bestseller *The Rosary* to charity, an act that is regarded as evidence of her sincere faith exercised in union with her vocation for writing.

BIOGRAPHICAL/CRITICAL SOURCES:

BOOKS

Bain, Virginia, Patricia Clements, and Isobel Grundy, *Feminist Companion to Literature in English: Women Writers from the Middle Ages to the Present,* Yale University Press (New Haven, CT), 1990, p. 59.
Book Review Digest, 1909, p. 24.
Vasudevan, Aruna, editor, *Twentieth-Century Romance and Historical Writers,* third edition, St. James Press, 1994, pp. 34-36.

PERIODICALS

Atlantic, May, 1913.
Boston Transcript, October 22, 1913, p. 24; October 14, 1914, p. 22.
Independent, June 13, 1912.
New York Times Book Review, November 24, 1912, p. 692; January 24, 1915, p. 27; November 27, 1932, p. 6.
Publishers Weekly, September 18, 1920, p. 660.
Spectator, January 18, 1913, p. 109; September 5, 1914, pp. 334-335.
Springfield Republican, January 27, 1918, p. 11.
Times Literary Supplement, November 1, 1917, p. 530.*

*   *   *

BECKER, Carl (Lotus) 1873-1945

PERSONAL: Born September 7, 1873, in Lincoln Township, Blackhawk County, IA; died April 10, 1945, in Ithaca, NY; son of Charles De Witt (a farmer) and Almeda (Sarvay) Becker; married Maude Ranney Hepworth, June 16, 1901; children: son Frederick De Witt Becker. *Education:* Attended a rural school in Blackhawk County, IA, and West Side High School, Waterloo, IA; attended Cornell College,

Mt. Vernon, IA, 1892-93; University of Wisconsin, B.L., 1896, Ph.D., 1907. *Politics:* Independent.

CAREER: American historian and educator. Pennsylvania State College, University Park, instructor in history, 1899-1901; Dartmouth College, Hanover, NH, instructor in history, 1901-02; University of Kansas, Lawrence, assistant professor of European history, 1902-07, associate professor, 1907, professor, 1908-16; University of Minnesota, Minneapolis, professor of history, 1916; Cornell University, Ithaca, NY, professor of history, 1917-22, John Stambaugh Professor of History, 1922-41, professor emeritus and university historian, 1941-45.

MEMBER: American Academy of Arts and Sciences, Institute of Arts and Letters, American Philosophical Society, American Historical Association (president, c. 1931-35), American Antiquarian Society, American Society of University Professors, Royal Historical Society, Town and Gown Club (Ithaca, NY).

AWARDS, HONORS: Columbia University fellowship in constitutional law, 1898-99; Honorary Litt.D., Yale University, 1932, Rochester University, 1938, and Columbia University, 1939.

WRITINGS:

The History of Political Parties in the Province of New York, 1760-1776 (doctoral dissertation), University of Wisconsin (Madison, WI), 1909.

The Beginnings of the American People, Houghton Mifflin (Boston), 1915.

The Eve of the Revolution: A Chronicle of the Breach with England, Yale University Press (New Haven, CT), 1918, Oxford University Press (London), 1920, Glasgow, Brook (Toronto, Canada), 1977.

The United States: An Experiment in Democracy, Harper (New York and London), 1920.

The Declaration of Independence: A Study in the History of Political Ideas, Harcourt, Brace (New York), 1922; new edition with introduction by Becker, Knopf (New York), 1942.

(With J. M. Clark and William E. Dodd) *The Spirit of '76 and Other Essays,* Brookings Graduate School (Washington, DC), 1927; edited and with an introduction by Louis Leonard Tucker, New York State American Revolution Bicentennial Commission (Albany, NY), 1971.

Modern History: The Rise of a Democratic, Scientific, and Industrialized Civilization, Silver, Burdett (New York), 1931.

The Heavenly City of the Eighteenth-Century Philosophers (lectures delivered at Yale University Law School, April, 1931), Yale University Press, 1932, reprinted, 1991.

Everyman His Own Historian (presidential address to American Historical Association), F. S. Crofts (New York), 1935, Quadrangle Books (Chicago), 1966.

Progress and Power (lectures given at Stanford University, April, 1935), Stanford University Press (Palo Alto, CA) and Oxford University Press (London), 1936; reprinted with an introduction by Leo Gershoy, Knopf (New York), 1949.

(With Frederic Duncalf) *The Story of Civilization,* Silver, Burdett, 1938.

Modern Democracy, Yale University Press and Oxford University Press, 1941.

New Liberties for Old, Yale University Press and Oxford University Press, 1941.

Cornell Traditions: Freedom and Responsibility (Messenger Lectures, Cornell University), 1943; published as *Cornell University: Founders and the Founding,* Cornell University Press (Ithaca, NY), 1943.

How New will the Better World Be?: A Discussion of Post-War Reconstruction, Knopf (New York), 1944, Books for Libraries Press (Freeport, NY), 1971.

Freedom and Responsibility in the American Way of Life: Five Lectures Delivered on the William W. Cook Foundation at the University of Michigan, December, 1944, with an introductory essay by George H. Sabine, Knopf, 1945, Vintage, 1955, Greenwood Press (Westport, CT), 1980.

Detachment and the Writing of History: Essays and Letters of Carl L. Becker, edited by Phil L. Snyder, Cornell University Press, 1958, Greenwood Press (Westport, CT), 1972.

"What Is the Good of History?": Selected Letters of Carl L. Becker, 1900-1945, edited and with an introduction by Michael Kammen, Cornell University Press, 1973.

Member of editorial board, *American Historical Review,* c. 1916-22. Author of the articles "Some Generalities that Still Glitter" (1940), "What Is Still Living in the Political Philosophy of Thomas Jefferson?" (1943), and "The Art of Writing," as well as more than seventy other scholarly articles and two hundred book reviews for journals, including *American Historical Review* and *Annals of the American Academy of Political and Social Sciences.* Author of entries on Benjamin Franklin, Samuel Adams, and Thomas Hutchinson for *Dictionary of American Biography,*

Scribners, 1928-44, and on Henry Adams, Samuel Adams, Benjamin Franklin, and "Progress," for *Encyclopedia of the Social Sciences,* Macmillan, 1930-35. Becker's papers are in the library of Cornell University.

SIDELIGHTS: Born on an Iowa farm, Carl Becker became one of the most prominent American historians of his generation, and, in addition, a widely recognized literary stylist. As well as being both a scholar and a writer, he was a teacher who, although uninspiring at the podium (according to former student William H. McNeill in a 1986 essay in *Mythistory and Other Essays*), prepared his lectures carefully in advance to compensate for his shyness. His writings typify the "public intellectual"—the academic thinker who interprets his specialized field for the general public. His books included highly successful history textbooks such as *The United States: An Experiment in Democracy* (1920), *Modern History: The Rise of a Democratic, Scientific, and Industrialized Civilization* (1931), and *The Story of Civilization* (1938); his ideas, and even some of his phrases, were adapted by writers of other textbooks as well. He resisted being labeled, but is considered to have been one of the earliest historical relativists of this century: that is, he believed that history was a matter of interpretation and revision.

The manifesto of Becker's relativism, in the opinion of many scholars, was his 1935 book *Everyman His Own Historian,* in which he said, "There are two histories: the actual series of events that once occurred; and the ideal series that we affirm and hold in memory. The first is absolute and unchanged . . . ; the second is relative, always changing. . . . [Historians] are . . . of that ancient and honorable company of wise men of the tribe . . . bards and story-tellers and minstrels . . . soothsayers and priests, to whom in successive ages has been entrusted the keeping of the useful myths." And any given myth, he went on to say, was eventually discarded. The speech to the American Historical Association in which he first said these words was greeted by his professional colleagues with an "electrifying response," according to Milton M. Klein in a 1985 essay, and has had an echoing effect on more recent historians.

It is perhaps not surprising that Becker saw historians as storytellers, for his initial literary ambition was to be a novelist. He pursued that aim quite seriously in college, keeping a private journal called the "Wild Thoughts Notebook" from 1894 to 1895, and assigning himself technical exercises in scene-writing. Through-

out his life, he read and studied the works of modern novelists such as Henry James and Virginia Woolf.

In keeping with the sense of ambiguity inherent in the label "relativist," Becker has been seen by many scholars as an enigmatic, ironic, and ambiguous figure, both personally and professionally. Historian Richard Nelson, in an essay for *Journal of the History of Ideas* in 1987, termed Becker "both a progressive and an anti-progressive . . . a relativist whose writing contained lessons on morality." Becker had referred to himself, as well, in idiosyncratic terms, calling himself a thinker about history rather than a historian. His references to his own professional career were sometimes puzzling in their apparent modesty. In fact, in 1935, after many years of thinking, teaching, and writing influentially about American history, he declined a prestigious offer of a visiting professorship on American history at Oxford on the grounds that he had not taught the subject.

The record of Becker's publications shows him to be more of a historian than he claimed. His 1907 doctoral dissertation, *The History of Political Parties in the Province of New York, 1770-1776,* produced under the guidance of the eminent historian Frederick Jackson Turner at the University of Wisconsin, pioneered the thesis that the American Revolution was a dual phenomenon: both a struggle between British and Americans, and between mercantile and working-class Americans. In 1922, Becker published *The Declaration of Independence: A Study in the History of Political Ideas,* a book to which he later added an introduction in response to World War II. The book, although partly a literary study of Jefferson's words, was primarily an intellectual study of the sources of the idea of the Rights of Man in the writings of John Locke and others. According to Milton M. Klein in the 1983 *Dictionary of Literary Biography,* Volume 17: *Twentieth-Century American Historians,* the book "received almost immediate acclaim, and it has been regarded as the definitive work on the subject until recently"; a 1952 poll of professional historians ranked it sixth among works on American history written between 1920 and 1935.

An even more influential book was the 1932 *The Heavenly City of the Eighteenth-Century Philosophers.* Becker, a lover of paradox, put forward the view that the philosophers of the Enlightenment, such as Voltaire and Diderot, who had helped overturn faith on behalf of reason, were themselves working on behalf of a faith—the faith in reason. The Enlightenment, in other words, as Wilson put it, "only existed on the inherited moral capital of Christianity." This idea has been heavily criticized since the book's publication, but, according to Fred Somkin in the *McGraw-Hill Encyclopedia of World Biography, The Heavenly City of the Eighteenth-Century Philosophers* endures as "a monument to Becker's literary artistry, a tour de force of high aphoristic wit, written in a spirit of masterful detachment." An instance of this attitude can be seen in a 1966 essay by Peter Gay; although taking Becker's ideas to task, Gay asserts that the book is "that rare thing, a work of scholarship that is also a work of literature—a masterpiece of persuasion that has done more to shape the current image of the Enlightenment than any other book."

Becker's literary skills were closely examined in a 1952 essay by Charlotte Watkins Smith published in the *William and Mary Quarterly.* "The high literary art of Carl Becker was a source of wonder to his contemporaries as it is to later generations," Smith averred, calling Becker's skill "a talent amounting to genius," and asking, "How could a man who never ceased to look like an Iowa farmer write with the urbanity of a Lord Chesterfield, as well as with the pithiness of a Benjamin Franklin?" Although Smith, after examining Becker's literary productions from his adolescence on, demurred from proposing any definitive answer, she felt that Becker had augmented natural talent with assiduous work. He rewrote heavily and was not satisfied with less than the most pleasing formulation of an idea. Childhood reading also played a part, Smith said: "The language of Shakespeare and the *King James Bible* had been so early deposited in Becker's mind and so completely assimilated that it became part of the very fabric of his prose." Becker himself, in an article entitled "The Art of Writing," had this to say about style: "Good style in writing is like happiness in living—something that comes to you, if it comes at all, only if you are preoccupied with something else: if you deliberately go after it you will probably not get it." He claimed to dislike the word *style* because "it tends to fix the attention on what is superficial and decorative whereas in reality the foundation of good writing is organic structure." Style, for Becker, was a byproduct of substantive thought.

BIOGRAPHICAL/CRITICAL SOURCES:

BOOKS

Gay, Peter, "Carl Becker's Heavenly City," *The Party of Humanity: Essays in the French Enlightenment,* Knopf, 1964, pp. 188-210.

McGraw-Hill Encyclopedia of World Biography, Volume 1, McGraw-Hill, 1973, pp. 444-445.
McNeill, William H., "Carl Becker," *Mythistory and Other Essays,* University of Chicago Press, 1986, pp. 147-173.
Wilson, Clyde N., editor, *Dictionary of Literary Biography,* Volume 17: *Twentieth-Century American Historians,* Gale, 1983, pp. 57-63.
Twentieth-Century Literary Criticism, Volume 63, Gale, 1996, pp. 59-119.

PERIODICALS

History Teacher, vol. 19, no. 1, November, 1985, pp. 101-109.
Journal of the History of Ideas, April-June, 1987, pp. 307-323.
William and Mary Quarterly, vol. IX, July, 1952, pp. 291-316.*

*   *   *

BECKER, Jurek 1937-1997

OBITUARY NOTICE—See index for *CA* sketch: Born September 30, 1937, in Lodz, Poland; died of cancer, March 14, 1997, in Frankfurt, Germany. Novelist, scriptwriter, and short story writer. Becker was a survivor of the Jewish ghetto of Warsaw and of the Nazi concentration camps at Ravensbruck and Sachsenhausen during World War II. He later became a member of the Communist Party and a citizen of East Germany, where he was educated at Humboldt University in Berlin and the Filmhochschule in Potsdam-Babelsberg. During the 1960s he wrote television scripts and published his first novel, *Jacob the Liar,* in 1969. His best-known work, the novel focuses on a Jewish prisoner who lifts the spirits of his fellow inmates in a concentration camp through a series of lies. Becker also adapted the story as a motion picture. He was embroiled in controversy during the mid-1970s when he protested decisions of the East German writers' association to exclude two other writers. Becker himself was dismissed from the group and publication of his next book was prohibited. He relocated to West Germany in 1977 and subsequently accepted a series of educational appointments at such institutions as Oberlin College, the University of Essen, Cornell University, the University of Texas at Austin, and Washington University in St. Louis. Among his numerous film and literary prizes are a Silver Bear from the Berlin Film Festival in 1974,

Adolf-Grimme Prizes in 1987 and 1988, a Bayer-ischer Fernsehpreis in 1990, the Bundesfilmpreis in 1991, and the Thomas Mann Award. His works include the novels *Sleepless Days* (1978) and *Bronstein's Children* (1986) as well as a volume of short stories published in 1980.

OBITUARIES AND OTHER SOURCES:

BOOKS

International Who's Who, 60th edition, Europa, 1996, p. 122.

PERIODICALS

New York Times, March 24, 1997, p. B7.

*   *   *

BEDFORD-JONES, H(enry James O'Brien) 1887-1949
(John Wycliffe, Allan Hawkwood, Gordon Keyne, and numerous other pseudonyms)

PERSONAL: Born April 29, 1887, in Napanee, Ontario, Canada; became a naturalized U.S. citizen; died May 12, 1949; son of William John Wicliff and Henrietta Louise (Roblin) Bedford-Jones; married (marriage ended); married Mary Bernardin McNally (a writer).

CAREER: Novelist and short story writer.

MEMBER: Cliff Dwellers Club (Chicago), Authors' Club (London).

WRITINGS:

NOVELS

The Cross and the Hammer: A Tale of the Days of the Vikings, David C. Cook (Elgin, IL), 1912.
Flamehair the Skald: A Tale of the Days of Hardrede, illustrated by Dan Sayre Groesbeck, A.C. McClurg (Chicago), 1913.
The Conquest, Cook, 1914.
The Myth Wawatam, or Alex, Henry Refuted, Being an Exposure of Certain Fictions, Hitherto Unsuspected of the Public; with which Are Also Found Some Remarks upon the Famous Old Fort Michillimackinnac, All of which Is Herein Written and

Publish'd from the Notes of Henry McConnell, Gent., privately published (Santa Barbara, CA), 1917.
The Mesa Trail, Doubleday, Page (Garden City, NY), 1920.
The Mardi Gras Mystery, Doubleday, Page, 1921.
(As John Wycliffe) *Against the Tide*, Dodd, Mead (New York), 1924.
The Star Woman, Dodd, Mead, 1924.
Rodomont: A Romance of Mont St. Michel in the Days of Louis XIV, Putnam's (New York City), 1926.
Saint Michael's Gold, Putnam's, 1926.
The Black Bull, Putnam's, 1927.
The King's Passport, Putnam's, 1928.
D'Artagnan, The Sequel to The Three Musketeers, Augmenting and Incorporating a Fragmentary Manuscript by Alexandre Dumas, pere, Covici, Friede (New York City), 1928.
Cyrano, Putnam, 1930.
The Shadow, The Fiction League (New York), 1930.
(With wife, Mary Bedford-Jones) *D'Artagnan's Letter*, Covici-Friede, 1931.
Drums of Dambala, Covici-Friede, 1932.

Also author of the novels *Splendour of the Gods*, 1924, *Son of Cincinnati*, 1925, *Centaur to Cross*, 1929, and *King's Pardon*, 1933; author, with uncredited co-author W. C. Robertson, of *The Temple of the Ten*, 1921.

Bedford-Jones's total written output includes more than one hundred novels in history, adventure, juvenile, fantasy, and science fiction genres.

"JOHN SOLOMON" SERIES; UNDER PSEUDONYM ALLAN HAWKWOOD; LATER PUBLISHED IN BOOK FORM

Solomon's Quest, originally published in *Argosy*, 1915.
Gentleman Solomon, originally published in *Argosy*, 1915.
Solomon's Carpet, originally published in *Argosy*, 1915.
John Solomon, originally published in *Argosy*, 1916.
John Solomon Retired, originally published in *Argosy*, 1917.
Solomon's Son, originally published in *Argosy*, 1918.
The Seal of Solomon, originally published in *Argosy*, 1924.
John Solomon, Supercargo, originally published in *Argosy*, 1924.
John Solomon, Incognito, originally published in *Argosy*, 1925.
The Shawl of Solomon, originally published in *Argosy*, 1925.

The Wizard of the Atlas, originally published in *Argosy,* 1928.

NONFICTION

The Fiction Business, [Evansville, IN], 1922, published as *This Fiction Business,* Covici, Friede, 1929.

The Graduate Fictioneer, with an introduction by Erle Stanley Gardner, Author & Journalist Publishing (Denver), 1932.

The Mission and the Man: The Story of San Juan Capistrano, with drawings by June Simonds, San Pasqual Press (Pasadena, CA), 1939.

OTHER

Author of the "Trumpets from Oblivion" series for *Blue Book,* including the short stories "The Stagnant Death," 1938, and "The Serpent People," 1939; author of the "Counterclockwise" series for *Blue Book,* including the short stories "Counterclockwise," 1943, and "The Gods Do Not Forget," 1944; author of the "Tomorrow's Men" series for *Blue Book,* including the short stories "Peace Hath Her Victories," 1943, "The Battle for France," 1943, "Sahara Doom," 1943, and "Tomorrow in Egypt," 1943; author of the "Quest, Inc." series for *Blue Book,* including the short stories "The Affair of the Drifting Face," 1943, and "The Final Hoard," 1945; also author of "The Adventures of a Professional Corpse" series for *Weird Tales,* 1940-41, the "Carson's Folly" series for *Blue Book,* 1945-46, and "The Sphinx Emerald" series for *Blue Book,* 1946-47.

Contributor of numerous uncollected short stories and short story series to magazines including *Blue Book, Magic Carpet, Golden Fleece, All-Star Weekly,* and *Weird Tales,* under pen name Gordon Keyne and more than fourteen other pseudonyms.

SIDELIGHTS: A mainstay of the pulp fiction industry during its heyday in the first half of the twentieth century, H. Bedford-Jones published, with enormous energy even for a prolific age, so many novels and short stories under so many pen names that many of his works have left little or no record apart from an intriguing title or a date of publication. Those that are fully accounted for, however, constitute sufficient publication credits to qualify Bedford-Jones as a busy professional writer. Some of his works, as was customary at the time, were published in serial form in magazines and later bound between covers.

A major series of books that helped established Bedford-Jones's professional career was a sequence of adventure novels that featured the protagonist John Solomon. Bedford-Jones published these in magazines (such as *Argosy*) under his own name, then in book form under the pseudonym Allan Hawkwood. These books are lost-world fantasies, according to the *Encyclopedia of Science Fiction,* and comprise ten titles. Notable among them are 1915's *Gentleman Solomon,* in which hero Solomon encounters a heretofore-unknown group of pygmies in the Middle East, and *The Seal of Solomon,* published in *Argosy* the same year, in which he finds a community inhabited by descendants of the Crusaders, who live in isolation in the deserts of Arabia.

A survey of Bedford-Jones' works in several genres gives an indication of his productivity and versatility. His 1921 mystery novel *The Mardi Gras Mystery* boasts a complex plot in which the exploits of a jewel thief, the "Midnight Masquer," turn out to be a decoy for the deeper espionage of protagonist Henry Gramont into oil property. Gramont traces the clues and arrests the members of a criminal organization, only to find that its leader, Fell, is an undercover operative. *New York Times* reviewer H. S. Gorman exclaimed of the novel that, "It will delight the soul of the lover of detective yarns that are well sustained to the last thrill." A contributor to the *Springfield Republican* opined, "The author not only tells a clever story but keeps his high card to play on the final trick"; and a critic for the *Literary Review,* in a similar mode, declared the book "a swift novel, full of action and improbability, and with a very satisfactory ending." In the same year, Bedford-Jones published *Mesa Trail,* a western adventure in which a middle-aged female prospector, Mrs. Mehitabel Crump, befriends a liquor-sodden actor, Thady Shea, who unwittingly betrays her interests in a mineral claim. Shea spends the remainder of the novel atoning successfully by saving the claim.

Moving ahead to Bedford-Jones' production for the year 1924, one finds *The Star Woman,* a well-received adventure yarn with fantasy overtones that focuses on the English and French in Hudson Bay, a historical setting that Bedford-Jones carefully researched. Hal Crawford, the hero, quests for Star Woman, a mystical female known to wear a star-shaped jewel on her breast; he undergoes a series of ordeals before finally finding this ideal love. Stella Heilbrunn of *International Book Review* wrote approvingly, "All the stuff of adventure is here. Historical facts support it." The critic added that, "Good writing adds beauty of word and scene. Could an adventure-lover ask for more?" While praising the author's style, Heilbrunn went on to offer the suggestion that a livelier, less "bookish" writing style might have been asked for, but that the novel contained plenty of action. A contributor to the *Saturday Review of Literature* also found reason to quarrel with Bedford-Jones' writing style. However, a *Literary Review* critic called *The Star Woman* "one of the outstanding novels of the year," and a reviewer for the *New York Times* also weighed in on the positive side, claiming that the book would appeal both to lovers of melodrama and to "those readers to whom mere melodrama does not appeal."

The tales of historical adventure that Bedford-Jones penned during the second half of the 1920s often found their source in France. The 1926 novel *Rodomont* is set on Mont St. Michel during the reign of Louis XIV. The Canadian hero, Rodomont, bears a letter to the monastery—a letter that, unknown to its bearer, orders his own imprisonment. After much turmoil, Rodomont escapes to England with a fellow Canadian. A *New York Times* reviewer praised the novel, saying that in spite of conventional genre apparatus, "the story is told with a zest and rapidity that keep the reader's interest constantly awake." A contributor to the *New York World* averred, "Few late adventure romances of our ken maintain their action throughout at so violent a pitch as one finds here. It is a vigorous, well written tale."

Bedford-Jones wrote a number of other adventures set in Europe, some around Mont St. Michel itself. The action of 1927's *Saint Michael's Gold* takes place during the French Revolution as the author's American hero tries unsuccessfully to save a treasure for the monastery, but does succeed in helping some royalists escape. The 1928 novel *The Black Bull* is set in Italy in the seventeenth century. Once again Bedford-Jones uses the device of introducing a hero from another country, this time, an Irish cavalier in pursuit of vengeance against an evil Italian duke. A critic for the *Boston Transcript* called *Black Bull* "a spirited tale full of the glamour of Old Italy." A *New York Times* contributor praised the author's dexterous handling of the flow of narrative, and a *New York Evening Post* reviewer compared the novel to a Verdi libretto.

Also in 1928, Bedford-Jones revived the classic tale of the Three Musketeers in *D'Artagnan,* a novel that incorporates a fragmentary text by Alexandre Dumas, pere. Praise came from a *New York Herald Tribune Books* critic, who called the attempt "high romantic

adventure of the right old heady flavor. . . . full of the proper spirit and stuffed with genuine thrills." Some reviewers found fault with the author's style and technique but enjoyed the novel's atmospheric adventure elements anyway: a *New York Times* reviewer called *D'Artagnan* "an entertaining, swiftly moving story," while a *Boston Transcript* critic noted that "Mr. Bedford-Jones has recaptured the spirit of *The Three Musketeers*." And a contributor to the *Saturday Review of Literature* continued to echo critical praise, dubbing the novel "a story full of action and fire."

The King's Passport was also about D'Artagnan, and involved Edmund Rostand's long-nosed fictional hero Cyrano de Bergerac to boot. Reviews of *The King's Passport* tended to take a line similar to that of reviews of *D'Artagnan*. A *New York Times* critic called the novel "a fine, galloping, vividly told yarn," while a *Saturday Review of Literature* contributor termed it "excellent reading. An intelligent, skillful novel of action." A reviewer for the *Times Literary Supplement* singled out the characters of Cyrano, Cardinal Richelieu, and the Cardinal's secretary, Mazarin, as well-drawn.

Then, in 1930, came Bedford-Jones' *Cyrano,* which a *New York Times* reviewer called "a lively, swashbuckling, swiftly moving tale." The *Times* critic alluded regretfully to a lack of plausibility, however, as did the *Books* contributor who also found the novel readably and enjoyably written. An *Outlook* critic solved the dilemma of excitement versus plausibility by calling *Cyrano* "an excellent cloak and sword romance."

Another Three Musketeers-based novel, *D'Artagnan's Letter,* was written by Bedford-Jones along with his wife, Mary, and published in 1931. It concerns the discovery, at an auction, of a letter supposedly written by D'Artagnan giving a clue to a missing fortune; the book centers on the search for that fortune. A *Boston Transcript* reviewer called this opus "a romantic tale with a happy ending, which moves swiftly with an adventure on almost every page."

In a 1932 solo effort Bedford-Jones moved his fiction back to the Western Hemisphere, with *Drums of Dambala,* a tale of voodoo and political intrigue that takes place in Haiti during the early 1800s. "Mr. Bedford-Jones has produced a thrilling yarn," raved Ward Greene in *Books,* specifying such ingredients as "vampires, drums, snake eyes, [and] slit gullets."

Published in 1933, Bedford-Jones' novel *King's Pardon* returned once again to France, but this time focuses its action during the reign of Henry IV. The hero, returning from a war in Hungary to find his lands seized, turns outlaw, serves the king, and wins a fair lady. "If sustained violence and bloodshed constitute the main essentials in a story of this kind," wrote a *New York Times* reviewer, "the book easily rates the rank of masterpiece."

An author capable of writing and publishing so many varied works of fiction was surely qualified to write a nonfiction book on the craft of writing; Bedford-Jones did so in 1922's *The Fiction Business,* which was reissued in 1929 as *This Fiction Business.* According to a *New York Times* review of the book, the author recommends a hard-headed, businesslike approach to writing. He advises the novice to determine what category of fiction he or she would prove best at and then proceed to acquire skill with words, characters, and technique through sheer diligence. According to a review in the *New York Times,* Bedford-Jones "is wholly practical in his viewpoint and in his defense of it he points to his own not inconsiderable commercial success as an author. . . . it must be admitted that he knows what he is talking about." A reviewer in Boston's *Herald Tribune Books* said, in a similar vein, that for prospective authors who felt an affinity for Bedford-Jones' commercial approach, "his advice is eminently practical and to the point. He knows his stuff."

Little of H. Bedford-Jones' fiction is available to the general reader today, but he and other writers like him were the bedrock of popular fiction in their own time, helping to maintain an enthusiastic readership for publishing houses and thriving magazines, and thus providing the climate in which more enduringly celebrated writers could flourish.

BIOGRAPHICAL/CRITICAL SOURCES:

BOOKS

Encyclopedia of Science Fiction, edited by Peter Nichols, Granada Publishing (London), 1993, pp. 101-02.

PERIODICALS

Booklist, May, 1932.
Books, May 11, 1930, p. 10; February 28, 1932, p. 14.
Boston Transcript, October 13, 1928, p. 7; October 15, 1927, p. 4; July 18, 1931, p. 8.

International Book Review, December 1924, p. 63.
Literary Review, May 28, 1921, p. 9; September 6, 1924, p. 9.
New York Evening Post, January 21, 1928, p. 14.
New York Herald Tribune Books, November 11, 1928, p. 20; August 25, 1929, p. 10.
New York Times, July 10, 1921, p. 11; September 14, 1924, p. 24; March 28, 1926, p. 22; November 27, 1927, p. 36; April 1, 1928, p. 24; November 25, 1928, p. 3; July 28, 1929, p. 8; April 13, 1930, p. 9; April 23, 1933, p. 16.
New York World, April 4, 1926, p. M7.
Outlook, April 2, 1930.
Saturday Review of Literature, October 4, 1924; January 1, 1927; August 25, 1928; October 13, 1928.
Springfield Republican, June 19, 1921, p. A9.
Times Literary Supplement, September 6, 1928, p. 634; June 16, 1932.*

* * *

BELL, Clare (Louise) 1952-
(Clare Coleman, a joint pseudonym)

PERSONAL: Born June 19, 1952, in Hitchin, Hertfordshire, England; immigrated to the United States, 1957; daughter of Ronald Lancelot Bell and Edna Kathleen (Wheldon) Steward; lives with M. Coleman Easton. *Education:* University of California, Santa Cruz, B.A., 1975; postgraduate studies at University of California, Davis, c. 1978; Stanford University, M.S. M.E., 1983. *Politics:* Green Party. *Avocational interests:* Electric cars, music, hiking, cycling, swimming.

ADDRESSES: Home & office—5680 Judith St., San Jose, CA 95123-2033. *Agent*—c/o Margaret K. McElderry Books, 866 3rd Ave., New York, NY 10022. *E-mail*—Ce96ed@aol.com.

CAREER: U.S. Geological Survey, Menlo Park, CA, field assistant, 1976-78; International Business Machines (IBM), San Jose, CA, test equipment engineer, 1978-89; freelance writer, c. 1983—. *Current EVents* (newsletter of Electric Auto Association), San Jose, CA, managing editor, c. 1995—.

MEMBER: American Civil Liberties Union, National Writers Union, Science Fiction Writers of America, Electric Vehicle Association, San Jose Peace Center.

AWARDS, HONORS: PEN Los Angeles Award and ALA's Best Book for Young People Award, both

1983, and International Reading Association's Children's Book Award, 1984, all for *Ratha's Creature*; ALA's Best Book for Young People Award, 1984, for *Clan Ground,* and 1990, for *Ratha and Thistle-Chaser.*

WRITINGS:

JUVENILE FANTASY NOVELS; RATHA SERIES

Ratha's Creature, Atheneum (New York City), 1983.
Clan Ground, Atheneum, 1984.
Ratha and Thistle-Chaser, M.K. McElderry (New York City), 1990.
Ratha's Challenge, M.K. McElderry, 1995.

OTHER NOVELS

Tomorrow's Sphinx (juvenile), M.K. McElderry, 1986.
People of the Sky, Tor (New York City), 1989.
(As Clare Coleman; with M. Coleman Easton) *Daughter of the Reef,* Jove (New York City), 1992.
The Jaguar Princess, Tor, 1993.
(As Clare Coleman; with Easton) *Sister of the Sun,* Jove, c. 1993.
(As Clare Coleman; with Easton) *Child of the Dawn,* Jove, 1994.

SIDELIGHTS: Clare Coleman began writing fantasy novels for children while she was still working as a test engineer for International Business Machines (IBM). Her first novel in the award-winning "Ratha" series about prehistoric sentient cats, *Ratha's Creature,* saw print in 1983. By 1989, her fiction was successful enough for her to leave engineering. In addition to three other books about Ratha and her friends, Coleman has penned fantasy novels for older audiences, including *People of the Sky* and *The Jaguar Princess.* She is also the co-author, with M. Coleman Easton, of two novels under the joint pseudonym Clare Coleman.

As Ratha's story begins in *Ratha's Creature,* Ratha is a year-old cat in a clan which calls themselves the Named. The Named herd and practice agriculture; their traditional enemies, the Unnamed, do not, and often live by raiding the herds of the Named. Ratha is due to become one of the clan's herders, but her discovery of how to harness fire threatens the leader of the Named, and she is exiled. She lives for a time with the Unnamed, and breeds with one of them, but the resulting kittens are unintelligent, and she and they are exiled yet again. She eventually persuades

the Named to accept her gift of fire, and becomes their Queen.

Booklist hailed *Ratha's Creature* as a "powerful, moving, and memorable story" and predicted it "will draw readers right in." Trev Jones in the *School Library Journal* praised it as well, noting that it "is charged with powerful emotions" and that "the characters will come vividly alive to readers." Mary Ellen Baker in *Voice of Youth Advocates* also felt that *Ratha's Creature* was "moving," and gave the novel that periodical's highest rating for quality.

In *Clan Ground,* Ratha's leadership is challenged by Shongshar, a male cat who turns the Named's use of fire into a strong and threatening religious cult. This sequel gained the favor of Hazel Rochman in the *School Library Journal,* who observed that "Bell creates characters that are authentically wild and feline and also sensitive, intelligent and complicated." In *Ratha and Thistle-Tail,* Ratha is reunited with the daughter that she tried to kill in a mistaken belief that she was a throwback to a more mindless race of cats. Instead, it turns out that Thistle-Tail and others like her are the next evolutionary step in sentient cats—kittens who take longer to come to maturity. By 1995's *Ratha's Challenge,* the mother and daughter are still creeping towards reconciliation, but they come together to deal with and understand another clan of sentient cats controlled by a communal song. Of *Ratha's Challenge,* Jeanne Triner declared in *Booklist* that "readers will find enough suspense, adventure, and even romance to satisfy them." Carolyn Polese, reviewing the same novel in the *School Library Journal,* lauded its "vivid descriptions of . . . life on the veldt," while Leslie A. Acevedo in *VOYA* concluded that the book's issues "are presented in a well-paced and thought provoking manner."

Bell stayed with the subject matter of cats for another book for young readers, *Tomorrow's Sphinx.* This explored the lives of two black cheetahs, one in Egypt during the reign of the pharaoh Tutankhamen, the other in a future devastated by environmental waste. Another novel of Bell's, *The Jaguar Princess,* is a historical fantasy set during the time of the Aztecs. This book concerns Mixcatl, a slave girl who turns out to be descended from a royal race of shape-changers. A *Kirkus Review* critic found *The Jaguar Princess* to be "thinly plotted," but a *Publishers Weekly* reviewer praised it as "vivid."

Daughter of the Reef, Bell's first collaboration with M. Coleman Easton as Clare Coleman, is set during ancient times on an island of the South Pacific. Tepua, the book's royal heroine, is washed away from the celebration of her own wedding by a tropical storm. In the place where she washes up, she must learn to fit in with a new society, and learns to dance for her new tribe. Her dancing also brings her a new love interest—Matopahu. *Publishers Weekly* assessed that the novel has "a dynamism that keeps it afloat."

BIOGRAPHICAL/CRITICAL SOURCES:

PERIODICALS

Booklist, March 15, 1983, pp. 956-957; January 1, 1995, pp. 814-816.
Kirkus Reviews, August 15, 1993, p. 1034.
Publishers Weekly, November 9, 1992, p. 78; October 4, 1993, p. 68.
School Library Journal, September, 1983, p. 130; October, 1984, p. 164; January, 1995, p. 134.
Voice of Youth Advocates, October, 1983, p. 196; June, 1995, p. 101.*

*   *   *

BELLAMY, Christopher (David) 1955-

PERSONAL: Born October 28, 1955, in Perivale, England; son of Peter (a banker) and Patricia (a teacher; maiden name, Buckland) Bellamy; married Heather Kerr, February 21, 1992. *Ethnicity:* "British." *Education:* Lincoln College, Oxford University, M.A. (history), 1976; King's College, London University, M.A. (war studies), 1978; University of Westminster, B.A. (Russian), 1987; University of Edinburgh, Ph.D., 1990.

ADDRESSES: Home—28 Meon Rd., London W3 8AN, England. *Office—Independent,* 1 Canada Sq., Canary Wharf, London E14 5DL, England. *E-mail—* C.Bellamy@independent.co.uk. *Agent*—Peters, Fraser & Dunlop, 503/4 The Chambers, London S.W.10, England.

CAREER: British Ministry of Defence, 1978-87; *Independent,* London, England, defense correspondent, 1990—. Institute of Linguists, associate, 1981. *Military service:* British Army, Royal Artillery, 1972-77; became second lieutenant.

MEMBER: Royal United Services Institute (fellow).

WRITINGS:

The Future of Land Warfare, Croom Helm (London), 1986, St. Martin's Press (New York), 1987.
Red God of War, Brassey's (London), 1987.
The Times Atlas of the Second World War, Times Books (London), 1989.
The Evolution of Modern Land Warfare, Routledge (New York), 1990.
Expert Witness, Brassey's (New York), 1993.
Knights in White Armour, Hutchinson (London), 1996.

*   *   *

BEN-DAVID, Joseph   1920-1986

PERSONAL: Born August 19, 1920, in Gyor, Hungary; emigrated to Palestine, 1941; died January 12, 1986, in Jerusalem, Israel; son of David and Gisela (maiden name, Mayer) Gross; married Miriam Sternberg, 1947; children: Aaron, B. Uriel, Gila. *Education:* London School of Economics, certificate in social administration, 1949; Hebrew University, M.A. in history and sociology of culture, 1950, Ph.D. in sociology, 1955.

CAREER: Sociologist, educator, editor, and author. Worked for the Israel National and Civil Service, 1942-51; Hebrew University, member of the faculty, 1951—, professor of sociology, 1970—. University of Chicago, research associate professor, 1968—.

Center for Advanced Study in Behavioral Sciences, Stanford University, fellow, 1957-58; Israel National Council for Research and Development, Prime Minister's Office, Jerusalem, member, 1962-64; University of California at Berkeley, visiting professor, 1964-65; Organization for Economic Co-operation and Development (OECD), Paris, France, temporary consultant, 1966-71; University of Chicago, visiting professor, 1968, 1969; National Board on Graduate Education, Washington, DC, member, 1972-75; Research Project on the Academic Profession, Harvard University, consultant; Institute for Advanced Study, Princeton University, member, 1976; Institute d'Histoire et de Sociopolitique des Science, University of Montreal, visiting professor, Roger Gaudry visiting professor, 1977.

MEMBER: American Academy of Arts and Sciences (fellow, honorary foreign member), Israel Sociological Association (chair, 1972-74), International Sociological Association, American Sociological Association, Israel Demographic Society, Research Committee on Sociology of Science (president), National Academy of Education (foreign associate).

AWARDS, HONORS: Borden Prize, American Council on Education, 1972; John Desmond Bernal Award, Society for the Social Study of Science, 1985.

WRITINGS:

(Editor) *Agricultural Planning and Village Community in Israel,* UNESCO (Paris), 1964.

Fundamental Research and the Universities: Some Comments on International Differences, Organization for Economic Co-operation and Development, 1968.

The Scientist's Role in Society: A Comparative Study, Prentice-Hall (Englewood Cliffs, NJ), 1971, revised edition published with the subtitle *A Comparative Study with a New Introduction,* University of Chicago Press, 1984.

American Higher Education: Directions Old and New, McGraw-Hill (New York, NY), 1972.

Centers of Learning: Britain, France, Germany, and the United States, McGraw-Hill, 1977, reprinted with a new introduction by Philip G. Altbach, Transaction Publishers (New Brunswick, NJ), 1992.

(Editor, with Terry Nichols Clark) *Culture and Its Creators: Essays in Honor of Edward Shils,* University of Chicago Press, 1977.

Trends in American Higher Education, University of Chicago Press, 1981.

Scientific Growth: Essays on the Social Organization and Ethos of Science, edited and introduced by Gad Gruedenthal, University of California Press (Berkeley, CA), 1991.

Contributed the bibliography to the International Sociological Association's *Professions in the Class System of Present-Day Societies,* Basil Blackwell (Oxford, England), 1964. Also conducted research and published in the fields of social stratification, comparative sociology, sociology of education, sociology of science, and sociological theory.

SIDELIGHTS: Joseph Ben-David, "master of a comparative historical approach to the sociology of science," according to reviewer D. Carmichael in *Choice,* was born in Hungary and emigrated to Palestine in 1941, where he was educated at Hebrew University in sociology and history. His historical approach to sci-

ence emphasizes the social and cultural factors affecting the growth of the sciences since the 1700s. Thus, Ben-David notes, the development of a new branch of science, such as psychology, may be dependent on such non-scientific factors as those that govern other organizations, such as the need for career opportunities among members of the profession.

"Ben-David viewed the modern sciences as particular forms of professional work organizations whose social structures influenced the ways in which scientific work gets done," Stephan Fuchs wrote in the professional journal *Contemporary Sociology.*

These ideas, and related musings on how the presence of competition influences the quality of the science emerging from, in particular, the university setting, were first set forth in Ben-David's *The Scientist's Role in Society,* which formed the basis for much of his later writing. *Culture and Its Creators,* an anthology dedicated to Edward Shils and co-edited by Ben-David and Terry Nichols Clark, examines the impact of ideology on the fields of sociology, economics, anthropology, and literature. Ben-David's own contribution focuses on the institutionalization of science. Though some complaint was made about gaps in Ben-David's and Clark's introduction, which lacks a biographical note on Shils and a "fuller review of Shils' own contributions to the sociology of culture," according to J. D. Y. Peel in the *Bulletin of Atomic Science,* Ben-David's *Culture and Its Creators* was warmly reviewed as a valuable contribution to the field of sociology. L. A. Coser in the *American Journal of Sociology* called it "an intellectual treat and a befitting tribute to the eminence of the man it is designed to honor."

Five years after Ben-David's death, twenty-five of his essays, compiled by editor Gad Freudenthal were published as *Scientific Growth: Essays on the Social Organization and Ethos of Science.* The book ranges over twenty-five year's worth of writings on such topics as the importance of the university to the growth of science, the potential for planning and directing this growth, and the problem of anti-scientism. The book's significance, according to Fuchs, is that it poses Ben-David's theories as a possible "bridge" between "the Mertonian paradigm and the constructivist sociology of scientific knowledge (SSK)"—the "two opposing camps" into which the sociology of science is divided. *Scientific Growth* includes a bibliography of Ben-David's works, and "will certainly prove to be the definitive collection of his works," concluded Carmichael in *Choice.*

BIOGRAPHICAL/CRITICAL SOURCES:

PERIODICALS

American Journal of Sociology, July, 1978, p. 182.
Bulletin of Atomic Science, March, 1978, p. 61.
Chicago Tribune, January 17, 1986.
Choice, May, 1992, p. 1414.
Contemporary Sociology, November, 1992, pp. 859-60.*

*   *   *

BENNETT, Clinton   1955-

PERSONAL: Born October 7, 1955, in Tettenhall, England; son of Howard (in business) and Joan (a nursing sister) Bennett; married Rekha Sarker (a social worker), April 12, 1996; children: George (stepson). *Education:* Victoria University of Manchester, B.A., 1978; University of Birmingham, M.A., 1985, Ph.D., 1990; Oxford University, M.Ed., 1996. *Avocational interests:* Fitness, running, cycling, walking, cooking.

ADDRESSES: Home—House No. 2, Westminster College, Oxford OX2 9AT, England. *Office*—Westminster College, Oxford OX2 9AT, England; fax 01-86-525-1847. *E-mail*—c.bennett@ox-west.ac.uk.

CAREER: Ordained Baptist minister, 1978; Government of New South Wales, Sydney, Australia, clerical officer, 1972-74; Baptist Missionary Society, Bangladesh, missionary, 1979-83; Birmingham Ethnic Education and Advisory Service, Birmingham, England, tutor, 1983-86; British Council of Churches, London, England, executive secretary, 1987-92; Westminster College, Oxford, England, senior lecturer, 1992—.

MEMBER: Royal Asiatic Society (fellow), Royal Anthropological Institute (fellow), British Association for the Study of Religions.

WRITINGS:

Victorian Images of Islam, Grey Seal, 1992.
In Search of the Sacred, Cassell (London, England), 1996.
(With C. Higgins and L. Foreman-Peck) *Researching Teaching Methods in Colleges and Universities,* Kogan Page, 1996.
Muhammad: An Interpretive Study, Cassell, 1997.

WORK IN PROGRESS: Research on Islam in Bangladesh and among Bangladeshis in Britain.

SIDELIGHTS: Clinton Bennett told *CA:* "Most academics will be familiar with the phrase 'publish or perish.' There is an expectation that we write. Research is also a contractual obligation. I would be less than honest to say that this does not contribute at all to my motivation for writing! I enjoy writing, however, and I only research and write in areas that I think are relatively neglected.

"My first book, *Victorian Images of Islam,* argued that some Western writers questioned the prevailing attitude of cultural and religious superiority that led to a belittling of everything non-European. My second book *In Search of the Sacred* combined my interest in methodology in religious studies generally with a specific focus on anthropology. This book, which seems to have filled a gap, was built on my teaching. My collaborative book *Researching Teaching Methods* drew on my use of small-scale, qualitative research that I performed because I wanted more exposure to social research methodology.

"I think that academic writing can be fun. I dislike dry, multiple-footnoted, impersonal prose. Clifford Geertz has influenced me enormously. So have postmodern writers, especially Michel Foucault and (dare I admit this?) Salman Rushdie. My new book on Muhammad explores the insider/outsider issue. Does any text have a single, true meaning that can be discussed, or are all of our readings mediated by the hermeneutical lenses we wear? I hope this book has something worthwhile to say."

*   *   *

BENSON, E(dward) F(rederic)   1867-1940

PERSONAL: Born July 24, 1867, in Wellington College, Shropshire, England; died February 29, 1940; son of E. W. (a clergyman who became Archbishop of Canterbury) and Mary Benson. *Education:* Attended Marlborough College, Wiltshire; graduated from King's College, Cambridge, with first-class honors, 1891. *Avocational interests:* Skating.

CAREER: Editor of the *Marlburian* while at Marlborough College; British School of Archaeology, Athens, Greece, staff member, 1892-95; Society for the Promotion of Hellenic Studies, Egypt, staff member,

1895; freelance writer, 1895-1940; mayor of Rye, Sussex, England, 1934-37.

AWARDS, HONORS: Named a Wortz student and a Prendergast and Craven student; named honorary fellow of Magdalene College, Cambridge, 1938.

WRITINGS:

NOVELS

Dodo, D. Appleton (New York, NY), 1893.
The Rubicon, 1894.
The Judgment Books, 1895.
Limitations, 1896.
The Babe, B.A., 1896; Garland (New York, NY), 1984.
The Vintage, 1898.
The Money Market, 1898.
The Capsina, 1899.
Mammon and Co., 1899.
The Princess Sophia, 1900.
The Luck of the Vails, 1901.
Scarlet and Hyssop, 1902.
The Book of Months, 1903.
The Valkyries, 1903.
The Relentless City, 1903.
An Act in a Backwater, 1903.
The Challoners, 1904.
The Angel of Pain, 1905.
The Image in the Sand, 1905.
Paul, 1906.
The House of Defence, 1906.
Sheaves, 1907.
The Blotting Book, 1908, Arno Press (New York, NY), 1976, Hogarth Press (London, England), c. 1987.
The Climber, 1908.
A Reaping, 1909.
Daisy's Aunt, 1910; also published as *The Fascinating Mrs. Halton,* 1910.
Margery, 1910.
The Osbornes, 1910.
Juggernaut, 1911.
Account Rendered, 1911.
Mrs. Ames, 1912; with introduction by Stephen Pile, Hogarth Press, 1984.
The Weaker Vessel, 1913.
Dodo's Daughter, 1913.
Thorley Weir, 1913.
Dodo the Second, 1914.
Arundel, 1914.
The Oakleyites, 1915.
David Blaize, Hodder and Stoughton (London, En-

gland), 1916; with introduction by Peter Burton, Hogarth Press (London, England), 1989.
Mike, 1916; also published as *Michael,* 1916.
The Freaks of Mayfair, 1916; illustrated by George Plank, Books for Libraries (Freeport, NY), 1971.
Robin Linnet, 1916.
An Autumn Sowing, 1916.
Mr. Teddy, 1917; also published as *The Tortoise,* 1917.
Up and Down, 1918.
David Blaize and the Blue Door, 1918.
Across the Stream, 1919.
Queen Lucia, 1920, with foreword by Micheal Mac Liammoir, Heinemann (London, England), 1970; with foreword by Nancy Mitford, Perennial Library (New York, NY), c. 1977.
Lovers and Friends, 1921.
Dodo Wonders, 1921.
Miss Mapp, 1922; with foreword by Mac Liammoir, Heinemann; with foreword by Mitford, Perennial Library, c. 1977.
Peter, 1922.
Colin, Hutchinson (London, England), 1923; with introduction by Peter Burton, Millivres (Brighton, England), 1994.
David of King's, 1924.
Alan, 1924.
Rex, 1925.
Colin II, 1925.
Mezzanine, 1926.
Pharisees and Publicans, 1926.
Lucia in London, 1927; Heinemann, 1968; foreword by Nancy Mitford, Perennial Library, 1987.
Paying Guests, 1929; introduction by Pile, Hogarth Press, 1984.
The Step, 1930.
The Inheritor, 1930.
Mapp and Lucia, 1931, Heinemann, 1967; Perennial Library, 1987.
Secret Lives, 1932.
Travail of Gold, 1933.
Ravens' Brood, 1934.
Lucia's Progress, 1935; Heinemann, c. 1967; also published as *The Worshipful Lucia,* 1935; with foreword by Nancy Mitford, Perennial Library, c. 1977.
Old London, 1937.
Trouble for Lucia, 1939; Heinemann, 1968; foreword by Mitford, Perennial Library, c. 1977.

SHORT STORY AND NOVEL COLLECTIONS

A Double Overture, 1894.
The Room in the Tower and Other Stories, 1912.

The Countess of Lowndes Square and Other Stories, 1920.

Visible and Invisible, G. H. Doran Co. (New York, NY), c. 1924.

Spook Stories, 1928; Arno Press (New York, NY), 1976.

More Spook Stories, 1934.

Make Way for Lucia (includes *Queen Lucia, Lucia in London, Mapp and Lucia, Miss Mapp, The Worshipful Lucia,* and *Trouble for Lucia*), Crowell (New York, NY), c. 1977; Harper & Row (New York, NY), 1986.

Dodo (contains *Dodo, Dodo the Second,* and *Dodo Wonders*), Crowell, c. 1978.

The Tale of an Empty House and Other Ghost Stories, edited by Cynthia Reavell, 1986.

The Flint Knife: Further Spook Stories, edited by Jack Adrian, 1988.

Lucia Rising (contains *Queen Lucia, Miss Mapp,* and *Lucia in London*), Penguin (London, England), 1991.

Desirable Residences and Other Stories, edited by Jack Adrian, Oxford University Press, 1991.

The Collected Ghost Stories, edited by Richard Dalby, Caroll & Graf (New York, NY), c. 1992.

Fine Feathers and Other Stories, selected and introduced by Adrian, Oxford University Press, 1994.

Also contributor of short stories to periodicals.

PLAYS

Aunt Jeannie, 1902.

Dodo: A Detail of the Day (adapted from his novel, *Dodo*), produced in 1905.

The Friend in the Garden, produced in 1906.

Westward Ho! (adapted from the novel by Charles Kingsley), with music by Philip Napier Miles, produced in 1913.

Dinner for Eight, (produced in 1915), 1915.

The Luck of the Vails (adapted from his novel), produced in 1928.

OTHER

Six Common Things, 1893.

(With E. H. Miles) *Daily Training,* 1902.

The Mad Annual, edited by E. H. Miles, 1903.

(Editor, with E. H. Miles) *A Book of Golf,* 1903.

(Editor, with E. H. Miles) *The Cricket of Abel, Hirst, and Shrewsbury,* 1903.

Two Generations, 1904.

(With E. H. Miles) *Diversions Day by Day,* 1905.

English Figure Skating, 1908.

Bensoniana, 1912.

Winter Sports in Switzerland, 1913.

Deutschland ueber Allah, 1917.

Poland and Mittel-Europa, 1918.

The White Eagle of Poland, 1918.

Crescent and Iron Cross, G. H. Doran (New York, NY), 1918.

Our Family Affairs, 1867-1896, 1920.

Mother, 1925.

Sir Francis Drake, 1927.

The Life of Alcibiades, 1928.

Ferdinand Magellan, 1929.

The Male Impersonator, 1929.

(Editor) *Henry James: Letters to A. C. Benson and Auguste Monod,* Scribner (New York, NY), 1930; Haskell House (New York, NY), 1969; Folcroft Library Editions (Folcroft, PA), 1973.

As We Were: A Victorian Peep-Show, 1930; Hogarth Press, c. 1986.

As We Are: A Modern Revue, 1932; Hogarth Press, c. 1986.

Charlotte Bronte, 1932; B. Blom (New York, NY), 1971.

King Edward VII, 1933.

The Outbreak of War, 1914, 1933.

Queen Victoria, 1935.

The Kaiser and English Relations, 1936.

Queen Victoria's Daughters, 1938.

Final Edition: Informal Autobiography, 1940.

ADAPTATIONS: The "Lucia" books were made into television films and aired on the British Broadcasting Corporation (BBC) in England and on the Public Broadcasting System (PBS) in the United States.

SIDELIGHTS: British author E. F. Benson had a long and prolific career, writing novels, plays, and short stories in several genres as well as biographies and other works of nonfiction. His first novel, *Dodo,* saw print approximately eight years before the end of Queen Victoria's reign, while his last, *Trouble for Lucia,* became available to readers as the Second World War was beginning. Several of Benson's books—including his biography of Victorian novelist Charlotte Bronte—have seen reprints during the last few decades, and new collections of his short stories were issued during the 1990s. Benson is probably best remembered, however, for his novels about the dominating socialite Emmeline Lucas, better known as Lucia. These titles include *Queen Lucia, Lucia in London,* and *Mapp and Lucia.* The novels—along with other "Lucia" tales—were published together by Crowell in one volume as *Make Way for Lucia* in 1977. "In these novels, written between 1920 and

1939," wrote Peter Matthews in *America,* "Benson has created a small world consisting of two British villages and populated that world with characters so idiosyncratic and so improbable that they must have been based on real people. . . . The result is compulsive reading."

The author was born Edward Frederic Benson into a distinguished English Victorian family in 1867. His father became the Archbishop of Canterbury, which is the highest office within the Anglican Church. His brothers, Arthur C. Benson and Robert Hugh Benson, were both writers of some note as well—Arthur composed the lyrics to the British patriotic song "Land of Hope and Glory," and Robert was a well-known Catholic apologist who wrote a famous history of Catholic martyrs in England during and after the reign of Elizabeth I. E. F. Benson, however, spent his early years after completing his university education working as a staff member of the British School of Archaeology in Athens, Greece, and the Society for the Promotion of Hellenic Studies in Egypt. He left both these organizations in 1895 to become a full-time author, having already published three books.

Benson never married, and most biographers have assumed that he was homosexual. There were many gay men among his friends and acquaintances, but as Francis King noted in the *Spectator:* "The question inevitably posed . . . is 'Did he or didn't he?'. . . . [The answer] can only be an equivocal 'Well, probably.'" King added that "where so much is surmise, it is difficult to give either an extended or a coherent account of Benson's personal life."

Dodo, Benson's first novel, was immediately and extremely popular when it was published in 1893. According to King, its heroine, Dodo (short for Dorothea) was based on the historical figure of Margot Asquith. The story details Dodo's adventures through two ill-fated marriages before she finally comes to her senses and weds her longtime friend Jack. Benson adapted the novel as a play in 1905, and followed *Dodo* with sequels, including *Dodo the Second* and *Dodo Wonders.*

The first is about Dodo's daughter, who nearly makes the same mistakes as her mother, and the second finds Dodo content with family and friends but anxious over the ways World War I has affected all of their lives. All three works were published in one volume under the title *Dodo* in 1978. There is some disagreement as to whether this trilogy of Benson's bears reading in our own time. A 1978 *Publishers Weekly*

review pointed out flaws in the books about Dodo, but also observed that they display "a fair measure of the irony, psychological penetration and glittering small talk for which the author is noted." A critic in the *New Yorker* the following year concluded that "the trilogy will always find, and deserve, new admirers."

The last Dodo novel overlapped the first about Lucia by a year. In 1920, Benson introduced what many agree to be his most memorable character. Lucia, according to Auberon Waugh in the *New York Times Book Review,* is "a superbly ridiculous woman" who "surrounds herself with a court of sycophants, charlatans, jealous neighbors and downright rivals." Waugh went on to explain that "it is from the dramas of their incredibly petty existence that Benson constructs a comedy that is as exquisite, in its way, as anything in English humorous literature." Also featured prominently in the "Lucia" series is the protagonist's best friend Georgie Pillson—an effeminate bachelor proficient in needlepoint and piano duets—and Miss Mapp, a social dominatrix far more evil and less sympathetic than Lucia herself.

In the course of the series, Lucia moves to the town of Tilling, which is Miss Mapp's domain and which is based on the town of Rye in Sussex, England. There, she overthrows Miss Mapp as the leading lady of society. Though Lucia and Georgie (after Lucia is widowed) eventually marry, "there is," in the words of Walter Clemons in *Newsweek,* "a finely gauged scene in which they sound each other out about a union without unwelcome 'connubialities.' Sex in these books is evaded by the characters, not ignored by the author." In addition to marrying Georgie, Lucia also eventually becomes the mayor of Tilling. In this way, her life somewhat parallels that of her creator; Benson served as the mayor of Rye from 1934 to 1937.

Great critical enthusiasm has greeted every reprint of the Lucia novels, both individually and as collected in *Make Way for Lucia.* Alan Brien, opining in a 1971 issue of the *New Statesman* on the subject of *Lucia's Progress,* asserted that the novel was "excellent light reading . . . whimsical but intelligent." Speaking of *Make Way for Lucia,* Waugh reported that "without this reissue I might have gone to my grave without ever knowing about Lucia or Miss Mapp. It is not a risk anyone should take lightly." Matthews pronounced: "Before we know it we have been snared; we develop a passionate interest in the characters, their activities, and even their gossip." Martin Seymour-Smith, reviewing *Lucia's Progress* and *Mapp and Lucia* in a 1967 issue of the *Spectator* lauded the author, praising "a trueness about his observations that makes them worth reading again." Speaking of a passage in which Lucia herself considers becoming a novelist but declines, thinking "perhaps there were enough geniuses already," Clemons concluded that "Benson was at least mildly infected by genius."

Other key works in Benson's oeuvre include 1912's *Mrs. Ames,* and the 1916 effort, *David Blaize.* Stephen Pile, who wrote the introduction to a 1984 edition of *Mrs. Ames,* labeled it *"Madame Bovary* played for laughs." Alan Brien in the *New Statesman* hailed *Mrs. Ames* as "undoubtedly Benson's masterpiece, a classic of discreetly barbed comedy."

Benson is also important in literary history for his contributions to the genres of mystery and horror fiction. A *Washington Post Book World* critic labeled Benson's *The Blotting Book,* first published in 1908, "one of the progenitors of . . . British mystery." Charlotte Mitchell, discussing *The Collected Ghost Stories* of Benson in the *Times Literary Supplement,* judged that "their charm comes out of the tension between an agreeable setting and a lurking anxiety."

BIOGRAPHICAL/CRITICAL SOURCES:

BOOKS

Benson, E. F., *Make Way for Lucia,* Crowell (New York, NY), c. 1977.
Benson, E. F., *Mrs. Ames,* Hogarth Press (London, England), 1984.
Masters, Brian, *The Life of E. F. Benson,* Chatto & Windus (London, England), 1991.

PERIODICALS

America, February 18, 1978, pp. 125-126.
New Statesman, August 20, 1971, p. 234; February 10, 1984, pp. 24-25.
Newsweek, July 4, 1977, p. 73.
New Yorker, February 12, 1979, p. 118.
New York Times Book Review, August 7, 1977, pp. 1, 27.
Publishers Weekly, October 30, 1978, p. 40.
Spectator, December 1, 1967, pp. 684-685; August 17, 1991, p. 27.
Times Literary Supplement, January 1, 1993, p. 18.
Washington Post Book World, June 28, 1987, p. 12.*

                                  —Sketch by Elizabeth Wenning

BENT, Timothy (David)   1955-

PERSONAL: Born November 9, 1955, in Cedar Rapids, IA; son of Fredrick T. (a professor) and Nancy P. (a college English teacher) Bent; married Lucinda Karter (a director of foreign rights), May 21, 1994. *Ethnicity:* "White." *Education:* Cornell University, A.B., 1978; Harvard University, A.M., 1980, Ph.D., 1986. *Politics:* Liberal. *Religion:* Unitarian-Universalist. *Avocational interests:* Travel.

ADDRESSES: Home—39 West 76th St., Apt. 5F, New York, NY 10023. *Office*—Arcade Publishing, 141 Fifth Ave., New York, NY 10010; fax 212-353-8148. *Agent*—Miriam Altshuler, R.R. 1, Box 5, 5 Old Post Rd., Red Hook, NY 12571.

CAREER: Penguin USA (publisher), New York City, assistant to the chief executive officer, 1990-91; Arcade Publishing, New York City, senior editor, 1991—.

WRITINGS:

(Translator) *Henry Miller: The Paris Years,* Arcade Publishing (New York City), 1996.
(Translator) *The Lost Museum,* HarperCollins (San Francisco, CA), 1997.

Co-translator of the book *Memoir in Two Voices,* Arcade Publishing.

                         *   *   *

BERDYAEV, Nicolas (Alexandrovitch)
   See BERDYAEV, Nikolai (Aleksandrovich)

                         *   *   *

BERDYAEV, Nikolai (Aleksandrovich)   1874-1948

PERSONAL: Name is pronounced "ber-*dya*-ef"; sometimes transliterated as Nicolas (Alexandrovitch) Berdyaev or Berdyayev; born March 19 (one source says March 6), 1874, in Kiev, Russia; immigrated to Clamart, France, in the 1920s; died March 23, 1948, in Paris, France; son of Princess Kudashev; married Lydia Yudifovna (some sources say Lydia Tushev or Lydia Troucheva), 1904. *Education:* Attended the Academy of Kiev and the University of Kiev, from which he was expelled in 1898.

CAREER: Philosopher. Co-editor, with Sergy Bulgakov, of *Novy'put* (title means "New Way"), a radical political and religious journal; established the Free Academy of Spiritual Culture in Moscow in 1918; appointed to the chair of philosophy at the University of Moscow in 1920; exiled from Russia in 1922; worked for the Y.M.C.A. in Berlin, Germany, and founded the Academy of Philosophy and Religion; emigrated to Paris in 1926, where he re-established his academy and started a review entitled *Putji* (title means "The Way"), serving as editor, 1926-39 (one source says 1925-40).

AWARDS, HONORS: Honorary Doctor of Divinity, Cambridge University, England, 1947.

WRITINGS:

Sub"ektivizm i individualizm v obshchestvennoi filosofii: Kriticheskii etiud o N.K. Mikhailovskom (title means "Subjectivism and Individualism in Social Philosophy: A Critical Study of N. K. Mikhailovskii"), O.N. Popova (St. Petersburg, Russia), 1901.

Novoe religioznoe sozdanie i obshchestvennost' (title means "The New Religious Work and the Public"), M.V. Pirozhkov, 1907.

Sub Specie Aeternitatis: Opyty filosopkie, sotsial'nye i literaturnye, 1900-1906 (title means "Sub Specie Aeternitatis: Philosophical, Social and Literary Essays, 1900-1906"), M.V. Pirozhkov (St. Petersburg), 1907.

Dukhovnyi krizis intelligentsii (title means "The Religious Crisis of the Intelligentsia"), Public Benefit Publishing House (St. Petersburg), 1910.

Aleksei Stepanovich Khomiakov, Put' (Moscow, Russia), 1912.

Filosofiia svobody (title means "The Philosophy of Freedom"), Put' (Moscow), 1912.

Dusha Rossii (title means "The Soul of Russia"), I.D. Sytin (Moscow), 1915.

Smysl tvorchestva: Opyt opravdaniia cheloveka, Leman and Sakharov (Moscow), 1916, published as *The Meaning of the Creative Act,* Harper (New York), 1954.

Nationalizm i imperializm (title means "Nationalism and Imperialism"), Leman and Sakharov (Moscow), 1917.

Nationalizm i messianizm (title means "Nationalism and Messianism"), Leman and Sakharov (Moscow), 1917.

Krizis iskusstva (title means "The Crisis in Art"), Leman and Sakharov (Moscow), 1918.

Sud'ba Rosii: Opyty po psikhologii voiny i nat- *sional'nosti* (title means "The Fate of Russia: Attempts at a Psychology of War and Nationality"), Leman and Sakharov (Moscow), 1918.

Filosofiia Dostoevskogo, Epokha (Petrograd, USSR), 1921, published as *Dostoevskii: An Interpretation,* Sheed and Ward (London, England), 1926.

Konets renessansa (title means "The End of the Renaissance"), Epokha (Petrograd), 1922.

Filosofiia neravenstva: Pis'ma k nedrugam po sotsial'noi filosofii (title means "The Philosophy of Inequality: Letters to My Foes on Social Philosophy"), Obelisk (Berlin, Germany), 1923.

Smysl istorii: Opyt filosofii cheloveckestkoi sud'by, Obelisk (Berlin), 1923, published as *The Meaning of History,* Scribner (New York), 1936.

Novoe srednevekov'e. Razmyshlenie o sud'be Rossii i evropy, Obelisk (Berlin), 1924, published as *The End of Our Time, Together with an Essay on the "General Line" of Soviet Philosophy,* Sheed and Ward (London and New York), 1933.

Konstantin Leont'ev, YMCA Press (Paris), 1926, translation by George Reavey published as *Leontiev,* Bles (London), 1940.

Filosofiia svobodnogo dukha, two volumes, YMCA Press (Paris), 1927-28, published as *Freedom and the Spirit,* Scribner (New York), 1935, new translation by Oliver Fielding Clarke, Books for Libraries Press (Freeport, NY), 1972.

O dostoinstve krhistianstva i nedostoinstve khristian (title means "On the Virtue of Christianity and the Unworthiness of Christians"), YMCA Press (Paris), 1928.

Marksizm i religiia. Religiia, kak orudie gospodstva i ekpluatatsii (title means "Marxism and Religion: Religion as an Instrument of Domination and Exploitation"), YMCA Press (Paris), 1929.

Krhistianstvo i klassovaia bor'ba, YMCA Press (Paris), 1931, published as *Christianity and Class War,* Sheed and Ward (London and New York), 1933.

O naznachenii cheloveka: Opyt paradoksal'noi etiki, Sovremennye Zapiski (Paris), 1931, published as *The Destiny of Man,* Harper (New York), 1937, translation by Natalie Duddington, Hyperion Press (Westport, CT), 1979.

O samoubiistve. Psikhologicheskii etiud (title means "On Suicide: A Psychological Study"), YMCA Press, 1931.

The Russian Revolution: Two Essays on Its Implications in Religion and Philosophy, Sheed and Ward (London and New York), 1931.

Russkaia religioznaia psikhologiia i kommunisticheskii ateizm (title means "Russian Religious Psychology and Communist Atheism"), YMCA Press (Paris), 1931.

(With others) *Vital Realities,* Macmillan (New York), 1932.

The Bourgeois Mind, and Other Essays, Sheed and Ward (London and New York), 1934.

Ia i mir ob"ektov: Opyt filosofii odinochestva i obshcheniia, YMCA Press (Paris), 1934, translation by George Reavey published as *Solitude and Society,* Scribner (New York), 1938.

Sud'ba cheloveka v sovremennom mire, YMCA Press (Paris), 1934, published as *The Fate of Man in the Modern World,* Morehouse (Milwaukee, WI), 1935.

Dukh i real'nost'. Osnovy bogochelovecheskoi dukhovnosti, YMCA Press (Paris), 1937, published as *Spirit and Reality,* Scribner (New York), 1939.

O rabstve i svobode cheloveka: Opyt personalisticheskoi filosofii, YMCA Press (Paris), 1939, published as *Slavery and Freedom,* Scribner (New York), 1939.

Russkaia ideia: Osnovnye problemy russkoi mysli XIX veka i nachala XX veka, YMCA Press (Paris), 1946, published as *The Russian Idea,* Bles (London), 1947, Macmillan (New York), 1948, new translation by R. M. French, Lindisfarne, 1992.

Opyt eskhatologicheskoi metafiziki: Tvorchestvo i ob"ektivatsii, YMCA Press (Paris), 1947, published as *The Beginning and the End: An Essay on Eschatological Principles,* Harper (New York), 1952; new translation by R. M. French, Greenwood Press (Westport, CT), 1976.

Au seuil de la nouvelle epoque, Bles (London), 1949, published as *Towards a New Epoch,* Norwood Editions (Norwood, PA), 1976.

The Divine and the Human, Bles (London), 1949.

Samopoznanie: Opyt filosofskoi avtobiografii, YMCA Press (Paris), 1949, published as *Dream and Reality: An Essay in Autobiography,* Bles (London), 1950, Macmillan (New York), 1951.

Tsarstvo dukha i tsarstvo kesaria, YMCA Press (Paris), 1949, translation by Donald A. Lowrie published as *The Realm of the Spirit and the Realm of Caesar,* Harper (New York), 1953.

Truth and Revelation, Harper (New York), 1953.

Istoki i smysl russkogo kommunizma, YMCA Press (Paris), 1955, published as *The Origin of Russian Communism,* Bles (London), 1955, University of Michigan Press, 1960.

Christian Existentialism: A Berdiaev Anthology, edited by Donald A. Lowrie, Harper (New York), 1965.

Sobranie sochinenii, YMCA Press (New York), 1983.

Aforizmy: entsiklopediia po Berdiaevu, Sam & Sam, 1985.

Eros i lichnost: filosofiia pola i liubbvi, Izd-vo Prometei (Moscow), 1989.

Tipy religioznoi mysli v Rossii, YMCA Press (Paris), 1989.

Dukhovnye osnovy russkoi revoliutsii; Filosofiia neravenstva, YMCA Press (Paris), 1990.

Teosofiia i antroposofiia v Rossii, Menedzher (Moscow), 1991.

N. A. Berdiaev o russkoi filosofii, Izd-vo Uralskogo universiteta (Sverdlovsk), 1991.

Filosofiia tvorchestva, kultury i iskusstva, Izd-vo Iskusstvo (Moscow), 1994.

Also contributor of articles to *Neue Zeit* (edited by Karl Kautsky); contributor to the anthology *Milestones* (1907).

SIDELIGHTS: Nikolai Berdyaev was a religious philosopher whose brand of Christian existentialism fell between what he considered the spiritual errors of atheistic existentialism and the social errors of Russian orthodoxy. Berdyaev was influenced by Marxism early in his life; he was attracted by its social activism and its utopian vision of an era at the end of history when the ills caused by class would be at an end. But he found that Marxism, like atheistic existentialism, traps humanity in history and in time by denying the spiritual element in human makeup. Soon after his adult conversion to the Russian Orthodox Church, however, Berdyaev realized that the church was rotten with a corrupt bureaucracy.

Because of these experiences, Berdyaev turned to other traditions for inspiration. The Christian God who animated Berdyaev's philosophy was borrowed from German Idealism, and thus is "more of an evolving moral principle than a transcendent deity," according to Douglas Kellogg Wood in *Men against Time.* Berdyaev's first book, *Subjectivism and Individualism in Social Philosophy* (1901), attempts to resolve the contradictions between the Marxist conception of history and an ethics based on a Christian god. The book was written while Berdyaev was in internal exile in Vologda, Russia, from 1898 to 1900, for the crime of participating in a large demonstration of Social Democrats. This was also the period of his move away from Marxism and toward a more spiritual orientation in his personal philosophy. This spiritual development culminated in what Wood describes as "a near-conversion to Russian Orthodoxy" in 1907.

But Berdyaev's ultimate conversion was short-lived, despite the influence of his long-time friend Sergy

Bulgakov, an important philosopher of Russian Ortho-doxy. Berdyaev "published a scathing polemic aimed at the hierarchy of the Holy Synod" in 1913, Wood recounted, and was charged with blasphemy, a crime that carried a sentence of life exile in Siberia. But the philosopher's trial was first delayed by the onset of World War I and later abrogated by the Russian Revolution. Berdyaev's support of the revolution, based on his beliefs in social justice, gained him both his freedom and a post at the University of Moscow. When he voiced objections to Lenin's version of Marxism, however, he was arrested and exiled from his homeland in 1922.

Berdyaev and his wife, Lydia Yudifovna, first fled to Germany, where he established his Academy of Philosophy and Religion. When the couple later moved to Paris, France, where they lived out the remainder of their lives, they reestablished the school there. In Paris between World War I and World War II, the author participated in numerous philosophical and religious discussion groups as his philosophy continued to evolve. It was also in France that he wrote most of the books upon which his mature reputation rests.

For his life-long interest in eschatology—an examination of the end of the world as humanity now knows it—Berdyaev is often considered an apocalyptic writer. According to Wood, Berdyaev "believed in the apocalypse because he felt that if the 'world' and 'history' did not come to an end, life would be 'devoid of meaning.'" It is that overarching quest for meaning in life that led Berdyaev to affirm the universal values of the spiritual realm in contrast to what he considered the deadly time-bound values of the atheism that attracted so many of his generation.

While not as well known as such atheistic existentialists as Jean-Paul Sartre, or as influential as Christian existentialist Soren Kierkegaard, Berdyaev nonetheless was considered one of the most important Christian philosophers of the twentieth century and gained a notable audience for his books and theories in Western Europe and the United States.

BIOGRAPHICAL/CRITICAL SOURCES:

BOOKS

Wood, Douglas Kellogg, *Men against Time: Nicolas Berdyaev, T.S. Eliot, Aldous Huxley, and C. G. Jung,* University Press of Kansas, 1982, pp. 27-64.*

BERDYAYEV, Nikolai (Aleksandrovich)
See BERDYAEV, Nikolai (Aleksandrovich)

*   *   *

BERNHARDT, Sarah (Henriette Rosine)   1844-1923

PERSONAL: Born October 22, 1844, in Paris, France; died March 26, 1923, in Paris, France; daughter of Youle Bernard (a seamstress and courtesan); married Jacques Damala, 1882 (separated, 1883); children: (by unknown partner) Maurice. *Education:* Attended convent school in Paris; studied acting at the Paris Conservatoire. c. 1860. *Religion:* Jewish.

CAREER: Actress, playwright, and author of memoirs. Debut on French stage, 1861, at Theatre de la Tour d'Auvergne; actress with Comedie-Francaise, 1862-63 and 1872-80, Gymnase Theatre, 1863-65, Theatre de l'Odeon, Paris, 1866-72, Theatre du Port Saint-Martin, 1882-90, Theatre de la Renaissance, 1893-98, and Theatre Sarah Bernhardt, 1899-1920. Toured the United States 1881, 1887, 1888, 1889, 1892, 1900, and 1916-18 (farewell tour); world tour, 1891-93; also toured Europe and played numerous London engagements through 1921. Co-manager, with son, Maurice, Theatre Ambigu, 1881; declared bankrupt, 1883; manager, Theatre du Porte Saint-Martin, 1883-86; manager, Theatre des Nations (renamed Theatre Sarah Bernhardt), 1899-1923. Organized hospital for wounded at Theatre de l'Odeon during siege of Paris, 1870; raised funds for the wounded in World War I.

Actress in silent films, including *Hamlet's Duel,* 1900, *Tosca,* 1908, *La Dame aux Camelias,* 1911, *Queen Elizabeth,* 1912, *Adrienne Lecouvreur,* 1913, *Jeanne Dore,* 1914, *Meres Francaises,* 1917, and *La Voyante,* 1923. Recordings include *Sarah Bernhardt & the Coquelin Brothers* (dramatic reading in French), 1903-18.

WRITINGS:

Dans les nuages; impressions d'une chaise; recit recueilli par Sarah Bernhardt, illustrated by Georges Clairin, G. Charpentier (Paris), 1878, translated as *In the Clouds,* G. Munro (New York City), 1880.
L'Aveu (one-act play), P. Ollendorff (Paris), 1888.
Adrienne Lecouvreur (six-act play), L'Illustration

(Paris), 1907, bilingual edition, with English translation by Charles Alfred Byrne, F. Rullman (New York), c. 1905.

Ma double vie: memoires de Sarah Bernhardt, Charpentier et Fasquelle (Paris), 1907, translated as *My Double Life: The Memoirs of Sarah Bernhardt,* Heinemann (London), 1907, as *The Memoirs of Sarah Bernhardt,* Appleton (New York City), 1907, as *The Memoirs of Sarah Bernhardt: Early Childhood through the First American Tour,* edited by Sandy Lesberg, Peebles Press (New York City), 1977.

Un Coeur d'homme (play), [Paris], 1911.

La Petite Idole (novel), [Paris], 1920, translated as *The Idol of Paris,* C. Palmer (London), 1921, translated by Mary Tongue, Macaulay (New York City), 1922.

Jolie Sosie (novel), [Paris], 1922.

L'Art du Theatre, edited by Marcel Berger and Georges Ribemont-Dessaignes, [Paris], 1924, translated by H. J. Stenning as *The Art of the Theatre,* preface by James Agate, G. Bles (London), 1924, Books for Libraries Press (Freeport, NY), 1969.

Sarah Bernhardt's Love-Letters to Sardou, translated by Sylvestre Dorian, Haldeman-Julius (Girard, KS), 1924.

Sarah Bernhardt's Philosophy of Love, translated by Sylvestre Dorian, Haldeman-Julius, 1924.

Sarah Bernhardt's Love-Letters to Pierre Berton, translated by Sylvestre Dorian, Haldeman-Julius, 1924.

Also contributor of short stories and articles to periodicals, including "A Christmas Story" for *The Strand Magazine,* December, 1893, and "Men's Roles as Played by Women" for *Harper's Bazaar,* December, 1900.

SIDELIGHTS: Sarah Bernhardt was perhaps the most acclaimed actress of her time, and remains one of the most legendary women to be associated with the stage during the last several centuries. In an age when playwrights such as Henrik Ibsen, George Bernard Shaw, and Anton Chekhov were alive, and esteemed actresses such as Eleanora Duse trod the boards, Bernhardt—"The Divine Sarah"—was indisputably the best-known theatrical personality. Her influence on the popular imagination of her time is paralleled today only, perhaps, by such figures as Marilyn Monroe, Elvis Presley, and the Beatles.

Among the famous men who admired her were Victor Hugo, both William and Henry James, Tchaikovsky,

and Oscar Wilde, who wrote his then-outrageous play *Salome* while under Bernhardt's spell. She herself, on a trip to Italy, inspired her younger rival Duse's choice of an acting career; later she would also experience the triumph of stealing Duse's lover, the Italian poet Gabriele D'Annunzio. Bernhardt was used as a character by Marcel Proust in his novel-cycle *Remembrance of Things Past.* She inspired Puccini, who turned one of the actress' stage roles, *La Tosca,* into a great opera. She made a lifelong impression upon the great British actor Sir John Gielgud, who saw her perform when he was fifteen. Sigmund Freud kept a photograph of Bernhardt on his desk. And American humorist Mark Twain said of her: "There are five kinds of actresses: bad actresses, fair actresses, good actresses, great actresses—and then there is Sarah Bernhardt." Novelist D. H. Lawrence, who saw Bernhardt as a sixty-something-year-old woman when he was twenty-three, wrote, "she is . . . the incarnation of wild emotion which we share with all live things. . . . She represents the primeval passions of woman, and she is fascinating to an extraordinary degree. I could love such a woman myself, love her to madness."

As an actress, Bernhardt was capable of playing both Hamlet—which she did in 1899—and Ophelia—which she had done in 1886. Her interpretation of Hamlet was innovative for presenting the "To be or not to be" speech as a contemplative murmur rather than a declaimed speech; indeed it has been said that the French did not truly appreciate Shakespeare until they saw Bernhardt perform his work. Yet the feelings she inspired transcended her acting; she was perhaps the first of that particularly modern type of celebrity, the person who is famous for being famous, and whose every private action, word, or gesture becomes potential public fodder. "She was the first of the goddesses of popular culture," wrote Ruth Brandon in her biography of the actress, titled *Being Divine.* "She used the media and was used by them in an entirely new way—a way that was to become a familiar feature of twentieth century life . . . but which in Sarah's day was a peculiarity all her own." Brandon goes on to point out that while Bernhardt was almost as well-known as Monroe, she accomplished this before the existence of radio, films, television, and airplanes: traveling by steamship, she appeared in person before millions of people throughout the world.

Significantly, though she came to represent France and French culture in the eyes of the world, Bernhardt was anything but a typical product of a French childhood. Her mother, Youle Bernard, grew up as a middle-class Jewish girl in Holland, but ran away, along with a sister, to find adventure. Youle became a popular, up-market courtesan whose salon attracted such luminaries as Alexandre Dumas, *pere,* and the opera composer Rossini; she also worked as a seamstress. Sarah was born in 1844, and although educated in local convent schools, returned home as a teenager, to join her mother in the family business.

Young Bernhardt had discovered the stage, however, and rather than become a paid prostitute, she used her mother's connection with the Duc de Morny to gain admission as an acting student to the Paris Conservatoire. Her early acting career was unpromising: her contract with the Comedie Francaise, the national theater of France, lasted only six months. A beautiful young woman, tall, slender, and dark-eyed, she used liaisons with men to support herself, a practice she continued even after becoming successful in her stage work.

A big break came at age twenty-two when George Sand, the greatest female novelist of France at that time, noticed Bernhardt and sponsored her at the Left Bank theater the Odeon. There, Bernhardt appeared in contemporary plays by the likes of Victor Hugo, Alexandre Dumas, *fils,* and Sand, as well as those by Racine, Moliere, and Shakespeare. A notable role was in Dumas' *La Dame aux Camelias,* in which she played an unhappy courtesan. Her growing fame enabled her to return to the Comedie Francaise as a star several years later. She would quit that prestigious venue, dissatisfied with the strictures of classical French staging, at age thirty-five, to found her own theater.

Bernhardt's interpretations of classical French plays were particularly influential, for she brought the characters of Racine and Moliere into the realm of romanticism—"thereby effectively changing the plays themselves," according to Eric Salmon in his introduction to *Bernhardt and the Theatre of Her Time.* Her title role in Racine's *Athalie* exemplifies this. Observes Philip Thody in the *International Dictionary of the Theatre,* "she quite renewed the interpretation of the character, playing her not as a violent, tempestuous, externally aggressive tyrant, but employing instead a cool sweetness that allowed Racinian poison to seep through every word."

Salmon, reviewing the contemporaneous accounts of Bernhardt not only by her admirers but by skeptical viewers such as George Bernard Shaw and Anton Chekhov, supposes that Bernhardt's acting was at times excessively melodramatic even for the tastes of the nineteenth century; he also discusses Bernhardt's tendency to use incantatory vocal quality as a means of attaining a kind of abstract beauty rather than a naturalistic portrayal of character. He quotes Shaw, who wrote of "the musical emptiness of Madame Bernhardt's habit of monotonously chanting sentences on one note." Salmon, thus, finds both romantic and classical aspects in Bernhardt's style. Trying to perceive her clearly from the distance of a half-century, he concludes, "She was not only an actress. . . . she was also the founder of a cult and the head of that cult."

The cult was propagated throughout the world by Bernhardt's energetic touring, which set the standard for other performers of that era. She first toured the United States in 1880, and attracted such phenomenal devotion that in six months she had earned a million dollars. In addition to a grueling acting schedule—twenty-seven performances, seven roles, in twenty-seven days—she met Thomas A. Edison and made a recording with him (she read from Racine's *Phedre*), as well as meeting other American celebrities. This was to be only the first of many American tours; the last was conducted during World War I, even though Bernhardt was then quite active in assisting the war effort in France.

The 1880s saw Bernhardt reach the peak of her fame in France in plays written by Victorien Sardou. In leading the traditional singing of "La Marseillaise," the French national anthem, at closing time each night, she moved audiences to tears. Her effect upon even the most sophisticated members of the public was such that, in Vienna in 1889, her performances caused court ladies to faint.

Bernhardt continued performing although her health declined in later years. The loss of her right leg—the result of a mishap that did not cause her to cease performing and touring—is legendary. She survived into the silent film era, enabling modern audiences to glean some inkling of her style even though its full power cannot be appreciated through celluloid. Her acting style, which contained broad, romantic, nineteenth-century gestures, heavily influenced the typical acting style of silent movies. (Duse's more restrained, intimate style is generally considered to be more modern.) Her voice, very imperfectly recorded by sound equipment of her time, was known for its clarity and perfect elocution. Today she is remembered as, in Thody's words, "a totally commanding presence on stage and a woman of considerable culture and independence of mind."

Bernhardt wrote two novels, *Le Petite Idole* and *Jolie Sosie,* neither of which has remained in print. More accessible to modern readers is her memoir, which has gone into several editions and remains a valuable source not only on her own life, but on French theater and the culture of *"la belle epoque."* Her essays on the art of the theater, which have been republished as recently as the 1970s, offer a highly individualistic, but influential expert's glimpse into the aesthetics and stagecraft of a past era. Bernhardt was also responsible for editing—usually by trimming—many of the plays she performed in, often to a play's advantage. She sculpted, she painted—and when she died, tens of thousands followed her funeral procession. Her name remains known as a symbol of the richness, the splendor, and the complacency of the Gilded Age before it fell before the destructive tide of World War I.

BIOGRAPHICAL/CRITICAL SOURCES:

BOOKS

Aston, Elaine, *Sarah Bernhardt: A French Actress on the English Stage,* Berg (Oxford), 1989.

Brandon, Ruth, *Being Divine: A Biography of Sarah Bernhardt,* Secker & Warburg (London), 1991.

Gold, Arthur, and Robert Fizdale, *The Divine Sarah: A Life of Sarah Bernhardt,* Knopf, 1991.

Richardson, Joanna, *Sarah Bernhardt and Her World,* Putnam, 1977.

Salmon, Eric, editor, *Bernhardt and the Theatre of Her Time,* Greenwood Press (Westport, CT), 1984.

Stokes, John, *Bernhardt, Terry, Duse: The Actress in Her Time,* Cambridge University Press (Cambridge), 1988.

Taranow, Gerda, *Sarah Bernhardt: The Art within the Legend,* Princeton University Press, 1972.

Verneuil, Louis, *The Fabulous Life of Sarah Bernhardt,* translated by Ernest A. Boyd, Greenwood Press, 1972.*

*   *   *

BESNER, Hilda F. 1950-

PERSONAL: Born October 30, 1950, in Lima, Peru; U.S. citizen; daughter of Jacob (self-employed; in business) and Hanna (a homemaker; maiden name, Silverman) Besner; married Mark Richard Krueger Colin (a dentist), April 14, 1984; children: Adriana, Hanna. *Ethnicity:* "Rumanian." *Education:* Attended

Duke University, 1968-69; University of Miami, Coral Gables, FL, B.S. (chemistry), 1971; Nova University, M.S. (psychology), 1972, Ph.D. (psychology of behavioral change), 1975. *Avocational interests:* Music, dance, tennis.

ADDRESSES: Office—915 Middle River Dr., Suite 204, Fort Lauderdale, FL 33304; fax 954-561-8331.

CAREER: Washington University, St. Louis, MO, intern in clinical psychology at Malcolm Bliss Mental Health Center, 1975-76; clinical psychologist in private practice, St. Louis, 1976; Bessette, Farinacci and Associates, Fort Lauderdale, FL, clinical psychologist, 1977-81; clinical psychologist in private practice, Fort Lauderdale, 1981—. Dade County Department of Youth and Family Development, clinical psychologist, 1977-78; Southeast Biosocial Institute, director of clinical internship, 1980-81; OptimaCare, vice president, 1994—. Nova University, adjunct professor at Florida School of Professional Psychology, 1979-82. Crisis Intervention Center, president and member of board of directors, 1976-78; Big Brothers/Big Sisters, volunteer, 1976-78; Foundation for Learning, member of board of directors, 1982-84; Sharon Solomon Foundation, member of board of trustees, 1987—.

MEMBER: American Psychological Association, Association for Applied Psychophysiology and Biofeedback, Biofeedback Society of Florida (founding member; past president), Florida Psychological Association, Biofeedback Society of Southeastern Florida (past president), Broward County Psychological Association (past president), Women's Executive Club.

AWARDS, HONORS: Named district woman of the year, National Business and Professional Women, 1983; award from Florida Psychological Association, 1993, for outstanding contribution by a psychologist for community service.

WRITINGS:

(With S. J. Robinson) *Understanding and Solving Your Police Marriage Problems,* C.C. Thomas (Springfield, IL), 1982.

(With A. Besner and T. L. Perez) *Rebuilding,* privately printed, 1992.

(With A. Besner and Perez) *After the Storm,* privately printed, 1992.

(With Charlotte I. Spungin) *Gay and Lesbian Students: Understanding Their Needs,* Taylor & Francis (Bristol, PA), 1995.

(With Spungin) *Training Professionals to Work with Gays and Lesbians in Educational and Workplace Settings* (tentative title), Taylor & Francis, 1997.

Author of "Heat," a monthly column published by Dade County Police Benevolent Association, 1985-86. Contributor to periodicals, including *Journal of Bio-Feedback, Psychotherapy in Private Practice,* and *Police Chief.* Guest reviewer, *Journal for Behavior Therapy and Experimental Psychiatry,* 1977-82.

BIOGRAPHICAL/CRITICAL SOURCES:

PERIODICALS

Contemporary Psychology, vol. 41, no. 10, 1996, p. 1025.

*   *   *

BEY, Pilaff
    See DOUGLAS, (George) Norman

*   *   *

BLAGA, Lucian 1895-1961

PERSONAL: Born May 9, 1895, in Lancram, Transylvania; died May 6, 1961, in Cluj, Romania; son of a Romanian Orthodox priest. *Education:* Graduated from Sibiu Orthodox Seminary; attended University of Vienna.

CAREER: Poet, dramatist, philosopher, and translator. Press attache in Vienna, 1932-39; University of Cluj, Cluj, Romania, professor of philosophy, 1939-49; worked as a librarian and translator, 1949-61. Also served as professor of the theory of culture at University of Sibiu.

AWARDS, HONORS: Awarded Nobel Prize for literature, 1956.

WRITINGS:

POETRY

Poemele luminii (title means "Poems of Light"), 1919, reprinted, edited by George Gana, Editura Prometeu (Bucharest), 1991.

In marea trecere, 1924, translation by Roy Mac-Gregor-Hastie published as *Poems of Light* (bilingual edition; includes partial translations of *In marea trecere* under title *In the Great Passage, Pasii profetulii* under title *In the Footsteps of the Prophet, Lauda somnului* under title *In Praise of Sleep, La cumpana apelor* under title *At the Watershed,* and *La curtile dorului* under title *In the Courtyard of Yearning*), English translations by Don Eulert, Stefan Avadanei, and Mihail Bogdan, Minerva (Bucharest), 1975.

Poezii, edited by Dorli Blaga, Minerva (Bucharest), 1981, translation by Afred Margul-Sperber, edited by Michael Taub, published as *Poezii/Poems,* Department of Romance Languages, University of North Carolina (Chapel Hill), 1983.

Poezii, collected by Marin Mincu, Allbatros (Bucharest), 1983.

At the Court of Yearning: Poems, English translation by Andrei Codrescu, Ohio State University Press (Columbus), 1989.

Also author of volumes of verse, including *Pasii profetului* (title means "In the Footsteps of the Prophet"), 1921; *The Great Transition,* Eminescu Publishing House (Bucharest), 1975; *Lauda somnului* (title means "In Praise of Sleep"), 1929; *La cumpana apelor* (title means "At the Watershed"), 1933; *La curtile dorului* (title means "In the Courtyard of Yearning"), 1938; *Poezii,* 1942; and *Nebanuitele trepte,* 1943.

DRAMA

Mesterul Manole: Drama, 1927, Univers si Teatrul National I. L. Caragiale (Bucharest), 1974.

Teatru, edited by Dorli Blaga, Minerva (Bucharest), 1984.

Teatru (includes *Zamolxe, Tulburarea apelor, Mesterul Manole, Avram Iancu,* and *Anton Pann*), Editura Minerva (Bucharest), 1987.

Also author of plays, including *Zamolxe,* 1921; *Tulbelarea,* 1923; *Daria,* 1925; *Avram Iancu,* 1934; *Opera dramatica,* 1942; *The Troubling of the Waters; Anton Pann; Noah's Ark; These Are Facts* (also titled *Ivanca*); and *The Children's Crusade.* Author of the pantomime *Resurrection.*

PHILOSOPHY

Trilogia culturii (includes *Orizont si stil, Spatiul mioritic,* and *Geneza metaforei si sensul culturii*), 1944, reprinted as *Trilogia culturii Cuvint inainte de Dumitru Ghise,* Editora pentru Literatura Universala (Bucharest), 1969.

Trilogia valorilor, 1946.

Despre constiinta filozofica, Facla (Timisoara), 1974.

Fiinta istorica, Dacia (Cluj-Napoca), 1977.

Incercari filosofice, Facla (Timisoara), 1977.

Also author of philosophy books, including *Orizont si stil,* 1935; *Spatiul mioritic,* 1936; *Genza metaforei si sensul culturii,* 1937; and *Trilogia cunoasterii,* 1943.

COLLECTED WORKS

Opere (title means "Works"), edited by Dorli Blaga, five volumes, Minerva (Bucharest), 1974-77.

Poezii (first of two-volume set), Editura Albatros (Bucharest), 1980.

Teatru [and] *Proza autobiografica* (second of two-volume set), Editura Albatros (Bucharest), 1980.

OTHER

(Compiler) *Antologie de poezie populara,* edited by George Ivascu, Editura pentru Literatura (Bucharest), 1966.

Gindirea romaneasca in Transilvania in secolui al XVIII-lea, Editura Stiintifica (Bucharest), 1966.

Zari si etape, edited by Dorli Blaga, Editura pentru Literatura (Bucharest), 1968.

Experimentul si spiritul matematic, Editura stiintifica (Bucharest), 1969.

Aspecte antropologice, Facla (Bucharest), 1976.

Elanul insulei: Aforisme si insemnari, Dacia (Cluj-Napoca), 1977.

Peisaj si amintire, Editura Sport-Turism (Bucharest), 1988.

Corespondenta, edited by Mircea Cenusa, Dacia (Cluj-Napoca), 1989.

Luntrea lui Caron: Roman, Humanitas (Bucharest), 1990.

Co-founder of the journal *Gindirea* (title means "Thought").

SIDELIGHTS: "Lucian Blaga—poet, philosopher, playwright, essayist, translator—holds a singular position in modern Romanian literature," stated Marcel Cornis-Pop in his afterword for *At the Court of Yearning: Poems,* "comparable to that of [T. S.] Eliot and [Ezra] Pound in the English-speaking countries." Awarded the Nobel Prize for literature in 1956, Blaga was prevented from publishing his own works for the last few years of his life by the Soviets in the Romanian government. Nonetheless, his writings proved influential among Romanian writers, and he is considered one of the great twentieth-century Romanian poets, dramatists, and thinkers. Blaga "belongs to the family of the great modern creators, destined to have a manysided commanding influence over the culture they belong to," declared Edgar Papu in *Romanian Review.* As Miguel de Unamuno and Okakura Kakuro did for Spanish and Japanese culture respectively, Blaga helped establish a literary picture of the modern Romanian character, basing his ideas not on "documents or charters, but [on] the investigation of the life and mythical traditions of the village," Papu continued. "With exceptionally subtle intuition," the reviewer concluded, "he applies to the Romanian people an original philosophy of culture."

Blaga's philosophy of culture is rooted in a deep sense of mystery and draws its essential characteristics from Romanian folk life rather than from classical Western civilization. "In Blaga," stated Dumitru Ghise in *Romanian Review,* "the concept of culture is divorced from and opposed to that of civilization, free from any causal explanation or objective determination, floating . . . mythically in a self-contained world whose scope can only be described by means of abysmal categories." The writer pictured life as a search for the source of all mystery and creation, which he termed the "Great Anonymous," and that culture—unique to each society, created from its environment—was humankind's creative response to that search.

Blaga was aware, Ghise asserted, that his philosophy lacked the sort of scientific basis demanded by Western thinkers and relied to a great extent on mysticism—"to go beyond philosophy proper into the obscure realm of mythosophy." For example, he traced the start of Romanian history from the departure of the Romans from the province of Dacia in the third century. "He claimed that the beginnings of the Romanian people coincided with their 'withdrawal from history' into an ahistorical world where . . . they led an organic existence with a rhythm all its own until the middle of the nineteenth century," explained Keith Hitchins in *Social Change in Romania: Debate on Development in a European Nation.* During this time, Hitchins continued, "there was a rich development in peasant art, village architecture, and popular poetry and music quite apart from the broader European cultural currents." At heart, Ghise avowed, Blaga "was a great humanist. Blaga did not share Spengler's view that culture is the parasitical product of a soul detached from man and subjugating him. On the contrary, Blaga argues that culture is closely linked to man's creative destiny, it is his fulfillment, his particular fine manner of being Man."

Critics find close links between Blaga's poetry and his philosophic views. "Like Siamese twins, with the same blood running in their veins," Ghise stated, "the poet and the philosopher are constantly joined together helping each other or disturbing each other." Although much of his verse is love poetry, the lyrics "are only casually aimed at the beloved," declared Andrei Codrescu in his introduction to *At the Court of Yearning: Poems,* "for their primary purpose is to induce an ecstatic joining with the primal state, a meta-orgasm." Others focus on discovering, understanding, and "a great desire to disappear in the mythic collective unconscious," Codrescu continued. "The emergence out from the mystical night, the reconversion of the nocturnal into light, through integration into the flux of nature," wrote Constantin Ciopraga in the preface to Blaga's *Poems of Light,* "demonstrates the way in which an exultation, characteristic of the Romanian spirit as a whole, triumphs in Blaga."

Blaga also won acclaim for his theatrical works, which echo his fascination with Romanian culture. A. Paleologu, writing in *Romanian Review,* called Blaga's plays works of "tragic genius." The critic pointed out that, although the writer's plays have been classified as Christian works and sometimes draw on Christian themes, in fact they rely primarily on Blaga's own nonchristian philosophy. "What is fundamental in Lucian Blaga's whole work, constituting its original kernel," Paleologu declared, "are its very 'heathen' elements, its heresies." Even in works that deal directly with Christian topics, such as *The Troubling of the Waters* and *The Children's Crusade,* Blaga emphasizes the distinctly Romanian differences—the heretic elements—over the Christian traditions. "The spiritual level of his experiences was a 'heathenism' similar to that of Goethe," Paleologu contended, "constituting the background of a philosophical pantheism analogous . . . to Goethe's."

Critics recognize Blaga's importance in modern Romanian literature and thought. "The presence of Blaga," Papu asserted, "marked one of the richest moments of Romanian culture from which there resulted a strong force of radiation which imparted to contemporary Romanian culture one of its powerfully pronounced directions." However, they also acknowledge that Blaga's influence transcends the Romanian culture he loved. "Blaga is one of the very few philosophers who are genuinely useful in bridging the gap between the Northern and Southern hemispheres of our planet," stated Virgil Nemoianu in *A Theory of the Secondary: Literature, Progress, and Reaction,* "as well as between the heretic, 'primitive,' and early historical modes of thinking and the mature empiricist or rationalist ones. As the globalization of intellectual discourse proceeds," he concluded, "Blaga's philosophy will grow in importance."

BIOGRAPHICAL/CRITICAL SOURCES:

BOOKS

Ciopraga, Constantin, author of preface, *Poems of Light* by Lucian Blaga, Minerva (Bucharest), 1975, pp. 37-58.

Codrescu, Andrei, author of introduction, *At the Court of Yearning: Poems* by Lucien Blaga, Ohio State University Press, 1989, pp. 11-19.

Contemporary Literary Criticism, Volume 75, Gale, 1993.

Cornis-Pop, Marcel, author of afterword, *At the Court of Yearning: Poems,* by Lucien Blaga, Ohio State University Press, 1989, pp. 189-202.

Jowitt, Kenneth, editor, *Social Change in Romania: Debate on Development in a European Nation,* University of California Press, 1978, pp. 140-173.

Nemoianu, Virgil, *A Theory of the Secondary: Literature, Progress, and Reaction,* Johns Hopkins University Press, 1989, pp. 153-70.

PERIODICALS

American Book Review, July-August, 1990, p. 25.

Poetics, April, 1984, pp. 149-69.

Romanian Review, vol. 24, no. 4, 1970, pp. 52-53, 62-64, 81-83, 83-87; vol. 40, no. 5, 1986, pp. 46-54.

Times Literary Supplement, August 24, 1984, p. 938.

World Literature Today, winter, 1977, p. 85; autumn, 1983, p. 625; winter, 1987, p. 89.*

* * *

BOETTICHER, Budd 1916-

PERSONAL: Born Oscar Boetticher, July 29, 1916, in Chicago, IL; son of Oscar Boetticher; married Mary Chelde, 1972. *Education:* Attended Culver Military Academy and Ohio State University. *Avocational interests:* Raising, training and exhibiting Portuguese Lusitano and Spanish Andalusian horses.

ADDRESSES: Office—P.O. Box 1137, Ramona, CA 92065. *Agent*—c/o Directors Guild of America, 7950 West Sunset Blvd., Hollywood, CA 90046.

CAREER: Director, writer, and producer of motion pictures. Assistant to director for Hal Roach Studios, 1941-44; feature director at Columbia Studios, beginning in 1944, at Eagle Lion Studios, beginning in 1954; films include *One Mysterious Night,* Columbia, 1944; *The Missing Juror,* Columbia, 1944; *Youth on Trial,* Columbia, 1944; *A Guy, a Gal, and a Pal,* 1945; *Escape in the Fog,* Columbia, 1945; *The Fleet That Came to Stay* (propaganda film), Paramount, 1946; *Well Done,* a film for President Truman to thank the troops following World War II; *Assigned to Danger,* Eagle Lion, 1948; *Behind Locked Doors,* Eagle Lion, 1948; *Black Midnight,* Monogram, 1949; *The Wolf Hunters,* Monogram, 1949; *Killer Shark,* Monogram, 1950; *The Bullfighter and the Lady,* Republic, 1951; *The Cimarron Kid,* Universal, 1951; *Bronco Buster,* Universal, 1952; *Red Ball Express,* Universal, 1952; *Horizons West,* Universal, 1952; *Blades of the Musketeers,* Howco, 1953; *City Beneath the Sea,* Universal, 1953; *The Man from the Alamo,* Universal, 1953; *Wings of the Hawk,* Universal, 1953; *East of Sumatra,* Universal, 1953; *Seminole,* Universal, 1953; *The Magnificent Matador* (released in England as *The Brave and the Beautiful*), Twentieth Century-Fox, 1955; *The Killer Is Loose,* United Artists, 1955; *Seven Men from Now,* Warner Bros., 1956; *The Tall T,* Columbia, 1957; *Decision at Sundown,* Columbia, 1957; *Buchanan Rides Alone,* Columbia, 1958; (and producer) *Ride Lonesome,* Columbia, 1959; *Westbound,* Warner Bros., 1959; *Comanche Station* (also produced), Columbia, 1960; *The Rise and Fall of Legs Diamond,* Warner Bros., 1960; *A Time for Dying,* Etoile, 1971; (and producer) *Arruza,* Avco Embassy, 1972; and *My Kingdom for . . .* (documentary), Lusitano Productions, 1985. Also director of numerous propaganda films. Traveled to Mexico to learn to torear (bullfight) under Lorenzo Garza and Fermin Espinosa, later served as technical director of bullfight sequences, *Blood and Sand,* Twentieth Century-Fox, 1941. Directed episodes of the television series *Maverick,* ABC, 1958-59. Played the role of Judge Nizetitch, *Tequila Sunrise,* Warner Bros., 1988, and appeared in *American Cinema* (television series), Public Broadcasting Service, 1995, and *Budd Boetticher: One on One* (biography), Sabado Productions, 1991. *Military service:* Served in U.S. military, 1945-47.

MEMBER: Directors Guild of America, Screenwriters Guild of America.

AWARDS, HONORS: Academy Award nomination for best original story, 1951, for *The Bullfighter and the Lady;* Gold Critic's Award, for *Arruza;* Los Angeles Film Critic's Award, for career achievement; Golden Boot Award, for westerns; Guardian Award, British Film Institute; Dallas Great Director Award; American Cinematheque Career Achievement Award; Great Cinema Award, Vienna. Honored with a fifteen week, twenty picture retrospective of Boetticher films in Lisbon, Madrid, Barcelona and Paris.

WRITINGS:

SCREENPLAYS

The Bullfighter and the Lady, Republic, 1951.
The Magnificent Matador, Twentieth Century-Fox, 1955.
Two Mules for Sister Sara, Universal, 1970.
A Time for Dying, Etoile, 1971.
Arruza, Avco Embassy, 1972.
My Kingdom for . . . (documentary), Lusitano Productions, 1982.

BOOKS

When in Disgrace (memoir), Neville, 1989.

WORK IN PROGRESS: Where Are the Elephants?, a memoir, in press; screenplay for *When In Disgrace;* directing as many as four films, including *A Horse for Mister Barnum.*

SIDELIGHTS: Budd Boetticher is known for having directed a series of motion pictures—mostly Westerns—during the 1950s, and for several films about bullfighting, including the fictional *The Bullfighter and the Lady* and the documentary *Arruza,* about the famous Mexican matador Carlos Arruza. That Boetticher became involved in motion pictures was quite accidental. During the late 1930s he attended Culver Military Academy and Ohio State University, starring on their athletic teams. While in Mexico recuperating from a football injury, Boetticher became interested in bullfighting, so much so that he studied the sport under matador Lorenzo Garza and became a professional matador.

Because of Boetticher's knowledge and experience in the bull ring, in 1940 he was asked to become the technical advisor for the motion picture *Blood and Sand,* starring Tyrone Power. This taste of Hollywood led Boetticher to want more, and for several years he worked as a messenger and later assistant to the director at several studios. In 1944 Boetticher began directing his first six films, the majority of them low-budget thrillers, which were released under his original name. These films were learning experiences for Boetticher and the one Western of the bunch appealed to him as a genre.

In 1950 Boetticher reached a turning point. For John Wayne and Republic Pictures, he authored the script and directed *The Bullfighter and the Lady,* which earned an Academy Award nomination for best original story. Based on Boetticher's experiences in the bull ring, the plot revolves around a young matador who is not yet ready for the bull ring, but insists that he must fight—the young man's mentor sacrifices his life to save him. Later the young bullfighter must redeem himself in the ring. The renowned director John Ford helped Boetticher edit the film, and the work was received favorably by critics. This success led to a contract at Universal-International. During this time Boetticher also worked for television on such projects as the pilot for *Maverick* and pilots of other series.

Seven Men From Now was Boetticher's first real commercial success and gained him a measure of critical recognition for its plot twists, irony, and photogenic use of scenery and horses. Boetticher, with Burt Kennedy, wrote and directed a series of Westerns as vehicles for Randolph Scott, who was a partner in the production company, Ranown. These motion pictures—*Seven Men from Now, The Tall T, Buchanan Rides Alone, Ride Lonesome,* and *Comanche Station*—have since become known as the Ranown films. They demonstrate variations on the themes of justice in the Wild West. Most of these films were made in a meager eighteen-day shooting schedule.

In *The Rise and Fall of Legs Diamond* Boetticher deviated from the norm to create a gangster movie set in New York City. He purposefully used lighting and filming techniques reminiscent of the 1920s. The result was a fresh look at the old story of a gangster reaching the top of the underworld heap, only to fall because he has cut all his ties to the past. Although the work was first ignored by critics, it gradually became recognized for its style.

That Boetticher was more than simply enamored by bullfighting was proven by his next step. While he had been working off and on for years on a documentary about the famous Mexican matador Carlos Arruza, in 1960 Boetticher took a great gamble. He went to Mexico to work full time on the film, which turned

into an eight-year ordeal that he later described in *When in Disgrace.* Even after Arruza and most of Boetticher's film crew were killed in an automobile accident, the persistent director turned down lucrative offers from Hollywood to finish his labor of love.

Upon his return to the United States, Boetticher found he was disillusioned with the film industry in Hollywood. His last commercial film was *A Time for Dying,* a Western which war hero and actor Audie Murphy produced. "The truth of the Audie Murphy picture has, much too long, been kept a secret," Boetticher told *CA.* "My dear pal Audie was in great trouble with some very unsavory characters in Las Vegas. Audie didn't drink, smoke or womanize, but he certainly did gamble. He needed a producer's credit, and salary to survive a serious threat. I supplied that for him with *A Time for Dying.* And I would do it again. He was a very special friend."

Boetticher reminisces at length about his colorful career in both the 1991 video *Budd Boetticher: One on One.* In *Booklist,* Candace Smith found *One on One* "an entertaining production" and "a delight for film buffs."

Boetticher told *CA:* "*Bullfighter and the Lady* was my first really successful picture. James Edward Grant's screenplay was completely discarded by both me and Robert Stack. We shot my seventy-eight page treatment. John Ford did not help me edit the completed picture; he destroyed it! I must tell you, immediately, that Jack Ford and I eventually became intimate pals until the day he died. I really learned to love him, but my half-pal/half-enemy John Wayne asked Mr. Ford to cut forty-two minutes out of it because he, and Grant, thought it was (the Duke's words) 'a piece of crap.' Ten years ago UCLA and the Washington Archives put all of those forty-two minutes back, and what you see on today's cassette is what I actually wanted.

"I was nominated for an Academy Award for the 'Best Original Story' of *Bullfighter and the Lady.* Ray Nazzaro typed the script from my hand-written pages, then registered it in both of our names. A great lesson for young writers. If 'we' had won the Oscar, I fully intended to throw Mr. Nazzaro into the bass drum.

"I sold my original screenplay of *Two Mules for Sister Sara* to Universal so that I could continue to work on my 'Arruza' project. Mr. Maltz's script had nothing to do with what I wrote. Mine was a love story. My 'nun' was a nun until the last scene in the picture.

I was seriously considering filming my version as one of my future projects. You wouldn't recognize it. My good friend, Martin Scorcese, asked what I intend to call it. I told him: 'Two Mules for Sister Sara RIGHT!'

"At Universal I never had one day off, except Sundays, during my two-year stint there. My forty week a year contract turned into fifty-two weeks a year. I think nine major films is some sort of a record. Universal was not a director's studio, and I got out of there as soon as I could. My films were very well received, but the studio executives weren't particularly happy with my desire to make each picture better than it should be. I would finish one show on Tuesday; begin a new one the following Friday. They considered my ambition a waste of time and money. Now that was my first real learning experience.

"Another big one was the directing of the film *Blades of the Musketeers*. I received a call from my friend Hal Roach, Jr., that he needed me to make a television show for Magnavox and Ford Motors, to be shown on Thanksgiving day. It was to run fifty-six minutes, and it was to be entitled *The Three Musketeers*. I asked him what chapter. He told me the whole thing; that it was to be scheduled for three days; it was eighty-four pages, and that he didn't have much money to pay me. I did the damn thing in three-and-one-half days, received five hundred dollars for my effort, then departed for Mexico to film *Magnificent Matador* with Anthony Quinn and Maureen O'Hara. When I returned, Universal called to tell me that three of my pictures, in first run, were playing 'right now' on Hollywood Boulevard, and that I, at least, should journey down the street and look at the marquees. It had never happened before. I took their suggestion; made the trip, and decided to go see Marlon Brando in *The Young Lions* playing across the street from my *Man from the Alamo* with Glenn Ford. To my shocked surprise, *Blades of the Musketeers* was the second feature. I telephoned my good friend the following day and suggested he mail me a check for thirty-four thousand, five hundred dollars, my established salary. He told me: 'A deal's a deal!' Then had the audacity to invite me to spend the next weekend on his new yacht—which I had 'bought.'

"Now onto the one thing I have never bothered to correct, and it really upsets me. I did not try to 're-kindle' my career in Hollywood upon my return to the United States (from working on *Arruza* in Mexico). I simply refused to make the kind of junk our beloved industry was turning out! I received seventy-seven shooting scripts the first six months I was home, and it was damn near impossible to finish reading any of them. I do not do filth, pornography, or explosions. Now I am busier than I've ever been in my life, and God willing, I will have four straight pictures to direct. And you can take your sons and daughters to them all.

"The most memorable compliment of my 'rediscovery' was the twenty picture retrospective of fifteen weeks of my films in Lisbon, Madrid, Barcelona and Paris. Mary and I gutted out six of those fifteen weeks, then hurried for home. We had both gotten pretty sick of Budd Boetticher."

BIOGRAPHICAL/CRITICAL SOURCES:

BOOKS

Boetticher, Budd, *When in Disgrace,* Neville, 1989.
Kitses, Jim, editor, *Budd Boetticher: The Western,* [London], 1969.
Kitses, Jim, *Horizons West: Anthony Mann, Budd Boetticher, Sam Peckinpah: Studies of Authorship within the Western,* Indiana University Press (Bloomington, IN), 1970.
Sherman, Eric, and Martin Rubin, *The Director's Event: Interviews with Five American Film-makers: Budd Boetticher, Peter Bogdanovich, Samuel Fuller, Arthur Penn, Abraham Polonsky,* Atheneum (New York), 1970.

PERIODICALS

Booklist, April 1, 1992, p. 1464.
Cinema (Beverly Hills), December, 1968.
Cinema (Los Angeles), fall, 1970.
Film Culture, March/April, 1955; spring, 1963.
Los Angeles Times, November, 29, 1992, pp. 4, 72, 76.
New Left Review, July/August, 1969.
Screen (London), July/August, 1969.
Variety, October 22, 1990, p. 16.

*   *   *

BOGARD, Travis (Miller) 1918-1997

OBITUARY NOTICE—See index for *CA* sketch: Born January 25, 1918, in San Francisco, CA; died of a stroke April 5, 1997, in Berkeley, CA. Professor and author. Bogard spent much of his career analyzing and commenting on the career of the playwright Eugene O'Neill. Educated at the University of California, Berkeley, as well as Princeton, Bogard served in the U.S. Army during World War II and returned to Berkeley, where he began teaching in 1948. Bogard's favorite subject both in teaching and writing was O'Neill. His works on the topic include (as editor) *The Later Plays of Eugene O'Neill* (1967), *Contour in Time: The Plays of Eugene O'Neill* (1972), and (with Jackson R. Byer) he also edited *Selected Letters of Eugene O'Neill,* a series of correspondence between the famed playwright and Kenneth Macgowan. Bogard also wrote *The Tragic Satire of John Webster* (1957), *Modern Drama: Essays in Criticism* (1965), and contributed to *Revels History of Drama in English* (1973). In addition to his writings, Bogard helped preserve the Tao House, O'Neill's former California home. He also formed the first doctoral program in dramatic art at Berkeley.

OBITUARIES AND OTHER SOURCES:

BOOKS

The Writers Directory: 1996-1998, St. James Press (Detroit, MI), 1995.

PERIODICALS

Los Angeles Times, April 11, 1997, p. A18.
New York Times, April 8, 1997, p. B10.

*   *   *

BOYLE, Alistair 1952-

PERSONAL: Born December 16, 1952; married.

ADDRESSES: Office—c/o Knoll Publishers, 200 West Victoria Street, Santa Barbara, CA 93101.

CAREER: Property manager in Los Angeles, CA; freelance writer, 1995—.

WRITINGS:

MYSTERY NOVELS; "GIL YATES" SERIES

The Missing Link, Knoll (Santa Barbara, CA), 1995.
The Con, Knoll, 1996.
The Unlucky Seven, Knoll, 1997.

WORK IN PROGRESS: More Gil Yates private investigator novels, including *Bluebeard's Last Stand,* due in 1998.

SIDELIGHTS: Mystery novelist Alistair Boyle was born in 1952 and serves as a property manager in the Los Angeles, California, area. His first book—and his first book to feature private investigator Gil Yates—is *The Missing Link,* published in 1995. Since then, Boyle has created two more mysteries around this protagonist, *The Con* and *The Unlucky Seven.*

In *The Missing Link,* Malvin Stark, a California man works for his dominating father-in-law and has to deal with a pushy wife. He gains relief from this dreary situation by inventing and fulfilling an exciting nighttime identity—Gil Yates, private investigator. As yet unlicensed, he nevertheless manages to obtain a client—an illegal arms dealer whose bulimic daughter is missing. The reader never meets the daughter, but she is integral to the plot, and one learns more and more about this missing person as Gil (or Malvin) puts together the details of her life. The reader does, however, meet the arms dealer's ex-wife, a waitress who excites Yates' romantic interest.

Several reviewers have observed Gil's resemblance to American humorist James Thurber's fictional character of Walter Mitty, well-known for his flights of fantasy. Others have enjoyed Gil's use of malapropisms such as "fit as a cello" and "the vegetables of my labor." Sybil S. Steinberg in *Publishers Weekly* hailed *The Missing Link* as "inventive, quirky and utterly implausible," further noting of Boyle that "charm oozes from his pages." Rex E. Klett in *Library Journal* lauded the novel as well, citing its humor and romance, and declaring it "a breeze to read."

By the time 1996's *The Con* opens, Stark has managed to acquire a license under the name of his alter ego, Gil Yates. As Yates, he is hired by the director of the Los Angeles Metropolitan Museum of Art to recover a stolen painting by nineteenth-century French Impressionist artist Claude Monet. Despite his continuing (other) life with his irritating wife Dorcas—whom he doesn't leave because he likes his kids—he manages to follow his investigation to exotic ports of call such as London, England, and Zurich, Switzerland with the help of a million-dollar advance from the director. In the course of his travels, Yates mingles, to his increasing confusion, with the often-crooked high stakes players of the art world. As chance would have it, he runs into the man a contributor to *Publishers Weekly* described as his "nemesis"—his first client from *The Missing Link,* the arms dealer Michael Hadaad.

Critical opinion of *The Con* varied somewhat. Brainard lamented that "the plot is really secondary to the Walter Mittyness of it all," and complained about Boyle's puns. A *Kirkus Reviews* critic, however, applauded the return of Gil Yates, and affirmed that *The Con* contained "enough twists, forgeries, double-crosses, and switcheroos to make your head rotate."

The third adventure of Stark/Yates, *The Unlucky Seven,* saw print in 1997. In this novel, Gil Yates is hired by a wealthy businessman who fears he is next on the list of mad bomber, who has been blowing up the world's power elite. A contributor to *Library Journal* noted that "the plot capitalizes on [Yate's] eccentric behavior, naively humorous predicaments, and lucky breaks." In *Booklist,* a reviewer noted that the "thriller . . . is sustained by a refreshingly quirky tone and an offbeat style." And a *Publishers Weekly* critic observed that *The Unlucky Seven* is "another light-hearted and amusing romp . . . Yates's fantasy life is geared just right for mystery fans."

Boyle told *CA:* "'Okay, I admit it. It was a crazy thing to do.'

"That is the start of my first book, *The Missing Link,* and it begins at a meeting of the Southern California Palm Society of which, as a collector of Palms and Cycads, I am a member. I did sit in the back row, and a guy did come up to talk to me while I was reading a *New Yorker.* The rest I made up from there, using bits of people in my acquaintance. The arms dealer is patterned after a man who deceived me in a business transaction. Writing is a stellar way of dealing with your demons.

"As for the part about being a henpecked husband with a wife I secretly refer to as Tyranny Rex—I'm not at liberty to discuss it. My wife won't let me."

BIOGRAPHICAL/CRITICAL SOURCES:

BOOKS

Boyle, Alistair, *The Con,* Knoll, 1996.

PERIODICALS

Booklist, April 15, 1997.
Kirkus Reviews, March 1, 1996, p. 340.

Library Journal, December, 1994, p. 137; March, 1997.
Publishers Weekly, November 21, 1994, p. 71; February 19, 1996, p. 207; February 3, 1997, p. 98.

*   *   *

BROWNING, Robert 1914-1997

OBITUARY NOTICE—See index for *CA* sketch: Born January 15, 1914, in Glasgow, Scotland; died March 11, 1997. Educator and author. Browning was a historian and classicist, whose special areas of interest included Byzantine and Hellenic studies. He was educated at Glasgow University and Balliol College of Oxford University, where he excelled in history and languages and was awarded numerous prizes for his scholarship. During World War II, Browning served as an intelligence officer with the Royal Artillery in Egypt, Italy, Bulgaria, and Yugoslavia. Following a brief stint at Merton College, in Oxford, Browning won appointment as a lecturer at University College, London. He maintained his association with that institution in various capacities until his retirement as professor emeritus of Birbeck College in 1981. During the 1980s and 1990s Browning served as a long-term fellow of the Center for Byzantine Studies, Dunbarton Oaks, in Washington, D.C. He wrote prodigiously throughout his academic career, and his works include articles, catalogs, historical studies, and reference texts. His *Medieval and Modern Greek* (1969; revised edition, 1983) traces the development of the Greek language and exemplifies his greatest academic passion, the study of Greek civilization. An active supporter of the restitution of the Parthenon marbles and vice president of the Association International des Etudes Byzantines, Browning also held leading positions in the Society for the Promotion of Hellenic Studies and the National Trust for Greece, and was a corresponding fellow of the Academy of Athens. In addition to his contributions to encyclopedias and academic journals, Browning served as editor of the *Journal of Hellenic Studies* from 1964 to 1974 and was a member of the editorial board of the Marxist periodical *Past and Present.* His biographical and historical writings include *Justinian and Theodora* (1971), *The Emperor Julian* (1976), *Studies in Byzantine History, Literature and Education* (1977), and *The Byzantine Empire* (1980; revised edition, 1992). Following his retirement from Birbeck College, Browning completed such works as the editorship of *The Greek World, Classical, Byzantine and Modern*

(1985), *History, Language and Literacy in the Byzantine World* (1989), and *Dated Greek Manuscripts from Cyprus,* a 1993 collaboration with C. N. Constantinides.

OBITUARIES AND OTHER SOURCES:

BOOKS

Who's Who, 148th edition, St. Martin's, 1996, p. 261.

PERIODICALS

Times (London), March 11, 1997, p. 27.

*   *   *

BURNETT, Ron 1947-

PERSONAL: Born May 24, 1947, in London, England; married Martha Aspler (a teacher), June 24, 1971; children: Maija, Katie. *Education:* McGill University, B.A. (English), 1968, M.A. (film and communications), 1971, Ph.D. (communications), 1981. *Avocational interests:* Photography.

ADDRESSES: Home—1236 Lakewood Dr., Vancouver, British Columbia, Canada V5L 4M4. *Office*—Emily Carr Institute of Art and Design, 1399 Johnston St., Vancouver, British Columbia, Canada V6H 3R9; fax 604-844-3884. *E-mail*—rburnett@eciad.bc.ca.

CAREER: McGill University, Instructional Communications Centre, Montreal, Quebec, television cameraman, 1968-69; Vanier College, Montreal, Quebec, professor of communications, 1970-82, founder and chair of media, fine arts, photography and theatre department, 1972-75 and 1977-80; LaTrobe University, Melbourne, Australia, professor of film studies, 1983-88; McGill University, Montreal, Quebec, associate professor of cultural studies, 1988-96, director of Graduate Program in Communications, 1990-96; Emily Carr Institute of Art and Design, Vancouver, British Columbia, president, 1996—. Director of documentary videotapes.

MEMBER: La Cinematheque Quebecoise, Film Studies Association of Quebec (founding member), Association des Critques du Cinema (founding member), International Institute of Communications, International Association of Mass Communications, Canadian Communications Association, Film Studies Association of Canada (founding executive member), Society for Cinema Studies, American Anthropology Association, Society for Visual Anthropology, Society for Cultural Anthropology, Asian Film Studies Association, Australia-New Zealand Society for Canadian Studies.

AWARDS, HONORS: Grants from Canada Council and Social Sciences and Humanities Research Council of Canada.

WRITINGS:

(Contributor) Barry Grant, editor, *In Film in the Undergraduate Curriculum,* M.L.A. (New York City), 1983.

(Contributor) Pierre Veronneau, editor, *A La Recherche d'Une Identite: Renaissance du Cinema d'Autuer Canadien-Anglais,* Cinematheque Quebecoise (Montreal, Quebec), 1991.

(Contributor) Real Larochelle, editor, *Quebec/Canada: L'enseignement du Cinema et de L'audiovisuel,* CinemaAction Books (Paris, France), 1991.

(Contributor) Nancy Thede and Alain Ambrosi, editors, *Video in the Changing World,* Black Rose Books (New York City), 1991.

(Editor and author of introduction) *Explorations in Film Theory,* Indiana University Press (Bloomington, IN), 1991.

(Contributor) William Dodge, editor, *Boundaries of Identity: A Quebec Reader,* Malcolm Lester (Toronto, Ontario), 1992.

(Contributor) Marc Glassman, editor, *Speaking Parts: Atom Egoyan,* Coach House Press (Toronto, Ontario), 1993.

Cultures of Vision: Images, Media and the Imaginary, Indiana University Press, 1995.

(Contributor) Janine Marchessault, editor, *Mirror Machine: Video in the Age of Identity,* XYZ Publications (Toronto, Ontario), 1995.

(Contributor) Michael Renov and Erika Suderberg, editors, *Resolutions: Essays on Contemporary Video Practices,* University of Minnesota Press (Minneapolis, MN), 1996.

(Contributor) George E. Marcus, editor, *Connected: Engagements with Media at the End of the Century,* University of Chicago Press (Chicago, IL), 1996.

Contributor to periodicals, including *Material History Review, On Track: Alliance for Community Media Journal, Zebra News, Basilisk Electronic Journal,*

Fifth Column, and *Canadian Journal of Communications.* Founder and editor in chief, *Cine-Tracts,* 1976-83; founding member of editorial board of the electronic journal *International Journal of Media and Communications;* member of editorial board, *Iris,* 1984-88, *Cinema Papers,* 1988-89, *Continuum,* 1989-92 and 1996—, *Canadian Journal of Film Studies,* 1990-93, Laval University's *Communications,* 1991—, *International Journal of Communications,* 1994—, and *ARENA Journal,* 1994—.

WORK IN PROGRESS: Countries of the Mind, a novel, completion expected in 1998; associate producer of a television mini-series, *The Prisoner,* based on an idea developed by Burnett; research on "telecommunities—culture and hypermedia."

SIDELIGHTS: Ron Burnett told *CA:* "My main motivation for writing is my love of the English language and my attachment to stimulating ideas. The main influences on my work are Italo Calvino, Roland Barthes, Milan Kundera, and Salman Rushdie. I believe there is room for informed debate on cultural issues through innovative writing. I am as comfortable with fiction as with the essay format."

*   *   *

BUSH, Ian (Elcock) 1928-1986

PERSONAL: Born May 25, 1928, in Bristol, England; immigrated to the United States, 1964; naturalized American citizen; died of cancer, November 1, 1986, in Hanover, NH; son of Gilbert B. and Jean Margaret (Elcock) Bush; married Alison Mary Pickard, August 26, 1951 (divorced, 1966); married Joan Morthland, September 16, 1967 (divorced, 1972); married Mary Calder Johnson, 1982; children: (first marriage) Charles Fabian, Philippa Seguineau, Caroline E.; (second marriage) Andrew E., Georgia. *Education:* University of Cambridge, M.A., 1949, Ph.D., 1952, M.B.B.Chir., 1957. *Avocational interests:* Music, chess, sailing, fishing, philosophy.

CAREER: St. Mary's Hospital, Boston, MA, research associate, 1952-53; St. Mary's Hospital Medical School, London, England, research associate, 1953-56; Oxford University, Oxford, England, graduate assistant and deputy regius professor of medicine, 1956-59; Medical Research Council, Oxford, member of scientific staff, 1959-61; University of Birmingham, Birmingham, England, department chair and

Bowman professor of physiology, 1960-64; Worchester Foundation for Experimental Biology, England, senior scientist, 1964-67; Medical College of Virginia, department chair and professor of physiology, 1967-70; Cybertek Inc., New York, vice-president and president and director of laboratories, 1970-71, president and chief executive officer, 1971-72; New York University School of Medicine, New York, professor of physiology, 1970-74; Dartmouth Medical School, Hanover, NH, senior research associate of neurology and psychiatry, 1974-77; Veteran's Administration Hospital, White River Junction, VT, resident professor of physiology and psychiatry and associate chief of staff for research and development, both 1977-86.

AWARDS, HONORS: Medical Research Council Scholar, Cambridge National Institute of Medical Research, 1949-52; Commonwealth fellow, University of Utah at Massachusetts General Hospital, 1952-53; honorary director of medical research council unit, Oxford, 1960, for research in chemical pathology of mental disorders.

WRITINGS:

The Chromatography of Steroids (nonfiction), Pergamon Press (New York), 1961.
The Siberian Reservoir (novel), Houghton Mifflin (Boston, MA), 1983.

Also contributor of articles to periodicals, including *Acta Endocrinologica, The Analyst, Biochemistry Journal, Biochemistry Society Symposia, British Medical Bulletin, Experientia, Journal of Biological Chemistry, Journal of Endocrinology, Journal of Physiology,* and *Nature.*

SIDELIGHTS: Physiologist and academician Ian Bush was born and educated in Great Britain, and spent the first portion of his career doing medical research in his homeland. In addition to contributing many articles to professional journals, he penned the 1961 reference work, *The Chromatography of Steroids.* Later, citing factors such as obsolete equipment, excessive paperwork and too many demands outside the laboratory, Bush immigrated to the United States. Several scientists followed Bush to the United States, a phenomenon known in mid-1960s Britain as "the brain drain." Bush eventually became a U.S. citizen and continued his research at such institutions as the Medical College of Virginia, and Dartmouth Medical School in Hanover, New Hampshire. Bush died of cancer in 1986, and was eulogized in the London

Times as "an outstanding scientist in the field of sex steroids."

Bush also produced noteworthy writings in other genres. Starting with an idea that occurred to him in his research, he plotted a novel of espionage, 1983's *The Siberian Reservoir*. In *The Siberian Reservoir*, the reader meets three main characters. One is Milstein, a triple agent who pretends to be a Polish defector. Part of his information includes clues about Soviet plans to develop a secret biological weapon; the two other characters—Central Intelligence Agency scientist Dr. Wallace Sharples and his assistant Jensen—figure out that this weapon is a form of the flu that will spread depression among the American people and eventually cause the collapse of the U.S. government. Milstein is sent back to Russia to make things difficult for Soviet intelligence, while Jensen travels to Prague (in what was then Czechoslovakia) to sabotage plans to vaccinate the Soviet people against the depression-causing flu.

Critics gave *The Siberian Reservoir* mixed reviews. While a *Kirkus Reviews* contributor conceded that the novel was "literate" and the author "talented," and predicted that "spy-readers with a taste for twisty unravelings will enjoy the first half," the reviewer judged the book to be ultimately "only half-engrossing." Barbara A. Bannon, reviewing *The Siberian Reservoir* in *Publishers Weekly,* remarked that while "there's at least one good spy thriller here," the volume "could have been profitably cut in half." Bush himself discussed *The Siberian Reservoir* in the *Library Journal*. According to Bush, the novel contains what he viewed as the traditional espionage themes of "treason and deception." In addition, he said he tried to "add two more" themes to *The Siberian Reservoir:* "the corrupting effect of bureaucracies, and the dangers of technological arrogance."

BIOGRAPHICAL/CRITICAL SOURCES:

PERIODICALS

Kirkus Reviews, November 15, 1982, p. 1248-49.
Library Journal, October 1, 1982, p. 1901.
Publishers Weekly, December 3, 1982, p. 47.

OBITUARIES:

PERIODICALS

New York Times, November 5, 1986.
Times (London), November 11, 1986.*

C

CAIDIN, Martin 1927-1997

OBITUARY NOTICE—See index for *CA* sketch: Born September 14, 1927, in New York, NY; died of thyroid cancer, March 24, 1997, in Tallahassee, FL. Novelist and nonfiction author. Caidin was a specialist in the subjects of space and aviation and is best known for his novels *Cyborg* (1972), which served as the basis of the 1970s television series *The Six-Million-Dollar Man*, and *Marooned* (1964), adapted as a theatrical motion picture starring Gregory Peck. While these novels brought Caidin fame, he had long been a prolific author of both fiction and nonfiction on aviation and space topics.

Caidin began his writing career at age sixteen as an associate editor for *Air News* and *Air Tech* and while still a teenager had been invited to join the Aviation Writers Association. He later served as a consultant on such subjects as nuclear warfare and aviation medicine to government agencies including the New York State Civil Defense Commission, the Air Force Missile Test Center in Cape Canaveral, Florida, and the Federal Aviation Agency. His career expanded to include broadcasting and appearances as a stunt pilot, and his *Maryjane Tonight at Angels Twelve* (1972) offers a fictionalized account of his flights simulating drug smuggling as a training exercise for narcotics agents. Caidin was the author of about two hundred books and several thousand magazine articles. His later works include *The Saga of Iron Annie* (1979), *Sun Bright* (1979), *Kill Devil Hill: Discovering the Secret of the Wright Brothers*, a 1979 collaboration with H. B. Combs, the novel *Manfrac* (1981), *Ragwings and Heavy Iron: The Agony and Ecstasy of Flying History's Greatest Warbirds* (1984), *Killer Station* (1985), *Zaboa* (1986), and *Prison Ship* (1989).

OBITUARIES AND OTHER SOURCES:

BOOKS

The Writers Directory: 1996-1998, St. James Press, 1995, p. 224.

PERIODICALS

Los Angeles Times, March 26, 1997, p. A18.
New York Times, March 14, 1997, p. D17.
Washington Post, March 27, 1997, p. D6.

* * *

CAMPBELL, Jo Ann (L.) 1958-

PERSONAL: Born July 26, 1958, in St. Paul, MN; daughter of Roger L. (an elementary school principal) and Ann Louise (a teacher; maiden name, Carlson) Campbell; companion of Laura Galloway (a college administrator). *Ethnicity:* "Caucasian." *Education:* Valparaiso University, B.A., 1980; Pennsylvania State University, M.A., 1984; University of Texas at Austin, Ph.D., 1989. *Politics:* Democrat. *Religion:* Unity.

ADDRESSES: Home—7509 Rodeo Dr., Ellettsville, IN 47429. *Office*—Center on Philanthropy, Indiana University, 550 West North St., Suite 301, Indianapolis, IN 46202; fax 317-684-8900. *E-mail*—jocampbe @indiana.edu.

CAREER: Indiana University, Bloomington, English department, assistant professor, 1989-96, Center on

Philanthropy, community service associate, Indianapolis, 1996—. Middle Way House (battered women's shelter), volunteer, 1996—.

MEMBER: National Society for Experiential Education.

WRITINGS:

(Editor) *Towards a Feminist Rhetoric: The Writing of Gertrude Buck,* University of Pittsburgh Press (Pittsburgh, PA), 1996.

WORK IN PROGRESS: Leaning into the Light: Essays on the Spiritual in Every Day.

SIDELIGHTS: Jo Ann Campbell told *CA:* "My primary motivation for writing *Toward a Feminist Rhetoric* was a desire to honor the work of Gertrude Buck, a remarkable woman professor at Vassar College from 1897 to 1922, whose theories of rhetoric and practices of writing have recently become more 'mainstream.'

"My position as a woman in higher education, the struggles I've had writing in what I perceived to be acceptable academic prose, challenges faced by students and colleagues, and contemporary debate on women's voices have led me to research the writing of the first generation of women to attend colleges and universities in the United States. I've conducted research in archives of women's colleges, finding student compositions, themes, letters, and diaries that explicitly address the issue of being taught to write in particular ways about certain subjects deemed appropriate to academe. Tied up in learning how to write in the academy are notions of what is considered intelligent, what's worthy of consideration, and what topics and ways of thinking are substandard. My questions throughout this research have been about what academia has lost in the process of creating a single acceptable way of thinking and expressing thought, and about how the entry of women into realms of higher education has changed the traditional rhetoric curriculum.

"My findings complicate the notion that women have been simply oppressed by writing processes or features that honor rational thought and linear logic in that the irony, play, and skill of these nineteenth-century essays reveal women's talent for writing within the confines of academic prose. While women are shaped by the traditions of academic writing, they also stretch, challenge, and reshape those traditions.

"Again and again I've found in writing academic prose that I face the very issue I'm writing about. So, if I'm addressing women's lack of authority, I struggle with my own authority to say anything on the topic. Or, for instance, when the subject is women's need to address issues in the margins of acceptable academic performance, the issues most important to me must be more central to the academic essay I'm drafting. Once I see how my own situation is mirrored in these older texts, I not only come to a new understanding of the writing context of the subjects, but also I add a perspective to contemporary debates that has been missing. In other words, I really believe that women working through writing blocks must come to value their experiences and bring those experiences to bear on the topic, especially in the realm of academic writing, in order to move through the block. As Victoria Nelson suggests, writing blocks and struggles are a gift from the psyche to alert the writer that compartmentalizing emotions, certain thoughts, and experiences denies the very source of the writer's contribution.

"With the publication of the last essay on this topic, I am turning my attention to non-academic writing, having found that the genre of the personal essay allows me greater freedom to address topics that matter to me. *Leaning into the Light* is a collection of essays first delivered as lessons at the Unity church of Bloomington. As the title suggests, these are meditations on moments in everyday life when all that's required of us is to lean into the light in order to embrace the spiritual and enjoy the everyday. I'm having a great deal of fun writing these pieces."

* * *

CAMPION, Dan(iel Ray) 1949-

PERSONAL: Born August 23, 1949, in Oak Park, IL; son of Raymond Edward (a retail manager) and Wilma Frances (a homemaker; maiden name, Dougherty) Campion; companion of JoAnn E. Castagna (a university administrator). *Education:* University of Chicago, A.B., 1970; University of Illinois—Chicago, M.A., 1975; University of Iowa, Ph.D., 1989. *Politics:* Independent.

ADDRESSES: Home—1700 East Rochester Ave., Iowa City, IA 52245. *Office*—ACT, 2201 North Dodge St., P.O. Box 168, Iowa City, IA 52243. *Agent*—c/o Associated University Presses, 440 Forsgate Dr., Cranbury, NJ 08512.

CAREER: Encyclopaedia Britannica, Inc., Chicago, IL, production editor, 1972-74; Follett Publishing Company, Chicago, children's book editor, 1977-78; University of Iowa, Iowa City, teaching and research assistant, 1978-84; ACT, Inc., Iowa City, test specialist and senior test editor, 1984—.

MEMBER: Modern Language Association, Midwest Modern Language Association, National Council of Teachers of English, Society for the Study of Midwestern Literature.

AWARDS, HONORS: Festival of the Arts Poetry Award from the University of Chicago, 1967; All-Nations Poetry Contest Award, from Triton College in River Grove, IL, 1975; Poetry Award from the Illinois Arts Council, 1979.

WRITINGS:

(Editor with Jim Perlman and Ed Folsom) *Walt Whitman: The Measure of His Song* (criticism), Holy Cow! Press (Minneapolis, MN), 1981.
Calypso (poetry), Syncline Press (Chicago, IL) 1981.
Peter De Vries and Surrealism (criticism), Bucknell University Press (Lewisburg, PA), c. 1995.

Contributor of poetry and articles to periodicals, including *Poetry, Light, Literary Magazine Review, Hispanic Journal, Rolling Stone, Chicago Tribune, Chicago Reader, Ascent, Poet Lore, The Spirit That Moves Us,* and *Poetry.*

SIDELIGHTS: Author and editor Dan Campion has had a varied writing and teaching career. He was born in Oak Park, Illinois, and raised on the West Side of Chicago. After obtaining his bachelor's degree from the University of Chicago, he worked for *Encyclopaedia Britannica* as a production editor. Then, after completing his master's degree at the University of Illinois—Chicago, he signed on with the Follett Publishing Company and became an editor of children's books. From there, he moved to Iowa City, Iowa, and while serving first as a teaching and research assistant at the University of Iowa, and then as a test specialist for ACT, a developer of academic and professional testing programs, he earned his doctorate in English from Iowa in 1989.

Campion's writings are mainly poetry and literary criticism. He has contributed to respected poetry anthologies and journals, including *Ascent, Light, Poetry,* and *The Spirit That Moves Us.* He also published a collection of poems, titled *Calypso,* in 1981. Campion has won several Illinois-area awards for his poetry, including a prize from the Illinois Arts Council.

Campion's literary criticism has been included in publications such as *Literary Magazine Review* and *Hispanic Journal.* With Jim Perlman and Ed Folsom, he edited in 1981 a volume of poems and essays written to and about American poet Walt Whitman—best known for his collection *Leaves of Grass*—entitled *Walt Whitman: The Measure of His Song.* In 1995, Campion published his study *Peter De Vries and Surrealism* under the auspices of Bucknell University Press.

As its title suggests, *Peter De Vries and Surrealism* places the novelist De Vries—known by many as a skeptic whose conflict with his early Calvinist upbringing colored his writing, vividly—within the literary tradition of surrealism. According to Ralph C. Wood, who reviewed *Peter De Vries and Surrealism* in the *Christian Century,* Campion successfully relates De Vries to French poet Andre Breton's founding concept of surrealism: the resolving of "conflicting states of dream and reality—of subjective fantasy and objective fact—into 'a kind of absolute reality, a *surreality.*'" Wood accepts that "De Vries was employing the surrealist methods he would never abandon" by the time he penned his first novel, *But Who Wakes the Bugler?* Wood paraphrased Campion by saying that De Vries "was engaging in a spiritual anarchism that would divorce people and things from their natural functions in order to place them in shocking new relations." *Peter De Vries and Surrealism,* Wood concludes, is a "carefully researched and deftly argued book," though he did not completely agree with Campion's conclusions about his novelist subject, feeling that De Vries' Calvinist upbringing was as strong an influence—in terms of producing a rebellion—as the surrealist movement. A, J. Griffith, reviewing *Peter De Vries and Surrealism* in *Choice,* remarks that "even readers who may take issue with all or part of Campion's thesis can be grateful for . . . probably the most detailed summary of De Vries' life available in any single book."

Campion told *CA:* "I write because it seems the most natural thing to do, owing, no doubt, to early encouragement from my parents and teachers. Writing permits me to imagine that I'm in collusion with my surroundings: 'To me the converging objects of the universe perpetually flow, / All are written to me, and I must get what the writing means' (Whitman); everyday life is a 'forest of signposts' awaiting the 'delirium of interpretation' (Breton).

"Writing about Peter De Vries is especially enjoyable for me because he fosters that sense of collusion (e.g., in various arcane literary allusions and verbal associations and by virtue of our shared Chicago background) while, paradoxically, humorously deflating pretensions to inside knowledge ('What I like to show,' he told the interviewer Douglas M. Davis, 'is something perfectly plain: that we're all absurd variations of one another'). Writing is for alertness."

BIOGRAPHICAL/CRITICAL SOURCES:

PERIODICALS

Choice, March, 1996, p. 1128.
Christian Century, September 11, 1996, pp. 871-873.

* * *

CANTWELL, Dennis P(atrick) 1940-1997

OBITUARY NOTICE—See index for *CA* sketch: Born February 28, 1940, in East St. Louis, IL; died of a heart attack April 14, 1997, in Woodland Hills, CA. Child psychiatrist and author. As a psychiatrist who advanced the study of adolescent mental illnesses such as eating disorders, attention deficit disorder and disruptive and suicidal behavior, Cantwell counted several well-known Hollywood youngsters among his patients. Educated at the University of Notre Dame and the Washington University School of Medicine, he worked at clinics in the United States and London before settling into a faculty position at the University of California, Los Angeles, in 1972. There, Cantwell brought an organized, clinical approach to treating communication and behavior disorders among children and teenagers. His writings on the subject include contributions to *The Community Mental Health Center: Strategies and Programs* (1972), *Annual Progress in Child Psychiatry and Child Development: 1972* (1973), *The Child Psychiatrist as Clinical Investigator* (1975), and *Studies on Childhood Psychiatric and Psychological Problems* (1977). He also edited *The Hyperactive Child: Diagnosis, Management and Current Research* (1975), and wrote (with P. E. Tanguay) *Basic Clinical Child Psychiatry: A Textbook for Medical Students and Students in Allied Disciplines* (1976).

Cantwell served as co-editor of *Child Psychiatry Newsletter* from 1972 to 1973, was a member of the editorial board of *Manual on Terminology and Classification*

in Mental Retardation, and a book reviewer for the *American Journal of Psychiatry,* the *Psychiatric Annals,* and *U.A.F. Bibliography in Mental Retardation.* The author of more than two hundred articles and papers, Cantwell was honored with several awards from the American Psychiatric Association and the Institute of the Living. He also received the lifetime achievement award from the Southern California Psychiatric Society.

OBITUARIES AND OTHER SOURCES:

BOOKS

American Psychiatric Association Biographical Directory, 1989.

PERIODICALS

Los Angeles Times, April 20, 1997, p. B3.
New York Times, April 27, 1997, sec. 1, p. 40.

* * *

CARAGIALE, Ion Luca 1852-1912

PERSONAL: Born January 30, 1852, in Haimanale, near Ploesti, Wallachia (now Romania); died June 9, 1912, in Berlin, Germany; son of Luca (an actor, lawyer, and judge) and Catinca (a peasant) Caragiale; married Alexandrina Burelly, 1889; children: (with Burelly) one son and two daughters; an illegitimate son. *Education:* Attended schools in Ploesti, 1857-68; studied in his uncle Iorgiu "Costache" Caragiale's acting, declamation, and mime classes, Conservatoire, Bucharest, 1868-70.

CAREER: Playwright. Held a variety of jobs, including court-copyist, proofreader, schools inspector, tobacco factory worker, and tavern manager. National Theatre, Bucharest, prompter, 1870; civil servant, Romanian Department of State Monopolies, 1899-1901. Contributor, *Ghimpele,* 1875; publisher, *Clapomul* (humorous periodical), 1877; theatre critic, *Romania libera,* 1877; contributor, *Timpul,* 1878-81, and *Vointa nationala,* 1895; director, National Theatre, Bucharest, 1888-89; contributor, *Constitutionalul,* 1889; founder and editor, *Moftul roman* (humor magazine), 1893, 1901; co-publisher, *Vatra,* 1894; settled in Berlin, 1904.

MEMBER: Conservative Party, *Junimea* (conservative literary and political group).

WRITINGS:

COLLECTIONS

Teatru (title means "Theatre"), [Bucharest], 1889.

Opere (collected works), [Bucharest], Volumes 1-2: *Nuvele si schite,* 1930-31; Volume 3: *Reminiscente si not critice,* 1932; Volume 4: *Notite critice, literatura si versuri,* 1938; Volume 5: *Articole politice si cronici dramatice,* 1938; Volume 6: *Teatru,* 1939; Volume 7: *Corespondenta,* 1942.

Opere (collected works), edited by A. Rosetti, S. Cioculescu, and Liviu Calin, [Bucharest], Volume 1: *Teatru,* 1959; Volume 2: *Momente; Schite; Notite critice,* 1960; Volume 3: *Nuvele; Povestiri; Amintiri; Versuri; Parodii; Varia,* 1962; Volume 4: *Publicistica,* 1965.

PLAYS

O noapte furtunoasa; sau, Namural 9 (produced in Bucharest, 1879), in *Teatru,* 1889, translated as *A Stormy Night* in *The Lost Letter and Other Plays,* 1956.

Conul Leonida fata cu reactiunea (produced in Bucharest c. 1884), in *Teatru,* 1889, translated as *Mr. Leonida and the Reactionaries,* in *The Lost Letter and Other Plays,* 1956.

O soacra (title means "A Mother-in-Law"), produced in Bucharest as *Soacra mea Fifina,* 1883.

Hatmanul Baltaq, from a story by N. Gane, with music by Eduard Caudell, produced in Bucharest, 1884.

O scricoare pierduta (produced in Bucharest in 1885), translated as *The Lost Letter* in *The Lost Letter and Other Plays,* 1956.

D'ale carnavalului (produced in Bucharest, 1885), in *Teatru,* 1889, translated as *Carnival Scenes* in *The Lost Letter and Other Plays,* 1956.

Napasta (title means "Injustice") produced in Bucharest, 1890.

1 Aprilie, produced 1896.

Incepem! (title means "We're Beginning!"), produced in Bucharest at Leon Popescu Theatre, 1909.

The Lost Letter and Other Plays (includes *Carnival Scenes, A Stormy Night,* and *Mr. Leonida and the Reactionaries*), translated by Frida Knight, Lawrence & Wishart, 1956.

Translator and producer of stage works for National Theatre, Bucharest, including (from French) *Roma Invinsa, Lucretia Borgia,* and *Rome Vaincue,* by Alexandre Parodi, all 1878.

FICTION

O faclie de Paste; Pacat; Om nu noroc, [Bucharest], 1892, translated by Joseph Ishill as *A Torch for Easter,* Oriole Press (Berkeley Heights, NJ), 1961.

Note si schite (title means "Notes and Sketches"), [Bucharest], 1892.

Moftul roman (title means "Romanian Nonsense"), [Bucharest], 1893.

Moftul roman, second series, [Bucharest], 1901.

Momente (stories), [Bucharest], 1901.

Kir Ianulea (title means "Lord Ianulea"), [Bucharest], 1909.

Schita nuoua (short stories; title means "New Sketches"), [Bucharest], 1910.

Sketches and Stories (selected works; bilingual edition) translated by E. D. Tappe, Cluj-Napoca (Dacia, Romania), 1979.

OTHER

Scrisori si acte (letters), [Bucharest], 1962.

1907, Din primavara in toamna (essays; title means "1907, from Spring to Autumn"), [Bucharest], 1907, portions translated as "Causes of the Peasant Revolt, 1907," in *Contrasts in Emerging Societies,* edited by D. Warriner, 1965.

SIDELIGHTS: Although generally recognized as the most significant of classic Romanian playwrights, and "unquestionably," in the words of Dennis Deletant in the *International Dictionary of the Theatre,* Romania's "most enduring author," Ion Luca Caragiale remains undeservedly little-known beyond the borders of his native country. During his lifetime, moreover, he was criticized and underrated by his own people to the extent that in middle age he went into voluntary exile in Germany. The twentieth century has seen a resurgence of Caragiale's reputation, however. During the Communist era, his plays were enjoyed as an "antidote," as Deletant terms it, to the oppressiveness of the regime; indeed they functioned so well in that capacity that performances of them were prohibited in the 1980s. After the toppling of dictator Nicolae Ceausescu's government in 1989, Caragiale's works served a satirical function in an era of unstable economic reform. "'Caragialean,'" notes Deletant, "has become a byword to describe the posturings, the verbiage, the vacuousness, and the insincerity of contemporary political life." Both as a playwright and as a writer of prose, Caragiale developed his gift for biting observations of human foibles, and for reproducing with comic exactitude the colloquial speech of ordinary people, causing him to be called by some the Mark Twain of Romania.

Caragiale's varied youthful experiences would provide a foundation for the future playwright's later comic creations, and provide a grounding in the world of the stage as well. Though his father left the theatre to settle into a legal career, his father's family were traveling actors and playwrights. An uncle led an acting school in Bucharest, the national capital, and in 1868, having previously gone through a patchy education in his home town of Ploesti, sixteen-year-old Caragiale left home to become one of his uncle's students. Two years later, Caragiale's father died, and the young man became responsible for supporting his mother and sister.

Economic necessity led him to work in such places as a beer garden and a tobacco factory, as well as in journalism. Although his job history shows a series of brief tenures and frequent switches, Caragiale was established as a Bucharest drama critic before his own plays were presented on stage. Financial difficulties did not end with his play-writing career, however; the demands of married life pressed him hard, and according to the *McGraw-Hill Encyclopedia of World Drama,* "he made more reputation than money." Although he was a respected playwright, he was still forced to take jobs in unrelated fields, such as civil service, during the years 1889 to 1904; he was an inspector of schools for several years after having been director of the National Theatre. Only in 1904, when he received a long-disputed inheritance from a deceased aunt, did Caragiale achieve financial independence; with it, he moved to Berlin, prompted to a great degree by the lack of appreciation his literary work had received in his homeland.

Neglect of Caragiale's works was sometimes punctuated by active opposition. Following the 1879 premiere of his first major play, *O noapte furtunoasa* (translated as *A Stormy Night*), protesters called the author unpatriotic and immoral. This play is organized around a love triangle consisting of a man, his wife, and the husband's assistant, who is the wife's lover. Like many of Caragiale's plays, this one is marked by frenetic action and agitated, tumultuous dialogue, its characters full of unbridled energy and yet unsuccessful in making their points. The 1880 play *Conul Leonida fata cu reactiunea,* known in English as *Mr. Leonida and the Reactionaries,* is a political comedy with a twist. Mr. Leonida, at bedtime, tells his wife the history of the extremely short-lived Romanian republic, and describes his own vi-

sion of a utopian society. That night, the Leonidas are awakened by gunshots; Mr. Leonidas, a republican, is convinced that reactionaries are after him—but it is only Shrovetide merriment conducted by the townspeople.

Caragiale's dramatic masterpiece, in the eyes of many, is the 1884 work *O scrisoare pierrduta,* usually translated as *The Lost Letter.* It is set in a provincial town where elections are to be held, and like *A Stormy Night,* it concerns a love triangle. The letter in question is a love letter from the wife of one candidate to the candidate's friend, an electoral official. The candidate's opponent tries to obtain the letter for purposes of raising a political scandal; the letter is lost and found more than once; and the two opposing candidates, meanwhile, band together to oppose a third candidate. It has been noted often that most of the characters in the play are unsympathetic figures, with the possible exception of Trahanache, the naive, trusting electoral official. The play's denouement is one of insincere reconciliation. Romanian audiences still identify with this play's cynical depiction of political life, "which," says Deletant, "has lost none of its validity . . . today." Writes Romanian scholar Ileana Popovici in *Romanian Review,* "Every culture possesses in its classical zone, icy cold peaks to which pilgrimages are undertaken, and burning hot sources, permanently connected with present-day circumstances by all manner of bridges and channels. For Romania, *A Lost Letter . . .* is a burning-hot source of this kind."

A later play, *D'Ale Carnavalului,* which was first produced in 1885, is a intricately plotted comedy set in Bucharest at carnival time. With the nonstop action of a farce, it portrays the romantic mixups of a group of low-life characters. Audiences at the time were shocked by the play's violence and crudity; it was cancelled after only two performances. In his last play, 1890's *Napasta,* the title of which can be translated as "Injustice," "False Witness," or "False Accusation," Caragiale turned to serious drama in a Dostoyevskyian vein. The main character, Anca, is the widow of a man who was killed by her present husband, Dragomir. Dragomir's associate, Ion, was convicted of the crime, and has escaped from the salt mines as the play opens. The main action concerns Anca's long-planned, melodramatic revenge against her husband Dragomir. Deletant, though finding aspects of Anca's vindictiveness "improbable," declares that "*Napasta* reveals as much of [Caragiale's] extraordinary perceptiveness as does his comic writing." The play was controversial in its time, and its themes have been compared to those of Leo Tolstoy's play *The Power of Darkness* as well as to those of Dostoyevsky's novel *Crime and Punishment*.

Having written *Napasta,* Caragiale turned his back on play writing. He continued to struggle to earn a living and in 1901 became embroiled in a psychologically painful plagiarism suit brought by a theatre critic. Ultimately absolved of all wrongdoing, he continued to write prose fiction and nonfiction for periodicals, and had two collections of short stories published in 1892. His stories were realistic, often ironic, treatments of Romanian life: the lives of clerks, peasants, and families. He also wrote comic sketches. One of his best short stories, in the opinion of critic E. D. Tappe in the *Columbia Dictionary of Modern European Literature,* "La Hanul lui Minjoala" ("Manjoala's Inn") was written between 1898 and 1899 and published in a 1901 collection of Caragiale's works. A "masterpiece of delicate irony," in Tappe's view, "Manjoala's Inn" depicts a man who stops at an inn run by a young widow who, it is implied, may be a witch; he tries to resist her charms by leaving, but is drawn back with the help of a severe storm. Says Tappe, "The descriptions of the ride, the inn, the storm, are remarkably vivid. Nowhere else, I think, does Caragiale create with such sustained delicacy."

A later, longer fictional masterpiece, the 1909 novella *Kir Ianulea* (title means "Lord Ianulea"), was a re-working of Niccolo Machiavelli's play *The Marriage of Belphagor.* Complicated in its plot and containing a wealth of details, the work depicts the fortunes of an imp who is sent to earth by the devil to investigate human women. In Bucharest, in the guise of the title character, who is a Greek merchant, the imp marries a shrew who bankrupts him; he is rescued by a man named Negoita, and rewards Negoita with wealth—whereupon even more complications ensue, till the imp returns exhausted to hell and the wife and Negoita go, at the imp's ironic request, to heaven.

Caragiale's achievement was considerable. He is considered by many critics to be Romania's first "objective writer" due to his unprecedented ability to bring the Romanian people's style of speech and national character to life. Rumanians in the twentieth century continue to honor him: the fiftieth anniversary of his death, in 1962, was the occasion for a week of performances of his works, and the name of a character from *The Lost Letter,* Catavencu, has become the title of a leading post-1989 Romanian satirical journal. Tappe, who appreciates Caragiale especially for his

detached irony and his fascination with the "cruel and monstrous," asserts, "At the very least, *Kir Ianulea* and 'Manjoala's Inn' deserve to rank among the classics of the world's literature." As Deletant puts it, Caragiale's works "possess a timelessness which ensures their continuing popularity with Romanian audiences."

BIOGRAPHICAL/CRITICAL SOURCES:

BOOKS

Columbia Dictionary of Modern European Literature, second edition, edited by Jean-Albert Bede and William B. Edgerton, Columbia University Press (New York City), 1980, p. 141.
Encyclopedia of World Theater, edited by Martin Esslin, translated by Stella Schmid, Scribner's (New York City), 1977.
European Authors, 1000-1900, edited by Stanley J. Kunitz and Vineta Colby, H. W. Wilson (New York City), 1967.
International Dictionary of Theatre, Volume 2: *Playwrights,* edited by Mark Hawkins-Dady, St. James Press (Detroit), 1994, pp. 165-167.
McGraw-Hill Encyclopedia of World Drama, first edition, McGraw-Hill, 1972, pp. 323-26.

PERIODICALS

American Slavic and East European Review, vol. XI, 1952, pp. 66-76.
Romanian Review, vol. 26, no. 3, 1972, pp. 103-108; vol. 41, no. 6, 1987.*

*   *   *

CARREL, Alexis (Marie Joseph Auguste Billiard) 1873-1944

PERSONAL: Born June 28, 1873, in Sainte-Foy-les-Lyon, France; son of Anne-Marie Ricard and Alexis Carrell Billiard (a textile manufacturer). Married Anne-Marie Laure Gourlez de la Motte de Meyrie, December 26, 1913. Died of heart failure in Paris on November 5, 1944. *Education:* Earned two baccalaureate degrees from Jesuit schools, 1889 (in letters) and 1890 (in science); University of Lyons, M.D., 1900. *Religion:* Roman Catholic. *Avocational interests:* Making annual pilgrimages to Lourdes, France; conducting research into such supernatural phenomena as miracles.

CAREER: Medical scientist. University of Lyons, instructor and researcher in medicine, 1900-04; University of Chicago, Hull Physiology Laboratory, assistant in physiology, 1904-06; Rockefeller Institute for Medical Research (now Rockefeller University), researcher, later director of Division of Experimental Surgery, 1906-39; Foundation for the Study of Human Problems, Paris, director, 1941-44. *Military service:* Served as an army surgeon in France's Alpine Chasseurs for one year, c. 1891; also served as director of a front-line army hospital for study and treatment of severely infected wounds, 1914-19.

AWARDS, HONORS: Nobel Prize in medicine and physiology, for developing successful technique in blood-vessel suturing and research in organ transplants in animals, 1912; Nordhoff-Jung Cancer Prize, for contributions to the study of malignant tumors, 1931.

WRITINGS:

Man, the Unknown, Harper & Brothers, 1935.
(With Charles A. Lindbergh) *The Culture of Organs,* Hoeber, 1938.
Prayer, Morehouse-Gorham, 1948.
Voyage to Lourdes, translated by Virgilia Peterson, Harper, 1950.
Reflections on Life, translated by Antonia White, H. Hamilton, 1952.

SIDELIGHTS: Alexis Carrel was an innovative surgeon whose experiments with the transplantation and repair of body organs led to advances in the field of surgery and the art of tissue culture . An original and creative thinker, Carrel was the first to develop a successful technique for suturing blood vessels together. For his work with blood-vessel suturing and the transplantation of organs in animals, he received the 1912 Nobel Prize in medicine and physiology. Carrel's work with tissue culture also contributed significantly to the understanding of viruses and the preparation of vaccines. A member of the Rockefeller Institute for Medical Research for thirty-three years, Carrel was the first scientist working in the United States to receive the Nobel Prize in medicine and physiology.

Carrel was born on June 28, 1873, in Sainte-Foy-les-Lyon, a suburb of Lyons, France. He was the oldest of three children, two boys and a girl, in a Roman Catholic family. His mother, Anne-Marie Ricard, was the daughter of a linen merchant. His father, Alexis Carrel Billiard, was a textile manufacturer. Carrel dropped his baptismal names, Marie Joseph Auguste,

and became known as Alexis Carrel upon his father's death when the boy was five years old. As a child, Carrel attended Jesuit schools. Before studying medicine, he earned two baccalaureate degrees, one in letters (1889) and one in science (1890). In 1891, Carrel began medical studies at the University of Lyons. For the next nine years, Carrel gained both academic knowledge and practical experience working in local hospitals. He served one year as an army surgeon with the Alpine Chasseurs, France's mountain troops. He also studied under Leo Testut, a famous anatomist. As an apprentice in Testut's laboratory, Carrel showed great talent at dissection and surgery. In 1900, he received his medical degree but continued on at the University of Lyons teaching medicine and conducting experiments in the hope of eventually receiving a permanent faculty position there.

In 1894, the president of France bled to death after being fatally wounded by an assassin in Lyons. If doctors had known how to repair his damaged artery, his life may have been saved, but such surgical repair of blood vessels had never been done successfully. It is said that this tragic event captured Carrel's attention and prompted him to try and find a way to sew severed blood vessels back together. Carrel first taught himself how to sew with a small needle and very fine silk thread. He practiced on paper until he was satisfied with his expertise, then developed steps to reduce the risk of infection and maintain the flow of blood through the repaired vessels. Through his careful choice of materials and long practice at various techniques, Carrel found a way to suture blood vessels. He first published a description of his success in a French medical journal in 1902.

Despite Carrel's growing reputation as a surgeon, he failed to acquire a faculty position at the university. His colleagues seemed indifferent to his research, and Carrel, in turn, was critical of the French medical establishment. The final split between Carrel and his peers came when Carrel wrote a positive account of a miracle he apparently witnessed at Lourdes, a small town famous since 1858 for its Roman Catholic shrine and often visited by religious pilgrims. In his article, Carrel suggested that there may be medical cures that cannot be explained by science alone, and that further investigation into supernatural phenomena such as miracles was required. This conclusion pleased neither the scientists nor the churchmen of the day.

In June, 1904, Carrel left France for the French-speaking city of Montreal, Canada; an encounter with French missionaries who had worked in Canada had sparked Carrel's interest in that country several years earlier. Shortly after his arrival, Carrel accepted an assistantship in physiology from the Hull Physiology Laboratory of the University of Chicago, where he remained from 1904 to 1906. The university provided him with an opportunity to continue the experiments he had begun in France.

Blood transfusion and organ transplantation seemed within reach to Carrel, now that he had mastered the ability to suture blood vessels. In experiments with dogs, he performed successful kidney transplants. His bold investigations began to attract attention not only from other medical scientists but from the public as well. His work was reviewed in both medical journals and popular newspapers such as the *New York Herald.* In the era of Ford, Edison, and the Wright Brothers, the public was easily able to imagine how work in a scientific laboratory could lead to major changes in daily life. Human organ transplantation and other revolutions in surgery did not seem far off.

In 1906, the opportunity to work in a world-class laboratory came to Carrel. The new Rockefeller Institute for Medical Research (now named Rockefeller University) in New York City offered him a position. Devoted entirely to medical research, rather than teaching or patient care, the Rockefeller Institute was the first institution of its kind in the United States. Carrel would remain at the institute until 1939. At the Rockefeller Institute, Carrel continued to improve his methods of blood-vessel surgery. He knew that mastering those techniques would allow for great advances in the treatment of disorders of the circulatory system and wounds. It also made direct blood transfusions possible at a time when scientists did not know how to prevent blood from clotting. Without this knowledge, blood could not be stored or transported. In the *Journal of the American Medical Association* in 1910, Carrel described connecting an artery from the arm of a father to the leg of an infant in order to treat the infant's intestinal bleeding. Although the experiment was a success, the discovery of anticoagulants soon made such direct transfer unnecessary. For his pioneering efforts, Carrel won the Nobel Prize in 1912.

Carrel's success with tissue cultures through animal experiments led him to wonder whether human tissues and even whole organs, might be kept alive artificially in the laboratory. If so, lab-raised organs might eventually be used as substitutes for diseased parts of the body. The art of keeping cells and tissue alive, and even growing, outside of the body is known as tissue culture. Successfully culturing tissue requires great technical skill. Carrel was particularly interested in perfusion—a procedure of artificially pumping blood through an organ to keep it viable. Carrel's work with tissue culture contributed greatly to the understanding of normal and abnormal cell life. His techniques helped lay the groundwork for the study of viruses and the preparation of vaccines for polio, measles, and other diseases. Carrel's discoveries, in turn, built upon the successes of, among others, Ross G. Harrison , a contemporary anatomist at Yale who worked with frog tissue cultures and transplants.

One of Carrel's experiments in tissue culture became the subject of a sensationalized news story and was viewed as a monstrosity by the public. In 1912, Carrel took tissue from the heart of a chicken embryo to demonstrate that warm-blooded cells could be kept alive in the lab. This tissue, which was inaccurately depicted as a growing, throbbing chicken heart by some newspapers, was kept alive for thirty-four years—outliving Carrel himself—before it was deliberately terminated. The *World Telegram,* a New York newspaper, annually marked the so-called chicken heart's "birthday" each January.

Though working in the United States, Carrel had not bought a house there, and did not become a U.S. citizen. Rather, he spent each summer in France, and on December 26, 1913, Carrel married Anne-Marie Laure de Meyrie, a widow with one son, in a ceremony in Brittany. They had met at Lourdes, where Carrel made an annual pilgrimage each August. Eventually, the couple bought some property on the island of Saint Gildas off the coast of Brittany, and lived in a stone house there. They had no children together.

When World War I began, Carrel was in France. The French government called him to service with the army, assigning him to run a special hospital near the front lines for the study and prompt treatment of severely infected wounds. There, Madame Carrel, his wife of less than one year and a trained surgical nurse, assisted him. In collaboration with biochemist Henry D. Dakin, Carrel developed an elaborate method of cleansing deep wounds to prevent infection. The method was especially effective in preventing gangrene, and was credited with saving thousands of lives and limbs. The Carrel-Dakin method, however, was too complicated for widespread use, and has since been replaced by the use of antibiotic drugs.

After an honorable discharge in 1919, Carrel returned to the Rockefeller Institute in New York City. He resumed his work in tissue culture, and began an investigation into the causes of cancer. In one experiment, he built a huge mouse colony to test his theories about the relationship between nutrition and cancer. But the experiment produced inconclusive results, and the Institute ceased funding it after 1933. Nevertheless, Carrel's tissue culture research was successful enough to earn him the Nordhoff-Jung Cancer Prize in 1931 for his contribution to the study of malignant tumors.

In the early 1930s, Carrel returned again to the challenge of keeping organs alive outside the body. With the engineering expertise of aviator Charles A. Lindbergh, Carrel designed a special sterilizing glass pump that could be used to circulate nutrient fluid around large organs kept in the lab. This perfusion pump, a so-called artificial heart, was germ-free and was successful in keeping animal organs alive for several days or weeks, but this was not considered long enough for practical application in surgery. Still, the experiment laid the groundwork for future developments in heart-lung machines and other devices. To describe the use of the perfusion pump, Carrel and Lindbergh jointly published *The Culture of Organs* in 1938. Lindbergh was a frequent visitor at the Rockefeller Institute for several years, and the Lindberghs and the Carrels became close friends socially. They appear together on the July 1, 1935, cover of *Time* magazine with their "mechanical heart."

Carrel's mystical bent, publicly revealed after his visit to Lourdes as a young man, was displayed again in 1935. That year Carrel published *Man, the Unknown,* a work written upon the recommendation of a loose-knit group of intellectuals that he often dined with at the Century Club. In *Man, the Unknown,* Carrel posed highly philosophical questions about mankind, and theorized that mankind could reach perfection through selective reproduction and the leadership of an intellectual aristocracy. The book, a worldwide best-seller and translated into nineteen languages, brought Carrel international attention. Carrel's speculations about the need for a council of superior individuals to guide the future of mankind was seen by many as anti-democratic. Others thought that it was inappropriate for a renowned scientist to lecture on fields outside his own.

Unfortunately, one of those who disliked Carrel's habit of discussing issues outside the realm of medicine was the new director of the Rockefeller Institute. Herbert S. Gasser had replaced Carrel's friend and mentor, Simon Flexner, in 1935. Suddenly Carrel found himself approaching the mandatory age of re-

tirement with a director who had no desire to bend the rules and keep him aboard. On July 1, 1939, Carrel retired. His laboratories and the Division of Experimental Surgery were closed.

Carrel's retirement coincided with the beginning of World War II in September, 1939. Carrel and his wife were in France at the time, and Carrel immediately approached the French Ministry of Public Health and offered to organize a field laboratory, much like the one he had run during World War I. When the government was slow to respond, Carrel grew frustrated. In May, 1940, he returned to New York alone. As his steamship was crossing the Atlantic, Hitler invaded France.

Carrel made the difficult return to war-torn Europe as soon as he was able, arriving in France via Spain in February, 1941. Paris was under the control of the Vichy government, a puppet administration installed by the German military command. Although Carrel declined to serve as director of public health in the Vichy government, he stayed in Paris to direct the Foundation for the Study of Human Problems. The Foundation, supported by the Vichy government and the German military command, brought young scientists, physicians, lawyers, and engineers together to study economics, political science, and nutrition. When the Allied forces reoccupied France in August, 1944, the newly restored French government immediately suspended Carrel from his directorship of the Foundation and accused him of collaborating with the Germans. A serious heart attack forestalled any further prosecution. Attended by French and American physicians, and nursed by his wife, Carrel died of heart failure in Paris on November 5, 1944. After his death, his body was buried in St. Yves chapel near his home on the island of Saint Gildas, Cotes-du-Nord.

Carrel's reputation remains that of a brilliant, yet temperamental man. His motivations for his involvement with the Nazi-dominated Vichy government remain the subject of debate. Yet there is no question that his achievements ushered in a new era in medical science. His pioneering techniques paved the way for successful organ transplants and modern heart surgery, including grafting procedures and bypasses.

BIOGRAPHICAL/CRITICAL SOURCES:

BOOKS

Durkin, Joseph T., *Hope for Our Times: Alexis Carrel on Man and Society,* Harper, 1965.

Edwards, William Sterling, *Alexis Carrel: Visionary Surgeon,* Thomas, 1974.

Malinin, Theodore I., *Surgery and Life: The Extraordinary Career of Alexis Carrel,* Harcourt, 1979.

May, Angelo M., and Alice G. May, *The Two Lions of Lyons: The Tale of Two Surgeons, Alexis Carrell and Rene Leriche,* Kabel Publishers (Rockville, MD), 1992.

Poole, Lynn, and Gray Poole, *Doctors Who Saved Lives,* Dodd, 1966, pp. 110-118.*

* * *

CARSON, Benjamin S(olomon) 1951-

PERSONAL: Born September 18, 1951, in Detroit, MI; son of Robert Solomon (a Baptist minister) and Sonya (Copeland) Carson; married Lacena (Candy) Rustin, July 6, 1975; children: Murray Nedlands, Benjamin Jr., Rhoeyce Harrington. *Ethnicity:* "African American." *Education:* Yale University, B.A. (psychology), 1973; University of Michigan, MD., 1977. *Religion:* Seventh Day Adventist.

ADDRESSES: Home—West Friendship, MD. *Office*—Associate Professor, Johns Hopkins Medical Institutions, Meyer 5-109, 600 North Wolfe, Baltimore, MD 21205.

CAREER: Neurosurgeon. Johns Hopkins University, Baltimore, MD, chief resident neurosurgery, 1982-83, assistant professor of neurosurgery, 1984—, assistant professor of oncology, 1984—, assistant professor of pediatrics, 1987—, associate professor, 1991—, director of pediatric neurosurgery, 1985-91; Queen Elizabeth II Medical Center, Perth, Australia, senior registrar of neurosurgery, 1983-84. Has appeared on television in numerous programs. Gives presentations, especially to adolescents, about fulfilling personal potential.

MEMBER: American Association for the Advancement of Science, National Pediatric Oncology Group, National Medical Association, Regional Red Cross Cabinet (honorary chair, 1987), Children's Cancer Foundation (medical advisory board, 1987—), Maryland Congress of Parents and Teachers, American Association of Neurological Surgeons, Congress of Neurological Surgeons, Academy of Pediatric Neurosurgeons.

AWARDS, HONORS: Citations for Excellence, Detroit City Council, 1987, Philadelphia City Council, 1987, Michigan State Senate, 1987, Detroit Medical Society, 1987, Pennsylvania House of Representatives, 1989; American Black Achievement Award, Business and Professional, Ebony and Johnson Publications, 1988; Clinical Practitioner of the Year, National Medical Association Region II, 1988; Certificate of Honor for Outstanding Achievement in the Field of Medicine, National Medical Fellowship Inc., 1988; Candle Award for Science and Technology, Morehouse College, 1989; Blackbook Humanitarian Award, Blackbook Publishing, 1991; numerous honorary doctor of science degrees, including honorary doctor of medical sciences from Yale University, 1996.

WRITINGS:

(With Cecil Murphey) *Gifted Hands, The Ben Carson Story,* Zondervan Publishing House (Grand Rapids, MI), 1990.

Think Big: Unleashing Your Potential for Excellence, Zondervan Publishing House, 1992.

(Editor with Craig R. Dufresne and S. James Zinreich) *Complex Craniofacial Problems: A Guide to Analysis and Treatment,* Churchill Livingstone (New York), 1992.

Contributor to periodicals. Member of editorial board, *Voices of Triumph,* Time-Life Books.

SIDELIGHTS: Benjamin S. Carson is an internationally acclaimed neurosurgeon best known for leading a surgical team in a successful operation to separate Siamese twins. He is also recognized for his expertise in performing hemispherectomies, where half the brain is removed to stop seizures. He is director of pediatric neurosurgery at Johns Hopkins University Hospital as well as assistant professor of neurosurgery, oncology, and pediatrics at the School of Medicine.

Born on September 18, 1951, Benjamin Solomon Carson came from a poor family in Detroit. He was the second son of Robert Solomon Carson, a Baptist minister, and Sonya Copeland Carson. His father was twenty-eight when he married, but his mother was only thirteen; she married in order to escape a difficult home situation. When Carson was only eight years old and his brother, Curtis, was ten, their parents divorced and his mother took them to live with relatives in a Boston tenement, while she rented out their house in Detroit. Working as many as three domestic jobs at a time, she earned enough money to move her family back to Detroit two years later.

Both Carson and his brother had a difficult time in school, and their low grades fanned the racial prejudice against them. But their mother took charge of their education, even though she herself had not gone past the third grade. By limiting the television they could watch and insisting they both read two books a week and report on them, she helped them raise their grades considerably. Carson discovered he enjoyed learning, and by the time he reached junior high school he had risen from the bottom to the top of his class.

But even then he continued to face racial prejudice; in the eighth grade, he listened to a teacher scold his class for allowing him, a black student, to win an achievement award. These early difficulties left Carson with a violent temper as a young man. He was often in fights: "I would fly off the handle," he told *People* contributors Linda Dramer and Joe Treen. Once he almost killed a friend in an argument. Carson tried to stab him in the stomach with a knife, but luckily the boy was wearing a heavy belt buckle, which stopped the blade. Only fourteen at the time, Carson was shocked at what he had almost done, and he saw the direction his life could have taken. This experience drove him more deeply into his religion—he is still a Seventh-Day Adventist—and his faith in God helped him control his temper.

Carson studied hard and did so well during high school that he won a scholarship to Yale University. He received his bachelor's degree from Yale in 1973. He had always dreamed of becoming a doctor and was very interested in psychiatry, but once in medical school at the University of Michigan, he realized he was good with his hands and set his sights on neurosurgery.

After completing medical school in 1977, Carson was one of the few graduates and the first black accepted into the residency program at Johns Hopkins Hospital in Baltimore. In 1983 because of a shortage of neurosurgeons in Australia, Carson was offered a chief neurosurgical residency at Queen Elizabeth II Medical Center in Perth, where he gained a great deal of operating experience. He returned to Johns Hopkins in 1984, and after a year he was promoted to director of pediatric neurosurgery, becoming one of the youngest doctors in the country to head such a division.

One of Carson's accomplishments was reviving the use of a procedure called hemispherectomy—an operation that removes half the patient's brain to cure

diseases such as Rassmussen's encephalitis, which causes seizures. These operations had been stopped because of their high mortality rate, but with Carson's skills the procedure has been highly successful.

But Carson's best known accomplishment was the operation he performed in September, 1987, to separate seven-month-old German Siamese twins, who were joined at the head. Carson was the lead surgeon on the team which performed "perhaps the most complex surgical feat in the history of mankind," as he described the operation in *Ebony*. There was a team of seventy medical staff members, including five neurosurgeons, seven pediatric anesthesiologists, five plastic surgeons, two cardiac surgeons, and dozens of nurses and technicians, and it took five months of preparation, including five three-hour dress rehearsals. A crowd of media people waited outside the operating room for Carson and his medical team to emerge, triumphant, at the end of the twenty-two-hour operation.

In 1988 Carson was awarded both the Certificate of Honor for Outstanding Achievement in the Field of Medicine by the National Medical Fellowship and the American Black Achievement Award. He has received honorary doctor of science degrees from several universities, and the Candle Award for Science and Technology from Morehouse College in 1989.

Carson married Lacena Rustin—whom he met at Yale—in 1975; she holds a M.B.A. degree and is an accomplished musician. They have three sons. Carson feels strongly about motivating young people to fulfill their potential, as he did, and he often lectures to students around the nation. He advises young people to "think big," and he has written a book by that title. Carson was also on the editorial advisory board of the Time-Life series *Voices of Triumph,* about the history and achievements of African Americans.

BIOGRAPHICAL/CRITICAL SOURCES:

BOOKS

Blacks in Science and Medicine, Hemisphere Publishing Co., 1990.

PERIODICALS

Ebony, January, 1988, pp. 52-58.
People, fall, 1991, p. 96.*

CASSIRER, Ernst 1874-1945

PERSONAL: Born July 28, 1874, in Breslau, Silesia, Prussia (now Wroclaw, Poland); died April 13, 1945, in New York, NY; became naturalized Swedish citizen, c. 1930s; son of Eduard and Jerry Cassirer; married Toni Bondy, 1902; children: two sons, one daughter. *Education:* Attended the *Gymnasium* in Breslau; University of Berlin, studied jurisprudence and German philosophy; also took courses at Universities of Leipzig, Munich, and Heidelberg; attended University of Marburg, 1886-89, Ph.D. in philosophy (summa cum laude), 1899; Glasgow University (Scotland), Ll.D.

CAREER: University of Berlin, lecturer, before World War I; University of Hamburg, professor, 1919-33, rector, 1930-33, resigned, 1933; All Souls College, Oxford University (England), lecturer, 1933-35; University of Goeteborg (Sweden), professor of philosophy, 1935-41; Yale University, visiting professor of philosophy, 1941-44; Columbia University, visiting professor of philosophy, 1944-45. *Military service:* Drafted for German civil service during World War I.

MEMBER: Svenska Vittesk Academy, Swedish Royal Academy of Science, Historic Academy (Stockholm, Bedford College, London (honorary member).

AWARDS, HONORS: Award from Berlin Academy for doctoral dissertation.

WRITINGS:

NONFICTION

Descartes' Kritik der mathematischen und naturwissenschaftlichen Erkenntnis, 1899.

Leibniz' System in seinen wissenschaftlichen Grundlagen, 1902.

Das Erkenntnisproblem in der Philosophie under Wissenschaft der neuren Zeit, three volumes, 1906-20; translated by William H. Woglom and Charles W. Hendel as *The Problem of Knowledge,* Yale University Press and Oxford University Press, 1950.

Substanzbegriff under Funktionsbegriff: Untersuchungen uber die Grundfragen der Erkenntniskritik, 1910; translated by William Curtis Swabey and Marie Colins Swabey as *Substance and Function, and Einstein's Theory of Relativity,* Open Court Publishing Co. (Chicago), 1923.

Freiheit und Form: Studien zur deutschen Geistesgeschichte, 1916.

Kants Leben und Lehre, 1918, translated by James Haden as *Kant's Life and Thought,* Yale University Press (New Haven, CT), 1981.

Idee und Gestalt: Funf Aufsatze (five essays), 1921.

Zur Kritik der Einsteinschen Relativitatstheorie, 1921; translated by William Curtis Swabey and Marie Collins Swabey as *Substance and Function, and Einstein's Theory of Relativity,* Open Court Publishing Co. (Chicago), 1923.

Die Begriffsform in mythischen Denken, 1922.

Philosophie der symbolischen Formen, three volumes, 1923-39; translated by Ralph Manheim as *The Philosophy of Symbolic Forms,* three volumes, with an introduction by Charles W. Hendel, Yale University Press, 1953-57; Volume 4 edited by John Michael Krois and Donald Philip Verene as *The Philosophy of Symbolic Fiorms, Volume 4: The Metaphysics of Symbolic Forms,* Yale University Press, 1996.

Die Philosophie der Greichen von den Anfangen bis Platon, 1925.

Sprache und Mythos: Ein Beitrag zum Problem der Gotternamen, 1925; translated by Susanne K. Langer as *Language and Myth,* Dover (New York), 1946.

Individuum und Kosmos in der Philosophie der Renaissance, 1927; translated and with an introduction by Mario Domandi as *The Individual and the Cosmos in Renaissance Philosophy,* B. Blackwell (Oxford, England), 1963, Harper & Row (New York) and Barnes & Noble (New York), 1964.

Goethe und die geschichtliche Welt: Drei Aufsatze (criticism), 1932.

Die Philosophie der Aufklarung, 1932; translated by Fritz C. A. Koelln and James P. Pettegrove as *The Philosophy of the Enlightenment,* Princeton University Press (Princeton, NJ), 1951, Beacon Press (Boston), 1955.

Die Platonische Renaissance in England und die Schule von Cambridge, 1932; translated by James P. Pettegrove as *The Platonic Renaissance in England,* Nelson, 1953, Gordian Press (New York), 1970.

Determinismus und Indeterminismus in der modernen Physik, 1936; translated by O. Theodor Benfey as *Determinism and Indeterminism in Modern Physics: Historical and Systematic Studies of the Problem of Causality,* with a preface by Henry Margenau, Yale University Press (New Haven, CT), 1956.

Axel Hagerstrom: Eine Studie zur swedischen Philosophie der Gegenwart, 1939.

Descartes: Lehre—Personlichkeit—Wirkung, 1939.

The Philosophy of Ernst Cassirer (with an autobiographical essay), edited by Paul A. Schilpp for *The Library of Living Philosophers,* Volume 6, Northwestern University Press (Evanston and Chicago), 1939.

Zur Logik der Kulturwissenschaften: Funf Studien, 1942; translated by Clarence Smith Howe as *The Logic of the Humanities,* Yale University Press (New Haven, CT), 1961; and as *Toward a Logic of the Humanities,* with a critical introduction by Howe, University Microfilms (Ann Arbor, MI), 1960.

An Essay on Man: An Introduction to a Philosophy of Human Culture, Yale University Press, 1944, reprinted, 1992.

Rousseau, Kant, Goethe: Two Essays (criticism), 1945, translated by James Gutmann, Paul Oskar Kristeller, and John Herman Randall, Jr., as *Rousseau, Kant, Goetthe: Two Essays,* Princeton University Press, 1945; republished with an introduction by Peter Gay, Harper & Row, 1963.

The Myth of the State, published in *Fortune* (magazine), June, 1944; Yale University Press, 1946, Greenwood Press (Westport, CT), 1983.

Erkenntnisproblem in der Philosophie, Volume 4, translated by William H. Woglom and Charles W. Hendel as *The Problem of Knowledge: Philosophy, Science, and History Since Hegel,* Yale University Press, 1950.

The Question of Jean-Jacques Rousseau, translated and with an introduction by Peter Gay, Columbia University Press and Oxford University Press, 1954, Indiana University Press (Bloomington, IN), 1963; second edition, with a new postscript by Gay, Yale University Press, 1989.

Symbol, Myth and Culture: Essays and Lectures of Ernst Cassirer, 1935-1945 (essays), edited by Donald Phillip Verene, Yale University Press, 1979.

EDITOR

(With Paul Oskar Kristeller and John Herman Randall, Jr.) *The Renaissance Philosophy of Man: Selections in Translation,* University of Chicago Press, 1948, reprinted, 1967.

Contributor to journals, including *Journal de Psychologie.*

SIDELIGHTS: Ernst Cassirer was among the foremost neo-Kantian German philosophers of the first half of the twentieth century. He was a profoundly humanistic thinker who placed human language and consciousness at the forefront of his investigations, and saw them as responsible for shaping the world.

Born in Breslau, Silesia, the son of a wealthy Jewish businessman, he was at first an indifferent student, but at age twelve, he acquired a passion for learning, under the tutelage of his scholarly grandfather. He studied philosophy at several German universities, doing his graduate work at the University of Marburg under the prominent neo-Kantian Hermann Cohen, who is supposed to have concluded, after Cassirer's first answers in class, that "this man had nothing to learn from me." Cohen, however, remained an influential mentor throughout Cassirer's early career.

Cassirer's early scholarly work, which included a dissertation on the philosopher Gottfried Wilhelm Leibniz, was considered brilliant, and after marrying in 1901, he set to work on his first major opus, a history of epistemology. The first of four volumes was published in 1906 under the title *Das Erkenntnisproblem in der Philosophie und Wissenschaft der Neuen Zeit* (known in English as *The Problem of Knowledge*). This work is known to scholars as a standard text for investigation into the history of human thought. Cassirer's 1910 essay, *Substance and Function,* is sometimes considered his first truly original work: it deals with the nature of concepts and the nature of generalization. Cassirer's greatest work, however, was the multi-volume *Philosophie der Symbolischen Formen,* translated as *The Philosophy of Symbolic Forms.* It was published between the years 1923 and 1929, and was the fruit of Cassirer's researches in mythology, folklore, and other forms of human symbol-making. This work, according to Daniel O'Connor in the *McGraw-Hill Encyclopedia of World Biography,* "subjected mythical thinking to detailed analysis and undertook to revise the Kantian accounts of scientific, moral, and esthetic thinking."

Cassirer's world-view is one in which the human symbol-making faculty is paramount, and is responsible for such cultural achievements as science and the arts. A contributor to the *Twentieth Century Authors* supplement commented, "His theory of language is thus a 'theory of mental activity' (to use Susanne Langer's phrase), which begins not with logic and the development of 'orderly thought about facts,' but with myth and with language, the symbolization of thought." As Leon Rosenstein put it in the 1973 essay "Some Metaphysical Problems of Cassirer's Symbolic Forms" (published in the journal *Man And World*), "The 'ultimate' in Cassirer's philosophy is the human spirit" as represented in culture as a center of meaning.

Cassirer, though interested in myths and in psychology, was not interested in these human phenomena for their own sake, but for the ways in which they pointed to the deep underlying symbolic functions of the mind; he believed, said Hazard Adams in the 1983 essay "Thinking Cassirer" (published in the journal *Criticism*), in "mythical thought as an independent configuring power of human consciousness." (Cassirer was influenced in this by the Renaissance Italian philosopher Vico.) Cassirer expressed this independent configuring power thusly: "The highest truth that is accessible to the spirit is ultimately the form of its own activity." Studying the external—psychiatric case histories, myths, poetic images, scientific theories—Cassirer found that it led him to the internal; as philosopher Susanne K. Langer put it in the 1949 essay "On Cassirer's Theory of Language and Myth" (published in the book *The Philosophy of Ernst Cassirer*), "Cassirer's greatest epistemological contribution is his approach to the problem of mind through a study of the primitive forms of conception."

Preferring scholarship to teaching, Cassirer delayed his entrance into the world of German academics, but did eventually receive an appointment as a professor at Berlin, and became a fine teacher, later serving with distinction at the University of Hamburg. Anti-Semitic feeling was on the rise, however, and with the accession of Hitler to power in 1933, Cassirer resigned his post immediately. He went to Oxford University in England, where he taught himself to speak English during three intensive months; then he went to Sweden, where he became a naturalized citizen. The outbreak of World War II found him in the United States, however, and he remained there, as a visiting professor, until his sudden death while walking to class on April 13, 1945.

Cassirer's post-World War I work had ventured beyond neo-Kantianism, and during World War II it became increasingly political. In the posthumously published (1946) *The Myth of the State*, he claimed, according to a contributor to *Twentieth Century Literary Criticism*, "that human beings often mythologize their political existence rather than embracing a rational basis for the state"—a thesis that surely was influenced by, and was evidenced by, the Nazi regime.

At his death, Cassirer was, as always, reading and writing in a variety of fields, ranging from the philosophy of science to literary criticism. The unifying thread throughout was his emphasis on the fundamental role played by symbolic forms in the human mind:

a "legacy," says O'Connor in the *McGraw-Hill Encyclopedia of World Biography*, "which has not yet been fully assimilated and exploited." After Cassirer's death, Swedish thinker Hajo Holborn mourned that "one of the great philosophical interpreters of human civilization has been taken from us." Cassirer's own self-description, quoted in the *Twentieth Century Authors* supplement, sheds an equally humane light on him: he described his life as an odyssey "that led me from one university to the other, from one country to the other. This Odyssey was rich in experiences—in human and intellectual adventures."

BIOGRAPHICAL/CRITICAL SOURCES:

BOOKS

Langer, Susanne K., "On Cassirer's Theory of Language and Myth," in *The Philosophy of Ernst Cassirer*, edited by Paul Arthur Schlipp, The Library of Living Philosophers, Inc., 1949, pp. 381-400.
McGraw-Hill Encyclopedia of World Biography, McGraw-Hill (New York), 1973, pp. 410-411.
Twentieth-Century Authors: A Biographical Dictionary of Modern Literature, First Supplement, edited by Stanley J. Kunitz, H. W. Wilson Co. (New York), 1955, pp. 179-180.
Twentieth-Century Literary Criticism, Volume 61, Gale (Detroit), 1996, pp. 37-122.

PERIODICALS

Criticism, vol. XXV, no. 3, Summer, 1983, pp. 181-195.
Man and World, vol. 6, no. 3, September, 1973, pp. 304-321.*

* * *

CAVENDISH, Peter
See HORLER, Sydney

* * *

CHADWICK, James 1891-1974

PERSONAL: Born October 10 (one source says October 20), 1891, in Bollington, England; died July 24, 1974, in Cambridge, England; son of John Joseph (owner of a laundry) and Ann Mary (Knowles) Chadwick; married Aileen Stewart-Brown, in 1925; children: two daughters (twins). *Education:* University of Manchester, graduated (with honors), 1911, M.Sc., 1913; Cambridge University, Ph.D., 1921.

CAREER: Physicist. Cavendish Laboratory, Cambridge University, Cambridge, England, research in physics, 1921-22, assistant director of research, 1922-35; University of Liverpool, Liverpool, England, coordinator of establishment of new research center and construction of a particle accelerator, beginning 1935; coordinator of atomic bomb experimental efforts at the universities of Birmingham, Cambridge, Liverpool, London, and Oxford, for the Ministry of Aircraft Production, during World War II; leader of British contingent of Manhattan Project; advisor for British representatives to the United Nations regarding the control of atomic energy.

AWARDS, HONORS: Fellow, Gonville and Caius College, 1921; Nobel Prize, 1935, for discovery of the neutron; knighthood, 1945; Medal of Merit, United States government, 1946; Copely Medal, Royal Society, 1950; several academic scholarships.

WRITINGS:

(With Ernest Rutherford and C. D. Ellis) *Radiations From Radioactive Substances,* University Press (Cambridge), 1930.
Radioactivity and Radioactive Substances, Pitman, 1934.

SIDELIGHTS: James Chadwick, who is remembered principally for his work in nuclear physics, received the Nobel Prize in 1935 for his discovery of the neutron. That discovery gave rise to new approaches and techniques in the physical sciences, new developments in the biological sciences, and a new form of warfare. Chadwick himself was actively involved with the development of the atomic bomb. Although he was shy and did not have the public visibility of other physicists of his time, his work in science, diplomacy, and administration left permanent marks in twentieth-century history. Knighted in 1945, Chadwick received the Medal of Merit from the United States government in 1946, and the Copley Medal of the Royal Society in 1950.

Chadwick was born in Bollington, not far from Manchester, England, on October 20, 1891, to John Joseph Chadwick and Ann Mary Knowles. Chadwick senior owned a laundry business in Manchester. At

the age of sixteen, Chadwick won a scholarship to the University of Manchester, where he had intended to study mathematics. However, because he was mistakenly interviewed for admittance to the physics program and was too shy to explain the error, he decided to stay in physics. Initially Chadwick was disappointed in the physics classes, finding them too large and noisy. But in his second year, he heard a lecture by experimental physicist Ernest Rutherford about his early New Zealand experiments. Chadwick established a close working relationship with Rutherford and graduated in 1911 with first honors. Chadwick stayed at Manchester to work on his master's degree. During this time he made the acquaintance of others in the physics department, including Hans Geiger and Niels Bohr. Chadwick completed his M.Sc. in 1913 and won a scholarship that required him to do his research away from the institution that granted his degree. At this time Geiger returned to Germany, and Chadwick decided to follow him.

Chadwick had not been in Germany long when World War I broke out. Unsure of his plans, he postponed leaving the country. Soon he was arrested and sat in a Berlin jail for ten days until Geiger's laboratory interceded for his release. Eventually Chadwick was interned for the duration of the war, as were all other Englishmen in Germany. Chadwick spent the war years confined at a race track, where he shared with five other men a stable intended for two horses. His four years there were quiet, cold, and hungry. To keep up his morale, he participated in a scientific society formed by a group of internees. He managed to maintain correspondence with Geiger, and he even persuaded his German captors to supply some basic scientific equipment. One such piece he obtained was a bunsen burner. However, it lacked a bellows, so Chadwick enlisted one of his fellow captives to blow air through a tube into the burner. Although the work he did under such harsh conditions was not very fruitful, Chadwick later believed that it helped greatly to keep up his spirits at the time. He also felt that the experience of internment contributed to his maturity. Moreover, when Chadwick returned to England, he found that no one else had made much progress in nuclear physics during his time away.

In 1919 Ernest Rutherford was appointed director of Cambridge University's Cavendish Laboratory, the leading research center for nuclear physics at the time. Rutherford brought Chadwick with him, and the two began a partnership that lasted sixteen years. Chadwick earned his Ph.D. in physics from Cambridge in 1921 and was made a fellow at Gonville and

Caius College, enabling him to continue working with Rutherford at the Cavendish lab. Rutherford had been working on atomic structure and had discovered many of the essential properties of the proton. One of Chadwick's first tasks was to help Rutherford establish a unit of measurement for radioactivity, to aid in experiments with the radiation of atomic nuclei. Chadwick then developed a method to measure radioactivity that required the observation of flashes, called scintillations, in zinc sulfide crystals under a microscope and in complete darkness. Although this method was difficult and prone to error, later experiments using newer detection techniques confirmed Chadwick's radiation measurements. In 1922 Chadwick became assistant director of research under Rutherford. In this post, Chadwick supervised all the research at the laboratory. Chadwick and Rutherford spent much time experimenting with the transmutation of elements, attempting to break up the nucleus of one element so that different elements would be formed. These experiments involved bombarding the nuclei of nitrogen and other elements with alpha particles (helium nuclei). This work eventually led to other experiments to gauge the size and map the structure of the atomic nucleus.

Throughout the years of work on the transmutation of elements, Chadwick and Rutherford struggled with an inconsistency. They saw that almost every element had an atomic number that was less than its atomic mass. In other words, an atom of any given element seemed to have more mass than could be accounted for by the number of protons in its nucleus. Rutherford initially thought that the extra mass was made up of proton-electron pairs, which would add mass but no additional charge to the nucleus. However, the nucleus did not seem to have room enough for such pairs. Rutherford then suggested the possibility of a particle with the mass of a proton and a neutral charge, but for a long time his and Chadwick's attempts to find such a particle were in vain.

For twelve years, Chadwick looked intermittently and unsuccessfully for the neutrally-charged particle that Rutherford proposed. In 1930 two German physicists, Walther Bothe and Hans Becker, found an unexpectedly penetrating radiation, thought to be gamma rays, when some elements were bombarded with alpha particles. However, the element beryllium showed an emission pattern that the gamma-ray hypothesis could not account for. Chadwick suspected that neutral particles were responsible for the emissions. Work done in France in 1922 by physicists Frederic Joliot-Curie and Irene Joliot-Curie supplied the answer. Studying

the hypothetical gamma-ray emissions from beryllium, they found that radiation increased when the emissions passed through the absorbing material paraffin. Although the Joliot-Curie team concluded that gamma rays emitted by beryllium knocked hydrogen protons out of the paraffin, Chadwick immediately saw that their experiments would confirm the presence of the neutron, since it would take a neutral particle of such mass to move a proton. He first set to work demonstrating that the gamma-ray hypothesis could not account for the observed phenomena, because gamma rays would not have enough energy to eject protons so rapidly. Then he showed that the beryllium nucleus, when combined with an alpha particle, could be transmuted to a carbon nucleus, releasing a particle with a mass comparable to that of a proton but with a neutral charge. The neutron had finally been tracked down. Other experiments showed that a boron nucleus plus an alpha particle results in a nitrogen nucleus plus a neutron. Chadwick's first public announcement of the discovery was in an article in the journal *Nature* with a title characteristic of his unassuming personality, "Possible Existence of a Neutron." In 1935 Chadwick was awarded the Nobel Prize in physics for this discovery. That same year, Chadwick took a position at the University of Liverpool to establish a new research center in nuclear physics and to build a particle accelerator.

Chadwick's discovery of the neutron made possible more precise examinations of the nucleus. It also led to speculations about uranium fission. Physicists found that bombarding uranium nuclei with neutrons caused the nuclei to split into two almost equal pieces and to release energy in the very large amounts predicted by Einstein's formula E=mc2. This phenomenon, known as nuclear fission, was discovered and publicized on the eve of World War II, and many scientists immediately began to speculate about its application to warfare. Britain quickly assembled a group of scientists under the Ministry of Aircraft Production, called the Maud Committee, to pursue the practicality of an atomic bomb. Chadwick was put in charge of coordinating all the experimental efforts of the universities of Birmingham, Cambridge, Liverpool, London, and Oxford. Initially Chadwick's responsibilities were limited to the very difficult and purely experimental aspects of the research project. Gradually, he became more involved with other duties in the organization, particularly as spokesperson.

Chadwick's work in evaluating and presenting evidence convinced British government and military leaders to move ahead with the project. Chadwick's involvement was broad and deep, forcing him to deal with scientific details of uranium supplies and radiation effects as well as broader issues of scientific organization and policy. His correspondence during this time referred to issues ranging from Britain's relationship with the United States to the effects of cobalt on the health of sheep. As the pressures of war became greater, the British realized that even with their theoretical advances, they did not have the practical resources to develop a working atomic bomb. In 1943 Britain and the United States signed the Quebec Agreement, which created a partnership between the two countries for the development of an atomic bomb. Chadwick became the leader of the British contingent involved in the Manhattan Project in the United States. Although he was shy and used to the isolation of the laboratory, Chadwick became known for his tireless efforts at collaboration and his keen sense of diplomacy. He maintained friendly Anglo-American relations despite a great variety of scientific challenges, political struggles, and conflicting personalities. On July 16, 1945, he witnessed the first atomic test in the New Mexico desert.

After the war Chadwick's work continued to focus on nuclear weapons. He was an advisor for the British representatives to the United Nations regarding the control of atomic energy around the world. He believed that the British had to have their own atomic weapons, and he pushed hard for Britain's atomic independence. This issue was particularly evident to him when the United States and Britain argued over an earlier agreement for dividing up the uranium supplies they had jointly accumulated during the development of the atomic bomb. Chadwick used his diplomacy to effect a compromise that enabled the British to reclaim the uranium needed for their own atomic projects. Chadwick's postwar involvement with nuclear energy was not limited to weapons. He also was interested in medical applications of radioactive materials, and he worked to develop ways of regulating radioactive substances.

Chadwick was a dedicated and tireless scientist who balanced his commitments to science with a commitment to his family. He and his wife, Aileen Stewart-Brown, whom he married in 1925, had twin daughters. Though he was shy and serious, he did not lack a sense of humor: to celebrate the operation of a new cyclotron (particle accelerator) at Liverpool, Chadwick passed around laboratory beakers full of champagne. Chadwick had an exacting sense of discipline and a tireless attention to detail. When he was at the Cavendish laboratory, all papers that went out for publication passed under his critical gaze. In an article in the *Bulletin of the Atomic Scientists,* Mark Oliphant, who had been a research student under Chadwick, remarked that "he was a severe critic of English usage and seemed to carry in his head the whole of Roget's *Thesaurus of English Words and Phrases.*"

Much of Chadwick's early career went toward searching for the neutron. When he found it, the physics community quickly seized on the prospect of developing from it the atomic bomb. Much of the rest of Chadwick's career was spent in assisting that development. Although he pushed for atomic policy issues as much as he pushed for scientific solutions, Chadwick eventually saw the uselessness of the atomic bomb. Margaret Gowing, in her article, "James Chadwick and the Atomic Bomb," quoted Chadwick as saying of the bomb, "Its effect in causing suffering is out of all proportion to its military effect." James Chadwick died in Cambridge, England, on July 24, 1974.

BIOGRAPHICAL/CRITICAL SOURCES:

BOOKS

Pais, Abraham, *Inward Bound,* Oxford University Press (Oxford), 1986.
Rhodes, Richard, *The Making of the Bomb,* Simon & Schuster (New York), 1986.

PERIODICALS

Bulletin of the Atomic Scientists, December, 1982, pp. 14-18.
Notes and Records of the Royal Society of London, January, 1993, pp. 79-92.
Physics World, October, 1991, pp. 31-33.
Time, August 5, 1974.*

*   *   *

CHAMELEON, A.
  See HARTMANN, Sadakichi

*   *   *

CHANCE, Britton 1913-

PERSONAL: Born July 24, 1913, in Wilkes Barre, PA; son of Edwin M. (a chemist and engineer) and

Eleanor (Kent) Chance; married Jane Earle, March 4, 1938 (divorced); married Lilian Streeter Lucas, November, 1956 (divorced); children: (first marriage) Eleanor, Britton, Jan, Peter; (second marriage) Margaret, Lilian, Benjamin, Samuel; stepchildren: (second marriage) Ann, Gerald B., A. Brooke, William. *Education:* University of Pennsylvania, B.S., 1935, M.S., 1936, Ph.D., 1940; University of Cambridge, Ph.D., 1942, D.Sc., 1952; Karolinska Institute, Stockholm, Sweden, M.D., 1962; attended Nobel Institute, Sweden, and Molteno Institute, England.

CAREER: Biochemist and biophysicist. E. R. Johnson Foundation, University of Pennsylvania, Philadelphia, acting director, 1940-41, assistant professor of biophysics and physical biochemistry, 1941-49, professor, 1947-49, director, 1949-83, chairperson of department of biophysics and physical chemistry, 1949-75; Massachusetts Institute of Technology, became head of Precision Components Group, associate head of Receiver Components Division, member of Steering Committee, 1941-46.

AWARDS, HONORS: Guggenheim fellow, 1946-48; Paul Lewis Award, 1950; Morlock Award, 1961; Genootschaps Medal, Dutch Biochemical Society, 1966; Franklin Medal, Franklin Institute, 1966; Harrison Howe Award, American Chemical Society, 1966; Nichols Award, 1970; Heineken Medal, 1970; Post-Cong Festschrift, 1973; Semmelweis Medal, 1974; National Medal of Science, 1974; Elizabeth Winston Lanier Award, 1986; honorary degrees from several universities, including Cambridge University, Semmelweise University, Hahnemann Medical College, Medical College of Ohio, University of Pennsylvania, University of Helsinki, and University of Dusseldorf.

WRITINGS:

EDITOR

Rapid Mixing and Sampling Techniques in Biochemistry, Academic Press (New York), 1964.
Waveforms, Dover Publications (New York), 1965.
(With Ronald W. Estabrook and John R. Williamson) *Control of Energy Metabolism,* Academic Press, 1965.
(With Estabrook and Takashi Yontani) *Hemes and Hemoproteins,* Academic Press, 1966.
Biological and Biochemical Oscillators, Academic Press, 1973.
Tunneling in Biological Systems, Academic Press, 1979.

(With Maurizio Brunori) *Cytochrome Oxidase: Structure, Function, and Physiopathology,* New York Academy of Sciences (New York), 1988.
Photon Migration in Tissues, Plenum Press (New York), 1989.
Time-Resolved Spectroscopy and Imaging of Tissues, SPIE (Bellingham, WA), 1991.
(With Ingrid Emerit) *Free Radicals and Aging,* Birheauser Verlag (Boston), 1992.
(With Robert R. Alfano) *Photon Migration and Imaging in Random Media and Tissues: 17-19 January, 1993, Los Angeles, California,* SPIE, 1993.

Contributor to journals and periodicals, including *Proceedings of the IEEE.*

SIDELIGHTS: Combining an interest in electronics with his specialties of chemistry and biology, Britton Chance developed new equipment and techniques for research in biochemistry and biophysics, including the invention of the double-beam spectrophotometer and the reflectance fluorometer and application of computer methods to the study of enzyme action and metabolic control. Furthermore, the experimental results he has obtained using his own innovative procedures are of major importance in such areas as determining the actions of narcotics and poisons on living cells.

Born in Wilkes-Barre, Pennsylvania, on July 24, 1913, Chance was the son of Edwin M. Chance, a chemist who was honored for research in mine gases and who worked with the Chemical Warfare Service during World War I. His mother was Eleanor Kent Chance. Both parents were from Philadelphia, Pennsylvania, and the family returned there after Britton's birth, with the senior Chance becoming an engineer. Summers were spent at Barnegat Bay, New Jersey, where the family kept a 100-foot cruiser that they sailed as far as the Caribbean and Europe.

After graduating from the Haverford School, Chance studied at the University of Pennsylvania, where he earned a B.S. degree in chemistry in 1935, and an M.S. the following year. His experience with sailing led him to an interest in navigation and automatic steering, which he thought could be improved using electronics; he found room in his curriculum to study enough physics and electrical engineering to pursue that interest. Under the guidance of Martin Kilpatrick, his chemistry mentor at Pennsylvania, Chance investigated rapid chemical reaction techniques. Using his knowledge of electronics, he developed better instrumentation for observing the small, quick changes in optical density that accompany reactions involving enzymes—proteins produced by living cells that stimulate such important functions as food digestion and the release of energy.

After receiving his master's degree, Chance traveled to England to supervise the installation of the marine electronic steering system he had invented, which was first used on a 12,000-ton ship. In 1938 he married his childhood sweetheart, Jane Earle, and they used the ship's trial cruise to Australia as their honeymoon. Upon returning to England, Chance enrolled as a research student at Cambridge University. He studied under F. J. W. Roughton, who had developed a fundamental procedure for observing rapid reactions, and G. A. Millikan, a physiologist. Millikan was using Roughton's technique to study muscle pigments, and Chance adapted the same procedure to reactions between small quantities of substances. Altering both the experimental technique and the equipment, Chance devised the "accelerated flow modification" procedure: reactants were simultaneously injected into a fine tube, where the changes in light absorption of the reacting material were continuously monitored with a highly sensitive oscilloscope. This important modification allowed experiments to be conducted more quickly, was more sensitive to reactions, and required less materials to complete experiments.

At the outbreak of World War II in 1939, Chance returned to the United States and joined the faculty at the University of Pennsylvania's Eldridge Reeves Johnson Foundation of Medical Physics. There, he finished developing his technique for measuring the reaction between hydrogen peroxide and the enzyme peroxidase. He was awarded a Ph.D. in physical chemistry in 1940 and became acting director of the Johnson Foundation. Two years later, he was awarded a Ph.D. in biology and physiology by Cambridge.

During World War II, Chance was invited to work on radar at the Massachusetts Institute of Technology's Radiation Laboratory. Between 1941 and 1946, he headed the Precision Components Group, served as associate head of the Receiver Components Division, and was one of the younger members of the laboratory's Steering Committee. Among the devices he helped develop were precision timing and computing circuits for bombing and navigation. In 1942, he applied advanced electronic circuits to measuring small changes in light absorption, and in 1943, he experimentally validated the Michaelis-Menton theory of enzyme action, which had first been proposed in 1913.

When the war ended, Chance devoted himself to the study of the nature of enzymes and won a Guggenheim Fellowship to study at the Nobel Institute in Sweden and the Molteno Institute in Great Britain from 1946 to 1948. His interest in boating continued; while in Europe, he and his wife (a skilled helmsman) won numerous races for Class E scows that were held in the Baltic Sea.

In 1949, Chance returned to the University of Pennsylvania as a professor, chairperson of the department of biophysics and physical biochemistry, director of the Johnson Foundation, and faculty adviser for the university yacht club. His research on enzymatic reactions in living systems directed him to the creation of the double-beam or dual-wavelength spectrophotometer, an optical device that was used to study mitochondria—those elements of the cell nucleus that produce energy—as well as cell suspensions and other biological systems. Adapting the double-beam spectrophotometer to living materials, he developed the reflectance fluorometer, an instrument that led, eventually, to a better understanding of the actions of narcotics, hormones and poisons on human cells.

In addition to his work with these ground-breaking devices, Chance began to apply analog and digital computers to his research in the 1940s, producing the first computer solution of the differential equations describing enzyme action. Beginning in 1955, Chance concentrated his studies on the control of metabolism, especially as it is related to mitochondria. Chance studied these energy-producing elements in the cell nucleus, attempting to determine their role as optical indicators of change within the cell. His work on the concentration of adenosinediphosphate (ADP) in tumor cells gave scientists a better understanding of the role of mitochondria in regulating the body's utilization of glucose.

During the next four decades, Chance developed increasingly sophisticated instruments for optical spectroscopy and imaging of tissues, particularly in living patients. In the area of tumor oxygenation, he found significant differences in hemoglobin oxygenation between the surface and deeper regions of solid tumors, which a 1992 article in *Proceedings of the IEEE* described as being "of great importance clinically, for example, in relation to the oxygen-dependent response to radiation therapy." In another study, he made time-resolved measurements of photon migration on the forehead of a patient with Alzheimer's disease, finding the scattering coefficient of the brain tissue in some regions to be one-half to one-third of normal values.

Recognition of Chance's fundamental contributions to biomedical electronics and other fields came from all over the world. His pioneering work with rapid enzyme reactions was described in a 1949 issue of *Nature:* "The value and scope of this experimental technique in the field of reaction kinetics can scarcely be overestimated." His achievements were further acknowledged in 1954 with his election to the National Academy of Sciences, and he became a life fellow in the Institute of Electrical and Electronics Engineers (IEEE) in 1961. He holds several honorary medical degrees, including an honorary M.D. from the Karolinska Institute of the University of Stockholm. Chance has also been honored with the Dutch Chemical Society's Genootschaps-Medaille and the Franklin Medal of the Franklin Institute. President Gerald Ford presented him with the National Medal of Science in 1974, and in 1976, the University of Pennsylvania named him university professor, its highest academic appointment. He retired from the university in 1983.

In 1956, Chance married for the second time, wedding Lilian Streeter Lucas. He has served as father to twelve children, including the four from his first marriage and four stepchildren.

BIOGRAPHICAL/CRITICAL SOURCES:

BOOKS

Modern Men of Science, McGraw-Hill, 1966, pp. 95-97.

PERIODICALS

Chemical and Engineering News, May 8, 1950.
Nature, April 9, 1949, pp. 558-559.*

                    *   *   *

CHANDRASEKHAR, Subrahmanyan 1910-

PERSONAL: Born October 19, 1910, in Lahore, India (now part of Pakistan); naturalized citizen, 1953 son of C. Subrahmanyan Ayyar and Sitalakshmi (Divan Bahadur) Balakrishnan; married Lalitha Doraiswamy, 1936. *Education:* Presidency College, Madras, India, B.A., M.A., 1930; Cambridge University, Ph.D., 1933, Sc.D., 1942; studied at Institut fur Theoretische Physik, Gottingen, Germany, 1931, under Max Born. *Avocational interests:* Literature and music (orchestral, chamber, south Indian).

CAREER: Astrophysicist and applied mathematician. Yerkes Observatory, Williams Bay, WI, research associate, 1937-38, assistant professor of astrophysics, 1938-52, professor, beginning in 1952; University of Chicago, Chicago, IL, associate professor of astrophysics, 1942-43, professor, 1943-46, Distinguished Service Professor, 1946-52, Morton D. Hull Distinguished Service Professor of Astrophysics, 1952-1980. Worked at the Aberdeen Proving Grounds in Maryland during World War II.

AWARDS, HONORS: Fellow, Trinity College, Cambridge, 1934; Adams Prize, Cambridge University, 1947; Bruce Medal, Astronomical Society of the Pacific, 1952; Gold Medal, Royal Astronomical Society, 1953; granted membership in National Academy of Sciences, 1955; Royal Medal, Royal Society of London, 1962; Srinivas Ramunujan Medal, Indian National Science Academy, 1962; National Medal of Science, United States Government, 1966; Padma Vibhushan Medal of India, 1968; Henry Draper Medal, National Academy of Sciences, 1971; Smoluchowski Medal, Polish Physical Society, 1973; Dannie Heineman Prize, American Physical Society, 1974; Nobel Prize for Physics, Royal Swedish Academy, 1983; Dr. Tomalla Prize, ETH, 1984; Copley Prize, Royal Society of London, 1984; R. D. Birla Memorial Award, Indian Physics Association, 1984; Vainu Bappu Memorial Award, Indian National Science Academy, 1985; Lincoln Academy Award, state of Illinois, 1993. Awarded a scholarship by the Indian Government, created especially for him, to study at Cambridge University, 1930.

WRITINGS:

An Introduction to the Study of Stellar Evolution, University of Chicago Press, 1939.
Principles of Stellar Dynamics, University of Chicago Press (Chicago), 1943.
Radiative Transfer, Clarendon Press (Oxford), 1950.
Plasma Physics, University of Chicago Press, 1960.
Hydrodynamic and Hydromagnetic Stability, Clarendon Press, 1961.
Ellipsoidal Figures of Equilibrium, Yale University Press (New Haven, CT), 1968.
Shakespeare, Newton, and Beethoven: or, Patterns of Creativity, University of Chicago, Center for Policy Study, 1975.
(Editor) *New Horizons of Human Knowledge: A Series of Public Talks Given at UNESCO,* Unesco Press (Paris), 1981.
The Mathematical Theory of Black Holes, Clarendon Press, 1983.

Eddington: The Most Distinguished Astrophysicist of His Time, Cambridge University Press (Cambridge, MA), 1983.

Truth and Beauty: Aesthetics and Motivations in Science, University of Chicago Press, 1987.

(Editor) *Proceedings of the Second Asia-Pacific Physics Conference, Bangalore, 1986,* World Scientific Pub. (Philadelphia, PA), 1987.

Stellar Structure and Stellar Atmospheres, University of Chicago Press, 1989.

Stochastic, Statistical, and Hydromagnetic Problems in Physics and Astronomy, University of Chicago Press, 1989.

Selected Papers (6 volumes), University of Chicago Press, 1989-90.

Relativistic Astrophysics, University of Chicago Press, 1990.

(Editor) *Classical General Relativity,* Oxford University Press (New York), 1993.

Newton's Principia for the Common Reader, Oxford University Press, 1995.

The Non-Radial Oscillations of Stars in General Relativity and Other Writings, University of Chicago Press, 1996.

Editor-in-Chief of *Astrophysical Journal* for almost twenty years. Contributor to journals and periodicals, including *Proceedings of the Royal Society* and *Review of Modern Physics.*

SIDELIGHTS: Subrahmanyan Chandrasekhar is an Indian-born American astrophysicist and applied mathematician whose work on the origins, structure, and dynamics of stars has secured him a prominent place in the annals of science. His most celebrated work concerns the radiation of energy from stars, particularly white dwarf stars, which are the dying fragments of stars. Chandrasekhar demonstrated that the radius of a white dwarf star is related to its mass: the greater its mass, the smaller its radius.

Chandrasekhar has made numerous other contributions to astrophysics. His expansive research and published papers and books include topics such as the system of energy transfer within stars, stellar evolution, stellar structure, and theories of planetary and stellar atmospheres. For nearly twenty years, he served as the editor-in-chief of the *Astrophysical Journal,* the leading publication of its kind in the world. For his immense contribution to science, Chandrasekhar has received numerous awards and distinctions, most notably, the 1983 Nobel Prize for Physics for his research into the depths of aged stars.

Chandrasekhar, better known as Chandra, was born on October 19, 1910, in Lahore, India (now part of Pakistan), the first son of C. Subrahmanyan Ayyar and Sitalakshmi nee (Divan Bahadur) Balakrishnan. Chandra came from a large family: he had two older sisters, four younger sisters, and three younger brothers. As the firstborn son, Chandra inherited his paternal grandfather's name, Chandrasekhar. His uncle was the Nobel Prize-winning Indian physicist, Sir C. V. Raman.

Chandra received his early education at home, beginning when he was five. From his mother he learned Tamil, from his father, English and arithmetic. He set his sights upon becoming a scientist at an early age, and to this end, undertook at his own initiative some independent study of calculus and physics. The family moved north to Lucknow in Uttar Pradesh when Chandra was six. In 1918, the family moved again, this time south to Madras. Chandrasekhar was taught by private tutors until 1921, when he enrolled in the Hindu High School in Triplicane. With typical drive and motivation, he studied on his own and steamed ahead of his class, completing school by the age of fifteen.

After high school, Chandra attended Presidency College in Madras. For the first two years, he studied physics, chemistry, English, and Sanskrit. For his B.A. honors degree he wished to take pure mathematics but his father insisted that he take physics. Chandra resolved this conflict by registering as an honors physics student but attending mathematics lectures. Recognizing his brilliance, his lecturers went out of their way to accommodate Chandra. Chandra also took part in sporting activities and joined the debating team. A highlight of his college years was the publication of his paper, "The Compton Scattering and the New Statistics." These and other early successes while he was still an eighteen-year-old undergraduate only strengthened Chandra's resolve to pursue a career in scientific research, despite his father's wish that he join the Indian civil service. A meeting the following year with the German physicist Werner Heisenberg, whom Chandra, as the secretary of the student science association, had the honor of showing around Madras, and Chandra's attendance at the Indian Science Congress Association Meeting in early 1930, where his work was hailed, doubled his determination.

Upon graduating with a M.A. in 1930, Chandra set off for Trinity College, Cambridge, as a research student, courtesy of an Indian government scholarship created especially for him (with the stipulation that upon his return to India, he would serve for five years in the Madras government service). At Cambridge, Chandra turned to astrophysics, inspired by a theory of stellar evolution that had occurred to him as he made the long boat journey from India to Cambridge. It would preoccupy him for the next ten years. He also worked on other aspects of astrophysics and published many papers.

In the summer of 1931, he worked with physicist Max Born at the Institut fur Theoretische Physik at Gottingen in Germany. There, he studied group theory and quantum mechanics (the mathematical theory that relates matter and radiation) and produced work on the theory of stellar atmospheres. During this period, Chandra was often tempted to leave astrophysics for pure mathematics, his first love, or at least for physics. He was worried, though, that with less than a year to go before his thesis exam, a change might cost him his degree. Other factors influenced his decision to stay with astrophysics, most importantly, the encouragement shown him by astrophysicist Edward Arthur Milne. In August 1932, Chandra left Cambridge to continue his studies in Denmark under physicist Niels Bohr. In Copenhagen, he was able to devote more of his energies to pure physics. A series of Chandra's lectures on astrophysics given at the University of Liege, in Belgium, in February 1933 received a warm reception. Before returning to Cambridge in May 1933 to sit for his doctorate exams, he went back to Copenhagen to work on his thesis.

Chandrasekhar's uncertainty about his future was assuaged when he was awarded a fellowship at Trinity College, Cambridge. During a four-week trip to Russia in 1934, where he met physicists Lev Davidovich Landau, B. P. Geraismovic, and Viktor Ambartsumian, he returned to the work that had led him into astrophysics to begin with, white dwarfs. Upon returning to Cambridge, he took up research of white dwarfs again in earnest.

As a member of the Royal Astronomical Society since 1932, Chandra was entitled to present papers at its twice monthly meetings. It was at one of these that Chandra, in 1935, announced the results of the work that would later make his name. As stars evolve, he told the assembled audience, they emit energy generated by their conversion of hydrogen into helium and even heavier elements. As they reach the end of their life, stars have progressively less hydrogen left to convert and emit less energy in the form of radiation.

They eventually reach a stage when they are no longer able to generate the pressure needed to sustain their size against their own gravitational pull and they begin to contract. As their density increases during the contraction process, stars build up sufficient internal energy to collapse their atomic structure into a degenerate state. They begin to collapse into themselves. Their electrons become so tightly packed that their normal activity is suppressed and they become white dwarfs, tiny objects of enormous density. The greater the mass of a white dwarf, the smaller its radius, according to Chandrasekhar. However, not all stars end their lives as stable white dwarfs. If the mass of evolving stars increases beyond a certain limit, eventually named the "Chandrasekhar limit" and calculated as 1.4 times the mass of the sun, evolving stars cannot become stable white dwarfs. A star with a mass above the limit has to either lose mass to become a white dwarf or take an alternative evolutionary path and become a supernova, which releases its excess energy in the form of an explosion. What mass remains after this spectacular event may become a white dwarf but more likely will form a neutron star. The neutron star has even greater density than a white dwarf and an average radius of about .15 kilometers. It has since been independently proven that all white dwarf stars fall within Chandrasekhar's predicted limit, which has been revised to equal 1.2 solar masses.

Unfortunately, although his theory would later be vindicated, Chandra's ideas were unexpectedly undermined and ridiculed by no less a scientific figure than astronomer and physicist Sir Arthur Stanley Eddington, who dismissed as absurd Chandra's notion that stars can evolve into anything other than white dwarfs. Eddington's status and authority in the community of astronomers carried the day, and Chandra, as the junior, was not given the benefit of the doubt.

Twenty years passed before his theory gained general acceptance among astrophysicists, although it was quickly recognized as valid by physicists as noteworthy as Wolfgang Pauli, Niels Bohr, Ralph H. Fowler, and Paul Dirac. Rather than continue sparring with Eddington at scientific meeting after meeting, Chandra collected his thoughts on the matter into his first book, *An Introduction to the Study of Stellar Structure,* and departed the fray to take up new research around stellar dynamics. An unfortunate result of the scientific quarrel, however, was to postpone the discovery of black holes and neutron stars by at least twenty years and Chandra's receipt of a Nobel Prize for his white dwarf work by fifty years. Surprisingly, despite their scientific differences, he retained a close personal relationship with Eddington.

Chandra spent from December 1935 until March 1936 at Harvard University as a visiting lecturer in cosmic physics. While in the United States, he was offered a research associate position at Yerkes Observatory at Williams Bay, Wisconsin, starting in January 1937. Before taking up this post, Chandra returned home to India to marry the woman who had waited for him patiently for six years. He had known Lalitha Doraiswamy, daughter of Captain and Mrs. Savitri Doraiswamy, since they had been students together at Madras University. After graduation, she had undertaken a masters degree. At the time of their marriage, she was a headmistress. Although their marriage of love was unusual, as both came from fairly progressive families and were both of the Brahman caste, neither of their families had any real objections. After a whirlwind courtship and wedding, the young bride and groom set out for the United States. They intended to stay no more than a few years, but, as luck would have it, it became their permanent home.

At the Yerkes Observatory, Chandra was charged with developing a graduate program in astronomy and astrophysics and with teaching some of the courses. His reputation as a teacher soon attracted top students to the observatory's graduate school. He also continued researching stellar evolution, stellar structure, and the transfer of energy within stars. In 1938, he was promoted to assistant professor of astrophysics. During this time Chandra revealed his conclusions regarding the life paths of stars.

During the Second World War, Chandra was employed at the Aberdeen Proving Grounds in Maryland, working on ballistic tests, the theory of shock waves, the Mach effect, and transport problems related to neutron diffusion. In 1942, he was promoted to associate professor of astrophysics at the University of Chicago and in 1943, to professor. Around 1944, he switched his research from stellar dynamics to radiative transfer. Of all his research, the latter gave him, he recalled later, more fulfillment. That year, he also achieved a lifelong ambition when he was elected to the Royal Society of London. In 1946, he was elevated to Distinguished Service Professor. In 1952, he became Morton D. Hull Distinguished Service Professor of Astrophysics in the departments of astronomy and physics, as well as at the Institute for Nuclear Physics at the University of Chicago's Yerkes Observatory. Later the same year, he was appointed managing editor of the *Astrophysical Jour-*

nal, a position he held until 1971. He transformed the journal from a private publication of the University of Chicago to the national journal of the American Astronomical Society. The price he paid for his editorial impartiality, however, was isolation from the astrophysical community.

Chandra became a United States citizen in 1953. Despite receiving numerous offers from other universities, in the United States and overseas, Chandra never left the University of Chicago, although, owing to a disagreement with Bengt Stromgren, the head of Yerkes, he stopped teaching astrophysics and astronomy and began lecturing in mathematical physics at the University of Chicago campus. Chandra voluntarily retired from the University of Chicago in 1980, although he remained on as a post-retirement researcher. In 1983, he published a classic work on the mathematical theory of black holes. Since then, he has studied colliding waves and the Newtonian two-center problem in the framework of the general theory of relativity. His semi-retirement has also left him with more time to pursue his hobbies and interests: literature and music, particularly orchestral, chamber, and South Indian.

During his long career, Chandrasekhar has received many awards. In 1947, Cambridge University awarded him its Adams Prize. In 1952, he received the Bruce Medal of the Astronomical Society of the Pacific, and the following year, the Gold Medal of the Royal Astronomical Society. In 1955, Chandrasekhar became a Member of the National Academy of Sciences. The Royal Society of London bestowed upon him its Royal Medal seven years later. In 1962, he was also presented with the Srinivasa Ramanujan Medal of the Indian National Science Academy. The National Medal of Science of the United States was conferred upon Chandra in 1966; and the Padma Vibhushan Medal of India in 1968. Chandra received the Henry Draper Medal of the National Academy of Sciences in 1971 and the Smoluchowski Medal of the Polish Physical Society in 1973. The American Physical Society gave him its Dannie Heineman Prize in 1974. The crowning glory of his career came nine years later when the Royal Swedish Academy awarded Chandrasekhar the Nobel Prize for Physics. ETH of Zurich gave the Indian astrophysicist its Dr. Tomalla Prize in 1984, while the Royal Society of London presented him with its Copley Prize later that year. Chandra also received the R. D. Birla Memorial Award of the Indian Physics Association in 1984. In 1985, the Vainu Bappu Memorial Award of the Indian National Science Academy was conferred upon

Chandrasekhar. In May 1993, Chandra received the state of Illinois's highest honor, Lincoln Academy Award, for his outstanding contributions to science.

While his contribution to astrophysics has been immense, Chandra has always preferred to remain outside the mainstream of research. He described himself to his biographer, Kameshar C. Wali, as "a lonely wanderer in the byways of science." Throughout his life, Chandra has striven to acquire knowledge and understanding, according to an autobiographical essay published with his Nobel lecture, motivated "principally by a quest after perspectives."

BIOGRAPHICAL/CRITICAL SOURCES:

BOOKS

Biographical Dictionary of Scientists, Astronomers, Blond Educational Company (London), 1984, pp. 36.
Chambers Biographical Encyclopedia of Scientists, Facts-on-File, 1981.
Goldsmith, Donald, *The Astronomers,* St. Martin's Press (New York), 1991.
Great American Scientists, Prentice-Hall (Englewood Cliffs, NJ), 1960.
Land, Kenneth R. and Owen Gingerich, editors, *A Sourcebook in Astronomy and Astrophysics,* Harvard University Press (Boston), 1979.
Modern Men of Science, McGraw-Hill (New York), 1966, p. 97.
Wali, Kameshwar C., *Chandra: A Biography of S. Chandrasekhar,* Chicago University Press (Chicago, IL), 1991.*

*   *   *

CHARPAK, Georges 1924-

PERSONAL: Born August 1, 1924, in Dabrovica, Poland; immigrated to France, 1929; became naturalized citizen, 1946; son of Maurice and Anna (Szapiro) Charpak; married Dominique Vidal, 1953; children: Yves, Nathalie and Serge. *Education:* Ecole des Mines de Paris, B.S., 1948; College of France, Ph.D., 1954. *Avocational interests:* Skiing, music, hiking.

ADDRESSES: CERN Lab for Particle Physics, CH 1211, Geneva, Switzerland.

CAREER: Physicist. Centre Nation de la Recherche Scientifique, professor, 1948-59; Centre Europeen pour la Recherche Nucleaire, Geneva, Switzerland, professor, 1959—; Ecole Superieure de Physique et Chimie de la Ville de Paris, Paris, France, Joliot-Curie professor, 1984—. Founder of the S.O.S. Committee at CERN.

AWARDS, HONORS: Croix de Guerre (military cross), 1939-40; Ricard Prize, European Physics Society, 1980; Commissariat prize of Atomic Energy, French Academy of Science, 1984; High Energy and Particle Physics Prize, 1989; Nobel Prize in Physics, 1992. Honorary degrees from universities, including University of Geneva, 1977; University of Thessalonica, Greece, 1993; Vrije University, Brussels, Belgium, 1994; University of Coimbra, Portugal, 1994; University of Ottawa, Canada, 1995.

WRITINGS:

(With Dominique Saudinos) *La Vie Aa Fil Tendu,* Editions O. Jacob (Paris), 1993.
Research on Particle Imaging Detectors, World Scientific (River Edge, NJ), 1995.

Contributor of articles to professional journals.

SIDELIGHTS: Georges Charpak received the Nobel Prize in physics in 1992 for his invention and development of particle detectors, most notably the multiwire proportional chamber. A number of his colleagues, who received the Nobel Prize before him, had used his invention to make important discoveries in physics. Charpak is credited with creating instrumentation that is used by thousands of other scientists at CERN, the European laboratory for particle physics located in Geneva, Switzerland, as well as by researchers in other prominent laboratories involved in the study of the nature of matter.

Born on August 1, 1924, in Dabrovica, Poland, to Maurice Charpak and Anna Szapiro, Charpak moved to France with his family in 1929. In 1943 the French Vichy government accused the young Charpak of being a terrorist and sentenced him to the concentration camp in Dachau, West Germany (now Germany). Charpak remained in the camp until its liberation in 1945. Upon his return to France, he completed a degree in civil engineering from the Ecole des Mines in Paris, and in 1946 he became a French citizen.

Two years later, as a graduate student in nuclear physics at the College de France in Paris, Charpak went to work in the laboratory of physicist Frederic Joliot-Curie. It was in this laboratory that Charpak began building the equipment he needed to perform his experiments (he constructed his own equipment out of necessity, as the laboratory had none). Charpak contends that he was not good at invention but had to learn in order to perform his experiments. In 1954 he received his Ph.D. from the College de France.

In awarding the Nobel Prize to Charpak, the Swedish Academy of Sciences traced the history of the development of detector devices in physics. The cloud chamber and the bubble chamber were two earlier inventions that had received recognition from the academy. Both relied on photographic techniques to capture particle events. In 1958 Charpak was invited by experimental physicist Leon Lederman, who had heard Charpak lecture in Padua, to come to CERN to work on sparking devices to detect particles. Though these devices were an improvement over existing techniques, they, too, relied on photographic recording, which was slow and cumbersome to analyze. Charpak turned to the problem of a spark chamber reading without photographic film, and built his first multiwire proportional tracking chamber in 1968.

The multiwire proportional chamber extended the technology of the Geiger-Muller tube, bubble chamber, and cloud chamber in two ways. The multiwire proportional chamber replaced the single positively charged wire of the Geiger-Muller tube, which attracts electrons in a chamber of ionized gas, with a multiwire device; it also replaced photographic analysis of a trail of bubbles with computerized electronic analysis of current produced in the wires as they attract electrons. Charpak credited his background in nuclear physics with the success of his invention.

Since liberating physics from dependence on film readings, Charpak has turned his interests to medicine and aerospace problems. Work he has done in the latter area makes it possible to produce an X-ray radiograph of turbine blades as they spin. In the field of medicine, his chamber is able to analyze the structure of a protein with X rays a thousand times faster than was previously possible. He also is working on imaging problems to identify receptors in the brain.

Charpak's particle work mimics the state of the universe as it was a fraction of a second after the Big Bang. It is believed that some of the particles have not existed in nature since that time, and the ability of physicists to study them will reveal and increase the understanding of the relationships among the forces of nature. Whereas Charpak built on the work of his predecessors with the bubble and spark chambers, others have used his invention to make their own contributions to the field of physics. A group led by Samuel Ting discovered the first manifestation of charmed quarks at Brookhaven in 1974, and Carlo Rubbia led a group to discover the W and Z particles. (Charmed quarks and W and Z particles are subatomic particles.)

As a survivor of a Nazi concentration camp, Charpak has worked on behalf of other scientists imprisoned by repressive governments. He is the founder of the SOS committee at CERN. This association worked diligently on the part of Soviet dissidents, such as Andrei Sakharov, Yuri Orlov, and Anatoly Sharansky, when they were deprived of their civil rights under the former Soviet Union.

Charpak married Dominique Vidal in 1953; they have two sons and one daughter. Some of Charpak's leisure interests include skiing, music, and hiking. He has been a member of the French Academy of Sciences since 1985. In addition to his continued association with CERN, Charpak is also the Joliot-Curie Professor at the Ecole Superieure de Physique et Chimie in Paris, a position he has held since 1984. In 1989 he received the High Energy and Particle Physics Prize from the European Physical Society. He has published numerous papers in scientific journals.

BIOGRAPHICAL/CRITICAL SOURCES:

BOOKS

Close, Frank, *The Particle Explosion,* Oxford, 1987.
Fernow, Richard C., *Introduction to Experimental Particle Physics,* Cambridge, 1986.
Sutton, Christine, *The Particle Connection: The Discovery of the Missing Links of Nuclear Physics,* Hutchinson, 1984.

PERIODICALS

Nature, October 22, 1992, p. 664.
New Scientist, October 24, 1992, p. 6.
New York Times, October 15, 1992, p. B14.
Physics Today, January, 1993, pp. 17-20.
Science, October 23, 1992, p. 543-544.*

CHESTNUT, Harold   1917-

PERSONAL: Born November 25, 1917, in Albany, NY; son of Harry and Dorothy (Schulman) Chestnut; married Erma Ruth Callaway, August 24, 1944; children: Peter Callaway, H. Thomas, Andrew T. *Education:* Massachusetts Institute of Technology, B.S., 1939, M.S., 1940; Case Western Reserve University, D.E. (honorary), 1966. Villanova University, honorary doctorate, 1972.

ADDRESSES: Home and office—1226 Waverly Place, Schenectady, NY 12308-2627.

CAREER: Electrical engineer. Affiliated with General Electric (GE), Schenectady, NY, 1940-83, worked in Aeronautics and Ordnance Department, c. 1943-56, worked in the Systems Engineering and Analysis Branch at GE's Advanced Technology Lab, 1956-66, manager of the Research and Development Center, 1966-71, consultant to GE on systems engineering, 1972-83. National Research Council, member of Commission on Sociotechnical Systems. 1975-78. Founder and president of SWIIS Foundation, Inc., 1983—.

MEMBER: Institute of Electrical and Electronics Engineers (served as vice president of tech. activities, 1970-71, vice president of regional activities, 1972, and president, 1973; served on executive committee, 1967-75) National Academy of Engineering, International Federation of Automatic Control (served as president, 1957-58), World Federalists Association (served on board, 1980-92, and on executive committee, 1984-90), American Automatic Control Council (served as president, 1962-63).

AWARDS, HONORS: Case Centennial Scholar, Case Western Reserve University, 1980; Honda Prize, 1981; Centennial Medal, 1984, and Richard M. Emberson Award, 1990, both from Institute of Electrical and Electronics Engineers; Bellman Control Heritage Award, 1985; American Association for the Advancement of Science, fellow.

WRITINGS:

(With Robert W. Mayer) *Servomechanisms and Regulating Systems Design,* Wiley, Volume 1, 1951, Volume 2, 1955, 2nd edition, 1959.
Systems Engineering Tools, Wiley, 1965.
Systems Engineering Methods, Wiley, 1967.
Influence of Technology on Modern World Evolution and Use of Dynamic Models of Macro-Economic
Systems in Development Planning (lecture), Accademia Nazionale dei Lincei (Rome), 1976.
(Editor, with others) *Supplemental Ways for Improving International Stability: Proceedings of the IFAC Workshop, Laxenburg, Austria, 13-15 September, 1983,* Pergamon Press (New York), 1984.
(Editor) *Contributions of Technology to International Conflict Resolution: Proceedings of the IFAC Workshop, Cleveland, Ohio, U.S.A., 3-5 June, 1986,* Pergamon Press (New York), 1987.
(Editor, with P. Kopacek and T. Vamos) *International Conflict Resolution Using System Engineering: Proceedings of the IFAC Workshop, Budapest, Hungary, 5-8 June, 1989,* Pergamon Press (New York), 1990.

Editor of the Pergamon Press journal *Automatica,* 1961-67. Editor of a systems engineering and analysis series published by John Wiley, 1965-85.

SIDELIGHTS: Harold Chestnut is a retired American engineer who, during a career with General Electric that spanned more than forty years, was active in systems engineering and analysis, a field that focuses on establishing the most efficient means for a system to accomplish a given task.

Chetsnut's research into systems includes investigations of adaptive (self-regulatory) control, system modeling and simulation, and the control of industrial businesses. He is also recognized as an expert in control systems analysis, especially as it applies to regulation of industrial, electric utility, and military systems. Since his retirement from General Electric, Chestnut has served as president of the SWIIS Foundation, Inc., a body he founded in 1983 whose task is to identify and implement ways for improving international political stability.

Chestnut was born on November 25, 1917, in Albany, New York. He took his B.S. degree in Electrical Engineering at the Massachusetts Institute of Technology, graduating in 1939. He remained at MIT to pursue an M.S. in Electrical Engineering, which he received in 1940. Following his graduation, Chestnut went to work for General Electric (GE) in Schenectady, New York, where he would remain for the rest of his career. Before being given any work assignments, Chestnut was obliged to continue his education. He became a student in General Electric's Advanced Engineering Program's Electrical Engineering Course, a three year commitment. During the latter part of the course, he gave tutorials to more junior students.

After finishing the program in 1943, Chestnut joined General Electric's Aeronautics and Ordnance Department. He was given responsibility for systems engineering and project work for a number of military aircraft, including the Mark 56 GFCS and the F-104, as well as some missile applications. Soon after beginning this post, Chestnut married Erma Ruth Callaway of Colorado Springs on August 24, 1944. The couple had three children—Peter Callaway, Harold Thomas, and Andrew Trammell.

Chestnut remained in the Aeronautics and Ordnance Department until 1956. That year, he became manager of the Systems Engineering and Analysis Branch of GE's Advanced Technology Lab. He was put in charge of working groups which investigated automatic control and information systems for various applications, such as rapid transit and the reliability systems for the space program's Apollo mission to the moon.

In 1961, Chestnut, in addition to working for GE, became editor of the Pergamon Press journal *Automatica;* he retained the post for the following six years. In 1965, he was appointed editor of a series by the John Wiley publishing company on systems engineering and analysis, a position he maintained until 1985. In 1972, he became a consultant to GE on systems engineering. One of his main responsibilities became the automation of electrical distribution systems, which regulate the flow and voltage of electricity. He continued in this role until 1983.

That year, Chestnut retired from General Electric. He did not remain idle for long, however. He quickly busied himself helping to establish the SWIIS Foundation Inc., a body whose mission is to identify and implement "supplemental ways to improve international stability." As the organization's president, Chestnut has been at the forefront of its efforts to set up a Cooperative Security System, whose purpose is to develop and lobby for a cooperative system of international security. By creating a security system that would protect nations equally, individual countries could feel safer, thereby increasing their political stability. Also in 1983, Chestnut became coeditor of the *International Federation of Automatic Control Proceedings on International Conflict Resolution.* He held the same position again in 1986 and in 1989.

Throughout his career, Chestnut has been active in the affairs of various professional engineering bodies. In 1957, he served on the founding committee for the International Federation of Automatic Control, and

was named its first president, from 1957 to 1958. He was elected a fellow of the Institute of Electrical and Electronics Engineers (IEEE) in 1962 for his "contribution to the theory and design of control systems." That same year, he was made chairman of the American Institute of Electrical Engineering's (AIEE) Schenectady branch.

Chestnut was president of the American Automatic Control Council between 1962 and 1964. He served as IEEE's treasurer from 1968 to 1969, and as vice president of its Technical Activities Board and Regional Activities Board. He became IEEE's president in 1973. In these various capacities, he has been active in promoting continuing education and cooperation amongst engineers.

Chestnut was elected a member of the National Academy of Engineering in 1974 and a fellow of the Instrument Society of America. He is also a member of the National Society of Professional Engineers, and a fellow of the American Association for the Advancement of Science. In 1980, he was made a Case Centennial Scholar.

In addition to holding many important offices, Chestnut has served on many technical committees, including as chairman of AIEE's technical committees on Automatic Control and Systems, Man, and Cybernetics. He has been a member of IEEE's board of directors and executive committee, and has chaired many of its committees on feedback control.

Between 1975 and 1978, Chestnut served as a member of the Commission on Sociotechnical Systems of the National Research Council. Chestnut received honorary doctorates of Engineering from Case Western Reserve University in 1966, and Villanova University in 1972. He was awarded the Honda Prize for ecotechnology in 1981, the Centennial Medal of the Institute of Electrical and Electronics Engineers in 1984, and the American Automatic Control Council's Bellman Control Heritage Award in 1985. Active in his church and community, Chestnut continues to live in Schenectady, New York, with his wife.*

*   *   *

CHEW, Geoffrey Foucar 1924-

PERSONAL: Born June 5, 1924, in Washington, DC; son of Arthur Percy (a journalist) and Pauline Lisette (a teacher; maiden name, Foucar) Chew; married Ruth Elva Wright (died, 1971); married Denyse Mettel, 1971; children: (with first wife) Beverly, Berkeley; with second wife, Pierre-Yves, Jean-Francois, Pauline. *Education:* George Washington University, B.S., 1944, University of Chicago, Ph.D., 1948.

*ADDRESSES: Home—*10 Maybeck Twin Dr., Berkeley, CA 94708-2037.

CAREER: Theoretical physicist. Los Alamos Science Laboratory, NM, junior theoretical physicist, 1944-46; Theoretical Physics Research Laboratory at the University of California, Berkeley, research physicist, 1948-49, assistant professor of physics, 1949, professor of physics, 1957—, chair of Physics Department, 1974-78, Miller Professor, 1981-82, dean of physical sciences, 1986-92, emeritus professor of physics and dean, 1993—; University of Illinois, Urbana, professor of physics, 1950-56; Princeton University, Princeton, NJ, visiting professor, 1970-71; University of Paris, visiting professor, 1983.

MEMBER: National Academy of Science, American Physical Society (fellow), American Academy of Arts and Sciences (fellow).

AWARDS, HONORS: Hughes Prize, American Physical Society, 1962; E. O. Lawrence Award, 1969; Alumni Achievement Award, George Washington University, 1973.

WRITINGS:

The S-matrix Theory of Strong Interactions, W. A. Benjamin, 1961.
The Analytic S-matrix: A Basis for Nuclear Democracy, W. A. Benjamin, 1966.
Lectures on Modeling the Bootstrap: Delivered at the Summer School in Theoretical Physics Held at Naina Tal, 1969, notes by P. Babu, S. M. Roy, and K. V. L. Sarma, Tata Institute of Fundamental Research (Bombay), 1970.

SIDELIGHTS: Geoffrey Foucar Chew works in the areas of elementary particle physics, scattering matrix (S-matrix) theory, topological bootstrap theory, and strong interactions. His most important contribution to particle physics is his "bootstrap hypothesis," which postulates that elementary particles' physical properties and interactions have an internal consistency that results from S-matrix theory. S-matrix theory is a table of probabilities that describes the possible outcomes of subatomic particle collisions. According to

S-matrix theory, subatomic particles are intermediate states in a network of interactions.

Chew was born in Washington, D.C., on June 5, 1924. His father, Arthur Percy Chew, was a journalist, and his mother, Pauline Lisette Foucar, was a teacher. Chew was educated at George Washington University and received his B.S. degree in 1944, the same year he became a junior theoretical physicist at Los Alamos Science Laboratory in New Mexico. In 1945, he married Ruth Elva Wright, with whom he had two children, Beverly and Berkeley.

From 1946 to 1948, Chew was a National Research Fellow at the University of Chicago, where he worked on his doctoral thesis under the supervision of American physicist Enrico Fermi. After receiving his Ph.D. in 1948, he worked as an assistant professor of physics at the Theoretical Physics Research Laboratory at the University of California, Berkeley, becoming an assistant professor of physics in 1949.

Chew left Berkeley to take up a position as professor of physics at the University of Illinois in 1950, but returned to Berkeley as professor of physics in 1957. He is also a senior research physicist at the Lawrence Berkeley Laboratory and occasionally heads the Laboratory's Theoretical Group.

After the death of his wife in 1971, Chew remarried later that year. He and his second wife, Denyse Mettel, have three children: Pierre-Yves, Jean-Francois, and Pauline. From 1981 to 1982, Chew was Miller Professor of Physics at Berkeley. He was a visiting professor of physics at the University of Paris between 1983 and 1984. In 1986, he became Dean of Physical Sciences at Berkeley, and is now a professor emeritus of physics.

Chew has received a number of honors, including the Hughes Medal of the American Physical Society in 1962, the Ernest O. Lawrence Award in 1969, and an Alumni Achievement Award from George Washington University in 1973. He is a member of the National Academy of Science and a Fellow of the American Physical Society and the American Academy of Arts and Sciences.

BIOGRAPHICAL/CRITICAL SOURCES:

BOOKS

A Passion for Physics: Essays in Honor of Geoffrey Chew, World Scientific (Philadelphia), 1985.*

CHILD, Charles Manning 1869-1954

PERSONAL: Born February 2, 1869, in Ypsilanti, MI; died December 19, 1954, of cancer; son of Charles Chauncey and Mary Elizabeth (Manning) Child; married Lydia Van Meter, August 15, 1899; children: Jeannette Manning. *Education:* Wesleyan University, Ph.D., 1890, M.S., 1892; University of Leipzig, Ph.D., 1894. *Avocational interests:* Hiking, mountain climbing.

CAREER: Zoologist. Naples Zoological Station, Naples, Italy, independent research, 1894-95; University of Chicago, Chicago, Illinois, faculty member, 1895-1934, became a full professor, 1916, zoology department chairperson, 1934-37. Duke University, Durham, NC, visiting professor, 1930; Rockefeller Foundation, Tohoku University, Sendai, Japan, visiting professor, 1930-31; guest lecturer at universities around the world.

WRITINGS:

Individuality in Organisms, University of Chicago Press (Chicago, IL), 1915.
The Origin and Development of the Nervous System from a Physiological Viewpoint, University of Chicago Press, 1921.
Patterns and Problems of Development, University of Chicago Press, 1941.

Founder and editor of *Physiological Zoology.*

SIDELIGHTS: Charles Manning Child was a nationally recognized zoologist who became a leader in the study of morphogenesis, which is the formation and differentiation of tissues and organs. His most important contribution to the field of zoology was the gradient theory, the concept that an organism's regenerative ability takes place in physiological stages along an axis, with each physiological stage being connected to and affecting those areas surrounding it. "In this gradient Child believed he had found the mechanism of correlation by which the mass of cells that constitutes an animal is maintained as a unified whole of definite form and construction. The chief factor in correlation is . . . each level dominates the region behind and is dominated by that in front," Libbie H. Hyman explained in *Biographical Memoirs of the National Academy of Sciences.*

Child received many honors in his lifetime and was highly respected in his field. While he was an able lecturer, Child was happiest and most proficient in the

area of research. He preferred to spend his time in the laboratory, where he trained many graduate students.

Child, the fifth and only survivor of five sons, was born to Mary Elizabeth Manning and Charles Chauncey Child on February 2, 1869, in Ypsilanti, Michigan. Although both families were of long-standing New England lineage, Mary Elizabeth traveled to Ypsilanti to be under the care of her father, a physician, at the time of Charles's birth. Mrs. Child and the infant returned to the family home in Higganum, Connecticut, shortly thereafter. Child's father was a fourth-generation descendant of Higganum shipbuilders who were forced to close their shipyard when the mechanization of shipping vessels appeared on the scene. The Childs lived in one of the family's three homes facing the Connecticut river on the grounds where the shipyard had been. His father also retained a small family-owned farm to be used primarily as a source of food.

Influenced by his parents' love of reading, Child became a fervent reader at a very early age. His interest in the natural sciences began at age ten when he became an avid collector of minerals from the granite hills around his boyhood home. Taught by his mother at home until he was nine, Child entered the formalized district school system in Higganum in 1878. From 1882 to 1886, Child attended high school in Middletown, Connecticut, graduating first in his class. Child then entered Wesleyan University in 1886 where his interest in both chemistry and zoology made choosing a major field of study difficult, but he finally decided on zoology. He was awarded the Seney scholarship for high academic achievement in all but his freshman year and was elected to the Phi Beta Kappa honor society. He graduated from Wesleyan University in 1890 with a Ph.D. and continued his studies there, receiving an M.S. in biology in 1892.

With his parents gone, Child sold the family home and went to the University of Leipzig in Germany. For a short time he studied psychology under Wilhelm Wundt and published his first original work in *American Naturalist.* In 1894 he completed his Ph.D. in zoology under Rudolf Leuckart. His doctoral dissertation on the insect sense organ was published in a leading German zoological journal and is still considered a standard in the field of entomology (a branch of zoology dealing with insects). Immediately following the completion of his Ph.D., Child conducted independent research at the Naples Zoological Station.

In 1895 Child returned to the United States and joined the staff of the University of Chicago, where he remained for his entire academic career. He achieved full professorship in 1916 and maintained that position until retirement in 1934. When he reached retirement age, Child was asked to stay on at the University of Chicago as chairman of the zoology department, which he accepted and maintained until 1937. During his summers at the University of Chicago, he conducted research at the Marine Biological Laboratory at Woods Hole, Massachusetts, at the Naples Zoological Station, and at various marine stations on the Pacific coast.

In 1899 Child married Lydia Van Meter, daughter of John Van Meter, the longtime dean and acting president of Goucher College in Baltimore. They had one daughter, Jeannette Manning Child. As a zoologist, Child's research and experimentation centered on animal organisms' reactivity and sensitivity as well as their developmental and reproductive problems. Child's colleagues criticized his controversial concept of the gradient theory, suggesting that his findings were too general since they were based on experiments with simple animals.

Still, his contribution to the field of morphogenesis was significant. In conjunction with the University of Chicago Press, Child founded the journal *Physiological Zoology* in 1928 and became its first editor. As his reputation grew, Child drew national and international attention. He was frequently asked to teach and lecture at colleges and universities around the world. In 1930 he was a visiting professor at Duke University, and from 1930 to 1931 he traveled to Japan, where he was invited as a visiting professor of the Rockefeller Foundation at Tohoku University, Sendai, Japan.

Child retired from his post at the University of Chicago in 1937 and, with his wife Lydia, moved to California. As impassioned about nature as he was about his work, Child frequently went hiking and mountain climbing. He had a special fascination for the Sierras. He also became a frequent visitor in the zoology department on the campus of Stanford University, where he often participated as a guest speaker and lecturer. Due to his reserved nature, Child was not an easy person to get to know. But when friendships did develop, they generally lasted a lifetime. Child died of cancer on December 19, 1954. He established very high standards for himself, standards he maintained throughout his personal life and professional career. He remained a committed scientist to the very end. Just prior to his death, Child was in the process of writing a book called *Physiological Factors in Organization and Reorganization,* which was a summation of his most important works as well as a synopsis of a previous volume, *Patterns and Problems of Development.* At the time of his death, the book remained unfinished, with only the placement of captions yet to be done.

BIOGRAPHICAL/CRITICAL SOURCES:

BOOKS

Biographical Memoirs, National Academy of Sciences Staff, Books on Demand (Ann Arbor, MI).*

*   *   *

CHURCH, Alonzo 1903-

PERSONAL: Born June 14, 1903, in Washington, DC; son of Samuel Robbins and Mildred Hannah (Letterman) Church; married Mary Julia Kuczinski, August 25, 1925; children: Alonzo, Mary Ann, and Mildred Warner. *Education:* Princeton University, A.B., 1924, Ph.D., 1927; attended Harvard University, 1927-28; attended University of Gottingen, Germany, 1928-29; attended University of Amsterdam, 1929.

CAREER: Mathematician and logician. Princeton University, Princeton, NJ, professor, 1929-67; University of California, Los Angeles, professor of philosophy and mathematics, 1967-90.

AWARDS, HONORS: Numerous honors, including induction into the National Academy of Science and the Academy of Arts and Sciences; fellow, Harvard University, 1927-29; honorary doctorates include: Case Western Reserve University, 1969; Princeton University, 1985; State University of New York, Buffalo, 1990.

WRITINGS:

The Calculi of Lambda-Conversion, Princeton University Press (Princeton, NJ), 1941.
Introduction to Mathematical Logic, Volume 1, Princeton University Press, 1956.
A Bibliography of Symbolic Logic, 1666-1935, Association for Symbolic Logic (Providence, RI), 1984.

Editor of *Journal of Symbolic Logic,* 1936-1979. Contributor to journals and periodicals, including *American Journal of Mathematics.*

SIDELIGHTS: Alonzo Church is an American mathematician and logician who provided significant innovations in number theory and in the decision theory that is the foundation of computer programming. His most important contributions focus on the degrees of decidability and solvability in logic and mathematics.

Church was born in Washington, D.C., on June 14, 1903, to Samuel Robbins Church and Mildred Hannah Letterman Church. He took his undergraduate degree from Princeton University in 1924. On August 25, 1925, he married Mary Julia Kuczinski. They had three children: Alonzo, Mary Ann, and Mildred Warner. Church completed his Ph.D. in mathematics at Princeton in 1927. After receiving his doctorate, he was a fellow at Harvard from 1927 to 1928. He studied in Europe from 1928 to 1929 at the University of Gottingen, a prestigious center for the study of mathematics and physics. He taught mathematics and philosophy at Princeton from 1929 to 1967. Among his Ph.D. students at Princeton was the British mathematician Alan Turing, who was to crack the German's World War II secret code, called Enigma, which played a key role in allowing the Western Allies to defeat Nazi Germany. Church was a professor of mathematics and philosophy at the University of California at Los Angeles from 1967 until his retirement in 1990. He also edited the *Journal of Symbolic Logic* from 1936 to 1979. His wife died in February, 1976.

Church's private life is very quiet and unremarkable. As Andrew Hodges said in his biography of Alan Turing (Church's famed student, who killed himself in 1954 after being arrested on homosexual charges), Church "[is] a retiring man himself, not given to a great deal of discussion."

One of the key problems in the foundations of mathematics was stated by the German mathematician David Hilbert (1862-1943): Is mathematics decidable? That is, as Andrew Hodges explains in his biography of Alan Turing, "did there exist a definite method which could, in principle, be applied to any assertion, and which was guaranteed to produce a correct decision as to whether that assertion was true"? Although Hilbert thought the answer would be yes, Church's answer was no. Church's theorem says in effect that there is no method to guarantee in advance that a mathematical assertion will be correct or incorrect.

Specific mathematical assertions may be found to be correct or incorrect, but there is no general method that will work in advance for all mathematical assertions.

What Church's proof—and the proofs of other mathematicians such as Kurt Friedrich Gobel—showed was that mathematics in general was not as tidy, logical, and airtight as people had always thought it was. And, to make matters worse, mathematics could never be perfectly tidy, logical, or airtight. There would always be some statements that were undecidable, inconsistent, and incomplete. Church and other mathematicians of his time showed that like everything else, mathematics was fallible.

For computer programs to run, programmers have to be able to reduce all problems to the kinds of simple binary logical (or on/off) statements that can be processed by the electronic circuits inside the computer. For a problem to be solvable by a computer, it must be possible to break it down into an operational set of rules and terms. Next it must be possible to apply these rules recursively—that is repeatedly—to the problem until it is solved in terms of the existing set of rules. In short, a computer's binary circuits can only solve a problem under three conditions: (1) if the problem can be expressed as a meaningful set of rules (i.e., meaningful to the computer); (2) if the result of each step is also meaningful in terms of the computer's predefined set of rules; (3) if the computer's set of rules can be applied repeatedly to the problem. For example, in a simple addition or subtraction computer program, it must be possible for a small number (e.g., 1) to be repeatedly added to or subtracted from a larger number (e.g., 100) to get some result, say 10 or 10,000. If any of these three conditions mentioned above is absent, then a computer program cannot solve the problem.

Church's contribution to the foundation of computer programming is that he discovered—as did Alan Turing and Emil Post simultaneously and independently—the importance of recursiveness in solving logical problems. That is, for calculations to take place, some actions (e.g. adding or subtracting) have to be repeated a certain number of times. Church's deceptively simple thesis (which is often called the Church-Turing thesis) is that a function is computable or calculable if it is recursive. That is, the idea of recursiveness (repeatability) is tightly bound up with computability. Church's thesis is important because the repetition of a simple action can result in significant changes. It also means that one simple action can be useful over a broad range of problems, and at different levels of a problem.

Church's contributions to decidability theory have led to many honors, including induction into the National Academy of Science and the American Academy of Arts and Sciences. He has received honorary doctorates from Case Western Reserve University in 1969, Princeton University in 1985, and the State University of New York at Buffalo in 1990.

BIOGRAPHICAL/CRITICAL SOURCES:

BOOKS

Hodges, Andrew, *Alan Turing: The Enigma,* Simon & Schuster, 1983.
Hofstadter, Douglas R., *Godel, Escher, and Bach: An Eternal Golden Braid,* Basic Books, 1979.*

*　　*　　*

CHVIDKOVSKI, Dmitri
　See SHVIDKOVSKY, Dimitri

*　　*　　*

CLARKE, Edith 1883-1959

PERSONAL: Born in 1883, in Ellicott City,MD; died in 1959, in Baltimore,MD; daughter of John Ridgely (a lawyer) and Susan Dorsey (Owings) Clarke. *Education:* Vassar College, A.B., 1908; attended University of Wisconsin, 1911-12; studied radio at Hunter College; Massachusetts Institute of Technology, M.S., 1919.

CAREER: Engineer. High school teacher (math and science) in San Francisco, CA, and later in Huntington, WV, c. 1909; American Telephone and Telegraph company (AT&T), New York City, computing assistant to research engineer George A. Campbell, during World War I led group of women who made calculations for the Transmission Department, later became engineer, 1922-45; Constantinople Women's College (now Istanbul American College), teacher of physics, 1921. University of Texas, associate professor in electrical engineering, 1946, professor, 1947, member of numerous committees and graduate student advisor.

AWARDS, HONORS: AIEE (now Institute for Electrical and Electronics Engineers, or IEEE) fellow, 1948.

WRITINGS:

Circuit Analysis of A-C Power Systems, Volume 1, 1943.

SIDELIGHTS: Edith Clarke is chiefly recognized for her contributions to simplifying and mechanizing the calculations required in power systems analysis. A pioneering female engineer, Clarke was the first woman granted an M.S. in electrical engineering from the Massachusetts Institute of Technology (MIT) and later became the first woman to deliver a technical paper before the American Institute of Electrical Engineers (AIEE).

Clarke was born on a farm near Ellicott City, Maryland, one of nine children of Susan Dorsey (Owings) and John Ridgely Clarke, a lawyer. She attended a nearby school until 1897, when she entered boarding school after the deaths of her parents. She returned home two years later with no ambition for a career. Clarke decided to study languages with a tutor, however, and entered Vassar College in 1904. There she studied mathematics and astronomy, graduating with an A.B. in 1908.

Clarke taught math and science in San Francisco and later in Huntington, West Virginia, before renewing her studies in 1911 at the University of Wisconsin. After one year of course work in civil engineering, she joined the American Telephone and Telegraph company (AT&T) in New York as a computing assistant to research engineer George A. Campbell. At the time, computing mathematical problems for engineers was considered an appropriate profession for women with advanced training in mathematics. During World War I, Clarke led a group of women who made calculations for the Transmission Department at AT&T. Concurrently, she studied radio at Hunter College and electrical engineering at Columbia University.

In 1919 Clarke became the first woman to graduate from the Massachusetts Institute of Technology (MIT) with an M.S. degree in electrical engineering. Even with such credentials, however, she was unsuccessful in acquiring a position as an engineer. She worked briefly as a computor for General Electric (GE) before accepting a post teaching physics at Constantinople Women's College (now Istanbul American College) in 1921. The following year, Clarke returned to GE—this time as an engineer. She analyzed electric power systems and researched special problems related to power-system operations.

Clarke remained with GE for twenty-six years. Chief among her contributions were innovations in long-distance power transmission and the development of the theory of symmetrical component and circuit analysis. Her method of regulating voltage on power transmission lines was patented in 1927. In 1932 she became the first woman to present a paper before the AIEE and garnered recognition for her work as the best paper of the year in the northern district. Her paper explored the use of multiple conductor transmission lines to increase power line capacity. While at GE, Clarke also published a textbook which covered circuit analysis of alternating-current power systems. Prior to World War II, Clarke devised calculating charts which greatly streamlined the computation process.

Clarke retired to Maryland in 1945 but was drawn back to engineering within a year, this time accepting an associate professorship in electrical engineering at the University of Texas. Gaining full professorship in 1947, Clarke also served on numerous committees and was a graduate student advisor, providing special assistance to foreign students. Clarke was elected a fellow of the AIEE (now the Institute for Electrical and Electronics Engineers, known as the IEEE) in 1948, the first woman to be so named. In 1957, at age seventy-four, Clarke retired a second time. She died two years later in Baltimore.

BIOGRAPHICAL/CRITICAL SOURCES:

BOOKS

Goff, Alice C., *Women Can Be Engineers*, Edwards Brothers, 1946, pp. 50-65.

PERIODICALS

IEEE Transactions on Education, November, 1985, pp. 184-89.
Society of Women Engineers Newsletter, December, 1959, p. 3.*

*   *   *

COHAN, George M(ichael) 1878-1942

PERSONAL: Born July 4, 1878 (some sources say July 3), in Providence, RI; died November 5, 1942,

in New York, NY; son of Jeremiah "Jerry" and Helen "Nellie" Cohan (vaudevillians); married Ethel Levey (a singer and actress), 1900 (divorced, 1907); married Agnes Nolan (a dancer), 1909.

CAREER: American entertainer, actor, songwriter, and playwright. Traveled with family troupe, "The Four Cohans," during childhood. Producer of his own and others' plays. With Sam Harris, produced more than forty-five plays by Cohan and others, 1904-20, and 1937. Starred in *Ah, Wilderness!* by Eugene O'Neill 1933, and as Franklin Delano Roosevelt in *I'd Rather Be Right,* by Richard Rodgers and Lorenz Hart 1937-38. Appeared in screen versions of several of his own plays.

AWARDS, HONORS: Medal of Honor, United States Congress, "in recognition of public service during World War I in composing the patriotic songs "Over There' and "A Grand Old Flag'".

WRITINGS:

PRINCIPAL PLAYS

The Governor's Son, 1901.
Running for Office (adaptation and expansion of Cohan's 1903 vaudeville sketch), 1903.
Little Johnny Jones, 1904.
Forty-Five Minutes from Broadway, 1906.
The Honeymooners, 1907.
George Washington, Jr., 1907.
The Talk of the Town, 1907.
Fifty Miles from Boston, 1908.
The Yankee Prince, 1908.
The Man Who Owns Broadway, 1909.
The Cohan and Harris Minstrels, 1909.
Get-Rich-Quick Wallingford, 1910.
The Little Millionaire, 1911.
Broadway Jones, 1912, S. French (New York), 1923.
Seven Keys to Baldpate (based on the novel by Earl Derr Biggers), 1913.
The Miracle Man, 1914.
Hello Broadway!, 1914.
Hit-the-Trail Holliday (based on a plot suggested by George Middleton and Guy Bolton), 1915, Cohan & Harris (New York), 1916.
The Cohan Revue of 1916, 1916.
The Cohan Revue of 1918 (includes songs by Irving Berlin), 1917.
A Prince There Was (from the story "Enchanted Hearts" by Darragh Aldrich), 1918, S. French (New York and London), 1927.
The Royal Vagabond, 1919.

The Meanest Man in the World, 1920.

The Tavern, 1920 (suggested by the play *The Choice of a Super-Man* by Cora Dick Grant), S. French (New York, London, Los Angeles), 1933.

Little Nellie Kelly, 1922.

The Song and Dance Man, 1923.

The Merry Malones, 1927.

Billie, 1928.

The Baby Cyclone, S. French (New York and London), 1929.

Fulton of Oak Falls, 1937.

The Return of the Vagabond, S. French (New York and Toronto),1940.

Pigeons and People, S. French (New York and Toronto), 1941.

OTHER

Twenty Years on Broadway, and the Years It Took to Get There: The True Story of a Trouper's Life from the Cradle to the "Closed Shop" (memoir) Harper and Brothers (New York), 1925.

ARTICLES

"Dance and Stay Young," *Liberty,* October 24, 1931, pp. 32-36.

"A Comedian Stops to Think," *Liberty,* October 31, 1931, pp. 26-32.

"Dirt for Dough's Sake," *Liberty,* June 6, 1936, pp. 21-24.

SOUND RECORDINGS

"I'm Mighty Glad I'm Living, That's All!" (78 rpm), Victor (Camden, NJ), 1911.

"Life's A Funny Proposition After All" (78 rpm), Victor, 1911.

"The Small Town Gal" (78 rpm), Victor, 1911.

"You Won't Do Any Business If You Haven't Got a Band" (78 rpm), Victor, 1911.

The Original Yankee Doodle Dandy (33 1/3 rpm), Old Shep (Boilow, ME).

SIDELIGHTS: Whether George M. Cohan was born on July Fourth, as he loved to claim, or on the third as more recent reviewers maintain, there is no doubt that he was a real "Yankee Doodle Dandy," to use a famous phrase from one of his earliest hit songs. "Never was a plant more indigenous to a particular part of the earth than was George M. Cohan to the United States of his day," wrote songwriter Oscar Hammerstein II in a 1957 tribute to Cohan. A legend-

ary figure in American musical theater, Cohan was literally born to show business. His parents were traveling vaudevillians on the small-city circuit; Cohan was carried onstage as an infant in a skit of his father's. "We were all small-town folks, when you get right down to it," Cohan wrote in a 1939 article for *The Rotarian* magazine. He played the violin in a vaudeville orchestra at age eight; at age nine, he spoke his first lines onstage. He began to write sketches at age eleven and songs at age thirteen; his first published song came at age sixteen. By then he was an old hand, having performed the lead role in *Peck's Bad Boy* from the age of twelve. His family, although successful, left vaudeville in 1900 because of a billing dispute with their manager, fomented by Cohan.

At this point, Cohan, who handled the family's business as well as wrote most of its material, was yearning for the bigger stage: Broadway. He wrote a musical comedy, *The Governor's Son* (1901), based on an earlier vaudeville sketch of his, for the family to perform, but it flopped in New York: the family was nervous, and Cohan sprained his ankle in the first scene. Undeterred, the Cohans took the show on the road for a successful run. A second play, *Running for Office,* was treated indifferently by New York audiences the following year. Digging in, Cohan formed a business partnership with Sam H. Harris in order to leave more of his own time for writing. By this time, Cohan's stage personality, which, according to the drama critic Brooks Atkinson "could not be ignored," had been developed through years of practice. As Atkinson describes it, "He rolled his eyes and dropped his eyelids with a confidential grimace that seemed to be directed at individual members of the audience; he sang through his nose, carried a jaunty cane, wore his hat on the side of his head, and danced exuberantly. Since he was a short man, he avoided standing near taller people and wore thick heel lifts. . . . He was overpoweringly loud and busy. He invented a type of musical show in which everybody talked at the top of his voice, everybody sang full out and danced ferociously." (Critic Arthur Ruhl, in 1910, summarized these qualities of enthusiasm as "childlike cocksureness.")

Cohan first impressed Broadway with this persona in the 1904 *Little Johnny Jones,* which contained the memorable songs "Give My Regards to Broadway" and "[I'm] A Yankee Doodle Dandy." Although its previews were unsuccessful, Cohan did some energetic rewriting on the road and brought the show back to New York for a moderately successful run that season. The plot, which concerned an American jockey unjustly accused of throwing a British horse race, was a "perfect vehicle," in Stanley Green's words, both for Cohan's brash charisma and for the newly rising patriotism of that era. Cohan's next show, *Forty-Five Minutes from Broadway,* a vehicle for popular singer-comedienne Fay Templeton, was also a hit. In the 1906 *George Washington, Jr.,* with the song "[You're] A Grand Old Flag" in the score, Cohan had a third success. Cohan's creative drive at that time was remarkable; Atkinson describes him as being capable of writing 140 pages of a script at one sitting, at night after performing a show, and of cutting it by almost two-thirds to fit into one act of a play.

Cohan's early shows marked the peak of his inventiveness as a creator of musical theater; in later efforts, although still writing hit songs at times, he tended to repeat his familiar plot formulas and rehash his attitudes. When he did, as in the early drama *Popularity,* he often failed. (He rewrote *Popularity,* adding songs, to turn it into the successful *The Man Who Owns Broadway.*) Yet he had made a permanent contribution to American musical theater by bringing a youthful new exuberance to it, and he reaped the rewards of that contribution for many years. In 1917, and not in the context of a show, he wrote one of his most influential songs, "Over There," a tremendously singable revamped bugle call which became perhaps the most familiar patriotic tune during two world wars. In 1919, however, Cohan's reputation took a downturn as a result of his choosing the wrong side in an important political issue, the Actors' Equity strike of that year. Although known primarily as a stage performer rather than a writer or businessman, Cohan identified with management and publicly vowed to fight the strikers with all the resources at his command. Actors' Equity was victorious.

After that point, not only did Cohan, who had previously been considered one of the most generous men in show business, have a horde of new enemies, but he could only appear on a Broadway stage by obtaining special permission from Equity (which Equity charitably gave). Bitter, Cohan renounced old friendships, quit the Friars and Lambs clubs, and dissolved his partnership with Harris. His creative verve diminished. He still wrote and performed in musicals, but less successfully and less often than before; the straight plays *The Tavern* (1920) and *The Song and Dance Man* (1923) were among his few, and small, successes of the post-1919 period. In addition to his political problems, Cohan found that his style of

songwriting and playwrighting had been surpassed by newer, more sophisticated stars such as Jerome Kern, Irving Berlin, and Rodgers and Hart. "I guess people don't understand me no more," he said, as quoted by David Ewen in *The Complete Book of the American Musical Theater,* "and I don't understand them." In 1932, he was notably snubbed by the cast and crew when he traveled to Hollywood to film a Rodgers and Hart musical, *The Phantom President.* Nevertheless, he was still rich, famous, and widely honored.

In 1925, he had a success in print with his autobiography, *Twenty Years on Broadway, and the Years It Took to Get There: The True Story of a Trouper's Life from the Cradle to the "Closed Shop,"*—the term "closed shop" in the subtitle referred to his acrid dispute with the actors' union. During the Depression he made his mark as a serious dramatic actor in the lead role in Eugene O'Neill's *Ah, Wilderness!* Using no makeup, he gave, in Atkinson's opinion, "a soft, winning, and memorable performance unlike anything he had done on his own." John Mason Brown described the performance this way: "He is his regulation self—with a difference. . . . He acts with a new depth; with a mellow poignancy born of the play he is adorning. . . . By his very refusal to steal the show the stage becomes his." Brown called Cohan's work in the play "this most brilliant of his characterizations." And Ruhl referred to Cohan's "more urbanely and authoritatively than ever before, taking the part of what might be described as not merely the American . . . but almost the 'universal' father."

Cohan had another stage success in the late 1930s when he played the part of President Franklin D. Roosevelt in Rodgers and Hart's musical, *I'd Rather Be Right.* Cohan was now an institution, though a controversial one. In 1936 he was awarded the Congressional Medal of Honor for his musical contributions to the World War I effort. In 1942, his life story was filmed as *Yankee Doodle Dandy,* with James Cagney starring in one of the most "brilliantly dramatized" impersonations in screen history, according to David Ewen. But Cohan was ailing. While convalescing from abdominal surgery, he convinced his nurse to drive around his Times Square 'neighborhood' and even to spend a few minutes at the Hollywood Theater to see a scene from *Yankee Doodle Dandy;* he died shortly after on October 5, 1942.

Cohan was hailed by critics, and by public figures such as President Roosevelt and New York mayor Fiorello La Guardia, as one of the greatest figures in

American theater. Throughout the years, other theatrical figures have continued to bear him tribute; an eight-foot-tall statue of him stands in Times Square, a singular honor within the profession. Hammerstein, as quoted by Atkinson, observed, "Cohan's genius was to say simply what everybody was subconsciously feeling." In his 1957 tribute article, Hammerstein attributed Cohan's success as an actor to "an extraordinary talent for listening to other characters. He would listen so eloquently that you would be more likely to be watching him than the actor who was speaking." Cohan himself had said, according to Atkinson, that "he wrote for Joe Blatz—his stereotype for an average audience," the customer with the "two-dollar heart." Cohan, wrote Atkinson, "said he "would rather make one man laugh than one thousand cry. He did exactly that in about fifty comedies and musical productions." And Hammerstein summed him up in these words: "He was an original. He had many imitators, no equals. He belonged to this country, no other. He belonged to his own time, no other. He gave us his talents, his energy, and . . . planted an image of himself in our hearts."

BIOGRAPHICAL/CRITICAL SOURCES:

BOOKS

Atkinson, Brooks, "For the Family and Its Tired Businessman," *Broadway,* revised edition, Macmillan, 1970, pp. 97-121.

Brown, John Mason, "Mr. Cohan in *Ah, Wilderness!,*" in *Two on the Aisle: Ten Years of American Theater in Performance,* Norton, 1938, pp. 235-236.

Ewen, David, Complete Book of the American Musical Theater, Holt, 1958, pp. 53-60.

Green, Stanley, "George M. Cohan," *The World of Musical Comedy,* Grosset & Dunlap, 1960, pp. 24-35.

Ruhl, Arthur, "A Minor Poet of Broadway: George M. Cohan," in *The American Theater as Seen By Its Critics,* edited by Montrose J. Moses and john Mason Brown, Norton, 1934, pp. 187-191.

Slide, Anthony, *Encyclopedia of Vaudeville,* Greenwood Press (Westport, CT), 1994, pp. 105-107.

Twentieth-Century Literary Criticism, Volume 60, Gale (Detroit), 1995, pp. 155-173.

PERIODICALS

New York Times Magazine, May 5, 1957, pp. 14, 72, 78.

Rotarian, September, 1939, pp. 10-13, 59-60.*

COLE, Johnnetta B(etsch) 1936-

PERSONAL: Born October 19, 1936, in Jacksonville, FL; daughter of John (an insurance company executive and entrepreneur) and Mary Frances (an educator, registrar, and insurance company vice president; maiden name, Lewis) Betsch; married Robert Cole (an economist), 1960 (divorced, 1982); married Arthur Robinson, Jr. (a public health administrator), December, 1988; children: (first marriage) David, Aaron, Ethan Che. *Education:* Attended Fisk University, 1952-53; Oberlin College, B.A., 1957; Northwestern University, M.A., 1959, Ph.D., 1967.

ADDRESSES: Home—1360 Beechwood Hills Court, N.W., Atlanta, GA 30327-3110.

CAREER: Washington State University, Pullman, assistant professor of anthropology and director of black studies, 1967-70; University of Massachusetts—Amherst, professor of anthropology and Afro-American studies, 1970-83, provost of undergraduate education, 1981-83; Hunter College of the City University of New York, New York City, Russell Sage Visiting Professor of Anthropology, 1983, professor of anthropology, 1983-87, director of Latin American and Caribbean studies, 1984-87; Spelman College, Atlanta, GA, president, 1987-97; writer. Founding member of board of directors of Points of Light Foundation.

MEMBER: National Council of Negro Women, American Anthropological Association (fellow).

AWARDS, HONORS: Elizabeth Boyer Award, 1988; award in education from *Essence* magazine, 1989; inducted into the Working Woman Hall of Fame; Jessie Bernard Wise Woman Award and American Woman Award, both 1990; Sara Lee's Frontrunner Award, 1992; also the recipient of forty honorary degrees.

WRITINGS:

NONFICTION

Conversations: Straight Talk with America's Sister President, Doubleday (New York), 1993.
Dream the Boldest Dreams: And Other Lessons of Life, Longstreet Press, 1997.

Author of columns in *McCall's,* 1990. Contributor to journals, including *Black Scholar* and *American Anthropologist.*

EDITOR

Anthropology for the Eighties: Introductory Readings,
    Free Press (New York), 1982.
All-American Women: Lines that Divide, Ties that
    Bind, Free Press (New York), 1986.
Anthropology for the Nineties: Introductory Readings,
    Free Press (New York), 1988.

OTHER

(Author of introduction) Mokubung Nkomo, *Student*
    Culture and Activism in Black South African Uni-
    versities: The Roots of Resistance, Greenwood
    (Westport, CT), 1984.
(Author of introduction) Dele Jegede, *Art by Meta-*
    morphosis: Selections of African Art from the
    Spelman College Collection, Spelman College Art
    Department (Atlanta, GA), 1988.

Project codirector of *Race and Representation,* an art
video for Hunter College Art Gallery, 1987.

SIDELIGHTS: Johnnetta B. Cole, president of
Spelman College, is a prominent figure in American
academia. Cole came to academic life at age fifteen
when she entered Fisk University in 1952. She stayed
at Fisk only into the following year, whereupon she
transferred to Oberlin College and assumed preparations for a career in the medical field. At Oberlin,
Cole found her career plans altered when she began
studying anthropology. Afterward, as she later told
Ms., it was "good-bye, premed and hello, anthropology!"

Cole conducted her graduate work in anthropology at
Northwestern University, from which she earned a
doctorate in 1967. She then began teaching at Washington State University, where she eventually helped
establish a black studies program. She served as initial director of that program until assuming a professorship at the University of Massachusetts—Amherst
in 1970. Throughout the next thirteen years Cole was
at the Amherst school. She taught in that school's
anthropology department and Afro-American studies
program, and she entered the administrative field by
becoming associate provost of undergraduate education.

In 1982 Cole moved to Hunter College of the City
University of New York, where she taught anthropology and directed the school's program in Latin
American and Caribbean studies. She also continued her interest in subjects such as inequality in Cuba

and Cape Verdean culture in the United States. In
1986 she saw publication of *All-American Women:*
Lines that Divide, Ties that Bind, in which she explored similarities and differences among American
women.

Cole left Hunter College for the presidency of
Spelman College in 1987, and in the ensuing years
she proved herself a commanding and inspirational
force in the academic world. While devoting a sizeable portion of her time and attention to fundraising,
Cole also remained an active teacher, leading one
course each spring term. In addition, she applied
herself to the development of new programs, including one that brings together particularly accomplished
students with leading corporation figures from the
school's Atlanta surroundings. In assessing Spelman's
value to students, Cole told *Dollars & Sense* that she
considered the school "the greatest women's college
in America."

While president of Spelman College, Cole issued
Conversations: Straight Talk with America's Sister
President. In this volume she engages in a conversation with African-American women (with all others invited to listen in) on such topics as racism,
sexism, education and community service. On June
30, 1997, Cole stepped down as president of Spelman
College.

BIOGRAPHICAL/CRITICAL SOURCES:

BOOKS

Bateson, Catherine, *Composing a Life,* Atlantic
    Monthly Press (New York), 1989.
Cole, Johnnetta B., *Conversations: Straight Talk with*
    America's Sister President, Doubleday (New
    York), 1993.
Contemporary Black Biography, Volume 5, Gale (De-
    troit), 1995, pp. 60-63.

PERIODICALS

Art in America, September, 1990.
Change, September/October, 1987.
Dollars & Sense, March, 1992.
Ebony, February, 1988.
McCall's, October, 1990.
Ms., October, 1987.
New York Times Book Review, February 28, 1993, p.
    28.
People, May 10, 1993.
Publishers Weekly, November 30, 1992, p. 45.

COLEMAN, Clare
  See **BELL, Clare (Louise)**

*   *   *

COLQUHOUN, Frank 1909-1997

OBITUARY NOTICE—See index for *CA* sketch: Born October 28, 1909, in Ventnor, Isle of Wight, England; died April 3, 1997, in England. Vicar of the Church of England, religious instructor, and writer. Colquhoun will likely be best remembered in the Church of England for his work with a new ordination course in Southwark in the 1950s and 1960s.

Colquhoun attended Durham University, where he graduated with a bachelor's degree in 1933, and the same year became a deacon at St. Faith's in Maidstone. Colquhoun's next stop was at Christ Church, New Malden, which was in the diocese of Southwark. In 1939 he was made vicar of St. Michael and All Angels but left the church after the war to become editorial secretary of the National Church League and *The Churchman*. But in 1954 he returned to the Southwark diocese and became vicar of the parish of Wallington, where he served until 1961. Colquhoun then joined the staff of Southwark Cathedral and helped create the new ordination course conceived by Bishop John Robinson. The course was different from established theological course work and welcomed women and both Methodist and United Reform members. Colquhoun wrote nearly thirty books, most of which dealt with ordination instruction.

The works include *Harringay Story: The Official Record of the Billy Graham Greater London Crusade* (1954), *The Fellowship of the Gospel: A New Testament Study in the Principles of Christian Cooperation* (1957), *Your Child's Baptism: A Book for Parents and Godparents Who Are Prepared to Think Seriously about Baptism* (1961), *The Gospels for the Sundays and the Principal Holy Days of the Church's Year* (1961), *The Catechism and the Order of Confirmation* (1963), *Christ's Ambassadors: The Priority of Preaching* (1965), *Total Christianity* (1965), *Parish Prayers* (1967), *Prayers for Every Occasion* (1974), *Contemporary Parish Prayers* (1975), *Hard Questions: A Discussion of Thirty-Eight Basic Christian Problems* (1976), and *Moral Questions* (1977). Colquhoun was made canon of Southwark and Norwich Cathedrals.

OBITUARIES AND OTHER SOURCES:

BOOKS

Who's Who, 149th edition, St. Martin's, 1997.

PERIODICALS

Times (London), April 15, 1997, p. 21.

*   *   *

COLWELL, Rita R. 1934-

PERSONAL: Born November 23, 1924, in Beverly, MA; daughter of Louis and Louise Di Palma Rossi; married Jack H. Colwell, May 31, 1956; children: Alison and Stacie. *Education:* Purdue University, B.S., 1956, M.S., 1958; University of Washington, Ph.D., 1961. *Avocational interests:* Jogging and competitive sailing.

CAREER: Marine microbiologist. University of Washington, Seattle, research assistant, 1961-64; Georgetown University, Washington D.C., visiting assistant professor, 1963-64, associate professor of biology, 1964-72; University of Maryland, professor, 1972—, director of Sea Grant College, 1977-83, vice-president of academic affairs, 1983-87, director of Biotechnology Institute. Consultant to various organizations, including the National Science Foundation and the Environmental Protection Agency. Producer of *Invisible Seas,* an award-winning film. Served as president of Sigma Xi, American Society for Microbiology, International Congress of Systematic and Evolutionary Biology, and American Association for the Advancement of Science.

AWARDS, HONORS: Phi Sigma Service Award, American Chemical Society, 1975; Outstanding Woman on Campus, University of Maryland, 1979; Certificate of Recognition, NASA, 1984; Fisher Award, American Society of Microbiologists, 1985; D.Sc., Heriot-Watt University, Edinburgh, Scotland, 1987; Alice Evans Award, American Society of Microbiology Committee on the Status of Women, 1988; Gold Medal, International Biotechnology Institute, 1990; Purkinje Gold Medal, Czechoslovakian Academy of Science, 1991; Scholar of the Year, Phi Kappa Phi, 1992; Andrew White Medal, Loyola College, 1994; D.Sc., University of Surrey, England, 1995.

WRITINGS:

(With L. H. Stevenson) *Estuarine Microbial Ecology,*
University of South Carolina Press, 1973.

(Editor) *The Role of Culture Collections in the Era of
Molecular Biology: ATCC 50th Anniversary Symposium, 23 September, 1975,* American Society
for Microbiology (Washington), 1976.

(Editor) *Vibrios in the Environment,* Wiley (New
York), 1984.

(Editor, with Anthony J. Sinskey and E. Ray Pariser)
Biotechnology in the Marine Sciences, Wiley,
1984.

(Editor, with Pariser and Sinskey) *Biotechnology of
Marine Polysaccharides,* Hemisphere (Washington), 1985.

(With Editor) *Biomolecular Data: A Resource in
Transition,* Oxford University Press (New York),
1989.

Contributor to journals and periodicals, including
Science.

SIDELIGHTS: Rita R. Colwell is a leader in marine
biotechnology, the application of molecular techniques to marine biology for the harvesting of medical, industrial and aquaculture products from the sea.
As a scientist and professor, Colwell has investigated
the ecology, physiology, and evolutionary relationships of marine bacteria. As a founder and president
of the University of Maryland Biotechnology Institute, she has nurtured a vision to improve the environment and human health by linking molecular biology
and genetics to basic knowledge scientists had gleaned
from life and chemistry in the oceans.

Rita Rossi was born in Beverly, Massachusetts, November 23, 1934, the seventh of eight children to
parents Louis and Louise Di Palma Rossi. Her father
was an Italian immigrant who established his own
construction company, and her mother was an artistic
woman who worked to help ensure her children would
have a good education. She died when her daughter
was just thirteen years old, but she had been proud of
her success in school. In the sixth grade, after Rossi
had scored higher on the IQ exam than anyone in her
school's history, the principal asked sternly whether
she understood that she had the responsibility to go to
college. Rossi had answered, "Yes, ma'am," and
eventually received a full scholarship from Purdue
University. She earned her bachelor of science degree
with distinction in bacteriology in 1956. Although she
had been accepted to medical school, Rossi chose
instead to earn a master's degree so that she could

remain at the same institution as graduate student Jack
Colwell, whom she married on May 31, 1956.

Colwell would have continued her studies in bacteriology, but the department chairman at Purdue informed her that giving fellowship money to women
would have been a waste. She instead earned her
master's degree in the department of genetics. The
University of Washington, Seattle, granted her a
Ph.D. in 1961 for work on bacteria commensal to
marine animals, which is the practice of an organism
obtaining food or other benefits from another without
either harming or helping it. Colwell's contributions
included establishing the basis for the systematics of
marine bacteria.

In 1964, Georgetown University hired Colwell as an
assistant professor, and gave her tenure in 1966.
Colwell and her research team were the first to recognize that the bacterium that caused cholera occurred
naturally in estuaries. They isolated the bacterium
from Chesapeake Bay and in ensuing years sought to
explain how outbreaks in human populations might be
tied to the seasonal abundance of the host organisms
in the sea, particularly plankton. In 1972, Colwell
took a tenured professorship at the University of
Maryland. Her studies expanded to include investigations on the impact of marine pollution at the microbial level. Among her findings was that the presence
of oil in estuarine and open ocean water was associated with the numbers of bacteria able to break down
oil. She studied whether some types of bacteria might
be used to treat oil spills. Colwell and her colleagues
also made a discovery that held promise for improving oyster yields in aquaculture—a bacterial film
formed on surfaces under water attracted oyster larvae to settle and grow.

In the spirit of using knowledge gained from the sea
to benefit humans and the environment, Colwell prepared a seminal paper on marine biotechnology published in the journal *Science* in 1983. It brought attention to the rich resources of the ocean that might be
tapped for food, disease-curing drugs, and environmental clean-up by the applications of genetic engineering and cloning. In order to realize the potential
of marine biotechnology as originally outlined in her
1983 paper, Colwell helped foster the concept and
growth of the University of Maryland Biotechnology
Institute, established in 1987. As president of the
U.M.B.I., she has formed alliances between researchers and industry and has succeeded in raising funds to
develop the center as a prestigious biotech research
complex.

In addition, Colwell has held numerous professional and academic leadership positions throughout her career and is a widely published researcher. At the University of Maryland, Colwell was director of the Sea Grant College from 1977 to 1983. She served as president of Sigma Xi, the American Society for Microbiology, and the International Congress of Systematic and Evolutionary Biology, and was president-elect of the American Association for the Advancement of Science. Colwell has written and edited more than sixteen books and over four hundred papers and articles; she also produced an award-winning film, *Invisible Seas*. Her honors included the 1985 Fisher Award of the American Society for Microbiology, the 1990 Gold Medal Award of the International Institute of Biotechnology, and the 1993 Phi Kappa Phi National Scholar Award.

Colwell is the mother of two daughters who pursued careers in science. She is an advocate for equal rights for women, and one of her long-standing aspirations is to write a novel about a woman scientist. Her hobbies include jogging and competitive sailing.

BIOGRAPHICAL/CRITICAL SOURCES:

PERIODICALS

Baltimore Sun, October 13, 1991.
Natural Science, May, 1991, pp. 304-310.
Warfield's, August, 1990.*

*   *   *

CONFER, Dennis W. 1941-

PERSONAL: Born January 13, 1941, in Pottstown, PA; son of John W. and Pearl H. (a homemaker) Confer; married Marlene W. Haddock (a company vice-president), March 3, 1962; children: Mark W., Keith A. *Ethnicity:* "Caucasian." *Education:* Syracuse University, B.S., 1967; Michigan State University, M.B.A., 1974, and doctoral study. *Politics:* Republican. *Religion:* Protestant. *Avocational interests:* Hunting, fishing, travel, collecting guns, consulting.

ADDRESSES: Home and office—2509 Kilkenny Circle, Anchorage, AK 99504-3422.

CAREER: U.S. Air Force, career officer, working as chaplain services supervisor, budget officer, auditor, and comptroller, 1959-80, retiring as major; Wily

Ventures (outfitters of big game hunters and fishers), owner and manager, 1981-94; Wily Ventures, Inc., Anchorage, AK, owner, publisher, hunting and business consultant, 1995—. Alyeska Pipeline, budget analyst, 1981-82; Municipality of Anchorage, worked as controller, management analyst, and executive, 1982-88.

MEMBER: National Rifle Association, Retired Officers Association, American Association of Retired People, Alaska Professional Sportsmen's Association (member of board of directors, 1986-89), Safari Club International, North American Hunting Club, American Legion, Veterans of Foreign Wars.

AWARDS, HONORS: Military: Meritorious Service Medal, two Air Force Commendation Medals, two Good Conduct Medals, National Defense Service Medal, and six general medals. *Other:* Alaska Sport Fish Trophy Certificates; Safari Club big game records.

WRITINGS:

Wily Ventures Equipment List, Wily Ventures (Anchorage, AK), 1982.
Hunt Alaska Now, Wily Ventures, 1982.
Hunt Alaska Now: Self-Guiding for Trophy Moose and Caribou, Wily Ventures, 1997.

Author of "Alaskan Hunting: Ninety-five Percent Hard Work, Five Percent Fun," a column in *Air Force Times,* 1975. Contributor to *Safari Club.*

WORK IN PROGRESS: The 53rd Buck of the Hunt, the story of a whitetail deer hunt in Mexico in 1997; a book of hunting, fishing, and humorous stories, for Wily Ventures, expected in 1998.

SIDELIGHTS: Dennis W. Confer told *CA:* "I did not particularly want to be an accountant, but I always loved counting game and fish and secretly dreamed of being an outfitter. The Air Force sent me to college and, through the Air Force, I was able to extend my hunting to the Far East, northern California, Minnesota and Saskatchewan, other midwestern states, eastern states, and finally Alaska. I had always wanted to live in Alaska to hunt and fish; it took us fifteen years before we made it.

"I retired from the Air Force in 1980, but went on to work for the Municipality of Anchorage until 1988. In 1981, I began outfitting big game hunters in Alaska. In fourteen years, I assisted more than eight-hundred happy (and a few not so happy) do-it-yourself hunters. The hunters thought these were once-in-a-lifetime hunts but, because I made them extremely affordable, sixty percent repeated, with many completing three to seven hunts. They had a very high success rate on trophy animals. My intent in this was to share my hunting with others in order to collect more stories through my hunters than I could by myself alone, because I had another secret goal: to write hunting stories.

"So, I've been a hunter and fisherman for over forty years. I have accounted for more time in the outdoors than most people, but less than some. I love hunting, hunters, and helping others. I combined thirty years of experience in research, finance, statistics, and organization with my forty years of hunting experience to formulate a method of helping hunters to share Alaska with me. I developed the do's and don'ts, the how to's and where to's, the mechanisms and cost savings for getting to and from, and a training program encompassing everything needed to be known for an Alaskan hunt. I converted hunts from ninety-five percent hard work and five percent fun to ninety-five percent fun and five percent moderate work that anyone could do. I started my outfitting business with no money down, and financed most everything from hunters' deposits. I was able to keep hunter costs low and make a good profit with no incremental cost to the hunters. Advertising was mainly by word of mouth from happy hunters.

"I could not have done much of anything without the encouragement and assistance of my wife Marlene. Fortunately, she loves most hunters. Every man needs a wife like her; she always encouraged me to do what I liked best, and she even bought most of my guns for me as presents. She did all of the cooking for the hunters; they stayed in our house two or three days during the course of their hunts. Most days there were four-to-eight hunters with us, but sometimes there were sixteen (not by my plans). She received a few marriage proposals and a lot of invites to the lower forty-eight (states). We never charged more than thirty dollars a day for all meals, accommodations, and snacks, and we made money at it. We thoroughly enjoyed sharing our lives and home with most of the guests.

"Marlene and I were getting older and tired and needed a change. It was good that we transferred the hunting operation when we did, as I had a heart attack in 1995. I resigned my guide license and restricted myself to personal hunting only, along with writing

and consulting. We have hunted in Africa, Mongolia, Mexico, and Canada, and traveled elsewhere. We've had good lives, great memories, and few regrets. We didn't postpone doing things; we did them. We blamed no one for not doing anything, and we have a lot to look forward to. We hope to be able to inspire others to experience some of what we have shared."

*   *   *

CONWAY, Lynn Ann 1938-

PERSONAL: Born January 2, 1938, in Mount Vernon, NY. *Education:* Columbia University, B.S., 1962, M.S. in electrical engineering, 1963. *Avocational interests:* Motocross racing.

ADDRESSES: Office—University of Michigan, ATL Bldg., Ann Arbor, MI 48109.

CAREER: Engineer. IBM Corporation, Yorktown Heights, NY, on research staff, 1964-68; Memorex Corporation, Santa Clara, CA, senior staff engineer, 1969-73; Xerox Corporation, Palo Alto, CA, on research staff, 1973-78, research fellow and manager of VLSI (very large scale integrated) systems area, 1978-82, research fellow and manager of knowledge systems area, 1982-83; Defense Advisory Research Projects Agency (DARPA), Arlington, VA, chief scientist and assistant director of Strategic Computing, 1983-85; University of Michigan, Ann Arbor, professor of electrical engineering and computer science, and associate dean of the College of Engineering, 1985—. Massachusetts Institute of Technology, Cambridge, MA, visiting associate professor, 1978-79. Served on United States Air Force Scientific Advisory Board, Executive Council of the American Association for Artificial Intelligence, and the Technical Council Society for Machine Intelligence.

AWARDS, HONORS: Harold Pender Award, University of Pennsylvania, 1984; John Price Wetherill Medal, Franklin Institute, 1985; Meritorious Civilian Service Award, Secretary of Defense, 1985; achievement award from Society of Women Engineers (SWE), 1990 for "essential contributions to very large scale integrated (VLSI) circuit and system design methodology, and for rapid propagation of the new innovations throughout the engineering community"; Major Educational Innovation Award from the Institute of Electrical and Electronics Engineers (IEEE); Electronics Magazine Achievement Award.

WRITINGS:

Introduction to VLSI Systems, Addison Wesley Publishing, 1980.

SIDELIGHTS: Lynn Ann Conway has been recognized for her pioneering work in very large scale integrated (VLSI) circuit and system design methodology. She helped simplify the way integrated computer circuit chips are designed, and then went on to develop a rapid means of prototype fabrication that fundamentally changed computer design methodology and contributed to an explosion of new hardware and software. A professor of electrical engineering and computer sciences and associate dean of the College of Engineering at the University of Michigan, Conway includes computer architecture, artificial intelligence, and collaboration technology among her research interests.

Born in Mount Vernon, New York, on January 2, 1938, Conway received an M.S. degree in electrical engineering from Columbia University in 1963 and worked as a staff researcher at IBM Corporation from 1964 to 1969. Conway then served as senior staff engineer at Memorex Corporation from 1969 to 1973, when she accepted a research position with Xerox Corporation at its Palo Alto Research Center in California. She founded the VLSI systems and Knowledge Systems research departments at Xerox and remained resident fellow and manager there until 1983, when she began two years of service as chief scientist and assistant director of Strategic Computing at the Defense Advisory Research Projects Agency (DARPA). In 1985 Conway accepted her current position at the University of Michigan's College of Engineering.

Conway is renowned for two major developments in circuitry. Her first, a joint effort with several colleagues, was the invention of a new approach to the design of integrated computer circuit chips. Previously, many designers, each with specialized skills, were needed in the laborious process of circuitry development. Conway helped create a unified structural methodology which allowed computer engineers with general backgrounds to design chips—demystifying the design process.

Her second major achievement, which she described in the textbook *Introduction to VLSI Systems,* was a new method of chip fabrication, whereby designers could very rapidly obtain prototypes with which to test their hardware and software inventions. Both this quick turnaround fabrication facility and Conway's earlier contribution to the design of integrated circuitry have added to the increased democratization of information in the computer field.

Conway has received extensive recognition for her work, including the John Price Wetherill Medal from the Franklin Institute in 1985; the Meritorious Civilian Service Award, given by the Secretary of Defense in 1985; and the Harold Pender Award, bestowed by the University of Pennsylvania in 1984. She was honored in 1990 with an achievement award of the Society of Women Engineers (SWE), presented for "essential contributions to very large scale integrated (VLSI) circuit and system design methodology, and for rapid propagation of the new innovations throughout the engineering community." She also received the Major Educational Innovation Award from the Institute of Electrical and Electronics Engineers (IEEE), and the Electronics Magazine Achievement Award.

Conway has held numerous consulting positions and was visiting associate professor of electrical engineering and computer sciences at the Massachusetts Institute of Technology from 1978 to 1979. She has served on such advisory panels as the United States Air Force Scientific Advisory Board, the Executive Council of the American Association for Artificial Intelligence, and the Technical Council Society for Machine Intelligence. Her love of adventure has led her to the hobby of motocross racing.

BIOGRAPHICAL/CRITICAL SOURCES:

BOOKS

Society of Women Engineers Achievement Awards, 1993.*

*   *   *

COOPER, Leon N.   1930-

PERSONAL: Born February 28, 1930, in New York, NY; son of Irving and Anna (Zola) Cooper; married Kay Anne Allard, May 18, 1969; children: Kathleen Ann, Coralie Lauren. *Education:* Columbia University, A.B., 1951, A.M., 1953, Ph.D., 1954.

CAREER: Physicist and neural scientist. University of Illinois, Urbana, research associate in physics, 1955-57; Ohio State University, Columbus, assistant professor, 1957-58; Brown University, Providence, RI, associate professor, 1958-62, professor of physics, 1962-66, Henry Ledyard Goddard university professor, 1966-74, co-chair of Center for Neural Sciences, 1973—, Thomas J. Watson, Sr. Professor of Science, 1974—; Institute for Brain and Neural Systems, 1992—. Visiting professor at various universities and summer schools; consultant to various government agencies, industrial and educational organizations. Co-founder and co-chair of Nestor, Inc., which applies neural network systems to commercial and military applications.

ADDRESSES: Office—Department of Physics, Brown University, Providence, RI 02912.

MEMBER: National Academy of Sciences, American Physical Society, American Academy of Arts and Science, American Philosophical Society, Federation of American Scientists, Society of Neuroscience, American Association for the Advancement of Science, Sigma Xi.

AWARDS, HONORS: National Science Foundation Postdoctoral Fellow, Institute for Advanced Study, 1954-55; fellow, Alfred P. Sloan resident, 1959-66; fellow, John Simon Guggenheim Memorial Foundation, 1965-66; Comstock Prize, National Science Academy, 1968; Nobel Prize, 1972; Award of Excellence, Graduate Faculties Alumni of Columbia University, 1974; Descartes Medal Academie de Paris, Universite Rene Descartes, 1977; John Jay Award, Columbia College, 1985. Honorary degrees from various universities, including Columbia University (1973), University of Sussex (1973), University of Illinois (1974), Brown University (1974), Gustavus Adolphus College (1975), Ohio State University (1976), and University of Marie Curie (1977).

WRITINGS:

(With Brian B. Schwartz) *The Physics and Application of Superconductivity,* Technology Forecasting Institute (New York), 1968.

An Introduction to the Meaning and Structure of Physics, Harper, 1968, short edition, 1970.

Physics: Structure and Meaning, University Press of New England (Hanover, NH), 1992.

How We Learn, How We Remember: Toward an Understanding of Brain and Neural Systems, World Scientific (River Edge, NJ), 1995.

Contributor to journals and periodicals, including *Physical Review, Physical Review, Physical Review,* *Physical Review Letters, New York Times, Review of the Week, Physics Today, Conference Proceedings, Science in the Service of Mankind, Daedalus, Contemporary Physics, Naval Research Reviews.*

SIDELIGHTS: Leon N. Cooper began his scientific career while in his early twenties with pioneering work on the theory of superconductivity, a specialized field of physics that studies the resistanceless flow of electricity through certain metals at very low temperatures. For his contributions to the discipline, Cooper was awarded the Nobel Prize in physics in 1972. In more recent years, he has directed his attention towards the neural and cognitive sciences, working toward an understanding of memory and other brain functions.

Cooper's interest in biology reflects his early pursuit of the study of science while living in New York City. He was born in 1930, the son of Irving and Anna (Zola) Cooper. Like many other students at the specialized Bronx High School of Science, which he attended, young Cooper entered the prestigious Westinghouse Science Talent Search as a senior. His independent research project for this competition analyzed how bacteria can become resistant to penicillin. He was selected as one of the forty national winners in the Westinghouse competition which has produced five Nobel laureates over its half-century duration.

Cooper then entered Columbia University where he spent seven years, earning his A.B. degree in 1951, his A.M. degree in 1953, and his Ph.D. degree in 1954 with a dissertation on the mu-mesonic atom. This latter work was done under the direction of Robert Serber, who was a friend of J. Robert Oppenheimer, a scientist instrumental in the creation of the atom bomb. Through this association, the young Cooper obtained a position as a National Science Foundation Postdoctoral Fellow at the Institute for Advanced Study in Princeton, New Jersey.

During a year-long stay at the institute, Cooper continued to investigate mu-mesonic atoms. His growing reputation in quantum field theory drew the attention of scientist John Bardeen, who was working on the phenomenon of superconductivity at the University of Illinois. Superconductivity had first been described by the Dutch physicist Heike Kamerlingh Onnes in 1911. Kamerlingh Onnes had reported that some metals lose all resistance to the flow of electrical current, becoming "superconductive," as they are cooled to temperatures close to absolute zero. The heightened conductivity derives from a free flow of electrons in the metal. Scientists were intrigued by this phenomenon for both theoretical and practical reasons. An understanding of superconductivity could potentially revolutionize the electronics industry. Every device that operates by means of an electric current wastes a huge amount of energy in overcoming electrical resistance. If superconducting materials could be used in those devices, virtually no energy would be lost to resistance. The practical problem posed by Kamerlingh Onnes's discovery was the low temperature required for superconductivity. In the intervening half century, scientists had been singularly unsuccessful in improving on his work. By the 1950s, the highest temperature at which superconductivity had been observed was still only about 20 kelvin, 20 degrees above absolute zero.

Bardeen needed a young physicist skilled in the latest theoretical techniques, and he invited Cooper to join him. Cooper served as a research associate at Illinois from 1955 to 1957. It was during those two years that Cooper, Bardeen and a third scientist, J. Robert Schrieffer, developed their Nobel Prize-winning theory of superconductivity. Cooper's notable contribution to superconductivity theory was the discovery of what became known as "Cooper pairs."

Cooper's own readings led to his conviction that research in the field needed to concentrate on the interaction between two electrons which normally repel each other but, when located among positive ions in a metal lattice, develop a small net attraction for each other. These "Cooper pairs" of electrons accumulate and sweep through the lattice all in the same direction, resulting in the resistanceless flow of electricity in the metal. The "Cooper pair" concept formed the heart of the BCS theory of superconductivity, named for its three originators: Bardeen, Cooper, and Schrieffer. The details of this theory were disclosed in a letter to the editor of *Physical Review,* and it was printed in the November 15, 1956 issue; another letter signed by the three collaborators was sent to the *Physical Review* editor early in 1957, followed by their comprehensive paper titled "The Theory of Superconductivity." It was this paper, printed in *Physical Review*'s December 1, 1957 issue, that earned Cooper and his two colleagues their claim to the Nobel Prize awarded to them fifteen years later.

In 1957 Cooper left Illinois to join the physics faculty at Ohio State University as an assistant professor. Here, he researched the properties of liquid Helium 3 (He 3) with Andrew Sessler and Robert Mills. Cooper was the first one to suggest that Helium 3 might be a

superfluid, and his work drew favorable attention. However, Cooper's own preference for the East Coast made him accept an offer as associate professor at Brown University in 1958, where he became a full professor in 1962. He was appointed Thomas J. Watson, Sr. Professor of Science in 1974 and has served as co-chair of Brown's Center for Neural Sciences since 1973. Cooper is also director of the university's Institute for Brain and Neural Systems.

While at Brown, Cooper continued his interest in theoretical physics. He even developed a physics course for liberal arts students and wrote a remarkable textbook in 1968 titled *An Introduction to the Meaning and Structure of Physics.* However, his breadth of interest and curiosity also led him into the study of history, philosophy and the classics, and he published papers on such varying subjects as the place of science in human experience; the role of values in scientific inquiry; how science can serve mankind; the source and limits of human intellect, faith and science; and the relationships between history, science and American culture.

Cooper was also very intrigued by learning and memory, and in 1973 he and his colleagues founded the Center for Neural Studies at Brown. The center's objective was to study animal nervous systems and the human brain, especially to determine how the brain's neural network modifies itself through experience. As co-chair of the center, Cooper served with an interdisciplinary staff drawn from the departments of applied mathematics, biomedical sciences, linguistics and physics. Drawing on the nearly twenty years of research by the Center for Neural Studies, Cooper founded the Institute for Brain and Neural Systems in 1992. This organization has brought together an international group of scientists, and its objective is to pave the way for the next generation of cognitive pharmaceutical and intelligent systems for use in electronics, automobiles and communications. Its research aims to traverse the boundaries of the traditional sciences, drawing on the fields of biology, psychology, mathematics, engineering, physics, linguistics and computer science. Cooper is also co-founder and co-chair of Nestor, Inc. an industry leader in applying neural network systems to commercial and military applications.

Cooper's work has been widely recognized, and he has earned numerous awards besides his Nobel Prize. He was a recipient of the Comstock Prize (with Schrieffer) from the National Academy of Sciences in 1968; the Award of Excellence from the Graduate

Faculties Alumni of Columbia University in 1974; the Descartes Medal Academie de Paris, from Universite Rene Descartes in 1977; and the John Jay Award of Columbia College in 1985. Cooper holds seven honorary degrees from universities in the United States and abroad as well as being a member of various scientific organizations, including the American Physical Society, American Academy of Arts and Sciences, American Philosophical Society, the National Academy of Sciences, the Sponsor Federation of American Scientists, the Society of Neuroscience, and the American Association for Advancement of Science. Cooper is married and the father of two children.

BIOGRAPHICAL/CRITICAL SOURCES:

BOOKS

Magill, Frank N., editor, *The Nobel Prize Winners: Physics,* Volume 3, 1968-1988, Salem Press (Englewood Cliffs, NJ), 1989.
Phares, Tom K., *Seeking and Finding Science Talent: A 50-Year History of the Westinghouse Science Talent Search,* Westinghouse Electric Corporation, 1990.
Weber, Robert L., *Pioneers of Science: Nobel Prize Winners in Physics,* second edition, Adam Hilger, 1988.*

*   *   *

CORLISS, Richard (Nelson) 1944-

PERSONAL: Born March 6, 1944, in Philadelphia, PA; son of Paul William and Elizabeth Brown (McCluskey) Corliss; married Mary Elizabeth Yushak (a museum curator), August 31, 1969. *Education:* St. Joseph's College, B.S., 1965; Columbia University, M.F.A., 1967. *Avocational interests:* Crossword puzzles, baseball statistics, songwriting.

ADDRESSES: Office—Time, Time-Life Building, Rockefeller Center, New York, NY 10020.

CAREER: National Review, New York City, film critic, 1966-70; Museum of Modern Art, New York City, staff member of film department, 1968-70; *Film Comment,* New York City, editor, 1970-89; *New Times,* New York City, film critic, 1975-78; Soho Weekly News, New York, film critic, 1980; *Time,* New York City, associate editor, 1980-85, senior

writer, 1985—. Member of the selection committee for the New York Film Festival, 1971-87.

MEMBER: National Society of Film Critics, New York Film Critics.

WRITINGS:

(Editor) *The Hollywood Screenwriters* (biography), Discus Books (New York), 1972.
Greta Garbo (biography), Pyramid Publications (New York), 1974.
Talking Pictures: Screenwriters in the American Cinema (nonfiction), preface by Andrew Sarris, Overlook Press (Woodstock, NY), 1974.
Lolita (monograph), British Film Institute (London), 1994.

Also contributor of articles to periodicals, including *National Review, Film Comment, New Times, Soho Weekly News,* and *Time.*

SIDELIGHTS: Author Richard Corliss has been a film critic since 1966, when he obtained his first professional position while still studying for a master's degree in fine arts at Columbia University in New York City. Originally from Philadelphia, Corliss stayed in New York after college and has continued working primarily for publications based there. He has served on the staff of such well-known magazines as the *National Review* and *Time*—where he rose to the position of senior writer in 1985—and previously held the editorship of *Film Comment* for nearly two decades. Corliss has been involved with several other aspects of the study and appreciation of film; he worked for the film department of New York's Museum of Modern Art during the late 1960s and was a member of the selection committee for the New York Film Festival during the 1980s. Corliss has also written or edited books about various aspects of film, including 1972's *The Hollywood Screenwriters,* 1974's *Talking Pictures: Screenwriters in the American Cinema,* and a biography of the now-deceased Swedish actress Greta Garbo published in the same year. In 1994, Corliss's monograph *Lolita* reached the market under the auspices of the British Film Institute in London, England.

The Hollywood Screenwriters, a compilation produced by the staff of *Film Comment* magazine and edited by Corliss, comprises a collection of sketches detailing the careers of film writers. The later *Greta Garbo* was part of a series, the "Pyramid Illustrated History of the Movies," for which Ted Sennett served as general editor. Corliss' biographical volume includes photographs and provides readers with a list of Garbo's many celebrated films—from the days of silent film past the advent of "talkies," to her reclusive retirement in 1941.

Talking Pictures: Screenwriters in the American Cinema, published in 1974 and perhaps Corliss' best-known book, includes a preface by film critic Andrew Sarris. Nearly four hundred pages in length, the work, discusses the films of such renowned motion picture writers as Ben Hecht, Jules Feiffer, Buck Henry, Terry Southern, and many others. The volume's comprehensiveness and "thorough scholarship" were highly praised by a *Publishers Weekly* reviewer, who went on to applaud Corliss's style of writing, including his humor and liveliness. *Talking Pictures* received even wider readership through its British release in 1975 and its republication in the United States in 1985.

In *Lolita,* a monograph of fewer than one hundred pages, Corliss utilized his critical expertise to encompass the flavor of both the novel by Russian-born author Vladimir Nabokov and the film it inspired. In a group review of British Film Institute monographs in the *Observer,* Corliss' *Lolita* was appraised as "up to scratch" and applauded for "ingeniously" examining the subject matter.

BIOGRAPHICAL/CRITICAL SOURCES:

PERIODICALS

Observer (London), January 8, 1995, p. 21.
Publishers Weekly, April 26, 1985, p. 81.*

*   *   *

CORNWELL, John

PERSONAL: Male.

ADDRESSES: Jesus College, Cambridge University, Cambridge CB5 8BL, England.

CAREER: Jesus College, Cambridge University, Cambridge, England, director of Science and Human Dimension Project.

WRITINGS:

(Editor) *Nature's Imagination: The Frontiers of Scientific Vision,* Oxford University Press, 1995.

SIDELIGHTS: John Cornwell, director of the Science and Human Dimension Project at Jesus College, Cambridge University, is editor of *Nature's Imagination: The Frontiers of Scientific Vision.* The volume is a compilation of scholarly essays that grew out of a 1992 symposium on reductionism in science. "Reductionism" refers to a method of scientific inquiry whereby a whole is studied by examining its parts, as well as the view that "all of nature is the way it is . . . because of simple universal laws, to which all other scientific laws may in some sense be reduced," explained Steven Weinberg in the *New York Review of Books.* The advantages and disadvantages of reductionism are vigorously debated in *Nature's Imagination,* which includes contributions by chemist Peter W. Atkins, philosopher Mary Midgley, mathematical physicist Roger Penrose, philosopher and computer scientist Margaret Boden, and science philosopher Freeman Dyson, "a fair collection of the big names in the expanding business of science commentary," according to *New Scientist* contributor Jon Turney.

The essays in *Nature's Imagination* address subjects such as the nature of the universe, the interaction between the mind and body, artificial intelligence, and computer mathematics. Peter Atkins contributes a defense of reductionism titled "The Limitless Power of Science," which sparks a response from Mary Midgley, "Reductive Megalomania." According to Turney, "Their opposing views make for the most entertaining chapters of the book." John L. Casti, writing in *Nature,* called Cornwell's book "a collection of intellectual vignettes welded together into a drama that anyone interested in complex systems and the philosophy of science will want to read and savour." Writing in *Booklist,* Brenda Grazis cautioned that the essays in *Nature's Imagination* were meant for specialists and "the lay reader may find many of the arguments impenetrable." Casti in *Nature,* however, was enthusiastic, commenting: "As the wise old sage Freeman Dyson states in the introductory chapter, 'Science is an art form and not a philosophical method.' This book is one of the strongest testaments to that belief. Read and enjoy."

BIOGRAPHICAL/CRITICAL SOURCES:

PERIODICALS

Booklist, April 15, 1995, p. 1461.
Kirkus Reviews, February 15, 1995, pp. 191-92.
Library Journal, April 15, 1995, p. 110.
Nature, April 27, 1995, p. 840.
New Scientist, June 24, 1995, p. 47.

New York Review of Books, October 5, 1995, pp. 39-42.*

* * *

COTES, Cecil V.
  See DUNCAN, Sara Jeannette

* * *

COURANT, Richard   1888-1972

PERSONAL: Born January 8, 1888, in Lublintz, Germany; died January 27, 1972; married, 1912 (divorced, 1916); married Nerina Runge, 1919; children: two sons, two daughters. *Education:* Attended University of Breslau, Germany, 1905-1907; University of Gottingen, Germany, Ph.D., 1910. *Avocational interests:* Skiing, hiking, playing the piano.

CAREER: Mathematician. University of Gottingen, Gottingen, Germany, research assistant, 1907-10, lecturer, 1912-14, 1919, professor and informal administrator, 1920-33, founder and director of the Mathematics Institute; University of Munster, Munster, Germany, lecturer, 1919-20; Cambridge University, Cambridge, England, visiting lecturer, 1933-34; New York University, New York, NY, lecturer, 1934-36, professor and head of mathematics department, 1936-58. Member of the Applied Mathematics Panel during World War II. *Military service:* German Army, 1910, became a noncommissioned officer, 1914-18.

AWARDS, HONORS: Navy Distinguished Public Service Award, 1958; Knight-Commander's Cross, 1958; Star of the Order of Merit, Federal Republic of Germany, 1958; distinguished service award, Mathematical Association of America, 1965, for mathematics.

WRITINGS:

(With Felix Klein) *Vorlesungen Euber die Entwicklung der Mathematik im 19. Jarhundert,* J. Springer (Berlin), 1926-27.
Vorlesungen Euber Differential- und Integralrechnung, J. Springer, 1927-29.
(With Herbert Robbins) *What Is Mathematics?, An Elementary Approach to Ideas and Methods,* Oxford University Press (New York), 1941.

(With Kurt O. Friedrichs) *Supersonic Flow and Shock Waves,* Springer-Verlag (New York), 1948.
Dirichlet's Principle, Conformal Mapping, and Minimal Surfaces, Interscience Publishers (New York), 1950.
(With David Hilbert) *Methods of Mathematical Physics,* (translation of *Methoden der mathematischen Physik*), two volumes, Interscience Publishers, 1953, 1962.
Differential and Integral Calculus, two volumes, Interscience Publishers, 1965, 1974.
(With Fritz John) *Introduction to Calculus and Analysis,* two volumes, Interscience Publishers, 1965.

Editor of the *Yellow Series,* a series of mathematics books. Contributor to journals and periodicals, including *Society for Industrial and Applied Mathematics (SIAM) Review* and *IBM Journal of Research and Development.*

SIDELIGHTS: Richard Courant received worldwide recognition as one of the foremost organizers of mathematical research and teaching in the twentieth century. Most of Courant's work was in variational calculus and its applications to physics, computer science, and other fields. He contributed significantly to the resurgence of applied mathematics in the twentieth century. While the Mathematics Institute in Gottingen, Germany, and the Courant Institute of Mathematical Sciences at New York University stand as monuments to his organizing and fund-raising abilities, his numerous honorary degrees and awards, as well as the achievements of his students, testify to his noteworthy contributions to mathematics and other sciences.

Courant, the first of three sons, was born on January 8, 1888, in Lublinitz, a small town in Upper Silesia that was then German but later Polish. The family moved to Glatz when he was three; when he was nine they moved to the Silesian capital, Breslau (now Wroclaw). He was enrolled in Breslau's Konig Wilhelm Gymnasium, preparing to attend a university. At the age of fourteen, Courant felt a need to become self-supporting and started tutoring students for the high-school math finals, which he himself had not yet taken. He was asked to leave the school for this reason in 1905, and he began attending lectures in mathematics and physics at the local university. He passed the high-school finals later that year and became a full-time student at the University of Breslau. Unhappy with the lecture methods of his physics instructors, Courant began to concentrate on mathematics.

In 1907 Courant enrolled at the University of Gottingen to take courses with mathematician David Hilbert, a professor there. Soon Courant became an assistant to Hilbert, working principally on subjects in analysis, an area of mathematics with a close relationship to physics. Under Hilbert, Courant obtained his Ph.D. in 1910 for a dissertation in variational calculus.

In the fall of 1910, Courant was called up for a year of compulsory military service, during which he became a noncommissioned officer. After Courant completed his tour of duty, Hilbert encouraged him to come back to Gottingen for the *Habilitation,* an examination that qualified him for a license as a *privatdozent,* an unsalaried university lecturer or teacher remunerated directly by students' fees. In 1912 Courant received his license to teach at Gottingen.

Two years of teaching and other mathematical work in Gottingen came to an abrupt halt when Courant received his orders to serve in the Army on July 30, 1914. The Kaiser declared war the next day. Courant, like many others, thought the war would be over quickly and was eager to serve. He believed that Germany's cause was right and that his country would be victorious. After about a year of fighting in the trenches, Courant was wounded and was subsequently deployed in the wireless communications department. Courant proposed that the use of mirrors to obtain visibility of what was going on above ground would help save lives. He also proposed the use of earth telegraphy, a means of communication that would use the earth as a conduit. Both ideas were utilized by the army.

About two weeks after the Armistice, which was signed November 11, 1918, in the midst of tremendous political turmoil, Courant managed to sign a contract with Ferdinand Springer to serve as editor for a series of mathematics books. Courant had made the original proposal for this series to Springer a year earlier. He envisioned timely mathematical treatises that would be especially pertinent to physics. These yellow-jacketed books became known worldwide as the *Yellow Series,* and their publication continued after Courant resigned as editor.

Courant returned to Gottingen in December of 1918 and resumed teaching as *Privatdozent* in the spring of 1919. During the summer of 1919, he completed a lengthy paper on the theory of eigenvalues of partial differential equations (of importance in quantum mechanics). After teaching at the University of Munster for a year, he returned as a professor to Gottingen in 1920; in addition to teaching, he was expected to take care of the informal administrative duties of the mathematics department. During the period from 1920 to 1925, Courant succeeded in making Gottingen an international center of theoretical and applied mathematics. Courant's emphasis on applied mathematics attracted physicists from all over the world, making the university a hub of research in quantum mechanics. His tireless efforts as a researcher, teacher, and organizer finally resulted in the creation of the Mathematics Institute of the University of Gottingen. Defining his vision of the future of mathematics, Courant said, "The ultimate justification of our institute rests in our belief in the indestructible vitality of mathematical scholarship. Everywhere there are signs to indicate that mathematics is on the threshold of a new breakthrough which may deepen its relationship with the other sciences and demand their mathematical penetration in a manner quite beyond our present understanding."

In the 1920s and 1930s, Courant worked with Hilbert on his most important publication, *Methoden der mathematischen Physik,* later translated into English as *Methods of Mathematical Physics.* The text was tremendously successful because it laid out the basic mathematical techniques that would play a role in the new quantum theory and nuclear physics. The Great Depression of the early 1930s created a need for university faculties to cut expenses, and there was an order to discharge most of the younger assistants. Courant successfully helped lead the fight of members of the mathematics and natural science faculty to pass a proposal that professors themselves pay the salaries of the assistants who were to be dismissed. He also helped students get scholarships and arranged for some to become part of his household to assist them financially. Those from wealthy families were encouraged to work without pay so that stipends could be available for needy students.

Courant took a leave of absence from Gottingen during the spring and summer of 1932 to lecture in the United States. His positions as professor and director of the Gottingen Mathematics Institute ended on May 5, 1933, when he and five other Gottingen professors received official word that they were on leave until further notice. The move reflected the National Socialist government's escalating campaign against German Jews as well as its displeasure with the university, which had become a locus of independent liberal thought. As Americans and other foreigners were leaving Gottingen at this time, Courant observed that the spirit of the institute had already been destroyed. During the 1933-1934 academic year he became a visiting lecturer at Cambridge in England. In January of 1934, he accepted an offer of a two-year contract with New York University.

In 1936, when his temporary position ended, he was appointed professor and head of New York University's mathematics department. In that position, he did for New York University what he had done for Gottingen by creating a center of mathematics and science of international importance. In recognition of his work, Courant was made director of the new mathematics institute at New York University, later named the Courant Institute of Mathematical Sciences. Courant's success as an organizer was largely due to his ability to attract promising young mathematicians. He was always available to them as a teacher, helped them to publish their work, and organized financial support for them if they needed it. His students often remained loyal to him for the rest of their lives and tended to stay in his orbit.

During World War II, Courant was a member of the Applied Mathematics Panel, which assisted scientists involved with military projects and contracted for specific research with universities throughout the country. While the group at New York University under contract with the panel made important contributions to the war effort, the contract in turn played a vital role in setting up a scientific center at New York University. Courant's mathematical work in numerical analysis and partial difference equations played a vital role in the development of computer applications to scientific work. Courant was also instrumental in getting the Atomic Energy Commission to place its experimental computer UNIVAC at New York University in 1953. Courant retired in 1958, the same year he was honored with the Navy Distinguished Public Service Award and the Knight-Commander's Cross and Star of the Order of Merit of the Federal Republic of Germany. In 1965, he received an award for distinguished service to mathematics from the Mathematical Association of America.

Married in 1912 to a woman he had tutored as an adolescent, Courant was divorced in 1916. In 1919 he married Nerina (Nina) Runge, and they had two sons and two daughters. He enjoyed skiing and hiking, and played the piano. In November of 1971, Courant suffered a stroke. He died on January 27, 1972, a few weeks after his eighty-fourth birthday. According to a *New York Times* obituary by Harry Schwartz, a Nobel laureate in physics once remarked that "every physicist is in Dr. Courant's debt for the vast insight he has given us into mathematical methods for compre-

hending nature and the physical world." At a memorial in Courant's honor, the mathematician Kurt O. Friedrichs said of him: "One cannot appreciate Courant's scientific achievements simply by enumerating his published work. To be sure, this work was original, significant, beautiful; but it had a very particular flavor: it never stood alone; it was always connected with problems and methods of other fields of science, drawing inspiration from them, and in turn inspiring them."

BIOGRAPHICAL/CRITICAL SOURCES:

BOOKS

Albers, Donald J., and G. L. Alexanderson, editors, *Mathematical People: Profiles and Interviews,* Birkhauser, 1985.

Beyerschen, Alan D., *Scientists under Hitler: In Politics and the Physics Community in the Third Reich,* Yale University Press, 1977.

Courant Anniversary Volume: Studies and Essays Presented to Richard Courant on his 60th Birthday, Interscience Publishers, 1948.

Reid, Constance, *Courant in Gottingen and New York: The Story of an Improbable Mathematician,* Springer-Verlag, 1976.

Struik, Dirk, J., *A Concise History of Mathematics,* Dover Publications, fourth revised edition, 1987.

PERIODICALS

Journal of Mathematical and Physical Sciences, a Journal of the Indian Institute of Madras, March, 1973, pp. i-iv.

New York Times, January 29, 1972, p. 32.

OTHER

"Richard Courant, 1888-1972: Remarks Delivered at the Memorial, February 18, 1972, and at the Meeting of the Graduate Faculty, March 15, 1972, New York University."

Richard Courant in Gottingen and New York, (video), The Mathematical *Association of America,* MAA Video Classics No. 4, 1966.*

* * *

COURNAND, Andre (Frederic) 1895-1988

PERSONAL: Born September 24, 1895, in Paris, France; immigrated to United States, 1930, naturalized citizen, 1941; died February 19, 1988, in Great Barrington, MA; son of Jules (a dentist) and Marguerite (Weber) Cournand; married Sibylle Blumer, 1924 (died 1959); married Ruth Fabian, 1963 (died 1973); married Beatrice Bishop Berle, 1975; children: four. *Education:* University of Paris, Sorbonne, B.A., 1913, M.D., 1930. *Avocational interests:* Philosophy, art.

CAREER: Physician. Bellevue Hospital, Columbia University College of Physicians and Surgeons, New York City, instructor, 1930-51, professor, 1951-64, member of faculty, 1964-88. *Military:* French Army, 1915-19, became auxiliary battalion surgeon.

AWARDS, HONORS: Lasker Award, 1942; joint Nobel Prize in physiology or medicine, 1956; elected to National Academy of Science, 1958.

WRITINGS:

Du Concept de la Conjonction de l'Air et du Sand dans le Poumon, Huber (Stuttgart, Germany), 1966.
(Editor with Maurice Laevy) *Shaping the Future: Gaston Berger and the Concept of Prospective,* Gordon and Breach Science Publishers (New York City), 1973.
From Roots to Late Budding: The Intellectual Adventures of a Medical Scientist, Gardner Press (New York City), c. 1986.

SIDELIGHTS: Andre Frederic Cournand shared the 1956 Nobel Prize in physiology or medicine with German surgeon Werner Forssmann and American physiologist Dickinson Woodruff Richards, Jr. for pioneering work in the field of cardiac and pulmonary physiology. Cournand helped develop the technique of cardiac catheterization, which permits blood samples to be obtained from the heart for determining cardiac abnormalities.

Cournand was born in Paris on September 24, 1895. His father, Jules Cournand, and his grandfather were both dentists. Cournand writes in his autobiography, *From Roots to Late Budding: The Intellectual Adventures of a Medical Scientist,* that his decision to study the sciences and medicine stemmed from his father's regrets of his own choice of dentistry over medicine. At age 15, young Andre began to accompany his parents to the salon of a physician friend where many internationally known scientists met and discussed issues of their day. Cournand's mother, Marguerite Weber Cournand, loved literature and learning and encouraged in her son a deep interest in philosophy

and art, which Cournand maintained even while pursuing his medical studies and research.

In 1913, Cournand received his bachelor's degree from the University of Paris-Sorbonne, where he also began his medical studies in 1914. But in that year the first World War broke out, and many medical professors enlisted in the army. In the spring of 1915, Cournand decided to postpone his studies. In July of that year he joined a surgical unit that provided emergency care on the front lines. By 1916 he was trained as an auxiliary battalion surgeon and was serving in the trenches. He didn't return to medical school until 1919. After serving as an intern, he received his M.D. in 1930.

Cournand had decided to specialize in upper respiratory diseases and, delaying his entry into private practice, pursued further training in the United States. He joined a residency program at the Tuberculosis Service of the Columbia University College of Physicians and Surgeons at Bellevue Hospital in New York City. He stayed at Columbia for the remainder of his career, rising from his initial position as investigator to a full professor in 1951. He became a naturalized citizen of the United States in 1941.

At Bellevue Cournand began what would become a long collaboration with Dickinson W. Richards. Together, they investigated the theories of a Harvard physiologist, Lawrence J. Henderson, who had postulated that the heart, lungs, and circulatory system are a functional unit designed to transport respiratory gases from the atmosphere to the tissues in the body and back out again.

In order to study respiratory gases and their concentrations in the blood as it passed through the heart, samples of blood from the heart had to be obtained. At this time, there was no established technique for this task. Catheters—flexible tubes intended to introduce and remove fluids from organs—had been used for the past 100 years, but only in animal experiments. The safety of catheter use in humans was doubtful. But Cournand was aware that in 1929 a German scientist, Werner Forssmann, had dramatically demonstrated the safety of cardiac catheterization by performing it on himself. He had inserted a catheter into one of his arm veins and then threaded it into his right atrium. Cournand became convinced of the safety of catheterization after speaking with one of his professors in Paris who had also performed a type of catheterization on himself, and subsequently scores of others, without any problems.

The Bellevue team experimented on animals for four years, working to standardize the procedure and perfect the equipment they were convinced was necessary for their studies of the cardiac system. When at last cardiac catheterization was used to obtain a sample of mixed venous blood in humans, what could previously be only vaguely determined by clinical observation could be physiologically described. Cardiac catheterization not only allows for samples of mixed venous blood to be collected, but it also measures blood pressure in various parts of the cardiac circulatory system—the right atrium, the ventricles, and the arteries—and measures total blood flow and gas concentrations. In short, the functions of the heart and the lungs can be fully specified through cardiac catheterization.

During World War II, Cournand led a team of physicians investigating the use of cardiac catheterization on patients suffering from severe circulatory shock resulting from traumatic injury. Obtaining physiological measurements of cardiac output in these patients helped identify the cause of shock—a fall in cardiac output and return. As a result of these findings, it was determined that the best treatment for shock was a total blood transfusion rather than simply replacing plasma, which had previously been used and was found to cause anemia.

After the war, Cournand applied the technique of cardiac catheterization to patients with heart and pulmonary diseases. The team continually worked to improve the technique and was able, at this time, to obtain simultaneous readings of blood pressure in the right ventricle and the pulmonary artery. This allowed for greater diagnostic accuracy of congenital defects as well as evaluations of treatment. Eventually these investigations led to increased understanding of acquired heart diseases and the relation between diseases of the lungs and cardiac function, thus opening up the field of pulmonary heart diseases.

Cournand began to be recognized for his research in the mid-1940s, when he was invited to speak at and lead various conferences. In 1949 he won the Lasker Award, and in 1952 he was invited by the National Institutes of Health to screen grant applications for the Lung, Heart and Kidney Study Section. Cournand's increasing recognition culminated in the fall of 1956 when he was awarded the Nobel Prize. In 1958 he was elected to the National Academy of Science.

During his years of research, Cournand remained interested and involved in the arts. While still in Paris, he had become a follower of the modern art movement and was friends with such painters as Jacques Lipschitz and Robert Delaunay and such writers as Andre Breton. In 1924 he married Sibylle Blumer, a daughter of Jeanne Bucher, who was a prominent gallery owner in Paris. They were married until her death in 1959. In 1963 Cournand married Ruth Fabian, who died in 1973. He was married again, to Beatrice Bishop Berle, in 1975. He had four children, three daughters and an adopted son.

Cournand retired in 1964 and devoted the years until his death to the study of the social and ethical implications of modern science. He died on February 19, 1988, in Great Barrington, Massachusetts.

BIOGRAPHICAL/CRITICAL SOURCES:

BOOKS

McGraw-Hill Modern Men of Science, McGraw-Hill, 1966, pp. 117-18.
Sourkes, Theodore L., *Nobel Prize Winners in Medicine and Physiology: 1901-1965,* revised edition, Abelard-Schuman, 1966.*

*   *   *

COX, Geraldine Vang 1944-

PERSONAL: Born January 10, 1944, in Philadelphia, PA; daughter of Karl Earling and Geraldine Florence (Oldroyd) Vang; married Walter George Cox, September 10, 1965. *Education:* Drexel University, B.S., 1966, M.S., 1967, Ph.D., 1970.

CAREER: Biologist. Raytheon Corporation, Portsmouth, RI, technical coordinator of environmental programs, 1970-76; U.S. Department of Labor, special assistant to the secretary, 1976-77; American Petroleum Institute, environmental scientist, Washington, 1977-79; Chemical Manufacturing Association, vice president and technical director, 1979-91; Fluor Daniel, Inc., Washington, vice president, 1991-93; Ampotech, Bristol, RI, chief executive officer, 1994—. Water Pollution Control Federation, program committee, 1974-79; Marine Quality Committee, founder, and chair, 1975-80; National Academy of Sciences, Environmental Measurement Panel of the National Bureau of Standards, 1977-80; Federation of Organizations for Professional Women, president, 1982-84; New Jersey Institute of Technology, board of governors, 1984-90.

AWARDS, HONORS: Rhode Island Governor's citation, 1975; White House fellowship, 1976; Achievement Award, Society of Women Engineers, 1984; Science and Engineering Award and Harriet E. Worrell Outstanding Alumna, Drexel University, 1987; Meritorious Service Award, U.S. Coast Guard, 1991.

WRITINGS:

(With Editor) *Oil Spill Studies: Strategies and Techniques,* American Petroleum Institute, Pathotox Publishers (Park Forest South, IL), 1977.

SIDELIGHTS: Geraldine V. Cox is a biologist whose specialty is environmental science. Her professional career has involved developing policy for the chemical industry in the fields of health and safety, water pollution, and hazardous waste management. She was granted a White House Fellowship in 1976, serving as Special Assistant to the Secretary of Labor.

Geraldine Anne Vang Cox is a native of Philadelphia, Pennsylvania, where she was born January 10, 1944. In 1970, she earned her doctorate degree in environmental sciences at Drexel University, where she had also completed her undergraduate studies and earned a master of science degree. She began her professional career at the Raytheon Company in 1970, where she served as Technical Coordinator of Environmental Programs until 1976. She then served as Special Assistant to the Secretary of the U.S. Department of Labor for one year.

In 1977, Cox joined the American Petroleum Institute as Environmental Scientist, a post she held until 1979, when she was named Vice President and Technical Director of Chemical Manufacturing Association. She held that position until 1991, when she joined Fluor Daniel as Vice President. Her contributions have reflected such specialties as marine and fresh water pollution, environmental health, and ecological damage assessment.

Cox was responsible for establishing the chemical industry's guidelines for community emergencies following the explosion of a plant in Bhopal, India. The result in 1985 was the establishment of CAER (Community Awareness and Emergency Response), which led to the adoption of a federal law, and later an international standard drafted by the United Nations—both based on Cox's model. She also developed guidelines for epidemiology studies and other community and worker health and safety standards.

Cox has held various posts concurrently. She was a member of the Program Committee of the Water Pollution Control Federation from 1974 to 1979; she founded the Marine Water Quality Committee and chaired it from 1975 to 1980; she was a member of the National Academy of Sciences Environmental Measurement Panel of the National Bureau of Standards from 1977 to 1980.

During the 1980s, Cox chaired the U.S. Coast Guard's Marine Occupational Safety and Health Committee and was a member of the Transportation Advisory Committee, for which she received the Coast Guard Meritorious Public Service Award in 1991. She served on the American Chemical Society's Committee on Science, and was President of the Federation of Organizations for Professional Women from 1982 to 1984. Cox has received numerous other honors, including the Society of Women Engineers Achievement Award in 1984, "for her contributions in the field of environmental management, in particular water pollution." In addition, Cox has been a member of the American Society for Testing and Materials, the Water Pollution Control Federation, and the American National Standards Institute.*

*   *   *

CRAM, Donald J(ames)   1919-

PERSONAL: Born April 22, 1919, in Chester, VT; son of William Moffet and Joanna (Shelley) Cram; married Jean Turner, 1940, marriage ended in 1968; married Jane Maxwell, November 25, 1969; *Education:* Rollins College, Florida, B.S., 1941; University of Nebraska, M.S., 1942; Harvard, Ph.D., 1947. *Avocational interests:* Surfing, downhill skiing, singing folk songs and playing the guitar.

CAREER: Research chemist in organic chemistry. Chemist with Merck and Company, 1942-45; research fellow, Harvard; assistant professor, 1947-56, and professor of chemistry, 1956-84, Saul Winstein Professor of Chemistry, 1985, professor emeritus, 1990, University of California, Los Angeles; consultant Upjohn, 1952-87; Union Carbide, 1961-87; Guggenheim Fellow, 1954-55. Eastman Kodak Company, 1981-90; Technicon Company, 1984-92; Institute Guido Donegani, Milan, Italy, 1988-91; State Department Exchange fellow to University of Mexico; guest lecturer and visiting professor in Mexico, Germany, Africa, and England.

AWARDS, HONORS: American Chemical Society Award, 1953 and 1965; Herbert Newby McCoy Award, 1965 and 1975; Society of Chemical Manufacturers Association Award, 1965; Arthur C. Cope Award from the American Chemical Association, 1974; R.C. Fuson Lecturer, University of Nevada, 1979; Willard Gibbs Award, 1985; Roger Adams Award, 1985; Nobel Prize in Chemistry, 1987; Beckman Lecturer, California Institute of Technology, 1988; Seaborg Medal, 1989; National Medal in Science, 1993. Honorary degrees awarded from Uppsala University, 1977, University of Southern California, 1983, Rollins College, 1988, and University of Nebraska and University of Western Ontario, both 1989.

WRITINGS:

(With George Hammond) *Organic Chemistry,* McGraw-Hill (New York City), 1964, 4th edition, 1980.
Fundamentals of Carbanion Chemistry, Academic Press, (New York City) 1965.
(With John H. Richards and Hammond) *Elements of Organic Chemistry,* McGraw-Hill, 1967.
(With James Hendrickson and Hammond) *Organic Chemistry,* Mcgraw-Hill, 1970.
(With Jane Maxwell Cram) *Essence of Organic Chemistry,* Addison-Wesley, 1978.
From Design to Discovery, American Chemical Society, 1990.

Contributor to journals and periodicals, including *CHEMTECH, Angewandte Chemie,* and *International Edition in English.*

SIDELIGHTS: Organic chemistry underwent profound changes in the second half of the twentieth century, and one of the scientists responsible for this progress is Donald J. Cram. When he entered the profession in the 1940s, organic chemistry was primarily concerned with clarifying molecular structure and with synthesizing new molecules by mixing reagents with organic compounds by a method that was more or less ad hoc. The mechanisms of reactions were infrequently exploited in directing reactions towards a desired product. In the years after World War II reaction mechanisms attracted new attention; the exact three-dimensional details of how molecules combine to form products became known, and chemists realized that compounds of very specific shapes could be constructed. This was called stereochemistry, and it had valuable applications for the discipline of making molecules that make other molecules—that is, building compounds that can hold other compounds in a

specific configuration, which in turn can lead to a specific reaction that would not otherwise have taken place. It was for his studies in this area, specifically his work in host-guest molecules, that Cram shared the Nobel Prize in 1987.

Cram was born April 22, 1919, in Chester, Vermont, the fourth child and only son of William and Joanna Shelley Cram, who had recently come from Ontario. The family moved to Brattleboro, Vermont, in 1921, and Cram's father died of pneumonia in 1923. Many years later, Cram recalled that this loss "forced me to construct a model for my own character that was composed of pieces taken from many different individuals; some being people I studied and others I lifted from books." He spent his childhood in Brattleboro, a curious, mischievous, bookish teenager who read through most of the standard classics but also played varsity sports. He supported himself and the family with a succession of odd jobs paid by barter, including receiving dental work in exchange for lawn mowing; these taught him self-discipline, but convinced him that he did not want to spend his life in a job that was repetitive and uninspiring. In 1935, when he was sixteen, his family dispersed and he entered Winwood, a small, private school on Long Island, where he finished his high school studies in 1937.

Cram received a scholarship to Rollins College in Florida, where he earned his B.S. in 1941. The chemistry department at Rollins College was small and underfunded, but it was here that Cram realized research could provide the ever new experience he had hoped to find in a career. He went on to receive an M.S. in chemistry at the University of Nebraska in 1942, and then spent the war years with Merck and Company, a pharmaceutical firm, in their penicillin program. Three years later, with a research fellowship and a strong recommendation from Merck's Max Tishler, he moved to Harvard University, where he received his Ph.D. under Louis Fieser in 1947. After a three-month postdoctoral stint with John D. Roberts at the Massachusetts Institute of Technology, Cram accepted an assistant professorship at the University of California at Los Angeles. He would remain here for the rest of his career, becoming a full professor in 1956 and Saul Winstein Professor of Chemistry in 1985.

Cram's research divides chronologically into two sections. In the first phase, from 1948 to about 1970, he concentrated on reaction mechanisms. He conducted his first mechanistic study on the substitution reaction of a compound with two adjacent asymmetric carbon atoms (carbons with four different groups attached, arranged in a specific order in space). As the asymmetry was preserved during the reaction, it was clear that something prevented rotation of the carbon atoms on their common bond in the transition state. Cram proposed that they were held in place by what he named a phenonium ion, formed by a phenyl (benzene-ring) group on one of the carbons; he believed this acted as a bridge between them in the transition state. Cram adduced other evidence to support the existence of this new ion, and he carried this kind of study to other organic molecules. The implications of such studies were particularly important in biological systems, where the greater number of large molecules contain asymmetric carbons.

Cram then turned to elimination reactions with the same sort of compound, containing two adjacent asymmetric carbon atoms. In an elimination reaction, an atom or group is removed from each carbon, creating a double bond between them, and the adjacent asymmetric carbon atoms show how the remaining groups will be arranged on the resulting double-bonded compound. He formulated his findings in what came to be called "Cram's rule." He went on to study many more molecules that formed a negative carbon atom in the transition state, and he showed that the associated positive ion could do many previously unsuspected things—including migrating to an adjacent carbon atom, or skating around a double-bond system and ending up on the other side of the carbon to which it was originally attached. At the same time that he performed his work on reaction mechanisms, Cram created and studied a new class of compounds, called the cyclophanes, in which two benzene rings are fastened together at each end by bridges of two or more carbon atoms. This brings the rings into close juxtaposition and also creates considerable angular strain.

Eventually, Cram decided that his research was becoming repetitive—precisely the situation he had resolved to avoid many years before. At age fifty he turned to a new field, the investigation of host-guest molecules. For his first host molecules he chose the "crown ethers" that had been synthesized by Charles John Pedersen of DuPont Chemical's research laboratories. Crown ethers are cyclic compounds in which oxygen atoms recur regularly around the ring, spaced apart by two or more carbons. In some conformations the oxygen atoms stick up like the points of a crown; hence the name. These atoms, which are polar and possess unbonded electron pairs, can form complexes with a variety of positive or incipiently positive atoms or molecules.

The simplest of these crown-ether structures was already known to form complexes with potassium ions by turning its oxygen atoms into the center to form what Cram called a corand. He discovered that a corand can be used to separate potassium from other ions. By constructing other corands and basket-shaped molecules he called cavitands, with interiors of carefully controlled size, Cram was able to select out each of the alkali metal ions (lithium, sodium, potassium, rubidium, cesium) from solution with a high degree of specificity. This had important applications in analytical chemistry, particularly in medical and biological systems. Other cavitands were synthesized that looked less and less like crown ethers, except that they had oxygen or nitrogen atoms in their interiors for complexation. Cram extended these studies to organic molecules. A special asymmetric compound was devised that could form complexes with either right- or left-handed amino acids; this was worked into a continuous mechanical separator for these asymmetric molecules.

The ultimate goal of those working with artificial enzymes has long been to produce large molecules. This has not yet been attained, but Cram's work has made great strides in this direction. For his research on host-guest molecules, he shared the 1987 Nobel Prize in chemistry with Pedersen and Jean-Marie Lehn of Strasbourg University. Cram delivered a lecture at the awards ceremony entitled "The Design of Molecular Hosts, Guests, and Their Complexes." Newspaper accounts emphasized the ramifications of his discoveries for both medical and industrial research, and it was observed that Cram had taught many of the chemists working on molecular recognition around the world.

Cram has co-authored an undergraduate textbook on organic chemistry, organized not by types of compounds (like nearly all other such works) but by types of reaction mechanism; it has gone through four editions and has been translated into thirteen languages. He also wrote another lower-level text, *Essence of Organic Chemistry,* with his second wife, Jane Maxwell Cram. These publications attest to his ongoing interest in undergraduate teaching. Cram's *Fundamentals of Carbanion Chemistry,* published in 1965, summarizes work in the field. In 1990, he produced the autobiographical *From Design to Discovery,* which contains relatively little personal information but is of great interest to chemists who want a review, with bibliography, of his research over four decades.

Other awards and honorary degrees have been presented to Cram in addition to the Nobel Prize. In 1974, he received the California Scientist of the Year award and the American Chemical Society's Arthur C. Cope Award. He was presented with the Richard Tolman Medal, the Willard Gibbs Award, and the Roger Adams Award, all in 1985. He also has received honorary doctorates from six institutions, including his undergraduate alma mater.

Cram has been married twice, first to Jean Turner from 1940 to 1968, and then in 1969 to Jane Maxwell, who is also a chemist. Both marriages have been childless. A man of abundant drive and energy, Cram spends his leisure time surfing and downhill skiing; he also sings folksongs and plays the guitar.

BIOGRAPHICAL/CRITICAL SOURCES:

BOOKS

James, Laylin K., editor, *Nobel Laureates in Chemistry, 1901-1992,* American Chemical Society, 1993, pp. 708-714.
Magill, Frank N., editor, *The Nobel Prize Winners: Chemistry,* Volume 3, Salem Press, 1990, pp. 1165-1176.

PERIODICALS

Science News, August 8, 1987, pp. 90-93.*

* * *

CROSBY, Elizabeth Caroline 1888-1983

PERSONAL: Born October 25, 1888, in Petersburg, MI; died July 28, 1983; daughter of Lewis Fredrick and Frances (maiden name, Kreps) Crosby; adopted child: Kathleen. *Education:* Adrian College, B.A. 1910; University of Chicago, M.S., 1912; Ph.D., 1915.

CAREER: Neuroanatomist; zoology, mathematics, and Latin instructor, principal, 1916, superintendent, 1918, Petersburg High School, Petersburg, Michigan; boys basketball coach; junior instructor, 1920, associate professor, 1929, full professor and consulting neurosurgeon, 1936-1960, University of Michigan; professor emeritus of anatomy, University of Alabama.

AWARDS, HONORS: Received ten honorary degrees from a variety of institutions, including Smith College, 1968; Woman's Medical College of Pennsylvania, 1968; and an honorary M.D. degree from the University of Groningen, Netherlands, 1958; inducted in to the Michigan and Alabama Women's Hall of Fame; Achievement Award of the American Association of Neurological Surgeons; Galen Award, 1956; first woman non-clinician honorary member of the Harvey Cushing Society; Henry Russel Lectureship, 1946, Distinguished Faculty Achievement Award, 1956, University of Michigan, (first woman to receive these awards); National Medal of Science, from President Jimmy Carter, c.1978.

WRITINGS:

The Forebrain of Alligator mississippiensis, [Philadelphia], 1917.
(With C. U. Ariens Kappers and G. Carl Huber) *The Comparative Anatomy of the Nervous System of Vertebrates, Including Man,* Volume I and II, Macmillan, 1936.
(Editor with H. N. Schnitzlein) *Comparative Correlative Neuroanatomy of the Vertebrate Telencephalon,* Macmillan, 1982.

SIDELIGHTS: Elizabeth Caroline Crosby was the first woman to be appointed a full professor at the University of Michigan's medical school. Her descriptive studies of reptilian and other vertebrate brains provided insight into their evolutionary history and helped lay the foundation for the science of comparative neuroanatomy. During a career spanning more than six decades, Crosby made important contributions to the male-dominated areas of science and medicine. Between 1920 and 1958 she taught neuroanatomy to an estimated 8,500 students and became known as the "angel of the medical school." Following her official retirement, Crosby continued her energetic pace, applying her comprehensive knowledge of the human brain to help neurosurgeons map brain surgery.

Crosby was born in Petersburg, Michigan, on October 25, 1888, the only child of Lewis Frederick and Frances Kreps Crosby. In the log house on their homestead, Crosby read adult books before she went to school. When she graduated from high school, her father promised her four years of college as a graduation present. Majoring in mathematics at nearby Adrian College, she completed the four-year program in three years, graduating in 1910. With one year left of her father's gift, she applied to C. Judson Herrick's anatomy program at the University of Chicago. At that time her only background for the course was one undergraduate course in zoology. Crosby was a diligent student. She stayed so late in the laboratory studying that, at one point, Herrick took away her key to force her to get some rest. When he saw her making her way home with her heavy reference books, microscope, and box of slides in her arms, however, he returned the key.

She received a master's degree in 1912 and was given a fellowship in the anatomy department. Her Ph.D. degree followed in 1915, and her dissertation, *The Forebrain of Alligator mississippiensis,* became an influential work. Prior to Crosby's study, little was known about reptilian brains. In 1918, Crosby and Herrick published *A Laboratory Outline of Neurology* with detailed instructions for brain dissection. Throughout her career, she received ten honorary doctorates, and her honorary M.D. from the University of Groningen in the Netherlands allowed her to add that designation behind her name.

With her parents' health failing, Crosby returned home to Petersburg, where she taught zoology, mathematics, and Latin in the high school, and coached the local boys' basketball team. She became principal of the school in 1916 and superintendent of schools in 1918. Her mother died that year, and in 1920, Crosby secured a job as junior instructor at the University of Michigan in Ann Arbor, thirty miles from Petersburg. There she taught histology and assisted G. Carl Huber, head of the anatomy department, with the neuroanatomy course. Crosby and Huber developed a close personal and working relationship. They continued her work on the alligator brain, then turned to descriptive studies of the brains of birds. After her father died in 1923, Crosby took several leaves to study at the University of London and the Central Institute for Brain Research in Amsterdam, the Netherlands.

C. U. Ariens Kappers, Crosby's colleague in Amsterdam, had published a comparative neurology textbook in German, and Huber and Crosby agreed to join him in preparing an English translation that incorporated more recent material. But because so much new descriptive information had accumulated, the book was almost a new effort; it ultimately became a ten-year project. Huber died of leukemia in 1934, and Crosby produced the book with little assistance. Although the two volumes of *The Comparative Anatomy of the Nervous System of Vertebrates, Including Man* list Crosby as the third author after Ariens Kappers and

Huber, it is essentially her work. The book was published in 1936, the same year that Crosby achieved the rank of full professor.

Spending the school year of 1939 to 1940 at Marischal College of the University of Aberdeen, Scotland, Crosby helped to organize the school's first course in histology and neuroanatomy. There she met a young girl, Kathleen, whom she later legally adopted.

The graduate research program at Michigan grew rapidly, and Crosby determined to continue the programs that she and Huber had begun. When she retired in 1958, thirty-eight students had received Ph.D. degrees under her direction, and many visiting scientists had come to Ann Arbor to work with her. Crosby often published with students and colleagues, and often deferred first authorship to them even when her contribution was great. Each year, the University of Michigan presents the Elizabeth C. Crosby Award to an outstanding medical student in the basic sciences.

Her work in comparative anatomy was fundamental. Prior to the intense descriptive period in which she worked, scientists had only crude knowledge of the interior of the brain. By the time Crosby had retired, she had gathered, according to *Time* magazine, "the largest collection of sub-mammalian and mammalian brains in the world." In addition to her research she had also taught an estimated 8,500 students; she was well-loved and known as an excellent teacher. In 1957, the Galens Society of the medical school established the Elizabeth C. Crosby Award for outstanding teaching in the basic sciences. According to a University of Michigan press release, Crosby believed that teachers "must do research. Teaching keeps you alert to the unanswered questions and by doing research you get your students interested. I learned a great deal from what my students needed to know."

As practicing physicians and neurologists brought their patients' problems to her, Crosby became more clinically oriented. She conferred on the wards, discussed cases at bedside, and consulted in operating rooms. In 1955 she collaborated with Edgar A. Kahn, Richard C. Schneider, and James A. Taren on *Correlative Neurosurgery.* In 1962, she published *Correlative Anatomy of the Nervous System* with Tryphena Humphrey and Edward Lauer.

In 1963 Humphrey, one of Crosby's first graduate students, took a position in the department of anatomy at the University of Alabama in Birmingham. As they continued their friendship and collaboration, Crosby became a frequent visitor to Alabama, sharing her talents with that school's faculty and students. The relationship was formalized with Crosby's appointment as professor emeritus of anatomy at Alabama's medical school. For eighteen years she commuted between Alabama and her consultantship at the University of Michigan, whose neurosurgery section named its research laboratories after her in 1982, the same year *Comparative Correlative Neuroanatomy of the Vertebrate Telencephalon* was published, co-edited with H. N. Schnitzlein of the University of South Florida. Crosby was inducted into both the Alabama and Michigan Women's Hall of Fame.

Over the years, numerous other honors were bestowed upon Crosby. In 1950, she received the Achievement Award of the American Association of University Women. She was the first non-neurosurgeon to be named an honorary member of the American Association of Neurological Surgeons, and was named the first woman non-clinician to become an honorary member of the Harvey Cushing Society. The University of Michigan honored her in 1946 with its Henry Russel Lectureship, and in 1956 with its Distinguished Faculty Achievement Award; in both cases she was the first woman to receive the award. In 1980, she received from President Jimmy Carter the federal government's highest honor for scientists, the National Medal of Science.

Although Crosby never married, she took pleasure in her adopted daughter's five children, whom she called her "pseudograndchildren," and to whom she was "auntie-grandma." She also considered her students her family, and former students passing through often contacted "Ma Crosby." She died on July 28, 1983, at age ninety-four.

BIOGRAPHICAL/CRITICAL SOURCES:

BOOKS

Rossiter, Margaret W., *Women Scientists in America: Struggles and Strategies to 1940,* Johns Hopkins University Press (Baltimore, MD), 1982, pp. 185, 188-89.

PERIODICALS

Anatomical Record, September, 1984, pp. 175-77.
Ann Arbor News, September 11, 1964.

Michigan Alumnus, May, 1966, pp. 14-15.
Research News, University of Michigan, August/September, 1983, pp. 3- 13, 16-17.
Time, July 21, 1958, p. 64.

OTHER

University of Michigan press release, August 17, 1978.*

*   *   *

CURTIS, Richard 1956-

PERSONAL: Born November 8, 1956, in Wellington, New Zealand; son of Anthony and Glyness Curtis; children: (with Emma Vallency Freud) Scarlett Kate Freud Curtis. *Education:* Attended American schools in Manila and Stockholm; attended Harrow and Oxford universities.

ADDRESSES: Agent—A. D. Peters, Peters, Fraser, and Dunlop, 503 The Chambers, Chelsea Harbor, London SW10 OXF, England.

CAREER: Writer for television and motion pictures. Writer for such television series as *Not the Nine O'Clock News,* BBC, 1981, *Blackadder,* BBC, 1989, and *Mr. Bean,* Tiger Television, 1992. Wrote and appeared in *The Tall Guy,* Virgin Vision, 1989; wrote and acted as coexecutive producer of *Four Weddings and a Funeral,* Gramercy, 1994.

AWARDS, HONORS: Writer's Guild Award, British Academy of Film and Television Arts Award, Academy Award nomination, best original screenplay, 1995, all for *Four Weddings and a Funeral;* several shared Emmy Awards, Cable ACE Awards, and British Academy of Film and Television Arts Awards, for *Blackadder.*

WRITINGS:

(With Simon Bell and Helen Fielding) *Who's Had Who: An Historical Rogister Containing Official Lay Lines of History from the Beginning of Time to the Present Day,* Faber and Faber (London), 1987, Warner Books (New York), 1990.
Four Weddings and a Funeral: Four Appendices and a Screenplay, Corgi (London), 1994; also published as *Four Weddings and a Funeral,* St. Martin's Griffin (New York), 1996.

SCREENPLAYS

The Tall Guy, Virgin Vision, 1989.

Bernard and the Genie, Twentieth Century-Fox Video, 1992.

Four Weddings and a Funeral, Gramercy, 1994.

TELEVISION SCRIPTS

(With others) *Not the Nine O'Clock News,* BBC, 1981.

Blackadder's Christmas Carol (special), BBC/Arts and Entertainment, 1989.

Rowan Atkinson: Not Just Another Pretty Face, Tiger Television/HBO Productions, 1992.

Mr. Bean, Tiger Television, 1992.

Also author of episodes (with Ben Elton) for the British television series *Blackadder.*

SIDELIGHTS: Since the early 1980s, Richard Curtis has made a career of writing humorous screenplays for motion pictures and television, including the motion picture *Four Weddings and a Funeral* and the satiric British television series *Blackadder.* Early in his career Curtis met comedian Rowan Atkinson at Oxford University, and he has continued to work with Atkinson on such projects as *Blackadder* and *Mr. Bean.* Curtis's first motion picture screenplay, *The Tall Guy,* demonstrated his "inventive dottiness," to use the words of Pauline Kael of the *New Yorker,* who described *The Tall Guy* as made up of a series of "leapfrogging" improvisations and one-liners that "spin about." According to Kael, *The Tall Guy* reveals Curtis as a "wizard at writing revue material that all fits together."

The romantic comedy *Four Weddings and a Funeral,* directed by Mike Newell and starring Hugh Grant, was filmed in London and became a major success with American moviegoers when it appeared in theaters in 1994. The plot of the movie revolves around a group of friends who attend the four weddings and funeral of the title. With the exception of a gay couple, each of the friends hopes to meet a future partner among the guests. By the movie's end, they have all found the love of their dreams.

While the film was a box office success, critics were not uniform in their assessment of the work. Several commentators remarked that the plot was too contrived, the writer too much visible through the dialogue, and the casting poorly done. Yet critics also found much to applaud. Describing the plot of *Four Weddings and a Funeral* as a "marvelous crossword puzzle," Richard Alleva, writing in *Commonweal,* gave the film qualified praise. "The great strength of Richard Curtis's script . . . isn't its dialogue (though there are many funny lines), nor its characterizations (which keep the plot humming but are rarely interesting in themselves), nor the passages of physical humor (only a cut above the better TV sitcoms). Curtis's special triumph here is in the sheer *arrangement* of the action, the crafting of a plot in which events and character quirks rhyme, contrast with, reverse, and echo one another." "At first it seems that Newell and Curtis have . . . engaged in Hollywood-style calculation, putting something in for everyone," commented David Denby in *Newsweek.* "But here's the surprise: The movie has a genuine good spirit, a democratic appreciation of erotic possibilities in unlikely situations. And Newell and Curtis convince us that the people in this odd group actually do like one another—certainly an immense change from the sour, chilblained nastiness that English movies have featured for years."

"Curtis provides a steadily ripening banter, and the actors take mighty bites," Denby remarked. Calling *Four Weddings and a Funeral,* "an immensely companionable movie," he added, "There is time for jokes, for nonsense, for old memories and a fine funeral speech. . . . Some of the sex play is crude, but none of it is mean-spirited." He concluded, "The movie doesn't always make sense, but it's still awfully pleasant."

BIOGRAPHICAL/CRITICAL SOURCES:

BOOKS

Contemporary Television, Film, and Theater, Volume 15, Gale (Detroit, MI), 1996.

PERIODICALS

Commonweal, May 6, 1994, pp. 17-18.
National Review, May 2, 1994, pp. 58-60.
New York, May 2, 1994, pp. 81-82.
New Yorker, September 24, 1990, pp. 101-02.*

D

DALE, Henry Hallett 1875-1968

PERSONAL: Born June 9, 1875, in London, England; died July 23, 1968; son of Charles (in business) and Frances (Hallet) Dale; married Ellen Harriett Hallett (a first cousin), 1904; children: one son, two daughters. *Education:* Attended Tollington Park College, London and Leys School, Cambridge University; Trinity College, Cambridge University, B.A., 1903, Ph.D., 1909; studied at St. Bartholomew's Hospital in London.

CAREER: Physiologist. University College, London, England, research under Ernest Henry Starling and William Maddock Bayliss, 1902-04; in Germany, research under Paul Ehrlich, 1904; Wellcome Physiological Research Laboratories, London, England, researcher, 1904-06, director, 1906-14; Medical Research Committee (later called Medical Research Council), National Institute for Medical Research, head of Department of Biochemistry and Pharmacology, 1914-42, director, 1928-42. Scientific Advisory Committee to the War Cabinet, chair, during World War II; Royal Society, elected fellow, 1914, secretary, 1925-35, president, 1940-45; Wellcome Trust, chair, 1938-60; Royal Institution of Great Britain, president, during the mid-1940s; British Association for the Advancement of Science, President, 1947; Royal Society of Medicine, president, 1948-50; British Council, president, during the 1950s.

AWARDS, HONORS: Knighted, 1932; Nobel Prize for Physiology or Medicine, 1936; Copely Medal, Royal Society, 1937; Knighted with Grand Cross Order of the British Empire, 1943; Order of Merit, 1944; Dale Medal created in his name to award excellence in research, Society for Endocrinology, 1959; Henry Dale professorship created, Wellcome Trust and Royal Society, since 1961.

WRITINGS:

Viruses and Heterogenesis, An Old Problem in a New Form, Macmillan and Co. (London), 1935.
An Autumn Gleaning: Occasional Lectures and Addresses, Pergamon, 1954.
Adventures in Physiology, with Excursions into Autopharmacology, Wellcome Trust, 1965.

Contributor to journals and periodicals, including *Proceedings of the Royal Society of Medicine, Journal of the Mount Sinai Hospital,* and *Perspectives in Biology and Medicine.*

SIDELIGHTS: Henry Hallett Dale was a British physiologist who devoted his scientific career to the study of how chemicals in the body regulate physiological functions. Although his work had many facets, the most significant was his collaborative effort with German pharmacologist Otto Loewi. In 1936 Dale and Loewi were jointly awarded the Nobel Prize in physiology or medicine for research demonstrating that nerve cells communicate with one another primarily by the exchange of chemical transmitters. In addition to his scientific work, Dale was a prominent figure in science and medicine in England at critical junctures in that nation's history. He was knighted in 1932.

Born June 9, 1875, in London, Dale was the second son of seven children born to Charles Dale, a London businessman, and his wife, Frances Hallett Dale. After graduating from Tollington Park College, London, and the Leys School, Cambridge, Dale entered

Trinity College at Cambridge University in 1894. His academic skills gained him first honors in the natural sciences and the Coutts-Trotter studentship at Trinity College. Dale's predecessor in the studentship was Ernest Rutherford, the physicist and chemist who would go on to win the Nobel Prize in chemistry in 1908.

Dale left Cambridge in 1900 to finish his clinical work in medicine at St. Bartholomew's Hospital in London. He received his bachelor's degree in 1903, and his medical doctorate in 1909. During this time, he also was awarded the George Henry Lewes studentship, which allowed him to pursue further physiological research. Later, Dale also received the Sharpey studentship in physiology at University College, London. Dale used these opportunities for research from 1902 to 1904, studying with Ernest Henry Starling and William Maddock Bayliss at University College. Starling and Bayliss identified secretin, a substance secreted by the small intestine, as the first hormone, and Dale collaborated with the pair in further studies on the impact of secretin on cells in the pancreas. Dale's work with Starling and Bayliss instilled in him the idea that physiological functions could be affected by such chemicals as hormones. It was also in this laboratory that Dale first met Otto Loewi, who at the time was visiting University College from Germany. Dale and Loewi would go on to become lifelong friends, collaborators, and co-recipients of the 1936 Nobel Prize.

In 1904 Dale spent three months working in the laboratory of the chemist Paul Ehrlich in Germany. Members of Ehrlich's laboratory were studying the relationship between the chemical structure of biological molecules and their effect on immunological responses, research that would garner for Ehrlich the 1908 Nobel Prize in physiology or medicine. As did the experience at Starling's laboratory in London, Ehrlich's research introduced Dale to the potential impact that chemicals can have on mediating biological and physiological processes.

After Dale returned to Starling's London laboratory, he was recommended to chemical manufacturer Henry Wellcome for a position with London's Wellcome Physiological Research Laboratories, a commercial laboratory. Established in the 1890s to produce an antitoxin for diphtheria, the laboratories, by the first decade of the 1900s, had begun to promote and pursue basic scientific research. Against the advice of colleagues who distrusted the commercial nature of the laboratory, Dale accepted the post. He reasoned that it would provide him the stability that would allow him to marry Ellen Harriett Hallett, his first cousin. (This marriage in 1904 would produce a son and two daughters; the older daughter, Alison, would go on to marry Alexander Todd, who would win the 1957 Nobel Prize in chemistry.) The post also provided a well-equipped laboratory, freedom from teaching and administrative duties, and the intellectual freedom to pursue his own course of research.

Once Dale had settled at Wellcome, the company suggested that he consider examining the therapeutic properties of ergot, a fungus being used by obstetricians to induce and promote labor. For the next decade, Dale devoted his research efforts to studying the properties of the drug. Although he failed at the stated purpose of his research—articulating the properties of ergot—accidental findings turned out to be of great significance, leading, for instance, to his discovery of the phenomenon of adrenaline (or epinephrine) reversal, in which the normally excitatory effects of these drugs are neutralized.

Dale's research on the effects of ergot also introduced him to ongoing efforts to study the central nervous system. T. R. Elliott, Dale's friend and colleague at Cambridge, postulated that epinephrine (a neurotransmitter or substance that transmits nerve impulses) when applied by itself could produce an effect similar to stimulating the sympathetic branch of the autonomic nervous system. The autonomic nervous system is responsible for involuntary physiological functions, such as breathing and digestion. This system's sympathetic branch affects such functions as increasing heart rate in response to fear and opening arteries to increased blood flow during exercise. Dale built on Elliott's research and showed, with the chemist George Barger, that epinephrine is one chemical in a class of such chemicals that has "sympathomimetic" properties.

Dale's serendipitous accomplishments drew the attention of Henry Wellcome, and Dale was promoted in 1906 to the directorship of the Wellcome Laboratories. After this promotion, Dale began to apply what he had learned while a student in the laboratories of Starling and Ehrlich. Dale understood that there are a number of active components in ergot. Wanting to understand the chemical mechanisms that underlie physiological functions, Dale began studies of the chemicals that operate in the posterior pituitary lobe of the brain. It is this area of the brain where ergot has its effects, since this area is responsible for inducing contractions of the uterine muscles.

Dale resigned from the Wellcome Laboratories in 1914, and joined the scientific staff of the Medical Research Committee; after 1920 this group came to be known as the Medical Research Council. The onset of World War I placed new demands on Dale's administrative and scientific skills. He joined the war effort by engaging in physiological studies of shock, dysentery, gangrene, and the effects of inadequate diet.

After the war, the Medical Research Council evolved to become the National Institute for Medical Research, and Dale served as the organization's first director from 1928 until 1942. Although he continued to perform physiological research, administrative and public duties for the Medical Research Council and the National Institute for Medical Research limited the time and energy that he could devote to the laboratory. His research efforts during the 1920s continued the work he began during the war—studying how histamine contributes to the swelling of tissue after traumatic shock. Dale demonstrated that histamine leads to the loss of plasma fluid into the tissues and produces swelling. This could lead to more serious problems, including decreased blood circulation, shock, and ultimately death.

Dale's study of histamine also contributed to his subsequent work on the nervous system. Histamine, like the neurotransmitter acetylcholine, dilates vascular tissue in the human body. Dale had long known from his work in Starling's laboratory that acetylcholine increases the diameter of vascular tissue. The question remaining for Dale was how this chemical produces the physiological effect.

In 1927 Dale collaborated with H. W. Dudley to isolate acetylcholine from the spleen of an ox and a horse. Having isolated the crucial compound, Dale sought to understand how and where acetylcholine plays its role in vasodilatation, or the widening of the cavities of blood vessels. Over the next decade, Dale worked with colleagues at the National Institute for Medical Research and concluded that acetylcholine serves as a neurotransmitter and that this is the chemical mediator involved in the transmission of nerve impulses. Dale's findings disproved the proposition of John Carew Eccles and other neurophysiologists who maintained that nerve cells communicate with one another via an electrical mechanism. Dale demonstrated that a chemical process and not an electrical one was the underlying mechanism for nerve transmission. A similar conclusion had been reached by Otto Loewi; as early as 1921 Loewi suggested that a chemical mediator was responsible for the conduction of nerve impulses; it would be Dale who would identify the mediator.

For their work, Dale and Loewi were jointly awarded the 1936 Nobel Prize in physiology or medicine. During the 1930s, Dale continued collaborative research with G. L. Brown, W. Feldberg, J. H. Gaddum, and M. Vogt at the National Institute for Medical Research. Their efforts produced more evidence that acetylcholine is a neurotransmitter involved in nerve impulses.

By the 1940s Dale was devoting much of his time to administrative duties in various organizations. During World War II, he served as chair of the Scientific Advisory Committee to the War Cabinet. Having been elected a fellow of the Royal Society in 1914, he served as secretary from 1925 to 1935, and as president from 1940 to 1945. His many other public affiliations included serving as president of various organizations, such as the Royal Institution of Great Britain during the mid-1940s, the British Association for the Advancement of Science in 1947, the Royal Society of Medicine from 1948 to 1950, and the British Council during the 1950s.

Other distinctions bestowed upon Dale include the Copley Medal from the Royal Society in 1937 and a knighthood with the Grand Cross Order of the British Empire in 1943. He also garnered the Order of Merit in 1944. Since 1959 the Society for Endocrinology has awarded the Dale Medal for the kind of excellence in research exemplified by Dale; and since 1961 the Wellcome Trust he chaired from 1938 until 1960 has endowed the Henry Dale Professorship with the Royal Society.

In later years Dale worked with Thorvald Madsen of Copenhagen directing an international campaign to standardize drugs and vaccines. The 1925 conference of the Health Organization of the League of Nations adopted such standards for insulin and pituitary products largely because of Dale's efforts. He repeated these efforts to see into law the Therapeutic Substances Act in England. His other political activities included promoting both the peaceful use of nuclear energy and the value of scientific research. Dale died on July 23, 1968, after a brief illness.

BIOGRAPHICAL/CRITICAL SOURCES:

BOOKS

Biographical Memoirs of Fellows of the Royal Society, Volume 16, Royal Society (London), 1970, pp. 77-174.

Dictionary of Scientific Biography, edited by Charles
    C. Gillispie, Scribner, 1978, pp. 104-107.
Pursuit of Nature, edited by A. L. Hodgkin and others,
    Cambridge University Press, 1977, pp. 65-83.

PERIODICALS

British Medical Journal, June 4, 1955, pp. 1359-1361.*

*   *   *

DALRYMPLE, G. Brent 1937-

PERSONAL: Born May 9, 1937, in Alhambra, CA;
son of Donald Inlow and Wynona Edith (Pierce)
Dalrymple; married Sharon Ann Tramel, June 28,
1959; children: Stacie Ann, Robynne Ann Sisco, and
Melinda Ann Dalrymple McGurer. *Education:* Occidental College, Los Angeles, A.B., 1959; University
of California, Berkeley, Ph.D., 1963. *Avocational
interests:* Downhill skiing, sailing.

ADDRESSES: Office—Oregon State University College of Oceanic and Atmospheric Science, Corvallis,
OR 97331-5503.

CAREER: Geologist. U.S. Geological Survey, Menlo
Park, CA, Branch of Theoretical Geophysics, research geologist, 1963-70, Branch of Isotope Geology,
1970-81, 1984-94, research geologist, assistant chief
geologist, western region, 1981-84; College of Oceanic
and Atmospheric Science, Oregon State University,
Corvallis, professor and dean, 1994—. Stanford University, visiting professor, lecturer, research associate, and
consulting professor since the 1970s; principle investigator for moon rocks collected by Apollo missions.

MEMBER: National Academy of Science, American
Institute of Physics (board of governors, 1991—),
AAAS, American Geophysics Union (president, 1990-
92), Geological Society of America, American Academy of Arts and Sciences.

AWARDS, HONORS: Fellow, National Science Foundation, 1961-63; Meritorious Service Award, U.S.
Department of the Interior, 1984; D.Sc. (honorary
degree), Occidental College, 1993.

WRITINGS:

(With Marvin A. Lanphere) *Potassium-Argon Dating:
    Principles, Techniques, and Applications to Geo-*

chronology, W. H. Freeman and Co. (San Fran-
    cisco), 1969.
*Irradiation Samples for 40Ar/39Ar Dating Using the
    Geological Survey TRIGA Reactor,* U.S. Govern-
    ment Printing Office (Washington, DC), 1981.
The Age of the Earth, Stanford University Press
    (Stanford, CA), 1991.
*49Ar/39Ar Age Spectra and Total-Fusion Ages of Tek-
    tites from Cretaceous-Tertiary Boundary Sedimen-
    tary Rocks in the Beloc Formation, Haiti,* U.S.
    Government Printing Office, 1993.
(With Lanphere and B. D. Turrin) *Abstracts of the
    Eighth International Conference on Geochronol-
    ogy, Cosmochronology, and Isotope Geology,*
    U.S. Geological Survey, Map Distribution
    (Washington, DC), 1994.
(With John W. M'Gonigle) *40Ar/39Ar Ages of Some
    Challis Volcanic Group Rocks and the Initiation
    of Tertiary Sedimentary Basins in Southwestern
    Montana,* U.S. Geological Survey, 1995.

Contributor to journals and periodicals, including
*Proceedings of the 63rd Annual Meeting, American
Association for the Advancement of Science, Pacific
Division,* and *Journal of Geophysical Research—Planets.*

SIDELIGHTS: G. Brent Dalrymple, a research geologist, holds the distinction of being a principal investigator for the moon rocks collected during the Apollo
11 and Apollo 12 lunar voyages, and later, the Apollo
15 and 17 lunar voyages. His research, clocking geologic time through isotopic dating methods and then
applying these findings to a range of geophysical
problems, has led to his reputation as one of the leading experts on the age of our planet. Dalrymple described the history of magnetic field reversals, which
led directly to the theory of Plate Tectonics, and he
demonstrated the hot spot origin of the Hawaiian-
Emperor volcanic chain. He is currently researching
lunar basin history.

Gary Brent Dalrymple, the son of Donald Inlow and
Wynona Edith Pierce Dalrymple, was born in Al-
hambra, California, on May 9, 1937. He married
Sharon Tramel in 1959, and the couple have three
daughters—Stacie, Robynne, and Melinda. Dalrymple
attended Occidental College, in his home state of
California, where he earned a B.A. in geology in
1959. He then moved to the University of California,
Berkeley, to do his graduate work. He earned his
Ph.D. in geology in 1963.

After graduation, Dalrymple began his career as a
research geologist with the U.S. Geological Survey

(USGS) in Menlo Park, California, in the Branch of Theoretical Geophysics. He remained there until the early 1970s, when he moved to the Branch of Isotope Geology. Between 1981 and 1984, he was assistant chief geologist for the Western Region of the USGS, during which time he was the principal contact within the USGS for the state geologists of the western states. Since 1984 he has served as a research geologist for the USGS.

One of Dalrymple's most significant investigations centers on his work in the 1960s, which proved that the earth's magnetic field reverses polarity. He and his colleagues Allan Cox and Richard Doell ascertained the time scale of these reversals over the past 3.5 million years. This work resulted in the theory of Plate Tectonics. Science historian William Glen writes of this work and its importance in his book *The Road to Jaramillo*. Another of Dalrymple's investigations confirmed the hypothesis that the volcanoes in the Hawaiian-Emperor volcanic chain, which extends from Hawaii to the Aleutian Trench near Siberia, were formed by the Pacific Plate's motion over a fixed source of lava in the earth's mantle.

Throughout his career Dalrymple has been involved in developing new methodology and instrumentation for determining the ages of rocks and minerals. His contributions include the development and refinement of potassium-argon dating methods and instruments. His interest in radiometric dating led to the publication of *Potassium-Argon Dating,* a guide to understanding the principles and techniques involved, which he co-authored with Marvin A. Lanphere in 1969. The book began as an abbreviated pamphlet, but was later expanded into a book by popular request. As the authors note in their preface, the book is not meant to be "a scholarly or comprehensive review" of the topic, but is instead intended to answer "practical questions of what the method can and cannot do." The authors begin with the basics, explaining about atoms, elements, and isotopes, before defining radioactivity. Then they explain how one form of potassium (K) decays, transforming into a form of argon (Ar), and how time measurements can be made by quantifying such changes. Although the book was published over twenty years ago, the potassium-argon method continues to be the primary means of radiometric dating, and the book remains the definitive work on this method of dating.

Another book, *The Age of the Earth,* published in 1991, resulted from Dalrymple's involvement in science education. Dalrymple's reputation as a leading authority on the age of the earth and radiometric dating has led to his involvement as an expert witness in court cases. He has served in cases involving creation "science" at both the state and federal levels. Dalrymple has also lectured and written several papers on the inappropriateness of including creation science in the science curriculum of public schools.

Dalrymple has been involved in two phases of research with moon rocks. "In our early investigations with the Apollo lunar rocks, we tried to understand how the stored energy from the trapped electrons in the rock, which can be released by heating to give off light, might be used to determine the rates and frequency of lunar surface processes," Dalrymple told contributor Patricia M. McAdams in an interview. "We eventually gave up because the results seemed to be reflecting small-scale impact phenomena that could not be correlated with the broader aspect of lunar history."

"We started working on moon rocks again a few years ago," Dalrymple explained. "Now we're using [Argon] methods to see if we can determine the history of lunar basin formation." Lunar basins, he notes, are the very big craters that form the face of the "man in the moon." Dalrymple and his colleagues have developed new methods of precisely measuring the age of tiny (sub-milligram) fragments of melt rocks that are created by basin-forming impacts of asteroid-sized objects into the lunar surface. "We are testing the hypothesis that the lunar basins were formed during a brief interval between 3.8 and 3.9 billion years ago, instead of over a prolonged interval between 4.5 and 3.8 billion years ago, as is the conventional wisdom," he said. "So far we have found no evidence for older basin-forming impacts in the rocks from the Apollo 15 or Apollo 17 missions."

In addition to his primary research at the U.S. Geological Survey, Dalrymple has served in various roles at Stanford University, including visiting professor, lecturer, research associate, and consulting professor in the school of earth sciences. His affiliation with Stanford was intermittent during the 1970s and 1980s, but has been continuous since 1990. He has also authored more than 150 journal articles, and dozens of other publications. In 1993 he was elected to the National Academy of Sciences, and received an honorary Doctor of Science degree from his undergraduate alma mater, Occidental College. He was elected to the American Academy of Arts and Sciences in 1992, and was the Distinguished Alumni Centennial Speaker at Occidental College in the 1980s. Other awards include the Meritorious Service Award of the Department of the Interior in 1984. In addition to his role as the president of the American Geophysical Union—a society thirty thousand strong—Dalrymple serves on the board of governors of the American Institute of Physics, and was elected to the executive committee of that institute in 1993. He served on the Council of Scientific Society Presidents between 1990 and 1992.

Dalrymple left the U.S. Geological Survey in 1994 and is now a dean and professor at Oregon State University. When he is not working, Dalrymple relaxes by downhill skiing or sailing with his family. He is also an instructor in celestial navigation.

BIOGRAPHICAL/CRITICAL SOURCES:

BOOKS

Glen, William, *The Road to Jaramillo,* Stanford University Press, 1982.

OTHER

Interview with Patricia M. McAdams, conducted September 24, 1993.*

*   *   *

DASGUPTA, Surendranath 1887-1952

PERSONAL: Born in Calcutta, India, October, 1887; died December 18, 1952; married Surama (an author and editor) Dasgupta. *Education:* Attended Calcutta University; Cambridge University (England), Ph.D.

CAREER: Philosopher and historian. Chittagong College, Senior Professor of Sanskrit, 1911-20; Cambridge University, Cambridge, England, lecturer, 1920-22; Indian Education Service Presidency College, Calcutta, professor of European philosophy, 1924-31; Sanskrit College, Calcutta, India, principal, 1933-42; Calcutta University, King George V Professor of Philosophy, 1942-45; Benares Hindu University, Life Professor of Philosophy, 1945-52. Harris Foundation Lecturer, University of Chicago, 1926; Stephanos Nirmalendu Ghosh Lecturer, Calcutta University, 1941.

MEMBER: Bengal Sanskrit Association (secretary, 1931-42).

AWARDS, HONORS: Griffith Memorial Prize, 1915, for *A Study of Patanjali;* Commander, Order of the British Empire, 1941; honorary doctorates from Calcutta University, Cambridge University, and University of Rome.

WRITINGS:

A Study of Pantanjali, University of Calcutta (Calcutta), 1920.
A Glimpse into the System of Education in Ancient India through an Old Sanskrit Institution of Modern Bengal, De (Chittagong), 1920.
A History of Indian Philosophy, Cambridge University Press, Volumes 1-4, 1922-49, Volume 5: *Southern Schools of Saivism,* completed and edited by wife, Surama Dasgupta, 1955, second edition, 1963, abridged by R. R. Agarwal and S. K. Jain, Kitab Mahal (Allahabad), 1969.
Yoga as Philosophy and Religion, Dutton (New York City), 1924.
Hindu Mysticism (lectures), Open Court (Chicago), 1927.
Yoga Philosophy in Relation to Other Systems of Indian Thought, University of Calcutta, 1930, Cambridge University Press, 1933.
Indian Idealism, Cambridge University Press, 1933.
Philosophical Essays, University of Calcutta, 1941.
Rabindranath, the Poet and Philosopher, Mitra & Ghosh (Calcutta), 1947.
(Editor with S. K. De.) *A History of Sanskrit Literature, Classical Period,* University of Calcutta, 1947, second edition, 1962.
Fundamentals of Indian Art, Bharatiya Vidya Bhavan (Bombay), 1952, second edition, 1960.
Religion and the Rational Outlook, Law Journal Press (Allahabad), 1954.
The Vanishing Lines (poems), Thacker Spink (Calcutta), 1956.
Natural Science of the Ancient Hindus, edited by Debiprasad Chattopadhyaya, Indian Council of Philosophical Research (New Delhi), 1987.
(Annotator) *The Mahabhasya of Patanjali: With Annotations: Ahrikas I-IV,* edited by Sibajiban Bhattacharyya, Indian Council of Philosophical Research (Calcutta), 1991.

Author of a comparative study of Italian philosopher Benedetto Croce, studies on Indian aesthetics, and books in Bengali on literary criticism and aesthetics.

Contributor of articles to anthologies, including *The Indian Mind, Comparative Studies in Philosophy,* and *Contemporary Indian Philosophy.*

SIDELIGHTS: Surendranath Dasgupta was a prominent Sanskrit scholar who, prior to his death in 1952, made major contributions to the study of Indian philosophy and aesthetics, and to the popularization of Yogic philosophy in the Western world. He possessed, according to Bimal Krishna Matilal in *Thinkers of the Twentieth Century,* a "rare combination of Sanskritic learning and philosophical acumen." Dasgupta's lifelong aesthetic bent is demonstrated, as well, by his posthumously published volume of poems, *The Vanishing Lines,* and his numerous works on aesthetics and literature in Bengali, his first language.

Dasgupta's career of scholarly publications began with his 1920 doctoral dissertation, *A Study of Patanjali,* which discussed that thinker's system of Yogic thought. His major work, however, was the massive, five-volume *A History of Indian Philosophy,* which emerged gradually over a period of more than thirty years and which Matilal hails as "a pioneering work" and "unique of its kind."

Dasgupta, unlike other historians of Indian philosophy before him, relied extensively on original Sanskrit sources and even unpublished Sanskrit manuscripts. Matilal calls him "a very painstaking scholar" with a "deep knowledge of the Sanskritic tradition." Assessing Dasgupta's own philosophical leanings through the multi-volume prism of the *History,* Matilal finds him "inclined toward a synthetic approach to Patanjala Yoga and Sankara's Advanta Vedanta"; he also, Matilal says, saw Buddhism through the lens of Vedanta, thus contributing to a trend among modern Indian scholars who have done likewise. Dasgupta was less interested, Matilal claims in "pramana epistemology and methodology of Nyaya, Mimamsa, Buddhism and Jainism."

On the initial publication of Volume One of Dasgupta's *History of Indian Philosophy,* Western reviewers were highly respectful. F. W. Thomas of the India Office, writing in the *Hibbert Journal,* applauded the comprehensiveness of Dasgupta's scope, singling out for special praise the section on Vedanta, the "good outline" of Jainism, and what he termed a "really admirable" introduction. "He is thoroughly at home in all the important and difficult texts," maintained Thomas. "His intelligence is alert and candid, and he has the historical sense. We can sincerely commend both his method . . . and his style, which is untrammeled, full, direct, and flowing."

Reviewer J. S. Mackenzie, in *Mind,* also commended upon Dasgupta's expertise, although he suggested that a fuller explanation of Sanskrit terms would be very useful for the Western reader. *Journal of Philosophy* reviewer Louis H. Gray also had some suggestions on format, namely, a formal bibliography and an index of technical terms. However, Gray also noted that Dasgupta's *History* would, "by its minute and exhaustive discussion of its theme, remain for some considerable time the standard study in this field." Edward J. Thomas, a reviewer for the *International Journal of Ethics,* noted admiringly of the first volume of Dasgupta's opus that "[w]e do not expect the philosopher to read works on medicine or grammatical commentaries. But this is what Dr. Dasgupta has done."

Like several other reviewers who found much to praise in the first volume of *The History of Indian Philosophy,* Thomas eagerly awaited the second volume, which due to its author's painstaking methods would not be published until 1932. The ten year gap in time, which was also partly the result of Dasgupta's health problems, did not diminish the stature of the work. Volume Two discussed, among other topics, the *Bhagavad Gita* and the philosophy of ancient Hindu medicine. In the *Journal of Philosophy,* George W. Briggs drew attention to Dasgupta's section on "Ethics of the Gita and Buddhist Ethics." Of the first two volumes in general, Briggs said the work "stands practically alone" in its field. He commended the work's "solidity and scope" and cited it as "thoroughgoing, clearly set forth, revealing the erudite and mature scholar." In the *International Journal of Ethics,* G. S. Brett called the first two volumes "masterly and very readable," but seemed to be overwhelmed by the weight of unfamiliar learning: "It is impossible to attempt any detailed account of its contents or to venture beyond the statement that it gives every student of ethics or any other branch of philosophy an encyclopedic statement of Indian thought which must sooner or later be considered as indispensable."

The third volume of Dasgupta's opus dealt with dualistic and pluralistic philosophies; the fourth and fifth, with Vallabha, Madhva and his followers, other schools of thought such as the Puranas and Tantras, legal and moral philosophy, and the religious philosophies of India's vernacular languages. Assessing Volume Four, which was published in 1949, *Eastern World* critic S. Bhattacharya found the author "at his best in the treatment of Madhva dialectics," and also commended Dasgupta's treatment of Vallabha. Bhattacharya complained, however, of oversimplification of some technical terms and of the references. The critic expressed the hope that Volume Five would be published in Dasgupta's lifetime, but that was not to be; it came out in 1955, edited by his wife. The shortest of the five volumes, it dealt with the Southern schools of Saivism, which may or may not have been influenced by the early Christianity of the Malabar Coast. Reviewer A. C. Bouquet, in *Philosophical Quarterly,* paid tribute both to the author—a "great scholar"—and his wife, a "constant and loving companion and disciple . . . who has regarded it as a great task and a sacred obligation to bring his labours to their due termination."

The five-volume history of Indian thought would have been a life's work for many, but Dasgupta published much besides. His six lectures on *Hindu Mysticism* were collected in a volume under that title in 1924. The lectures deal with six different types of Indian mysticism: Vedic sacrifice, Upanishad Mysticism, Yoga, Buddhism, classical forms of mysticism, and popular mysticism such as that of Bakhti. Edward J. Thomas, reviewing the work for *Mind,* applauded "the moderation and dignity and sense of spiritual values with which he has treated the subject. . . . His words ring absolutely true." Dasgupta, Thomas wrote, had "an unrivalled knowledge of all stages of the literature and the living religions."

An interesting and prescient review was written in 1927 by the great U.S. critic H. L. Mencken for his *American Mercury.* In the acid, satirical style that evoked the adjective "Menckenesque," the caustic iconoclast used the opportunity to throw darts at American believers in Eastern thought. "Here is a little book," he wrote, "which offers salubrious reading to those persons who still labor under the delusion that the Hindus are privy to a store of wisdom hidden from Western eyes, and that their religion is, in some vague way, more refined and civilized than Christianity." Mencken went on to hurl witticisms at the Vedas and, especially, at Yoga, whose American practitioners, he observed, were "chiefly concentrated in Los Angeles the damned" but were spreading to such places as Kansas City and Dallas. The author's presentation, Mencken maintained of *Hindu Mysticism,* was so lucid as to reveal the lack of lucidity in the beliefs it discussed: "Unfortunately, Dr. Dasgupta's book is too intelligent."

A particularly influential book of Dasgupta's has been his 1924 *Yoga as Philosophy and Religion,* which has been reissued several times on both sides of the Atlantic. *International Journal of Ethics* reviewer Edward J. Thomas called yoga "the one Indian system that has real parallels with modern scientific thought," and called Dasgupta's guidebook "an authoritative

exposition . . . by one who is a complete master of all the original authorities." A more scholarly volume, issued in 1930, was *Yoga Philosophy in Relation to Other Systems of Indian Thought.* Dasgupta's specialized thesis here was that yoga is a genuine philosophy rather than a practical mystical system tacked on to a pre-existing Sankhya philosophy. For the general philosophy reader, as James Bissett Pratt put it in his review of the work for the *Journal of Philosophy,* the book was valuable for its "sound scholarship . . . clear exposition and . . . real philosophical insight." Reviewers for *Monist* and for the *International Journal of Ethics* expressed—along with admiration for the author's work—the wish that the *Yoga Philosophy* had been accompanied by full explanations of technical terms. But Alban G. Widgery wrote in his review for *Philosophical Review* that *Yoga Philosophy* was a book "[n]o one seriously interested in Indian thought can afford to neglect."

Another valuable book of Gasgupta's was 1933's *Indian Idealism,* in which he attempted, within the space of little more than two hundred pages, to summarize aspects of Vedic, Upanishadic, Vedantic, and Buddhist thought. The book was a slight revision of the Readership Lectures that Dasgupta had given at Patna University. F. Otto Schrader, writing for *Philosophy,* noted some sketchiness of treatment, and took up the gauntlet of regretting the presence of unexplained Sanskrit terms; overall, however, he said that "[e]very reader . . . will draw profit from this highly interesting work, the use of which is facilitated by an excellent summary covering seventeen pages." This last fact indicates that Dasgupta was thinking of his audience. It was a wider audience than he perhaps anticipated, and his intellectual influence was wider as well: the 1960s counterculture philosopher Mircea Eliade was a student of Dasgupta's in Calcutta in the 1930s. Thus, Dasgupta helped till the soil that would become so fruitful for Eastern religions as their influence spread to the United States a generation after him.

BIOGRAPHICAL/CRITICAL SOURCES:

BOOKS

Turner, Roland, editor, *Thinkers Of The Twentieth Century,* second edition, St. James Press (Chicago), 1987, pp. 169-70.

PERIODICALS

American Mercury, October 1927, p. 253.
Eastern World, September 1949, pp. 25-26.

Hibbert Journal, March 1922, pp. 796-799.
International Journal of Ethics, July 1924, pp. 403-405; April 1925, p. 324; April 1931, pp. 402-404; October 1934, pp. 102-107.
Journal of Philosophy, January 31, 1924, pp. 77-80; October 13, 1932, pp. 575-81; February 12, 1931, pp. 106-107; February 1, 1934, p. 79.
Mind, January 1923, pp. 93-100; October 1927, p. 520.
Monist, January 1928, p. 160; April 1931, p. 315.
Philosophical Quarterly, January 1958, pp. 79-80.
Philosophical Review, May 1932, p. 325.
Philosophy, October 1934, pp. 493-494.*

*   *   *

DAVID, Joseph Ben
    See BEN-DAVID, Joseph

*   *   *

DE DUVE, Christian (Rene) 1917-

PERSONAL: Born October 2, 1917, in Thames-Ditton, England, to Belgian parents; moved to Belgium with parents, 1920; became Belgian citizen; son of Alphonse and Madeleine (Pungs) de Duve; married Janine Herman, September 30, 1943; children: Thierry, Anne, Francoise, Alain. *Education:* Catholic University of Louvain, M.D., 1941, Ph.D., 1945, M.Sc., 1946; additional study at the Medical Nobel Institute, Stock-holm, Sweden and Washington University School of Medicine, St. Louis, MO.

CAREER: Biochemist and cell biologist. Catholic University of Louvain, instructor in physiological chemistry at the medical school, 1947, promoted to full professor of biochemistry, 1951. Joined Rockefeller Institute (now Rockefeller University), 1962, while still teaching at Louvain; worked with numerous research groups at both institutions. Formed the International Institute of Cellular and Molecular Pathology, 1971.

MEMBER: American Society for Cell Biology (founding member), United States National Academy of Sciences (elected foreign associate, 1975).

AWARDS, HONORS: 1974 Nobel Prize in physiology or medicine (shared with Albert Claude and George

Palade); various awards from Belgian, French, and British biochemical societies.

WRITINGS:

Glucose, Insuline, et Diabete, [Paris], 1945.
A Guided Tour of the Living Cell, W. H. Freeman, 1985.
Blueprint for a Cell: The Nature and Origin of Life, Carolina Biological Supply Co., 1991.
Vital Dust: Life as a Cosmic Imperative, Basic Books, 1995.

Contributor to journals and periodicals, including *International Review of Cytology, Proceedings of the Royal Society: Biological Sciences B, Journal of Cell Biology,* and *Scientific American.*

SIDELIGHTS: Christian de Duve's ground-breaking studies of cellular structure and function earned him the 1974 Nobel Prize in physiology or medicine (shared with Albert Claude and George Palade). However, he did much more than discover the two key cellular organelles—lysosomes and peroxisomes—for which the Swedish Academy honored him. His work, along with that of his fellow recipients, established an entirely new field, cell biology. De Duve introduced techniques that have enabled other scientists to better study cellular anatomy and physiology. De Duve's research has also been of great value in helping clarify the causes of and treatments for a number of diseases.

De Duve's parents, Alphonse and Madeleine (Pungs) de Duve, had fled Belgium after its invasion by the German army in World War I, escaping to safety in England. There, in Thames-Ditton, Christian Rene de Duve was born on October 2, 1917. De Duve returned with his parents to Belgium in 1920, where they settled in Antwerp. (De Duve later became a Belgian citizen.) As a child, de Duve journeyed throughout Europe, picking up three foreign languages in the process, and in 1934 enrolled in the Catholic University of Louvain, where he received an education in the "ancient humanities." Deciding to become a physician, he entered the medical school of the university.

Finding the pace of medical training relaxed, and realizing that the better students gravitated to research labs, de Duve joined J. P. Bouckaert's group. Here he studied physiology, concentrating on the hormone insulin and its effects on uptake of the sugar glucose. De Duve's experiences in Bouckaert's laboratory convinced him to pursue a research career when he graduated with an M.D. in 1941. World War II disrupted his plans, and de Duve ended up in a prison camp. He managed to escape and subsequently returned to Louvain to resume his investigations of insulin. Although his access to experimental supplies and equipment was limited, he was able to read extensively from the early literature on the subject. On September 30, 1943, he married Janine Herman, and eventually had four children with her: Thierry, Anne, Francoise, and Alain. Even before obtaining his Ph.D. from the Catholic University of Louvain in 1945, de Duve published several works, including a four-hundred page book on glucose, insulin, and diabetes. The dissertation topic for his *Agrege de l'Enseignement Superieur* was also insulin. De Duve then obtained an M.Sc. degree in chemistry in 1946.

After graduation, de Duve decided that he needed a thorough grounding in biochemical approaches to pursue his research interests. He studied with Hugo Theorell at the Medical Nobel Institute in Stockholm for eighteen months, then spent six months with Carl Ferdinand Cori, Gerty Cori, and Earl Sutherland at Washington University School of Medicine in St. Louis. Thus, in his early postdoctoral years he worked closely with no less than four future Nobel Prize winners. It is not surprising that, after this hectic period, de Duve was happy to return to Louvain in 1947 to take up a faculty post at his alma mater teaching physiological chemistry at the medical school. In 1951, de Duve was appointed full professor of biochemistry. As he began his faculty career, de Duve's research was still targeted at unraveling the mechanism of action of the anti-diabetic hormone, insulin. While he was not successful at his primary effort (indeed the answer to de Duve's first research question was to elude investigators for more than thirty years), his early experiments opened new avenues of research.

As a consequence of investigating how insulin works in the human body, de Duve and his students also studied the enzymes involved in carbohydrate metabolism in the liver. It was these studies that proved pivotal for de Duve's eventual rise to scientific fame. In his first efforts, he had tried to purify a particular liver enzyme, glucose-6-phosphatase, that he believed blocked the effect of insulin on liver cells. Many enzymes would solidify and precipitate out of solution when exposed to an electric field. Most could then be redissolved in a relatively pure form given the right set of conditions, but glucose-6-phosphate stubbornly remained a solid precipitate. The failure of this elec-

trical separation method led de Duve to try a different technique, separating components of the cell by spinning them in a centrifuge, a machine that rotates at high speed. De Duve assumed that particular enzymes are associated with particular parts of the cell. These parts, called cellular organelles (little organs) can be seen in the microscope as variously shaped and sized grains and particles within the body of cells. It had long been recognized that there existed several discrete types of these organelles, though little was known about their structures or functions at the time.

The basic principles of centrifugation for separating cell parts had been known for many years. First cells are ground up (homogenized) and the resultant slurry placed in a narrow tube. The tube is placed in a centrifuge, and the artificial gravity that is set up by rotation will separate material by weight. Heavier fragments and particles will be driven to the bottom of the tube while lighter materials will layer out on top. At the time de Duve began his work, centrifugation could be used to gather roughly four different fractions of cellular debris. This division proved to be too crude for his research, because he needed to separate out various cellular organelles more selectively.

For this reason, de Duve turned to a technique developed some years earlier by fellow-Belgian Albert Claude while working at the Rockefeller Institute for Medical Research. In the more common centrifugation technique, the cells of interest were first vigorously homogenized in a blender before being centrifuged. In Claude's technique of differential centrifugation, however, cells were treated much more gently, being merely ground up slightly by hand prior to being spun to separate various components.

When de Duve used this differential centrifugal fractionation technique on liver cells, he did indeed get better separation of cell organelles, and was able to isolate certain enzymes to certain cell fractions. One of his first findings was that his target enzyme, glucose-6-phosphatase, was associated with microsomes, cellular organelles which had been, until that time, considered by cell biologists to be quite uninteresting. De Duve's work showed that they were the site of key cellular metabolic events. Further, this was the first time a particular enzyme had been clearly associated with a particular organelle.

De Duve was also studying an enzyme called acid phosphatase that acts in cells to remove phosphate groups (chemical clusters made up of one phosphorus and three oxygen atoms) from sugar molecules under acidic conditions. The differential centrifugation technique isolated acid phosphatase to a particular cellular fraction, but measurements of enzyme activity showed much lower levels than expected. De Duve was puzzled. What had happened to the enzyme? He and his students observed that if the cell fraction that initially showed this low level of enzyme were allowed to sit in the refrigerator for several days, the enzyme activity increased to expected levels. This phenomenon became known as enzyme latency.

De Duve believed he had a solution to the latency mystery. He reasoned that perhaps the early, gentle hand-grinding of differential centrifugation did not damage the cellular organelles as much as did the more traditional mechanical grinding. What if, he wondered, some enzymes were not freely exposed in the cells' interiors, but instead were enclosed *within* protective membranes of organelles. If these organelles were not then broken apart by the gentle grinding, the enzyme might still lie trapped within the organelles in the particular cell fraction after centrifugation. If so, it would be isolated from the chemicals used to measure enzyme activity. This would explain the low initial enzyme activity, and why over time, as the organelles' membranes gradually deteriorated, enzyme activity would increase.

De Duve realized that his ideas had powerful implications for cellular research. By carefully observing what enzymes were expressed in what fractions and under what conditions, de Duve's students were able to separate various enzymes and associate them with particular cellular organelles. By performing successive grinding and fractionations, and by using compounds such as detergents to break up membranes, de Duve's group began making sense out of the complex world that exists within cells.

De Duve's research built on the work of other scientists. Previous research had clarified some of the roles of various enzymes. But de Duve came to realize that there existed a group of several enzymes, in addition to acid phosphatase, whose primary functions all related to breaking down certain classes of molecules. These enzymes were always expressed in the same cellular fraction, and showed the same latency. Putting this information together, de Duve realized that he had found an organelle devoted to cellular digestion. It made sense, he reasoned, that these enzymes should be sequestered away from other cell components. They functioned best in a different environment, expressing their activity fully only under acidic conditions (the main cell interior is neutral). More-

over, these enzymes could damage many other cellular components if set loose in the cells' interiors. With this research, de Duve identified lysosomes and elucidated their pivotal role in cellular digestive and metabolic processes. Later research in de Duve's laboratory showed that lysosomes play critical roles in a number of disease processes as well.

De Duve eventually uncovered more associations between enzymes and organelles. The enzyme monoamine oxidase, for example, behaved very similarly to the enzymes of the lysosome, but de Duve's careful and meticulous investigations revealed minor differences in when and where it appeared. He eventually showed that monoamine oxidase was associated with a separate cellular organelle, the peroxisome. Further investigation led to more discoveries about this previously unknown organelle. It was discovered that peroxisomes contain enzymes that use oxygen to break up certain types of molecules. They are vital to neutralizing many toxic substances, such as alcohol, and play key roles in sugar metabolism.

Recognizing the power of the technique that he had used in these early experiments, de Duve pioneered its use to answer questions of both basic biological interest and immense medical application. His group discovered that certain diseases result from cells' inability to properly digest their own waste products. For example, a group of illnesses known collectively as disorders of glycogen storage result from malfunctioning lysosomal enzymes. Tay Sachs disease, a congenital neurological disorder that kills its victims by age five, results from the accumulation of a component of the cell membrane that is not adequately metabolized due to a defective lysosomal enzyme.

In 1962 de Duve joined the Rockefeller Institute (now Rockefeller University) while keeping his appointment at Louvain. In subsequent years, working with numerous research groups at both institutions, he has studied inflammatory diseases such as arthritis and arteriosclerosis, genetic diseases, immune dysfunctions, tropical maladies, and cancers. This work has led, in some cases, to the creation of new drugs used in combatting some of these conditions. In 1971 de Duve formed the International Institute of Cellular and Molecular Pathology, affiliated with the University at Louvain. Research at the institute focuses on incorporating the findings from basic cellular research into practical applications.

De Duve's work has won him the respect of his colleagues. Workers throughout the broad field of cellular biology recognize their debt to his pioneering studies. He helped found the American Society for Cell Biology. He has received awards and honors from many countries, including more than a dozen honorary degrees. In 1974, de Duve, along with Albert Claude and George Palade, both also of the Rockefeller Institute, received the Nobel Prize in physiology or medicine, and were credited with creating the discipline of scientific investigation that became known as cell biology. De Duve was elected a foreign associate of the United States National Academy of Sciences in 1975, and has been acclaimed by Belgian, French, and British biochemical societies. He has also served as a member of numerous prestigious biomedical and health-related organizations around the globe.

BIOGRAPHICAL/CRITICAL SOURCES:

BOOKS

Magill, F. N., editor, *The Nobel Prize Winners: Physiology or Medicine,* Volume 3: *1970-1990,* Salem Press, 1991, pp. 1177-1187.

PERIODICALS

Journal of Cell Biology, vol. 91, 1981, pp. 66-76.*

*   *   *

DE FOREST, Lee 1873-1961

PERSONAL: Born August 26, 1873; died June 30, 1961; son of Henry Swift (a minister) and Anna (Robbins) De Forest; married Lucile Sheardown, c. 1907 (divorced, 1907); married Nora Stanton Blatch (a civil engineer; divorced, 1911); married Mary Mayo (a singer), December, 1912 (divorced, 1929); married Marie Mosquini (an actress), 1930; children: (from second marriage) Harriot Stanton de Forest; (from third marriage) two daughters, one son. *Education:* Yale University, B.A. 1896, Ph.D. 1899.

CAREER: Engineer and inventor. Founded the De Forest Wireless Telegraph Company, 1902, also founded the DeForest Phonofilm Corporation and several other companies.

WRITINGS:

Television Today and Tomorrow, Dial, 1942.
Father of Radio, Wilcox & Follett, 1950.

SIDELIGHTS: Lee de Forest was one of several scientists who contributed to the development of radio. A controversial and litigious man who seemed nearly as much concerned with fame as with science, de Forest is generally credited with the invention of the triode, or three-electrode vacuum tube, which he called the Audion. This tube made possible the amplification of electrical energy by introducing a third element into the existing two-electrode vacuum tube, allowing control over the flow of electrons, or ions, through ionized gas in the tube. De Forest's invention paved the way for radio signals to be received through the airwaves, without wires.

De Forest was born August 26, 1873, the son of the Reverend Henry Swift De Forest (he retained the capital D in his name, while his son preferred the lowercase) and the former Anna Robbins. His father, president of Talladega College in Alabama, had hoped that his son would also become a minister, but early in life Lee had shown an intense interest in inventing. As preparation for what his father hoped would be a religious career, de Forest was enrolled at Mount Hermon school in Massachusetts. The school's emphasis on hard work (students did most of the chores in order to defray the expenses) left de Forest little time for inventing, and he was unhappy there. Nevertheless, after graduation he was able to convince his parents to allow him to attend the Sheffield Scientific School at Yale University.

An unpopular and unsociable youth (he was voted the "homeliest boy in school"), de Forest was deeply concerned, perhaps even obsessed, with receiving recognition from his peers. Unlike many of his classmates, de Forest had to work to supplement his scholarship money, and still was often in debt. In an attempt to raise his status, de Forest sought money and fame by inventing several devices which he hoped to sell to companies or enter in contests with large prizes. Although none of his inventions were accepted, de Forest was certain of future success; he wrote in his diary that "I must be brilliant, win fame, show the greatness of genius and to no small degree," as Tom Lewis related in *Empire of the Air.*

De Forest received his bachelor's degree in 1896 and went on to receive a Ph.D. in physics from Yale in 1899; his dissertation, "Reflection of Hertzian Waves from the Ends of Parallel Wires," was a pioneering study of a phenomenon of radio waves . By 1902 he had founded the de Forest Wireless Telegraph Company, based on his invention of an improved wireless receiver. The company was the first of a series of businesses that were to fail, largely because of questionable practices by de Forest's business partners.

Despite his creativity, de Forest seemed to be weak in theoretical understanding; he frequently did not see the potential in his inventions and often misunderstood why they worked. De Forest's triode was based on the Fleming valve, which was itself a variation on inventor Thomas Edison's incandescent lamp. Edison had noticed that the insides of his incandescent lamps tended to blacken, as if particles were being emitted from the carbon filament. When he inserted a metal plate into the lamp and connected it to the "positive" side of the filament, he found that current somehow flowed to the positively charged plate. At this time nothing was known of the existence of electrons, the negatively charged particles of electricity, and Edison did not pursue this line of research, although he did receive a patent for the two-element lamp in 1883.

The emission of particles to the plate, known as the "Edison effect," became the focus of experiments by J. Ambrose Fleming, an engineer who recognized that current flowed in only one direction, from the filament to the plate, and could therefore convert an input of alternating current (AC), or current continuously switching polarity, to an output of direct current (DC). The Fleming valve, invented in 1903, was physically no different from Edison's two-element lamp, but unlike Edison, Fleming understood both its operation and its potential.

In the meantime, de Forest was working on an improved detector for wireless telegraph signals. Existing detectors used a gas flame to ionize gas; by employing a filament in a partially evacuated vacuum tube instead of an open flame, he found that he could create a more stable detector. His tube differed from Fleming's chiefly in that it retained some gas in the tube, on the theory that this residual gas was necessary for ionization. This tube, the first of two to which he gave the name Audion, became the subject of litigation by Fleming, although de Forest claimed that his source was the gas-flame detector, not Fleming's valve.

De Forest's further modification of this tube, however, was his own work, and it was to be his most significant development; this was the triode, created by the addition of a third element, the grid, between the two existing components of the vacuum tube, the filament and the plate. When current was applied to this grid, the current received by the plate was strengthened, or amplified, allowing weak telegraph

signals—and, after engineer Ernst F. W. Alexanderson's development of Reginald Fessenden's high-frequency alternator, radio signals—to be heard more easily. De Forest did not fully understand how this tube worked; he believed, mistakenly, that the operation of the triode was dependent on the presence of gas (ions) within the tube. He failed to realize that the presence of gas limited the tube's life, weakened its signal, and generated noise, making it only marginally useful as an amplifier. It was not until 1912 that other scientists showed that the total evacuation of the tube produced a stronger, less noisy tube that had potential not only as an amplifier of weak radio signals but as an oscillator—a necessary component in the construction of a radio transmitter. By this time it was too late for de Forest to take full advantage of his invention; others with a clearer understanding of the technology had left him behind.

De Forest clearly had foresight, however, in his understanding of the potential of radio broadcasting as a public service—an opportunity to bring educational, cultural, and informational material to a wide spectrum of people. Once it was demonstrated (by 1906) that high-frequency radio signals could carry sound—of music and of the human voice—the possibilities of radio as a tool for communication unfolded. De Forest's vision for the medium frequently exceeded its existing technical capabilities, but he created a compelling popular image of what radio could achieve. On January 13, 1910, he attempted the first live broadcast from the stage of the Metropolitan Opera House in New York City, a performance of Mascagni's *Cavalleria rusticana* featuring Emmy Destinn and Enrico Caruso. The medium was still primitive—employing an antenna strung across the roof of the opera house, an arc generator to provide the radio-frequency signal, and a telephone transmitter to send the signal out over the airwaves—and the broadcast could be heard only at a few locations in the city, its sound quality compromised by heavy background noise. Nevertheless, it represented an attempt to use radio to raise the cultural level of Americans. De Forest also made what may have been the first news broadcast, an inaccurate announcement of the outcome of the 1916 presidential election.

De Forest continued producing inventions related to radio, but none had the importance of the triode. In 1912 he developed a method for transmitting two signals over a single line—a diplex system. That same year he developed a cascade amplifier circuit, which fed the output of one triode into the input of another. It increased the amplification by a factor of three; a series of three tubes thus produced twenty-seven times the original signal.

A more significant outcome of this research was the feedback, or regenerative, circuit. In this circuit, the output of one triode was fed back to become its own input. This not only increased the output even further, but it allowed the tube to produce oscillations, that is, alternating current (AC). This enabled the tube to be used as a transmitter. But de Forest did not realize the true potential of this discovery; by the time he applied for a patent on the feedback circuit in 1915, the device had been patented by inventor E. Howard Armstrong. Litigation over the patent dragged on until 1934; although the courts found in de Forest's favor, the industry did not; it viewed the feedback circuit as Armstrong's invention and credited de Forest only with the invention of the triode.

Even the Audion triode, de Forest's most successful invention, did not produce the financial rewards he sought. Although American Telephone and Telegraph showed interest in the tube, the firm feared legal action by the giant Marconi companies, which owned the rights to the Fleming valve, of which the Audion was still seen as a possible patent infringement. De Forest did eventually sell the rights to the Audion to AT&T, but for a low sum; he had been advised to do so by one of his partners who, unknown to de Forest, was associated with AT&T.

During the early 1920s, de Forest turned his attention to sound recording, intending to develop a method for recording sound using electricity—based on his Audion—as opposed to the purely mechanical methods then in use. He succeeded in recording sound on magnetic wire, which had been done by engineer Valdemar Poulsen in 1898, but without the advantage of de Forest's Audion. He later succeeded in recording sound on film using what were, in effect, photographed sound waves read by a photoelectric cell; this, too, was derivative of an earlier inventor's work—Eugen Lauste had made recordings using light as early as 1903—but again, the Audion provided the amplification lacking in the earlier device.

It was a small conceptual step from this idea to that of recording sound directly on motion picture film—avoiding the synchronization problems of the existing sound films using disk recordings—a goal he achieved by 1921, which he called "Phonofilm." A series of sound films followed, and theaters began to be equipped with Phonofilm equipment by 1924, a full three years before Warner's Vitaphone sound-on-disk

method produced *The Jazz Singer,* the first full-length film using sound and the one usually credited with launching the sound film era. Inadequate interest by Hollywood studios, de Forest's lack of expertise as a producer, his decision to make only short films, and legal troubles with the inventor of the photoelectric cell used in the process all contributed to the demise of the de Forest Phonofilm Corporation by 1925. Ironically, this light-on-film soundtrack method was eventually adopted by the motion picture industry.

After 1925 de Forest developed a television system. This was a mechanical (rather than purely electronic) device for transmitting and receiving pictures over the airwaves. Later, in 1946, he developed a color television system; this was also a mechanical system, and it could not compete with the all-electronic color television developed by RCA in the early 1950s. As with radio, de Forest believed that television had the potential to raise the level of civilization. He became severely critical of the radio and television programming of his time, however, feeling that it perpetuated the lowest forms of entertainment.

De Forest's life was punctuated with business reverses and long-running litigation that gave him as much notoriety in the radio industry as fame. In his private life as well, de Forest encountered considerable difficulty. There was a series of failed marriages. The first, to Lucile Sheardown, lasted barely a month before they separated; they were divorced in 1907. His second wife was Nora Stanton Blatch, a civil engineer at Cornell University who was the granddaughter of Elizabeth Cady Stanton and daughter of suffragist Harriot Stanton Blatch. Nora had a strong interest in electrical engineering—she had studied under the inventor Michael Pupin—and she worked alongside her husband in his laboratory. This did not conform with de Forest's idea of a woman's place, however, and relations between them became strained. A daughter, Harriot Stanton de Forest, was born in 1909, but by this time her parents had separated, their divorce becoming final in 1911. De Forest married his third wife, singer Mary Mayo, in December 1912. Apparently depressed about giving up her stage career, and suffering from severe rheumatism, she became an alcoholic. After three difficult pregnancies—two daughters survived, but the third child, the son for whom de Forest had long hoped, died after two days—Mayo left her husband; they were divorced in 1929. His fourth and final marriage, to Marie Mosquini, a motion picture actress, took place in 1930.

Throughout his life, de Forest held to the belief that he was the "father of radio"—in fact, this was the title of his autobiography, published in 1950. He could not understand why he did not receive this recognition, and he saw his life as a series of hurdles placed in his path by business partners and other scientists in an effort to rob him of the glory he felt was his due. Others in the industry, however, found engineer Guglielmo Marconi or Fleming as more deserving of the appellation "father of radio," pointing out that de Forest's inventions were adaptations of others' and, in any case, that he did not completely understand how they worked. Radio was not the invention of a single person; rather, it evolved from the separate, sometimes overlapping, inventions of several people, including Edison's incandescent lamp, Marconi's wireless telegraph, Fleming's valve, and Fessenden's electrolytic detector. De Forest died of heart failure on June 30, 1961, and is remembered not as the "father of radio," as he intended, but as one of several contributors to its development.

BIOGRAPHICAL/CRITICAL SOURCES:

BOOKS

Hijiya, James A., *Lee de Forest and the Fatherhood of Radio,* Lehigh University Press, 1992.
Lewis, Tom, *Empire of the Air: The Men Who Made Radio,* Edward Burlingame, 1991.
Maclaurin, W. Rupert, *Invention and Innovation in the Radio Industry,* Macmillan, 1949.
Read, Oliver, and Walter L. Welch, *From Tin Foil to Stereo,* Howard W. Sams, 1976.

PERIODICALS

Opera News, November, 1993, pp. 30-36, 61.*

*   *   *

DE GENNES, Pierre-Gilles 1932-

PERSONAL: Born in 1932, in Paris, France; son of Robert de Gennes and Yvonne Morin-Pons; married Anne-Marie Rouet, 1954. *Education:* Centre d'Etudes Nucleaires de Saclay, Ph.D., 1959. *Avocational interests:* Kayaking, windsurfing, drawing.

CAREER: Physicist. University of Paris, Orsay, professor of solid-state physics, 1961-71; Ecole de Physique et Chimie, Paris, France, director, beginning in 1976; Rhone-Poulenc, science director for chemical physics, beginning in 1988.

AWARDS, HONORS: Wolf Prize in Physics, 1990; Nobel Prize for physics from Royal Swedish Academy of Sceinces, 1991.

WRITINGS:

Superconductivity of Metals and Alloys, translated by P. A. Pincus, W. A. Benjamin, 1966.
The Physics of Liquid Crystals, Clarendon, 1974, second edition with J. Prost, Clarendon, 1994.
Scaling Concepts in Polymer Physics, Cornell, 1979.
Introduction to Polymer Dynamics, Cambridge University Press, 1990.
Simple Views on Condensed Matter, World Scientific, 1992.
(With J. Badoz) *Fragile Objects: Soft Matter, Hard Science, and the Thrill of Discovery,* Springer Verlag, 1996.
Soft Interfaces: The 1994 Dirac Memorial Lecture, Cambridge University Press, 1997.

Contributor to journals and periodicals, including *Science.*

SIDELIGHTS: The winner of the 1991 Nobel Prize for physics, Pierre-Gilles de Gennes has been called the "Isaac Newton of our time." He succeeded in marrying chemistry and physics by means of mathematics and has a rare talent for recognizing unlikely relationships between problems. De Gennes concentrated on liquid crystals and polymers, areas most physicists avoided as intractable. He was able to untangle the physics of polymers by comparing them to simpler systems. During his career, he brought together several groups of scientists from different disciplines and was able to successfully explain a number of important phenomenon with extraordinary simplicity.

De Gennes was born in Paris, France, in 1932, to Robert de Gennes and Yvonne Morin-Pons. His early education was in the Ecole Normale Superieure, and he received his Ph.D. as a research scientist from the Centre d'Etudes Nucleaires de Saclay, which he attended from 1955 to 1959. His association with academic institutions included his professorship of solid-state physics at the University of Paris, Orsay, for a decade from 1961 to 1971.

His early research was in the areas of magnetism and superconductivity, the disappearance of electrical resistance in a substance, especially at very low temperatures. By the 1960s, de Gennes turned to a neglected subject that had been discovered in the 1920s—liquid crystals. They have been called "nature's delicate phase of matter" because their molecules can be arranged in many ways, and the arrangements can be easily disturbed by weak magnetic or electrical fields. A familiar use of liquid crystals is in pocket calculators and digital watches.

Another description of liquid crystals is that they are soaplike. In this phase, the molecules flow only in two dimensions and in parallel layers. An industrial interest in this property of liquid crystals has come about with the development of "flat" television screens. By the end of the 1960s, de Gennes had formed the liquid crystal group at Orsay. His team comprised both theoreticians and experimenters. His book, *The Physics of Liquid Crystals,* was published in 1974 and became the standard work in the field.

De Gennes's shift into liquid crystals came after he had completed substantial work in the area of superconductivity. In 1966 he had published *Superconductivity of Metals and Alloys.* He had also organized a group of scientists in the 1960s at Orsay, and they became widely known and respected throughout the worldwide scientific community for their experiments. As the field became more technically sophisticated, de Gennes began working with liquid crystals, a field in which he was able to work on simpler experiments. De Gennes earned the Nobel Prize for his interest in studying order in simple systems and generalizing the findings to more complex forms of matter.

The general problem in physics of trying to explain how systems behave in their transition from order to disorder is one that de Gennes addressed in his work with polymers. Work on polymers has been described by physicists as "messy" and called "dirt physics, dirt chemistry." The ordinary rules of physics were difficult to apply to the complexities posed by a beaker of molten plastic. Made up of long chains of repeating units, polymers have been compared on the molecular level to clumps of spaghetti.

While their properties and behavior had been described by chemical laws, it was de Gennes who analyzed polymers using the laws of physics. He was able to compare polymers to systems that were simpler, like magnets, liquid crystals, and superconductors, whose mysteries he already understood. De Gennes discovered mathematical relationships that were shared by all these systems and was able to demonstrate that the thickness of the polymer chain

was a function of its length. He was also able to calculate the length of the polymer chain using the same mathematics that defines the size of bubbles when liquid is boiled.

De Gennes's work on polymers is considered invaluable because the knowledge he brought to the understanding of their nature makes it possible to control the important properties of the material when it is being used. William Graessley, a chemical engineer, remarking on de Gennes's work in a *Science* interview said that he "[has] brought a lot of fresh insights. His work has had dramatic effects in chemistry, materials science, and chemical engineering."

Others have commented on de Gennes's willingness to veer off into unconventional areas and to learn new fields. He has been praised for his insatiable curiosity and his desire to see unifying principles. De Gennes won the American Chemical Society's Award in Polymer Chemistry in 1988, one of many honors that he has received during his career. His work on polymers has led him to investigations into some fields that had been considered engineering disciplines. One such field is tribology, the study of the design, friction, wear, and lubrication of interacting surfaces in motion, such as gears or bearings.

In 1976 de Gennes became the director of the Ecole de Physique et Chimie in Paris and in 1988 he became the science director for chemical physics at Rhone-Poulenc. The STRASACOL was a joint project with physicists and chemists from Strasbourg, Saclay, and the College de France that de Gennes formed for polymer studies. He describes this period of his work in his book, *Scaling Concepts in Polymer Physics,* published in 1979. The Royal Swedish Academy of Sciences noted in its announcement of the Nobel Prize to de Gennes that he "has shown that even 'untidy' physical systems can be described in general terms."

De Gennes married Anne-Marie Rouet in 1954. He enjoys the outdoor sports of kayaking and windsurfing and the indoor hobby of drawing in his leisure time. In 1990 de Gennes was one of two recipients of the Wolf Prize in Physics, cited for his pioneering contributions to the understanding of complex systems.

BIOGRAPHICAL/CRITICAL SOURCES:

PERIODICALS

Chemical and Engineering News, October 21, 1991, p. 5.

Nature, October 24, 1991, p. 689.
New Scientist, October 26, 1991, pp. 14-15.
Physics Today, June, 1990, p. 91; December, 1991, pp. 17-19.
Science, October 25, 1991, p. 518.

OTHER

Royal Swedish Academy of Sciences, announcement of Nobel Prize award to Pierre-Gilles de Gennes, October 16, 1991.*

* * *

DEISENHOFER, Johann 1943-

PERSONAL: Born September 30, 1943, in Zusamaltheim, Bavaria, Germany; son of Johann (a farmer) and Thekla Magg (a farmer) Deisenhofer; married Kirsten Fischer Lindahl (a scientist), in 1989. *Education:* Attended the Technical University of Munich; Max Planck Institute, Munich, Germany, Ph.D., 1974. *Avocational interests:* Music, history, skiing, swimming, chess.

CAREER: Biochemist and biophysicist. Conducted research at the Max Planck Institute of Munich, Germany, 1971-1987. University of Texas Southwestern Medical Center, Dallas, TX, Virgnia and Edward Linthicum Distinguished Chair in Biomolecular Science, 1987—.

MEMBER: American Crystallographic Association, German Biophysical Society, Academia Europa, American Association for the Advancement of Science (fellow).

AWARDS, HONORS: Biological Physics Prize from American Physical Society (shared with Hartmut Michel), 1986; Otto-Bayer Prize (shared with Michel), 1988; Nobel Prize for Chemistry from Royal Swedish Academy of Sciences (shared with Michel and Robert Huber), 1988; Knight Commander's Cross from the order of Merit of the Federal Republic of Germany; Bavarian Order of Merit.

WRITINGS:

(With James P. Norris) *The Photosynthetic Reaction Center,* Academic Press, 1993.
(With B. Chance and S. Ebashi) *Synchrotron Radiation in the Biosciences,* Clarendon Press, 1994.

Contributor to journals and periodicals, including *Embo j.*

SIDELIGHTS: Johann Deisenhofer is a biochemist and biophysicist whose career has been devoted to analyzing the composition of molecular structures. An expert in the use of X-ray technology to analyze the structure of crystals, he became part of a team of scientists in the 1980s who were studying photosynthesis—the process by which plants convert sunlight into chemical energy. In 1988, he shared the Nobel Prize for Chemistry with Robert Huber and Hartmut Michel, awarded for their work in mapping the chemical reaction at the center of photosynthesis.

Deisenhofer was born September 30, 1943, in Zusamaltheim, Bavaria, approximately fifty miles from Munich, Germany. He was the only son of Johann and Thekla Magg Deisenhofer; his parents were both farmers and they expected him to take over the family farm, as was the tradition. It was clear from an early age, however, that Deisenhofer was not interested in agriculture, and his parents sent him away to school in 1956. Over the next seven years, Deisenhofer attended three different schools, graduating from the Holbein Gymnasium in 1963. He then took the *Abitur,* an examination German students must take in order to qualify for university. He passed the exam and was awarded a scholarship. He then spent eighteen months in the military, as was required for young German men, before enrolling at the Technical University of Munich to study physics. His interest in physics had been developed through reading popular works on the subject, and he had an early passion for astronomy. Deisenhofer soon found himself doing an increasing amount of work in solid-state physics, which concerns the structures of condensed matter or solids. He secured a position in the laboratory of Klaus Dransfeld, and there he narrowed his interests further to biophysics, the application of the principles of the physical sciences to the study of biological occurrences. In 1971, Deisenhofer published his first scientific paper and received his diploma, roughly equal to a master's degree. He then began work on his Ph.D. in biochemistry at the Max Planck Institute in Munich under the direction of Robert Huber. Here, Deisenhofer began using a technique known as X-ray crystallography, which had first been demonstrated by Max von Laue in 1912.

A crystal is a solid characterized by a very ordered internal atomic structure. The structural base of any crystal is called a lattice, which is defined by M. F. C. Ladd and R. A. Palmer in *Structure Determination by X-ray Crystallography* as "a regular, infinite arrangement of points in which every point has the same environment as any other point." Crystallography, the study of crystals, is considered a field of the physical sciences, and X-ray crystallography is the study of crystals using radiation of known length. When X rays hit crystals, they are scattered by electrons. Knowing the wavelength of the X rays used, and measuring the intensities of the scattered X rays, the crystallographer is able to determine first the specific electron structure of the crystal and then its atomic structure.

Deisenhofer finished work for his Ph.D. in 1974. He chose to remain in Huber's laboratory and continue his work with X-ray crystallography, first on a postdoctoral basis, and later as a staff scientist. At the same time, he was developing computer software to be used in the mapping of crystals. While working on his doctorate, Deisenhofer had embarked on a collaborative effort with Wolfgang Steigemann; they studied crystallographic refinement of the structure of Bovine Pancreatic Trypsin Inhibitor, and their findings were published in *Acta Crystallographica* in 1975.

In 1979, Hartmut Michel joined Huber's laboratory. He had been studying photosynthesis for several years and was trying to develop a method for a detailed analysis of the molecules essential to this reaction. Photosynthesis is a very complicated process, about which much is still not known. The photosynthetic reaction center, which is a membrane protein, is considered a key to understanding the process, since it is here the electron receives the energy which drives the reaction. In 1981, Michel discovered a way to crystallize the photosynthetic reaction center from the purple bacterium *Rhodopseudomonas viridis*. Once Michel had developed this technique, he turned to Huber for help in analyzing it. Huber directed Michel to Deisenhofer, and a four-year collaboration began.

Deisenhofer, with Kunio Miki and Otto Epp, used his X-ray crystallography techniques to determine the position of over 10,000 atoms in the molecule. They produced the first three-dimensional analysis of a membrane protein. *New Scientist* magazine, as quoted in *Nobel Prize Winners Supplement 1987-1991,* called the combined efforts "the most important advance in the understanding of photosynthesis for twenty years." The Royal Swedish Academy of Sciences awarded the 1988 Nobel Prize for Chemistry jointly to Huber, Michel, and Deisenhofer for this work. Their findings opened the possibility of creating artificial reaction centers, but the scientists were credited with more than an increase in knowledge of photosynthesis. Their findings will aid efforts to increase the

scientific understanding of other functions, such as respiration, nerve impulses, hormone action, and the introduction of nutrients to cells. Deisenhofer and Michel were also recipients of the 1986 Biological Physics Prize of the American Physical Society and the 1988 Otto-Bayer Prize.

In 1987, Deisenhofer accepted the Virginia and Edward Linthicum Distinguished Chair in Biomolecular Science at the University of Texas Southwestern Medical Center at Dallas; his goal there is to establish a major center for X-ray crystallography. He has continued his research interests in the areas of protein crystallography, macromolecules, and crystallographic software. Deisenhofer has been awarded the Knight Commander's Cross of the Order of Merit of the Federal Republic of Germany, as well as the Bavarian Order of Merit. He is a fellow of the American Association for the Advancement of Science and a member of the American Crystallographic Association, the German Biophysical Society, and Academia Europa. In 1993, Deisenhofer, with James R. Norris of the Argonne National Laboratory, published a two-volume book called *The Photosynthetic Reaction Center,* based on work that grew out of Diesenhofer's collaboration with Michel.

Deisenhofer was married in 1989 to a fellow scientist, Kirsten Fischer Lindahl. He enjoys music, history, skiing, swimming, and chess in his free time. After Diesenhofer won the Nobel Prize, Dr. Kern Wildenthal, president of the Southwestern Medical School, described him to the *New York Times* as "very shy" and a man whose "life was his work." Wildenthal further observed that the scientist is "quiet, peaceful and calm. But beneath that exterior, he is scientifically fearless."

BIOGRAPHICAL/CRITICAL SOURCES:

BOOKS

Ladd, M. F. C., and Palmer, R. A., *Structure Determination by X-Ray Crystallography,* Plenum Press, 1977.
McGuire, Paula, editor, *Nobel Prize Winners Supplement 1987-1991,* H. W. Wilson, 1992.

PERIODICALS

Chemical and Engineering News, October 24, 1988, pp. 4-5.
New York Times, October 20, 1988, p. B13.
Physics Today, February, 1989, pp. 17-18.

Science, November 4, 1988, pp. 672-673.
Time, October 31, 1988, p. 65.*

* * *

DE LA SALLE, Innocent
See HARTMANN, Sadakichi

* * *

DENG, Francis Mading 1938-

PERSONAL: Born January 1, 1938, in Abyei, Sudan;
son of Majok Deng (a Paramount chief); married
Dorothy Ludwig; children: Donald, Daniel, David,
Dennis. *Education:* Khartoum University, LL.B.
(with honors), 1962; Yale Law School, LL.M. 1965,
JS.D., 1967; attended graduate courses at King's
College and School of Oriental and African Studies in
Jurisprudence and African Law, Islamic and Civil
Procedure, 1962-64.

ADDRESSES: Home—708 Highland Ave., NW, Washington, DC 20012. *Office*—The Brookings Institution,
1775 Massachusetts Ave., NW, Washington, DC
20036.

CAREER: Sudanese Ambassador to Scandinavia, 1972-
74; Sudanese Ambassador to the United States, 1974-
76; Minister of State for Foreign Affairs (Sudan),
Khartoum, Sudan, 1976-80; Sudanese Ambassador to
Canada (Minister of State), 1980-83; Brookings Institution, Washington, D.C., senior fellow, 1988—.
Yale Law School, visiting lecturer; representative of
the United Nations Secretary-General on Internally
Displaced Persons, 1992—.

MEMBER: African Studies Association, African-
American Institute, SYNERGOS Institute, African
Leadership Forum, Yale Club of New York, Cosmos
Club (Washington, DC).

AWARDS, HONORS: Excellence in Publishing Award,
Association of American Publishers, 1990.

WRITINGS:

AS FRANCIS MADING DENG

Tradition and Modernization: A Challenge for Law

among the Dinka of the Sudan, Yale University
Press (New Haven, CT), 1971.
The Dinka of the Sudan, Holt (New York, NY), 1972.
The Dinka and Their Songs, Clarendon Press (Oxford,
England), 1973.
*Dynamics of Identification: A Basis for National Inte-
gration in the Sudan,* Khartoum University Press
(Khartoum, Sudan), 1973.
Dinka Folktales: African Stories from the Sudan,
Africana (New York, NY), 1974.
*Africans of Two Worlds: The Dinka in Afro-Arab
Sudan,* Yale University Press, 1978.
Dinka Cosmology, Ithaca Press (London), 1980.
Recollections of Babo Nimir, Ithaca Press, 1982.
Seed of Redemption: A Political Novel, Lilian Barber
Press (New York), 1986.
*The Man Called Deng Majok: A Biography of Power,
Polygyny, and Change,* Yale University Press,
1986.
(Editor with Prosser Gifford) *The Search for Peace
and Unity in the Sudan,* Wilson Center Press
(Washington, DC), 1987.
Cry of the Owl (novel), Lilian Barber Press, 1989.

AS FRANCIS M. DENG

Security Problems: An African Predicament, Indiana
University (Bloomington, IN), 1981.
(Editor with Robert O. Collins) *The British in the
Sudan, 1898-1956: The Sweetness and the Sor-
row,* Macmillan (London), 1984.
(With M. W. Daly) *Bonds of Silk: The Human
Factor in the British Administration of the Sudan,*
Michigan State University Press (Lansing, MI),
1990.
(Editor with Ahmed An-Naim) *Human Rights in Af-
rica: Cross-Cultural Perspectives,* Brookings In-
stitution (Washington, DC), 1990.
(Editor with I. William Zartman) *Conflict Resolution
in Africa,* Brookings Institution, 1991.
(With Larry Minear) *The Challenges of Famine Re-
lief: Emergency Operations in the Sudan,* Brook-
ings Institution, 1992.
*Protecting the Dispossessed: A Challenge for the In-
ternational Community,* Brookings Institution,
1993.
War of Visions: Conflict of Identities in the Sudan,
Brookings Institution, 1995.
*Sovereignty as Responsibility: Conflict Management in
Africa,* Brookings Institution, 1996.

Contributor of numerous articles to periodicals, including *Current, Middle East Journal,* and *Brookings
Review.*

WORK IN PROGRESS: Internally Displaced Persons: An Agenda for Protection, Assistance and Development, and *Sovereignty, Responsibility and Accountability: An African Challenge.*

SIDELIGHTS: During his career Francis Mading Deng has served in several ambassadorial positions for Sudan, including representing Sudan in the United States and in Canada. In 1988 he became a senior fellow at the Brookings Institution in Washington, DC. Deng has contributed regularly to such journals as the *Brookings Review, Current,* and the *Middle East Journal,* as well as editing and authoring a number of books on Africa in general and Sudan in particular.

Deng's prolific and varied output of writing includes both fiction and nonfiction. In 1986 his novel of the Sudanese Civil War, *Seeds of Redemption,* was published. David Dorsey in *World Literature Today* called the book "an honorably biased account of Sudanese politics since independence. . . . effective and original, with romantic idealism, well-crafted suspenseful episodes, cyclical plot·patterns, subtle humor, and delayed revelations of authorial irony." Bernard D. Williams, writing in *Best Sellers,* called the *Seeds of Redemption* "a realistic account . . . of the political developments of the civil war in the Sudan."

In Deng's 1990 nonfiction work *Bonds of Silk: The Human Factor in the British Administration of the Sudan,* which he coauthored with M. W. Daly and which is based on a collection of interviews, Deng investigated the nationalist movement in Sudan.

Deng's 1992 volume, *The Challenge of Famine Relief: Emergency Operations in the Sudan,* coauthored with international development specialist Larry Minear, is a study of two famines in Sudan during the 1980s— one drought-induced, the other conflict-related—and the efforts by various non-governmental relief organizations and government agencies to alleviate the suffering. In a review of *Famine Relief, African Studies Review* contributor Carl C. Mabbs-Zeno maintained: "The strength of this book lies in the compelling insights shared by two, well informed perspectives on the process of relief." He concluded, "The challenge of coordinating a wide variety of relief initiatives is covered particularly well by this book."

Deng has also written several books on the law, culture, and folklore of Sudan's Dinka people, including a biography of his own father, who was one of their important leaders. Reviewing *The Man Called Deng Majok,* Lina Fruzetti in *Africa Today* wrote: "Enter-

ing the world of Deng Majok, the reader is confronted with levels of contradictions, some of which are delicately balanced by the author."

BIOGRAPHICAL/CRITICAL SOURCES:

PERIODICALS

Africa Today, vol. 35, no. 1, 1988; vol. 36, nos. 3 and 4, 1989.
African Studies Review, September, 1995, pp. 150-52.
Best Sellers, February, 1987, p. 414.
Choice, March, 1992, p. 1150.
Foreign Affairs, March/April, 1994, pp. 141-142.
Times Literary Supplement, March 8, 1991, p. 8.
World Literature Today, summer, 1987, p. 483.

* * *

de ROXAS, Juan Bartolome
    See RUBIA BARCIA, Jose

* * *

DIAZ, Henry Frank 1948-

PERSONAL: Born July 15, 1948, in Santiago de Cuba, Oriente, Cuba; naturalized U.S. citizen; son of Francisco (an attorney) Diaz and Maria Vias; married Marla Cremin, 1969; children: Christopher, Susana. *Education:* Florida State University, B.S., 1971; University of Miami, M.S., 1974; University of Colorado, Boulder, Ph.D., 1985.

CAREER: Meteorologist. National Oceanic and Atmospheric Administration, Washington, DC, meteorologist, 1974-75, assigned to National Climatic Data Center, Climate Analysis Division, Asheville, NC, 1975-83, Environmental Research Laboratory, Climate Research Program, 1983-85, acting director, 1985-86, Climate Monitoring and Diagnostic Laboratory, Climate Research Division, 1988-93, Climate Diagnostic Center, 1993—. University of Colorado, Boulder, geography teacher; Scripps Institution of Oceanography, La Jolla, CA, visiting scholar, 1982; University of Massachusetts, Amherst, visiting scholar, 1988-89.

MEMBER: American Meteorological Society, American Geophysical Union, American Quarternary Association, Cooperative Institute for Research in Environmental Sciences (CIRES).

AWARDS, HONORS: Achievement Award, National Oceanic and Atmospheric Administration, 1977, 1978, 1982, 1988, 1989, 1992, and 1993.

WRITINGS:

A Long Record of Weather Observations at Cooperstown, New York, 1854-1977, National Climatic Center (Asheville, NC), 1978.

Ninety-One Years of Weather Records at Yellowstone National Park, Wyoming, 1887-1977, National Climatic Center, 1979.

Atlas of Mean Winter Temperature Departures from the Long-term Mean Over the Contiguous United States, 1895-1979, National Climatic Center, 1980.

A Long Record of Weather Observations in Southeastern Iowa, 1839-1979, National Climatic Center, 1980.

Inventory of Sources of Long Term Climatic Data in Microfilm and Publication Form, National Climatic Center, 1982.

El Nino: Historical and Paleoclimatic Aspects of the Southern Oscillation, Cambridge University Press, 1992.

(With Malcolm K. Hughes) *The Medieval Warm Period,* Kluwer Academic Publishers (Boston, MA), 1994.

(With Roger S. Pulwarty) *Hurricanes: Climate and Socioeconomic Impacts,* Springer (New York City), 1997.

Contributor to journals and periodicals, including *Science, Nature, Monthly Weather Review,* and *Journal of Geophysical Research.*

SIDELIGHTS: A distinguished atmospheric scientist, Henry F. Diaz has written extensively on climatic variability and global and regional climate analysis. He has also co-edited a book on the phenomenon of El nino, a periodic warming of Pacific ocean currents that has the potential to affect weather conditions worldwide.

Born in Santiago de Cuba on July 15, 1948, Diaz is the son of Francisco Diaz, an attorney of Spanish and French descent, and Maria Vias. He became interested in geography and tropical weather after moving to Havana in 1959. During the early 1960s, Diaz immigrated to the United States, attending high school in Miami and later college at Florida State University in Tallahassee. After earning an undergraduate degree in meteorology, he matriculated at the University of Miami and received a master's degree in atmospheric science in 1974.

Following graduation, Diaz found employment as a meteorologist with the National Oceanic and Atmospheric Administration (NOAA) in Washington, D.C. A year later, he moved with his wife, Marla Cremin, and his son to Asheville, North Carolina, where he had accepted a position in the Climate Analysis Division of NOAA's National Climatic Data Center. In 1980, intrigued by the phenomenon of climatic variability, Diaz enrolled at the University of Colorado in Boulder on a NOAA scholarship. He received his doctorate in geography with a specialization in climatology five years later.

During his twenty-year career with NOAA, Diaz has published numerous articles, atlases, and technical reports on climatic fluctuation; he is best known, however, for his 1992 study *El Nino: Historical and Paleoclimatic Aspects of the Southern Oscillation.* Diaz presently works for NOAA in Boulder and has received several awards for his work. His professional associations include membership in the Cooperative Institute for Research in Environmental Sciences (CIRES) of the University of Colorado, where he also teaches geography. An avid outdoorsman, Diaz has been honored as a visiting scientist by the Scripps Institution of Oceanography (summer, 1982) and the University of Massachusetts (1988-89).*

*   *   *

Di BLASI, Debra 1957-

PERSONAL: Born May 27, 1957, in Kirksville, MO; daughter of Donald Eugene (a cattle rancher and crop farmer) and Donna Marlene (a registered nurse; maiden name, Aby) Pickens; married Carlos Roberto Di Blasi, 1984 (divorced, 1989). *Ethnicity:* "Caucasian (English, Welsh, Scottish, German, Jewish, Native American, Swiss)." *Education:* Attended University of Missouri—Columbia, 1975-78; Kansas City Art Institute, B.F.A., 1985; attended San Francisco State University, 1989. *Politics:* "Flexible." *Religion:* "Flexible." *Avocational interests:* Music and sound composition, science, painting, hiking, softball, basketball, comparative theology, opera, film, theater.

ADDRESSES: Home—Kansas City, MO. *Office*—Kansas City Art Institute, 4415 Warwick Blvd., Kansas City, MO 64111. *E-mail*—ddiblasi@gvi.net.

CAREER: Robert Half of Northern California, San Francisco, advertising manager, 1986-89; *MacWeek,*

San Francisco, advertising production manager, 1989; Accessible Arts, Inc., Kansas City, KS, assistant to the executive director, 1990-92; Spring Communications, Kansas City, MO, senior secretary in International Network Design and Engineering Department, 1992-95; Kansas City Art Institute, Kansas City, MO, writing tutor, 1994, learning specialist, 1995—. River of Words National Poetry Competition, judge, 1997; *SOMA,* associate guest editor; gives lectures and readings from her works.

MEMBER: National Geographic Society, Writers Place, Kansas City Art Institute Alumni Circle.

AWARDS, HONORS: Eyster Prize for Fiction, *New Delta Review,* 1991, for the short story "An Interview with My Husband;" Austin Heart of Film Screenwriters Competition, finalist, 1996, for "The Walking Wounded."

WRITINGS:

Drought and Say What You Like (novellas), New Directions (New York City), 1997.

Author of the screenplays *The Season's Condition,* based on her own story, Breathing Furniture Films, 1993; and *Drought,* a Lisa Mancure production based on her novella, 1997. Author of short stories in anthologies, including *Lovers: Writings by Women,* 1992, and *Exposures: Essays by Missouri Women,* 1997. Author of short stories in periodicals, including *Moondance, Cottonwood, Potpourri, New Letters, Sou'wester, New Delta Review, AENE, Colorado-North Review,* and *Transfer.*

Contributor of essays, articles, and reviews to periodicals, including *SOMA* and *New Art Examiner.*

WORK IN PROGRESS: Prayers of an Accidental Nature, a collection of short stories, publication by Coffee House Press expected in 1999; *Moments before Dying,* a collection of stories and essays, completion expected in 1998; *Reprise: Reprisal,* a novel and an accompanying compact disc; two plays, *Drowning Hard* and *An Interview with My Husband,* adapted from her short stories; three screenplays, *Lucid,* a science fiction thriller, *Sandman and Messiah,* a futuristic thriller, and *Corporate Trilogy,* including a drama, a thriller, and a comedy, 1998. Research on music, weather, militia, mercenaries, guerilla warfare, crows, the history of experimental fiction, quantum physics, synchronicity, lucid dreaming, and comparative theology.

SIDELIGHTS: Debra Di Blasi told *CA:* "Growing up in the 1960s and 1970s, in an environment of social cynicism and political skepticism, I began writing with the intent of becoming an investigative reporter in the vein of Woodward and Bernstein. I wanted to rip the smiling mask off the face of the world and reveal what I suspected to be the grotesque truths beneath.

"Then I discovered poetry.

"Truth took on a larger meaning, and language became something much more significant than merely a means to an end. It was a means to a means. I fell in love with the writing process and thus became a literary bigamist: married to both language and truth. Of course, art and truth should never be separated. I have learned this through poetry, through fiction, through painting, through living.

"Although journalism no longer beckons me, I am still interested in masquerades—the lies we tell ourselves and each other—and the dark, sometimes terrifying shape at our core: raw, ignoble, violent emotions safely tethered—or not. It is really the 'not' to which I am most intimately drawn at this point in my career. I am drawn to folks of a desperate nature, who wrestle with and, for whatever reasons, surrender to their darker passions. It is their hearts I wish to expose, slice open, anatomize, report.

"It takes a great deal of empathy to enter into the mind of a society snob, a child abuser, a racist, a suicide, a killer—anyone whose core appears weak or flawed. My protagonists often bear the markings of antagonists, yet they are us: the writer and reader. Perfection and righteousness do not interest me, for they too are lies or, at best, incomplete truths. This society does not teach us compassion. Rather it teaches us (masqueraders, all) to judge, loathe, condemn—to weigh the dark against the light and ignore the many shades of gray in between. Tragedy, as well as triumph, occurs in the gray. In the gray squats the honesty of fiction.

"Likewise, I am drawn to fiction writers whose literary investigations appear similar to mine and whose use of language is, if not innovative, then aurally exciting. Oddly, works in translation appeal to me the most. Something happens during the translation—an emotional distancing from the origin, I suppose, that creates a heightened omniscience I find intellectually and aesthetically seductive. To say that such fiction bears the strongest influence on my writing would lack wisdom; I am influenced by everything I read, and I read diversely: from fiction and poetry to science and theology, to military manuals and fashion slicks. All of it finds its way into my subconscious, and my subconscious finds its way into my fiction."

* * *

DICKE, Robert H(enry) 1916-1997

OBITUARY NOTICE—See index for *CA* sketch: Surname is pronounced *Dick*-ee; born May 6, 1916, in St. Louis, MO; died of complications from Parkinson's disease, March 4, 1997, in Princeton, NJ. Physicist, educator, and author. Highly respected for his contributions to the study of physics, astrophysics, and cosmology, Dicke was an early believer in the Big Bang theory of the creation of the universe and postulated that an echo of that event could still be detected through radio waves. However, before he could confirm his theory, the echo was verified by two other scientists working in a related area, and Dicke was excluded—unfairly in the view of some commentators—from sharing in the Nobel Prize that they were awarded in 1978 as a result of the finding.

A longtime professor at Princeton University, Dicke conducted numerous experiments in gravity and in his unsuccessful challenge of Albert Einstein's general theory of relativity. Dicke held approximately fifty patents for his discoveries, many of them pertaining to the development of radar. He was named the Albert Einstein University Professor of Science at Princeton University in 1975, becoming emeritus in 1984. His books include *An Introduction to Quantum Mechanics* (1960), *The Theoretical Significance of Experimental Relativity* (1964), and *Gravitation and the Universe* (1970).

OBITUARIES AND OTHER SOURCES:

BOOKS

Who's Who in America, 51st edition, Marquis, 1997, p. 1062.

PERIODICALS

Los Angeles Times, March 6, 1997, p. A22.
New York Times, March 5, 1997, p. B9.
Washington Post, March 8, 1997, p. B4.

DIENER, Theodor Otto 1921-

PERSONAL: Born February 28, 1921, in Zurich, Switzerland; immigrated to U.S., 1949; became U.S. citizen, 1955; son of Theodor Emanuel (a postal employee) and Hedwig Rosa (an accountant; maiden name, Baumann) Diener; married Shirley Baumann, 1950 (divorced, 1966); married Sybil Mary Fox, May 11, 1968; children: (from first marriage) Theodor W., Robert A., Michael S. *Education:* Swiss Federal Institute of Technology, diploma, 1946, D.Sc., 1948. *Avocational interests:* Aviation.

ADDRESSES: Home—Beltsville, MD.

CAREER: Plant pathologist. Swiss Federal Experimental Station, Waedenswil, Switzerland, plant pathologist, 1949-50; University of Rhode Island, Kingston, RI, assistant professor, 1950; Washington State University, Prosser, WA, assistant plant pathologist, 1950-55, associate plant pathologist, 1955-59; U.S. Department of Agriculture (Agricultural Research Service), Beltsville, Maryland, plant pathologist, 1959-88; University of Maryland, College Park, distinguished professor in the department of botany and acting director at the Center for Agricultural Biotechnology, 1988—. Lecturer at leading universities around the United States, as well as at numerous institutions around the world.

MEMBER: New York Academy of Sciences, U.S. National Academy of Sciences, American Academy of Arts and Sciences, German Academy of Natural Scientists, Leopoldina.

AWARDS, HONORS: Campbell Award, American Institute of Biological Sciences, 1968; Ruth Allen Award, American Phytopathological Society, 1976; Wolf Award in Agriculture, 1987; National Medal of Science, 1987; inducted into USDA Science Hall of Fame, 1988.

WRITINGS:

Viroids and Viroid Diseases, Wiley, 1979.
(Editor) *The Viroids,* Plenum (New York City), 1987.

Contributor to journals and periodicals, including *Virology* and *Scientific American.* Served as editor of *Virology,* 1964-66 and 1974-76.

SIDELIGHTS: Theodor Otto Diener has achieved international recognition as the discoverer of viroids, the smallest known agents of infectious disease. The identification of these tiny RNA molecules, which are only about one-thousandth the size of the smallest virus, sparked new interest in pathogens other than microorganisms and viruses. For this accomplishment, which has been compared with the discovery of bacteria, Diener received the National Medal of Science in 1987.

Diener was born on February 28, 1921, in Zurich, Switzerland, the son of Theodor Emanuel Diener, a postal employee, and Hedwig Rosa Baumann Diener, an accountant. From an early age, Diener was fascinated by nature. As he related to contributor Linda Wasmer Smith, "As a boy, I always kept animals at home: turtles, salamanders, frogs, white mice, hamsters, etc. Whereas my parents exhibited a large dose of tolerance to this, neighbors often did not. . . . Later, my interests fortunately gravitated toward smaller and smaller animals, particularly after I had invested money earned by sorting mail at the Christmas/New Year holiday in an old Leitz microscope."

When Diener eventually entered the Swiss Federal Institute of Technology in Zurich, it was with the intention of studying science. He was awarded a diploma in natural sciences—equivalent to a master's degree—by that institution in 1946. Two years later, he earned a doctoral degree in biology. During this time, Diener first came under the influence of Ernst Gaumann, a pioneer in the emerging specialty of plant pathology. Diener credits his choice of career field to Gaumann's inspirational teaching style.

During his last three years of college, Diener gained valuable experience as a research assistant in the botany department. After completing his studies, he first took a post as a plant pathologist at the Swiss Federal Experimental Station in Waedenswil. Then in 1950 he came to the United States to accept a short-term position as an assistant professor at the University of Rhode Island. In that same year he moved on to Washington State University, where he worked at the Irrigation Experiment Station in Prosser for a decade. Diener became an American citizen in 1955. Finally, in 1959, he began what proved to be a long and highly productive career in experimental plant pathology for the Agricultural Research Service of the U.S. Department of Agriculture in Beltsville, Maryland. This association lasted even beyond Diener's formal retirement in 1988; he continues to collaborate with USDA scientists in ongoing investigations.

It was not until Diener was fifty years old that he made his greatest contribution to science. At the time,

he was studying spindle tuber disease in potatoes, an infection that causes the tubers to grow gnarled, elongated, and cracked. While it was known that the disease spread easily from plant to plant, no bacteria or other microorganisms were consistently associated with it, and attempts to isolate a viral cause had also ended in failure. Yet Diener noted that infected tissues did contain very small molecules of an unusual form of RNA, or genetic ribonucleic acid. Healthy plants of the same species did not exhibit these molecules, but if they were introduced, the plants soon developed symptoms. Diener concluded that these tiny particles were the causative agent. In 1971 he coined the term viroids for this novel class of plant pathogens.

In later work Diener further explored the nature and role of viroids. Before their physical and chemical properties could be studied, however, it was necessary to separate viroids from the nucleic acids of cells they infected. The low concentration of viroid RNA, as compared with host RNA, made this challenging. But using the leaves of tomato plants Diener and his colleagues eventually developed new separation and purification techniques for the purpose. Once purified viroid preparations were available, it became possible to study the molecule's structure. Scientists elsewhere soon identified two viroid forms: long, threadlike molecules and circular ones. Diener and his associates were able to show that both types are infectious and present in diseased plants.

Viroids have thus far been found only in higher plants, including potatoes, tomatoes, cucumbers, avocados, coconuts, and chrysanthemums. But Diener reasoned that they might also be responsible for some diseases in human beings and other animals for which no other cause had been identified. Among the most promising candidates seemed to be a group of degenerative brain diseases including kuru and Creutzfeldt-Jakob disease in man and scrapie in sheep and goats.

Although these conditions were commonly attributed to slow viruses, no causative agent had yet been found. Furthermore, the pathogens apparently had several characteristics, such as extreme insensitivity to ultraviolet rays, that are either unknown or unusual in conventional viruses. Diener's 1972 proposal that viroids might be involved prompted a flurry of activity in labs around the world. Diener himself ultimately rejected this hypothesis after it was demonstrated that the responsible pathogens, unlike viroids, contained protein. Nevertheless, his suggestion had opened other avenues of important research, including work on small protein particles called prions. In addition, a viroidlike RNA has since been discovered that is a component of hepatitis delta virus, which does infect humans. Diener has participated in a number of conferences on this topic.

In 1988 Diener moved to the University of Maryland, where he soon assumed concurrent posts as distinguished professor in the department of botany and acting director at the Center for Agricultural Biotechnology. Not surprisingly, he has been honored on several occasions by his former employer, the USDA, including induction into that organization's Science Hall of Fame in 1988. In addition, he received the Campbell Award of the American Institute of Biological Sciences in 1968, the Ruth Allen Award of the American Phytopathological Society in 1976, and the Wolf Award in Agriculture in 1987. The latter, presented before Israel's Knesset, carried a stipend of $100,000. Among other Wolf honorees that year was violinist Isaac Stern. As Diener recalled to Linda Wasmer Smith, "I still vividly remember the animated conversations we had relating to the similarity of the sciences and the arts as different expressions of the human spirit."

Diener has been elected a fellow or member of such organizations as the New York Academy of Sciences; the U.S. National Academy of Sciences; the American Academy of Arts and Sciences; and the German Academy of Natural Scientists, Leopoldina. For several years, he also served as an editor of the journal *Virology,* where many of his most influential papers appeared. A popular lecturer, he has presented approximately two hundred talks and seminars at leading universities around the United States, as well as at numerous institutions around the world.

In his leisure time Diener is an avid private pilot who has had a lifelong interest in aviation. Diener's first marriage in 1950 to Shirley Baumann produced three sons: Theodor, Robert, and Michael. That union ended in divorce in 1966, and Diener was married to Sybil Mary Fox on May 11, 1968, in Winchester, Virginia. The pair make their home in Beltsville, Maryland, the site of Diener's greatest scientific triumphs.

BIOGRAPHICAL/CRITICAL SOURCES:

BOOKS

Berberich, Stephen M., *The Naked Intruder: USDA and the Discovery of the Viroid,* (booklet), U.S. Department of Agriculture, April, 1989.

PERIODICALS

Agricultural Research, May, 1989, pp. 4-7.
Science, June 26, 1987, p. 1621.

OTHER

Diener, Theodor Otto, letters to Linda Wasmer Smith written on January 3 and 14, 1994.
Interview with Linda Wasmer Smith, conducted on January 6, 1994.*

*   *   *

DIETZ, Lew 1907-1997

OBITUARY NOTICE—See index for *CA* sketch: Born May 22, 1907, in Pittsburgh, PA; died April 26, 1997, in Rockport, ME. Author. A writer who appealed to both young and old readers, Deitz's favorite subject was his adopted home of Maine. After working as a copywriter for Crowell Publishing in New York, Dietz moved to Maine and became editor of the *Camden Herald* from 1948 to 1949. Many of his books center on oceanside and outdoor life. One of his best-selling books is *A Seal Called Andre* (1975; written with Harry Goodridge), the story of an orphaned baby seal who became a star attraction in Maine. His books for children included the *Jeff White* series—*Jeff White: Young Woodsman* (1949), *Jeff White: Young Trapper* (1950), *Jeff White: Young Guide* (1952), *Jeff White: Young Lumberjack* (1954), and *Jeff White: Forest Fire Fighter* (1956). His other titles include *Pines for the King's Navy* (1958), *Wilderness River* (1961), *Savage Summer* (1964), *The Allagash* (1968), *Touch of Wildness* (1970), *The Year of the Big Cat* (1970). In addition, Dietz was assistant editor of the *Maine Coast Fisherman* from 1959 to 1961 and assistant editor of *Outdoor Maine* from 1961 to 1962. He also wrote articles for *Collier's, Saturday Evening Post, Field and Stream, Sports Illustrated* and *Ford Times.*

OBITUARIES AND OTHER SOURCES:

BOOKS

The Writers Directory: 1984-1986, St. James Press, 1983.

PERIODICALS

New York Times, March 3, 1997, p. 14.

Di FILIPPO, Paul 1954-

PERSONAL: Born October 29, 1954, in Woonsocket, RI; son of Frank (a manager of a textile firm) and Claire Louise (a bookkeeper; maiden name, St. Amant) Di Filippo; married Deborah Newton (a designer). *Education:* Attended Rhode Island College.

ADDRESSES: Home and office—2 Poplar St., Providence, RI 02906. *E-mail*—AC038@osfn.rhilinet.gov.

CAREER: Writer.

MEMBER: Science Fiction Writers of America.

AWARDS, HONORS: British Science Fiction Award, best short story of 1994, for "The Double Felix."

WRITINGS:

The Steampunk Trilogy, Four Walls Eight Windows (New York City), 1995.
Ribofunk (stories), Four Walls Eight Windows, 1996.
Fractal Paisleys, Four Walls Eight Windows, 1997.

Work represented in anthologies, including *Best Science Fiction of the Eighties,* edited by Hayakawa; and *What Might Have Been,* Volume 2, edited by Benford. Contributor of about a hundred stories and articles to magazines, including *Amazing, Science Fiction Age, Pirate Writings, Interzone, Shock Waves,* and *Fantasy and Science Fiction.*

*   *   *

DIJKSTRA, Edsger W(ybe) 1930-

PERSONAL: Born May 11, 1930, in Rotterdam, The Netherlands; son of Douwe Wijbe (a chemist, inventor, and president of the Dutch Chemical Society) and Brechtje Cornelia (a mathematician; maiden name, Kluyver) Dijkstra; married Maria Cornelia Debets, April 23, 1957; children: Marcus Joost, Femke Elisabeth, Rutger Michael. *Education:* University of Leyden, The Netherlands, Candidaats degree, 1951, doctoral degree, 1956; University of Amsterdam, Ph.D., 1959; Queen's University, Belfast, honorary doctorate, 1976.

ADDRESSES: Home—6602 Robbie Creek, Austin, TX 78750-8138. *Office*—University of Texas, Computer Science Dept., Austin, TX 78712.

CAREER: Computer scientist. Mathematics Center, Amsterdam, The Netherlands, staff member, 1952-62; Technical University, Eindhoven, The Netherlands, professor of mathematics, 1962-73; Burroughs Corporation, Nuenen, The Netherlands, research fellow, 1973-84; University of Texas, Austin, professor and Schlumberger Centennial Chair in Computer Science, 1984—.

MEMBER: Royal Netherlands Academy of Arts and Sciences, American Academy of Arts and Sciences.

AWARDS, HONORS: British Computer Society, Distinguished Fellow; Turing Award from Association for Computing Machinery, 1972; Harry Goode Memorial Award, 1974, for achievements in the field of information processing.

WRITINGS:

A Primer of ALGOL 60 Programming, together with Report on the Algorithmic Language ALGOL 60, Academic Press, 1962.
(With O. J. Dahl, and C. A. R. Hoare) *Notes on Structured Programming,* Academic Press, 1972.
A Discipline of Programming, Prentice Hall, 1976.
Selected Writings on Computing: A Personal Perspective, Springer-Verlag (New York), 1982.
Formal Development of Programs and Proofs, Addison-Wesley, 1990.
Predicate Calculus and Program Semantics, Springer-Verlag, 1990.

Contributor to journals and periodicals, including *Communications of the ACM.* Served as editor for *Acta Informatica.*

SIDELIGHTS: Edsger W. Dijkstra has highly influenced the manner in which computer programs, the sets of instructions that tell computers what to do, are constructed. His persuasive support for the concept and practice of *structured programming* permanently changed the way computer programs are written. It was once assumed that bugs or program errors were inevitably introduced into programs during their development and that, as a consequence, programs had to be debugged in order to work properly. Dijkstra argued that this was not necessarily so; he convinced the scientific community that computer programs could be correctly constructed from the initial stages of design.

Dijkstra was born in Rotterdam, The Netherlands, on May 11, 1930. He was the third of four children. His father, Douwe W. Dijkstra, was a chemist and inventor who had been president of the Dutch Chemical Society, and his mother, Brechtje Cornelia Kluyver, was a mathematician. Dijkstra originally intended to study law, but his scientific talents came to light following his final exams at the gymnasium in 1948. His exam grades were better than most of his teachers had ever seen, and he was convinced, as he recalled in a written interview with contributor Frank Hertle, "that it would be a pity if I did not devote myself to science." Dijkstra enrolled at Leyden University to study mathematics and physics.

It was during his early years at Leyden that Dijkstra was introduced to computers. As a reward for his academic performance, in 1951 his father offered him the opportunity to attend a three-week computer programming course (for the Electronic Delay Storage Automatic Calculator, or EDSAC) in Cambridge, England. Dijkstra, who then had plans to become a theoretical physicist, thought it would be a good idea to learn more about computers. When A. van Wijngaarden, the director of the computation department at the Mathematical Center in Amsterdam, heard by chance of Dijkstra's plans to attend this course, he interviewed him and offered him a job. Dijkstra began working part-time at the Mathematical Center in 1952 and took a full-time position there in 1956. In 1957, Dijkstra married Maria Cornelia Debets; they would eventually have three children together.

While at the Mathematical Center, Dijkstra worked with Bram J. Loopstra and Carel S. Scholten on the design and construction of a computer, known as the ARMAC. He was primarily responsible for the software, and they for the hardware, and his involvement included writing the programming manual that was to contain a complete functional description of the machine. The document served as a "contract" between Dijkstra and the two other men: they knew what they had to build and Dijkstra knew what he would build upon. This project had an important influence on the course of his career. Dijkstra already sensed that computers would be a permanent and important part of the modern world and had become convinced of the need to program them accurately. From this point forward, he felt personally challenged to develop a methodology for constructing programs that could be proven correct before being run on a computer.

During this period, Dijkstra designed some of his first computer algorithms—sequences of instructions designed to perform specific mathematical tasks.

Dijkstra developed one of his most famous algorithms—the Shortest Path (to find the shortest distance between two cities on a map)—over coffee on a cafe terrace in Amsterdam, and without paper and pencil.

When Loopstra and Scholten set out to design their next machine, they wanted it to be able to respond to what is known as a real-time interrupt. A real-time interrupt is a spontaneous event originating outside the computer that influences the action that the program running in the computer will take. Dijkstra devised a solution to this problem; he called it a real-time interrupt handler, and it became his doctoral thesis. In 1959 he received a Ph.D. from the University of Amsterdam, but he remained at the Mathematical Center, where he worked with J. A. Zonneveld designing an ALGOL 60 compiler. The project frequently took him outside of The Netherlands and gave him the opportunity to begin polishing his English. The ALGOL implementation took eight months to complete and was done in August of 1960, more than a year before their nearest competitor. This work helped establish Dijkstra's reputation among computer scientists in America.

In 1962, Dijkstra became professor of mathematics at the Technical University in Eindhoven, The Netherlands. His work there included a collaboration that produced a multiprogramming operating system (called "THE Multiprogramming System") for the university's computer, an Electrologica X8. THE Multiprogramming System was to influence the design of nearly all later operating systems.

It was while at Eindhoven that Dijkstra challenged one of the most basic techniques of programming at that time: the abrupt transfer of control from one point in a flow of computer instructions to some other point in the program. This technique was called a GOTO statement, and programmers were using them to interrupt sequences of computer instructions in order to perform a different instruction or set of instructions. GOTO is a generic term for an instruction that causes a program to "go to" some location within itself for its next instruction. GOTO statements, also called "branches" or "transfers," were commonly used in early computer program designs.

In a famous 1968 letter to the editor of *Communications of the ACM,* Dijkstra argued that the ability of programmers to read and understand programs written in high-level languages was severely compromised by the number of GOTO statements in these programs. High-level languages (meant to resemble written English or mathematical statements) are to a certain degree self-documenting; this means that the reader should be able to understand the flow of operations simply by reading the programming statements. The use of GOTO statements interrupts the logical flow, and the composition and interpretation of a program (especially a large one) becomes more difficult as the number of GOTO statements increases. In his letter, entitled by the ACM editors "Go To Statement Considered Harmful," Dijkstra termed the statements as "primitive" in high-level programming languages, calling them "too much an invitation to make a mess of one's program."

The alternative Dijkstra offered he called structured programming. It is a style, or methodology, of programming in which a program is put together by connecting a number of smaller structured programs or program segments. It is easiest to understand structured programming if one thinks of an English sentence containing several difficult words; these words are like GOTO statements. The reader must look up these words in order to understand the sentence, but taking the time to find a word in the dictionary is an interruption, and one tends to lose track of the meaning of the original sentence. If the same sentence were written in a structured fashion, each difficult word would be replaced by an expression that defined it, thus ending the need to look elsewhere for clarification. While it is generally agreed that the idea of structuring programs had supporters before Dijkstra's letter, there is no question that his arguments brought everyone's attention to the issue and led the way to the wide implementation of structured programming.

In 1972 Dijkstra contributed to the book *Notes on Structured Programming,* in which he wrote that "program testing can be used to show the presence of bugs, but never to show their absence!" He advanced the idea that "it is not only the programmer's task to produce a correct program but also to demonstrate its correctness in a convincing manner." In order to provide the proof, the program must be "usefully structured." In Dijkstra's view, every effort must always be made to design programs to be as error-free as possible from the beginning; he believed that this method of design made programs easier to construct and understand. The easier it was to write and comprehend a program, he argued, the easier it was to avoid introducing errors or bugs into it.

Dijkstra left Eindhoven in August of 1973 to accept a position as a research fellow with the Burroughs Corporation. Even though the company was headquar-

tered in Detroit, Michigan, Dijkstra's position allowed him to continue to work and live in his home in Nuenen, a village near Eindhoven in The Netherlands. Burroughs gave Dijkstra great latitude in the use of his time, and he traveled widely during his years with the company, lecturing all over the world and frequently visiting the United States.

In the early 1980s, the intellectual climate at Burroughs changed: the company became more concerned with short-term profits and Dijkstra's colleagues became disenchanted and began to leave. Additionally, Dijkstra's interests were shifting from computers and programming to mathematical methodology in general. He felt it appropriate to return to a university environment, and the University of Texas offered him the Schlumberger Centennial chair in Computer Science.

The vocabulary of computer programmers is far richer for the influence of Dijkstra. He introduced and popularized a number of terms including *go-to-less programming, structured programming, semaphore, guarded command,* and *deadly embrace.* Semaphores are elements used to coordinate the activities of two or more simultaneously running programs that share data. Guarded commands are those that execute conditionally, that is, only when some condition that can be tested for is satisfied. A deadly embrace (also called a deadlock) occurs when a program cannot continue because it is waiting for some event that will never happen.

Dijkstra's philosophy can perhaps best be summarized by a passage from *Notes on Structured Programming:* "My point is that a program is never a goal in itself; the purpose of a program is to evoke computations and the purpose of the computations is to establish a desired effect." He goes on to say that "although the program is the final product made by the programmer, the possible computations evoked by it . . . are the true subject matter of his trade." Programs, in other words, are not ends in themselves but rather means to ends, those ends being correct computations and outcomes. The elegance of a program should increase the ease with which the program can be comprehended and maintained.

In 1972 Dijkstra was presented with the Turing Award. This award is made each year by the Association for Computing Machinery (ACM) as a memorial to A. M. Turing. The award recognized Dijkstra's tremendous influence on programming methodology. In 1974, Dijkstra received the Harry Goode Memorial

Award as recognition of his achievements in the field of information processing.

BIOGRAPHICAL/CRITICAL SOURCES:

BOOKS

Beauty Is Our Business: A Birthday Salute to Edgser W. Dijkstra, edited by W. H. J. Feijen, Springer-Verlag (New York), 1990.
Encyclopedia of Computer Science and Engineering, Van Nostrand Reinhold, 1983, pp. 508, 877-878, 1311, 1348.
Macmillan Encyclopedia of Computers, Macmillan, 1992, pp. 100-101.

OTHER

Dijkstra, E. W., written response to interview questions from Frank Hertle on December 7, 1993.*

*   *   *

DONALD, Diana   1938-

PERSONAL: Born June 3, 1938, in Guildford, England; daughter of Charles (an advertising manager) and Muriel (a homemaker; maiden name, Tucker) Butler; married Trevor Donald (a schoolmaster), February 9, 1963; children: Paul Frederick, Alice Penelope. *Ethnicity:* "White." *Education:* Courtauld Institute of Art, University of London, B.A., 1959. *Politics:* Labour. *Religion:* None. *Avocational interests:* Country walking, natural history.

ADDRESSES: Home—18 Parkfield Rd. S., Manchester M20 6DH, England. *Office*—Department of Art History and Design, Manchester Metropolitan University, Manchester M15 6BG, England; fax 01-61-247-6393.

CAREER: Department of History of Art and Design, Manchester Metropolitan University, Manchester, England, department head, 1986—, professor of art history and design, 1990—. Yale University, visiting fellow at Center for British Art, 1987. Manchester University Press, member of editorial board. Higher Education Funding Council, panelist, 1996.

MEMBER: Royal Society of Arts (fellow), Association of Art Historians, British Society for Eighteenth-Century Studies.

AWARDS, HONORS: Leverhulme fellow, 1990.

WRITINGS:

The Age of Caricature: Satirical Prints in the Reign of George III, Yale University Press (New Haven, CT), 1996.

Contributor to journals, including *Art History.*

WORK IN PROGRESS: Editing *Gillroy Observed,* publication by Cambridge University Press (Cambridge, England) expected in 1998; research for a major book on attitudes to animals in eighteenth-century England.

SIDELIGHTS: Diana Donald told *CA:* "I came to research and publication late in my career, which has been interrupted by family responsibilities. An avid interest in eighteenth-century history combined with my interest in the history of cartooning produced *The Age of Caricature,* which was the result of about ten years of thought on the subject. I found it surprising that caricaturists as brilliant as Gillroy and Rowlandson should have been so little discussed and interpreted, and I went back to the earliest commentaries on their prints and to other primary records of the period in order to gain insight into contemporary attitudes and responses to their work.

"My principal aim is to understand the characteristics of visual art in a historical and political light, and I enjoy working between disciplines and across a broad cultural field. I am now embarking on research, on attitudes to the animal kingdom from about 1750 to 1830, which will embrace aspects such as natural history and science, exploration, the history of reforming movements and humane societies, and will attempt to relate these to visual expression and style in paintings, prints, and scientific illustrations."

*   *   *

**DORRIS, Michael (Anthony)   1945-1997
(Michael A. Dorris)**

OBITUARY NOTICE—See index for *CA* sketch: Born January 30, 1945, in Louisville, KY; died following an apparent suicide, April 11, 1997, in Concord, NH. Author, essayist, and educator. Dorris' award-winning 1989 book, *The Broken Cord: A Father's Story,* which detailed his son's battle with fetal alcohol syndrome, brought international attention to the problem and led to new alcohol labeling laws. But the educated man who worked to improve the lives of others killed himself in a New Hampshire motel after learning that he was the target of a sex abuse investigation in Minneapolis and charges were likely. His estranged wife, author Louise Erdrich, told the *New York Times* that Dorris had a secret depression problem, hardly slept the last year of his life and had attempted suicide before the investigation. Dorris was educated at Georgetown and Yale University and founded Dartmouth College's Native American Studies Program. He was also a professor and department chair at Dartmouth. Dorris was of mixed Native American, Irish, and French ancestry and his first two books—*Native Americans: Five Hundred Years After* (1977) and (as Michael A. Dorris, along with Arlene Hirschfelder and Mary Gloyne Byler) *A Guide to Research on North American Indians* (1983)—dealt with the subject of his studies and teaching. His first novel, *A Yellow Raft in Blue Water* was published in 1987. But his breakthrough book, *The Broken Cord: A Father's Story* (1989), was a nonfiction work of a personal nature—his adopted son's lifelong struggle of living with brain damage brought on by his mother's drinking. It won the National Book Award, among others, and inspired Congress to draft legislation requiring warning labels on alcoholic beverages. Dorris and his wife also found literary success together with their co-written books *Route Two and Back* and *The Crown of Columbus* (both in 1991). For young adults, Dorris wrote *Morning Girl* (1992) and *Guests* (1995). His other works included *Rooms in the House of Stone, Working Men* (both in 1993), and *Paper Trail: Collected Essays, 1967-1992* (1994). He had been working on a follow-up to *Broken Chord* entitled *Matter of Conscience*. Besides his teaching and writing career, Dorris also served on the U.S. Advisory Committee on Infant Mortality, was a member of the National Indian Education Association, the American Association for the Advancement of Science and was a board member of the Save the Children Foundation. He was also a consultant to the National Endowment for the Humanities. *Broken Chord* was made into a television movie and Dorris appeared on numerous radio and television programs.

OBITUARIES AND OTHER SOURCES:

PERIODICALS

Los Angeles Times, April 15, 1997, p. A18.
New York Times, April 15, 1997, p. B11; April 16, 1997, p. A12; April 18, 1997, p. A14.

DORRIS, Michael A.
See DORRIS, Michael (Anthony)

* * *

DOUGLAS, (George) Norman   1868-1952
(Normyx, a joint pseudonym; Pilaff Bey, a pseudonym)

PERSONAL: Born December 8, 1868, in Thuringen, Vorarlberg, Germany; died February 9, 1952, in Capri, Italy; son of John Sholto (a manager of cotton mills) and Vanda (von Poelnitz) Douglass; married Elizabeth Theobaldina FitzGibbon in 1898 (divorced, 1904); children: Robin, one other son. *Education:* Attended Karlsruhe Gymnasium, Germany, 1883-89. *Avocational interests:* Travel, music, natural history.

CAREER: British novelist, travel writer, and memoirist. Entered British Foreign Office in 1893; appointed to British Embassy, St. Petersburg, Russia, 1894-96, becoming Third Secretary. Assistant editor of *English Review,* 1912-15.

WRITINGS:

NOVELS, UNLESS OTHERWISE NOTED

(With wife, Elizabeth Douglas, as Normyx) *Unprofessional Tales* (stories), [London], 1901.
South Wind, M. Secker (London), 1917, Dodd, Mead (New York City), 1928, with an introduction by Dorothy Scarborough, Macmillan (New York City), 1929.
They Went, Chapman & Hall (London), 1920, Dodd, Mead, 1921.
In the Beginning, [London], 1927, John Day (New York City), 1928.
The Angel of Manfredonia, Windsor Press (San Francisco), 1929.

TRAVEL

Siren Land, Dutton (New York City), 1911, with *Fountains in the Sand,* Secker & Warburg (London), 1957.
Fountains in the Sand: Rambles among the Oases of Tunisia, M. Secker, 1912, Oxford University Press (New York City), 1986, with *Siren Land,* Secker & Warburg, 1957.
Old Calabria, Houghton (Boston), 1915, with an introduction by John Davenport, Penguin (London),

1962, with an introduction by Jonathan Keates, Picador Travel Classics, (London), 1984.

Alone, Chapman & Hall (London), 1921.

Together, Chapman & Hall, 1923.

One Day, [London], 1929, published in *Three of Them,* Chatto & Windus (London), 1930.

Nerinda, John Day, 1929, published in *Three of Them,* Chatto & Windus, 1930.

Three of Them (includes "On the Herpetology of the Grand Duchy of Baden," "Nerinda," and "One Day"), Chatto & Windus, 1930.

Summer Islands, Ischia and Ponzo, Colophon (New York City), 1931.

Footnotes on Capri, with photographs by Islay Lyons, Sidgwick & Jackson (London), 1952.

Contributor of travel articles and essays to journals, including *Zoologist.*

OTHER

(As G. Norman Douglass) *On the Darwinian Hypothesis of Sexual Selection* (originally published in *Natural Science,* Volume 7, numbers 45 and 46, 1895), Rait, Henderson & Co. (London), 1896.

London Street Games, St. Catherine Press (London), 1916, revised and enlarged, Chatto & Windus, 1931, Singing Tree Press (Detroit), 1968.

D. H. Lawrence and Maurice Magnus: A Plea for Better Manners, privately published (Florence, Italy), 1924, Haskell House (New York City), 1973.

Experiments (essays, sketches, and short stories; includes *D. H Lawrence and Maurice Magnus: A Plea for Better Manners*), R. M. McBride (New York City), 1925.

Birds & Beasts of the Greek Anthology, privately published (Florence, Italy), 1927, Chapman & Hall, 1928, J. Cape/H. Smith (New York City), 1929.

How about Europe?, privately published (Florence, Italy), 1929, as *Good-Bye to Western Culture: Some Footnotes on East and West,* Harper & Brothers (New York City), 1929.

Paneros: Some Words on Aphrodisiacs and the Like, privately published (Florence, Italy), 1930, Chatto & Windus, 1931, R. M. McBride, 1932.

Materials for a Description of Capri (monographs), privately published, 1930, published as *Materials for a Description of the Island,* [London], 1931.

Looking Back: An Autobiographical Excursion (autobiography), Chatto & Windus, 1934, Harcourt, Brace, 1971.

Late Harvest, L. Drummond (London), 1946, AMS Press (New York City), 1977.

(Editor, as Pilaff Bey) *Venus in the Kitchen, or Love's Cookery Book,* Heinemann (London), 1952, as *Lovers' Cookbook,* with an introduction by Graham Greene, New English Library (London), 1971.

(Compiler) *The Norman Douglas Limerick Book: Collected for the Use of Students, & Ensplendour'd with Introduction, Geographical Index, and with Notes Explanatory and Critical* (bawdy verse), Blond (London), 1969, as *Some Limericks, Collected for the Use of Students, & Ensplendour'd with Introduction, Geographical Index, and with Notes Explanatory and Critical,* Grove Press (New York City), 1970.

SIDELIGHTS: Norman Douglas is known primarily for his bestselling novel *South Wind,* which, with its sophisticated, ironic view of the leisure class of Europe in the years just prior to World War I, presaged the novels of disillusionment that became fashionable after the war. A few other works from his varied *oeuvre,* however, are considered to stand at least equal to *South Wind,* especially the Mediterranean travel books that he wrote during the 1910s. All Douglas's works reflect the complex life of a widely traveled man who was born to privilege but sometimes fell into poverty, who was ahead of his time in his mores, and who maintained an aristocratic sense of standards.

The author was born George Norman Douglass in the city of Thuringen, Germany, in 1868. Noble bloodlines characterized both sides of his family: his mother was the daughter of a German baron, and his father was a son of John Douglass, fourteenth laird of Tilquhillie, Scotland. There was affluence, too: Douglas's father engaged in the lucrative occupation of managing cotton mills in Germany for his father. Douglas (he dropped the second *s* in his surname, as well as the first name George, when he was about forty), spoke German before he learned English. When he was six years old, his father was killed in an accident; after his mother remarried, the family moved to the British Isles. This change of culture did not sit well with young Douglas; rebelling against the English public school system, he was sent back to Germany for "gymnasium" (high school), where he entertained a passion for natural history as well as pursuing a traditional curriculum in the classics and the arts. After leaving school in 1888, twenty-year-old Douglas toured Italy. This would be the author's first of many visits to Capri, the island off the Neapolitan coast where he was to spend many years of his life.

Douglas's initial choice of career was the Foreign Service, and under its auspices he moved to St. Petersburg, the Russian capital, in 1894, and eventually attained the rank of Third Secretary. While in the Foreign Service Douglas produced an official report criticizing child labor practices in Italy, which he later claimed had a major effect on eliminating child labor abuses in that country. He resigned from the Foreign Service after three years, and bought an Italian villa in Posillipo, on the Bay of Naples. He was married in 1898 to his cousin Elizabeth, known as Elsa. The couple would have two sons.

Douglas's first literary book, a collaboration between he and his wife, was the 1901 work *Unprofessional Tales,* published under the pen name Normyx. The couple also traveled together in Tunisia and India before divorcing in 1904. By now approaching forty years of age, Douglas then moved to Capri, where he spent several stressful years. In 1907, three years after his divorce from Elsa, he experienced a severe financial loss. In response, he sold his Capri property and embarked on a serious writing career.

Douglas wrote travel articles about Italy and Tunisia, which were collected in three books that have since become minor classics: *Siren Land* (1911), *Fountains in the Sand* (1912), and *Old Calabria* (1915), which deal respectively with the Sorrentino peninsula of Italy, with Tunisia, and with Calabria, the "toe" of Italy's "boot." According to D. M. Low in the *Dictionary of National Biography 1951-1960,* this triptych is "generally recognized as his finest achievement," owing to the extensive personal and research-based knowledge that Douglas brought to bear upon his subjects. Low discerns the character of Douglas clearly in these works, and describes the central feature of that character as "anti-asceticism and a ruthless denunciation of 'crooked thinking.'"

Douglas's three travel books were not commercially successful upon their initial publication—Low points out that *Siren Land* was published only with the help of recommendations from authors Joseph Conrad and Edward Garnett—but the books helped their author obtain an assistant editorship at the prestigious *English Review.* While at the *Review,* he met several literary figures, including D. H. Lawrence, with whom he later quarreled, prompting the occasion for Douglas' slim 1924 book, *D. H. Lawrence and Maurice Magnus,* which contains, according to Low, "brilliant invective." Another nonfiction book Douglas issued during his London years was *London*

Street Games, a 1916 work on childhood whose topic is precisely what the title advertises.

Douglas left England in 1916 and went to Capri to begin work on a novel that would become *South Wind.* At this point he was living the life of an exile or expatriate. He was, as Low describes him from personal knowledge, tall, distinguished, fastidious in dress and manners: a lover of the good life, whose charm appealed to both men and women. Sometimes, however, this adventurous lifestyle, which did not include a regular, paying job, left Douglas without sustenance for periods of time, such as the two years he spent in France after the completion of his novel. Indeed, although *South Wind* was an instant hit upon its publication in 1917, its author was not able to reap the financial rewards at first; Low comments, "he was unable [in 1918] to continue his next novel . . . for want of food." Nevertheless, fame and fortune caught up to him soon enough.

South Wind became the talked-about novel of 1918. It depicts a group of flamboyant characters on the imaginary Mediterranean island of Nepenthe; through this cast of eccentrics, Douglas satirically examines the differences between Northern and Southern Europe. The novel provided, according to the *Cyclopedia of World Authors,* "escape literature of a highly sophisticated kind," marked by "polish, urbanity, and a gentle cynicism." Douglas's name was made, and he soon found himself in the financial position to begin work on a second novel, which would be published in 1920 as *They Went.*

The following year, a travel book, *Alone,* emerged—it was Douglas' favorite book, according to Low. *Alone* was followed by 1923's *Together,* a reminiscence of Douglas' German childhood, and then a collection of occasional nonfiction and fiction pieces, the 1925 work *Experiments.* Reviewing the latter volume for the *Yale Review,* Joseph Warren Beach discerned Douglas' traits of "abhorrence of the commonplace," as well as "learning and irony . . . pithiness and downrightness of expression, and an enthusiasm for honesty, intelligence, and beauty, which give flavor to everything he writes."

Although Beach saw *Experiments* as a mixed bag, he singled out some pieces as worthy additions to English literature: a review of Charles Doughty's classic *Travels in Arabia Deserta,* a group of reviews titled "Theology," the booklet on Lawrence and Magnus, and three short stories, notably "At the Forge." Beach asserted that although Douglas was indifferent to principles of fictive craftsmanship, the inherent strength of his tales overcame that weakness.

Now living in Florence in the company of a devoted friend, Giuseppe (Pino) Oriloi, who also published Douglas' works in limited editions, the novelist entered a period of relative calm, which was to last till 1937. He became acquainted with numerous well-known writers, and published an autobiography, 1933's *Looking Back.* Douglas left Florence for France in 1937, fled to Lisbon in 1940—presumably, according to his biographers, to escape the war—returned to England, and finally settled again on his beloved Capri from 1946 until his death in 1952.

Douglas' postwar books included *Late Harvest,* a largely autobiographical commentary on the world as the aging Douglas experienced it. Douglas never recaptured the high popular peak of *South Wind,* but that novel remains available in many public libraries and has been reissued—as have some of his nonfiction titles—repeatedly over the years. His work and his personality, which formed a whole, remain memorable, for, as Low puts it, "His great humanity made him a foe to all cruelty and stupidity, and he won the friendship of the most diverse types of people."

BIOGRAPHICAL/CRITICAL SOURCES:

BOOKS

Leary, Lewis, *Norman Douglas,* Columbia University Press, 1968.

Magill, Frank, editor, *Cyclopedia of World Authors,* Harper, 1958, pp. 311-312.

Tomlinson, Henry, *Norman Douglas,* M. S. G. House (London), 1974.

Williams, E. T., and Helen M. Palmer, editors, *Dictionary of National Biography 1951-1960,* Oxford University Press, 1971, pp. 307-08.

Woolf, Cecil, *A Bibliography of Norman Douglas,* R. Hart-Davis (London), 1954.

PERIODICALS

Cornhill Magazine, summer 1955.

D. H. Lawrence Review, vol. 9, 1976, pp. 283-95.

Journal of Modern Literature, vol. 2, 1972, pp. 342-56.

Kenyon Review, autumn 1952, p. 660.

Sewanee Review, vol. 15, 1932, pp. 55-67.

South Atlantic Quarterly, April 1950, p. 226.

Spectator, vol. 117, 1946, p. 684.

Yale Review, vol. 16, 1926, p. 378; January 1927, pp. 378-81.*

DRAPER, Charles Stark 1901-1987

PERSONAL: Born October 2, 1901, in Windsor, MO; died July 25, 1987, in Cambridge, MA; son of Arthur (a dentist) and Martha Washington (a former school teacher; maiden name, Stark) Draper; married Ivy Willard, September 7, 1938; children: James, Martha, Michael, John. *Education:* Attended University of Missouri, 1917, and Herald's Radio College; Stanford University, B.A. (psychology); Massachusetts Institute of Technology, B.S. (electrochemical engineering), 1926, M.S., 1928, D.Sc., 1938.

CAREER: Aeronautical engineer and educator. Instrumentation Laboratory (now Charles Stark Draper Laboratory), Massachusetts Institute of Technology, Cambridge, MA, director, 1939-73, professor 1939-51, chair of aeronautical engineering department, 1951-66, senior scientist, 1973-87.

AWARDS, HONORS: Sylvanus Albert Reed award, 1945; National Medal of Science, 1964; Foundation Medal, National Academy of Engineering, 1970; Holley Medal, American Society of Mechanical Engineers, 1971.

WRITINGS:

(With Sidney Lees and Walter McKay) *Instrument Engineering,* McGraw-Hill, 1952.
(With Walter Wrigley and John Hovorka) *Inertial Guidance,* Pergamon, 1960.

SIDELIGHTS: Charles Stark Draper was a pioneering engineer who developed advanced weapons technologies and sophisticated navigational and guidance systems. His most important scientific contribution was in the field of automatic control systems for piloting, specifically his inertial guidance system. This system successfully implemented completely automatic navigation, with applications that reached from the depths of the oceans in the Polaris submarine to the Apollo moon mission. An avid private pilot, Draper was first drawn to engineering by his navigator's interest in flight instrumentation. During World War II, Draper and colleagues in his lab at the Massachusetts Institute of Technology (MIT) developed the Mark 14 gun sight for use on U.S. battleships. Using gyroscopes to correct for target motion in flight, the gun sight is credited with successfully thwarting attacks of Japanese Kamikaze pilots. Draper spent almost his entire career at MIT and took great pride in his role as an educator who spurred his students on to significant scientific research efforts. Despite his stolid appearance as a bespectacled engineer, Draper was, at least academically, a free thinker. His interests in a variety of subjects gave rise to an MIT legend that he had taken more courses for credit than anyone else in the school's history.

Draper was born on October 2, 1901, in Windsor, Missouri, a small town near Kansas City. His father, Arthur Draper, was a dentist; his mother, Martha Washington (Stark) Draper, was a former schoolteacher. After graduating from the Windsor public school system, Draper enrolled in the University of Missouri in Columbia in 1917 with intentions of studying medicine. When Draper's parents moved to California, Draper transferred to Stanford University, where he obtained his bachelor of arts degree in psychology. But instead of enrolling in medical school, Draper decided to become a ship's radio operator and enrolled in Herald's Radio College. After finishing at Herald's, he traveled back East with a friend who was going to Harvard University. Draper liked Cambridge, Massachusetts, and decided to enroll at MIT.

In 1926, Draper earned his bachelor of science degree in electrochemical engineering at MIT. Still, he hesitated to commit himself to one field of study. His wide-ranging interests included mathematics, chemistry, physics, metallurgy, and aeronautical engineering. In 1928, despite not having earned enough credits in any one field for a master's degree, the university awarded him a master of science degree without departmental specification. The following year the university appointed him as a research assistant in aeronautical engineering. As he became more focused, Draper's superior intellect began to shine. Continuing his studies in pursuit of a doctorate, Draper took a new course in hydro- and aerodynamics conducted by Julius A. Stratton. "It would be difficult to say whether it was teacher or student in the course of that winter who learned most from the other," said Stratton in *Air, Space, and Instruments,* a volume of essays that celebrated Draper's sixtieth birthday.

Draper continued to pursue a wide range of interests and gained renown at MIT as the person to take the most credits ever at the school without receiving a doctorate. Eventually, MIT insisted that Draper finish his doctoral studies. In 1938, he received his doctor of science degree, twenty-one years after he first enrolled at a college.

In addition to his studies at MIT, Draper had gained his private pilot's license through the Army Air Corps reserve flight school in 1926. Draper's early interest

in flying combined with his diligence and "bulldog" tenacity in thinking a problem through led him to make many inroads into aeronautical engineering. In *Air, Space, and Instruments,* Stratton recalled one particularly harrowing demonstration in which Draper finally convinced his instructor to fly with him in an open cockpit as he demonstrated how more sophisticated airplane instrumentation could prevent stalling and spinning in blind flying. To prove his point, Draper nosed the plane up to make it stall and then took it on a nose dive. "It occurred to me that I had left a good many things undone and that the Department would be hard put to find someone to teach mechanics," Stratton recalled. Fortunately for both men, Draper's "practical demonstration" was a success as the plane leveled out and the two safely concluded their flight.

The year after he received his doctorate, Draper was appointed a professor and given the helm of MIT's Instrumentation Laboratory. Working with Jimmy Doolittle, Elmer Sperry, and the Sperry Gyroscope Company, which provided support for his research, Draper completed a project to develop a new gyroscopic rate of turn indicator for navigational purposes. Despite the project's success, the indicator did not seem to have immediate practical applications. However, when the United States entered World War II, Draper's rate-of-turn indicator proved to be the stepping stone for a high-tech gyroscopic gun sight. In *The Eagle Has Returned,* Brigadier General Robert Duffy wrote that Draper's "gun sight would correct for 'Kentucky Windage,' or target motion in flight, and became the basis for the new technological field of aided tracking fire control."

Based on high-precision rate-measuring gyros, Draper used "damping," or rotors immersed in viscous fluid, to develop the Mark 14 gun sight, which semiautomatically adjusted for range, wind, and ballistics relying on deck coordinates as reference axes rather than complicated gyro-stabilized references. Draper's "black box" gun sight with moving cross-hairs proved to be an effective antiaircraft gun sight for ships and was used on a wide variety of antiaircraft weaponry. Draper's Instrumentation Laboratory was staffed by several hundred people at the height of World War II. For his engineering efforts during the war, Draper was awarded the Sylvanus Albert Reed Award in 1945. After the war, Draper continued to work on control systems for military purposes, including a sight control system for U.S. Air Force F-86 fighter planes during the Korean War in the early 1950s; he later also worked on missile fire control systems.

As Draper systematically improved upon his control systems, primarily through advances in gyroscopic instrumentation, he began to pursue his long-held belief that these gyroscopic-based systems could be used to develop a revolutionary guidance system. Working with the Air Force Armament laboratory, Draper and his colleagues at the Instrumentation Laboratory began work on an inertial guidance system. This ultimate navigational system would require no outside reference points, such as radio signals or celestial guides. In addition to increasing safety by effectively eliminating many aeronautical guidance problems due to such circumstances as bad weather conditions, the system would become a vital development for space exploration.

Draper's diverse background at MIT served him well as he oversaw a group of researchers and doctoral students in interdisciplinary research that combined geometry, kinematics, and dynamics with aerodynamics, electronics, and mechanics. Based on his gun sight systems of World War II, which used the single-degree-of-freedom integrating gyro floating in a viscous fluid, Draper developed an improved gyro accelerometer that could accurately measure acceleration and velocity, as well as distance, or position. Essentially, the inertial guidance system used three friction-free gyros that responded to motion on one axis only to develop a computerized system that could measure and "remember" a plotted course, taking into account such factors as the earth's rotation. Draper's device, sometimes referred to as "astronomy in a closet" was ultimately connected to instruments that recorded the plane's altitude and direction, thus effectively creating a self-contained system for guidance.

Draper's inertial guidance system could be applied both to naval and aeronautical craft. Despite Draper's engineering credentials, many engineers and others doubted whether his invention would really work; after all, it represented a virtual revolution in the ancient art of navigation. With a flair for the dramatic, to which Draper's early teacher Stratton could attest, Draper set out on a flight from Bedford, Massachusetts, to Los Angeles, California, using only his inertial navigation system to guide the plane on its journey. With an Air Force piloting crew and seven other MIT engineers, Draper took off on February 8, 1953, in a B-29 for a twelve-hour flight that amazed all those aboard. Without anyone touching the controls, the plane flew across the continental United States, adjusting for altitude and direction as it sped across the Midwest, over the Rocky Mountains, and to within ten miles of the Los Angeles International Airport, where the crew took over.

Because of the significant military applications of his system, the general public did not learn of the historic flight until 1957. But during those intervening years, the military supported Draper as he developed more sophisticated inertial guidance systems for submarines, missiles, and manned aircraft. The submarine inertial navigation system (SINS) was unveiled in 1954 and was eventually used to guide the Navy's Polaris submarines as well as the Polaris missiles. Further development of SINS and SPIRE (Space Inertial Reference Equipment) brought about even more sophisticated inertial guidance systems for use in military craft, including bombers, jet fighters, and submarines. By the 1970s commercial aircraft were also being equipped with inertial guidance systems.

The most dramatic use of Draper's guidance system, however, was initiated in 1961 when Draper and colleagues in his laboratory at MIT began designing a guidance and control system for the Apollo spacecraft missions to the moon. Despite his success with the system so far, many doubted Draper's ability to devise such a system for space flight. Despite his advancing years, Draper proposed that he would be the logical choice to go on an Apollo mission, since he had the most intimate knowledge of the system. Although NASA turned down his offer to go along on the flight (reportedly arousing Draper's anger), the entire world was witness to Draper's engineering genius as millions watched the televised landing of a man on the moon and the safe splashdown of the capsule that returned the astronauts to earth.

In honor of Draper, the MIT Instrumentation Laboratory was renamed the Charles Stark Draper Laboratory, and the National Academy of Engineering created the Charles Stark Draper Prize in 1988. Draper's career in MIT included an appointment as chairman of the aeronautical engineering department from 1951 to 1966. He was appointed a senior scientist at the laboratory in 1973. Among his many honors were the Holley Medal of the American Society of Mechanical Engineers in 1971, the National Medal of Science in 1964, and the Foundation Medal of the National Academy of Engineering in 1970.

Draper married Ivy Willard on September 7, 1938, and had four children: James, Martha, Michael, and John. He died on July 25, 1987, in Cambridge, Massachusetts.

BIOGRAPHICAL/CRITICAL SOURCES:

BOOKS

Current Biography, H. W. Wilson, 1965, pp. 130-32.

Duffy, Robert, *The Eagle Has Returned,* American Astronautical Society, 1976.

Lees, Sidney, editor, *Air Space, and Instruments,* McGraw-Hill, 1963.

McGraw-Hill Modern Engineers and Scientists, McGraw-Hill, 1980, pp. 307-308.

Wolko, Howard S., *In the Cause of Flight: Technologists of Aeronautics and Astronautics,* Smithsonian Institution, 1981, pp. 112-13.

PERIODICALS

Readers Digest, 1957, vol. 73, pp. 63-67.*

*   *   *

DRESSELHAUS, Mildred S.   1930-

PERSONAL: Born November 11, 1930, in Brooklyn, NY; daughter of Meyer and Ethel (Teichteil) Spiewak; married Gene F. Dresselhaus, May 25, 1958; children: Marianne Dresselhaus Cooper, Carl Eric, Paul David, Eliot Michael. *Education:* Hunter College, New York City, A.B. (with high honors), 1951; attended Cambridge University (Fulbright fellow), 1951-52; Radcliffe College, Cambridge, MA, A.M., 1953; University of Chicago, Ph.D., 1958.

CAREER: Physicist. Massachusetts Institute of Technology, Cambridge, MA, staff member of Lincoln Laboratory, 1960-67, professor, 1967—, associate department head of electrical science and engineering, 1972-83, director of Center of Material Science and Engineering, 1977-83, professor of physics, 1983—, institute professor, 1985—. National Research Council, Committee on the Education and Employment of Women in Science and Engineering, member; National Academy of Sciences, Executive Committee of Physics and Math Sciences, 1975-78, English section, chairperson, 1987-90; National Bureau of Standards, Steering Committee Evaluation Panels, chairperson, 1978-83; American Physical Society, president, 1984. Visiting professor at numerous universities and colleges, including: University of Campinas, Brazil, 1971; Technion Israel Institute of Technology, Haifa, 1972; Nihon and Aoyama Gakuin Universities, Tokyo, 1973; IVIC, Caracas, Venezu-

ela, 1977; and University of California, Berkeley, 1985.

MEMBER: National Academy of Engineering, Society of Women Engineers.

AWARDS, HONORS: Fellow, National Science Foundation, 1958-60; Abby Rockefeller Mauze Visiting Professor, M.I.T., 1967; Hall of Fame, Hunter College, 1972; Alumnae medal, Radcliffe College, 1973; Achievement Award, Society of Women Engineers, 1977; Graffin Lecturer, 1982; Killian Faculty Achievement award, 1986-87; Hund-Klemm lecturer, Max Planck Institute, 1988; Annual Achievement Award, Engineering Society of New England, 1988; National Medal of Science, 1990; numerous honorary doctorates from universities, including Worcester Polytechnic Institute, Smith College, New Jersey Institute of Technology, University Catholique de Louvain, Rutgers University, University of Connecticut, University of Massachusetts, Princeton University, Colorado School of Mines, Technion Israel Institute of Technology, Johannes Kepler University, and Harvard University.

WRITINGS:

(With others) *Intercalated Graphite,* North-Holland (New York), 1983.

Intercalation in Layered Materials, Plenum Press (New York), 1986.

(With Gene Dresselhaus, K. Sugihara, I. L. Spain, and H. A. Goldberg) *Graphite Fibers and Filaments,* Springer-Verlag (New York), 1988.

(With R. Kalish) *Ion Implantation in Diamond, Graphite, and Related Materials,* Springer-Verlag, 1992.

(With G. Dresselhaus and P. C. Eklund) *Physical Properties of Fullerenes,* Academic Press (San Diego), 1993.

(With G. Dresselhaus and P. C. Eklund) *Science of Fullernes and Carbon Nanotubes,* Academic Press, 1996.

Contributor of articles to periodicals.

SIDELIGHTS: Born during the Depression to a poor immigrant family, Mildred S. Dresselhaus possessed a natural intelligence and love of science that brought her recognition in the field of solid state physics. She has contributed a great deal of new knowledge about the electronic properties of many materials, particularly semi-metals such as graphite, and was the recipient of the National Medal of Science in 1990. Her public service includes work on behalf of the National Research Council and the National Science Foundation.

Mildred Spiewak Dresselhaus was born on November 11, 1930, in Brooklyn, New York; her father was a journalist. As a child, she worked in sweatshops and factories to help with family expenses. At age eleven, she spent one year teaching a mentally retarded child how to read and write. In helping the child, she found her first insight into her future—in education. Dresselhaus' ambition then was to become an elementary school teacher. Her other love was music, and she and her talented brother received free violin lessons from philanthropic organizations which served as an introduction to the world of education.

Dresselhaus' parents encouraged her natural love of learning, and she studied diligently for an entrance exam for Hunter College High School—a girls' preparatory school associated with Hunter College in New York. She not only passed the exam, she did so with a perfect score in mathematics. Dresselhaus struggled at the school initially because her prior education was meager. She also had a difficult time socially among upper-middle-class schoolmates and their families. But her drive, intelligence and wit carried her through these early challenges. She excelled in high school and, with the help of a state scholarship, entered Hunter College, where she was graduated with highest honors in 1951. By that time, she was preparing for a career in physics.

Dresselhaus then accepted a Fulbright Fellowship and performed graduate studies at Newnham, the women's college of Cambridge University. After returning from England, where she had benefited from her studies as well as the new friendships she formed, she earned a master of science degree in physics from Radcliffe College in Massachusetts. Upon her graduation from Radcliffe in 1953, Dresselhaus entered the prestigious doctoral program in physics at the University of Chicago. Solid state physics, the specialty which addresses matter in a condensed state, was in its infancy. The transistor had just been developed, and pioneers in the field were researching practical applications of semiconductors. In her graduate research, Dresselhaus explored the activities of superconductors. She found that some materials are excellent conductors of current at extremely low temperatures. She wrote two papers, "Magnetic Field Dependence of High-Frequency Penetration into a Super-Conductor" and "Magnetic Field Dependence of the Surface Impedance of Superconducting Tin," in 1958

and 1959, respectively, which were significant contributions to an area that few had begun to investigate.

Soon after receiving her doctorate degree, she married a colleague, solid state physicist Gene Dresselhaus. In 1958, she accepted a postdoctoral appointment as a National Science Foundation Fellow at Cornell University, while he became a junior faculty member there. Two years later, following the birth of her first child, Dresselhaus accepted a staff position at Lincoln Laboratory, a part of Massachusetts Institute of Technology that at that time specialized in semiconductors. Her husband also obtained a position there. Around that same time, a revolutionary development occurred in physics: the invention of integrated circuits, which would later be used in computers, automobile electronics, and entertainment systems. Dresselhaus began focusing on this area, examining the transport of electrons in high magnetic fields.

While at Lincoln Laboratory, where she remained until 1967, Dresselhaus resumed her study of low temperature superconductors. She researched the behavior of various materials at temperatures as low as negative 250 degrees Celsius—the point at which hydrogen gas liquifies. She inquired into why semiconductors carry electrical current at room temperature, and applied what she discovered to further study. Dresselhaus also embarked on a study of semimetals—materials such as arsenic and graphite. These semimetals were shown to have properties in common with semiconductors and even superconductors. Dresselhaus' work on the structure of graphite (a form of pure carbon) was extremely original and earned her the respect of her colleagues. Apart from her academic life, Dresselhaus had three more children during the 1960s.

Dresselhaus was named Abby Rockefeller Mauze Visiting Professor in 1967, and the following year received a full professorship at M.I.T. She served as associate department head of electrical science and engineering from 1972 to 1974, and director of the Center of Material Science and Engineering from 1977 to 1983. In 1973, she became permanent holder of the Abby Rockefeller Mauze Chair, and in 1983, she was named professor of physics. Two years later, she was named institute professor, a lifetime honor conferred on no more than twelve active professors at M.I.T. Beginning in the 1980s she and her associates investigated the properties of carbon, finding it to harbor hollow clusters, each containing sixty atoms. Today scientists are experimenting with these clusters—known as Buckminster Fullerenes, or "Bucky-balls," on account of their shape—for their potential use as a delivery system for drugs, and as an extremely strong form of wire tubing.

The challenges Dresselhaus faced as a prominent physicist and mother of four children caused her to become an advocate of women scientists. When her children were small, she had met with a lack of support from her male colleagues, and as a result she worked with other female colleagues at M.I.T. to expand the admission opportunities for women at the Institute. She also began a Women's Forum to explore solutions for difficulties faced by working women. Her initiative in this forum led to her appointment to the Committee on the Education and Employment of Women in Science and Engineering, part of the National Research Council's Commission on Human Resources.

Concurrent with her work at M.I.T., Dresselhaus has held numerous advisory and service positions. She was a member of the National Academy of Sciences' Executive Committee of Physics and Math Sciences from 1975 to 1978. She chaired the Steering Committee Evaluation Panels of the National Bureau of Standards from 1978 to 1983. She served as President of the American Physical Society in 1984. She chaired the English Section of the National Academy of Sciences from 1987 to 1990, and is a member of the National Academy of Engineering, as well as a senior member of the Society of Women Engineers.

Dresselhaus has received many honors. In 1977, she received the Society of Women Engineers Annual Achievement Award "for significant contributions in teaching and research in solid state electronics and materials engineering." In addition, she was a visiting Professor at the University of Campinas in Brazil in 1971, and at the Technion Israel Institute of Technology in Haifa. She also was Hund-Klemm Lecturer at the Max Planck Institute in Stuttgart, Germany, and received the Annual Achievement Award from the English Societies of New England, both in 1988. In 1990, Dresselhaus was awarded the prestigious National Medal of Science.

Her lifetime of achievements in the field of solid state physics might have surprised some who knew of her early circumstances, but Dresselhaus has no regrets. "All the hardships I encountered," she has said, as quoted in Iris Noble's *Contemporary Women Scientists of America,* "provided me with the determination, capacity for hard work, efficiency, and a posi-

tive outlook on life that have been so helpful to me in realizing my professional career."

BIOGRAPHICAL/CRITICAL SOURCES:

BOOKS

Noble, Iris, *Contemporary Women Scientists of America,* Julian Messner, pp. 138-51.

PERIODICALS

Lear's, March, 1994, pp. 56-61, 82-83.*

*   *   *

DRUCKER, Daniel Charles 1918-

PERSONAL: Born June 3, 1918, in New York, NY; son of Moses Abraham (a civil engineer) and Mabelle (Breschel) Drucker; married Ann Bodin, August 19, 1939; children: R. David, Mady Upham. *Education:* Columbia University (New York City), B.S., 1937, C.E., 1938, Ph.D., 1940.

CAREER: Mechanical engineer. Cornell University, Ithaca, New York, instructor in engineering, 1940-43; Armour Research Foundation, Illinois Institute of Technology, Chicago, supervisor of mechanics of solids, 1943-45, assistant professor of mechanics, 1946-47; Brown University, 1947-64, became full professor, 1950, chair of Division of Engineering, 1953-59, chair of Physical Sciences Council, 1961-63, L. Herbert Ballou University Professor, 1964-68; University of Illinois, Urbana-Champaign, Dean of College of Engineering, 1968-84; University of Florida, Gainesville, graduate research professor of aerospace, 1984—. U.S. National Committee on Theoretical and Applied Mechanics, chair. *Military service:* Served briefly in U.S. Army Air Corps.

MEMBER: American Academy of Arts and Sciences, National Academy of Engineering, American Society of Mechanics, International Union of Theoretical and Applied Mechanics, American Society for Engineering Education, American Society of Mechanical Engineers, AAAS.

AWARDS, HONORS: Guggenheim Fellow, 1960-61; von Karman Medal, American Society of Civil Engineers, 1966; Lamme Medal, 1967, Hall of Fame, 1993, both from American Society for Engineering

Education; Max M. Frocht Award, Society for Experimental Stress Analysis, 1967; Thomas Egleston Medal, Columbia University School of Engineering and Applied Science, 1978; Gustave Trosenster Medal, University of Liege, Belgium, 1979; Timoshenko Medal, American Society of Mechanical Engineers, 1983; National Medal of Science, 1988; ASME Medal, 1992. Awarded several honorary degrees from universities, including: Lehigh University, 1976; Israel Institute of Technology, 1983; Brown University, 1984; Northwestern University, 1985; and University of Illinois, Urbana, 1992.

WRITINGS:

(Editor with J. J. Gilman) *Fractures of Solids; Proceedings of an International Conference Sponsored by the Institute of Metals Division, American Institute of Mining, Metallurgical, and Petroleum Engineers,* Gordon & Breach, 1963.
Introduction to the Mechanics of Deformable Solids, McGraw-Hill (New York), 1967.
Exceptional Lie Algebras and the Structure of Hermitian Symmetric Spaces, American Mathematical Society (Providence, RI), 1978.
(Editor with Ren Wang) *Constitutive Relations for Finite Deformation of Polycrystalline Metals,* Springer-Verlag (New York), 1992.

Technical editor of the American Society of Mechanical Engineers' *Journal of Applied Mechanics,* 1956-84. Contributor to technical books, scientific journals, and academic papers.

SIDELIGHTS: Daniel Charles Drucker is an American engineer and researcher in applied mechanics whose ingenuity has revealed important new ways of determining stress. His field of expertise is materials engineering and stress analysis. His best known work concerns photoelasticity—the change in light-transmitting properties of solids (such as glass) caused by stress—in particular, photoelastic analysis of the interior of complex bodies which are under a stress load. He has also carried out important research in soil mechanics, plasticity, and the mechanics of metal cutting and deformation processing. He pioneered a method of classifying materials according to their degree of stability, now known as "Drucker's postulate." In the latter part of his career, he turned his attention to materials research, including research at the level of the optical and electron microscopes.

Drucker was born in New York City on June 3, 1918, the son of a civil engineer. From an early age, he realized his ambition was to be a design engineer. He was educated at New York's Columbia University, and received his B.S. degree in 1937. He remained at the University to pursue further studies in engineering, and received his C.E. degree in Engineering in 1938. He then went on for doctoral studies, and was awarded his Ph.D. in 1940. The previous August, he had married Ann Bodin. The couple has two children, R. David Drucker and Mady Upham.

After completing his education, Drucker was offered a position as instructor in Engineering at Cornell University in Ithaca, New York. He then served as supervisor of mechanics of solids at the Armour Research Foundation. Drucker spent a short time in the U.S. Army Air Corps, then returned to academic life to become assistant professor at the Illinois Institute of Technology. In 1947, Drucker transferred to Brown University in Rhode Island, where he spent the next twenty-one years; he became a full professor in 1950, and served as the L. Herbert Ballou University Professor from 1964 to 1968. In 1953 he became chair of the department of Engineering, and he was chair of the university's Physical Sciences Council between 1961 and 1963.

Drucker moved to the University of Illinois at Urbana-Champaign as Dean of the College of Engineering in 1968. He remained in that position until 1984, when he accepted a post as Graduate Research Professor of Aerospace at the University of Florida in Gainesville. That same year, 1984, he retired the technical editorship of the *Journal of Applied Mechanics* of the American Society of Mechanical Engineers, which he had held since 1956.

During his career, Drucker has developed many innovative engineering techniques. In collaboration with engineer H. Tachau, he designed a simple wire rope that is protected against fatigue failure. The development of "Drucker's postulate," a means of classifying materials according to their stability, gave rise to a general method for dealing with varying classes of stress-strain relations for metals and alloys. In addition, the postulate led to a general theorem for the analysis and design of engineering structures in the important range of relatively small displacement. Finally, using optical and electron microscopes, Drucker hypothesized—correctly, it turned out—that tiny precipitates, rather than grain size, determine the flow strength of steel and aluminum alloys. He also outlined some of the properties of various iron-alloy steels and of sintered carbides, carbides that have been formed by heating without melting.

Drucker is a member of many learned societies, including the American Academy of Arts and Sciences, to which he was elected in 1955; the National Academy of Engineering, of which he became a member in 1967; and the American Society of Mechanics. In addition, he served as chair of the U.S. National Committee on Theoretical and Applied Mechanics, was a member of the General Committee of the International Council of Scientific Unions between 1976 and 1986; was the first vice president and chair of the Engineering College Council of the American Society for Engineering Education, and was a member of the National Science Board beginning in 1988. Drucker has also held some honorary lectureships, including the Marburg Lectureship of the American Society for Testing and Materials in 1966, the W. M. Murray Lectureship of the Society for Experimental Stress Analysis in 1967, and Washington University's Raymond R. Tucker Memorial Lectureship in 1967.

Drucker's career has been saluted many times. He served as a Guggenheim Fellow from 1960 to 1961. He has been awarded an honorary Doctorate of Engineering by Lehigh University in 1976 and an Honorary Doctorate of Science in Technology by the Israel Institute of Technology. He won the Max M. Frocht Award of the Society for Experimental Stress Analysis in 1967 and the Lamme Award of the American Society for Engineering Education the same year. In 1978, he was presented with the Egleston Medal of the Engineering Alumni Association of Columbia University. Drucker remains active in engineering research and in stress analysis. He also devotes a good deal of his time to teaching at the University of Florida in Gainesville.

BIOGRAPHICAL/CRITICAL SOURCES:

BOOKS

McGraw-Hill Modern Scientists and Engineers, Volume 1, McGraw-Hill, 1980, pp. 310.*

* * *

DULBECCO, Renato 1914-

PERSONAL: Born February 22, 1914, in Catanzaro, Italy; naturalized U.S. citizen, 1953; son of Leonardo (a civil engineer) and Maria (Virdia) Dulbecco; married Gulseppina Salvo, June 1, 1940 (divorced, 1963); married Maureen Muir, 1963; children: (first mar-

riage) Peter Leonard (deceased), Maria Vittoria; (second marriage) Fiona Linsey. *Education:* University of Turin, M.D., 1936.

CAREER: Virologist. University of Turin, assistant researcher, 1940-47; University of Indiana, Bloomington, research associate, 1947-49; California Institute of Technology, Pasadena, senior research fellow, 1949-52, associate professor, professor of biology, 1952-63; Salk Institute, La Jolla California, senior research fellow, 1963-71, distinguished research professor, 1977—, president, 1982-92, professor emeritus, 1993—; Imperial Cancer Research Fund, London, England, assistant director of research, 1971-74, deputy director, 1974-77; University of California at San Diego Medical School, La Jolla, professor of pathology and medicine, 1977-81. Elected city councilor of Turin, Italy, 1945. *Military service:* Served in Italian army as physician, 1936-38, recalled in 1939; also served in French and Russian armies.

AWARDS, HONORS: Kimble Methodology Award, Public Health Laboratories, 1959; GHA Clowes memorial Lecturer, American Association of Cancer Research, 1961; Albert and Mary Lasker Award, 1964; Howard Taylor Ricketts Award, 1965; Paul Ehrlich-Ludwig Darmstaedter Prize, 1967; Louisa Gross Horwitz Prize, Columbia University, 1967; Prather Lecturer, Harvard University, 1969; Dunham Lecturer, Harvard University, 1972; Leeuwenhoek Lecturer, Royal Society, 1974; Selman A. Waksman Award in Microbiology, National Academy of Sciences, 1974; Nobel Prize for medicine or physiology, 1975; Targa d'oro Villa San Giovanni, 1978; Mandel Golden Medal, Czechoslovakian Academy of Science, 1982; Culling Memorial Lecturer, 1983; Gold Public Health Medal, Italian Government, 1985; honorary degrees include: Yale University, 1968; University of Glasgow, 1970; Vrije University, 1978; and Indiana University, 1984.

WRITINGS:

(With Harold S. Ginsberg) *Virology,* Harper and Row (Hagerstown), 1980.
The Design of Life, Yale University Press, 1987.
(With Harold S. Ginsberg) *Virology,* 2nd edition, Lippincott, 1988.
Scienza, Vita e Avventura, Sperling and Kupfer (Milan), 1989.
(Editor-in-chief) *Encyclopedia of Human Biology,* Academic Press (San Diego), 1991.
I Geni e Il Nostro Futuro: la Scommessa del Progetto Genoma, Sperling and Kupfer, 1995.

SIDELIGHTS: Renato Dulbecco was a pioneer in the field of virology, the study of viruses. He began as a practicing physician in the military service of his native Italy during World War II and continued to practice as physician with partisan units fighting the German occupation of that country near the end of the war. It was only with his immigration to the United States in 1947 that he began his lengthy and highly distinguished second career in scientific research. Dulbecco developed the plaque assay technique which allowed scientists to quantify the number of viral units in a laboratory culture, thus making possible most of the later major discoveries in virology. He then went on to devote most of his life to the study of viruses that could cause cancer in animals and human beings. For his work in this field, Dulbecco shared the Nobel Prize in medicine or physiology for 1975 with microbiologist David Baltimore and oncologist Howard Temin.

Dulbecco was born in Catanzaro, a town in the southernmost part of Italy, on February 22, 1914, the son of Leonardo Dulbecco, a civil engineer, and Maria Virdia Dulbecco. His father was called into military service during World War I, and his mother moved the children to northern Italy, where they lived in Turin and Cuneo. After the war, the family relocated to Imperia, where Dulbecco received his primary and secondary education. He developed an interest in physics and built an electronic seismograph, one of the earliest of its kind. He considered going into physics, but his mother persuaded him to study medicine when he entered the University of Turin in 1930 at the age of sixteen. By the end of his first year of study, he realized that he was more interested in biology than in medicine per se, so he went to work as an assistant in the laboratory of Giuseppe Levi, a professor of anatomy and an expert on nerve tissue, where he learned histology (the study of plant and animal tissue structure at the microscopic level) and the techniques of cell culture. His fellow students included microbiologist Salvador Edward Luria and neurologist Rita Levi-Montalcini, both of whom were to be Nobel Prize winners and were to influence Dulbecco's scientific career.

Dulbecco received his doctorate of medicine in 1936 and was soon drafted into the Italian army as a physician. He was discharged in 1938 but was recalled in 1939 at the outset of World War II. He married Giuseppina Salvo in 1940; they eventually had a son, Peter Leonard Dulbecco, and a daughter, Maria Vittoria Dulbecco. After Italy, led by dictator Benito Mussolini, became a belligerent in 1940, Dulbecco served in France and then in Russia. A serious wound in Russia in 1942 hospitalized him for several months, after which he went home. Following the fall of Mussolini's government, Dulbecco went into hiding in a small village near Turin and became a physician to the local partisan units resisting the German occupation. After the end of the war in 1945, he was elected a city councilor of Turin but soon gave up the position to return to scientific study and research at the University of Turin. In 1946 Luria invited Dulbecco to join his research group at the University of Indiana at Bloomington. Dulbecco and Levi-Montalcini both immigrated to the United States the following year. He became an American citizen in 1953.

At Indiana, Dulbecco experimented with bacteriophage, viruses that invade and kill bacteria cells. His principal discovery at this time was that bacteriophage previously rendered inactive by exposure to ultraviolet light could be reactivated by exposure to white light of short wavelength. This work attracted the attention of Max Delbruck, a German-born physicist-turned-microbiologist. Delbruck invited Dulbecco to join him at the California Institute of Technology (Caltech) in Pasadena. Dulbecco and his family traveled from Indiana to California in an old car with a trailer in the summer of 1949. The beauty and size of the country and the kindness of its people made a strong impression on him, and he was especially attracted to the climate and life of southern California. Dulbecco became a research fellow and later a professor of biology at Caltech, where he remained until 1963.

In his first years at Caltech, Dulbecco continued his studies of bacteriophage. In the early 1950s, however, Delbruck suggested to him that animal virology, that is, the study of the viruses that invade animal cells, might be a fruitful field for investigation. Dulbecco plunged into the new subject with enthusiasm. His first important contribution in the field was his development of a method for determining the number of units of a given virus in a culture of animal cell tissue. This method, called the plaque assay technique, enabled the researcher to count the viral units in a culture by examining the number of plaques, or clear spots, in the culture, where the viruses had killed the host cells. This method was the basis for many of the later important advances made in animal virology. One spectacular practical result of the use of the plaque assay technique was the development of physician Albert Sabin's polio vaccine, developed from a living virus, used to prevent poliomyelitis, a paralyzing and sometimes lethal disease. This vaccine eventually superseded the vaccine produced earlier by physician Jonas Salk, which was made with a virus killed by formaldehyde.

In the late 1950s Dulbecco's interest shifted to the study of animal viruses that could cause cancerous tumors. His research over the next twenty years was devoted to an investigation of the precise manner in which particular viruses could transform host cells in such ways that the cell was either killed or multiplied indefinitely (that is, became cancerous). After working for a while with a virus that causes tumors in chickens, he and his colleagues concentrated primarily on the polyoma virus, which causes tumors in mice. They eventually discovered that the virus's DNA (deoxyribonucleic acid) combined with the DNA of the host cell and remained there as a provirus (a virus that is integrated with a cell's genetic material and that can be transmitted without causing disintegration when the cell reproduces) which controlled the genetic mechanism of the cell. In a process called cell transformation, the virus could induce a cancer-like state, causing the cell to multiply endlessly in a tissue culture environment in the laboratory. In an animal body, the same process of cell transformation and subsequent cell multiplication led to the growth of cancerous tumors.

In 1963 several important changes occurred in Dulbecco's life. During that year, he was divorced from his first wife and married Maureen Muir; Renato and Maureen later had one daughter, Fiona Linsey Dulbecco. In 1963 he also left Caltech to become one of the original fellows of the Salk Institute, a research organization founded by Salk in La Jolla, California. There Dulbecco continued his research on animal tumor viruses.

In 1972 Dulbecco moved to London to become assistant (later deputy) director of research at the Imperial Cancer Research Fund. He was by then involved in the study of cancer in human beings, concentrating on breast cancer. It was while he was in London that he, Baltimore, and Temin were jointly awarded the Nobel Prize in medicine or physiology for their work on tumor virology.

In his Nobel Prize lecture Dulbecco, after first outlining the research that had led to his award, made a strong plea for the governments of the world to ban or otherwise remove cancer-causing substances from the environment. He especially called upon them to prevent the use of tobacco. While scientists spent their lives asking questions about the nature of cancer and finding ways to prevent or cure it, he said, "society merrily produces oncogenic [tumor-causing] substances and permeates the environment with them."

Dulbecco returned to his beloved southern California in 1977 to become a distinguished research professor at the Salk Institute. He became president of the institute in 1982 and held that position until his retirement in 1992. In addition, during the late 1970s Dulbecco taught at the University of California in San Diego.

BIOGRAPHICAL/CRITICAL SOURCES:

BOOKS

McGraw-Hill Modern Scientists and Engineers, McGraw (New York), 1980, p. 315.
Nobel Lectures: Physiology or Medicine, 1971-1980, World Scientific Publishing (River Edge, NJ), 1992, pp. 229-40.

PERIODICALS

Science, November 14, 1975, pp. 650, 712, 714.*

* * *

DUNCAN, Sara Jeannette 1861-1922
(Cecil V. Cotes, Jane Wintergreen, Garth Grafton, pseudonyms)

PERSONAL: Born December 22, 1861, in Brantford, Ontario, Canada; died July 22, 1922, in Ashmead, England; eldest daughter of Charles (a merchant) and Jane (Bell) Duncan; married Everard Charles Cotes (a museum official, newspaper editor, and Reuters correspondent), in Calcutta, India, 1891; lived in India much of her life thereafter. *Education:* Attended school in Brantford, Ontario, and the Toronto Normal School, Toronto, Canada.

CAREER: Canadian journalist and novelist. *Washington Post,* 1885-1886, book reviewer and editorial writer; *Toronto Globe,* columnist, author of "Woman's World," 1886-87; *Montreal Star,* columnist, "Bric-a-Brac," 1887, parliamentary correspondent, beginning 1888. Also contributed to periodicals, including the *Washington Post, Washington Star, London (Ontario) Advertiser, Memphis Appeal,* and to *Week* (a literary journal).

WRITINGS:

A Social Departure: How Orthodocia and I Went Round the World by Ourselves (novel), Appleton (New York) and Chatto & Windus (London, England), 1890.

An American Girl in London (novel), Appleton, 1891, and Chatto & Windus, 1891.

(As Cecil V. Cotes) *Two Girls on a Barge* (novel), Appleton, 1891.

The Simple Adventures of a Memsahib (novel), Appleton, 1893, and Chatto & Windus, 1893.

A Daughter of Today (novel), Appleton, 1894, and Chatto & Windus, 1894.

The Story of Sonny Sahib (novel), Macmillan (London, England), 1894, Appleton, 1895.

Vernon's Aunt: Being the Oriental Experiences of Miss Lavinia Moffat (novel), Chatto & Windus, 1894, Appleton, 1895.

His Honour, and a Lady (novel), Appleton, 1896, Chatto & Windus, 1896.

Hilda: A Story of Calcutta (novel), Stokes (New York), 1898; as *The Path of a Star,* Methuen (London, England), 1899.

A Voyage of Consolation (Being in the Nature of a Sequel to Experiences of "An American Girl in London" (novel), Appleton, 1898, Methuen, 1898.

The Crow's Nest (memoir), Dodd, Mead (New York), 1901; published as *On the Other Side of the Latch,* Methuen, 1901.

Those Delightful Americans (novel), Appleton, 1902, Methuen, 1902.

The Pool in the Desert (short stories), Appleton, 1903, Methuen, 1903.

The Imperialist (novel), Appleton, 1904, Constable (London, England), 1904; republished, 1961.

Set in Authority (novel), Doubleday, Page (New York), 1906, Constable, 1906.

Cousin Cinderella (novel), Macmillan, 1908, Methuen, 1908; also published as *A Canadian Girl in London,* Methuen, 1908.

(As Jane Wintergreen) *Two in a Flat* (memoir), Hodder & Stoughton (London, England), 1908.

The Burnt Offering (novel), Methuen, 1909, Lane (New York), 1910.

The Consort (novel), Paul (London, England), 1912.

His Royal Highness (novel), Appleton, 1914.

Title Clear (novel), Hutchinson (London, England), 1922.

The Gold Cure (novel), Hutchinson, 1924.

Selected Journalism (journalism), edited by Thomas E. Tausky, Tecumseh (Ottawa, Ontario, Canada), 1978.

Author of several commercially unsuccessful plays. Contributor to periodicals, including *Week* (sometimes under the pseudonym Garth Grafton).

Duncan's manuscripts are in the library of the University of Western Ontario.

SIDELIGHTS: Sara Jeannette Duncan was both a seminal Canadian novelist of the turn of the century and one of the first female Canadian journalists. Born and raised in Brantford, Ontario, she dreamed in childhood of becoming a writer. She got her start professionally at age twenty-three, when she traveled to New Orleans with the purpose of writing and selling freelance articles on the Cotton Centennial of 1884. She achieved that purpose, and on returning to Canada, got steady work with prominent newspapers in Toronto and Montreal.

In her early articles, Duncan began to show a flair for analyzing social mores and a pride in the achievements of independent women. "One cannot help but be impressed by the range, originality, and vigor of Duncan's journalism, which deserves to be better known," wrote Canadian literary critic Thomas E. Tausky in *Dictionary of Literary Biography: Canadian Writers, 1890-1920.* (Tausky is also the editor of Duncan's *Selected Journalism,* published in 1978.) "As early as in her New Orleans articles, she had the ability to turn a shrewd piece of observation into a telling and often sardonic commentary on an entire social system."

Duncan first put these gifts into book form in the 1890 novel *A Social Departure: How Orthodocia and I Went Round the World by Ourselves,* a fictionalized version of a trip Duncan took in 1888. The book deals with Canada, England and India, three settings that would later figure prominently in Duncan's work, but according to Tausky, "the real heart of the book is the account of Japan," a country that Duncan fell in love with. In India, however, she fell in love with Everard Cotes, an official in the Indian Museum of Calcutta; she married him, and spent much of the rest of her life by his side in India, with periodic lengthy vacations in England.

In 1891, Duncan published two novels set in England: *Two Girls on a Barge* and *An American Girl in London.* "*An American Girl in London* is genuinely witty and consistently entertaining," in Tausky's view. It presents an international theme of the type made famous by Henry James: Duncan's ingenuous American heroine, Mamie Wick, goes to England, where she is treated as a provincial but, in turn, sees through the artificiality and snobbism of upper-class British life.

An American Girl in London was one of Duncan's most popular books in her lifetime; *A Social Departure* was perhaps her single most popular. Never a bestselling author, she consistently achieved a level of moderate sales appeal and critical approval that allowed her to establish herself as a publishable Canadian author for the duration of her career. Her later novels were often about India and Anglo-Indians (British colonists in that country). An example is the 1893 *The Simple Adventures of a Memsahib,* in which two English women, young Helen Browne and older Mrs. Perth Macintyre, are used as foils for each other, with Macintyre's "delicate and subtle narration," in Tausky's words, illuminating both the younger girl's personality and the suffocating colonial social scene.

Three novels of the turn of the century—*His Honour, and a Lady* (1896), *Set in Authority* (1906), and *The Burnt Offering* (1909)—deal with sociopolitical aspects of the relationship between British colonists and Indian natives. The fundamental ethical question in all three books is the dilemma between principle and expediency. Perhaps a more interesting novel for the Western audience a century later is *A Daughter of Today* (1894). Here Duncan deals with the theme of personal independence, both for women and for artists. Using a love triangle between a male painter, a conventional female novelist, and a bohemian female painter, the novel tries to steer a middle path, showing the bohemian feminist as too extreme but criticizing the surrounding society as too conformist. In this "ambitious but flawed" work, opines Tausky, "neither the bohemian artist nor the bourgeois artist really wins in the end. . . . The result is a work that is powerful in feeling, but also overly moralistic and schematic."

Duncan would limn similar conflicts between convention and artistic rebellion in a long short story, "An Impossible Ideal," which was collected in the 1903 *The Pool in the Desert,* and which Tausky describes as "the best story in an uneven collection." In this story, says the *Dictionary of Literary Biography* critic, "the idea that the artist is inherently uneasy with society . . . is given a carefully controlled, psychologically subtle treatment."

It was in 1904 that Duncan published what is regarded as her finest novel, *The Imperialist.* It has repeatedly been compared with Stephen Leacock's 1912 *Sunshine Sketches of a Little Town,* and like Leacock's book, it is affectionately admired as a portrait of small-town Canadian life before World War I. It is more than a work of regionalism, however; it is "Duncan's most personal book," Tausky avers, and beyond that, a commentary on a society in miniature. The title character is Lorne Murchison, a young Canadian lawyer who believes in closer ties with imperial England. Engaged both in an electoral battle and in a romantic quest (for the daughter of a political opponent), he suffers a breakdown but is repaired to health by novel's end. *The Imperialist* received mixed reviews on first publication: Canadian reviewers did not respond heartily, and British periodicals apparently felt that the subject of provincial Canadian life was unworthy of serious fiction. On the positive side, the *New York Times* (quoted by Tausky) called it "perhaps the most worthwhile [story] which has come out here in some time."

Since the novel's republication in 1961, Duncan's centennial year, *The Imperialist* has attracted considerable attention from Canadian literary scholars. Carole Gerson, writing in *Canadian Literature* in 1975, said, "*The Imperialist* has unfortunately suffered the neglect accorded to much literature based on a topical political situation. . . . But once made accessible, the book reveals itself to be one of the most sophisticated and penetrating Canadian novels written before World War I. Sara Jeannette Duncan's scheme of levels of vision, her ability to work ideas into the structure of her narrative, and her detached sympathy for both her idealists and her common-sense characters raise *The Imperialist* above the local and the historical into the universal concerns of literature."

George Woodcock, in a 1983 essay published in *The Yearbook of English Studies,* wrote, "*The Imperialist* is as much a social as a political novel, and a great deal of its lasting appeal in Canada lies in the nostalgic vividness with which Sara Duncan recreates, in the small town of Elgin, the Brantford in which she spent her childhood and her youth." Peter Allen, in a 1984 *Studies in Canadian Literature* essay, observed that Duncan's "theme is the ambiguity of Canadian identity and especially the mixture of excitement and skepticism or apathy with which we viewed our role in the British Empire. . . . In both her certainty and her uncertainty, in her realism and occasional lapses from it, Duncan is an eloquent and important witness to the ambiguity of our developing national identity."

A follow-up novel, *Cousin Cinderella,* is generally ranked second among Duncan's novels. Planned immediately after the writing of *The Imperialist* but published in 1908, *Cousin Cinderella* is set in England, but gives a distinctly Canadian view of the mother country through its heroine, Mary Trent. Mary and her brother Graham, offspring of a Canadian lumber baron, achieve only mixed success in British society, and thus come to view it with a blend of admiration and criticism that illuminates both their host country and their homeland. In this novel as in others, Britain is shown as too conventional. In contrast, Duncan viewed the United States as excessively individualistic. Canada, for her, was the promising synthesis of these two mighty social forces. As Misao Dean puts it in a 1985 *Journal of Canadian Studies* essay, "Canada emerges as a *via media,* a middle way, between the extreme of freedom and tradition those nations represent." Having explored this issue skillfully in two novels that are, according to Tausky, "among the enduring classics of Canadian fiction," Duncan is seen as a noteworthy predecessor to such later female Canadian writers as Alice Munro, Margaret Atwood, and Carole Shields, who have used provincial Canadian life as material in works that have achieved the heights of international acclaim.

More than a social novelist, however, Duncan was a capable creator of people and scenes. Enthuses Tausky, "F. Scott Fitzgerald once said that he wanted 'to recapture the exact feel of a moment in time and space.' The best passages in Sara Jeannette Duncan's work, the passages that mark her as a clever observer of manners, realize that ambition."

BIOGRAPHICAL/CRITICAL SOURCES:

BOOKS

Dictionary of Literary Biography: Canadian Writers, 1890-1920, Volume 92, edited by W. H. New, Gale (Detroit), 1990, pp. 97-104.

Tausky, Thomas E., "Sara Jeannette Duncan as a Novelist," *Sara Jeannette Duncan: Novelist of Empire,* P. D. Meany Publishers, 1980, pp. 73-90.

Twentieth-Century Literary Criticism, Volume 60, Gale (Detroit), 1995, pp. 174-256.

PERIODICALS

Canadian Literature, autumn, 1961, pp. 72-77; winter, 1974, pp. 30-37; winter, 1975, pp. 73-80; autumn, 1983, pp. 117-119; spring, 1992, pp. 16-30, 82-93.

Journal of Canadian Fiction, vol. II, no. 3, summer. 1973, pp. 205-210; vol. III. no. 4, 1975, pp. 74-84.

Journal of Canadian Studies, vol. 12, no. 2, spring, 1977, pp. 38-49; vol. 20, no. 2, summer, 1985, pp. 132-149.

Journal of Commonwealth Literature, vol. XXVI, no. 1, 1991, pp. 215-228.

Literary Criterion, nos. 3-4, 1984, pp. 93-104.

Studies in Canadian Literature, vol. 9, no. 1, 1984, pp. 41-60.

World Literature Written in English, vol. 16, no. 1, April, 1977, pp. 71-81.

Yearbook of English Studies, vol. 13, 1983, pp. 210-227.*

*   *   *

DUNLAP, David W.

PERSONAL: Male.

ADDRESSES: Office—New York Times, 229 West 43rd St., New York, NY 10036.

CAREER: New York Times, New York City, reporter.

WRITINGS:

(And photographer) *On Broadway: A Journey Uptown over Time,* Rizzoli, 1990.

Contributor to periodicals.

SIDELIGHTS: David W. Dunlap is a *New York Times* reporter specializing in the history of architecture and land developments in the vicinity of New York City. In addition to covering such subjects as Times Square renovation projects, he wrote *On Broadway: A Journey Uptown over Time,* in which he relates the history of New York City's prominent performing-arts thoroughfare from its origin as a Native American trail to its current prominence as a boulevard that is lined with residential housing, stores, and theatres. Here, Dunlap provides background on the seventeen-mile street's many notable structures, such as the Woolworth Building, which features a Gothic tower, and the United Church-Science of Living Institute (formerly Loew's 175th St. Theatre), which incorporates a melange of architectural styles, including, according to Dunlap, rococo and Byzantine elements.

In *On Broadway,* Dunlap also speculates on the street's continued existence and maintenance and advocates increased care for the historic route, which he characterizes as a link between America's rural past and its chaotic, urban present. *On Broadway* has been acknowledged as an important work on its subject. John Tauranac, in a review for the *New York Times,* deemed Dunlap's book "a major contribution to New York's architectural history," and he described it as an informational "gold mine." And Tony Hiss, writing in the *New York Times Book Review,* declared that Dunlap "commandingly unites his professional and personal passions" and proves himself Broadway's "herald, its lexicographer, its guardian." Hiss added that *On Broadway* constitutes "an arresting and authoritative . . . history book."

BIOGRAPHICAL/CRITICAL SOURCES:

PERIODICALS

New York Times, December 20, 1990, p. C18.
New York Times Book Review, December 2, 1990, p. 11.*

* * *

DURAND, William F. 1859-1958

PERSONAL: Born March 5, 1859, in Bethany, CT; died August 9, 1958; son of William L. (a business person) and Ruth (a business person, maiden name Coe) Durand. *Education:* U.S. Naval Academy (Annapolis, MD), B.A., 1880; Lafayette College, Ph.D., 1888.

CAREER: Aeronautical engineer. Professor of mechanical engineering at the Agricultural and Mechanical College of Michigan (now Michigan State University), 1888-91; professor of marine engineering, Cornell University, Ithaca, NY, 1891-04; Stanford University, Stanford, CA, professor of mechanical engineering (created aeronautical engineering curriculum), beginning 1904. Served on Advisory Board of Engineers, Boulder Dam Project, 1929, and Navy Department Special Committee on Airship Design and Construction, beginning 1935.

MEMBER: National Advisory Committee for Civil Aeronautics, Morrow Board, and National Research Council.

AWARDS, HONORS: Presidential Award of Merit, 1946.

WRITINGS:

The Resistance and Propulsion of Ships, Wiley, 1898.
Practical Marine Engineering, Marine Engineering, Inc., 1901.
Motor Boats, International Marine Engineering, 1907.
Hydraulics of Pipe Lines, Van Nostrand, 1921.
Robert Henry Thurston: A Biography, The Record of a Life of Achievement as Engineer, Educator, and Author, American Society of Mechanical Engineers, 1929.
(With Editor) *Aerodynamic Theory,* six volumes, J. Springer, 1934-36.
Selected Papers, California Institute of Technology, 1944.
Adventures: In the Navy, In Education, Science, Engineering, and In War: A Life Story, American Society of Mechanical Engineers and McGraw-Hill, 1953.

SIDELIGHTS: William F. Durand was an internationally known teacher and researcher in aeronautical propulsion during the first half of the twentieth century. He made enormous contributions to the development of flight, fired the enthusiasm of the first generation of aeronautical engineers involved in aviation research, and virtually created the aeronautical engineering program at Stanford University. During a career spanning more than five decades of aircraft research and development, he helped establish the principles of propulsion used on aircraft reciprocating engines and later on jet aircraft.

William Frederick Durand was born on March 5, 1859, in Bethany, Connecticut, the son of William L. and Ruth Coe Durand, local business people. Educated in the public schools, Durand entered the U.S. Naval Academy at Annapolis in 1876, long before aviation became a technological possibility. He did well at Annapolis, graduating second in his class in 1880. He immediately entered the Naval Engineering Corps, where he worked on the problems of marine engineering. Adept in his duties, he was sent by the Navy to work on a Ph.D. in engineering. Durand graduated from Lafayette College in 1888, though he had resigned his naval commission a year earlier to accept a post as professor of mechanical engineering at the Agricultural and Mechanical College of Michigan. He remained there until 1891, when he moved to Cornell University to teach marine engineering.

In 1904, Durand moved to Stanford University on the West Coast, ostensibly to teach mechanical engineering. He soon became involved in the new technology of airplanes—the Wright brothers had made their historical flight the previous year—and began studying the problems of flight. Over the next several years, Durand created an aeronautical engineering curriculum at Stanford that became one of the best in the nation. By 1915, both Durand personally and his department at Stanford collectively had been recognized as leaders in solving the problems of flight.

The United States government recognized the importance of fostering aeronautical development by establishing the National Advisory Committee for Aeronautics (NACA) in 1915. Its purpose, as set forth in the Naval Appropriations Act of 1915, was "to supervise and direct the scientific study of the problems of flight, with a view to their practical solution." Governed by a committee of largely non-government experts, the NACA became an enormously important government research and development organization for the next half century, materially enhancing the development of aeronautics. Durand served as a member of the committee from 1915 until 1933, and again between 1941 and 1945. He also chaired the committee from 1917 to 1918, during World War I. Over the years, most of the research conducted under NACA auspices was done in its own facilities, but until the first of those facilities was constructed in 1918, the committee let contracts to educational institutions. Durand's research team at Stanford led all other contractors with its NACA-funded experimentation with propellers. This would have been considered a conflict of interest at a different time, but in the midst of World War I, and given the lax regulatory environment of the era, no one questioned it. This and other contracts paid off; the NACA's research on aircraft engines was the first major success of the organization and helped develop the Liberty Engine, the major contribution the United States made to aeronautics during World War I.

On September 12, 1925, President Calvin Coolidge established the Morrow Board to study the use of aircraft in national defense. Among its members was William Durand, who lent considerable experience and expertise in aeronautics to its deliberations. The board held hearings and found that there was little agreement as to how many usable aircraft the Army Air Service had. While it rejected the most strident claims for air power, its report of November 30, 1925, recommended the appointment of two additional airmen as brigadier generals, one to head procurement and the other to command the flying schools. The board also recommended increased appropriations for the training of airmen and the development of

modern airplanes, and suggested changing the name of the Army Air Service to Air Corps. In response, Congress passed the Air Corps Bill of 1926 to formalize many of these recommendations, setting the stage for the creation of the modern military air arm that would emerge during World War II.

In addition to serving on the Morrow Board, Durand participated in numerous other technical committees and advisory boards employed by a wide range of government entities. For instance, in 1929 he was a member of the advisory board of engineers for the Boulder Dam project, a significant effort that brought greatly increased supplies of water and electricity to the American southwest. He was also a member of the National Research Council between 1915 and 1945, and chair of the Navy Department's Special Committee on Airship Design and Construction in 1935.

Perhaps no technological innovation has been more significant in the development of aviation than the turbojet engine. Although it is relatively simple in its principles, its development required a unique combination of metallurgical capability, cooling and velocity control, and an unconventional understanding of Newton's third law of motion. By the 1930s and 1940s, no American researchers had solved the jet propulsion problem, leaving the nation far behind Great Britain and Germany in jet development during those crucial years. The United States had to make an enormous effort in the 1940s and get help from the British in order to catch up with developments elsewhere.

In March, 1941, at the request of Hap Arnold, chief of staff of the Army Air Forces, the NACA created a special committee to study jet propulsion. Under Durand's leadership, this special committee met seven times in five months, finally recommending that the military award industrial firms contracts to study jet propulsion. Allis Chalmers, Westinghouse, and General Electric were chosen for their promising ideas on the subject. Durand's efforts as both engineer and advisor were important for the development of the jet engine and its application to military aircraft near the end of World War II.

While Durand had been recognized as a leading authority in aeronautics since the early 1900s, he was especially revered as the sage of the discipline in the postwar era. Durand received numerous awards from government, industry, and foundations for his contributions to the development of aviation in America, including the Presidential Award of Merit in 1946. He died at age ninety-nine on August 9, 1958, just as the space age was dawning.

BIOGRAPHICAL/CRITICAL SOURCES:

BOOKS

Constant, Edward W. II, *The Origins of the Turbojet Revolution,* Johns Hopkins University Press, 1980.
Maurer, *Aviation in the U.S. Army,* Office of Air Force History, 1987.
Nicolson, Harold, *Dwight Morrow,* Harcourt, 1935.
Rae, John B., *Climb to Greatness: The American Aircraft Industry, 1920-1960,* MIT Press, 1968.
Roland, Alex, *Model Research: The National Advisory Committee for Aeronautics, 1915-1958,* two volumes, NASA SP-4301, 1985.

PERIODICALS

Prologue: The Journal of the National Archives, winter, 1992, pp. 361-73.*

E

EARLE, Sylvia A. 1935-

PERSONAL: Born August 30, 1935, in Gibbstown, NJ; daughter of Lewis Read and Alice Freas (maiden name Richie) Earle; married Graham Hawkes, divorced. *Education:* Florida State University, B.S., 1955; Duke University, M.A., 1956, Ph.D., 1966.

ADDRESSES: Home—12812 Skyline Boulevard, Oakland, CA 94619-3125. *Office*—Deep Ocean Engineering, 1431 Doolittle Drive, San Leandro, CA 94577-2225.

CAREER: Research marine biologist and oceanographer. Cape Haze Marine Laboratories, Sarasota, FL, resident director, 1966; Radcliffe Institute, research scholar; Farlow Herbarium, Harvard University, Cambridge, MA, research fellow, 1975; California Academy of Sciences, research biologist and curator, 1976; Natural History Museum, University of California, Berkeley, fellow, 1976; National Oceanic and Atmospheric Administration (NOAA), chief scientist, 1990-92; Deep Ocean Technology and Deep Ocean Engineering, Oakland, CA, founder, president, and CEO, 1981-90.

MEMBER: World Wildlife Fund (trustee, 1976-82); World Wildlife Fund, International, (trustee 1979-81); Charles A. Lindbergh Fund (president, 1990—); Center for Marine Conservation, (trustee, 1992—); Perry Foundation, (chairman, 1993—); International Union for Conservation of Nature; Woods Hole Oceanographic Institute; National Advancement Commission on Oceans and Atmosphere; International Phycological Society; Phycological Society of America; American Society of Ichthyologists and Herpetologists; American Institute of Biological Scientists; Brit-ish Phycological Society, Ecology Society of America; International Society of Plant Taxonomists; Explorer's Club.

AWARDS, HONORS: Conservation Service Award, United States Department of Interior, 1970; Woman of the Year, Los Angeles Times, 1970; Boston Sea Rovers Award, 1972 and 1979; Nogi Award, Underwater Society of America, 1976; Order of Golden Ark, Prince, Netherlands, 1980; Lowell Thomas Award, Explorer's Club, 1980; Scientist of the Year, California Museum of Science and Industry, 1981; Conservation Service Award, California Academy of Science, 1989; David B. Stone Medal, New England Aquarium, 1989; Gold medalist, Society of Women Geographers, Radcliffe College, 1990; Pacon International Award, 1992; Directors Award, Natural Resources County Administration, 1992. Fellow, AAAS, Marine Technological Society, California Academy of Scientists. Honorary degrees conferred from Monterey Institute of International Studies, 1990; Ball State University, 1991; George Washington University, 1992; D.Sc., Duke University, 1993; Ripon College, 1994; and University of Connecticut, 1994.

WRITINGS:

Humbrella, a New Red Alga of Uncertain Taxonomic Position From the Juan Fernandez Islands, Harvard University Press (Cambridge), 1969.

(With Joyce Redemsky Young) *Siphonoclathrus, A New Genus of Chlorophyta (Siphonales: Codiaceae) from Panama,* Harvard University Press, 1972.

(Editor with Bruce C. Collette) *Results of the Tektite Program: Ecology of Coral Reef Fishes,* Natural History Museum (Los Angeles), 1972.

(Editor with Robert J. Lavenberg) *Results of the Tektite Program, Coral Reef Invertebrates and Plants,* Natural History Museum (Los Angeles, CA), 1975.

(With Al Giddings) *Exploring the Deep Frontier: The Adventure of Man in the Sea,* National Geographic Press, 1980.

Sea Change: A Message of the Oceans, G.P. Putman and Sons (New York City), c. 1995.

SIDELIGHTS: Sylvia A. Earle is a former chief scientist of the National Oceanic and Atmospheric Administration (NOAA) and a leading American oceanographer. She was among the first underwater explorers to make use of modern self-contained underwater breathing apparatus (SCUBA) gear, and identified many new species of marine life. With her former husband, Graham Hawkes, Earle designed and built a submersible craft that could dive to unprecedented depths of three thousand feet.

Sylvia Alice (Reade) Earle was born in Gibbstown, New Jersey on August 30, 1935, the daughter of Lewis Reade and Alice Freas (Richie) Earle. Both parents had an affinity for the outdoors and encouraged her love of nature after the family moved to the west coast of Florida. As Earle explained to *Scientific American,* "I wasn't shown frogs with the attitude 'yuk,' but rather my mother would show my brothers and me how beautiful they are and how fascinating it was to look at their gorgeous golden eyes." However, Earle pointed out, while her parents totally supported her interest in biology, they also wanted her to get her teaching credentials and learn to type, "just in case."

She enrolled at Florida State University and received her Bachelor of Science degree in the spring of 1955. That fall she entered the graduate program at Duke University and obtained her master's degree in botany the following year. The Gulf of Mexico became a natural laboratory for Earle's work. Her master's dissertation, a detailed study of algae in the Gulf, is a project she still follows. She has collected more than twenty thousand samples. "When I began making collections in the Gulf, it was a very different body of water than it is now—the habitats have changed. So I have a very interesting baseline," she noted in *Scientific American.*

In 1966, Earle received her Ph.D. from Duke University and immediately accepted a position as resident director of the Cape Haze Marine Laboratories in Sarasota, Florida. The following year, she moved to Massachusetts to accept dual roles as research scholar at the Radcliffe Institute and research fellow at the Farlow Herbarium, Harvard University, where she was named researcher in 1975. Earle moved to San Francisco in 1976 to become a research biologist at and curator of the California Academy of Sciences. That same year, she also was named a fellow in botany at the Natural History Museum, University of California, Berkeley.

Although her academic career could have kept her totally involved, her first love was the sea and the life within it. In 1970, Earle and four other oceanographers lived in an underwater chamber for fourteen days as part of the government-funded Tektite II Project, designed to study undersea habitats. Fortunately, technology played a major role in Earle's future. A self-contained underwater breathing apparatus had been developed in part by Jacques Cousteau as recently as 1943, and refined during the time Earle was involved in her scholarly research. SCUBA equipment was not only a boon to recreational divers, but it also dramatically changed the study of marine biology. Earle was one of the first researchers to don a mask and oxygen tank and observe the various forms of plant and animal habitats beneath the sea, identifying many new species of each. She called her discovery of undersea dunes off the Bahama Islands "a simple Lewis and Clark kind of observation." But, she said in *Scientific American,* "the presence of dunes was a significant insight into the formation of the area."

Though Earle set the unbelievable record of freely diving to a depth of 1,250 feet, there were serious depth limitations to SCUBA diving. To study deep-sea marine life would require the assistance of a submersible craft that could dive far deeper. Earle and her former husband, British-born engineer Graham Hawkes, founded Deep Ocean Technology, Inc., and Deep Ocean Engineering, Inc., in 1981, to design and build submersibles. Using a paper napkin, Earle and Hawkes rough-sketched the design for a submersible they called *Deep Rover,* which would serve as a viable tool for biologists. "In those days we were dreaming of going to thirty-five thousand feet," she told *Discover* magazine. "The idea has always been that scientists couldn't be trusted to drive a submersible by themselves because they'd get so involved in their work they'd run into things." *Deep Rover* was built and continues to operate as a mid-water machine in ocean depths ranging 3,000 feet.

In 1990, Earle was named the first woman to serve as chief scientist at the National Oceanic and Atmospheric Administration (NOAA), the agency that conducts underwater research, manages fisheries, and monitors marine spills. She left the position after eighteen months because she felt that she could accomplish more working independently of the government.

Earle, who has logged more than six thousand hours under water, is the first to decry America's lack of research money being spent on deep-sea studies, noting that of the world's five deep-sea manned submersibles (those capable of diving to twenty thousand feet or more), the U.S. has only one, the *Sea Cliff.* "That's like having one jeep for all of North America," she said in *Scientific American.* In 1993, Earle worked with a team of Japanese scientists to develop the equipment to send first a remote, then a manned submersible to 36,000 feet. "They have money from their government," she told *Scientific American.* "They do what we do not: they really make a substantial commitment to ocean technology and science." Earle also plans to lead the ten million-dollar deep ocean engineering project, Ocean Everest, that would take her to a similar depth.

In addition to publishing numerous scientific papers on marine life, Earle is a devout advocate of public education regarding the importance of the oceans as an essential environmental habitat. She is currently the president and chief executive officer of Deep Ocean Technology and Deep Ocean Engineering in Oakland, California, as well as the coauthor of *Exploring the Deep Frontier: The Adventure of Man in the Sea.*

BIOGRAPHICAL/CRITICAL SOURCES:

PERIODICALS

Discover, February, 1986, pp. 60-67.
Scientific American, April, 1992, pp. 37-40.*

*   *   *

EDDINGTON, Arthur Stanley 1882-1944

PERSONAL: Born December 28, 1882, in Kendal, Westmorland, England; died November 22, 1944; son of Arthur Henry (a teacher and headmaster) and Sarah Ann (Shout) Eddington. *Education:* Owens College (now University of Manchester), degree in physics, 1902; Trinity College, Cambridge University, degree, 1905. *Religion:* Quaker.

CAREER: Astronomer. Royal Observatory, Greenwich, England, chief assistant, 1906-13; Cambridge University, Plumian Professor of Astronomy and Experimental Philosophy, 1906-44, director of university observatory, 1907-44. Royal Astronomical Society, president, 1921-23; International Astronomical Union, president.

AWARDS, HONORS: Gold medal, Royal Astronomical Society, 1924; knighted, 1930; Order of Merit, 1938; numerous honorary degrees from universities and colleges; Eddington Medal created by Royal Astronomical Society, 1947, for outstanding work on theoretical astronomy.

WRITINGS:

Stellar Movements and the Structure of the Universe, Macmillan (London), 1914.
Report on the Relativity Theory of Gravitation, Fleetway Press (London), 1918.
Space, Time, and Gravitation, Cambridge University Press (London), 1920, Harper (New York), 1959.
The Mathematical Theory of Relativity, Cambridge University Press, 1923, Chelsea Publishing (New York), 1975.
The Internal Constitution of the Stars, Cambridge University Press, 1926.
Stars and Atoms, Yale University Press (New Haven, CT), 1927.
The Nature of the Physical World, Macmillan (New York), 1928.
Science and the Unseen World, Macmillan, 1929.
The Expanding Universe, Macmillan, 1933.
New Pathways in Science, Cambridge University Press, 1935.
Relativity Theory of Protons and Electrons, Macmillan, 1936.
The Philosophy of Physical Science, Macmillan, 1939.
Fundamental Theory, Edmund T. Whittaker, editor, Cambridge University Press, 1946.
(Contributor) *Freedom of Action in a Mechanistic Universe* by Donald M. Mackay, Cambridge University Press, 1967.

SIDELIGHTS: Arthur Stanley Eddington is considered to be one of the greatest astronomers of his age. During his career he led theoretical investigations into the structure of stars and the formation of the solar system and established the mass-luminosity law, which relates a star's brightness to its mass. He explained how Cepheid variable stars, which are at the edge of stability, could exist and was one of the first to understand the importance—and implications—of Einstein's theories of relativity.

Born on December 28, 1882, at Kendal, Westmorland, England, Eddington was the son of Arthur Henry Eddington and Sarah Ann (Shout) Eddington. From 1878 to 1884, the elder Eddington was the proprietor and headmaster of Stramongate School in Kendal. Upon his death, Mrs. Eddington took young Arthur, who was just two years old, and his six-year-old sister, Winifred, to Weston-super-Mare, Somerset. Mrs. Eddington's ancestors had been north-country Quakers for seven generations, and she raised her children as Quakers.

Eddington received a first-rate education. During the day he attended Brynmelyn School, where three exceptionally gifted teachers gave him a love for natural history, fine literature, and mathematics—all of which he would use during his life to make his impact on the world. (His great knowledge of science and mathematics, mixed with the lively ability to write, would make him one of the first "popularizers" of astronomy.) In the evening he received additional instruction at home.

Before he was sixteen years old, he won an entrance scholarship to Owens College (now the University of Manchester), where he had the good fortune to receive instruction from Horace Lamb in mathematics and Arthur Schuster in physics. Eddington graduated with a degree in physics in 1902 and won an entrance scholarship to Trinity College in Cambridge, where he distinguished himself in mathematics. (Mathematician Alfred North Whitehead was one of his teachers.) He was at the head of his class in 1904, became the first second-year student to achieve the coveted position of "First Wrangler," and graduated in only three years, receiving his degree in 1905.

Following his graduation, Eddington was appointed chief assistant at the Royal Observatory at Greenwich. During the next seven years, from 1906 to 1913, he received extensive training in practical astronomy. He also made two long voyages; the first, in 1906, was to Malta, where he determined the latitude of the geodetic station there; the second was to Brazil, in 1912, where he was the leader of an expedition to observe a total solar eclipse. Returning to Cambridge after the eclipse expedition, Eddington became Plumian Professor of Astronomy and the director of the observatory. He remained there for the next thirty-one years.

During his career at Greenwich, his investigations into theoretical astronomy made Eddington the leader in astronomical research. His first topic of investigation was the proper (actual) motion of the stars through the sky. He also examined the distribution of stars of different spectral classes, observed planetary and gaseous nebulae, and studied open star clusters and globular clusters.

Eddington's first book, *Stellar Movements and the Structure of the Universe* (1914), a collection of fifteen papers, is considered to be a paradigm of clear scientific discourse. In it he summarized the celestial knowledge of his era, defined the most pressing problems facing astronomy, and stated his personal preference that the spiral nebulae were not a part of the Milky Way, but located far outside our galaxy (later researchers proved this belief correct). In the final chapter, called "Dynamics of the Stellar System," Eddington set the stage for the founding of a very important branch of research.

Eddington's major contribution to astronomy began in 1916, when he chose to penetrate deep into stars and attempt to determine what kept them from collapsing under their own force of gravity. He also hoped to establish how stellar energy was transported to the surface of celestial bodies. Astronomers had been plagued for years over the question of how a star could be a stable object. Since it was nothing more than a big ball of gas, why didn't all stars collapse and become white dwarf stars?

Eddington determined that three forces had to be taken into account: gravitation, gas pressure, and the pressure of radiation. He hypothesized that the inward crush of gravitation is offset by the pressure of the gases within the star and the force of stellar energy radiating outward. The concept of radiation force was very controversial: Scientists had believed that convection forces were responsible for stellar energy, but Eddington, using his radiation theory, established his own equation showing how stars maintained stability.

Eddington suggested that gravitational pull increases as one moves further toward the center of a star. Hence, he hypothesized, radiation pressure moving outward must increase in order for a star to maintain stability. The only way for an increase in radiation pressure to occur would be if the star's temperature was greater toward the center of the star. Therefore, the hottest region of the star had to be closest to its core, where the temperature would reach into the millions of degrees. As Hans Bethe would show later, temperatures of great magnitude were required to initiate the nuclear fusion that powered the stars. As the pressure, radiation and temperature increased, so did the star's luminosity (brightness). From this, Eddington determined his mass-luminosity law in 1924. The relation between these two factors makes it possible to estimate the mass of a star based on its luminosity.

For stars with more mass than the sun, the increase in radiation pressure was remarkable. Eddington concluded that very few stars could exist if they were more than ten times the mass of the sun, and it would be very rare for a star with fifty times the sun's mass to exist; it would have so much radiation pressure, the star would be blown apart. Although there are extremely large stars, as far as volume goes, they are comprised of rarefied gasses which do not exceed Eddington's limit for mass. Cepheid variable stars (stars which pulse, physically changing their diameter), are at the very limit of stability, and Eddington devised a theoretical explanation for their behavior that is still accepted at present.

After applying his calculations to Sirius B, a companion star of Sirius (Canis majoris), Eddington, in the summer of 1920, calculated the diameters of several red giant stars. That December he received a letter from George Ellery Hale, one of the founders of astrophysics. The correspondence, part of which is reprinted in the *Dictionary of Scientific Biography,* conveyed that a measurement of the red supergiant star Betelgeuse, in Orion (Orionis), was "in close agreement with your theoretical value and probably correct within about ten percent." This was confirmation that Eddington's calculations were more than just "theory."

An unexpected side effect to Eddington's work was how it affected the two main theories regarding the origin of the solar system. On one side of the question was Thomas C. Chamberlin, who held that, following the collapse of the rotating cloud which formed the sun, the material that remained behind accumulated into planets. On the other side was Sir James Jeans, who believed that a star had passed close to the sun eons ago. The gravitational pull of this star had drawn material out of the sun which condensed into planets.

Eddington's theory suggested that the material within the sun was under such great pressure, that had it been drawn out it would have exploded violently, not condensed. Jeans was not pleased to have his theory debunked, especially by such an illustrious man as

Eddington, and a strong professional enmity developed between the two.

When World War I broke out, Eddington received an exemption as a conscientious objector because of his Quaker beliefs. While the war raged, he singlehandedly finished transit observations to complete the zodiacal catalogue. In the meantime, another uproar had been unleashed; this one was the result of the work of Albert Einstein, who had published his general theory of relativity in 1915 (the special theory of relativity had been issued in 1905).

Einstein's theories have been listed among the greatest intellectual achievements of the twentieth century. When first proposed, there were very few practical applications for them. More recently, however, the theories have become paramount in understanding such phenomena as quasars, pulsars and black holes. Eddington was one of the few people who could not only understand Einstein's theories but also realize their implications. He immersed himself in the study of the "new" mathematics, learned absolute differential calculus, became an expert in the use of tensors, and proceeded to develop his own concepts of relativity. His "Report on the Theory of Gravitation," issued in 1918, was the first comprehensive account of general relativity written in English. Eddington would introduce an entire generation of adults and children to Einstein, making the difficult concepts comprehensible. Einstein considered Eddington's 1923 book, *The Mathematical Theory of Relativity,* the finest presentation of relativity in any language.

The theories of relativity went far beyond Isaac Newton's laws of gravitation, and there was considerable controversy surrounding them. Einstein himself suggested three, and only three, observational tests to verify his theories—all of which had to do with astronomical phenomena. These included two gravitational effects on starlight, involving both a stretching of starlight waves called the redshift effect and a bending of the waves as they traveled through space. The third proof involved the hypothesis that Mercury's perihelion—the point where the planet would be closest to the sun—would continually advance.

According to Einstein, relativity would cause Mercury's perihelion to advance a tiny bit more than what Newton's law of gravity expected. Since the predicted amount was a minuscule 43 arc-seconds, it would take about thirty thousand years for the axis of Mercury's orbit to make a complete rotation. With that kind of time frame, it seemed unlikely that such a tiny measurement could be made, yet discrepancies in Mercury's orbit had been noticed, and Einstein's prediction accounted for what was observed.

The investigation was on to verify Einstein's two other tests. In a paper smuggled out of Germany during World War I, Einstein suggested an excellent, and rare, opportunity for an experiment; a total eclipse of the sun on May 29, 1919, would permit a test for the bending of starlight by gravity. During the brief period of totality, stars would be visible near the sun's position. As the starlight passed the sun, the sun's gravitational attraction should cause the light to bend. Unfortunately, the eclipse would not be visible from Europe or North America. As is often the case, the observers would have to travel a considerable distance to observe it, and travel conditions in 1919 were only for the adventurous.

Realizing that local weather conditions at the eclipse site would be a major concern, Eddington organized not one, but two expeditions to observe the eclipse—one on the island of Principe, off the coast of West Africa, and the second across the Atlantic Ocean at Sobral, in North Brazil. The weather at both sites was frustratingly troublesome, but each expedition was able to take some photographs of the sky. These were compared with photographs of the same area of the sky which had been made at another time of the year, obviously when the sun was nowhere near.

Starlight near the sun during the eclipse was, indeed, displaced, and the shift agreed with the theory of relativity's prediction. This resulted in making Einstein a celebrity around the globe, although Eddington, in a second edition of his book, warned the theory still had not met the test of the gravitational redshift.

To understand the redshift of light, consider sound waves: When an automobile drives by, sounding its horn, a noticeable change in pitch is heard because the sound waves are stretched out. Einstein predicted that gravity would stretch out light waves. As the waves were lengthened, a shift in color, toward the low (red) end of the spectrum, would be observed.

In order to provide the third proof for Einstein's theory, Eddington observed Sirius B, which had qualities which would made it a likely candidate for redshifting. Eddington wrote to W. A. Adams at the Mount Wilson Observatory and asked him to make a measurement of the spectrum of Sirius B. Adams immediately set to work and eventually was able to obtain a measurement in 1924 that closely matched

prediction. The test of gravitational redshift was not only the third confirmation of Einstein's theories, it also verified density measures which Eddington had determined for Sirius B.

During the years, Eddington published extensively. His works include *The Nature of the Physical World* (1928), *The Expanding Universe* (1933), *New Pathways in Science* (1935), and *The Philosophy of Physical Science* (1939). Although some of these books had ponderous titles, all were written in an extremely lively, imaginative, and humorous manner, introducing new ideas and new ways of thinking. During his last years he threw all his energy into realizing his dream: calling it "Bottom's dream," it was nothing less than the unification of quantum physics and relativity. This is a topic that has yet to be resolved.

In the autumn of 1944, Eddington underwent a major surgical procedure from which he did not recover. He was only 61 years old when he died on November 22. Devoting his life to the advancement of knowledge, he had never married (when he moved into the Cambridge Observatory House in 1913, be brought his mother and sister along). His genius had been honored the world over; he had been elected to the Royal Astronomical Society in 1906 and the Royal Society in 1914. He received honoraria from many universities and was knighted in 1930, but his greatest honor was receiving the Order of Merit in 1938. In the same year he became president of the International Astronomical Union. Following his death an annual Eddington Memorial Lectureship was created, and the Eddington Medal was struck for annual presentation.

In 1945 astrophysicist Edward Arthur Milne wrote, as noted in the *Dictionary of Scientific Biography,* that Eddington brought the understanding of the structure of stars "all to life, infusing it with his sense of real physics and endowing it with aspects of splendid beauty. . . . Eddington will always be our incomparable pioneer." Judged in today's light, many of Eddington's great advances in understanding the structure of stars may seem very elementary. But for his day they were revolutionary.

BIOGRAPHICAL/CRITICAL SOURCES:

BOOKS

The Eddington Memorial Lectures, Cambridge University Press, 1975-82.

Abbott, David, *Biographical Dictionary of Scientists, Astronomers,* Peter Bedrick, 1984.

Abell, George, et al, *Exploration of the Universe,* 6th Edition, Saunders College Press, 1991.

Chandrasekhar, Subrahmanyan, *Eddington, the Most Distinguished Astrophysicist of His Time,* Cambridge University Press (New York), 1983.

Chandrasekhar, *Truth and Beauty: Aesthetics and Motivations in Science,* University of Chicago Press, 1987.

Dingle, Herbert, *Reflections on the Philosophy of Sir Arthur Eddington,* Cambridge University Press (London), 1948.

Gillispie, Charles Coulston, editor, *Dictionary of Scientific Biography,* Scribner, 1971.

Kilmister, C. W., and B. O. J. Tupper, *Eddington's Statistical Theory,* Clarendon Press (Oxford), 1962.

Kilmister, *Sir Arthur Eddington,* Pergamon Press (New York), 1966.

Kilmister, *Eddington's Search for a Fundamental Theory: a Key to the Universe,* Cambridge University Press, 1994.

Ritchie, Arthur David, *The Sources of Eddington's Philosophy,* Cambridge University Press, 1954.

Witt-Hansen, Johannes, *Exposition and Critique of the Conceptions of Eddington Concerning the Philosophy of Physical Science,* G.E.C. Gad (Copenhagen), 1958.*

*   *   *

EDWARDS, Cecile Hoover 1926-

PERSONAL: Born October 26, 1926 in East St. Louis, IL; daughter of Ernest (an insurance manager) and Annie (a schoolteacher; maiden name, Jordan); married Gerald Alonzo; children: Gerald, Adrienne, Hazel. *Education:* Tuskegee Institute, B.A., 1946, M.A., 1947; Iowa State University, Ph.D., 1950.

ADDRESSES: Office—Department of Nutritional Sciences, College of Allied Health Sciences, Howard University, 2400 6th Street NW, Washington, DC 20059.

CAREER: Nutritional researcher. Research Awards project director, 1951; White House Conference Panel on Community Nutrition chair, 1969; Tuskegee Institute, Tuskegee, AL, faculty and research associate, 1950-56, head of department of foods and nutrition, beginning 1952; School of Human Ecology, Howard University, Washington, DC, curriculum designer, 1970-74, Dean of the School of Human Ecol-

ogy, 1974-87; National Institute of Child Health and Human Development, director of the study of nutritional medical, psychological socioeconomic, and lifestyle factors, 1985; *Journal of Nutrition,* editor, 1994.

MEMBER: American Institute of Nutrition; Southeastern Conference of Teachers of Foods and Nutrition, 1971; National Institute of Health, 1972-75; Expert Committee on Nitrates, Nitrites and Nitrasamines, 1975-79; consultant, University of Khartoum Sudan Ford Foundation, 1978; project director, training program for residents of public housing, 1982; chair, National Conference on Black Youth Unemployment, 1983; project director, Nutrition, Other Factors and the Outcomes of Pregnancy, 1985; American Institute of Nutrition; National Institute of Science.

AWARDS, HONORS: Outstanding Achievement Award, National Council of Negro Women, 1963; Citation for outstanding contribution to education, City of East St. Louis, 1964; Scroll of Honor, Outstanding Achievement in Nutrition and Research the Links Inc., 1970; Home Economics Centennial Alumni Award, Iowa State University, 1971; Alumni Achievement Award Iowa State University, 1972; Alumni Merit Award Tuskegee Institute, 1974; Citation from House of Representatives, State of Illinois, for Devotion to Eliminating Poverty, 1980; Proclamation by Governor of Illinois, Cecile Hoover Edwards Day.

WRITINGS:

(Editor with others) *Current Knowledge of the Relationships of Selected Nutrients, Alcohol, Tobacco, and Drug Use, and Other Factors to Pregnancy Outcomes,* School of Human Ecology, Howard University (Washington, DC), 1988.

(Editor with others) *Human Ecology: Interactions of Man with His Environments,* Kendall-Hunt, 1991.

Contributor to journals and periodicals, including *Journal of Nutrition, American Journal of Clinical Nutrition, Journal of Negro Education, Human Ecology Monograph.*

SIDELIGHTS: Cecile Hoover Edwards, a nutritional researcher and educator, devoted her career to improving the nutrition and well-being of disadvantaged people. In recognition of her achievements, she was cited by the National Council of Negro Women for outstanding contributions to science and by the Illinois House of Representatives for "determined devotion to the cause of eliminating poverty through the creation of a quality environment."

Edwards was born in East St. Louis, Illinois, on October 26, 1926. Her mother, Annie Jordan, was a former schoolteacher and her father, Ernest Hoover, was an insurance manager. Edwards enrolled at Tuskegee Institute, the college made famous by Booker T. Washington and George Washington Carver, at age fifteen, and entered a home economics program with minors in nutrition and chemistry. "I knew from the first day that I had no interest in dietetics," Edwards told Laura Newman in an interview. "My real interest was in improving nutrition through research." Edwards was awarded a bachelor of science degree with honors from Tuskegee in 1946. With a fellowship from Swift and Co. she conducted chemical analyses of an animal source of protein. In 1947, she earned a master's degree in chemistry from Tuskegee. Edwards received a Ph.D. in nutrition from Iowa State University in 1950. Edwards's doctoral dissertation was a study of methionine, an essential amino acid that she said has "not only the good things needed to synthesize protein, but also has sulfur, which can be given to other compounds and be easily released." Edwards wrote at least twenty papers on methionine.

After completing her doctorate, Edwards returned to Tuskegee as a faculty member and a research associate of the Carver Foundation, remaining there for six years. "Staying in nutrition at Tuskegee seemed like an opportunity," said Edwards. "I felt obligated to pay back the opportunity Tuskegee had given me." In 1952 she became head of Tuskegee's department of foods and nutrition. Edwards's nutritional research later expanded to studies of the amino acid composition of food, the utilization of protein from vegetarian diets, and the planning of well-balanced and nutritious diets, especially for low-income and disadvantaged populations in the United States and developing countries.

Designing a new curriculum for the School of Human Ecology at Howard University, Washington, D.C., in the 1970s was a high point of Edwards's career. Just before she came to Howard, in 1969, Arthur Jensen had argued in his paper, "How Much Can We Boost IQ," that blacks were inherently inferior, and that providing education, nutrition, and other resources could not bring them equality. Disproving the Jensen hypothesis became a major goal for Edwards. Howard's School of Human Ecology conducted research and evaluated work in providing resources for low-income people so that they could help themselves. It taught parenting, childcare, nutrition, budgeting, job skills, and other skills useful in overcom-

ing obstacles. In 1974, Edwards was appointed Dean of the School of Human Ecology, a position she held until 1987.

In 1985 Edwards became director of a five-year project sponsored by the National Institute of Child Health and Human Development to study the nutritional, medical, psychological, socioeconomic, and lifestyle factors which influence pregnancy outcomes in low-income women. In 1994 she served as editor of the *Journal of Nutrition* May supplement on "African American Women and Their Pregnancies." A humanitarian and prolific writer who published numerous scientific papers, Edwards helped to establish a family resource development program in her birthplace, East St. Louis, Illinois.

BIOGRAPHICAL/CRITICAL SOURCES:

PERIODICALS

Interview with Laura Newman, conducted March 12, 1994.*

*   *   *

EGOYAN, Atom 1960-

PERSONAL: Surname is pronounced "Eh-*goy*-en"; born July 19, 1960, in Cairo, Egypt; immigrated to Canada, 1962; naturalized Canadian citizen; son of Joseph (a furniture store manager) and Shushan (a furniture store manager; maiden name, Devletian) Egoyan; married Arsinee Khanjian (an actress); children: Arshile (son). *Education:* Trinity College, University of Toronto, B.A., 1982. *Avocational interests:* Classical guitar.

ADDRESSES: Home—Toronto, Ontario Canada. *Office*—Ego Film Arts, 80 Niagara St., Toronto, Ontario M5V 1C5, Canada.

CAREER: Director, producer, film editor, actor, and writer. Associated with Playwrights Unit in Toronto, Ontario, Canada. Director of Ego Film Arts in Toronto, 1982—. Director of films, including *Howard in Particular,* 1979; *After Grad with Dad,* 1980; *Peep Show,* 1981; (and producer and editor) *Next of Kin,* 1984; *Men: A Passion Playground,* 1985; (and producer and editor) *Family Viewing,* 1987; *The Final Twist,* 1987; *Speaking Parts,* Cinephile, 1989; (and producer) *The Adjuster,* Orion Classics, 1991; "En passant" in *Montreal vu par,* 1991; (and producer and coeditor) *Calendar,* Zeitgeist, 1992; (and producer) *Exotica,* Miramax, 1994. Director of television movies, including *Open House* (broadcast as part of *Canadian Reflections* series), Canadian Broadcasting Corporation (CBC), 1982; *In This Corner,* 1985, *Looking for Nothing,* 1989, and *Gross Misconduct,* CBC, 1992; director of episodes of television shows such as *Alfred Hitchcock Presents* and *Twilight Zone;* director of stage productions, including Salome, 1996. Actor in motion pictures, including *Next of Kin,* 1984; *La boite a soleil,* 1988; *Calendar,* Zeitgeist, 1992; and *Camilla,* Miramax, 1994. Member of jury for Cannes International Film Festival, 1996.

MEMBER: Academy of Canadian Television and Radio Artists, Directors Guild of Canada.

AWARDS, HONORS: Grant from University of Toronto's Hart House Film Board; prize from Canadian National Exhibition's film festival, for *Howard in Particular;* grants from Canadian Council and Ontario Arts Council; Gold Ducat Award, Mannheim International Film Week Festival, 1984, for *Next of Kin;* Toronto City Award for excellence in a Canadian production, Toronto Film Festival, 1987, International Critics Award for Best Feature Film, Uppsala Film Festival, 1988, and Priz Alcan from Festival du Nouveau Cinema, 1988, all for *Family Viewing;* prize for best screenplay, Vancouver International Film Festival, 1989, for *Speaking Parts;* Special Jury Prize, Moscow Film Festival, Golden Spike, Vallodolid Film Festival, Toronto City Award, Toronto Film Festival, and award for best Canadian film, Sudbury Film Festival, all 1991, all for *The Adjuster;* Golden Gate Award, San Francisco Film Festival, 1992, for *Gross Misconduct;* prize for best film in "new cinema," International Jury for Art Cinema and prize from Berlin International Film Festival, both 1994, both for *Calendar;* Genie awards for best picture, best director, and best writer, International Film Critics Award, Cannes Film Festival, Prix de la Critique for best foreign film, and Toronto City Award, Toronto International Film Festival, all 1994, all for *Exotica.*

WRITINGS:

SCREENPLAYS

(And director, producer, and editor) *Next of Kin,* 1984.
(And director, producer, and editor) *Family Viewing,* 1987.

(And director) *Speaking Parts,* Cinephile, 1989.
A Fortified City, 1990.
(And director and producer) *The Adjuster,* Orion Classics, 1991.
(And director, producer, and coeditor) *Calendar,* Zeitgeist, 1992.
(And director and producer) *Exotica,* Miramax, 1994.

Also director and writer of short films, including *Howard in Particular,* 1979, and *Open House* (broadcast as part of *Canadian Reflections* series), Canadian Broadcasting Corporation, 1982. Director and writer of the segment "En passant" for the film *Montreal vu par,* 1992.

OTHER

Speaking Parts (essays, interviews, and the script for *Speaking Parts*), Coach House Press, 1993.
Exotica (includes interview with Egoyan and script for *Exotica*), introduction by Geoff Pevere, Coach House Press, 1995.

Author of plays, including *The Doll.*

WORK IN PROGRESS: Libretto for composer Rodney Sharman's opera *Elsewhereness.*

SIDELIGHTS: Atom Egoyan is a prominent independent filmmaker whose works reflect some of the more peculiar and alienating aspects of modern life. Egoyan was born in 1960 in Egypt and moved with his family to Canada when he was only two years old. He studied at the University of Toronto's Trinity College, where he turned to filmmaking. His works at that time included the short films *Howard in Particular* and *Open House.* Egoyan graduated from college in 1982 and subsequently joined a playwright's group in Toronto. The appeal of filmmaking, however, proved too great for Egoyan, and after earning grants from Canadian arts councils he undertook the writing and directing of *Next of Kin,* his first feature film.

In *Next of Kin,* a listless Canadian youth leaves his troubled home and poses as the missing son of an Armenian couple, who respond by welcoming him into their lives. *Next of Kin*'s themes of alienation and identity—coupled with Egoyan's technical precision, particularly his use of the camera as an overtly voyeuristic device—earned Egoyan the Gold Ducat Award from the Mannheim International Film Week Festival in 1984, but he otherwise received little attention as a new filmmaker.

Egoyan fared better with his second film, *Family Viewing,* which he completed after directing various episodes of atmospheric television shows such as *Alfred Hitchcock Presents* and *The Twilight Zone.* Like these programs, and Egoyan's own *Next of Kin, Family Viewing* is an often unnerving drama. It features a troubled husband who determines to eliminate evidence of his past by replacing home videos with footage of him and his lover engaged in sexual acts. In the course of these and other questionable activities, the protagonist runs afoul of his teenage son, who undertakes a scheme to restore the family to at least a modest degree of harmony and stability. Brian D. Johnson, who profiled Egoyan in *Maclean's,* described *Family Viewing* as a film that "explored video as a literal metaphor for distressed, disembodied memory," and he noted that the film brought attention to Egoyan "at film festivals around the world."

Speaking Parts, Egoyan's next film, shares with *Next of Kin* notions of deception and voyeurism. Here a hotel maid finds herself so obsessed with a coworker that she regularly watches films in which he appeared as a mere extra player. The aspiring actor, in turn, attempts to endear himself to a screenwriter who is staying at the hotel. The screenwriter, however, is preoccupied with the status of a script already submitted to a prospective film producer. *New Statesman and Society* reviewer Suzanne Moore, noting Egoyan's own preoccupation with "the isolation of modern life and the proliferation of media images," declared that *Speaking Parts* "confirms [Egoyan] as a filmmaker of dark originality."

Egoyan followed *Speaking Parts* with *The Adjuster,* a characteristically peculiar drama in which an otherwise alienated insurance adjuster connects profoundly with his clients, many of whom he has placed together in a nearby motel, by tending their needs even as he draws out their stay by delaying the resolutions of their cases. The central character's wife, meanwhile, is a government censor who regularly absconds with the pornographic films she is supposed to be censoring. *Nation* reviewer Stuart Klawans deemed the movie "one of the very best nonmall films now playing."

In 1992 Egoyan completed *Calendar,* another sex-and-videotape drama in which a photographer is accompanied by his wife to Armenia, where he intends to photograph churches for inclusion in a calendar. In Armenia, the protagonist is dismayed by his own inability to connect to the land and culture of his ancestors. His wife, however, is less troubled, and manages to enter into a love affair with their tour guide. Interactions between the hero's wife and the tour guide are ironically preserved by the very video camera that the photographer is using to capture the Armenian imagery. Like Egoyan's previous films, *Calendar* fared well at film festivals, winning prizes from both the International Jury for Art Cinema and the Berlin International Film Festival.

Exotica, Egoyan's 1995 drama, has more of a mysterious tone than either *The Adjuster* or *Calendar. Exotica* details the interactions, and memories, of various figures gathering regularly at a striptease club. Among this band of loners is a customer preoccupied with both his daughter's death and the wellbeing of a particular dancer, an announcer equally concerned with the dancer, and the dancer herself, who had been both the dead daughter's babysitter and the forlorn announcer's lover. The relationships between these and still other characters are slowly disclosed as the film proceeds, although the final sequences serve to deepen, rather than diminish, the characters' personal secrets and obsessions. An *Entertainment Weekly* reviewer described *Exotica* as "an elaborate shell game" and added that it is "a gorgeous tease."

The scripts for both *Speaking Parts* and *Exotica* have been published in volumes that also feature commentaries on Egoyan's life and work.

BIOGRAPHICAL/CRITICAL SOURCES:

PERIODICALS

Entertainment Weekly, March 24, 1995, pp. 46-47.
Film Comment, November-December, 1995, p. 73.
Maclean's, October 3, 1994, pp. 45-47.
Nation, July 13, 1992, p. 64; March 21, 1994, pp. 190-92.
New Statesman and Society, September 22, 1989, p. 43.*

*   *   *

EHRENFEST, Paul   1880-1933

PERSONAL: Born January 18, 1880, in Vienna, Austria-Hungary (now Austria); died September 25, 1933, following suicide; son of Sigmund (owner of a grocery store) and Johanna (Jellinek) Ehrenfest; married Tatyana Alexeyevna Afanassjewa (a mathematician), December 21, 1904; children: Tatyana Pavlovna,

Anna, Paul Jr. and Vassily. *Education:* Attended the University of Gottingen; Vienna Technische Hochschule, Ph.D., 1904.

CAREER: Physicist. University of Leiden, Amsterdam, The Netherlands, professor of theoretical physics, 1912-32.

WRITINGS:

(With wife, Tatyana Ehrenfest) *The Conceptual Foundations of the Statistical Approach in Mechanics,* Cornell University Press, 1959.
Collected Scientific Papers, Interscience, 1959.

SIDELIGHTS: Paul Ehrenfest is best known as a profound, yet engaging teacher who popularized and explained many new ideas in physics, particularly in the categories of quantum theory and relativity. His own research and collaborations with his wife served to solidify existing concepts in physics, while his personal devotion to science forged bonds between himself and the likes of physicists Max Planck and Albert Einstein. Ehrenfest succeeded Hendrik Lorentz as professor of theoretical physics at the University of Leiden, where he remained until his death in 1933.

Paul Ehrenfest was born in Vienna (in what was then Austria-Hungary), on January 18, 1880. His parents—Sigmund Ehrenfest and the former Johanna Jellinek—had moved to Vienna in the 1860s from the small village of Loschwitz in Moravia. Although very poor at the time of this move, the Ehrenfests had used Johanna's dowry to establish a grocery store in Vienna. By the time Paul (the youngest of five sons) was born, the business had become a successful enterprise and the family was living comfortably. Ehrenfest's interest in science was the result of his elder brother Arthur's encouragement and instruction, and it was a pursuit that offset an adolescence impaired by consistently poor health and the persistent and powerful anti-Semitic atmosphere that prevailed in Vienna at the time. The loss of Ehrenfest's mother, when he was ten, and his father, when he was sixteen, contributed to his sense of depression and a lack of confidence which would plague him throughout his life.

After completing his primary education in 1890, Ehrenfest entered the Akademisches Gymnasium, graduating nine years later. Throughout this period, his formal schooling was supplemented by the education he received at home from his four older brothers. In the fall of 1899, Ehrenfest enrolled at the Vienna

Technische Hochschule, where he was at first interested in majoring in chemistry. He soon changed his mind, however, after attending lectures on the mechanical theory of heat given by the famous Ludwig Boltzmann. Eventually taking a close personal interest in Ehrenfest, Boltzmann later supervised the thesis that earned his student a doctoral degree in 1904.

Two years after entering the Technische Hochschule, Ehrenfest decided to spend a year at the University of Gottingen, where he was exposed to some of the most brilliant minds in science and mathematics. He also met his future wife, Tatyana Alexeyevna Afanassjewa, a mathematics student from Russia. The two soon fell in love and were married on December 21, 1904. They eventually had four children together, Tatyana Pavlovna, Anna, Paul Jr., and Vassily. The husband-and-wife team of Paul and Tatyana Ehrenfest would later produce a number of scholarly papers, primarily in the field of statistical mechanics. They lived at first in Vienna, then in Gottingen, and finally in St. Petersburg, moves necessitated by the fact that between 1904 and 1911, Ehrenfest was unable to obtain a permanent teaching appointment.

Ehrenfest's fortunes took a turn for the better in May, 1912, when he received a letter from Lorentz, the prominent Dutch physicist. Retiring as professor of theoretical physics at the University of Leiden, Lorentz offered to suggest Ehrenfest as his successor. Delighted with the offer, Ehrenfest moved to Leiden in October, 1912, where he remained for the next two decades. During his tenure at Leiden, Ehrenfest became one of the most highly respected members of the world scientific community. His fame came not from any great contribution, but primarily because of his skills as a teacher and through his role in disseminating coherently the new developments in physics. In a memorial to Ehrenfest, published in *Out of My Later Years,* Einstein wrote of the Dutch physicist: "He was not merely the best teacher in our profession whom I have ever known; he was also passionately preoccupied with the development and destiny of men, especially his students." George Uhlenbeck, discoverer of electron spin and one of Ehrenfest's students, called him "one of the really great teachers," in a 1956 article in the *American Journal of Physics.*

Ehrenfest contributed greatly in clarifying the modern concepts of physics. Throughout the early 1900s, many tenets of classical physics were being overthrown and replaced by new concepts governing quantum mechanics, relativity, and other fields. However, technical expositions of "the new physics" were often internally inconsistent and difficult to understand—in many cases, to both scientists and non-scientists. Ehrenfest had the remarkable ability to sort out what was going on at the frontiers of research and summarize it in a way that could be more easily understood. Unfortunately, the accolades of his students and colleagues were not enough to overcome his deep-rooted sense of inferiority and insecurity. Those feelings were compounded in the early 1930s by both personal and professional problems. He was partially estranged from his wife, whom he loved with a passion the likes of which, Einstein observed, "I have not often witnessed in my life." In addition, Ehrenfest took very personally the growing threat posed to his fellow scientists by the rise of the Nazi party in Germany. Finally, he seems to have felt overwhelmed and inadequate to deal with the continuing changes taking place in physics during the early 1930s. All of these factors appear to have contributed to his decision to end his own life in Amsterdam, The Netherlands, on September 25, 1933.

BIOGRAPHICAL/CRITICAL SOURCES:

BOOKS

Einstein, Albert , *Out of My Later Years,* Philosophical Library, 1950, pp. 236-39.
Gillispie, Charles Coulson, editor, *Dictionary of Scientific Biography,* Volume 4, Scribner, 1975, pp. 292-94.
Klein, Martin J., *Paul Ehrenfest,* Volume 1: *The Making of a Theoretical Physicist,* North-Holland Publishing, 1970.

PERIODICALS

American Journal of Physics, vol. 24, 1956, pp. 431-33.*

*   *   *

EISNER, Thomas 1929-

PERSONAL: Born June 25, 1929, in Berlin, Germany; naturalized United States citizen, 1952; son of Hans Edouard (a chemist) and Margarete (a painter; maiden name, Heil); married Maria Lobell (a social scientist and entomologist), June 10, 1952; children: Yvonne Maria, Vivian Martha and Christina Margaret. *Education:* Harvard University, B.A., 1951, Ph.D., 1955.

CAREER: Entomologist and biologist. Cornell University, Ithaca, NY, assistant professor, became full professor, 1957-75, Jacob Gould Schurman Professor of Biology, 1976--. University of Florida, visiting professor, 1977-78; Hopkins Marine Lab, Stanford University, visiting professor, 1979-80; University of Zurich, visiting professor, 1980-81. Department of Entomology, School of Agriculture, Netherlands, visiting scientist, 1964-65; affiliated with Smithsonian Tropical Resident Laboratory, 1968, and Center for Conservation Biology, Stanford University, 1983. World Environment and Resources Program, MacArthur Foundation, consultant, 1987.

AWARDS, HONORS: Founder's Memorial Award, Entomology Society of America, 1969; Archie F. Carr Medal, 1983; Proctor Prize, Sigma Xi, 1986; Karl Ritter von Frisch Medal, German Zoological Society, 1988; Centennial Medal, Harvard University, 1989; Tyler Prize, 1990; Esselen Award, 1991; Silver Medal, International Society of Chemical Ecology, 1991; National Medal of Science, 1994. Guggenheim fellow, 1964 and 1972; fellow, American Academy of Arts and Sciences, Royal Society of Arts, Animal Behavioral Society, and Entomological Society.

WRITINGS:

(Editor with E. O. Wilson) *Animal Behavior: Readings from Scientific American,* W. H. Freeman, 1975.
(Editor with E. O. Wilson) *The Insects: Readings from Scientific American,* W. H. Freeman, 1977.
The Defensive World of Insects, American Chemical Society, 1981.
Chemische ekologie, Territorialiteat, Gegenseitige Versteandigung, G. Fischer (Stuttgart, Germany, and New York City), 1986.
(With Bert Heolldobler and Martin Lindauer) *Chemical Ecology: The Chemistry of Biotic Interaction,* National Academy Press (Washington, DC), 1996.

Contributor to journals and periodicals, including *Insectes sociaux, Nature and Science, Science, GEO, Science News,* and *Issues in Science and Technology.* Coauthor of several books including, *Animal Adaptation,* 1964, and *Life on Earth,* 1973.

SIDELIGHTS: Thomas Eisner is one of the world's foremost authorities on the role of chemicals in the behavior and survival of insects. He has also played an active role in the crusade to preserve the world's endangered rain forests and other threatened lands. Eisner was born in Berlin, Germany, on June 25, 1929, the second of two children. His father, Hans E. Eisner, was a chemist, and as a hobby made perfumes, lotions, and home remedies. The intriguing odors that filled their home caused Eisner to develop an early interest in both chemistry and the art of "sniffing." His mother, Margarete Heil Eisner, a painter, instilled in him an appreciation for nature's beauty.

Eisner's father was Jewish and in 1933, when Eisner was only four years old, the family fled Nazi Germany. They settled for a few years in Barcelona, Spain, and there the young Eisner began to develop a fascination with insects. One day, while sitting in a sand box playing with pill bugs (wood lice), a violent explosion shook the neighborhood. Eisner's recollection, according to a *Scientific American* profile in 1991, was that he was annoyed rather than frightened. The commotion had interrupted the fun he was having with his insects. The explosion was a harbinger of the Spanish Civil War. Its violence caused the Eisners to flee again, this time for France, aboard a freighter carrying diseased cattle and hordes of refugees. They settled in Paris for half a year, and there the family rented a piano. It was Eisner's first introduction to the instrument on which he would eventually become accomplished. In 1937, with the threat of World War II looming, the Eisner family left Europe altogether and set off for South America, eventually finding a home in Uruguay. There was much insect life in his new environment, and as a young boy Eisner made collections of the beetles, tropical moths, and ants he encountered. His fascination with insects was rivaled only by his enjoyment of music. He considered becoming a professional pianist, but eventually chose the sciences.

In 1947 Eisner's family moved again, this time to New York City. He enrolled in Champlain College in Plattsburg, New York, but two years later transferred to Harvard University, where he received the B.A. degree in 1951. In 1952 he became a naturalized U.S. citizen, and that same year he married Maria Lobell. Originally trained in social work, she went on to become an entomologist and occasional research collaborator with Eisner. Together they had three daughters, Yvonne Maria in 1954, Vivian Martha in 1957, and Christina Margaret in 1959.

During Eisner's senior year at Harvard he had taken a course in entomology, an experience that led him to realize it was possible to make a career out of study-

ing insects. He went on to enroll in the entomology department at Harvard and received his Ph.D. in 1955. While a graduate student he discovered, by performing delicate microscopic surgery, an unusual valve in the digestive tract of certain ants. The valve enables the ants to ingest enormous amounts of food that they later regurgitate and feed to other ants. During the two years following his graduate work, Eisner did postdoctoral research at Harvard on insect physiology. In 1957 he accepted an appointment as an assistant professor at Cornell University, in Ithaca, New York.

Eisner has remained on the faculty at Cornell University since 1957, rising through the ranks to full professorship in 1966. Since 1976 he has held the title of Jacob Gould Schurman Professor of Biology. At Cornell Eisner's research interests shifted from insect physiology to the chemical aspects of insect behavior. Since then his scientific work has focused on the intricate and unusual ways in which insects use chemistry to court, communicate, defend themselves, and remain healthy. A pioneer in his field, he is considered the father of chemical ecology, the study of chemical relationships among living things.

Using high-speed photography and microscopic lenses, he has detected previously unknown insect strategies for capturing prey and repelling enemies. Many of these strategies involve the use of chemicals. Eisner is perhaps best known for his discovery of the unusual defensive behavior of the bombardier beetle. At the tip of the beetle's abdomen is a gland that operates like a gun turret, firing rounds of scalding hot poison at a rate of five hundred pulses per second. Eisner has helped decipher the flash code of "femme-fatale fireflies" and documented the use of disguise by green lacewing larvae to gain access to their prey, woolly alder aphids. He is intrigued by the chemical odors that insects give off, and employs the olfactory skills he developed in his youth to detect chemical communication among his research subjects. Many of Eisner's practical discoveries have been the result of collaborative efforts with his colleague, Cornell University chemist Jerrold Meinwald. Together they have discovered nerve drugs in millipedes, cardiac stimulants in fireflies, and cockroach repellents in an endangered mint plant.

Eisner's interest in insect life has led naturally to a broader concern for preservation of natural habitats. He has taken a leadership role in the conservation movement, testifying before United States Senate subcommittees on the Endangered Species Act, helping to publicize the effects of overpopulation on the environment, and serving on the advisory council of the World Resources Institute. He was responsible for convincing the pharmaceutical firm of Merck & Company to strike a deal with the Costa Rican government that preserves their rain forest and provides chemical prospecting rights to Merck. Eisner's research and activism have increased public awareness about the benefits of biodiversity.

Eisner has received numerous awards for his conservation efforts and other achievements, including the Karl Ritter von Frisch Medal from the Deutsche Zoologische Gesellschaft and the Tyler Prize for Environmental Achievement. He has held two Guggenheim fellowships. He became a member of the National Academy of Sciences in 1969. He has been awarded honorary doctorate degrees from colleges and universities in the United States, Germany, Switzerland, and Sweden.

In his spare time, Eisner continues to pursue his love of music, conducting an amateur Cornell University orchestra called BRAHMS, an acronym for Biweekly Rehearsal Association of Honorary Musicians. His insect laboratory at the university is equipped with an upright piano.

BIOGRAPHICAL/CRITICAL SOURCES:

PERIODICALS

New Yorker, August 17, 1992, pp. 34-54.
Scientific American, December, 1991, pp. 60-64.*

*   *   *

ELDREDGE, Niles 1943-

PERSONAL: Born August 25, 1943, in Brooklyn, NY; son of Robert L. (an accountant) and Eleanor R. Eldredge; married Michelle J. Wycoff, June 6, 1964; children: Douglas and Gregory. *Education:* Columbia University, New York City, A.B. (summa cum laude), 1965, Ph.D., 1969. *Avocational interests:* Birdwatching, collecting trumpets and coronets.

CAREER: Paleontologist. Geology Department, Columbia University, New York, adjunct assistant professor, 1969-72, adjunct associate professor of geology, 1975—; Department of Invertebrate Paleontology, American Museum of Natural History, New York, assistant curator, 1969-74, associate curator of invertebrate paleontology, 1974-79, curator, 1979—; City University, New York City, adjunct professor of biology, 1972-80.

MEMBER: Paleontological Society, British Paleontological Association, Society of the Study of Evolution, AAAS.

AWARDS, HONORS: Schuchert Award, Paleontological Society, 1979.

WRITINGS:

(With Harold B. Rollins and Judith Spiller) *Gastropoda and Monoplacophora of the Solsville Member (Middle Devonian, Marcellus formation) in the Chenango Valley, New York State,* American Museum of Natural History (New York), 1971.
Systematics and Evolution of Phacops rana (Green, 1832) and Phacops Iowensis Delo, 1935 (Trilobita) from the Middle Devonian of North America, American Museum of Natural History, 1972.
Systematics of Lower and Lower Middle Devonian Species of the Trilobite Phacops Emmrich in North America, American Museum of Natural History, 1973.
Revision of the Suborder Synziph Osurina (Chelicerata, Merostomata): With Remarks on Merostome Phylogeny, American Museum of Natural History, 1974.
(With Roy E. Plotnick) *Revision of the Pseudoniscine Marostome Genus Cyamocephalus Currie,* American Museum of Natural History, 1974.
(With Joel Cracraft) *Phylogenetic Analysis and Paleontology,* Columbia University Press, 1979.
(With Cracraft) *Phylogenetic Patterns and the Evolutionary Process: Method and Theory in Comparative Biology,* Columbia University Press, 1980.
(With Leonardo Braniesa) *Calmoniid Trilobites of the Lower Devonian Scaphiocoelia Zone of Bolivia: With Remarks on Related Species,* American Museum of Natural History, 1980.
(With Ian Tattersall) *The Myths of Human Evolution,* Columbia University Press, 1982.
The Monkey Business: A Scientist Looks at Creationism, Washington Square Press (New York), 1982.
(With Steven M. Stanley) *Living Fossils,* Springer Verlag (New York), 1984.
Time Frames, the Rethinking of Darwinian Evolution and the Theory of Punctuated Equilibria, Simon & Schuster (New York), 1985.

Unfinished Synthesis: Biological Hierarchies and Modern Evolutionary Thought, Oxford University Press (New York), 1985.

Life Pulse: Episodes from the Story of the Fossil Record, Facts on File (New York), 1987.

The Natural History Reader in Evolution, Columbia University Press, 1987.

Macroevolutionary Dynamics: Species, Niches, and Adaptive Peaks, McGraw-Hill (New York), 1989.

The Fossil Factory: A Kid's Guide to Digging Up Dinosaurs, Exploring Evolution, and Finding Fossils, Addison-Wesley (Reading, MA), 1989.

Fossils: The Evolution and Extinction of Species, H. N. Abrams (New York), 1991.

The Miner's Canary: Unraveling the Mysteries of Extinction, Prentice Hall (New York), 1991.

Systematics, Ecology, and the Biodiversity Crisis, Columbia University Press, 1992.

(With Marjorie Green) *Interaction: the Biological Context of Social Systems,* Columbia University Press, 1992.

Reinventing Darwin, The Great Debate at the High Table of Evolutionary Theory, Wiley (New York), 1995.

Dominion, H. Holt (New York), 1995.

Co-editor of *Systematic Zoology,* 1973-76. Contributor to journals and periodicals, including *Evolution, New Republic, Nature.*

SIDELIGHTS: Niles Eldredge is a paleontologist best known for a theory he developed with fellow paleontologist Stephen Jay Gould called punctuated equilibrium, an evolutionary theory that challenged Darwinian gradualism and changed the way scientists interpret the fossil record. A curator of invertebrate paleontology at the American Museum of Natural History in New York, Eldredge has used the fossil record to improve current theories of evolution, and he has applied some of these theories to better understanding the problems faced by living species. He has been a staunch opponent of the so-called "scientific creationism" movement, and he remains a prolific author.

Eldredge was born in Brooklyn, New York, on August 25, 1943, to Robert and Eleanor Eldredge. His father was an accountant and his mother a homemaker. As a young boy growing up in the northern suburbs of New York City, he would sometimes venture into the city and visit the American Museum of Natural History. "That was definitely formative, no question about it," he told John Spizzirri in an interview. Having done well in Latin in high school, Eldredge planned to study classics when he entered

Columbia University in 1961; he intended to become a lawyer but discovered himself increasingly fascinated with academic research.

Eldredge met his future wife, Michelle J. Wycoff, at Columbia University; she introduced Eldredge to various members of the anthropology department and he began taking courses in this subject. His participation in an ethnographic study turned his attention toward evolution. In the summer of 1963, he served as a trainee with anthropologists studying in a Brazilian fishing village, and he began collecting invertebrate (having no spinal column) fossils from the surrounding reef. After taking courses in paleontology and geology the following semester, Eldredge recalled in his book *Fossils: The Evolution and Extinction of Species,* how he then "embarked on a lifetime career of trying to make some sense of the fossil record of the history of life." On June 6, 1964, he married Wycoff, with whom he would have two sons. He received his bachelor's degree in anthropology in 1965, graduating summa cum laude.

While still an undergraduate, Eldredge met Stephen Jay Gould, who was then a graduate student two years his senior. They both shared an interest in scrutinizing the fossil record of invertebrates at the species level. By the time Eldredge began graduate studies at Columbia University, his interest in invertebrate paleontology had turned to the Paleozoic era, and it was from this era that he chose the subject for his Ph.D. thesis, trilobites. Trilobites lived between 530 and 245 million years ago and they represent one of the earliest groups of arthropods—invertebrate animals with jointed limbs. Fossil evidence has been collected from all over the world which establishes that they existed in a diverse range of environments over an extremely long period of time.

After receiving his Ph.D. in geology from Columbia University in October of 1969, Eldredge assumed the post of adjunct assistant professor in Columbia's geology department, while simultaneously holding a position as an assistant curator in the American Museum of Natural History's department of invertebrate paleontology. By 1971, his work on Paleozoic invertebrates had led to a rethinking of the evolutionary process; he published his theory in the journal *Evolution.* Frustrated that he could find no evolutionary changes in his trilobites despite their wide distribution over time and space, Eldredge conducted a more detailed examination of his specimens. "Then I started noticing these very slight patterns of differences between the eyes in different populations," he told

Spizzirri. "I looked at these in terms of where they were distributed on a map, and how they were distributed in time, and saw that there were these great periods of stability that were interrupted at varying intervals by small, but definitive change, and the change seemed to be concentrated at these short intervals." The following year, Gould contributed to Eldredge's hypothesis. Republished in the collection, *Models in Paleobiology,* their theory of "punctuated equilibrium" seemed to contradict certain fundamental elements of Darwinian evolution.

Darwin argued that evolution was gradual and continuous, but his concept of a gradual progression of species over time was often marred by gaps in the fossil record, although he believed these would eventually be filled by later research. In the early 1940s, the American paleontologist George Gaylord Simpson suggested that these gaps were not necessarily the result of a poor fossil record and speculated that evidence of continuous evolution might never be found. He went on to delineate the circumstances in which abrupt changes could occur, but he limited the scope of his research to the larger groups, like whales and bats, because he believed that specific species, the individual constituents of groups, were not important to this process. Eldredge and Gould redefined Simpson's theories by concentrating on species, where they were able to incorporate aspects of speciation theories that suggested that the branching off, or budding, of lineages served as the primary mechanism for abrupt change. In the theory proposed by Eldredge and Gould, change is only abrupt relative to geological time and the long history of evolution. "Most anatomical change in the fossil record," Eldredge told Neil A. Campbell in the *American Biology Teacher,* "seems to be concentrated in relatively brief bursts punctuating longer periods of relative stability." The theory of punctuated equilibrium initially met with mixed reviews and still has its opponents, though leading evolutionary biologists tend to agree that stasis plays an integral role in the process of evolution.

In 1972, Eldredge became adjunct professor of biology at the City University of New York; in 1974, he advanced to associate positions at Columbia University and the American Museum of Natural History, where he was named curator of the department of invertebrate paleontology in 1979. As an extension of his work on species, Eldredge began to look at the hierarchical relationships of living systems, working to define the interactive nature of organisms and their environments within successively larger systems. "Large scale entities—ecosystems, species, social systems—are real entities in and of themselves composed of parts," Eldredge explained to Spizzirri. "Just like organisms are composed of parts and organisms are parts of populations, populations are parts of these larger scale systems."

In the early 1980s, Eldredge unwillingly became the subject of controversy over scientific creationism. Creationist leader Luther Sunderland co-opted the theory of punctuated equilibrium and, using the ideas of stasis and gaps in the fossil record, he claimed it could disprove evolution. After conducting an interview with Eldredge under the guise of being a consultant for the New York State Board of Regents, Sunderland apparently referred to Eldredge as an advocate for the simultaneous teaching of evolution and creationism in the classroom. Embarrassed and angry, Eldredge wrote an article for the *New Republic,* denouncing claims of scientific creationism as bad science, if even science at all. He later expanded the article into the book *The Monkey Business: A Scientist Looks at Creationism,* and he has written other critical pieces against the movement.

Eldredge has continued to study events of the geologic past, with a particular interest in the connections between environmental change and speciation and extinction, as well as the role these events play within living systems. Looking at the mass extinctions of the past, Eldredge has tried to derive from them answers that might help solve modern concerns about biodiversity. Examples from the past have shown that when habitats are radically and abruptly altered and organisms are unable to find similar or suitable habitats elsewhere, they will become extinct. He believes extinction has played a critical role in the emergence of new species, particularly humans, as he told Neil A. Campbell in the *American Biology Teacher:* "There is nothing inevitable in the system that human beings would emerge. And that is where the importance of extinction really is—it reshuffles the deck." But he argues that evolution is not necessarily good, and he believes that our survival depends on the survival of other species in the complex global ecosystem.

Eldredge co-edited the publication *Systematic Zoology* from 1973 to 1976, and has written over 160 articles, books, and reviews. The recipient of the Schuchert Award from the Paleontological Society in 1979, he is a lecturer on issues concerning evolutionary theory and biodiversity. Besides his hobby as a bird-watcher, which he says "has real implications for my professional career," he plays and collects trumpets and cornets.

BIOGRAPHICAL/CRITICAL SOURCES:

BOOKS

Gould, Stephen Jay, *Hen's Teeth and Horse's Toes,* Norton, 1983, pp. 253-62.

Gould, Stephen Jay, *The Panda's Thumb,* Norton, 1983, pp. 179-85.

PERIODICALS

American Biology Teacher, May, 1990, pp. 264-67.

OTHER

Interview with John Spizzirri, conducted February 18, 1994.*

* * *

ELLIOTT, Melinda 1947-

PERSONAL: Born November 6, 1947, in Phoenix, AZ; daughter of Richard H.(an attorney) and Maxine (a homemaker; maiden name, Yeatmau) Elliott; married Michael R. Snouffer (a carpenter and photographer), May 6, 1978 (divorced January 3, 1990). *Education:* Occidental College, B.A., 1969; Stanford University, M.A., 1977; license in massage therapy.

ADDRESSES: Home and office—2442 Cerrillos Rd., Ste. 262, Santa Fe, NM 87505. *Agent*—Maggie Duval, P.O. Box 515, Tesuque, NM 87574.

CAREER: Writer, journalist, licensed massage therapist.

WRITINGS:

The School of American Research: A History: The First Eighty Years, The School (Santa Fe, NM), 1987.

(With Rick Dillingham) *Acoma and Laguna Pottery,* edited by Joan Kathryn O'Donnell, School of American Research Press (Santa Fe, NM), 1992.

Great Excavations: Tales of Early Southwestern Archaeology, 1888-1939, School of American Research Press, 1995.

Contributor to periodicals, including *Denver Post, Boston Globe,* and *Massage and Bodywork Magazine.*

SIDELIGHTS: Melinda Elliott told *CA:* "My first home was a ten-acre farm in Phoenix, Arizona, the town where I was born on November 6, 1947. I grew up in that green, leafy rural space, in a house surrounded by olive, fig, and pecan trees. My family named this little farm 'Few Acres.' Here my grandfather, who died just before my birth, had raised chickens and later my grandmother rented our big pasture to a Mexican cowboy named Jose. My Dad and my Aunt helped me to buy a horse when I was twelve, and after that I spent lots of time riding through orange groves and cotton fields on rich farmland now covered with shopping malls.

"My writing career began when I started sending letters home from Heide, Germany, where I was an American Field Service (AFS) high school exchange student in 1964. My B.A. is from Occidental College in Los Angeles, where I majored in German after spending my junior year at Heidelberg. Eight years after I received my B.A. in 1969, I managed to come up with an M.A. from Stanford in journalism; then I moved to Santa Fe, New Mexico, with my husband-to-be, Michael Snouffer, who was then a carpenter and photographer. (Somewhere in there I also spent two semesters at the American Graduate School of International Management—I like going to school.)

"In Santa Fe my first job was in the publications department of an anthropological center called the School of American Research. Eighteen years later, having worked for the school as an independent contractor for years, I gave the publications department there the manuscript of my first major book. This project, six years in the writing, was an adventure story covering the romance and science of southwestern archaeology—*Great Excavations: Tales of Early Southwestern Archaeology, 1888-1939.* It was published in September '95, and the reviews have been great. (A few years previous, the school had also published *Acoma and Laguna Pottery,* a beautifully illustrated volume for which I received a "with" credit, while Rick Dillingham was listed as the primary author.)

"In between my arrival in Santa Fe and the publication of these two books were hours and hours of writing for newspapers and magazines—notably the *Boston Globe* and *Denver Post.* I covered the colorful and fascinating people, places, history, and culture of the Southwest, and especially the Four Corners region.

"While *Great Excavations* was in press, the greatest events of my writing career were taking place—I visited Hawaii, *and* I went swimming with dolphins in the Caribbean Sea, *and* I became a licensed massage therapist with a specialty in aquatic bodywork. Now I write regularly for *Massage and Bodywork Magazine,* and I am working on a book compiling all of my articles on in-water massage. The future of my work as a writer and therapist lies in those amazing experiences of the connection between mind, body and natural world."

*   *   *

ENGLADE, Ken(neth Francis) 1938-

PERSONAL: Born October 7, 1938, in Memphis, TN; son of Joseph George and Sara (Schneider) Englade; married Sharon Flynn, November 27, 1960 (divorced, February, 1971); married Sara Elizabeth Crews, February 29, 1980 (divorced, September, 1991); married Heidi Hizel, January 3, 1997; children: (first marriage) Dennis Alan, Michelle Suzanne, Mark Andrew. *Education:* Louisiana State University, B.A., 1960. *Politics:* Democrat. *Religion:* Roman Catholic.

ADDRESSES: Office—P.O. Box 3148, Corrales, NM 87048.

CAREER: LaFourche Comet (newspaper), Thibodaux, LA, reporter, 1960-63; United Press International, reporter, bureau manager, correspondent, Baton Rouge, LA, 1963-64, New Orleans, LA, 1964-67, Edinburgh, TX, 1967-68, Albuquerque, NM, 1968-71, New York, NY, 1971-72, Saigon, Vietnam, 1972-73, Hong Kong, 1973-75, and Dallas, TX, 1975-77; freelance writer, 1977-79; *Florida Times Union,* Georgia capital correspondent 1980-83; freelance writer, 1983—.

MEMBER: American Society of Journalists and Authors, Authors Guild, Southwest Writers.

AWARDS, HONORS: Edgar Award nomination, Mystery Writers of America, 1991, for *Beyond Reason: The True Story of a Shocking Double Murder, a Brilliant and Beautiful Virginia Socialite, and a Deadly Psychotic Obsession.*

WRITINGS:

Cellar of Horror (crime nonfiction), St. Martin's (New York City); 1989.

Murder in Boston (crime nonfiction), St. Martin's (New York City); 1990.

Beyond Reason: The True Story of a Shocking Double Murder, a Brilliant and Beautiful Virginia Socialite, and a Deadly Psychotic Obsession (crime nonfiction), St. Martin's (New York City), c. 1990.

Deadly Lessons (crime nonfiction), St. Martin's, 1991.

A Family Business (crime nonfiction), St. Martin's, 1992.

To Hatred Turned: A True Story of Love and Death in Texas (crime nonfiction), St. Martin's, c. 1993.

Hoffa (film novelization), HarperCollins (New York City), c. 1993.

Blood Sister (crime nonfiction), St. Martin's, 1994.

Hot Blood: The Millionairess, the Money, and the Horse Murders (crime nonfiction), St. Martin's, 1996.

People of the Plains (novel; part of "Tony Hillerman's Frontier, People of the Plains" series), HarperCollins, 1996.

The Tribes (novel; part of "Tony Hillerman's Frontier, People of the Plains" series), HarperCollins, 1996.

The Soldiers (novel; part of "Tony Hillerman's Frontier, People of the Plains" series), HarperCollins, 1996.

Battle Cry (novel; part of "Tony Hillerman's Frontier, People of the Plains" series), HarperCollins, 1997.

WORK IN PROGRESS: Brothers in Blood.

SIDELIGHTS: Ken Englade had a career in newspaper journalism during the 1960s and 1970s. His first reporting job was for the *LaFourche Comet,* a paper in Thibodaux, Louisiana. After three years, however, Englade took a position with United Press International, and worked for them in various locations, including New Orleans, Louisiana, New York City, Saigon, Vietnam, and Dallas, Texas. He left to try his hand as a freelance writer in 1977; a little over a decade later, his first book in the genre of true crime, *Cellar of Horror,* was published. Since then, Englade has penned other volumes of true crime, including *Beyond Reason: The True Story of a Shocking Double Murder, a Brilliant and Beautiful Virginia Socialite, and a Deadly Psychotic Obsession, To Hatred Turned: A True Story of Love and Death in Texas,* and *Hot Blood: The Millionairess, the Money, and the Horse Murders.*

In *Beyond Reason,* Englade provides readers with the facts behind a gruesome double murder which took place in Virginia in 1985. A retired married couple was found murdered in their home, and at first, the circumstances were so bizarre that the police suspected that some strange cult had been behind the act. Eventually, however, the trail led to the couple's own daughter, and to her German-born boyfriend—both extremely disturbed individuals. *Publishers Weekly* declared that the author "ably narrates a complex case, showing how difficult it was to defeat the wiles" of the young murderous pair. Peter Robertson in *Booklist* noted the "pleasure" available to readers of Englade's narrative, and further explained that the author "works hard at exposing the psychotic underpinnings" of the crime's perpetrators.

Englade's 1993 book, *To Hatred Turned,* tells a story that began with the murder of a woman in Dallas, Texas, in 1983. The victim was the mistress of a contractor, and police investigated him in connection with the murder, but no evidence could be found to link him to the crime. The contractor reconciled with his wife, Joy, but three years later, the pair were back upon the brink of divorce, and an attempt was made upon the man's life. Two years later, Joy's sister gave a tip to the police that Joy had paid for the first murder; eventually Joy—along with her sister's estranged husband—was linked to the assault upon the contractor as well.

"Englade here treats a complex . . . murder case with a master's touch," declared a reviewer in a *Publishers Weekly* review. Sue-Ellen Beauregard in *Booklist* expressed a wish that the writer would have delved deeper into the personalities of "the principal players," but concluded that "true-crime junkies . . . should relish Englade's even-handed reporting."

For his 1996 effort, *Hot Blood,* Englade explores the mysterious circumstances surrounding the disappearance of Helen Voorhees Brach, the heiress of Brach's Candy company, as well as the murders of expensive show horses. Though the complete truth of her disappearance and probable death have never been uncovered, Englade makes it clear that the main suspect was Richard Bailey, a Chicago con man who got Brach to buy a racehorse at a price far higher than its actual worth. Bailey was tried and convicted of conspiring to murder Brach. The Bailey investigation also uncovered a wide-spread practice of horse owners who have their animals murdered for the insurance money—the "horse murders" referred to in *Hot Blood*'s subtitle. Several others were involved in the scam as well, including George Lindemann, Jr., who tried out for the equestrian portion of the U.S. Olympic team.

A reviewer for *Publishers Weekly* stated that "Englade is at his best when detailing the life and crimes of Bailey, a colorful if detestable human being." Gregor A. Preston in the *Library Journal* predicted that *Hot Blood* "will appeal to both true-crime and horse buffs," while Patricia Hassler in *Booklist* concluded that the volume "proves that not only is truth stranger than fiction but sometimes it's more intriguing, too." In the *Los Angeles Times Book Review* Dick Roraback stated, "Sorting out the disparate elements of parallel narrative, whose only commonality is surpassing greed is the job of a pro. Ken Englade, investigative reporter and true-crime author, is a pro. No similes, no metaphors, no frangipani. Just a story told well and true."

In addition to his nonfiction works about crime, Englade is also responsible for the novelization of the 1993 film about the long-missing Teamster union leader, Jimmy Hoffa. According to Sean Wilentz, who expressed his dislike of the motion picture in the *New Republic,* "here and there, Englade does try to make his story conform more closely than the movie to the known facts about Hoffa."

Englade told *CA:* "Moving from nonfiction to fiction has been a real challenge, and it is something I hope to do more of in the future."

BIOGRAPHICAL/CRITICAL SOURCES:

PERIODICALS

Booklist, April 1, 1990, p. 1511; November 1, 1993, p. 487; July, 1996, p. 1783.
Library Journal, June 1, 1996, p. 126.
Los Angeles Times Book Review, September 1, 1996.
New Republic, February 1, 1993, pp. 53-60.
Publishers Weekly, April 6, 1990, p. 109; October 25, 1993, pp. 52-53; June 17, 1996, p. 56.

—*Sketch by Elizabeth Wenning*

*   *   *

ERICKSON, Robert 1917-1997

OBITUARY NOTICE—See index for *CA* sketch: Born March 7, 1917, in Marquette, MI; died April 24, 1997, in Encinitas, CA. Composer, educator, and author. Erickson was an experimental composer who often invented instruments for his modern sounds and wrote two books on music. He's also credited with writing California's official anthem, Sierra. After serving in the U.S. Army in World War II and earning degrees in composition from Hamline University in St. Paul, Minnesota, Erickson taught at the College of St. Catherine in St. Paul, the University of California, Berkeley, and the San Francisco Conservatory of Music before moving to the University of California, San Diego, where he spent the rest of his career. The unusual nature of his music, a mix of tones and lyrics, wasn't immediately popular in San Diego, but Erickson's work was admired by his colleagues. Among his awards were grants from the American Academy and Institute of Arts and the National Endowment for the Arts, and the Fried-heim Award for chamber music. His two books on music include The Structure of Music: A Listener's Guide (1957) and Sound Structures in Music (1975). His compositions were commissioned and performed by the Minneapolis, Oakland, San Francisco and Los Angeles orchestras and the American Composers Orchestra.

OBITUARIES AND OTHER SOURCES:

BOOKS

International Who's Who in Music and Musicians' Directory, 12th edition, Melrose, 1990.

PERIODICALS

Los Angeles Times, May 2, 1997, p. A30.

*   *   *

ERLANGER, Joseph 1874-1965

PERSONAL: Born January 5, 1874, in San Francisco, CA; died December 5, 1965, of heart failure; son of Herman (a merchant) and Sarah (Galinger) Erlanger; married Aimee Hirstel; children: Margaret, Ruth Josephine, and Hermann. Education: College of Chemistry, University of California, Berkeley, B.S., 1895; Johns Hopkins University School of Medicine, Baltimore, M.D. (graduated second in his class), 1899. Avocational interests: Walking, camping, and the outdoors.

CAREER: Physiologist. Johns Hopkins Medical School, histology laboratory, research associate, 1896-1901, assistant professor of physiology, 1901-06; University

of Wisconsin Medical School, Madison, first professor of physiology, 1906-10; Washington University School of Medicine, St. Louis, professor of physiology and department chairman, 1910-46. Continued to work part-time following retirement, conducting research and assisting graduate students.

AWARDS, HONORS: Nobel Prize for physiology or medicine, 1944; elected member of National Academy of Sciences, Association of American Physicians, American Philosophical Society, American Physiological Society; honorary doctorates from universities, including California, Michigan, Pennsylvania, Wisconsin, Johns Hopkins, Washington, and Free University of Brussels.

WRITINGS:

(With Herbert S. Gasser) *Electrical Signs of Nervous Activity,* University of Pennsylvania Press (Philadelphia), 1937.

Contributor to journals and periodicals, including *Johns Hopkins Hospital Reports, American Journal of Physiology, American Journal of Physiology,* and *Annual Review of Physiology.*

SIDELIGHTS: Joseph Erlanger was an American physiologist whose pioneering work with his collaborator, Herbert Spencer Gasser, helped to advance the field of neurophysiology. For their work, Erlanger and Gasser shared the 1944 Nobel Prize in medicine or physiology. The prize committee cited their work on "the highly differentiated functions of single nerve fibers." Although unstated, the awarding of the Nobel Prize to Erlanger and Gasser also recognized their roles in developing the most basic tool in modern neurophysiology, the amplifier with cathode-ray oscilloscope. The prize culminated for Erlanger a distinguished career in medical education and physiological research.

Erlanger was born on January 5, 1874, in San Francisco, California. His father, Herman Erlanger, had immigrated to the United States in 1842 at the age of sixteen from his home in Wurtemberg, in Southern Germany. After struggling as a peddler in the Mississippi Valley, he went to California during the Gold Rush. Unsuccessful at mining, Erlanger turned to business and became a moderately successful merchant. In 1849, he married Sarah Galinger, also an immigrant from Southern Germany and the sister of his business partner. Joseph was the sixth of seven children, five sons and two daughters.

From an early age, Erlanger showed an interest in the natural world, a fact that led his older sister to give him the nickname "Doc." In 1889, he entered the classical Latin curriculum at the San Francisco Boys' High School. After graduating in 1891, he began studies in the College of Chemistry at the University of California at Berkeley, receiving a bachelor's degree in 1895. It was at Berkeley that Erlanger performed his first research—studying the development of newt eggs. He then enrolled at the Johns Hopkins University School of Medicine in Baltimore and earned a medical degree in 1899, fulfilling his childhood aspirations of becoming a doctor. Erlanger excelled as a student while at Johns Hopkins, graduating second in his class. This distinction allowed him to work as an intern in internal medicine for William Osler, the renowned physician and teacher.

After arriving in Baltimore, Erlanger decided that medical research and not medical practice would be his life's pursuit. In the summer of 1896, he worked in the histology laboratory of Lewellys Barker, demonstrating his zeal for research by studying the location of horn cells in the spinal cord of rabbits. The following summer, he undertook a different project—determining how much of a dog's small intestine could be surgically removed without interfering with its digestive processes. This study led to Erlanger's first published paper in 1901, and to his appointment as assistant professor of physiology at Johns Hopkins by William H. Howell, one of America's most important physiologists and head of the department. He was later promoted to associate professor of physiology.

Erlanger spent the next several years exclusively at Johns Hopkins except for a six week trip in the summer of 1902 to study biochemistry at the University of Strassburg in Germany. His career to that point was exceptional for two reasons. Unlike the generation of scientists that preceded him, Erlanger did not migrate to Europe to study. This decision reflected the improving standards of medical education and scientific research in the United States at the close of the nineteenth century. Second, Erlanger, although he was a trained physician, chose to pursue a full-time career in research instead of medical practice. Physician-scientists before Erlanger could devote only part of their time to research, as the rest was spent on patient care.

During his career at Johns Hopkins, Erlanger studied a number of problems that were important in medicine. In 1904, he designed and constructed a sphygmomanometer, a device that measures blood pressure.

Erlanger improved on previous designs by making it sturdier and easier to use. Later that year, he used the device to find a correlation between blood pressure and orthostatic albuminuria, wherein proteins appear in the urine when a patient stands. His last few years at Johns Hopkins were spent studying electrical conduction in the heart, particularly the activity between the auricles and the ventricles that is responsible for the consistent beating of the heart. Using a clamp of his own design, he was able to determine that a conduction blockage, or heart block, in the bundle of His, a connection between the auricles and ventricles, was responsible for the reduced pulse and fainting spells associated with Stokes-Adams syndrome.

On June 21, 1906, Erlanger married Aimee Hirstel, a fellow San Franciscan. Their marriage of more than fifty years was a strong and vibrant one, and produced three children, Margaret, Ruth Josephine, and Hermann. The personalities of Joseph and Aimee Erlanger complemented one another. He was reserved, quiet, and introverted; she was effusive, active, and extroverted. Their mutual love of walking, camping, and the outdoors stayed with them throughout Erlanger's lengthy professional career.

In 1906, Erlanger left Johns Hopkins and moved to the University of Wisconsin, where he became the first professor of physiology at the university's medical school. Though the university's administration recruited Erlanger to build and equip a physiological laboratory, his efforts were continually hampered by a lack of funds. This situation contributed to his decision to leave Wisconsin in 1910 for the Washington University School of Medicine, in Saint Louis. The medical school at Washington had been newly reorganized and had sufficient funds to meet Erlanger's needs. He worked at Washington for the remainder of his career, serving as professor of physiology and department chairman. Even after his retirement in 1946, Erlanger continued to work part-time performing research and helping graduate students in their work.

After arriving at Washington University, Erlanger devoted much of his time and energy to the formidable task of helping to reorganize the medical school. Erlanger and the other department heads constituted the new school's executive faculty which oversaw administration and offered significant input into the construction and design of the new medical school buildings. In 1917, the United States' entry into World War I drew Erlanger's attention away from his administrative duties, presenting him with the opportunity to return to the laboratory and to his research on cardiovascular physiology. He participated with other physiologists in the study of wound shock and helped to develop therapeutic solutions that were used by the United States Army in Europe. He also continued the work that he had begun at Johns Hopkins, studying the sounds of Korotkoff, the sound one hears in an artery when measuring blood pressure with a stethoscope.

Although Erlanger would remain interested in cardiovascular physiology throughout his career, he experienced an intellectual transition in the early 1920s, when he took up questions of neurophysiology. The arrival at Washington University of Herbert Spencer Gasser, a student of Erlanger's from Wisconsin and a fellow Johns Hopkins graduate, spurred this change. Erlanger and Gasser would collaborate at Washington University until Gasser's departure in 1931 for the Cornell Medical College. Understanding how nerves transmit electrical impulses preoccupied Erlanger and Gasser during the 1920s. The difficulty in studying nerves was that the electrical impulses were too weak and too brief to measure them accurately. In 1920, one of Gasser's former classmates, H. Sidney Newcomer, developed a device that would amplify nerve impulses by some 100,000 times, allowing physiologists to measure and study the subtle changes that occur during nerve transmission. A year later, Erlanger and Gasser, based on advances made at the Western Electric Company, constructed a cathode-ray oscilloscope that could record the nerve impulse. The cathode-ray oscilloscope with amplifier was a technological breakthrough that permitted neurophysiologists to overcome the barrier posed by the subtlety and brevity of nerve activity. Erlanger and Gasser went on to study the details of nerve transmission. Their most significant contribution derived from these researches was their conclusion that larger nerve fibers

conducted electrical impulses faster than smaller ones. Also, they demonstrated that different nerve fibers can have different functions.

Erlanger and Gasser's work on nerve physiology increased Erlanger's already important role in American physiology. Not only had he made significant contributions to the science of physiology, but his career—based on a wholly American education and consisting of a full-time research effort—represented a new generation of American physiologists. For his scientific efforts, Erlanger was elected a member of the National Academy of Sciences, the Association of American Physicians, the American Philosophical Society, and the American Physiological Society. He also received honorary degrees from universities of California, Michigan, Pennsylvania, Wisconsin, and Johns Hopkins University, Washington University, and the Free University of Brussels. His highest honor came when he shared, with Gasser, the 1944 Nobel Prize for physiology or medicine. Erlanger died of heart failure on December 5, 1965, one month before his ninety-second birthday.

BIOGRAPHICAL/CRITICAL SOURCES:

BOOKS

Advances in American Medicine: Essays at the Bicentennial, edited by John Z. Bowers and Elizabeth F. Purcell, Josiah Macy, Jr., Foundation (New York), 1976.

PERIODICALS

National Academy of Sciences Biographical Memoirs, vol. 41, 1970, pp. 111-39.
Perspectives on Biology and Medicine, vol. 26, 1983, pp. 613-36.*

F

FARON, Fay 1949-

PERSONAL: Born February 27, 1949, in Kansas City, MO; daughter of Albert D. and Geraldine M. Faron. *Education:* Attended Arizona State University, 1968-71, and University of Arizona, 1971-72.

ADDRESSES: *Office*—Rat Dog Dick Detective Agency, P.O. Box 470862, San Francisco, CA 94147; fax 415-882-4456. *E-mail*—ratdog@sprint.com. *Agent*—Scovil Chichak Galen, 381 Park Ave. S., Suite 1020, New York, NY 10016.

CAREER: Rat Dog Dick Detective Agency, San Francisco, CA, owner, 1982—. Creighton-Morgan Publishing Group, owner, 1987—; Elder Angels, founder, 1997.

MEMBER: National Association of Bank Investigators, Professionals Against Confidence Crimes.

WRITINGS:

The Instant National Locator Guide, Creighton-Morgan Publishing (San Francisco, CA), 1991.
A Private Eye's Guide to Collecting a Bad Debt, Creighton-Morgan Publishing (San Francisco, CA), 1995.
Missing Persons, Writers Digest (Cincinnati, OH), 1997.
Congames, Writers Digest (Cincinnati, OH), 1998.

Author of "Ask Rat Dog," a column syndicated by King Features, 1994—.

WORK IN PROGRESS: *Lily Kills Her Client,* a mystery novel.

SIDELIGHTS: Fay Faron told *CA:* "Why do I write? Aside from the money, I like to take life's little mysteries and try to make some sense of them. My 'Ask Rat Dog' column exposes me to other people's experiences, so I don't have to go through all these ordeals myself. That is a good thing. From this safe distance I can figure out what makes criminals tick, why our laws can't seem to contain them, even what it feels like to be adopted.

"Other writers I emulate? Jack Olsen, of course, the dean of true crime. He's my hero and personal mentor."

                    *   *   *

FASSETT, John D. 1926-

PERSONAL: Born January 30, 1926, in East Hampton, NY; son of Howard J. and Irene (Darby) Fassett; married Betty Conrad, August 4, 1947; children: Ellen Joy Mermin, John D. Jr., Lora Jean Mason. *Ethnicity:* "WASP." *Education:* University of Rochester, B.A. (cum laude), 1948; Yale University Law School, J.D. (cum laude), 1953, then LL.B. *Politics:* Republican. *Religion:* Protestant. *Avocational interests:* Competitive tennis, collecting biographies of Supreme Court justices.

ADDRESSES: *Home*—5108 Brittany Dr. S., Apt. 605, St. Petersburg, FL 33710.

CAREER: United States Supreme Court, Washington, DC, law clerk, 1954-55; Yale University, New Haven, CT, lecturer, 1955-56; Wiggin and Dana (law firm), New Haven, partner, 1954-73; United Illuminating Co. (electrical utility), New Haven, president and chair of board, 1973-85. Former director of United Illuminating Co., New Haven Savings Bank, Barnes Group, Inc., Northeast DataCom, Inc., Jackson Newspapers, Inc., Edison Electric Institute, National Association of Electric Companies, Electric Council of New England, New England Powerpool, Connecticut Yankee Atomic Company. New Haven Chamber of Commerce, chair, 1979-81; Connecticut Public Expenditure Council, chair, 1979-81; New England Council, director; Quinnipiac Council, Boy Scouts of America, director; Visiting Nurses Association, director; University of New Haven, trustee. Also associated with many other commissions and boards in New Haven, 1954-73. *Military service:* Army Air Corps, 1943-46; recalled to Army, 1950-51; became first lieutenant.

MEMBER: Supreme Court Historical Society, Lakewood Country Club.

AWARDS, HONORS: Charles Ellis Caldwell Prize, 1948; best work in department of English citation, University of Rochester; Edward D. Robbius Prize, 1953; Yale University Law School, highest grades in class in examinations.

WRITINGS:

United Illuminating: History of an Electric Company (corporate history), privately published, 1990.
(Contributor) *The Supreme Court Justices: Illustrated Biographies, 1789-1993,* edited by Clare Cushman, Congressional Quarterly (Washington, DC), 1993.
New Deal Justice: The Life of Stanley Reed of Kentucky (biography), Vantage Press (New York, NY), 1994.

Contributor to periodicals, including *Journal of Supreme Court History.*

WORK IN PROGRESS: "None, except articles on aspects of Supreme Court."

SIDELIGHTS: John D. Fassett told *CA:* "Upon retirement in 1985 as CEO of a large electric company, other members of the board urged me to undertake a corporate history in order to preserve the story of one of the very early power companies.

"Shortly after I retired, I wrote an article for the *Journal of Supreme Court History* titled 'Justice Reed and Brown v. the Board of Education' (1986). As a result, I was asked to write the chapter on Justice Reed when the Supreme Court Historical Society (SCHS) sponsored publication by Congressional Quarterly of *The Supreme Court Justices: Illustrated Biographies, 1789-1993,* recently updated by a second edition. My research for the chapter disclosed that not only had Justice Reed been neglected by biographers, but considerable information regarding his career in other biographies and histories was erroneous. Encouraged by the SCHS, I decided to undertake a biography, but had not expected to find the large volume of records which the justice's sons had deposited in the archives at the University of Kentucky. The result was a very long tome which was originally scheduled for publication by a university press. Rather than make further cuts in historical details as requested by that press, I opted to have the book published by Vantage Press and I was pleased with the quality of their production work."

*   *   *

FERMI, Enrico 1901-1954

PERSONAL: Born September 29, 1901, in Rome, Italy; immigrated to the United States, 1939; became U.S. citizen, July 11, 1944; died November 30, 1954, of stomach cancer; son of Alberto (a railroad worker) and Ida (a school teacher, maiden name, de Gattis) Fermi; married in Italy (wife's name, Laura). *Education:* Attended Reale Scuola Normale, Pisa, 1918; University of Pisa, Ph.D. (magna cum laude), 1924.

CAREER: Physicist. Professor of physics at University of Gottingen, University of Leiden, and University of Florence; University of Rome, Italy, chair of theoretical physics, 1926; Columbia University, New York City, professor of physics, 1938; University of Chicago, IL, professor of physics, 1942, Charles H. Swift Distinguished Service Professor of Physics, 1945-91; Argonne National Laboratory, Chicago, IL, research scientist; Manhattan Project, Hanford, WA, design consultant for plutonium processing plant; consultant for nuclear bomb construction at Los Alamos, NM.

AWARDS, HONORS: Nobel Prize for Physics, 1938; Civilian Medal of Merit, 1946, for the Manhattan Project; Franklin Medal from the Franklin Institute, 1947; Transenter Medal from the University of Liege, Belgium, 1947; recipient of honorary doctorate degrees awarded by institutions, including Washington

University, Yale University and Harvard University. Posthumously awarded the first Enrico Fermi Award from the United States Atomic Energy Commission; element number 100 on the periodic table was named *fermium* in his honor, as was *fermimeter,* a nuclear dimension unit of measure.

WRITINGS:

Fisica per i Licei, N. Zanichelli (Bologna), 1929.

Introduzione all Fisica Atomica, N. Zanichelli, 1929.

Molecole e Cristalli, N. Zanichelli, 1934, (translated by Ferro-Luzzi) W.A. Benjamin, 1966.

Thermodynamics, Prentice-Hall, 1937, Dover (New York City), 1957.

Fisica per Istituti Tecnici Commerciali, N. Zanichelli, 1938.

Nuclear Physics, University of Chicago Press, 1950.

Elementary Particles, Yale University Press, 1951.

Collected Papers, University of Chicago Press, 1962-65.

Notes on Thermodynamics and Statistics, University of Chicago Press, 1966.

Significato di una Scoperta: il Navigatore Italiano Sbarcato nel Nuovo Mondo, (translated by Bianca Franco), Roma, 1982.

SIDELIGHTS: Enrico Fermi's fame rests on accomplishments in the fields of both theoretical and experimental physics. At the age of twenty-five, he developed a statistical method for describing the behavior of a cloud of electrons that later came to be known as Fermi-Dirac statistics. In combination with another system of mathematics, Bose-Einstein statistics, it provides a method for analyzing any system of discrete particles, such as photons, electrons, or neutrons. Fermi also devised an explanation for the process of beta decay, an event in which an atomic nucleus emits an electron and changes into a new nucleus. Fermi's major experimental contributions involved the study of nuclear changes brought about as a result of neutron bombardment of nuclei. This field of research eventually led to Fermi's participation in the Manhattan Project, during which the first controlled fission reactions were carried out. For his work on neutron bombardment, Fermi was awarded the 1938 Nobel Prize for Physics.

Fermi was born in Rome on September 29, 1901. His father, Alberto Fermi, was employed by the Italian state railway system, while his mother, Ida de Gattis, had been a school teacher before her marriage. The Fermis had two other children, a son, Giulio, and a daughter, Maria. Giulio died when Enrico was four-

teen, with apparently traumatic effects on the younger brother. Fortunately, Enrico soon made the acquaintance of a young man, Enrico Persico, who was to become his best friend and a close professional colleague for the rest of his life.

Fermi exhibited unusual intellectual talents at an early age. He did well in school but also read a great deal on his own. A friend of his father, Adolfo Amidei, assumed some responsibility for Fermi's intellectual development, arranging to have books on mathematics and physics given to him in the proper sequence. According to his friend and colleague, Emilio Sergre, Fermi knew as much classical physics by the time he graduated from high school as did the typical university graduate student. That knowledge had come not only from books, but also from experiments designed and carried out by Fermi and Persico.

In November, 1918, Fermi applied for a scholarship at the Reale Scuola Normale in Pisa. His entrance essay dealt with the mathematics and physics of vibrating reeds and convinced the examiners that he was a candidate of unusual promise. Six years later, Fermi was granted his doctorate in physics, *magna cum laude,* from Pisa. His thesis dealt with experiments he had conducted using X rays.

Since the scientific community was not then well developed in Italy, Fermi set out for Northern Europe to continue his studies. He spent seven months with Max Born at the University of Gottingen and then returned to Rome. He taught mathematics for one year in Rome before traveling north again, this time to the University of Leiden. There he studied with the great Dutch physicist Paul Ehrenfest and became close friends with Samuel A. Goudsmit and George Uhlenbeck, both of whom later immigrated to the United States.

Fermi returned to Italy in 1925, hoping to be appointed to a chair in mathematical physics. When this opportunity was offered to another man instead, Fermi accepted a teaching position at the University of Florence. During his first year at Florence, Fermi wrote a paper that was to establish his name among physicists almost immediately. The paper dealt with an application of Wolfgang Pauli's Exclusion principles, discovered earlier the same year, to the atoms in a gas. Pauli's Exclusion principles restrict the possible location of electrons. Fermi postulated that the same rules developed by Pauli for electrons might also be applied to the atoms in a gas. The mathematical system he invented, later developed independently by Paul Dirac, has become known as Fermi-Dirac statistics.

This accomplishment came about at a propitious time for Fermi. In Rome, Orso Mario Corbino had just begun a campaign to revitalize Italian science, which had been in a long period of decline. Corbino, as both chairman of the physics department at the University of Rome and a powerful figure in the Italian government, obtained authorization to create a new chair of theoretical physics at Rome, a position that he immediately offered to Fermi. In 1926, Fermi left Florence to assume his new position in Corbino's department. Over the next half dozen years, Corbino's dreams were realized as a number of first class physicists and young students were attracted to Rome.

During that period, Fermi and his colleagues concentrated on the latest developments in atomic theory. Along with many other chemists and physicists, they were working out the implications of quantum and wave mechanics, relativity, and uncertainty to atomic theory. By the turn of the decade, however, many of those problems had been solved, and Fermi began to look elsewhere for challenges. He, like many others, settled on the atomic nucleus as a new focus of research.

One of the first problems to which he turned was beta decay. Beta decay is the process by which a neutron in an atomic nucleus breaks apart into a proton and electron. The electron is then emitted from the nucleus as a beta particle. The mechanics of beta decay appeared to violate known physical principles and were, therefore, the subject of intense study in the early 1930s. Wolfgang Pauli had suggested, for example, that the apparent violation of conservation laws observed during beta decay could be explained by assuming the existence of a tiny, essentially massless particle, also released during the event. Fermi was later to name that particle the *neutrino* ("little neutron"). In 1933, Fermi proposed a theory for beta decay. He said that the event occurs because a neutron moves from a state of higher energy to one of lower energy as it undergoes conversion to a proton and electron. To explain the process by which this occurs, Fermi postulated the existence of a new kind of force, a force now known as the *weak force*.

Fermi's interest in the nucleus also prompted him to return to the laboratory and to design a number of experiments in this field. An important factor motivating this research was the recent discovery of artificial radioactivity by Irene Joliot-Curie and her hus-

band, Frederic Joliot-Curie. The Joliot-Curies had found that bombarding stable isotopes with alpha particles would convert the original isotopes into unstable, radioactive forms. Fermi reasoned that this type of experiment might be even more effective if neutrons, rather than alpha particles, were used as the "bullets." Neutrons have no electrical charge and are, therefore, not repelled by either the negatively charged electrons or the positively charged nuclei in an atom.

Beginning in 1934, Fermi and his colleagues systematically submitted one element after another to bombardment by neutrons. Progress was slow until a key discovery was made. In contrast to previous expectations, it turned out that slow neutrons—neutrons that have been slowed by passing through substances containing hydrogen—are more effective in bringing about nuclear changes than are fast neutrons. After revising his experimental procedure based on this discovery, Fermi had greater success. Over a period of months, he was able to show that 37 of the 63 elements he studied could be converted to radioactive forms by neutron bombardment.

The element among all others that especially intrigued Fermi was uranium. He knew that one reaction that could reasonably be expected as the result of neutron bombardment of uranium was the production of a new element with an atomic number one greater than that of uranium. But no such element exists naturally. So, the successful bombardment of uranium with neutrons might well result in the formation of the first synthetic element.

When this experiment was actually performed, the results were ambiguous. Fermi did not feel that he had enough evidence to announce the preparation of a new element. His sponsor, Corbino, had no such reluctance, however. Motivated by a desire to exalt the "new Italian science," Corbino reported that Fermi had indeed discovered element 93 and suggested that it be named *italium*.

In fact, Fermi did not recognize the revolutionary nature of his experimental results. Bombardment of uranium with neutrons had resulted not in a simple nuclear transformation, but in nuclear fission, a process during which the uranium atom is split, unleashing tremendous amounts of energy. The true nature of this reaction was later elucidated by Lise Meitner and Otto Robert Frisch.

As the 1930s came to a close, Fermi's future became more uncertain. Fascist influences were growing, not only in Hitler's Germany, but also in Mussolini's Italy. These political changes troubled Fermi in a number of ways. For one thing, they threatened the nature of his scientific work since political factors now determined what was "correct" research and what was not. In addition, Fermi's family felt threatened since his wife was Jewish and subject, therefore, to the dangers of state-enforced anti-Semitism.

Fortunately, a solution for his dilemma presented itself in November of 1938 when Fermi was informed that he had won the Nobel Prize for Physics. The award had been given for his research on the bombardment of elements by slow neutrons. The Fermis and a few friends decided that their trip to Stockholm to accept the prize would be a one-way passage. After the ceremony, he would defect to the West. On January 2, 1939, he arrived in the United States and assumed a new post as professor of physics at Columbia University.

The timing of Fermi's arrival in the United States was indeed fortuitous. At almost the same time, Niels Bohr was delivering to American physicists news of the discovery of nuclear fission by Otto Hahn and Fritz Strassmann in Germany. The significance of this discovery was immediately apparent to Fermi and his colleagues. A movement was soon under way to inform the U.S. government of the political and military implications of the Hahn-Strassmann discovery. That movement culminated in the famous August 2, 1939 letter to President Franklin D. Roosevelt, written by Leo Szilard and signed by Albert Einstein, that discussed the importance of nuclear research.

Fermi's immediate future was now laid out for him. He became involved in the Manhattan Project to determine whether a controlled nuclear chain reaction was possible and, if so, how it could be used in the construction of a nuclear weapon. Although his initial work was carried out at Columbia, Fermi eventually moved to the University of Chicago. He began work there in April, 1942, with a team of the nation's finest physicists attempting to produce the world's first sustained nuclear fission reaction.

That effort came to a successful conclusion under the squash courts at the university on December 2, 1942. At 3:21 p.m., instruments indicated that a self-sustaining chain reaction was taking place in the world's first atomic "pile," a primitive nuclear reactor. The message sent to Washington confirming this event stated, "The Italian navigator has landed in the New World." In response to that message, James Conant,

director of the project, asked, "Are the natives friendly?" indicating that the team was ready to go ahead with further research. The reply from Fermi's team was, "Yes, very friendly," and the race to build a bomb was on its way.

For the next two years, Fermi continued his research on nuclear fission at the Argonne National Laboratory outside Chicago. Toward the end of that work, on July 11, 1944, Fermi and his wife became naturalized citizens of the United States. A few weeks later, Fermi left for Hanford, Washington, where he briefly assisted in the design and construction of a new plutonium processing plant. In September, he moved on to Los Alamos, New Mexico, where final assembly of the first nuclear weapons was to occur. There Fermi was placed in charge of his own special division (the F division) whose job it was to solve special problems as they arose during bomb construction.

After the first successful tests at Los Alamos, on July 16, 1945, and after the bombs were dropped on Japan a month later, Fermi concluded his work with the Manhattan Project. He returned to the University of Chicago, where he became Charles H. Swift Distinguished Service Professor of Physics and a member of the newly created Institute for Nuclear Studies. He remained at Chicago for the rest of his life, a period during which he received many honorary degrees and other awards. Included among the former were honorary doctorates from Washington University, Yale, and Harvard. He also received the Civilian Medal of Merit in 1946 for his work on the Manhattan Project, the Franklin Medal from the Franklin Institute in 1947, and the Transenter Medal from the University of Liege in Belgium in 1947.

Fermi's health began to fail in 1954, and exploratory surgery showed that he had stomach cancer. He refused to give up his work, however, and continued his research almost until he died, in his sleep, on November 30, 1954. He was buried in Chicago. Shortly after his death, he was posthumously awarded the first Enrico Fermi Award, given by the U.S. Atomic Energy Commission. Since his death, Fermi has received additional honors, including the naming of element #100, *fermium,* after him and the choice of the unit *fermimeter* for nuclear dimensions.

In addition to his great mental genius, Fermi was a highly respected and well-loved person. His long-time colleague, Segre, has written of Fermi's special pleasure in working with younger colleagues, a tendency that helped maintain his own youthful spirit.

BIOGRAPHICAL/CRITICAL SOURCES:

BOOKS

Fermi, Laura, *Atoms in the Family: My Life with Enrico Fermi,* University of Chicago Press, 1954.

Gillispie, Charles Coulson, editor, *Dictionary of Scientific Biography,* Volume 4, Scribner, 1975, pp. 576-583.

Jaffe, Bernard, *Men of Science in America,* Simon and Schuster, 1958.

McGraw-Hill Modern Men of Science, Volume 1, McGraw-Hill, 1984, pp. 168-169.

Segre, Emilio, *Enrico Fermi, Physicist,* University of Chicago Press, 1970.*

* * *

FIESER, Louis F(rederick) 1899-1977

PERSONAL: Born April 7, 1899, in Columbus, OH; died July 25, 1977, in Cambridge, MA; son of Louis Frederick and Martha Victoria (Kershaw) Fieser; married Mary A. Peters, 1932; children: none. *Education:* Williams College, B.A., 1920; Harvard University, Ph.D., 1924; graduate work at University of Frankfurt am Main, 1924-25, and Oxford University, 1925.

CAREER: Organic chemist. Bryn Mawr College, Bryn Mawr, PA, instructor, 1925-30; Harvard University, Cambridge, MA, assistant professor of chemistry, beginning 1930, became Sheldon Emery Professor of Organic Chemistry, 1939-68. Writer, lecturer, and researcher. Served on the Surgeon General's Advisory Committee on Smoking and Health. *Military service:* Served in U.S. Army during World War I.

AWARDS, HONORS: Elected to National Academy of Sciences, 1940; Katherine Berkan Judd Prize from Memorial Hospital, 1941, for work on cancer; Manufacturing Chemists' Association Award, 1959; Norris Award, 1959, for teaching skills; American Chemical Society Award in Chemical Education, 1967.

WRITINGS:

Experiments in Organic Chemistry, Heath (Boston and New York), 1941.

(With Mary Peters Fieser) *Organic Chemistry,* Wiley, 1944.

Introduction to Organic Chemistry, Heath, 1946.

(With Mary Peters Fieser) *Steroids,* Reinhold (New York), 1959.

(With Mary Peters Fieser) *Style Guide for Chemists,* Reinhold (New York), 1960.

(With Mary Peters Fieser) *Advanced Organic Chemistry,* Reinhold (New York), 1961.

(With Mary Peters Fieser) *Topics in Organic Chemistry,* Reinhold (New York), 1963.

(With Mary Peters Fieser) *Chemistry in Three Dimensions,* [Cambridge, MA], 1963.

(With Mary Peters Fieser) *Current Topics in Organic Chemistry,* Reinhold (New York), 1964.

Organic Experiments, Heath (Boston), 1964.

(Editor with Mary Peters Fieser) *Reagents for Organic Synthesis,* Volumes 1-8, Wiley, 1967.

Organic Experiments, Raytheon Education Co. (Lexington, MA), 1968.

(With Kenneth L. Williamson) *Organic Experiments,* Heath (Lexington, MA), 1975.

(With Kenneth L. Williamson) *Organic Experiments,* Heath (Lexington, MA), 1979.

(With Kenneth L. Williamson) *Organic Experiments,* Heath (Lexington, MA), 1983.

(With Kenneth L. Williamson) *Organic Experiments,* Heath (Lexington, MA), 1987.

Contributor to journals and periodicals, including *Science* and *Scientific American.*

SIDELIGHTS: Louis F. Fieser was a renowned educator, researcher, and author. In addition to writing numerous research papers, reference books, and textbooks, he developed methods of synthesizing various compounds including an antimalarial drug, vitamin K, and carcinogenic (or cancer-causing) chemicals for use in medical research. He also invented napalm, and he played a key role in developing the drug cortisone for treating arthritis. Among the many awards he received for his contributions was the American Chemical Society's Award in Chemical Education, which recognized his thirty years of innovative and inspiring teaching at Harvard University.

Louis Frederick Fieser was born on April 7, 1899, in Columbus, Ohio, to Louis Frederick and Martha Victoria (Kershaw) Fieser. The younger Fieser earned an A.B. degree from Williams College in 1920, and went on to earn a Ph.D. in chemistry from Harvard in 1924. The following year he spent in Frankfurt, Germany, and at Oxford University in England doing postgraduate work with a Harvard travel fellowship. On his return to the United States in 1925, he accepted a teaching position at Bryn Mawr College. Initially leery of teaching at an all-women's college, his expectation of intellectually inferior students proved groundless, and he remained there until 1930. It was here that he met a chemistry student named Mary Peters, whom he married in 1932. Mary Peters Fieser would collaborate with him on numerous research projects, as well as many books.

Fieser joined the chemistry department at Harvard in 1930 as assistant professor. There he became known for his well-organized, entertaining, and imaginative lectures, and especially for his ability to inspire interest in laboratory work. In 1939, he became the Sheldon Emery Professor of Organic Chemistry. He retained this post until 1968, and after his retirement devoted his time to writing, lecturing, and performing laboratory research.

One of Fieser's most famous accomplishments was developing a method of synthesizing vitamin K, a blood coagulant, in the laboratory. During the 1930s, biochemist Henrik Dam of Copenhagen discovered that a substance (later called "Koagulations-Vitamin") found in certain green plants, especially alfalfa, prevented hemorrhages. Although other researchers succeeded in isolating the vitamin, the amount available from natural sources was too small to be of practical use. As Fieser explained in a 1939 lecture he gave to the Boylston Chemical Club at Harvard (as quoted in *Science*), the work of his research team "culminated in the establishment of the structure by a synthesis . . . which has the merit of providing a practical method for the production of the pure material in quantity." Vitamin K also proved useful in prenatal care and for other therapeutic anti-hemorrhagic purposes.

Fieser headed a chemistry research team at Harvard that investigated a number of other important topics in the field of chemistry. During the 1930s, he conducted research on the chemical causes of cancer and developed methods of synthesizing various carcinogens (cancer-causing agents) for use in medical research. During World War II, the Japanese invasion of the East Indies blocked the Allies, including the United States, from access to most of the world supply of quinine, a major antimalarial medicine. As part of his work on the chemistry of quinones in general, Fieser investigated the use of naphthoquinones as a substitute. His research team eventually synthesized the drug lapinone, which proved to be effective against malaria.

One of Fieser's most controversial accomplishments was also invented during wartime. In 1941, the Na-

tional Defense Research Committee contracted with Fieser to develop napalm, the jellied gasoline substance used in bombs and flame-throwers. Fieser and his research team also discovered a civilian use for napalm—it was an effective crabgrass killer, as it burned away crabgrass seeds without harming grass roots needed for lawns. But it was the military application that received the most attention. During and after World War II, Fieser received letters from many who credited the invention with saving thousands of American lives. But during the Vietnam Conflict, public reaction to napalm was quite different. Many criticized it as an immoral weapon whose use was intended to harm Vietnamese civilians. Fieser again received letters about his invention, this time critical of him and his work. He maintained, however, that he felt no guilt about inventing napalm. He believed scientists could not be held responsible for how other people used their discoveries. "You don't know what's coming," he said in an interview reported in the *New York Times*. "That wasn't my business. . . . I was working on a technical problem that was considered pressing." In *Time*, he maintained that he would "do it again, if called upon, in defense of the country."

In contrast to his work on napalm, public reaction to Fieser's contributions to the development of synthetic cortisone was consistently positive. Cortisone, one of the hormones secreted by the cortex (outer layer) of the adrenal glands, was found to be useful in treating rheumatoid arthritis and related diseases. Other researchers had discovered most of the necessary steps in synthesizing cortisone. In 1951, Fieser played a key role in the completion of this process by his discovery of a missing portion of the cortisone molecule.

Fieser was elected to the National Academy of Sciences in 1940. For his work on cancer, Fieser was awarded the Katherine Berkan Judd Prize from Memorial Hospital in 1941. In addition to an award from the American Chemical Society, he received the Manufacturing Chemists' Association Award in 1959 and the Norris Award, also in 1959, for his teaching skills. He later served on the Surgeon General's Advisory Committee on Smoking and Health that issued the 1964 report linking cigarette smoking with cancer.

A prolific writer, Fieser published over three hundred research papers, and he wrote or co-wrote numerous chemistry textbooks and reference books with his wife, Mary Peters Fieser. Although he avoided making any public comments about the Vietnam War despite the controversy over napalm, he did take an active role in trying to reduce hostilities in another part of the world. In 1967, he joined four other scientists in initiating a public statement, addressed to U.S. President Lyndon B. Johnson and signed by eighty prominent Americans, urging the United States to pursue a peace settlement in the Middle East between Israel and the Arab countries. Fieser died in Cambridge on July 25, 1977, at age seventy-eight.

BIOGRAPHICAL/CRITICAL SOURCES:

BOOKS

Modern Men of Science, McGraw Hill, 1968, pp. 153-156.

PERIODICALS

Journal of Chemical Education, March, 1985, pp. 186-191.
New York Times, September 16, 1944, p. 22; September 21, 1946, p. 21; September 19, 1967, p. 2; December 27, 1967, p. 8; July 27, 1977, p. B2.
Time, January 5, 1968, pp. 66-67.*

* * *

FIRST, Philip
  See WILLIAMSON, Philip G.

* * *

FISCHER, Ernst Otto 1918-

PERSONAL: Born November 10, 1918, in Solln, Germany; son of Karl Tobias (a physics professor) and Valentine (Danzer) Fischer. *Education:* Technique Hochscule, Germany, Ph.D., 1952. *Avocational interests:* Art, travel, history.

CAREER: Inorganic chemist. Technique Hochscule, Munich, Germany, assistant researcher, 1952-54, assistant professor, 1954-57, director of Institute for Inorganic Chemistry, 1964—; University of Munich, Germany, professor, 1957-64. Visiting professorships in U.S., 1971-73. *Military service:* Served two years compulsory service in German army in addition to wartime service.

MEMBER: American Academy of Arts and Sciences (honorary member), German Academy of Scientists.

AWARDS, HONORS: Gottingen Academy Prize, 1957; Alfred Stock Memorial Prize, Society of German Chemists, 1959; Nobel Prize for Chemistry, 1973. Various honorary degrees from universities, including Munich, 1972; Strathclyde, 1975; Erlangen, 1977; Veszprem, 1983.

WRITINGS:

(With H. Werner) *Metal (pi)-Complexes,* Elsevier (New York), 1966.
Gas Installation. Ein Leitfaden feur die Praxis, Verlag feur Bauwesen (Berlin), 1966.
(With Karl Heinz Dotz and others) *Transition Metal Carbene Complexes,* Verlag Chemie (Deerfield Beach, FL), 1983.
(With A. G. Davies and O. A. Reutov) *Organometallic Chemistry Reviews,* Elsevier (New York), 1988.

Contributor to journals and periodicals, including *Zeitzschrift fur Naturforschung, Journal of Inorganic and Nuclear Chemistry,* and *Pure and Applied Chemistry.*

SIDELIGHTS: The field of organometallic chemistry, the study of compounds of metal and carbon, is tremendously important not only to an understanding of such basic structures as the B vitamins, but also to the chemical industry as a whole. The growth of plastics as well as the refining of petroleum hydrocarbons all involve at some stage the metal-to-carbon bond which is at the heart of organometallic chemistry. Ernst Otto Fischer has played a crucial role in the pioneering of this science. Co-recipient of the 1973 Nobel Prize in Chemistry for his X-ray analysis of the structure of a particular iron-to-carbon bond in so-called "sandwich compounds," Fischer, working with members of his research laboratory in Munich, was also on the cutting edge of transition-metal research, synthesizing totally new classes of compounds.

Fischer was born on November 10, 1918, in the Munich suburb of Solln. The third child of Valentine Danzer Fischer and Karl Tobias Fischer, a physics professor at Munich's Technische Hochschule, Fischer attended the Theresien Gymnasium (high school), graduating in 1937. Following this, Fischer spent two years compulsory service in the German army, a stint which was extended with the outbreak of World War II in 1939. Between serving in Poland, France, and Russia, Fischer was able, in the winter of 1941-42, to begin his studies in chemistry at the Technische Hochschule in Munich. Captured by the Americans, he was held in a prisoner of war camp until repatriation in the fall of 1945. He renewed his chemistry studies in Munich in 1946, studying under Walter Hieber, well known for his early work on combining metals with molecules of carbon and oxygen, or metal-carbonyl chemistry. Fischer earned his Ph.D. degree in 1952 for research on carbon-to-nickel bonds; his course was well set by this time for a career in the new field of organometallic chemistry.

After earning his doctorate, Fischer stayed at the Technische Hochschule, working as an assistant researcher. He and his first research students were drawn to a puzzling compound reported by the chemists T. Kealy and P. Pauson. In an attempt to link two cyclopentadiene (five-carbon) rings together, these scientists discovered an unknown compound which they believed involved an iron atom linked between two consecutive longitudinal rings of carbon. The intervening iron atom seemed to join with a carbon atom on each of the rings. That such metal-to-carbon bonds exist was not the surprising thing. In fact, such unstable bonds are necessary for catalytic processing of such compounds. What was interesting about this compound (initially called dicyclopentadienyl iron) was that it was not unstable at all. It was in fact highly stable both thermally and chemically. Such stability made no sense to Fischer given the nature of the proposed structure of the compound, and he theorized that it was in fact an entirely new sort of molecular complex.

An English chemist, Geoffrey Wilkinson, soon proposed an alternate structure to the compound (now renamed ferrocene). He described ferrocene as made up of an atom of iron sandwiched between two parallel rings, one on top of the other rather than in a line on the same plane. Thus the iron formed bonds not just with a single atom on each ring, but with all of the atoms and also with the electrons within the rings, accounting for its stability. From this description came the term "sandwich compounds." Meanwhile, Fischer and his research team, including W. Pfab, carried out meticulous X-ray crystallography on ferrocene, elucidating the compound's structure and proving Wilkinson's theory correct. The examination and discovery of the structure of ferrocene was a watershed event in the field of organometallic chemistry, spawning a new generation of inorganic chemists.

From ferrocene, Fischer and his team went on to determine the structure of, as well as synthesize,

other transition metals—those substances at a stage in between metal and organic—especially dibenzenechromium, an aromatic hydrocarbon. Such substances are termed aromatic not because of smell, but because of structure. They are hydrocarbons in closed rings which are capable of uniting with other atom groups. Fischer showed dibenzenechromium to be another sandwich compound with two rings of benzene joined by an atom of chromium. This bit of research earned him world-wide renown in scientific circles, as the neutral chromium molecule and neutral benzene molecules had been thought to be uncombinable. Fischer's rise in academia parallelled the swift advance of his research: by 1954 he was an assistant professor at the Technische Hochschule; by 1957, a full professor at the University of Munich; and in 1964 he came back to the Technische Hochschule—by now called the Technische Universitat or Technical University—as director of the Institute for Inorganic Chemistry, replacing the retiring director and his former mentor, Professor Hieber.

Fischer's laboratory, equipped with all the latest equipment for spectrographic and structural analysis, soon became a center for worldwide organometallic research, and Fischer, whose talents at lecturing were equal to those in research, soon became the leading spokesperson for the new study. He also began lecturing around the world, and spent two visiting professorships in the United States in 1971 and 1973.

In 1973 Fischer was awarded the Nobel Prize, sharing it with the English Wilkinson for their "pioneering work, performed independently, on the chemistry of the organometallic, so-called sandwich compounds." At about this same time, Fischer and his team at Munich's Technical University were successfully synthesizing both the first carbene complexes and carbyne complexes (carbon atoms triply joined to metal atoms) which heralded an entirely new class of metal complexes of a transitional sort and spurred research in the field.

In addition to the Nobel, Fischer, a life-long bachelor, has also won the Gottingen Academy Prize in 1957 and the Alfred Stock Memorial Prize of the Society of German Chemists in 1959, as well as honorary membership in the American Academy of Arts and Sciences and full membership in the German Academy of Scientists. Among the many commercial and industrial spin-offs of his work is the creation of catalysts employed in the drug industry and also in oil refining, leading to the manufacture of fuels with low lead content.

BIOGRAPHICAL/CRITICAL SOURCES:

BOOKS

Biographical Encyclopedia of Scientists, Facts on
    File, 1981, Volume 1, pp. 264-265.
*Hinduja Foundation Encyclopedia of Nobel Laureates
    1901-1987,* Konark Publishers, 1988, pp. 486-487.

PERIODICALS

Science, November 16, 1973, pp. 699-701.*

*   *   *

FISCHER, Tibor 1959-

PERSONAL: Born November 15, 1959, in Stockport,
England; son of George and Margaret (Fekete) Fischer. *Education:* Attended Cambridge University, England.

ADDRESSES: Agent—Elizabeth Ziemska, Nicholas
Ellison Inc., 55 Fifth Ave., New York, NY 10003.

CAREER: Freelance journalist and novelist.

AWARDS, HONORS: Betty Trask Award for Best of
Young British Novelists, and nomination for the
Booker Prize, both 1993, for *Under the Frog.*

WRITINGS:

Under the Frog (novel), Polygon (Edinburgh, Scot-
    land), 1992; published in the United States as
    Under the Frog: A Black Comedy, New Press
    (New York City), 1994.
The Thought Gang (novel), Polygon, 1994, New
    Press, 1995.
The Collector Collector: A Novel, Holt (New York
    City), 1997.

SIDELIGHTS: British journalist and novelist Tibor
Fischer came to fame with his first novel, *Under the
Frog,* published in 1992. This tale of the exploits of
a Hungarian basketball team caught up in the anti-
communist revolution of 1956 garnered the author
1993's Betty Trask Award for the Best of Young
British Novelists, and also received a nomination for
that year's Booker Prize—one of the most prestigious
literary awards in Great Britain. In the same year that
Under the Frog was published in the United States,

Fischer's second book, *The Thought Gang,* appeared
on bookstore shelves in his native land.

Under the Frog's title comes from an old Hungarian
expression that loosely means things couldn't get any
worse—"under a frog's arse down a coalmine," as an
Observer reviewer quoted the novel. Heroes Gyuri
and Pataki are pleased to be on a basketball team in
communist Hungary, because it means they do not
have to work. They travel throughout their homeland
and have many sexual adventures along the way.
Though this may sound like a lighthearted romp, the
hardships and ironies of life under communism are
depicted as rock-solid, just under the surface of the
protagonists' quest for amusement. For instance,
there is the plight of Pataki's father, described by
Robert A. Morace in *Contemporary Novelists:* "Arrested in 1951, the elder Pataki must endure interro-
gation and torture before being released to face a
different kind of humiliation, 'having been judged too
dull' to be a conspirator." After having a Polish girlfriend die because of what Morace labeled her commitment "to justice and freedom," Gyuri eventually
escapes Hungary, but not without regret.

A *Washington Post Book World* contributor hailed
Under the Frog as a "picaresque tale" and com-
plimented the author's use of black humor. Larry
Wolff, a reviewer for the *New York Times Book
Review,* applauded the novel as "fully a work of
dynamic historical imagination."

The Thought Gang is about Eddie Coffin, a lazy
Cambridge professor of philosophy who leaves his
university position and moves to France with a large
portion of stolen academic grant money. When the
money goes up in flames in an automobile accident,
Eddie teams up with Hubert, a disabled French bank
robber. Together they decide to give each of their
robberies a philosophical theme—on one occasion, for
instance, they commit the crime wearing mask like-
nesses of nineteenth-century German philosopher
Friedrich Nietzsche. On another, they distribute cus-
tomized t-shirts to victims and bystanders. They always succeed, and they become folk heroes to the
French people.

Morace commented in *Contemporary Novelists* on *The
Thought Gang:* "The entire novel may be read as a
weirdly angled takeoff on Boethius's *Consolation of
Philosophy,* with opening gambit adapted from [Franz]
Kafka's *The Trial,* plot from [the film] *Bonnie and
Clyde,* title from [George] Orwell's *1984,* parts of the
structure from Nietzsche's *The Will to Power,* and

additional material from the Keystone Kops, Charlie Chaplin, and Francois Rabelais, among others."

Ron Loewinsohn, critiquing *The Thought Gang* in the *New York Times Book Review* declared that "Fischer's very funny tale . . . manages to be intelligent and irreverent, original and conventional, entertaining and tedious all at the same time." He went on to compare the *The Thought Gang* to eighteenth-century English novelist Laurence Sterne's famed *Tristam Shandy*. David L. Ulin in the *Nation* compared it to John Kennedy Toole's *A Confederacy of Dunces,* and labeled it "a lampoon with a soul as dark as night." He also observed that "Fischer evolves a unique structure for the novel that allows . . . digressions to become as fundamental to the texture of his story as they are to the iconoclastic cast of Eddie's mind" and praised the book as "exhilarating . . . daring by magic to turn philosophy into the substance of art." Novelist John Updike, reviewing *The Thought Gang* in the *New Yorker,* concluded that "it is the kind of novel that used to come out of Eastern Europe, in which the protagonist's chaotic, drunken, horny, self-careless behavior functioned as a piece of subversion, an adverse comment upon an oppressive and ridiculous government."

BIOGRAPHICAL/CRITICAL SOURCES:

BOOKS

Contemporary Novelists, St. James Press, 1996.

PERIODICALS

Nation, July 10, 1995, pp. 66-67.
New Yorker, August 21, 1995, pp. 105-114.
New York Times Book Review, August 28, 1994, p. 10; June 25, 1995, p. 11.
Observer, October 3, 1993.
Washington Post Book World, April 30, 1995, p. 12.

OTHER

http://www.books.com/scripts/view, May 1997.

*   *   *

FISH, Joe
  See WILLIAMSON, Philip G.

FISHER, Ronald A(ylmer) 1890-1962

PERSONAL: Born February 17, 1890 in East Finchley, London, England; died July 29, 1962 in Adelaide, Australia; son of George Fisher (a partner in a fine arts auction firm); married Ruth Eileen Guinness, 1917 (later separated); children: eight. *Education:* Studied mathematics and theoretical physics at Gonville and Caius College, Cambridge; graduated in 1912, and continued study for another year.

CAREER: Statistician and geneticist. Worked briefly as a farm laborer in Canada. Mercantile and General Investment Company, London, England, statistician, 1913-15; public school teacher, 1915-19; Rothamsted Agricultural Research Institute, researcher, 1919-33; University College, London, Galton Chair of Eugenics, 1933-43; Cambridge University, Balfour Professor of Genetics, 1943-57; Commonwealth Scientific and Industrial Research Organization, Adelaide, Australia, statistical researcher, 1959-62. Iowa State College (now University), lecturer, summers, 1931 and 1936.

AWARDS, HONORS: Became Fellow of the Royal Society, 1929 (president 1952-54); received several medals from the Royal Society and the Royal Statistical Society; knighted in 1952.

WRITINGS:

Statistical Methods for Research Workers, 1925, Hafner, 1973.
The Genetical Theory of Natural Selection, Clarendon (London), 1930, 2nd edition, Dover (New York), 1958.
Design of Experiments, [London], 1935, seventh edition, Oliver and Boyd (Edinburgh), 1960.
Contributions to Mathematical Statistics, Wiley, 1950.
The Design of Experiments, Revised eighth edition, Hafner, 1974.
Statistical Methods, Experimental Design, and Scientific Inference, Oxford University Press, 1990.

Contributor to journals and periodicals, including *Philosophical Transactions of the Royal Society* and *Annals of Science.*

SIDELIGHTS: Sir Ronald A. Fisher was a prominent mathematician who formalized and extended the field of statistics and revolutionized the concept of experimental design. He worked for fourteen years as a research statistician and later held professorships in genetics, another field to which he made significant contributions. He wrote some three hundred papers and seven books throughout his prodigious career.

The son of George Fisher, a partner in a fine arts auction firm, Ronald Aylmer Fisher was born on February 17, 1890, in the north London suburb of East Finchley. The youngest of seven children, Fisher was a precocious child. In her biography, *R. A. Fisher: The Life of a Scientist,* Fisher's daughter Joan Fisher Box describes an incident that occurred when the scientist was about three years old: he engaged his nurse in a breakfast-table conversation about the successive halving of the number two; after she answered the first three questions of his series, he concluded that "half of a sixteenth must be a thirty-toof."

During his school years at Stanmore Park and Harrow schools, Fisher developed a facility for visualizing complex geometrical relationships in his mind. Because of his poor eyesight, he was not allowed to read or write under artificial light, so he often listened to lectures without taking notes and solved problems mentally. This ability later proved fruitful, when his geometrical interpretation of statistics led him to new results.

In 1909, Fisher earned a scholarship to attend Gonville and Caius College in Cambridge, where he concentrated on mathematics and theoretical physics, while also pursuing interests in biometry and genetics. As an undergraduate, he published his first scholarly paper, discussing an absolute criterion for fitting frequency curves. Following his graduation in 1912, he continued his studies for another year, investigating statistical mechanics, quantum theory, and the theory of errors.

During his first six years after college, he searched for an occupation that would suit him, even working briefly as a farm laborer in Canada. Primarily, however, he worked as a statistician for the Mercantile and General Investment Company in London (1913-15) and as a public school teacher (1915-19). Although he was unhappy and apparently ineffective as a teacher, he was nonetheless recognized as a brilliant thinker who had some difficulty explaining his ideas to others. In 1917, he married Ruth Eileen Guinness, the daughter of a doctor; they had eight children and eventually separated.

Even though his jobs did not support research opportunities, Fisher published several notable papers. One of his earliest accomplishments in statistics (published in 1915) was to establish, in mathematical terms, an exact method of sample measurement in statistics. A child of the upper class, he also wrote two papers on eugenics, the science of improving the human race through selective mating. His concern that the—as he thought—less talented lower classes produced offspring at a faster rate than the—in his mind—more capable upper classes influenced his personal choice to have a large family. This was, in addition to being jingoistic, a risk on his part considering his own genetic shortcomings regarding his poor vision, a trait he could have engendered to several large generations of Fishers. His 1918 paper on Gregor Mendel's theory of inherited characteristics laid the foundation for his later work on the statistical analysis of variance.

His growing reputation as a mathematician brought Fisher two promising job offers in 1919. One, from the noted statistician Karl Pearson (with whom he developed a lifelong feud), was to work at the Galton Laboratory in London's University College under Pearson's close supervision. Recognizing a better opportunity to conduct his own research, Fisher accepted a second offer from Sir John Russell at the Rothamsted Experimental Station, about twenty-five miles north of London. Established in 1843, this agricultural research laboratory had accumulated a sixty-six-year backlog of statistical data; it would be Fisher's job to analyze this material. For the next fourteen years, Fisher took advantage of the huge data resources at Rothamsted to derive new analysis techniques as well as agricultural results. On the theoretical side, he formulated the analysis of variance. Now a fundamental tool of statistical analysis, it isolates the effects of several variables in an experiment, showing what contribution each made to the results. Subsequently, he advocated factorial experimentation, in which several factors are varied simultaneously, rather than varying one factor at a time. This approach not only speeds results by gathering information on the effects of several factors, but it also accounts for the possibility that the effect of a factor may be influenced by interaction with other factors.

In another innovation of experimental design, Fisher advocated the random arrangement of samples receiving different treatments. Traditional agricultural experiments arranged samples according to elaborate placement schemes on checkerboard plots to avoid bias from extraneous factors such as variations in soil and exposure to weather. Fisher showed that assigning these positions randomly, rather than according to a systematic pattern, facilitated statistical analysis of the results. His 1925 textbook *Statistical Methods for Research Workers* is considered a landmark work in this field, although it is so difficult to read that, as Fisher's friend and colleague M. G. Kendall wrote in *Studies in the History of Statistics and Probability,* "Somebody once said that no student should attempt to read it unless he had read it before."

During the course of his career, Fisher's theoretical work also included improvements to different tests of statistical significance. He refined the Helmert-Pearson chi-square test (including the addition of degrees of freedom) and the t-distribution test, also developing what would eventually be called the F-distribution test after Fisher himself. He introduced the concept of the null hypothesis to designate random processes. Deviations from the null hypothesis indicate significant correlations in statistical samples. Fisher developed procedures for determining when results deviate from the null hypothesis sufficiently to justify an assumption that correlations are significant. He derived the distributions of numerous statistical functions, including partial and multiple correlation coefficients and the regression coefficient in analyses of covariance. Covariance is a term used to describe samples in which statistical results are influenced by different factors. Regression analysis allows the statistician to screen out the effect of all factors other than the one whose significance is being tested. In his 1922 paper "On the Mathematical Foundations of Theoretical Statistics," he analyzed and formalized existing knowledge in the field.

Fisher became a Fellow of the Royal Society in 1929. That same year he published a paper on sampling moments that would provide the foundation for future development of that topic. During the 1930s, he wrote several substantial papers on the logic of inductive inference, building on earlier work on the maximum likelihood estimate.

In the agrarian setting of Rothamsted, Fisher also pursued his interest in genetics by breeding various animals such as mice, snails, and poultry, even in his own home. He applied his mathematical prowess to Mendel's work on inheritance, resulting in the 1930 publication of *The Genetical Theory of Natural Selection.* In it, he showed that Mendelian selection always favors the dominance of beneficial genes and concluded that Mendel's results were mathematically compatible with Charles Darwin's theory of natural selection. His work solidified the growing consensus among theorists of evolution that the Darwinian

model, favoring selection over genetic mutation as the explanation for evolutionary change, best fit the available data. Fisher left Rothamsted in 1933 to occupy the Galton Chair of Eugenics at University College, a position he held until 1943. In 1935, he established a blood-typing department in the Galton Laboratory, which developed important information on the inheritance of rhesus blood groups.

That same year, he published *Design of Experiments,* another landmark text in statistical science. The following year, he published his first presentation on discriminant analysis, an approach to statistical samples in which several factors influence outcomes; this is now used in such areas as weather forecasting, medical research, and educational testing. During a 1936 summer lectureship at Iowa State College's agricultural research center at Ames (where he had also taught during the summer of 1931), Fisher established contacts that helped popularize his techniques among American educators and psychologists, as well as agriculturalists.

In 1943, he joined Cambridge University as Balfour Professor of Genetics. He was knighted in 1952 and served as president of the Royal Society from 1952 until 1954. Both the Royal Society and the Royal Statistical Society awarded him several prestigious medals during his tenure at the University of Cambridge. He formally retired in 1957, but continued working until a successor was found in 1959. In 1950, Fisher published *Contributions to Mathematical Statistics,* an annotated collection of forty-three of his most significant papers, many of which had originally appeared in rather obscure journals. During the late 1950s, he wrote several articles criticizing the presumption of a cause-and-effect relationship between smoking and cancer based only on the establishment of a correlation between them. When he left Cambridge in 1959, he moved to Adelaide, Australia, to join several of his former students as a statistical researcher for the Commonwealth Scientific and Industrial Research Organization. He died on July 29, 1962, as a result of an embolism following an intestinal disorder.

BIOGRAPHICAL/CRITICAL SOURCES:

BOOKS

Box, Joan Fisher, *R. A. Fisher: The Life of a Scientist,* Wiley, 1985.
Fienberg, Stephen E., *R. A. Fisher, An Appreciation,* Springer-Verlag, 1990.

Gillespie, Charles Coulston, editor, *Dictionary of Scientific Biography,* Volume 5, Scribner, 1974, pp. 7-11.

Pearson, E. S. and M. G. Kendall, editors, *Studies in the History of Statistics and Probability,* Hafner Press, 1970, pp. 439-53.

Tankard, James W., *The Statistical Pioneers,* Schenkman, 1984, pp. 111-33.*

*   *   *

FRANKLIN, Carl (Mikal) 1930-

PERSONAL: Born April 11, 1930. *Education:* Attended University of California at Berkeley and American Film Institute. *Avocational interests:* Poetry.

ADDRESSES: Agent—Rifkin-David Artists Management, 9615 Brighton Way, Beverly Hills, CA 90210.

CAREER: Director, actor, and scriptwriter. Director of films, including *Eye of the Eagle II: Inside the Enemy,* Concorde, 1989; *Nowhere to Run,* Concorde, 1989; *Full Fathom Five,* Concorde, 1990; *One False Move,* I. R. S., 1992; and *Devil in a Blue Dress,* TriStar, 1995. Director of television special, *Punk* (also known as *Alive T.V.*), PBS, 1989; also director of television miniseries, *Laurel Avenue* (also known as *Rondo: Scenes of a Weekend*), HBO, 1993. Actor in television series, including *Streets of San Francisco,* ABC, 1974; *Cannon,* CBS, 1974 and 1975; *Caribe,* ABC, 1975; *Barnaby Jones,* CBS, 1975; *Good Times,* CBS, 1976; *Most Wanted,* ABC, 1976; *Fantastic Journey,* NBC, 1977; *White Shadow,* CBS, 1980; *Trapper John, M.D.,* CBS, 1980; *Joshua's World,* CBS (pilot), 1980; *Lou Grant,* CBS, 1980; *McClain's Law,* NBC, 1981-82; *A-Team,* NBC, 1984; *Cover-Up,* CBS, 1985; *MacGyver,* ABC, 1985; *Riptide,* NBC, 1985; *Frank's Place,* CBS, 1987; *Alf,* NBC, 1987; and *Steel Magnolias,* CBS (pilot), 1990. Actor in television movies, specials, and miniseries, including *It Couldn't Happen to a Nicer Guy,* ABC, 1974; *Monkey in the Middle,* 1976; *Battle of the Network Stars II,* ABC, 1977; *Loose Change* (miniseries; also shown as *Those Restless Years*), NBC, 1977; *Legend of the Golden Gun,* NBC, 1979; *One Cooks, the Other Doesn't,* CBS, 1983; *A Smoky Mountain Christmas,* ABC, 1986; *Too Good to Be True,* NBC (also shown as *Leave Her to Heaven*), 1988; and *Flying Blind,* NBC, 1990. Actor in films, including *Five on the Black Hand Side* (as Carl Mikal Franklin), United Artists, 1973; *The Laughing Police-*

man, 1974; *Eye of the Eagle II: Inside the Enemy,* Concorde, 1989; *Last Stand at Lang Mei,* 1989; *Full Fathom Five,* Concorde, 1990; *Eye of the Eagle 3,* Concorde, 1992; and *In the Heat of Passion,* Concorde, 1992. Appeared as himself in documentaries, including *A Personal Journey with Martin Scorsese through American Movies,* Miramax, 1995; and *American Cinema,* PBS, 1995.

AWARDS, HONORS: Independent Spirit Award, best director, Independent Feature Project/West, 1993, for *One False Move.*

WRITINGS:

SCREENPLAYS

Last Stand at Lang Mei, 1989.
Eye of the Eagle II: Inside the Enemy, Concorde, 1989.
(With Bart Davis) *Full Fathom Five,* adapted from the novel by Brad Davis, Concorde, 1990.
Eye of the Eagle 3, Concorde, 1992.
Devil in a Blue Dress, adapted from the novel by Walter Mosley, TriStar, 1995.

TELEPLAYS

Punk, PBS, 1989; also shown as *Alive TV,* 1993.

POETRY

Portrait of Man, Exposition Press, 1952.

SIDELIGHTS: Beginning his entertainment career as a television actor in the 1970s, Carl Franklin successfully expanded into directing and writing for both television and theatrical motion pictures. He has often worked within the action and mystery genres, but his credits include directorial work for the dramatic miniseries *Laurel Avenue* and acting in the critically acclaimed series *Frank's Place.* Franklin's early writing and directing efforts produced 1989's *Last Stand at Lang Mei* and *Eye of the Eagle II: Inside the Enemy.* In 1989 he also wrote and directed the television special *Punk* for PBS. *Nowhere to Run,* a 1989 action movie that Franklin directed, starred David Carradine and Jason Priestley, and the 1990 action picture *Full Fathom Five,* which Franklin cowrote and directed, starred Michael Moriarty.

In 1992, Franklin directed the low-budget independent release *One False Move.* This crime-spree movie about a cocaine-snorting, mixed-race femme fatale and her two male accomplices (one white, one black), with a script by actor Billy Bob Thornton and Tom Epperson, is loaded with "suspense and surprise," according to Donald Lyons in *Film Comment*. Lyons called it "a tightly wound movie," and added that "[d]irector Carl Franklin keeps his camera in the pores; he hugs faces and likes to inch up folks' bodies." James Bowman, writing in *The American Spectator* at the time of the film's release, suggested that *One False Move* was receiving "so much attention" in part because it shows evil as "simply evil" rather than explaining it away in sociopsychological terms. Critic John Simon, in the *National Review,* wrote that "*One False Move* is a modest B picture, but, wonder of wonders, it tells a real story." While Simon noted a lack of clarity in the beginning of the film, he asserted that the writers and director are "adept at creating suspense and at conveying brutality and horror in a way that reaches the precise last limit of the bearable." Richard Alleva in a 1995 review of *Devil in a Blue Dress* for *Commonweal,* looked back on *One False Move* as "the best American movie" of 1992.

Laurel Avenue, the 1993 HBO miniseries directed by Franklin and shown in two ninety-minute segments, struck a very different note. The miniseries portrays the lives of a working-class African American family—three generations in four households—in St. Paul, Minnesota. The family members try to solve their own and their relatives' problems, which include cocaine addiction, drinking, and involvement with organized crime. Critics praised the show for its realism and its avoidance of sentimentality; Richard Zoglin, in *Time,* called it "almost a breakthrough . . . honest but not exploitative, affirmative without sappy TV 'uplift,'" and specified that it was "tautly directed" by Franklin. *People* magazine declared that in *Laurel Avenue,* Franklin "proves again . . . that he has an uncommon ability to capture the psychology of ordinary people . . . who find their world twisted out of shape by pressures they haven't anticipated and don't understand." *New York* magazine reviewer John Leonard, pointing out that the miniseries had "the best cast of African-American actors since *Frank's Place*" (in which Franklin had performed), praised Franklin, the writer, and producers for portraying the Arnett family "as individuals, not as victims, object lessons, or pathologies."

The year 1995 saw Franklin cowriting and directing the theatrical film *Devil in a Blue Dress,* starring Denzel Washington and based on a novel by the acclaimed crime writer Walter Mosley. *Devil in a Blue*

Dress is one of a series of novels centering on protagonist Easy Rawlins, an African American homeowner in 1940s Los Angeles who becomes a private detective despite himself. The film, and Washington's performance, were widely praised for their subtle complexity and their exploration of moral ambiguities. Alleva, in *Commonweal,* compared Franklin's directorial style to that of John Huston, applying James Agee's description of Huston's work to Franklin's: "His style is practically invisible as well as practically universal in its possible good uses; it is the most virile movie style I know of." Writing in *Nation,* Stuart Klawans compared the depiction of evil in *One False Move* with the treatment of that subject in *Devil in a Blue Dress,* concluding that "unlike the film world's multitude of sensationalists, Franklin also knows why some acts are evil; they're evil because people are worth caring about. And that's why Franklin is a filmmaker worth caring about."

BIOGRAPHICAL/CRITICAL SOURCES:

PERIODICALS

American Spectator, October, 1992, p. 54.
Commonweal, November 3, 1995, pp. 16-17.
Film Comment, September-October, 1992, pp. 8-9.
Nation, October 23, 1995, pp. 480-81.
National Review, August 31, 1992, pp. 70-71.
New York, July 12, 1993, p. 55.
People, July 12, 1993, pp. 12-13.
Time, July 12, 1993, pp. 60-61.*

*   *   *

FREEDMAN, Jonathan (Borwick) 1950-

PERSONAL: Born April 11, 1950, in Rochester, NY; son of Marshall Arthur and Betty (Borwick) Freedman; married Maggie Locke, May 4, 1979; children: Madigan, Nicholas. *Education:* Columbia College, A.B. (cum laude), 1972. *Religion:* Jewish. *Avocational interests:* Skiing, tai chi, Brazilian music, travel.

ADDRESSES: Home and office—7144 Monte Vista Ave., La Jolla, CA 92037; fax (619) 551-1694. *Agent*—Charlotte Sheedy, 65 Bleeker St. New York, NY 10012.

CAREER: Associated Press reporter in Sao Paulo and Rio de Janeiro, Brazil, 1974-75; *Tribune,* San Diego,

CA, editorial writer, 1981-90; Copley News Service, San Diego, syndicated columnist, 1987-89; freelance opinion and editorial writer for both the *Los Angeles Times* and the *New York Times,* 1990-91; freelance columnist and author of books. Member of the U.S.-Japan journalists exchange program of the International Press Institute, 1985; board of directors of the Schools of the Future Commission, San Diego, 1987; moderator for Public Broadcasting System, San Diego, 1988; visiting lecturer at San Diego State University, 1990—.

MEMBER: Society of Professional Journalists, National Conference of Editorial Writers, Authors Guild, Phi Beta Kappa.

AWARDS, HONORS: Cornell Woolrich writing fellowship, Columbia University, 1972; Copley Ring of Truth Award and Sigma Delta Chi Award, both 1983; San Diego Press Club Award, 1984; special citation, Columbia Graduate School of Journalism, and Distinguished Service Award, Society of Professional Journalists, both 1985; Eugene C. Pulliam Editorial Writing fellowship, Sigma Delta Chi Foundation, and Distinguished Writing Award, American Society of Newspaper Editors, both 1986; Pulitzer Prize in Distinguished Editorial Writing, Columbia University Graduate School of Journalism, for editorials urging the passage of new immigration laws, 1987; media fellowship, Hoover Institution, 1991.

WRITINGS:

(Also illustrator) *The Man Who'd Bounce the World: A Story* (juvenile fiction), Turtle Island Press, 1979.
The Editorials and Essays of Jonathan Freedman, 1988.
The Pulitzer Prizes, Volume One, 1987, (anthology), Simon and Schuster (New York City), 1988.
From Cradle to Grave: The Human Face of Poverty in America (nonfiction), Atheneum, 1993.

Contributor of articles and editorials to periodicals, including the *New York Times, Chicago Tribune, San Francisco Examiner, Oakland Tribune, Los Angeles Times,* and the San Diego *Tribune.*

SIDELIGHTS: Jonathan Freedman has been a journalist since the 1970s. In the 1980s editorial writing became his predominant work, and his series of editorials in the San Diego *Tribune* in support of immigration reform garnered him a Pulitzer Prize in 1987. Since then his free-lance articles have appeared in many prominent newspapers, including the *Los Angeles Times,* the *New York Times,* and the *Chicago Tribune.* Freedman is also the author of both a children's story and a well-received nonfiction volume, *From Cradle to Grave: The Human Face of Poverty in America.* His juvenile fiction work, *The Man Who'd Bounce the World,* concerns a protagonist who gave away all of his money on the streets of Harlem in New York City; Freedman's 1993 study, *From Cradle to Grave,* focuses on real-life efforts toward community improvement. According to Linnea Lannon of the *Detroit Free Press,* the book also suggests "that it is increasingly the middle class that is falling through the so-called safety net of social programs." *From Cradle to Grave* recounts the stories of individuals dealing with poverty issues, and, as the title implies, they range in age from newborn babies to the elderly. Calling Freedman a "beautiful prose stylist [and] . . . a very persuasive writer," Patricia A. O'Connell noted in *Commonweal* that he discusses several programs that are doing a good job of helping people and "offers a theoretical plan for overhauling social services and health care."

BIOGRAPHICAL/CRITICAL SOURCES:

PERIODICALS

Commonweal, November 5, 1993, pp. 35-36.
Detroit Free Press, October 17, 1993.*

*   *   *

FREY, Darcy

PERSONAL: Male. *Education:* Graduated from Oberlin College.

ADDRESSES: Home—Boston, MA. *Office*—c/o Houghton Mifflin, 222 Berkeley St., Boston, MA 02116.

CAREER: Journalist. Worked for business and law magazines following graduation; staff editor at *Harper's* for a year.

AWARDS, HONORS: National Magazine Award, for article on college basketball recruiting.

WRITINGS:

The Last Shot: City Streets, Basketball Dreams (nonfiction), Houghton Mifflin (Boston, MA), 1994.

Also contributor of articles to periodicals, including *Harper's* and *Rolling Stone*.

SIDELIGHTS: Journalist Darcy Frey turned his award-winning article on college basketball recruiting into the critically acclaimed 1994 volume *The Last Shot: City Streets, Basketball Dreams.* In the book, Frey explores the issue in much greater depth, studying the lives of four high school basketball stars in order to expose the darker truths behind the myth of escaping from the slums via professional basketball. As Brent Staples explained in the *New York Times Book Review:* "Fewer than one percent of the half-million young men who play high school ball will win scholarships. A depressing number of those who do will never graduate. Fewer than one in a hundred of those who play in college will go on to careers in professional basketball. Of this final, golden few, most, through injury, insufficient skill or defects in personality, will last no longer than four years—has-beens at the age of twenty-six."

The Last Shot profiles four basketball superstars from Coney Island, New York's Lincoln High School. Once a proud, academically oriented institution, it is now surrounded by slums. Two of the students Frey portrays miss their goal because they lack the academic scores for admission to four-year colleges. One succeeds at Seton Hall University, while another has bloomed so early in his basketball skills that Frey's narrative ends while he is still in high school, hounded by college recruiters who are encouraged by his ambitious father.

In the course of the book, Frey follows the most successful boy to a Nike-sponsored basketball camp, a place James North in *Chicago Tribune Books* described as "swarming with college coaches." North judged *The Last Shot* to be "outstanding," while Staples asserted that the book was "compellingly written, with elegance, economy and just the right amount of outrage." John Skow in *Time* praised the volume as "thoughtful" and "sharply observed," while Evan Thomas in *Newsweek* hailed it as "an achingly good book."

BIOGRAPHICAL/CRITICAL SOURCES:

PERIODICALS

Chicago Tribune Books, November 27, 1994, p. 5.
Kirkus Reviews, September 1, 1994, p. 1185.
Newsweek, November 21, 1994, p. 101.
New York Times, November 7, 1994, p. C18.

New York Times Book Review, November 13, 1994, pp. 3, 66-67.
Publishers Weekly, September 12, 1994, p. 74.
Time, November 28, 1994, p. 91.

OTHER

http://www.yale.edu/ydn/paper/4.12.96storyno.AD.html*

* * *

FREY, Stephen W.

PERSONAL: Male.

ADDRESSES: Office—Westdeutsche Landesbank, 1211 Avenue of the Americas, 24th Floor, New York, NY 10036-8701.

CAREER: Westdeutsche Landesbank, New York City, vice-president of corporate finance. Worked previously in the mergers and acquisitions department, J. P. Morgan & Company.

WRITINGS:

The Takeover, Dutton (New York City), 1995.
The Vulture Fund, Dutton, 1996.

ADAPTATIONS: The film rights for both *The Takeover* and *The Vulture Fund* have been sold to Paramount.

SIDELIGHTS: After reading the suspense novels of John Grisham, Tom Clancy, and Scott Turow, Wall Street banker Stephen W. Frey decided he could do the same. The result of Frey's first foray into the world of publishing was released in 1995 as *The Takeover.* In this Wall Street thriller, the Sevens (a secret society of powerful Harvard Business School alumni) set in motion an elaborate scheme to oust the ultra-liberal U.S. president currently in office because his policies do not support the wealthy. In accomplishing their objective the Sevens put young mergers-and-acquisitions specialist Andrew Falcon in a position to manage the takeover of a major bank. Unbeknownst to Falcon, the Sevens rig the takeover so that the bank will collapse just weeks before the presidential election. By the time Falcon realizes what is going on, it may be too late to save either the bank or himself.

Describing *The Takeover* in a *USA Today* review, John H. Healy writes that "John Grisham meets Robert Ludlum on Wall Street in this fast-paced novel. "A *Publishers Weekly* contributor agrees: "Frey's plotting requires leaps of faith, and his characters are cartoonish," adding, however, that the novel does have all the elements a fan of the thriller genre would enjoy. "Looking to vicariously live the life of a financier on Wall Street?," Healy asks. "This is the roller coaster that will take you there."

BIOGRAPHICAL/CRITICAL SOURCES:

PERIODICALS

Chicago Tribune, August 20, 1995, section 14, p. 4.
Library Journal, June 15, 1995, p. 93.
New York Times Book Review, August 13, 1995, pp. 3, 24.
Publishers Weekly, January 23, 1995, p. 44; June 5, 1995, p. 49.
USA Today, August 30, 1995, p. 4B.
Wall Street Journal, September 8, 1995, p. A7.

OTHER

http://www.penguin.com/usa/takeover.*

*   *   *

FROOKS, Dorothy   1899-1997

OBITUARY NOTICE—See index for *CA* sketch: Born February 12, 1899, in Saugerties, NY; died April 13, 1997, in New York, NY. Lawyer, suffragist, and author. She spoke out for the suffragist movement at age eleven, conceived of the small claims court, participated in well-publicized trials and was the first full-time lawyer for the Salvation Army. In between,

Frooks found time to write several books and serve her country in both World Wars. The daughter of a well-to-do East Coast businessman, Frooks was recruited by one of her mother's friends to make speeches for the suffragist movement. As a teenager, she also recruited men for the service in World War I and was invited by President Woodrow Wilson to serve in the U.S. Navy. Her first book, *The American Heart,* was published in 1919. She then earned her law degree from Hamilton Law School in Chicago and a master's degree from New York University. While in New York, she set up free legal aid clinics and was the Salvation Army's first full-time attorney.

In 1920, Frooks began writing a column titled "My Day" for the *New York World,* which lasted until 1932. Frooks also wrote *Love's Law* (1928), *All in Love* (1932), *Over the Heads of Congress* (1935), *The Olympic Torch* (1946), *Are You a Happy American?* (with brother Richard Frooks in 1970), and *Lady Lawyer* (with Cay Dorney in 1974). Frooks also spent much of her early career in New York fending off marriage proposals from Mayor Fiorello La Guardia, though she convinced him to sign a law establishing small claims courts. She also pushed for legislation for aid to dependent children. During World War II, Frooks served in the Judge Advocate office in the U.S. Army. Despite her devotion to women's causes, she opposed the Equal Rights Amendment in the 1970s. In 1986, she married Jay P. Vanderbilt.

OBITUARIES AND OTHER SOURCES:

BOOKS

Who's Who of American Women, 17th edition, Marquis, 1991.

PERIODICALS

New York Times, April 19, 1997, p. 48.

G

GAGARIN, Yuri A(lekseevich) 1934-1968

PERSONAL: Born March 9, 1934, in Klushino, U.S.S.R. (now Russia); died March 27, 1968, during MiG-15 flight training maneuvers; son of Aleksey Ivanovich (a carpenter) and Anna (a dairymaid, maiden name, Ivanovich) Gagarin; married Valentina Ivanova Goryacheva (a biomedical researcher and medical doctor) in 1957; children: a daughter and a son. *Education:* Saratov Industrial Technical School, graduated, 1955; flight school, pilot's license, 1955; attended Soviet Air Force flight training school, 1957.

CAREER: Cosmonaut and first human in space; Vostok I, commander of cosmonaut team; deputy director of cosmonaut training center; chair of the Soviet-Cuban Friendship Society; served on the Council of the Union and the Supreme Soviet Council of Nationalities. *Military service:* Soviet Air Force, moved through the ranks, eventually reaching the rank of major.

AWARDS, HONORS: Tsiolkovsky Gold Medal of the Soviet Academy of Sciences, Gold Medal of the British Interplanetary Society, and two awards from the International Aeronautical Federation; posthumously, the cosmonaut training center, his hometown, a space tracking ship, and a lunar crater were renamed in his honor, 1968; awarded the Order of Lenin. Named a Hero of the Soviet Union and a Hero of Socialist Labor. Became an honorary citizen of fourteen cities in six countries.

WRITINGS:

Road to the Stars, translated by G. Hanna and D. Myshne, Foreign Languages Publishing House, 1962.

(With Vladimir Lebedev) *Survival in Space,* translated by Gabriella Azrael, Bantam Books, 1969.

SIDELIGHTS: Yuri A. Gagarin was the first human in space. In 1961, this boyish-looking Soviet cosmonaut captured the attention of the world with his short flight around the Earth. "He invited us all into space," American astronaut Neil Armstrong said of him, as quoted in *Aviation Week and Space Technology.* Gagarin died in 1968 when the jet that he was flying crashed, as he was preparing to return to space.

The third of four children, Yuri Alekseevich Gagarin was born on a collective farm in Klushino, U.S.S.R., on March 9, 1934. His father, Aleksey Ivanovich Gagarin, was a carpenter on the farm and his mother, Anna, a dairymaid. Gagarin grew up helping them with their work. Neither of his parents had much formal education, but they encouraged him in his schooling. During World War II, the family was evicted from their home by invading German troops, and Gagarin's older brother and sister were taken prisoner for slave labor, though they later escaped.

After the war, Gagarin went to vocational school in Moscow, originally intending to become a foundry worker, and then he moved on to the Saratov Industrial Technical School. He was still learning to be a foundryperson, although his favorite subjects were physics and mathematics. In 1955, during his fourth and final year of school, he joined a local flying club. His first flight as a passenger, he later wrote in *Road to the Stars,* "gave meaning to my whole life." He quickly mastered flying, consumed by a new determination to become a fighter pilot. He joined the Soviet Air Force after graduation. The launch of Sputnik—

the first artificial satellite sent into space—occurred on October 4, 1957, while he pursued his military and flight training. He graduated with honors that same year and married medical student Valentina Ivanova Goryacheva. They would have two children, a daughter and a son.

Gagarin volunteered for service in the Northern Air Fleet and joined the Communist Party. He followed closely news of other Sputnik launches; although there had been no official announcement, Gagarin guessed that preparations for manned flights would soon begin and he volunteered for cosmonaut duty. Gagarin completed the required weeks of physical examinations and testing in 1960, just before his twenty-sixth birthday. He was then told that he had been made a member of the first group of twelve cosmonauts. The assignment was a secret, and he was forbidden to tell even his wife until his family had settled into the new space-program complex called Zvezdniy Gorodok (Star Town), forty miles from Moscow. An outgoing, natural leader, the stocky, smiling Gagarin stood out even among his well-qualified peers. Sergei Korolyov, head of the Soviet space program and chief designer of its vehicles, thought Gagarin had the makings of a first-rate scientist and engineer, as well as being an excellent pilot. In March of 1961, Korolyov approved the selection of Gagarin to ride Vostok I into orbit.

Senior Lieutenant Gagarin made history on April 12, 1961, when a converted ballistic missile propelled his Vostok capsule into Earth orbit from the remote Baikonur Cosmodrome. "Off we go!" the cosmonaut exclaimed. The Vostok was controlled automatically, and Gagarin spent his time reporting observations of the Earth and his own condition. He performed such tasks as writing and tapping out a message on a telegraph key, thus establishing that a human being's coordination remained intact even while weightless in space. Proving that people could work in space, he also ate and drank to verify that the body would take nourishment in weightlessness. He commented repeatedly on the beauty of the earth from space and on how pleasant weightlessness felt.

Gagarin rode his spacecraft for 108 minutes, ejecting from the spherical reentry module after the craft reentered the atmosphere just short of one complete orbit. Ejection was standard procedure for all Vostok pilots, although Gagarin dutifully supported the official fiction that he had remained in his craft all the way to the ground—a requirement for international certification of the flight as a record. Cosmonaut and

capsule landed safely near the banks of the Volga River.

After doctors proclaimed him unaffected by his flight, Gagarin was presented to the public as an international hero. He received an instant promotion to the rank of major and made appearances around the world. He was named a Hero of the Soviet Union and a Hero of Socialist Labor, and he became an honorary citizen of fourteen cities in six countries. He received the Tsiolkovsky Gold Medal of the Soviet Academy of Sciences, the Gold Medal of the British Interplanetary Society, and two awards from the International Aeronautical Federation. The flight had many implications for international affairs: American leaders extended cautious congratulations and redoubled their own efforts in the space race, while the Soviet media proclaimed that Gagarin's success showed the strength of socialism.

Gagarin became commander of the cosmonaut team. In 1964 he was made deputy director of the cosmonaut training center at the space program headquarters complex—where he oversaw the selection and training of the first women cosmonauts. He served as capsule communicator—the link between cosmonauts and ground controllers—for four later space flights in the Vostok and Voskhod programs. At various times during this period, he also held political duties; chaired the Soviet-Cuban Friendship Society and served on the Council of the Union, and the Supreme Soviet Council of Nationalities.

Gagarin always wanted to venture back to space, and in 1966 he was returned to active status to serve as the backup cosmonaut to Vladimir Komarov for the first flight of the new Soyuz spacecraft. When the Soyuz 1 mission ended and Komarov died due to a parachute malfunction, Gagarin was assigned to command the upcoming Soyuz 3. But Gagarin himself did not live to fly the Soyuz 3 mission. On March 27, 1968, he took off for a routine proficiency flight in a two-seat MiG-15 trainer. He and his flight instructor became engaged in low-level maneuvers with two other jets. Gagarin's plane crossed close behind another jet and was caught in its vortex; he lost control and the jet crashed into the tundra at high speed, killing both occupants instantly.

Gagarin was given a hero's funeral. The cosmonaut training center was renamed in his honor, as were his former hometown, a space tracking ship, and a lunar crater. His wife continued to work as a biomedical laboratory assistant at Zvezdniy Gorodok, and Gagarin's office there was preserved as a museum; a huge statue of him was erected in Moscow. His book *Survival in Space* was published posthumously. Written with space-program physician Vladimir Lebedev, the work outlines Gagarin's views on the problems and requirements for successful long-term space flights. On April 12, 1991, thirty years after Gagarin's flight, his cosmonaut successors, along with eighteen American astronauts, gathered at Baikonur to salute his achievements.

BIOGRAPHICAL/CRITICAL SOURCES:

BOOKS

Hooper, Gordon R., *The Soviet Cosmonaut Team,* GRH Publications, 1986.
Oberg, James E., *Red Star in Orbit,* Random House, 1981.

PERIODICALS

Aviation Week and Space Technology, April 8, 1991, p. 7.*

*   *   *

GALL, Lothar   1936-

PERSONAL: Born December 3, 1936, in Loetzen, Poland. *Education:* Attended Universities of Mainz and Munich; earned Ph.D., 1960; University of Cologne, Habilitation, 1967.

ADDRESSES: Office—History Seminar, University of Frankfurt, Senckenberganlage 31, Postfach 11 19 32, D-60054 Frankfurt am Main, Germany.

CAREER: University of Giessen, Giessen, Germany, faculty member, 1968; Free University of Berlin, Berlin, Germany, faculty member, beginning in 1969; Oxford University, Oxford, England, guest professor, 1972-73; University of Frankfurt, Frankfurt, Germany, professor of contemporary history, 1975—. Institute for European History, Mainz, Germany, chairperson of academic advisory council; member of Committee for the History of Parliamentarism and of Political Parties, Committee for German History in Berlin, Committee for the History of the German Land Hessen, and Committee for the History of the Land Baden-Wuerttemberg. German Historical Museum, chairperson of academic advisory council; Historical Commission of Frankfurt, chairperson.

MEMBER: Association of German Historians (chairperson, 1992-96), Deutsche Forschungsgemeinschaft (vice president), Bayerische Akademie der Wissenschaften, Society for Business History (member of board of directors).

AWARDS, HONORS: Gottfried Wilhelm Leipniz-Preis, Deutsche Forschungsgemeinschaft, 1987; Herbert Quandt Medienpreis, 1990; Global Business Book Award, 1996, for *Die Deutsche Bank.*

WRITINGS:

Bismarck: d. weisse Revolutionear, Propyleaen (Vienna, Austria), 1980, translation by J. A. Underwood published as *Bismarck, the White Revolutionary,* Allen & Unwin (Boston, MA), 1986.

UNTRANSLATED WORKS

Fragen an die deutsche Geschichte: Ideen, Kreafte, Entscheidungen von 1800 bis z. Gegenwart, Kohlhammer (Mainz, Germany), 1974.
(Editor) *Liberalismus,* Kiepenheuer & Witsch (Cologne, Germany), 1976.
(Editor) Otto Feurst von Bismarck, *Die grossen Reden,* Severin & Siedler (Berlin, Germany), 1981.
(Editor with Rainer Koch) *Der Europeaische Liberalismus im 19. Jahrhundert: Texte zu seiner Entwicklung,* Ullstein (Frankfurt am Main, Germany), 1981.
Europa auf dem Weg in die Moderne, 1850-1890, R. Oldenbourg (Muenster, Germany), 1984.
(Editor with others) *Enzyklopeadie deutscher Geschichte,* R. Oldenbourg (Munich, Germany), 1988-96.
Beurgertum in Deutschland, Siedler (Berlin), 1989.
(Editor) *Stadt und Beurgertum im 19. Jahrhundert,* R. Oldenbourg (Munich, Germany), 1990.
(With Karl-Heinz Jeurgens) *Bismarck: Lebensbilder,* G. Leubbe (Bergisch-Gladbach, Germany), 1990.
(Editor) *Vom alten zum neuen Beurgertum: Die mitteleuropeaische Stadt im Umbruch, 1780-1820,* R. Oldenbourg (Munich, Germany), 1991.
(Editor) *Neuerscheinungen zur Geschichte des 20. Jahrhunderts,* R. Oldenbourg (Munich, Germany), 1992.
Von der steandischen zur beurgerlichen Gesellschaft, R. Oldenbourg (Munich, Germany), 1993.
(Editor) *Stadt und Beurgertum im e Ubergang von der traditionalen zur modernen Gesellschaft,* R. Oldenbourg (Munich, Germany), 1993.
Germania, eine deutsche Marianne?, Bouvier (Bonn, Germany), 1993.

(Editor with Dieter Langewiesche) *Liberalismus und Region: Zur Geschichte des deutschen Liberalismus im 19. Jahrhundert,* R. Oldenbourg (Munich, Germany), 1995.

(With Gerald D. Feldman, Harold James, and others) *Die Deutsche Bank, 1870-1995,* Beck (Muenster, Germany), 1995.

(Editor) *Frankfurter Gesellschaft fuer Handel, Industrie, und Wissenschaft: Casino-Gesellschaft von 1802,* Societeats-Verlag (Frankfurt am Main, Germany), 1995.

(Editor) *Die Grossen Deutschen unserer Epoche,* Propyleaen Verlag (Berlin, Germany), 1995.

Editor in chief, *Historische Zeitschrift,* R. Oldenbug Verlag (Munich, Germany, 1975—).

WORK IN PROGRESS: A history of the Krupp steel company.

* * *

GARDNER, Craig Shaw 1949-

PERSONAL: Born July 2, 1949, in Rochester, NY. *Education:* Attended Boston University.

ADDRESSES: Home and office—P.O. Box 458, Cambridge, MA 02238. *Agent*—Merrilee Heifetz, Writers House, 21 W. 26th St., New York, NY 10010.

CAREER: Science fiction and fantasy novelist.

MEMBER: Horror Writers of America (president, 1990—).

WRITINGS:

"EBENEZUM" SERIES

A Malady of Magicks, Ace (New York City), 1986.
A Multitude of Monsters, Ace (New York City), 1986.
A Night in the Netherhells, Ace (New York City), 1987.
The Exploits of Ebenezum (includes all three novels), Nelson Doubleday (Garden City, NY), 1987.

"WUNTVOR" SERIES

A Difficulty with Dwarves, Ace (New York City), 1987.

An Excess of Enchantment, Ace (New York City), 1988.
A Disagreement with Death, Ace (New York City), 1989.
The Wanderings of Wuntvor (includes all three "Wuntvor" novels), Nelson Doubleday (Garden City, NY), 1989.

"CINEVERSE" SERIES

Slaves of the Volcano God, Ace (New York), 1989.
Bride of the Slime Monster, Ace, 1990.
Revenge of the Fluffy Bunnies, Ace, 1990.
Cineverse Cycle (includes all three novels), Guild America (New York), 1990.

"ARABIAN NIGHTS" SERIES

The Other Sinbad, Ace (New York), 1991.
A Bad Day for Ali Baba, Ace, 1992.
The Last Arabian Night, Ace, 1993.

"DRAGON" SERIES

The Dragon Circle: Dragon Sleeping, Ace (New York), 1994.
The Dragon Circle: Dragon Waking, Ace, 1995.
The Dragon Circle: Dragon Burning, Ace, 1996.

NOVELIZATIONS

The Lost Boys: A Novel, Berkley (New York), 1987.
Wishbringer (novelization of a computer game), Avon (New York), 1988.
Back to the Future, Part II: A Novel, Berkley (New York), 1989.
Batman, Warner (New York), 1989.
The Batman Murders, Warner (New York), 1990.
Back to the Future, Part III: A Novel, Berkley (New York), 1990.

SIDELIGHTS: Craig Shaw Gardner has written several series of fantasy novels for young adults; some branch out from the genre into actual science fiction. Nearly all win praise for moving beyond the serious gothic mood common to this area of young-adult fiction and instead boasting a heavy dose of humor. Gardner's first cycle of books arrived as the "Ebenezum" series, which depicts the exploits of a luckless wizard (the title character) who becomes allergic to magic. Perpetually battling his archenemy, the demon and rhymemaster Guxx, Ebenezum's tales stretch through *A Malady of Magicks, A Multitude of Monsters,* and *A Night in the Netherhells,* all published in the mid-1980s; all three were collected and issued in 1987's *The Exploits of Ebenezum.*

Gardner followed up the cycle with a second, related series: the "Wuntvor" novels. Wuntvor is Ebenezum's apprentice, and in a battle to rescue his master's powers and save their land, which is now under the same dire curse from Guxx, Wuntvor must do battle with an array of foes. Assisting him is his love, a witch named Norei. Toxic fog and a cult who kills disbelievers through immersion in custard are only two of the situations Gardner makes his protagonists to endure. The trio of Wuntvor novels, *A Difficulty with Dwarves, An Excess of Enchantment,* and *A Disagreement with Death,* were published in the late 1980s, issued again in collected form in *The Wanderings of Wuntvor* in 1989.

In 1989 Gardner began another series, this time focusing on the exploits of public-relations man Roger Gordon. In *Slaves of the Volcano God, Bride of the Slime Monster,* and *Revenge of the Fluffy Bunnies,* Gordon enters the Cineverse, a world that resembles bad Hollywood movies. The hero traverses back and forth with the help of a secret decoder ring and visits a variety of shlock film scenarios where beach-party fruggers evolve into the disco age and biker gangs run amok; meanwhile, Gordon's girlfriend is being held captive by a slime monster. All three works were published in a single volume in 1990's *Cineverse Cycle.*

In the early 1990s Gardner reworked the legendary Arabian Nights tales into fantasy humor. *The Other Sinbad* introduces a second Sinbad—not the mythic sailor, but a porter who narrates the epic tale revolving around an eighth journey not "included" in the original. In its sequel, *A Bad Day for Ali Baba,* readers again encounter heroes from the Arabian Nights tales, in this case the poor woodcutter Ali Baba. His bad day begins when he meets forty thieves, who take him along on a fantastical adventure. Ali Baba's brother, who has been sliced into six pieces but survives, accompanies them. In the third installment of the series, *The Last Arabian Night,* loose ends are tied up by Scheherazade, another character from the original Middle Eastern legend; her long-winded stories are designed to keep her husband from killing her.

In his fifth series, Gardner skewers middle-class suburbia by launching one such community into a strange netherworld after a particularly bad storm. Families are separated and teenagers learn new skills to do battle with the soldiers, wizards, and monsters who serve as their new local governors. One teenager, Nick, emerges as a hero in *The Dragon Circle: Dragon Sleeping* and its sequels, *Dragon Waking* and *Dragon Burning.* Throughout all three there looms a sleeping, malevolent dragon. Coveted jewels imbued with special powers are known as dragon's eyes and a tree-like figure name Oomgosh assists the more upstanding members of the transplanted society. All three "Dragon" novels were published in the mid-1990's.

BIOGRAPHICAL/CRITICAL SOURCES:

BOOKS

Encyclopedia of Science Fiction: An Illustrated A to Z, edited by Peter Nicholls, Granada Publishing (London), 1979, p. 448.
Twentieth-Century Science-Fiction Writers, third edition, edited by Noelle Watson and Paul E. Schellinger, St. James Press, 1991, p. 920.

PERIODICALS

Washington Post Book World, February 23, 1986, p. 12.*

*   *   *

GARTH, Will
  See KUTTNER, Henry

*   *   *

GEORGI-FINDLAY, Brigitte 1956-

PERSONAL: Born December 15, 1956, in Ellwangen, Germany; married Jay Findlay (a writer). *Education:* University of Heidelberg, M.A., 1981, Ph.D., 1985.

ADDRESSES: Office—Institut fuer Anglistik/Amerikanistik, Technische Universitaet Dresden, D-01062 Dresden, Germany; fax 011-49-351-463-7733.

CAREER: Free University of Berlin, Berlin, Germany, assistant professor of American literature at John F. Kennedy Institute, 1988-95; University of Bremen, Bremen, Germany, associate professor of American studies, 1995-97; University of Dresden, Dresden, Germany, professor of North American studies, 1997—. University of Arizona, visiting scholar, 1991-93.

MEMBER: German Association of American Studies, American Studies Association.

AWARDS, HONORS: Fellow, American Council of Learned Societies, 1991-92.

WRITINGS:

The Frontiers of Women's Writing: Women's Narratives and the Rhetoric of Westward Expansion, University of Arizona Press (Tucson, AZ), 1996.

WORK IN PROGRESS: Research on North American travel writing, gender, and national identity.

*   *   *

GINSBERG, (Irwin) Allen 1926-1997

OBITUARY NOTICE—See index for *CA* sketch: Born June 3, 1926, in Newark, NJ; died of liver cancer (some sources say stroke), April 5, 1997, in Manhattan, NY. Political activist and poet. Ginsberg gained fame as the poet laureate of the Beat Generation, a group of artists and writers known for their anti-establishment political leanings. Other Beats, as they were called during the 1950s and 1960s, included Jack Kerouac, Lawrence Ferlinghetti, and William S. Burroughs. Ginsberg protested many causes of the day—American involvement in Vietnam and American ties to the Shah of Iran—or supported movements running against mainstream societal beliefs—transcendental mysticism, use of hallucinogenic drugs, and homosexuality.

Before becoming the counterculture icon and coining the term "flower power," Ginsberg held many different jobs as diverse as a welder for the Brooklyn Naval Yard, a dishwasher at a local cafeteria, and worker on cargo ships. He was a book reviewer for *Newsweek* in 1950, conducted market research, and taught at the University of British Columbia. As the protege of poet William Carlos Williams, Ginsberg issued his first major work, *Howl!,* in 1956. The book was initially considered pornographic by many due to its eroticism and homosexual content; its publisher, Ferlinghetti, was brought to trial but the obscenity charges against him were dismissed when the judge

deemed the work was not without "social importance." Ginsberg, who wrote hundreds of poems and contributed to many other written works and audio recordings, lectured frequently. His list of honors and awards include the Golden Wreath Prize, a National Book Award, and a Pulitzer Prize nomination, among others. His major works include *Kaddish and Other Poems, TV Baby Poems, The Gates of Wrath: Rhymed Poems, 1948-1952, Collected Poems, Snapshot Poetics, Notes After an Evening with William Carlos Williams, Take Care of My Ghost, Ghost* (with Kerouac), *Cosmopolitan Greetings: Poems, 1986-1992,* and *Journals: 1954-1958.*

OBITUARIES AND OTHER SOURCES:

BOOKS

Who's Who in America, 51st edition, Marquis, 1997.

PERIODICALS

Los Angeles Times, April 6, 1997, p. A1.
New York Times, April 6, 1997, pp. A1, A42; April 7, 1997, pp. B1, B3; April 8, 1997, p. B10.
Times (London), April 7, 1997.
Washington Post, April 6, 1997, p. B8.

OTHER

CNN Interactive (website), April 5, 1997.
MSNBC (website), April 7, 1997.

*   *   *

GIVEN, David R(oger) 1943-

PERSONAL: Born November 8, 1943, in Nelson, New Zealand; son of Bruce (a research scientist) and Brenda Given; married, wife's name Karina C. (a secondary schoolteacher); children: Bronwyn, Andrew, Craig. *Ethnicity:* "New Zealander." *Education:* University of Canterbury, B.Sc. (with honors), 1965, Ph.D. (botany), 1970; Moore College, Sydney, Australia, Certificate in Theology, 1975; attended Christchurch Polytechnic, 1992. *Religion:* Christian. *Avocational interests:* History, mountaineering, exploration.

ADDRESSES: Home and office—101 Jeffreys Rd., Christchurch 5, New Zealand; fax 64-3-351-6069. *E-mail*—givend@lincoln.ac.nz.

CAREER: New Zealand Department of Scientific and Industrial Research, research scientist, 1965-92, herbarium keeper, 1974-87; self-employed environmental consultant, 1992—. Christchurch College, resident dean of students, 1967; University of Otago, Tennant Lecturer, 1991; Lincoln University, lecturer, 1993-95, honorary lecturer, 1996—; New Zealand Bible College, member of Canterbury regional board, 1994—. National Museum of Natural Sciences, Ottawa, Ontario, postdoctoral research fellow, 1973-74. Southern Heritage Expeditions, lecturer and tour guide, 1992-95. International Union for the Conservation of Nature, executive member of Species Survival Commission, 1977; member of New Zealand Historic Places Trust and Queen Elizabeth Trust. North Canterbury Conservation Board, member, 1983-96; Christchurch Agenda 21 Committee, member, 1993—. Federation International d'Arte Photographique, *artiste,* 1990.

MEMBER: International Association of Pteridologists, World Wildlife Fund, World Wide Fund for Nature (life member), Society for Conservation Biology, Natural Areas Association, Nelson Fern Society, Royal Society of New Zealand, Royal New Zealand Institute of Horticulture (Sir Joseph Banks Lecturer, 1986; associate of honor, 1993), Royal New Zealand Forest and Bird Protection Society, New Zealand Botanical Society, New Zealand Ecological Society (member of council, 1978-81), New Zealand Photographic Society, New Zealand Alpine Garden Society, Indian Society of Conservation Biology, Pacific Science Association, Canterbury Botanical Society, Wellington Botanical Society, Christchurch Photographic Society, Linnean Society of London (fellow), Friends of Christchurch Botanic Gardens (president, 1994—).

AWARDS, HONORS: Fellow, National Research Council of Canada, 1973-74; Bronze Medals, Christchurch International Photographic Exhibition, 1976, and New Zealand International Photographic Exhibition, 1977; fellow, Commonwealth Science Council, 1980, 1981; Loder Cup, New Zealand Ministry for Conservation, 1995.

WRITINGS:

The Arctic-Alpine Element of the Vascular Flora of Lake Superior, National Museums of Canada, 1981.
(With G. A. Williams) *New Zealand Red Data Book,* Nature Conservation Council, 1981.
Rare and Endangered Plants of New Zealand, A. H. and A. W. Reed, 1981.

(Editor) *Conservation of Plant Species and Habitats,* Nature Conservation Council, 1983.
(With P. A. Williams) *Conservation of Chatham Islands Flora and Vegetation,* Department of Scientific and Industrial Research (DSIR), 1984.
(With C. Wilson) *Guide to Threatened Plants of New Zealand,* DSIR, 1990.
(With Warwick Harris) *Methods of Ethnobotany,* Commonwealth Secretariat (London, England), 1984.
Principles and Practice of Plant Conservation, Timber Press (Portland, OR), 1994.

Contributor of more than one hundred-fifty articles and numerous photographs to scientific journals and periodicals.

WORK IN PROGRESS: A book on biodiversity.

SIDELIGHTS: David R. Givens told *CA:* "I write quite simply because of an innate desire to communicate and to change the world by doing so. I love words, their nuances, and their evolution.

"My writing process is simple. Sit down at the word processor and *write*—then go through a honing process in which something elegant develops from the rough-hewn block. I was brought up in a world of books and have married a wife whose fondness for books and reading is shared."

*   *   *

GLICKMAN, James (A.) 1948-

PERSONAL: Born December 29, 1948, in Davenport, IA; son of Eugene D. (in business) and Elaine Jeanne (Ginsberg) Glickman; married Elissa Deborah Gelfand (a professor of French), October 14, 1982; children: Daniel Gelfand. *Education:* Yale University, B.A. (magna cum laude), 1970; University of Iowa Writer's Workshop, M.F.A., 1972.

ADDRESSES: Home—51 McGilpin Road, Sturbridge, MA 01566-1230. *Agent*—Molly Friedrich, Aaron Priest Literary Agency, 708 Third Ave., 23rd Fl., New York, NY 10017-4103. *E-mail*—jaglickman @aol.com.

CAREER: University of Arizona Law School, Tucson, instructor, 1972; Community College of Rhode Island, Lincoln, English teacher, 1972—; Radcliffe

Seminars, Cambridge, MA, faculty member, 1985-88; writer.

WRITINGS:

Sounding the Waters (novel), Crown (New York City), 1996.

Contributor of short stories to periodicals, including *Kansas Quarterly, Redbook, Ladies Home Journal,* and *Worcester Review.*

WORK IN PROGRESS: The Crossing Point, a historical novel, publication expected in 1999.

SIDELIGHTS: James Glickman's first novel, *Sounding the Waters,* revolves around the construction of characters and their human weaknesses set against the background of a political campaign. Lieutenant governor Bobby Parrish is running for the U.S. Senate, and he asks his old friend Ben Shamas to help him. Past secrets come to the forefront during a dirty campaign as Ben and Bobby try to prevail on election day.

Many critics have praised the author's writing style. "Glickman is a sound craftsman who fills in all the necessary details," related Merle Rugin, writing in *Christian Science Monitor,* "making this a richly rewarding, agreeably old-fashioned sort of novel with complex, believable characters who develop in the course of engaging in vividly and intelligently rendered experiences." James Polk in the *New York Times Book Review* called *Sounding the Waters* "frequently shrewd and arresting." *Los Angeles Times* contributor Michael Harris stated that *Sounding the Waters* is "taut and involving, written so cleanly it squeaks."

Glickman, who studied under Robert Penn Warren, told *CA:* "My preoccupation in most of my writing seems to be about something William Faulkner wrote in *A Requiem for a Nun,* 'The past is not dead. It isn't even past.'"

BIOGRAPHICAL/CRITICAL SOURCES:

PERIODICALS

Booklist, March 15, 1996, p. 1239.
Christian Science Monitor, May 8, 1996, p. 15.
Library Journal, February 15, 1996, p. 176.
Los Angeles Times, April 14, 1996, p. 8.
New York Times Book Review, May 26, 1996, p. 15.
Winston-Salem Journal, July 14, 1996.

GLISERMAN, Martin 1945-

PERSONAL: Born September 19, 1945, in Winthrop, MA; son of Phillip (a pharmacist) and Nora (a secretary; maiden name, Silverman) Gliserman; married Susan Elmer, June, 1967 (died, June, 1973); married Marilyn Rye, May 16, 1982; children: Nicholas. *Education:* Colby College, B.A., 1967; Indiana University, Ph.D., 1973; Center for Modern Psychoanalytic Studies, Psychoanalyst, 1993. *Politics:* "Socialist." *Avocational interests:* Photography, dogs (Tibetan terriers).

ADDRESSES: Home—112 North Second Ave., Highland Park, NJ 08904-2421. *Office*—Department of English, Rutgers University, P.O. Box 5054, New Brunswick, NJ 08903-5054; fax: 908-932-1150. *E-mail*—gliserma@rci.rutgers.edu.

CAREER: Rutgers University, New Brunswick, NJ, associate professor of English, 1971—; psychoanalyst, Highland Park, NJ, 1987—. Editor in chief, *American Imago.*

MEMBER: Modern Language Association of America, National Association for Accreditation in Psychoanalysis.

AWARDS, HONORS: Lieber teaching award, Indiana University, 1971; Distinguished service fellow award, Rutgers University, 1976.

WRITINGS:

Psychoanalysis, Language, and the Body of the Text, University Press of Florida (Gainesville, FL), 1997.

WORK IN PROGRESS: Research on the history of the body in the novel.

*　　*　　*

GODEL, Kurt Friedrich 1906-1978

PERSONAL: Born April 28, 1906 in Brunn, Moravia (became Brno, Czech Republic); died January 14, 1978, in the United States, of complications from malnutrition; son of Rudolf and Marianne (Handschuh) Godel; married Adele Porkert Nimbursky (a dancer), September 20, 1938. *Education:* University of Vienna, Ph.D., 1930.

CAREER: Mathematician. Conducted research at Princeton University's Institute for Advanced Study, beginning c. 1933.

AWARDS, HONORS: Einstein award, 1951; National Medal of Science, 1975. Honorary degrees from Yale University, 1951, and Harvard University, 1952. Honorary doctorate from the University of Vienna, awarded posthumously.

WRITINGS:

Collected Works, edited by Solomon Feferman and others, 4 volumes, Oxford University Press, 1986.

SIDELIGHTS: Kurt Friedrich Godel was a mathematical logician who proved perhaps the most influential theorem of twentieth-century mathematics—the incompleteness theorem. Although he was not prolific in his published research and did not cultivate a group of students to carry on his work, his results have shaped the development of logic and affected mathematics and philosophy, as well as other disciplines. The philosophy of mathematics has been forced to grapple with the significance of Godel's results ever since they were announced. His work was as epoch-making as that of Albert Einstein, even if the ramifications have not been as visible to the general public. Gregory H. Moore, in *Dictionary of Scientific Biography,* related that in May of 1972 mathematician Oskar Morgenstern wrote that Einstein himself said that "Godel's papers were the most important ones on relativity theory since his own [Einstein's] original paper appeared."

Godel was born in Brunn, Moravia (now Brno, Czech Republic), on April 28, 1906, the younger son of Rudolf Godel, who worked for a textile factory in Brunn, and Marianne Handschuh. Godel had an older brother, Rudolf, who would study medicine and become a radiologist. The Godels were part of the German-speaking minority in Brunn, which subsequently became one of the larger cities in the Czech Republic. The family had no allegiance to the nationalist sentiments around them, and all of Godel's educational experience was in German-speaking surroundings. He was baptized a Lutheran and took religion more to heart than the rest of his family.

Godel began his education in September, 1912, when he enrolled in a Lutheran school in Brunn. In the fall of 1916 he became a student in a gymnasium, where he remained until 1924. At that point he entered the University of Vienna, planning to major in physics. In 1926, influenced by one of his teachers in number theory, he changed to mathematics; he did, however, retain an interest in physics, which he expressed in a number of unpublished papers later in life. He also continued his studies in philosophy and was associated with the Vienna Circle, a gathering of philosophers of science that had great influence on the English-speaking philosophical community. Godel never was one, however, to follow a party line, and he went his own way philosophically. He felt that his independence of thought contributed to his ability to find new directions in mathematical logic.

Godel's father died in February of 1929, and shortly thereafter his mother and brother moved to Vienna. Godel completed the work for his dissertation in the summer of that year. He received his doctorate in February of 1930 for his proof of what became known as the completeness theorem. The problem that Godel had considered was the following: Euclidean geometry served as an example of a kind of branch of mathematics where all the results were derived from a few initial assumptions, called axioms. However, it was hard to tell whether any particular list of axioms would be enough to prove all the true statements about the objects of geometry. Godel showed in his dissertation that for a certain part of logic, a set of axioms could be found such that the consequences of the axioms would include all true statements of that part of logic. In other words, the collection of provable statements and the collection of true statements amounted to the same collection. This was a reassuring result for those who hoped to find a list of axioms that would work for all of mathematics.

In September of 1930, however, mathematical logic changed forever when Godel announced his first incompleteness theorem. One of the great accomplishments of mathematical logic earlier in the century had been the work of two British mathematicians, Alfred North Whitehead and Bertrand Russell. Their three-volume work *Principia Mathematica* (Latin for "mathematical principles" and based on the title of a work by Isaac Newton), tried to derive all of mathematics from a collection of axioms. They examined some areas very thoroughly, and though few mathematicians bothered to read all the details, most were prepared to believe that Whitehead and Russell would be able to continue their project through the rest of mathematics.

Godel's work was written up under the title "On Formally Undecidable Propositions of *Principia*

Mathematica and Related Systems." In this paper, which was published in a German mathematical journal in 1931, Godel introduced a new technique which enabled him to discuss arithmetic using arithmetic. He translated statements in logic into statements involving only numbers, and he did this by assigning numerical values to symbols of logic. It had long been known that there were problems involved in self-reference; any statement that discussed itself, such as the statement "This statement is false," presented logical difficulties in determining whether it was true or false. The assumption of those who hoped to produce an axiomatization of all of mathematics was that it would be possible to avoid such self-referring statements.

Godel's method of proof enabled him to introduce the technique of self-reference into the very foundations of mathematics; he showed that there were statements which were indisputably true but could not be proved by axiomatization. In other words, the collection of provable statements would not include all the true statements. Although the importance of Godel's work in this area was not immediately recognized, it did not take long before those seeking to axiomatize mathematics realized that his theorem put an immovable roadblock in their path. The proof was not obvious to those who were not used to thinking in the terms that he introduced, but the technique of Godel numbering rapidly became an indispensable part of the logician's tool kit.

Of the schools of mathematical philosophy most active at the time Godel introduced his incompleteness theorem, at least two have not since enjoyed the same reputation. Logicism was the belief that all mathematics could be reduced to logic and thereby put on a firm foundation. Formalism claimed that certainty could be achieved for mathematics by establishing theorems about completeness. In the aftermath of Godel's work, it was even suggested that his theorem showed that man was more than a machine, since a machine could only establish what was provable, whereas man could understand what was true, which went beyond what was provable. Many logicians would dispute this, but no philosophy of mathematics is imaginable which does not take account of Godel's work on incompleteness.

Godel was never a popular or successful teacher. His reserved personality led him to lecture more to the blackboard than to his audience. Fortunately, he was invited to join the Institute for Advanced Study at Princeton, which had opened in the fall of 1933,

where he could work without teaching responsibilities. Despite the attractions of the working environment in Princeton, Godel continued to return to Austria, and it was there that he lectured on his first major results in the new field to which he had turned attention, the theory of sets.

Set theory had been established as a branch of mathematics in the last half of the nineteenth century, although its development had been hindered by the discovery of a few paradoxes. As a result, many who studied the field felt it was important to produce an axiomatization that would prevent paradoxes from arising. The axiomatization which most mathematicians wanted was one which would capture the intuitions they had about the way sets behaved without necessarily committing them to points about which there was disagreement. Two of the statements about which there were disagreement were the axiom of choice and the continuum hypothesis. The axiom of choice said that for any family of sets there is always a function that picks one element out of each set; this was indisputable for finite collections of sets but was problematic when infinite collections of sets were introduced. The continuum hypothesis stated that, although it was known that there were more real (rational and irrational) numbers than whole numbers (integers), there were no infinite sets in size between the real numbers and the whole numbers.

Godel's major contribution in set theory was the introduction of what are known as constructible sets. These objects formed a model for the standard axiomatization of set theory. As a result, if it could be shown that the axiom of choice and the continuum hypothesis applied to the constructible sets, then those disputed principles had to be at least consistent with the standard axiomatization. Godel successfully demonstrated both results, but this still left open the question of whether the two statements could be proved from the standard axiomatization. One of the major accomplishments of set theory in the second half of the century was the demonstration by Paul Cohen that neither the axiom of choice nor the continuum hypothesis could be proved from the standard axiomatization.

Godel had suffered a nervous breakdown in 1934 which aggravated an early tendency to avoid society. He married Adele Porkert Nimbursky, a nightclub dancer, on September 20, 1938. He had met his wife when he was twenty-one, but his father had objected to the match, based on the difference in their social standing and the fact she had been married before. After his marriage, his domestic situation was something of a comfort in the face of the deteriorating political situation in Austria, especially after the union of Austria and Germany in 1938, when Adolf Hitler was in power. When he returned to Vienna from the United States in June of 1939, he received a letter informing him that he was known to move in "Jewish-liberal" circles, not an attractive feature to the Nazi regime. When he was assaulted by fascist students that year, he rapidly applied for a visa to the United States. It was a sign of his stature in the profession that at a time when so many were seeking to escape from Europe, Godel's request was promptly granted. He never returned to Europe after his hasty departure.

Godel was appointed an ordinary member of the Institute for Advanced Study in Princeton, where he would remain for the rest of his life. His closest friends were Einstein and Oskar Morgenstern, and he took frequent walks in Einstein's company. Einstein and Godel were of opposing temperaments, but they could talk about physics and each respected the other's work. Morgenstern was a mathematical economist and one of the founders of the branch of mathematics known as game theory. Godel and his wife were content with this small social circle, remaining outside the glare of publicity which often fell on Einstein.

After his arrival in Princeton, Godel started to turn his attention more to philosophy. His mathematical accomplishments guaranteed his philosophical speculations a hearing, even if they ran counter to the dominant currents of thought at the time. Perhaps the most popular philosophical school then was naturalism —the attempt to ground mathematics and its language in terms of observable objects and events of the everyday world. Godel, however, was a Platonist and he believed that mathematics was not grounded in the observable world. In two influential published articles, one dealing with Bertrand Russell and the other with the continuum hypothesis, Godel argued that mathematical intuition was a special faculty which needed to be explored in its own right. Although the bulk of mathematical philosophers have not followed him, they have been obliged to take his arguments into account.

Although Godel moved away from mathematics in his later years, he contributed occasionally to the field. One of his last mathematical articles, published twenty years before his death, dealt with the attempt to formalize the approach to mathematical philosophy known as intuitionism. Godel himself was not partial

to that approach, but his work had wide influence among the intuitionists. American mathematician Paul Cohen was also careful to bring his work on the axiom of choice and the continuum hypothesis to him for his approval.

In his years at the Institute for Advanced Study, awards and distinctions began to accumulate. In 1950, Godel addressed the International Congress of Mathematicians and the next year received an honorary degree from Yale; in 1951, he also received the Einstein award and delivered the Gibbs lecture to the American Mathematical Society. Harvard gave him an honorary degree in 1952 and in 1975 he received the National Medal of Science. That same year he was scheduled to receive an honorary degree from Princeton, but ill health kept him from the ceremony. By contrast, Godel refused honors from Austria, at least as long as he lived; however, the University of Vienna gave him an honorary doctorate posthumously.

Godel had a distrust of medicine that amounted in his later years to paranoia. In late December of 1977 he was hospitalized and he died on January 14, 1978 of malnutrition, brought on by his refusal to eat because of his fear of poisoning. His wife survived him by three years; they had no children. Godel's heirs were the mathematical community to which he left his work and the challenge of understanding the effects of his results. The year after his death Douglas Hofstadter's book *Godel, Escher, Bach* became a best-seller, illustrating Godel's ideas in terms of art and music.

BIOGRAPHICAL/CRITICAL SOURCES:

BOOKS

Dawson, John W., Jr. , *Logical Dilemmas,* A & K Peters, 1995.

Gillespie, Charles Coulson, editor, *Dictionary of Scientific Biography,* Volume 17, Scribner, 1990, pp. 348-357.

Hofstadter, Douglas R., *Godel, Escher, Bach,* Basic Books, 1979.

Nagel, Ernest, and J. R. Newman, *Godel's Proof,* New York University Press, 1958.

Van Heijenoort, Jean, editor, *From Frege to Godel,* Harvard University Press, 1967.

Yourgrau, Palle, *The Disappearance of Time,* Cambridge University Press, 1991.

PERIODICALS

Philosophy, 1961, pp. 120-124.*

GODWIN, Parke 1929-

PERSONAL: Born January 28, 1929, in New York, NY; son of Harold P. and Consuelo (Hawks) Godwin. *Ethnicity:* "Anglo-Irish." *Education:* Attended American University for one year. *Politics:* Democrat.

ADDRESSES: Home and office—736 Auburn Ravine Terrace, No. 535, Auburn, CA 95603. *Agent*—Writers House, 21 West 26th St., New York, NY 10010.

CAREER: Writer. *Military service:* Six years as Army staff sergeant.

AWARDS, HONORS: World Fantasy Award, 1982, for novella "The Fire When It Comes."

WRITINGS:

NOVELS; EXCEPT AS NOTED

(With Marvin Kaye) *The Masters of Solitude* (first volume of "Solitude" trilogy), Doubleday (Garden City, NY), 1978.

Firelord (first volume of "Arthurian" series), Doubleday, 1980.

(With Kaye) *Wintermind* (second volume of "Solitude" trilogy), Doubleday, 1982.

A Memory of Lions, 1983.

(With Kaye) *A Cold Blue Light* (first volume of "Cold Blue Light" series), Charter Books (New York), 1983.

Beloved Exile (second volume of "Arthurian" series), Bantam (Toronto), 1984.

The Fire When It Comes (novella and short stories), Doubleday, 1984.

The Last Rainbow (third volume of "Arthurian" series), Bantam, 1985.

A Truce with Time (A Love Story with Occasional Ghosts), Bantam, 1988.

(Editor) *Invitation to Camelot: An Arthurian Anthology of Short Stories,* Ace (New York), 1988.

Waiting for the Galactic Bus (first volume in "Snake Oil Wars" series), Doubleday, 1988.

The Snake Oil Wars; or, Scheherazade Ginsberg Strikes Again (second volume in "Snake Oil Wars" series), Doubleday, 1989.

Sherwood (first volume in "Robin Hood" series), Morrow (New York), 1991.

Robin and the King (second volume in "Robin Hood" series), Morrow, 1993.

Limbo Search, Avo-Nova, 1995.

The Tower of Beowulf, Morrow, 1995.

ADAPTATIONS: Sherwood was adapted as a sound recording by Audio Partners (Auburn, CA), 1991.

SIDELIGHTS: Fantasy and science fiction author Parke Godwin did not publish his first novel until he was almost forty-five years old but has become, in the words of the *Encyclopedia of Science Fiction,* "a figure whose relative obscurity is fully undeserved." That first novel, cowritten with Marvin Kaye, was *Masters of Solitude,* the beginning of a projected trilogy by that name. The novel postulates a post-apocalyptic future America divided into two societies at odds: a rural portion believing in an altered form of Christianity, and a science-oriented urbanopolis. In the second volume of the series, 1982's *Wintermind,* the scale is narrowed to that of the novel's protagonist, a half-breed between the two societies. (A third volume was not issued.) One year later, with Kaye, Godwin produced a novel about ghosts, *A Cold Blue Light,* again the first volume in a projected series. The second volume was written by Kaye alone.

Godwin's solo ventures have made him known for fantasy rather than science fiction, and the fantasy has often been centered in traditional British lore. First came *Firelord* (1980), a novel about King Arthur. Although it contains fantasy elements, *Firelord* is based on current historical and archeological research; it attempts to lend realism to the Arthurian legend by presenting Artos (Godwin's name for Arthur) as a fifth-century tribal leader of the Celts, battling against the Saxons. Politics is a focus of the plot, and magic is demythologized, for the Faerie, Arthur's allies, are shown to be diminutive Stone Age nomads. Shelly Cox, writing in *Library Journal,* approved of Godwin's balance of romance and realism, calling the historical aspects of the novel "psychologically believable and genuinely tragic." High praise was given by Craig Shaw Gardner in *Washington Post Book World:* in a review of *Beloved Exile* (1984), he recalled its predecessor, *Firelord,* as "a wonderful book, fit to stand alongside [Frederik Pohl's] *Gateway,* John Crowley's *Little, Big* and Gene Wolfe's *The Shadow of the Torturer* as one of the most fully realized fantasy novels written in the last decade." *Beloved Exile,* second in Godwin's Arthurian cycle, is in fact a Guenevere novel: the text comprises the queen's memoir, beginning the day Arthur dies. According to fantasy writer Colin Greenland, reviewing the book for the *New Statesman, Beloved Exile* is "[e]ven more striking than *Firelord* for its rigorous eschewal of mysticism and glamour," and Godwin's Guenevere is "a thoroughly explored and wholly compelling character." A *Publishers Weekly* reviewer commended Godwin for departing imaginatively from Sir Thomas Malory's vision of Guenevere. Instead of retiring to a convent as Malory's Guenevere does, Godwin's heroine fights to regain Arthur's lands, is defeated and sold into slavery, and mellows into maturity during her captivity. The *Publishers Weekly* commentator called *Beloved Exile* "a compelling character study," in which "Guenevere fascinates the reader as she betrays herself in every phrase of Godwin's supple, sensual yarn." Reviewer Michael M. Levy, in *Fantasy Review,* chimed in with similar praise but found the last sixteen pages of the novel faulty for their "black comedy."

The next major work by Godwin was a short story collection, *The Fire When It Comes,* the title novella of which had won a World Fantasy Award in 1982. "The Fire When It Comes" is a ghost story told from the point of view of the ghost: a deceased actress haunting New York's Upper West Side. A reviewer in *Publishers Weekly* called it "a cheery, life-and love-affirming tale." Also singled out within the collection were "Stroke of Mercy," a "stunning and provocative" (in the words of the *Publishers Weekly* reviewer) story that spans a number of European and American wars, and "The Last Rainbow," a comic take on the legend of the Holy Grail. Godwin, in an afterword, said that the story inspired him to write *Firelord.* Godwin's third Arthurian novel, also titled *The Last Rainbow* though its material is different from that of the short story, concentrates on the Faerie, the nomads whose folkways are misunderstand as sorcery by the Celtic farmers. The protagonist is a Romanized priest named Patricius, who later is to become St. Patrick. Tortured and left to die by enemies, he is rescued by Dorelei, a queen of the Faerie; he becomes one of the nomads, and the teachings of two faiths are exchanged in the process. Colby Rodowsky, in *Washington Post Book World,* called *The Last Rainbow* "well-paced" and "a moving love story"; *Publishers Weekly* commented that "[a]s in his other books, Godwin's strength is his vibrant portrayal of human nature in a rich, witty, sensual prose that captures some of the rhythm and the pungency of older forms of English." Frances Deutsch Louis, writing in the *Christian Science Monitor,* called the novel "a moving and loving tribute to our lost and imaginary innocence, and a painful, often illuminating examination of what faith means."

Godwin changed pace with 1988's *A Truce with Time (A Love Story with Occasional Ghosts).* This novel is "perhaps only by courtesy fantasy," according to Tom Easton in *Analog.* It presents Pat Landry, a fiftyish fantasy novelist who wishes to escape his genre and who is haunted—perhaps literally, perhaps only in his imagination—by the ghosts of dead relatives. Easton, expressing pleasant surprise, termed it "a marvelous book, warm and witty and soul-illuminating." Harry Baldwin, in the *Los Angeles Times Book Review,* found weaknesses in the sections of the novel that deal with the New York publishing world. But with regard to Landry and his "ghost" relatives, Baldwin wrote, "By telling a traditional tale in an untraditional way, Godwin has created an often funny, occasionally moving drama of what it really means to be haunted by a family's past." Also in the late 1980s, Godwin turned to a pair of broad satires about religion: *Waiting for the Galactic Bus* (1988) and *The Snake Oil Wars: or, Scheherazade Ginsberg Strikes Again.* The premise of the sequence is that life on earth was created as the result of a prank by two drunken intergalactic college students, Barion and Coyul, who eventually became God and the Devil. That myth is recounted in the first volume, while the second depicts an afterlife containing debunked versions of Abraham Lincoln, Dorothy Parker, and various contemporary evangelists. Some critics found these novels hard to take, but Easton assured the reader of *Waiting for the Galactic Bus,* "You'll have fun."

Godwin returned to medieval Britain as the setting of his 1991 novel, *Sherwood,* a retelling of the Robin Hood legend that a *Publishers Weekly* reviewer called "highly satisfying" and commended for "carefully etched characterizations of Normans and Saxons." Although keeping many of the traditional Robin Hood trappings, Godwin set the legend not in the time of Richard I but a century earlier, in the time of William the Conqueror. This worked toward demythologizing the legend—an intention on the author's part that Sue Martin, in the *Los Angeles Times Book Review,* both lauded for realism and regretted for the loss of magic. Martin called *Sherwood* "a hefty, thoughtful novel that puts you squarely into the muck and smoke of 11th-century villages and sieges." A sequel, *Robin and the King,* appeared in 1993. It depicts Robin and Marian settled into marriage with two children and on friendly terms with the Sheriff of Nottingham. Robin gets into trouble at court when he tries to save Sherwood Forest from conversion into a royal hunting preserve; after a struggle, he not only regains favor, but alters British history through his powers of persuasion. A *Publishers Weekly* commentator called *Robin and the King* "Not just a first-rate adventure," but "also a fascinating account of everyday life in the 11th century"; the reviewer drew attention to "[d]eft characterizations, superb battle scenes and more than a little wit." *LOCUS* contributor Faren Miller wrote, "As a historical novel, *Robin and the King* merits my strongest possible recommendation."

Although he published a space opera, *Limbo Search,* in 1995, Godwin's major effort that year was the retelling of still a third medieval British legend: that of Beowulf's defeat of the monster Grendel. A *Publishers Weekly* contributor found *The Tower of Beowulf* "greatly refreshing" for its insights into spirituality and the nature of the hero, and for "vivid and heart-wrenching" characterizations. Roland Green, writing in *Booklist,* found similar virtues, saying, "Both Beowulf and his world are magnificently realized, fully comprehensible, and absorbing."

BIOGRAPHICAL/CRITICAL SOURCES:

BOOKS

Clute, John, and Peter Nicholls, editors, *Encyclopedia of Science Fiction,* St. Martin's Press (London), 1993, p. 503.
Reginald, Robert, *Science Fiction and Fantasy Literature, 1975-1991,* Gale (Detroit, MI), 1992, p. 377.

PERIODICALS

Analog, November, 1988, pp. 134-35; February, 1989, pp. 179-80.
Booklist, September 1, 1995, p. 39.
Christian Science Monitor, May 16, 1986, p. 24.
Fantasy Review, September, 1984, p. 29.
Library Journal, October 1, 1980, p. 2106.
Locus, August, 1993, pp. 17, 49.
Los Angeles Times Book Review, July 31, 1988, p. 8; August 4, 1991, pp. 2-3, 8.
New Statesman, October 10, 1986, pp. 28-29.
Publishers Weekly, March 9, 1984, p. 101; May 25, 1984, p. 57; June 14, 1985, p. 70; June 7, 1991, p. 58; May 24, 1993, p. 71; July 24, 1995, p. 51.
Washington Post Book World, June 24, 1984, p. 6; July 14, 1985, p. 9.

*   *   *

GOEHLERT, Robert 1948-

PERSONAL: Born December 1, 1948, in Springfield, MA. *Education:* Participated in a Russian language program in the Soviet Union, organized by Oberlin College, 1969; University of Massachusetts, B.A.,

1970; Indiana University, M.A., 1972, M.L.S., 1976, Ph.D., 1981.

ADDRESSES: Home—4519 East Deckard Drive, Bloomington, IN 47408. *Office*—Indiana University Library, Bloomington, IN 47405.

CAREER: Indiana University, Bloomington, archivist at Political Science Data Archive and Computing Library, 1971-72, assistant instructor, 1973, research and editorial assistant, 1973-74, and instructor, 1975—; University Library, assistant to librarian for economics and political science, 1973-74, subject specialist for political science, economics, and criminal justice, 1974—, assistant head of subject and area librarians, 1974—, acting head for Interlibrary Services, 1985-86; Honor's Division, assistant instructor, 1974; School of Library and Information Science, adjunct faculty, 1985—. Guest lecturer for the School of Library and Information Science, Indiana University, 1975—; visiting librarian at the Commonwealth of Australia Parliamentary Library and Australian National University's Menzies Library, 1984; Chairman of various Indiana University Library committees, 1978-96.

MEMBER: Beta Phi Mu.

AWARDS, HONORS: Departmental honors, Department of Political Science, University of Massachusetts, 1970; graduate fellowship, Department of Political Science, Indiana University, 1971-72; teaching fellowship, Indiana University Honor's Division, 1974; development grant, Office of Learning Resources, Indiana University, 1976; research grant, President's council on International Programs, Indiana University, 1984; research grant, President's Council on the Social Sciences, Indiana University, 1984; grant-in-aid of research, Indiana University, 1985; "Outstanding Academic Book", *Choice,* for *Policy Analysis and Management: A Bibliography, The Presidency: A Research Guide, The American Presidency: A Bibliography, The U.S. Supreme Court: A Bibliography,* and *The United States Congress: An Annotated Bibliography 1980-1993.*

WRITINGS:

NONFICTION, WRITTEN WITH FENTON MARTIN

The Parliament of Great Britain: A Bibliography, Lexington Books, 1982.
Policy Analysis and Management: A Bibliography, ABC-Clio Press (Santa Barbara, CA), 1984.

The Presidency: A Research Guide, ABC-Clio Press (Santa Barbara, CA), 1984.

The American Presidents: A Bibliography, Congressional Quarterly (Washington, DC), 1988.

The U.S. Supreme Court: A Bibliography, Congressional Quarterly (Washington, DC), 1990.

How to Research the Supreme Court, Congressional Quarterly (Washington, DC), 1992.

The United States Congress: An Annotated Bibliography 1980-93, Congressional Quarterly (Washington, DC), 1995.

(With John Sayre) *Members of Congress: A Bibliography,* Congressional Quarterly (Washington, DC), 1996.

How to Research Congress, Congressional Quarterly (Washington, DC), 1996.

How to Research the Presidency, Congressional Quarterly (Washington, DC), 1996.

Political Science Journal of Information, American Political Science Association (Washington, DC), 1997.

American Government and Politics: A Guide to Books for Teachers, Librarians and Students, Congressional Quarterly (Washington, DC), 1997.

OTHER

(With Thomas Michalk) *Reform of Local Government Structures in the United States 1945-1971: A Microfiche Library,* Johnson Associates (Greenwich, CT), 1976.

Presidential Campaigns: A Cartoon History 1789-1976, Indiana University (Bloomington, IN), 1977.

Directory of Librarians and Information Specialists in Political Science, American Political Science Association (Washington, DC), 1979.

(With Paula Baker and Elinor Ostrom) *Metropolitan Reform: An Annotated Bibliography,* Workshop in Political Theory and Policy Analysis (Bloomington, IN), 1979.

(With John Sayre) *The United States Congress: A Bibliography,* Free Press (New York), 1982.

(With Fred Musto) *State Legislatures: A Bibliography,* ABC-Clio Press (Santa Barbara, CA), 1985.

(With Elizabeth Hoffmeister) *The Department of State and American Diplomacy: A Bibliography,* Garland (New York), 1986.

(With Nels Gunderson) *Government Regulation of Business: An Information Sourcebook,* Onyx Press (Phoenix, AZ), 1987.

The Parliament of Australia: A Bibliography, Department of Parliamentary Library (Canberra, Australia), 1988.

(With Hugh Reynolds) *The Executive Branch of the U.S. Government: A Bibliography,* Greenwood Press (Westport, CT), 1988.

Congress and Law-making: Researching the Legislative Process, ABC-Clio Press (Santa Barbara, CA), 1989.

(With Marian Shaaban) *The European Community: Basic Resources,* West European Studies National Resource Center (Indiana University), 1991.

(With Marian Shaaban) *UN Documentation: A Basic Guide,* Indiana Center on Global Change and World Peace (Bloomington, IN), 1992.

(With Anthony C. Stamatoples) *The Chinese Economy: A Bibliography of Works in English,* Borgo Press (San Bernadino, CA), 1995.

Contributor to anthologies, including *International Review of Administrative Processes,* Volume 41, 1975; *Library Acquisitions: Practice and Theory,* Volume 3, 1979; *Government Publications Review,* 1980; *Government Documents Review,* 1980; *Information Processing and Management,* 1980; *Managing the Legislative Workload: Lessons From the United States,* Department of Parliamentary Library (Canberra, Australia), 1984; *The Selection of Library Materials: Guides to Sources and Strategies,* American Library Association (Chicago), 1985; *The Reader's Advisor,* Volume 3, Bowker (New York), 1985; *Encyclopedia of the United States Congress,* Volume 1, Simon and Schuster (New York), 1995. Contributor to periodicals, including *Electoral Studies, News for Teacher of Political Science: A Publication of the American Political Science Association, College and Research Libraries News, Journal of Religious Thought, ULA Quarterly, Journal of Education for Librarianship, Journal of Academic Librarianship, Teaching Political Science,* and *Special Libraries.*

*   *   *

GOLDFRANK, Esther S(chiff) 1896-1997

OBITUARY NOTICE—See index for *CA* sketch: Born May 5, 1896, in New York, NY; died April 23, 1997, in Mamaroneck, NY. Anthropologist and author. Goldfrank became widely known for her anthropological field work with the Pueblo Indians in the southwestern United States. In 1919, she accompanied Franz Boas to New Mexico. While there she interviewed and recorded members of the Pueblo, including Carolyn Quintana of the Conchiti tribe. She later moved into the pueblo to continue her research and eventually wrote *The Social and Ceremonial Organization of Conchiti.* Later field research took her to Alberta, Canada, to study the Blackfoot, which resulted in *Changing Configurations in the Social Organization of a Blackfoot Tribe During the Reserve Period: The Blood of Alberta, Canada.* In 1943, Goldfrank joined the staff at the University of Washington for its Chinese history project. In 1978, she published her memoirs in *Notes on an Undirected Life: As One Anthropologist Tells It.* She contributed numerous articles to journals and also edited the monograph *The Artist of Isleta Paintings in Pueblo Society* (1962) by Elsie Clews Parsons.

OBITUARIES AND OTHER SOURCES:

BOOKS

Who's Who in America, 45th edition, Marquis, 1988.

PERIODICALS

New York Times, May 25, 1997, sec. 1, p. 38.

*   *   *

GOUDSMIT, Samuel A(braham) 1902-1978

PERSONAL: Born July 11, 1902, in The Hague, Netherlands; died of a heart attack, December 4, 1978, in Reno, NV; son of Isaac (in business) and Marianne (in business; maiden name, Gompers) Goudsmit. *Education:* University of Leiden, Ph.D. (physics), 1927.

CAREER: Physicist. University of Michigan, academic appointment, c. 1925-40; conducted secret research on radar at Massachusetts Institute of Technology, c. 1940; associated with Project Alsos (secret intelligence mission), 1944; associated with Northwestern University, 1946-48; Brookhaven National Laboratory, member of staff, c. 1948-50, chair of physics department, 1950-78; University of Nevada at Reno, distinguished visiting professor, 1974-78. *Physical Review* (American Physical Society), editor, 1952-74.

AWARDS, HONORS: Medal of Freedom; Order of the British Empire.

WRITINGS:

(With Linus Pauling) *The Structure of Line Spectra,* McGraw-Hill (New York), 1930.

(With R. F. Bacher) *Atomic Energy States,* Greenwood Press (New York), 1932.

Alsos, H. Schuman, 1947.

(With Robert Claiborne and others) *Time,* Time-Life (New York), 1966.

Contributor to journals and periodicals, including *Nature, Bulletin of the Atomic Scientists,* and *Physics Today.*

SIDELIGHTS: A prominent figure in American physics, Samuel A. Goudsmit was an authority on atomic energy and nuclear research, and was the co-discoverer of the electron spin. Goudsmit was educated in the Netherlands, where he received his Ph.D. in physics from the University of Leiden in 1927. While still a graduate student, Goudsmit, in collaboration with fellow physics student George Uhlenbeck, made the discovery for which he is most famous: electron spin. That discovery explained some important theoretical predictions by physicists Wolfgang Pauli and Paul Dirac as well as a number of anomalies in the existing atomic theory. Nobel Prize winner and physics professor I. I. Rabi was quoted by Daniel Lang in *New Yorker* as observing that the discovery "was a tremendous feat. Why those two men never received a Nobel Prize for it will always be a mystery to me." During World War II, Goudsmit led a group of physicists and military personnel in a search through war-torn Europe, in an attempt to locate German scientist Werner Heisenberg and determine what the Germans had accomplished in terms of their atomic bomb research. For this mission he received the Medal of Freedom and the Order of the British Empire.

Samuel Abraham Goudsmit was born in The Hague, Netherlands, on July 11, 1902. His father, Isaac Goudsmit, was a prosperous dealer in bathroom fixtures, and his mother, Marianne Gompers Goudsmit, was the owner of a fashionable hat store called Au Louvre. Young Samuel developed a passionate interest in the millinery business early in life. He was excited by the tales his mother told of life in Paris, and he loved the challenge of trying to predict six months in advance what kind of hats the women of The Hague would be wearing.

Goudsmit's first introduction to the sciences came when he was eleven years old and off-handedly picked up his older sister's physics textbook. He was intrigued by a discussion on spectroscopic phenomena—the theory that the elements of the earth and the stars are identical. Although interested, Goudsmit developed no particular on-going curiosity about science until, after graduation from high school in 1919, he was influenced by a physics teacher. At the University of Leiden, Goudsmit decided to major in physics—he had earned his best grades in science and mathematics—and found himself in a class taught by Paul Ehrenfest. Ehrenfest recognized in Goudsmit an inquiring intellect combined with an infallible intuition, and took a particular interest in helping his young student to develop those qualities. Goudsmit's moderate interest in physics soon became a passionate pursuit under the guidance of his new teacher. As a result of Ehrenfest's encouragement, Goudsmit published his first scientific paper in 1921 on the fine structure of atomic spectra.

That topic was one of immense importance in the 1920s. The quantum model of atomic structure proposed by Niels Bohr in 1913 had been an extraordinary breakthrough and solved many problems in the field of atomic theory. But a number of important questions remained. One of these concerned the nature of atomic spectra produced when atoms are placed within a magnetic field. In particular, the spectra produced in such instances always contain twice as many lines as were predicted by Bohr's theory. The answer to that puzzle came in 1925, shortly after Goudsmit met George Uhlenbeck, another of Ehrenfest's students. The two were assigned to spend the summer working together on the problem of double spectral lines.

The match of the two young students turned out to be nearly ideal. According to Goudsmit's biographer, Stanley Goldberg, in *Dictionary of Scientific Biography,* "Goudsmit supplied the intuitions necessary to recognize and summarize regularities not immediately obvious in the data . . . [while] Uhlenbeck was more analytically oriented, more readily able to make connections between formal synthesis and traditional physical concepts."

As a result of this collaboration, Goudsmit and Uhlenbeck realized that the problem of double lines could be solved by assuming that the electron spins on its axis as it travels around the atomic nucleus. The two possible directions of spin—clockwise and counterclockwise—could then explain two different orientations of an electron in a magnetic field and, hence, two spectral lines that are very close together in all other respects. Scientists immediately recognized the significance of this bold hypothesis. Only a few months earlier, Pauli had proposed his "exclusion principle," according to which no two electrons in an atom can have exactly the same set of quantum num-

bers. A condition of that theory, however, was that a fourth quantum number was necessary to describe any given electron, a quantum number that could have the values of plus or minus one-half. Pauli made no guess as to what this quantum number might represent physically, but the Goudsmit-Uhlenbeck hypothesis immediately answered that question. The values of plus or minus one-half corresponded, they pointed out, to the two possible directions of electron spin. The discovery led to a fundamental change in the mathematical structure of quantum mechanics, as scientists recognized that spin is an integral property not only of electrons but also of protons and neutrons.

Goudsmit and Uhlenbeck no sooner announced their theory of electron spin before they were both offered appointments at the University of Michigan. For Goudsmit, the decision to leave the Netherlands was a difficult one. He hated leaving behind family, friends, Ehrenfest, and his other European colleagues. But he accepted the Michigan offer nonetheless. A few years later, Goudsmit referred to himself during an interview as a "has-been," he was quoted as saying by Daniel Lang in *New Yorker.* His remarks suggested that his greatest accomplishment was behind him, and he could look forward only to a rather mundane career in the future. "As a physicist's career goes . . . a scientist can do useful work all his life, but if he is to carry learning one big step forward, he usually does so before he is thirty. Youth has the quality of being radical, in the literal sense of the word—of going to the root. . . . Obviously, if one hits on something through this approach, it may well be outstanding. After a scientist passes his creative peak, it seems to me the most useful thing he can do is teach the status quo to youngsters."

While he continued to remain active in research throughout the rest of his life, Goudsmit continued to teach—with one abrupt, but eventful interruption—until his death in 1978.

The interruption was World War II. At the outbreak of war, Goudsmit left the University of Michigan to conduct a secret research project at the Massachusetts Institute of Technology (MIT) to test the theory of radar. In 1944 General Leslie R. Groves asked the physicist to serve as part of a secret intelligence mission. The project—code-name "Alsos"—was an effort to find out what German scientists had been able to discover about nuclear weapons and atomic-bomb research during the war. Goudsmit was placed in charge of a group of about one hundred men, six of whom were scientists, sent to Europe to track down Werner

Karl Heisenberg, head of the German atomic weapons project. Goudsmit's team successfully found Heisenberg near Munich at the end of the war in Europe. Later, Goudsmit wrote a popular book titled *Alsos* describing his experience.

Goudsmit's participation with the Alsos project engendered an important change in his outlook on the future. In a 1951 interview with *New Yorker* writer Daniel Lang, Goudsmit explained that he felt he could not simply go back to the routine of university life again, but needed to "take an active part in scientific developments in order to—yes, at the time I perhaps meant it literally—to help save the world." As a consequence, after a brief stay at Northwestern University (1946 to 1948), he accepted an appointment at the Brookhaven National Laboratory, where he was promoted to chair of the physics department in 1950.

During his years at Brookhaven, Goudsmit became very active in the political aspects of scientific research, including the development of scientific policy, the funding of research, and the defense of science against the attacks of McCarthyism—the extreme governmental opposition to communism which swept the United States in the 1940s and 1950s.

In the two decades between 1952 and 1974, Goudsmit took on another important responsibility with the editorship of the American Physical Society's *Physical Review*. During his long term of office, Goudsmit oversaw the expansion of the journal from a single publication of about five thousand pages per year, to a group of five related journals with a combined size of more than twenty-five thousand pages per year. He also recommended the creation of—and then put into production—an important new journal, *Physical Review Letters,* in 1958.

Goudsmit retired from his editorial work in 1974 and accepted a position as distinguished visiting professor at the University of Nevada at Reno. His only teaching assignment there was a large general education course in "physics appreciation." He was found dead of a heart attack in Reno on December 4, 1978.

BIOGRAPHICAL/CRITICAL SOURCES:

BOOKS

Holmes, Frederic L., *Dictionary of Scientific Biography,* Volume 17, Scribner, 1982, pp. 362-368.
McGraw-Hill Modern Scientists and Engineers, Volume 1, McGraw-Hill, 1980, pp. 452-453.

PERIODICALS

New Yorker, November 7, 1953, p. 46; November 14, 1953, p. 47.*

*   *   *

GRAFTON, Garth
 See DUNCAN, Sara Jeannette

*   *   *

GRANGER, Percy   1945-1997

OBITUARY NOTICE—See index for *CA* sketch: Born August 8, 1945, in Ithaca, NY (two sources say Norman, OK); died after suffering cardiac arrest, March 10, 1997, in New York, NY. Playwright and screen writer. Granger was best known for his short, satirical plays but also wrote screenplays and scripts for television soap operas. Educated at Harvard University, where he graduated magna cum laude in 1967, Granger tried to break into acting but quickly switched to writing. One of his early plays, *The Complete Works of Studs Edsel* (1972), set the tone for his career with its one-act format and witty satire. Granger's other plays include *Eminent Domain* (first performed in 1981 at the Eugene O'Neill Theater Center in Waterford, Connecticut), *Vivien* (1981), *Unheard Songs* (1982), *The Dolphin Position* (1984), *Scheherazade* (1992), and *Coyote Hangin' on a Barbed Wire Fence* (1993). Granger wrote the screenplays *My Brother's Wife* and *A Dime to Dance.* For television, he wrote *The Comeback* and *Vital Signs* (both in 1986) and was a script writer for the ABC soap opera *Loving* and the CBS soap opera *As the World Turns.* His career was curtailed by a heart attack in 1992. In 1977, Granger won an award at the National Playwrights Conference.

OBITUARIES AND OTHER SOURCES:

BOOKS

Writers Directory: 1996-1998, St. James Press, 1995.

PERIODICALS

Los Angeles Times, March 13, 1997, p. A20.

New York Times, March 13, 1997, p. D22.
Washington Post, March 15, 1997, p. D7.

* * *

GREEN, Terence M(ichael) 1947-

PERSONAL: Born February 2, 1947, in Toronto, Canada; son of Thomas and Margaret (Radey) Green; married Merle Casci, September 2, 1994; children: Conor, Owen. *Education:*University of Toronto, B.A., 1967, B.Ed., 1973; University College, Dublin, M.A., 1972.

ADDRESSES: Home—Toronto, Canada. *Agent*—c/o Tor/Forge, 175 Fifth Ave., New York, NY 10010.

CAREER: Science fiction writer. English teacher at East York Collegiate Institute, Toronto, Canada, 1968—. Served as juror for the Philip K. Dick Award, 1995.

MEMBER: Science Fiction Writers of America, Writers' Union of Canada, Crime Writers of Canada.

AWARDS, HONORS: Recipient of Canada Council grants and Ontario Arts Council grants; participant in Harborfront Festival of Authors; four-time finalist for the Aurora Award.

WRITINGS:

The Woman Who Is the Midnight Wind (short stories), Pottersfield Press (Porters Lake, Nova Scotia, Canada), 1987.
Barking Dogs (novel), St. Martin's (New York), 1988.
Children of the Rainbow (novel), McClelland & Stewart (Toronto), 1992.
Shadow of Ashland (novel), Tor/Forge (New York), 1996.
Blue Limbo (novel), Tor (New York), 1997.

Contributor of short stories, articles, interviews, reviews and poetry to periodicals, including *Globe and Mail, Books in Canada, Quarry, Magazine of Fantasy and Science Fiction, Isaac Asimov's SF Magazine, Twilight Zone, Unearth, Thrust, SF Review, SF Chronicle, Poetry Toronto,* and *Leisure Ways.* Contributor to anthologies, including *Northern Stars, Northern Frights, Ark of Ice, Dark Visions, Conversations with Robertson Davies, Tes-* *seracts, The Writer's Voice 2,* and *Aurora: New Canadian Writing.*

WORK IN PROGRESS: The Redemption of Martin Radey, a novel.

SIDELIGHTS: Canadian science fiction writer Terence M. Green has been praised throughout his career for his quiet, restrained style. A *Science Fiction Chronicle* reviewer, discussing Green's first collection of stories, *The Woman Who Is the Midnight Wind,* theorized that such a style, however worthy, would not establish the author's fame until a substantial body of work had been built up. The reviewer further stated that while not yet widely known, Green's writing "is extraordinary and indicates a great talent masquerading as simplicity." Reviewer Joel Yanofsky wrote in *Books in Canada,* "it's Green's restrained and understated prose style that makes his fiction work." Yanofsky approved of the fact that the short stories in Green's collection deal with universal human emotions as much as with the trappings of science-fiction. In some of the stories, for instance, futuristic technology allows characters to speak with their dead relatives; Green uses this scenario to explore the emotional ramifications of such communication. "Green's vision of the future," Yanofsky asserted, "is of a world, not unlike our own, that has progressed too much and gotten too smart for the people who inhabit it."

Green's first novel, *Barking Dogs,* is a futuristic, violent thriller, in a style "aimed, as Green has stated, at the American market," reported Darlene James in *Maclean's.* The novel's hero is police officer Mitch Helwig of the Canadian city of Toronto, Ontario, who takes revenge on criminals after his partner is murdered. The cop's equipment includes a kind of portable super-lie-detector called a "barking dog." Reviewers in both *Maclean's* and *Books in Canada* compared the tale with *Rambo* movies; *Books in Canada*'s Douglas Hill observed that "the dialogue is snappy and sharp-edged."

More favorably received was Green's 1992 novel, *Children of the Rainbow,* a time-travel novel that centers on a character named Fletcher Christian IV—a descendant of the hero of *Mutiny on the Bounty.* The plot focuses on a hypothetical New Inca Church in the 2070s that is run by a leader who discovers a way to send people one hundred years back in time. This device allows Green to move his narrative through different historical periods—from the Norfolk Island penal colony in 1835 to French nuclear tests in 1972.

Quill and Quire reviewer R. John Hayes found *Children of the Rainbow* too self-consciously clever for its own good and thought the nuclear testing/Greenpeace subplot unnecessary, but added that Green "draws his characters very well and manages the frequent temporal shifts, which might have been disconcerting, brilliantly." Barbara Canfield, analyzing the novel as suitable for ages fourteen and up in *Canadian Materials,* approved of the Greenpeace aspect of the plot, and of the book in general; a *Science Fiction Chronicle* reviewer found it "a very quiet, introspective work." In *Canadian Forum,* Douglas Barbour called Green "very good at showing the psychological disruption the time shifts create in his two central characters" and singled out the long conversations between twenty-first-century Fletcher Christian IV and the nineteenth-century penal colony commandant as the best parts of the book, capturing "perfectly the intelligent incomprehension of [the commandant]." *Books in Canada* contributor John Degen labeled *Children of the Rainbow* "gracefully and authoritatively written . . . a questioning novel, a book that wonders as much about the lessons of our past as about our possible future." In an afterword to the novel, Green himself said, "writing *Children of the Rainbow* gave me the opportunity to revisit the magic of the stories of my youth. Everyone should be so lucky."

Four years after the release of *Children of the Rainbow,* Green produced the novel *Shadow of Ashland.* The story is set in Ashland, Kentucky, a town that was also the setting of a story in *The Woman Who Is the Midnight Wind.* In the novel, protagonist Leo Nolan takes up his mother's deathbed request to find her long-lost brother Jack. Letters from Jack written in 1934 have mysteriously been arriving in the mail; Leo not only traces them back to Ashland, Jack's old stomping ground, but finds himself in the year 1934, mixed up in a crime hatched by Jack. In the *New York Times Book Review,* Malachy Duffy regretted a "clumsy" subplot, but deemed the work an overall success because of the author's "dedication to exploring its underlying themes of redemption, resolution and homecoming." George Needham, in *Booklist,* was still more enthusiastic, declaring, "This is a jewel of a novel, sensitively told and filled with fascinating characters."

With *Blue Limbo* Green returned to the style of the futuristic thriller, and to hero Mitch Helwig. Out to avenge the murder of his partner (and a murder attempt on his own life and his captain's), Helwig finds himself on suspension from the police force—"a

rogue cop," according to a *Publishers Weekly* contributor. Coinciding with Helwig's violent mission is a twenty-first-century medical breakthrough, a technique known as "Blue Limbo," used for reviving the recently dead back to consciousness. "What separates Green's thrillers from conventional ones is his concern for the emotional lives of his characters," commented Douglas Barbour in the Edmonton *Journal.* In *Publishers Weekly,* a reviewer described *Blue Limbo* as "a high tech action cop thriller, albeit one sensitively drawn." Barbour concluded in the *Journal* that the novel "is a solid entertainment, with more than a bit of heart."

Green told *CA:* "*The Redemption of Martin Radey* is a follow-up to *Shadow of Ashland,* spinning off one of the characters mentioned in that novel. Both books use as their starting points real people and incidents in my own family. (In *Shadow of Ashland,* a major character, Jack Radey, is the real name of an uncle of mine who disappeared in the 1930s; *The Redemption of Martin Radey* is based on the life of my maternal grandfather, whose name is in fact Martin Radey.) They illustrate my growing interest in exploring the intricacies of family in fiction, a kind of blend of genealogy, drama, mythologizing, and personal resolution."

BIOGRAPHICAL/CRITICAL SOURCES:

PERIODICALS

Booklist, February 1, 1996, p. 917.
Books in Canada, June-July 1987, pp. 18-19; June-July 1988, p. 35; summer 1992, p. 52.
Canadian Forum, July/August 1992, p. 30.
Canadian Materials, September 1992, p. 220.
Journal (Edmonton), August 11, 1996, p. C6; January 11, 1997; February 23, 1997, p. D5.
Maclean's, June 27, 1988, p. 53.
New York Times Book Review, September 15, 1996, p. 30.
Publishers Weekly, December 30, 1996.
Quill and Quire, May 1992, p. 23.
Science Fiction Chronicle, February 1988, pp. 43-44; October 1992, p. 33.

*   *   *

GREGOR-DELLIN, Martin 1926-

PERSONAL: Born June 3, 1926, in Naumburg, Germany; married Annemarie Dellin (a writer), November 9, 1951; children: Katja. *Education:* Graduated from Oberrealschule Weissenfels, in Saale, 1944; attended University of Leipzig. *Religion:* Evangelical.

ADDRESSES: Home—Kochelseestrasse 57, D-8038 Gorbenzell bei Munchen, Germany.

CAREER: Writer and editor in Halle and Munich, 1951-58 and 1962-66; writer for radio, Frankfurt am Main, 1961-62; freelance novelist, editor, biographer and poet, 1966—. *Military service:* 1944-45.

MEMBER: German Academy for Language and Literature, Bavarian Academy of Fine Arts, Association of German Writers, PEN Centre.

AWARDS, HONORS: Forderpreis zum Andreas-Gryphius Preis, 1963; Ehrengabe des Kulturkreises im BdI, 1963; Ostdeutscher Schrifttimuspreis, 1963; Stereo Radio Play Prize, 1967; Munich Literary Prize, 1971; Critics Prize, "Die Goldene Feder," 1972; Grand Prix de la critique musicale francaise, 1982; Fernseh-Kulturpreis der Eduard-Rhein-Stiftung, 1984; Federal Cross of Merit, first class.

WRITINGS:

Catherine (narration), Mitteldeutscher Verlag (Halle, Germany), 1954.

Jakob Haferglanz (novel), Mitteldeutscher Verlag, 1956.

Der Mann Mit der Stoppuhr (poetry), Mitteldeutscher Verlag, 1957.

Funf Kleine Stuecke (poetry), Verlag der Telegramm-Gruppe, 1957.

Wagner und Kein Ende (essay), Edition Musica, 1958.

Der Nullpunkt (novel), Desch Verlag, 1959.

Der Kandelaber (novel), Walter Verlag (Duesseldorf, Germany), 1962; republished in 1980 by Schneekluth (Munich, Germany).

(Editor) *Stories der Welt* (anthology), Deutscher Taschenbuch-Verlag (Munich), 1963.

(Editor) *24 Erzaehler der Welt* (anthology), Nymphenburger Verlagshandlung (Munich), 1964.

Einer (novel), Walter Verlag, 1965.

Aufbruch ins Ungewisse, Baden-Baden, Signal-Verlag, 1968.

(Editor) Klaus Mann, *Preufungen; Schriften zur Literatur,* Nymphenburger Verlagshandlung, 1968.

Das Kleine Wagnerbuch, Residenz Verlag. (Salzburg, Germany), 1969.

(Editor) Richard Wagner, *Mein Leben,* List (Munich), 1969.

(Editor) Klaus Mann, *Die Heimsuchung des Europeaischen Geistes: Aufseatze,* Deutscher Taschenbuch-Verlag, 1973.

Richard Wagner, *Die Revolution als Oper,* Hanser (Munich), 1973.

(Editor) Klaus Mann, *Briefe und Antworten,* Edition Spangenberg im Ellermann-Verlag (Munich), 1975.

(Editor) *Deutsche Erzeahlungen aus drei Jahrzehnten: Deutschsprachige Prosa seit 1945,* Erdmann (Basel, Switzerland), 1975.

Das Riesenrad: Erzeahlungen, R. Piper (Munich), c. 1976.

(Commentary) Cosima Wagner, *Die Tagebeucher,* Piper (Munich), 1976-77.

(Editor with Wolfgang, R. Langenbucher, and Volker Schleondorff) *Das Andere Bayern: Lesebuch zu e. Freistaat,* Nymphenburger Verlagshandlung, 1976.

(Editor) Klaus Mann, *Abenteuer des Brautpaars,* Edition Spangenberg (Munich), 1976.

(Editor) Bruno Frank, *Trenck: Roman e. Geunstlings,* Nymphenburger Verlagshandlung, 1977.

(Editor with Dietrich Mack) Cosima Wagner, *Cosima Wagner's Diaries,* translation by Geoffrey Skelton, Harcourt Brace Jovanovich (New York City), 1978-80.

(Editor) Deutsches P.E.N., *PEN Bundesrepublik Deutschland: Seine Mitglieder, Seine Geschichte, Seine Aufgaben,* Goldmann (Munich), 1978.

(Editor) Bruno Frank, *Cervantes: Roman,* Nymphenburger Verlagshandlung, 1978.

(Editor) *Die Grosse Gespenstertruhe: D. Buch d. Phantast. Literatur,* Nymphenburger Verlagshandlung, 1978.

(Editor) *Deutsche Schulzeit: Erinnerungen u. Erzeahlungen aus 3 Jahrhunderten,* Nymphenburger Verlagshandlung, 1979.

Im Zeitalter Kafkas: Essays, Piper, 1979.

(Editor) Bruno Frank, *Die Monduhr: Erzeahlungen,* Nymphenburger Verlagshandlung, 1979.

Richard Wagner: *Sein Leben, Sein Werk, Sein Jahrhundert,* R. Piper, c. 1980, translation by J. Maxwell Brownjohn, published in U.S. as *Richard Wagner, His Life, His Work, His Century,* Harcourt Brace Jovanovich, c. 1983.

(Editor) Klaus Mann, *Woher Wir Kommen Und Wohin Wir Meussen: Freuhe und Nachgelassene Schriften,* Edition Spangenberg, c. 1980.

Schlabrendorf, oder, Die Republik, Piper, c. 1982.

(Editor) P.E.N.—*Schriftstellerlexikon Bundesrepublik, Deutschland,* Piper, c. 1982.

Richard Wagner: Eine Biographie in Bildern, R. Piper and Co. Verlag (Munich), c. 1982.

(Editor) *Deutsche Erzeahlungen Aus Vier Jahrzehnten: Deutschsprachige Prosa seit 1945,* Edition Erdmann (Teubingen, Germany), c. 1982.

Luther: Eine Anneaherung, Nymphenburger (Munich), c. 1983.

(With Michael von Soden) *Richard Wagner: Leben, Werk, Wirkung,* Econ (Duesseldorf, Germany), 1983.

Heinrich Scheutz: Sein Leben, Sein Werk, Seine Zeit, Piper, c. 1984.

Was ist Greosse?: Sieben Deutsche und ein Deutsches Problem, Piper, c. 1985.

Italienisches Traumbuch, Piper, c. 1986.

Pathos und Ironie: Ein Lesebuch von und Euber Martin Gregor-Dellin, edited by Elisabeth Endres, Piper, 1986.

(Contributor) *Ludwig II: Die Tragik des "Mearchenkeonigs",* by Martin Gregor-Dellin, et al., F. Pustet (Regensburg, Germany), c. 1986.

(Editor) *Die Botschaft Heor' Ich Wohl: Schriftsteller zur Religion,* Kreuz (Stuttgart, Germany), c. 1986.

(Editor) Carl Christian Bry, *Der Hitler-Putsch: Berichte und Kommentare Eines Deutschland-Korres-pondenten, 1922-24,* Greno (Neordlingen, Germany), 1987.

Also author of radio plays *Jakob Haferglanz,* 1961, *Blumen oder keine,* 1962, *Suche nach einem Zeugen,* 1965, *Geordnete Verhaltnisse,* 1967, *Markwerben—Konstruktion einer Landschaft,* 1967, *Ferdinand wird totgeredet,* 1971, *Das Gastehaus,* 1972. Author of television documentaries, "Klaus Mann. Zeitgenosse zwischen den Fronten," 1978, "Deutsch in Ost und West," 1978, and "Ich bin wie Othello—mein Tagwerk ist vorbei," 1983. Contributor of essays and poetry to numerous anthologies.

SIDELIGHTS: While Martin Gregor-Dellin is a prolific novelist whose works are well known in his native Germany, in the United States he is largely known for his nonfiction books on music, which include an edition of the diaries of Cosima Wagner, and the biographies *Richard Wagner, Sein Leben, sein Werk, sein Jahrhundert (Richard Wagner: His Life, His Work, His Century)* and *Heinrich Schutz: Sein Leben, sein Werk, seine Zeit.* Cosima Wagner was the wife of the famous German composer Richard Wagner, and her diaries, which were long kept from publication by German scholars, have shed light on the life and thought of her husband. After commenting that "reading Cosima's diaries is remarkably like having breakfast with Richard Wagner, day after day, for years on end," Joseph McLellan of the *Washington*

Post Book World remarked, "They have been edited most scrupulously, with detailed notes to explain the many obscure passages in the text."

In the twentieth century many biographies of Richard Wagner have been published in both English and German; yet many of these take either a rabid anti-Wagner or pro-Wagner position. That Gregor-Dellin attempted a more balanced view in *Richard Wagner* attracted the attention of critics. Writing in the *Washington Post Book World,* George C. Schoolfield maintained, "A clever man, Gregor-Dellin deals from his own strengths: his genuine scholarship and his ability as a practiced narrator. It must immediately be added that he neither heaps footnote on footnote nor stoops to such novelist's devices as the imaginary conversation. . . . He tries hard not to over-dramatize or to ironize. . . . Gregor-Dellin keeps to a sober yet fascinating objectivity." Michael Tanner, in the *Times Literary Supplement* called Gregor-Dellin's "a fluent, pleasing style," with "a remarkable range of cultural reference and a very balanced view of things." Tanner added, "His book is notable for its cool (in the best sense) tone, and its general lack of partisanship."

While asserting that *Richard Wagner* "falls a little short, perhaps, in one way; Gregor-Dellin accords the music itself only routine attention," Schoolfield declared, "For an American audience . . . there is probably no better introduction to the life, in all its vitality, and the world, in all its variety." Several critics remarked that the English translation is an abridged version, a fact that the publishers did not make clear to the American readership. Tanner went so far as to say that "Gregor-Dellin's book has been ruined" by the poor editing and translation. Nevertheless, Tanner concluded that for its breath and objectivity, "It is not surprising that it has been widely hailed as *the* book on Wagner that we've been waiting for."

In *Heinrich Schutz* Gregor-Dellin attempted to present a picture of the man behind the music. "He has done this on the basis of minute and loving knowledge of historical detail," Leonard Forster wrote in the *Times Literary Supplement.* "This combination is potentially a very strong one, and indeed what comes across is a compelling picture." While Forster called Gregor-Dellin's range of knowledge "impressive" and added that "the book as a whole does the job it sets out to do," he expressed reservations about historical and literary details. Thus he concluded, "The master work on Schutz has yet to be written. Meanwhile this will deservedly gain him many friends."

BIOGRAPHICAL/CRITICAL SOURCES:

PERIODICALS

New York Times, January 25, 1981, p. 9.
New York Times Book Review, May 31, 1981, p. 15.
Times Literary Supplement, June 14, 1985, p. 670;
    June 17, 1996, p. 620.
Washington Post Book World, January 4, 1981; April
    3, 1983, pp. 9, 11.

*   *   *

GRODIN, Charles 1935-

PERSONAL: Born April 21, 1935, in Pittsburgh, PA;
son of Ted (in sales) and Lana (a volunteer for disabled veterans) Grodin; married Julia (divorced, c.
1969); married Elissa, March, 1985; children: Marion.
Education: Attended University of Miami, 1953;
graduated from Pittsburgh Playhouse School, 1956;
studied acting with Lee Strasberg and Uta Hagen in
New York City.

ADDRESSES: Home—Connecticut.   *Office*—c/o Jim
Berkus, Leading Artists, 445 North Bedford Dr.,
Penthouse, Beverly Hills, CA 90210.

CAREER: Actor, director, producer, and writer. Host
of the television talk show *Charles Grodin,* CNBC,
1995—.

Appeared in roles for films, including, Bob, *Sex and
the College Girl,* Entertainment Enterprises, 1964;
Dr. Hill, *Rosemary's Baby,* Paramount, 1968; Aard-
vark, *Catch-22,* Paramount, 1970; Lenny Cantrow,
The Heartbreak Kid, Palomar/Twentieth Century-
Fox, 1972; Chesser, *11 Harrowhouse* (also known as
Anything for Love), Twentieth Century-Fox, 1974;
Fred Wilson, *King Kong,* Paramount, 1976; Martin
Cramer, *Thieves,* Brut/Paramount, 1977; Tony Abbott,
Heaven Can Wait, Paramount, 1978; Warren Yeager,
Real Life, Paramount, 1979; Jake, *Sunburn,* Tuesday/
Paramount, 1979; Homer, *It's My Turn,* Rastar-Mar-
tin Elfand/Columbia, 1980; Ira, *Seems Like Old
Times,* Columbia, 1980; Nicky Holiday, *The Great
Muppet Caper,* Universal, 1981; Vance Kramer, *The
Incredible Shrinking Woman,* Lija/Universal, 1981;
All of Me, Universal, 1984; Warren Evans, *The
Lonely Guy,* Universal, 1984; Buddy, *The Woman in
Red,* Woman in Red Productions/Orion, 1984; Herb
Derman, *Movers and Shakers,* Metro-Goldwyn-Mayer
(MGM)/United Artists (UA), 1985; George Lollar,
The Last Resort, Concorde-Cinema Group-Trinity,
1986; *Club Sandwich,* 1986; *Greetings from LA,*
1987; Jim Harrison, CIA agent, *Ishtar,* Columbia/
Delphi V, 1987; Jonathan Mardukas, *Midnight Run,*
Universal, 1988; George Maitlin, *The Couch Trip,*
Orion, 1988; Mr. Glerman, *You Can't Hurry Love,*
Lightning Pictures, 1988; *Taking Care of Business,*
Disney, 1990; George Newton, *Beethoven,* Universal,
1992; George Newton, *Beethoven's 2nd,* Universal,
1993; Murray Blum, *Dave,* Warner Bros., 1993;
Harrison Winslow, *Heart and Souls,* Universal, 1993;
commandeered car driver, *So I Married an Axe Mur-
derer,* TriStar, 1993; Martin Daniels, *Clifford,* Orion,
1994; old man, *It Runs in the Family,* MGM, 1994.
Producer of films, including *Sorceress,* New World
Pictures, 1983; and (with William Asher, Richard
Carrothers, and Dennis D. Hennessey), *Movers and
Shakers,* MGM/UA, 1985.

Appeared in roles for television series, including Matt
Crane, *The Young Marrieds,* ABC, 1964-66. Appeared in the television episodes "Black Monday,"
Play of the Week, syndicated, 1961; "Autumn Garden," *Sunday Showcase,* CBS, 1966; and "Rotten
Island," *Shelley Duvall's Bedtime Stories* (as narrator;
animated), Showtime, 1992. Appeared in roles for
television movies, including Michael, *Just Me and
You,* NBC, 1978; and Jim Benson, *The Grass Is Always Greener over the Septic Tank,* CBS, 1978. Appeared in roles for television miniseries, including
Cane Kensington, *Fresno,* CBS, 1986. Appeared in
television specials, including *Paradise* (as Bill Foster), CBS, 1974; *The Paul Simon Special,* NBC,
1977; *Love, Sex . . . and Marriage* (as Him), ABC,
1983; *Charley's Aunt* (as Lord Fancourt Babberly),
syndicated, 1988; *Donahue: The 25th Anniversary,*
NBC, 1992; *Lassie Unleashed: 280 Dog Years in TV*
(also known as *Lassie: A Dog Star—40 Years in Television*), ABC, 1994; *Sesame Street's All-Star 25th
Birthday: Stars and Street Forever!* (as Chaz), ABC,
1994; and *Talk Back America III,* syndicated, 1995.

Also appeared as Jake, *Grown Ups,* 1985. Also ap-
peared in *Night of 100 Stars,* 1982; *King Kong: The
Living Legend,* 1986; *The American Comedy Awards,*
1989; *What's Up Dr. Ruth,* 1989; *The Muppets at
Walt Disney World,* 1990; and *Jessica Lange: It's
Only Make-Believe,* 1991. Also appeared in *The De-
fenders,* CBS; *Camera Three,* CBS; *Armstrong Circle
Theatre,* NBC; *The Nurses,* CBS; *My True Story,*
CBS; *Love of Life,* CBS; *Trials of O'Brien,* CBS; *My
Mother the Car; The FBI; Guns of Will Sonnett;* and
The Big Valley.

Television producer and director of episodes of *Candid Camera;* the special *Acts of Love and Other Comedies,* ABC, 1973; and *Paradise,* CBS, 1974. Also director, *Songs of America,* 1969.

Appeared in stage performances, including (Broadway debut) Robert Pickett, *Tchin-Tchin,* Plymouth Theatre, 1962; Perry Littlewood, *Absence of a Cello,* Ambassador Theatre, New York City, 1964; Tandy, *Steambath,* Truck and Warehouse Theatre, New York City, 1970; George, *Same Time Next Year,* Brooks Atkinson Theatre, New York City, 1975; and *Night of 100 Stars,* Radio City Music Hall, New York City, 1982. Toured as George, *Same Time Next Year,* U.S. cities. Directed stage performances, including *Hooray! It's a Glorious Day . . . and All That,* Theatre Four, New York City, 1966; *Lovers and Other Strangers,* Brooks Atkinson Theatre, 1968; *Thieves* (and producer), Broadhurst Theatre, New York City, 1974; and *Unexpected Guests* (and producer), Little Theatre, New York City, 1977.

MEMBER: American Federation of Television and Radio Artists, Actors Equity Association, Screen Actors Guild.

AWARDS, HONORS: Golden Globe Award, 1973, for *The Heartbreak Kid;* Outer Critics Circle Award, 1975, for *Same Time, Next Year;* Actors Fund Award of Merit, 1975; Emmy Award, Academy of Television Arts and Sciences, for outstanding writing in a comedy-variety or music special, for *The Paul Simon Special.*

WRITINGS:

(With Maurice Teitelbaum) *Hooray! It's a Glorious Day . . . And All That* (play), produced at Theatre Four, 1966.
The Opening (play), produced in Nyack, New York, 1972, revised version debuted in New York in 1992 as *One of the All-Time Greats,* published by S. French, (New York), 1992.
(With Jeffrey Bloom) *11 Harrowhouse* (screenplay; adapted from the novel of the same name; also released as *Anything for Love*) Twentieth Century-Fox, 1974.
Movers and Shakers (screenplay), Metro-Goldwyn-Mayer/United Artists, 1985.
It Would Be So Nice If You Weren't Here: My Journey Through Show Business (memoir), Morrow (New York), 1989.
Price of Fame (play), produced at Roundabout Theater, New York City, 1990, S. French (New York), 1991.

How I Get Through Life: A Wise and Witty Guide (book), Morrow (New York), 1992.
Freddie the Fly (children's book), illustrated by Sal Murdocca, Random House (New York), 1993.
We're Ready for You, Mr. Grodin: Behind the Scenes at Talk Shows, Movies, and Elsewhere (memoir), Macmillan (New York), 1994.

Also wrote material for the television program *Candid Camera* as well as the 1977 NBC presentation *The Paul Simon Special* and the 1983 ABC special *Love, Sex . . . and Marriage.*

SIDELIGHTS: Though Charles Grodin's greatest successes as a film actor have come from portraying a wry, sincere type of character, his thirty-year career has suffered the vagaries of show business and studio politics. As a result, his less successful endeavors on both stage and screen have yielded material for a written body of work that includes screenplays, plays, and nonfiction books.

At the beginning of his career during the early 1960s, Grodin aimed at building a meaningful career on the New York stage; a graduate of the Pittsburgh Playhouse School, Grodin also studied acting with luminaries Lee Strasberg and Uta Hagen. Moving behind the wings, Grodin debuted as a director and co-author of *Hooray! It's a Glorious Day . . . And All That,* a satire on the Broadway musical that debuted in 1966 to less-than-enthusiastic reviews. Around this same time, Grodin became one of the most infamous also-rans when he almost secured the role of Benjamin Braddock in 1967's *The Graduate;* he lost out to a young Dustin Hoffman when Grodin expressed insult at the low salary producers were offering for the lead. He next appeared as Mia Farrow's closet Satanist doctor in *Rosemary's Baby,* and two years later in a role in the film version of Joseph Heller's *Catch-22.*

Yet despite these high-profile Hollywood successes, Grodin still pursued a career on the stage, and as he recounted in an article he wrote for the *New York Times* in 1990, claimed he "became a writer in self-defense." Because of some difficult experiences in an equally competitive Broadway star system, "I had nightmares about being fired for weeks. . . . There was nothing left to do but invent some work for myself, since no one else was." Based on his experiences with *Hooray! It's a Glorious Day,* Grodin wrote a play about a bumbling director of a stage production doomed to failure before opening night, and called it *The Opening.* It debuted in Nyack, New York, in

1972 to rave reviews, but one obstacle after another prevented it from heading to Broadway.

Returning to his film career, that same year Grodin starred in *The Heartbreak Kid* opposite Cybill Shepherd to laudatory reviews. Back on Hollywood's A-list, Grodin was next cast in *11 Harrowhouse,* for which he also wrote the screenplay with Jeffrey Bloom; the duo adapted a novel of the same name. The 1974 jewel-heist tale starred Grodin with Candice Bergen but failed to attract an audience.

Grodin found better success with Warren Beatty's 1978 movie *Heaven Can Wait,* and again returned to favor among Hollywood executive circles. That year, he was handed a plum project—Paramount had bought the rights to the classic how-to manual, *The Joy of Sex,* and gave Grodin the job of turning it into a screenplay. He pitched studio executives an idea about a hot-topic screenplay that fictional Hollywood brass can't seem to figure out what to do with; Paramount was originally supportive, but then backed out. Grodin managed to get the film made starring both himself and Walter Matthau; it appeared in 1985 as *Movers and Shakers* to mixed reviews. Vincent Canby of the *New York Times* asserted it "has no real story or screenplay," but a *Time* contributor allowed that the film "is a nice idea not as well executed as it could have been."

Grodin continued to act in films but also made another effort at writing for the stage. For his play *Price of Fame,* which debuted at the Roundabout Theater in New York City in 1990, Grodin addressed the morals and posturings inside celebritydom and the entertainment business. The play takes place on the set of a movie as a reporter comes to interview an aging actor; the two fall in love briefly, despite the fact that Grodin's character knows she will be writing a harsh piece on him. "What's missing from both acts is any serious introspection" on the part of the characters who, wrote the *New York Times*'s Frank Rich, are "on their way to a jerry-built sentimental resolution of their various crises." John Simon, critiquing it for *New York,* noted that while Grodin's charms as an actor are considerable, "even he cannot make a nothing play seem charming." *New Yorker* writer Edith Oliver was less critical in her review of *Price of Fame* and called it "a neat, harmless little comedy that tells a credible story in a credible setting."

Grodin continued his career as a playwright with a revised version of *The Opening,* which premiered as *One of the All-Time Greats* in New York in 1992. He added an entire act, but the story remained essentially the same: the torturous rehearsal path of a doomed play. The central characters are the producer and director, along with their wives, who meet at a Chinese restaurant nightly to formulate new strategies prior to opening night. Their fictional "Thunder Road" ends before the disastrous reviews put a stop to it, but *One of the All-Time Greats* was not let off the hook so easily. David Richards of the *New York Times* called it "flat and colorless."

In 1989 Grodin ventured into memoir writing with the publication of *It Would Be So Nice If You Weren't Here: My Journey Through Show Business.* As its title implies, the book begins with the earliest days of Grodin's career—in summer stock theater—and takes the reader through his roller-coaster of a career. He recounts *The Graduate* episode, and the reason that *Hooray! It's a Glorious Day* received such poor reviews in 1966—an angry costume sewer stole the garments before opening night, delaying the curtain several hours.

Grodin's next book was *How I Get Through Life: A Wise and Witty Guide,* which appeared in 1992. The brief book is comprised of page-long anecdotes on a variety of topics ranging from museums to marriage.

Grodin also penned a children's book, *Freddie the Fly,* published in 1993, before chronicling another aspect of his career in 1994's *We're Ready for You, Mr. Grodin: Behind the Scenes at Talk Shows, Movies, and Elsewhere.* Throughout his career as an actor, Grodin was known for being an outrageous guest on the banal-by-nature talk show circuit. His bullying once induced Johnny Carson to admit he was "just here to scoop up the money and take it home," as Philip Weiss reported in *Esquire.*

Later, Grodin's appearances on David Letterman became legendary; he appeared angry and uncooperative, unwilling to promote his latest movie or book, the ostensible reason for his being there. In *We're Ready for You, Mr. Grodin,* the actor recounts experiences on both the *Tonight Show* and *Late Night* sets, and reveals what many viewers suspected—that his hosts played along with the hostile act. "In print," asserted Peter Keepnews in the *New York Times Book Review,* "Grodin comes across as more bemused than angry. He also comes across as smart, likable and, as Mr. Carson once described him, a first-rate storyteller." In 1995 Grodin premiered on the cable channel CNBC with his own talk show.

BIOGRAPHICAL/CRITICAL SOURCES:

BOOKS

Contemporary Theatre, Film, and Television, Volume 9, Gale (Detroit), pp. 185-186.

PERIODICALS

Celebrity Register, 1990, pp. 180-181.
Esquire, January, 1994, p. 76.
Los Angeles Times, June 2, 1985, p. C18; January 9, 1995, p. F1.
New York, July 18, 1988, p. 34; June 25, 1990, p. 58.
New York Times, May 3, 1985, p. C5; June 30, 1989; June 10, 1990, sec. 2, p. 7; June 14, 1990; April 17, 1992, p. C3; May 17, 1992.
New York Times Book Review, November 13, 1994, p. 73.
New Yorker, June 25, 1990, p. 71.
People, October 30, 1989, p. 22; November 14, 1994, p. 152.
Time, May 13, 1985, p. 69.
Variety, May 8, 1985, p. 24.*

* * *

GROSS, Bertram M(yron) 1912-1997

OBITUARY NOTICE—See index for *CA* sketch: Born December 25, 1912, in Philadelphia, PA; died of congestive heart failure, March 12, 1997, in Walnut Creek, CA. Political scientist, economist, educator, and author. Chiefly remembered as an economic adviser to presidents Franklin D. Roosevelt and Harry S. Truman from 1938 to 1953, Gross contributed substantially to the development of legislation regarding employment and wages and was a strong advocate for federal programs to create jobs. He attended the University of Pennsylvania, receiving a bachelor's degree in 1933 and a master's degree in 1935. He joined the United States Housing Authority in 1938 and went on to such government appointments as research and hearing director of the Senate Committee on Small Business from 1942 to 1943, staff director of the Senate Military Affairs Subcommittee on War Contracts during 1943 and 1944, economic adviser to the Senate Banking and Currency Committee from 1945 to 1946, and executive secretary of the Council of Economic Advisers to the President from 1946 to 1951. Leaving Washington in 1953, Gross served as

an economic adviser to the government of Israel and taught at Hebrew University in Jerusalem. He returned to the United States in 1956, when he assumed a visiting professorship at Syracuse University's Maxwell School of Citizenship and Public Affairs. He was later the director of the Urban Studies Center at Wayne State University in Detroit and Distinguished Professor of Urban Affairs at Hunter College of the City University of New York. A contributor to anthologies and periodicals on various topics of economics and politics, Gross was the author of *The Legislative Struggle: A Study in Social Combat* (1953), and such legislation as the "Employment Act of 1946" and the "Humphrey-Hawkins Full Employment Act of 1978."

OBITUARIES AND OTHER SOURCES:

PERIODICALS

New York Times, March 15, 1997, p. 31.

* * *

GUEST, Christopher 1948-

PERSONAL: Born February 5, 1948, in New York, NY; son of Peter Haden (a baron) and Jean Guest; married Jamie Lee Curtis (an actress), December 18, 1984; children: (a son and a daughter). *Education:* Graduate of New York City's High School of Music and Art; attended Bard College, 1967, and New York University, 1968-70.

ADDRESSES: Office—Creative Artists Agency, 9830 Wilshire Blvd., Beverly Hills, CA 90212.

CAREER: Actor, writer, and director. Appeared in stage plays, including *Little Murders,* 1969; *Room Service,* Edison Theater, New York, NY, 1970; appeared with the Arena Stage, Washington, DC, 1971-72; *Moonchildren,* Royale Theater, New York, 1972; (also co-writer of music and lyrics) *National Lampoon's Lemmings,* Village Gate Theater, New York, 1973; *East Lynne,* Manhattan Theater Club, New York, 1975.

Appeared in films, including *The Hot Rock* (also known as *How to Steal a Diamond in Four Easy Lessons;* appeared as a policeman), Twentieth Century-Fox, 1972; *Death Wish* (appeared as patrolman Reilly), Paramount, 1974; *The Fortune* (appeared as a boy lover), Columbia, 1975; (voice) *La Honte de la jungle* (animated; also known as *Jungle Burger*), Entertainment Film Distributors, 1975; *Girlfriends* (appeared as Eric), Warner Bros., 1978; *The Last Word* (also known as *Danny Travis;* appeared as Roger), International, 1979; *The Long Riders* (appeared as Charlie Ford), United Artists, 1980; (voice) *The Missing Link* (animated), SND, 1980; *Heartbeeps* (appeared as Calvin), Universal, 1981; (also co-writer of script, music, and lyrics) *This is Spinal Tap* (also known as *Spinal Tap;* appeared as Nigel Tufnel), Embassy, 1984; *Little Shop of Horrors* (appeared as the first customer), Warner Bros., 1986; *Beyond Therapy* (appeared as Bob), New World, 1987; *The Princess Bride* (appeared as Count Rugen), Twentieth Century-Fox, 1987; *Sticky Fingers* (appeared as Sam), Spectrafilm, 1988; *A Few Good Men* (appeared as Dr. Stone), Columbia, 1992; (also co-writer and director) *Waiting for Guffman* (appeared as Corky St. Claire), Sony Pictures, 1996.

Appeared on television in series, specials, pilots, and films, including *Saturday Night Live With Howard Cosell* (appeared as a regular), American Broadcasting Company (ABC), 1975; (also co-writer) *The Lily Tomlin Special,* ABC, 1975; *Billion Dollar Bubble* (appeared as Al Green), National Broadcasting Corporation (NBC), 1977; *All in the Family* (appeared as Jim), Columbia Broadcasting System (CBS), 1977; *It Happened One Christmas* (appeared as Harry Baily), ABC, 1977; *How to Survive the 70s and Maybe Even Bump Into Happiness,* CBS, 1978; *Blind Ambition* (appeared as Jeb Stuart Magruder), CBS, 1979; *The TV Show,* ABC, 1979; *Haywire,* CBS, 1980; *Million Dollar Infield* (appeared as Bucky Frische), CBS, 1982; *A Piano for Mrs. Cimino* (appeared as Philip Ryan), CBS, 1982; *Close Ties* (appeared as Ira), Entertainment Channel, 1983; *Saturday Night Live* (appeared as a regular), NBC, 1984-85; *Martin Short Concert for the North Americas,* Showtime, 1985; *Billy Crystal—Don't Get Me Started* (appeared as Chip), Home Box Office (HBO), 1986; *Saturday Night Live 15th Anniversary,* NBC, 1989; *I, Martin Short, Goes Hollywood,* HBO, 1989; *Billy Crystal: Midnight Train to Moscow,* HBO, 1989; *Partners in Life* (appeared as El Supremo), CBS, 1990; (also co-writer and co-producer) *A Spinal Tap Reunion,* NBC, 1992; and (also director and songwriter) *Attack of the 50-Ft. Woman,* HBO, 1993.

Director of additional television films, programs, pilots, series, and specials, including *Tall Tales and Legends,* Showtime; *The Sad Professor,* Public Broadcasting System (PBS), 1989; (and executive producer, and composer of theme) *Morton & Hayes,* CBS, 1991; appeared on radio comedy programs and comedy albums with the National Lampoon, with Spinal Tap, and with comedian Billy Crystal; went on concert tour as his *This Is Spinal Tap* character musician Nigel Tufnel.

AWARDS, HONORS: Emmy Award for best writing for a comedy special, 1976, for *The Lily Tomlin Special.*

WRITINGS:

SCREEN AND TELEPLAYS

(With others) *The Lily Tomlin Special,* ABC, 1975.
(With Michael McKean and Harry Shearer; and co-composer of music and lyrics, and actor) *This is Spinal Tap,* Embassy, 1984.
(With McKean and Michael Varhol; and director, and composer of song) *The Big Picture,* Columbia, 1989.
(With others; and co-producer) *A Spinal Tap Reunion,* NBC, 1992.
(With others; and director and actor) *Waiting for Guffman,* Sony Pictures, 1997.

Also wrote lyrics and music for *National Lampoon's Lemmings,* Village Gate Theater, New York, NY, 1973.

SIDELIGHTS: Actor, director, and writer Christopher Guest has had a varied and fruitful career in the entertainment field. His debut as a stage performer came in 1969. Four years later he had his first big success in *National Lampoon's Lemmings,* a comedic musical for which he composed the music and wrote the lyrics. Guest won an award—an Emmy—for his next major writing task, collaborating with several others on the script for *The Lily Tomlin Special* in 1975.

Guest appeared in several films, including *Death Wish, Girlfriends, The Long Riders,* and *Heartbeeps,* before achieving popular success in 1984 with the comedic spoof on rock documentaries, *This Is Spinal Tap.* He was not only one of the film's three principal stars, but he co-wrote the script with the other two stars, Michael McKean and Harry Shearer. The trio also composed the music and penned the lyrics for the amusing pseudo-hits performed by the pseudo-band. The concept was revived for the 1992 television special *A Spinal Tap Reunion,* and Guest and his co-stars also released two albums as Spinal Tap.

Guest made his big-screen directorial debut with another of his screenplays, 1989's *The Big Picture*. He returned to the mock-documentary format with 1997's *Waiting for Guffman*, a comedy about the trials of a would-be Broadway director working with small-town actors in Missouri. Other film appearances for Guest include roles in 1987's *The Princess Bride* and 1992's *A Few Good Men*.

Guest's television credits are numerous. He appeared on an episode of the acclaimed television series *All in the Family*, and was a regular on NBC's *Saturday Night Live* in 1984 and 1985. He has also had guest roles on the comedy specials of such performers as Billy Crystal and Martin Short. He has directed and produced for the small screen as well; his titles in this area include the short-lived television series *Morton & Hayes*. He also directed an episode of *Tall Tales and Legends* for cable's Showtime network, and the cable remake of the 1950s science fiction film *Attack of the 50-Foot Woman* for Home Box Office (HBO).

Guest penned 1989's *The Big Picture* with *This Is Spinal Tap*'s McKean, and also with Michael Varhol. The story, which Guest created himself, concerns a young student filmmaker who is "discovered" by Hollywood after his first motion picture. With a professional agent, and big studios interested in his next project, he is in great danger of being corrupted to the point where his second film will bear no relation to his original idea for it but will instead be filled with Hollywood gimmicks. As Terrence Rafferty, reviewing *The Big Picture* in the *New Yorker*, revealed, however, the film's protagonist "learns to be a nice guy again, and finally gets to make his picture, his way."

The Big Picture did not meet with as much success as *This Is Spinal Tap*, and critics handed it mixed reviews. Peter Travers in *Rolling Stone* liked *The Big Picture*'s basic theme but lamented that "you keep rooting for this Hollywood sendup to make it, even as the bad ideas start gaining on the good." Rafferty labeled the film's satire "distressingly mild," though he cites "a handful of funny lines." A reviewer in the *Nation* praised the scenes in *The Big Picture* which depict story conferences as "all-too-plausible," but felt that the film's star, Kevin Bacon, was miscast as the young filmmaker. The critic conceded that "you'll get all the jokes even if you've never set foot in Los Angeles." One aspect of *The Big Picture*, however, drew raves from both Rafferty and Travers—comedian Martin Short's performance as the protagonist's

overly-slick agent. Travers labeled Short's presentation as "one for the comedy time capsule," while Rafferty declared: "Every time he's on the screen, you're on the floor."

The band Spinal Tap was reunited for a television special in 1992, and, as he had with the big-screen version, Guest co-wrote the program's script, lyrics, and music. In addition to portraying Nigel Tufnel once more, he co-produced the special as well. Its premise is that the band have reunited after a nasty break-up in order to tour and to promote their latest album, *Break Like the Wind*—an album of heavy-metal parody that was actually released in the same year that the special aired. The show also included mock-interviews with celebrities such as Robin Williams, Mel Torme, and Graham Nash, who discuss Spinal Tap's impact on the music field. John Leonard, reviewing the television show in *New York* disqualified himself as a judge, saying that his reverent feelings toward rock documentaries had been hurt by the original film: "About rock music we aren't supposed to be ironic; it hurts too much. Would you laugh at your own childhood: so many pimples, so little sex?" *Entertainment Weekly* was more enthusiastic, lauding the whole concept of the pseudo-band as "gratifyingly supple." That periodical also called the parody songs "pretty funny," but labeled the interviews with the band members and with celebrity commentators as "the strongest material."

Guest turned to the world of community theater for his next motion picture mock-documentary, 1997's *Waiting for Guffman*. The film's protagonist is the somewhat effeminate Corky St. Claire, who has come from New York to the fictional town of Blaine, Missouri to teach high school drama. He is put in charge of a stage show commemorating Blaine's sesquicentennial, from its founding to its rise to fame as a manufacturer of stools. Corky has no one to cast but talentless yokels, including hammy travel agents who sing "Midnight at the Oasis," a dentist with crossed eyes, a girl who works at the Dairy Queen counter, and a retired taxidermist. He also wants a hundred-thousand-dollar budget for the show when the budget for the town as a whole is only fifteen thousand. Nevertheless, Corky dreams of having his presentation of "Red, White, and Blaine" discovered by Guffman, a Broadway critic.

David M. Kimmel, who saw an early screening of *Waiting for Guffman* at a Boston, Massachusetts, film festival, reviewed it in *Variety* and felt that it was better-suited for the small screen, "especially on an irreverent showcase like Comedy Central." David Ansen in *Newsweek,* however, had much greater praise for the film. He observed that the parodic songs of *Waiting for Guffman* "straddle the thin and hilarious line between competence and catastrophe," and that Guest's performance as Corky "is a triumph, a queenly stereotype invested with such enthusiastic conviction it transcends offensiveness." Ansen summed up *Waiting for Guffman* as "from start to finish, a hoot."

Though born in New York City in 1948, Guest became a baron by inheriting his father's title in 1996. He is married to actress Jamie Lee Curtis, and the couple have one daughter and one son.

BIOGRAPHICAL/CRITICAL SOURCES:

BOOKS

Contemporary Theatre, Film, and Television, Volume 7, Gale, 1989.

PERIODICALS

Entertainment Weekly, December 18, 1992, p. 50.
Nation, October 9, 1989, p. 398.
Newsweek, February 10, 1997.
New York, January 4, 1993, p. 44.
New Yorker, September 18, 1989, pp. 103-104.
Rolling Stone, October 5, 1989, p. 36.
Variety, September 16, 1996, p. 71.*

*   *   *

GURDJIEFF, G(eorge) I(vanovich)   1877(?)-1949

PERSONAL: Name is sometimes rendered Georgei Ivanovitch Gurdjieff; born in 1877 (some sources say 1872, others 1869) in Alexandropol, Armenia; immigrated to France in 1922; died, October 29, 1949, in Paris, France; son of a carpenter and *ashokh,* a village poet and storyteller; married Countess Ostrowska (a lady-in-waiting), about 1914 (deceased, 1927); fathered several children according to one source. *Education:* Studied with the dean of the Russian Military Cathedral.

CAREER: Established the Institute for the Harmonious Development of Man in Constantinople, 1917-21; relocated to Fountainbleau, France, 1922-36. Teacher, mystic, author.

WRITINGS:

The Herald of Coming Good, 1933.
All and Everything: Ten Books, in Three Series, of Which This Is the First, Harcourt (New York), 1950.
Meetings with Remarkable Men, translated by Alfred R. Orage, Dutton (New York), 1963.
Beelzebub's Tales to His Grandson: An Objectively Impartial Criticism of the Life of Man, NAL-Dutton, 1973, revised edition, Viking Arkana, 1992.
Life Is Real Only Then, When "I Am," 1975, Viking Penguin, 1991.
Views from the Real World: Early Talks in Moscow, Essentuki, Tiflis, Berlin, London, Paris, New York and Chicago, as Recollected by His Pupils, Dutton, 1973, Viking Penguin, 1991.

SIDELIGHTS: G. I. Gurdjieff created a philosophy or occult religion based on an amalgam of Sufi and Buddhist teachings, combined with his own emphasis on self-knowledge and strenuous physical activity. He placed a great emphasis on awakening the individual out of what he believed was the prisonhouse of habitual reactions so that the person's true essence might be revealed. In pursuit of this goal with students at his Institute for the Harmonious Development of Man, he relied upon surprise, intense frustration, humiliation, and impelling individuals to do what seemed contrary to their natures. "At the Institute delicately nurtured ladies and fragile intellectuals were put to hard dirty physical work. Devoted disciples were abused and insulted, moved from luxurious rooms to bare attics," a writer for the *Times Literary Supplement* noted. Although much has been written about Gurdjieff's thought and method, it is difficult to pin down, being at base "a method, not a doctrine," as Gurdjieff himself insisted, according to the reviewer. "It could be learnt only in practice."

While many found him an intensely charismatic individual, Gurdjieff was said to offend or repel nearly as many as he attracted by his mysterious and unpredictable demeanor and his penchant for exposing others' weaknesses in public. "It was his function to disturb and to destroy complacency wherever he found it," explained Kenneth Walker in *The Saturday Book.* "Nobody ever came into contact with him without being in some way ruffled." Kathleen Riordan in an essay for *Transpersonal Psychologies* characterized Gurdjieff's habit of holding others up for public examination of their flaws: "These celebrations of individual personality weaknesses were part of the attempt, carried on by Gurdjieff on many fronts simultaneously, to invalidate and detoxify patterns of conditioning so that the student's more essential nature could begin to appear."

The aura of mystery that surrounds Gurdjieff's life began with the man himself, who was said to be deliberately vague or self-contradictory in the matter of autobiography, particularly about his early years. What is known with some confidence about Gurdjieff's life starts after 1922, when he and his followers arrived in France and set up the Institute for the Harmonious Development of Man at a chateau near Fountainbleau. The first fifty years of his life—depending on which date of birth one accepts—are shrouded in mystery. "The conflicting details [of his early life story] invite . . . apocryphal interpretations which becloud yet enlarge the man himself," B. A. St. Andrews observed in the *University of Windsor Review*. Born around 1877 or before on the border between Armenia and Russia to a Greek father and an Armenian mother, Gurdjieff was educated in the Greek Orthodox Church and at the knee of his father, a travelling storyteller whose tales and poems were both history and art to the people of the Asiatic hinterlands. Some biographers place the young Gurdjieff's fascination with his father's stories, and their ancient origins, at the root of his lifelong quest for ancient, universal truths.

As a young man, Gurdjieff reputedly traveled through Persia, Afghanistan, China, and Tibet, seeking the origins of the wisdom he had found in the legends his father had taught him. As part of a band of likeminded individuals known as Seekers of the Truth, "[t]hey talked to wandering dervishes and religious hermits, stayed in old monasteries, were admitted to ancient world brotherhoods and followed up every clue that seemed to lead them towards the object of their search," Walker recounted. Gurdjieff incorporated into his own philosophy dances, music, and ritualized movements he had learned on these travels, which along with hard physical labor and intense self-scrutiny, served as a foundation of his method. A somewhat parabolic rendering of these early years is found in his *Meetings with Remarkable Men*.

Another rendition of Gurdjieff's youth was offered by a contributor to the *Times Literary Supplement* in a 1980 review article of several biographies of the mysterious leader: "What probably is true is that he grew up as a bazaar mountebank, small trader, traveller, with an extraordinary power to dominate others,

a strong interest in hypnotism, and a propensity to absorb a miscellany of thaumaturgic baggage from the numerous sects and creeds that abounded in the southern Caucasus at that time. No doubt he travelled a good deal in wild places." The Sufi origins of much of what he taught, and the affinities of his method with Zen Buddhism and the Cabala, are widely acknowledged. In addition, the undeniable attraction of Gurdjieff's method for some seems to have been at least in part a symptom of the times in which he lived, a time of great spiritual seeking which some believe was a reaction to the Industrial Revolution and the rise of science.

Gurdjieff settled in Russia and began teaching, healing, and attracting followers around the turn of the twentieth century. Other mystics gained popularity as well, most famously Madame Helena Petrovna Blavatsky. By 1914 he had met his future wife, a former lady-in-waiting to the tsarina, and his most important acolyte, Peter Ouspensky, a journalist whose proselytizing and writings Gurdjieff relied upon to spread the word of his teachings abroad. Gurdjieff soon opened the first Institute for the Harmonious Development of Man in St. Petersburg, but because of World War I and the onset of the Russian Revolution, he was forced to relocate to the Caucasus, then to Tiflis, Constantinople, and Berlin before finally settling in Paris in 1922. "The decade from 1923 to 1933 was spent in intense work with students at the Institute," wrote Riordan, "during which time Gurdjieff tested and revised a system of study, self-observation, physical work, and exercise aimed toward the reconciliation and union of the three basic human functions of thinking, feeling, and physical activity."

The 1920s and 1930s were decades of intense productivity for Gurdjieff, who began to write down and circulate privately a series of manuscripts which directly and indirectly extolled his philosophy. Published after his death, they include *All and Everything*, which many consider his magnum opus, and which Riordan describes as "an encyclopedic commentary on the most urgent questions facing every individual"; *Meetings with Remarkable Men*, which is considered far more approachable in style though some question the status of its putatively factual account of Gurdjieff's early travels; and *Life Is Real Only Then, When "I Am,"* a work which remained in fragmentary form at the end of the author's life.

Each of Gurdjieff's writings is marked by an obscure prose style, one which some find incomprehensible, though others consider it a means of throwing the reader off balance so that a new avenue of understanding may be reached. The obscurantism of Gurdjieff's *Beelzebub's Tales to His Grandson,* is somewhat meliorated, according to *Parabola* reviewer Chris Thompson, by the improved translation of the 1992 edition. Dennis Fry, who wrote the entry on Gurdjieff for *Makers of the Modern Culture,* warned, however, against a too heavy reliance on the many accounts of Gurdjieff's followers of the master's teachings: "[T]here is a sharp contrast between Gurdjieff's own writing and these accounts; they appear over-systematized and intellectualized when compared with, for example, *All and Everything,* which is difficult to read, being full of unusual constructions and neologisms, but makes a great impact on the reader."

In the years following his death in 1949, Gurdjieff continued to be influential, thanks in great part to the extensive writings of his followers. The mystery surrounding his charismatic personality grew. "Condemned by some, extolled by others, Gurdjieff remains enigmatic," St. Andrews remarked in 1988; "the stories about him provide a portrait of a pompous man, an independent one; an inspiring personality, an insulting one. Gurdjieff is charlatan and saint, shyster and sage." Kathleen Riordan Speeth and Ira Friedlander in the introduction to their *Gurdjieff: Seeker of the Truth* noted: "Gurdjieff was deeply compassionate, yet he was not angelic. He was a man who behaved with understanding and could change his mood at any time, sit down, listen and talk, helping another out of confusion with accuracy. As the dervishes say, he had learned how to be in this world but not of it. . . . In his presence people were awakened for a moment."

BIOGRAPHICAL/CRITICAL SOURCES:

BOOKS

Makers of Modern Culture, edited by Jim Wintle, Facts on File, 1981, pp. 214-15.
Riordan, Kathleen, "Gurdjieff," in *Transpersonal Psychologies,* edited by Charles T. Tart, Harper, 1975, pp. 281-328.
Speeth, Kathleen Riordan, and Ira Friedlander, *Gurdjieff: Seeker of the Truth,* Harper, 1980, pp. 13-24.

PERIODICALS

Bulletin of Bibliography, October, 1971, pp. 117-18.

Parabola, February, 1993, pp. 97-99.
Saturday Book, volume 10, 1951, p. 86-91.
Times Literary Supplement, June 13, 1980, pp. 665-66.
University of Windsor Review, vol. 21, no. 2, 1988, pp. 46-51.*

* * *

GUTENBERG, Beno   1889-1960

PERSONAL: Born June 4, 1889, in Darmstadt, Germany; died in 1960, in Pasadena, CA; son of Hermann (in manufacturing) and Pauline (Hachenburger) Gutenberg. *Education:* Attended Realgymnasium and Technische Hochschule, Darmstadt; University of Goettingen, Ph.D., 1911.

CAREER: Seismologist. International Seismological Association, Strasbourg, France, assistant, 1911-18; University of Frankfurt-am-Main, Germany, privatdozent, 1918-26, professor of geophysics, 1926; manager of family business, 1926-1930; California Institute of Technology, Pasadena, professor, 1930-47; Carnegie Institution, director of Seismological Laboratory, 1947-58. *Military service:* Army service in World War I.

WRITINGS:

(Editor and contributor) *Internal Constitution of the Earth,* McGraw Hill, 1939.
(With Charles Francis Richter) *Seismicity of the Earth,* The Society, 1941.
The Physics of the Earth's Interior, International Geography Series, Volume 1, [New York], 1959.

Contributor to journals and periodicals, including *Beitraege zur Geophysik.*

SIDELIGHTS: German-born seismologist Beno Gutenberg investigated and determined most of the currently accepted causes of microseismic disturbances, and he improved methods of epicenter and depth determinations. He worked with noted seismologist Charles F. Richter to derive more accurate travel time curves for earthquakes and to clarify the relationships among magnitude, intensity, energy and acceleration of vibrations in the earth. His research began in Germany and continued at the California Institute of Technology, where he held the position of director of the Seismological Laboratory from 1947 to 1958.

Born in Darmstadt, Germany, on June 4, 1889, Gutenberg was the son of Hermann Gutenberg and Pauline Hachenburger Gutenberg. He studied at the Realgymnasium and the Technische Hochschule in Darmstadt, completing course work in physics, chemistry and mathematics. While attending the University of Goettingen, his passion shifted from mathematics and physics to climatology. He also took courses with Emil Wiechert, a learned seismologist who taught Gutenberg practically everything then known in the field of seismology. Gutenberg decided to carry out his doctoral studies in the area of microseisms—weak, recurring vibrations of the earth's crust. He was awarded a doctoral degree in 1911.

From 1911 to 1918, Gutenberg worked as an assistant at the International Seismological Association in Strasbourg, except for a period of army service during World War I. In 1918 he became *Privatdozent* at the University of Frankfurt-am-Main, until he gained a professorship of geophysics in 1926. In that same year, Gutenberg's father died, and he took over the management of the family's soap manufacturing business. In 1930 Gutenberg accepted a position as professor at the California Institute of Technology, which gave him the opportunity to utilize the resources of the Seismological Laboratory of the affiliated Carnegie Institution.

At the time Gutenberg began studying microseisms, the field baffled most seismologists. Through his research, Gutenberg identified numerous sources for these disturbances, and much of his work still stands. His most important research in microseismic disturbances provided important insights into the internal constitution of the earth. Investigations carried out in the 1930s on the travel time of waves enabled him to establish the existence of a solid terrestrial core which propagates waves more slowly than does the more viscous mantle, the region between core and crust containing molten matter. He calculated the core to lie at a depth of 2,900 kilometers, a calculation of such accuracy that it has yet to be improved upon.

Gutenberg employed recently perfected instruments to develop superior methods of epicenter detection and depth determination. In research performed jointly with Charles Richter, Gutenberg enhanced travel time curves for earthquakes, and was able to quantify the relationships between magnitude, intensity, energy and acceleration of compressional waves disturbing the tranquility of the earth's interior. The two scientists also worked together to redetermine the epicenters, or origins, of all major earthquakes, establishing the patterns and geometry of major seismic disturbances. In addition, Gutenberg further developed Richter's magnitude scale, extending it to include deep-focus shocks.

In 1947 Gutenberg was appointed director of the Seismological Laboratory at the Carnegie Institution. Besides carrying out his administrative duties, he also continued his own research in seismology. Studying the variation in the amplitude of waves, Gutenberg found evidence that the earth has more superficial layers, through which waves travel relatively slowly. Further measurements of the focal depth of waves made possible a more precise determination of the location of these layers in the upper mantle, at a depth between one hundred and two hundred kilometers. This low-velocity channel later turned out to play an important role in plate tectonics (the movement of the earth's crust that is responsible for continental drift and causes volcanic activity and earthquakes).

Rather than confining his studies to the field of seismology, Gutenberg also maintained an interest in meteorology, a not uncommon secondary research focus for seismologists. His researches in the structure of the upper atmosphere led him to observe ring zones of silence surrounding profound air blasts. From this data he was able to deduce temperature patterns in the upper atmosphere.

Gutenberg retired from the directorship of the Seismological Laboratory in 1958 and died in Pasadena in 1960. Much of his work on earthquake travel times can be found in his 1939 publication, *Internal Constitution of the Earth*. Gutenberg's landmark work, "On Seismic Waves," published in four parts in the 1930s, elucidates his studies of the various phases of earthquake arrivals.

BIOGRAPHICAL/CRITICAL SOURCES:

PERIODICALS

Quarterly Journal of the Royal Astronomical Society, vol. 1, 1960, pp. 239-42.*

H-J

HAECKEL, Ernst Heinrich (Philipp August) 1834-1919

PERSONAL: Born February 16, 1834, in Potsdam, Brandenburg, Germany; died August 9, 1919, in Jena, Thuringia, Germany; son of Carl (an administrative advisor for religious and educational affairs in Merseburg, Germany) and Charlotte (Sethe) Haeckel; married Anna Sethe, 1862 (died, 1864); married Agnes Huschke, 1867. *Education:* Attended Dom-gymnasium, Merseburg, 1852; studied medicine at Berlin, Wurzburg, and Vienna; University of Berlin, M.D., 1857; passed state medical examination, 1858. *Avocational interests:* Travel, painting, botany.

CAREER: German biologist and author. Practiced medicine for one year. University of Jena, Jena, Germany, Faculty of Medicine, lecturer in comparative anatomy, 1861-62, Faculty of Philosophy, associate professor of zoology, 1862-65, full professor and director of Zoological Institute, 1865-1909. Founded Phyletic Museum at Jena; bequeathed Ernst Haeckel Haus, which contains his books, papers, and memorabilia.

MEMBER: Leopoldine Academy, Bavarian Academy of Sciences, Imperial Academy of Sciences (Vienna), Royal Academy of Sciences (Italy), Royal Swedish Academy of Sciences, Royal Lombard Institute of Sciences and Letters, American Philosophical Society, Royal Society of Edinburgh, Royal Academy of Sciences of the Institute at Bologna, more than eighty other learned societies and scientific organizations.

WRITINGS:

Uber die Gewebe des Flusskrebses (doctoral dissertation), [Berlin], 1857.

Die Radiolarien (Rhizopoda radiaria), [Berlin], 1862.

Generelle Morphologie der Organismen, two volumes, G. Reimer (Berlin), 1866, published as *Principien der Generellen Morphologie der Organismen,* 1906.

Naturliche Schopfungs-Geschichte, [Berlin], 1868, as *Naturliche schopfungeschichte. Gemeinverstanliche wissenschaftliche vortrage uber die entwickelungslehre im allgeimeinen und diejenige von Darwin, Goethe, und Lamarck im besonderen,* G. Reimer, 1874, translation revised by E. Ray Lankester as *The History of Creation: or, The Development of the Earth and its Inhabitants by the Action of Natural Causes: A Popular Exposition of the Doctrine of Evolution in General, and of that of Darwin, Goethe and Lamarck in Particular,* H. S. King & Co. (London), 1876.

Zur entwicklungsgeschichte der siphonoren, C. van der Post Jr. (Utrecht, Netherlands), 1869.

Anthropogenie: oder, Entwickelungsgeschichte des Menschen. Keimes-und Stammes-Geschichte, W. Engelmann (Leipzig), 1874, translated as *The Evolution of Man: A Popular Exposition of the Principal Points of Human Ontogeny and Phylogeny,* D. Appleton (New York City), 1878.

Das protistenreich. Eine populare uebesicht uber das formengebiet der niedersten lebewesen, E. Gunther (Leipzig), 1878.

Freie wissenschaft und freue lehre, E. Schweizerbart (Stuttgart), 1878, translated as *Freedom in Science and Teaching,* D. Appleton, 1879.

Das System der Medusen, G. Fischer (Jena), 1879.

Indische Reisebriefe (travel), [Jena], 1883, Gebruder Paetel (Berlin), 1893, translated by Clara Bell as *A Visit to Ceylon,* Kegan Paul (London), 1883, translated by S. E. Boggs as *India and Ceylon,* J. W. Lovell (New York City), 1883.

Plankton-studien. Verleichende untersuchungen uber die bedeutung und zusammensetzung der pelagischen fauna und flora, G. Fischer, 1890, translated by George Wilton Field as *Planktonic Studies: A Comparative Investigation of the Importance and Constitution of the Pelagic Fauna and Flora,* Government Printing Office (Washington, DC), 1893.

Der monismus als band zwischen religion und wissenschaft, E. Strauss (Bonn), 1893, translated by J. Gilchrist as *Monism as Connecting Religion and Science: The Confession of Faith of a Man of Science,* A. & C. Black (London), 1895, as *The Confession of Faith of a Man of Science,* 1903.

Systematische Phylogenie, Entwurf eines naturlichen Systems der Organismen auf Grund ihrer Stammesgeschichte, three volumes, [Berlin], 1894-96.

Die amphorideen und cystoideen; beitrage zur morphologie und phylogenie der echinodermen, W. Engelmann (Leipzig), 1896.

On Our Present Knowledge of the Origin of Man, Smithsonian Institution (Washington, DC), 1898, revised as *The Last Link: Our Present Knowledge of the Descent of Man,* with notes, biographical sketches, and glossary by Hans Gadow, A. & C. Black (London), 1899.

Die Weltrathsel. Gemeinverstandliche Studien uber monistiche Philosophie, E. Strauss (Bonn), 1899, translated by Joseph McCabe as *The Riddle of the Universe: At The Close of the Nineteenth Century,* Harper & Brothers, 1900.

Aus Insulinde; mayalische reisebriefe (travel), E. Strauss, 1901.

Kunstformen der Natur (watercolor plates with text), Verlag der Bibliographischen Instituts (Leipzig and Vienna), 1899-1904, translated as *Art Forms in Nature* (with captions replacing original text), Dover Publications (New York City), 1974.

Lebenswunder (supplementary volume to *Die Weltrathsel*), translated by Joseph McCabe as *The Wonders of Life: A Popular Study of Biological Philosophy,* Harper & Brothers, 1905.

Last Words on Evolution: A Popular Retrospect and Summary, translated by Joseph McCabe, A. Owen & Co. (London), 1906.

The Answer of Ernst Haeckel to the Falsehoods of the Jesuits, Catholic and Protestant, from the German Pamphlet "Sandolion," and "My Church Departure"; Being Haeckel's Reasons, as Stated by Himself, for his Late Withdrawal from the Free Evangelical Church, with Comments by Joseph McCabe and Thaddeus Burr Wakeman, The Truth-Seeker Co. (New York City), 1911.

Englands blutsculd am weltkriege, O. Kayser (Eisenach, Germany), 1914.

Funfzig Jahre Stammesgeschichte. Historische-kritische Studien uber die Resultate der Phylogenie, [Jena], 1916.

Eternity: World-War Thoughts on Life and Death, Religion, and the Theory of Evolution, translated by Thomas Seltzer, The Truth-Seeker Co., 1916.

Kristallseelen, Studien uber das anorganische Leben, [Leipzig], 1917.

(Contributor) *Evolution in Modern Thought* (contains "Charles Darwin as an Anthropologist"), Boni & Liveright (New York City), 1917.

The Story of the Development of a Youth: Letters to His Parents, 1852-1856, translated by G. Barry Gifford, Harper & Brothers, 1923.

Gemeinverstandliche werke. herausgegeben von Heinrich Schmidt-Jena (collected works), edited by Heinrich Schmidt, A. Kroner (Leipzig), 1924.

Franziska von Altenhausen, ein roman aus den leben eines beruhnten mannes in briefen aus den jahren 1898-1903; aus einem echten briefwechsel gestaltet von Johannes Werner, Koehler & Amelang (Leipzig), 1927, translated by Ida Zeitlin as *The Love Letters of Ernst Haeckel, Written between 1898 and 1903, Arranged from the Correspondence by Johannes Werner,* Harper & Brothers, 1930.

Der gerechtfertigte Haeckel. Einblicke in seine Schriften aus Anlass des Erscheinens seines Hauptwerkes "Generelle Morphologie der Organismen" vor 100 Jahren (anthology on the 100th anniversary of publication of *Generelle Morphologie der Organismen*), edited and with an introduction by Heinrich Schmidt, G. Fischer (Stuttgart, Germany), 1968.

OTHER

Contributor to periodicals, including *Jenaische Zeitschrift fur Naturwissenschaft* and *Monist.*

SIDELIGHTS: The nineteenth-century German biologist Ernst Haeckel was a strong supporter of British naturalist Charles Darwin's views and a major contributor to the Darwinian generation's theorizing about evolution. Although his specific answers to evolutionary questions have not, on the whole, held up to later research, they had enormous influence in their time; Haeckel remains respected as one who asked provocative questions and who championed evolutionism in an embattled era. His views find resonance today among those who attempt to connect scientific and philosophical or religious thought.

Anyone who has ever used the word "ecology" owes a debt to Haeckel, for he was the one who coined the word. First using it in 1869, he defined ecology as "the body of knowledge concerning the economy of nature—the investigation of the total relationship of the animal both to its organic and inorganic environment." Thus, Haeckel helped lay the groundwork for a science which did not even exist in his day. A less widely known, but also still valid, concept which Haeckel invented was that of chorology, or, in his words, "the entire science of the spatial distribution of organisms, that is, of their geographical and topographical extension over the earth's surface."

More famous, during Haeckel's lifetime and for decades afterward, was his theory that "ontogeny recapitulates phylogeny." This "recapitulation theory" or "biogenetic law," as it was sometimes called, posits a parallel between the development of the individual embryo and the evolutionary history of its species. Haeckel, who was influenced in this matter by fellow German scientist Karl von Beer, believed that the embryo grows through stages that resemble its species' ancestors. Anyone who has ever looked at pictures of a human embryo's development and discerned fishlike or amphibian-like structures in its early weeks, can be intrigued by this theory—but it is not valid except, in the words of a contributor to the *Biographical Dictionary of Psychology,* for "certain aspects of morphology." As part of Haeckel's pursuit of the recapitulation theory, however, he made drawings of the evolutionary family trees of animal species; he was the first scientist to do so. The practice remains widespread in textbooks today, and according to an *Environmental Encyclopedia* contributor, some of Haeckel's own drawings are still used in textbooks.

Another intellectual result of Haeckel's recapitulation theory was the cultural recapitulation theory of psychologist G. Stanley Hall, in which individual cultures were believed to repeat a worldwide pattern of cultural evolution. Hall's theory remains an unproven hypothesis.

By temperament, Haeckel was a unifier: he sought to regularize the world by providing single explanations for the varied aspects of life. His philosophy was monism, the belief that the world is a unified whole, and he contributed several articles to the *Monist,* a prominent journal of thought expressing the ideas of that school. One example of Haeckel's unifying tendency was his view that human evolution can be analyzed in the same way as animal evolution, a view which the vast majority of scientists today would sup-

port. For example, Haeckel believed that the most important advance in early human evolution was the development of the larynx, allowing the production of speech.

Haeckel attempted to regularize evolutionary theory by setting forth a series of "laws" of heredity—laws that have not held up to scrutiny, and which were not based on experimentation as Gregor Mendel's laws of heredity were. Haeckel distinguished between what he called "conservative" heredity—i. e., genetic inheritance—and "progressive" heredity—i.e., the inheritance of acquired characteristics. Both types of heredity interacted to produce evolution, he thought. The idea of the inheritance of acquired characteristics, first popularized by the French biologist Jean Lamarck in the early 1800s, was widespread in its time and still has a hold on the popular imagination, but is viewed by almost all scientists as a misconception.

In his effort to unify the laws of nature, Haeckel applied Darwin's ideas of natural selection to the very first organisms arising from lifeless organic molecules. Darwin himself had not applied natural selection to such primitive life-forms, but Haeckel saw a continuum from inorganic matter to complex organic molecules to living things. Indeed, he believed that even lifeless matter is "ensouled"; his monism verged on being a kind of pantheism or monotheism, in which God is manifest in natural law and present in all of nature. He discussed this concept in his first major work, the *Generelle Morphologie der Organismen* (1866), and continued to develop it throughout his life; it provides the major thesis of his final book, 1917's *Kristallseelen.* His three ideals, Haeckel wrote, were "the True, the Good, and the Beautiful."

On the taxonomic level—the level of classification of living species—Haeckel's attempt at unifying nature produced long-lived fruit. He developed the idea of the phylum, the evolutionary group that is one step less inclusive than the kingdom. He defined the phylum as "the totality of all the organisms existing at present, or that are extinct, that are descended from one and the same common progenitor." The term "phylum" is now standard. More speculatively, Haeckel thought that the earliest forms of life were lumps of undifferentiated plasma: he called such a lump a Moner, and thought that one or more Moners may have given rise to the first life-forms. He also hypothesized the prehistoric existence of something he called a *Gastrea,* a two-layered creature that was ancestral to all later organisms. George Uschmann, writing in the *Dictionary of Scientific Biography,* says that while Haeckel's assumptions in the Gastrea theory were false, Haeckel undertook "a problem that has since been the subject of an extensive literature." Additionally, Haeckel was the first scientist to distinguish one-celled organisms (protozoa) from many-celled (metazoa). This distinction, of course, has endured.

Haeckel's blending of scientific and philosophical inclinations can be seen in his early life as well as in his later intellectual development. His father, Carl Haeckel, was an official in the religious administration of his town of Merseburg, in Germany. Haeckel was a nature lover from an early age; he kept a herbarium as a schoolboy, and noticed that the plants in his herbarium varied more than he had been taught at school. (His several herbaria, which are still consulted by scientists, are maintained in the Ernst Haeckel Haus in Jena and in the herbarium of Freidrich Schiller University in that city.) He loved to draw and paint—activities which he later joined to his work in classifying natural species—and was an avid youthful collector and classifier of plants.

Although Haeckel's early ambition was to study pure science and to participate in botanical expeditions such as those he read about in the works of Darwin, Alexander von Humboldt, and others, his parents influenced him to enter medical school. After resisting for a while, he turned parental pressure to his own advantage when he realized that medical training would provide him a foundation for scientific research. At the university in Berlin, he came under the influence of the marine zoologist Johannes Muller; at Wurzberg, where he also studied, he encountered the views of materialistic scientists. It was in testing his own Christian upbringing against materialism that Haeckel would arrive at the monist compromise which remained his lifelong philosophy.

After completing his doctoral work, and in the aftermath of the death of his mentor Muller, the young scientist found shelter under the wing of the anatomist Karl Gegenbauer, who encouraged Haeckel in making an 1859 to 1860 expedition to the Mediterranean to study *radiolaria,* a form of invertebrate marine life. Haeckel discovered one hundred forty-four new radiolarian species and wrote a monograph, *Die Radiolarien* (1862), in which he first discussed his evolutionist views, having read Darwin's *Origin of Species* in German in 1859. Then, in 1866, in *Generelle Morphologie der Organismen,* Haeckel made a much more ambitious attempt to apply Darwinist thought to life as a whole. Haeckel's contribution to the debate on evolution which raged at that time was in the area

of morphology, or the forms which organisms take. His later work continued to refine and fill out the theories he developed in the *Generelle Morphologie.*

As a zoologist of marine invertebrates, Haeckel described more than four thousand new species and helped establish that now-thriving discipline. His theorizing on the evolution of vertebrate species, including humankind, was controversial among scientists in his own day and has not been generally accepted; but his popularizations, including essays, lectures, and books, were well-received by the public.

In 1899 his book *Die Weltrathsel,* known in English as *The Riddle of the Universe: At The Close of the Nineteenth Century,* explained Haeckel's beliefs in their most unified form for the general audience. The book was a major success with readers at the time and was widely translated during the early years of the twentieth century. In this and in other popularizations, he earned antagonism both from religious believers and from scientists, since he attacked church dogmas but attempted to replace them with a scientific philosophy that was, in Uschmann's words, "insecurely grounded." Uschmann feels that Haeckel's attempt at purveying a science-based monist spiritualism answered a need of his era, when evolutionism was making major inroads against traditional religious views. Many people a century later feel that the same need persists, and that Haeckel's example, therefore, if not his specific theories, has something to teach us.

In his private life, Haeckel lived fully. He married his cousin, Anna Sethe, in 1862; Anna died in 1864. In 1867 Haeckel married Agnes Huschke, whose father was the anatomist Emil Huschke. Haeckel, a strong, athletic man, loved swimming and hiking, though arthritis limited his activity at times. He traveled widely and drew and painted what he saw; his books on his journeys to India and Ceylon (now Sri Lanka) were published and translated, as were his love letters to a woman to whom he gave a fictional name. In these things, as well as in his scientific work, he exemplified an era whose thought could be profoundly speculative and whose energy of output was remarkable.

BIOGRAPHICAL/CRITICAL SOURCES:

BOOKS

Environmental Encyclopedia, Gale (Detroit), 1994, pp. 399-400.
Dictionary of Scientific Biography, edited by Charles Coulson Gillispie, Scribner's, 1970-76, pp. 6-11.

World of Scientific Discovery: Scientific Milestones and the People Who Made Them, Gale, 1994.

Zusne, Leonard, *Biographical Dictionary of Psychology,* Greenwood Press (Westport, CT), 1984.*

* * *

HALPERIN, James L(ewis) 1952-

PERSONAL: Born October 31, 1952, in Boston, MA; son of Edward B. and Audrey B. Halperin; married Gayle Zaks (a professor of dance), August 5, 1984; children: David, Michael. *Education:* Attended Harvard University. *Politics:* Independent. *Religion:* "Jewish/agnostic." *Avocational interests:* Collecting art by Maxfield Parrish and Harriet Frishmuth, *Mad* magazine memorabilia, EC comic books, investing.

ADDRESSES: Office—Heritage Rare Coin Galleries, 100 Highland Park Village, Dallas, TX 75205; fax 214-520-7108. *E-mail*—jim@heritagecoin.com. *Agent*—Joel Gotler, Renaissance, 8523 Sunset Blvd., Los Angeles, CA 90069.

CAREER: Heritage Rare Coin Galleries, Dallas, TX, co-chairperson, 1982—.

WRITINGS:

How to Grade U.S. Coins, Ivy Press, 1990.
The Truth Machine (novel), Ballantine/Del Rey (New York City), 1996.
The First Immortal (novel), Ballantine/Del Rey, 1997.

WORK IN PROGRESS: Beginner's Luck (Anfaengerglueck), an alternative history, expected in 1998; two novels, *Said the Walrus* and *Spontaneous Combustion.*

SIDELIGHTS: James L. Halperin told *CA:* "I want to write novels that impel readers to think about ideas and issues they have never thought about before. I guess this must be the result of some long-forgotten childhood trauma, don't you think?"

* * *

HANFF, Helene 1916-1997

OBITUARY NOTICE—See index for *CA* sketch: Born April 15, 1916, in Philadelphia, PA; died of pneumonia, April 9, 1997, in New York, NY. Screenwriter and author. Hanff dedicated her entire career to writing, first as a manuscript reader for Paramount Pictures and later as a television scriptwriter for Columbia Broadcasting System (CBS) and National Broadcasting Company (NBC). While she also established herself as a prolific author of children's books, she gained critical and popular acclaim with her 1970 work, *84, Charing Cross Road.* The book originated as a series of letters that Hanff exchanged with an antiquarian bookseller's chief buyer, Frank Doel, and other staff in London. In an effort to further educate herself by reading classic literature, Hanff ordered books from the store, located on Charing Cross Road, and often wrote of her opinions to Doel. She exchanged witty letters with Doel and the staff, and she also sent some goods to them during wartime rationing overseas. The correspondence continued for some twenty years until Doel's death. The book *84, Charing Cross Road* was later adapted for film, television, and the stage. Hanff ultimately visited the shop herself upon learning of Doel's passing. Her travels were the basis for her later book *The Duchess of Bloomsbury Street.*

Hanff initially began pursuing a career in writing in 1938 after winning a Bureau of New Plays fellowship. Later, she gained experience by working with the Theater Guild. She wrote numerous plays, which were never produced, and later described this early part of her career in *Underfoot in Show Business.* Her television work, which flourished in the 1950s, included writing for *Hallmark Hall of Fame* and *The Adventures of Ellery Queen.* From 1978 to 1985 she provided monthly radio broadcasts for the British Broadcasting Corporation's *Woman's Hour.* Her 1992 book, *Letter from New York,* contained excerpts from those broadcasts. Among her other books were history texts for young readers such as *The Day the Constitution Was Signed* and *The Movers and Shakers.*

OBITUARIES AND OTHER SOURCES:

BOOKS

Who's Who, St. Martin's Press, 1997.

PERIODICALS

Los Angeles Times, April 13, 1997, p. B3.
New York Times, April 11, 1997, p. B12.
Times (London), April 11, 1997.
Washington Post, April 13, 1997, p. B6.

HARBOTTLE, Michael (Neale) 1917-1997

OBITUARY NOTICE—See index for *CA* sketch: Born February 7, 1917, in Littlehampton, England; died April 30, 1997. Soldier and writer. Harbottle gained prominence as the British Brigadier General who founded the Centre for International Peacebuilding and Generals (Retd) for Peace and Disarmament. He began his thirty-year military career in 1937 with the British Army, Oxfordshire and Buckingham Light Infantry, serving in Italy during World War II. Throughout his military career, he commanded the 1st Battalion Royal Green Jackets and commanded the garrison at Aden before taking his last assignment in Cyprus as Chief of Staff of the United Nations Peacekeeping Force. When he retired in 1968, he had risen to the rank of Brigadier General and had received the Order of the British Empire. After a short stint as chief of security for the British-owned Sierra Leone Selection Trust Ltd., a diamond mining company, Harbottle became a visiting lecturer for several universities speaking on his involvement with peacekeeping operations and the need for peace and disarmament. He authored several books, including *The Impartial Soldier, The Knaves of Diamonds,* and *The Blue Berets.* He also collaborated on *The Thin-Blue Line: International Peacekeeping and Its Future, New Roles for the Military, Reflections on Security in the Nuclear Age,* and *Peacekeeper's Handbook.*

OBITUARIES AND OTHER SOURCES:

BOOKS

Who's Who, 149th edition, St. Martin's, 1997.

PERIODICALS

Times (London), May 7, 1997.

* * *

HARDING, Mildred Davis 1916-

PERSONAL: Born October 2, 1916, in Jacksonville, FL; daughter of Richard Brayton (in wholesale grocery) and Maude (a homemaker; maiden name, Davis) Davis; married John Boman Adams (a professor of anthropology), 1939 (divorced 1963); married Robert Douglas Harding (a yacht captain), 1973 (divorced 1991); married Robert V. Frey (in insurance and investments), 1991; children: Branwen Adams

Denton, John Brayton Adams. *Ethnicity:* "White." *Education:* Agnes Scott College, Decatur, GA, B.A. (Latin), 1938; Columbia University, M.A. (English and comparative literature), 1939, Ph.D. (English and comparative literature), 1960; attended University of Chicago, post-Master's studies in English, 1940-42. *Politics:* "Critical Democrat." *Religion:* "Esoteric Anglican Christian." *Avocational interests:* "Music, psychology, philosophy, comparative religion, history, living abroad (especially Wales), looking at what's left of 'nature.'"

ADDRESSES: Home—6075 Shore Blvd., Apt. 501 (Town Shores), Gulfport, FL 33707.

CAREER: Writer and teacher of English. Fishweir Elementary School, Jacksonville, FL, cadet teacher, 1933-34; New Jersey College for Women (now Douglass College), New Brunswick, NJ, English instructor, 1943-44; Stephens College, Columbia, MO, literature teacher, 1945-46; Washington University, St. Louis, MO, English instructor, 1946-47; Shurtleff College, Alton, IL, assistant professor of English, 1947-49; Stetson University, Deland, FL, English instructor, 1950-51; American University at Cairo, Egypt, assistant professor of English, 1952-54; Queen Aliya College, Baghdad, Iraq, assistant professor of English, 1955-56; Beirut College for Women, Lebanon, assistant professor of English, 1956-57; American University of Beirut, Lebanon, assistant professor of English, 1956-61; Shimer College, Mt. Carroll, IL, literature teacher, 1961-62; University of South Florida, Tampa, FL, assistant professor of English, 1962-67; University of Maryland abroad at Wurzburg, Germany, assistant professor of English, 1966; Keene State College, Keene, NH, associate professor of English, 1967-73; International Academy, Rhodes, Greece, humanities teacher, 1969; College of Boca Raton, FL, associate professor of English and philosophy, 1974-76; Florida Junior College, Jacksonville, FL, adjunct teacher of English, 1976-80; Phelps-Stokes Program for African Refugees, Pottstown, PA, teacher of English as a second language, 1980; Lutheran Refugee Services, teacher and program coordinator of English as a second language, 1980-82; University of Maryland abroad at Okinawa, Japan, associate professor of English, 1984-85. Has worked as a free-lance editor, including *Archives* (American Medical Association), 1939-40; assistant book editor, *Coronet* (magazine), 1943; and University of Pennsylvania Press, 1989-92.

MEMBER: Phi Betta Kappa, Eta Sigma Phi.

AWARDS, HONORS: Mortar Board and Quennelle-Harold fellowship, Agnes Scott College; three fellowships from Columbia University.

WRITINGS:

Air-Bird in the Water: The Life and Works of Pearl Craigie (John Oliver Hobbes), Fairleigh Dickinson University Press (Cranbury, NJ), 1996.

Contributor to periodicals, including *Agnes Scott Alumnae Quarterly, Yale Literary Magazine, South Asian Review, Chronicles,* and *Turn-of-the-Century Women.*

WORK IN PROGRESS: "New article on Pearl Craigie for Oxford University Press's *New (Revised) Dictionary of National Biography;* further research on Pearl Craigie."

SIDELIGHTS: Harding told *CA:* "I began writing for publication late in life, after about forty years of college teaching in English, comparative literature, and the humanities. For better or worse, my mind was steeped in the great literary works of Western civilization from Homer to the present, and my values and tastes were permanently formed by them. Amidst the dizzying cultural changes of these last decades, I have remained a Christian humanist, a romanticist *and* a classicist, and so (some would say) an elitist.

"Naturally, then, I grieve for the deterioration in our culture ('the revolt of the masses' in language, education, publishing, popular entertainment, manners, morality, etc.) and especially for the contribution that many writers and other artists have made to that deterioration through their capitulation to the tyranny of the majority and the power of 'big bucks.' I look for and delight in 'the saving remnant.'

"When I finally began to write for publication it was not for money. It was because I was stirred to speak out from personal experience against certain important misconceptions. 'My Black Mountain,' a memoir, was evoked by popular adulation of Black Mountain College; 'Waking Up in Egypt' (still unpublished), by the widespread ignorance of Americans about the Middle East. Next, feeling that two topics in my doctoral dissertation on George Moore—his debt to Schopenhauer, and the author Pearl Craigie, with whom Moore had been in love—deserved better treatment than I had given them, I wrote a long article on the first and two articles on the second. Convinced by then that my attempt to rescue Craigie/Hobbes

from near oblivion required a comprehensive book, I wrote *Air-Bird in the Water: The Life and Works of Pearl Craigie (John Oliver Hobbes)*—an eight years' labor of love.

"Favorable response to that book has led me to further work (now in progress) on Craigie/Hobbes: an essay for Oxford University Press's *New Dictionary of National Biography,* and research in two sources of information, in England, that were not available to me when I wrote the book.

"What next? Publication of an almost completed double autobiography, tentatively entitled *Love, Mildred*: Lloyd Houser's memoirs woven around my letters to him. Probably also short stories, memoirs, and essays.

"My advice to aspiring writers? Don't be obsessed by 'the Market'! *Feed* on excellent writings; analyze the technique that makes them good. Live intensely; be (as Henry James put it) 'one upon whom nothing is wasted.' Trust *your* vision, write from your heart, rewrite with your head."

BIOGRAPHICAL/CRITICAL SOURCES:

PERIODICALS

Choice, December, 1996, p. 613.
Nineteenth-Century Literature, March, 1997, p. 558.

*   *   *

HARSHAV, Barbara 1940-

PERSONAL: Born in 1940.

ADDRESSES: Agent—c/o HarperCollins, 1000 Keystone Industrial Park, Scranton, PA 18512.

CAREER: Translator and editor.

WRITINGS:

TRANSLATOR

(With Benjamin Harshav, Kathryn Hellerstein, Brian McHale, and Anita Norich; and editor with Harshav) *American Yiddish Poetry: A Bilingual Anthology,* University of California Press (Berkeley, CA), 1986.

Avigdor Dagan, *The Court Jesters* (novel), Jewish Publication Society (Philadelphia, PA), 1989.

(With Harshav) Yehuda Amichai, *Even a Fist Was Once an Open Palm with Fingers: Recent Poems,* HarperPerennial (New York), 1991.

(With Harshav) Abraham Sutzkever, *A. Sutzkever: Selected Poetry and Prose,* University of California Press, 1991.

Yehudit Katzir, *Closing the Sea* (short stories), Helen and Kurt Wolff/Harcourt (New York), 1992.

(And editor) Yitzhak Zuckerman ("Antek"), *A Surplus of Memory: Chronicle of the Warsaw Ghetto Uprising,* University of California Press, 1993.

(With Harshav) Yehuda Amichai, *Yehuda Amichai: A Life of Poetry, 1948-1994,* HarperCollins (New York), 1994.

(And editor) Simha Rotem ("Kazik"), *Memoirs of a Warsaw Ghetto Fighter: The Past within Me,* Yale University Press (New Haven, CT), 1994.

Meir Shalev, *Esau: A Novel,* HarperCollins, 1994.

Lucjan Dobroszycki, *Reptile Journalism: The Official Polish-Language Press under the Nazis,* Yale University Press, 1995.

Israel Zamir, *Journey to My Father, Isaac Bashevis Singer* (memoir), Arcade (New York), 1995.

SIDELIGHTS: Barbara Harshav is a prominent translator who has won acclaim for her English-language renderings of various Yiddish and Hebrew texts. Her first work, *American Yiddish Poetry: A Bilingual Anthology,* is a collaborative effort that was published in 1986. Three years later she solely translated *The Court Jesters,* Czech-Israeli diplomat and writer Avigdor Dagan's novel about four Jewish prisoners who survive a Nazi concentration camp by serving as entertainers for the sadistic camp commander. Reviewing the work in the *New York Times Book Review,* Avery Rome remarked that this modern fairy tale that explores profound questions arising from the Holocaust was "translated with sensitivity."

In 1991 Harshav again collaborated on translations, this time on *A. Sutzkever: Selected Poetry and Prose* and Yehuda Amichai's *Even a Fist Was Once an Open Palm with Fingers: Recent Poems.* The following year *Closing the Sea,* a debut collection of four novellas by Israeli writer Yehudit Katzir, was published. Writing in the *New York Times Book Review,* Cathy A. Colman praised Harshav for her "flawless translation" of Katzir's work, whose stories offer commentary on contemporary Israeli society.

Among Harshav's more widely known achievements is the editing and translation of Yitzhak Zuckerman's

A Surplus of Memory: Chronicle of the Warsaw Ghetto Uprising, a memoir by one of the few surviving fighters among the Warsaw Jews who rebelled, with disastrous consequences, against the Nazis in 1943. In addition to recounting the uprising, Zuckerman's volume records his endeavors on behalf of other survivors.

Irving Howe, writing in *New Republic,* proclaimed that *A Surplus of Memory* "can stand together with [Nadezhda Mandelstam's] *Hope Against Hope* as revelations of what it meant to live and to die in the totalitarian age" and called attention to Harshav's accomplishment of "superbly" translating and editing the work, as she "provides almost all the auxiliary information a reader might need."

Harshav followed *A Surplus of Memory* with a translation of *Esau: A Novel,* Meir Shalev's wide-ranging saga of sibling rivalry and deception set in modern-day Prague, Israel, and the United States. In 1994 Harshav also collaborated on the translation and editing of *Yehuda Amichai: A Life of Poetry, 1948-1994* and served in the same capacities for Simha Rotem's *Memoirs of a Warsaw Ghetto Fighter: The Past within Me.* Rotem was among the Warsaw Jews who managed to evade the Nazis by fleeing through the sewers and finding safety in the houses of sympathizers and in the countryside. In 1995 Harshav translated another work about the plight of Poles during World War II, Lucjan Dobroszycki's *Reptile Journalism: The Official Polish-Language Press under the Nazis.*

Harshav is also the translator of *Journey to My Father, Isaac Bashevis Singer.* This memoir recalls Israel Zamir's search for his father, Nobel Prize-winning writer Isaac Bashevis Singer. Singer abandoned Zamir and his mother in the mid-1930s, immigrated to the United States, and eventually remarried. Singer and Zamir did not meet again until the mid-1950s. Zamir documents the father-son relationship in *Journey to My Father,* described as a "bittersweet memoir" by Roger Kamenetz in the *New York Times Book Review.*

BIOGRAPHICAL/CRITICAL SOURCES:

PERIODICALS

New Republic, May 3, 1993, pp. 29-36.
New York Times Book Review, November 12, 1989, p. 55; May 17, 1992, p. 35; December 10, 1995, p. 35.*

HART, W. D. 1943-

PERSONAL: Born February 18, 1943, in Ithaca, NY; son of W. D. (an engineer) and Ruth H. Hart; married Faith Brabenec, July 20, 1974; children: Luke. *Ethnicity:* "White." *Education:* Harvard University, B.A. (summa cum laude), 1964, Ph.D., 1969.

CAREER: Writer.

WRITINGS:

The Engines of the Soul, Cambridge University Press (Cambridge, England), 1988.
(Editor and contributor) *The Philosophy of Mathematics,* Oxford University Press (Oxford, England), 1996.

* * *

HARTER, H(arman) Leon 1919-

PERSONAL: Born August 15, 1919, in Keokuk, IA; son of Harman T. (a farmer) and Mary Josie (Hough) Harter; married Alice Lauretta Madden, October 23, 1943. *Ethnicity:* "German, Scotch-Irish, English." *Education:* Carthage College, A.B. (mathematics), 1940; University of Illinois at Urbana-Champaign, A.M. (mathematics), 1941; Purdue University, Ph.D. (mathematical statistics), 1949. *Politics:* Democrat. *Religion:* Christian (Disciples of Christ). *Avocational interests:* Reading, church work, sports (baseball fan).

ADDRESSES: Home—203 North McKinley Ave., Champaign, IL 61821-3251.

CAREER: Missouri Valley College, Marshall, professor of physics, 1943-44; Purdue University, West Lafayette, IN, instructor in mathematics, 1946-48; Michigan State College (now University), East Lansing, assistant professor of mathematics, 1949-52; Aerospace Research Laboratories, Wright-Patterson Air Force Base, civilian mathematical statistician, 1952-64, senior scientist, 1964-75; Air Force Flight Dynamics Laboratory, civilian mathematician, 1976-78; Wright State University, Dayton, OH, research professor of mathematics and statistics, 1979-84; self-employed consultant and writer, 1984—. Air Force Institute of Technology, Wright-Paterson Air Force Base, distinguished visiting professor, 1982-84. *Military service:* U.S. Navy, radio technician, 1944-46.

MEMBER: International Statistical Institute, Institute of Mathematical Statistics (fellow), American Statistical Association (fellow; chairperson, 1964; member of council, 1963-64, 1972-79), Society for Industrial and Applied Mathematics (president of Dayton section, 1959-60), National Association of Retired Federal Employees (legislative officer).

WRITINGS:

New Tables of the Incomplete Gamma-Function Ratio and of Percentage Points of the Chi-Square and Beta Distributions, U.S. Government Printing Office (Washington, DC), 1964.
(With F. N. David, D. E. Barton, and others) *Normal Centroids, Medians, and Scores for Ordinal Data,* Cambridge University Press (London, England), 1968.
Order Statistics and Their Use in Testing and Estimation, Volume 1: *Tests Based on Range and Studentized Range of Samples from a Normal Population,* Volume 2: *Estimates Based on Order Statistics of Samples from Various Populations,* U.S. Government Printing Office, 1970.
(Editor with D. B. Owen) *Selected Tables in Mathematical Statistics,* Volume 1, Markham (Chicago, IL), 1970, Volume 2, American Mathematical Society (Providence, RI), 1974, Volume 3, American Mathematical Society, 1975.
The Chronological Annotated Bibliography of Order Statistics, Volume 1: *Pre-1950,* U.S. Government Printing Office, 1978, revised edition, American Sciences Press (Columbus, OH), 1983, Volume 2: *1950-1959,* American Sciences Press, 1983, Volume 3: *1960-1961* and Volume 4: *1962-1963,* both American Sciences Press, 1991, Volume 5: *1964-1965,* Volume 6: *1966-1967,* and Volume 7: *1968-1969,* all American Sciences Press, 1992, Volume 8: *Indices, with a Supplement on 1970-1972* (supplement by N. Balakrishnan), American Sciences Press, 1993.
(With Balakrishnan) *The CRC Handbook of Tables for the Use of Order Statistics in Estimation,* CRC Press (Boca Raton, FL), 1996.
(With Balakrishnan) *The CRC Handbook of Tables for the Use of Range,* CRC Press, 1997.

Contributor to books. Contributor of more than sixty articles to journals.

SIDELIGHTS: H. Leon Harter told *CA:* "At the Aerospace Research Laboratories at Wright-Patterson Air Force Base, in the 1950s and 1960s, my mentors Paul R. Rider and Gertrude Blanch aroused and stimulated my interest in order statistics and in numerical analysis and computation. I was also greatly influenced by the pioneering work of E. S. Pearson and H. O. Hartley and that of A. E. Sarhan and B. G. Greenberg, as well as that of contemporaries Herbert A. David, John W. Tukey, David B. Duncan, and A. Clifford Cohen. My interest in history and bibliography has been shared with Stephen M. Stigler and Oscar Sheynin. I have also benefited greatly from collaboration with Donald B. Owen, Albert H. Moore, and N. Balakrishnan.

"As early as 1960, I began making preparations to write a book on order statistics. My first book was a by-product of this effort. Continued research during the 1960s, much of it in collaboration with Albert H. Moore, led to expansion to two volumes and then to three. The first two volumes on theory and tables were published in 1970. The proposed third volume (a bibliography) grew to eight volumes, published between 1978 and 1993. Meanwhile, with Donald B. Owen, I edited the first three volumes of *Selected Tables in Mathematical Statistics.*

"My eight-volume bibliography of order statistics is intended to facilitate research by providing a chronological listing of publications on the subject. It includes brief summaries and lists of references and citations to aid in tracing ideas both backward and forward in time.

"Prepared under the auspices of the Institute of Mathematical Statistics, the series of *Selected Tables in Mathematical Statistics,* of which I was a founding co-editor, was designed to provide a vehicle for the publication of useful tables of intermediate length (too long to be accepted by a journal, but too short to be published separately in book form)."

*   *   *

HARTMANN, Sadakichi 1867-1944

(Sadakichi, Sidney Allan, Sydney Allan, Sidney H. Allen, Innocent De La Salle, Klingsor the Magician, A. Chameleon, S. H., pseudonyms)

PERSONAL: Born November 8, 1867, on Deshima island, near Nagasaki, Japan; immigrated to U.S., June, 1882; became U.S. citizen, 1894; died November 21, 1944, in St. Petersburg, FL; son of Carl Herman Oscar Hartmann (a German government

and business official) and Osada; married Elizabeth Blanche Walsh (a nurse and, as Elizabeth Breuil, a screenplay writer), 1891; marriage ended, c. 1910; lived with Lillian Bonham (an artist), 1912-18; children: five by first marriage, seven by second relationship; daughters include Atma and Wistaria. *Education:* Educated by private tutors; attended boarding school in Steinwaerden, Germany; attended naval academy, Kiel, Germany (left school after three months). *Religion:* Baptized, 1871.

CAREER: Art and photography critic, poet, playwright, publisher, painter, and lecturer. Held various jobs: "Active in Philadelphia as spittoon and window cleaner, press feeder, lithographic stippler, clerk in a tombstone factory, perfume peddler, and negative retoucher" (according to Hartmann in *White Chrysanthemums*); secretary to poet Walt Whitman, 1884; freelance writer for Boston and New York newspapers, c. 1880s-90s; apprentice in royal theater, Munich, Germany, 1885; moved to Boston, 1887; traveled in Europe, 1887-88; moved to Greenwich Village, New York City, 1889; moved to Paris, 1890; wintered in Canada, 1892; journalist on special assignment in Paris for McClure Syndicate, 1892; returned to Boston and New York, 1892; publisher, *The Art Critic* (Boston), three issues, November, 1893-March, 1894; popular lecturer on art, from 1895; librarian for McKim, Mead, and White, architects, 1896.

Publisher, *Art News* (New York), four issues, March, 1897-June, 1897; staff writer, *Criterion,* 1898; columnist, *Musical America,* 1898, and *New Yorker Staats-Zeitung,* 1898; staff writer, *Camera Notes,* 1899-1901; writer, *Camera Work,* 1901-04, 1907-08; touring lecturer on photography, 1905-10; Carnegie Institute, assistant to director John Beatty, 1906; publisher, *The Stylus* (New York), three issues, December, 1909-February, 1910; moved to Roycroft Inn, East Aurora, NY, 1911; moved to San Francisco, 1912; moved to North Carolina and New Jersey, 1921-23; moved to Los Angeles and Beaumont, CA, 1923; Hollywood columnist, *The Curtain* (London), c. mid-1920s; moved to shack, Catclaw Siding, on Morongo Indian Reservation in Banning, CA, 1938. Traveled extensively across U.S., c. 1910s-1930s. Appeared in film *The Thief of Baghdad,* 1924, as Court Magician.

WRITINGS:

ON ART

(As Sadakichi) *Conversations with Walt Whitman,* E. P. Colby & Co. (New York), 1895, Gordon Press

(New York), 1972, Folcroft Library Editions (Folcroft, PA), 1973, Haskell House Publishers (New York), 1973, Norwood Editions (Norwood, PA), 1977; included in *The Whitman-Hartmann Controversy,* edited by George Knox and Harry Lawton, with an introduction by Knox, Herbert Lang (Bern), 1976.

Shakespeare in Art, L.C. Page & Co. (Boston), 1901, AMS Press (New York), 1973.

A History of American Art, two volumes, Page, 1902, revised edition, Tudor Publishing (New York), 1934.

(Editor) *Modern American Sculpture,* Paul Wenzel (New York), 1902, Architectural Book (New York), 1914.

Winter, photographs by Rudolf Eickmeyer, Jr., with introduction by Hartmann, R. H. Russell (New York), 1903.

(As Innocent De La Salle) *Japanese Art,* Page, 1904, Horizon Press (New York), 1971, reprinted as *The Illustrated Guidebook of Japanese Painting: From Primitive Art to the 18th Century,* American Classical College Press (Albuquerque, NM), 1978.

(As Sidney Allan) *Composition in Portraiture,* Edward L. Wilson (New York), 1909, Arno Press (New York), c. 1970s.

Landscape and Figure Composition, Baker and Taylor (New York), 1910, later reprinted by Arno Press, c. 1970s.

The Whistler Book: A Monograph of the Life and Position in Art of James McNeill Whistler Together with a Careful Study of His More Important Works, Page, 1910.

A Note on the Portraits of Walt Whitman (pamphlet), At the Sign of the Sparrow (New York City), 1921.

Strands and Ravelings of the Art Fabric (pamphlet), Author's Edition (Hollywood), 1940.

White Chrysanthemums: Literary Fragments and Pronouncements, edited by George Knox and Harry Lawton, Herder and Herder (New York), 1971.

The Valiant Knights of Daguerre: Selected Critical Essays on Photography and Profiles of Photographic Pioneers, edited by Harry Lawton and George Knox, with Wistaria Hartmann Linton; foreword by Thomas F. Barrow; bibliography compiled by Michael Elderman, University of California Press (Berkeley), 1978.

Sadakichi Hartmann: Critical Modernist: Collected Art Writings, edited and with an introduction by Jane Calhoun Weaver, University of California Press, 1991.

PLAYS, POETRY, FICTION, AUTOBIOGRAPHY

Christ: A Dramatic Poem in Three Acts, Boston, 1893, republished in *Buddha, Confucius, Christ: Three Prophetic Plays,* edited by Lawton and Knox, Herder and Herder, 1971.

A Tragedy in a New York Flat: A Dramatic Episode in Two Scenes, [New York], 1896.

Buddha: A Drama in Twelve Scenes, [New York], 1897, republished in *Buddha, Confucius, Christ: Three Prophetic Plays,* 1971.

"Leitmotif," a prose-poem introduction by Hartmann in *Whisperings of a Wind-Harp* by Anne Throop, 1897.

Schopenhauer in the Air: Seven Stories, [New York], 1899, enlarged as *Schopenhauer in the Air: Twelve Stories,* Stylus Publishing (Rochester, NY), 1908.

Drifting Flowers of the Sea and Other Poems to Elizabeth Blanche Walsh, 1904.

My Rubaiyat, Mangan Printing (St. Louis), 1913, revised edition, Bruno Chap Books (San Francisco), 1916.

Tanka and Haiku: Fourteen Japanese Rhythms, Bruno Chap Books (San Francisco), June, 1915, revised edition, 1920, revised again as *Japanese Rhythms,* 1926 and 1933.

The Last Thirty Days of Christ, privately printed (New York), 1920.

Confucius: A Drama in Two Acts, privately printed (Los Angeles), 1923, republished in *Buddha, Con-fucius, Christ: Three Prophetic Plays,* 1971.

Passport to Immortality, Beaumont, CA, 1927.

Seven Short Stories, Cloister Press (Beaumont, CA), 1930.

My Crucifixion: Asthma for Forty Years, Cloister Press of Hollywood (Tujunga, CA), 1931.

Moses: A Drama in Six Episodes, 1934.

Esthetic Verities, an unpublished manuscript, c. 1927-31, is held by the Manuscripts Division, Pennsylvania Historical Society, Philadelphia, PA.

PERIODICAL CONTRIBUTIONS

Frequent contributor to the *Bulletin of Photography* "Modern Portrait" series, March 31, 1915-May 26, 1915, and "Masterpieces of American Portraiture" series (as Sidney Allan), June 2, 1915-August 25, 1915; to *Camera Notes* vols. 2-6, 1898-1902; to *Camera Work* (some as Sidney Allan or as Klingsor the Magician), nos. 1-7, 1903-04, (as unsigned) no. 10, April, 1905, and (some as S. H., A. Chameleon, Klingsor the Magician, or unsigned), nos. 21, 26, and 28-39; to *The Criterion,* December 25, 1897-November 22, 1898; to the *Curtain,* January, 1925-January,

1932; to *The Daily Tatler,* November 18, 1896-November 20, 1896; to the "Studio Talk" column in *International Studio* (as S. H.), vol. 28, 1906-vol. 29, 1907; to *Musical America,* vol. 1, no. 1, October 8, 1898-no. 11, December 17, 1898; to "The Ten Leading Styles of Portraiture" series, and the "Pictorial Aims of Modern Portraiture" series, November, 1913-October, 1914, January, 1918-December, 1918, both in *Portrait*; to *The Theatre,* March 8, 1890-December 5-20, 1890; to the "Masters in Portraiture" series (as Sidney Allan), August, 1909-February, 1913, as well as the articles "Alvin Langdon Coburn—Secessionist Portraiture," vol. 44, no. 606, June, 1907, "The Chances of Moving-Picture Portraiture," vol. 51, no. 9, September, 1914, "Charles Rohlfs: A Worker in Wood," vol. 49, no. 662, February, 1912, "E. S. Curtis, Photo Historian," no. 44, August, 1907, "A Few American Portraits," vol. 49, no. 670, October, 1912, "In the Proletarian Interest: Elias Goldensky," no. 43, December, 1905, "International Exhibition of Pictorial Photography—Albright Art Gallery," no. 48, 1911, "A Painter Photographer—J. H. Garo," no. 43, March, 1906, "Painters and the Public," February, 1907, "The Portrait Print—Its Significance in Interior Decoration," no. 47, December, 1910, "Portraiture at the Buffalo Exhibition," no. 47, December, 1910, and "A Visit to the Chicago Art Institute," no. 48, 1911, all in *Wilson's Photographic Magazine.* Served as publisher for *The Art Critic, Art News,* and *Stylus.* Also contributed to *Smith's Magazine, Leslie's Weekly, Brush and Pencil, Magazine of Art, Photographic Times,* and *The British Art Journal of Photography*

OTHER

Hartmann's Papers are located in the Department of Special Collections at the Rivera Library, University of California, Riverside, and in the Alfred Stieglitz Archive, Collection of American Literature, Beinecke Rare Book and Manuscript Library, Yale University.

SIDELIGHTS: "Artists must not become too respectable," said Sadakichi Hartmann, "because their mission is to teach the play phase of life." The art and photography critic, poet, and playwright lived up to that credo, leading a quintessentially artistic life of bohemian wandering; he has been called, in fact, "The First Hippie" by Richard Hill in an article in *Swank International.* And during his Greenwich Village days, in 1915, he was called "The King of Bohemia," although—and perhaps fittingly—he was not even a fulltime resident of the Village. Hartmann

was the son of a German father living in Japan and a Japanese mother. He was schooled in Germany, where he was sent as an infant with his older brother Taru to live with a rich uncle. (It is not clear whether Hartmann's mother died a few months after his birth, as he claimed, or a few years later.) The uncle, Ernst Hartmann, introduced Sadakichi to the visual arts, a field which would inform his life's work. When Hartmann's father returned to Germany to marry a widow with two daughters, Hartmann was sent to a naval academy, from which he ran away to Paris after only three months. Disinherited by his father, he made the ocean voyage to the United States and landed, with three dollars in his pocket, in June, 1882. He moved in with relatives in Philadelphia, who are described by Jane Calhoun Weaver in *Sadakichi Hartmann: Critical Modernist* as "puritanical"; he moved out the following year and proceeded to support himself by a wide variety of jobs, and to educate himself by reading at the Mercantile Library in Philadelphia. From 1884, with the help of a small allowance from his grandmother, he was able to devote more of his time to his self-education; but money would be a lifelong problem. Hartmann was artistic by temperament, scarred by a peripatetic childhood, plagued by severe asthma, and subject to racial prejudice as a Eurasian in turn-of-the-century America and even afterward.

In 1884, the young Hartmann got up the nerve to visit Walt Whitman, who was living in Camden, New Jersey, across the river from Philadelphia. The childless, unmarried, old poet and the rootless "orphan-immigrant" (in his own words) developed a solid friendship, with Hartmann visiting Whitman often between 1884 and 1891. The friendship was marred by an unsuccessful attempt on Hartmann's part to establish a Walt Whitman Society, and by his 1889 publication, in the *New York Herald,* of a fantasy interview with Whitman in which the poet made unkind remarks about his contemporaries. Whitman was angry but forgiving, remarking, according to memoirist Horace Traubel in *With Walt in Camden,* "He is away from home—helpless—a poor enough creature—yet I have a soft spot for him . . . poor boy!" The relationship was deep enough for the poet to present Hartmann with Whitman's own personal copy of the 1876 edition of *Leaves of Grass*—a copy which Hartmann apparently sold during one of his periods of financial hardship. Another result of the Hartmann-Whitman connection was Hartmann's 1895 book, *Conversations with Walt Whitman,* which has been the subject of scholarly and popular debates outlined in *The Whitman-Hartmann Controversy,* edited by George Knox and Harry Lawton.

Perpetually on the move, Hartmann traveled to Boston and New York in the late 1880s, joining the younger artistic circles in his three years in the latter city. Then he went to France as a foreign correspondent with his wife, Elizabeth Blanche Walsh, a nurse whom he had met in the hospital after an 1891 suicide attempt. Among the artists he met in Paris were James Abbott McNeill Whistler and Claude Monet, as well as a variety of French poets, including the symbolist Stephane Mallarme and his circle. Back in Boston, Hartmann enrolled 750 artists, including some of the most prominent in America, as subscribers to his new venture, a magazine called *Art Critic*. "Although the periodical lasted only three issues," comments Weaver, "the contents present a startling amalgam of fin de siecle commentary and militant American art criticism," aimed at developing a national art. Ironically, Hartmann's budding career as a dramatist threatened his role as publisher: *Art Critic* folded in the bankruptcy following the scandal that erupted upon the introduction of Hartmann's 1893 play, *Christ*. (He was arrested by the Watch and Ward Society of Boston, and spent Christmas in jail.) But after returning to New York, Hartmann picked up his critical career anew, becoming a prolific reviewer and writer of articles for art publications in that city. He founded two more art magazines over the years, *Art News* and *Stylus*, and though each was short-lived, each left its mark in the form of pithy critical articles by Hartmann.

Hartmann was indefatigably social within the art world of turn-of-the-century New York; he frequented cafes and private and public galleries, and was acquainted with eminent artists such as Thomas Eakins and Robert Henri. However, publication was not always easy for him, as can be seen by the fact that many of his critical and creative writings have been gathered by later editors from relatively obscure serial publications. According to Weaver, his style could be at times too erudite, at times too flippant for his American audience; he had difficulty establishing the kind of tone—the just-right level of assumed prior knowledge—which readers wanted. More seriously, Hartmann was neither a skillful businessman nor an untroublesome social presence. "Hartmann's social problems became legendary," writes Weaver, "as did his asocial proclivity to seek financial support from friends, acquaintances, business associates, and artistic colleagues. For that reason, most of his New York peers (Alfred Steiglitz being a notable exception) later came to shun him." Hence, Hartmann was little mentioned in those people's

memoirs, and thus is underrepresented in cultural histories of that era, according to Weaver.

Steiglitz, the influential American photographer and gallery owner who was later to mentor and marry the painter Georgia O'Keeffe, became the most profound artistic presence in Hartmann's life after Whitman. Steiglitz and Hartmann hit it off rather quickly, and established a close friendship that lasted more than thirty years. Both were German immigrants who spoke German fluently; both felt themselves somewhat misunderstood in America; both had reputations for being difficult; both were brilliant and are now considered ahead of their time. Steiglitz was to reminisce that Hartmann—who was better-known that Steiglitz at the time of their first meeting—was his most important artistic influence before 1907, when Steiglitz met Max Weber. Steiglitz, for his part, gave Hartmann a major boost as a photography critic by publishing Hartmann's writing in his magazine *Camera Work*. Hartmann became on the world's first professional critic of photography. Much of Hartmann's work for Steiglitz's magazine was written under the pen name Sidney Allan; during his career he used several other pen names as well, some of them humorous, such as A. Chameleon and Klingsor the Magician. (Weaver speculates that pseudonyms were an aid to productivity—they enabled Hartmann to publish more articles in a given space of time.) His most important contributions to photography journals, according to Weaver, are twenty-two articles appearing between October, 1898, and December, 1902, in *Camera Notes,* and thirty-five essays and poems appearing between January, 1903, and July, 1912, in *Camera Work*. (Hartmann and Steiglitz were estranged for a period between 1906 and 1908, but Hartmann returned to the magazine when the rift healed.)

In these early essays, Hartmann put forward a critical model for the new art form: he warned against retouching, championed the "straight negative," advised photographers to cultivate their knowledge and taste in the arts and to study artistic composition. He also predicted that photography would become a popular illustrational and decorative form. He was instrumental in the fight to obtain for photography the status of an art, worthy of critical consideration and of serious collecting. About 1911, however, Hartmann inexplicably felt that his career as an art critic was waning; he distanced himself from the New York art world in order to concentrate on lecture tours and on travel to the West, particularly to California. Partly in order to assuage his asthma, he moved to Southern California during the 1920s and began a new, equally bohemian round of socializing. First accepted by European emigres, he then gravitated to the wild party sessions of film stars such as John Barrymore and W. C. Fields, who saw him, Weaver reports, as "an aged, alcoholic jester in the ragged intellectual garb of a distant, suspect past." The escapades of this Hollywood coterie are recounted, with variable accuracy, in *Minutes of the Last Meeting,* by Gene Fowler (1954), a book that began as a biography of Hartmann and then expanded to include his wide circle of acquaintances. He continued traveling, often by bus across the U.S., and appeared in a famous silent film, *The Thief of Baghdad,* with Douglas Fairbanks, Sr. (He capitalized on the experience by writing magazine articles about it.) In later years, Hartmann built a one-room shack on the Morongo Indian reservation in the California desert, near the Palm Springs area where his daughter Wistaria lived. Even there, however, he maintained his intellectual and artistic activity, painting with pastels and corresponding with the likes of poet Ezra Pound and philosopher George Santayana. (Pound wrote about Hartmann in Canto 80 of the 1948 *Pisan Cantos* as the leader of a "lost legion" of the unjustly forgotten.) Of his later writings, Weaver singles out a "brilliant" 1930 essay on the Russian film director Sergei Eisenstein; Eisenstein's visit to Hollywood to learn American technique prompted Hartmann to ironically declare the Russian silent cinema to be more powerful than the American, because of the former's adherence to an artistic ideal.

Although Hartmann is "primarily remembered" as a photography critic, asserts Weaver, he was "above all a knowledgeable, perceptive critic of painting and sculpture whose brilliant intuition of an emerging modernism illuminates American art in the decades on either side of 1900." In his columns for periodicals, Hartmann offered insightful, witty commentary on the art of his time; notable was the October 19, 1895 essay in *Musical America* in which he called Thomas Eakins and Winslow Homer America's greatest artists —an opinion unorthodox in its time, but borne out by history. Hartmann put many of his separately published critical pieces together, with some revisions, for his two-volume *A History of American Art,* published in 1902. His creed in these volumes was a "virile" American art, a vigorous realism, much like that propagandized for by Whitman; in addition to Eakins and Homer, Albert Pinkham Ryder exemplified that art for Hartmann. "For a view of Hartmann's own time," states Weaver, "the book is invaluable." In this history and in later writings, such as 1910's *The Whistler Book,* Hartmann expounded on the virtues of "suggestive" or "evocative" art, and

made popular the label "suggestivism" to describe a new American style of painting, influenced somewhat by French Impressionism, somewhat by Japanese art, somewhat by German naturalism, and somewhat by the French Barbizon school, but applied to American subjects and American ideals. "It was not so much things as feelings that they tried to suggest," he clarified in *A History of American Art,* referring to his favorite new American painters.

Hartmann throughout his life was also a prolific writer of plays, poems, and other literary works. His most ambitious venture was a multi-volume series of symbolist plays on the lives of major religious figures; in addition to the three subjects of *Buddha, Confucius, Christ: Three Prophetic Plays,* edited by Harry Lawton and George Knox in 1971, he wrote plays, published and unpublished, about Moses, Mohammed, and Mary Baker Eddy. Other plays, now lost, include "Abraham Lincoln," "The Flute Maker," a one-act drama, and "Mademoiselle Bb," a play about a child. Of Hart-mann's dramatic works, Weaver, from the vantage point of one interested primarily in art history, singles out *Buddha,* specifically its final scene, which is dedicated to "Students of Color Psychology" and was praised by Mallarme; she describes it as "an imaginary fantasy for productions of the future that incorporates fireworks and lighting effects . . . to be staged in an enormous field eight hundred feet long." Hartmann, in short, anticipated the stadium rock concert by almost a century.

Hartmann's early poetry was strongly marked by the influence of Whitman and by that of French symbolism, a movement which Hartmann, in his critical writings, helped bring to the attention of the American public. (An early short story, in the 1899 collection *Schopenhauer in the Air,* is entitled "The Wife of the Symbolist.") The Whitman influence had disappeared from view in Hartmann's 1904 volume of verse, *Drifting Flowers of the Sea and Other Poems,* according to Marshall Van Deusen in *Dictionary of Literary Biography.* The "closely patterned" verse deals with such traditionally poetic themes as lost love and innocence, nostalgia, and the sea. At this time, Hartmann had begun studying Japanese *tanka* and *haiku* forms, and included some adaptations of Japanese poems in *Drifting Flowers,* as well as writing at least one article on Japanese poetry ("The Japanese Conception of Poetry," *Reader Magazine,* 1904). His next collection, a chapbook of Japanese-style verse, was *Tanka, Haikai, Fourteen Japanese Rhythms* (mistakenly calling *haiku* by the name of *haikai,* another

Japanese verse form). "He was in the vanguard in the United States in making available foreign forms of art and seeking to domesticate them in the New World," writes Van Heusen. Another such venture was the long poem *My Rubaiyat* (1913), inspired by the *Rubaiyat of Omar Khayam.* In this work, Hartmann tries to combine—in the words of his preface— "Whitman's free rhymeless rhythm . . . and the vague alliteration of sound in quarter tones, characteristic of Japanese poetry." *My Rubaiyat,* set in a Romantic landscape that alternates between gloomy forests and smoke-choked cities, protests against militarism, affirms women's rights, speaks up for the sick and aged, and, less topically, laments the passing of youth and love.

Notable among Hartmann's works of fiction is the short novel *The Last Thirty Days of Christ* (published in 1920), which was praised by Ezra Pound. It describes the relationship between Jesus and Judas. During these post-World War I years, Hartmann was traveling between California and New York, hanging out with Jack London and others in San Francisco, and playing sometimes the clown, sometimes the mentor, for California artists. (Generally speaking, he was more admired by younger artists, while older, more well-established figures humorously tolerated him.) He never "made it" in Hollywood, as Van Heusen puts it, but remained a colorful and eccentric local figure for many years. He dabbled in a little theater in San Francisco, producing Henrik Ibsen's play *Ghosts,* and wrote a 300,000-word philosophical statement, *Esthetic Verities,* a culmination of his views, which is in the Ridgway Library in Philadelphia. In 1930, he published a volume of seven short stories culled from among the forty or fifty he had published in magazines over the years; in 1931 came a pamphlet on his experiences as an asthma sufferer, entitled *My Crucifixion: Asthma for Forty Years.* On April 17, 1937, Pound paid him the following unique tribute, scrawled on a postcard: "If one hadn't been one's self it w[oul]d have been worth while being Sadakichi, meaning that life won't have been a dead loss." In the 1940's Hartmann was occasionally subject to FBI surveillance and was the object of an unsuccessful attempt to intern him and his family in a World War II camp for Japanese-Americans. His 1940 book, *Strands and Ravelings of the Art Fabric,* is, in Van Heusen's view, "a waspish attack on abstractionism and surrealism." He died while visiting a daughter, Atma, in Florida, in 1944, and did not live to see the destruction of his birthplace by a nuclear weapon. His reputation has always been tenuous, his name veering in and out of the limelight. In 1922, a writer named Gorham Munson, in an article

for *Broom* magazine, wrote of him as having joined "The Limbo of American Literature." Yet Weaver, in 1991, did much to revive Hartmann's reputation, calling attention to his "remarkable ability to identify the artists and ideas that would become the primary forces of twentieth-century American art." To scholars of art history, she gave notice that "a reading of the 1890-1915 era in American art is virtually impossible without recourse to Hartmann's writings."

BIOGRAPHICAL/CRITICAL SOURCES:

BOOKS

Browne, Turner, and Partnow, Elaine, *Macmillan Biographical Encyclopedia of Photographic Artists and Innovators,* Macmillan (New York), 1983, p. 263.
Fowler, Gene, *Minutes of the Last Meeting,* Viking (New York), 1954.
Hart, James D., *Oxford Companion to American Literature,* sixth edition, pp. 275-276.
Quartermain, Peter, editor, *Dictionary of Literary Biography, Volume 54: American Poets, 1880-1945,* two parts, Gale, 1987, pp. 154-163.
Traubel, Horace, *With Walt Whitman in Camden,* several volumes, Small, Maynard (Boston), 1906-14.
Weaver, Jane Calhoun, editor, *Sadakichi Hartmann: Critical Modernist: Collected Art Writings,* University of California Press, 1991.

PERIODICALS

Broom, June, 1922, pp. 250-260.
Sadakichi Hartmann Newsletter, English Department, University of California, Riverside, fall, 1969-spring, 1973; East Texas State University, fall, 1973-spring, 1975.
Swank International, April, 1969, pp. 16-18.*

*   *   *

HASSEL, Odd 1897-1981

PERSONAL: Born May 17, 1897 in Kristiana (now Oslo), Norway; son of Ernst (a gynecologist) and Mathilde (Klaveness) Hassel; died May 15, 1981, in Oslo, Norway. *Education:* University of Oslo, graduated 1920; University of Berlin, Ph.D., 1924.

CAREER: K. Fajans Laboratory, Munich, Germany, physical chemist, 1922; Kaiser Wilhelm Institute, Berlin, Germany, researcher 1922-24; University of

Oslo, Norway, professor of physical chemistry, 1925-43, and 1945-64; editor of *Acta Chimica Scandinavia,* Norway, 1947-57.

AWARDS, HONORS: Fridtjof Nansen Award, 1946; Gunnerus Medal, Royal Norwegian Academy of Sciences, 1964; Nobel Prize for Chemistry, 1969; recipient of Guldber and Waage Law of Mass Action Memorial, and honorary fellow, Norwegian Chemical Society; British Chemical Society, fellow; fellow of Royal Danish Academy of Science, Royal Norwegian and Royal Swedish Academies of Sciences.

WRITINGS:

Kristallchemie, [Dresden], 1934, translation by R. C. Evans published as *Crystal Chemistry,* 1935.

SIDELIGHTS: Through twenty-five years of painstaking work, Norwegian physical chemist Odd Hassel confirmed the long-suspected three-dimensional nature of organic molecules, and his work in this field, called conformational analysis, altered the perception of chemistry. He received the Nobel Prize for chemistry in 1969, which he shared with the English chemist Derek H. R. Barton. Although other Norwegians had won the prize before him, Hassel's win was a special source of pride for his countrymen, for he was the first winner whose work had been carried out almost entirely in Norway.

One of a set of twins, Odd Hassel was born May 17, 1897, in Kristiana (now Oslo), Norway. His father Ernst was a gynecologist. His mother, Mathilde Klaveness Hassel, raised her four sons and one daughter alone after her husband died when Odd was eight years old. While his brothers, including his twin Lars, entered law and civil engineering, Hassel chose a different route. He had disliked school except for mathematics and science. The interest he developed in chemistry during high school evolved into his major area of study at the University of Oslo, which he entered in 1915.

Hassel toured France and Italy for a year after his graduation in 1920, a common practice at the time. In 1922 he worked at K. Fajans's laboratory in Munich where he discovered adsorption indicators, organic dyes used in the analysis of silver and halide ions for greater accuracy. He returned to school to study at the University of Berlin, a center for chemistry and physics, where he was recommended for and received a Rockefeller scholarship. He earned his doctorate in 1924.

While in Berlin, Hassel worked at the Kaiser Wilhelm Institute, and learned the technique known as X-ray crystallography. In this method of analysis the atomic structure of a substance can be determined by striking a pure crystal of the substance with X-rays. After passing through the crystal, the rays are bent, or diffracted; the pattern of this diffraction is captured on photographic film and, when analyzed, reveals the arrangement of the atoms within the substance.

In 1925 Hassel returned to the University of Oslo as an instructor, and a year later was named associate professor of physical chemistry. In 1930 he began to investigate the three-dimensional structure of molecules, particularly ring-shaped carbon molecules. Many important organic molecules, including several carbohydrates and steroids, are built on a ring-shaped base. Although it was widely believed that all the carbon atoms in these molecules were arranged in one plane (rather like a doughnut lying on a plate), the possibility that they were actually three-dimensional had been proposed in 1885. Molecules having six or more carbon atoms, reasoned German chemist Johann Friedrich Wilhelm Adolf von Baeyer, would be under too much strain to lie flat; in 1890 chemist Ulrich Sachse suggested two configurations of cyclohexane (a six atom carbon ring). One, the boat form, was represented as four atoms framing the "sides" laying in the same plane with the remaining atoms in the plane above them, like the bow and stern of a canoe. The second, or chair configuration, resembled a reclining shape having four atoms in the central plane, with one end atom above, and one below. In the absence of more conclusive experiments, however, most scientists maintained that cyclohexane resembled a doughnut on a plate.

Hassel's work was to correct that view. His primary investigations used the X-ray crystallography technique he had learned in Berlin; the drawback however, was that the technique could be used only with solids. A technique called dipole measurement, the analysis of positive and negative charges in a molecule, was also used. But electron diffraction proved to be the best method to investigate the structure of molecules because it could be used with gases and free molecules. By 1938 Hassel's laboratory was able to afford an electron diffraction unit, and he devoted the next five years to studying cyclohexane. Not only did he confirm that the boat and chair forms did indeed exist as predicted nearly fifty years before, Hassel also discovered that the molecules oscillated between the boat and chair forms at an enormous rate, with the latter form occurring predominantly. His investigations made it possible to predict the chemical properties of many organic substances whose base was cyclohexane. He also determined that the hydrogen atoms bonded to the carbon atoms either perpendicular to the four-atom plane (axial) or parallel (equatorial). These observations further deepened the behavioral chemistry of cyclohexanes and their related compounds—substituted cyclohexanes.

Hassel continued his work on cyclohexane even after Germany invaded Norway in 1940. He refused to publish his papers in German scientific journals, which limited the dissemination of his ideas. Some of his most important research was first reported in small Norwegian-language journals not circulated outside of Norway. In 1943, the Germans shut down the University of Oslo. Hassel, along with the other faculty members and scholars, was sent to a concentration camp at Grini, near Oslo. During his two years of imprisonment Hassel carried on his work, teaching physical chemistry without the consent of his captors. Despite his shy, reticent nature, he enlisted other scientists to work with him, including Per Andersen, and Ragnar Frisch, who remained a good friend and later received the Nobel Prize for economics the same year Hassel received one for chemistry. They were freed from Grini in November of 1944.

During the 1950s Hassel turned his attention to the physical structure of charge-transfer compounds. In such a compound, one part "donates" an electron to the other part, which "accepts" it. Because many of these compounds were too unstable to study in gaseous form, Hassel studied the solid forms with X-ray crystallography. He concluded that many of the theories about how these molecules worked were incorrect, and devised a new, simple set of rules that would inform the arrangement and size of the molecular bonds.

Hassel retired from the University of Oslo in 1964, but continued to research and publish until 1971. In the course of his career he published over 250 scientific papers, as well as *Kristallchemie* (1934), the first modern review of work in crystal chemistry. It was quickly translated into English, as *Crystal Chemistry,* and Russian. The book became a standard reference work for crystallographers and chemists throughout the field. From 1947 to 1957 Hassel was also the Norwegian editor of *Acta Chimica Scandinavica.* During his long career Hassel received numerous honors for his contributions to science. Apart from being honored with the Fridtjof Nansen Award in 1946, the Gunnerus Medal from the Royal Norwegian

Academy of Sciences was awarded him in 1964, as well as the Guldber and Waage's Law of Mass Action Memorial from the Norwegian Chemical Society, of which he was an honorary fellow. In addition, he was a fellow of the Royal Norwegian Academy of Sciences, the Royal Swedish Academies of Sciences, and the Royal Danish Academy of Science. An honorary fellow of the British Chemical Society besides, Hassel received honorary degrees from the University of Copenhagen (1950) and the University of Stockholm (1960). He was made a knight of the Order of Saint Olav. In 1969, he shared the Nobel Prize for Chemistry with Derek Barton "for their contributions to the development of the concept of conformation and its application in chemistry." Speaking of the award to the *New York Times,* Hassel commented, "I had been among the chemistry candidates before, but did not expect to get the prize now. It was indeed very pleasing." He had doubts about going to Stockholm to accept the prize, however, saying, "I detest public appearances and have to think it over thoroughly." Hassel rarely attended international conferences and never married. "He prefers molecules," noted one of his students. After his twin brother died in 1980, Hassel reportedly lost his "zest for life." On May 15, 1981, Hassel died in Oslo, just two days before his eighty-fourth birthday.

BIOGRAPHICAL/CRITICAL SOURCES:

BOOKS

Magill, Frank, editor, *The Nobel Prize Winners: Chemistry,* Volume 3: *1969-1989,* Salem Press, 1990.

PERIODICALS

New York Times, October 31, 1969, p. 20.
Science, November 7, 1969, pp. 718-720.*

*   *   *

HATFIELD, Kate
See WRIGHT, Daphne

*   *   *

HAWKINS, Anthony Hope
See HOPE, Anthony

HAWKWOOD, Allan
  See BEDFORD-JONES, H(enry James O'Brien)

HERITAGE, Martin
  See HORLER, Sydney

*   *   *

*   *   *

HECKSCHER, August 1913-1997

HERZOG, Chaim 1918-1997

OBITUARY NOTICE—See index for *CA* sketch: Born September 16, 1913, in Huntington, Long Island, NY; died of heart failure, April 5, 1997, in New York, NY. Education, journalist, civil servant, and author. Heckscher had a varied career that began when he joined the faculty of Yale University as an instructor from 1939 to 1941. During World War II he held a post with the Coordinator of Information, and he was also sent to North Africa for service with the Office of Strategic Services. Following World War II, he was editor at the *Auburn Citizen Advertiser* and later became an editorial writer with the *New York Herald Tribune*. From 1956 to 1967 he was director of New York City's Twentieth Century Fund. During that time he was chosen to be President John F. Kennedy's cultural matters coordinator. He also acted as a special consultant to the president concerning matters of art.

In 1967 Heckscher became the City Parks Commissioner and Administrator of Recreation and Cultural Affairs. Among the popular events staged in the parks while he was commissioner were the 1967 Barbra Streisand concert and the first New York City Marathon. He rounded out his career with work as chair of the general committee of the New York City Office of Cultural Affairs. He also served as a member of the New York State Council on the Arts. In addition, he wrote and edited books, including *These Are the Days, The Politics of Woodrow Wilson, Diversity of Worlds* (with Raymond Aron), *Open Spaces: The Life of American Cities,* and *St. Paul's: The Life of a New England School.* Among the honors bestowed on him were the rank of Chevalier of the French Legion of Honor.

OBITUARIES AND OTHER SOURCES:

BOOKS

Who's Who in America, 51st edition, Marquis, 1997.

PERIODICALS

New York Times, April 7, 1997, p. B9.

OBITUARY NOTICE—See index for *CA* sketch: Born Vivian Herzog, September 17, 1918, in Belfast, Northern Ireland; immigrated to Palestine, 1935; died of heart failure, April 17, 1997, in Tel Aviv, Israel. Soldier, politician, diplomat, author. Herzog gained worldwide acclaim as president of Israel from 1983 to 1993. He was born in Northern Ireland and educated in England and Palestine. After relocating to Palestine in 1935, he returned to England to join the British Army during the early days of World War II. He participated in the Normandy Invasion in 1944 and assisted in the liberation of Nazi concentration camps at the close of the war. He also interrogated Gestapo Chief Heinrich Himmler, shortly before returning to Palestine. He joined Haganah, the Jewish underground, also known as the Israeli Defense Force, and was instrumental in the formation of the state of Israel. He served as Israel's director of military intelligence from 1948 to 1950 and again from 1959 to 1962. Shortly after the Six-Day War, he became governor of the newly acquired West Bank territory. Herzog hosted a series of radio broadcasts during both the Six-Day War and the Yom Kippur War (1973) and established himself as a military analyst.

Herzog held numerous posts in diverse fields, including managing an industrial firm, practicing law, and eventually holding the post of Israel's Ambassador to the United Nations. Later, in 1981, he was elected to the Knesset, Israel's Parliament. Once president, Herzog was seen as controversial. Many of his actions were criticized by the media and the public alike; he pardoned members of the Shin Bet, Israel's security force, for executing militant Palestinians in the 1980s before the alleged criminals had been tried. He also visited West Germany. Herzog wrote numerous volumes on Israel's history and on his personal experiences, including *The War of Atonement, Israel's Finest Hour, Heroes of Israel: Profiles of Jewish Courage,* and *The Arab-Israeli Wars: War and Peace in the Middle East* (later released as *The Arab-Israeli Wars: War and Peace in the Middle East, from the War of Independence through Lebanon*). He also contributed to *Final Letters: From Victims of the Holocaust,* edited by Yehudit Kleiman.

OBITUARIES AND OTHER SOURCES:

BOOKS

Who's Who, 149th edition, St. Martin's, 1997.

PERIODICALS

Chicago Tribune (electronic), April 17, 1997.
Chicago Tribune, April 18, 1997, sec. 2, p. 12.
Los Angeles Times, April 18, 1997, p. A30.
New York Times, April 18, 1997, p. A20.
Times (London; electronic), April 19, 1997.
Washington Post, April 18, 1997, p. B4.

OTHER

CNN (website), April 17, 1997.
Israel Ministry of Foreign Affairs (website), April 18, 1997.
MSNBC (website), April 17, 1997.

*   *   *

HEYWARD, (Edwin) DuBose 1885-1940

PERSONAL: Born August 31, 1885, in Charleston, SC; died of a heart attack on June 16, 1940, in Tryon, NC; buried in St. Philip's Episcopal Church in Charleston; son of Edwin Watkins ("Ned"; worker in a rice mill) and Janie DuBose (maiden name, Screven; a poet who ran a boardinghouse, sewed, and wrote poetical advertisements for a printing company) Heyward; descendant of Thomas Heyward, Jr. (a signer of the Declaration of Independence); married Dorothy Hartzell Kuhns (a playwright), September 22, 1923; children: Jenifer. *Education:* Attended public schools until age fourteen. *Politics:* Democrat. *Religion:* Episcopalian.

ADDRESSES: Home—Charleston, SC, and Hendersonville, NC.

CAREER: Novelist, poet, and playwright. Sold newspapers at age nine; other early jobs included hardware store clerk, warehouse clerk, cotton checker on the Charleston waterfront, and insurance salesman by age 21. With John Bennett and Hervey Allen, established the Poetry Society of South Carolina, 1920, becoming editor of its *Year Book,* 1921-24, and president, 1924.

MEMBER: National Institute of Arts and Letters,

Poetry Society of America, MacDowell Colony, honorary Phi Beta Kappa.

WRITINGS:

(With Hervey Allen) *Carolina Chansons: Legends of the Low Country* (poetry), Macmillan (New York, NY), 1922.
Skylines and Horizons (poetry), Macmillan, 1924.
Porgy (novel), Doran (New York, NY), 1925.
Angel (novel), Doran, 1926.
(With Dorothy Heyward) *Porgy: A Play in Four Acts,* Doubleday, Doran (Garden City, NY), 1928.
Mamba's Daughters: A Novel of Charleston, Doubleday, Doran, 1929.
The Half Pint Flask (short story), Farrar & Rinehart (New York, NY), 1929.
Brass Ankle: A Play in Three Acts, Farrar & Rinehart, 1931.
Jasbo Brown and Selected Poems, Farrar & Rinehart, 1931.
Peter Ashley, Farrar & Rinehart, 1932.
(Librettist, and lyricist with Ira Gershwin) *Porgy and Bess* (opera), music by George Gershwin, Gershwin Publishing Corporation (New York, NY), 1935.
Lost Morning (novel), Farrar & Rinehart, 1936.
(With Herbert Ravenel Sass) *Fort Sumter,* Farrar & Rinehart, 1938.
The Country Bunny and the Little Gold Shoes: As Told to Jenifer (children's story), illustrated by Marjorie Flack, Houghton Mifflin (Boston, MA), 1939.
(With Dorothy Heyward) *Mamba's Daughters: A Play,* Farrar & Rinehart, 1939.
Star Spangled Virgin (novel), Farrar & Rinehart, 1939.

Author of screenplay for *Emperor Jones,* adapted from Eugene O'Neill's play of the same title, United Artists, 1933; co-editor and co-author of the forewords with Hervey Allen to *Year Book of the Poetry Society of South Carolina,* Poetry Society of South Carolina (Charleston, SC), 1921, 1922, 1923, 1924; essays appear in *Library of Southern Literature,* no. 1, edited by Edwin A. Alderman and Charles A. Smith, Martin & Hoyt (Atlanta, GA), 1923, and *The Carolina Low-Country,* edited by Augustine T. Smythe and others, Macmillan (New York, NY), 1932; contributed the foreword to Samuel Gaillard Stoney and Gertrude Mathews Shelby, *Black Genesis: A Chronicle,* Macmillan, 1930, and to E.T.H. Shaffer, *Carolina Gardens,* Huntington Press (New York, NY), 1937; periodical publications include *Poetry, Reviewer,*

Bookman, Southwest Review, Publishers Weekly, Stage, Magazine of Art, and *National Geographic.*

SIDELIGHTS: A respected poet and novelist of the 1920s, DuBose Heyward is now remembered mainly for his contribution to the opera *Porgy and Bess.* Heyward's 1925 novel, *Porgy,* on which the opera is based, tells the story of a crippled African-American man who falls in love with a prostitute in turn-of-the-nineteenth-century Charleston, South Carolina. Urged on by his wife, playwright Dorothy Heyward, who roughed out the dramatic structure of the novel as a play, the husband and wife team wrote *Porgy: A Play in Four Acts,* which was first produced in 1927, and enjoyed successful runs in both New York and London. The play came to the attention of Ira and George Gershwin, who replaced the traditional folk songs of the play with their own music, and lyrics co-written by the Heywards who contributed the libretto. The result was the opera *Porgy and Bess,* which, while initially less successful than its dramatic predecessor, grew in popularity through revivals starting in the post-World War II era, eventually becoming a worldwide sensation.

Born to an impoverished branch of an old, aristocratic Charleston family, DuBose lost his father while still a toddler and, despite bouts of ill health that periodically plagued him, began contributing to the family's finances before the age of ten. The boy's responsibilities apparently distracted him from his studies, for he was an indifferent student and left school at age fourteen. He worked a series of jobs until at age twenty-five he became a founding partner in an insurance company that brought him wealth and returned him to the high place in Charleston society to which his grandparents' generation had belonged. With the leisure time his newfound affluence gave him, "he wrote and acted in amateur theatricals," according to Harlan Greene in *Dictionary of Literary Biography,* "and the local press praised his efforts extravagantly." Heyward soon began writing seriously and chose his hometown, particularly its unique pre-World War I character, as his recurring subject and setting. Indeed, wrote Anthony Harrigan in the *Georgia Review* more than a decade after Heyward's death: "His great strength was that he wrote so completely and convincingly of the place in which he was born and lived and died."

With his mentors John Bennett, a children's book author, artist, and poet, and Hervey Allen, who later wrote a popular novel, *Anthony Adverse,* Heyward founded the Poetry Society of South Carolina, and

eventually toured the lecture circuit on its behalf. His first book was published in 1922, a collection of poetry called *Carolina Chansons,* co-authored by Allen. His second book, a solo effort, also poetry, *Skylines and Horizons,* earned positive responses from such critics as Allen Tate, who praised Heyward as an important Southern poet of the era. Heyward's philosophy of poetry, according to Greene, was anti-aristocratic: "Poetry, he said, was not to be introspective, subjective, or obscure; it was to provide the common man access to beauty."

Heyward shortly turned to writing novels, giving up the insurance business in 1924 and producing *Porgy,* his first and best-loved novel, in 1925. His marriage in 1923 to a young playwright he had met at the MacDowell Colony in New Hampshire gave him an incentive to turn his attentions to the theater, and Heyward had several plays produced, most successfully his and wife Dorothy's adaptation of Heyward's first novel. Though rarely produced after it was further adapted to the opera form by the Gershwin brothers, *Porgy: A Play in Four Acts,* was a rarity in the artistic world of the American 1920s. If the 1925 book was one of the first American novels to treat American black culture seriously, the play was likewise the first authentic depiction of African-American culture in the theater.

Heyward's interest in representing South Carolina's African-American residents is often attributed both to a stint as a cotton checker on the Charleston wharf in the years before he turned to the insurance business, and to the influence of his mother, who had also written verse and stories featuring black characters and a faithful rendering of the Gullah dialect which is unique to the region. Though not African-American himself, Heyward's success during his lifetime came from *Porgy* and *Mamba's Daughters* and their dramatic adaptations, works which center on African-American characters. Though most of his novels, poems, and plays are now considered less worthy of critical attention than is *Porgy and Bess,* Heyward is still recognized as the first white author to treat American blacks realistically and sympathetically, and the first to accurately render the Gullah dialect in fiction.

BIOGRAPHICAL/CRITICAL SOURCES:

BOOKS

Contemporary Authors, Vol. 108, Gale (Detroit, MI), 1983, pp. 218.

Dictionary of Literary Biography, Gale, Volume 7, 1981, pp. 296-301; Volume 45, 1986, pp. 190-96.

Something about the Author, Vol. 21, Gale, 1980, pp. 66-69.

Twentieth-Century Literary Criticism, Vol. 59, Gale, 1995, pp. 83-110.

PERIODICALS

Georgia Review, Fall, 1951, pp. 335-344.*

* * *

HOLMES, Diana 1949-

PERSONAL: Born January 28, 1949, in Preston, Lancashire, England; daughter of Maurice Frederick and Marie (Newsham) Holmes; married Nicolas W. Cheesewright, June 18, 1983; children: Thomas, Martha. *Ethnicity:* "White." *Education:* University of Sussex, B.A. (with honors), 1971, D.Phil., 1977; attended la Nouvelle Sorbonne, Universite de Paris III, 1972. *Politics:* "Labour (left)." *Religion:* None.

ADDRESSES: Home—151 Compton Rd., Wolverhampton, West Midlands WV3 9JT, England. *Office*—Department of Modern Languages, Keele University, Keele, Staffordshire ST5 5BG, England; fax 01-78-258-4078. *E-mail*—mla28@cc.keele.ac.uk.

CAREER: Wolverhampton Polytechnic (now University of Wolverhampton), Wolverhampton, England, lecturer in French, 1975-80; North London Polytechnic, London, England, part-time lecturer in French, 1981-84; Wolverhampton Polytechnic, senior lecturer, 1984-90, principal lecturer in French, 1990; Keele University, Keele, England, lecturer, 1992-94, senior lecturer, 1994-95, professor of French and head of French studies, 1995—. University of Birmingham, visiting lecturer, 1986-87; speaker at educational institutions, including Thames Valley University, University of Sheffield, and St. John's College, Oxford, 1994, Fitzwilliam College, Cambridge, University of Warwick, and University of Wales, University College, Cardiff, 1995.

MEMBER: Association for the Study of Modern and Contemporary France (member of executive committee, 1987-91), Women in French.

WRITINGS:

(Contributor) J. Bridgford, editor, *France: Image and Identity,* Newcastle Publications (Newcastle upon Tyne, England), 1986.

Colette, St. Martin's Press (New York, NY), 1991.

(Contributor) R. Gunther and J. Windebank, editors, *Violence and Conflict in French Culture,* Sheffield University Press (Sheffield, England), 1995.

Women in Context: French Women Writers, 1848-1994, Athlone Press (London, England), 1996.

(Contributor) Alex Hughes and Kate Ince, editors, *French Erotic Fiction: Women's Desiring Writing, 1880-1990,* Berg (Oxford, England), 1996.

Co-editor of the series "French Film Directors," Manchester University Press (Manchester, England). Contributor to periodicals, including *Cross-Currents.* Editor, *Modern and Contemporary France,* 1996—.

WORK IN PROGRESS: A critical study of the films of Truffaut, with R. A. Ingram, for Manchester University Press; a book on Rachilde, for Berg.

SIDELIGHTS: Diana Holmes told *CA:* "I developed an interest in women's writing when I was completing a doctoral thesis on *images* of women in France in the inter-war period. While most of the thesis dealt with the socio-political context of the period and the work of male authors, the final chapter was on the work of Colette, and Colette's writing (particularly the way she wrote about gender) was a revelation.

"After some years, preoccupied mainly with juggling the beginning of a university teaching career with having babies, I wrote a feminist critical study of Colette's work. Teaching at Wolverhampton Polytechnic, I worked with women colleagues to set up both undergraduate and postgraduate interdisciplinary courses in women's studies and to establish the Centre for Women's Studies. Within my own discipline of French studies, I have taught a variety of courses in nineteenth and twentieth century French culture. I developed an interest in film and wrote a series of articles and chapters on French women writers. After moving to Keele University, I published a study of French women writers from 1848 to 1996, with an emphasis on the socio-political contexts of women's lives. The authors studied range from the well-known to those who have been lost from, or have not yet entered, literary history.

"My next book is a study of the films of Francois Truffaut, based on work that rose out of teaching film to undergraduates. After that, I will return to one of the little-known authors from *French Women Writers:* Rachilde, the only woman writer of the *fin-de-siecle* Decadent movement."

*   *   *

HOLTZMAN, Elizabeth 1941-

PERSONAL: Born August 11, 1941, in New York, NY; daughter of Sidney (an attorney) and Filia (a college professor) Holtzman. *Education:* Radcliffe College, A.B. (magna cum laude), 1962; Harvard University, J.D., 1965. *Politics:* "Democratic." *Religion:* Jewish.

ADDRESSES: Home—180 Bergen St., Brooklyn, NY 11217. *Office*—Herrick, Feinstein, LLP, 2 Park Ave., New York, NY 10016; fax 212-889-7577. *E-mail*—eholtz@herrick.com. *Agent*—Jennifer Lyons, Joan Daves Agency, 21 West 26th St., New York, NY 10010.

CAREER: U.S. House of Representatives, Washington, DC, representative of the 16th District, Brooklyn, NY, 1973-81; Kings County, district attorney, Brooklyn, 1982-90; City of New York, comptroller, 1990-93; currently with Herrick, Feinstein, LLP, New York City. Member of Select Commission on Immigration Policy, 1979-80, Helsinki Watch Committee, 1981—, Lawyers Committee on International Human Rights, 1981-88, American Jewish Commission on the Holocaust, and President's Commission on the U.S. Observance of International Women's Year. Harvard University, member of board of overseers, 1976-82.

MEMBER: National Women's Political Caucus, Bar Association of the City of New York.

AWARDS, HONORS: Faith and Humanity Award, National Council of Jewish Women; Elizabeth Cutler Morrow Award, Young Women's Christian Association; Award of Remembrance, Warsaw Ghetto Resistance Organization; honorary degrees from Smith College, Skidmore College, Simmons College, and St. Regis College; awards from American Civil Liberties Union, New Jersey and Los Angeles chapters.

WRITINGS:

(With Cynthia C. Holtzman) *Who Said It Would Be Easy?* (memoir), Arcade Publishing (New York City), 1996.

*   *   *

HOPE, Anthony 1863-1933

PERSONAL: Full name, Anthony Hope Hawkins; born February 9, 1863, in London, England; died July 8, 1933, at Heath Farm, in Walton-on-the-Hill, Surrey, England (some sources say Tadworth, England); son of Edwards C. (a clergyman and headmaster) and Jane Isabella (Grahame) Hawkins; married Elizabeth Somerville, 1903; children: two sons, one daughter. *Education:* Balliol College, Oxford University, first class degrees in classical moderations, 1882, and in *literae humanitiores,* 1885.

CAREER: British novelist and barrister. Called to the Bar, 1887; practiced law in London, 1887-94; full-time writer, 1894-1933. Liberal Parliamentary candidate for South Buckinghamshire, 1892. *Wartime service:* Editorial and Public Branch Department (later known as Ministry of Information), 1914-18.

MEMBER: Authors' Society (member of committee for twelve years; chair of committee, 1900-03, 1907).

AWARDS, HONORS: Knighted for wartime service, 1918.

WRITINGS:

NOVELS

A Man of Mark, Remington (London), 1890, Holt (New York), 1895.
Father Stafford, Cassell (London and New York), 1891.
Mr. Witt's Widow, United States Book Co. (New York), 1892.
A Change of Air, Methuen (London), 1893, Holt (New York), 1894.
Half a Hero, Harper (New York), 1893.
The Dolly Dialogues (reprinted from the *Westminster Gazette*), Holt (New York), 1894, published with illustrations by Howard Chandler Christy, Books for Libraries Press (Freeport, NY), 1970.
The God in the Car, Appleton (New York), 1894.
The Indiscretion of the Duchess, Holt (New York), 1894.
The Lady of the Pool, Appleton (New York), 1894.

The Prisoner of Zenda, Holt (New York), 1894, published with *Rupert of Hentzau* and illustrated by Charles Dana Gibson, Dover (New York), 1961, published as a limited edition with illustrations by Paul Geiger, Franklin Library (Franklin, PA), 1984.

The Chronicles of Count Antonio, Appleton (New York), 1895.

Phroso, Stokes (New York), 1897.

Rupert of Hentzau, Holt (New York), 1898, published with *The Prisoner of Zenda* and illustrated by Charles Dana Gibson, Dover (New York), 1961, published with illustrations by Michael Godfrey, Dent, Dutton Children's Illustrated Classics, 1963.

Simon Dale, Stokes (New York), 1898.

The King's Mirror, Appleton (New York), 1899.

Quisante, Stokes (New York), 1900.

Captain Dieppe, Doubleday (New York), 1900.

Tristram of Blent, McClure (New York), 1901.

The Intrusions of Peggy, Harper (New York), 1902.

Double Harness, Stokes (New York), 1904.

A Servant of the Public, Stokes (New York), 1905.

Sophy of Kravonia, with illustrations by Fred Pegram, Harper (New York), 1906.

Helena's Path, McClure (New York), 1907.

Tales of Two People, Methuen (London), 1907.

The Great Miss Driver, McClure (New York), 1908.

Second String, Doubleday (New York), 1910.

Mrs. Maxon Protests, Harper (New York), 1911.

A Young Man's Year, Appleton (New York), 1915.

Beaumaroy Home from the Wars, Methuen (London), 1919, published as *The Secret of the Tower,* Appleton (New York), 1919.

Lucinda, Appleton (New York), 1920.

Little Tiger, Doran (New York), 1925.

SHORT STORY COLLECTIONS

Sport Royal and Other Stories, Innes (London), 1893, Holt (New York), 1895.

Lover's Fate, and a Friend's Counsel, Neely (Chicago), 1894.

Frivolous Cupid, Platt Bruce (New York), 1895.

Comedies of Courtship, Scribner (New York), 1896.

The Heart of Princess Osra and Other Stories, Stokes (New York), 1896.

A Man and His Model (includes "An Embassy"), Merriam (New York).

A Cut and a Kiss, Brown (Boston), 1899.

Love's Logic and Other Stories, McClure (New York), 1908.

PLAYS

The Adventure of Lady Ursula (produced in New York and London, 1898), Russell (New York), 1898.

(With Edward Rose) *When a Man's in Love,* produced in London, 1898.

Rupert of Hentzau (adaptation of Hope's novel of the same name), produced in Glasgow, 1899, produced in London, 1900.

(With Rose) *English Nell* (adaptation of Hope's novel *Simon Dale*), produced in London, 1900.

Pilkerton's Peerage (produced in London, 1902), French (London), 1909.

(With Harrison Rhodes) *Captain Dieppe* (adaptation of Hope's novel of the same name), produced in New York, 1903, produced in London, 1904.

(With Cosmo Gordon-Lennox) *Helena's Path* (adaptation of Hope's novel of the same name), produced in London, 1910.

In Account with Mr. Peters, published in *Windsor Magazine* (London), December 1914.

Love's Song, produced in London, 1916.

The Philosopher in the Apple Orchard: A Pastoral, French (London), 1916.

NONFICTION

Dialogue (address), privately printed, 1909.

The New—German—Testament: Some Texts and a Commentary, Methuen (London), 1914, Appleton (New York), 1915.

Militarism, German and British, Darling (London), 1915.

Why Italy Is with the Allies, Clay (London), 1917.

Memories and Notes, Hutchinson (London), 1927, Doubleday (New York), 1928.

OTHER

Selected Works, ten volumes, Harrap (London), 1925.

SIDELIGHTS: Those familiar with the work of Anthony Hope (the pen name by which Anthony Hope Hawkins is known) are most likely to have read *The Prisoner of Zenda,* his popular adventure novel set in the mythical Balkan kingdom of Ruritania. *Zenda* was a landmark adventure-romance novel, becoming a best-seller and inspiring decades of similar works. Hope was the first to utilize the locale of the Balkans, a device that became a standard used by other romance writers for many years.

Born the son of a British clergyman and headmaster, Hope was an outstanding sprinter at school and an honored student at Balliol College, Oxford. Hope, who lived with his widowed father for seventeen years, was uncertain at first about a choice of profession; he was torn between law, literature, and politics. In the end, he chose to pursue all three. He practiced law successfully for six years, in the midst of which, in 1892, he ran an unsuccessful campaign for Parliament as a Liberal in a traditionally Conservative district. Meanwhile, he had begun writing, publishing five novels by 1893—the first of which, *A Man of Mark* (1890), he printed at his own expense.

According to legend, it was while walking from the courthouse after winning a case on November 29, 1893, that the idea for *The Prisoner of Zenda* suddenly came to him. He began writing it the next day, and within one month he had completed the most successful work of his career. The plot of *Zenda* concerns Rudolf Rassendyll, a dashing English gentleman in Ruritania, who thwarts a plot against that nation's king by impersonating him at his coronation. Chivalric adventures, including the love of a princess, make up much of the novel, and a pleasantly unrealistic atmosphere prevails.

Published in April of 1894, *The Prisoner of Zenda* was a groundbreaking best-seller; it set the pattern for adventure-romances set in Balkan kingdoms, a staple of popular fiction for the next half-century. Other writers were quick to take notice of his work. Such famous authors as Richard Harding Davis would follow Hope's footsteps in this genre, and the renowned romancer Robert Louis Stevenson sent Hope a congratulatory telegram from Samoa after the novel's publication.

Another success for Hope in 1894 was his series of sketches in the comedy-of-manners mode, *The Dolly Dialogues,* which were first published in a magazine, then gathered in a book. The sketches take the form of conversations among the characters of Dolly, Lady Mickleham, and Samuel Carter, conveying the language and manners of the fashionable of that time period. A. E. W. Mason, writing in the *Dictionary of National Biography,* felt that *The Dolly Dialogues* are valuable for being "so truthfully set in the London season of their day that the social historian would be unwise to neglect them."

These two successes convinced Hope of his calling. He quit his law practice on July 4, 1894, sending a letter to that effect to his clients. He then proceeded to turn out a long string of works that have not lasted as well as his two 1894 hits. John M. Munro, in the

Reference Guide to English Literature, even asserted that "in a sense it is unfortunate that Hope turned professional, for in his evident determination to make a decent living by his pen, much of the spark went out of his writing." As an example, Munro cited the 1898 sequel to Zenda, *Rupert of Hentzau,* which is still available a century later, sometimes bound with its predecessor. Munro felt the sequel was marred by solemnity of purpose and theatricality of narrative, adding that the novel is enlivened by "occasional flashes of mild cynicism." Hope himself thought the 1899 *The King's Mirror* and the 1904 *Double Harness* his best work. Many of his other novels, however, were essentially recastings of the mold of Zenda.

Hope also wrote some more realistic novels, upon which he bestowed more labor than his popular adventures. Among these novels are a study of an empire builder, *The God in the Car* (1894), a portrait of a politician, *Quisante* (1900), and the story of an actress, *A Servant of the Public* (1905). *The Great Miss Driver* (1908) is notable for its portrayal of a woman's struggle for independence. Critics praised this novel about a masterful, wealthy woman narrated by her ambitious secretary. *Bookman* contributor T. Cooper called it "easily the biggest, best rounded, and altogether worthiest story [Hope] has ever written." An *Independent* reviewer stated, "The ease and politeness of manner with which the story is told may be compared with that of an intelligent, cultivated man who tells a story fascinatingly, yet with a certain deprecatory air, as if he said, 'But do not let me tire you,' and the reader's response is, 'Pray go on, sir; you could not tire me if your tale lasted till morning.'" Other critics, while praising the characterization of Jenny Driver, found the workings of the plot too mechanical, or the novel a bit too long.

Hope married in 1903, and fathered three children; living in London at first, he later moved to the Surrey countryside for health reasons. During World War I he worked for the Editorial and Public Branch Department, producing books on the wartime crisis; he was knighted for these efforts in 1918. He also wrote and co-wrote plays, some of which were adaptations of his novels; the most notable of the plays was the 1902 satire *Pilkerton's Peerage.*

His last published book was *Memories and Notes* in 1927. Here, he mused fondly over his Victorian youth, his days at public school and Oxford, and his acquaintances with prominent literary figures such as Thomas Hardy, Oscar Wilde, and George Meredith. A *Saturday Review of Literature* critic called it "a pleasant, gossipy work . . . and always readable" and singled out the Oxford chapter as a highlight. Harriet Sampson, writing in the *New York Evening Post,* told readers, "All the portraits are drawn with geniality and graciousness. . . . And always his manners are impeccable."

BIOGRAPHICAL/CRITICAL SOURCES:

BOOKS

Dictionary of National Biography, 1931-1940, edited by L. G. Wickham Legg, Oxford University Press, 1949, pp. 408-9.

Mallet, Charles E., *Anthony Hope and His Books: Being the Authorized Life of Sir Anthony Hope Hawkins,* Hutchinson & Co. (London, England), 1935, Kennikat Press (Port Washington, NY), 1968.

Reference Guide to English Literature, edited by D. L. Kirkpatrick, second edition, St. James Press (Detroit, MI), 1991, pp. 742-43.

PERIODICALS

Bookman, December 1908.
Independent, October 29, 1908.
New York Evening Post, February 25, 1928, p. 12.
Outlook, October 17, 1908.
Saturday Review (of Literature) September 26, 1908, sup. 6; March 10, 1928.
Spectator, October 24, 1908.*

*   *   *

HORLER, Sydney 1888-1954
(Peter Cavendish, Martin Heritage, pseudonyms)

PERSONAL: Born July 18, 1888, in Leytonstone, Essex, England; died October 27, 1954; married. *Education:* Attended Redcliffe and Colston schools, Bristol, England. *Avocational interests:* Collecting pipes.

CAREER: Novelist and journalist. *Western Daily Press,* Bristol, England, reporter, 1905-11; E. Hulton, Ltd., Manchester, England, special correspondent; London *Daily Mail* and London *Daily Citizen,* reporter, both before 1918; *John O'London's Weekly,* sub-editor, 1919; also worked for Newnes publications. *Wartime service:* Propaganda Section of Air Intelligence, 1918.

WRITINGS:

CRIME NOVELS

The Breed of the Beverleys, Odhams Press (London), 1921.
Love, the Sportsman, Hodder and Stoughton (London), 1923, published as *The Man with Two Faces,* Collins (London), 1934.
The Mystery of No. 1, Hodder and Stoughton (London), 1925, published as *The Order of the Octopus,* Doran (New York), 1926.
False-Face, Doran (New York), 1926.
The House of Secrets, Hodder and Stoughton (London), 1926, Doran (New York), 1927.
The Black Heart, Hodder and Stoughton (London), 1927, Doubleday (New York), 1928.
In the Dark, Hodder and Stoughton (London), 1927, published as *A Life for Sale,* Doubleday (New York), 1928.
Vivanti, Doran (New York), 1927.
Chipstead of the Lone Hand, Hodder and Stoughton (London), 1928, Holt (New York), 1929.
The Curse of Doone, Hodder and Stoughton (London), 1928, Mystery League (New York), 1930.
The 13th Hour, Readers' Library (London), 1928.
Miss Mystery, Hodder and Stoughton (London), 1928, Little, Brown (Boston), 1935.
Heart Cut Diamond, Hodder and Stoughton (London), 1929.
Lady of the Night, Hodder and Stoughton (London), 1929, Knopf (New York), 1930.
The Secret Service Man, Hodder and Stoughton (London), 1929, Knopf (New York), 1930.
Checkmate, Hodder and Stoughton (London), 1930.
Danger's Bright Eyes, Hodder and Stoughton (London), 1930, Harper (New York), 1932.
The Evil Chateau, Hodder and Stoughton (London), 1930, Knopf (New York), 1931.
Peril!, Mystery League (New York), 1930; published as *Cavalier of Chance,* Hodder and Stoughton (London), 1931.
Adventure Calling!, Hodder and Stoughton (London), 1931.
The Man Who Walked with Death, Knopf (New York), 1931.
The Murder Mask, Readers' Library (London), 1931.
Princess after Dark, Hodder and Stoughton (London), 1931; published as *The False Purple,* Mystery League (New York), 1932.
The Spy, Hodder and Stoughton (London), 1931.
The Temptation of Mary Gordon, Newnes (London), 1931.
Vivanti Returns, Hodder and Stoughton (London), 1931.

Wolves of the Night, Readers' Library (London), 1931.

Gentleman-in-Waiting, Benn (London), 1932.

High Stakes, Collins (London), 1932, Little, Brown (Boston), 1935.

Horror's Head, Hodder and Stoughton (London), 1932.

My Lady Dangerous, Collins (London), 1932, Harper (New York), 1933.

The Formula, Long (London), 1933, published as *The Charlatan,* Little, Brown (Boston), 1934.

Harlequin of Death, Little, Brown (Boston), 1933.

Huntress of Death, Hodder and Stoughton (London), 1933.

The Menace, Little, Brown (Boston), 1933.

Tiger Standish, Doubleday (New York), 1933.

The Man from Scotland Yard, Hutchinson (London), 1934.

The Prince of Plunder, Little, Brown (Boston), 1934.

The Secret Agent, Little, Brown (Boston), 1934.

S.O.S., Hutchinson (London), 1934.

Tiger Standish Comes Back, Hutchinson (London), 1934.

The Lessing Murder Case, Collins (London), 1935.

Lord of Terror, Collins (London), 1935, Curl (New York), 1937.

The Mystery of the Seven Cafes: The Novel of the Famous Wireless Play, Hodder and Stoughton (London), 1935.

The Vampire, Hutchinson (London), 1935, Bookfinger (New York), 1974.

Death at Court Lady, Collins (London), 1936.

The Grim Game, Little, Brown (Boston), 1936.

The Traitor, Little, Brown (Boston), 1936.

The Hidden Hand, Collins (London), 1937.

Instruments of Darkness, Hodder and Stoughton (London), 1937.

They Called Him Nighthawk, Hodder and Stoughton (London), 1937.

Dark Journey, Hodder and Stoughton (London), 1938.

The Destroyer, and The Red-Haired Death, Hodder and Stoughton (London), 1938.

The Evil Messenger, Hodder and Stoughton (London), 1938.

A Gentleman for the Gallows, Curl (New York), 1938.

Here Is an S.O.S., Hodder and Stoughton (London), 1939.

The Man Who Died Twice, Hodder and Stoughton (London), 1939.

The Phantom Forward, Hodder and Stoughton (London), 1939.

Terror on Tip-Toe, Hodder and Stoughton (London), 1939.

Tiger Standish Takes the Field, Hodder and Stoughton (London), 1939.

The Enemy within the Gates, Hodder and Stoughton (London), 1940.

The Return of Nighthawk, Hodder and Stoughton (London), 1940.

Tiger Standish Steps on It, Hodder and Stoughton (London), 1940.

Enter the Ace, Hodder and Stoughton (London), 1941.

Nighthawk Strikes to Kill, Hodder and Stoughton (London), 1941.

Tiger Standish Does His Stuff (two novelettes), Hodder and Stoughton (London), 1941.

Danger Preferred, Hodder and Stoughton (London), 1942.

Fear Walked Behind, Hale (London), 1942.

The Man in White, Staples Press (London), 1942.

The Night of Reckoning, Eyre and Spottiswoode (London), 1942.

High Hazard, Hodder and Stoughton (London), 1943.

The Hostage, Quality Press (London), 1943.

The Man Who Preferred Cocktails, Crowther (London), 1943.

Murder Is So Simple, Eyre and Spottiswoode (London), 1943.

The Lady with the Limp, Hodder and Stoughton (London), 1944.

The Man with Dry Hands, Eyre and Spottiswoode (London), 1944.

Nighthawk Mops Up, Hodder and Stoughton (London), 1944.

A Bullet for the Countess, Quality Press (London), 1945.

Dark Danger, Mystery House (New York), 1945.

Terror Comes to Twelvetrees, Eyre and Spottiswoode (London), 1945.

Virus X, Quality Press (London), 1945.

Great Adventure, and Out of a Dark Sky (two novelettes), Hale (London), 1946.

Corridors of Fear, Quality Press (London), 1947.

Ring Up Nighthawk, Hodder and Stoughton (London), 1947.

The Closed Door, Pilot Press (London), 1948.

Exit the Disguiser, Hodder and Stoughton (London), 1948.

The House with the Light, Hodder and Stoughton (London), 1948.

The Man Who Did Not Hang, Quality Press (London), 1948.

A Man of Affairs, Pilot Press (London), 1949.

The Man Who Loved Spiders, Barker (London), 1949.

Master of Venom, Hodder and Stoughton (London), 1949.

They Thought He Was Dead, Hodder and Stoughton (London), 1949.

Whilst the Crowd Roared, Archer Press (Stoke on Trent, England), 1949.

The Blanco Case, Quality Press (London), 1950.

The High Game, Redman (London), 1950.

The House of the Uneasy Dead, Barker (London), 1950.

Nap on Nighthawk, Hodder and Stoughton (London), 1950.

Scarlett—Special Branch, Foulsham (London), 1950.

The Devil Comes to Bobolyn, Marshall (London), 1951.

The House of Jackals, Hodder and Stoughton (London), 1951.

The Man in the Cloak, Eyre and Spottiswoode (London), 1951.

The Man of Evil, Barker (London), 1951.

Murderer at Large, Hodder and Stoughton (London), 1951.

The Mystery of Mr. X, Foulsham (London), 1951.

Scarlett Gets the Kidnapper, Foulsham (London), 1951.

These Men and Women, Museum Press (London), 1951.

The Blade is Bright, Eyre and Spottiswoode (London), 1952.

The Face of Stone, Barker (London), 1952.

Hell's Brew, Hodder and Stoughton (London), 1952.

The Man Who Used Perfume, Wingate (London), 1952.

The Mocking Face of Murder, Hale (London), 1952.

The Web, Redman (London), 1952.

The Cage, Hale (London), 1953.

The Dark Night, Hodder and Stoughton (London), 1953.

Death of a Spy, Museum Press (London), 1953.

Nighthawk Swears Vengeance, Hodder and Stoughton (London), 1954.

The Secret Hand, Barker (London), 1954.

The Man in the Hood, Redman (London), 1955.

The Man in the Shadows, Hale (London), 1955.

The Dark Hostess, Eyre and Spottiswoode (London), 1955.

OTHER NOVELS

Standish of the Rangeland: A Story of Cowboy Pluck and Daring, Newnes (London), 1916.

Goal! A Romance of the English Cup Ties, Odhams Press (London), 1920.

A Legend of the League, Hodder and Stoughton (London), 1922.

McPhee, Jenkins (London), 1922, published as *The Great Game,* Collins (London), 1935.

The Ball of Fortune, Aldine Press (London), 1925.

School! School!, Partridge (London), 1925.

The Man Who Saved the Club, Aldine Press (London), 1926.

On the Ball!, Blackie (London), 1926.

The Fellow Hagan!, Cassell (London), 1927.

(Under pseudonym Martin Heritage) *The House of Wingate,* Hurst and Blackett (London), 1928; published as *A House Divided,* Macaulay (New York), 1929.

(Under pseudonym Peter Cavendish) *Romeo and Julia,* Hodder and Stoughton (London), 1928.

The Exploits of Peter, Collins (London), 1930.

A Pro's Romance, Newnes (London), 1930.

Song of the Scrum, Hutchinson (London), 1934.

The Man Who Stayed to Supper: A Comedy, Jenkins (London), 1941.

Now Let Us Hate, Quality Press (London), 1942.

Springtime Comes to William, Jenkins (London), 1943.

Marry the Girl, Jenkins (London), 1945.

High Pressure, Jenkins (London), 1946.

Oh, Professor!, Jenkins (London), 1946.

The Man with Three Wives, Jenkins (London), 1947.

Man Alive, Jenkins (London), 1948.

The Beacon Light, Jenkins (London), 1949.

Haloes for Hire, Jenkins (London), 1949.

Wedding Bells, Jenkins (London), 1950.

Dr. Cupid, Jenkins (London), 1951.

Girl Trouble, Jenkins (London), 1951.

SHORT STORIES

The Worst Man in the World, Hodder and Stoughton (London), 1929.

The Screaming Skull and Other Stories, Hodder and Stoughton (London), 1930.

The Mystery Mission and Other Stories, Hodder and Stoughton (London), 1931.

Beauty and the Policeman, Hutchinson (London), 1933.

The Man Who Shook the Earth, Hutchinson (London), 1933.

Dying to Live and Other Stories, Hutchinson (London), 1935.

The House in Greek Street, Hodder and Stoughton (London), 1935, revised edition, Crowther (London), 1946.

The Stroke Sinister and Other Stories, Hutchinson (London), 1935.

Knaves & Co., Collins (London), 1938.

Tiger Standish Has a Party, Todd (London), 1943.

Murder for Sale, Vallancey Press (London), 1945.

PLAYS

The House of Secrets (adaptation of Horler's novel of the same name), produced in London, 1927.

Oh! My Aunt, produced in Birmingham, England, 1928.

Midnight Love (produced in London, 1931), Jenkins (London), 1931.

Death at Court Lady, produced in London, 1934.

The Man Who Died Twice, Nelson (London), 1941.

The Man Who Mislaid the War, Muller (London), 1943.

NONFICTION

Black Soul, Jarrolds (London), 1931.

Writing for Money, Nicholson and Watson (London), 1932.

Excitement: An Impudent Autobiography, Hutchinson (London), 1933.

London's Underworld: The Record of a Man's Sojourn in the Crime Centres of the Metropolis, Hutchinson (London), 1934.

Strictly Personal: An Indiscreet Diary, Hutchinson (London), 1934.

More Strictly Personal: Six Months of My Life, Rich and Cowan (London), 1935.

Malefactor's Row: A Book of Crime Studies, Hale (London), 1940.

I Accuse the Doctors, Being a Candid Commentary on the Hostility Shown by the Leaders of the Medical Profession Towards the Healing Art of Osteopathy, and How the Public Suffers in Consequence, Redman (London), 1949.

SIDELIGHTS: It has been said that to transcribe all of the musical scores of the composer Wolfgang Amadeus Mozart would take the average person a lifetime. It might be said, similarly, that just to read all of Sydney Horler's more than 150 novels—not to mention his short stories, plays, and nonfiction books—would take more time than the average reader possesses. To have actually written them, therefore, is an astonishing feat. Between the years 1925 and 1953, Horler never published fewer than three books of fiction in any year. Three books, in fact, was a markedly slow year for him: he only sank to that level in 1940, the year of the blitz in England in World War II, when three Horler novels emerged, and in 1946, when he issued two novels and a book of paired novelettes. In 1931 he produced an astonishing seven novels and a book of short stories, but he topped himself in 1951 with ten novels, eight of which were crime thrillers. Horler boasted that he dictated 25,000 words, about 100 pages, per week. Known as an enthusiastic self-promoter, he was evidently pleased to become a virtual brand name, advertised by his publisher with the slogan, "Horler for Excitement."

His thrillers were often series novels, and the names of the heroes provide a piquant glimpse into the varying settings, tones, and atmospheres of the different types of novels he wrote. His main characters ranged from the aristocratic Sir Harker Bellamy or Sir Brian Fordinghame and the exotic Baron Veseloffsky, to the pulp-chic thievery of the Nighthawk, the science-and-supernatural tinge of the novels featuring Paul Vivanti, the jocosely named H. Emp, and the almost generic The Ace.

Horler made most of his money and reputation with thrillers. He was a competitor—although a later entrant into the field—of the more enduring but equally productive Edgar Wallace. Horler was extremely popular in his lifetime, but his reputation has sunk and he is read very little today; one reason, perhaps, is Horler's tendency to, in his own words, "give old man coincidence's arm a frightful twist." His books star larger-than-life heroes—dashing society burglars, secret agents, and the like—who become involved in plot machinations that defy credibility.

Critical opinion of Horler's works during his lifetime was divided. Quite frequently, the same book would draw high praise from one critic, while receiving strong opprobrium from another. A case in point is the 1929 novel, *The Mystery of No. 1,* published in the United States as *The Order of the Octopus.* The first of Horler's Vivanti novels, the mystery features a plot that concerns a statesman's nephew, Peter Foyle, who, scouting clues to an apparent criminal plot by Vivandi, is swept into Vivandi's gang. A subplot involving Peter's lady love, Sylvia Fowke, is set in a country house, and the two plots eventually intertwine. Reviewer E. N. Sachs in the *New York Herald Tribune Books* called the confection "an absorbing adventure story" that "absorbs your brain while you're losing precious sleep to finish it, and you forget it promptly, which speaks well for any vice." A critic in the *Literary Review* deemed it "an interesting and thrilling tale" in which "something stirring happens almost every hour of the day and night." But a *New York Times* writer put a negative spin on those qualities, saying the book was "never for a moment convincing. Mr. Horler has been content simply to put a thrill in every chapter and to set a continuously fast pace . . . sacrificing the reader's credulity in order to preserve his interest."

Despite the mixed criticism of these early reviews, the Vivanti novels and stories, some of which verge on science fiction, are probably Horler's most enduring works. In addition to *The Mystery of No. 1,* the series consists of *The Screaming Skull, and Other*

Stories (1930), *The Worst Man in the World* (1930), *The Man Who Shook the Earth* (1933), *Lord of Terror* (1935), and *Virus X* (1945). These works are notable for the use of such science fiction elements as death rays and the occult; the short story "The Man Who Shook the Earth" features a scientist who discovers the secret of atomic power and tries to blackmail the world with it.

Horler's personal qualities can be discerned between the lines of some of his works. The secondary character Jerry Hartsell in the 1928 *The Curse of Doone* is a farmer with poor eyesight who likes to write; Horler's own poor vision had kept him from being a Royal Air Force pilot in World War I. Horler's moralistic streak, along with a special abhorrence for the French Riviera, appears in the Nighthawk novels, in which crack jewel thief Gerald Frost, nicknamed Nighthawk, writes the word "wanton" in lipstick on the pillowcases of society women from whom he steals. According to Marvin Lachman in *Twentieth Century Crime and Mystery Writers,* Horler's revulsion for what he considered effeminacy is visible in numerous passages through the works, in which the author takes special care to emphasize the manliness of his heroes. Thus, his most popular protagonist, the Honourable Timothy Overbury "Tiger" Standish, possesses "all the attributes of a thoroughly likable fellow . . . he likes his glass of beer, he is a confirmed pipe smoker, he is always ready to smile back into the face of danger." The Horler hero would not have been an Italian or a Jew, however, for "Tiger" Standish expresses certain prejudices in that line, which, in Lachman's opinion, echo the prejudices of the author himself.

Horler also wrote novels of school life, sports, and romance, often aimed at the juvenile audience. His best football (soccer) novel, according to *The Men behind Boys' Fiction,* was the 1920 *Goal! A Romance of the English Cup Ties,* which was issued in book form after magazine publication. Later titles, such as *School! School!* (1925), *On the Ball!* (1926), *Marry the Girl* (1945), *Oh, Professor!* (1946), *Wedding Bells* (1951), and *Dr. Cupid* (1951), convey the overall coloration of this side of Horler's career. Genre versatility is visible in his first published novel, the 1916 *Standish of the Rangeland: A Story of Cowboy Pluck and Daring,* but Westerns apparently did not do well for Horler; after his second novel, *Goal!,* came out a full four years later, he left the Western genre behind.

During the mid-1930s Horler wrote a series of nonfiction books expressing his own viewpoints and experi-

ences directly: *Excitement: An Impudent Autobiography* (1933), *Strictly Personal: An Indiscreet Diary* (1934), and *More Strictly Personal: Six Months of My Life* (1935). His career received a fitting epitaph, however, from Lisle Bell, in her review of his 1936 crime novel *The Traitor* in *New York Herald Tribune Books:* "Mr. Horler is an adroit spinner of plot and juggler of suspense, thus fulfilling the primary functions of his job."

BIOGRAPHICAL/CRITICAL SOURCES:

BOOKS

Clute, John, and Nicholls, Peter, *The Encyclopedia of Science Fiction,* St. Martin's Press (New York), 1993, p. 585.

Henderson, Lesley, *Twentieth-Century Crime and Mystery Writers,* third edition, St. James Press (Detroit), 1991, pp. 566-68.

Lofts, W. O. G., and D. J. Adley, *The Men behind Boys' Fiction,* Howard Baker Publishers (London), 1970, p. 196.

McCormick, Donald, and Fletcher, Katy, *Spy Fiction: A Connoisseur's Guide,* Facts on File (New York), 1990, pp. 138-39.

PERIODICALS

Bookman, March, 1927.
Boston Transcript, March 23, 1927, p. 6; December 13, 1933, p. 2.
Independent, September 10, 1927.
Literary Review, July 17, 1926, p. 6.
New York Evening Post, May 7, 1932, p. 7.
New York Herald Tribune Books, May 9, 1926, p. 21; August 26, 1928, p. 10; June 16, 1935, p. 10; March 8, 1936, p. 19.
New York Times, June 13, 1926, p. 9; July 3, 1932, p. 10; December 3, 1933, p. 22; March 15, 1936, p. 22; September 18, 1938, p. 18; January 28, 1945, p. 22.
Saturday Review of Literature, August 25, 1928; November 23, 1933; June 8, 1935.
Times Literary Supplement, August 27, 1938, p. 558.*

*   *   *

HORSEFIELD, J(ohn) Keith 1901-1997

OBITUARY NOTICE—See index for *CA* sketch: Born October 14, 1901, in Bristol, England; died March

25, 1997. Educator, historian, civil servant, and author. Horsefield's contributions to the study of monetary history earned him recognition worldwide. He began his career at London's Prudential Assurance Company as a clerk in 1919, and he continued this employment until 1937, when he received his B.A. from the University of Bristol. In 1939 and 1940, he lectured in banking at the London School of Economics, then joined the British Civil Service. He served at the Ministry of Aircraft Production and with the Ministry of Supply during World War II.

In 1947 Horsefield began a lengthy association with the International Monetary Fund in Washington, D.C., first as a division chief, then later as chief editor, and finally as historian. In 1952 he became the deputy assistant secretary general for economics and finance with the North Atlantic Treaty Organization (NATO). He served briefly on the Iron and Steel Board as supply and development officer in 1954, before he became director of finance and accounts at the Post Office. An honorary treasurer at the Carisbrooke Castle Museum from 1971 to 1992, he also wrote books including *British Monetary Experiments 1690-1710, The International Monetary Fund 1945-1965,* and *The Real Cost of War.*

OBITUARIES AND OTHER SOURCES

BOOKS

Who's Who, 146th edition, St. Martin's, 1994.

PERIODICALS

Times (London; electronic), April 24, 1997.

*   *   *

HOSSACK, Joei Carlton 1944-

PERSONAL: Born February 11, 1944, in Montreal, Quebec, Canada; daughter of Fred and Zelda Schertzer; married Paul Gordon Hossack, April 10, 1976 (died June 26, 1992). *Education:* Los Angeles City College, graduated, 1967; National Academy for Law Enforcement, graduated, 1967. *Avocational interests:* Crafts (with awards for knitting, needlepoint, weaving, and crewel).

ADDRESSES: Home—Sarasota, FL. *Office*—c/o Skeena Press, P.O. Box 19071, Sarasota, FL 34276-2071.

CAREER: Kraft Foods, office worker and sales representative in Montreal, Quebec, 1974-78, and Toronto, Ontario, 1978-80; Joei's Place (wool and craft store), Toronto, owner, 1980-89. Volunteer for theaters, marine laboratories, and the opera.

MEMBER: Toastmasters International.

WRITINGS:

Restless from the Start (travel essays), Skeena Press (Sarasota, FL), 1997.

Contributor to magazines and newspapers, including *Reminisce.*

WORK IN PROGRESS: Everyone's Dream, Everyone's Nightmare, for Skeena Press.

SIDELIGHTS: Joei Carlton Hossack told *CA:* "In 1989 my husband and I, living in Toronto, quit, sold and stored everything, and went traveling. In June of 1992, in northern Germany, my husband died of a heart attack. That is the subject of my next book, *Everyone's Dream, Everyone's Nightmare.*

"In 1994 I answered an ad on the back of *Modern Maturity.* Although they did not publish the travelogue I wrote on Turkey, that was the start of my writing career. A local newspaper published it two days before my fifty-first birthday, and everything I have written and submitted has been published since that time.

"My first book has been available since April, 1997, and I have started my lectures. This is the start of my new life, and I love the prospects."

*   *   *

HOWARD, Rhoda E. 1948-

PERSONAL: Born September 3, 1948, in Aberdeen, Scotland; daughter of Michael and Mary Howard; married Peter McCabe (an economist), May 20, 1978; children: Patrick. *Ethnicity:* "Mixed." *Education:* McGill University, B.A. (political science), 1969, M.A., 1972, Ph.D., 1976. *Religion:* None. *Avocational interests:* Music, films, literature, travel, swimming.

ADDRESSES: Home—60 Homewood Ave., Hamilton, Ontario, Canada L8P 2M4. *Office*—Department of

Sociology, McMaster University, Hamilton, Ontario, Canada L8S 4M4; fax 905-522-2642. *E-mail*—howardr @mcmaster.ca.

CAREER: McMaster University, Hamilton, Ontario, professor of sociology, 1976—. Hamilton Mayor's Committee against Racism and Discrimination, member, 1991-96.

MEMBER: Royal Society of Canada (fellow).

WRITINGS:

Colonialism and Underdevelopment in Ghana, Croom Helm (London, England), 1978.
Human Rights in Commonwealth Africa, Rowman & Littlefield (Lanham, MD), 1986.
(Editor with Jack Donnelly) *International Handbook of Human Rights,* Greenwood Press (Westport, CT), 1987.
Human Rights and the Search for Community, Westview (Boulder, CO), 1995.

WORK IN PROGRESS: To Be a Canadian: Citizenship, Human Rights, and the Search for Identity.

*   *   *

HOWARD, Robert E(rvin) 1906-1936

PERSONAL: Born January 22, 1906, in Peaster, TX; died June 12, 1936, from a self-inflicted gunshot wound; son of Isaac Mordecai (a doctor) and Hester Jane (Ervin) Howard. *Education:* Attended Howard Payne Commercial School, c. 1927. *Avocational interests:* Boxing, history.

CAREER: Writer of fantasy and adventure stories. Creator of the characters Conan the Cimmerian, Kull of Atlantis, Breckenridge Elkins, Solomon Kane, Sailor Steve Costigan, Francis X. Gordon, and Bran Mak Morn. Contributor of short stories and novellas to pulp magazines, including *Spicy Adventure, Action Stories, Thrilling Adventures, Weird Tales, Top Notch, Strange Detective, Oriental Stories, Fight Stories,* and *Argosy.*

WRITINGS:

"CONAN" FANTASY NOVELS

Conan the Conqueror, Gnome Press, 1950, published as *The Hour of the Dragon,* 1977.

"CONAN" SHORT-STORY COLLECTIONS

The Sword of Conan, Gnome Press, 1952.
The Coming of Conan, Gnome Press, 1953.
King Conan, Gnome Press, 1953.
Conan the Barbarian, Gnome Press, 1954.
(With L. Sprague de Camp) *Tales of Conan,* Gnome Press, 1955.
(With de Camp) *Conan the Adventurer,* Lancer, 1966.
(With de Camp and Lin Carter) *Conan,* Lancer, 1967.
(With de Camp) *Conan the Warrior,* Lancer, 1967.
(With de Camp) *Conan the Usurper,* Lancer, 1967.
(With de Camp) *Conan the Freebooter,* Lancer, 1968.
(With de Camp and Carter) *Conan the Wanderer,* Lancer, 1968.
(With others) *Conan the Avenger,* Lancer, 1968.
(With de Camp and Carter) *Conan of Cimmeria,* Lancer, 1969.
Conan: The Tower of the Elephant, Grosset & Dunlap, 1975.
Conan: The People of the Black Circle, edited by Karl Edward Wagner, Putnam, 1977.
The Conan Chronicles, 1989.

Contributor of Conan stories to periodicals, including *Weird Tales.*

WESTERN SHORT STORIES

A Gent from Bear Creek, Jenkins, 1937, selections published as *The Pride of Bear Creek,* Grant, 1966.
The Vultures; Showdown at Hell's Canyon, Fictioneer, 1973.
Vultures of Whapeton, Zebra, 1975.
The Last Ride, Berkley, 1978.

Contributor of western stories to periodicals, including *Argosy, Cowboy Stories,* and *Zane Grey Western.*

OTHER NOVELS

Almuric, Ace, 1964.
A Witch Shall Be Born, illustrations by Alicia Austin, Grant, 1975.

OTHER SHORT-STORY COLLECTIONS

Skull-Face and Others, Arkham House, 1946, published as *Skull-Face Omnibus,* Spearman, 1976, published in England as *The Valley of Worms and Others,* 1976, and as *The Shadow Kingdom,* 1976.

The Dark Man and Others, Arkham, 1963.

With Lin Carter) *King Kull,* Lancer, 1967, material by Howard published separately as *Kull, the Fabulous Warrior King,* 1978.

Wolfshead, Lancer, 1968.

Red Shadows, Grant, 1968.

Bran Mak Morn, 1969.

(With Tevis Clyde Smith) *Red Blades of Black Cathay,* illustrations by David Karbonik, Grant, 1971.

Marchers of Valhalla, illustrations by Robert Bruce Acheson, Grant, 1972.

The Sowers of the Thunder, illustrations by Roy G. Krenkel, Grant, 1973.

The Incredible Adventures of Dennis Dorgan, introduction by Darrell C. Richardson, Fax, 1974.

The Lost Valley of Iskander, illustrations by Michael William Kaluta, Fax, 1974.

The People of the Black Circle, Grant, 1974.

Tigers of the Sea, Grant, 1974.

Worms of the Earth (includes *Bran Mak Morn*), Grant, 1974.

Red Nails, illustrations by George Barr, Grant, 1975.

Swords of Shahrazar, illustrations by Michael William Kaluta, Fax, 1976.

Black Vulmea's Vengeance, and Other Tales of Pirates, illustrations by Robert James Pailthorpe, Grant, 1976.

The Devil in Iron, illustrations by Dan Green, Grosset & Dunlop, 1976.

Rogues in the House, Grant, 1976.

Son of the White Wolf, illustrations by Marcus Boas, Fax, 1977.

The Hour of the Dragon, Putnam, 1977.

The People of the Black Circle, Berkley, 1977.

The Hour of the Dragon, edited by Karl Edward Wagner, Berkley, 1977.

Sword Woman, 1977.

Black Canaan, 1978.

Queen of the Black Coast, Grant, 1978.

The Gods of Bal-Sagoth, 1979.

Hawks of Outremer, edited by Richard L. Tierney, illustrations by Rob MacIntyre and Chris Pappas, Grant, 1979.

The Road to Azrael, illustrations by Roy G. Krenkel, Grant, 1979.

Lord of the Dead, illustrations by G. Duncan Eagleson, Grant, 1981.

The Last Cat Book, illustrations by Peter Kuper, Dodd, Mead, 1984.

Pool of the Black One, Grant, 1986.

Cthulhu: The Mythos and Kindred Horrors, 1987.

Shadows of Dreams, edited by David A. Drake, 1989.

OTHER OMNIBUS VOLUMES

The Book of Robert E. Howard, 1976.

The Second Book of Robert E. Howard, 1976.

The Robert E. Howard Omnibus, 1977.

The Dark Barbarian: The Writings of Robert E. Howard, edited by Don Herron, Greenwood Press, 1984.

POETRY

Always Comes Evening: The Collected Poems of Robert E. Howard, Arkham, 1958.

Etchings in Ivory, Glenn Lord, 1968.

Singers in the Shadows, illustrations by Marcus Boas, Grant, 1970.

Echoes from an Iron Harp, illustrations by Alicia Austin, Grant, 1972.

A Song of the Naked Lands, Squires, 1973.

The Gold and the Grey, Squires, 1974.

ADAPTATIONS: Howard's fictional character Conan has been featured in tales by writers such as Bjorn Nyberg, L. Sprague de Camp, Lin Carter, Andrew J. Offutt, Robert Jordan, and Steve Perry; in addition, the character has been featured in the Marvel comics *Conan the Barbarian* and *The Savage Sword of Conan* and in such films as *Conan the Barbarian* and *Conan the Destroyer.* Marvel comics has also adapted Kull of Atlantis, Solomon Kane, and other characters to a comic book format. Howard's stories have been adapted for television, including "Pigeons from Hell" for *Boris Karloff's Thriller.*

SIDELIGHTS: Robert E. Howard ranks among the most prominent, and prolific, writers in the genre of fantastic, sword-and-sorcery fiction, and he is widely known as the creator of the heroic barbarian character Conan. Howard was born in 1906 in Peaster, Texas. Without siblings or many playmates, Howard spent much of his childhood reading, but after repeated victimization by gangs he devoted himself to physical fitness as well. Unable to afford a college education, Howard pursued financial independence by writing. In 1924, when he was still in his teens, he sold his first story, "Spear and Fang," to *Weird Tales.* This magazine would prove to be the principal publisher of Howard's writings throughout the brief remainder of his life.

Howard quickly showed himself to be a speedy and imaginative writer whose best stories were inevitably propelled by action. Many of these fast-paced tales featured recurring heroes. In the late 1920s, for instance, he produced stories centering on Solomon Kane, a morose figure dedicated to the eradication of evil. During that same period, Howard also wrote about Steve Costigan, a vigorous sailor with considerable prowess as a boxer. And in the sword-and-sorcery genre he had already written several atmospheric tales featuring King Kull, an adventurer hailing from the underwater kingdom Atlantis. Notable among the Kull tales, which H. P. Lovecraft, quoted in his *Selected Letters: 1934-1937,* summarized as "a weird peak" in Howard's canon, are "The Mirrors of Tuzun Thune" and "Kings of the Night."

In 1932 Howard introduced Conan the Barbarian to *Weird Tales* readers with "By This Ax I Rule!" and "The Phoenix and the Sword." In these tales, and the many that followed, Conan roams the primitive lands of Cimmeria, where all manner of helpless maidens, evil sorcerers, and gruesome serpents might be found. Conan himself is a crude figure whose powers in combat far outweigh his prowess as a reasoning individual, and in dangerous situations he inevitably favors brutal retaliation over deliberation. Howard, as quoted in *The Last Celt: A Bio-Bibliography of Robert Ervin Howard,* described Conan as "a combination of a number of men I have known." He added that he "took the dominant characteristics of various prize-fighters, gunmen, bootleggers, oil field bullies, gamblers, and honest workmen . . . and combining them all produced . . . Conan the Cimmerian."

"[Howard's heroes were] wish projections of himself," observed H. R. Hays in the *New York Times.* "All of the frustrations of his own life were conquered in a dream world of magic and heroic carnage. . . . The problem of evil is solved by an impossibly omnipotent hero."

It was in the Conan series that Howard produced what he described in *The Last Celt* as "the bloodiest and most sexy weird story I ever wrote." That tale, "Red Nails," featuring the strong-willed female warrior Red Sonja, is among the most prominent of the Conan series, which also includes such titles as "The Hour of the Dragon," "The Tower of the Elephant," "The Slithering Shadow," "The People of the Black Circle," and "Beyond the Black River."

In 1936, depressed by news of his mother's grave illness, Howard killed himself. In the ensuing decade Howard's stories would seem to have been largely forgotten. But in 1950 "The Hour of the Dragon" was published as *Conan the Conqueror,* and two years later a collection of Conan tales were published as

The Sword of Conan. By the middle of the decade Howard's Conan tales were back in print. And the Conan revival continued, for fantasy writer L. Sprague de Camp had obtained Howard's incomplete manuscripts and notes and had completed many of the stories. The de Camp continuations appeared in such 1960s volumes as *Conan the Adventurer, Conan the Warrior,* and *Conan the Usurper.*

In the following years Conan has been featured in sword-and-sorcery fiction by other writers, including de Camp, Lin Carter, Andrew J. Offutt, Robert Jordan, and Steve Perry. In addition, he has appeared in the comic books *Conan the Barbarian* and *The Savage Sword of Conan* and in such films as *Conan the Barbarian* and *Conan the Destroyer.*

While the Conan tales remain most prominent among Howard's writings, westerns, detective tales, and even poetry also hold a place in his collected works. His verse, for example, is featured in several publications, including *Always Comes Evening: The Collected Poems of Robert E. Howard, Etchings in Ivory, Singers in the Shadows, Echoes from an Iron Harp,* and *The Gold and the Grey.*

"Howard was, in my opinion, a writer of superior ability," commented Darrell Schweitzer, summing up the author's vast body of work, "who only sometimes wrote as well as he could, due mainly to haste and sheer laziness." Jessica Amanda Salmonson, in the 1982 essay "Dark Agnes: A Critical Look at Robert E. Howard's 'Swordsmen'" published in *American Fantasy,* stated, "Howard was a great storyteller. Perhaps not a skilled writer in technical terms, but nonetheless, his fiction is powerful in an awkward, honest, direct manner—not unlike many of his heroes." Salmonson noted that Howard "could do what few adventure writers can do even today; that is, depict a strong woman. Further, he did it in an atmosphere of rank misogyny: the male-defined pulp era of writing."

de Camp noted in his book *Literary Swordsmen and Sorcerers: The Makers of Heroic Fantasy,* "Howard's stories . . . bid fair to be enjoyed for their action, color, and furious narrative drive for many years to come."

BIOGRAPHICAL/CRITICAL SOURCES:

BOOKS

de Camp, L. Sprague, *Literary Swordsmen and Sorcerers: The Makers of Heroic Fantasy,* Arkham, 1976.

Lord, Glenn, editor, *The Last Celt: A Bio-bibliography of Robert E. Howard,* Berkley, 1976.

Schweitzer, Darrell, *Conan's World and Robert E. Howard,* Borgo Press, 1978.

Twentieth-Century Literary Criticism, Volume 8, Gale (Detroit), 1982.

PERIODICALS

American Fantasy, February, 1982, pp. 4-6.

New York Times Book Review, September 29, 1934; May 29, 1946, p. 34; April 30, 1978, p. 75.

Starlog, June, 1982, pp. 16-21.*

* * *

HSU, Madeleine (DeMory) 1938-

PERSONAL: Born September 20, 1938; U.S. citizen; children: Yann, Olen. *Education:* Ecole Normale de Musique, Paris, Diploma in Pedagogy, 1960, Diploma in Musicology, 1961; Warsaw Conservatory, Diploma, 1965; Juilliard School, B.Mus., 1970, M.S., 1971; New York University, Ph.D., 1984; studied with Alfred Cortot, Wilhelm Kempff, Zbigniev Drzewiecki, Rosina Lhevinne, and Martin Canin. *Avocational interests:* Swimming, art.

ADDRESSES: Office—Department of Music, Morrison Center for the Performing Arts, Boise State University, 1910 University Dr., Boise, ID 83725; fax 208-385-3006.

CAREER: Teacher at a private studio in Paris, France, 1955-64; Ecole Magda Tagliaferro, Paris, private instructor, 1960-63; teacher at private studios in Rio de Janeiro, Brazil, 1965-66, and New York City, 1966-71; Boise State University, Boise, ID, professor of piano, 1971—. Yale University, visiting Hendon fellow, 1996. Professional pianist, 1952—; performed in solo, with orchestras, and on radio and television broadcasts in the United States, Europe, Africa, and South America. Bronx House Music School, piano instructor, 1968-70; Usdan Center for the Performing Arts, piano instructor and accompanist, summers, 1968-69; teacher at private studios in Boise, 1971—, and Sun Valley, ID, 1993—.

MEMBER: Music Teachers National Association (certified master teacher), American Liszt Society, National Federation of Music Clubs.

AWARDS, HONORS: Silver Medal, Viotti International Piano Competition, 1961; prize, Maria Canals International Piano Competition, 1962; Polish government grant for Warsaw, 1964-65; Silver Medal, Guanabara International Piano Competition, 1965; French government grant for the United States, 1966-67; Josef Lhevinne Memorial Award, 1970; Canadian government grant, 1988; Governor's Award for Excellence in the Arts, State of Idaho, 1990; Idaho Commission on the Arts, grant, 1994, fellowship, 1995; fellow of National Endowment for the Arts, 1995, 1996, and Idaho Humanities Council, 1996.

WRITINGS:

Olivier Messiaen, the Musical Mediator: A Study of the Influence of Liszt, Debussy, and Bartok, Associated University Presses (Cranbury, NJ), 1996.

Contributor to periodicals, including *Journal of the American Liszt Society, Piano Guild Notes, Clavier,* and *American Music Teacher.*

SIDELIGHTS: Madeleine Hsu told *CA:* "Music is neither game nor recreation for the true performer: it is an uncompromising synthesis of intellect and soul. It is a fearful and magnificent exercise in authenticity and perseverance. I urge my students to demand more from themselves than they would otherwise dare, to know themselves beneath the skin, to strip their surfaces until they have found their core. I teach my students to express themselves, as individual men and women; to embrace music as their personal act; to reach the heart and intellect of their audience; to explore their own selves in order that they may hear their innermost dreams and render their music with life. I teach them to transcend prosaism as we merge with the greatest minds of the musical world. As performers, we feel elevated beyond our own humanity. Our audiences receive offerings from our world of the spirit. The performer and the listener, through these offerings, find emotional renewal, each excavating new truths from within the other.

"Technique is not a question of practicing seven hours a day. It is in the mind and depends on intelligence. For this reason, I teach my students to be aware of their bodies, to study carefully their reactions, and to control their motions through their brains with care, sensitivity, and a heightened awareness of their biological composition. Musical spirit lies in the synthesis of mind and body.

"We approach each composer with humility. I lead my students toward writings on and by the composers themselves in order that the students may understand the composer's thinking, his world of emotions, and his spirit. In striving to understand the mind of the composer, we must also tune our introspection. It is at the center of our introspection that we find the most wonderful part of ourselves: the part that does not belong to us. We reach the innermost part of human experience, and there, through our music, we collectively meet.

"As performers, we embrace the composer's spirit as our own, and in offering it to our audiences through music, we temporarily dissolve ourselves and let the composer speak through us. The performer is the in-between, the audience's guide to the collective part of our minds that allows music to be the language we all understand.

"I guide my students to be wise with this language. I teach them to be poets, to examine subtlety and nuance, and to discipline their musical ear. The world of emotions awaits them, but opens only to those whose honesty is absolute. This honesty can be a devastating thing; it is treacherous at times to examine one's own naked soul. Some students, afraid to look too deeply into their own eyes, prefer to turn away instead. It is so much more comfortable to look away, and so much easier to demand little of oneself. For them, my studio has little to offer. Others, however, find a hint of truth in what I have to say; these students remain. They probe their hearts and intellects, and they learn to reach the rigorous honesty that surpasses the artist's ego. They learn to discover within themselves the most sublime of human emotions, and to offer them humbly to the world."

*   *   *

ISERSON, Kenneth Victor 1949-

PERSONAL: Born April 8, 1949, in Washington, DC; son of Isadore Irving and Edith (Swedlow) Iserson; married Mary Lou Sherk (a C.P.A.), June 16, 1973. *Education:* University of Maryland, College Park, B.S., 1971; University of Maryland School of Medicine, M.D., 1975; studied surgical practice at Mayo Clinic, 1975; studied emergency medicine at University of Cincinnati College of Medicine, 1976-78; University of Phoenix, M.B.A. (valedictorian), 1986. *Politics:* Liberal. *Religion:* Jewish.

ADDRESSES: Office—Arizona Bioethics Program, University of Arizona, College of Medicine, Box 245057, 1501 North Campbell Ave., Tucson, AZ 85724.

CAREER: Cincinnati General Hospital, OH, emergency medicine residency, 1976-78, chief resident, 1977-78; Community Mercy Hospital, Onamia, MN, general practice, 1976; Division of Emergency Medicine, Texas A&M University College of Medicine, clinical associate professor and chairman, 1980-81; University of Arizona College of Medicine, section of emergency medicine, department of surgery, emergency physician, 1981—, assistant professor, 1981-85, associate professor, 1985-92, professor, 1992—. Senior fellow in Bioethics, University of Chicago, 1990-91. *Modern Medicine,* specialty advisory board, 1988—; Arizona Emergency Services Council (appointed by governor), 1990-91; Arizona Legislative Committee on Advance Directives (appointed by governor), 1991-92; *ER* (television show), ethics advisor, 1994—. *Military service:* U.S. Air Force, 1978-80, became captain and director of emergency medicine.

MEMBER: American College of Emergency Physicians, American Medical Association, Emergency Medicine Foundation, European Society for Philosophy of Medicine and Health Care, Society for Academic Emergency Medicine, Society for Bioethics Consultation, Society for Health and Human Values, Southern Arizona Rescue Association (medical director), Wilderness Medical Society, Arizona Bioethics Network, University Medical Center Bioethics Committee (chair), American Medical Association Section on Medical Schools (faculty representative), Arizona Bioethics Program (director), Department of Surgery Promotion and Tenure Committee, Society of Teachers of Emergency Medicine (now SAEM; president, 1982-83), American Society for Law, Medicine, and Ethics, American Association of Bioethics, Arizona Medical Association, Literary Guild, American Philosophical Association, Society of Southwestern Authors.

AWARDS, HONORS: Diplomate, American Board of Emergency Medicine, 1980; fellow, American College of Emergency Medicine, 1982; senior fellow in bioethics, Center for Clinical Medical Ethics, University of Chicago, 1990-91; Arizona Emergency Medical Services Council, appointed by governor, 1990-91; Arizona Legislative Committee on Advance Directives, appointed by governor, 1991-92; award for best reference books, New York Public Library, 1994, for *Death to Dust: What Happens to Dead Bodies?*

WRITINGS:

(Editor with A. B. Sanders, D. R. Mathieu, and A. E. Buchanan) *Ethics in Emergency Medicine,* Williams and Wilkins (Baltimore, MD), 1986.

Getting into Residency: A Guide for Medical Students, Camden House (Columbia, SC), 1988, second edition, 1990; third edition and fourth editions published by Galen Press (Tuscon, AZ), 1993 and 1996.

Death to Dust: What Happens to Dead Bodies?, Galen Press (Tucson, AZ), 1994.

(Editor with A. B. Sanders and D. R. Mathieu) *Ethics in Emergency Medicine,* Galen Press (Tucson, AZ), 1995.

Get into Medical School!: A Guide for the Perplexed, Galen Press (Tucson, AZ), 1997.

Non-standard Medical Electives in the U.S. and Canada, Galen Press (Tucson, AZ), 1997.

Also author of over 150 professional journal articles, textbook chapters, and other publications. Reviewer for medical journals, including *Annals of Emergency Medicine, American Journal of Emergency Medicine, American Journal of Diseases in Children, Journal of the American Medical Association, Archives of Internal Medicine, Pediatrics* and *Journal of Clinical Ethics.* Editor for *Journal of Emergency Medicine, Hospital Ethics Committee Forum,* and *Cambridge Quarterly.*

WORK IN PROGRESS: Scripting a videotape which will teach physicians practical ethics, planning new book projects, and helping to draft new ethics-related statutes.

SIDELIGHTS: Ken Iserson wrote, *Death to Dust: What Happens to Dead Bodies?* for two reasons. He told *CA* that he hopes not only to inform the public and professional world of post-death procedures that a body may undergo but also to promote organ and tissue donation. "Corpses deteriorate, no matter what," Iserson commented. "There is no reason not to donate organs and tissues 'the last, best gift a person can leave behind.'" The book itself is laid out in a question and answer format with information ranging from common questions about burial and cremation, funeral costs, and organ donation to more unusual possibilities, such as cryogenic preservation and scientific study. Iserson also devotes sections of his book to bizarre practices such as head-shrinking and grave-robbing. Not included in the book is a discussion of the afterlife, since, as Iserson tells *CA,* he "leaves the spiritual side to others, although the reli-

gious rites practiced throughout human history and across cultures comprises a fascinating part of my books and talks."

The critical success of *Death to Dust* has led to the author's guest appearances on radio talk shows and speaking engagements at national meetings. "A most curious volume," remarked a critic from *Choice,* adding that the book "should help individuals make more informed choices concerning autopsy, organ donation, and funeral arrangements. The peculiar facts and stories about the dead have a captivating appeal."

Among Iserson's other books are *Ethics in Emergency Medicine* and *Getting into a Residency: A Guide For Medical Students.* Iserson says of the first, "It is still the only book dealing with unique ethical issues faced by emergency physicians, emergency nurses, and ambulance personnel. My unique background in medicine and ethics and the exciting list of case commentators, brings an interesting flavor to this casebook." *Getting into Residency* was the best-selling non-clinical book in medical education in its third edition, according to Iserson, who refers to it as "'The Bible' for medical students seeking a postgraduate position. It gives a step-by-step method for getting through the process intact."

Iserson continues to be an active part of the emergency medical system in addition to teaching, speaking, writing articles, and performing various administrative duties and offices; he uses his spare time to write books. The author says he "firmly believes in the saying, 'It is harder to wear out than to rust out.'" He adds that he does not plan on donating his organs and tissues anytime soon (although the card has been signed and next-of-kin notified).

BIOGRAPHICAL/CRITICAL SOURCES:

PERIODICALS

Choice, November, 1994, p.479.

                    *   *   *

JOHNSON, Una E.   1905-1997

OBITUARY NOTICE—See index for *CA* sketch: Born in 1905, in Dayton, IA; died April 28, 1997, in Manhattan, NY. Curator and author. Johnson is credited with building the print collection at the Brooklyn Museum of Art and organizing the National Print Exhibition at the museum for more than twenty years. She began her career at the Cleveland Museum of Art in 1931. In 1937, she accepted a curatorial position at the Brooklyn Museum of Art; she retired in 1968 and from 1969 to 1971 became the curator of collections at the Storm King Art Center in Mountainville, New York. She was a contributor to many art and literary journals and wrote numerous books. They include *Isabel Bishop: Prints and Drawings, 1925-1964, Ambroise Vollard, Editeur: Prints, Books, Bronzes, Twentieth Century Drawings, American Prints and Printmakers: A Chronicle of over Four Hundred Artists and Their Prints from 1900 to the Present, What Is a Modern Print, The American Woodcut: 1670-1950,* and *Georges Rouault and His Prints.*

OBITUARIES AND OTHER SOURCES:

BOOKS

Who's Who in American Art, 20th edition, Bowker (New Providence, NJ), 1993.

PERIODICALS

New York Times, May 4, 1997, p. 45; May 5, 1997, p. B11.

*   *   *

JOHNSON, Whittington B. 1931-

PERSONAL: Born April 29, 1931, in Miami, FL; son of Joseph Blake (a mattress maker) and Lucille Marie (a domestic worker; maiden name, Bain; present surname, Milton) Johnson; married Juanita Simkins, September, 1955 (divorced, March, 1959); married Vivian Page, May, 1959 (divorced, June, 1966); married Imogene Smith, June 26, 1966; children: Terrance (deceased), Toni Thomas, Traci-Leigh, Todd. *Ethnicity:* "African American." *Education:* West Virginia State College, B.S., 1953; Indiana University—Bloomington, M.A.T., 1957; University of Georgia, Ph.D., 1970. *Politics:* Democrat. *Religion:* Episcopalian.

ADDRESSES: Home—Miami, FL. *Office*—Department of History, University of Miami, Coral Gables, FL 33124.

CAREER: Edward Waters College, Jacksonville, FL, instructor in social science, 1957-62; Savannah State College (now University), Savannah, GA, assistant professor of social science, 1962-67; University of Miami, Coral Gables, FL, associate professor, 1970-95, professor of history, 1995—, department head, 1976-77, director of Afro-American Studies Center, 1972-73. Wisconsin State University (now University of Wisconsin—Superior), guest lecturer, 1972. Civil Rights Museum, Savannah, member of board of directors. *Military service:* U.S. Army, airborne marksman, 1953-55; became first lieutenant.

MEMBER: Society for Historians of the Early American Republic, Southern Historical Association, Phi Kappa Phi (president, 1986-87), Omicron Delta Kappa, Phi Alpha Theta, Golden Key, Iron Arrow.

AWARDS, HONORS: Recipient of plaque for dedicated service to education, Dade County Commission, 1972; Educator of the Year, Zeta Phi Beta Sorority, 1975; Professor of the Year, Phi Eta Sigma Freshman Honorary Fraternity, 1979; Max Orovitz summer fellow, 1981, 1987, 1988; Social Science Professor of the Year, 1984; Professor of the Year, College of Arts and Sciences Alumni Association, 1984; Southern Regional Education fellow, 1988; Mac Lamore summer award, 1995.

WRITINGS:

The Promising Years, 1750-1830: The Emergence of Black Labor and Business, Garland Publishing (New York City), 1993.
Black Savannah, 1788-1864, University of Arkansas Press (Fayetteville, AR), 1996.

Contributor of articles and reviews to periodicals, including *Journal of the Early American Republic, Gulf Coast Historical Review, Journal of Negro History, Georgia Historical Quarterly, Southern University Law Review,* and *Journal of the Bahamas Historical Society.*

WORK IN PROGRESS: Race Relations in the Bahamas, 1784-1834.

SIDELIGHTS: Whittington B. Johnson told *CA:* "I entered graduate school at the University of Georgia in the fall of 1967 with the goal of earning a doctorate and returning to Savannah State College, where I worked, to continue teaching history to students who may enroll at that institution. By the time I had completed my course work, however, I knew that just teaching history would not be enough for me; I want to both teach and write history, because creating knowledge is as important to me as disseminating it. In short, I write history to contribute to the corpus of knowledge on the subject. In this small way, I hope to justify the time God has given to me, on this wonderful planet we call earth."

* * *

JONES, Thom 1945(?)-

PERSONAL: Born c. 1945; children: one daughter. *Education:* Attended the University of Iowa Writer's Workshop.

ADDRESSES: Home—Olympia, WA. *Agent*—Little, Brown, 34 Beacon St., Boston, MA 02108.

CAREER: Writer. Has worked variously as a boxer, an ad copywriter, and a janitor. *Military service:* U.S. Marines; discharged for medical reasons, 1963.

AWARDS, HONORS: O. Henry Award, 1993, for *The Pugilist at Rest;* National Book Award nomination, 1993, for *The Pugilist at Rest.*

WRITINGS:

SHORT STORIES

The Pugilist at Rest, Little, Brown (Boston), 1993.
Cold Snap: Stories, Little, Brown, 1995.

Contributor to periodicals, including *Playboy* and *New Yorker.*

WORK IN PROGRESS: A novel.

SIDELIGHTS: The author of short story collections *The Pugilist at Rest* and *Cold Snap,* Thom Jones writes autobiographical short stories that have been noted for their pessimism, straightforward prose, and tough characters. "Often I will hear something in passing, perhaps as I walk through a room, and then a couple weeks later I'll remember the line," the author once explained in describing the writing process in *Contemporary Literary Criticism Yearbook* (*CLC Yearbook*). "I often begin that way, with just a single line of speech which I write, and then a story begins to take shape. I don't really plan it, I just get the first draft out, which seems to flow automati-

cally." Jones added that "The stories in *The Pugilist at Rest* . . . are partly autobiographical, about people who meant a great deal to me. I was writing from the heart with a lot of emotion—they were magical stories that just seemed to pour out."

Some critics have noticed an obsessive quality in Jones's characters, and in his interview in *CLC Yearbook* he described himself in similar terms: "Writing is more important to me than my own life—I never really wanted to do or be anything other than a writer. And yet . . . I was lazy about it. I suppose if you're serious about something and you fail, then you have to acknowledge that you're a failure. By being lazy, you can excuse yourself—there's always the possibility that you *could* be successful if you really tried."

Other critics have emphasized the machismo expressed by some of Jones's characters, and have questioned his frequent references to the philosophy of Friedrich Nietzsche and Arthur Schopenhauer in his pessimistic tales. In his *CLC Yearbook* interview, Jones responded: "The strange thing is that I really don't like Nietzsche that much. My background probably also influenced the concern with masculinity in those stories. As a child I had conflicts with my father and stepfather, and I've never liked people—particularly men—pushing me around. This is probably why I got into boxing. I got fired from jobs because I refused to take orders and if I felt threatened, I was prepared to react in an extreme manner. A lot of those emotions and conflicts are revealed in the writing. I suppose it was kind of cathartic to write those stories. Recently, since I've received some recognition, the tone of my work has been shifting, becoming a bit more positive and upbeat."

Several of the stories in 1993's *The Pugilist at Rest* feature a young marine as he goes though boot camp, then a tour of duty in Vietnam, and then is returned home, full of anger and the knowledge of the violence of which he is capable. B. G. Preston, contributor to *Details* magazine, described this protagonist and his buddies as "more than a little brave; these guys are gung ho and psycho." But as Ted Solotaroff of the *Nation* wrote, "there are several interactive furies in the writing persona of Thom Jones." In another story, "Mosquitos," Jones's protagonist is an emergency-room surgeon obsessed with rescuing his weak brother from a domineering wife. In "As of July 6th, I Am Responsible for No Debts Other Than My Own," a teenage boy's stoical grandmother helps him struggle with his contempt for his stepfather. "I Want to Live!" was often singled out for comment as many critics found the story heartrending in its realistic portrayal of the quick but painful death of a cancer patient. Critical reaction was more mixed for Jones's only story with a female narrator, "Unchain My Heart," which concerns an ambitious but bored magazine editor who skips work to go deep-sea diving with her muscle-bound boyfriend and is fired as a result.

Jones's own experiences of boxing for a living and of suffering with a form of epilepsy due to injuries inflicted in the ring inform several of the stories in *The Pugilist at Rest*. In the title story, which was awarded the O. Henry Award for short fiction in 1993, an unnamed protagonist serving in the military during the Vietnam War defends a weaker buddy by smashing in the skull of a bully during boot camp. The narrators of both "The Black Lights," and "Rocket Man" identify themselves as boxers, the former who is recovering from a blow to the head in a Marine psychiatric ward. While *Nation* critic Ted Solotaroff criticized Jones's relentlessly masculine protagonists, he joined other critics in finding a depth in the author's otherwise one-dimensional characters. "Jones is more than just another talented young writer who is a pushover for himself and muscular male values," Solotaroff wrote. "What he understands deeply as well as clinically is pain and mortality, the validating elements of his balefulness."

"Part of what Jones manages in these eleven stories (besides declaring his arrival as an audacious and powerful talent) is to keep us laughing, albeit in the dark growls of one offended," wrote *Los Angeles Times Book Review* critic Fred Schruers. Other critics remarked on Jones's ability to add a comedic touch to the depressing scenarios he invokes without degrading the sympathy one should feel for his hard-pressed characters. Judith Wynn of *Tribune Books* emphasized the author's tendency to take a seemingly hopeless situation and turn it into a source of wisdom: "Thom Jones takes the events of what seems to have been a rough-and-tumble life and sets them to the deeper rhythms of reflection and self-insight." Many critics expressed the sentiment contained in novelist Thomas McGuane's review of *The Pugilist at Rest* in the *New York Times Book Review:* "Writers as good as Thom Jones appear but rarely. The original poetry of his fictional world is irresistible, and the sense that he knows this world absolutely has cleansed his prose and produced an affectless sheen."

BIOGRAPHICAL/CRITICAL SOURCES:

BOOKS

Contemporary Literary Criticism Yearbook 1993, Volume 81, Gale (Detroit), 1994.

PERIODICALS

Commonweal, October 6, 1995, pp. 24-26.
Details, August 1993, p. 134.
Los Angeles Times Book Review, August 1, 1993, pp. 2-3.
Nation, September 6, 1993, pp. 254-257.
New York Times Book Review, June 13, 1993, p. 7; June 4, 1995, p. 8.
Publishers Weekly, May 15, 1995, p. 56.
Time, June 19, 1995, p. 60.
Tribune Books, July 25, 1993, p. 6.*

K

KALISH, Betty McKelvey 1913-1997

OBITUARY NOTICE—See index for *CA* sketch: Born September 30, 1913, in Minneapolis, MN; died of pneumonia, April 28, 1997, in Falls Church, VA. Author. A journalist by trade, Kalish accompanied her husband on foreign assignments and found inspiration for two children's books while living abroad. A graduate of the University of Wisconsin, Kalish was a reporter, state editor, and society editor for the *Green Bay Press-Gazette* from 1935 to 1940 and a reporter for the *Milwaukee Journal* from 1940 to 1941. She then moved to Washington, D.C., after marrying Stanley Edward Kalish, who worked for the United States Information Agency. She continued freelance writing and contributed articles to *Foreign Service Journal, American Home* and *Popular Aviation.* Kalish also wrote scripts for the United States Information Agency from 1964 to 1965. Her travels to England, France, Austria, Indonesia and Pakistan while her husband was in the Foreign Service led to her two children's novels, *Siti's Summer* (1964), and *Eleven! Time to Think About Marriage, Farhut* (1970). She also contributed to *Fodor Guide to Austria.*

OBITUARIES AND OTHER SOURCES:

PERIODICALS

Washington Post, May 10, 1997, p. B4.

*   *   *

KEYNE, Gordon
See BEDFORD-JONES, H(enry James O'Brien)

KHAN, Hasan-Uddin 1947-

PERSONAL: Born November 28, 1947, in Hyderabad, India; son of Naser-Ud-Deen and Bilquis (Jehan) Khan; married Karen Longeteig; children: Ayesha, Zehra. *Education:* Attended Chichester School of Art, 1965-66; Architectural Association School of Architecture, graduated, 1971, graduate study, 1971-72. *Politics:* Liberal. *Religion:* Islamic.

ADDRESSES: Home—143 Concord Ave., Lexington, MA 02173. *Office*—Department of Architecture, Building 10-390, Massachusetts Institute of Technology, 77 Massachusetts Ave., Cambridge, MA 02139. *E-mail*—huk@mit.edu.

CAREER: Payette Associates, Inc., Boston, MA, assistant architect in London office, 1972-73; Gerald Shenstone and Partners, London, England, project architect, 1973-74; Unit 4 Architects and Planners, Karachi, Pakistan, partner, 1974-76; Aga Khan Award for Architecture (now Aga Khan Trust for Culture), Philadelphia, PA, assistant convenor, 1977-79, convenor, 1980; consultant in Jakarta, Indonesia, 1981-84; Secretariat of the Aga Khan, Gouvieux, France, head of architectural activities, 1984-91; Institute of Ismaili Studies, London, consultant, 1994-95; Massachusetts Institute of Technology, Department of Architecture, Cambridge, visiting associate professor, 1994—. Architect and home renovator. Concept Media Ltd. (publishing company), member of board of directors, 1981-87; Zamana Gallery Ltd., member of board of directors, 1985-92; Baltit Heritage Trust, member of board of trustees, 1990-94; Aga Khan Trust for Culture, director of special projects and public education, 1991-94; consultant to Rockefeller Foundation.

MEMBER: International Committee of Architectural Critics, Architectural Association (London), Royal Institute of British Architects, Architects Institute of Pakistan, Royal Overseas League (London).

WRITINGS:

Charles Correa (monograph), Concept Media (Singapore, China), 1987.

(Contributor) H. Salam, editor, *Expressions of Islam in Buildings,* Aga Khan Trust for Culture (Geneva, Switzerland), 1991.

(Editor with Martin Frishman, and contributor) *The Mosque: History, Architecture, Development, and Regional Diversity,* Thames & Hudson (London, England), 1994.

Contemporary Asian Architects (trilingual in English, French, and German), Benedikt Taschen (Cologne, Germany), 1995.

(With Renata Holod) *Contemporary Mosques: Clients, Designs, and Processes since 1950* (monograph), Thames & Hudson, 1997.

Internationalist Architecture, 1925-1965 (in English, German, Dutch, and French), Benedikt Taschen, 1997.

Contributor of articles and reviews to architecture journals and other periodicals, including *Journal of Architectural Education, Criticism in Architecture, Architecture U.S.A.,* and *Space.* Founder and editor in chief, *Mimar: Architecture in Development,* 1981-92.

WORK IN PROGRESS: Research on North American mosques and on pluralism and its cultural expressions.

SIDELIGHTS: Hasan-Uddin Khan told *CA:* "My primary motivation for writing is a desire to help promote a dialogue about architecture in Asia and Africa. This is neglected in general architectural discourse. We need to build bridges between people of the 'west' and the 'east.' My perspective is that of an international nomad and a man of both east and west—a cultural hybrid.

"Having been very lucky in my wide set of experiences, I feel the need to communicate them and the ideas I have developed, partly as a way of sorting them out for myself.

"I have been influenced by various architectural writers and actual practitioners, but by no one in particular more than others."

KIBERD, Declan   1951-

PERSONAL: Born May 24, 1951, in Dublin, Ireland; son of Fred and Eithne (maiden name, Keegan) Kiberd. *Education:* St. Pauls College, Trinity College, Dublin; Oxford University.

ADDRESSES: Office—J203 Department of English, University College, Dublin, Ireland.   *Agent*—c/o Harvard University Press, 79 Garden St., Cambridge, MA 02138.

CAREER: Literary critic and educator. University College, Dublin, lecturer in English. Professor of Anglo-Irish Literature and Drama.

WRITINGS:

Synge and the Irish Language (literary criticism), Rowman & Littlefield (Totowa, NJ), 1979.

Men and Feminism in Modern Literature (literary criticism), St. Martin's Press (New York City), 1985.

(Editor with Susan Dick), *Omrium Satlerum: Essays for Richard Ellmann,* Colin Smythe (Serrards Cross), 1989.

(Editor, with Gabriel Fitzmaurice) *An Crann Faoi Bhlath/The Flowering Tree: Contemporary Irish Poetry with Verse Translations,* Wolfhound (Dublin), 1991.

(Editor) *The Student's Annotated Ulysses,* Penguin Classics (Harmondsworth), 1992.

Idir Dha Chultur, (literary criticism), Coisceim (Dublin), 1993.

Inventing Ireland: The Literature of the Modern Nation (literary criticism), Harvard University Press (Cambridge, MA), 1996.

SIDELIGHTS: Declan Kiberd is a literary historian and critic whose area of specialization is Irish literature of the twentieth century. In addition to his critical reexamination of the works of influential Irish playwright J. M. Synge, whose *The Playboy of the Western World* caused riots upon its premiere production at Dublin's Abbey Theatre in 1907, Kiberd is the author of *Men and Feminism in Modern Literature,* a study of how six male modernists respond in their writings to the image of the "New Woman." Co-editor of an anthology of Gaelic verse, with English translations, Kiberd has also produced the critically praised anti-revisionist literary history, *Inventing Ireland,* a work that considers the ways in which a great variety of writers and cultural commentators reshaped a modern Irish identity.

In his first book, 1979's *Synge and the Irish Language,* Kiberd aspires to broaden Irish playwright J. M. Synge's reputation as a great Anglo-Irish writer to include an evaluation of his use of literary material from the Gaelic tradition. In this pursuit Kiberd examines Synge's published and unpublished works for evidence of that author's knowledge of Gaelic and Old and Middle Irish dialects and literature. Ulick O'Connor, writing in the *Irish Independent* described the work as a "magisterial and splendid study." And Patricia Craig in her *New Statesman* review, asserts that the book "is informative, but uneven in tone" because of the author's attempt "to amass all the facts relating to his . . . specialised subject." A commentary in *Choice,* on the other hand, called *Synge and the Irish Language* "an invaluable book," and praised the author for "opening up this important avenue of inquiry." *Synge* became popular reading again, when in 1993 Macmillan of London republished it in paperback edition, at which time Eileen Battersby saluted its return in the *Irish Times,* calling it "*the* classic book on J.M. Synge."

Kiberd's next publication, *Men and Feminism in Modern Literature,* is considered an exploration of the concept of "anima" in the work of leading male modernists. One of the earliest critics to deal with the topic of feminism, Kiberd explores female characters in the works of Henrik Ibsen, August Strindberg, Thomas Hardy, William Butler Yeats, James Joyce, and D. H. Lawrence, authors whom he perceives as rejecting the turn-of-the-century's emancipatory New Woman in favor of a more androgynous equality between the sexes as exemplified in some of their male characters. "When he is considering role-reversal simply as a theme in Fin-de-Siecle literature, Kiberd is clear and helpful," remarked Elaine Showalter in the *London Review of Books.* However, Showalter continued, "For Kiberd 'feminism' appears to mean something like 'female dominance', and thus, despite his support for equal pay, and his care to call women 'Ms,' he seems strikingly ambivalent about the women's movement."

Kiberd returned to the subject of Irish literature in his third book, *An Crann Faoi Bhlath/The Flowering Tree,* an anthology of Gaelic poetry accompanied by English verse translations, which Kiberd co-edited with Gabriel Fitzmaurice. Gaelic poetry didn't come into its own in the twentieth century until the mid-1940s, according to Patricia Craig of the *Times Literary Supplement.* But "poets and other writers in Irish ever since have been at pains to show themselves as no less amenable to the avant-garde than anyone else," Craig continued, and *The Flower Tree* gives a good idea of what has been happening in Gaelic poetry over the past forty-odd years."

Kiberd is also the author of *Inventing Ireland,* a highly praised examination of what is known as the Irish Literary Revival, the period in the early part of the twentieth century when Ireland produced a large number of world-class writers. Inherently connected to the Irish nationalist movement, which agitated to remove the British from power in Ireland, the Irish Literary Revival has been subjected to a revisionist analysis by several critics, according to Terry Eagleton, writing in the *New Statesman & Society.* "Declan Kiberd's spirited blockbuster . . . is thus courageously unfashionable," Eagleton continued. "Few Irish critics know this astonishingly fertile period as well as he does, and few love it so unashamedly." Like Eagleton, the *New York Times Book Review*'s Thomas Flanagan praised Kiberd's prose style, dubbing *Inventing Ireland* "a critical study laced with wit, energy and an unrelenting adroitness of discourse." In addition, Kiberd "possesses a special gift for patient exploration of works of art in relationship to their surroundings," Flanagan remarked. Finally, Flanagan, again like Eagleton, praised Kiberd's obvious delight in his subject: "It is heartening," Flanagan concluded, "to find an academic critic talking about masterpieces and writing in celebration of them."

A lecturer in English literature at University College, Dublin, Kiberd is widely acknowledged as an expert on Irish literature and writers who write in Gaelic. However, his work in other areas has sometimes been seen as controversial, particularly his critique of feminist literary criticism in *Men and Feminism in Modern Literature.* Kiberd's scholarly commentaries on playwright Synge and the Irish Literary Revival, however, have been cited as important contributions to our understanding of Irish literature in the first half of the twentieth century. Influential literary critic Terry Eagleton summed up Kiberd's style in a review of *Inventing Ireland* as follows: "Kiberd's brand of criticism is a mite too zesty and robust, and it doesn't always give a sense of plumbing the depths. But there are moments . . . when it shifts into a register that is both moving and wise."

Kiberd told *CA:* "My main interest as a writer has been the attempt to show that traditions often taken to be opposed may, at a deeper level, be secret doubles of one another.

"I take as a motto the statement of Giordano Bruno that 'every power in nature must evolve its own opposite in order to achieve itself—but from that opposition may spring eventual reunion.' For me words are both a means of describing the majesty of great works of art and an alternative way of seizing cultural power."

BIOGRAPHICAL/CRITICAL SOURCES:

PERIODICALS

Choice, May 1980, p. 388.
Irish Independent, c. 1979.
Irish Times, c. 1993.
London Review of Books, March 20, 1986, p. 8.
New Statesman, November 23, 1979, pp. 813-14.
New Statesman & Society, November 24, 1995, p. 40.
New York Times Book Review, March 17, 1996, p. 6.
Times Literary Supplement, June 21, 1991, p. 18.
Women's Review of Books, February 1981, p. 17.

* * *

KIRK, Pauline (M.) 1942-

PERSONAL: Born April 14, 1942, in Birmingham, England; daughter of Benjamin James (an electrician) and Edith Florence (Hill) Marlow; married Peter Geoffrey Kirk (a civil servant), April 4, 1964; children: Jo Goldby, Geoff. *Ethnicity:* "Caucasian." *Education:* University of Nottingham, B.A. (with honors), 1963; University of Sheffield, Diploma in Education (with distinction), 1964; Monash University, M.A., 1970.

ADDRESSES: Home and office—Leeds, England. *Agent*—David Grossman, David Grossman Literary Agency Ltd., 110-114 Clerkenwell Rd., London EC1M 5SA, England.

CAREER: Methodist Ladies College, Melbourne, Australia, teacher, 1965-66; Open University, began as tutor, became counselor and assistant senior counselor, 1969-89; Department of Social Services, Leeds, England, senior officer and voluntary resource coordinator for city council, 1988-95; writer, 1995—. Tutor in adult education at Universities of London, Reading, and Leeds, 1969-89. Fighting Cock Press, partner. Performance poet and leader of creative writing workshops; judge of short story and poetry competitions; organizer of community arts festivals, 1980—.

MEMBER: Society of Authors, Pennine Poets.

AWARDS, HONORS: Grant from Yorkshire Arts, 1980; New Beginnings Award, Yorkshire and Humberside Arts Association, 1994-95.

WRITINGS:

Scorpion Days (poems), Rivelin Press, 1982, second edition, Medal Poets (Australia), 1986.
Red Marl and Brick (poems), Littlewood Press, 1985.
Waters of Time (novel), Century Hutchinson, 1988.
Rights of Way (poems), Unibird Press, 1990.
Travelling Solo (poems), KT Publications, 1995.
The Keepers (novel), Virago Press (London, England), 1996.
(Author of introduction) *Scathed Earth: The Collected Poems of Mabel Ferrett,* University of Salzburg (Salzburg, Austria), 1996.
Return to Dreamtime (poems), Fighting Cock Press, 1996.

Work represented in anthologies, including *Purple and Green,* Rivelin Grapheme, 1985; *Yesterday's Yorkshire,* David and Charles, 1991; and *Cleopatra,* Edizioni Universum (Italy), 1994. Contributor of poems and articles to magazines and newspapers, including *Acumen, She, Sheaf, Pennine Platform,* and *Mobius.* Member of editorial board, *Teaching at a Distance,* 1974-79, and *Aireings,* 1982—.

WORK IN PROGRESS: Collected Poems; two novels, tentatively titled *Blackthorn* and *Ellahnah,* completion expected in 1998; research on family history.

SIDELIGHTS: Pauline Kirk told *CA:* "I am one of those odd people who have always wanted to write. Education gave me chances denied to my parents. I studied literature at the University of Nottingham, afterwards training to be a teacher of English. I married while still a student and moved to Australia, where I spent four years. I have retained connections with colleagues from that time, and the scenery of Australia—its vast distances, history, and attitudes—have had a formative effect on my work.

"Like many writers, I found academic study initially dried up my inspiration. For the first ten years of my writing career, I published articles and research papers, mostly related to continuing education. Following the birth of my second child, I began to write poetry, but it was only after moving to Leeds in 1979 that I gained confidence. Yorkshire has a rich cultural life, and groups such as the Pennine Poets gave me invaluable stimulus and criticism.

"As part of my work as a tutor in adult education, I edited a series of booklets on local history subjects. The idea of time came to fascinate me and is an important theme in both my novels. *Waters of Time* moves into the past, and then returns to the present. It felt natural to consider the future in my second novel, *The Keepers.* By setting the narrative two hundred years from now, I was free to imagine anything, so long as it was logically possible.

"The book is not a science fiction novel in the usual sense. It portrays people living two hundred years from now—our descendants—and considers what their lives might be like if present trends continue to develop. The story opens as England is recovering from a period of civil war, under the control of a faceless, unidentifiable group that enforces peace and happiness at any cost. The central character, Esther, risks life and love to break free.

"I have always been interested in ideas of freedom, human endurance, and dignity, but this was increased by my employment from 1989 to 1995 by the Leeds Department of Social Services. In 1995 an award from the Yorkshire and Humberside Arts Association enabled me to give up this post and become a full-time writer, but I am still involved with issues of caregivers and community arts."

*   *   *

KLINGSOR THE MAGICIAN
See HARTMANN, Sadakichi

*   *   *

KOHL, James Vaughn 1951-

PERSONAL: Born November 7, 1951, in Napoleon, OH; son of Verland LaVon Kohl (in sales) and Laura Kathryn Grayson Kohl Boyer; married Bernadette Shardt, 1970 (divorced, 1976); married Terri Denbo, 1980 (divorced, 1982); married Cheerie R. Farris (a bookkeeper), February 22, 1992. *Ethnicity:* "Caucasian." *Education:* Attended Clark County Community College, North Las Vegas, NV; attended Midwestern University, Wichita Falls, TX; attended University of Nevada, Las Vegas. *Politics:* Republican. *Religion:* Protestant. *Avocational interests:* Music.

ADDRESSES: Home—2621 Seashore Dr., Las Vegas, NV 89128. *Office*—Simtex, 2950 East Flamingo, Las Vegas, NV 89121; fax: 702-255-3127. *E-mail*—jkohl@vegas.infi.net.

CAREER: Partell Medical Center, Las Vegas, NV, clinical laboratory scientist, 1980-95. *Military service:* U.S. Air Force, 1970-1977.

MEMBER: American Medical Technologists; American Society for Clinical Laboratory Science; MENSA; Association for Chemoreception Sciences; Society for the Scientific Study of Sexuality.

WRITINGS:

(With Robert T. Francoeur) *Scent of Eros* (nonfiction), Continuum (New York), 1995.

Also author of internet website, *http://www.pheromones.com.* Contributor of articles to periodicals, including *Hormones and Behavior.*

WORK IN PROGRESS: Research on olfaction and hormones in human sexuality.

SIDELIGHTS: Author James Vaughn Kohl has been a laboratory scientist in Las Vegas, Nevada, for two decades. In the process of his work, he became interested in what he described in an interview with *Amazon.com* as "the link between sexual 'chemistry' and sexual behavior." He had already begun to write on other topics; as a member of Mensa, the organization for people with high intelligence quotients, he penned a spoof of advice columns for a Las Vegas chapter's publication, *Mind Bets.* He also had experience writing speeches, so he decided to try his hand at writing a book on his subject of interest. The result, coauthored with Robert T. Francoeur, was the 1995 volume, *The Scent of Eros: Mysteries of Odor in Human Sexuality.* Its purpose, Kohl told *Amazon.com,* was to "encourage others to acknowledge the role that natural human body odors, i.e., pheromones, play in human sexuality." Kohl also told the electronic publication that he was inspired to write *The Scent of Eros* for a general audience (rather than for his colleagues within the scientific community) by such works as Helen Fisher's *Anatomy of Love,* Anthony Walsh's *The Science of Love,* and Timothy Perper's *Sex Signals: The Biology of Love.*

Kohl told *CA:* "Recent human studies strongly suggest that natural body odor is very important to the development of human sexuality."

BIOGRAPHICAL/CRITICAL SOURCES:

PERIODICALS

Hormones and Behavior, vol. 30, 1996, pp. 333-353.

OTHER

http://www.amazon.com, 1996.

* * *

KRAMER, Aaron 1921-1997

OBITUARY NOTICE—See index for *CA* sketch: Born December 13, 1921, in Brooklyn, NY; died April 7, 1997, in Long Island, NY. Educator, translator, poet, and author. A poet himself, Kramer contributed significantly to the study of verse through numerous books on the subject, including the forthcoming *Neglected Aspects of American Poetry,* as well as *The Prophetic Tradition in American Poetry: 1835-1900* and *Poetry the Healer* (written with others). He began work as an educator at the New York Guild for the Jewish Blind in 1955, and he eventually became the Guild's dramatics director. From 1959 to 1961, he taught high school in Bogota, New Jersey, before beginning a lengthy association with Dowling College in New York. He rose to the rank of graduate professor of English by 1975. Among the other schools that benefitted from his teaching were Queens College of the City University of New York and the University of Guanajuanto.

Kramer also established a poetry therapy program at Hillside Hospital in Glen Oaks and directed similar programs at Cleary School for the Deaf and the Central Islip State Hospital. In addition, he produced radio poetry programs and was a judge in various competitions. An accomplished poet himself, his verse was published in volumes such as *Roll the Forbidden Drums!, The Tune of the Calliope, Carousel Parkway, The Burning Bush, On the Way to Palermo, Indigo and Other Poems,* and *Regrouping.* An editor and translator as well, he published *The Last Lullaby: Poems of the Holocaust, Rilke: Visions of Christ, Poetry Therapy* (with others), *Der Kaiser von Atlantis,* and *Dora Teitelboim: Selected Poems.*

OBITUARIES AND OTHER SOURCES:

BOOKS

Who's Who in America, 51st edition, Marquis, 1997.

PERIODICALS

New York Times, April 12, 1997, p. 28.

* * *

KRAUSE, Shari Stamford
See STAMFORD KRAUSE, Shari

* * *

KUTTNER, Henry 1915-1958
(Will Garth, Lewis Padgett, Jack Vance, and numerous other pseudonyms)

PERSONAL: Born April 7, 1915, in Los Angeles, CA; died February 3, 1958, after a heart attack; married Catherine Lucille Moore (a writer), June 7, 1940. *Education:* University of Southern California, Los Angeles, B.A., 1954.

CAREER: Writer. Worked at a literary agency before becoming a freelance writer. *Military service:* U.S. Army Medical Corps; served during World War II.

WRITINGS:

NOVELS

(As Will Garth) *Lawless Guns,* Dodge (New York City), 1937.
(As Will Garth) *Dr. Cyclops,* Phoenix Press, 1940.
(With wife, C. L. Moore) *Fury,* Grosset & Dunlap (New York City), 1950, published as *Destination Infinity,* Avon (New York City), 1958.
(As Jack Vance) *The Dying Earth,* Hillman (New York City), 1950.
(As Jack Vance) *Vandals of the Void,* Winston (Philadelphia), 1953.
The Murder of Ann Avery, Permabooks (New York City), 1956.
The Murder of Eleanor Pope, Permabooks, 1956.
(As Jack Vance) *To Live Forever,* Ballantine (New York City), 1956.

Murder of a Mistress, Permabooks, 1957.

Murder of a Wife, Permabooks, 1958.

Man Drowning, Harper (New York City), 1961.

(With C. L. Moore) *Earth's Last Citadel,* Ace (New York City), 1964.

(With C. L. Moore) *Valley of the Flame,* Ace, 1964.

(As Jack Vance) *Future Tense,* Ballantine, 1964.

(With C. L. Moore) *The Time Axis,* Ace, 1965.

(With C. L. Moore) *The Dark World,* Ace, 1965.

The Creature from Beyond Infinity, Popular Library, 1968.

(With C. L. Moore) *The Mask of Circe,* Ace, 1971.

The Time Trap, published in *Evil Earths,* edited by Brian Aldiss, Futura (London), 1976.

Clash by Night, published with *The Jungle,* by David Drake, Tom Doherty Associates (New York City), 1991.

Author of numerous short stories for periodicals, including *Marvel Science Stories, Startling Stories,* and *Weird Tales,* often under a variety of pseudonyms.

WITH C. L. MOORE; UNDER PSEUDONYM LEWIS PADGETT

The Brass Ring (novel), Duell (New York City), 1946, published as *Murder in Brass,* Bantam (New York City), 1947.

The Day He Died (novel), Duell, 1947.

A Gnome There Was (short stories), Simon & Schuster (New York City), 1950.

Tomorrow and Tomorrow, and the Fairy Chessmen (novels), Gnome Press (New York City), 1951, published as *The Far Reality,* Consul (London), 1963, *The Fairy Chessmen* published separately as *Chessboard Planet,* Galaxy (New York City), 1956.

Well of the Worlds (novel), Galaxy, 1953.

Mutant (short stories), Gnome Press, 1953.

Beyond Earth's Gates (novel), Ace, 1954.

Line to Tomorrow (short stories), Bantam, 1954.

SHORT STORIES

(As Lewis Padgett) *Robots Have No Tails,* Gnome Press, 1952, published under name Henry Kuttner as *The Proud Robot: The Complete Galloway Gallegher Stories,* Hamlyn (London), 1983.

Ahead of Time, Ballantine, 1953.

Remember Tomorrow, American Science Fiction (Sydney, Australia), 1954.

Way of the Gods, American Science Fiction, 1954.

(With C. L. Moore) *No Boundaries,* Ballantine, 1955.

As You Were, American Science Fiction, 1955.

Sword of Tomorrow, American Science Fiction, 1955.

Bypass to Otherness, Ballantine, 1961.

Return to Otherness, Ballantine, 1965.

The Best of Kuttner, two volumes, Mayflower (London), 1965-66.

The Best of Henry Kuttner, Doubleday (Garden City, NY), 1975.

(With C. L. Moore) *Clash by Night and Other Stories,* edited by Peter Pinto, Hamlyn, 1980.

(With C. L. Moore) *Chessboard Planet and Other Stories,* Hamlyn, 1983.

Elak of Atlantis, Gryphon (New York City), 1985.

The Best of Henry Kuttner (contains "Mimsy Were the Borogroves," "Two-handed Engine," "The Proud Robot," "The Misguided Halo," "The Voice of the Lobster," "Exit the Professor," "The Twonky," "A Gnome There Was," "The Big Night," "Nothing but Gingerbread Left," "The Iron Standard," "Cold War," "Or Else," "Endowment Policy," "Housing Problem," "What You Need," and "Absalom"), Doubleday, 1987.

Kuttner Times Three (contains "The Old Army Game," "Bamboo Death," and "The Wolf of Aragon"), V. Utter (Modesto, CA), 1988.

Also the author of fiction under the pseudonyms Edward J. Bellin, Paul Edwards, Noel Gardner, James Hall, Keith Hammond, Hudson Hastings, Peter Horn, Kelvin Kent, Robert O. Kenyon, C. H. Liddell, Hugh Maepenn, K. H. Maepenn, Scott Morgan, Lawrence O'Donnell, Woodrow Wilson Smith, and Charles Stoddard.

ADAPTATIONS: Kuttner's story "Don't Look Now" was dramatized and recorded on video by Bob Cooley, Agency for International Television (Bloomington, IN), 1983.

SIDELIGHTS: In all his guises, Henry Kuttner contributed to the pulp fiction and science fiction publications of the 1930s and 1940s. During this period, known as the Golden Age of Science Fiction, Kuttner and his wife, Catherine Lucille Moore (C. L. Moore), collaborated to varying degrees on numerous imaginative works. Unlike such of his contemporaries as Isaac Asimov and Robert A. Heinlein, who stressed technology in their science fictional works, Kuttner emphasized the sociological. He often wrote about mutants, children, and pioneers of new worlds who must adapt to new physical environments and societies.

Kuttner's reputation faltered in the decades following his premature death in 1958 at age forty-four. This decline is thought to be in part due to the number of pen names he employed, the many genres in which he wrote, his versatility of style, and in some cases the unevenness of his work. While some critics have described Kuttner as a derivative writer who never found a voice of his own, others recognized his technical mastery and depth of imagination. Over the years, Kuttner's best stories have entertained many and have been included in several anthologies for new generations of science fiction fans; they also served to influence the younger writers of his own era, including Ray Bradbury.

Although today Kuttner is remembered as a science fiction writer, he wrote an enormous number of works in a wide variety of genres—westerns, adventure, sword-and-sorcery, supernatural horror, and detective works—under more than a dozen pen names. His first published story, "Graveyard Rats," was a horror tale in the vein of H. P. Lovecraft that appeared in the magazine *Weird Tales* in March of 1936. Kuttner, like many writers of speculative fiction, published widely in pulp magazines. In fact, it was the writer's own literary agent who suggested that Kuttner try science fiction. Though he was reluctant because his science background was limited, Kuttner wrote *When Earth Lived* and saw it published in *Thrilling Stories* in 1937, launching his career as a writer of science fiction.

In 1940 Kuttner married Catherine Moore, an established writer of fantasy, and began a fruitful collaboration. The two were able to work so well together that it was said that one could pick up at the typewriter where the other had left off. During World War II, Kuttner received a lucky break—while other, better known science fiction writers were serving in the military, Kuttner was tapped to write for *Astounding Science Fiction* and *Unknown Worlds*. According to William P. Kelly, writing in the *Dictionary of Literary Biography,* Kuttner was as popular as authors Isaac Asimov, A. E. van Vogt, or Murray Leinster by war's end. Using the G.I. bill to resume his education, which had been stalled by the Great Depression, Kuttner enrolled at the University of Southern California, from which he earned a bachelor's degree in 1954. Tragically, while attending classes part time to complete his master's degree, Kuttner succumbed to a sudden heart attack. He died in February of 1958.

Among Kuttner's best-known works are the short stories "The Twonky" and "Mimsy Were the Borogroves" and the novels *Tomorrow and Tomorrow* and the *Fairy Chessmen*. *A Gnome There Was,* a collection of short stories published in 1950 under the pseudonym Lewis Padgett, contained "The Twonky"

and "Mimsy." This "twonky" is a radio-console from the future that has been accidentally sent into the past. Like a robot, it aids the owner of the home, but in the end it destroys him. In "Mimsy" Kuttner suggested that children are really aliens, one of the author's favorite notions. In the tale, a time-traveler from the future sends toys into the past to teach children how to manipulate space and time. *A Gnome There Was* elicited positive reviews. "This collection is just enough off the beaten track of 'space stories' to make it most intriguing," wrote a *Library Journal* reviewer. Likewise, a critic in the *New York Times Book Review* noted, "There could be few better introductions to what one of the better practitioners can do. Some of the themes have been handled by other writers, but rarely more skillfully."

In 1951 *Tomorrow and Tomorrow* and *The Fairy Chessmen* appeared in a joint volume under the Padgett pen name. J. F. McComas, writing in the *New York Times,* gave the work qualified praise. "There's a sharp contrast in the quality of these two novels. . . . *Tomorrow and Tomorrow,* while good, competent science fiction, offers nothing new. . . . Happily, however, *The Fairy Chessmen* gives us Padgett's imagination at its brilliant best." "Both short novels are excellent examples of what science fiction can be in the hands of an accomplished writer," declared Don Fabun in the *San Francisco Chronicle.*

A reissue of the author's 1950 novel *Fury* in the early 1970s, along with the publication of *The Best of Henry Kuttner* in 1975 and *The Startling Worlds of Henry Kuttner* in the mid-1980s, have helped to keep Kuttner's art alive. Writing for the *New York Times Book Review,* a commentator called *Fury,* a tale that takes place on Venus after the destruction of the Earth in a nuclear holocaust, a "white-hot, fast-paced legend." "Well plotted and constantly suspenseful, in the best tradition of top quality sci-fi," remarked a reviewer for *Publishers Weekly.* Calling *The Startling Worlds of Henry Kuttner* "an excellent introduction to the grand vistas of space opera," Roberta Rogow of *Voice of Youth Advocates* found the three stories collected in the volume, which all feature men drawn into alternate universes, to be "heavy with atmosphere (of all kinds). . . . [They] deserve re-reading again and again."

In his introduction to *The Best of Henry Kuttner,* Ray Bradbury maintained that the prolific novelist has been "unfairly neglected" and compared the best of Kuttner's work favorably to that of J. R. R. Tolkien,

Lovecraft, Robert Heinlein, Theodore Sturgeon, H. G. Wells, Jules Verne, George Orwell, and Kurt Vonnegut. Kelly too found much to validate Kuttner's claim for recognition by posterity. "The best of Kuttner's science fiction reflects both a highly personal vision and a capacity to address meaningfully the psychic needs of his audiences," wrote Kelly. "In these works Kuttner offers a balanced view of the human condition that at once acknowledges man's capacity for self-destruction and his potential for unlimited growth."

In *Voices for the Future: Essays on Major Science Fiction Writers,* James Gunn extended much deserved credit to Kuttner's wife and co-author. The critic described Catherine Moore and Henry Kuttner's joint contribution to science fiction in terms of the literary quality of their work. "What the Kuttners brought to science fiction, which broadened it and helped it evolve, was a concern for literary skill and culture," Gunn maintained. "The Kuttners expanded the techniques of science fiction to include techniques prevalent in the mainstream; they expanded its scope to include the vast cultural tradition available outside science fiction." Gunn concluded, "The significance of the Kuttners' work rests in the fact that much of the development in science fiction over the past twenty years has come along the lines they pioneered."

BIOGRAPHICAL/CRITICAL SOURCES:

BOOKS

Aldiss, Brian W., *Billion Year Spree: The True History of Science Fiction,* Doubleday, 1973.
Bradbury, Ray, "Introduction," *The Best of Henry Kuttner,* Doubleday, 1987.
Carter, Lin, *Imaginary Worlds: The Art of Fantasy,* Ballantine, 1973.
Dictionary of Literary Biography, Volume 8: *Twentieth-Century American Science Fiction Writers,* Gale (Detroit), 1981.
Gunn, James, *Voices for the Future: Essays on Major Science Fiction Writers,* Popular Press (Bowling Green, OH), 1976.
Moskowitz, Sam, *Seekers of Tomorrow: Masters of Science Fiction,* World Publishing, 1961.
Rose, Mark, *Alien Encounters: Anatomy of Science Fiction,* Harvard University Press (Cambridge, MA), 1981.
Twentieth-Century Literary Criticism, Volume 10, Gale, 1983.
Twentieth-Century Science-Fiction Writers, third edition, St. James Press (Chicago), 1991.
Utter, Virgil, and Gordon Benson Jr., *Catherine Lucille Moore and Henry Kuttner: A Marriage of Souls and Talent: A Working Bibliography,* V. Utter (Modesto, CA), 1986.

PERIODICALS

Christian Century, September 23, 1953, p. 1082.
New Republic, September 23, 1946, p. 358.
New Statesman and Nation, October 30, 1954, pp. 554-56.
New Yorker, September 28, 1946, pp. 103-04; August 30, 1947; August 16, 1952, p. 91.
New York Times Book Review, October 13, 1946, p. 40; September 7, 1947, p. 36; December 17, 1950, p. 18; February 10, 1952, p. 21; June 22, 1952, p. 11; July 27, 1952, p. 17; September 5, 1953, p. 13.
Riverside Quarterly, vol. 5, no. 2, 1972.
San Francisco Chronicle, October 6, 1946, p. 40; February 4, 1951, p. 17; December 16, 1951, p. 20.
Saturday Review, August 2, 1952, p. 34.
Washington Post Book World, September 14, 1975, pp. 4-5.*

L

LAI, Larissa 1967-

PERSONAL: Born September 13, 1967, in La Jolla, CA; daughter of Tyrone (a university professor) and Yuen-Ting (an independent scholar; maiden name, Tsui) Lai. *Ethnicity:* "Chinese-Caucasian-American." *Education:* University of British Columbia, B.A. (with honors), 1990.

ADDRESSES: Home—20-12 West 10th Ave., Vancouver, British Columbia, Canada V5Y 1R6.

CAREER: Writer. Eric Cumine and Associates (architects and engineers), apprentice, 1989; CITR-Radio, host and producer of the series *Air Aware,* 1989; On Edge Productions, assistant curator, 1990; SAW Video Cooperative, coordinator, 1991; Banff Centre for the Arts, television and video associate in media arts department, 1992; Top Dollar Sisters, production manager for the film *My Sweet Peony,* 1992; *Western Front Society,* editor, 1994-95; Vancouver Art Gallery, gallery animateur, 1996-97.

Cottages at Hedgebrook, resident, 1995; University of Calgary, Markin-Flanagan Distinguished Writer in Residence, 1997-98. Gives readings from her works. Filmmaker and videographer.

MEMBER: Asian Canadian Writers Group.

AWARDS, HONORS: Awards from Canada Council and Multiculturalism and Citizenship Canada, 1993; Canada Council grant, 1994; Emerging Writers Award, Astraea Foundation, 1995; grant from British Columbia Cultural Services Branch, 1996; award from Cultures and Heritage Canada, 1996.

WRITINGS:

(Contributor) P. Wong, editor, *Yellow Peril: Reconsidered,* On Edge Productions (Vancouver, British Columbia), 1990.
When Fox Is a Thousand (novel), Press Gang Publishers (Vancouver), 1995.
(Contributor) *Bringing It Home: Women Talk about Feminism in Their Lives,* Arsenal Pulp Press (Vancouver), 1996.

Work represented in anthologies, including *Pearls of Passion,* edited by M. Silvera and C. A. Lee, Sister Vision Press (Toronto, Ontario), 1994; *Eye Wuz Here,* edited by S. Cooley, Douglas & McIntyre (Vancouver), 1996; and *Into the Fire: Asian American Prose,* edited by S. Watanabe and C. Bruchac, Greenfield Review Press (New York City), 1996. Contributor of stories, poems, articles, and reviews to magazines, including *Kinesis, Absinthe, West Coast Line, Asian American Journal, Capilano Review,* and *Harbour: Magazine of Art and Everyday Life.* Editor, *Front,* 1994-95.

SIDELIGHTS: Larissa Lai told *CA:* "Although it might not be apparent at first glance, *When Fox Is a Thousand* comes very much out of a history of activist work around questions of race and representation. Of course, as I worked on it, the story became very much more than that. It took on a life of its own. The questions that instigated the story were questions about history, identity, and belonging. It was part of a project to carve out a homespace for myself in a place where I felt, living between cultures as I do, that I had none, or that the space I had was, of necessity, a hybrid space. I also wanted to write from a place that was intentionally not biographical in the direct sense of the word. I believe that 'historically accurate' works are important because they articulate a history which, until quite recently, has been completely invisible in Canada. However, I sometimes feel that, in a lot of ways, our lives as Chinese Canadians have been largely anthropologized, and that if we don't branch out and have a lot of different kinds of work, our work becomes artifactual, and then it is easily stereotyped and exoticized.

"As an English-speaking, assimilated woman, very much touched by histories of colonialism and migration, my relationship with my own history is highly mediated. The only way in which I can access my own history, beyond the stories told by family members, is through English texts. These texts, however, are heavily inscribed with the West's expectations and understandings of 'the Orient.' It may be, in fact, that these expectations are all that those works convey. That is, perhaps, an overly cynical take on the situation, but not without a grain of truth.

"At the time in which I started seriously writing fiction, around 1992, questions of authenticity and appropriation were at the top of the list in cultural debates taking place in Vancouver, at least in certain circles. It was a time when a new generation of antiracist activists and artists were beginning to clarify for themselves and others the way in which systemic racism has suppressed us and our work in Canada. It was incredibly empowering to be a part of those discussions. I began to think about questions of power and history in ways I had not before.

"One of the things that interested me about those discussions was the way many of us often assumed a kind of utopic place of origin which we, or our ancestors, inhabited some time in the distant past before the advent of European colonialism. I think we knew that there had never been any such thing, that we all come out of particular troubled histories of our own, just as the Europeans did when they crossed the Atlantic to come to the Americas. The desire for that utopia was overwhelming, precisely because it pinpointed what we felt was lacking in this society. That was how I first started thinking about *When Fox Is a Thousand*. I didn't want to pass judgment on the imagination of that utopia. I wanted to flesh it out, to create a little, literary, utopic world where my weary brothers and sisters could retire when they were exhausted from more confrontational types of work.

"I also wanted to engage the question of myth. It is something which I feel has been largely abandoned by

the Chinese society I know, in favor of more pragmatic types of knowledge. I am thinking particularly of Hong Kong, which is where my roots are.

"This is where the character of the Poetess comes from. *When Fox is a Thousand* is a novel in three voices of which she is one. She is based on a woman who actually lived during the T'ang dynasty. She was a poet and a courtesan, with a strong and very critical mind. Many of the versions of her story which I uncovered on my travels portray her as evil, but I refuse to believe them. I see that portrayal as the combined efforts of male Chinese scholar's sexism and the racism and sexism of the Western translators and anthologists. They all accuse her of having murdered a young woman who worked for her, out of jealousy. All but one—this one particular source suggests very clearly that she was framed by an official who did not like her active, critical mind, or the way in which she insisted on living outside the system, refusing to register herself as courtesan although she worked as one.

"Realizing how biased all these various so-called historical records were was actually very freeing for me. I thought that if all the truths I can find are already ideologically determined, what harm is there in producing another one, true to my own quirky sense of the world. I also believe that, while exact histories can get lost or buried under false or biased renderings, our histories run very much in our blood, and that we can remember their emotional content, if not precisely what transpired during events long past.

"My 'utopia of origins' could not, of course, be maintained. The second voice in the novel, a contemporary, twentieth-century voice which largely documents the life of a young Chinese-Canadian woman called Artemis Wong, began as a series of letters to the Poetess. It eventually evolved into a voice on its own. Elliptically, Artemis's misadventures show up in the unreality of the Poetess's utopia in a way that is often troubling and disturbing. To an extent, these sections come out of my own observations and experiences of my late teens and early twenties. I wanted to illuminate how a young woman in what I call a "pre-political state" negotiates the very complex tensions of race, class, gender and sexuality which infuse contemporary society. So, for instance, you have Artemis' infatuation with a bright, articulate, but ultimately untrustworthy Chinese-Canadian woman called Diane. You have her troubled relationship with a young white man trying to come out of the closet and clinging to her as a figure of "difference," but one much safer than the "other" that he desires. In a lot of ways, my writing of that section was a response to the backlash against some of the more blatantly political writings of other women of color in this country. I wanted to show what the world was like for us without the political analysis that is currently available, if you know where to look. I believe that a lot of young women growing up today still don't have access to those ideas and writings. They don't know where to look, or they are influenced by the backlash not to look. I don't think that is a good thing.

"The character of the Fox is my way of transcending those neatly packaged definitions of Asian women's identity, which, because they have been used against us we must often articulate along the path of our own liberation. In that re-articulation, we run the danger of re-inscription. The Fox is a creature of transformation. She has the power to transform herself into a woman. But the way she does it is not entirely savory. The Fox goes into the graveyard at night looking for the corpse of a young woman who has died before her time. She breathes life into the corpse and enters it, and then comes up to the surface of the earth to wreak havoc in the lives of others. I suppose you could read this as a journey out of the troubled locations of the other two main characters, Artemis and the Poetess.

"I got the impetus for the Fox from reading a lot of old Chinese folklore, in translation of course. The most useful was a popular book by Pu Songling, called *Strange Tales of Liaozhai*. It deals with all kinds of supernatural characters, from foxes to tigers, from ghosts to flowers that turn into young girls after dark. It was ostensibly produced as a collection of popular stories of the time (sixteenth century by Western reckoning), but it was also a witty critique of government corruption and the Confucian patriarchy, as well as the foibles of human nature: jealousy, sloth, greed, ungratefulness and so on.

"The Fox has much earlier roots, going back to the third century as far as I have been able to ascertain. She was, at least in the records that have come through the troubled channels that I described earlier, an archetype of the evil, lascivious woman. However, there are enough oddities about her to make me suspect that she was a figure of something much more complicated and interesting that got obliterated along the way. In the stories that remain, she is always a villain, out to cheat men—usually scholars or young monks—away from their pious purposes. But in a number of stories, including Pu's, the Fox becomes more complex, teaching lessons and doing good deeds in unexpected ways.

"By the time of my grandparents generation, her role has once again been simplified. My mother tells me that, when she was growing up in Hong Kong, people would use the word 'fox' the way we in the West use the word 'slut.' The fox crops up again in popular Hong Kong cinema, but again it is not in a flattering way. I wanted to reclaim her and take her to late twentieth-century Vancouver and see what she would do. I gave her just a tinge of a feminist consciousness and set her free."

BIOGRAPHICAL/CRITICAL SOURCES:

PERIODICALS

Advocate, December 26, 1995.
Books in Canada, February, 1996.
Canadian Literature, summer, 1996.
Focus on Women, September, 1996.
Pacific Current, November-January, 1995-1996.
Rice Paper, winter/spring, 1996.
World Journal (Vancouver), February, 1996.

*   *   *

LAMPMAN, Robert James 1920-1997

OBITUARY NOTICE—See index for *CA* sketch: Born September 25, 1920, in Plover, WI; died of lung cancer, March 4, 1997, in Madison, WI. Economist, educator, and author. A specialist in measuring income distribution, Lampman is best remembered for his work during the early 1960s as an economic adviser to President John F. Kennedy. His contributions to Kennedy's Council of Economic Advisers included research and recommendations on poverty that later provided the outline for the antipoverty strategy employed by the administration of President Lyndon B. Johnson throughout the 1960s. Lampman completed his undergraduate studies at the University of Wisconsin in 1942. Following wartime service as an air navigator in the U.S. Navy, he returned to the University of Wisconsin to pursue a graduate degree in economics, completing a Ph.D. in 1950. Lampman taught economics at the University of Washington in Seattle from 1948 until 1958, when he returned to the University of Wisconsin in Madison as a professor of economics. While Lampman remained a Wisconsin faculty member for the duration of his academic career, he also served as visiting professor at such institutions as the University of the Philippines and Cornell University. Lampman wrote and edited books and articles on issues of income, poverty, and social welfare. His written works include such studies as *The Low Income Population and Economic Growth* (1959), *The Share of Top Wealth-Holders in National Wealth, 1922-1956* (1962), and *Ends and Means of Reducing Income Poverty* (1971).

OBITUARIES AND OTHER SOURCES:

PERIODICALS

New York Times, March 8, 1997, p. 52.

*   *   *

LECKIE, Ross 1957-

PERSONAL: Born June 5, 1957, in Scotland; son of Joseph (a minister of religion) and Hannah (a teacher; maiden name, Matthews) Leckie; married Vera Wolfing (divorced, April, 1992); children: Douglas, Xenia, Patrick, Alexia. *Ethnicity:* "Scottish." *Education:* Corpus Christi College, Oxford, M.A. (classics), 1980; attended Royal Agricultural College, Cirencester, England, 1980-81.

ADDRESSES: Agent—Shiel Land, 43 Doughty St., London WC1N 2LF, England.

CAREER: Farmer, Perthshire, Scotland, 1981-83; Odeco, "roughneck" on North Sea oil rigs, 1983-85; freelance journalist and copywriter, Edinburgh, Scotland, 1986-96; Martin Currie Investment Management, Edinburgh, head of corporate communications, 1996—.

MEMBER: Speculative Society (president, 1985-87), Hellenic Society, Society of Antiquaries of Scotland (fellow).

WRITINGS:

Bluff Your Way in the Classics, Ravette Books (West Sussex, England), 1989.
Grampian, Canongate Publishing (Edinburgh, Scotland), 1991.
The Gourmet's Companion, EPC, 1994.
Hannibal (historical novel), Canongate Publishing, 1995.
Scipio (historical novel, a sequel to *Hannibal*), Canongate Publishing, 1997.

Reviewer, *Times* (London), 1993—.

WORK IN PROGRESS: Carthage, a sequel to *Scipio,* publication by Canongate Publishing expected in 1998; research on Alaric the Visigoth.

SIDELIGHTS: Ross Leckie told *CA:* "My primary motivation is a love of language and the struggle of trying to produce prose that demonstrates clarity, lucidity, and euphony. I am also moved to try to recreate a vanished world and show how what it learned is still relevant to us, to show what is enduring in human nature.

"My influences are the classics, which have been my love since I started Greek and Latin at age five; Herodotus and Polybius, the historians, and Livy, too; of the poets, Homer and Vergil and the Greek lyricists—Sappho, Aechilochus, and Pindar, in particular. In the twentieth century, Patrick White and Mary Renault have influenced me, as has the poetry of R. S. Thomas and Iain Crichton-Smith.

"In my writing process, I read everything I can find on my subject and take notes. I digest the notes, then throw them away and begin writing. I have a broad synopsis in mind, but I let the story unfold of itself. I am at long last comfortable typing my work. I write best in the morning and work from six until ten o'clock. In the evenings I revise and edit, prune, and refine.

"The idea of a novel on Hannibal came to me in a dream. My general interest in that period began when I was very young, through reading Livy. I gain further motivation to write about the classics because they are dying out. I want to try and help to keep them alive. The classics have not merely influenced western civilization; they are part of its essence."

*   *   *

LEE, Ang 1954-

PERSONAL: Born October 23, 1954, in Taiwan, son of a high school principal; married Jane Lin (a microbiologist); children: Han, Mason. *Education:* University of Illinois, B.F.A., 1978; New York University, 1984. *Military Service:* Served two years in the Taiwanese military.

ADDRESSES: Office—c/o Good Machine, 526 West 25th St., New York, NY 10001.

CAREER: Director of films, including *Fine Line* (student film), 1985; *Pushing Hands,* Good Machine, 1991; *Wedding Banquet,* Central Motion Picture (Taiwan), 1993; *Eat Drink Man Woman,* Central Motion Picture (Taiwan), 1994; and *Sense and Sensibility,* Columbia, 1995.

AWARDS, HONORS: Best Student Film Award, New York University, for *Fine Line,* 1985; Asian Pacific Film Festival, Best Film Honors, for *Pushing Hands,* 1992; *Pushing Hands* was nominated for Golden Horse Award in Taiwan and received a Special Jury Prize; Sixteenth Asian American International Film Festival, Asian American Media Award, and Berlin Film Festival, Golden Bear Award, both for *Wedding Banquet,* 1993; *Wedding Banquet* and *Eat Drink Man Woman* were nominated for an Academy Award for Best Foreign Language Film, in 1993 and 1994, respectively.

WRITINGS:

SCREENPLAYS

Pushing Hands, Good Machine, 1991.
(With Neil Peng and James Schamus) *The Wedding Banquet,* Central Motion Picture (Taiwan), 1993.
(With Hui Ling Wang and James Schamus) *Eat Drink Man Woman,* Central Motion Picture (Taiwan), 1994.

WORK IN PROGRESS: A film of *The Ice Storm,* based on the novel by Rick Moody.

SIDELIGHTS: Taiwanese born Ang Lee is the director and screenwriter of such critically acclaimed motion pictures as *The Wedding Banquet* and *Eat Drink Man Woman,* and the director of *Sense and Sensibility,* a highly praised adaptation of the novel by Jane Austen. Lee approaches filmmaking with a sense of balance and interest in domestic drama that, in the opinion of some reviewers, too many directors lack and which the director himself described to Sarah Kerr of *New York* as a "weird mixture of drama and anti-drama."

The son of a high school principal, Lee was born and raised in Taiwan. After he failed the entrance examination for the national university, Lee enrolled in the Taiwan Academy of Art, where he became interested in acting. After serving a mandatory two-year stint in the Taiwanese army, Lee emigrated to the United States in 1981 to study acting at the University of Illinois at Urbana-Champaign. It was an eye-opening experience for Lee. "From the study in the theater, I

realized that the Western world emphasizes letting emotion out," Lee informed Kerr in *New York.* "Conflict. It's very Judeo-Christian. A man and a woman, the loss of Eden. All that stuff. It's very dramatic."

Because of his poor English, Lee was limited in the roles he could perform. Thus he delved deeply into the history of film and decided that he wanted to direct motion pictures. Lee pursued further studies at the New York Film School. For his student thesis he wrote and filmed the short *Fine Line,* in which an Italian American husband tries to take revenge on his wife's lover and in the process befriends a young Taiwanese woman who is trying to avoid the Immigration and Naturalization Service. In 1985 the film, which Kerr described in *New York* as a "charming, clever caper," won the New York University Tisch School of the Arts Award for film. The award did not guarantee success, however; for the next six years Lee tried to pitch various projects to producers with no success.

The duo of James Schamus and Ted Hope, founders of the low-budget film production company Good Machine, had seen *Fine Line* and sought out Lee in 1991. After Lee told the duo about his idea for a film to be called *Pushing Hands,* about a Taiwanese man whose father comes to live with him in New York City, Schamus and Hope knew they had found their director. *Pushing Hands* was filmed on a budget of 200,000 dollars and although it was not seen by many in the United States, the film was hugely successful in Taiwan.

The success of *Pushing Hands* led a Taiwanese production company to sponsor the filming of the costlier *The Wedding Banquet,* which Lee co-authored with Neil Peng and James Schamus. *The Wedding Banquet* tells the story of Wai Tung, a successful Taiwanese immigrant to the United States. As a real-estate tycoon, he has everything he wants—including a homosexual lover—but his peace of mind is rankled by the constant prodding of his parents in Taiwan who want him to marry (they don't know he is gay). Wai decides to fake a marriage to one of his female tenants, a beautiful Chinese artist who will use the marriage to obtain a green card which will allow her to remain in the United States. When Wai's relieved parents learn of the wedding, they make a surprise visit to New York and the elaborate wedding ceremony and banquet goes awry.

"The lovely Taiwanese American comedy *The Wedding Banquet* begins as a classically structured farce and ends as a serious, almost heartrending embrace of patriarchal responsibility. And, it does this without going soft. This small, delicate independent movie has perfect balance," remarked David Denby in *New York*. The reviewer pointed out that "*The Wedding Banquet* is consistently funny in an unforced, almost glancing style: Ang Lee sets up his cross-cultural and cross-erotic currents and then he observes. His touch is sure and light, the jokes securely planted but never fussed over." Writing for *Entertainment Weekly* Ty Burr commented, "*The Wedding Banquet* is really more concerned with the collision of generations than of cultures: With a comic knowingness, Lee shows us the contortions that adult children go through to live up to their parents' image of them."

Lee's next film for Good Machine was *Eat Drink Man Woman*, a light social farce that observes the lives of a widower and his three daughters, all of whom have lost their appetite for life. Like *The Wedding Banquet*, *Eat Drink Man Woman* garnered positive reviews. The film "benefits enormously from its sitcom factor, the fact that once it strays from its rather restrictive central metaphor, it has plenty of strands to keep you interested, and not just the noodles," quipped Jonathan Romney of *New Statesman*. In his review for the *New Republic*, Stanley Kauffmann called the film "quite enjoyable," adding that while the stories of the main characters are "basically commonplace," the quality of the camerawork, the acting, and the "wonderful appearance" of some one hundred dishes prepared for the film hold the viewer's attention. "As a statement about modern Taiwan, by a director grappling with his own cosmopolitanism *Eat Drink Man Woman* displays a gentle touch," Romney commented in the *New Statesman*. "It's enjoyable from start to finish, with an unashamedly feel-good ending that even cynics can relish."

Lee described *Pushing Hands, The Wedding Banquet*, and *Eat Drink Man Woman* as a trilogy of life experiences. "It's firsthand life experience," he told Kerr in *New York*. "After thirty years of age, you suddenly start to look back. You see beginning, middle, end—like a process, you see parents getting older, children getting stronger." Lee added, "The first time that became my theme, I dug into it, and it's treacherous ground. It's the secret about the most secret. I always make movies in the family bathroom, in the master bedroom. A puking scene, or the kitchen gets smashed. The world is falling apart."

Lee's interest in domestic drama was evident to Lindsay Doran, the producer of *Sense and Sensibility*, who considered about fifteen directors before settling on Lee. According to Kerr in *New York*, when Lee told Doran that he wanted the movie "to break people's hearts so badly that they'll still be recovering from it two month's later," Doran was convinced Lee was the right choice. The plot of *Sense and Sensibility* is based on the novel of the same name written by the nineteenth-century English novelist Jane Austen. It follows the romances of two sisters, Elinor and Marianne, who have been left in dire straits after the death of their father because, by law, they cannot inherit his estate. Thus they must marry well to secure their future. While Elinor, the eldest, appears to find her true love too late, Marianne becomes infatuated with a cad.

Commentators praised the film, which was a major box office success and earned several Academy Awards for lead actress and screenwriter Emma Thompson. Lisa Schwarzbaum in *Entertainment Weekly* called it "perfectly realized," adding that it is "proof of what power can come of a great book given inspired filmmaking." Richard Alleva, after explaining in *Commonweal* that Jane Austen was "a genius at characterization and plotting" but less talented at physical description, maintained that this deficit "puts the burden on the director to supply the visual equivalent of the novelist's sensibility." In doing so, "Ang Lee triumphs," stated Alleva. "He never permits his camera to be a tourist of the English countryside but uses the settings to support the emotions of any given scene. . . . Lee's subtle directorial touches can be relished at second, even third viewings."

Although Lee's films have shown his sensitive and philosophical side, he would also like to direct a more mainstream work. "I think there's a range of audience there that needs to watch movies with content, with more sophisticated thinking—but not necessarily artsy-fartsy or stuffy," Lee told Kerr. "But sometimes, you want to be mainstream. You don't want to be odd or special from everybody else You want your heart to go out like *everybody!*"

BIOGRAPHICAL/CRITICAL SOURCES:

BOOKS

Notable Asian Americans, Gale (Detroit), 1995.

PERIODICALS

America, March 9, 1996, pp. 20-21.
American Spectator, November, 1993, p. 70.

Commonweal, March 8, 1996, pp. 15-17.

Entertainment Weekly, September 10, 1993, p. 50; August 16, 1996, pp. 54-55.

National Review, January 29, 1996, p. 67.

New Republic, September 5, 1994, p. 36; January 8, 1996, pp. 34-36.

New Statesman, January 20, 1995, p. 33; February 23, 1996, p. 43.

Newsweek, December 18, 1995, pp. 66-69.

New York, August 30, 1993, p. 136; April 1, 1996, pp. 42-47.

New Yorker, December 18, 1995, pp. 124-27.

New York Review of Books, February 1, 1996, pp. 13-16.

Premiere, February, 1996, pp. 17-19.

Time, December 18, 1995, pp. 72-74.*

*   *   *

LEGANY, Dezso 1916-

PERSONAL: Born January 19, 1916, in Szombathely, Hungary; son of Dezso (a professor) and Erzsebet (a pianist; maiden name, Serenyi) Legany; married Erzsebet Hegyi, September 23, 1961; children: Zsolt, Denes. *Education:* Studied composition with Janos Viski, folk music with Zoltan Kodaly, musical history with Bartha and Szabolcsi at the Budapest Academy of Music; University of Pecs, LL.D., 1937; Hungarian Academy of Sciences, awarded Doctor of Musical Sciences, 1981. *Religion:* Lutheran.

ADDRESSES: Home—Apahida u. 11, Budapest H-1112, Hungary.

CAREER: Liszt Academy of Music, Budapest, Hungary, professor, 1951-58; Bartok Conservatory of Music, Budapest, professor, 1958-73; Institute for Musicology of Hungarian Academy of Sciences, head of Hungarian Music department, beginning 1973; writer.

MEMBER: International Kodaly Society, Hungarian Kodaly Society, Musicological Commission of Hungarian Academy of Sciences, Association of Hungarian Musicians, American Liszt Society, International Liszt Centre (Stockholm).

AWARDS, HONORS: Grand Prix, Hungarian Art Foundation, 1982; Award for Excellence, American Liszt Society, 1984; Gold Medal of Labour, 1987; Erkel Prize, 1988.

WRITINGS:

Henry Purcell, Gondolat Kiado (Budapest), 1959, second edition, 1981.

A magyar zene kronikaja: zenei muvelodesunk ezer eve dokumentumokban (title means "Chronicle of Hungarian Music: One Thousand Years of Documentation on Musical Culture"), Zenemukiado (Budapest), 1962.

Erkel Ferenc muvei es korabeli tortenetuk (title means "Ferenc Erkel's Works and Their Contemporary History"), Editio Musica (Budapest), 1975.

Liszt Ferenc Magyarorszagon. 1869-1873, Corvina Kiado (Budapest), 1976, translated by Gyula Gulyas as *Ferenc Liszt and His Country, 1869-1873,* Corvina Kiado, 1983.

Letters by Z. Kodaly, Zenemukiado, 1982.

Franz Liszt. Unbekannte Presse und Briefe aus Wien 1822-1886, Corvina Kiado (Budapest), 1983.

Liszt Ferenc Magyarorszagon. 1874-1886, Corvina Kiado (Budapest), published as *Liszt and His Country 1874-1886,* Occidental Press, 1992.

Contributor to reference books, including *Grove's Dictionary of Music, Concise Oxford Dictionary of Opera,* and *Music and Letters.* Contributor to journals, including *Bulletin of the International Kodaly Society.*

SIDELIGHTS: The son of an academic father and a pianist mother, Dezso Legany would combine these two disciplines to become a leading musicologist, a professor of Hungarian music, and an authority on such European composers as Ferenc (Franz) Liszt and Zoltan Kodaly.

Of Legany's major work, 1976's *Ferenc Liszt and His Country, 1869-1873, Times Literary Supplement* critic Alan Walker declared: "Thanks to the tireless efforts of [the author], we have a book which is worthy of its subject, and which is bound to take its place in the permanent Liszt literature." Calling *Ferenc Liszt* "a masterpiece of musicological research," Walker went on to say that Legany's work is a "well documented, thoroughly researched and attractively written" book that "may be confidently recommended to all serious Liszt researchers."

BIOGRAPHICAL/CRITICAL SOURCES:

PERIODICALS

Times Literary Supplement, November 11, 1983.

LEROY, Gilles 1958-

PERSONAL: Born December 28, 1958, in Paris, France; son of Andre and Eliane (Mesny) Leroy. *Education:* Attended Hypokhange, Khagne.

ADDRESSES: Office—c/o Mercure de France SA, Subsidiary of Editions Gallimard, 26, rue de Conde, F-75006 Paris, France.

CAREER: Writer.

AWARDS, HONORS: Prix de la Nouvelle, Nanterre, 1992, for *Les Derniers seront les premiers.*

WRITINGS:

Habibi (novel), Michel de Maule, 1987.
Maman est morte (nonfiction; title means "Mother Is Dead"), Michel de Maule, 1990.
Les Derniers seront les premiers (stories; title means "The Last Shall Be the First"), Mercure de France (Paris), 1991.
Madame X (novel), Mercure de France (Paris), 1992.

WORK IN PROGRESS: L'Aviateur, a novel and *Forget Me Not,* to be published by Roman.

SIDELIGHTS: Gilles Leroy has drawn from his childhood growing up in a middle-class family in the suburbs of Paris to create novels and short stories. His first novel, *Habibi,* revolves around the tragic passions of two adolescent boys. It was followed three years later by the nonfiction work *Maman est morte,* an account of the author's grief over the death of his mother. Rene de Ceccatty of *Le Monde* remarked on the "disconcerting tone" of the work and called it notable for its mixture of "surgical coldness and vibrant emotion during mourning." "*Maman est morte* is an unusual book, for it says something truly new: allegory has given way to the feelings that exist beyond the facts. Without sadness somehow, Gilles Leroy has written an astonishing book," lauded Gerard-Julien Salvy in *Le Figaro Magazine.* Asserting that *Habibi* and *Maman est morte* did not receive the attention they deserved, Ceccatty maintained, "A close reading will reveal the talent of the novelist, who sometimes hesitates between lyricism and detachment, passion and disillusioned mistrust, which are evidently two parts of the writer's personality."

In *Les Derniers seront les premiers,* a collection of nine short stories, Leroy portrays the marginalized in society: children and adolescents, the lonely elderly, little-known writers, the poor, and singers of forgotten songs. Leroy explained to a contributor to *Figaroscope,* "In less than ten years, I lost my entire family. I wanted to pay my respects to all of the people I loved. They became the characters in my book. I wanted to reconstruct a sort of legacy." In the title story, the narrator is a reporter assigned to interview stars whose careers are on the wane; in "Les Coups et blessures" (Blows and Wounds) Leroy describes the relationship of two teenagers, and in "Hors la loi" (Beyond the Law) he recounts what happens when a father discovers his son shoplifting. In "La Chiennerie de la vie" (Life's a Bitch) he depicts two young women sharing their secrets with each other while riding a train home from market, then describes them many years later when they accidentally encounter each other and find that their roles of 'needy' and 'satisfied' have been reversed. *Les Derniers seront les premiers* garnered good reviews. "This is a sensitive collection—grim, tense, and compassionate. With a knowing eye and sparkling style, Leroy has created a spellbinding work," declared Laurence Vidal in *Le Figaro.* "It's in the most condensed and saddest stories, such as the title story or "Les Coups et blessures," that the emotions come across best to the reader," Ceccatty remarked in *Le Monde.* J.M. Mi also praised the work in his review for *Lire,* stating that "the stories of these characters whose fate is sealed are very moving. Gilles Leroy proves here that he is a talented writer."

The short novel *Madame X* revolves around an aging prostitute who holds court in a dilapidated movie theater in Paris and the narrator who becomes her client and friend, known only as the Sentimental One. At one point, the two meet for drinks at a bar and the narrator invites Madame X to a bowling alley, where she tells the story of her lost true love, an American businessman. According to Ceccatty, "In a condensed and striking theatrical format, *Madame X* attempts to answer the question: 'Why don't we love the people we are supposed to love?'" James Kirkup, writing in the *Times Literary Supplement,* called *Madame X* both "extraordinary" and "strange and unclassifiable, with a subject at once pathetic and shocking." He concluded, "This is a sharply observed little tale about the death of our simple human joys; its language, like its heroine, is discreet, classic and poignant."

Leroy told *CA:* "I spent my childhood reading all the books I could get my hands on. When I was ten years old, I discovered literature with *The Red and the Black* by Stendhal, which I read in a single night. I believe that night I began to write, without setting a pencil to paper, without even being aware of my desire to write. Ten years later, I made another important discovery: William Faulkner and his novel *Sanctuary*. Several days later, I wrote my first novel. Was there a link between these two aesthetic 'shocks' and the books I write? I don't know. I believe they have in common the search for truths that neither the sciences nor ethics can teach us. These truths take the form of violence and metaphor: Julien Sorel's crushed head in *The Red and the Black* and the cornstalk sword in *Sanctuary* are what might be called unforgettable images, and perhaps for me the foundations of writing.

"A book is always wrested from chaos. To write is to engage in a battle to create a part of the world, to take from it some flashes of insight. The chaos in my life was to have lost my entire family in several years. I found myself still a young man and all alone, deprived of my origins, which are also social references, landmarks from which to move forward. I felt as if I were not the heir but the depository of a history that while inevitably personal was also the history of the century. It is a concrete history, lived by people 'without history' as anonymous lives are called.

"Both sides of my family lived this century in Paris, in the outlying, rural suburbs that are part of the suburbs today. Among them were small business people—furriers, butchers—and workers in metal, clothes manufacturing, and printing. Inspired by their circumstances and destinies, I felt the need to create in my last two books a certain world: my own topography (imaginary settings, a little like Yoknapatawpha county in Faulkner's works) and my own 'society' of people who go from one work to another. This is still the kind of novel that I write today and should be with *Les Derniers seront les premiers* and *Madame X,* the final part of a trilogy.

"Finally, I want to say that I do not believe in the idea of a 'writing career.' Today that is the greatest danger for anyone who writes books. Writing is a vocation, not a job. To want to make a career, which many authors do, is to take part in spite of oneself in the system that wants to make the book a product of consumption like any other. In my novel *L'Aviateur* I evoked the life of one of my great-aunts, who worked in a printing factory. Sometimes she brought home from work books that were damaged or soiled and thus couldn't be sold, so they were left for the workers. She solemnly put them in her library to give to me later. She was very proud of her library and realized, I think, that she belonged to a sort of worker's

aristocracy that took part in the development of knowledge. It was as if the product of her labor transcended her modest condition. And for me, who received these works, the feeling of respect was too strong for me to be able today to call the books products, that is, to imagine readers as clients. The only true danger for a writer is to want to please."

BIOGRAPHICAL/CRITICAL SOURCES:

PERIODICALS

Le Figaro, June 1, 1990.
Le Figaro Magazine, June 1, 1990.
Figaroscope, November 13, 1991.
Lire, December, 1991, p. 122.
Le Monde, October 18, 1991, p. 21; November 9, 1991.
Times Literary Supplement, February 5, 1993, p. 12.

*   *   *

LEWIS, (Percy) Wyndham 1882(?)-1957

PERSONAL: Born November 18, 1882 (some sources say 1884 or 1886), on a ship anchored at Amherst, Nova Scotia, Canada; emigrated to England, 1888; died March 7, 1957, in London, England; son of Charles (a former American army officer) and Anne (Prickett) Lewis; married Gladys Anne Hoskyns, 1930; children: fathered and abandoned five illegitimate children. *Education:* Attended the Slade School of Art, 1898-1901.

CAREER: Artist, poet, literary critic, and novelist. Taught at Assumption College in Windsor, Ontario, 1943-44.

AWARDS, HONORS: Awarded a Civil List Pension by the British government, 1952; received honorary doctorate from Leeds University, 1952.

WRITINGS:

The Ideal Giant, Little Review (London), 1917.
Tarr (novel), Knopf (New York), 1918.
The Caliph's Design, Egoist (London), 1919.
Harold Gilman, Chatto & Windus (London), 1919.
The Art of Being Ruled, Harper (New York), 1927.
The Lion and the Fox: The Role of the Hero in the Plays of Shakespeare, Harper (New York), 1927.
Time and Western Man, Harcourt, Brace (New York), 1927.

The Wild Body, Chatto & Windus (London), 1927, Harcourt, Brace (New York), 1928.

The Childermass, Covici Friede (New York), 1928.

Paleface: The Philosophy of the "Melting Pot", Chatto & Windus (London), 1929, Haskell House (New York), 1969.

The Apes of God (novel), Arthur (London), 1930, Robert McBride (New York), 1932.

Satire and Fiction, Chatto & Windus (London), 1930, Folcroft Library (Folcroft, PA), 1975.

Hitler, Chatto & Windus (London), 1931, Gordon (New York), 1972.

The Diabolical Principle and The Dithyrambic Spectator, Chatto & Windus (London), 1931, Haskell House (New York), 1971.

The Doom of Youth, Robert McBride (New York), 1932.

Filibusters in Barbary (travelogue), National Travel Club (New York), 1932.

Enemy of the Stars (play), Harmsworth (London), 1932.

Snooty Baronet (novel), Cassell (London), 1932, Haskell House (New York), 1971.

The Old Gang and the New Gang, Harmsworth (London), 1933, Haskell House (New York), 1972.

One-Way Song (poetry), Faber & Faber (London), 1933.

Men Without Art, Cassell (London), 1934, Russell & Russell (New York), 1964.

Left Wings Over Europe: or, How to Make a War About Nothing (essay), Cape (London), 1936, Gordon (New York), 1972.

Count Your Dead: They Are Alive! (essay), Dickson (London), 1937, Gordon (New York), 1972.

The Revenge for Love, Cassell (London), 1937, Regnery (Chicago), 1952.

Blasting and Bombardiering, Eyre & Spottiswoode (London), 1937, University of California Press (Berkeley), 1967.

The Mysterious Mr. Bull, Hale (London), 1938.

The Jews, Are They Human?, Allen & Unwin (London), 1939, Gordon (New York), 1972.

Wyndham Lewis the Artist from Blast to Burlington House, Laidlaw & Laidlaw (London), 1939, Haskell House (New York), 1971.

The Hitler Cult, Dent (London), 1939, Gordon (New York), 1972.

America, I Presume, Howell, Soskin (New York), 1940.

Anglosaxony: The League That Works, Ryerson (Toronto), 1941.

The Vulgar Streak, Hale (London), 1941, Jubilee (New York), 1973.

America and the Cosmic Man, Nicholson & Watson (London), 1948, Doubleday (Garden City, NY), 1949.

Rude Assignment, Hutchinson (London), 1950.

Rotting Hill (short stories), Methuen (London), 1951, Regnery (Chicago), 1952.

The Writer and the Absolute, Methuen (London), 1952, Greenwood (Westport, CT), 1975.

Self Condemned (novel), Methuen (London), 1954, Regnery (Chicago), 1955.

The Demon of Progress in the Arts, Methuen (London), 1954, Regnery (Chicago), 1955.

Monstre Gai, Methuen (London), 1956.

Malign Fiesta, Methuen (London), 1956.

The Red Priest, Methuen (London), 1956.

The Letters of Wyndham Lewis, edited by W. K. Rose, Methuen (London), 1963, New Directions (Norfolk, CT), 1964.

A Soldier of Humor, edited with an introduction by Raymond Rosenthal, New American Library (New York), 1966.

Wyndham Lewis on Art, edited with an introduction by Walter Michel and C. J. Fox, Funk & Wagnalls (New York), 1969.

Wyndham Lewis: An Anthology of His Prose, edited with an introduction by E. W. F. Tomlin, Methuen (London), 1969.

Unlucky for Pringle: Unpublished and Other Stories, edited with an introduction by Fox and Robert Chapman, David Lewis (New York), 1973.

The Roaring Queen, Liverlight (New York), 1973.

Enemy Salvoes: Selected Literary Criticism, edited with an introduction by Fox, general introduction by C. H. Sisson, Barnes & Noble (New York), 1976.

Mrs. Dukes' Millions, Coach House Press (Toronto), 1977.

Collected Poems and Plays, edited by Alan Munton, introduction by Sisson, Carcanet (Manchester, England), 1979.

SIDELIGHTS: The circles in which Wyndham Lewis moved were home to some of the most celebrated writers, painters, and social critics of his day, yet Lewis himself remains an obscure figure in twentieth-century intellectual history. A painter, poet, novelist, and essayist, he drew upon some of the most revolutionary currents in art and philosophy then gaining currency among European intelligentsia during his era, but his political views often placed him at odds with the more liberal leanings of his peers. Moreover, Lewis's difficult temperament and cutthroat talent for mercilessly skewering fellow writers and artists earned him more than a few enemies. "Lewis's provocative and even insulting attacks established his ferocious public image, antagonized his enemies, and alienated nearly everyone who was in a position to help him," wrote Jeffrey Meyers in the *Dictionary of Literary Biography*. As a result, he toiled in poverty for long stretches of his career, and often found himself in court as the defendant in libel suits.

"Wyndham Lewis was one of those originals whose genius as a filibuster in paint and prose is dispersed over so wide a ground that one does not know where to have him," wrote V. S. Pritchett in the *New Statesman*. His unusual heritage testifies to that range. He was born in the 1880s on a vessel in Canadian waters off the coast of Nova Scotia to an English mother and an American Civil War veteran, which gave him a Canadian passport that he was compelled to use somewhat reluctantly later in life. His parents' marriage ended when he was eleven, and he grew up in England with his mother. As a young man, he attended London's Slade School of Art before alighting on the continent to experience life in various European capitals. In 1909 Lewis returned to England and began a career in earnest as a painter, becoming a leading proponent of what would become known as Vorticism, England's first abstract art movement to be linked with Cubism and Futurism. In the *Dictionary of Literary Biography,* Meyers offered a definition of Vorticism: "It emphasized the importance of African and Polynesian sculpture; employed hard geometrical lines; represented machinery and the city; used iron control and underlying explosiveness, classical detachment and strident dynamics."

Gaining in status as a young, challenging artist of his day, Lewis developed friendships among the literati of the era in Britain; he counted Rebecca West, Ford Madox Ford, and Ezra Pound as friends. With Pound, he began a collaboration in 1914 on a literary review they called *Blast*. The radical look of its typography and layout mirrored its content, and *Blast* took its influences from the socio-political currents underlying the Cubist and Futurist art movements and offered readers some vociferous opinions. The sole two issues of *Blast* (the last appeared in July of 1915) made Lewis a feted figure on the intellectual scene. That milieu, however, was sundered with the outbreak of World War I; Lewis enlisted and served as a gunner in the Royal Artillery, and witnessed some horrific battles. Scholars of his work assert the miseries of the battlefield Lewis experienced later found outlet in his politically-charged works, in which he argued for a strong militarism in a "peacekeeping" effort to avoid further bloodshed on such a mass scale.

Blast had expanded Lewis's talents from the canvas to the printed page, and in 1918 his first novel, *Tarr,* was published. Set in Paris's bohemian Montparnasse quarter, it drew heavily among Lewis's own somewhat romantic days as a young man there in its tale of the parallel lives of two artists. The Englishman "Tarr" enjoys success in his career and dallies with German and Russian mistresses; the German Otto Kreisler "represents a recurring Lewis theme: the difficult life of the would-be artist, without sufficient talent or money, living under the strain of poverty and fear of failure," opined Meyers in the *Dictionary of Literary Biography*. In its rejection of equality between the sexes, *Tarr*'s themes mirrored Lewis's own turbulent personality; he had numerous affairs throughout his life and fathered, then abandoned, at least five children outside of his childless marriage to Gladys Anne Hoskyns, whom he met in 1918 and wed in 1930. Furthermore, with its neat themes of English-vs.-German dominance, it would appear that Lewis wrote *Tarr* as a timely reflection of the conflicts of World War I, yet he claimed to have begun it much earlier.

After the war, Lewis's father died but he was cheated out of an inheritance; this, combined with the devastating combat experiences, left him somewhat embittered. He came to see the war as a disastrous event in civilization, and took a hiatus from writing for a time. Instead he read extensively, kept painting, and continued to socialize with the era's best-known literary figures, including James Joyce and Ernest Hemingway. By 1926 Lewis's ruminations on civilization and politics came to the fore in his nonfiction treatise *The Art of Being Ruled*. In it, he postulates that an authoritarian society, one in which artists are allowed an exalted and compensated status, is the antidote for the disjointedness and dysfunction of modern times. He draws from the writings of Friedrich Nietzsche and Bertrand Russell, excoriates Marxism, parliamentary politics, jazz, post-impressionist art, and feminism. Though *New York Times Book Review* critic William MacDonald called it "formless and inconclusive," he granted that "Lewis perceives certain trends and has the courage to speak his mind about them, and courageous writing, even when it is irritating, is always to be praised."

The second of Lewis's magnum opuses of the 1920s was *Time and Western Man,* published in 1927. It marked the beginning of Lewis's no-holds-barred criticism of his contemporaries; he lambasted both Joyce and Pound, calling the latter an "intellectual eunuch." The book's primary theme, however, was the denunciation of what Lewis called the "cult of time," and, relatedly, the unfavorable changes wrought upon civilization by the advent of mass advertising and cinematic arts; *Time and Western Man* was illustrated with examples to support these theories. A *Times Literary Supplement* contributor found it provocative and asserted the book's "merit is to have singled out a vital idea and presented it with that kind of power which makes you wonder why no one has seen it so before."

Lewis's other significant novel of this era was *The Childermass,* published in 1928. It was to be part of trilogy entitled *The Human Age,* and its plot follows two men "who welter in imbecility and drivel," as a *Times Literary Supplement* critic explained. At the gates of heaven, they set off on a walk to pass the time before judging is to commence; along the way they meet fearsome dragons and queer embryonic life forms who jeer at them, while landmarks mysteriously vanish upon approach. The farcical mood also introduces characters who are weak disguises for leading figures both past and present, including Marcel Proust and Albert Einstein. At their judging, their trial is interrupted by a raucous chorus of elitists, who despise the "common" man represented by the duo. Lawrence S. Morris, reviewing *The Childermass* in the *New Republic,* faulted what he called Lewis's "mannered, self-conscious style," but commended the novel and the way in which its author "leaps from metaphysics to politics to literature, so full of combativeness that he has not yet had time to think any one of his thoughts through. And, in a pinch, he will sacrifice all of them for a slashing phrase."

From 1927 to 1929 Lewis edited and wrote much of the literary review *The Enemy.* The "enemy" was a literary persona he "found particularly congenial to his irascible temperament," noted an essay on Lewis in the *Encyclopedia of World Literature in the 20th Century.* Yet some of his contentions were perceived as sympathetic to Fascism, which by then was well-established in Mussolini's Italy and gaining ground in Spain and Germany as well. These leanings would flourish after Lewis was sent on assignment to Berlin by a magazine and came back and wrote *Hitler.* The 1931 work, its jacket adorned with swastikas, was brought out by Lewis's respected London publishing house Chatto & Windus. Attempting to walk a thin line between outright approval of the Nazi Party leader in the years before he assumed power in Germany and resolute dismissal of reactionary fascist tactics, Lewis called his subject a "Man of Peace," and predicted the anti-Semitic foment which the Nazis

had whipped up would eventually fade away. His pro-fascist leanings were also evident in two pamphlets published in the mid-1930s, *Left Wings Over Europe* and *Count Your Dead: They Are Alive!*

These works, and Lewis's dalliance with the British Association of Fascists, would later serve as one of the pillars of his ostracism. The biggest nail in his coffin, however, seemed to be his 1930 novel *The Apes of God.* The 625-page self-illustrated work chronicled the exploits of an eager young man in his introduction to contemporary bohemian terrain. Lewis managed to skewer an array of acquaintances, from his patrons to T. S. Eliot to Gertrude Stein to the entire Bloomsbury group. Only thinly disguised by aliases, their foibles and pretensions were savagely illuminated by Lewis's sharp pen. "It is a farcical magnification of inanity that employs linguistic virtuosity and the technique of overkill to demolish its victims," noted Meyers in the *Dictionary of Literary Biography.* "It is also a bitter comedy, a deliberately cruel personal attack, and a savage roman a clef. The satire expresses Lewis's moral and aesthetic values as well as his caustic character, records his friendships and feuds, and gives a lively if biased account of the literary history of the 1920s."

Not surprisingly, *The Apes of God* caused a stir. Fred T. Marsh, critiquing it for the *New York Times Book Review,* noted that "Lewis applies his lash fiercely for hours upon end" but called the book "a satire of unusual originality and power." Most reviewers concurred that the novel was overwritten, with Henry Bamford Parkes of the *New Republic* terming it "unbearably monotonous." Yet Parkes, like the other critics, found some passages marvelous, and noted, "parts of the book have an originality of observation and a power of expression unequaled by any other English writer of the twentieth century. . . . If it is not a genuine masterpiece, it is from a lack of discipline." Lewis also ventured into poetry. *One Way Song,* published in 1933, poked fun at the new breed of society poets of the 1930s. *Spectator* critic and literary figure Stephen Spender, himself skewered mercilessly as the character Dan Boleyn in *The Apes of God,* termed it "full of dislike for democracy and democratic ideals."

Misfortune plagued Lewis through the 1930s. He suffered from an array of health problems, some of them the result of venereal disease. Libel suits were filed, and Chatto & Windus recalled *The Doom of Youth* and *Filibusters in Barbary,* both published in 1932; later, the house sued Lewis for breach of contract after he tried to sell works to other publishers before completing the other two novels in *The Human Age* cycle. His 1934 work *Men Without Art* contained an essay deriding Hemingway entitled "The Dumb Ox"; in it, Lewis compared the writer with "a dull-witted, bovine, monosyllabic simpleton, a lethargic and stuttering dummy." In response, Hemingway pilloried Lewis in *The Movable Feast,* opining he "had the eyes of an unsuccessful rapist," according to Meyers in the *Dictionary of Literary Biography.* The Royal Academy rejected his portrait in 1938, an unambiguous snub.

Lewis managed to reverse the backslide of his reputation with his 1937 memoir, *Blasting and Bombardiering.* Set in the years from 1914 to 1926, the work covers his wartime experiences and political evolution and treats his former targets more gently, even commenting favorably upon Joyce and Pound. It was written in Lewis's typical, adjective-laden exhausting prose, prompting *Spectator* reviewer and acclaimed novelist Anthony Burgess to fault its author's powers of over-observation: "Seeing a sardine on toast, he acts as though commissioned to paint its portrait," remarked Burgess. Around the same time, Lewis also reconsidered his fascist sympathies and wrote essays critical of Nazi Germany in *The Jews, Are They Human?* and *The Hitler Cult,* both published in 1939.

The year 1939 also marked the onset of World War II with Hitler's surprise invasion of Poland on September 1. The next day, Lewis and his wife sailed for the United States, where he was to execute a portrait commission; a day later, war was declared and they were stranded. Low on funds, his reputation now tarnished, Lewis wound up waiting out the war in a run-down hotel in Toronto, then a far cry from the cosmopolitan hub into which it would later evolve. His hatred of these years and of the provincial-minded city would surface in later novels. The only respite Lewis seemed to have enjoyed during these years was from a teaching stint at Assumption College in Windsor, where he engaged in intellectual repartee with its Roman Catholic priests. It was here Lewis also came to know a young Marshall McLuhan, and the elder's theories of humankind and its relationship to time, advertising, and the mass media—as expounded upon in Lewis's 1927 work *Time and Western Man*—made a unquestionable impact on McLuhan.

After the war, Lewis and his wife were on the first passenger ship sailing to England in August of 1945. He resumed his career as a painter and writer, achieving some restoration of his former status. He became the art critic for *The Listener* in 1946, but five years later his increasing loss of vision caused him to re-

sign. The following year, some of his financial burdens were eased when the British government awarded him a Civil List Pension, commonly given to artists and writers who have made significant cultural contributions during their career. He continued to write books despite his disability, at first writing his drafts on a board that rested on his knees by means of a pen attached to a wire; his wife and a former mistress, who now helped take care of him, transcribed his longhand; he later used a Dictaphone. In 1954 his novel *Self Condemned* was published, a work some scholars consider to be Lewis's most outstanding. It follows the travails of an English couple—the husband a history professor—in their self-imposed exile in "Momaco"; its author's derision of Toronto and Canada is vehement. Adam Mars-Jones, writing in the *Times Literary Supplement* in 1982, pointed out that the novel "put [Toronto] on the map, but only so that thinking persons might be aware of its location on the planet, and successfully avoid it."

Lewis was felled by the brain tumor that had brought on his blindness, and died in March of 1957. Meyers, writing in the *Dictionary of Literary Biography,* remarked that other lauded, similarly modernist writers of Lewis's era like Eliot and Pound also entertained somewhat unsavory political views—but never suffered the scholarly rebuff that Lewis did, who, Meyers pointed out, "remained self-condemned." Occasional volumes of Lewis's prolific output have appeared intermittently in the years since his death, most notably *The Letters of Wyndham Lewis,* published in 1963, and *Enemy Salvoes: Selected Literary Criticism,* issued in 1976. In 1989, *The Art of Being Ruled* was reissued and *Times Literary Supplement* critic Julian Symons found Lewis's theories surprisingly enduring. "After reading the chapters here about feminism and homosexuality, the cult of youth and the opposition between races, one may look disbelievingly at the publication year of the book, for these are 'wars' going on today in full force," declared Symons, who concluded: "More than sixty years after its publication, this book remains the most valuable guide available to the cant and absurdities of the attitudes about sex, race, 'elitism' and 'prejudice' prevalent in liberal Western society, and to their basic meanings."

BIOGRAPHICAL/CRITICAL SOURCES:

BOOKS

Dictionary of Literary Biography, Volume 15: *British Novelists, 1930-1959,* edited by Bernard Olsey, Gale, 1983.

Encyclopedia of World Literature in the 20th Century, revised edition, edited by Leonard S. Klein, Continuum Publishing, 1993, p. 65.

PERIODICALS

Canadian Literature, winter, 1992, p. 154.
Christian Century, November 30, 1955, pp. 1400-01.
Commonweal, July 13, 1932, pp. 294-295; January 6, 1956, p. 356.
London Review of Books, June 22, 1989, pp. 19-20.
Modern Fiction Studies, summer, 1983, p. 237; winter, 1992, pp. 845-869.
Nation, April 20, 1927, p. 446; December 21, 1932, p. 623; September 3, 1949, p. 234; March 27, 1974.
New Republic, September 22, 1926, p. 124; March 7, 1928, p. 102; December 12, 1928, p. 111; June 8, 1932, p. 105; August 22, 1934.
New Statesman, December 24, 1927, pp. 358-359; July 7, 1928, p. 426-427; January 5, 1952, pp. 18-19; January 8, 1955, pp. 48-49; July 28, 1967, pp. 119-120; April 14, 1972, p. 498; February 20, 1976, p. 234; April 27, 1979, p. 598.
New York Times Book Review, October 10, 1926; November 20, 1927, p. 9; July 15, 1928, p. 2; April 17, 1932, p. 2; June 12, 1932, p. 11; September 25, 1932, p. 12; June 19, 1949, p. 8; August 9, 1964, p. 5; February 10, 1985, p. 29.
New Yorker, June 4, 1955.
Observer, November 14, 1993, p. 22.
Saturday Review, June 18, 1955, p. 16; April 4, 1964, p. 29.
Spectator, August 13, 1932, pp. 210-211; December 1, 1933, p. 812; December 14, 1951, p. 832; May 20, 1966, pp. 640-642; July 7, 1967, pp. 15-16; January 31, 1976, p. 14; October 21, 1989, p. 39.
Time, September 2, 1940, p. 64; July 4, 1949, p. 70; May 23, 1955, p. 102.
Times Literary Supplement, April 8, 1926, p. 258; February 10, 1927, p. 89; October 27, 1927, p. 760; December 8, 1927, p. 930; July 19, 1928, p. 531; July 7, 1932, p. 490; August 4, 1932, p. 553; March 15, 1934, p. 185; December 7, 1951, p. 777; April 5, 1963, p. 232; August 3, 1973, p. 893; February 6, 1976, p. 128; June 30, 1978, p. 726; December 3, 1982, p. 1934; November 8, 1985, p. 1259; April 10, 1987, p. 381; May 12, 1989, p. 517; September 22, 1989, p. 1024; June 15, 1990, p. 628.
Voice Literary Supplement, December, 1983, p. 13.
Washington Post Book World, September 30, 1973, p.

15; September 27, 1981, p. 12; May 29, 1983, p. 12; November 12, 1989, p. 16.*

—Sketch by Carol Brennan

*   *   *

LISBOA, Maria Manuel   1963-

PERSONAL: Born November 17, 1963, in Mozambique; Portuguese citizen; daughter of Eugnio and Maria Antonieta (Gabao) Lisboa; married Michael Brick (a painter), May 11, 1993; children: Laura Caroline. *Education:* University of London, B.Sc., 1985; University of Nottingham, M.A., Ph.D., 1988.

ADDRESSES: Office—St. John's College, Cambridge University, Cambridge CB2 1TP, England; fax 01-22-333-7720. *E-mail*—MMGL100@cam.ac.uk.

CAREER: University of Newcastle upon Tyne, Newcastle upon Tyne, England, lecturer in Portuguese and Brazilian literature, 1988-93; Cambridge University, St. John's College, Cambridge, England, lecturer in Portuguese, Brazilian, and African (Lusopaone) literature, 1993—. Guest lecturer at University of Leeds, University of St. Andrews, University of Hamburg, Institute of Romance Studies, London, and University of Reading.

WRITINGS:

(Contributor) Jon Davies, editor, *Ritual and Remembrance: Responses to Death in Human Societies,* Sheffield University Press (Sheffield, England), 1994.
(Contributor) Sarah M. Hall, editor, *Reference Guide to World Literature,* Gale (London, England), 1995.
Machado de Assis and Feminism: Re-Reading the Heart of the Companion, Edwin Mellen (Lewiston, NY), 1996.
(Contributor) Georgiana Colville, editor, *Other Women's Voices/Other Americas,* Edwin Mellen (Lewiston, NY), 1996.
(Contributor) Naomi Segal and Nicholas White, editors, *Scarlet Letters: Fictions of Adultery from Antiquity to the 1990s,* Macmillan (Basingstoke, England), 1997.

Contributor of stories, translations, articles, and reviews to periodicals, including *Portuguese Studies,*

Letras e Letras, Journal of the Institute of Romance Studies, Journal of Hispanic Research, and *Revista Arca.*

WORK IN PROGRESS: A book of essays on themes of national identity and origin in Portugal from the nineteenth century to the present; a book of essays on Brazilian romanticism, examining both colonial and post-colonial themes.

*   *   *

LISLE, Holly 1960-

PERSONAL: Born in October, 1960, in Salem, OH. *Education:* Richmond Community College, associate degree in nursing, 1982.

ADDRESSES: Agent—Russell Galen, Scovil, Chichak, Galen Literary Agency, 381 Park Ave. S., Suite 1020, New York, NY 10016. *E-mail*—Holly.Lisle@sff.net.

CAREER: Writer. Worked as an advertising representative for a newspaper, sang in restaurants, taught guitar, did commercial artwork, and worked as a registered nurse for ten years, primarily in emergency and critical care units; became full-time writer, 1993—.

MEMBER: Science Fiction Writers of America.

AWARDS, HONORS: Compton Crook Award for Best First Novel, 1993; finalist for John W. Campbell Award for Best New Writer, 1993 and 1994.

WRITINGS:

"ARHEL" NOVELS

Fire in the Mist, Baen (Riverdale, NY), 1992.
Bones of the Past, Baen, 1993.
Mind of the Magic, Baen, 1995.

"GLENRAVEN" NOVELS

(With Marion Zimmer Bradley) *Glenraven,* Baen, 1996.
(With Marion Zimmer Bradley) *Glenraven: In the Shadow of the Rift,* in press.

"DEVIL'S POINT" NOVELS

Sympathy for the Devil, Baen, 1996.

(With Walter Spence) *The Devil and Dan Cooley,* Baen, 1996.
(With Ted Nolan) *Hell on High,* Baen, 1997.

"BARD'S TALE" NOVELS

(With Aaron Allston) *Thunder of the Captains,* Baen, 1996.
(With Aaron Allston) *Wrath of the Princes,* Baen, 1997.
Curse of the Black Heron, Baen, in press.

OTHER NOVELS

Minerva Wakes, Baen, 1993.
(With Mercedes Lackey) *When the Bough Breaks,* Baen, 1993.
(With S. M. Stirling) *The Rose Sea,* Baen, 1994.
(With Chris Guin) *Mall, Mayhem and Magic,* Baen, 1995.
Hunting the Corrigan's Blood, Baen, 1997.

Contributor of short stories to anthologies, including *Women at War,* edited by Lois McMaster Bujold, Tor, 1992; *The Enchanter Reborn,* edited by L. Sprague de Camp and Christopher Stasheff, Baen, 1992; and *Chicks in Chainmail,* edited by Esther Friesner, Baen, 1995.

WORK IN PROGRESS: "Mirror of the Dead," a trilogy: *Diplomacy of Wolves, Vengeance of Dragons,* and *Courage of Falcons.*

SIDELIGHTS: Holly Lisle is an author of fantasy novels that often center on female protagonists who possess or come under the influence of magical powers. In her first novel, 1992's *Fire in the Mist,* Lisle presents the story of Faia, a young shepherdess who exhibits a natural talent for magic. She joins a group of more advanced practitioners in order to develop her abilities but ultimately rebels against the strict social arrangement of the society, in which men and women reside separately and celibately. Carolyn Cushman, reviewing *Fire in the Mist* in *Locus,* called the novel "exceptionally well-crafted and readable," concluding that the work is "a real page-turner that should be highly popular with genre fans."

In 1993's *Minerva Wakes,* protagonist Minerva Kiakra inadvertently gains possession of a wedding ring with magical powers, setting off a series of fantasy adventures that include an encounter with a dragon, the abduction of Minerva's children, and a trip to an alternate universe. Susan E. Chmurynsky, reviewing

Lisle's second novel in *Kliatt,* called *Minerva Wakes* "a good natured and breezy tale that moves along at a rapid clip."

In *Mind of the Magic,* published in 1995, Lisle returns to the saga of Faia, the protagonist of *Fire in the Mist,* who has grown into adulthood and is now the mother of a five-year-old child. The novel centers on circumstances that evolve when all the inhabitants of the town of Arhel suddenly develop magical abilities, then just as suddenly lose their magical gifts, leaving the town in a nightmarish state of ruin. Through Faia the community is reborn and establishes harmonious contacts with the Klaue, nonhuman beings who cohabit the region. Commenting on *Mind of the Magic,* Sister Avila Lamb in *Kliatt* wrote that "there are instances of very fine writing. . . . Readers will be charmed by the delightful characters."

Coauthored with Chris Guin, Lisle's young adult fantasy novel *Mall, Mayhem, and Magic* was published in 1995. In the work, magic wreaks havoc in the local mall when a bookstore clerk attempts to cast a love spell on the girl he admires. Karen S. Ellis, reviewing *Mall, Mayhem, and Magic* in *Kliatt* noted that coauthors Lisle and Guin "have created an interesting combination of fantasy, horror and humor." Ellis called the pace of the novel "quick and exciting."

In *Sympathy for the Devil,* published in 1996, a young woman's wish that all those in Hell receive a second chance at redemption brings the condemned back to earth. "This clever tale gives a down-to-earth look at religious 'fates,'" remarked Lesley S. J. Farmer, reviewing *Sympathy for the Devil* in *Kliatt.* "Character development is well done, and the tone is actually light-hearted."

Glenraven, coauthored with noted fantasy writer Marion Zimmer Bradley and published in 1996, follows the adventures of two women who visit Glenraven, a fictitious country that harbors secrets of "Europe's mystical forgotten past." Recommending *Glenraven* in a review in *Library Journal,* a critic noted that "Bradley and Lisle expertly juxtapose contemporary women and a medieval, magical culture."

BIOGRAPHICAL/CRITICAL SOURCES:

PERIODICALS

Kliatt, March 1994, p. 18; September 1995, p. 23; November 1995, p. 17; May 1996, p. 18.

Library Journal, August 1996, p. 120.
Locus, July 1992, p. 33.

*   *   *

LOFAS, Jeannette 1940-

PERSONAL: Born June 5, 1940, in New York, NY; daughter of Gerhard and Elissa Kullack; married October 2, 1980; children: Lars. *Ethnicity:* "German." *Education:* Attended University of Vienna, and University of Geneva; University of Michigan, B.A., 1960; Fordham University, M.S.W., 1990, and C.S.W. *Avocational interests:* Skiing, body surfing, horses.

ADDRESSES: Home—333 West End Ave., New York, NY 10023. *Office*—The Stepfamily Foundation, Inc., 333 West End Ave., New York, NY 10023; fax: (212) 362-7030. *Agent*—Gloria Mosesson. *E-mail*—stepfamily@aol.com.

CAREER: Atlas Magazine, New York City, cofounder and associate editor, 1959-61; Radio Free Europe, New York City, reporter, 1961-69; ABC-TV, New York City, on-air reporter, 1969; Ivan Tors Films, independent producer, 1970; Snowmass Arts Foundation, Aspen, CO, executive director, 1971-72; *Family Matters* cable television show, host, 1972-73; Stepfamily Foundation, Inc., New York City, founder and president, 1975—. Also worked at KWTV, Oklahoma City, OK, as a television reporter and film critic; Metro Media, New York City, as on-air reporter. Whitney Museum, New York City, cofounder of New American Film Series. Public speaker on the topic of stepfamilies; has made guest appearances on a number of television programs, including *The Today Show, Good Morning America, CBS This Morning, The Oprah Winfrey Show, Geraldo Rivera, Larry King, Sally Jesse Raphael,* and *Prime Time Live.* Has also worked as a corporate consultant.

MEMBER: AMFT, Milton Erikson Society.

AWARDS, HONORS: Honorary Ph.D., University of Oklahoma, 1971; Southwest Film Award, 1978; National Parents' Day Award presented to the Stepfamily Foundation, 103rd United States Congress, 1995, for "your efforts in strengthening step relationships in families across America and thus contributing to effective parenting"; Woman of the Month, *Good Housekeeping* magazine.

WRITINGS:

(With Ruth Roosevelt) *Living in Step* (nonfiction), Stein and Day (New York), 1976.

(With Dawn B. Sova) *Stepparenting* (nonfiction), Zebra Books (New York), 1985; revised edition, Kensington Books (New York), 1995.

(With Joan MacMillan) *He's OK, She's OK: Honoring the Differences between Men and Women* (psychology), Tzedakah Publications (Sacramento, CA), 1995.

Also the creator of the audio book *How to be a Stepparent,* Nightingale-Conant Audio Book, 1986.

WORK IN PROGRESS: The House Rules.

SIDELIGHTS: Jeannette Lofas is the coauthor of several books examining stepfamily relationships and the differences between men and women. The founder of the Stepfamily Foundation, Inc., Lofas, together with Ruth Roosevelt, wrote the family guidebook *Living in Step* in 1976. This work was followed in 1985 by *Stepparenting,* which was revised and updated in 1995. In the book, Lofas and Dawn B. Sova "[set] forth the principles for stepfamilies to live by," according to Kay Brodie in *Library Journal.* The program advocated by Lofas and Sova in *Stepparenting* emphasizes open communication within the family and suggests that a set of "job descriptions," or expectations, be created for each member of the blended family.

He's OK, She's OK: Honoring the Differences between Men and Women, which Lofas authored with Joan MacMillan, was published in 1995. An examination of sex roles as well as psychological and communication differences between the sexes, the work outlines the impact of these differences on male/female relationships in personal, social, and business situations.

While Denise Perry Donavin suggested in *Booklist* that generalizations about typical behavior patterns rendered *He's OK, She's OK* less helpful to "those who do not readily conform to a mold," she nevertheless concluded that there was "plenty to ponder" for both male and female readers.

BIOGRAPHICAL/CRITICAL SOURCES:

PERIODICALS

Booklist, June 1, 1995, p. 1702.
Library Journal, June 1, 1995, pp. 150, 152.

LOGAN, Michael F. 1950-

PERSONAL: Born September 22, 1950, in Tucson, AZ. *Education:* University of Arizona, B.A. (history and journalism), 1981, M.A., 1990, Ph.D., 1994.

ADDRESSES: Home—516 South Ramsey St., Stillwater, OK 74074. *Office*—Department of History, 501 Life Sciences W., Oklahoma State University, Stillwater, OK 74078. *E-mail*—mfl4925@okway.okstate.edu.

CAREER: University of Arizona, Tucson, history teacher, 1990-94; Oklahoma State University, Stillwater, assistant professor of history, 1994—. Pima Community College, teacher, 1992-94.

MEMBER: American Historical Association, American Society for Environmental History, Western History Association.

WRITINGS:

Fighting Sprawl and City Hall: Resistance to Urban Growth in the Southwest, University of Arizona Press (Tucson, AZ), 1995.

Contributor of articles and reviews to periodicals, including *Journal of American Culture, Locus,* and *Journal of Arizona History.*

*   *   *

LOPES, Dominic (M. McIver) 1964-

PERSONAL: Born July 3, 1964, in England; son of Anthony D. (a physician) and Anita C. (a writer; maiden name, Macfarlane) Lopes; married Anne M. Blackburn, August, 1988 (divorced, 1995). *Ethnicity:* "South Asian, British, and Hispanic." *Education:* McGill University, B.A. (with honors), 1986; Oxford University, D.Phil., 1992.

ADDRESSES: Office—Department of Philosophy, Indiana University at Kokomo, 2300 South Washington St., Kokomo, IN 46904-9003; fax 765-455-9528. *E-mail*—dlopes@indiana.edu.

CAREER: Indiana University at Kokomo, associate professor of philosophy, 1992—.

MEMBER: American Philosophical Association, American Society for Aesthetics, British Society of Aesthetics.

WRITINGS:

Understanding Pictures, Clarendon Press (New York City), 1996.
(Editor with Damian Lopes) *A Handful of Grams: Goan Proverbs,* Caju Press (Toronto, Ontario), 1996.

Editor, *American Society for Aesthetics Newsletter.*

WORK IN PROGRESS: Getting in Touch with Pictures: Pictures and the Blind, completion expected in 1999.

M

MACKENNEY, Richard 1953-

PERSONAL: Born April 2, 1953, in Aylesbury, Buckinghamshire, England. *Education:* Queens College, Cambridge, B.A. (with honors), 1975, graduate study, 1976-80; University of Edinburgh, Ph.D., 1982.

ADDRESSES: Office—Department of History, University of Edinburgh, William Robertson Building, George Square, Edinburgh EH8 9JY, Scotland. *Agent*—Bruce Hunter, David Higham Associates, 5-8 Lower John St., Golden Square, London W1R 4HA, England.

CAREER: Historian and educator. University of Edinburgh, Edinburgh, Scotland, senior lecturer in history.

AWARDS, HONORS: Graduate fellow, Rotary Foundation of Rotary International, 1975-76; Royal Historical Society fellow, 1988—.

WRITINGS:

Tradesmen and Traders: The World of the Guilds in Venice and Europe, c. 1250-c. 1650, Barnes & Noble (New York City), 1987.
The City-State, 1500-1700: Republican Liberty in an Age of Princely Power, Macmillan (London), 1989.
Sixteenth-Century Europe: Expansion and Conflict, St. Martin's Press (New York City), 1993.
Renaissance Italians, 1300-1600, Macmillan, 1997.

Also the author of various specialized articles on Renaissance Venice.

WORK IN PROGRESS: A project on the Spanish conspiracy against Venice in 1618.

SIDELIGHTS: Examining a different section of Venetian society than most historians of the Italian Renaissance, Richard Mackenney describes the city's lower middle class of small manufacturers and storekeepers in *Tradesmen and Traders: The World of the Guilds in Venice and Europe, c. 1250-c. 1650.* During the thirteenth, fourteenth, and fifteenth centuries these working-class Venetians belonged to guilds that brought together both tradesmen and traders in one organization. In his study, Mackenney asserts that the commercial prosperity of the city was a direct result of such guilds, which boasted a widespread membership throughout Venice and encouraged the acceptance of capitalist ideas. "The strength of this pioneering book is its embarrassing emphasis on a vast array of subjects which lie at the very heart of Venetian history and yet have been consistently ignored by historians," maintained David Abulafia, reviewing the work in the *Times Literary Supplement.* "Mackenney's achievement," the critic continued, "is not so much that of finding answers to fundamental questions about how the city really functioned, as that of indicating which questions need to be asked and where clues to an answer might lie."

A lecturer in history at the University of Edinburgh, Mackenney began his writing career after his general historical interests grew more specialized, a result of research he was conducting on Venetian guilds, the origins of capitalism, and the development of the modern state. Mackenney told *CA:* "The study of Venice in Western history has raised the unsettling notion that history is a Western disease, an obsession with change in a culture which makes its ideals—Plato's Republic, [Thomas] More's Utopia, Renaissance Venice—places where change simply does not happen. The writers who have most influenced me are Jacob Burckhardt, Kenneth Clark, Hugh Trevor-Roper and John Roberts. All of them offer history which is general and which makes sense of the contemporary world in relation to the past. This is not self-consciously popular history, but it offers an alternative to what Burckhardt called 'the devastation of the mind by newspapers and novels.'"

BIOGRAPHICAL/CRITICAL SOURCES:

PERIODICALS

Times Literary Supplement, June 5, 1987, p. 599.

*   *   *

MAHONEY, Thomas H(enry) D(onald) 1913-1997

OBITUARY NOTICE—See index for *CA* sketch: Born November 4, 1913, in Cambridge, MA; died of a stroke, April 21, 1997, in Palo Alto, CA, as he returned to Massachusetts after giving a speech in Korea. Historian, educator, politician, and author. Mahoney embarked on two careers during his lifetime in addition to writing and editing books. His first career was in education with stints at schools such as Boston College, Massachusetts Institute of Technology, and College of the Holy Cross. His work at MIT spanned 1945 to 1984 and saw Mahoney teach history and serve as section head. His second career was in politics; he would ultimately be elected to offices eleven times. Among the positions he held were school committeeperson, state representative, and founding chairperson of the ethics committee. Later, he was appointed to the post of First Secretary of Elder Affairs for Massachusetts by Governor Edward King.

Mahoney's work in bringing issues regarding aging into the public eye took him to various parts of the globe to lecture. He also found time to get his doctorate in public affairs in 1989 from the John F. Kennedy School of Government at Harvard. He was seventy-five when he received the degree. He wrote and edited a number of books, including *Edmund Burke and Ireland, The United States in World History, Edmund Burke: The Enlightenment and the Modern World,* and *Aging in Urbanization.*

OBITUARIES AND OTHER SOURCES:

BOOKS

Who's Who in America, 51st edition, Marquis, 1997.

PERIODICALS

New York Times, April 27, 1997, sec. 1, p. 40.
Washington Post, April 28, 1997, p. B4.

*   *   *

MAIZELS, John 1945-

PERSONAL: Surname is pronounced May-*zells;* born January 4, 1945, in London, England; son of Alfred (an economist) and Joan (a sociologist) Maizels; married Margaret Jones, May, 1968; children: Jennie, Lucy. *Education:* Chelsea College of Art, London, England, B.A., 1967. *Politics:* "Progressive Anarchist." *Religion:* "Yogic." *Avocational interests:* Outsider art.

ADDRESSES: Home—Hertfordshire, England. *Office*—Raw Vision, P.O. Box 44, Watford, Hertfordshire WD2 8LN, England; fax 01-92-385-9798. *E-mail*—rawvis@dial.pipex.com.

CAREER: Freelance artist, 1967—. *Raw Vision,* Watford, England, editor and publisher, 1989—. Member of board of trustees, Outsider Archive, London, England, and British Friends of American Visionary Art Museum, Baltimore, MD.

WRITINGS:

Raw Creation: Outsider Art and Beyond, Phaidon (London, England), 1996.

WORK IN PROGRESS: Research on visionary Indian artist Nek Chand.

SIDELIGHTS: John Maizels told *CA:* "I have been involved in the study of 'outsider art' for many years. I have been overwhelmed by its truth and power, especially when compared to the paucity of so much contemporary art. As a result of this involvement, I decided to write a 'guidebook' to outsider art that would take the reader through the various discoveries and developments of the century and point to many aspects for further research and inquiry."

MAKAVEJEV, Dusan 1932-

PERSONAL: Born October 13, 1932, in Belgrade, Yugoslavia; married Bojana Marijan, 1964. *Education:* Earned a degree in psychology from Belgrade University, 1955; attended the Academy for Theatre, Radio, Film, and Television, Belgrade.

ADDRESSES: Home—Paris, France. *Agent*—c/o Cannon Pictures, 8200 Wilshire Blvd., Beverly Hills, CA 90212.

CAREER: Film director and screenwriter. Director of the film *The Coca-Cola Kid* (screenplay by Frank Moorhouse), released by Cinecom International/Film Gallery, 1985; worked variously as a reviewer, film editor, and producer/director of shorts and documentary films. *Military service:* Served in the Yugoslavian Army, 1959-60.

AWARDS, HONORS: Ford Foundation Grant, 1968.

WRITINGS:

SCREENPLAYS; AND DIRECTOR

Covek Nije Tijka, published as *Man Is Not a Bird,* Grove Press, 1966.
Ljubavni Slucaj, ili tragedija sluzbenice P.T.T. (also known as *Love Affair: Or the Case of the Missing Switchboard Operator* and *An Affair of the Heart),* Brandon, 1967, released in the United States in 1968.
Nevinost bez zatite (also known as *Innocence Unprotected*), Grove Press, 1968, released in the United States by Avala/Grove Press, 1971.
W. R. Misterite organizma (also known as *W. R.—Mysteries of the Organism*),Yugoslavija Film/ Cinema V, 1971.
Sweet Movie, Biograph, 1974.
(With Bon Jonsson, Donald Arthur, Arnie Gelbert, Branko Vucicevic, and Bojana Marijan) *Montenegro* (also known as *Montenegro, or Pigs and Pearls*), New Realm/Atlantic, 1981.
The Coca-Cola Kid, Cinecom International/Film Gallery, 1985.
Manifesto (also known as *Pour une nuit d'amour* and *For One Night of Love*), Cannon Releasing, 1988.
The Gorilla Bathes at Noon, Balfour Films, 1993.
Hole in the Soul, 1995.

Also directed and wrote short films and documentaries, including *Jatagan Mala,* 1953; *Pecat* (also known as *The Seal*), 1955; *Antonijevo razbijeno ogledalo* (also known as *Anthony's Broken Mirror*), 1957; *Spomenicima ne treba verovati* (also known as *Don't Believe in Monuments*), 1958; *Slikovnica pcelara* (also known as *Beekeeper's Scrapbook*), 1958; *Prokleti praznik* (also known as *Damned Holiday*), 1958; *Boje sanjaju* (also known as *Colors Are Dreaming*), 1958; *Sto je radnicki savjet?* (also known as *What Is a Workers' Council?*), 1959; *Eci, pec, pec* (also known as *One Potato, Two Potato*), 1961; *Pedagoska bajka* (also known as *Educational Fairy Tale*), 1961; *Osmjeh 61* (also known as *Smile 61*), 1961; *Parada* (also known as *Parade*), 1962; *Dole plotovi* (also known as *Down with the Fences*), 1962; *Ljepotica 62* (also known as *Miss Yugoslavia 1962*), 1962; *Film o knjizi A.B.C.* (also known as *Film about the Book*), 1962; *Nova igracka* (also known as *New Toy*), 1964; *Nova domaca zivotinja* (also known as *New Domestic Animal*), 1964.

SIDELIGHTS: Dusan Makavejev became interested in filmmaking as a university student at the University of Belgrade, and while serving in the Yugoslavian Army he wrote several scripts about military psychology. His initial films, *Man Is Not a Bird, Love Affair,* and *Innocence Unprotected,* were made within the restrictions of the state-run Yugoslavian film industry, which prohibited certain political views and overt sexuality. Makavejev left Yugoslavia for France in the early 1970s to escape these restrictions. Operating outside of his native country, he was able to create films according to his true artistic vision and present them in more receptive venues.

At the Cannes Film Festival, Makavejev's 1971 film *W. R.—Mysteries of the Organism* earned popular and critical accolades, but more importantly it brought the filmmaker's talents to the attention of international film financiers. Makavejev's benefactors have not always been entirely pleased with the filmmaker's results, however. When shooting a film, he often improvises scenes as the mood strikes him, and the blatant sexuality of his films has caused an outcry in several countries—his 1975 offering, *Sweet Movie,* was banned in England, Canada, and South Africa. To appease the censors and make his films available to a wider audience, Makavejev has on occasion edited his films to meet the rating standards of other countries. His explicit films have earned him a reputation as an original and true voice in filmmaking— albeit one whose work is uneven and intentionally provocative. This fact has caused consternation among some critics, causing speculation that the filmmaker has traded the intuitive emotional resonance of his earlier films for the calculated heavy-handedness of his later works.

"From his very first movie," wrote Andrew Sarris in *Village Voice,* Makavejev "revealed himself as a talented trouble-maker, the worst kind. *Man Is Not a Bird* is nothing if not dialectical, but dialectics turned upside down and inside out by a disenchanted intellectual and disoriented sensualist. . . . We do not merely see, we feel as well, for there is mercy and beauty in Makavejev's vision, and humor too. But as we look at the very delicate balance between fiction and documentary in *Man Is Not a Bird,* we realize that Makavejev will never again be this appealing to a general audience. His later films will seem more explicit, more schematic, more theoretical, more cerebral, less intuitive, less delirious, less inspired, and, hence, less affecting."

Other critics have found problems with other aspects of Makavejev's work. *Nation* reviewer Robert Hatch, who called *Sweet Movie* "prolific with cliches," took the director to task for his filmmaking technique. "I don't want to put Makavejev down—he's a talented man with a great deal on his mind. But I think he makes the mistake of supposing that if he gets the cameras rolling and his brain free-associating, his ideas will somehow shape themselves into a communicable statement. If he were a mural painter, it might work." Hatch concluded, "I have no opinion about the originality or profundity of Makavejev's ideas, but I'm reasonably sure he has not discovered how to convey them."

Made in Sweden, *Montenegro* boasts an international cast and an English script. The plot revolves around a Swedish businessman's wife who is losing her sanity. "Like some improbable blend of Maxim Gorky and Preston Sturges, Makavejev has made a psycho-social political farce, with mythic undertones, about the clash of cultures and psyches in this mongrelized world," remarked Jack Kroll in *Newsweek.* "It's a funny, disquieting film—spicy, sweet and sorrowing like all his work." "Mr. Makavejev makes movies so full of routinely decodable images that one attends to them not as if they were a movie but somewhat garbled telegrams," commented Vincent Canby in the *New York Times.* "[*Montenegro*] is less a film than a series of illustrated slogans that proclaim the decadence of capitalism, the sterility of Freudian psychiatry and the joys of unrepressed sexuality. Though Mr. Makavejev has liberated himself, his films have grown smaller, more precious, more ponderously didactic than they were when he was working in Yugoslavia." Stanley Kauffmann of *New Republic* saw Makavejev's work since *Love Affair* as suffering a disintegration in quality: "Labored cleverness has

replaced elan, heavy sexual symbolism has smothered erotic understanding, and the satire on Marxism has been dreadful." About *Montenegro* specifically, Kauffmann maintained, "Makavejev's varicose virtuosity lames the whole enterprise," and concluded, "If Makavejev could spend seven years looking for a sponsor and then come up only with a film as mannered, as strained for trite angst, as this one, it's difficult to hope further for him."

After viewing *Manifesto* at a sneak preview during the Cannes Film Festival, *Variety* critic Strat described the film as "a chirpy, quirky, erotic and visually lush charmer. Mellow in tone, it contains many of this director's most characteristic ideas about sex and revolution, and though not as tough as his very best work, still looms as a good arthouse bet."

The Gorilla Bathes at Noon depicts a Russian soldier's wanderings after the fall of the Berlin Wall and his subsequent abandonment by his army. Noting that the film manifests compelling spiritual longing, which famed Russian director Andrei Tarkovsky asserted is an essential condition for the emergence of art, James M. Wall commented in *The Christian Century,* "The great political conflicts that led to 'the fall of Berlin' and to today's chaos in [the former] Yugoslavia are all struggles of absurdity, in which people suffer on behalf of leaders who lack vision or the will to resolve conflicts. Makavejev looks at this absurdity and invites the audience to laugh at it."

BIOGRAPHICAL/CRITICAL SOURCES:

PERIODICALS

Chicago Tribune, August 11, 1985.
Nation, November 1, 1975.
New Republic, November 25, 1981.
New Statesman, May 13, 1988.
Newsweek, November 16, 1981.
New York Times, November 15, 1981.
Variety, June 1, 1988; October 19, 1988.
Village Voice, February 21, 1974.*

*   *   *

MALONE, James Hiram   1930-

PERSONAL: Born March 24, 1930, in Winterville, GA; son of Ralph (a laborer) and Sarah Lena (a homemaker; maiden name, Echols) Malone; married

Mary Louise Liebaert (a school teacher), 1972 (divorced, 1982); children: Andrew Ralph, Matthew Martin. *Education:* Morehouse College, A.A., 1951; Center for Creative Studies College of Art and Design, A.A., 1962. *Politics:* Democrat. *Religion:* Unitarian. *Avocational interests:* Poetry, photography, tennis, woodworking, reading.

ADDRESSES: Home and office—1796 North Ave. N.W., Atlanta, GA 30318-6441.

CAREER: Author and illustrator. K-Mart International Headquarters, Troy, MI, senior graphics designer, 1980-83; *Atlanta Journal and Constitution,* Atlanta, GA, ad promotions creative director, 1983-90; Bianco Art Collections of Atlanta, fine art producer/painter, 1990-92; *Atlanta News Leader,* author of "Street Beat" column and artist, 1992—; freelance cartoonist for periodicals. Guest author, reader, lecturer, and storyteller at schools, festivals, conferences, and coffee houses. Active in many civic, public, and community organizations, including Neighborhood Planning, Black Artists Network and Advocacy, Literacy Action of Atlanta, and Atlanta Arts Council. Volunteer at Atlanta's Homeless Association, Inc., and for Christmas in July (for homeless children). Has exhibited fine art paintings at art galleries, museums, art festivals, malls, and parks. *Military service:* U.S. Army, 1950-59; became Sergeant First Class.

MEMBER: International Black Writers Association (president, 1997), First World Writers Association (vice president, 1993-94), Visual Vanguard Art Group (board member), High Museum of Art, Writers Resource Center (consultant), Nexus Art Association, Center for Creative Studies College of Art and Design Alumni Association.

AWARDS, HONORS: Scholastic Magazine National Scholastic Art Award, 1949; Atlanta University Art Award, 1949; Famous Artists Art Award, National Cartoonists Society, 1956; National Newspaper Publishers Association Award, 1973; Michigan's Artists Book Award, Willis Gallery, 1980, for *Brother; Atlanta Journal and Constitution* Creative Ad Awards, 1984-87; Atlanta Symphony Poster Contest Award, 1985; United Way Human Support Awards and Helping Hand Awards, 1985, 1986, 1988; Atlanta newspapers publishing grant, 1986; Center for Creative Studies Alumni Art Award, 1986; Bronze Jubilee Community Art Award, 1986; Atlanta Employer's Voluntary Employment Association Task Force on Youth Motivation Awards, 1987, 1988, 1989; Southern Drawl Exhibition Award, Mobile College, 1993; Interna-

tional Black Writers Association Merit Award, 1994; Nexus Family History Artbook Project Youth Motivation Award, 1994; Windsor Hills School honor, 1997.

WRITINGS:

SELF-ILLUSTRATED

Here and There Poetry, Hilltop Press, 1954.
Blues Poetry, Hilltop Press, 1954.
Grandma Sarah's Closet, Funtime Books, 1960.
Brother, Jamlou Publishers, 1970.
Malone's Atlanta, Impressive Press, 1986.
Say Literacy Guide, Writeway, 1986.
No-Job Dad, Victory Press, 1992.
Jone's Family Cart, Ahkeelah's Press, 1997.

Also author and illustrator of *Y'All Come Back,* 1988, and *Atlanta, the Democrats Are Coming,* 1988. Author and illustrator of the cartoon strip *Ralph,* 1970s.

OTHER

(Contributor) *The Total Cartoonist,* Prentice-Hall, 1983.

Contributor to *Word Up Anthology,* 1990. Contributor of writings and illustrations to over 350 periodicals, including *Famous Artists Magazine, Illustrator, Bledsonian Banner, Dunlap Tribune, Atlanta Pictorial Reporter, Jackson Journal, Army Times, Soul, Detroit Free Press, Ebony, Liberator, Michigan Chronicle, Atlanta Journal and Constitution, Intown Extra, Catalyst,* and *Atlanta News Leader.* Coauthor of song lyrics for recordings, including *Talk to Your Child, Willie Lives in the Streets,* 1986, and *Homeless Hope,* 1987. Co-author of song lyrics for *Tap,* performed in Atlanta, GA, 1995.

WORK IN PROGRESS: Malone Art Journal, a self-illustrated autobiography; research for a book on storefront churches, illustrated with photographs; *If I Lives an' Nuthin' Happen,* a novel.

SIDELIGHTS: James Hiram Malone commented: "I remember when I was a barefoot toddler living in Atlanta's Fourth Ward District being a busy-bee little wall scribbler. As high as my arms could reach I decorated walls, woodwork, furniture, and any place that boy and crayons got together. At that age I was an artist and I had a story to tell. And I told it.

"In the first grade, my free-hand drawing of the three bears eating was at a very slanted table. Even the chair rungs wouldn't meet in the right places. But what I remember best is Miss Barnette, my teacher, saying to me, 'My, my, young man, that is very good!" This encouragement helped build Malone's image of himself, as did the stories his mother told and the drawings she created as she told them.

"Along with my mother's natural talent of building my self-esteem, I also relied on the neighborhood movie house," Malone explained. "I lived for the Saturday afternoon matinees, because at this young age I lived in fantasy land and fairytale land to escape from poverty realization. My first creative writings were all just daydreams of being like a hero on the movie screen. It was sometime later before anything was put on paper. I borrowed my friend's shoeshine box and learned early to shine shoes for movie fare.

"During my youthful years of movie-going, all of what most of my friends cared about were full-of-action, fast-motion, and sometimes funny happenings. However, what I wondered about was, 'Where were the colored heroes?' Even the cowboy hats were white. Being aware of this trend, later I reflected on this policy in my writings and artwork. *Here and There Poetry* and *Blues Poetry* (both 1954) are bittersweet efforts to really understand society. And I found out that keeping up with news headlines is a challenge to any writer and especially a writer of color."

While he spent his weekends at the movie theater, Malone became active in various school activities during the week, including the high school newspaper and the yearbook. Proud to be a part of these projects, Malone still found himself bothered by the disparity between his school supplies (including textbooks) and the supplies at the suburban schools. "I kept my sanity by tuning out this mundane situation by dreaming up stories I wanted to write about as I sat there in the classroom," he remembered. "I had an amazing memory, didn't have to make notes because my resources were constant, plus I always 'wrote' in my head before applying it to paper. I was daydream writing; 'writing' about my cousin who lived around the corner from me, my aunt, down the street from my other cousin and across the street from my uncle. These memory pieces were later freelanced to periodicals. Slices of life that started at adolescence and were my survival kit all through high school; living in the same neighborhood, family ties. Modern family ties dissolved after desegregation and families moved to the suburbs. Closer living was closer togetherness."

More schooling and the army set Malone on his freelance writing and illustrating career, during the course of which he has published in numerous magazines and newspapers. And all of this writing and illustrating eventually led to his self-illustrated children's books. "*Grandma Sarah's Closet,* my juvenile picture book effort of 1960, was inspired by my Grandmother Sarah and how she related to her grandchildren," Malone commented. "This was a very limited edition experiment to get the feel of the marketplace and to challenge my production capabilities. Working on this book paved the way for better understanding and smoother sailing for my later efforts."

One of Malone's latest efforts in this genre is *No-Job Dad,* which relates the story of a young boy, Joey, who is afraid to ask his father to school on career day. Despite the fact that he is unemployed at the moment, the father comes to school and puts his son's fears to rest. "How I got my concept of *No-Job Dad* was thinking about what kind of book I wanted to do, a juvenile picture book. After this, how many characters. It had to be mainstream and simple, something kids would like.

"At that time, the economy wasn't anything to brag about, either, so *No-Job Dad* could relate to society as a whole. Deciding on three characters, Joey, the son and student, and his mother and father, I then thought of a conflict. I always wondered what would happen if a parent of a student was invited to career day at school and the parent didn't have a job at that time. So, now I had my plot, theme, and conflict all rolled into one. And this has to be, because juvenile picture books are based on simplicity, simplicity, simplicity.

"My youth and childhood came out in the production of *No-Job Dad;* I had to think young to write young. Yep, I had to smile all the while like a juvenile! Yeah."

BIOGRAPHICAL/CRITICAL SOURCES:

PERIODICALS

Atlanta Journal and Constitution, May, 1994; June, 1994.
Center Line (Detroit), winter, 1997.
Creative Loafing (Atlanta), September, 1995; March, 1997.
Impresario Magazine, November/December, 1972.
Wave Newspapers (Los Angeles), March, 1995.

MANLEY, Michael Norman 1924-1997

OBITUARY NOTICE—See index for *CA* sketch: Born December 10, 1924, in Kingston, Jamaica; died of prostate cancer, March 6, 1997, in Kingston, Jamaica. Politician and author. Manley was a trade union activist, member of Parliament, and senator, who rose to become one of the most notable figures in Caribbean politics and was three times elected to the office of Prime Minister of Jamaica. He was born into one of Jamaica's most prominent families. His father, Norman Washington Manley, was the founder of the People's National Party (PNP) and the island's Prime Minister from 1955 to 1962. Following wartime service with the Royal Canadian Air Force, Manley studied at the London School of Economics. While in London he contributed to "Caribbean News" broadcasts for the British Broadcasting Corp. and wrote articles for the *Observer*. He returned to Jamaica in 1951 and entered politics, becoming active in both the National Workers Union and the political party headed by his father. From 1962, when Jamaica was granted independence from Great Britain, to 1967 Manley was an appointed member of the senate; from 1967 to 1972 he served as an elected member of parliament representing central Kingston. He succeeded his father as the leader of the PNP in 1969. Manley became Prime Minister in 1972, a position to which he was reelected in 1976. These first two terms were characterized by socialist domestic policies, political alignment with Fidel Castro, and anticapitalist economic policies that discouraged foreign investment. Manley was ousted from power in 1980, when his party was defeated by the Jamaican Labor Party (JLP), led by Edward P. G. Seaga. His party boycotted the 1983 election, and until his return to power in 1989 Manley worked on behalf of the international Socialist movement. When he won election again, however, he espoused capitalism and sought improved relations with the United States. He resigned from office in 1992 due to ill health. Manley's writings include works on politics, labor relations, and the history of cricket in the West Indies. His *Poverty of Nations* was published in 1991.

OBITUARIES AND OTHER SOURCES:

BOOKS

Who's Who, 148th edition, St. Martin's, 1996.

PERIODICALS

Los Angeles Times, March 8, 1997, p. A22.

New York Times, March 8, 1997, p. 52.
Washington Post, March 8, 1997, p. B4.

*   *   *

MARTENS, Lorna 1946-

PERSONAL: Born December 28, 1946. *Education:* Attended Paedagogische Hochschule Braunschweig, 1965-66, and University of Goettingen, 1966-67 and 1969-70; Reed College, B.A. (German literature), 1969; Yale University, M.Phil., 1973, Ph.D. (comparative literature), 1976; attended University of Konstanz, 1974-76.

ADDRESSES: Home—128 Observatory Ave., Charlottesville, VA 22903. *Office*—Department of Germanic Languages and Literatures, 108 Cocke Hall, University of Virginia, Charlottesville, VA 22903; fax 804-924-6700.

CAREER: Yale University, New Haven, CT, instructor, 1973, acting instructor, 1973-74 and 1976, assistant professor, 1976-83, associate professor of Germanic languages and literatures, 1983-87; University of Virginia, Charlottesville, associate professor of Germanic languages and literatures, 1988—.

MEMBER: Phi Beta Kappa.

AWARDS, HONORS: Woodrow Wilson fellow, 1969-70; Fulbright grant for Germany, 1969-70, senior fellow, 1994-95; fellow in Germany, German Academic Exchange Service, 1974-75; Morse fellow, 1981-82; fellow of Summer Institute for the Study of Avant-Gardes, Harvard University, 1987; Guggenheim fellow, 1987-88.

WRITINGS:

The Diary Novel, Cambridge University Press (Cambridge, England), 1985.
Shadow Lines: Austrian Literature from Freud to Kafka, University of Nebraska Press (Lincoln, NE), 1996.
(Contributor) Janet Lungstrum and Elizabeth Sauer, editors, *Agonistics: Arenas of Creative Contest,* State University of New York Press (Albany, NY), 1997.

Contributor of articles and reviews to periodicals, including *Comparative Literature, Modern Austrian*

Literature, PMLS, Hebrew University Studies in Literature, Stanford Literature Review, and *German Quarterly.*

WORK IN PROGRESS: The Promised Land?, a book on feminism and socialism in German women writers.

*   *   *

MARTIN, Fenton S(trickland) 1943-

PERSONAL: Born November 3, 1943, in Topeka, KS; daughter of Charles Kenneth (an attorney) and Fenton (Wambersie) Strickland; married second husband, Richard L. Pacelle, Jr. (a professor of political science), February 11, 1995; children: (first marriage) Russell A., Craig E. *Ethnicity:* "White." *Education:* Florida State University, B.S., 1964; Indiana University—Bloomington, M.L.S., 1970. *Avocational interests:* Jogging, raising poodles, following baseball, travel.

ADDRESSES: Home—721 East First St., Bloomington, IN 47401. *Office*—Political Science Library, Woodburn 200, Indiana University—Bloomington, Bloomington, IN 47401; fax 812-855-2027. *E-mail*—martinf@indiana.edu.

CAREER: Indiana University—Bloomington, head librarian at Political Science Library, 1971—.

MEMBER: American Library Association, American Political Science Association, Midwest Political Science Association, Indiana University Librarians Association, Beta Phi Mu.

AWARDS, HONORS: Outstanding Academic Books Award, *Choice,* 1985-86, for *Policy Analysis and Management* and *The Presidency,* 1987-88, for *The American Presidency,* and 1991-92, for *The U.S. Supreme Court;* Outstanding Reference Sources Award, *Choice,* 1995, for *The United States Congress, 1980-1990.*

WRITINGS:

WITH ROBERT GOEHLERT

The Parliament of Great Britain: A Bibliography, Lexington Books (Lexington, MA), 1982.
Political Science Journal Information, American Political Science Association (Washington, DC), revised edition, 1984, fourth edition, 1997.

The Presidency: A Research Guide, American Bibliographical Center-Clio Press (Santa Barbara, CA), 1985.
Policy Analysis and Management: A Bibliography, American Bibliographical Center-Clio Press, 1985.
The American Presidents: A Bibliography, Congressional Quarterly Books (Washington, DC), 1987.
The American Presidency: A Bibliography, Congressional Quarterly Books, 1987.
Congress and Lawmaking: A Research Guide, 2nd edition, American Bibliographical Center-Clio Press, 1989.
The U.S. Supreme Court: A Bibliography, Congressional Quarterly Books, 1990.
How to Research the Supreme Court, Congressional Quarterly Books, 1992.
The United States Congress, 1980-1990: An Annotated Bibliography, Congressional Quarterly Books, 1994.
Members of Congress: A Bibliography, Congressional Quarterly Books, 1995.
How to Research the Presidency, Congressional Quarterly Books, 1996.
How to Research Congress, Congressional Quarterly Books, 1996.
Bibliography of American Government, Congressional Quarterly Books, 1997.

WORK IN PROGRESS: Congressional and Presidential Elections: An Annotated Bibliography, 1960-1996, with Robert Goehlert, publication by Congressional Quarterly Books expected in the year 2000.

*   *   *

MARTIN, Sam
See MOSKOWITZ, Sam

*   *   *

MARTINSON, Ida M(arie) 1936-

PERSONAL: Born November 8, 1936, in MI; daughter of Oscar (a farmer) and Maruel (a homemaker; maiden name, Nelson) Sather; married Paul Varo Martinson, March 31, 1962; children: Anna Marie, Peter V. *Ethnicity:* "White." *Education:* University of Minnesota—Twin Cities, B.S., 1960, M.S.N., 1962; University of Illinois at the Medical Center,

Ph.D., 1972. *Politics:* Democrat. *Religion:* Lutheran. *Avocational interests:* Skiing, reading.

ADDRESSES: Home—Flat 12B, Pak Sui Yuen, 17 Science Museum Rd., Tsim Sha Tsui East, Hong Kong. *Office*—Department of Health Sciences, Hong Kong Polytechnic University, Hong Kong; fax 85-22-363-6217. *E-mail*—hsida@polyu.edu.hk.

CAREER: Hong Kong Polytechnic University, Hong Kong, professor of health sciences and head of department. Ohio University, nursing scholar, 1986; Foo Yin Junior College of Nursing and Midwifery, visiting professor, 1987; consultant to Taiwan's National Defense Medical Center School of Nursing and National Cheng-Kung University. Shriners Hospitals, member of national nursing advisory committee, 1981-83; Veterans Administration Central Office, member of geriatrics and gerontology advisory committee, 1981-85; American Bureau for Medical Advancement in China, member of nursing committee, 1981—; International Work Group on Dying and Bereavement, member and chairperson of work groups, 1982—; Harvey L. Lapides, Jr. Family-Centered Home Care Hospice Program, member of board of advisers, 1983-85; Children's Hospice International, honorary member of advisory council, board of directors, and executive committee, 1985, president, 1986-88, co-chairperson, 1988-89, member, 1989—; Childhood Cancer Foundation, Taipei, Taiwan, co-founder, 1986, advisor, 1986—; Kaleidoscope, member of board of directors, 1995—; honorary adviser for Hong Kong Society for Nursing Education, Institute of Advance Nursing Studies, and College of Nursing.

MEMBER: American Nurses Association, National Hospice Organization, Professional Nurses Network Association, Foundation of Thanatology, Society of Chinese Bioscientists in America, Association of Pediatric Oncology Nurses, Society of Pediatric Nursing, California Hospice Association, Arizona Nurses Association, Sigma Theta Tau.

WRITINGS:

(Editor and contributor) *Home Care for the Dying Child: Professional and Family Perspectives,* Appleton-Century-Crofts, (New York City), 1976.

(With G. R. Kepner) *Mathematics for Health Professionals,* Springer Publishing (New York City), 1977.

(Editor with Diane K. Kjervik) *Women in Stress: A Nursing Perspective,* Appleton-Century-Crofts, 1979.

(Editor with D. Kjervik, and contributor) *Women in Health and Illness: Life Experiences and Crises,* Saunders (Philadelphia, PA), 1986.

(Editor with T. Krulik and B. Holaday, and contributor) *The Child and Family Facing Life Threatening Illness: A Tribute to Eugenia Waechter,* Lippincott (Philadelphia), 1987.

(Editor with C. L. Gilliss, B. L. Highley, and B. M. Roberts, and contributor) *Toward a Science of Family Nursing,* Addison-Wesley (Menlo Park, CA), 1989.

(Editor with A. Widmer, and contributor) *Home Health Care Nursing,* Saunders, 1989.

(Contributor) I. Coreless, B. Germino, and M. Pittman, editors, *Dying, Death, and Bereavement,* Jones & Bartlett (Boston, MA), 1994.

(Contributor) D. Adams and E. Deveau, editors, *Childhood Cancer,* Baywood Press, 1995.

(Editor with J. Fitzpatrick) *Selected Writings of Rosemary Ellis: In Search of the Meaning of Nursing Science,* Springer Publishing, 1996.

(Contributor) Fitzpatrick and D. Modley, editors, *Developing Home Care Nursing Services: International Lessons,* Springer Publishing, 1997.

Contributor of more than a hundred articles to nursing, health, and medical journals, including *Pediatric Nursing, Death Studies, Cancer Nursing, International Healthcare for Women, Western Journal of Medicine, Allied Health Journal, American Journal of Nursing, Pediatrics, Journal of Nursing, Nursing Times, Journal of Gerontological Nursing,* and *Journal of Community Health Nursing.*

BIOGRAPHICAL/CRITICAL SOURCES:

BOOKS

Brooten, D. A., L. L. Hayman, and M. G. Naylor, editors, *Leadership for Change,* Lippincott, 1989.

PERIODICALS

Lutheran Woman Today, September, 1990, pp. 30-32.

*   *   *

McAULEY, Paul J. 1955-

PERSONAL: Born April 23, 1955, in Stroud, Gloucestershire, England. *Education:* Bristol University, B.Sc., 1976, Ph.D., 1980.

ADDRESSES: Agent—MBA Literary Agents, 45 Fitzroy St., London, England, W1P 5HR.

CAREER: Biologist, writer, and editor. Cell biologist at Oxford University, University of California, Los Angeles, and University of St. Andrews.

AWARDS, HONORS: Philip K. Dick Memorial Award for Best New Novel, 1989, for *Four Hundred Billion Stars;* Arthur C. Clarke Award for Best British Novel, 1995, for *Fairyland;* Sidewise Award, 1995, for *Pasquale's Angel;* British Fantasy Society Short Story Award, 1995, for "The Temptation of Dr. Stein."

WRITINGS:

Four Hundred Billion Stars (novel), Victor Gollancz (London), 1988.
Secret Harmonies (novel), Victor Gollancz (London), 1989; published in the United States as *Of the Fall,* Ballantine (New York), 1989.
Eternal Light (novel), Victor Gollancz (London), 1991.
The King of the Hill, and Other Stories (short stories), Victor Gollancz (London), 1991.
(Editor, with Kim Newman) *In Dreams* (anthology), Victor Gollancz (London), 1992.
Red Dust (novel), Victor Gollancz (London), 1993, Avon, 1994.
Pasquale's Angel (novel), Victor Gollancz (London), 1994, Avon, 1995.
Fairyland (novel), Victor Gollancz, 1995 (London), Avon 1995.
The Invisible Country (short stories), Victor Gollancz (London), 1996.
Child of the River (part one of "The Confluence Trilogy"), Victor Gollancz (London), 1997.
Ancients of Days (part two of "The Confluence Trilogy"), Victor Gollancz (London), in press.

Contributor of short stories to *Amazing, The Magazine of Fantasy and Science Fiction, Interzone,* and *IASFM.*

WORK IN PROGRESS: Ship of Fools, the third part of "The Confluence Trilogy," to be published by Gollancz.

SIDELIGHTS: Paul J. McAuley is an English biologist and science fiction novelist whose works combine hard biological science with such genre conventions as space opera plots, interstellar warfare, genetic engineering, and alien colonization. McAuley's first

novel, *Four Hundred Billion Stars,* won the Philip K. Dick Memorial Award for best new novel in 1988. His sixth novel, *Fairyland,* won the Arthur C. Clarke Award for Best British Novel of 1995.

During the mid-1980s, McAuley's short fiction began appearing in magazines devoted to the science fiction genre, and these works were later collected in 1991's *The King of the Hill, and Other Stories.* His first novel, *Four Hundred Billion Stars,* was published in 1988. In it McAuley depicts a setting several hundred years in the future, when humans have colonized alien worlds. The plot centers on the discovery of an ancient form of alien life that destroys the colonists' notion of the development of life, in particular the development of humanity. Tom Easton, in *Analog Science Fiction/Science Fact,* found *Four Hundred Billion Stars* "interesting," in part because "McAuley, as a biologist, has a somewhat different view of utopia than many."

McAuley's second novel, *Secret Harmonies,* which was published in the United States as *Of the Fall,* depicts a revolution that ensues in an alien world when contact between Earth and human colonists is severed. Reviewing the novel in *Analog Science Fiction/Science Fact,* Easton observed, "Like almost all [science fiction], McAuley has a point to make, a moral to state, and he sets that point up with immense care. The final effect is a satisfied reader."

Eternal Light, published in 1991, continued McAuley's consideration of the nature of the universe. Dorothy Yoshida, a telepath who also served as the protagonist of *Four Hundred Billion Stars,* is joined in this story by a disparate group of colleagues who travel deep into space where they make significant discoveries about alien life and the history of the galaxy. A reviewer in *Publishers Weekly* ultimately found *Eternal Light* "disappointing" but did praise the author's ability to depict "awe-inspiring starscapes and grand cosmological theories with impeccable scientific detail." David V. Barrett, offering a mixed review in the *New Statesman & Society,* praised the novel as "well-written," but complained that it "doesn't quite pull off the blend of science and mysticism central to the story."

The science fiction anthology *In Dreams,* issued in 1992 and edited by McAuley with Kim Newman, contains contributions by twenty-seven science fiction writers on the subject of the 45 RPM record. *In Dreams* won praise in *Publishers Weekly* as "a collection that unnerves and provokes while it entertains."

Set six hundred years in the future, McAuley's 1993 novel *Red Dust* recounts the adventures of Wei Lee, an agronomist attempting to release the water necessary to revitalize the barren Martian landscape. Gerald Jonas offered a favorable review of *Red Dust* in the *New York Times Book Review*. According to Jonas, "The story . . . is not so much a straight-line narrative as a meandering quest for enlightenment, both personal and global. It is a quest well worth sharing."

Representing a departure from McAuley's earlier space operas, *Pasquale's Angel*, published in 1994, presents an alternate history. Set in Renaissance Florence, where the fine arts have been supplanted by engineering as the dominant force in cultural life, the work details a sixteenth-century industrial revolution, complete with air pollution and oppressive working conditions. The plot of the novel concerns the investigation by Pasquale, an apprentice painter, and his mentor, the journalist Niccolo Machiavegli, into a series of murders involving politics and technology. Janice M. Eisen in the *Washington Post Book World* commented that "the consideration of aesthetic and metaphysical questions makes this book more than an alternate history and more than an action-packed thriller, though it can be enjoyed on those levels, too."

McAuley told *CA:* "The future is an unknown country that minute by minute becomes the present. I'm honored to be one of the advance party which maps its possible hazards and wonders."

BIOGRAPHICAL/CRITICAL SOURCES:

PERIODICALS

Analog Science Fiction/Science Fact, February 1989, p. 183; February 1990, pp. 183-184.
New Statesman & Society, August 23, 1991, p. 39.
New York Times Book Review, November 13, 1994, p. 62.
Publishers Weekly, August 16, 1993, p. 91; October 11, 1993, p. 84; October 10, 1994, pp. 65-66; May 22, 1995, p. 52.
Washington Post Book World, May 28, 1995, p. 10.

*   *   *

McBRIDE, Jim   1941-

PERSONAL: Born September 16, 1941, in New York, NY; married Tracy Tynan (a costume designer); chil-

dren: three sons. *Education:* Attended New York University.

ADDRESSES: Agent—Daniel Ostroff Agency, 9200 Sunset Blvd., Suite 402, Los Angeles, CA 90069.

CAREER: Screenwriter and director. Director of motion pictures, including *The Big Easy,* 1987, *The Wrong Man,* 1993, *Pronto,* 1997, and *The Informant,* 1997. Director for television productions, including *The Twilight Zone,* 1985, and *Fallen Angels,* 1995.

AWARDS, HONORS: Grand Prizes from Manheim Film Festival and Pesaro Film Festival, both 1967, both for *David Holzman's Diary.*

WRITINGS:

SCREENPLAYS, AND DIRECTOR

David Holzman's Diary, Grove Press (New York), 1967.
My Girlfriend's Wedding, Paradigm, 1969.
(With Lorenzo Mans and Rudy Wurlitzer) *Glen and Randa,* UMC, 1971.
Hot Times, William Mishkin, 1974.
(With L. M. Kit Carson) *Breathless* (adapted from the film directed by Jean-Luc Godard), Orion, 1983.
(With Jack Baran) *Great Balls of Fire* (adapted from the book by Myra Lewis and Murray Silver Jr.), Orion, 1989.
Blood Ties, Shapiro Entertainment, 1991.
Uncovered, CIBY UK/Filmania, 1994.

SIDELIGHTS: Jim McBride is an accomplished screenwriter and director who is known for his vivid, freewheeling films. He came to fame in the late 1960s with his first film, *David Holzman's Diary,* which concerns a young movie fan's efforts to stabilize his life by filming it and, in effect, produce a cinematic diary. Holzman believes that by filming his own activities he will realize a degree of self-knowledge that will otherwise elude him. But the sequences he films fail to elevate his self-awareness. Rather, they serve as further evidence of his growing madness. Indeed, the monomaniacal persistence with which Holzman vainly pursues his filmmaking endeavor is symptomatic of his instability. Peter Hogue, writing in *Film Comment,* described *David Holzman's Diary* as "that rare thing, an American film that has absorbed the breakthroughs of European-style self-reflexiveness in a viable, coherent form of its own."

Although *David Holzman's Diary* has come to be recognized as a classic independent—even avant-garde—film, it hardly produced a ripple within the United States' profit-driven movie business. And although McBride managed to continue as a filmmaker after completing *David Holzman's Diary,* his other early efforts, including *My Girlfriend's Wedding, Glen and Randa,* and *Hot Times,* are even less well known.

After completing *Hot Times* in 1974, nine years passed before McBride returned to commercial film-making with *Breathless,* an overtly Americanized adaptation of French master Jean-Luc Godard's New Wave classic from the late 1950s. In McBride's film, actor Richard Gere assumes the lead as a comically narcissistic fellow who runs afoul of the law after shooting—perhaps inadvertently—a police officer. Gere's character soon seduces a fetching student who eventually joins him as he attempts to elude pursuing lawmen.

Breathless failed to impress a substantial number of film reviewers, some of whom may have been perplexed by the work's offbeat humor and Gere's absurd garb. However, it managed to serve as evidence that McBride could maintain his own style, characterized by unlikely humor, unusual characters, and technical exuberance, while working within a somewhat more commercial framework.

After making *Breathless,* McBride served as director of *The Big Easy,* a thriller written by Daniel Petrie Jr. and Jack Baran about corruption among law enforcement officials in the city of New Orleans. Largely on the strength of the considerable sexual rapport between lead performers Dennis Quaid and Ellen Barkin, *The Big Easy* brought McBride a greater measure of recognition as a capable, if somewhat iconoclastic, filmmaker.

McBride next wrote (with Jack Baran) and directed *Great Balls of Fire,* which featured Dennis Quaid as Jerry Lee Lewis, the rock-and-roll pianist and singer who enjoyed particular prominence in the 1950s before he became notorious for marrying his thirteen-year-old cousin. *Great Balls of Fire,* which deals with both the period of Lewis's greatest fame and his courting of his young cousin, was described by *Newsweek* reviewer David Ansen as "brash, bold and broad."

In the years that have passed since the release of *Great Balls of Fire,* McBride has continued working, but his ensuing films have not realized similar mainstream play. He directed the made-for-television

thrillers *Blood Ties* and *The Wrong Man* and both wrote and directed the European thriller *Uncovered.* Perhaps most notable among these later films is *The Wrong Man,* an atmospheric, sexually charged suspense drama in which an American in Mexico is implicated in a crime and finds himself tracked by the police there. The suspect falls into the company of an unlikely American couple traveling in the foreign land. Soon enough the hero, played by Jason Patric, is drawn to the wife, a crudely seductive woman, played by Rosanna Arquette, who seems an ill match for her older, boorish husband. As the three characters come to acknowledge their unusual relationship, the law officials close in. *Variety* reviewer Todd McCarthy deemed *The Wrong Man* "sultry" and noted the film's "offbeat scenes, potent atmosphere and overt sexuality."

BIOGRAPHICAL/CRITICAL SOURCES:

BOOKS

Contemporary Theatre, Film, and Television, Volume 8, Gale (Detroit, MI), 1988.

PERIODICALS

Film Comment, November/December, 1993, pp. 2-4.
Newsweek, July 10, 1989, p. 72.
Rolling Stone, August 10, 1989, p. 33.
Time, July 10, 1989, p. 67.
Variety, May 24, 1993, pp. 46-47.*

* * *

McCORD, David (Thompson Watson) 1897-1997

OBITUARY NOTICE—See index for *CA* sketch: Born November 15, 1897, in New York, NY; died April 13, 1997, in Boston, MA. Editor, executive, educator, poet, and author. McCord is best remembered for his children's poetry that appeared in works such as *Take Sky: More Rhymes of the Never Was and Always Is, Every Time I Climb a Tree, The Star in the Pail, One at a Time,* and *Mr. Bidery's Spidery Garden.* The National Council of Teachers of English acknowledged his contributions to children's verse by giving him its first national award for excellence. McCord had a varied career, first serving as associate editor and later editor of the *Harvard Alumni Bulletin.* During five years with the *Boston Evening Transcript,* he also began nearly forty years with the Harvard Fund

Council as its executive director. He found time to work as Phi Beta Kappa poet at schools like Tufts College, Massachusetts Institute of Technology, and Colby College. In addition to his children's poetry, he wrote verse for adults that appeared in works such as *Odds Without Ends, And What's More, The Crows,* and *Remembrance of Things Passed.* He edited books, including *What Cheer: An Anthology of American British Humorous and Witty Verse,* and he wrote *The Language of Request: Fishing with a Barbless Hook* and *The Fabric of Man: Fifty Years of the Peter Bent Brigham Hospital.* The recipient of numerous honorary degrees, he was the first to be named Harvard's honorary doctor of humane letters.

OBITUARIES AND OTHER SOURCES:

BOOKS

Twentieth-Century Children's Writers, 4th edition, St. James Press, 1995.

PERIODICALS

New York Times, April 16, 1997, p. D22.
Washington Post, April 20, 1997, p. B6.

*   *   *

McCOURT, Frank 1930-

PERSONAL: Born August 19, 1930, in Brooklyn, NY; immigrated to Ireland for several years during childhood before returning to the United States; son of Malachy and Angela (a homemaker; maiden name, Sheehan) McCourt. *Education:* Attended New York University.

ADDRESSES: Home—New York, NY. *Agent*—c/o Scribner Educational Publishers, 866 3rd Ave., New York, NY 10022.

CAREER: Co-starred in his own vaudeville act; taught writing in the New York Public School system for several years, including stints at McKee Vocational and Technical on Staten Island, as well as Peter Stuyvesant High School; freelance writer, c. 1996—.

AWARDS, HONORS: National Book Critics Circle Award in biography/autobiography, and Pulitzer Prize in biography, both 1997, for *Angela's Ashes.*

WRITINGS:

Angela's Ashes (autobiography), Scribner (New York, NY), 1996.

SIDELIGHTS: Frank McCourt taught writing in the New York Public School system for several years, but waited until he had retired to pen his first book, 1996's *Angela's Ashes.* An autobiography, *Angela's Ashes* tells the story of McCourt's poverty stricken childhood in Ireland. The volume has become a critically acclaimed bestseller, and garnered McCourt both a National Book Critics Circle Award and the Pulitzer Prize.

McCourt was born in 1930 in Brooklyn, New York, to parents who had recently immigrated from Ireland. When McCourt was about four years old, his father decided to move the family back to Ireland. As outlined in *Angela's Ashes,* the elder McCourt—Malachy—had experienced difficulties holding down a job in the United States due to a drinking problem. He had even greater difficulties once he returned to his native soil. Malachy occasionally found work as a laborer in the depressed Irish town of Limerick, but would often spend an entire Friday night drinking in a pub. As a result, he would be too hung over to show up for work on Saturday; ultimately he would be fired. Between Malachy's sporadic jobs, the family would exist on the scant Irish version of welfare, but Malachy would often spend this meager amount entirely upon drink. In his book, McCourt recounts all of this—plus his mother Angela's efforts to keep the family alive and together by economizing, borrowing from family, and begging from parish charity. He describes how his baby sister and two twin brothers died of disease because their family was too poor to ensure proper sanitation and adequate medical care. McCourt himself contracted typhoid as a child and had to be hospitalized for several weeks. There, from the books available in the hospital, he first encountered the works of English playwright William Shakespeare, and he developed a love of literature that would later guide his work.

Several critics reviewing *Angela's Ashes* concluded that McCourt rightfully placed the blame for his family's poverty upon his father's drunken shoulders. However, McCourt also details his father's sobriety during the week. "I'm up with him early every morning with the whole world asleep," McCourt recalls in *Angela's Ashes.* "He lights the fire and makes the tea and sings to himself or reads the paper to me in a whisper that won't wake up the rest of the family."

Michiko Kakutani of the *New York Times* surmised that "[t]here is not a trace of bitterness or resentment in *Angela's Ashes*." Devon McNamara in the *Christian Science Monitor* reported that "what has surprised critic and reader alike is how a childhood of poverty, illness, alcoholism, and struggle, in an environment not far removed from the Ireland of [eighteenth-century English writer Jonathan] Swift's 'A Modest Proposal,' came to be told with such a rich mix of hilarity and pathos." McCourt himself told McNamara: "I couldn't have written this book fifteen years ago because I was carrying a lot of baggage around . . . and I had attitudes and these attitudes had to be softened. I had to get rid of them, I had to become, as it says in the Bible, as a child." He explained further: "The child started to speak in this book. And that was the only way to do it, without judging."

Angela's Ashes also discusses McCourt's return to the United States at the age of nineteen, with one of his surviving brothers. The pair made a living with their own vaudeville show for a time, before Frank McCourt turned to teaching. "The reader of this stunning memoir can only hope," declared Kakutani, "that Mr. McCourt will set down the story of his subsequent adventures in America in another book. *Angela's Ashes* is so good it deserves a sequel." Denis Donoghue, discussing the book in the *New York Times Book Review,* asserted: "For the most part, his style is that of an Irish-American raconteur, honorably voluble and engaging. He is aware of his charm but doesn't disgracefully linger upon it. Induced by potent circumstances, he has told his story, and memorable it is." John Elson in *Time* wrote favorably of *Angela's Ashes* as well, observing that "like an unpredicted glimmer of midwinter sunshine, cheerfulness keeps breaking into this tale of Celtic woe." Paula Chin in *People* hailed it as "a splendid memoir," while McNamara concluded it to be "a book of splendid humanity."

BIOGRAPHICAL/CRITICAL SOURCES:

BOOKS

McCourt, Frank, *Angela's Ashes,* Scribner, 1996.

PERIODICALS

Christian Science Monitor, December 4, 1996, p. 13; March 21, 1997, p. 4.
New York Times, September 17, 1996.
New York Times Book Review, September 15, 1996, p. 13.

People, October 21, 1996, p. 42.
Time, September 23, 1996, p. 74.*

*   *   *

McFARLANE, Alexander C. 1952-

PERSONAL: Born May 27, 1952, in South Australia; son of John Preiss and Nancy Douglas (Robertson) McFarlane; married Catherine Mary Houen, June 25, 1977; children: James Alexander, David Anthony, Anna Catherine. *Ethnicity:* "Caucasian." *Education:* University of Adelaide, M.B., B.S., 1976, Diploma of Psychotherapy, 1983, FRANZCP, 1983, M.D., 1990.

ADDRESSES: Home—Torrens Park, Australia. *Office*—Department of Psychiatry, Queen Elizabeth Hospital, University of Adelaide, Woodville Rd., Woodville, South Australia 5011; fax 61-88-222-6515. *E-mail*—amcfarla@pulse.health.adelaide.edu.au.

CAREER: Flinders University, clinical professor, 1991—; head of psychiatry at Queen Elizabeth Hospital, 1995—; University of Adelaide, Woodville, Australia, professor of psychiatry, 1990—; University of Sydney, Department of Rheumatology, Sydney, Australia, visiting research fellow, 1985—; National Health and Medical Research Council, assessor; consultant to the government of Kuwait. *Military service:* Royal Australian Air Force, Active Reserve.

MEMBER: International Society for Traumatic Stress Studies (member of board of directors, 1993—), Royal Australian and New Zealand College of Physicians (fellow; representative to Australian National Disaster Relief Committee), Australian Society for Traumatic Stress Studies (vice president, 1996-97).

AWARDS, HONORS: Herbert John Wilkinson Memorial Prize, Wood Jones Scalpel, 1972; Junior Roche Prize, Smith Kline and French Prize, Dr. Davies-Thomas Scholarship, 1973; Keith Sheridan Prize, Mead Johnson Pediatric Prize, 1974; Everard Scholarship, William Gardner Scholarship and Prize, Thomas L. Borthwich Memorial Prize, 1975; H. K. Fry Memorial Prize for Psychological Medicine, 1975, for an essay; Organon Junior Research Award, 1986.

WRITINGS:

(Contributor) Steven E. Hobfall and Marten W. de Vries, editors, *Extreme Stress and Communities,* Kluwer Academic, 1995.

(Contributor) R. J. Kleber, C. R. Figley, and B. P. R. Gersons, editors, *Beyond Trauma: Cultural and Societal Dynamics,* Plenum (New York City), 1995.

(Co-editor and contributor) *Traumatic Stress: The Effects of Overwhelming Experience on Mind, Body, and Society,* Guilford (New York City), 1996.

(Contributor) A. J. Marsella, M. J. Friedman, and other editors, *Ethno-Cultural Aspects of Post Traumatic Stress Disorders: Issues Research and Clinical Applications,* American Psychological Association (Washington, DC), 1996.

Contributor of more than a hundred articles to medical journals and other periodicals, including *Medicine and War, International Journal of Eating Disorders, Veterans Health,* and *Disasters.*

SIDELIGHTS: Alexander C. McFarlane told *CA:* "Psychological trauma is the lifeblood of much literature. The attempt to convert the unspeakable into a narrative is a major cultural function of literature. Perhaps more than in any other field, an understanding of the basic workings of the mind and the way in which psychologically traumatic experiences are processed needs to be understood in the formation of this narrative. My recent work is an attempt to summarize the burgeoning knowledge in the field of traumatic stress.

"The study of trauma has been remarkably capricious, with major fluctuations in interest. A new wave of research and clinical interest emerged in 1988, when a specific set of diagnostic criteria was endorsed by the American Psychiatric Association. This has provided the foundation for the blossoming of a substantial and sophisticated knowledge that has largely lain quiescent for much of this century, except in the period around the end of the two world wars.

"The challenge in reviewing any scientific literature is to do more than to take account of the consensus views. The challenge for any field of knowledge is to deal with the inconsistencies and contradictory observations. A major challenge of my recently published book was to provide a balance between these two representations of knowledge.

"My interest in the field emerged from living in a region affected by a major brush fire disaster. In this context, the personal, social, and clinical issues surrounding a disaster-affected population led to a series of research projects. This created many links with the international research community embraced by the International Society for Traumatic Stress Studies. Our edited volume brings together many of the collegial relationships that exist among trauma-related researchers."

* * *

McINTYRE, Ian (James) 1931-

PERSONAL: Born December 9, 1931, in Banchory, Kincardineshire, Scotland; son of Hector Harold and Annie Mary Michie (Ballater) McIntyre; married Leik Sommerfelt Vogt, 1954; children: Andrew, Neil, Anne, Katherine. *Education:* Attended Prescot Grammar School; St. John's College, Cambridge, B.A., 1953; M.A., 1960; attended College of Europe, Bruges, Belgium, 1953-54.

ADDRESSES: Home—Spylaw House, Newlands Ave., Radlett, Hertfordshire, England WD7 8EL.

CAREER: Commissioned in the Intelligence Corps, 1955-57; British Broadcasting Corporation (BBC), 1957-61 and 1970-87, began as current affairs talks producer, 1957, served in various capacities, including writer and broadcaster, 1970-76, controller of BBC Radio 4, 1976-78, and controller of BBC Radio 3, 1978-87; *At Home and Abroad,* editor, 1959; Independent Television Authority, program services officer, 1961; *Times* (newspaper), London, England, associate editor, 1989-90. Staff of the Conservative Party in Scotland, 1962-70; director of Information and Research.

MEMBER: Beefsteak Club, Cambridge Union.

WRITINGS:

NONFICTION

The Proud Doers: Israel After Twenty Years, British Broadcasting Corp. (London, England), 1968.

(Editor and contributor) *Words: Reflections on the Uses of Language,* British Broadcasting Corp (London, England), 1975.

Dogfight: The Transatlantic Battle over Airbus, Praeger (Westport, CT), 1992.

The Expense of Glory: A Life of John Reith, Harper-Collins (New York, NY), 1993.

Dirt and Deity: A Life of Robert Burns, Harper-Collins, 1996.

Also contributor of articles to periodicals, including the *Listener,* the *Times,* and the *Independent.*

WORK IN PROGRESS: A biography of David Garrick, eighteenth-century actor and manager.

SIDELIGHTS: Scottish journalist and author Ian McIntyre has had a long and distinguished career with the British Broadcasting Corporation (BBC). He has served that network in many capacities, including broadcaster as well as controller of two of its radio channels. After leaving the BBC in 1987, McIntyre spent a year as an associate editor of the London *Times,* responsible for its "leader page." In addition to these achievements, McIntyre has penned several books during the course of his career, including biographies of BBC founder John Reith and eighteenth-century Scottish poet Robert Burns.

McIntyre's first book, however, was a study of the nation of Israel published in 1968. *The Proud Doers: Israel After Twenty Years* was published soon after Israel surprised the world by swiftly defeating her Arab neighbors in the Middle East War of 1967. Peter Mansfield, reviewing the work in the *Listener,* questioned McIntyre's objectivity—the critic felt the author accepted Israel's positions on many disputes with the Arabs too easily. Mansfield did, however, praise *The Proud Doers* as being "of the highest standard of intelligent and perceptive reporting."

The author edited one book and authored another, *Dogfight: The Transatlantic Battle over Airbus,* before his 1993 effort, *The Expense of Glory: A Life of John Reith,* reached appreciative readers. Reith was the first Director-General of the BBC, and established many of the high standards in programming for which the corporation has become known. Reith's own diary was published after his death, but only in a greatly edited form. For his biography of Reith, however, McIntyre had access to the unabridged manuscript. He reveals much about Reith's personal vindictiveness, a possible homosexual affair in his youth with a younger boy named Charlie Bowser, and odd infatuations during his later years with a series of female secretaries and personal assistants. *The Expense of Glory* has been widely praised by reviewers. "McIntyre's biography," declared John Dugdale in the *New Statesman & Society,* "besides vividly depict-

ing a personality as mesmerisingly complex as any hero of twentieth-century fiction—is an important tool for those who seek to shape the post-Reithian future" of the BBC. An *Economist* critic added that McIntyre "has a good clear style and an eye for detail," though he expressed the wish that the author had given more attention to Reith's government work under Prime Minister Winston Churchill. E. S. Turner, opining in the *Times Literary Supplement,* concluded that *Expense of Glory* was a "judicious and unblinking book."

In 1996, McIntyre's *Dirt and Deity: A Life of Robert Burns* was published. Burns was one of Scotland's most famous and revered poets, but, as an *Economist* reviewer noted while discussing McIntyre's book, previous biographies have generally tried to emphasize only one side of a widely versatile writer and claim that side as the true Burns. Burns penned both haunting love ballads and bawdy verse; lines filled with political passion and cynical practicality. He was also a womanizer who fathered many children, both legitimate and illegitimate. The *Economist* praised *Dirt and Deity* as "cheeringly level-headed. . . . McIntyre glides over none of the shame. . . . But he isn't stabbing or demolishing, and his judgments are just."

BIOGRAPHICAL/CRITICAL SOURCES:

PERIODICALS

Economist, September 25, 1993, pp. 102, 105-106; February 10, 1996, p. 85.
Listener, February 20, 1969, pp. 243-244.
London Review of Books, October 21, 1993, p. 9.
New Statesman & Society, September 24, 1993, p. 54.
Times Literary Supplement, October 8, 1993, p. 31.

*   *   *

McLEAN, Alan A(ngus)   1925-

PERSONAL: Born August 18, 1925, in Fenchow, China. *Education:* Downstate Medical College, State University of New York, M.D., 1948.

ADDRESSES: Home—17 Wakeman Pl., Westport, CT 06880.

CAREER: Seattle General Hospital, Seattle, WA, intern, 1948-49; Western State Hospital, Ft. Steilacoom, WA, general psychiatry resident, 1950-51; Oregon State Hospital, Salem, general psychiatry resident,

1951; Cornell University Medical Center, New York City, psychiatry fellow, 1952-53, 1954-56, instructor, 1954-63; U.S.P.H.S. Hospital, Lexington, KY, deputy chair psychiatrist, 1953-54; New York Hospital, psychiatrist to O.P.D., 1954-63; International Business Machines Corp., Armonk, NY, chief psychiatric consultant, 1957-67, manager of medical program 1967-70, Eastern area medical director, New York City, 1970-85; New York University, clinical assistant professor, 1963-66; University Hospital, New York City, assistant attending psychiatrist, 1963-66; New York Hospital, White Plains, NY, assistant attending psychiatrist, 1966-68, associate attending psychiatrist, Westchester Division, 1967-85; Cornell University Medical College, New York City, clinical assistant professor of psychiatry, 1966-68, head of the Center for Occupational Mental Health, beginning 1967, clinical associate professor, beginning 1968; private practice as occupational psychiatrist/consultant, Westxport, CT, beginning 1985. Member of committee on occupational psychiatry, 1956-67, chair, 1963-67; member of committee on confidentiality, beginning 1976; chair of Task Force on Psychiatry and Industry, 1981-85. *Military service:* U.S. Naval Reserve, 1949-50; U.S.P.H.S., 1953-54, surgeon.

MEMBER: Group for the Advancement of Psychiatry, American Occupational Medical Association, American Academy of Occupational Medicine (president, 1978-79).

AWARDS, HONORS: Health Achievement in Industry, American Occupational Medical Association, 1975.

WRITINGS:

(With Graham C. Taylor) *Mental Health in Industry,* McGraw-Hill (New York City), 1958.
Occupational Mental Health: An Emerging Art, National Clearinghouse for Mental Health Information, 1966.
(Editor) *To Work Is Human: Mental Health and the Business Community,* Macmillan (New York), 1967.
(Editor) *Cornell Occupational Mental Health Conferences, Westchester Division of New York Hospital-Cornell Medical Center,* Rand McNally (New York City), 1970.
(Editor) *Mental Health and Work Organizations,* Rand McNally, 1970.
(Editor) *Occupational Stress,* Thomas, 1974.
(Editor-in-chief) *Reducing Occupational Stress: Proceedings of a Conference, May 10-12, 1977, Westchester Division, New York Hospital-Cornell Medical Center,* The Institute, 1978.

Work Stress, Addison-Wesley (Reading, MA), 1979.
High Tech Survival Kit: Managing Your Stress, Wiley (New York City), 1986.

Contributor to books, including *American Handbook of Psychiatry,* Basic Books, 1974; *Comprehensive Textbook of Psychiatry,* edited by H. Kaplan, A. Freedman, and B. Sadock, Williams & Wilkins, 1975; and *Man & Work in Society,* Van Nostrand Reinhold, 1975. Contributor to periodicals, including *American Journal of Psychiatry* and *Industrial Medicine and Surgery.*

SIDELIGHTS: In his 1986 work *High Tech Survival Kit: Managing Your Stress,* psychiatrist Alan A. McLean focuses on work-related stress encountered by employees who must constantly adapt to changes resulting from new technologies. Much of the book deals with McLean's tripartite model of stress, which states that "the overlap of personal vulnerability, context, and specific stressors produces the greatest possibility of perceived stress and stress symptoms," according to Monty L. Lynn in a review for *Personnel Psychology.* To demonstrate his points, McLean uses several detailed cases of workers in stressful situations, but Lynn maintains that these vignettes lose their potential effectiveness because the author fails to offer any coping strategies for the stresses described. And although Lynn observed that *High Tech* "is well written, and the ideas presented are easily understood," he goes on to conclude that McLean's lack of coping mechanisms and "the lack of substantial additional material in the author's analysis of the readers' surveys" cause the work to fall short of offering enough to the average employee trying to deal with stress in high-tech situations. "*High Tech* serves as a good primer but would not be appropriate for someone already introduced to the basic concepts of stress," assessed Lynn.

BIOGRAPHICAL/CRITICAL SOURCES:

PERIODICALS

Personnel Psychology, spring, 1987, pp. 190-92.*

*   *   *

MICHAELS, Anne 1958-

PERSONAL: Born April 15, 1958, in Toronto, Ontario, Canada; daughter of Isaiah and Rosalind Michaels. *Education:* University of Toronto, B.A. (English), 1980.

ADDRESSES: Home—Toronto, Canada. *Office*—McClelland & Stewart, 481 University Ave., Suite 900, Toronto, Ontario M5G 2E9, Canada.

CAREER: Poet and novelist.

MEMBER: League of Canadian Poets.

AWARDS, HONORS: Epstein Award, 1980; Commonwealth Prize for the Americas, 1986; Canadian Authors' Association Award for Poetry, 1991; National Magazine Award (Gold) for Poetry, 1991; nominated for the Governor General's Award, 1991; nominated for the Giller Award, 1996; The Martin and Beatrice Fisher Award, 1997; Trillium Award, 1997; nominated for the Chapters First Novel Award, 1997; nominated for the Orange Prize (U.K.), 1997.

WRITINGS:

The Weight of Oranges, Coach House (Toronto), 1985.
Miner's Pond: Poems, McClelland & Stewart (Toronto), 1991.
Fugitive Pieces, McClelland & Steward, 1996.

Contributor of poems to anthologies, including *Poets 88,* edited by Ken Norris and Bob Hilderley, Quarry (Kingston, Ontario), 1988; *Poetry by Canadian Women,* edited by Rosemary Sullivan, Oxford (Don Mills, Ontario), 1989; and *Sudden Miracles: Eight Women Poets,* edited by Rhea Tregebov, Second Story Press (Toronto), 1991. Also contributor to *Contemporary Poems in English, When We Were Young,* and *Worst Journeys.*

SIDELIGHTS: Winning awards for her poetry while still in her twenties, Anne Michaels' first book of poetry, 1985's *The Weight of Oranges,* explores common poetic themes of love, loss, and human struggle. Louise Longo explained in *Books in Canada,* "There is more than a tinge of mortality to these poems, but Michaels's superb use of language and her emotionally-weighted insight keep them from stumbling into the morbid." Light and falling are recurring images, "explored intuitively in various contexts, from varying perspectives, with shadings and gravity, subtlety and grace," expressed Paul Dutton in *Quill & Quire.*

Six years later, describing Michaels as a borrower of other lives, Fraser Sutherland remarked in *Canadian Literature* that in Michaels' second book of poetry,

Miner's Pond: Poems, "a fine painterly touch is present." While one poem includes Michael's brothers, most of the poems in *Miner's Pond* portray writers, painters, and others from history, such as the seventeenth-century German astronomer, Johannes Kepler. "An intelligent and inquisitive mind is at work here," declared Charlene Diehl-Jones in *Books in Canada,* "wrestling with problems of language and memory, history and desire, and the body in art and in the world." Fortunately, notes at the end of the book identify such figures as Russian poets Marina Tsvetaeva, Osip Mandelstam, and Anna Akhamatova; German novelist Alfred Doeblin; Danish novelist Isak Dinesen; and French painter Pierre-Auguste Renoir—since not all the names mentioned in the work are familiar to readers. Rhea Tregebov, in *Quill & Quire,* asserted, "Michaels' dramatic monologues are an intriguing test of the limits of the poetic imagination."

In 1996 Michaels tried her hand at a novel, *Fugitive Pieces;* despite the different form she does have her character, Jakob Beer of Poland—a survivor of Nazi persecution during World War II—decide to be a poet. Athos Roussos, a Greek geologist who discovered Jakob, hid him during the war. Roussos raised the boy in Toronto with stories connected to his knowledge of geology. He encourages Jakob to "write to save yourself, and someday you'll write because you've been saved." Kate Moses, in the on-line magazine *Salon,* applauded *Fugitive Pieces,* commenting, "a story of decency, compassion and hope under extraordinary duress, it is above all an argument for the healing power of words."

BIOGRAPHICAL/CRITICAL SOURCES:

PERIODICALS

Books in Canada, May 1986, p. 43; October 1991, pp. 49-50.
Canadian Literature, Winter 1992, p. 177.
Quill & Quire, January 1987, p. 32; June 1991, p. 39.
Salon (on-line magazine), March 19, 1997; http://www.salonmagazine.com/march97/sneaks/sneak970320.html.*

*   *   *

MIDDLETON, Darren J. N. 1966-

PERSONAL: Born October 6, 1966, in Nottingham, England; son of Alan (a coal miner) and Joan (a medical receptionist) Middleton; married Elizabeth Hill Flowers (a seminarian), April 2, 1994. *Ethnicity:* "White." *Education:* Victoria University of Manchester, B.A. (with honors), 1989; Oxford University, M.Phil., 1991; University of Glasgow, Ph.D., 1996. *Politics:* Labour. *Religion:* Anglican. *Avocational interests:* Cricket, chess, photography, soccer.

ADDRESSES: Home—2926 Tishomingo Lane, Memphis, TN 38111-2627. *Office*—Department of Religious Studies, Rhodes College, 2000 North Parkway, Memphis, TN 38112-1624; fax 901-843-3727. *E-mail*—DMiddleton@rhodes.edu.

CAREER: Rhodes College, Memphis, TN, instructor, 1993-94, assistant professor of religion and literature, 1995—. Guest speaker at colleges and universities, including University of Memphis and Chester College of Higher Education, Chester, England. WEVL-FM Radio, volunteer programmer for community radio station; volunteer with Habitat for Humanity and Amnesty International.

MEMBER: American Academy of Religion, Modern Greek Studies Association, Center for Process Studies, Center for the Study of Literature and Theology.

AWARDS, HONORS: British Academy Scholar, Oxford University, England 1990-91; Owen Chadwick Philosophical Theology Prize, University of Manchester, England, 1990.

WRITINGS:

(Editor with Peter A. Bien, and contributor) *God's Struggler: Religion in the Writings of Nikos Kazantzakis,* Mercer University Press (Macon, GA), 1996.
(Contributor) Angela M. Nelson, editor, *This Is How We Flow: Rhythm in Black Cultures,* University of South Carolina Press (Columbia, SC), in press.

Contributor of articles and reviews to periodicals, including *Midwest Quarterly, Modern Believing, Notes in Contemporary Literature, Journal of Modern Greek Studies,* and *Modern Churchman.* Abstracts editor, *Process Studies;* book review editor and member of editorial board, *Christianity and the Arts.*

WORK IN PROGRESS: Understanding Nikos Kazantzakis, publication by University of South Carolina Press expected in 1998; editing *Process Thought and Literature,* an anthology of essays devoted to the in-

terface of process thought and literary theory and fiction, for State University of New York Press (Albany, NY).

SIDELIGHTS: Darren J. N. Middleton told *CA:* "In the tradition of Nikos Kazantzakis and Graham Greene, I view writing as a spiritual vocation. Themes of religious struggle, de-conversion, and the evolving character of God are important to my work. While I am a devout Anglican theologian, I am particularly fascinated by men and women caught on the borderlands between belief and unbelief. My writing is an attempt to help others to map and navigate this arduous terrain. In addition to Greene and Kazantzakis, I have been influenced by the work of Soeren Kierkegaard, Dietrich Bonhoeffer, Toni Morrison, and David Lodge."

*   *   *

MILLER, George   1945-

PERSONAL: Born March 3, 1945, in Brisbane (one source says Cinchilla, Queensland), Australia. *Education:* University of New South Wales, M.D., 1970.

ADDRESSES: Office—Kennedy Miller Productions, 30 Orwell St., Kings Cross, Sydney 2011, Australia. *Agent*—International Creative Management, 8942 Wilshire Blvd., Beverly Hills, CA 90211.

CAREER: St. Vincent's Hospital, Sydney, Australia, physician; screenwriter of motion pictures, 1971—. Director of motion pictures, including *Twilight Zone: The Movie,* 1982, and *The Witches of Eastwick,* 1987.

AWARDS, HONORS: Nomination for Academy Award for best original screenplay, Academy of Motion Picture Arts and Sciences, 1992, for *Lorenzo's Oil;* nomination for Academy Award for best adapted screenplay, 1996, for *Babe.*

WRITINGS:

"MAD MAX" SCREENPLAYS, AND DIRECTOR

(With James McCausland) *Mad Max,* American International, 1979.
(With Terry Hayes and Brian Hannat) *The Road Warrior: Mad Max II,* Warner Bros., 1982.
(With Hayes; director with George Oglivie) *Mad Max: Beyond the Thunderdome,* Warner Bros., 1985.

OTHER SCREENPLAYS, AND DIRECTOR

(With Byron Kennedy) *Violence in the Cinema, Part One* (short), 1971.
Devil in Evening Dress (documentary), 1973.
(With Nicholas Enright) *Lorenzo's Oil,* Universal, 1992.
40,000 Years of Dreaming, 1996.

OTHER SCREENPLAYS

(With Christ Noonan) *Babe* (adapted from Dick King-Smith's children's book *The Sheep-Pig;* also published as *Babe, the Gallant Pig*), MCA/Universal, 1995.

SIDELIGHTS: George Miller is a versatile Australian filmmaker who has won acclaim for a range of films. Miller began his filmmaking career in the early 1970s after working as a physician at a hospital in Sydney, Australia. His first film was a short work, *Violence in the Cinema, Part One,* which he wrote with Byron Kennedy. Miller followed this film with *Devil in Evening Dress,* a documentary that he completed in 1973.

Miller first won significant widespread recognition with *Mad Max,* a gripping action drama released in 1979. In this film, which Miller wrote with James McCausland, a motorcycling law officer exacts considerable revenge against a biker gang responsible for the deaths of his wife and child. With its exhilarating handheld camerawork and staggering stuntwork, *Mad Max* brought a new level of technical proficiency and recklessness to the ostensibly superficial action genre.

In 1982, Miller wrote *The Road Warrior: Mad Max II* with Terry Hayes and Brian Hannat. The film exceeded the earlier Max film by featuring even more astonishing stuntwork and dizzying camerawork. In *The Road Warrior,* the hardened Max comes upon a biker gang committing rape and murder. Once again, he opposes an entire gang, which includes several extremely large and frightening hoodlums. And, once again, Max manages to triumph over the evil bikers, despite the accompaniment of a loony aviator whose involvement in the conflict more often constitutes interference rather than assistance.

Miller completed the Mad Max saga in 1985 with *Mad Max: Beyond the Thunderdome,* an appropriately disturbing, and exciting, action drama. In this film, Max comes upon a tribe devoted to pitting humans against one another in death battles, which are held in an appropriately unsettling arena replete with screaming hordes. Spurred by the desire to rescue a sizeable group of children, Max enters into the competition, which is supervised by a notably sadistic villainess played by pop singer Tina Turner. Max, as usual, emerges victorious, despite unlikely odds.

While making the Mad Max films, Miller also contributed an episode to the three-part *Twilight Zone: The Movie.* Miller's episode, last of the three main stories, was generally considered the most accomplished. In it, an anxious airline passenger discovers that a gnome is destroying a wing of the plane as it flies through a thunderstorm. The film concentrates on the passenger's increasing anger and panic as he fails to convince airline personnel of the impending disaster.

After completing the final Mad Max film, Miller was again drawn to horrific material. He served as director of the grim comedy *Witches of Eastwick,* which was released in 1987. This film, adapted by Michael Cristofer from John Updike's novel, concerns three women who befriend the devil after he arrives in town posing as an obnoxious philanderer. When the women realize that he has seduced all three of them, they exact a measure of revenge, though it is not without a price.

Miller's next important film is *Lorenzo's Oil,* a moving drama about a married couple striving to develop a cure for their son's lethal brain disease. *New Statesman and Society* reviewer Jonathan Romney, who noted that Miller "made his name with three fender-bending pieces of apocalyptic roadhoggery in the Mad Max films," contended that with *Lorenzo's Oil* the filmmaker was "still playing hit-and-run with the audience, co-opting soft hearts and hard facts into an emotional collision derby." *Commonweal*'s reviewer, meanwhile, hailed *Lorenzo's Oil* as "a great enterprise." Miller and screenwriting collaborator Nicholas Enright received an Academy Award nomination for best original screenplay for *Lorenzo's Oil.*

Babe, Miller's next screen credit, is among his less likely endeavors. This film, which Miller wrote with director Chris Noonan, comes from Dick King-Smith's children's book *The Sheep-Pig* (also published as *Babe, the Gallant Pig*), which details the escapades of a young pig on a farm. The pig aspires to be a sheep herder like the border collie already on the premises, and some of the greatest humor in the film derives from Babe's misguided efforts to dominate the sheep. *Babe,* which employs impressive special effects in depicting talking animals, was hailed by *New Yorker*'s Terrence Rafferty as "a lovely, stubbornly idiosyncratic fable of aspiration and survival" and he described the film as "imaginative, hilariously eventful." Miller and Noon's screenplay for *Babe* received an Academy Award nomination for best adaptation.

BIOGRAPHICAL/CRITICAL SOURCES:

PERIODICALS

Commonweal, March 12, 1993, pp. 12-15.
Entertainment Weekly, March 22, 1996, p. 80.
New Statesman and Society, February 26, 1993, pp. 33-34.
New Yorker, September 4, 1995, pp. 99-101.*

*   *   *

MITCHARD, Jacquelyn 1953-

PERSONAL: Born December 10, 1953, in Chicago, IL; daughter of Robert G. and Mary M. Dvorak; married Dan Allegretti (a journalist), 1981 (died, 1993); children: five. *Education:* Rockford College, B.A. in English literature, 1973.

ADDRESSES: Home—Madison, WI.   *Agent*—Jane Gelfman, Gelfman, Schneider Literary Agents Inc., 250 West 57th St., New York, NY 10107.

CAREER: High school English teacher, 1974-76; *Pioneer Press,* Chicago, IL, managing editor and reporter, 1976-79; *The Capital Times,* Madison, WI, 1979-84; *Milwaukee Journal,* Milwaukee, WI, metro reporter and columnist, 1984-88; speechwriter for Donna Shalala, 1989-90; author of nationally syndicated column "The Rest of Us" (Tribune Media Services); author of nonfiction and fiction.

AWARDS, HONORS: Maggie Award for public service magazine journalism, 1993 and 1994; Parenting Network Public Awareness Award, 1997; Milwaukee Press Club Headliner Award, 1997, for exceptional service to the community; Ragdale Foundation Fellow for three years; Anne Powers Award, Council of Wisconsin Writers, 1997, for book of fiction.

WRITINGS:

Mother Less Child: The Love Story of a Family, W.W. Norton (New York), 1985.

Jane Addams: Pioneer in Social Reform and Activist for World Peace, Gareth Stevens Children's Books (Milwaukee), 1991.
(With Barbara Behm) *Jane Addams: Peace Activist,* Gareth Stevens Children's Books (Milwaukee), 1992.
The Deep End of the Ocean, Viking (New York), 1996.

Also author (with Amy Paulsen) of the screenplays *The Serpent's Egg* and *Typhoid Mary.* Also author of essays, including "Mother to Mother," anthologized in *The Adoption Reader,* Seal Press (Seattle, WA), 1995.

ADAPTATIONS: A movie option, for *The Deep End of the Ocean,* was sold to Peter Guber's Mandalay Entertainment, in conjunction with Michelle Pfeiffer's production company, Via Rosa.

WORK IN PROGRESS: A collection of essays, *The Rest of Us: Dispatches from the Mother Ship,* to be published by Viking Penguin, and a novel, *The Most Wanted,* to be published by Viking.

SIDELIGHTS: Heralded as a first-rate storyteller, Jacquelyn Mitchard of Madison, Wisconsin, sold her 1996 book *The Deep End of the Ocean* after writing a mere one hundred pages for a two-book contract worth five hundred thousand dollars. The story is about a Midwestern family, the Cappadoras, that collapses in on itself after three-year-old Ben Cappadora is kidnapped from a hotel lobby in Chicago. Before Mitchard's success as a novelist, she worked as a newspaper columnist for the *Milwaukee Journal-Sentinel.*

Her strong desire to have children, a nearly fatal tubal pregnancy, and her efforts to cope with her inability to conceive and overcome the emotional and psychological aspects of infertility compelled Mitchard to write an account of her ordeal in *Mother Less Child: The Love Story of a Family.* In *Publishers Weekly,* Genevieve Stuttaford advised, "The casual reader may feel she covers the material too thoroughly, but those faced with a similar reality will empathize with the couple's plight. Mitchard writes frankly and well of a painful subject that haunts all too many."

In 1993, when her husband, journalist Dan Allegretti, died of cancer, Mitchard was determined to keep freelancing. She used her competence as a reporter and columnist to write "*everything* for *anybody* to pay the bills. I wrote warning labels: 'Don't point the paint-sprayer at your face while operating.' I put up with a lot of horrible rejection, but I wouldn't give in," she related to Jeff Giles in *Newsweek*. That persistence paid off in a big way. The success of *The Deep End of the Ocean* has provided financial security for Mitchard and her five children. The novel was the first selection for Oprah Winfrey's television book club and went on to become a number one *New York Times* bestseller.

The heart-squeezing anxiety of *The Deep End of the Ocean* is enhanced by intriguing characters, including Ben's brother Vincent and his parents Beth and Pat. Donna Seaman wrote in *Booklist,* "[Mitchard] describes [Ben's mother] Beth's unraveling with clinical finesse, then proceeds to chronicle every aspect of the high-profile search for the missing child, the media feeding frenzy over this ideal prime-time tragedy, and the psychological toll such a cruel and mysterious disappearance exacts."

Nine years pass in the suspenseful plot, giving adequate time to explore the various family member's feelings, especially those of teenage Vincent Cappadora, who at age seven was put in charge of Ben in the crowded hotel lobby while his mother Beth checked them in. During these years, Beth has neglected Vincent, baby daughter Kerry, and husband Pat.

Reviewer Sybil S. Steinberg, in *Publishers Weekly,* declared that Mitchard's plot in *The Deep End of the Ocean* is permeated with "disturbingly candid" revelations regarding familial relationships. Mitchard delves into all the relationships. Jeff Giles insisted in *Newsweek,* "Don't bother predicting the end: there's a plot twist that'll spin you around no matter which way you're looking."

BIOGRAPHICAL/CRITICAL SOURCES:

PERIODICALS

Booklist, March 15, 1985, p. 1019; April 1, 1996, p. 1324.
Choice, October 1991, p. 245.
Kirkus Reviews, January 15, 1985, p. 81; March 15, 1996, p. 400.
Library Journal, March 15, 1985, p. 67; April 15, 1996, p. 123.
Newsweek, June 3, 1996, pp. 72-74.
Publishers Weekly, February 1, 1985, p. 353; April 1, 1996, p. 54.

MIYAZAWA Kenji 1896-1933

PERSONAL: Born August 27, 1896, in Hanamaki, Iwate Prefecture, Japan; died September 21, 1933, in Hanamaki, Japan; son of a pawnbroker specializing in used clothing. *Education:* Attended agricultural schools in Hanamaki and Nichiren Buddhist school in Tokyo. *Religion:* Hokke Buddhist. *Avocational interests:* Local theater and music ensembles, collecting recordings of classical music.

CAREER: Poet and author of children's stories. Taught science and agronomy at agricultural schools; agricultural worker, beginning 1926.

WRITINGS:

POETRY

Haru to Shura, four volumes, privately printed, 1924-c. 1932, selections translated by Gary Snyder in *Back Country,* New Directions (New York City), 1968, selections translated by Hiraoki Sato as *Spring and Asura: Poems of Kenji Miyazawa,* with an introduction by Burton Watson, Chicago Review Press (Chicago), 1973, selections translated and introduced by Sato in *Ten Japanese Poets,* Granite (Hanover, NH), 1973.
A Future of Ice: Poems and Stories of a Japanese Buddhist (poems and prose tales), translated and with an introduction by Sato, North Point Press (San Francisco), 1989.

STORIES

Ginga tetsudo no yoru, privately printed, c. 1922, translated by Sarah M. Strong as *Night of the Milky Way Railway,* with illustrations by Bryn Barnard, M. E. Sharpe (Armonk, NY), 1991.
Winds and Wildcat Places, translated by John Bester, illustrated by Rokuro Taniuchi, Kodansha International (Palo Alto, CA), 1967.
Winds from Afar, translated by John Bester, Kodansha International (Tokyo), 1972.
Nametokoyama no kuma, translated and adapted by Helen Smith as *Kojuro and the Bear,* illustrated by Junko Morimoto, Collins (Sydney, Australia), 1986.
The Night Hawk Star, Random House (New York City), 1991.
Once and Forever: The Tales of Kenji Miyazawa, translated by John Bester, Kodansha International (London), 1993.

Collected Works, Chikjuma shobo (Japan), eleven
    volumes, 1967, expanded into twelve volumes,
    1968.
Miyazawaka Kenji Zenshu, [Japan], fifteen volumes,
    1973-77, revised as *Miyazawa Kenji Zenshu,* six-
    teen volumes, 1979-80.

OTHER

Works by Miyazawa Kenji have been translated and
published in periodicals, including *Chicago Review,*
and anthologies, including *Penguin Book of Japanese
Verse,* edited by Geoffrey Bownas and Anthony
Thwaite, Penguin (London), 1964; and *Modern Japanese Poets and the Nature of Literature,* by Makoto
Ueda, Stanford University Press, 1983.

SIDELIGHTS: Almost unknown to the reading public
during his lifetime, Miyazawa Kenji has become
revered since his death as one of the greatest Japanese poets of the twentieth century. Indeed, he is
regarded in some quarters as an almost saintly figure because of the self-effacing simplicity and al-
truistic hard work that marked his life and contributed to his early death.

Born of an affluent family in the poor agricultural
region of Iwate, where crop failures were frequent,
Miyazawa studied at two local agricultural schools
with an eye toward helping the peasants. His strict
Buddhist beliefs led him to study at a religious school
in Tokyo, but he returned to his birthplace to be
present during the final illness of his beloved sister
Toshiko. After her death, he remained in Iwate,
which was known as "the Tibet of Japan" because of
its harsh topography and poor soil. He dedicated himself to a life of hard work, first teaching agronomy
and science, then resigning his job in 1926 in order to
work directly with the peasants at their own labors. A
devout follower of the Lotus Sutra, he overworked
himself for others and sustained himself on an even
poorer diet than was customary for the local people.

The peasants viewed Miyazawa as a saintly character,
according to J. Thomas Rimer in *A Reader's Guide to
Japanese Literature;* however, Hiraoki Sato, Miyazawa specialist and translator, leavens this image by
saying that many of the peasants viewed the poet as
a do-gooder who was trying to change their time-
honored farming methods with his newfangled scientific ideas. Sato also points out that some of Miyazawa's poems, such as "Hateful Kuma Eats His
Lunch," sound ruefully comic, and that Miyazawa
was apparently plagued by a sense of failure.

Miyazawa's single most famous poem has been translated as "November Third," although the author left
it untitled; the title refers to the date in 1933—two
months before the poet's death—when the work was
composed. According to Burton Watson in his introduction to *Spring and Asura,* this poem is printed on
cloth and hung as a sampler in Japan; "almost any
Japanese" can recite it by heart and identify it as by
Miyazawa, who is known as "the saint of northern
Japan"—"Kenji *busatsu,*" or "the saintly Kenji," was
his nickname. The thirty-line poem was found in
Miyazawa's pocket notebook after his death; according to Sato, in his introduction to *A Future of Ice,* it
was probably intended more as a prayer than as a
poem.

As translated by Makoto Ueda in *Modern Japanese
Poets and the Nature of Literature,* the revered work
begins, "Neither rain / nor wind / nor snow nor
summer's heat / will affect this robust body." It goes
on to describe a man who exists on a quart of rice per
day supplemented by some vegetables and miso (soy-
bean paste), who keeps a calm smile on his face, is
not concerned with himself, observes the world carefully, helps others, lives in a small thatched hut, and
is considered a bum by others. "I should like to become / such a man," the speaker concludes.

Ueda, noting that "November Third" has become a
staple of Japanese textbooks and a model of that
nation's ideals, also points out some controversies
surrounding the work, such as the fact that during
World War II, Japanese militarists used the poem as
propaganda for their own brand of self-effacing dedication. Others, today, brand the poem as too passive
in its response to poverty, although readers of the
middle of the poem, where the character is described
as tending a sick child and carrying a bundle for a
tired mother, might dispute that. Readers who only
know Miyazawa from this one lyric and from ideal-
ized summaries of his life might come away with "an
image of Miyazawa as the sort of pious wimp you
would want to avoid," says Sato, in his introduction
to *A Future of Ice,* but in fact the poet was much
more than that. His personal ideal was that of the
asura, a Sanskrit word in Buddhist terminology meaning a freewheeling, rough-natured, sometimes malevolent giant whose place is somewhere between
those of humans and animals.

Miyazawa himself, rather than being purely self-deny-
ing, loved to observe nature: his poems are filled with
technically precise descriptions of the natural phenomena around him. He delighted in long walks,

during which he wrote his poems with a pencil that hung from a string tied around his neck. His nature poems, even when up to eight hundred lines long (as in "Koiwai Farm," in which he describes, in reverse chronology, a walk from a train station to a farm) are not mere catalogues, according to Sato, because of the extraordinarily free visual imagination that could encompass a huge landscape or a microscopic speck within a few lines, and which amounted almost to a hallucinatory quality. Drama, humor, religious faith, and understanding of science blended to create, in Sato's words, "a unique poetic world that is at once intense and light, joyful and moving. It is a world yet to be matched by another Japanese poet, ancient or modern."

Rimer also finds in Miyazawa's poetry a "fierce affection" for the poet's sister, and a vulnerability to her death," that is balanced by the poet's affirmative belief in the healing power of nature; Rimer finds the poems "often resistant to comprehension," with images that are often "easier to feel than to understand," but adds, "the totality provides a special species of spiritual clarity, one that is virtually unique." According to Geoffrey O'Brien in the *Village Voice,* Miyazawa "is devotional without ever being didactic," and his poems represent a fragmentation or exhaustion of the self. Writes O'Brien in a review of *A Future of Ice:* "The 'I' of Miyazawa's diaristic voice charts its own disintegration into its compound elements: lava slopes, mineral deposits, parched reeds, foreign scientific terms, Sanskrit mantras, imaginary vistas . . . apparitions . . . abstract patterns of line and color." In real life, Miyazawa disintegrated all too soon, dying at age thirty-seven "of what can only be called chronic exhaustion," according to William E. Naff in the *Journal of the American Oriental Society.*

Miyazawa's poems are available in English in a few translations, some of them published in anthologies. The premier single-volume edition is Sato's *A Future of Ice,* which greatly expands upon and supersedes that translator's *Spring and Asura.* Fine translations of eighteen of the poems are to be found in Beat poet Gary Snyder's 1968 collection *Back Country.* Watson, himself a prominent translator from Japanese, calls Snyder's renditions "striking and deeply sympathetic." To Sato's versions, he gives the encomium, "extraordinarily successful in capturing and bringing over both the sharply observed, often dazzling imagery of Miyazawa's poetry, and the relaxed, almost prosy matrix in which it is characteristically set. . . . Mr. Sato . . . has with great taste and fidelity rendered both the strangeness and the simplicity of Miyazawa's poetry, both its intense individuality and its passionate concern for transcendent values and the celebration of all the manifold aspects of creation."

A lesser, though still major, strand in Miyazawa's work consists of his stories, fable-like pieces which are often published as illustrated children's books. The most famous of these was translated into English by Sarah M. Strong in 1991 as *Night of the Milky Way Railway.* In her "guide" to the volume, Strong explains that the story concerns young Giovanni, who flees from the taunts of his classmates to the sanctuary of a hillside which turns out to be a cosmic pillar. A sort of celestial railroad then takes Giovanni and his friend Campanella on a tour of the Milky Way galaxy. Campanella's jacket, strangely, is wet, and Giovanni eventually realizes that his friend has drowned: the railroad is a ferry to the afterlife, and Giovanni is the only passenger who has a round-trip ticket.

Night of the Milky Way Railway, claims the translator, "stands with boyish exuberance in the small but elite company of great fantasies of the afterlife." Reviewer Robert Omar Khan, in the *San Francisco Review of Books,* notes that the book is "immensely popular in Japan." It appeals, he says, both to lovers of children's books and to adults who approach its allegory "with a more philosophical eye." Strong's edition, he writes, "is ideal for both approaches" because of its "well-translated" text, "attractive" illustrations, and backup material, including the guide and variant chapters.

Both in his fiction and in his poetry, Miyazawa was a restless reviser who continued to refine his poems in notebook after notebook, and whose personal esthetic viewed the work of literature as a fluid thing, capable of undergoing continual change and improvement. Many of his poems exist in variant versions. The "honesty, sincerity, and intensity," as Ueda terms them, of both his life and work, however, are immutable: "He not only conceived a unique view of poetry; he lived it."

BIOGRAPHICAL/CRITICAL SOURCES:

BOOKS

Rimer, J. Thomas, *A Reader's Guide to Japanese Literature,* Kodansha International, 1988, pp. 145-8.

Sato, Hiraoki, introduction to *A Future of Ice* by Miyazawa Kenji, North Point Press, 1989, pp. xiii-xvii.

Strong, Sarah M., introduction to *Night of the Milky Way Railway* by Miyazawa Kenji, M. E. Sharpe, 1991.

Ueda, Makoto, *Modern Japanese Poets and the Nature of Literature,* Stanford University Press (Stanford, CA), 1983, pp. 184-231.

Watson, Burton, introduction to *Spring and Asura* by Miyazawa Kenji, Chicago Review Press, 1973, pp. xv-xix.

PERIODICALS

Japanese Quarterly, vol. 9, 1968, p. 263.

Journal of the American Oriental Society, July/September, 1978, pp. 300-301.

Journal of Asian Studies, February, 1975, pp. 535-538.

Journal of Intercultural Studies, vol. 2, 1975.

San Francisco Review of Books, fall, 1991, pp. 58-59.

Village Voice, December 5, 1989, pp. 757-76.*

*   *   *

MOOKERJEE, Ajit 1915-
(Ajitcoomar Mookerjee)

PERSONAL: Born December 29, 1915, in Nalia, Faridpur, Bengal (now Bangladesh); son of Anath B. and Prabahka Mookerjee; married, wife's name, Sudha; children: Priya, Parvati (daughters). *Education:* Calcutta University, M.A. (ancient Indian history and culture), 1939; University of London, M.A. (history of art), 1942; received training in museology from the Victoria and Albert Museum and the Horniman Museum, London, 1939-42.

ADDRESSES: Home—2 Wayland Ave., London E8 2HP, England; 44 (A10) Amrita Shergil Marg, New Delhi 110003, India. *Office*—c/o Thames & Hudson Ltd., 30-34 Bloomsbury St., London 4C1B 3QP, England.

CAREER: Indian Institute of Art in Industry, Calcutta, India, director, 1946-59; Crafts Museum, New Delhi, India, director, 1959-75. All India Handicrafts Board, chief executive officer and development commissioner for handicrafts. Member, art purchasing committee, Calcutta College of Art. Calcutta University, lecturer in museology, 1958-59. Consultant on Indian arts and crafts to various museums or museum departments, including the Smithsonian Institution. Has made guest appearances on the subject of Indian art to organizations, including the British Broadcasting Corporation (BBC). Served as a delegate to numerous international conferences for organizations including the U.N. Educational, Scientific, and Cultural Organization (UNESCO) and the Smithsonian Institution. Lecturer to various groups; delivered the "Indian Art through the Ages" lecture series to numerous U.S. audiences, 1950, and the "Tantric Art" lecture series at various English locations, 1971. Founder and donor, Tantra Museum, New Delhi.

MEMBER: Indian National Committee for ICOM (UNESCO), Museum Association of India.

AWARDS, HONORS: Ghosh Travelling fellow, Calcutta University, 1940; fellow, Royal Anthropological Institute of Great Britain and Ireland, 1941; Rockefeller Foundation study grant, 1955; Watumull Foundation Award, 1962, for research on Tantra art; awarded British Council Travel grant.

WRITINGS:

UNDER NAME AJITCOOMAR MOOKERJEE

Folk Art of Bengal: A Study of an Art for, and of, the People, foreword by Sir William Rothenstein, University of Calcutta, 1939.

Art of India, Oxford Book & Stationery (Calcutta), 1949, revised and enlarged edition published as *The Arts of India: From Prehistoric to Modern Times,* Tuttle (Rutland, VT), 1966.

Folk Toys of India, Oxford Book & Stationery, 1956.

Modern Art in India, Oxford Book & Stationery, 1956.

Indian Primitive Art, Oxford Book & Stationery, 1959.

UNDER NAME AJIT MOOKERJEE

Tantra Art: Its Philosophy and Physics, Ravi Kumar (New York City), 1966.

Indian Dolls and Toys, Crafts Museum (New Delhi), 1968.

Tantra Asana: A Way to Self-Realization, Wittenborn (New York City), 1971.

Crafts Museum, Crafts Museum, All India Handicrafts Board, Ministry of Foreign Trade, Government of India (New Delhi), 1971.

Yoga Art, New York Graphic Society (Boston), 1975.

Tantra Magic, afterword by Mulk Raj Anand, Arnold-Heinemann (London), 1977.

(With Madhu Khanna) *The Tantric Way: Art, Science, Ritual,* Thames & Hudson (London), 1977.

Kundalini: The Arousal of the Inner Energy, Destiny Books (New York City), 1982.

Ritual Art of India, Thames & Hudson (New York), 1985.

Folk Art of India, Clarion (New Delhi), 1985.

Kali: The Feminine Force, Destiny Books (New York), 1988.

EDITOR; UNDER NAME AJIT MOOKERJEE, EXCEPT AS NOTED

(Under name Ajitcoomar Mookerjee) *Designs in Indian Textiles,* Indian Institute of Art in Industry, 1953.

(Under name Ajitcoomar Mookerjee) *Five Thousand Designs and Motifs,* Indian Institute of Art in Industry, 1958, Dover (Mineola, NY), 1996.

Cire Perdue Casting in India, [New Delhi], 1961.

Banaras Brocades, Crafts Museum, 1966.

Temple Terracottas of Bengal, [New Delhi], 1972.

Editor of quarterly journal *Art in Industry;* member of editorial board, *Roop-Lekha* (publication of All-India Fine Arts and Crafts Society); contributor to numerous periodicals.

Author's works have been translated into French.

SIDELIGHTS: Indian scholar Ajit Mookerjee has had a long and distinguished career as an expert in the field of traditional Indian art. In addition to his directorial posts at museums dedicated to this subject, he has written numerous scholarly books during his three decades of professional activity. Educated in both Calcutta and London, Mookerjee first headed Calcutta's Indian Institute of Art in Industry and later moved to New Delhi to oversee the Crafts Museum there. In addition to Mookerjee's prodigious amount of academic writings about Indian art, he has traveled the globe to give lecture tours and appear at formal conferences. Mookerjee's first book, *Folk Art of Bengal: A Study of an Art for, and of, the People,* was published in 1939 when its author was still in his early twenties.

In the midst of World War II, Mookerjee embarked upon a quasi-exile world tour, living first in London and studying museum practice at England's eminent Victoria and Albert Museum, and later traveling in sometimes dangerous circumstances through Africa and South America. During his subsequent directorship of New Delhi's Crafts Museum, he would be instrumental in developing that institution's holdings, while beginning to write and edit a number of schol-

arly works, including *The Arts of India: From Prehistoric to Modern Times* and *Folk Toys of India.*

Mookerjee has become best known for his study of Tantrism, an Indian philosophy, and its relationship to the folk art of his native country. He has written extensively on Tantric philosophy and its relationship to Indian folk art, and his books have been translated into several other languages. Mookerjee describes the Tantric set of beliefs as a way of viewing the universe as well as a scientific method to uncover one's own spirituality. One of Mookerjee's many volumes on this subject is Tantra Art: Its Philosophy and Physics, first published in 1966. In it, the author attempts to define and analyze the Eastern philosophy for a Western-minded audience; ample color illustrations of Indian art serve to assist the reader in understanding Mookerjee's theses.

One pillar of the Tantra philosophy is that the human body is a microcosmic form of a greater macrocosm: the universe. In its artistic manifestation, this awareness of the corporeal lends itself to a healthy regard for human sexuality that is sometimes perceived as slightly pornographic to the Western eye. As Mookerjee notes, the Tantric view of the world and its attempt to redefine it through a specific set of symbolic imagery can be found in certain movements of modern art in Western culture. A *Times Literary Supplement* reviewer praised *Tantra Art* and stated that its author "does his very best to guide us through the intricacies of his subject."

In his research, Mookerjee has amassed a large personal collection of objects that showed how Tantric spiritual beliefs have often been visually manifested in common items. His collection became part of an exhibition that traveled to numerous European museums. Mookerjee wrote more about the subject of Tantrism in *Tantra Asana: A Way to Self-Realization,* published in 1971, and *Yoga Art* in 1975. Two volumes appeared in 1977—*Tantra Magic* and *The Tantric Way: Art, Science, Ritual,* co-authored with Madhu Khanna. *Kundalini: The Arousal of the Inner Energy,* a 1982 work, was followed by *Ritual Art of India,* a 1986 volume in which Mookerjee attempts to present the many ways in which art is a part of everyday life in India. The author defines ritual art in India as a tangible object that brings together certain components to make an offering to a god, and discusses the strong ties between spirituality and decorative elements in Indian households and the public strata. In the illustrated volume Mookerjee offers evidence in support of his theories regarding the spiritual in Indian life, from the decoration of common household objects to the elaborateness of a wedding ceremony.

BIOGRAPHICAL/CRITICAL SOURCES:

PERIODICALS

New York Times Book Review, December 12, 1971, p. 37.
Publishers Weekly, January 17, 1986, p. 56.
Times Literary Supplement, October 19, 1967, p. 976.
Village Voice, December 13, 1976.
Washington Post Book World, December 7, 1986, p. 14.

* * *

MOOKERJEE, Ajitcoomar
See MOOKERJEE, Ajit

* * *

MORRISON, Arthur 1863-1945

PERSONAL: Born November 1, 1863, in London, England; died December 4, 1945, in Chalmont St. Peter, Buckinghamshire, England; son of Richard (an engine fitter) and Jane Cooper Morrison; married Elizabeth Adelaide Thatcher, 1892; children: Guy. *Education:* Self-educated. *Avocational interests:* Boxing, cycling, collecting Asian art.

CAREER: British fiction writer, journalist, and art historian. Clerk, People's Palace (charitable institution), 1886-90; subeditor, *Palace Journal,* 1889-90. Freelance journalist, 1890-1913; briefly on staff of the London *Globe.* Collection of Japanese and Chinese paintings acquired by the British Museum, 1913. *Wartime Service:* Chief inspector of Special Constabulary of Epping Forest, Essex, during World War I.

MEMBER: Royal Society of Literature fellow, 1924, member of the council, 1935.

WRITINGS:

NOVELS

A Child of the Jago, Methuen (London) and Stone (Chicago), 1896; reprint with biographical sketch by P. J. Keating, MacGibbon & Kee (London), 1969, Boydell Press (Suffolk, England), 1969.
To London Town, Methuen, 1899, and Stone, 1899.
Cunning Murrell, Methuen, 1900, and Doubleday (New York), 1900.
The Hole in the Wall, Methuen, 1902, and McClure Phillips (New York), 1902.
The Red Triangle, Being Some Further Chronicles of Martin Hewitt, Investigator, Nash (London) and Page (Boston), 1903.

SHORT STORIES

The Shadows Around Us: Authentic Tales of the Supernatural, Simkin & Marshall (London), 1891.
Tales of Mean Streets, Methuen, 1894, Roberts (Boston), 1895; with a preface by Michel Krzak, Boydell Press, 1983.
Martin Hewitt, Investigator, Ward Lock (London) and Harper (New York), 1894.
Zig-Zags at the Zoo, Newnes (London), 1895.
Chronicles of Martin Hewitt, Ward Lock, 1895, Appleton (New York), 1896.
Adventures of Martin Hewitt, Ward Lock, 1896.
The Dorrington Deed-Box, Ward Lock, 1897.
The Green Eye of Goona: Stories of a Case of Tokay, Nash, 1904; as *The Green Diamond,* Page, 1904.
Divers Vanities, Methuen, 1905.
Green Ginger, Hutchinson (London) and Stokes, 1909.
Short Stories of Today and Yesterday (includes selected stories from *Tales of Mean Streets, Divers Vanities,* and *Green Ginger*), Harrap (London), 1929.
Fiddle O'Dreams, Hutchinson, 1933.
The Best Martin Hewitt Detective Stories, selected and with an introduction by E. F. Bleiler, Dover Publications (New York), 1976.

PLAYS

(With Herbert C. Sargent) *That Brute Simmons,* adaptation of the story by Morrison, produced in London, 1904; French (London), 1904.
(With Richard Pryce) *The Dumb-Cake,* adaptation of a story by Morrison; produced in London, 1907; French, 1907.
(With Horace Newte) *A Stroke of Business,* produced in London, 1907.

NONFICTION

The Painters of Japan, 2 volumes, Jack (London), and Stokes (New York), 1911.

SIDELIGHTS: A prominent realistic novelist and short story writer of the 1890s and early 1900s and a succcessful writer of detective stories, Arthur Morrison was circumspect about his own life to the point that the London *Times* obituary of him, in 1945, has been described by scholar Vincent Brome as "a bewildered piece of writing"; and P. J. Keating, perhaps the foremost Morrison specialist of modern times, has doubted in print that a full biography of Morrison can ever be written. Some facts are known, however, and some educated surmises have been made. He was born on one of the two John Streets in the poverty-stricken East End of London in 1863, according to his birth certificate, and his father was an engine fitter; but he claimed to have been born in Kent, the son of an engineer—a contradiction that perhaps indicates a sense of shame about his origins. The facts of his education are unknown; he probably was an autodidact, reading his way into self-education. The idea that he was enthusiastic about boxing and cycling has developed from passages in his work and from his friendship with writer William Ernest Henley, a known boxing enthusiast. In his twenties, Morrison was a clerk at a charitable institution, the People's Palace, run by Walter Besant in the Mile End Road, London; he also had the opportunity to help edit the institution's newsletter, and he credited Besant with teaching him much of the technique of writing.

Morrison's early short stories drew on his People's Palace observations to a considerable extent. His first story, in *Macmillan's Magazine,* drew the attention of Henley, who invited him to join the contributors to Henley's *National Observer,* a group that included Robert Louis Stevenson, Rudyard Kipling, Thomas Hardy, and James M. Barrie. Morrison was also briefly a staff member of the *Globe.* He married Elizabeth Adelaide Thatcher in 1892; their only child, Guy, was born in 1893 and died in 1921 of complications of malaria contracted during service in World War I. Supporting himself as a freelance journalist and writer, Morrison moved to Loughton in Essex, apparently at some point between 1892 and 1896, then to High Beech, in Epping Forest, also in Essex. At age fifty, in 1913, he retired to concentrate on collecting Asian art, an interest that had already borne fruit in the publication of his well-regarded two-volume survey, *The Painters of Japan* (1911). His later fiction volumes were publications and selections of stories written earlier. During World War I he was chief inspector for the Special Constabulary of Essex, and "had the curious distinction," as Brome puts it, "of telephoning the warning of the first Zeppelin raid

on London." He moved back to London after the war, where he lived in Cavendish Square, off Regent Street; he moved to a home in Chalmont St. Peter, Buckinghamshire, in 1930, and died there in 1945. At his request, his wife burned all his manuscripts, letters, and papers after his death.

His lasting literary reputation rests primarily on two novels, *A Child of the Jago* (1896) and *The Hole in the Wall* (1902), and a book of short stories, *Tales of Mean Streets* (1894). Other works of interest include the novel *To London Town* (1899), his selected stories in the 1929 *Short Stories of Today and Yesterday,* and the detective fiction in three short-story collections about detective Martin Hewitt—*Martin Hewitt, Investigator* (1894), *Chronicles of Martin Hewitt* (1895), and *Adventures of Martin Hewitt* (1896)—one novel about the same character, *The Red Triangle: Being Some Further Chronicles of Martin Hewitt, Investigator* (1903), and stories about a criminal-turned-amateur-sleuth named Dorrington in *The Dorrington Deed-Box* (1897). The 1904 crime novel *The Green Eye of Goona: Stories of a Case of Tokay,* "a light detective fantasy," is, in the opinion of E. F. Bleiler in *Twentieth Century Crime and Mystery Writers,* "successful in combining topical humor and mystery." Additionally, the work on Japanese art was warmly welcomed on first publication and is still highly thought of; Jocelyn Bell, in her 1952 "A Study of Arthur Morrison," calls it "a leading work on the subject."

Tales of Mean Streets first attracted significant attention to Morrison. According to Robert Calder's "Arthur Morrison: A Commentary with an Annotated Bibliography of Writing About Him," it garnered words of praise from *Athenaeum* ("absolutely convincing"), *Bookman* ("scrupulously truthful"), and the *Spectator* ("great power"). Morrison intended to take a further step in realism than his predecessors Charles Dickens, Emile Zola, and George Gissing; he tried to record slum life as it was rather than to moralize, melodramatize, or plead for improved conditions: to show working-class life from inside rather than outside. His "descriptive method is direct photography—a recording of things as they are," says Bell. Morrison's own words on the subject, as quoted by Bell, were: "In my East End stories, I determined that they must be written in a different way from the ordinary slum story. They must be done with austerity and frankness, and there must be no sentimentalism, no glossing over. I felt that the writer must never interpose himself between his subject and his reader. . . . For this I have been abused as hard and unsympathetic, but I can assure you it is far more painful for me to write stories than for you to read them." Whether contemporary readers will feel that Morrison was entirely successful is a matter of opinion; several critics, both at the time of publication and afterward, have complained that in emphasizing crime and violence rather than everyday existence, and in omitting working-class humor, Morrison was, as Brome puts it, "an inverted romantic rather than a realist." Of the stories in *Tales of Mean Streets,* "Lizerunt" was singled out at the time for its violence; futhermore, it was a direct inspiration on W. Somerset Maugham's first novel, the 1897 *Liza of Lambeth.* Other stories in the collection, as P. J. Keating points out in his "Biographical Study" and as Calder summarizes, are less marked by violence than by "a mixture of "realistic observation and quiet despair," or by "hopeless monotony." Monotony and violence, say Keating and Caler, combine with a third quality, the striving for a dull respectability, to form a triad of lower-class attitudes prevalent among Morrison's characters.

The British public was most actively attracted to Morrison's view of slum life when he presented it in his 1896 novel, *A Child of the Jago.* "The Jago" was Morrison's fictional name for a real London slum: "that part of Shoreditch," directs Bell, "known as the Nichol, from the name of Old Nichol Street. . . [comprising] the Boundary Lane area skirted by the Shoreditch High Street and the Bethnal Green Road." Morrison was drawn to the area when a local minister, Rev. A. Osborne Jay, wrote him a complimentary letter after reading *Tales of Mean Streets.* Investigating the area at Jay's behest, Morrison lived there for eighteen months, talking with the residents and taking notes. Slum clearance had been under way since 1891 (contrary to some Morrison adherents' claims that his novel was responsible for the reform); when he moved in, said Morrison to the London *Daily News,* it was "on the point of being pulled down," and when he completed *A Child of the Jago* in 1896, "the last houses were coming down." The novel, in which "the Jago itself is a major character," according to critic Derek Severn, describes a heroine, Sally Green, who fights with broken glass bottles; a boy, Dicky Perrott, whose thieving father and weak mother help rob him of any chance in life; a fence, Aaron Weech, who exploits the boy; a missionary, Father Sturt, who tries to get him a job in a shop. The novel ends with Dicky's father hanging for the murder of Weech, and Dicky himself stabbed to death in a street fight. Severn, appraising the novel in 1980 for *London Magazine,* calls it "a work of horrifying power," and attributes to it "three outstanding qualities—Morrison's

steadiness of vision, his accuracy of observation, and the assurance with which he handles each of his major scenes." On the negative side, he finds some flaws of craftsmanship typical of youthful novels: episodic plot, simplistically drawn characters, intrusive irony, and excessive concentration on squalor. Other critics have noted a lingering debt to Dickens in some of the characters, such as Weech, who is reminiscent of Fagan in *Oliver Twist.* Bell observes eloquently: "His very feeling about his subject blunts his vision, leading him to record rather than interpret his experience." She cites a lack of selectivity, a reliance on repetition, and a thinness of characterization as problems: "[I]t is the old confusion between realism and reality." She assesses the novel thusly: "It is as a sidelight on social history rather than as a novel that it is now valuable." Both Bell and Severn compare Morrison's *Jago* to British painter William Hogarth's *Gin Lane.* A noteworthy contemporaneous review of *A Child of the Jago* was written by H. D. Traill for the *Fortnightly Review* in 1897; as summarized by Calder, Traill compares Morrison's narrative gifts favorably with those of Stephen Crane, but says the novel "gives the impression of extraordinary unreality, as if one visited some 'fairyland of horror'"; Morrison, he wrote, had created an "idealisation of ugliness," and "like many 'realists,' falls backs on sentimental sham when he needs pathos." Traill, setting a controversy in motion, went so far as to enlist the signatures of nine "experts" vowing that the slums were not as bad as Morrison had portrayed them to be. But H. G. Wells, reviewing *A Child of the Jago* for the *Saturday Review,* praised the book's "extraordinary faithfulness" and Morrison's "really artistic sense of effect," though regretting the author's narrowness of focus and lack of emphasis on the origins of poverty.

Morrison turned to a less violent aspect of East End life in *To London Town,* a novel about a lower-middle-class family in which the mother is a widowed shopkeeper and her son is apprenticed to an engineering firm. Critic John R. Greenfield, in *Dictionary of Literary Bioraphy,* says that "the general consensus about this novel is that Morrison is not as successful in portraying the problems of the petite bourgeoisie as he is with the desperate characters and dramatic situations of the slums"; Greenfield disparages *To London Town* in relation to Wells' *Tono-Bungay* and *The History of Mr. Polly.* Keating, in *The Working Classes in Victorian Fiction,* puts a sharp finger on the problem: "So long as Morrison is dealing with working-class characters in extreme situations, then his fiction comes vividly alive, but the same is not true of his treatment of the more ordinary, less sensational, aspects of working-class life." Brome, in different words, makes the same point on page sixteen of his *Four Realist Novelists.*

Morrison returned to extreme situations in his novel of slum crime, *The Hole in the Wall,* and Brome calls it "his best." The title was also the name of "a public house in the notorious Radcliffe Highway of the East End," Brome notes; the novel is about a boy, Stephen, brought up by his grandfather—a fence named Nat—in its atmosphere of corruption and squalor. For this novel, Morrison uses a shifting narrative viewpoint, alternating between Stephen's first-person voice and a third-person narrator, a technique borrowed from Dickens' *Bleak House.* Brome finds this technique "clumsy," but praises the characterizations in contrast to those in *A Child of the Jago:* "[I]n *The Hole in the Wall* they are more complex and the novel, in consequence, more sophisticated." Severn makes a similar point about the characters even more enthusiastically, raving, "Nothing about them, not a flicker of an eye or an inflection of the voice, escapes Morrison's notice. They are not controlled by the plot; they create it." He says of this "superbly accomplished" thriller, "Without hurry, and without the least sign of strain, Morrison has achieved what few novelists ever achieve, a book in which all the elements—scene, action, character and moral problem—are woven into a seamless fabric. . . . It is a work of classic quality, and deserves a permanent place in English literature." Eminent twentieth-century fiction writer and critic V. S. Pritchett sounded a similar note in his 1967 book *The Living Novel and Later Appreciations:* "*The Hole in the Wall* strikes me as being one of the minor masterpieces of the last sixty years."

Morrison's decline after the triumph of *The Hole in the Wall* has puzzled more than one critic. Bell, Brome, and Keating hypothesize possible reasons: that his strength was craftmanship rather than artistic creation, that he was too busy doing other work, or that he simply wasn't ambitious—that he hadn't viewed himself as a fulltime novelist in the first place. He continued to write short stories and detective fiction, and to co-author plays, after *The Hole in the Wall,* but that was his last realistic novel. His detective fiction ranks "second only to [Sir Arthur Conan] Doyle's work in the period 1890-1905," according to Bleiler in *Twentieth-Century Crime and Mystery Writers.* Morrison's stories about detective Martin Hewitt began to appear in the *Strand Magazine* in the mid-1890s, "as an unwelcome suprise" to lovers of his realistic fiction, Bleiler asserts. "They were

skilled commercial work, but without the power of Morrison's serious fiction." Morrison's Hewitt is as infallible in deduction as Sherlock Holmes, but more of "a plain fellow," as Bell puts it: "in detective fiction he marks a distinct break-away from the established eccentric type of crime-investigator." The crimes he solves in the eighteen stories are more ordinary, too, in Bell's opinion, although Bleiler calls the stories "ingenious in concept, well-written, and entertaining. If they lack the idiosyncratic snap of Doyle's works," he writes, "they are smoother and more relaxed." And to Bell's mind, "Morrison's sound style and good craftsmanship was a solid contribution to a genre which was too readily debased by third-rate hack writing."

Having contributed significant work both to turn-of-the-century realistic fiction and to detective fiction, Morrison apparently turned his back on the literary world and embraced that of a country gentleman. Literary history, in turn, has to an extent overlooked Morrison, perhaps because he kept his own personality a mystery. Later working-class writers have usually given him a nod of approval—but not always, as can be seen in Alan Sillitoe's comment that Morrison purveyed a stereotype that still haunts British fiction. But Morrison's best works are still written about and occasionally reprinted.

BIOGRAPHICAL/CRITICAL SOURCES:

BOOKS

Bell, Jocelyn, "A Study of Arthur Morrison," in *Essays and Studies 1952,* collected by Arundell Esdaile, John Murray (London), 1952, pp. 77-89.

Benstock, Bernard, and Thomas F. Staley, editors, *Dictionary of Literary Biography, volume 70: British Mystery Writers, 1860-1919,* Gale, 1988, pp. 212-218.

Bleiler, E. F., introduction to *Best Martin Hewitt Detective Stories,* Dover Publications (New York), 1976, pp. vii-xiv.

Brome, Vincent, *Four Realist Novelists,* Longmans, Green (London), 1965, pp. 7-19.

Greene, Hugh, editor and author of introduction, *The Rivals of Sherlock Holmes: Early Detective Stories,* Pantheon (New York), 1970.

Henderson, Lesley, *Twentieth-Century Crime and Mystery Writers,* third edition, St. James Press, 1988, pp. 782-783.

Keating, P. J., *The Working Classes in Victorian Fiction,* Barnes & Noble (New York), 1971, pp. 167-198.

Krzak, Michel, "Arthur Morrison's East End of London," in *Victorian Writers and the City,* edited by Jean-Paul Hulin and Pierre Coustillas, Publications de L'Universit de Lille III, pp. 145-180.

Magill, Frank N., *Critical Survey of Mystery and Detective Fiction,* volume 3, Salem Press (Pasadena, CA), 1988, pp. 1241-1245.

Pritchett, V. S., *The Living Novel and Later Appreciations,* Vintage, 1967, pp. 207-212.

Sillitoe, Alan, introduction to *The Ragged Trousered Philanthropists,* by Robert Tresall, Panther (London), 1965, p. 8.

Thesing, William B., *Dictionary of Literary Biography, vol. 135: British Short Fiction Writers, 1880-1914: The Realist Tradition,* Gale, 1994, pp. 247-254.

PERIODICALS

Athenaeum, November 24, 1894, pp. 712-713.
Bookman, January, 1895, pp. 121-122.
English Literature in Transition 1880-1920, vol. 28, no. 3, 1985, pp. 276-297.
Fortnightly Review, January, 1897, pp. 65-73.
London Magazine, February, 1980, pp. 62-67.
Novel, Spring, 1992, pp. 302-320.
Saturday Review, November 28, 1896, p. 573.
Spectator, March 9, 1895, pp. 329-330.*

*   *   *

MOSKOWITZ, Sam 1920-1997
(Sam Martin)

OBITUARY NOTICE—See index for *CA* sketch: Born June 30, 1920, in Newark, NJ; died of heart failure, April 15, 1997, near Newark, NJ. Truck driver, educator, editor, publisher, and author. Moskowitz was recognized around the globe as one of the planet's foremost authorities on science fiction. He claimed to collect every science fiction magazine and fanzine appearing in English, taught the first course in the genre at City College (now City College at the City University of New York) in 1953, and wrote various histories and published collections in the field. Moskowitz's interest in science fiction began when he was twelve and read his first sci-fi stories. His first career position was driving a truck, delivering produce. He also dabbled in science fiction writing and was a co-organizer of the initial World Science Fiction Convention (now World Con) in 1939. However, Moskowitz became increasingly interested in science

fiction as a reader, and he would later write and edit books about the genre itself. In the early 1940s he worked as a literary agent before becoming a salesman with Hazel Specialty Company, a grocery wholesaler. In 1952 he was hired by Gernsback Publications, which specialized in science fiction. Moskowitz served as managing editor of *Science-Fiction Plus* until 1954 when he held the same position on *Frosted Food Field.* In 1955 he became editor of *Quick Frozen Foods* and *Quick Frozen Foods International* for E.W. Williams Publications. He was the company's vice president for the next seventeen years. He continued to edit the frozen food publications with Harcourt Brace Jovanovich and also worked as a publisher. A prolific author, Moskowitz wrote many books, some as Sam Martin. Among his volumes were *The Immortal Storm: A History of Science Fiction, Seekers of Tomorrow: Masters of Modern Science Fiction, A. Merritt: Reflections in the Moon Pool, After All These Years* (memoir), *The Haunted Pampero, H. P. Lovecraft and Nils H. Frome,* and *Terrors of the Sea.* He edited books, including *Masterpieces of Science Fiction, Vortex Blasters, The Man Who Called Himself Poe,* and *Horrors Unseen.* He was inducted into the Science Fiction Hall of Fame in 1972 and into the New Jersey Hall of Fame in the late 1970s. A president of the H.G. Wells Society for many years, he was also awarded honors by the Eastern Science Fiction Association and the New Jersey Institute of Technology.

OBITUARIES AND OTHER SOURCES:

BOOKS

Who's Who in America, 1996.

PERIODICALS

New York Times, April 25, 1997, p. B12.
Washington Post, April 27, 1997, p. B6.

*   *   *

MYERS, L(eopold) H(amilton) 1881-1944

PERSONAL: Born September 6, 1881, in Cambridge, England; died from a drug overdose, April 8, 1944; son of F. W. H. (a writer and Cambridge University don) and Eveleen (a photographer; maiden name, Tennant) Myers; married Elsie Palmer, 1908; children: two daughters. *Education:* Attended Eton College, 1894-99; educated in Germany, 1899-1900; attended Trinity College, Cambridge, 1900-01.

CAREER: Poet and novelist. Served as a clerk in the British Foreign Office trade department during World War I; visited Ceylon, 1925.

AWARDS, HONORS: James Tait Black memorial prize, 1936; Femina-Vie Heureuse prize, 1936.

WRITINGS:

(Editor) *Human Personality and Its Survival of Bodily Death* by F. W. H. Myers, 1907.
Arvat (dramatic poem), 1908.
The Orissers (novel), Putnam's (London), 1922, Scribners (New York), 1923.
The Clio (novel), Putnam's (London) 1925, Scribners (New York), 1925.
The Near and the Far (novel), Cape (London), 1929, Harcourt, Brace (New York), 1930.
Prince Jali (novel), Cape (London), 1931, Harcourt, Brace (New York), 1931.
The Root and the Flower (novels; contains revised versions of *The Near and the Far, Prince Jali,* and the previously unpublished *Rajah Amar*), Cape (London), 1935, Harcourt, Brace (New York), 1935.
Strange Glory (novel), Putnam's (London), 1936, Harcourt, Brace (New York), 1936.
The Pool of Vishnu (novel), Cape (London), 1940, Harcourt, Brace (New York), 1940.
The Near and the Far (novels; contains *The Near and the Far, Prince Jali, Rajah Amar,* and *The Pool of Vishnu*), Cape (London), 1943; republished as *The Root and the Flower,* Harcourt, Brace (New York), 1947.

SIDELIGHTS: A novelist concerned with both spiritual transcendence and social equality, L. H. Myers is best known for *The Near and the Far,* a tetralogy set in sixteenth-century India. Briefly active with the Bloomsbury Group, Myers rejected what he deemed its members' insufficient regard for spiritual matters; in his own fiction, he insisted upon the importance of the soul as a link to the eternal. Myers also repudiated the insularity, elitism, and socially irresponsible aesthetics that he associated with the Bloomsbury coterie, particularly after the 1930s, when he became convinced that only communism could free people from the social constraints imposed by class affiliation.

Born in Cambridge, England, in 1881, Myers was descended from two liberal and intellectually accom-

plished families. His mother, Evelyn Tennant Myers, maintained a photography studio in the family home. His father, F. W. H. Myers, was a classicist and poet who founded the Society for Psychical Research, and as a child Myers participated in a number of the seances through which his father sought to establish the immortality of the soul.

The young Myers attended Eton, graduating in 1899 and spending a year in Germany before he entered Trinity College, Cambridge; he left the university without taking a degree when his father died in 1901. To console his mother, Myers accompanied her on a visit to America, where he fell in love with a young heiress, Elsie Palmer. Upon his return to Cambridge, Myers received a legacy from his godfather that left him financially independent. Although he continued to travel and socialize extensively, he also undertook several intellectual projects, editing his father's long work, *Human Personality and Its Survival of Bodily Death,* and composing a verse play, *Arvat,* published in 1908.

After his marriage to Elsie Palmer that year, Myers began work on his first novel, *The Orissers,* which took him ten years to complete. Published to considerable acclaim in 1922, *The Orissers* was followed three years later by *The Clio.* In 1929 Myers published *The Near and the Far,* the first volume in a series set in India during the Mogul era and focusing on a young man's spiritual quest. *Prince Jali,* the second novel in the series, appeared in 1931. Four years later, Myers published *The Root and the Flower,* which contained *The Near and the Far, Prince Jali,* and a new novel, *Rajah Amar.* During the late 1930s Myers's sympathy for Russian communism manifested itself in *Strange Glory* (1936), and *The Pool of Vishnu* (1940). The latter novel concluded his Indian series, the four volumes of which were published in 1943 under the collective title *The Near and the Far.* Myers committed suicide the following year.

In *Arvat,* his blank verse drama, Myers disparages the corruption that ensues, in his view, from material ambition, and this theme permeates all of his later work. In the words of critic Robert Grant, writing in the *Cambridge Quarterly,* the play is "of no merit whatsoever, but notable for Hamletizing scepticism and world weariness and for embodying the first of many antithesis between the religious and humanist positions."

The novel *The Orissers* takes place during the 1920s in a remote district of Wales, where two families are vying to possess Eamor, the country estate that one of the families has owned for five hundred years. Compared to Emily Bronte's *Wuthering Heights* for its inquiry into the relationship between love and sexual desire, and to E. M. Forster's *Howards End* for its examination of how individuals must mute their passions to survive in a social order, *The Orissers,* according to G. H. Bantock, "exhibits the characteristic preoccupations of Myers in a somewhat raw and undigested state." According to L. A. G. Strong in *Personal Remarks,* "*The Orissers* was by any standards a distinguished first novel. It caught brilliantly a certain limited section of the world of the early nineteen-twenties, and it showed that a fastidious and discerning intelligence had been contemplating, with faint distaste, the predicaments and perplexities which beset sensitive people who had money and intelligence and sufficient leisure to brood on their emotional difficulties."

Myers criticized the decadent materialism that he identifies with the privileged classes once again in *The Clio,* another contemporary work concerning a wealthy Englishman dying of malaria aboard a steam yacht on the Amazon. In a 1934 essay for *Scrutiny,* D. W. Harding praised Myers' body of novels, stating that they "present characters and situations with which you are invited to enter imaginatively into full and subtle social relationships." He excepted *The Clio,* however, pointing out that it "lacks richness and importance."

The Root and the Flower, which consists of the first three novels of Meyers' Indian series, was influenced by Arthur Waley's translation of Lady Murasaki's *The Tale of Genji,* then being published serially. However, while Myers adopted Murasaki's setting, an Asian court, *The Root and the Flower* is more concerned than *The Tale of Genji* with appraising different means to spiritual enlightenment. In representing the young Prince Jali's quest for peace, Myers exposes him to characters who espouse Hinduism, Christianity, Buddhism, and various other religious and philosophical schemas, incorporating psychological symbolism drawn from Sigmund Freud and Carl Jung, and drawing as well upon memories of the numerous mediums he met during his own childhood. More interested in exploring philosophical issues relevant to modern readers than in scrupling to achieve historical verisimilitude, Myers castigates the amoral aestheticism that he associated with Bloomsbury in *The Root and the Flower,* wherein he portrays a colony of insular and hedonistic aesthetes. In *Personal Remarks,* Strong commented that "*The Root*

and the Flower . . . was a sudden and staggering manifestation of maturity from a writer whose previous work gave no promise of anything so profound." Mark Van Doren referred to the trilogy in his *The Private Reader: Selected Articles and Reviews* as "superb."

Strange Glory, Myers's final novel set during the twentieth century, depicts Paulina, an American-born heiress who returns to Louisiana after her marriage to an English lord ends in divorce. Visiting the bayou annually, she meets two men. Tom Wentworth, the elder, is a mystic; Stephen, the younger, is a social reformer whose wife and child live in Russia. With Wentworth's help, Paulina achieves oneness with a primordial unconscious, which Myers derived from Carl Jung and embodied in the bayou. Paulina falls in love with Stephen, and, when he and his wife die, she travels to Russia to care for their orphaned child.

The Pool of Vishnu, the fourth and concluding novel of Myers's Indian series, is far longer than the three preceding novels. It introduces a new protagonist, the Guru, who believes in the essential goodness of man and advocates transforming the social order by dispossessing the propertied class. Like *Strange Glory, The Pool of Vishnu* attests to Myers's enthusiasm for a society based on personal affection rather than one determined by class, and the Guru repeatedly endorses this sentiment.

Myers' works fell out of sight shortly after the author's death, a fact some critics consider reflective less of the inherent merit of his generally acknowledged "masterpiece," the trilogy *The Root and the Flower,* than to a failure to find favor with the literary establishment, whose critical attentions tend to keep interest in a writer alive long after his or her death.

Bantock has described Myers as "more interested in 'ideas' than in people," and critics have contended that many of his characters function as mouthpieces for various philosophical creeds, while others are not sufficiently differentiated from one another or from the narrator. The latter charge may result from Myers's predilection for what W. D. Harding terms "quasi-musings, half soliloquy from a character and half author's comment." "At its worst," Harding maintains, Myers's style could be "stilted" and "ponderous." A related critique faults Myers's penchant for elaborating his themes without dramatizing them. "Mr. Myers," R. P. Blackmur wrote of the tetralogy, "is nowhere able to resort to the great advantages of plot."

Myers has also been criticized for the vagueness and irrelevance of his settings; in his fiction, Christopher Gillie notes, the "material environment is indistinct." In *Strange Glory* and, especially, *The Pool of Vishnu,* Myers drew additional fire from critics who charged that he was more prone to oversimplify and proselytize following his espousal of communism. Yet almost all of Myers's critics commend the philosophical seriousness that distinguishes his fiction, particularly *The Near and the Far,* which has been unanimously praised as his most successful work.

Numerous scholars have lauded the novelist's accurate, sympathetic portrayal of Buddhism in this series, while others have praised the knowledge of Freudian and Jungian psychology that informs it. In the estimation of L. P. Hartley, the tetralogy "is a unique work: there is nothing like it in the field of English fiction."

BIOGRAPHICAL/CRITICAL SOURCES:

BOOKS

Bantock, G. H., "Strange Glory," *L. H. Myers: A Critical Study,* University College and Jonathan Cape, 1956, pp. 116-127.

Blackmur, R. P., *The Expense of Greatness,* Peter Smith, 1958, pp. 176-198.

Dictionary of Literary Biography: British Novelists, 1930-1959, Volume 15, *Part 2: M-Z,* Gale (Detroit), 1983.

Hartley, L. P., introduction, *The Near and the Far* by L. H. Myers, 1943, reprinted by Jonathan Cape, 1956, pp. iv-ix.

Prescott, Orville, *In My Opinion: An Inquiry into the Contemporary Novel,* Bobbs-Merrill, 1952, pp. 235-48.

Strong, L. A. G., *Personal Remarks,* Liveright, 1953, pp. 193-209.

Van Doren, Mark, *The Private Reader: Selected Articles and Reviews,* Henry Holt, 1942, pp. 208-210.

PERIODICALS

Cambridge Quarterly, vol. VI, no. 3, 1975, pp. 214-240.

Dial, no. 75, July, 1923, p. 97.

Revue des langues vivantes, vol. XXXVII, no. 1, 1971, pp. 64-74.

Scrutiny, vol III, no. 1, June, 1934, pp. 44-63.

Southern Review, vol. II, no. 2, autumn, 1936, pp. 399-418; winter, 1941, pp. 610-628.*

N-O

NEALE, R(onald) S(tanley) 1927-1985

PERSONAL: Born February 3, 1927, in London, England; died in 1985, in London, England; son of Horace Stanley (a carpenter) and Alice (Johnson) Neale; married Margaret Mary Turner (a teacher), July 2, 1949; children: Anne Elizabeth, Patrick John, Andrew Charles, Katharine Jane. *Education:* University College, Leicester, B.Sc., 1951, Dip.Ed., 1952; Bristol University, M.A., 1963. *Politics:* Socialist.

CAREER: City of Bath Technical College, Bath, England, lecturer in history, 1952-64; University of New England, Armidale, New South Wales, Australia, began as lecturer, became professor of history, 1964-85. Vice-president of the Bath Labour Party, 1963-64. *Military service:* British Royal Marines, 1944-47, served with the No. 45 Royal Marine Commando, 1945-47, attained rank of Lance-Corporal.

MEMBER: Economic History Society, Australian Historical Association, Australian and New Zealand Economic History Society.

WRITINGS:

NONFICTION

Class and Ideology in the Nineteenth Century, Routledge & Kegan Paul (London), 1972.
(Editor with Eugene Kawenka) *Feudalism, Capitalism, and Beyond,* Edward Arnold, 1975.
Bath 1680-1850: A Social History, Routledge & Kegan Paul, 1981.
Class in English History, 1680-1850, Basil Blackwell (Oxford), 1981.

(Editor) *History and Class: Essential Readings in Theory and Interpretation,* Basil Blackwell, 1983.
Writing Marxist History: British Society, Economy and Culture since 1700, Basil Blackwell, 1985.

WORK IN PROGRESS: Writing a two-volume Marxist history of Britain since 1680.

SIDELIGHTS: British-born scholar R. S. Neale has taught history both in his native England and in New South Wales, Australia. He has written or edited several books about English history from a Marxist perspective; his first, *Class and Ideology in the Nineteenth Century,* was published in 1972. Neale is also the author of *Bath 1680-1850: A Social History* and *Writing Marxist History: British Society, Economy and Culture since 1700.*

In *Class and Ideology in the Nineteenth Century,* Neale replaces the traditional three class model of British Victorian society with a division into five classes. In addition to the better known upper, middle, and working classes, Neale posits a "middling class," which was on the low end of enfranchisement and which was responsible for much of the radical political movement of the time. Neale further divides the traditional working class into two groups, "with unskilled labourers and most women at the bottom," as a *Times Literary Supplement* reviewer explained. That critic was unconvinced of the need for Neale's five class model but asserted that the essays which comprise *Class and Ideology* "are almost all worth reading, and often provide useful correctives and open up further discussion on too-easily accepted theses."

Class in English History, 1680-1850, Neale's 1981 effort, "examines some of the claims made by social historians . . . when they use the concepts of class and class consciousness in their attempts to explain the history of England in the eighteenth and nineteenth centuries," according to Peter Carey in the *Times Literary Supplement.* Carey further noted that Neale's purpose is "to start a debate which will help to define procedures in social history and delineate more clearly the nature of the social historian's task." The critic concluded by praising *Class in English History* as "exceedingly stimulating and challenging," and by judging that it will "at the very least . . . provoke just the sort of debate which [Neale] hopes for."

In *Bath 1680-1850: A Social History,* Neale focuses on the development of the famed British resort town where he himself taught for a time. Noting wistfully that until the 1981 publication of *Bath 1680-1850,* "Bath . . . had somehow survived . . . almost untouched by radical historiography," Pat Rogers in the *Times Literary Supplement* still hailed the volume as "engrossing." Adam Fergusson, the *Times* reviewer, differed, calling the work "dull," while Isabel Colegate, holding forth in the *Spectator,* praised the "considerable research" evidenced in *Bath.*

In 1985's *Writing Marxist History: British Society, Economy and Culture since 1700,* Neale provides essays on related subjects both general and specific. For instance, he examines eighteenth-century British novelist Jane Austen's *Mansfield Park* in the light of class conflict and as an anti-industrialization tract. He also, noted Sidney Pollard in the *Times Literary Supplement,* begins *Writing Marxist History* "with a quotation from [eighteenth-century British novelist Lawrence Stern's] *Tristam Shandy.*" Pollard went on to declare that "like that book," Neale's volume "is self-indulgent, chaotic, aggravating, well written and a pleasure to read." A *Virginia Quarterly Review* critic admired *Writing Marxist History* as well, and congratulated Neale on offering the reader "some good chuckles along with his rather exotic history."

BIOGRAPHICAL/CRITICAL SOURCES:

PERIODICALS

Spectator, June 6, 1981, pp. 22-23.
Times [London], June 23, 1981.
Times Literary Supplement, May 25, 1973, p. 592; July 3, 1981, p. 767; August 7, 1981, p. 911; May 23, 1986, p. 572.
Virginia Quarterly Review, autumn, 1986, p. 121.*

NERNST, (Hermann) Walther   1864-1941

PERSONAL: Born June 25, 1864, in Briesen, West Prussia (now Wabrzezno, Poland); died November 18, 1941, in Zibelle, Oberlausitz (near the German-Polish border), Poland; son of Gustav (a judge) and Ottilie (Nerger) Nernst; married Emma Lohmeyer, c. 1890; children: three daughters, two sons. *Education:* Attended the universities of Zurich, Berlin, Graz; University of Wurzburg, Ph.D. (summa cum laude), 1887.

CAREER: Chemist and educator. University of Leipzig, assistant to Friedrich Wilhelm Ostwald, 1887; University of Gottingen in Leipzig, instructor, c. 1890, promoted to full professor, 1894; University of Berlin, professor of physical chemistry, c. 1905-22 and 1924-34. President of the Physikalisch-technische Reichsanstalt, c. 1922-24.

AWARDS, HONORS: Nobel Prize for Chemistry, 1920.

WRITINGS:

Theoretische Chemie vom Standpunkte der Avogadroschen Regel und der Thermodynamik (title means "Theoretical Chemistry from the Standpoint of Avogadro's Rule and Thermodynamics"), [Gottingen], 1893.
(With A. Schonflies) *Einfuhrung in die mathematische Behandlung der Naturwissenschaften-Kurzgefasstes Lehrbuch der Differential- und Integralrechnung mit besonderer Berucksichtigung der Chemie,* [Leipzig], 1895.
Die Ziele der physikalischen Chemie, [Gottingen], 1896.
Experimental and Theoretical Applications of Thermodynamics to Chemistry, [London], 1907.
Die Theoretischen und experimentellen Grundlagen des Neuen Warmesatzes, [Halle-Salle], 1918.

Contributor to journals and periodicals, including *Nachrichten von der Gesellschaft der Wissenschaften zu Gottingen.*

SIDELIGHTS: Walther Nernst made a significant breakthrough with his statement of the Third Law of Thermodynamics, which holds that it should be impossible to attain the temperature of absolute zero in any real experiment. For this accomplishment, he was awarded the 1920 Nobel Prize for chemistry. He also made contributions to the field of physical chemistry. While still in his twenties, he devised a mathematical expression showing how electromotive force is dependent upon temperature and concentration in a galvanic, or electricity-producing, cell. He later developed a theory to explain how ionic, or charged, compounds break down in water, a problem that had troubled chemists since the theory of ionization was proposed by Svante A. Arrhenius.

Born Hermann Walther Nernst in Briesen, West Prussia (now Wabrzezno, Poland), on June 25, 1864, he was the third child of Gustav Nernst, a judge, and Ottilie (Nerger) Nernst. He attended the gymnasium at Graudenz (now Grudziadz), Poland, where he developed an interest in poetry, literature, and drama. For a brief time, he considered becoming a poet. After graduation in 1883, Nernst attended the universities of Zurich, Berlin, Graz, and Wurzburg, majoring in physics at each institution. He was awarded his Ph.D. summa cum laude in 1887 by Wurzburg. His doctoral thesis dealt with the effects of magnetism and heat on electrical conductivity.

Nernst's first academic appointment came in 1887 when he was chosen as an assistant to professor Friedrich Wilhelm Ostwald at the University of Leipzig. Ostwald had been introduced to Nernst earlier in Graz by Svante Arrhenius. These three, Ostwald, Arrhenius, and Nernst, were to become among the most influential men involved in the founding of the new discipline of physical chemistry, the application of physical laws to chemical phenomena.

The first problem Nernst addressed at Leipzig was the diffusion of two kinds of ions across a semipermeable membrane. He wrote a mathematical equation describing the process, now known as the Nernst equation, which relates the electric potential of the ions to various properties of the cell.

In the early 1890s, Nernst accepted a teaching position appointment at the University of Gottingen in Leipzig, and soon after married Emma Lohmeyer, the daughter of a surgeon. The Nernsts had five children, three daughters and two sons. In 1894, Nernst was promoted to full professor at Gottingen. At the same time, he also received approval for the creation of a new Institute for Physical Chemistry and Electrochemistry at the university.

At Gottingen, Nernst wrote a textbook on physical chemistry, *Theoretische Chemie vom Standpunkte der Avogadroschen Regel und der Thermodynamik* ("Theoretical Chemistry from the Standpoint of Avogadro's Rule and Thermodynamics"). Published in 1893, it

had an almost missionary objective: to lay out the principles and procedures of a new approach to the study of chemistry. The book became widely popular, going through a total of fifteen editions over the next thirty-three years.

During his tenure at Gottingen, Nernst investigated a wide variety of topics in the field of solution chemistry. In 1893, for example, he developed a theory for the breakdown of ionic compounds in water, a fundamental issue in the Arrhenius theory of ionization. According to Nernst, dissociation, or the dissolving of a compound into its elements, occurs because the presence of nonconducting water molecules causes positive and negative ions in a crystal to lose contact with each other. The ions become hydrated by water molecules, making it possible for them to move about freely and to conduct an electric current through the solution. In later work, Nernst developed techniques for measuring the degree of hydration of ions in solutions. By 1903, Nernst had also devised methods for determining the pH value of a solution, an expression relating the solution's hydrogen-ion concentration (acidity or alkalinity).

In 1889, Nernst addressed another fundamental problem in solution chemistry: precipitation. He constructed a mathematical expression showing how the concentration of ions in a slightly soluble compound could result in the formation of an insoluble product. That mathematical expression is now known as the solubility product, a special case of the ionization constant for slightly soluble substances. Four years later, Nernst also developed the concept of buffer solutions—solutions made of bases, rather than acids—and showed how they could be used in various theoretical and practical situations.

Around 1905, Nernst was offered a position as professor of physical chemistry at the University of Berlin. This move was significant for both the institution and the man. Chemists at Berlin had been resistant to many of the changes going on in their field, and theoretical physicist and eventual Nobel Prize winner Max Planck had recommended the selection of Nernst to revitalize the Berlin chemists. The move also proved to be a stimulus to Nernst's own work. Until he left Gottingen, he had concentrated on the reworking of older, existing problems developed by his predecessors in physical chemistry. At Berlin, he began to search out, define, and explore new questions. Certainly the most important of these questions involved the thermodynamics of chemical reactions at very low temperatures.

Attempting to extend the Gibbs-Helmholtz equation and the Thomsen-Berthelot principle of maximum work to temperatures close to absolute zero—the temperature at which there is no heat—Nernst eventually concluded that it would be possible to reach absolute zero only by a series of infinite steps. In the real world, that conclusion means that an experimenter can get closer and closer to absolute zero, but can never actually reach that point. Nernst first presented his "Heat Theorem," as he called it, to the Gottingen Academy of Sciences in December of 1905. It was published a year later in the *Nachrichten von der Gesellschaft der Wissenschaften zu Gottingen*. The theory is now more widely known as the Third Law of Thermodynamics. In 1920, Nernst was awarded the Nobel Prize in chemistry in recognition of his work on this law.

The statement of the Heat Theorem proved to be an enormous stimulus for Nernst's colleagues in Berlin's chemistry department. For at least a decade, the focus of nearly all research among physical chemists there was experimental confirmation of Nernst's hypothesis. In order to accomplish this objective, new equipment and new techniques had to be developed. Nernst's Heat Theorem was eventually integrated into the revolution taking place in physics, the development of quantum theory. At the time he first proposed the theory, Nernst had ignored any possible role of quantum mechanics. A few years later, however, that had all changed. In working on his own theory of specific heats, for example, Albert Einstein had quite independently come to the same conclusions as had Nernst. He later wrote that Nernst's experiments at Berlin had confirmed his own theory of specific heats. In turn, Nernst eventually realized that his Heat Theorem was consistent with the dramatic changes being brought about in physics by quantum theory. Even as his work on the Heat Theorem went forward, Nernst turned to new topics. One of these involved the formation of hydrogen chloride by photolysis, or chemical breakdown by light energy. Chemists had long known that a mixture of hydrogen and chlorine gases will explode when exposed to light. In 1918, Nernst developed an explanation for that reaction. When exposed to light, Nernst hypothesized, a molecule of chlorine will absorb light energy and break down into two chlorine atoms. A single chlorine atom will then react with a molecule of hydrogen, forming a molecule of hydrogen chloride and an atom of hydrogen. The atom of hydrogen will then react with a molecule of chlorine, forming a second molecule of hydrogen chloride and another atom of chlorine. The process is a chain reaction because the remaining atom of chlorine allows it to repeat.

In 1922, Nernst resigned his post at Berlin in order to become president of the Physikalisch-technische Reichsanstalt. He hoped to reorganize the institute and make it a leader in German science, but since the nation was suffering from severe inflation at the time, there were not enough funds to achieve this goal. As a result, Nernst returned to Berlin in 1924 to teach physics and direct the Institute of Experimental Physics there until he retired in 1934.

In addition to his scientific research, Nernst was an avid inventor. Around the turn of the century, for example, he developed an incandescent lamp that used rare-earth oxide rather than a metal as the filament. Although he sold the lamp patent outright for a million marks, the device was never able to compete commercially with the conventional model invented by Thomas Alva Edison. Nernst also invented an electric piano that was never successfully marketed.

The rise of the Nazi party in 1933 brought an end to Nernst's professional career. He was personally opposed to the political and scientific policies promoted by Adolf Hitler and his followers and was not reluctant to express his views publicly. In addition, two of his daughters had married Jews, which contributed to his becoming an outcast in the severely anti-Semitic climate of Germany at that time.

Nernst was one of the geniuses of early twentieth-century German chemistry, a man with a prodigious curiosity about every new development in the physical sciences. He was a close colleague of Einstein, and was a great contributor to the organization of German science—he was largely responsible for the first Solvay Conference in 1911, for example. In his free time, he was especially fond of travel, hunting, and fishing. Nernst also loved automobiles and owned one of the first to be seen in Gottingen. Little is known about his years after his retirement. Nernst died of a heart attack on November 18, 1941, at his home at Zibelle, Oberlausitz, near the German-Polish border.

BIOGRAPHICAL/CRITICAL SOURCES:

BOOKS

Concise Dictionary of Scientific Biography, Macmillan, 1981, pp. 499-501.
Farber, Eduard, editor, *Great Chemists,* Interscience, 1961, pp. 1203-1208.
Gillispie, Charles Coulson, editor, *Dictionary of Scientific Biography,* Volume 15, Scribner, 1975, pp. 432-53.

Mendelsohn, Kurt, *The World of Walther Nernst: The Rise and Fall of German Science, 1864-1941,* Pittsburgh, 1973.

PERIODICALS

Journal of the American Chemical Society, 1953, pp. 2853-72.
Scientific Monthly, February, 1942, pp. 195-196.*

*   *   *

NETTERVILLE, Luke
   See O'GRADY, Standish (James)

*   *   *

NIGHTINGALE, Pamela 1938-

PERSONAL: Born October 17, 1938, in Greenfield, Yorkshire, England; daughter of Victor Saxon Bottoms (an engineer) and Marion Jane Leyland; married John Stuart Nightingale, July 12, 1962; children: Giles Edward John, Sophia Elizabeth Mary Winters, Eleanor Jane Matilda. *Education:* Newnham College, Cambridge, B.A., 1960, M.A., Ph.D., 1964. *Religion:* Catholic. *Avocational interests:* Music, gardening, interior decorating.

ADDRESSES: Home—20 Beaumont Buildings, Oxford, OX1 2LL, England.

CAREER: Archivist, 1963-66; research assistant to the Reverend Honorable Lord Glendevon, 1967-69; Open University, tutor, 1972-79; Worker's Educational Association, lecturer, 1972-79. Honorable Librarian, Buckinghamshire Archaeological Society, 1974-80; chair, Historical Association, Buckinghamshire branch, 1974-80; Fellow of the Royal Historical Society.

AWARDS, HONORS: Walker Krewer Lord Prize, Royal Commonwealth Society, 1962.

WRITINGS:

Trade and Empire in Western India, 1784-1806, Cambridge University Press, 1970.
(With Clarmont Slerine) *Macartney at Kashgar: New Light on British, Chinese and Russian Activities*
in *Singkiang, 1890-1918,* Methuen (London), 1973.
Fortune and Integrity: A Study of Moral Attitudes in the Indian Diary of George Paterson, 1769-74, Oxford University Press (Delhi), 1985.
A Medieval Mercantile Community, Yale University Press (New Haven, CT), 1995.

Contributor of academic articles on medieval economic and monetary history to scholarly journals.

WORK IN PROGRESS: Academic articles, research on English medieval monetary economy.

*   *   *

NORMAN, Dorothy 1905-1997

OBITUARY NOTICE—See index for *CA* sketch: Born March 28, 1905, in Philadelphia, PA; died April 12, 1997, in East Hampton, Long Island, NY. Civil rights advocate, photographer, and writer. Norman gained prominence as a patron of the arts who believed in social change. In the 1920s, Norman accepted a position with the American Civil Liberties Union (ACLU) conducting research. She also became involved with the Planned Parenthood Association, an organization that was then in its early development stage. In 1938 she published and edited a literary journal called *Twice a Year,* and in 1942 she began a weekly column for the *New York Post* entitled "A World to Live In," which ran for seven years. Her association with photographer Alfred Stieglitz brought her into the world of picture taking; her photographs have appeared in numerous museums around the United States, including the Boston Museum of Fine Arts and the J. Paul Getty Museum. She was a founding member of Americans for Democratic Action and founded the American Citizens' Committee for Economic Aid Abroad and American Emergency Food Committee for India. Her work in India culminated in her writing *Indira Gandhi: Letters to an American Friend* and *Nehru: The First Sixty Years.* Her other written works include *The Hero: Myth, Image, and Symbol, Alfred Stieglitz: An American Seer,* and *Encounters: A Memoir.*

OBITUARIES AND OTHER SOURCES:

BOOKS

Who's Who in American Art, 1991-1992, 19th edition, Bowker, 1990.

PERIODICALS

New York Times, April 14, 1997, p. B9.

*   *   *

NORMYX
  See DOUGLAS, (George) Norman

*   *   *

NORWICH, William 1954-

PERSONAL: Name originally William Goldberg; born July 18, 1954, in Norwich, CT. *Education:* Hampshire College, B.A., 1976; Columbia University, M.F.A.

ADDRESSES: Home—New York, NY. *Office—New York Observer,* 54 East 64th St., New York, NY 10021.

CAREER: New York Daily News, New York City, columnist, beginning in 1985; *New York Observer,* New York City, columnist; *Vogue,* New York City, editor-at-large; author.

WRITINGS:

Learning to Drive (novel), Atlantic Monthly Press (New York City), 1996.

Author of column in *Harper's & Queen,* 1989—. Contributor to periodicals, including *House and Garden, Interview, Premiere, Redbook,* and *Vanity Fair.*

SIDELIGHTS: William Norwich is a New York City newspaper columnist and novelist. In 1985 he became the society columnist for the *New York Daily News,* where he had been recommended by syndicated columnist Liz Smith. At the *Daily News,* Norwich showed himself to be a witty, urbane social observer with a particular flair for charting the activities of Great Britain's royal family. Norwich eventually proved similarly skilled as the gossip columnist for the *New York Observer,* while also becoming editor-at-large for the popular fashion magazine *Vogue.* In addition, he has contributed to periodicals ranging from *House and Garden* to *Interview.*

In 1996 Norwich published his first novel, *Learning to Drive.* This narrative concerns Julian Orr, a middle-aged, homosexual society columnist who is encouraged by his psychiatrist to obtain a driver's license so that he can visit the grave sites of his deceased parents in rural Connecticut. Ensuing portions of the novel alternate details of Orr's troubled childhood with accounts of his daily professional and personal activities, including his endeavor to master automobile driving. Drama builds when Orr is suddenly abducted by his deranged instructor, Hector, who takes the columnist on a harrowing journey that culminates in acts of murder and related mayhem.

Learning to Drive won Norwich attention as a notable personality even within New York City's considerable literary community. Susan Bolotin, writing in the *New York Times Book Review,* noted that Norwich, whom she described as "perennially effusive," had "New Yorkers . . . tripping over one another to get close enough to . . . congratulate him on his first novel." Bolotin added that *Learning to Drive* is "one literary gamble . . . that pays off."

BIOGRAPHICAL/CRITICAL SOURCES:

PERIODICALS

Entertainment Weekly, May 24, 1996, pp. 88-89.
New York Times Book Review, June 16, 1996, p. 11.
Publishers Weekly, April 8, 1996, p. 55.*

*   *   *

O'CONNELL, Laurence J. 1945-

PERSONAL: Born May 12, 1945, in Chicago, IL; son of Joseph J. (an engineer) and Eleanor Margaret (Coleman) O'Connell; married Angela Schneider; children: Coleman Brian. *Education:* Loyola University, B.A., 1969; Catholic University of Louvain, B.A., 1969, M.A., 1970, S.T.B., 1970, S.T.L. (magna cum laude), 1972, Ph.D. (magna cum laude), 1976, S.T.D., 1976. *Religion:* Roman Catholic. *Avocational interests:* Skiing, sailing, art, music.

ADDRESSES: Home—507 West Barry St., Chicago, IL 60657. *Office*—The Park Ridge Center, 211 East Ontario, Suite 800, Chicago, IL 60611.

CAREER: The Park Ridge Center for Health Faith and Ethics, Chicago, IL, president and CEO, 1989—;

affiliated with St. Louis University, St. Mary of the Lake, and The Catholic Health Association.

AWARDS, HONORS: Outstanding Young Man of the Year Award, 1978; St. Louis Speakers Award, 1979; Fellow, Institute of Medicine, 1992; Golden Eurydice Award, 1996.

WRITINGS:

(Translator with Angela M. Schneider) W. A. de Pater, *Reden van Gott: Reflexionen sur analytischen Philosophie der religioesen Sprache,* Linguista Biblica Bonn (Bonn), 1974.

(Editor with Robert Craig and Karl Middleton) *Ethics Committees: A Practical Approach,* Catholic Health Association Press (St. Louis, MO), 1986.

(Editor with Edwin Dubose and Ronald Hamel) *A Matter of Principles?: Ferment in U.S. Bioethics,* Trinity Press International (Valley Forge, PA), 1994.

(Editor with Renee Fox and Stuart Youngner) *Organ Transplantation: Meanings and Realities,* University of Wisconsin Press (Madison), 1996.

Contributor of articles, collaborative reports, letters, prefaces, forewords, and reviews to journals and periodicals, including *Health Progress, Crain's Chicago Business, Healthcare Executive, Healthcare Ethics Committee Forum, Western Journal of Medicine, Journal of Medicine and Philosophy, Medical Humanities Review, Cambridge Quarterly of Healthcare Ethics, New York Newsday, Chicago Tribune, New Dictionary of Catholic Spirituality, Interhealth Links, Trustee, Journal of Clinical Ethics, Critic, St. Louis Review, Theology Digest, Journal of the American Academy of Religion,* and *Chicago Studies.*

*   *   *

O'GRADY, Standish (James) 1846-1928
(Luke Netterville)

PERSONAL: Born September 18, 1846, in Castletown Berehaven, County Cork, Ireland; died May 18, 1928, in Shanklin, Isle of Wight, England; son of Viscount Guillamore (a theologian); married c. 1872, wife's maiden name, Fisher; children: three sons. *Education:* Trinity College, Dublin, B.A., 1868.

CAREER: Journalist, historian, folklorist, fiction writer, and political commentator. Called to the Irish Bar, 1872. Owned and edited a small-town newspa-

per, the *Kilkenny Moderator;* printer and publisher of books; publisher of a literary weekly, *All Ireland Review,* 1900-06.

WRITINGS:

NONFICTION

Early Bardic Literature of Ireland (history), Sampson Low & Co. (London), 1879.

History of Ireland: Critical and Philosophical (history), Sampson Low & Co., 1881.

The Crisis in Ireland (political essay), E. Ponsonby (Dublin), 1882.

Toryism and the Tory Democracy (political essay), Chapman & Hall (London), 1886.

Red Hugh's Captivity: A Picture of Ireland, Social and Political in the Reign of Queen Elizabeth, Ward & Downey (London), 1889.

The Story of Ireland (history), Methuen, (London), 1893.

All Ireland (political essay), Sealy, Bryers & Walker (Dublin), 1898.

Also author of *History of Ireland: The Heroic Period,* 1878, and *History of Ireland: Cuculain and His Contemporaries,* 1880.

FICTION

Finn and His Companions (novel), Children's Library, 1892.

The Bog of Stars (stories), New Irish Library, 1893.

The Coming of Cuculain: A Romance of the Heroic Age of Ireland (novel), Methuen, 1894.

Lost on Du Corrig; or, 'Twixt Earth and Ocean (novel), Cassell, 1894.

The Chain of Gold: A Tale of Adventure on the West Coast of Ireland (novel), T. F. Unwin (London), 1895; also published as *The Chain of Gold; or, In Crannied Rocks: A Boys' Tale of Adventure on the Wild West Coast of Ireland,* Dodd, Mead (New York), 1895.

In the Wake of King James; or, Dun-Randal on the Sea (novel), J. M. Dent (London), 1896.

Ulrick the Ready; or, The Chieftain's Last Rally (novel), Downey, (London), 1896; also published as *Ulrick the Ready: A Romance of Elizabethan Ireland,* Dodd, Mead, 1896.

The Flight of the Eagle (novel), Lawrence & Bullen (London), 1897.

(As Luke Netterville) *The Queen of the World; or, Under the Tyranny* (fiction), Lawrence & Bullen, 1900.

The Departure of Dermot (novel), Talbot Press, 1917.
In the Gates of the North (novel), Talbot Press, 1919.
The Triumph and Passing of Cuculain (novel), Talbot Press, 1919.

OTHER

Selected Essays and Passages (bibliography, folklore, history, political essays, criticism, and fiction), Talbot Press (Dublin), 1918.

SIDELIGHTS: An Irish historian, novelist, folklorist, and journalist, Standish O'Grady is generally considered the founder of the Irish Literary Renaissance of the late nineteenth and early twentieth centuries. His most important works include the multi-volume *History of Ireland,* which comprises a compilation of ancient Irish legends. A magazine publisher and political commentator as well, O'Grady also wrote a series of novels drawing on Irish history of the heroic age and of the Elizabethan era.

O'Grady was born in Castletown Berehaven, County Cork, where his father was the parish rector. Educated at Trinity College in Dublin and prepared for a career in law, O'Grady was called to the Irish Bar in 1872. In 1869 he read O'Halloran's *History of Ireland* and was subsequently inspired to preserve the ancient legends by reintroducing them to modern readers. O'Grady wrote *History of Ireland: The Heroic Period* in 1878 and the companion volume, *History of Ireland: Cuculain and His Contemporaries,* two years later. Together these works formed a catalyst for the Irish Literary Renaissance, which encompassed such events as the founding of the Abbey Theatre in Dublin and included such notable participants as the poet W. B. Yeats and the playwright J. M. Synge, among others.

Norreys Jepson O'Conor, writing in his *Changing Ireland: Literary Backgrounds of the Irish Free State, 1889-1922,* commented that "O'Grady's great achievement is that from the obscure, confused, incoherent narrative of most of the early Irish texts he has made a connected story with a beginning, a middle, and an end." Some scholars, however, have faulted O'Grady's versions of the tales as unfaithful to the original Gaelic texts. For instance, O'Grady purged or purified explicit sexual content to render the tales inoffensive to the Victorian moral sensibility. Nevertheless, according to Richard Fallis, writing in *The Irish Renaissance,* "O'Grady's work provided a model for a way to deal with the Gaelic inheritance of heroic legend, the way of imaginative re-creation."

Fallis further noted that "the publication of Standish O'Grady's *History of Ireland: The Heroic Period* . . . demonstrated that it was possible to combine the work of the scholars with the techniques of popularization and so produce a work which would become part of the living Irish imagination."

In addition to compiling Gaelic legends, O'Grady eventually reworked several of the tales as historical novels set either in the heroic age or in Elizabethan Ireland. Of these, W. B. Yeats praised *Finn and His Companions* (1892) as "delightful" and *The Coming of Cuculain: A Romance of the Heroic Age of Ireland* (1894) as "memorable" in a *Bookman* review. In his study *Ireland's Literary Renaissance,* Ernest Boyd wrote that "the finest qualities of the historian are revealed by [O'Grady's] treatment of the story of Cuculain. Step by step this heroic and lordly nature is unfolded before us with the skill and sympathy which come of deep understanding coupled with a power of vision and expression." Another of the novels, *The Flight of the Eagle* (1897), focuses on the heroic exploits of Irish chieftain Red Hugh O'Donnell, a champion of Irish nationalism during the Elizabethan period. Boyd noted that "in *The Flight of the Eagle* [O'Grady] gave to Irish literature one of its most spirited and beautifully written romances."

A third group of O'Grady's writings focuses on contemporary politics and social issues. Although he did not speak Gaelic, O'Grady promoted Irish arts through his publication the *All Ireland Review* and as the owner and editor of the *Kilkenny Moderator.* His most significant political essay, *Toryism and the Tory Democracy* (1886), called for cooperation between tenants and land owners to revitalize the Irish economy, a collaboration that to O'Grady's disappointment was not forthcoming. In the introduction to the 1920 edition of *The Coming of Cuculain,* a writer identified as "A. E." concluded that O'Grady's "political and social writings will remain to uplift and inspire and to remind us that the man who wrote the stories of heroes had a bravery of his own and a wisdom of his own."

However, O'Grady's significance in Irish literature rests primarily on his popularization of the ancient texts and the extent to which his works inspired Irish writers to draw on the mythic history of Ireland in forging a national identity through literature at a time when political nationalism was at the forefront of Irish social life. A. E., writing in *Irish Literature,* noted that "O'Grady's finest achievement has been to rescue for us the great pagan virtues and to bring them with a living force into modern Ireland."

BIOGRAPHICAL/CRITICAL SOURCES:

BOOKS

A. E., *Irish Literature,* Volume VII, edited by Justin McCarthy, John D. Morris, 1904, pp. 2737-40.
Boyd, Ernest, *Ireland's Literary Renaissance,* revised edition, Barnes & Noble, 1922, pp. 26-54.
Fallis, Richard, *The Irish Renaissance,* Syracuse University Press, 1977, pp. 55-72.
O'Conor, Norreys Jepson, *Changing Ireland: Literary Backgrounds of the Irish Free State, 1889-1922,* Harvard University Press, 1924, pp. 179-85.
O'Grady, Standish, *The Coming of Cuculain,* introduction by A. E., Frederick A. Stokes Co., 1920.

PERIODICALS

Bookman, February, 1895, p. 153.*

*   *   *

OLSSON, Jennifer 1959-

PERSONAL: Born May 20, 1959, in Long Beach, CA; daughter of Jack (an attorney) and Barbara (Decker) Miller; married 1984 (divorced, 1993); married Lars-Ake Olsson (an author and riverkeeper), January 28, 1995; children: (first marriage) Peter; stepchildren: (second marriage) Magnus, Frank. *Education:* Vassar College, B.A., 1981. *Avocational interests:* Cross country skiing, Big Brothers/Big Sisters organization.

ADDRESSES: Home and office—P.O. Box 132, Bozeman, MT 59771; fax (406) 585-9625. *E-mail*—jolsson @montana.net.

CAREER: KBOZ (radio station), Bozeman, MT, radio announcer and copywriter, 1982-84; Computerland, Bozeman, salesperson, 1984-85; owner of High Country Angler, a fly shop in Bozeman, 1984-87; fly fishing guide, author, and speaker, 1985—. Has appeared on radio and television shows in the United States and in Sweden; appeared in CD-ROM program *Great Rivers of the West* and in video *Women and Fly Fishing.*

MEMBER: Trout Unlimited, Federation of Fly Fishers, Northwest Outdoor Writers Association.

AWARDS, HONORS: Named 1990 National Big Sister by the Big Brothers/Big Sisters of America.

WRITINGS:

Cast Again: Tales of a Fly-Fishing Guide, Lyons & Burford (New York), 1996.

Contributor to the books *Uncommon Waters: Anthology,* Seal Press (Seattle, WA), 1991; *The World's Best Trout Flies: Anthology,* Boxtree Ltd., 1994; and *A Different Angle: Anthology,* Seal Press, 1995. Also contributor of articles to periodicals, including the World Wide Web's *Virtual Fly Shop.*

WORK IN PROGRESS: Coming to the Village: A Woman's Journey to the Forest Country of Sweden.

SIDELIGHTS: Jennifer Olsson makes much of her living as a fly-fishing guide in Bozeman, Montana. She has attained a high status in the sport of fly-fishing and was the first woman in her profession to be endorsed by the Scott Fly Rod Company. Olsson also has lectured on fly-fishing in the country of Sweden. She has put much of her knowledge and experience into writing, contributing to anthologies on the sport including *The World's Best Trout Flies, A Different Angle,* and *Uncommon Waters.* Olsson's first book of her own, *Cast Again: Tales of a Fly-Fishing Guide,* saw print in 1996.

As the title implies, Olsson has filled the volume with stories from her years as a professional fishing guide. In one of the stories, however, what takes place is not a fishing expedition but a shopping excursion. In another, she describes catching a cut-throat trout by applying a piece of cheese and a piece of bread to the fly's hook. Brian Baise, reviewing *Cast Again* for the *Big Sky Journal,* gave it high praise, noting that Olsson shows her reader the unpleasant and messy sides of the sport. He asserted that for Olsson, discussing fly-fishing "is not an excuse to be lyrical," and, speaking of both the sport's problems and its "transcendental moments of clarity and sanctity," the critic concluded that "in *Cast Again,* you'll find a little of both."

Olsson told *CA:* "I write because I want to share. The craft of writing is a challenge that I can't seem to leave alone. Life as a fly fishing guide has inspired me to write about people and their interactions with each other and with rivers. Because I divide my time between the United States and Scandinavia, the landscapes of Montana and the forest country of Sweden are the settings for my stories. I have been influenced by the writings of western women authors: Mary Clearman Blew, Linda Hasselstrom, Terry Tempest Williams, Pam Houston, Teresa Jordon, Gretel Erlich.

"The mysterious process of writing directs me more than I direct it. While in the midst of a conversation, event, or adventure, a story may present itself and want to be told. Sometimes looking back over certain events I see stories that have been hiding from me for years. Telling them gives me pleasure.

"For the first time in our history, a woman's voice speaking about her life in the outdoors—as a wife, mother, lover, adventurer—is being heard in record numbers. It is important to me to participate in this effort."

BIOGRAPHICAL/CRITICAL SOURCES:

PERIODICALS

Big Sky Journal, fall 1996, p. 97.

*　　*　　*

OTWAY-WARD, Patricia
　　See WEENOLSEN, Patricia

P

PADGETT, Lewis
See KUTTNER, Henry

*   *   *

PARISH, Steven M. 1953-

PERSONAL: Born November 29, 1953, in LaCrosse, WI; son of Lyle D. (a farmer and factory worker) and Alice (a nurse) Parish; married Rita Shakya, 1985. *Education:* University of Oregon, B.A., 1978; University of California, San Diego, M.A., 1981, Ph.D., 1987.

ADDRESSES: Office—Department of Anthropology, University of California, San Diego, 9500 Gilman Dr., La Jolla, CA 92093. *E-mail*—sparish@ucsd.edu.

CAREER: Boston University, Boston, MA, assistant professor of anthropology, 1988-93; independent scholar and consultant, Boston, 1994-96; University of California, San Diego, La Jolla, assistant professor of anthropology, 1996—.

MEMBER: American Anthropological Association, Society for Psychological Anthropology.

WRITINGS:

Moral Knowing in a Hindu Sacred City, Columbia University Press (New York City), 1994.
Hierarchy and Its Discontents, University of Pennsylvania Press (Philadelphia), 1996.

SIDELIGHTS: Steven M. Parish told *CA:* "As a writer and ethnographer, I explore lived cultural worlds. My first book is a study of self in culture, an exploration of a moral world and its cultural psychology. My second book is about untouchables in the caste system of Nepal and India; it attempts to bring to light their psychological struggles and the cultural politics of their consciousness.

"I see people, their lives and self-awareness, as grounded in society; yet, I see them as struggling with the society and culture that shapes them. Writing about moral consciousness, I found that culture and identity often emerge out of the existential pain of social life. I have explored ways that people experience and resist social definition, the ways people are constructed by society and find themselves congealed in those constructions: '. . . bound, first without, then within,' as James Baldwin put it. The power of society to define and limit the person is undeniable, yet I detected something squeezed painfully and creatively between the monolith of what society thinks of those it stigmatizes and the unwilled acceptance of this as self-image by those stigmatized. A kind of raw nerve runs there, agonized, sensitive, emitting rejections of society, ambivalent, humming with self-assertion. Here, at this nerve point, I found the notion of the autonomy of the self developed and put into eccentric motion by ordinary people.

"They struggled with the images society created for them and made them embody, trying to reconcile them with the possibilities of a selfhood that would be their own. People, I found, may seek to transcend the limits of their cultures. The project of converting pain into hope seems likely to fail in most cases, but it is surely a perennial human project, one worth any writer's and scholar's effort to understand. Out of their pain and struggles, people generate visions of self and society in counterpoint to dominant cultural conceptions. Identity emerges from a politics of consciousness in which men and women are active agents, not the passive subjects of society and culture.

"Trying to do a little justice to this very human process means writing against powerful intellectual currents that reduce persons to social constructions, render them flat, one-dimensional discourses, or even reduce them to empty, passive 'sites' for such discourse. This obscures the pain and dynamics of being human in any culture, obscures human agency and people's efforts to make lives for themselves. As James Baldwin reminded us, evading the complexity of others diminishes us all: for the complexity of others resonates with "the disquieting complexity of ourselves." Along with others, I have tried to write a more robust sense of the person into contemporary anthropology and social theory.

"I believe those of us who struggle to understand society, culture, and history should not ignore those who struggle to live in society and culture, who confront history with their lives. Social theorist C. Wright Mills wrote that we must locate society into the flow of history, and human lives in society. We need to ask about the experience and identity of people, to explore their quandaries and lives and selves. Such questions guide my work and writing.

"What I write is ethnography. That is, I try to describe and say something meaningful about cultural worlds and the lives of those who inhabit those worlds. In the contemporary scene, ethnography has emerged as an important and controversial genre of writing—one centrally involved in debates about society. Yet I believe it has yet to develop fully its potential for illuminating the cultural and psychological life of persons-in-society.

"My books are my contribution to the unfinished task of developing forms of ethnography that do justice to persons-in-society, to their cultural experience, their agency, their lives. I believe the painstaking ethnography of persons can make a crucial contribution to human understanding. By taking account of what it shows us, we can engage social and psychological theory in critical and constructive ways. By showing us how people exist, how they are aware of themselves, and how they make (or fail to make) lives for themselves, person-centered ethnography forces us to contemplate the terms of our own existence, and it invites reflection on society, history, and culture."

PARIZEAU, Alice (Poznanska) 1930-1990

PERSONAL: Born July 25, 1930, in Luniniec, Poland; immigrated to France, 1945; immigrated to Canada, 1955; died of cancer, 1990; daughter of Stanislaus Poznanski (an industrialist) and Bronislawa Poznanska (a concert pianist); married Jacques Parizeau (an economist and politician), 1976. *Education:* Educated in Paris; received baccalaureat es lettres, 1948, and certificate in political science and law degree, 1953.

CAREER: Writer, journalist, and lawyer. Universite de Montreal, Montreal, Quebec, Canada, Secretaire Generale du Centre International de Criminologie Comparee, 1972-79; Salon du Livre, Paris, France, delegate, 1983.

MEMBER: Union of Authors, American Authors Guild.

AWARDS, HONORS: Canadian Women's Press Club, Montreal, 1966; Prix Europeen de l'Association des ecrivains de langue francais, 1982, for *Les Lilas fleurissent a Varsovie.*

WRITINGS:

Voyage en Pologne (travel), Editions du Jour (Montreal), 1962.
Fuir (novel), Deom (Montreal), 1963.
Survivre (novel), Cercle du Livre de France (Montreal), 1964.
Une Quebecoise en Europe "rouge" (travel), Fides (Montreal), 1965.
Rue Sherbrooke ouest (novel), Cercle du Livre de France, 1967.
(With Denis Szabo and Denis Gagne) *L'Adolescent et la societe* (nonfiction), Dessart (Brussels), 1972.
(With Marc-Andre Delilse) *Ces jeunes qui nous font peur* (nonfiction), Ferron (Montreal), 1974.
Les Militants (novel), Cercle du Livre de France, 1974.
L'Envers de l'enfance: Recits (fiction), La Presse (Montreal), 1976.
(With Szabo) *Le Traitement de la criminalite au Canada* (nonfiction), Presses de l'Universite de Montreal (Montreal), 1977, translated, revised, and edited by Dorothy R. Crelinsten as *The Canadian Criminal-Justice System,* Lexington Books (Lexington, MA), 1977.
Protection de l'enfant, echec? Famille, etat de droits de l'enfance (nonfiction), Presses de l'Universite de Montreal, 1979, translated by Crelinsten as *Parenting and Delinquent Youth,* Lexington Books (New York), 1980.

Les Lilas fleurissent a Varsovie (novel), Pierre Tisseyre (Montreal), 1981, translated by A. D. Martin-Sperry as *The Lilacs Are Blooming in Warsaw,* New American Library (New York), 1985.

Le Charge des sangliers (novel), Pierre Tisseyre, 1982.

Cote-des-neiges (novel), Pierre Tisseyre, 1983.

Ils se sont connus a Lwow (novel), Pierre Tisseyre, 1985.

L'amour de Jeanne (novel), Pierre Tisseyre, 1986.

Blizzard sur Quebec (novel), Quebec/Amerique (Montreal), 1987.

Nata et le professeur (novel), Quebec/Amerique, 1988.

Une femme (diary), Lemeac (Montreal), 1991.

Contributor to periodicals, including *Chatelaine, Ecrits du Canada Francais, La Presse, Le Devoir, Revue de Droit Penal et de Criminologie,* and *Vie des Arts.*

SIDELIGHTS: Alice Parizeau was a Polish-born Canadian journalist and novelist who drew on the grim circumstances of her childhood in wartime Poland, her experiences as a student in Paris, and her life as an immigrant in Canada to produce a variety of travel books and novels examining themes of alienation and exile.

During the 1960s Parizeau wrote three novels that found inspiration in her own life. In *Fuir* (1963), a woman returns to Paris, where she had been a student ten years earlier. *Survivre* (1964) traces maneuvers of the underground in Poland during World War II, and the protagonist Yves—like Parizeau herself, who was held at Bergen-Belsen concentration camp—ends up a German prisoner. In the third work, *Rue Sherbrooke ouest* (1967), Yves moves to Canada. Also during this period, Parizeau completed the travel accounts *Voyage en Pologne* (1962) and *Une Quebecoise en Europe "rouge"* (1965).

During the 1970s Parizeau held the position of secretary general of the Centre International de Criminologie Comparee at the University of Montreal. While there she coauthored several studies, including *Protection de l'enfant, echec? Famille, etat de droits de l'enfance* (translated as *Parenting and Delinquent Youth,* 1980), an examination of the role of community intervention in preventing delinquency.

Following her term at the University of Montreal, Parizeau again turned to writing fiction, and her novel *Les Lilas fleurissent a Varsovie (The Lilacs Are Blooming in Warsaw)* was published in 1981. By far

Parizeau's most acclaimed work, *The Lilacs Are Blooming in Warsaw* won the prestigious Prix Europeen as the best French novel of the year written by a non-native speaker. Set in Poland, the novel portrays the lives of several survivors of the Second World War as they attempt to reconcile themselves to the conflict's aftermath. Wanda Urbanska, writing in the *Los Angeles Times Book Review,* called *The Lilacs Are Blooming in Warsaw* "lively," but noted that "despite a certain uplifting quality, the author's obvious love of Poland and its people undermines her purpose in building realistic fiction." A negative appraisal was registered by *Books in Canada* reviewer I. M. Owen, who complained that the novel is "mechanical, amateurish, lifeless, and written in a flat style." More favorable assessments included a review in *World Literature Today* by Armand B. Chartier, who found that by "[c]arefully orchestrating a multitude of vignettes, episodes, moments of crisis and scenes of daily life, the author has created many viable characters and has ably balanced the factual and the fictional." A reviewer in the *West Coast Review of Books* concluded that the novel "offers telling insights into one of the world's most tragic nations as seen through the eyes of its people."

Parizeau's later works include *La Charge des sangliers* (1982), which comprises a sequel to *The Lilacs Are Blooming in Warsaw,* the novel *Nata et le professeur* (1988), which combines Parisian and Polish settings to explore themes of alienation and exile, and *Une femme* (1991), the diary Parizeau maintained throughout her two year battle with terminal cancer.

BIOGRAPHICAL/CRITICAL SOURCES:

PERIODICALS

Books in Canada, November, 1985, pp. 24-25.

Los Angeles Times Book Review, September 22, 1985, p. 4.

Social Science Quarterly, June, 1982, p. 398.

West Coast Review of Books, November/December, 1985, p. 29.

World Literature Today, autumn, 1983, p. 601.*

* * *

PAXSON, Diana L(ucile) 1943-

PERSONAL: Born February 20, 1943, in Detroit, MI; daughter of Edwin W. Paxson and Mary (maiden name, Herrington) Paxson; married Donald C. Studebaker (Jon De Cles, a writer), 1968; children: Ian, Robin. *Ethnicity:* Anglo-German. *Education:* Mills College, B.A., 1964; University of California, Berkeley, M.A., 1968. *Politics:* Green. *Religion:* Pagan. *Avocational interests:* Costuming, folkharp, gardening.

ADDRESSES: Home—c/o Box 472, Berkley, CA 94701. *E-mail*—d.studebake1@Genie.com.

CAREER: Writer; community college English and Composition teacher and developer of educational materials, 1971-81; illustrator of books, including *Folk Tales from Persia,* A. S. Barnes, 1971, and *Folk Tales from Portugal,* A. S. Barnes, 1972, both by Alan S. Feinstein; ordained minister, Fellowship of the Spiral Path, 1982; chairman, president, board member, and instructor of 'Clergy in Training,' Center for Non-Traditional Religions (now The Fellowship of the Spiral Path), 1981-86, president, 1986-89; editor of the journal *Idunna,* 1996—; western regional director of the Board of Science Fiction Writers of America, 1990-96, served on grievance committee, 1992; elder, Covenant of the Goddess; elder, Ring of Troth, presents workshops on 'Oracular Seidh' (a Norse magic rite). Elected to High Rede (Board of Directors) Ring of Troth, 1995.

MEMBER: Aquarian Order of the Restoration, Dark Moon Circle, Equinox (founding member), Hrfnar (founding member), Covenant of the Goddess (first officer, 1987-89).

WRITINGS:

FANTASY NOVELS

Brisingamen, Berkeley (New York City), 1984.
White Mare, Red Stallion, Berkeley, 1986.
The Paradise Tree, Ace (New York City), 1987.
The White Raven, Morrow (New York City), 1988.
The Serpent's Tooth, Morrow, 1991.
The Wolf and the Raven, Morrow, 1993.
The Dragons of the Rhine, AvonNova, 1995.
The Lord of Horses, AvonNova, 1996.

"WESTRIA" SERIES; FANTASY NOVELS

Lady of Light, Pocket Books (New York City), 1982, published with *Lady of Darkness,* New English Library (London), 1990.
Lady of Darkness, Pocket Books, 1983, published with *Lady of Light,* New English Library, 1990.

Silverhair, the Wanderer, Tor/Tom Doherty Associates, 1986.
The Earthstone, Tor/Tom Doherty Associates, 1987.
The Sea Star, Tor/Tom Doherty Associates, 1988.
The Wind Crystal, Tor/Tom Doherty Associates, 1990.
The Mistress of the Jewels (includes *Lady of Light* and *Lady of Darkness*), Tor (New York City), 1991.

"FIONN MAC CUMHAIL" SERIES; FANTASY NOVELS; WITH ADRIENNE MARTINE-BARNES

Master of Earth and Water, AvonNova, 1993.
The Shield between the Worlds, AvonNova, 1994.
Sword of Fire and Shadow, AvonNova, 1995.

OTHER

Also contributor of columns on Goddesses to *Sagewoman* magazine and to *GreenMan;* author of fantasy short stories.

WORK IN PROGRESS: Hallowed Isle, (an Arthurian novel) and *Walking Into The Sunrise,* on the spirituality of menopause.

SIDELIGHTS: Diana L. Paxson is both a prominent Neo-Pagan figure in the San Francisco area and a prolific fantasy writer. She published her first fantasy novel, *Lady of Light,* in 1983. This volume, the first of six works known collectively as the "Westria" chronicles, concerns a royal leader, Westria's King Jehan, who endeavors to find himself a bride capable of using powerful jewels that magically maintain his kingdom's stability. In the second Westria volume, *Lady of Darkness,* King Jehan has died and his widow, Queen Faris, must contend with an ambitious sorcerer as she struggles to master the four jewels essential to the Westrians' wellbeing. *Lady of Light* and *Lady of Darkness,* which were published together as *The Mistress of Jewels,* were followed in the Westria series by *Silverhair, the Wanderer, The Earthstone, The Sea Star,* and *The Wind Crystal,* which record the efforts of their son, Julian, to reclaim the jewels and the kingdom.

Since completing the Westria series, Paxson has focused on historical fantasy. In the mid-1980s she produced two of the earliest contemporary urban fantasies: *Brisingamen,* the story of an academic who restores an ancient necklace that unleashes the power of the Norse Goddess Freyja, and is opposed by the Norse god Loki, who soon begins wreaking havoc at the University of California in Berkeley. Reviewing the novel in *West Coast Review of Books,* Neil K.

Citrin noted that Paxson "depicts her characters skillfully, tells an entertaining yarn, and handles the mythological materials well."

In 1986 came *The Paradise Tree,* featuring computers, drugs and kublalah. Paxson turned to the Celtic legend of Tristan and Iseult for *The White Raven,* which chronicles that couple's doomed love. Among Paxson's other novels from the 1990s are *The Serpent's Tooth,* a re-telling of the King Lear legend in which an aging king foolishly divides his domain between two conniving daughters while banishing his third daughter, the only one of the three who actually loves him.

In the early-1990s Paxson teamed with Adrienne Martine-Barnes to produce three volumes relating the escapades of Irish folk hero Fionn Mac Cumhal. This series is comprised of *Master of Earth and Water, The Shield between the Worlds,* and *Sword of Fire and Shadow.* These volumes were derived by Paxson and Martine-Barnes from actual Irish legends. At the same time she was writing the *Wodan's Children* trilogy, dealing with the Germanic Nibelungen legend. *The Wolf and the Raven,* a re-telling of Norse mythology's saga of Siegfried and Brunhilde (here called Siegfrid and Brunahild), two courageous figures who become lovers; *The Dragons of the Rhine,* which continues the tale of Siegfrid and Brunahild by recounting Siegfrid's unwitting betrayal of Brunahild and the destruction that ensues, and the conclusion, *The Lord of Horses,* in which Siegfrid's widow is married to Attilla the Hun and all the characters find both justice and redemption.

BIOGRAPHICAL/CRITICAL SOURCES:

PERIODICALS

Fantasy Review, March 1984, p. 34.
Los Angeles Times Book Review, February 17, 1988, p. 12.
Publishers Weekly, February 22, 1993, p. 82; July 24, 1995, p. 52; February 5, 1996, p. 80.
Voice of Youth Advocates, August 1983, p. 150; April 1985, p. 56; February 1992, p. 386.
West Coast Review of Books, May/June, 1985, p. 51.

*   *   *

PEATMAN, John Gray 1904-1997

OBITUARY NOTICE—See index for *CA* sketch: Born March 16, 1904, in Centerville, IA; died of cancer, March 9, 1997, in Norwalk, CT. Statistician, psychologist, educator, and author. Peatman was a pioneer in developing scientific methods for the study of broadcast audiences. In the 1940s he surveyed the responses of listeners to radio broadcasts and from this data developed a system that was later used to estimate audience share for both radio and television programs. Peatman was educated at Columbia University, completing a bachelor's degree in 1927, a master's degree in 1928, and a Ph.D. in 1931. He joined the faculty of the City College of New York in 1929 and served as dean of the psychology department from 1952 to 1963. He also held teaching posts at such institutions as Columbia University and St. Mark's Hospital in Manhattan during the nearly four decades until his retirement in 1970.

In addition, Peatman served as an educational consultant to the United States Air Force from 1949 to 1950 and presided over arbitration hearings for the American Society of Composers, Authors, and Publishers (ASCAP) during the mid-1950s. His writings include the textbooks *Descriptive and Sampling Statistics* (1947), *Geographical Sampling in Testing Appeals of Radio Broadcasts* (1950), and *Introduction to Applied Statistics* (1963).

OBITUARIES AND OTHER SOURCES:

BOOKS

Who's Who in the East, 24th edition, Marquis, 1992.

PERIODICALS

New York Times, March 31, 1997, p. B5.

*   *   *

PEERY, Janet 1948-

PERSONAL: Born July 18, 1948, in Wichita, KS; daughter of Walter A. and Joyce (Davis) Sawhill; married William Peery, January 23, 1976 (divorced, 1988); married Cy Bolton, November 5, 1994; children: (with Peery) Joanna, Gretchen, Bridget. *Education:* Wichita State University, B.A. (speech pathology and audiology), 1975, M.F.A. (fiction), 1992.

ADDRESSES: Agent—Leigh Feldman, Darhansoff and Verrill Literary Agency, 179 Franklin St., New York, NY 10013.

CAREER: Short story writer, novelist, and book reviewer. Worked as teacher of fiction at Sweet Briar College, Warren Wilson M.F.A. for Writers program, Cumberland Writers Conference, and Old Dominion University M.F.A. program.

AWARDS, HONORS: Writers at Work fellowship, 1990; National Endowment for the Arts fellowship, 1990; Goodheart Prize, Washington and Lee University, 1991 and 1992; story chosen for Pushcart Prize, 1991 and 1992; Seaton Award, *Kansas Quarterly,* 1992; Mrs. Giles Whiting Foundation Writers Award, 1993; Rosenthal Award, American Academy of Arts and Letters, 1993; work selected for *Best American Short Stories,* 1993, and cited for being among "100 Distinguished Stories," 1993 and 1994; National Book Award finalist, 1996, for *The River beyond the World.*

WRITINGS:

Alligator Dance (short stories), Southern Methodist University Press (Dallas), 1993.
The River beyond the World (novel), Picador (New York), 1996.

Contributor of short stories to periodicals, including *New Virginia Review, Shenandoah, Black Warrior Review, Chattahoochee Review, Kansas Quarterly, Southwest Review,* and *Quarterly West.* Contributor of book reviews to periodicals, including *Los Angeles Times* and *Washington Post Book World.*

The River Beyond the World has been translated into German.

WORK IN PROGRESS: The Daughters of the Mighty Nile, a novel set in Oklahoma in 1962.

SIDELIGHTS: At the beginning of her literary career, fiction writer Janet Peery had garnered the acclaim that many better-known authors have yet to attain. Her first collection of short stories, *Alligator Dance,* which was published simultaneously in hardback and paperback by Southern Methodist University Press in 1993, was extolled in the most enthusiastic terms by fiction writer Dorothy Allison in the *New York Times Book Review.* Allison noted Peery's penchant for having her characters muse introspectively about the large issues of their lives; she found this quality in the female narrators of the stories "Mountains, Road, the Tops of Trees" and "Job's Daughters." As Allison pointed out, Peery presents her characters—such as the racist young girl in "The Waco Wego"—at points

at which they suddenly glimpse the past and present trends of their lives and, sometimes, the possibility of future change. Peery's stories, set in the Southwest, "pull you in," said Allison, "startle you, stay with you long after you have finished the book; you are left feeling, as the author puts it, 'stunned before the complex living heart of grace.'" Calling Peery's work "the product of a thoroughly engaged intellect, one that listened to her insides, one that has the blessing of both insight and a sense of humor," Allison declared *Alligator Dance* to be "one of the best first collections I have ever read."

The collection was also praised highly by writer Jeanne Schinto in *Belles Lettres.* Schinto, calling the collection "excellent," praised Peery's gift for language: "Here is an author with not only a voice, but also an ear." Language itself, Schinto noted, plays a role in many of the collection's stories. Otherness, observed the critic, is also a recurring theme in Peery's work: the otherness of a disfigured boy in the title story, or of a confused Mexican domestic worker in the United States in "Nosotros."

The logical next step in Peery's literary career was a novel, and Allison, in her review of *Alligator Dance,* expressly looked forward to the one that Peery was then writing. The novel, *The River beyond the World,* was published in 1996 and became a finalist for a National Book Award. Focusing on the long-term relationship between two women—a Mexican housekeeper and her American employer—the novel is a meditation on the two cultures as well as a story driven by complex personalities.

As Louise Redd commented in the Austin *American-Statesman,* "The expertly woven plot is a delight, but the real strength of *The River beyond the World* is in its fully realized characters; they linger in the mind long after the book is finished." In the *Los Angeles Times,* Richard Eder stated that "Peery is charting the mutual distrust and mutual need of two nations and two national characters; yet in the main she does it with fictional grace through her stubbornly individual personages." Eder noted that, while *The River beyond the World* is not a "polemic," it "replies to the current anti-immigration fanfare. It is not the labor of immigrants that the United States needs but the humanizing dimensions of their culture." Remarking on Peery's switch to composing longer works of fiction, Redd observed that "*The River beyond the World* achieves both the tense compression of a short story and the expansive vision of a novel."

BIOGRAPHICAL/CRITICAL SOURCES:

PERIODICALS

American-Statesman (Austin), October 27, 1996, pp.
   E6-E7.
Belles Lettres, summer 1994, pp. 12-14.
Los Angeles Times, October 7, 1996.
New York Times Book Review, January 9, 1994, p. 9.

*   *   *

PETRY, Ann (Lane)   1908-1997

OBITUARY NOTICE—See index for *CA* sketch: Born October 12, 1908, in Old Saybrook, CT; died April 28, 1997, near Old Saybrook, CT. Pharmacist, journalist, educator, and author. Petry is best known for her work as a novelist, particularly for her 1946 work, *The Street,* which described life in Harlem. The daughter of a pharmacist, Petry grew up in the resort town of Old Saybrook, Connecticut, being among the few black families to live in the predominantly white town. She attended the University of Connecticut and received her degree in pharmacy and later attended Columbia University. From 1931 to 1938 she worked at James' Pharmacy. In 1938, after a move to New York City, she began writing and selling ads for the *Amsterdam News.* From 1941 to 1944, she served as a reporter and editor of the *People's Voice* women's page. In the mid-1970s she taught English at the University of Hawaii. She also worked with New York City's American Negro Theatre as a teacher and actress. Her novel *The Street* was written after she moved with her husband, George Petry, to Harlem. She penned the novel, which became a critical and popular success, while her husband was serving in the military during World War II. She wrote other novels, such as *The Narrows* and *Country Place.* She also penned stories and biographies for children and young adult readers, including *Harriet Tubman: Conductor on the Underground Railroad, The Drugstore Cat, The Common Ground,* and *Tituba of Salem Village.* Among the honors bestowed on her was a distinguished writer award in 1994.

OBITUARIES AND OTHER SOURCES:

BOOKS

Who's Who Among African Americans, Gale, 1996.

PERIODICALS

New York Times, April 30, 1997, p. B9.

*   *   *

PHILLIPS, Kate   1966-

PERSONAL: Born July 30, 1966, in Pomona, CA; daughter of Richard (a professor of chemical engineering) and Joan (a teacher's aide) Phillips. *Education:* Dartmouth College, B.A. (summa cum laude), 1988; Harvard University, M.A. (English), 1992, Ph.D. (history of American civilization), 1997.

ADDRESSES: Agent—Ann Borchardt, Georges Borchardt Literary Agency, 136 East 57th St., New York, NY 10022.

CAREER: Writer. Beijing Normal University, Beijing, China, teacher, 1988-89; Irish Immigration Center, Boston, grant writer and newsletter editor, 1992-95.

WRITINGS:

White Rabbit, Houghton Mifflin (Boston), 1996.

White Rabbit has been translated into German.

WORK IN PROGRESS: A novel, tentatively titled *The Shadow Life;* a nonfiction study of Helen Hunt Jackson's literary career.

SIDELIGHTS: Unlike many other young writers, Kate Phillips created a character decades older than herself in her highly praised debut novel, *White Rabbit.* Begun after a period of traveling and teaching in China—Phillips was an English teacher at Beijing Normal University at the time of the tragic 1989 Tiananmen Square crack-down—*White Rabbit* is viewed by its Southern California-born author as part of a literary tradition composed of works by such writers as Joan Didion, Nathanael West, and John Steinbeck that, as Phillips noted, "explore the underside of the California dream." Remarking that Phillips "saddles herself with an unpromising conceit," *Philadelphia Inquirer* critic Mark Robinson praised her first novel's stylistic abilities, commenting of *White Rabbit,* "It's funny, touching, and represents a confident leap for a young, first-time novelist."

Beginning at 5:25 in the morning, the story follows eighty-eight-year-old Ruth Caster Armstrong Hubble through her daily routines on what turns out to be the last day of her life. Because it is the first day of the month, she has visions of a snow-colored rabbit, conjured up by the game she plays with family and friends; they call each other up and the first one to say "White Rabbit" will be blessed with good luck for the rest of the month, while the losers need to watch their step. Throughout the day, this ritual seems to call up many memories for Ruth of events and people that played an important role in her life. At the same time, she sticks to the rigid daily activities that her stubborn demeanor dictates. When the day is over, Ruth crawls onto her bed as usual, her imminent death having provided some special wisdom to her.

"Phillips' captivating first novel is a poignant slice of Ruth's daily habits," described Joseph Olshan in *Entertainment Weekly*. Richard Eder, writing in the *Los Angeles Times Book Review*, also focused on the way Phillips portrays the character of Ruth: "The vitality, shrewdness and even a touch of nobility (along with the cantankerousness and fog patches) of Ruth in her old age are rendered subtly and sometimes thrillingly. Something has burnt away the foliage, leaving branches that are bare though gnarled with crotchets. Phillips has too much class to pronounce whether this is life triumphing or death approaching; there is no demarcation."

Pointing out to readers that Phillips is at the beginning of her own life, a *Publishers Weekly* contributor concluded that "deftly balancing humor with difficult questions . . . Phillips . . . has managed to write a perceptive and sophisticated novel about a woman at the end of hers."

BIOGRAPHICAL/CRITICAL SOURCES:

PERIODICALS

Chicago Tribune, February 15, 1996, p. 3.
Entertainment Weekly, February 16, 1996, pp. 56-57.
Los Angeles Times (Orange County edition), March 1, 1996, pp. E1-2.
Los Angeles Times Book Review, January 21, 1996, p. 3.
New York Times, January 25, 1996, p. C19.
Philadelphia Inquirer, January 14, 1996, p. H2.
Publishers Weekly, October 16, 1995, p. 42.
Washington Post, January 10, 1996, p. D2.

PICCARD, Auguste 1884-1962

PERSONAL: Born on January 28, 1884, in Basel, Switzerland; died March 25, 1962, in Lausanne, Switzerland; son of Jules (chair of the chemistry department at the University of Basel) and Helene (Haltenhoff) Piccard; children: Jacques. *Education:* Federal Institute of Technology in Zurich, Switzerland, B.S., Ph.D., 1907.

CAREER: Physicist. Professor, University of Basel, Switzerland, 1907-20; professor of physics, Brussels Polytechnic Institute, Brussels, Belgium, 1920-54. *Military Service:* Swiss Army Ballonists, 1913-15.

AWARDS, HONORS: Gold Medal of the Belgian Aero Club.

WRITINGS:

Audessus des nuages, B. Grasset (Paris), 1933.
Entre terre et ciel, Editions d'Ouchy (Lausanne), 1946, translation by Claude Apcher published as *Between Earth and Sky,* Falcon Press, 1950.
Au fond des mers en bathyscaphe, Arthaud (Paris), 1954, translation by Christina Stead published as *In Balloon and Bathyscaphe,* Cassell, 1956, and as *Earth, Sky, and Sea,* Oxford University Press, 1956.

SIDELIGHTS: Auguste Piccard earned his fame by exploring higher into the Earth's atmosphere and deeper into its oceans than any person had before him. He and his twin brother both earned doctorates in engineering, became professors, and collaborated in a variety of research projects. In 1931, Piccard and a colleague traveled in a balloon to an altitude of about ten miles, more than three miles higher than any human had ever gone before. Shortly after this feat, Piccard became interested in the exploration of the ocean depths and designed a new vehicle—the bathyscaphe—by which they could be explored.

Piccard and his twin brother Jean Felix were born in Basel, Switzerland, on January 28, 1884. The Piccard family had a long and notable history in the area. Auguste and Jean Felix's grandfather had been chief commissioner of the region in which the family lived, and their uncle owned the Piccard-Pictet Company in Geneva, manufacturers of hydroelectric turbines. The twins' mother was Helene Haltenhoff Piccard, and their father Jules Piccard was the chair of the department of chemistry at the University of Basel.

After graduation from the local high school, the twins entered the Federal Institute of Technology in Zurich where Auguste majored in mechanical engineering and Jean Felix majored in chemical engineering. They both received their bachelor of science degrees and then went on to complete doctorates in their respective fields. Between 1907 and 1920, Auguste taught in Zurich. He then accepted an appointment as professor of physics at the Brussels Polytechnic Institute, a post he held until his retirement in 1954.

One of Piccard's earliest interests was the Earth's upper atmosphere and the cosmic rays to be detected there. He was not alone, of course, in this interest. As early as 1783, scientists had been using lighter-than-air balloons to carry themselves and their instruments into the atmosphere to study its properties. In 1804, for example, the French physicist Joseph Louis Gay-Lussac had ridden a balloon 23,000 feet into the atmosphere where he collected samples of air for later analysis. Auguste and Jean Felix made their own first balloon ascension from Zurich in 1913, after which, in 1915, they both joined the balloon section of the Swiss army for a period of service.

The use of balloons to study the atmosphere involved an inherent risk and limitation, however. At a certain altitude, the air becomes so thin that humans can no longer function. In 1862, the English meteorologist James Glashier lost consciousness as his balloon reached an altitude of 29,000 feet. He survived only because his companion was able to maneuver the balloon back to earth. Such occurrences made it clear that open-air balloons could be used only below certain altitudes.

One solution to this limitation was developed by the French meteorologist Leon Philippe Teisserenc de Bort. Teisserenc de Bort decided that unmanned balloons carrying instruments could more safely record the data that humans had been collecting previously. Between 1899 and 1902, he launched dozens of automated balloons that brought back information about the atmosphere. One discovery he made was the existence of layers in the atmosphere, the first evidence for the presence of the stratosphere. Piccard's view was that unmanned ascents could never provide the quality of data that could be obtained from balloons in which humans could travel. He resolved, therefore, to design a pressurized gondola in which observers could travel well beyond the 29,000 foot level that had marked the previous barrier to manned flight.

By 1930, his first design was ready for testing. The gondola was made of an air-tight aluminum shell that could be pressurized to sea-level pressures and was then suspended from a hydrogen-filled balloon. On May 27, 1931, Piccard and a colleague, Paul Kipfer, took off in their airship from Augsburg, Germany. They eventually reached an altitude of 51,775 feet, by far the highest altitude so far attained by human researchers. About fifteen months later, on August 18, 1932, Piccard made another record-breaking ascent, this time to a height of 53,139 feet after departing from Zurich. His companion on this flight was Max Cosyns.

Piccard made more than two dozen more balloon ascensions before he retired from the activity in 1937. During that time, he collected valuable new information on atmospheric electricity and radioactivity, as well as cosmic radiation. Probably more important, he continued to improve on the design of his aircraft, making the kinds of improvements that would eventually allow other scientists to reach altitudes of more than 100,000 feet. In recognition of his many accomplishments in balloon flight, Piccard was awarded the Gold Medal of the Belgian Aero Club.

In the late 1930s, Piccard shifted his attention to a new challenge: the ocean depths. He became convinced that the same techniques used to study the thin upper atmosphere could be used in the high-pressure depths of the oceans. He began work on the design of a *bathyscaphe,* or "ship of the deep." The bathyscaphe consisted of two parts. The lower portion of the vessel was an air-tight steel sphere, built to withstand pressures of 12,000 pounds per square inch, where researchers rode. The upper part of the bathyscaphe consisted of a 5,200 cubic foot metal tank containing heptane that provided the vessel with buoyancy. The bathyscaphe operated under its own power and could rise or sink by having seawater pumped into the flotation chamber or iron pellets dumped from the same chamber.

The first test of the bathyscaphe took place in 1948, but the vessel was able to dive no deeper than about a mile below sea level, far less than Piccard had hoped. He continued to modify the design of his vessel, however, and a second test five years later was more successful. In 1953, he and his son Jacques traveled to a depth of 10,335 feet off the coast of Capri, a depth three times as great as the previous record set by William Beebe in his bathysphere in 1934. The Piccards also built another bathyscaphe, the *Trieste,* which was sold to the U.S. Navy for research use. The *Trieste* was used in a 1960 expedition that took Jacques Piccard and U.S. Navy lieutenant Don Walsh to a depth of 35,802 feet in the Mariana Trench off the coast of Guam. Piccard and his son Jacques were working on yet another modification of the bathyscaphe design—to be called a mesoscaphe—when Piccard died on March 25, 1962, in Lausanne, Switzerland.

BIOGRAPHICAL/CRITICAL SOURCES:

BOOKS

Field, Adelaide, *Auguste Piccard, Captain of Space, Admiral of the Abyss,* Houghton Mifflin, 1969.
Honour, Alan, *Ten Miles High, Two Miles Deep: The Adventures of the Piccards,* Whitlesey House, 1957.
Malkus, Alida, *Exploring the Sky and Sea: Auguste and Jacques Piccard,* Kingston, 1961.*

*   *   *

PLAUT, Joshua Eli 1957-

PERSONAL: Born April 4, 1957, in New York, NY; son of Walter H. (a rabbi) and Hadassah (a teacher; maiden name, Yaweh) Plaut; married Lori Epstein (a lawyer), April 7, 1995. *Education:* Beloit College, B.A., 1979; attended Hebrew University of Jerusalem, 1981; University of California, Los Angeles, M.A., 1982; Hebrew Union College-Jewish Institute of Religion, Cincinnati, OH, rabbinic ordination and M.H.L., 1986; attended Oxford Centre for Postgraduate Hebrew Studies, Oxford, England, 1989; doctoral study at New York University. *Religion:* Jewish.

ADDRESSES: Home—P.O. Box 692, Vineyard Haven, MA 02568. *E-mail*—rjplaut@mit.edu.

CAREER: Jerusalem Center for Public Policy, Jerusalem, Israel, archivist, 1977; U.S. Department of State, Washington, DC, analyst of investment aid, 1978; rabbinic intern, Selma, AL, 1983-84, Sydney, Australia, 1984, and Jonesboro, AR, 1984-86; Congregation Kol Haverim, Rabbi, Glastonbury, CT, 1986-93; Martha's Vineyard Hebrew Center, Vineyard Haven, MA, rabbi, 1993—. Trinity College, Hartford, CT, B'nai B'rith Hillel director, 1986-93; Massachusetts Institute of Technology, Hillel Jewish chaplain, 1993—. U.S. Holocaust Memorial Museum, visiting lecturer; creator of photographic documentaries and exhibitions on Jewish life in various countries and culture.

AWARDS, HONORS: Grants from Lucius N. Littauer Foundation, American Jewish Archives, Joseph Myerhoff Fund, Skirball Foundation, Scheuer Foundation, Baron de Hirsch Fund, Memorial Foundation for Jewish Culture, Union of American Hebrew Congregations, and National Federation of Temple Sisterhoods.

WRITINGS:

Greek Jewry in the Twentieth Century, 1913-1983: Patterns of Jewish Survival in the Greek Provinces before and after the Holocaust, Fairleigh Dickinson University Press (Madison, NJ), 1996.

BIOGRAPHICAL/CRITICAL SOURCES:

PERIODICALS

Bulletin of Judaeo-Greek Studies, winter, 1996, pp. 27-29.
Erensia Sefardi, summer, 1996, pp. 10-11.

*   *   *

POLLACK, Rachel (Grace) 1945-

PERSONAL: Born in 1945.

ADDRESSES: Agent—c/o HarperCollins Publishers, 8 Grafton St., London W1X 3LA, England.

CAREER: Writer.

AWARDS, HONORS: Arthur C. Clarke Award for best British science fiction novel, 1988, for *Unquenchable Fire;* Nebula Award finalist, 1995, for *Temporary Agency.*

WRITINGS:

NOVELS

Golden Vanity, Berkley (New York City), 1980.
Alqua Dreams, F. Watts (New York City), 1987.
Unquenchable Fire, Century (London), 1988, Overlook (Woodstock, NY), 1992.
Temporary Agency, St. Martin's Press (New York City), 1994.
Godmother Night, St. Martin's Press (New York City), 1996.

NONFICTION

Seventy-Eight Degrees of Wisdom: A Book of Tarot (two volumes), Aquarian Press (Wellingborough, Northamptonshire, England), 1980-83, Borgo Press (San Bernardino, CA), 1986.

Salvador Dali's Tarot, Salem House (Salem, NH), 1985.

A Practical Guide to Fortune Telling: Palmistry, The Crystal Ball, Runes, Tea Leaves, The Tarot, Sphere/Rainbird (London), 1986, published as *Teach Yourself Fortune Telling,* Holt (New York City), 1986.

Tarot: The Open Labyrinth, Aquarian Press, 1986, Borgo Press, 1989.

The New Tarot, Aquarian Press, 1989, Overlook Press, 1990.

Tarot Readings and Meditations, Aquarian Press, 1990.

(With Cheryl Schwartz) *The Journey Out: A Guide for and about Lesbian, Gay, and Bisexual Teens,* Viking (New York City), 1995.

EDITOR

(With Caitlin Matthews) *Tarot Tales,* Legend (London), 1989.

(With Mary K. Greer) *New Thoughts on Tarot: Transcripts from the First International Newcastle Tarot Symposium,* Newcastle Publishing (North Hollywood, CA), 1989.

OTHER

Author of short stories, including "Angel Baby," "The Protector," and "The Malignant One."

SIDELIGHTS: Rachel Pollack has used her interest in the occult to establish literary careers both as a Tarot expert and as a science fiction novelist, while also taking time to co-author a practical guide for teenagers dealing with questions of sexual identity. Pollack's first novel, *Golden Vanity,* was published in 1980, but it attracted little attention—David V. Barrett, in *Twentieth-Century Science-Fiction Writers,* called it "neglected." It would be another seven years before Pollack published her second entry in the genre, *Alqua Dreams.*

Golden Vanity, according to Barrett, is a traditional science-fiction yarn with New Age overtones: while describing first contact between earthlings and aliens, it also delves into the terrain of meditation and religious self-deception. Pollack's *Alqua Dreams* also

establishes a traditional science-fiction premise, in this case an interstellar trader's attempt to establish trading links with a new planet in order to obtain an intelligent mineral used in spaceship drives. However, Pollack's second novel's ambitious underlying philosophical theme is, in Barrett's words, "the age-old debate between Platonic and Aristotelian life-views." *Analog* magazine reviewer Tom Easton termed this "a complex, difficult subtext of epistemological puzzling." In the framework of the plot, the space trader, Jaimi Cooper, visits Keela, a world whose inhabitants believe they are dead and that nothing is real—and who therefore believe that Cooper's desire to trade with them is also unreal. In order to trade successfully, Cooper must convince them to abandon their beliefs. A *Publishers Weekly* critic enjoyed the novel's premise but felt that it might have been explored more effectively as a short story. Barrett appreciated the "encyclopedic knowledge of religion and myth" which author Pollack brings to *Alqua Dreams,* and considered the book, although not entirely successful, a worthy and intriguing study of its philosophical subject. Indeed, not since Philip Jose Farmer's *Night of Light,* a generation earlier, had Barrett found a more "disturbing and believable" exposition of an alien religion in a science fiction work.

Pollack's next novel, *Unquenchable Fire,* brought her the highest critical acclaim of any of her fiction to that point. Even so, the novel took several years to find a U.S. publisher, even after winning the Arthur C. Clarke Award for best British science fiction novel of 1988. Reviewer Gregory Feeley, in the *Washington Post Book World,* speculated that the delay in acceptance by U.S. bookmakers resulted from Pollack's use of eclectic forms of magic as the basis for the book's fantasy, rather than the fairy tales and European folklore that underlie most novels in this genre. Aspects of the plot are familiar to fantasy and science fiction readers, however, as *Publishers Weekly* pointed out, for the book describes a future United States (Dutchess County, New York, to be specific) in which the laws of the universe have changed and magic reigns. The twist is that the original sense of wonder has fallen away, and magic now seems routine.

The main character of *Unquenchable Fire,* Jennifer Mazdan, finds herself pregnant with a child who, according to magical signs, may reawaken the lost sense of wonder at magic powers. This main plot is interwoven with tales of other aspects of life in the magical United States of America. Feeley found the novel's interpolations difficult and didactic, but thought the main story "witty, absorbing and frequently funny." John Clute, reviewing the novel for the *Observer,* went further and called it "dense, supple, and hilarious, by far her finest novel to date," and *Publishers Weekly* dubbed Pollack's third novel "compelling, surrealistic fantasy." Encyclopedist Barrett shared this critical consensus, but departed from Feeley by esteeming the interpolated tales more highly. "It's by no means an easy book," Barrett wrote, "but it is a very powerful and stimulating examination of the spiritual life"—one written with a depth, Barrett surmised, that might prevent its author from becoming widely popular.

Pollack's next novel, 1994's *Temporary Agency,* is actually two linked novellas, and acts as something of a sequel to *Unquenchable Fire* in that it assumes a knowledge of the magical beings who ran human affairs in the earlier book. In the title novella, the main characters, becoming involved with a being called a Malignant One, discover, according to *Publishers Weekly,* "what people will do in the name of pragmatism." In the second piece, "Benign Adjustments," two of the same characters, Ellen and Alison, find out "how the most benign intentions can be adulterated by human frailties." The settings of the novellas include a Manhattan advertising agency, Westchester, and the floor of the New York Stock Exchange—a place where, in Pollack's alternate world, traders obtain assistance from magical robes and dolls.

Publishers Weekly called *Temporary Agency* "a first-rate work" and commended it for combining rational speculation with an awareness that "the key to good fiction is people and what happens to them." *Library Journal* hailed the book as a "brilliant extrapolation of a spiritually awakened society" that "bears witness to her [Pollack's] potent literary imagination." Science fiction novelist Maureen F. McHugh, assessing *Temporary Agency* for the *Washington Post Book World,* praised the novel for being unsentimental and "full of ambiguity and loss." Pollack, McHugh concluded, "has written a fantasy book for grown-ups." *Temporary Agency* was rewarded with finalist status in that year's Nebula Award competition.

Pollack's next novel, *Godmother Night,* explored a different fantasy world, one that exists on the back of a giant turtle as if in fulfillment of an ancient myth. The main characters in this 1996 work are two young women, Laurie and Jaqe, who are lovers. Meeting Mother Night, who is really Death, enable the couple to overcome social obstacles in their path, but at the price of the early death of one of the women soon after a child has been born to them. Mother Night then becomes a godmother figure to the child, easing its passage through life. *Publishers Weekly* noted the "resourceful and original" quality of this plot, and called the novel "another fine outing by one of the most gifted and sensitive fantasists working today."

Pollack's simultaneous careers as an occultist and nonfiction writer have also won her acclaim. She has written a text for a Tarot deck illustrated by surrealist painter Salvador Dali, and has authored *The New Tarot,* which in "delightful and richly illustrated" fashion, according to Barrett, examines more than seventy commercial Tarot decks of the past generation. In 1986, Pollack published *A Practical Guide to Fortune Telling: Palmistry, the Crystal Ball, Runes, Tea Leaves, the Tarot,* which was issued in the United States as *Teach Yourself Fortune Telling.*

Reviewing the work for the *Voice Literary Supplement,* Stacey D'Erasmo began by stating: "I've been waiting for this book my whole life." Pollack's wide-ranging introduction to divination deals with palmistry, tea-leaf reading, Tarot, and other methods of foretelling the future from the standpoint of character analysis rather than fortune telling in the strict sense. The author's thesis is that hidden patterns underlie the seemingly random events that occur in individuals' lives; examining the apparent randomness, whether in a shuffled deck of cards or in the arrangement of leaves or in other phenomena, will unveil these patterns. D'Erasmo called Pollack "a gentle and learned guide" and singled out the Tarot section, the book's longest, for praise, saying, "amidst the flood of Tarot decks and guides now on the market, Pollack's is remarkably clear and free of gooeyness."

The same qualities of clarity, informativeness, and lack of sentimentality that characterize Pollack's other work are found in a book of hers on a very different topic, 1995's *The Journey Out: A Guide for and about Lesbian, Gay, and Bisexual Teens,* written with Cheryl Schwartz. The authors combine advice, which *Publishers Weekly* called "frank, reassuring" and "authoritative," with quotes from gay or bisexual teens, "extensive" informational listings, and forthright, helpful discussion of sexually transmitted diseases. *School Library Journal* reviewer Claudia Morrow called the book a "gentle, informative, well-written guide. . . . An antidote to isolation for despairing kids," and a "hopeful, kind book" that encourages self-acceptance, understanding, and love.

BIOGRAPHICAL/CRITICAL SOURCES:

BOOKS

Watson, Noelle, and Paul E. Schellinger, editors, *Twentieth-Century Science-Fiction Writers,* third edition, St. James Press, 1991, pp. 631-32.

PERIODICALS

Analog, September 1988, pp. 181-82.
Library Journal, August 1994, p. 139.
Observer, December 18, 1988, p. 43.
Publishers Weekly, October 2, 1987, p. 87; March 23, 1992, p. 64; July 25, 1994, p. 38; November 27, 1995, p. 70; August 26, 1996, p. 78.
School Library Journal, January 1996, p. 136.
Voice Literary Supplement, July/August 1993, p. 20.
Washington Post Book World, April 26, 1992, p. 6; September 25, 1994, p. 14.*

* * *

POPE, Dudley (Bernard Egerton) 1925-1997

OBITUARY NOTICE—See index for *CA* sketch: Born December 29, 1925, in Ashford, Kent, England; died April 25, 1997, in Marigot, St. Martin, French West Indies. Naval historian and author. Pope gained wide acclaim as the prolific author of the "Ramage" saga, a series of novels chronicling the life and exploits of Lt. Nicholas Ramage, a ship's commander in the British Navy during parts of the 1700s and 1800s. Pope enlisted in the British Merchant Navy in 1941 at the age of sixteen. He was wounded in 1942 and released in 1943. In 1944, he accepted a post with London's *Evening News* as a naval correspondent, a position he held until 1959. From that time on, Pope devoted himself to writing works, including *Graf Spee: The Life and Death of a Raider, Life in Nelson's Navy,* and *The Devil Himself.*

Pope also spent much of his time writing novels about life on the high seas. He received an honorable mention from the Mark Twain Society in 1976. Along with the eighteen-tome Ramage series, Pope also wrote many other books, including a series on the seagoing Yorke family. Among his works are *Galleon, Ramage at Trafalgar, Ramage and the Freebooters, Corsair, Ramage's Devil,* and *Ramage and the Saracens.*

OBITUARIES AND OTHER SOURCES:

BOOKS

Who's Who, 149th edition, St. Martin's, 1997.

PERIODICALS

New York Times, May 5, 1997, p. B11.

* * *

POWELL, Cecil Frank 1903-1969

PERSONAL: Born November 5, 1903, in Tonbridge, Kent, England; died August 9, 1969, at Bellano, Lake Como, Italy; son of Frank (a gunsmith) and Elizabeth Caroline (Bisacre) Powell; married Isobel Therese Artner, 1932; children: two daughters. *Education:* Sidney Sussex College, Cambridge University, degree in physics, 1925, Ph.D., 1927.

CAREER: Physicist. University of Bristol, England, research assistant, then lecturer, then reader, 1927-48, Melville Wills professor of physics, 1948-63, Henry Overton Wills professor of physics, 1964-69, vice-chancellor, 1964-69, H. H. Wills Physics Laboratory, director, 1964-69. British Atomic Energy Project, member, c. 1940-45; Association of Scientific Workers, president, 1952-54; World Federation of Scientific Workers, president, 1956-69; European Center for Nuclear Research (CERN), organizer, 1961, Science Policy Committee, chair, 1961-63; Pugwash Movement for Science and World Affairs, founding member.

AWARDS, HONORS: Hughes medal, 1949; Nobel Prize in physics, 1950; Royal medal, Royal Society, 1961; Rutherford medal and prize, 1961; Lomonosov gold medal, Soviet Academy of Sciences, 1967; Guthrie prize and medal, Institute of Physics and Physical Society, 1969.

WRITINGS:

(With G. P. S. Occhialini) *Nuclear Physics in Photographs,* Oxford University Press, 1947.
(With others) *The Preparation of High-Purity Boron,* Rand Corporation (Santa Monica, CA), 1950.
(With P. H. Fowler and D. H. Perkins) *The Study of Elementary Particles by the Photographic Method,* Pergamon, 1959.

Selected Papers of Cecil Frank Powell, edited by E. H. S. Burhop, W. O. Lock, and M. G. K. Menon, North-Holland Publishing (Amsterdam, Netherlands), 1972.

SIDELIGHTS: Cecil Frank Powell's research into cloud chambers and the detection of subatomic particles led to his development of photographic emulsion systems to detect and identify fast-moving particles, especially those found in cosmic rays. This enabled him to discover the pi-meson, a particle formed from nuclear reactions within cosmic rays. Powell was awarded the 1950 Nobel Prize in physics for his work in this area. He also was a member of the British Atomic Energy Project during World War II, though in his later years he became an advocate for nuclear disarmament.

Powell was born on November 5, 1903, at Tonbridge, Kent, England. His father, Frank Powell, was a gunsmith, and his mother, Elizabeth Caroline Bisacre, came from a family of skilled technicians. Powell developed an interest in science at an early age after becoming captivated by a chemistry book he saw in a store. Inspired by the book to conduct his own chemistry experiments, he eventually convinced his family to let him purchase the makings of a home chemistry set.

In 1914 Powell won a scholarship to the Judd School in Tonbridge. Upon graduation from Judd, he earned two more scholarships that allowed him to attend Sidney Sussex College at Cambridge University. He graduated in 1925 with a degree in physics but turned down a teaching job to continue his graduate work at Cambridge.

At the time Ernest Rutherford, the Nobel-Prize winning physicist who had determined the structure of the atom, was the director of the Cavendish Laboratories at Cambridge. It was under C. T. R. Wilson, the inventor of the cloud chamber, that Powell conducted his doctoral research, a study of condensation phenomena in cloud chambers, for which he was awarded his Ph.D. in 1927. Cloud chambers are devices that reveal ionized particles by producing a trail of water droplets from air saturated with water. Powell accepted an appointment as research assistant to A. M. Tyndall at Bristol College. In succession he became lecturer in physics, a reader in physics, the Melville Wills Professor of Physics (1948), the Henry Overton Wills Professor of Physics and director of the H. H. Wills Physics Laboratory (1964), and vice chancellor of the University at Bristol (1964).

Powell's initial work at Bristol involved the study of ion mobility in gases—the way electrically charged atoms behave in gases. By 1938, however, Powell became interested in particle detection devices. That interest, which first developed while he was studying cloud chambers, was rekindled when he learned that photographic emulsions could be used to detect particles in the atmosphere. For a number of years, Wilson's cloud chamber had been the instrument of choice for detecting subatomic particles, such as those produced in radioactive reactions and cosmic rays. However, the cloud chamber possessed one serious disadvantage—it required a brief resting phase each time it was used. In contrast, photographic emulsions were ready at all times to record events.

Like other scientists, Powell had been aware of the potential of photographic emulsions for this purpose, but no one had yet used them successfully. The main problem was that emulsions were not sensitive enough to be used for detection purposes, so Powell decided to find a way to overcome this limitation. His first year of research proved disappointing. He found that neither the emulsions nor the microscopes available were of sufficient quality to obtain the results he wanted. His research was interrupted by World War II, and he became involved with the British Atomic Energy Project for its duration. After the war, he again tackled the technical challenges of using photographic emulsions for detection purposes, this time with much greater success.

In 1946 at Powell's request, Ilford Ltd., a photographic company, developed a new emulsion that could more clearly record particle tracks. Powell and his colleagues used this new detection system to study cosmic radiation at altitudes of up to nine thousand feet. These studies resulted in the discovery of a new particle, the pion (or pi-meson), that had been predicted by the Japanese physicist Hideki Yukawa in 1935. The pion proved to be a cohesive force within the atomic nucleus, as was the K-meson, another particle discovered by Powell shortly thereafter. It was partly for these discoveries that Powell was awarded the 1950 Nobel Prize in physics. Over the next decade Powell continued his studies of cosmic radiation. As balloon technology improved, he launched his detectors higher into the atmosphere, in some cases reaching and maintaining altitudes of ninety thousand feet for many hours. A key element in the success of this research program was the collaborative effort among scientists, technicians, and laypersons throughout Europe who collected and monitored his equipment. That experience proved to be especially helpful in the early 1960s, when Powell became involved in organizing the European Center for Nuclear Research (CERN) in Geneva, Switzerland. Powell served as chairman of CERN's Science Policy Committee from 1961 to 1963.

During the 1950s Powell became increasingly concerned about social problems related to scientific and technological development. He served as president of the Association of Scientific Workers from 1952 to 1954, and as president of the World Federation of Scientific Workers from 1956 until his death. A founding member of the Pugwash Movement for Science and World Affairs, he lent his signature to Bertrand Russell's 1955 petition calling for nuclear disarmament.

Powell was married in 1932 to Isobel Therese Artner, with whom he had two daughters. He died on August 9, 1969, at Bellano, Lake Como, Italy, while on vacation to celebrate his retirement from Bristol a few months earlier. Powell's awards in addition to the Nobel Prize included the Hughes Medal in 1949 and the Royal Medal of the Royal Society in 1961, the Rutherford Medal and Prize in 1961, the Lomonosov Gold Medal of the Soviet Academy of Sciences in 1967, and the Guthrie Prize and Medal of the Institute of Physics and Physical Society in 1969.

BIOGRAPHICAL/CRITICAL SOURCES:

BOOKS

Biographical Memoirs of Fellows of the Royal Society, Volume 17, Royal Society (London), 1971, pp. 541-63.
McGraw-Hill Modern Scientists and Engineers, Volume 2, McGraw-Hill, 1980, pp. 436-37.*

*   *   *

PRITCHARD, Allan (Duncan) 1928-

PERSONAL: Born August 8, 1928, in Comox, British Columbia, Canada. *Education:* University of British Columbia, B.A., 1951; University of Toronto, Ph.D., 1958.

ADDRESSES: Home—609-1159 Beach Dr., Victoria, British Columbia, Canada V8S 2N2.

CAREER: University of British Columbia, Vancouver, lecturer in English, 1955-58; University of Toronto, Toronto, Ontario, began as lecturer, became professor of English, 1958-91, professor emeritus, 1991—.

WRITINGS:

(Editor) Abraham Cowley, *The Civil War,* University of Toronto Press (Toronto, Ontario), 1973.
(Coeditor) *The Collected Works of Abraham Cowley,* Volume I, University of Delaware Press (Newark, DE), 1989.
(Editor) *Vancouver Island Letters of Edmund Hope Verney, 1862-65,* University of British Columbia Press (Vancouver, British Columbia), 1996.

Contributor to literature journals in England, Canada, and the United States.

*   *   *

PRITCHETT, V(ictor) S(awdon) 1900-1997

OBITUARY NOTICE—See index for *CA* sketch: Born December 16, 1900, in Ipswich, England; died from complications following a stroke, March 20, 1997, in London, England. Short story writer, literary critic, novelist, essayist, biographer, and journalist. One of England's foremost contemporary literary figures, Pritchett is ranked among the modern masters of the short story and the world's most respected literary critics. His short stories—published throughout the nearly six decades of his literary career—have won praise for a style that relies on economy of language while revealing astute powers of observation and comic discernment. As a literary critic Pritchett wrote in the conversational tone of the familiar essay, approaching literature from the viewpoint of a lettered but not overly scholarly reader. Largely self-educated, Pritchett left school at the age of fifteen and worked in the leather trade before traveling to France, Ireland, Spain, Morocco, and the United States. He began a journalistic career as a freelance contributor to the *Christian Science Monitor* and other publications, and his travels abroad provided material for his first books, including 1928's nonfiction work *Marching Spain* and the 1930 short story collection *The Spanish Virgin, and Other Stories.* Returning to England, Pritchett began contributing to the *New Statesman* in 1926 and was the author of the weekly review column "Books in General" for many years. He advanced to the position of director of *New Statesman* in 1951. In addition to collections of his literary essays, Pritchett's books include critical biographies of the Russian writers Anton Chekhov and Ivan Turgenev and the French novelist Honore de Balzac. He won both the Royal Society of Literature Award and the Heinemann Award for *A Cab at the Door: A Memoir* (1968), an account of his unorthodox upbringing, which included numerous moves as a result of his father's failed businesses. Pritchett remained active as a writer well into his eighties. He edited the *Oxford Book of Short Stories* in 1981 and published his highly-regarded biography of Chekhov in 1988. Pritchett, who was made Commander of the British Empire in 1968, was knighted for his services to literature in 1975 and won designation as a Companion of Honor in 1993. His last published works include the collections *The Complete Short Stories* (1990), *Lasting Impressions* (1990), and *The Complete Essays* (1991).

OBITUARIES AND OTHER SOURCES:

BOOKS

Who's Who, 148th edition, St. Martin's, 1996.

PERIODICALS

Los Angeles Times, March 23, 1997, p. B3.
New York Times, March 22, 1997, p. 14.
Washington Post, March 22, 1997, p. C4.

*   *   *

PROKHOROV, Aleksandr Mikhailovich 1916-

PERSONAL: Born June 28, 1916, in Atherton, Australia; raised in Russia; son of Mikhail Ivanovich and Mariya Ivanovna Prokhorov; married Galina Alekseyevna Shelepina, 1941; children: Kiril. *Education:* graduated from Leningrad State University, 1939; Soviet Academy of Sciences, Moscow, Ph.D. (physical and mathematical sciences), 1951.

ADDRESSES: Office—Russian Academy of Sciences, Department of Physics, Ulitsa Vavilova 38, 117942 Moscow, Russia.

CAREER: Physicist. Oscillation Laboratory, Lebedev Institute of Physics, Russian Academy of Sciences, Moscow, U.S.S.R., assistant director, 1946-72, deputy director, 1972-83, director, 1983—; Moscow State University, Moscow, U.S.S.R., professor, 1959—.

Great Soviet Encyclopedia, editor-in-chief, 1969—; Moscow Physics and Technical Institute, head, 1971—; General Physics and Astronomy branch, U.S.S.R. Academy of Sciences, academician-secretary, 1973-91. *Military service:* Soviet Army, 1941-44.

MEMBER: Academy of Arts and Sciences of the Americas, Russian Academy of Sciences (formerly Soviet Academy of Sciences), National Commission of Soviet Physicists (chair).

AWARDS, HONORS: Lenin prize, 1959; Nobel Prize in physics (with Nikolai G. Basov and Charles H. Townes), 1964; Hero of Socialist Labor, 1969 and 1986; Lomonosov gold medal, Soviet Academy of Sciences, 1988.

WRITINGS:

Problems in Solid-State Physics, translated by Ram S. Wadhwa, Mir Publishers (Moscow, Russia), 1984.
(With others) *Laser Heating of Metals,* A. Hilger (Philadelphia, PA), c. 1990.
(Editor-in-chief) *Coherent Radiation Generation and Particle Acceleration,* American Institute of Physics (New York, NY), c. 1992.
(Editor with Evgeny M. Solotov) *Guided-Wave Optics,* International Society for Optical Engineering (Bellingham, WA), c. 1993.

Contributor to journals and periodicals.

SIDELIGHTS: Aleksandr Prokhorov, a pioneer in the field of quantum electronics, began his scientific career by studying radio wave propagation. His application of these studies to the theoretical design of a molecular generator and amplifier in 1952 formed the basis for the invention of both masers and lasers. For his work in quantum electronics Prokhorov shared the 1964 Nobel Prize in physics with his colleague, Nikolai G. Basov, and the American physicist Charles H. Townes.

Prokhorov was born on June 28, 1916, in Atherton, Australia. His parents, Mik-hail Ivanovich and Mariya Ivanovna Prokhorov, had fled from Siberia to Australia in 1911 because of Mikhail's involvement in revolutionary activities. The family returned to the Soviet Union in 1923, and Prokhorov entered Leningrad State University, receiving his baccalaureate degree in 1939.

Prokhorov embarked on his graduate studies at the P. N. Lebedev Institute of Physics of the Soviet Academy of Sciences in Moscow. His research dealt with the propagation of radio waves and their use in studying the upper atmosphere of earth. In June 1941 the German invasion of Russia interrupted his studies and he was called to military service. Prokhorov was wounded in battle twice before being discharged in 1944. He then completed his research for the candidate's degree (comparable to a master's degree) with a thesis on nonlinear oscillators. In 1951 he was awarded a Ph.D. in physical and mathematical sciences for his research on the radiation produced by electrons in the high-energy orbits of the synchrotron, a circular particle accelerator that uses electrical and magnetic fields to propel the components of atoms to extremely high speeds. Prior to receiving his degree, Prokhorov had been appointed assistant director of the Oscillation Laboratory at the Lebedev Institute. He continued his research on the uses of radar and radio waves and applied them to the study of molecular structure and properties. In connection with this work, he came into contact with Nikolai G. Basov, with whom he was to collaborate on some of his most important work.

Prokhorov and Basov soon became involved in the stimulated emission of radiation from gas molecules. Three decades earlier in 1917, Albert Einstein had studied the effects of radiation on atoms. Using quantum mechanics, Einstein confirmed earlier hypotheses that electrons in an atom tend to absorb small amounts of energy and jump to higher energy levels in the atom. They then re-emit the absorbed radiation and return to lower, less energetic orbitals. But Einstein also discovered that in some instances an electron in a higher energy level can, simply by virtue of being exposed to radiation, jump to a lower energy level and emit a photon of a wavelength identical to that of the external radiation. This process became known as stimulated emission.

Prokhorov and Basov saw in Einstein's analysis a way of using molecules to amplify the energy of a given beam of radiation. Radiation could be used to stimulate the emission of more photons of the same wavelength within an atom, creating a domino effect among other atoms, thus stimulating the emission of more photons. This cascade of energy emission could result in a mechanism for generating more and more

intense beams of radiation with a very narrow range of wavelengths. Later researchers used these findings to develop masers (microwave amplification by stimulated emission of radiation) and lasers (light amplification by stimulated emissions of radiation).

Prokhorov and Basov announced the discovery of their molecular generator in a paper read before the All-Union Conference on Radio Spectroscopy in May, 1952. However, they did not publish their results for more than two years, by which time the American physicist Charles H. Townes had built a working maser and published his conclusions in *Physical Review*. In awarding the 1964 Nobel Prize in physics, the Nobel committee recognized the contributions of all three physicists. The discovery of the molecular generator provided the theoretical basis for the development of both masers and lasers, on which Prokhorov has concentrated his research efforts since the mid-1950s.

In 1941 Prokhorov married the former Galina Alekseyevna Shelepina, with whom he had one son, Kiril. He was appointed professor at Moscow State University in 1959 and eventually returned to the Lebedev Institute, where he was appointed deputy director in 1972. He has also been editor-in-chief of the *Great Soviet Encyclopedia* since 1969 and was made a corresponding (associate) member of the Soviet Academy of Sciences in 1960 and an academician (full member) in 1966. Prokhorov was awarded the Lenin Prize in 1959 and the Lomonosov Gold Medal of the Soviet Academy of Sciences in 1988.

BIOGRAPHICAL/CRITICAL SOURCES:

BOOKS

Nobel Prize Winners, H. W. Wilson, 1987, pp. 839-41.
Weber, Robert L., *Pioneers of Science: Nobel Prize Winners in Physics,* American Institute of Physics, 1980, pp. 199-200.

PERIODICALS

Science, November 13, 1964, pp. 897-99.
Science News, November 7, 1964, p. 295.*

R

RAWN, Melanie (Robin) 1954-

PERSONAL: Born June 12, 1954, in Santa Monica, CA; daughter of Robert Dawson and Alma Lucile (Fisk) Rawn. *Ethnicity:* "German, Irish, English, French, Scots, Welsh, Italian, Dutch; all ancestors emigrated to America before 1750." *Education:* Scripps College, B.A. (history), 1975; attended graduate school at University of Denver, 1975-76; California State University at Fullerton, teacher credentials, 1980.

ADDRESSES: Home—Los Angeles, CA. *Agent*—Russell Galen, Scovil Chichak Galen, Inc., 381 Park Avenue S., New York, NY 10016.

CAREER: Writer.

MEMBER: Science Fiction and Fantasy Writers of America.

WRITINGS:

FANTASY NOVELS

Dragon Prince (first volume of "Dragon Prince" trilogy), DAW (New York City), 1988.
The Star Scroll (second volume of "Dragon Prince" trilogy), DAW, 1989.
Sunrunner's Fire (third volume of "Dragon Prince" trilogy), DAW, 1990.
Stronghold (first volume of "Dragon Star" trilogy), DAW, 1990.
The Dragon Token (second volume of "Dragon Star" trilogy), with map by Marty Siegrist, DAW, 1992.
Skybowl (third volume of "Dragon Star" trilogy), DAW, 1993.

The Ruins of Ambrai (first volume of "Exiles" trilogy), DAW, 1994.
(With Jennifer Roberson and Kate Elliot) *The Golden Key,* DAW, 1996.
The Mageborn Traitor (second volume of "Exiles" trilogy), DAW, 1997.

WORK IN PROGRESS: The Diviner, a prequel to *The Golden Key,* for DAW; *Keftiu,* a novel of Minoan Crete in the Bronze Age, for Avon Books.

SIDELIGHTS: Popular fantasy novelist Melanie Rawn published her first novel, *Dragon Prince,* in 1988, beginning a succession of trilogies and also beginning a long-lasting association with a single publisher, New York City's DAW Books. The prince of the "Dragon Prince" trilogy is Rohan. In the series' opening novel, Rohan's father, Zehava, has recently died, leaving their desert kingdom open to threats from High Prince Roelstra, whose seventeen daughters give him considerable leverage in concluding alliances with nearby domains. Dragons are included in the adventures too, as is love in the person of an orphaned acolyte, Sioned. Commenting on the length and extravagance of this romantic saga, a *Publishers Weekly* critic felt it would appeal to readers of specific tastes, adding, "Rawn moves her large cast swiftly and colorfully through their expected motions."

The second volume in the trilogy, *The Star Scroll,* finds Prince Rohan settled into peaceful rulership of his realm fourteen years after the conflicts of the first novel have been resolved. This peace is mistaken for weakness by some, who wish for a change of leadership. A new conflict arises through a star scroll which discloses the magic techniques of an ancient people who were able to control starlight. Two reviewers, Karen S. Ellis in *Kliatt* and John Christensen in *Voice of Youth Advocates,* cautioned that a reading of *Dragon Prince* was necessary to an understanding of the complicated feuds and character relationships in *The Star Scroll;* but both reviewers enjoyed the book on its own terms as well. Ellis called it "involved fantasy fare" in which "[t]he characters . . . are all woven together by intrigue and magic." Christensen labelled it a "struggle of good against evil. . . . The main characters," he continued, "are well developed and it is a very compelling fantasy."

The "Dragon Prince" trilogy ended in 1990 with *Sunrunner's Fire,* and Rawn's sequel-trilogy, "Dragon Star," began that same year with *Stronghold.* A change of generations takes place, with Prince Rohan dying, his son Pol taking charge of the kingdom, and the kingdom's stronghold being destroyed. In the trilogy's second volume, 1992's *The Dragon Token,* Pol must deal with an attack from an army of unidentified invaders; to do so, he returns to his desert roots and consults the wise dragons who live there (and who communicate by means of color). Sally Estes, in *Booklist,* found the dragon-human relationship in *The Dragon Token* to be one of its most interesting aspects, both in itself and in comparison to dragon-human relationships in other works of fantasy. Writing that "Rawn demonstrates a fine sense of world building and characterization," Estes called the novel "challenging fantasy well worth the effort." The effort she referred to was the effort of keeping track of a huge cast of characters and interrelationships, many of them from Rawn's four previous novels. Reviewer Margaret Miles, in *Voice of Youth Advocates,* offered the same caveat to readers. However, Miles, like Estes, gave the novel a clear thumbs-up, opining that Rawn's "fully imagined historical and cultural backgrounds, and her absorbing systems of Sunrunners' and sorcerers' magic all give this series a tremendous and well-deserved appeal." Similar views were voiced by a critic for *Publishers Weekly,* who called *The Dragon Token* "unusually sophisticated" for its genre. The reception for the trilogy's finale, *Skybowl,* was less enthusiastic, as critics in both *Publishers Weekly* and *Kirkus Reviews* complained of the 1993 novel's massive length and intricate cast of characters. Estes, in *Booklist,* was once again on the positive side, saying that the novel was a fully satisfying wrap-up to the series—briskly paced, involving, and boasting a gripping denouement.

Rawn's next fantasy series, "Exiles," takes the reader to a different land, Lenfell, which was colonized in the distant past by a population of mages who gained control of—and polluted through warfare—the natural environment. *The Ruins of Ambrai,* the 1994 opening volume of the series, brings the reader up-to-date on this matriarchal society's past and introduces three orphaned sisters: Glennin, Sarra, and Cailet. Raised apart from one another, each sister has different strengths and attitudes and each separately, and together, has the potential to affect the planet's future. *Voice of Youth Advocates* reviewer Rosemary Moran praised the author's "great attention to detail," and called *The Ruins of Ambrai* "engrossing." She especially appreciated Rawn's delineation of the structure of a matriarchy, as did *Kliatt* reviewer Judith H. Silverman, who, despite complaining of the novel's length and complexity, said, "Fantasy readers hungry for a good matriarchy will not be disappointed."

Rawn's career took a turn in 1996, when she collaborated with two other fantasy writers, Jennifer Roberson and Kate Elliott, to create a three-generation novel that aimed to preserve both novelistic unity and authorial individuality. Set in the fantasy duchy of Tira Virte, *The Golden Key* examines the relationship among art, love, and magic, for this is a world in which paintings constitute the recorded history of the society, and some of the paintings—those made by the magical Grijalva family—can actually affect history. The Grijalva artists, called Limners, are sterile, and insert their vital essence into the paintings, at the cost of the painters' early, painful deaths. *Booklist* reviewer Roland Green found the novel not only "original in concept and superior in execution," but clearly the best work any of its three authors had produced to that point. "The romance justifies every one of its nearly eight hundred pages," Green declared, marking a welcome departure from some previous reviewers who had thought Rawn's novels too long.

BIOGRAPHICAL/CRITICAL SOURCES:

BOOKS

Reginald, Robert, *Science Fiction and Fantasy Literature, 1975-1991,* Gale (Detroit), 1992, p. 797.

PERIODICALS

Booklist, March 15, 1992, p. 1344; February 15, 1993, p. 1041; September 1, 1996, p. 69.
Kirkus Reviews, December 15, 1992, p. 1542.
Kliatt, September 1989, p. 20; March 1996, p. 20.
Library Journal, October 15, 1994, p. 90.

Publishers Weekly, October 28, 1988, p. 74; December 6, 1991, pp. 60-61; November 30, 1992, pp. 38-39; October 9, 1995, p. 83; August 19, 1996, p. 57.

Voice of Youth Advocates, December 1989, p. 291; August 1992, p. 179; February 1995, p. 351.

*　　*　　*

RAY, Clyde H.　1938-

PERSONAL: Born August 30, 1938, in Waynesville, NC; son of Clyde H. (in business) and Caroline (an author) Ray; first marriage, wife's name Susie (divorced); married July 9, 1982, wife's name Doris (a teacher); children: Clyde H., IV. *Education:* Western Carolina University, B.A., 1966; East Tennessee State University, M.A., 1973; attended University of Tennessee, 1975-78. *Politics:* "Democratic." *Religion:* Roman Catholic. *Avocational interests:* Genealogy.

ADDRESSES: Home—276 Purple Mountain Rd., Sylva, NC 28879.

CAREER: Western Carolina University, Cullowhee, NC, senior research associate, 1979-95; Southwestern Community College, Sylva, NC, teacher, 1994—; Jackson County Schools, Sylva, teacher, 1995—; Haywood Community College, Clyde, NC, teacher, 1997—. Haywood County, served on school board, 1976-80.

MEMBER: Pi Gamma Mu.

WRITINGS:

Across the Dark River (novel), Parkway Publishers, 1996.

Contributor to periodicals, including *Appalachian Heritage* and *Appalachian Studies.*

WORK IN PROGRESS: A Haunting on Dark Hollow, a novel.

SIDELIGHTS: Clyde H. Ray told *CA:* "Historical analysis traditionally works toward objectivity, avoiding such intangibles as emotion, the measurement and place of which in history are relatively ignored. However, any historical account that ignores emotion is an inexact record in itself, when emotion, whether in congressional debates or wars, is often a pivotal concern.

"This is where the imaginative process has a legitimate role, recreating the emotion in prose or verse. If it is true to the time, setting, and character, then it lends authenticity and truth to the record. When emotion was present in the original event, then that same emotion must be present in the record too, for lacking that, the record remains incomplete, and perhaps even false as well."

*　　*　　*

RAZ, Simcha　1931-

PERSONAL: Birth-given name, Rakover Simcha, name legally changed, 1958; born August 15, 1931, in Jerusalem, Palestine (now Israel); son of Chaim and Chana (Mandelbaum) Rakover; married Colleen Nurok, 1962; children: Esther, Chana, Abraham. *Education:* Yeshiva of Harav Kook, ordained rabbi, 1951; Institute of Public Administration, qualified Public Administrator.

ADDRESSES: Home—111 Uziel St., Bayet Vegan, Jerusalem, Israel 96431.

CAREER: World Hebrew Union, Jerusalem, Israel, general director, 1960-78; Cape Board of Jewish Education, Cape Town, South Africa, general director, 1978-82; Centre of Guidance for Public Libraries, Jerusalem, assistant director, beginning in 1982. Radio lecturer on Judaism. *Military service:* Israeli Defence Force, rabbi, 1951-53; became captain.

MEMBER: B'nai B'rith.

AWARDS, HONORS: S. Meretz Prize, 1972; Aminoach Prize, 1987; Tzytlin Prize, 1988.

WRITINGS:

A Tzaddik in Our Time: The Life of Rabbi Aryeh Levin, translated by Charles Wengrow, Feldheim (New York), 1977.
Judaism in a Nutshell: Basic Concepts and Terms, Biblas, 1981.
Hasidic Sayings (in Hebrew), Keter Publishing (Jerusalem), 1981.
Hasidic Sayings of Rabbi Nachman of Bratslav (in Hebrew), Keter Publishing, 1986.

Jerusalem in Aggadah and Midrash (in Hebrew), Keter Publishing, 1987.

(Editor) *The Sayings of Menahem Mendel of Kotzk,* translated by Edward Levin, J. Aronson (Northvale, NJ), 1995.

Other books include *The Face of Israel; Chapters in Israeli History; The History of Rabbi Akiva; The History of Hillel;* and *Yahadut alRegel Ahat.* Contributor to newspapers.

SIDELIGHTS: Simcha Raz told *CA:* "In my books, I have tried to present Jewish sources, concepts, and thoughts to the contemporary secular public."

*   *   *

REDGRAVE, Deirdre 1939-

PERSONAL: Born in 1939; (maiden name, Hamilton-Hill); married Corin Redgrave (an actor); divorced; children: two.

ADDRESSES: Office—c/o HarperCollins, 77-85 Fulham Palace Rd, Hammersmith, London W6 8JB, England.

CAREER: Writer.

WRITINGS:

(With Danae Brook) *To Be a Redgrave* (memoir), Simon and Schuster (New York), 1982.
Me and My Shadow (memoir), HarperCollins (London), 1995.

SIDELIGHTS: To Be a Redgrave, as told to journalist Danae Brook, is the inside story of Corin and Deirdre Redgrave's life together and Deirdre's attempts to create an identity separate from the Redgrave name. When the pretty, middle-class Deirdre Hamilton-Hill met the handsome and intellectual Corin Redgrave, she was blinded by love. After the couple lived together for some time, they married and had two children. In this memoir Deirdre looks upon the events of her life with the more certain eye of hindsight. She describes the various members of the Redgrave family—known for talent as actors as well as radical politics—and comments on such topics as the banalities of family life and her own attempt to run an antique clothing store. Of her husband's political activities, she said little. Initially Deirdre was interested

in the radical political causes that Corin and sister Vanessa Redgrave so ardently supported. During her fourteen years of marriage, however, Deirdre became disillusioned with politics, particularly the Workers' Revolutionary Party to which Corin was committed, and she sued for divorce. While several commentators found the work to be self-indulgent, a reviewer for *Publishers Weekly* remarked, "One admires the candor and lack of rancor" Deirdre shows in revealing her story. In 1995 Deirdre Redgrave described her fight against cancer in the memoir *Me and My Shadow.*

BIOGRAPHICAL/CRITICAL SOURCES:

PERIODICALS

Los Angeles Times Book Review, January 2, 1983, p. 5.
Publishers Weekly, June 25, 1982, p. 96.
Spectator, May 7, 1983, p. 25.*

*   *   *

REDGRAVE, Lynn (Rachel) 1943-

PERSONAL: Born in 1943, in London, England; daughter of Michael (an actor) and Rachel (an actress; professional name, Rachel Kempson) Redgrave; married John Clark (a producer and director), April 2, 1967; children: Benjamin, Kelly, Annabel. *Education:* Attended the Central School of Speech and Drama, London.

ADDRESSES: Office— c/o John Clark, PO Box 1207, Topanga, CA 90290-1207.

CAREER: Actress. Made stage debut as Helena, *A Midsummers Night's Dream,* Royal Court Theatre, London, 1962. Made Broadway debut as Carol Melkett, *Black Comedy,* Ethel Barrymore Theatre, 1967. Appeared on stage in *The Merchant of Venice,* 1962; *The Tulip Tree,* 1962; *Hamlet,* 1963; *Saint Joan,* 1963; *The Recruiting Officer,* 1963; *Andorra,* 1964; *Hay Fever,* 1964; *Much Ado about Nothing,* 1965; *Mother Courage,* 1965; *Love for Love,* 1965; *Zoo, Zoo, Widdershins Zoo,* 1969; *Slag,* 1971; *A Better Place,* 1972; *Born Yesterday,* 1973; *My Fat Friend,* 1974; *Mrs. Warren's Profession,* 1976; *Knock Knock,* 1976; *Saint Joan,* 1977; *Circle,* 1977; *Twelfth Night,* 1978; *The Actor's Nightmare,* 1982; *Sister Mary Ignatius Explains It All for You,* 1982; *Aren't*

We All?, 1985; *Sweet Sue*, 1987; *Les Liaisons Dangereuses*, 1988; *A Little Hotel on the Side*, 1992; *The Masterbuilder*, 1992; and *Shakespeare for My Father*, 1993.

Made film debut as Susan, *Tom Jones*, United Artists, 1963. Appeared in films, including *The Girl with the Green Eyes*, 1964; *Georgy Girl*, 1966; *Smashing Time*, 1967; *The Virgin Soldiers*, 1970; *The Last of the Mobile Hot-Shots*, 1970; *Every Little Crook and Nanny*, 1972; *Everything You Always Wanted to Know about Sex** (**but were afraid to ask*), 1972; *The National Health, or Nurse Norton's Affair*, 1973; *Don't Turn the Other Cheek*, 1974; *The Happy Hooker*, 1975; *The Big Bus*, 1976; *Morgan Stewart's Coming Home*, 1987; *Getting It Right*, 1989; and *Shine*, 1996.

Made television debut in *The Power and the Glory*, ABC (British Television), 1963. Appeared on television in *Not For Women Only*, 1972; *Turn of the Screw*, 1974; *Vienna 1900: Games with Love and Death*, 1975; *Sooner or Later*, 1979; *Beggarman, Thief*, 1979; *House Calls*, 1979; *Gauguin the Savage*, 1980; *The Seduction of Miss Leona*, 1980; *Rehearsal for Murder*, 1982; *Teachers Only*, 1982-83; *My Two Loves*, 1986; *A Conversation with Dinah*, 1989; *Chicken Soup*, 1989; *Jury Duty: The Comedy*, 1990; *What Ever Happened to Baby Jane?*, 1991; and *Calling the Shots*, 1993.

Redgrave has played roles on a wide variety of television shows, including hosting many specials and awards shows, and has made numerous sound recordings.

MEMBER: The Players.

AWARDS, HONORS: Golden Globe Award, New York Film Critics Award, Independent Film Importers and Distributors of America Award, and Academy Award nomination, all Best Actress, 1967, for *Georgy Girl;* Antoinette Perry Award nomination, Best Actress in a Play, 1976, for *Mrs. Warren's Profession;* Sarah Siddons Awards, Best Stage Actress in Chicago, 1977 and 1978; also Emmy Award nomination for *House Calls;* Antoinette Perry Award and Drama Desk nominations, Elliot Award, 1993, for *Shakespeare for My Father.*

WRITINGS:

This Is Living: How I Found Health and Happiness, Dutton (New York), 1991.
Diet for Life, Penguin (London), 1993.

SIDELIGHTS: In both *This Is Living: How I Found Health and Happiness* and *Diet For Life,* actress Lynn Redgrave lets readers into her secret past of compulsive eating and dieting, which was a product of her childhood upbringing and exacerbated by her stressful career. Delighting in her triumph over these bad habits with the help of the Weight Watchers weight control program, for which she was the television spokesperson from 1984 to 1992, Redgrave shares useful information about the program, relates how it affected her health and happiness, and lists her favorite Weight Watchers recipes and menu plans.

In the first half of the *This Is Living*, Redgrave describes how it was difficult for her—the shy and chubby youngest child—to live in the shadow of her naturally thin and outgoing siblings, Vanessa and Corin, who would become well-known actors like their parents. She also remarks on how the English diet is replete with fatty dishes, such as roast beef and pudding made with lard, and on her own secret overeating habits.

Redgrave talks about her career as an actress, which gained momentum when she accepted the title role in the film *Georgy Girl*, about a plump young woman who is starved for affection. She had spent years trying to get away from that "lumpy" image, both on the stage and screen and in real life. Finally after years of abusing her body with fad diets, slimming drugs, and overeating binges, Redgrave joined Weight Watchers using her married name Lynn Clark, and a transformation began. After some years and much success in the program, Redgrave became the program's television spokesperson. About *This Is Living,* a reviewer for *Publishers Weekly* remarked, "The book has occasional glints of the sunny charm and humor that have endeared Redgrave to audiences."

BIOGRAPHICAL/CRITICAL SOURCES:

BOOKS

Contemporary Theatre, Film, and Television, Volume 7, Gale (Detroit), 1989.

PERIODICALS

Books, March/April, 1993, p. 20.
Commonweal, June 2, 1989, p. 338.
Interview, February, 1991, p. 121.
Library Journal, July, 1992, p. 145.
Publishers Weekly, April 26, 1991, p. 62.
Time, March 1, 1993, p. 71.*

REMER, Gary 1957-

PERSONAL: Born November 22, 1957, in Los Angeles, CA; son of Natan (a hardware wholesaler) and Jacqueline (a homemaker) Remer; married Karen Weissbecker, June 23, 1997; children: Amos. *Ethnicity:* "White." *Education:* University of California, Los Angeles, B.A., 1978, M.A., Ph.D., 1989. *Religion:* Jewish. *Avocational interests:* Reading, hiking, travel.

ADDRESSES: Home—5115 Baronne St., New Orleans, LA 70115. *Office*—Department of Political Science, Tulane University, New Orleans, LA 70118; fax 504-862-8745. *E-mail*—gremer@mailhost.tcs.tulane.edu.

CAREER: California State University, Long Beach, lecturer in political science, 1989-90; Tulane University, New Orleans, LA, associate professor of political science, 1990—.

MEMBER: American Political Science Association, Renaissance Society of America, Western Political Science Association.

AWARDS, HONORS: Outstanding Academic Book Award, *Choice,* 1996, for *Humanism and the Rhetoric of Toleration.*

WRITINGS:

(Contributor) *Difference and Dissent: Theories of Toleration in Medieval and Early Modern Europe,* edited by Cary Nederman and Chris Laursen, Rowman & Littlefield (Lanham, MD), 1996.
Humanism and the Rhetoric of Toleration, Pennsylvania State University Press (University Park, PA), 1996.
(Contributor) *Religious Toleration in Europe before the Enlightenments,* edited by Cary Nederman and Chris Laursen, University of Pennsylvania Press (Philadelphia, PA), 1997.

Contributor of articles and reviews to journals and periodicals, including *Review of Politics, Journal of Armenian Studies, Polity,* and *History of Political Thought.*

WORK IN PROGRESS: Deliberation and the Absent Orator: Deliberative Democracy's Neglect of the Rhetorical Tradition.

RIFKIN, Adam 1972(?)-

PERSONAL: Born c. 1972.

CAREER: Filmmaker and writer. Director of films, including *Never on Tuesday,* Cinema Group, 1988; *Tale of Two Sisters,* Vista Street Entertainment, 1989; *The Dark Backward,* Greycat Films, 1991; *The Nutty Nut,* Connexion American Media, 1992; *The Chase,* Twentieth-Century Fox, 1994; and *The Nutt House,* Triboro, 1995. Director of films under pseudonym of Rif Coogan, including *Psycho Cop II: Psycho Cop Returns,* Film Nouveau, 1992.

WRITINGS:

SCREENPLAYS

The Dark Backward, Greycat Films, 1991.
The Chase, Twentieth-Century Fox, 1994.

Played a role in the film *The Disturbed,* 1991.

SIDELIGHTS: Director Adam Rifkin is the creative force behind the motion pictures *The Dark Backward* and *The Chase,* for which he wrote the screenplays. Rifkin wrote the surrealist comedy *The Dark Backward* when he was nineteen years old and filmed the work six years later. The plot revolves around a nerdy standup comic, Marty Malt, who cannot give up his day job as a garbage man until something unusual happens. A strange lump on his back grows into a third arm. Though he is still a poor comedian, with his unusual appendage, Marty gains some success on the novelty act circuit. "Rifkin has much fun with the central concept of his freakish occurrence, drawing it out in a series of blackly amusing scenes," commented a reviewer in *Variety.* Yet the critic continued that despite inspired bursts of lunacy, the film "leaves the possibilities dangling."

The Chase is just what it sounds like, a long car chase involving an escaped convict and a kidnapped heiress. Accompanied by a soundtrack of heavy metal rock and roll, almost the entire action of the film takes place in a shiny red BMW, with the convict and heiress earning a grudging respect for each other. While the plot twists are limited in scope, Rifkin lampoons the local police forces and the television news media who try to scoop each other. According to Brian Lowry in *Variety, The Chase* offers "some surprisingly big, if lowbrow, laughs," and "Rifkin exhibits some wit in his clever skewering of TV news."

BIOGRAPHICAL/CRITICAL SOURCES:

PERIODICALS

Entertainment Weekly, June 30/July 7, 1995, pp. 108-09.
Rolling Stone, August 22, 1991, p. 73.
Variety, August 2-8, 1989, p. 21; March 18, 1991,
    pp. 84-85; March 7-13, 1994, p. 60.*

*   *   *

RING, Nancy G. 1956-

PERSONAL: Born December 24, 1956, in Irvington,
NJ. *Education:* Attended Boston Museum School of
Fine Arts, 1975-76; Syracuse University School of
Visual Arts, B.F.A. (cum laude), 1978.

ADDRESSES: Home—115 West 86th St., No. 9E,
New York, NY 10024. *Office*—c/o Dumont-Landis
Fine Art Inc., Deer Park Dr., Ste. H-2, Princeton
Corporation Plaza, Monmouth Junction, NJ 08852.

CAREER: Guest lecturer and resident artist, Montalvo
Center for the Arts, Montalvo, Saratoga, CA, 1987,
and Skidmore College, Saratoga, NY, 1988; artist-in-
residence, Zebra Art Gallery, Baleares, Spain, 1988,
and Djerassi Foundation, Woodside, CA, 1989. Exhibitions include "Selections 14," Drawing Center,
New York, 1981; "New Drawing in America," Drawing Center, New York, 1982; "68th Annual Exhibition," Hudson River Museum, Yonkers, New York
City, 1983; "Works on Paper," Gallery Henoch, New
York City, 1986; "Unique Investigations," PS 122,
New York City, 1988; "Visual Impact," Selena Gallery, Brooklyn, NY, 1988; "Recent Works on Paper," Limner Gallery, New York, 1989; "Women
Figure," School 33 Gallery, Baltimore, MD, 1990.

MEMBER: Foundation for Community Artists (New
York), Artists Equity.

AWARDS, HONORS: Monticello Fellowship, Montalvo
Center for the Arts, Saratoga, CA, 1987; Fellowship
in Drawing, New York Foundation for Arts, 1987;
Fellowship for "Works on Paper," MidAtlantic Arts
Foundation/National Endowment for the Arts, 1988.

WRITINGS:

New Drawing in America (exhibition catalog), Draw-
    ing Center (New York), 1982.

Walking on Walnuts, Bantam (New York), 1996.

SIDELIGHTS: Painter, poet, and pastry chef Nancy
Ring has written a memoir called *Walking on Walnuts*
in which she describes how she supported herself in
New York City by waiting tables and later baking for
fine restaurants in order to pursue her career as an
artist. The daughter of Jewish immigrants who settled
in New Jersey, Ring learned her baking skills and
recipes from the members of her large family. In
Walking on Walnuts, Ring's account ranges from her
work in restaurants to her creative process in the studio to her romance with another chef/artist. She also
includes information about the folklore surrounding
walnuts and some favorite family recipes, including her
great-grandmother's recipe for *taiglach. Walking on
Walnuts* received mixed reviews. A *Publishers Weekly*
critic found Ring a "talented writer" and the memoir
"a cornucopia of good reading and eating," although
the reviewer acknowledged that the walnut imagery is
overdone. Despite its flaws, "readers will nosh her
book with delight," the critic declared. Likewise, a
commentator for *Kirkus Reviews* found the work to be
"often engaging" but flawed by an "injudicious use of
baking similes." Writing for *Booklist,* George Cohen
stated that the work is an "unforgettable portrait of
one woman's family and her determination to succeed."

BIOGRAPHICAL/CRITICAL SOURCES:

PERIODICALS

Booklist, July, 1996, p. 1799.
Kirkus Reviews, May 15, 1996, pp. 733-34.
Publishers Weekly, May 27, 1996, p. 57.*

*   *   *

ROHAN, Michael Scott 1951-
    (Mike Scott Rohan; Michael Scot, a joint pseud-
    onym)

PERSONAL: Born January 22, 1951, in Edinburgh,
Scotland; son of Renaud-Philippe (a doctor and dental
surgeon) and Vera (maiden name, Forrest) Rohan;
married Deborah (an instructor in archival conservation). *Ethnicity:* "Breton-Scots passing for English."
Education: Oxford University, M.A., 1973. *Politics:*
"Highly suspect." *Religion:* "Sympathetic agnostic, with
fire insurance." *Avocational interests:* Music, home entertainment technology, anthropology, paleontology, ar-
chery, travel.

ADDRESSES: Home—Cambridge, England. *Agent*—c/o Maggie Noach Literary Agency, 21 Redan Street, London W14 0AB, England. *E-mail*—mike.scott.rohan@asgard.zetnet.co.uk.

CAREER: Writer. Entered publishing as a reference book editor and became senior editor of two general encyclopedias, as well as other publications; also runs Asgard, an editorial company specializing in international reference titles, with two other senior editors. Worked for a short time as a technical author.

AWARDS, HONORS: All Time Great Fantasy Short Story, Gamesmaster International, 1991, for "Findings"; William F. Crawford Award for Best First Fantasy Novel, International Association for the Fantastic Arts, 1991, for the "Winter of the World" trilogy.

WRITINGS:

FANTASY NOVELS

(With Allan Scott) *Fantastic People,* Pierrot (London), 1980, NAL/Dutton (New York), 1981.
(With Scott, under joint pseudonym Michael Scot) *The Ice King,* New English Library (London), 1986, published as *Burial Rites,* Berkley (New York City), 1987.
(With Scott) *A Spell of Empire: The Horns of Tartarus,* Orbit (London), 1992.
The Lord of Middle Air, Gollancz (London), 1994.

FANTASY NOVELS; "WINTER OF THE WORLD" SERIES

The Anvil of Ice, Morrow (New York City), 1986.
The Forge in the Forest, Morrow, 1987.
The Hammer of the Sun, Morrow, 1988.

FANTASY NOVELS; "SPIRAL" SERIES

Chase the Morning, Morrow, 1990.
The Gates of Noon, Morrow, 1992.
Cloud Castles, Morrow, 1993.
Maxie's Demon, Little, Brown (New York), 1997.

SCIENCE-FICTION NOVELS

(Under name Mike Scott Rohan) *Run to the Stars,* Arrow (London), 1983, Ace (New York), 1986.

NONFICTION

(With Scott) *The Hammer and the Cross,* Alder (Oxford), 1980.

!/!, Arrow, 1982.
First Byte: Choosing and Using a Home Computer, E. P. Publishing, 1983.
(With Scott and Phil Gardner) *The BBC Micro Add-On Guide,* Collins (London), 1985.
(Editor) *The Classical Video Guide,* Gollancz, 1994.

OTHER

Work represented in anthologies, including *Aries 1* and *Andromeda 2.* Author of various computer titles. Translator of various German and French works, including a number of arts and crafts books. Contributor of articles, columns, and reviews to magazines and newspapers, including *Opera Now, Times, Classic CD, Gramophone,* and *Music.* Author of the short story "Findings."

WORK IN PROGRESS: Castle of the Winds, in press for Little, Brown, a prequel to the "Winter of the World" series; a sequel to *Maxie's Demon,* tentatively titled *The Cabinet of Dr. Maxie.*

SIDELIGHTS: Michael Scott Rohan has published both science-fiction and fantasy novels. Notable among his fantasy writings is the "Winter of the World" trilogy comprised of *The Anvil of Ice, The Forge in the Forest,* and *The Hammer of the Sun.* This trilogy, published in the late 1980s, concerns the classic conflict between good and evil during an Ice Age replete with wizards, knights, and strange creatures. Among the many memorable characters in these volumes are Alv (later known as Elof), a foundling trained by the sinister necromancer Mylio, who eventually becomes Alv's foe, and Kermorvan, a great warrior who joins Alv in his battle against Mylio. There are also—in addition to Mylio—a host of villains, including hordes of demonic Ekwesh who seek to overcome all who conduct their lives in opposition to the evil Ekwesh ways.

Rohan is also the author of the "Spiral" trilogy comprised of *Chase the Morning, Gates of Noon,* and *Cloud Castles.* In this series, which appeared in the early 1990s, Rohan writes of Stephen Fisher, an inventor and prominent businessperson who discovers the Spiral, a supernatural world in which mythology is real. Fisher embarks on various adventures in each of the "Spiral" tales. In *The Gates of Noon,* which a *Publishers Weekly* reviewer called "a welcome change from standard sword-and-sorcery quests," he and a band of pirates undertake a perilous journey that leads them into conflict with supernatural forces attempting to undermine Fisher's shipping business. In

Cloud Castles, Fisher travels across a futuristic Europe as he attempts to return the magical lance associated with the Holy Grail, also the origin of worldwide benevolence. Fisher's journey, as one might expect, is hardly an uneventful one, for neo-fascists threaten to cause political and social instability throughout the lands, and the spear itself is sought by evil powers.

Among Rohan's other writings are *First Byte: Choosing and Using a Home Computer* and, with Allan Scott and Phil Gardner, *The BBC Micro Add-On Guide.* In addition, Rohan has translated and edited Agnes Marie-Therese Masias's *Painting on China,* as well as many other French and German titles, and edited *The Classical Video Guide,* published in 1994.

Rohan told *CA:* "I try to write, above all, the kinds of books I want to read myself. I love knowledge and scholarship. I love hard science, wild myth and legend, and the possibilities of the imagination. Above all, I love weaving all of these together. Music feeds my imagination, music of all kinds, the more timeless the better, whether it is Wagner, Basin Street or ancient folk melodies. My literary heroes range from Shakespeare and Chaucer to Goethe, the great Edinburgh men Robert Louis Stevenson and Sir Arthur Conan Doyle, the late Fritz Leiber, Avram Davidson, Mikhail Bulgakov, and, of course, J. R. R. Tolkien.

"What I write may be escapist; but I believe escape is a necessary function which every author of fiction must to some extent fulfill, and which can often allow us to confront our condition with greater clarity. Ask yourself, as Tolkien said to C. S. Lewis, 'Who is most interested in preventing escape?—Jailers.'"

BIOGRAPHICAL/CRITICAL SOURCES:

BOOKS

Encyclopedia of Science Fiction, edited by John Clute and Peter Nicholls, St. Martin's Press (New York City), 1993, p. 1024.

PERIODICALS

Kliatt, November 1992, p. 18.
Locus, October 1992, p. 56; January 1994, p. 48.
Publishers Weekly, August 22, 1986, p. 83; October 9, 1987, p. 81; June 7, 1993, p. 57; August 8, 1994, p. 392.
School Library Journal, February 1987, p. 99.
Voice of Youth Advocates, April 1995, pp. 38-39.

ROHAN, Mike Scott
See ROHAN, Michael Scott

*   *   *

ROSS, Ronald   1857-1932

PERSONAL: Born May 13, 1857, in Almora, Nepal; died September 16, 1932; son of Campbell Claye Grant (a British officer) and Matilde Charlotte (Elderton) Ross; married Rosa Bessie Bloxam, April 25, 1889; children: Charles, Dorothy, Sylvia, Ronald. *Education:* St. Bartholomew's Hospital, London, England, M.D., 1879.

CAREER: Physician and parasitologist. Anchor Line ships, London and New York City, ship's doctor, c. 1875; Indian Medical Service, India, doctor, 1881-99; School of Tropical Medicine, Liverpool, England, lecturer, 1899-1917; King's College Hospital, London, physician of tropical diseases, 1917-26; Ross Institute and Hospital for Tropical Diseases, London, director, 1926-32.

AWARDS, HONORS: Parke gold medal, 1895; Cameron prize, 1901; Nobel Prize in physiology or medicine, 1902; Royal medal, Royal Society, 1909; knighted, England, 1911.

WRITINGS:

Memoirs with a Full Account of the Great Malaria Problem, Keynes Press, 1888.
The Deformed Transformed, Chapman and Hall, 1892.
The Prevention of Malaria, J. Murray, 1910.
The Setting Sun, J. Murray, 1912.
The Revels of Orsera, J. Murray, 1920.
Poems, E. Matthews and Marrot, 1928.
Studies on Malaria, J. Murray, 1928.

Contributor to journals and periodicals, including *British Medical Journal.*

SIDELIGHTS: Ronald Ross is best known for his discovery of the method by which malaria is transmitted, research for which he was awarded the 1902 Nobel Prize in physiology or medicine. However, Ross's true passion was the arts, and he became a doctor only because of his father's insistence. Ross's interest in bacteriology led him to study the causes of malaria, a disease that was widespread in India where he lived.

His determination that the affliction was transmitted through a parasite common to mosquitos led to more advanced treatments for the condition and more effective means of preventing it. In addition to his Nobel Prize and other honorary awards, Ross was knighted in 1911. Born in Almora, Nepal, on May 13, 1857, Ross was the first of ten children of General Sir Campbell Claye Grant Ross, a British officer stationed in India, and the former Matilde Charlotte Elderton. General Ross was described by Paul DeKruif in his book *Microbe Hunters* as "a ferocious looking border-fighting English general with belligerent side-whiskers, who was fond of battles but preferred to paint landscapes."

In 1865 at the age of eight, Ross was sent to England for his schooling. When he returned to his family in India, he declared to his father that he wanted to pursue a career in the arts. General Ross's view was that the arts were a legitimate vocation but not a sensible career for a young man. Instead, he insisted that his son plan for a medical career in the Indian Medical Service. Ross returned to England in 1874 and began his medical education at St. Bartholomew's Hospital in London. He did poorly in his classes because he spent most of his time writing novels and reading. His father became so upset with his grades that he threatened to withdraw his son's financial support. In response, Ross took a job as a ship's doctor on Anchor Line ships plying the London-New York City route. DeKruif reports that Ross spent much of his time aboard ship "observing the emotions and frailties of human nature," which gave him more material for his novels and poems. In 1879 Ross completed his course at St. Bartholo-mew's and was awarded his medical degree. He returned to India and held a series of posts in Madras, Bangalore, Burma, and the Andaman Islands. He soon became more interested in research than in the day-to-day responsibilities of medical practice and spent long hours working out new algebraic formulas.

An important turning point in Ross's life came with his first leave of absence in 1888. He returned to England and became interested in research on tropical diseases, many of which he had seen during his years in India. Ross took a course in bacteriology offered by E. Emanuel Klein and earned a diploma in public health. During this furlough he also met Rosa Bessie Bloxam, whom he married on April 25, 1889, just prior to returning to India. The Rosses later had four children: Charles Claye, Dorothy, Sylvia, and Ronald.

With his new-found knowledge of bacteriology, Ross turned his attention to what was then the most serious health problem in India: malaria. In 1880 the French physician Alphonse Laveran had discovered that malaria is caused by a one-celled organism called plasmodium. Two decades of research had produced further data on the organism's characteristics, its means of reproduction, and its correlation with disease symptoms, but no one had determined how the disease was transmitted from one person to another. Ross's original research led him to question Laveran's discovery, but for five years he made little progress in his studies. Then, on a second leave of absence in England during 1894, he met Patrick Manson, an English physician particularly interested in malaria. During Ross's year in England, he studied with Manson and became convinced that Laveran's theory was correct and that the causative agent for malaria was transmitted by mosquitoes.

When Ross returned to India in March of 1895, he was prepared to take up an aggressive research program on the mosquito-transmission theory. However, he was frustrated by working conditions in India—especially the lack of support from his superiors and the primitive equipment available to him—but with Manson's constant letters of support and encouragement, he eventually succeeded. The key discovery came on August 20, 1897, when Ross first observed in the stomach of an anopheles mosquito a cyst with black granules of the type described by Laveran. Ross worked out the life cycle of the disease-causing agent, including its reproduction within human blood, its transmission to a mosquito during the feeding process, its incubation within the mosquito, and then its transmission to a second human during a second feeding (a "bite") by the mosquito. Ross's work, however, was complicated by several factors. For example, in the midst of his research he was transferred to Rajputana, a region in which human malaria did not exist. He spent his time there instead working on the transmission of another form of the disease that affects birds. In addition, Ross was continually distracted by his passion for writing, and he produced a number of poems when he could no longer work on his battle against malaria.

Adding to Ross's frustration was the news he received late in 1898 that an Italian research team led by Battista Grassi had published reports on malaria closely paralleling his own work. Although little doubt exists about the originality of the Italian studies, Ross called Grassi's team "cheats and pirates." The dispute was later described by DeKruif as similar to a spat between "two quarrelsome small boys." To some extent, the dispute was resolved in 1902 when the Nobel Prize committee awarded Ross the year's prize in physiology or medicine. By that time, Ross had retired from the Indian Medical Service and returned to England as lecturer at the new School of Tropical Medicine in Liverpool. There he worked for the eradication of the conditions (such as poor sanitation) that were responsible for the spread of malaria. In 1917, after eighteen years at Liverpool, Ross was appointed physician of tropical diseases at King's College Hospital in London. In 1926 he became director of a new facility founded in his name, the Ross Institute and Hospital for Tropical Diseases near London. He remained in this post until his death on September 16, 1932. Among the honors granted to Ross were the 1895 Parke Gold Medal, the 1901 Cameron Prize, and the 1909 Royal Medal of the Royal Society. He was knighted in 1911.

BIOGRAPHICAL/CRITICAL SOURCES:

BOOKS

DeKruif, Paul, *Microbe Hunters,* Harcourt, 1926.
Kamm, Jacqueline, *Malaria Ross,* Methuen, 1963.
Megroz, Rodolphe L., *Ronald Ross: Discoverer and Creator,* Allen & Unwin, 1931.

PERIODICALS

Bulletin of the New York Academy of Medicine, August, 1973, pp. 722-35.
Scientific Monthly, August, 1916, pp. 132-50.*

*   *   *

ROY, Brandon
See BARCLAY, Florence L(ouisa Charlesworth)

*   *   *

ROYKO, Mike 1932-1997

OBITUARY NOTICE—See index for *CA* sketch: Born September 19, 1932, in Chicago, IL; died of heart failure following surgery for a brain aneurysm, April 29, 1997, in Evanston, IL. Journalist. Proclaimed by some of his colleagues as the best columnist in the United States, Royko wrote a popular column in Chicago that epitomized the voice of the common man. Syndicated in several hundred newspapers, the column earned Royko accolades, including a Pulitzer Prize in 1972, a National Press Club Lifetime Achievement Award in 1990, and the Damon Runyon Award in 1995. Royko used the column to remark on politics, social concerns, and general observations. At times, his views were controversial with some of his readers, especially in his later years. Royko decided on pursuing writing while serving in the U.S. Air Force during the Korean conflict. He sought a job on the O'Hara Field base newspaper and was soon running the publication. After his discharge in 1956, he found work as a reporter with the Chicago North Side Newspapers. After a three-year stint with the Chicago City News Bureau, he joined the staff of the *Chicago Daily News.* He remained with the organization from 1959 to 1978. From 1978 to 1984 he was a columnist for the *Chicago Sun-Times.* Royko continued his column with the *Chicago Tribune* after leaving the *Sun-Times* when it was acquired by media mogul Rupert Murdoch. Royko had resigned saying that "no self-respecting fish" would want to be wrapped in one of Murdoch's newspapers. During his career, Royko also wrote an unauthorized biography about one of Chicago's mayors, entitled *Boss: Richard J. Daley of Chicago.* The work was highly critical of Daley's political machine. Among Royko's other books were collections of columns such as *Slats Grobnik and Some Other Friends, Sez Who? Sez Me, Like I Was Sayin',* and *Dr. Kookie, You're Right!* Slats Grobnik and Dr. Kookie were two fictionalized characters that Royko sometimes pretended to have debates or conversations with in his columns.

OBITUARIES AND OTHER SOURCES:

BOOKS

Who's Who in America, 51st edition, Marquis, 1997.

PERIODICALS

Chicago Tribune (electronic), April 29, 1997.
Detroit Free Press (electronic), April 30, 1997.
Detroit News (electronic), April 30, 1997.
Los Angeles Times, April 30, 1997.
New York Times (electronic), April 30, 1997.
USA Today (electronic), April 29, 1997, p. A3.
Washington Post, April 30, 1997, p. B9; May 1, 1997, pp. C1, C4.

OTHER

CNN Interactive (website), April 29, 1997.
MSNBC (website), April 30, 1997.

RUBIA BARCIA, Jose 1914-1997
(Juan Bartolome de Roxas)

OBITUARY NOTICE—See index for *CA* sketch: Born July 31, 1914, in Galicia, Spain; became American citizen, 1957; died April 6, 1997, in Los Angeles, CA. Educator, translator, and author. Rubia Barcia is remembered for his co-translation of *Cesar Vallejo: The Complete Posthumous Poetry,* which earned him and Clayton Eschleman a National Book Award in 1979. Rubia Barcia began his career as an educator at the University of Granada in 1935. However, he soon found himself involved in the Spanish Civil War fighting against Franco. After fleeing to Cuba, he worked at the University of Havana from 1939 to 1943 before venturing to the United States to teach at Princeton University for one year. For a time, he dubbed films in Hollywood for Warner Bros., then he began nearly forty years at the University of California—Los Angeles. He eventually became professor of contemporary Spanish literature in 1949 and then professor emeritus in 1985. Among his books were *A Bibliography and Iconography of Valle Inclan, 1866-1936; Americo Castro and the Meaning of Spanish Civilization,* edited with Selma Margaretten; and *Unamuno: Creator and Creation,* edited with M. A. Zeitlin. His works in Spanish include *Lengua y Cultura* and also *Tres en Uno: Auto Sacramental a la Usanza Antigua,* written under the pseudonym Juan Bartolome de Roxas. Rubia Barcia was also the recipient of the Premio Jose Vasconcelos Prize.

OBITUARIES AND OTHER SOURCES:

PERIODICALS

Los Angeles Times, April 8, 1997, p. A20.

* * *

RUSCH, Kris
See RUSCH, Kristine Kathryn

* * *

RUSCH, Kristine Kathryn 1960-
(Sandy Schofield, Kris Rusch)

PERSONAL: Born June 4, 1960, in Oneonta, NY; daughter of Carrol E. (a math professor) and Marian M. (a homemaker; maiden name, Beisser) Rusch; married Dean Wesley Smith (a writer), December 20, 1992. *Education:* University of Wisconsin, B.A., 1982. *Avocational interests:* History, music, film, theater, needlework.

ADDRESSES: Home—Lincoln City, OR. *Agent*—Merrilee Heifetz, Writers House, 21 West 26th St., New York, NY 10010.

CAREER: Freelance author, 1987—; co-founder with Dean Wesley Smith of Pulphouse Publishing, Eugene, OR, 1987—, and editor of *Pulphouse: The Hardback Magazine,* 1987-91; editor of *Magazine of Fantasy & Science Fiction,* 1991-97.

AWARDS, HONORS: World Fantasy Award (with Dean Wesley Smith), 1989, for work with Pulphouse Publishing; John W. Campbell Award for Best New Writer, 1990; *Locus* Award for Best Nonfiction (with Dean Wesley Smith), 1991, for *Science Fiction Writers of America Handbook: The Professional Writer's Guide to Writing Professionally; Locus* Award for Best Novella, 1992, for *Gallery of His Dreams;* Hugo Award for Best Editor, 1994.

WRITINGS:

PULPHOUSE ANTHOLOGIES

Pulphouse, the Hardback Magazine: Issues One and Two, Pulphouse Publishing (Eugene, OR), 1988.
Pulphouse, the Hardback Magazine: Issues Three, Four and Five, Pulphouse Publishing, 1989.
Pulphouse, the Hardback Magazine: Issues Six, Seven, Eight and Nine, Pulphouse Publishing, 1990.
Pulphouse, the Hardback Magazine: Issues Ten and Eleven, Pulphouse Publishing, 1991.
The Best of Pulphouse: The Hardback Magazine, St. Martin's (New York, NY), 1991.

OTHER

(Editor with Dean Wesley Smith) *Science Fiction Writers of America Handbook: The Professional Writer's Guide to Writing Professionally,* Pulphouse Publishing, 1990.
The Gallery of His Dreams (short novel), Axolotl Press, 1991, reprinted in *The Year's Best Science Fiction: Ninth Annual Collection,* edited by Gardner Dozois, St Martin's Press, 1992.
The White Mists of Power (novel), Roc (New York, NY), 1991.

(With Kevin J. Anderson) *Afterimage* (novel), Roc, 1992.

(Written under the pseudonym Sandy Schofield, with Dean Wesley Smith) *Star Trek: Deep Space Nine: The Big Game* (novel), Pocket Books, 1993.

Traitors (novel), Roc, 1993.

Heart Readers (novel), Roc, 1993.

Facade (novel), Dell Abyss, 1993.

Alien Influences (novel), Millenium (Great Britain), 1994.

(Editor with Edward L. Ferman) *The Best From Fantasy & Science Fiction: A 45th Anniversary Anthology,* St. Martin's, 1994.

Sins of the Blood (novel), Dell (New York, NY), 1994.

(With Dean Wesley Smith) *Star Trek: Voyager: The Escape* (novel), Pocket Books, 1995.

(Written under the pseudonym Sandy Schofield, with Dean Wesley Smith) *Aliens: Rogue* (novel), Bantam/Dark Horse, 1995.

The Fey: The Sacrifice (novel), Millenium (Great Britain), 1995, Bantam, 1996.

(With Dean Wesley Smith) *Star Trek: Deep Space Nine: The Long Night* (novel), Pocket Books, 1996.

(With Dean Wesley Smith) *Star Trek: Klingon!* (novel), Pocket Books, 1996.

(With Dean Wesley Smith) *Klingon Immersion Studies* (CD-ROM), Simon and Schuster Interactive, 1996.

(With Dean Wesley Smith) *Star Trek: Rings of Tautee* (novel), Pocket Books, 1996.

(With Dean Wesley Smith) *Star Trek: The Next Generation: Invasion! Soldiers of Fear* (novel), Pocket Books, 1996.

The Devil's Churn (novel), Dell, 1996.

Star Wars: The New Rebellion (novel), Bantam (New York, NY), 1996.

The Sacrifice: The First Book of the Fey (novel), Bantam, 1996.

The Fey: The Rival (novel), Bantam, 1997.

(Under the pseudonym Sandy Schofield, with Dean Wesley Smith) *Quantum Leap: The Loch Ness Monster* (novel), Ace, 1997.

(With Dean Wesley Smith) *Star Trek: Day of Honor—Book Four* (novel), 1997.

(Under the pseudonym Kris Rusch) *Hitler's Angel* (novel), St. Martin's Press, 1997.

The Fey: The Resistance (novel), Bantam, in press.

(With Dean Wesley Smith and Nina Kiriki Hoffman) *Star Trek: Voyager: Echoes* (novel), in press.

Also author of several short booklets about writing style; contributor to periodicals, including *Magazine of Fantasy & Science Fiction* and *Alfred Hitchcock's Mystery Magazine.*

SIDELIGHTS: Kristine Kathryn Rusch has had a great deal of influence on the genres of science fiction and fantasy writing since the late 1980s. In that year, her first story was published in *Aboriginal Science Fiction,* but more importantly, with Dean Wesley Smith, she co-founded Pulphouse Publishing. For many years, Pulphouse's primary project was the publication of *Pulphouse: The Hardback Magazine,* which was a book-length anthology that came out quarterly. They also published other projects within or about the speculative fiction field, including a collaboration between Rusch and Smith on the nonfiction *Science Fiction Writers of America Handbook: The Professional Writer's Guide to Writing Professionally,* which garnered them an award from *Locus* magazine.

After *Pulphouse: The Hardback Magazine* went on hiatus—to return briefly in the mid-1990s in a more conventional magazine format—Rusch served as the editor of another popular outlet for speculative fiction, the *Magazine of Fantasy & Science Fiction,* until the middle of 1997. In 1991, she published her first full-length novel, *The White Mists of Power.* Since then, Rusch has penned several other novels and edited several anthologies.

In the same year that Rusch won Best New Writer acclaim, her novella *The Gallery of His Dreams* was published by Pulphouse. This tale, some eighty pages in length, concerns the historical figure Mathew Brady, famed for his photographic record of the U.S. Civil War. In his dreams, Brady travels through time to photograph the horrors of more modern wars, such as the atomic bombing of Hiroshima, Japan, and the massacre at My Lai in Vietnam. Tom Easton, reviewing *The Gallery of His Dreams* in *Analog Science Fiction & Fact,* observed that Rusch "is quite explicit in contrasting Brady's vision of his work as the production of cautionary documents with the visions of his contemporaries, of his photographs of death and destruction as commercial commodities . . . of those photographs as art."

In the same article, Easton also reviewed *The Best of Pulphouse: The Hardback Magazine,* an anthology which Rusch edited during roughly the same period. He hailed it as "good stuff, the best of a good series. Often outrageous and provocative. Always interesting." Edward Bryant in the *Bloomsbury Review* gave it his stamp of approval as well, labeling it "a fine anthology." In a previous issue of *Analog,* Easton offered his opinion of Rusch's nonfiction collaboration with Smith, *Science Fiction Writers of America Handbook,* praising its "thorough, useful discussions" of issues pertaining to writers in the genre.

In *The White Mists of Power,* readers become acquainted with Bard Byron, who is really the long-lost prince of Kilot, and his traveling companion Seymour, an inexpert magician. War in Kilot between the upper and lower classes is predicted by the magical being Cache Enos, but young Byron has a plan to preserve his country despite the fact that his father, the king, dies before Byron can be identified as the true prince. *The White Mists of Power* was well received by many, including Denice M. Thornhill who reported in *Voice Of Youth Advocates:* "I just loved this book and have raved about it to several people." She went on to applaud the story's "good characters that grow," and called it "a must buy." *Publishers Weekly* liked *The White Mists of Power* as well, citing Rusch's "beguiling characters" and hailing it as "a fine first novel."

Rusch collaborated with Kevin J. Anderson on the 1992 novel, *Afterimage.* The plot of this tale hinges on the existence of shape shifters who can help people jump from one body to another. One such being is able to save the life of Rebecca, left for dead after being assaulted and raped by the Joan of Arc killer. Unfortunately, she is spirited into the body of the last image left upon her mind—that of her attacker. She must conceal her temporary form from the police while she seeks a way to return to her old body. Jody K. Hanson in *Kliatt* declared *Afterimage* to be "an excellent, thoroughly enjoyable book," though she did caution readers about the graphic rape scenes. Hanson felt, however, that these were not gratuitous depictions, but rather that they helped readers understand "the horror of these crimes."

Traitors, Rusch's next novel, became available to readers in 1993. Its protagonist, Diate, reluctantly gives up his talent for dance, a compromise he makes in order to live in safety among the island people of Golga. On Golga he waits for the right time to seek revenge upon the rulers of his native land, whom he believes slaughtered all his family members. Observing that the novel contains "elements both modern and medieval," Joseph R. DeMarco in *Kliatt* declares that "what [Diate] does to fulfill his desire for revenge is laid out neatly" by Rusch. A *Science Fiction Chronicle* reviewer gave *Traitors* favorable notice as well, assessing it as "entertaining" and "a well concocted mix."

With Edward L. Ferman, the previous editor of the *Magazine of Fantasy and Science Fiction,* Rusch edited 1994's *Best From Fantasy and Science Fiction.* Gary K. Wolfe in *Locus* recalled lovingly that the magazine from which the anthology sprang "was bending traditional genre boundaries decades before . . . others broadened the scope of the competition," cited many stories as worthy of attention, and finished: "In all, this latest addition to a distinguished series honors both the magazine's rich tradition and its interesting new directions." Deborah A. Feulner, writing in *Voice Of Youth Advocates,* asserted that "readers . . . will be pleased with the variety of stories presented."

Rusch tried her hand at vampire fiction in the 1994 novel *Sins of the Blood.* In the United States as portrayed in this book, all acknowledge the existence of vampires. In some states, they are treated as victims of disease; in others, they are legally hunted down and killed, primarily through the efforts of bounty hunters. One such killer is the protagonist in *Sins of the Blood,* a woman whose own father is a vampire. During the course of the novel, she seeks to find her long-estranged brother, and protect him from joining the vampiric world. *Science Fiction Chronicle* praised "the well delineated central character" of *Sins of the Blood,* and described Rusch's vampire world as "tantalizing."

In 1996, Rusch began an epic work about an evil people known as the Fey with the novel, *The Sacrifice.* In this volume, the target of the Fey is the magical Blue Isle, and Prince Rugar, the son of the Black King of the Fey, leads the attack. Because of the Blue Isle's magic, the attackers are repulsed by its denizens, but the Fey are unlikely to give up their quest for world domination. Though she warned readers about what she saw as "gruesome" warfare descriptions, Karen S. Ellis in *Kliatt* recommended *The Sacrifice,* and asserted that "the diversity of characterization, as shaped by contrasting cultures, is fascinating."

In the same year that *The Sacrifice* hit bookstands, Rusch also published a novel in the popular *Star Wars* series created by filmmaker George Lucas. Titled *The New Rebellion,* the story takes familiar characters such as Princess Leia Organa Solo into the first year that former leaders of the evil empire are allowed to hold seats in the Senate. Roland Green in *Booklist* assured readers that "everybody snatches triumph from the jaws of disaster in the nick of time and in the approved fashion."

BIOGRAPHICAL/CRITICAL SOURCES:

PERIODICALS

Analog Science Fiction & Fact, September, 1991, p. 168; May, 1992, pp. 164-165.
Bloomsbury Review, December, 1991, p. 27.
Booklist, October 1, 1996, p. 292.
Kliatt, November, 1992, pp. 18-19; January, 1995, p. 19; March, 1996, p. 20.
Locus, October, 1994, p. 58.
Publishers Weekly, October 4, 1991, p. 84.
Science Fiction Chronicle, October, 1993, p. 36; February, 1995, p. 38.
VOYA, April, 1992, pp. 46-47; December, 1994, pp. 282-283.

—*Sketch by Elizabeth Wenning*

*   *   *

RUSSELL, Frederick S(tratten) 1897-1984

PERSONAL: Born November 3, 1897, in Bridport, England; died June 5, 1984; son of William and Lucy (Binfield) Russell; married; wife's name, Gweneth (died 1978); children: a son. *Education:* Gonville and Caius College, Cambridge University, degree, 1922.

CAREER: Marine biologist. Government of Egypt, marine biologist, 1922-24; Plymouth laboratory, Marine Biological Association, Plymouth, England, staff member, 1924-40, director, 1945-65. *Military service:* Royal Naval Air Service, 1916-1918, served in France, received Distinguished Service Cross, Distinguished Flying Cross, and Croix de Guerre; Royal Air Force, 1940-45, intelligence officer.

AWARDS, HONORS: Elected to the Royal Society of London, 1938; Gold medal, Linnean Society, 1961; Knighted, England, 1965.

WRITINGS:

(With C. M. Yonge) *The Seas: Our Knowledge of Life in the Sea and How It Is Gained,* Frederick Warne and Company (New York, NY), 1928, reprinted as *The Seas: An Introduction to the Study of Life in the Sea,* Frederick Warne and Company, 1975.
The Medusae of the British Isles, two volumes, Cambridge University Press, 1953, 1970.

The Eggs and Planktonic Stages of British Marine Fishes, Academic Press (New York, NY), 1976.

Journal of the Marine Biological Association, editor, 1945-65; *Advances in Marine Biology,* founding editor, 1963-67, advising editor, 1967-84.

SIDELIGHTS: Marine biologist Frederick Stratten Russell linked the distribution of planktonic organisms to water masses and the intensity of light in the seas off the British Isles. His work helped explain the long-term changes in the ecosystem of the English Channel. Russell was fascinated by the larval stages of fishes and the life histories of certain types of jellyfish, which he studied in great detail. He wrote and illustrated several books on his findings. Colleagues J. H. S. Baxter, A. J. Southward, and C. Maurice Yonge characterized Russell as possessing "an old world courtesy" as well as "great personal charm and friendliness."

The youngest son of William and Lucy Binfield Russell, he was born on November 3, 1897, in Bridport, England, on the coast of the English Channel. Russell attended university at Cambridge and planned to study medicine at Gonville and Caius College. But after World War I broke out, he left school to serve in the Royal Naval Air Service in France from 1916 to 1918. He served with distinction, earning the Distinguished Service Cross, the Distinguished Flying Cross, and the Croix de Guerre. After the war he returned to school, earning his degree in 1922.

That year, Russell was assigned to the Egyptian government to study the eggs and larvae of marine fishes. Before embarking on his trip to Egypt, Russell went to the laboratory of the Marine Biological Association in Plymouth, where he studied the early stages in the life histories of fish with R. S. Clark and E. Ford. There, Russell's lifelong interest in marine biology was sparked. When Russell returned from Egypt in 1924 he joined the Plymouth laboratory as a staff member. He continued to study fish larvae and other plankton. Using a special net that allowed him to filter large columns of water, Russell collected plankton, noting their vertical distributions. He built on this initial data over the next fifty years, observing how the composition of the species changed seasonally and over the long term.

Russell's work gained international attention when he showed that the depth at which fish plankton were found was related to the intensity of light in the water. He used photoelectric cells to measure the light, finding that the plankton moved up and down the water column in a daily cycle. Seasonal variations in light intensity also affected the migrations. In 1928, C. Maurice Yonge, with whom Russell had co-authored the book *The Seas: Our Knowledge of Life in the Sea and How It Is Gained,* led the Great Barrier Reef expedition to Australia. Russell and his wife, Gweneth, joined the one-year expedition. Russell compared the distribution of plankton in tropical waters there with that of more temperate regions.

After returning to Plymouth, Russell studied in detail the biology of the torpedo-shaped marine worm, sagitta. Finding that the abundance of different species of sagitta varied from year to year, he traced the cause to the movement of water masses in the English Channel and the North Sea. For example, one species preferred the warmer Atlantic water masses to the Arctic water masses. Russell was able to use sagitta as an indicator species, since other planktonic organisms associated with them. His work helped explain long-term changes in the English Channel ecosystem, including the varying abundance of herring. With a colleague, W. J. Rees, Russell began to study another indicator species, a type of jellyfish, medusae. Little was known about its early life stages. Russell and Rees raised medusae in captivity, studying the early hydroid stages. In 1938, he was elected a fellow of the Royal Society of London.

The outbreak of World War II interrupted Russell's work on a massive text on the medusae that was to contain nearly a thousand illustrations. Russell left Plymouth in 1940 to serve as an intelligence officer for the Royal Air Force. Returning to the Marine Biological Laboratory as director in 1945, he supervised the growth of the laboratory after the war. He also completed his text on the medusae, struggling to remember the finer details of his research before it had been interrupted by the war. The first volume of the book, called *The Medusae of the British Isles,* was finally published in 1953. Russell then devoted more time to different types of jellyfish, including the large scyphomedusae. He also studied a red jellyfish from the Bay of Biscay that gave birth to live young. Russell named it stygiomedusa fabulosa. Russell's studies led to his being honored with the Gold Medal of the Linnean Society in 1961. He was knighted in 1965, the same year he retired.

Continuing his studies even in retirement, at age seventy-eight Russell published a definitive work, *The Eggs and Planktonic Stages of British Marine Fishes,* in which he described in detail the development of fish eggs and larvae. In his later years, after his wife Gweneth passed away in 1978, Russell moved from Plymouth to live near his son in Reading. Russell died on June 5, 1984. He had left his influence on the *Journal of the Marine Biological Association,* which he had edited for twenty years, from 1945 to 1965. He had also been the founding editor of the journal *Advances in Marine Biology,* and had participated in its editing and publishing until shortly before his death.

BIOGRAPHICAL/CRITICAL SOURCES:

PERIODICALS

Advances in Marine Biology, vol. 21, 1984, pp. vii-ix.
Times (London), June 6, 1984.*

S

SADAKICHI
See HARTMANN, Sadakichi

* * *

SAKHAROV, Andrei D(mitrievich) 1921-1989

PERSONAL: Born May 21, 1921, in Moscow, U.S.S.R. (now Russia); died December 14, 1989, in Moscow, U.S.S.R. (now Russia), after suffering a heart attack; son of Dmitri (a physicist) and Ekaterina Sofiano (a gymnastics teacher); married Klavdia (Klava) Vikhireva (a laboratory assistant; died 1969), July 10, 1943; married Yelena Bonner (an Armenian-Siberian Jewish dissident and M.D.), January, 7, 1972; children: (first marriage) Tanya, Lyuba, Dmitri. *Education:* Moscow State University, B.S., 1942, Ph.D. 1947.

CAREER: Theoretical physicist. On staff of P.N. Lebedev Institute of Physics of the Soviet Academy of Science; worked on H-Bomb team, 1945-63; lecturer at Moscow Energetics Institute and Kurchatov Institute.

AWARDS, HONORS: Nobel Peace Prize, 1975; Stalin Prize; Order of Socialist Labor Award (three times); elected full member, Soviet Academy of Sciences; American Academy of Arts and Sciences, 1969; National Academy of Sciences, 1972; Eleanor Roosevelt Peace Award from SANE (Committee for a Sane Nuclear Policy), 1973; Cino del Duca Prize, Chicago University and Rheinhold Niebuhr Prize, 1974; Fritt Ord Prize, 1980; foreign associate of the French Academy of Science, 1981.

WRITINGS:

Reflections on Progress, Peaceful Coexistence, and Intellectual Freedom, self-published, 1968, published as *Progress, Peaceful Coexistence, and Intellectual Freedom,* Norton, 1968.
Sakharov Speaks, Knopf, 1974.
My Country and the World, Knopf, 1975.
Alarm and Hope, Knopf, 1979.
Collected Scientific Works, Dekker, 1982.
Memoirs, Knopf, 1990.
Moscow and Beyond, 1986 to 1989, Vintage Book, 1992.

SIDELIGHTS: Russian nuclear physicist Andrei Sakharov was a well known Soviet dissident and human rights advocate who played an important role in the development of the hydrogen bomb. The so-called "father of the H-Bomb" won the 1975 Nobel Peace Prize for his calls for detente between the U.S.S.R. and the United States and for an end to the arms race. Once fully committed to the Soviet Union's development of a hydrogen bomb in the belief that nuclear parity between the superpowers would prevent a nuclear war, Sakharov had a change of heart and became active in the fight for nuclear disarmament. He was exiled to the city of Gorky in 1980 as a punishment for his outspokenness. With the rise to power of Mikhail Gorbachev and the introduction of *perestroika* (a policy of moderate political and economic "restructuring"), Sakharov and his wife Yelena Bonner were permitted to return to Moscow in 1986.

Sakharov was born in Moscow, Russia, on May 21, 1921, into a family of intellectuals. His father, Dmitri Sakharov, a physicist who wrote popular textbooks about physics and taught at the Lenin Pedagogical

Institute, was also a talented pianist. Andrei's mother, Ekaterina Sofiano, a teacher of gymnastics before her marriage, was the daughter of a professional soldier. Sakharov had one brother, Georgy, known to the family as Yura. The Sakharovs shared a communal apartment with five other families, including four sets of relatives. The immediate family shared two rooms, equal to three hundred square feet, among its four members. Despite these straitened circumstances, by Soviet standards Sakharov's family was reasonably well off—they were able to rent rooms in a country house during the summer—thanks to the extra income generated by Dmitri's writing.

Sakharov taught himself to read when he was about four. His childhood favorites among the mostly pre-revolutionary books that filled his parents' and relatives' libraries were the works of Hans Christian Andersen, Jules Verne, Charles Dickens, Mark Twain, H. G. Wells, Jack London, Leo Tolstoy, Jonathan Swift, Aleksander Pushkin, and Nikolai Gogol. He was educated primarily at home until he was about thirteen, in math and physics by his father and in geography, history, biology, chemistry, and Russian language and literature by private tutors. Late in 1934, he entered the Third Model School. At home, in the meantime, he carried out simple physics experiments in electrostatics and optics. He also became interested in photography, and built a crystal radio based on his father's design. His reading progressed to include science fiction and science books, including those of Yakov Perelman, Sir James Jean's *The Universe Around Us,* and Max Valier's *Space Travel as a Technical Possibility.*

Sakharov graduated from high school as one of only two honors students in his class. In 1938 he enrolled in Moscow State University's physics program. During his third year, Germany invaded the Soviet Union, and Sakharov's work became geared towards the war effort. He repaired radio equipment for the army and invented a magnetic device for locating shrapnel in injured horses. During his fourth year, the faculty was moved to Ashkhabad, capital of the Turkmen Republic in Central Asia. He graduated in 1942.

After finishing college, Sakharov was invited to remain on as a graduate student of theoretical physics. He refused the offer, preferring to join in the war effort. He was assigned to work at a cartridge factory in Ulyanovsk, a city on the Volga. Before long, he transferred to the central laboratory's metallurgical department, where he devised a novel method of test-

ing the armor-piercing steel cores of 14.5 mm bullets for antitank guns.

November 10, 1942, the day he started work at the laboratory, was also the day he met his first wife, Klavdia (Klava) Vikhireva, a laboratory assistant in the chemical department. They were married on July 10 of the following year. They had three children—Tanya, Lyuba, and Dmitri.

In 1945, Sakharov was invited to join the staff of the P. N. Lebedev Institute of Physics of the Soviet Academy of Science. There, he worked closely with the Russian physicist Igor Tamm, who went on to win the 1958 Nobel Prize for Physics jointly with Il'ya Frank and Pavel Cherenkov for their work on radiation. Sakharov produced papers on the generation of a hard component of cosmic rays, on the interaction of electrons and positrons, and on the temperature of excitation in plasma of a gaseous discharge. He also lectured in nuclear physics, relativity theory, and electricity at the Moscow Energetics Institute for three semesters, and for half a year at the Kurchatov Institute's workers night school. In his *Memoirs,* Sakharov described the hardships of these years. He and his family were forced to move house every two months; "at one point, we found ourselves without money even to buy milk," he says. Even more frustrating were the restrictions on his professional freedom: his scientific and technical articles were censored, as was all published material. In 1947, at age twenty-six, he was awarded a Candidate of Doctor of Science degree—equivalent to an American doctorate—for his research into cosmic ray theory.

Despite his straitened circumstances, Sakharov turned down an offer to work for the government and continued working with Tamm. In 1948, they jointly published a paper outlining a principle for the magnetic isolation of high temperature plasma which was to change the entire course of Soviet thermonuclear physics. That was the last the mainstream scientific establishment heard from either of them for the next twenty years, as the pair went underground to work on the hydrogen bomb project. Although Sakharov had no real choice in the matter, he later admitted that he had welcomed the opportunity to work on what he described as "superb physics" and that he had believed his work to be "essential." He firmly believed that strategic parity in the great powers' nuclear arsenals would prevent a war.

In June, 1948, Sakharov and the rest of the H-bomb team were transferred to the "Installation," a secret city where he spent the next eighteen years of his life. By 1950, he and Tamm had come up with a theoretical basis for controlled thermonuclear fusion, that is, a method of using thermonuclear power for peaceful means, such as the generation of electricity. But their work was also geared toward more belligerent ends. By 1953, they were in a position to carry out the first test explosion of a Soviet hydrogen bomb. Although the United States had tested an H-bomb the previous November, the Soviets were the first to explode a compact device deliverable by plane or rocket. Sakharov was credited with developing an essential triggering device that used a fission explosion to set off the process of hydrogen fusion that released the bomb's destructive energy.

Sakharov was richly rewarded for these services. He received the Stalin Prize and three orders of Socialist Labor, all in top secret. In 1953, he became the youngest man to be elected a full member of the Soviet Academy of Sciences. He was given the relatively enormous salary of 2,000 rubles a month (equivalent to about $27,000 a year at current exchange rates), privileged housing, a chauffeured car, access to black-market consumer goods, a bodyguard, and other perks.

By the end of the 1950s, however, Sakharov began to question the morality of some of his scientific work. He first publicly aired his opposition to the Soviet government in 1958, in an article published in *Pravda* jointly with Yakov B. Zeldovich on the subject of education. In it, he decried the Soviet educational system and called for reform. Some of his recommendations were adopted by the government. Soon afterwards, he unsuccessfully opposed the government's plan to resume nuclear testing, which it had briefly suspended. This experience changed him profoundly. He also joined with two agricultural scientists, V. P. Efroimson and F. D. Schhepotyev, to denounce the attacks being made on Mendelian genetics.

Sakharov's scientific interests shifted in the 1960s, from thermonuclear energy to the structure of the universe. He published a paper on the appearance of non-uniformity in the distribution of matter in 1965, and one on quarks in 1966. He continued to write on non-scientific subjects, including nuclear disarmament, intellectual freedom, and the need to establish civil liberties in the Soviet Union. His manifesto *Reflections on Progress, Coexistence, and Intellectual Freedom,* self-published in 1968 in the form of a *samizdat* (an illegal, typewritten book), brought Sakharov a wider audience. In it, he discussed various threats facing humankind, including widespread famine, wars, environmental catastrophe, and the danger of nuclear annihilation, and laid out his vision of a less frightening and threatening world based on convergence between socialism and capitalism and rapprochement between the U.S.S.R. and the United States. He called for disarmament, condemned repression in the Soviet Union, and castigated Stalin. The essay was widely circulated both in the U.S.S.R. and abroad; reportedly eighteen million copies in all were published.

Sakharov's complete break with the military-industrial complex came in 1968 with the Soviet invasion of Czechoslovakia. Sakharov and some of his friends had seen the Czechoslovakia of the "Prague Spring" as a model of democratic socialism. Sakharov appealed directly to Soviet President Yuri Andropov to exercise leniency towards the people who had been arrested for demonstrating against the invasion in Red Square. Soon after, he was released from his official duties at the Installation. That year, his wife became seriously ill with gastric hemorrhages. In October, they both moved to the Council of Ministers' sanitarium in Zheleznovodsk. Doctors examining Sakharov found a cardiovascular disorder. In December, his wife was diagnosed with terminal stomach cancer. She died on March 8, 1969.

In 1970, Sakharov came further into conflict with the authorities when he joined other Soviet scientists in forming the Committee for Human Rights to promote the principles espoused in the Universal Declaration of Human Rights. His "Manifesto II" was also published that year in the form of an open address to President Leonid Brezhnev. Written with physicist Valentin F. Turchin and historian Roy A. Medvedev, it accused the government of having failed the people and of having failed to meet the challenges of the modern world. It urged the government to embark on an urgent course of democratization. As the 1970s advanced, Sakharov continued to publish controversial works on these themes, including *Sakharov Speaks* in 1974, *My Country and the World* in 1975, and *Alarm and Hope* in 1979. These writings won him universal acclaim. He was elected a foreign member of the American Academy of Arts and Sciences in 1969, and of the National Academy of Sciences in 1972. He received the Eleanor Roosevelt Peace Award from SANE (Committee for a Sane Nuclear Policy) in 1973; Chicago University's Cino del Duca Prize and Rheinhold Niebuhr Prize in 1974; and the Fritt Ord Prize in 1980. He became a foreign associate of the French Academy of Science in 1981.

In the meantime, Sakharov had remarried. He wed Yelena Bonner, an Armenian-Siberian Jewish dissident, on January 7, 1972. His bride's mother had spent sixteen years in Stalinist gulags. Bonner herself had served as a nurse's aide during World War II, being promoted to lieutenant in the medical corps. Afterwards, she had become a doctor and an activist. She was divorced, with two children.

Sakharov's outspokenness on a range of issues—from the exile of the Tartar people of the Crimea to the government's use of punitive psychiatry—brought him into increasing conflict with the government throughout the 1970s, and he was prevented from traveling to Norway to accept the 1975 Nobel Peace Prize. Sakharov was especially vocal in his opposition to the 1979 Soviet invasion of Afghanistan. In consequence, in January, 1980, he was stripped of his titles and honors and exiled to Gorky, a town of one million that is closed to foreigners. He was forbidden contact with foreigners and most other visitors and kept under constant surveillance. In addition, he was continually harassed. His apartment was repeatedly ransacked by the KGB, and twice he had important manuscripts and documents stolen. He eked out a precarious living on a pension provided by the Academy of Sciences. Sakharov's family also suffered; his stepdaughter was dismissed from Moscow University's journalism school, her husband lost his job, and Sakharov's stepson was denied admission to Moscow University.

On November 21, 1981, Sakharov and Bonner began a seventeen-day hunger strike to protest the Soviet government's refusal to issue an exit visa for Liza Alexeyeva, who wanted to join her fiance, Bonner's son Alexi Semyonov, in the United States. Their protest attracted worldwide attention, and the Soviet government eventually capitulated. In 1984, Sakharov again staged a hunger strike when Bonner was convicted of "slandering the Soviet system," sentenced to internal exile, and prevented from traveling to Moscow. He was detained against his will in Gorky's Semashko Hospital and force-fed. He went on a hunger strike again on July 25, 1985, to protest the government's refusal to allow Bonner an exit visa so that she could go to the United States for medical treatment and to visit her children. Once again he was taken to hospital and force-fed. He ended his strike only when his wife was finally given permission to leave in late October.

In February, 1986, Sakharov wrote to Gorbachev, calling for the release of prisoners of conscience. In October, he wrote yet again, asking that he and Bonner be released from Gorky. He told the General Secretary that he had been exiled illegally, and promised to cease speaking out on public affairs, except when "he could not remain silent." On December 16, 1986, the phone rang in the Sakharov apartment. Mikhail Gorbachev was on the line. He told Sakharov that he and Bonner were at last free to return to Moscow.

On November 6, 1988, Sakharov traveled abroad for the first time in his life. In the United States he met with President George Bush and British Prime Minister Margaret Thatcher. In France for the fortieth anniversary of the Universal Declaration of Human Rights, he met President Francois Mitterrand, Polish president Lech Walesa, and Javier Perez de Cuellar, the United Nations secretary general. In February, he and Yelena Bonner traveled to Italy, where they met with Bettino Craxi, the president of the Italian Socialist Party; Alessandro Pertini, the former president of Italy; and the Pope. Afterwards, they visited Canada. In the summer of 1989, shortly after addressing the first Congress of People's Deputies, Sakharov and Bonner traveled to the United States to visit Bonner's children. Sakharov died of a heart attack on December 14, 1989, in Moscow.

BIOGRAPHICAL/CRITICAL SOURCES:

BOOKS

Babyonyshev, Alexander, editor, *On Sakharov,* Knopf, 1982.
Bonner, Yelena, *Alone Together,* Knopf, 1986.
Medvedev, Zhores A. , *Soviet Science,* Norton, 1978.
Parry, Albert , *The Russian Scientist,* Macmillan, 1973, p. 172.

PERIODICALS

Chicago Tribune, December 17, 1989.
Los Angeles Times, December 15, 1989.
New York Times, December 16, 1989; December 18, 1989; December 19, 1989.
Washington Post, December 16, 1989; December 18, 1989; December 19, 1989.*

*   *   *

SALAM, Abdus 1926-

PERSONAL: Born January 29, 1926, in Jhang, Pakistan; son of Hajira and Muhammed Hussain. *Education:*

Attended Government College, Lahore, Pakistan, 1938-46; St. John's College, Cambridge University, B.A. (mathematics and physics, with highest honors), 1949, Ph.D. (theoretical physics), 1952.

ADDRESSES: Office—International Center for Theoretical Physics, P.O. Box 586, 34100 Trieste, Italy.

CAREER: Physicist. Government College, Lahore, Pakistan, professor, 1951-54; University of Punjab, Lahore, professor and head of math department, 1951-54; St. John's College, Cambridge University, England, fellow, 1951-54, lecturer, 54-56; Imperial College of Science and Technology, London, professor of theoretical physics, 1957-93, senior research fellow, 1994—. United Nations, science and technology advisory committee, member, 1964-75; International Center for Theoretical Physics, founder and director, 1964-93, president, 1994—; Third World Academy of Sciences, founder and president, 1983-94, honorary president, 1995—; Third World Network of Science Organizations, founder and president, 1988-94, honorary president, 1995—.

MEMBER: Stockholm International Peace Research Institute.

AWARDS, HONORS: Hopkins prize, Cambridge University, 1957; Adams prize, 1958; Maxwell medal and prize, London Physics Society, 1961; Atoms for Peace prize, 1968; Oppenheimer prize and medal, 1971; Guthrie medal and prize, Institute of Physics, London, 1976; John Torrence Tate medal, American Institute for Physics, 1978; Nobel Prize in physics (with Sheldon Glashow and Steven Weinberg), 1979.

Einstein award, United Nations Educational, Scientific, and Cultural Organization (UNESCO), 1979; Peace medal, Charles University, Prague, 1981; Gold medal, Czechoslovak Academy of Sciences, 1981, for outstanding contributions to physics; Lomonosov gold medal, U.S.S.R. Academy of Sciences, 1983; Erice Science Peace prize, 1989; Catalunya international prize, 1990; International Leoncino d'Oro prize, Italy, 1993; numerous honorary doctorates.

WRITINGS:

Symmetry Concepts in Modern Physics, edited by Fayyazuddin and M. A. Rashid, Atomic Energy Centre (Lahore, Pakistan), 1966.
On Renormalization Constants and Inter-Relation of Fundamental Forces, International Centre for Theoretical Physics (Trieste), 1970.

(Editor with E. P. Wigner) *Aspect of Quantum Mechanics,* Cambridge University Press, 1972.
Ideas and Realities: Selected Essays of Abdus Salam, World Scientific (Singapore), 1987.
Science in the Third World, Edinburgh University Press (England), c. 1989.
(Editor with Ergin Sezgin) *Supergravities and Diverse Dimensions,* World Scientific/Elsevier Science, 1989.
Renaissance of Sciences in Islamic Countries, edited by H. R. Dalafi and M. H. A. Hassan, World Scientific, c. 1994.
Selected Papers of Abdus Salam, edited by A. Ali, et. al., World Scientific, 1994.

Contributor to journals and periodicals, including *Physical Sciences.*

SIDELIGHTS: Abdus Salam's major field of interest in the 1950s and 1960s was the relationship between two of the four basic forces governing nature then known to scientists: the electromagnetic and weak forces. In 1968, Salam published a theory showing how these two forces may be considered as separate and distinct manifestations of a single more fundamental force, the electroweak force. Experiments conducted at the European Center for Nuclear Research (CERN) in 1973 provided the empirical evidence needed to substantiate Salam's theory. For this work, Salam shared the 1979 Nobel Prize in physics with physicists Sheldon Glashow and Steven Weinberg, who had each independently developed similar theories between 1960 and 1967. Salam's long-time concern for the status of science in Third World nations prompted him in 1964 to push for the establishment of the International Center for Theoretical Physics (ICTP) in Trieste, Italy. The Center provides the kind of instruction for Third World physicists that is generally not available in their own homelands.

Salam was born on January 29, 1926, in the small rural town of Jhang, Pakistan, to Hajira and Muhammed Hussain. Salam's father worked for the local department of education. At the age of sixteen, Abdus Salam entered the Government College at Punjab University in Lahore, and, in 1946, he was awarded his master's degree in mathematics. Salam then received a scholarship that allowed him to enroll at St. John's College at Cambridge University, where he was awarded a bachelor's degree in mathematics and physics, with highest honors, in 1949.

Salam remained at Cambridge as a graduate student for two years, but felt an obligation to return to Pakistan. Accepting a joint appointment as professor of mathematics at the Government College of Lahore and head of the department of mathematics at Punjab University, Salam soon discovered that he had no opportunity to conduct research. "To my dismay," he told Nina Hall for an article in the *New Scientist,* "I learnt that I was the only practicing theoretical physicist in the entire nation. No one cared whether I did any research. Worse, I was expected to look after the college soccer team as my major duty besides teaching undergraduates."

As a result, Salam decided to return to Cambridge, from which he had received a Ph.D. in theoretical physics in 1952. He taught mathematics for two years at Cambridge and, in 1957, was appointed professor of theoretical physics at the Imperial College of Science and Technology in London. He has held that post ever since.

Beginning in the mid-1950s, Salam turned his attention to one of the fundamental questions of modern physics, the unification of forces. Scientists recognize that there are four fundamental forces governing nature—the gravitational, electromagnetic, strong, and weak forces—and, that all four may be manifestations of a single basic force. The unity of forces would not actually be observable, they believe, except at energy levels much greater than those that exist in the everyday world, energy levels that currently exist only in cosmic radiation and in the most powerful of particle accelerators.

Attempts to prove unification theories are, to some extent, theoretical exercises involving esoteric mathematical formulations. In the 1960s, three physicists, Salam, Steven Weinberg, and Sheldon Glashow, independently derived a mathematical theory that unifies two of the four basic forces, the electromagnetic and weak forces. A powerful point of confirmation in this work was the fact that essentially the same theory was produced starting from two very different beginning points and following two different lines of reasoning.

One of the predictions arising from the new electroweak theory was the existence of previously unknown weak "neutral currents," as anticipated by Salam and Weinberg. These currents were first observed in 1973 during experiments conducted at the CERN in Geneva, and later at the Fermi National Accelerator Laboratory in Batavia, Illinois. A second prediction, the existence of force-carrying particles designated as W+, W-, and Z0 bosons was verified in a later series

of experiments also carried out at CERN in 1983. By that time, Salam, Glashow, and Weinberg had been honored for their contributions to the electroweak theory with the 1979 Nobel Prize in physics.

Theoretical physics has been only one of Salam's two great passions in life. The other has been an on-going concern for the status of theoretical physicists in Third World nations. His own experience in Pakistan has been a lifelong reminder of the need for encouragement, instruction, and assistance for others like himself growing up in developing nations. His concern drove Salam to recommend the establishment of a training center for such individuals. That dream was realized in 1964 with the formation of the ICTP in Trieste, Italy, which invites outstanding theoretical physicists to teach and lecture aspiring students on their own areas of expertise. In addition, the Center acts, according to *New Scientist*'s Nina Hall as a "sort of lonely scientist's club for Brazilians, Nigerians, Sri Lankans, or whoever feels the isolation resulting from lack of resources in their own country." Salam has also served as a member of Pakistan's Atomic Energy Commission (from 1958 to 1974) and its Science Council (from 1963 to 1975), as Chief Scientific Advisor to Pakistan's President (from 1961 to 1974) and as chairman of the country's Space and Upper Atmosphere Committee (from 1962 to 1963).

Salam, director of ICTP since its founding, has been involved in a host of other international activities linking scientists to each other and to a variety of governmental agencies. He was a member (from 1964 to 1975) and chairman (from 1971 to 1972) of the United Nations Advisory Committee on Science and Technology, vice president of the International Union of Pure and Applied Physics (from 1972 to 1978), and a member of the Scientific Council of the Stockholm International Peace Research Institute (1970—). Salam has been awarded more than two dozen honorary doctorates and has received more than a dozen major awards, including the Atoms for Peace Award for 1968, the Royal Medal of the Royal Society in 1978, the John Torrence Tate Medal of the American Institute of Physics in 1978, and the Lomonosov Gold Medal of the U.S.S.R. Academy of Sciences in 1983.

BIOGRAPHICAL/CRITICAL SOURCES:

BOOKS

Nobel Prize Winners, H. W. Wilson, 1987, pp. 914-16.

Weber, Robert L., *Pioneers of Science: Nobel Prize Winners in Physics,* American Institute of Physics, 1980, pp. 263-64.
The Way of the Scientist, Simon & Schuster, 1962, pp. 67-76.

PERIODICALS

New Scientist, October 18, 1979, pp. 163-64; January 27, 1990, p. 31.
Physics Today, December, 1979, pp. 17-19.
Science, December 14, 1979, pp. 1290-91.*

*   *   *

SANCHEZ, David A. 1933-

PERSONAL: Born January 13, 1933, in San Francisco, CA; son of Cecilio and Concepcion Sanchez; married Joan Patricia Thomas, December 28, 1957; children: Bruce, Christina. *Education:* University of New Mexico, B.S. (mathematics), 1955; University of Michigan, M.S., 1960, Ph.D. (math), 1964. *Avocational interests:* Fishing, bridge, fiction writing.

ADDRESSES: Office—Academic Affairs, Texas A & M University, College Station, TX 77843-1138.

CAREER: Mathematician. University of Chicago, Chicago, IL, math instructor, 1963-65; University of California, Los Angeles, assistant professor, then professor of math, 1965-77; University of New Mexico, Albuquerque, professor of math, 1977-86, chair of department of math, 1983-86; Lehigh University, Bethlehem, PA, vice president and provost, 1986-90; National Science Foundation, Washington, DC, assistant director of mathematical and physical sciences, 1990-92; Los Alamos National Laboratory, NM, deputy associate director for research and education, 1992-93; Texas A & M System, College Station, vice chancellor of academic affairs, 1993—. University of Manchester, visiting lecturer, 1965-66; Brown University, visiting assistant professor, 1970; Mathematics Research Center, University of Wisconsin, visiting associate professor, 1973-74. *Military Service:* U.S. Marine Corps, 1956-59.

MEMBER: American Mathematical Society, Mathematical Association of America, Society of Industrial and Applied Mathematics, Society for the Advancement of Chicanos and Native Americans in Science.

WRITINGS:

Ordinary Differential Equations and Stability Theory: An Introduction, W. H. Freeman and Co. (San Francisco, CA), 1968.
(With William D. Lakin) *Topics in Ordinary Differential Equations: A Potpourri,* Prindle, Weber and Schmidt (Boston, MA), 1970.
(With Richard. C. Allen and Walter. T. Kyner) *Differential Equations: An Introduction,* second edition, Addison Wesley (Reading, MA), 1988.

Contributor to journals and periodicals, including *Texas A & M Fortnightly.*

SIDELIGHTS: David A. Sanchez is a mathematics scholar with international teaching experience whose recent positions have led him into science administration and academic research program development. Through his study of calculus during his early career, Sanchez developed a particular interest in using ordinary differential equations to create mathematical models for the study of population growth and competing populations. More recently, he has been actively interested in minority participation in academics, and as the vice chancellor for academic affairs of the Texas A & M University System, he provides leadership and coordination to a system of seven universities with an enrollment of over 75,000 students.

David Alan Sanchez was born in San Francisco, California, on January 13, 1933, to Cecilio and Concepcion Sanchez. After obtaining his bachelor of science degree in mathematics from the University of New Mexico in 1955, Sanchez entered the U.S. Marine Corps in 1956. In 1959 he left the Corps as a lieutenant to attend the University of Michigan, where he earned his M.S. in 1960 and his Ph.D. in 1964. During those graduate school years, he also worked as a research assistant in the Radar Laboratory of the university's Institute of Science and Technology, where he investigated signal processing and battlefield simulations for U.S. Army applications. In 1963 he accepted an instructor's position at the University of Chicago; he remained there until 1965 when he became a visiting professor for a year at Manchester University in Manchester, England. In 1966 he returned to the United States, becoming an assistant professor at the University of California at Los Angeles (UCLA). In 1970 he took another year as visiting assistant professor, this time at Brown University in Providence, Rhode Island, and then returned to UCLA as associate professor. After spending a school year during 1973 and 1974 as visiting associate professor at the University of Wisconsin's Mathematics Research Center, Sanchez became a full professor at UCLA in 1976. In 1977 he returned to his alma mater, accepting a professorship at the University of New Mexico. He remained there until 1986, serving as chair of the department of mathematics and statistics from 1983 to 1986. He took time during 1982 to teach at the University of Wales in Aberystwyth.

During this period, Sanchez developed an interest in biomathematics—math that can be applied to the study of biology. He began using mathematical models to study population growth and competing populations. In his study on an ordinary game bird, the sand hill crane, for instance, Sanchez used a mathematical model to predict the effect of an external force that reduces a population, in this case by hunting. He wanted to formulate a simple mathematical equation that could predict the point at which the crane population would face extinction because it was being hunted at a rate faster than it could reproduce and grow. In this and other research studies, Sanchez constructed mathematical models that have implications for the study of human populations.

In 1986, Sanchez made a career switch and accepted a position as vice president and provost at Lehigh University in Bethlehem, Pennsylvania. After four years of administrative experience there, he became the assistant director for mathematical and physical sciences for the National Science Foundation in Washington, D.C. In 1992 he changed from administering science funds to helping to run a federal laboratory, joining the Los Alamos National Laboratory in New Mexico as deputy associate director for research and education. On November 1, 1993, he became vice chancellor for academic affairs for the Texas A & M University System. This large state system, which is composed of seven universities and eight agencies, has an enrollment of over 75,000 students, employs more than 19,000 people, and has operations in each of the 254 counties in Texas. In a *Texas A & M Fortnightly* article, university chancellor William Mobley said that Sanchez's extensive experience with academic and research program development both at the university and at the federal level made him capable of providing the long-range academic planning and linkages needed by its vast university system.

Sanchez is a member of the American Mathematical Society, the Mathematical Association of America, the Society of Industrial and Applied Mathematics, and the Society for the Advancement of Chicanos and Native Americans in Science. A specialist in differential equations, he has published more than fifty articles in professional and technical journals and also is the author of three books on mathematics. He has served on several boards of governors, directors, advisory boards, and policy committees. Always interested in minority participation in academics, he served on the American Mathematical Society's Committee on Opportunities in Mathematics for Disadvantaged Groups, and the Committee on Minority Participation in Mathematics for the Mathematics Association of America.

Sanchez married Joan Patricia Thomas in 1957, and they have two children, Bruce and Christina. Besides mathematics and administration, Sanchez enjoys fishing, bridge, and fiction writing and has published articles in *Flyfishing News* and *The Steamboat Whistle*.

BIOGRAPHICAL/CRITICAL SOURCES:

PERIODICALS

Texas A & M Fornightly, September 27, 1993.

OTHER

Sanchez, David A., interview with Donna Olendorf, April 20, 1994.*

*   *   *

SANDAY, Peggy Reeves 1937-

PERSONAL: Born July 9, 1937, in Long Island, NY; children: two. *Education:* Columbia University, B.A., 1960; University of Pittsburgh, Ph.D. (anthropology), 1966.

ADDRESSES: Office—Department of Anthropology, University of Pennsylvania, Philadelphia, PA 19104.

CAREER: Carnegie-Mellon University, Pittsburgh, PA, assistant professor of anthropology and urban affairs, 1969-72; University of Pennsylvania, Philadelphia, associate professor of anthropology, 1972—.

WRITINGS:

(Editor) *Anthropology and the Public Interest: Fieldwork and Theory*, Academic Press (New York City), 1976.

Female Power and Male Dominance: On the Origins of Sexual Inequality, Cambridge University Press (Cambridge), 1981.

Divine Hunger: Cannibalism as a Cultural System, Cambridge University Press (Cambridge), 1986.

(Editor with Ruth Gallagher Goodenough) *Beyond the Second Sex: New Directions in the Anthropology of Gender,* University of Pennsylvania Press (Philadelphia), 1990.

Fraternity Gang Rape: Sex, Brotherhood, and Privilege on Campus, New York University Press (New York City), 1990.

A Woman Scorned: Acquaintance Rape on Trial, Doubleday (Garden City, NY), 1996.

SIDELIGHTS: Anthropologist Peggy Reeves Sanday has issued several books, among them *Anthropology and the Public Interest: Fieldwork and Theory,* which she edited. This book is a study of the vast influence of anthropology on society, and it contains chapters dealing with the role of the anthropologist in various aspects of American culture, including language planning and public policy.

For her second book, *Female Power and Male Dominance: On the Origins of Sexual Inequality,* Sanday culled anthropological data from some one hundred and fifty societies, studying the history of men's and women's roles in various cultures. In this book, the author analyzes male and female roles in two types of societies: those with inner orientation and those with outer orientation. Inner-oriented societies, Sanday sets forth, are those in which inhabitants live in harmony with nature and with one another. A society that has inner orientation has an abundant food supply, with little need for hunting, and there is no threat of attack or oppression from neighboring societies. The creation story of a society with inner orientation most often finds its god in nature and portrays god as either a woman or a couple.

On the other hand, Sanday demonstrates, societies that have outer orientation offer a more difficult way of life. The scarcity of food forces the men to become hunters and, as food suppliers, men are considered to be more valuable than women. Women in outer-oriented cultures are more apt to be beaten and dominated by their men, and often treated as slaves. The deity of a society that has outer orientation is generally portrayed as a male, supernatural god, who competes with nature.

Sanday's study reports an increase in the number of outer-orientation societies with the advent of western

colonization. Discussing Sanday's report, critics Paula England and Dana Dunn explain Sanday's findings about outer- and inner-orientation in their assessment of *Female Power and Male Dominance* for the *Women's Review of Books:* "Sanday argues that societies with an inner orientation have [far] more egalitarian relationships between men and women. . . . Where an inner orientation prevails men and women share more activities. . . . women have more control over the distribution of goods and services beyond the household and more political power. And where an inner orientation prevails there is less emphasis on male toughness, less wife-beating, less rape, and less frequent raiding of alien groups to take women captive."

Sanday issued her next book, *Divine Hunger: Cannibalism as a Cultural System,* in 1986. In this volume the author looks at fifteen societies that practice, or have previously practiced, cannibalism. Contrary to widespread belief that cannibalism results from food shortages, Sanday's findings indicate that there are spiritual and practical aspects of cannibalism. Kinsmen, for example, often eat the body of a dead loved one in order to bond with the deceased, while others maintain internal order by consuming invasive outsiders. Reviewing *Divine Hunger* in the *New York Times Book Review,* Deborah Gewertz deemed Sanday's work a "lucid and intellectually compelling book [that] demonstrates that cannibals and, in most cases, their victims are likely to regard the torture and consumption of human flesh as entirely appropriate if not essential."

Two of Sanday's later books examine another form of human injustice. *Fraternity Gang Rape: Sex, Brotherhood, and Privilege on Campus* and *A Woman Scorned: Acquaintance Rape on Trial* are the anthropologist's studies of rape and its effect on society. The first of these looks specifically at a gang rape that occurred in a fraternity house on a college campus in 1983. The victim, referred to as "Laurel," was one of the author's students at the time of the rape and told her story to Sanday several weeks after the incident. According to Sanday's account, Laurel had used LSD and was drinking heavily when she attended a fraternity party. After falling down a flight of stairs, Laurel fell asleep, waking later to find herself unclothed and being carried to a room where five or six fraternity brothers raped her. Although the men involved admitted having had relations with Laurel, they insisted that she seduced them and was a willing participant in the incident. The university sided with the fraternity brothers, believing their story that Laurel consented to sex that evening. The brothers were ordered to do some assigned reading and community service assignments as penance, while Laurel was paid a sum of money to settle the issue.

Sanday's book on the fraternity rape focuses on the views of the men involved regarding rape, as well as the opinions of other male college students. The men who raped Laurel did not perceive the incident as rape; on the contrary, they said they were merely taking advantage of a situation, not of a person. They cited her drunkenness as the reason she was so easily victimized, and they refused to admit to rape because they did not have to use force to have sex with her.

Sanday's interviews of male college students reveal the prevalence of gang rape on American campuses. The fraternity brothers who raped Laurel reported that similar incidents occur several times a month at their particular university, as fraternities use gang rapes to prove their prowess, even making participation in gang rapes a segment of hazing rituals for fraternity pledges. This domination of women perpetuates, Sanday asserts, as the fraternity introduces each succeeding generation of pledges to its demoralizing ritual of rape. Still, most of the men interviewed refuse to recognize themselves as rapists.

Sanday further explores society's reaction to rape in *A Woman Scorned,* which traces the history of beliefs about the sexual domination of women, while indicating how those beliefs influence cases of acquaintance rape. *Publishers Weekly* reviewer Peggy Reeves praised *A Woman Scorned,* finding that Sanday's "analysis of past and present attitudes toward acquaintance rape is insightful and persuasive."

BIOGRAPHICAL/CRITICAL SOURCES:

PERIODICALS

Choice, November 1976, p. 1176; November 1981, p. 412; January 1987, p. 791; March 1991, p. 1178.
New York Times Book Review, May 3, 1987, p. 39; April 28, 1991, p. 16.
Publishers Weekly, February 5, 1996, p. 73.
Reviews in Anthropology, vol. 22, no. 3, 1993, pp. 175-84.
Signs, winter 1983, p. 304; winter 1994, p. 527.
Washington Post, September 5, 1991, p. D3.
Women's Review of Books, June 1985, pp. 14-15; February 1991, pp. 8-9.*

SCHAWLOW, Arthur L(eonard) 1921-

PERSONAL: Born May 5, 1921, in Mount Vernon, NY; son of Arthur (an insurance agent) and Helen (Mason) Schawlow; married Aurelia Keith Townes, May 19, 1951; children: Arthur Keith, Helen Aurelia, Edith Ellen. *Education:* University of Toronto, B.A., 1941, M.A., 1942, Ph.D., 1949, L.L.D. (with honors), 1970.

ADDRESSES: Office—Department of Physics, Stanford University, Stanford, CA 94305-4060; fax: 1-(415)-725-2376.

CAREER: Physicist. Columbia University, New York City, research associate, 1949-51; Bell Telephone Labs, Murray Hill, NJ, research physicist, 1951-61; Stanford University, Stanford, CA, professor of physics, 1961-91, department chair, 1966-70, J. G. Jackson/C. J. Wood Professor of Physics, 1978-91.

AWARDS, HONORS: Carbide and Carbon Chemicals scholarship, 1941; Ballantine Medal, Franklin Institute, 1962; Thomas Young Medal and Prize, Physical Society of London and Institute of Physics, 1963; Morris Liebmann Memorial Award, Institute of Electricians and Electrical Engineers, 1964; California Scientist of the Year, 1973; Frederick Ives Medal, Optical Society of America, 1976; Marconi International fellow, 1977; Nobel Prize in Physics, 1981; Schawlow Medal, Laser Institute of America, 1982; National Medal of Science, 1991. Honorary degrees from various universities, including University of Ghent, University of Toronto, University of Bradford, University of Alabama, Trinity College, Dublin, University of Lund, and Victoria University, Toronto.

WRITINGS:

(With C. H. Townes) *Microwave Spectroscopy,* McGraw-Hill, 1955.
(Contributor) *Lasers and Light; Readings from Scientific American,* W. H. Freeman (San Francisco), 1969.

Contributor to journals and periodicals, including *Physical Review* and *Physical Review Letters.*

SIDELIGHTS: Arthur L. Schawlow's contribution to physics lies in his Nobel Prize-winning research regarding the use of laser and maser spectroscopy, which is the examination of spectra shown under the amplification of either a laser or a maser, in order to discover properties of the targeted material. Schawlow is also recognized as an important professor, lecturer, and highly visible member of the scientific community.

Schawlow was born on May 5, 1921, in Mount Vernon, New York. His father, Arthur Schawlow, was an insurance agent who had come to the United States from Latvia circa 1910, and his mother, the former Helen Mason, was a citizen of Canada. After the Schawlow family moved to Toronto, Canada, in 1924, young Arthur was educated at the Winchester Elementary School, the Normal Model School, and the Vaughan Road Collegiate Institute, all in Toronto.

After graduating from high school at the age of sixteen in 1937, Schawlow entered the University of Toronto. He had originally planned to major in radio engineering, but the only scholarship he was able to find was one in physics and mathematics. Thus, it was in these fields that he studied for his bachelor's degree, which he received in 1941. Schawlow also found time during his student days to pursue his favorite hobby, jazz music. A biographer, Boris P. Stoicheff, reports in *Science* that Schawlow "distinguished himself in certain Toronto circles as a clarinetist playing Dixieland jazz at a time when his idols were Benny Goodman and 'Jelly Roll' Morton."

Shortly after Schawlow received his bachelor's degree, Canada and the United States became involved in World War II. His assignment for the next three years was to teach physics to military personnel at the University of Toronto. At the same time, he was able to complete the work necessary for his M.A. degree, which he received in 1942. At the war's conclusion, Schawlow returned to his graduate studies full time. In 1949 he was awarded his Ph.D. in physics for research completed under the supervision of Malcolm F. Crawford.

In 1941 Schawlow was awarded a Carbide and Carbon Chemicals scholarship that allowed him to spend two years as a postdoctoral researcher at Columbia University. While there, Schawlow met Charles H. Townes, who was later to win the 1964 Nobel Prize in physics for his work on the development of the maser. A maser (microwave amplification by stimulated emission of radiation) is a device for amplifying microwave signals. Schawlow and Townes began a long and productive collaboration on the subjects of masers, lasers, and laser spectroscopy. One product of that collaboration was a book, *Microwave Spectroscopy,* published in 1955. Also, towards the end of his postdoctoral work at Columbia, on May 19, 1951,

Schawlow married Townes's sister, Aurelia. The couple later had three children, Arthur Keith, Helen Aurelia, and Edith Ellen.

In 1951 Schawlow accepted a job as a research physicist at the Bell Telephone Laboratories in Murray Hill, New Jersey. He worked on a variety of topics there, including superconductivity and optical and microwave spectroscopy. But he also remained interested in a problem he and Townes had been investigating, an optical maser.

The first maser had been designed and built in the mid-1950s by Townes and two Russian physicists, Nikolai Gennadiyenich Basov and Aleksandr Prokhorov. Following that achievement, a number of physicists had explored the possibility of extending the maser principle to the optical region of the electromagnetic spectrum. After much discussion, Schawlow and Townes developed a proposal for building such an instrument, one that was later given the name laser, for light amplification by stimulated emission of radiation. They published their ideas in the December, 1958, issue of *Physical Review*.

Their next step was to attempt the actual construction of a laser. Unfortunately for Schawlow and Townes, they took a somewhat more difficult approach than was necessary and were to see their concept brought to reality by a fellow physicist, Theodore Maiman, who built the first successful laser in 1960. Schawlow and Townes were not far behind in constructing their own laser, however, and put the new device to use in a number of ways.

One of the most productive uses of laser technology has been in the area of laser spectroscopy, a field in which Schawlow has become one of the world's authorities. In laser spectroscopy, a laser beam is directed at a material to be studied. The wavelengths absorbed and then reemitted by the sample are determined by the electron energy levels and chemical bonds present in the material. By studying the spectra produced by laser analysis, a researcher can determine a number of fundamental properties of a material as well as the changes that take place within the material. For his contributions to the design of the laser and to its applications in laser spectroscopy, Schawlow (along with Nicolaas Bloembergen and Kai M. Siegbahn) was awarded a share of the 1981 Nobel Prize in physics.

In 1961 Schawlow left Bell Laboratories to accept a post as professor of physics at Stanford University.

He served as chair of the department from 1966 to 1970 and in 1978 became J. G. Jackson-C. J. Wood Professor of Physics. Schawlow has been honored not only for his accomplishments as a researcher, but also for his skills as a teacher. Boris Stoicheff's report on the 1981 Nobel Prize in *Science* referred to Schawlow and fellow Nobel laureate Bloembergen as "celebrated teachers, possessed of a characteristic flair and combination of talents that have marked them as outstanding scientists and gifted lecturers."

Schawlow has been a highly visible scientist also, having appeared on Walter Cronkite's television series *The 21st Century,* Don Herbert's *Experiment* series, and on a variety of other U.S. and British educational programs. Among his many awards are the Ballantine Medal of the Franklin Institute (1962), the Thomas Young Medal and Prize of London's Physical Society and Institute of Physics (1963), the Morris Liebmann Memorial Award of the Institute of Electricians and Electrical Engineers (1964), and the Frederick Ives Medal of the Optical Society of America (1976).

BIOGRAPHICAL/CRITICAL SOURCES:

BOOKS

Weber, Robert L., *Pioneers of Science: Nobel Prize Winners in Physics,* American Institute of Physics, 1980, pp. 275-276.
Yen, William M., and Marc D. Levenson, *Lasers, Spectroscopy, and New Ideas: A Tribute to Arthur L. Schawlow,* Springer-Verlag, 1987.

PERIODICALS

Physics Today, December, 1981, pp. 17-20.
Science, November 6, 1981, pp. 629-633.*

*   *   *

SCHOFIELD, Sandy
See RUSCH, Kristine Kathryn

*   *   *

SCHRAEPLER, Hans-Albrecht 1934-

PERSONAL: Born July 23, 1934, in Stolp, Germany; married Christiane Megret de Devise, 1967; children:

Manfred, Anne-Jacqueline, Marc. *Education:* Attended Universities of Tuebingen, Bonn, and Dijon. *Religion:* Protestant.

ADDRESSES: Home—14 Wielandstrasse, 53173 Bonn, Germany. *Office*—German Embassy, 01 BP 1900, Abidjan O1, Ivory Coast; fax 225-32-47-29.

CAREER: Foreign Minister, Bonn, Germany, ambassador to the Ivory Coast; served as head of information for Council of Europe, member of the Royal College of Defense Studies, London, and member of NATO Defense College, Rome, Italy; represented the German Embassy in Jakarta, Saigon, Peking, Paris, Rome, London, and Bamako. Federal Institute of Security Policy Studies, Bonn, past vice president.

AWARDS, HONORS: French and Vietnamese merit awards.

WRITINGS:

European Handbook of Organisations, Whurr Publishers (London, England), 1993.
Organisations Internationales et Europeennes, Economica (Paris, France), 1995.
Taschenbuch der Internationalen Organisationen, Beck (Muenster, Germany), 1995.
Directory of International Organizations, Georgetown University Press (Washington, DC), 1996.

Also author of *International Organizations* (in Russian), Mezjdunarodnye otnosjenija, Russian Federation (Moscow).

WORK IN PROGRESS: Directory of International Economic Organizations, for Georgetown University Press;

SIDELIGHTS: Hans-Albrecht Schraepler told *CA:* "I compiled my books to meet the citizen's need for a practical and concise source of information on international organizations responding to the growing political, economic, and cultural interdependence of countries. The global transition since the collapse of the ideological barrier between East and West has evolved into a redistribution of political and economic cards, in a multidimensional nature of political and economic challenge, in a restrengthened dynamic international cooperation, all of which underline the necessity for such publications. The increasing numbers of natural disasters call additionally for integrated international operations.

"During my work in the German diplomatic service, I noticed that no readily usable source of information was available. The 'fact sheet' style of the data used in my books facilitates immediate understanding and use, both professional and private, of each individual organization and its position within the network of increasing international cooperation. The books are intended to be used by government officials, international organizations, bureaucracies and associations, students, and the general reader."

* * *

SCOT, Michael
  See ROHAN, Michael Scott

* * *

SEMENOV, Nikolai N(ikolaevich) 1896-1986

PERSONAL: Born April 16, 1896, in Saratov, Russia; died in 1986; son of Nikolai Alex and Elena (Dmitrieva) Semenov; married Natalia Nikolaevna Burtseva, September 15, 1924; children: Yurii Nikolaevich, Ludmilla Nikolaevna. *Education:* University at Petrograd, graduated, 1917. *Avocational interests:* Hunting, gardening, architecture.

CAREER: Physical chemist and physicist. Instructor of physics, Siberian University, Leningrad Institute of Physics and Technology, 1920-31; Head Institute of Physical Chemistry of the Soviet Academy of Sciences, 1931-62; head of department of chemical kinematics, University of Moscow.

AWARDS, HONORS: Stalin Prize; Order of the Red Banner of Labor; Order of Lenin (seven times); Nobel Prize in chemistry (with Cyril Hinshelwood), 1956.

WRITINGS:

Chain Reactions, Clarendon Press, 1935.
Chemical Kinetics and Chain Reactions, Clarendon Press, 1935.
Problems of Chemical Kinetics and Reactivity, Princeton University Press, 1958-1959.

Contributor to journals and periodicals, including *Bulletin of the Atomic Scientists.*

SIDELIGHTS: Nikolai N. Semenov was a physical chemist and physicist who was the first Soviet citizen living in Russia to win the Nobel Prize. His scientific work focused on chain reactions and their characteristic "explosiveness" during chemical transformations. This influenced the development of greater efficiency in automobile engines and other industrial applications where controlled combustion was involved, such as jet and rocket engines. Enjoying important academic success, he also played a significant role as a spokesperson for the Soviet scientific community. He was instrumental in establishing institutions where physical chemistry could be studied, and he collaborated in creating a journal dedicated to the field. In addition, he actively participated in scientific conferences dealing with physical chemistry.

Semenov was born on April 16, 1896, in Saratov, Russia, to Nikolai Alex and Elena (Dmitrieva) Semenov. He graduated from Petrograd University (later renamed Leningrad; now called St. Petersburg, its original name) in 1917, the year of revolution that led to the establishment of Communism in Russia. Semenov had shown an interest in science from the time he entered Petrograd University at age sixteen in 1913 to study physics and mathematics. He published his first paper at the age of twenty on the subject of the collision of molecules and electrons. After graduation from Petrograd, Semenov accepted a post in physics at the Siberian University of Tomsk, but in 1920, he returned to Petrograd where he was associated with the Leningrad Institute of Physics and Technology for eleven years. In 1928, Semenov organized the mathematics and physics departments at the Leningrad Polytechnical Institute. He became the head of the Institute of Physical Chemistry of the Soviet Academy of Sciences in 1931, where he remained for more than thirty years. In 1944, Semenov became the head of the department of chemical kinematics at the University of Moscow.

The branch of physical chemistry concerned with the rates and conditions of chemical processes, called chemical kinetics, dominated Semenov's research from his earliest studies. His work led to the understanding of the sequence of chemical reactions and provided insight into the conversion of substances into products. Along with some of his colleagues, Semenov felt that physics held the key to understanding chemical transformations. The branch of science referred to as chemical balances was a consequence of their work.

Semenov was awarded the Nobel Prize in chemistry in 1956 with English chemist Cyril Hinshelwood for their researches into the mechanism of chemical reactions. Both scientists had worked independently for twenty-five years on chemical chain reactions and their importance in explosions. There is wide agreement in the scientific community that Semenov and Hinshelwood were responsible for the development of plastics and the improvement of the automobile engine. There remains some controversy over whether their work on chain reactions contributed to atomic research.

Other experiments by Semenov had culminated in his theory of thermal explosions of mixtures of gases. As a result of this research, he increased the understanding of free radicals—highly unstable atoms that contain a single, unpaired electron. Semenov demonstrated that when molecules disintegrate, energy-rich free radicals are formed. His extensive works on this subject were published first in Russian in the 1930s and later in English.

In subsequent research, Semenov found that the walls of an exploding chamber can influence a chain reaction as well as the substances within the chamber. This concept was particularly beneficial in the development of the combustion engine in automobiles. Semenov's chemical chain reaction theory and his observations on the inflammable nature of gases informed the study of how flames spread, and had practical applications in the oil and chemical industries, in the process of combustion in jet and diesel engines, and in controlling explosions in mines. This work was based on Semenov's earlier investigations of condensation of steam on hard surfaces and its reaction under electric shock.

Semenov made substantial contributions to the development of Soviet scientific institutions and journals. He was active in the training of Soviet scientists and the organizing of important institutions for scientific research in physical chemistry. His long association with the Academy of Sciences of the U.S.S.R. earned him an appointment as a full member in 1932. When the Academy moved to Moscow in 1944, Semenov began teaching at Moscow University. Semenov's theories of combustion, explosion, and problems of chemical kinetics, along with a bibliography of his work by the Academy, were published during the 1940s and 1950s and helped secure his role in his field.

Semenov was not immune to the politics of his country. He became a member of the Communist Party in 1947, and he was the person who answered criticism of the Soviet Union from the *Bulletin of the Atomic Scientists,* a publication of the United States. The *Bulletin* challenged Soviet scientists to protest against Soviet restrictions on release of scientific publications from the country. Semenov replied that there were no such restrictions and accused the American scientists of ignoring their own government restrictions. It was discovered later that some Soviet publications had been arriving regularly at the Library of Congress in Washington, D.C.

In his own country, Semenov was highly regarded. He had received the Stalin Prize, the Order of the Red Banner of Labor, and the Order of Lenin, the latter seven times. He served his country in the political capacity of deputy in the Supreme Soviet in the years 1958, 1962, and 1966, and he was made an alternate to the Central Committee of the Communist Party in 1961. While he was a loyal Soviet citizen, he did work diligently for freedom in scientific experimentation.

On September 15, 1924, he married Natalia Nikolaevna Burtseva, who taught voice, and they had a son, Yurii Nikolaevich, and a daughter, Ludmilla Nikolaevna. Semenov enjoyed hunting, gardening, and architecture in his leisure time. He died in 1986.

BIOGRAPHICAL/CRITICAL SOURCES:

BOOKS

Current Biography, H. W. Wilson, 1947, pp. 498-500.
Prado and Seymour, *McGraw-Hill Encyclopedia of World Biography,* Jack Heraty & Associates, 1973, pp. 504-505.*

*   *   *

S. H.
  See HARTMANN, Sadakichi

*   *   *

SHEINWOLD, Alfred   1912-1997

OBITUARY NOTICE—See index for *CA* sketch: Born January 26, 1912, in London, England; moved to the United States in 1921; naturalized citizen, 1940; died following a stroke, March 8, 1997, in Sherman Oaks, CA. Columnist and contract bridge theorist. Known to many as the "King of Bridge," Sheinwold was one of the foremost authorities on the card game, and his syndicated column on bridge theory appeared in more than two hundred newspapers. A native of England, Sheinwold was brought to the United States as a child and lived in Brooklyn, New York. He began playing bridge while studying economics at the City College of New York and, as a player, won such prestigious tournaments as the North American Open Team Championship, the North American Men's Championship, and the North American Mixed Pair Championship. He led several teams in international competitions, including the 1985 North American team that won the world championship. In addition to his regular column, which he had produced for nearly forty years, Sheinwold was a contributor to leading bridge magazines and had written thirteen books on the subject, including 1959's best-selling work, *Five Weeks to Winning Bridge.* In 1996 Sheinwold was inducted into the Bridge Hall of Fame in Philadelphia, Pennsylvania.

OBITUARIES AND OTHER SOURCES:

BOOKS

Who's Who in America, 47th edition, Marquis, 1992.

PERIODICALS

Los Angeles Times, March 9, 1997, p. B3.
New York Times, March 10, 1997, p. B9.
Washington Post, March 10, 1997, p. D4.

* * *

SHVIDKOVSKY, Dimitri 1959-

PERSONAL: Some sources transliterate the name Dmitri Chvidkovski; born May 14, 1959, in Moscow, U.S.S.R. (now Russia); son of Oleg (a professor of architectural history) and Vera (a professor of architectural history; maiden name, Kalmykova) Shvidkovsky; married Ekaterina Chozban (an art historian), January 6, 1987. *Ethnicity:* "Russian." *Education:* Moscow Institute of Architecture, M.A., 1982; State Institute for Art History, Moscow, Ph.D., 1983. *Religion:* Russian Orthodox.

ADDRESSES: Home—Kv. 90 dom 7/2, B. Dorogomilovskaya Str., Moscow 121 151, Russia. *Office*—

Department of the History of Architecture, Moscow Institute of Architecture, 11 Rojdestvenka, Moscow, Russia; fax 095-921-5190.

CAREER: Moscow Institute of Architecture, Moscow, Russia, professor of architectural history and head of department, 1991—. Academy of Art of the Russian Federation, senior research fellow at Institute for the History and Theory of Art, 1986—.

MEMBER: Society of Architectural History, State Academy of the Fine Arts of the Russian Federation.

WRITINGS:

St. Petersburg (in French), Menges (Paris, France), 1995, English translation published by Abbeville Press (New York City), 1996.
The Empress and the Architect: Architecture and Gardens at the Court of Catherine the Great, Yale University Press (New Haven, CT), 1996.
Moscow: A Guide for Architects, Flammarion (Paris), 1997.
The Moscow Mansions, Trilistnik Publishing (Moscow, Russia), 1997.

Member of editorial board, *Nashe Nasledie* (a Russian heritage magazine)

WORK IN PROGRESS: The History of Russian Architecture in Its Relation to the West.

SIDELIGHTS: Dimitri Shvidkovsky told *CA:* "I was born into a family of architectural historians and couldn't imagine any other occupation than to write about the history of architecture. But, frankly, history was always more of a passion for me than architecture. I am trying only to show how architecture reflects history.

"I am always in a hurry to write something, but writing is a painful process for me. I'm still writing by hand and use an old lady to type everything. She even became able to read my handwriting!"

* * *

SHYER, Christopher 1961-

PERSONAL: Born May 9, 1961, in New Rochelle, NY; son of Robert M. (a business executive) and Marlene (a writer; maiden name, Fanta) Shyer.

Ethnicity: "Caucasian." *Education:* University of Vermont, B.A., 1983; Columbia University, M.B.A., 1987. *Avocational interests:* Skiing, travel.

ADDRESSES: Home—Sleepy Hollow, NY. *E-mail*—Ichabodz@ix.netcom.com. *Agent*—c/o Alice Martell, Martell Agency, 555 Fifth Ave., New York, NY 10017.

CAREER: Zyloware Corporation (suppliers of eyeglasses and sunglasses), Long Island City, NY, vice president, 1989—.

MEMBER: NYACN, MBAQ, NetGALA, Columbia Club.

AWARDS, HONORS: Washington Irving Book Selection, Westchester Library Association, 1997, for *Not Like Other Boys.*

WRITINGS:

(With mother, Marlene Fanta Shyer) *Not Like Other Boys* (nonfiction), Houghton (Boston, MA), 1996.

* * *

SIKORSKY, Igor I(van) 1889-1972

PERSONAL: Born May 25, 1889, in Kiev, Russia (now Ukraine); emigrated to the U.S., 1919; became U.S. citizen, 1928; died of a heart attack, October 26, 1972, in Easton, CT; son of Ivan (a professor of psychology) and Zinaida (a medical school graduate; maiden name, Temrouk-Tcherkoss) Sikorsky; married (marriage ended); married Elizabeth A. Semion, January 27, 1924; children: four sons and a daughter. *Education:* Attended Russian Naval Academy, 1903-06; attended Mechanical College of Polytechnic Institute (Kiev), 1906-08. *Religion:* Russian Orthodox.

CAREER: Aeronautical engineer. Inventor in Russia, 1909-17; teacher in the U.S., c. early 1920s; founder of Sikorsky Aero Engineering Corporation, Long Island, NY, 1923; director of Sikorsky Aeronautical Division (subsidiary of United Aircraft Corporation), 1929-57; consultant; lecturer on aeronautical development to government organizations and universities.

AWARDS, HONORS: Wright Memorial Trophy, 1967, for contributions to aeronautics; National Medal of Science, 1968.

WRITINGS:

Story of the Winged-S, Dodd, 1938.
The Message of the Lord's Prayer, Scribner, 1942.
The Invisible Encounter, Scribner, 1947.
Recollections and Thoughts of a Pioneer, 1964.

Contributor to journals and periodicals, including *Air Force.*

SIDELIGHTS: Igor I. Sikorsky was one of the most significant aeronautical engineers and aircraft designers of the twentieth century. He was a leader in the design of four-engine bombers in World War I and large passenger-carrying seaplanes in the interwar years, but he is best known for designing the first single-rotor helicopters. During and after World War II the Sikorsky Aircraft Division of United Aircraft Corporation became synonymous with a multitude of helicopter designs used for everything from military operations to forest firefighting.

In some respects, Sikorsky's career in the United States was a rags-to-riches story. After gaining a reputation for aeronautical design in Russia, he fled the country following the Bolshevik Revolution and arrived nearly penniless in New York City in 1919. Teaching mathematics to other Russian emigres to make ends meet, he soon obtained financial backers and formed an aeronautical engineering company on Long Island in 1923. Within a decade he had established a central place in the expanding American aviation industry, a place he maintained until his death in 1972.

Perhaps Sikorsky's fascination with helicopters throughout his long life is an appropriate metaphor for his own experience. The search for freedom, whether in flight or in his personal life, motivated much of Sikorsky's career. Sikorsky said he fled Russia for freedom's sake, and he founded his own company and pursued helicopter design for the same reason. According to *Air Force* magazine, in a speech Sikorsky gave in 1967 when he received the Wright Memorial Trophy for his contributions to aeronautics, he summarized his beliefs by emphasizing the importance of "individual initiative, individual work, and total freedom" in the accomplishment of great tasks.

Sikorsky was born on May 25, 1889, in Kiev, Russia, and was the youngest of Ivan and Zinaida Temrouk-Tcherkoss Sikorsky's five children. His family was prominent in Tsarist Russia, where his father was a professor of psychology at St. Vladimir

University in Kiev and his mother was a medical school graduate. Well educated, the young Sikorsky learned about and was fascinated by fifteenth-century Italian artist Leonardo da Vinci's aeronautical studies, especially his drawings of a helicopter-like flying machine.

At age fourteen Sikorsky entered the Imperial Naval College in St. Petersburg and, after graduating in 1906, entered the Mechanical College of the Polytechnic Institute in Kiev. During his two years at the Mechanical College, he concentrated on the new science of aviation. There Sikorsky learned everything he could about early aviators Wilbur and Orville Wright and their experiments in the United States. He also studied the work of Count Ferdinand von Zeppelin, who developed lighter-than-air craft in Germany. In 1909 Sikorsky went to Paris, considered the mecca of aeronautics in Europe at the time, to study the latest design efforts.

Even during that early part of his career, Sikorsky was already studying the possibilities of building a helicopter. He purchased in Paris, for instance, a small 25-horsepower engine to power the rotor on his planned helicopter. For almost two years after his return to Russia, Sikorsky concentrated on designing and building helicopters, but the two prototypes he constructed were unable to lift their own weight. While the designs were sound, the engines needed to be more powerful. As a result, Sikorsky turned to more conventional, winged aircraft, on which a larger body of technical knowledge was available. In 1911 he produced the S-5 racer, which set a speed record of seventy miles per hour. The next year Sikorsky's S-6A design earned an award at a military competition and on the basis of these efforts the Russo-Baltic Railroad Car Works hired him to design a bomber for the Imperial Army.

Sikorsky responded with a huge four-engine aircraft, the *Ilya Mourometz,* which first flew on May 13, 1913. Its four engines each generated from 100 to 220 horsepower, its crew of five had sleeping compartments in the rear fuselage, and it was protected from air attack by either three or four machine guns. The most advanced variant of the *Ilya Mourometz* could remain aloft for five hours at an altitude of approximately nine thousand feet and a speed of eighty-five miles per hour. It could carry a bomb load of between 992 and 1,543 pounds, depending on other operational factors. The aircraft also enjoyed a sixty percent bombs-on-target rating because of precise bombsights and excellent training of bombardiers.

During World War I, Russian Major-General M. V. Shidlovski, commanding the *Eskadra Vozdushnykh Korablei* (Squadron of Flying Ships), equipped his unit with the *Ilya Mourometz.* Formed specifically to exploit the weakness in the air of the Central Powers on the Eastern Front early in the war, Shidlovski made his squadron into a self-contained force with its own test operations, training, and other activities. He first employed it in combat on February 15, 1915, when it left from its base at Jablonna, Poland, and raided a German base in East Prussia. Between this time and November of 1917, Shidlovski's unit made more than four hundred bombing raids over Germany and the Baltic states.

Sikorsky's *Ilya Mourometz* was a rugged airplane. Its only casualty from air attack occurred on September 12, 1916, but only after the aircraft's gunners had shot down three German fighters. Two other bombers were lost in crashes, but the force was not crippled until February of 1918, when thirty planes were destroyed by the Russians at Vinnitza to prevent capture by an advancing German army.

When the Bolshevik Revolution was successful in Russia in 1917, Sikorsky's career as the tsar's bomber designer came to an abrupt end. Not only was Sikorsky targeted as an enemy of Communist revolutionaries because of his family's prominence, but also because of his importance to the tsar as the designer of the *Ilya Mourometz.* Sikorsky abandoned his business and land holdings and went to France, where he was commissioned to build a bomber for the Allied forces still fighting in World War I. The aircraft had not yet progressed beyond the design stage when the Armistice was signed in 1918, and the French cancelled his contract. The next year he came to the United States and lived for a time in New York City, where he existed hand-to-mouth.

Soon after arriving in the United States, Sikorsky tried to obtain a military contract to produce an aircraft, but the War Department declined. It was not until four years later that he found sufficient financial backing to set up the Sikorsky Aero Engineering Corporation on a farm near Roosevelt Field, Long Island.

Immediately after starting his own company, Sikorsky began work on an all-metal passenger monoplane. It became known as the S-29, a twin-engine, fourteen-passenger aircraft with a top speed of 115 miles per hour. In 1925 he organized the Sikorsky Manufacturing Corporation to build the S-29 and combined the engineering and manufacturing companies into the Sikorsky Aviation Corporation in 1928. A string of successful designs that reestablished Sikorsky as a leading aeronautical designer followed. The most important of his designs was the S-38, ten-passenger amphibian, sold to Juan Trippe's Pan American Airways. It was in this business arrangement that Sikorsky first met Charles A. Lindbergh, who had gained international fame for making a solo flight nonstop over the Atlantic in 1927. The two eventually became good friends and sometime business associates.

Sikorsky eventually turned out more than one hundred S-38 seaplanes, and they were used extensively in opening the airline connections between North and South America. Because of this success, in 1929 Sikorsky was bought out by the United Aircraft Corporation, although he continued to direct his operation as a subsidiary. More advanced variations on the S-29 seaplane appeared throughout the 1930s, among them the S-40, called the *American Clipper,* a four-engine amphibian that became a standard vehicle for international flights in the 1930s.

By the mid-1930s Sikorsky had persuaded United Aircraft to allow him to develop a helicopter, and it invested a reported 300,000 dollars in the effort. On September 14, 1939, he flew the first true single-rotor helicopter, the VS-300, a strange configuration of welded pipes and open-air cockpit powered by a seventy-five-horsepower engine that turned a three-bladed rotor by means of an automobile fanbelt. Sikorsky was elated when it flew. He wrote in his autobiography, *Recollections and Thoughts of a Pioneer,* "It is a dream to feel the machine lift you gently up in the air, float smoothly over one spot for indefinite periods, move up or down under good control, as well as move not only forward or backward but in any direction."

Recognizing that this new air vehicle had military potential, the U.S. Army purchased its first helicopter from Sikorsky in 1941. Two years later it ordered the production of the R-4 helicopter, a VS-300 variant. Several years elapsed before the helicopter became a military staple—few of them were used during World War II—but by the time of the Korean War (1950 to 1953) several different designs were being routinely used for observation, transportation of wounded, and movement of high priority cargo and passengers into areas without airfields. In acknowledgment of this use, American helicopter manufacturers received the 1951 Collier Trophy, given annually to the person or group making the most significant contribution to

American aviation. U.S. President Harry S. Truman chose Sikorsky to accept the award on behalf of the industry. Since that time the military has found increasingly sophisticated uses for helicopters, including as gunships, transport vehicles for its "air cavalry" units, and rescue and recovery and commando craft.

Sikorsky was especially delighted with the business and humanitarian uses found for the helicopter during the same era. For instance, in January of 1944 his helicopters were called upon to carry vital blood plasma from New York to Sandy Hook, New Jersey, for the victims of a steamship explosion. Sikorsky recalled in his autobiography, "It was a source of great satisfaction to all the personnel of our organization, including myself, that the helicopter started its practical career by saving a number of lives and by helping man in need rather than by spreading death and destruction."

In the latter 1940s other uses were found for Sikorsky's helicopter, including as an air mail carrier and as air buses transporting passengers from airports to the hearts of major cities. By the early 1960s they were also being routinely used for traffic observation, forest firefighting, crop dusting, rescue, and a host of other practical jobs.

The Sikorsky Aeronautical Division built a succession of helicopters for various purposes during the 1940s and 1950s. After the VS-300 and the R-4 military production model, Sikorsky's helicopters grew in size and complexity. The S-55 was the first certified transport helicopter in the United States, while the twin-engine S-56 was capable of carrying fifty combat troops. An important breakthrough design was the economical S-58, which could carry twelve passengers and was excellent for moving people short distances. Subsequent incarnations of the helicopter included the S-62, an amphibious helicopter with a flying-boat hull, and the S-61 twin-turbine helicopter, used for antisubmarine warfare. Sikorsky also developed the giant S-64 "Skycrane" helicopter, which could haul cargoes of up to ten tons suspended from its belly.

Sikorsky retired from active involvement in aircraft design and production in 1957 but continued as a consultant to his company. Furthermore, after his retirement, Sikorsky enjoyed the role of aviation sage. He was in the spotlight on numerous public occasions, as when he received the National Medal of Science from U.S. President Lyndon B. Johnson in

1968. He also lectured widely on aeronautical development to government organizations, at universities, and within the industry. In every case, Sikorsky spoke of his quest for freedom and his commitment to both technological and personal excellence.

Sikorsky was a deeply religious man, a member of the Russian Orthodox Church and author of two books on Christianity—*The Message of the Lord's Prayer* and *The Invisible Encounter.* He died of a heart attack on October 26, 1972, at the age of eighty-two in his home in Easton, Connecticut. His second wife, Russian-born Elizabeth A. Semion, whom he married in 1924, survived him. Additionally, he had four sons and a daughter, some of whom followed him into the aviation business.

BIOGRAPHICAL/CRITICAL SOURCES:

BOOKS

Finne, K. N., *Igor Sikorsky: The Russian Years,* edited by Carl J. Bobrow and Von Hardesty, Smithsonian Institution Press, 1987.

PERIODICALS

Air Force Magazine, December, 1972, pp. 26-27.
Christian Science Monitor, September, 1963.

OTHER

"The Aviation Careers of Igor Sikorsky," exhibit at the National Air and Space Museum, Smithsonian Institution, Washington, DC, 1990.

Letter from Thurman H. Bane, Engineering Division, Air Service, to Jerome C. Hunsaker, Navy Department, U.S. War Department document, 1919.*

*   *   *

SIMMEL, Georg   1858-1918

PERSONAL: Name is pronounced *Zim*-el; born March 1, 1858, in Berlin, Germany; son of a businessman; died on September 26, 1918. *Education:* University of Berlin, Ph.D., 1881.

CAREER: Sociologist, philosopher, educator, writer. University of Berlin, lecturer, 1885-1900, professor extraordinary, 1900-14; University of Strasbourg, in-

structor, 1914-18. Co-founder, with Max Weber, of the German Sociological Association, 1910.

WRITINGS:

TRANSLATED WORKS

Die Probleme der Geschichtsphilosophie: Eine erkenntnistheoretische studie (philosophy), Duncker & Humblot (Leipzig, Germany), 1892, revised edition, 1905, *The Problems of the Philosophy of History: An Epistemological Essay,* translated and edited with an introduction by Guy Oakes, Free Press (New York), 1977.

Philosophie des Geldes (sociology), Duncker & Humblot, 1900, *The Philosophy of Money,* translated by Tom Bottomore and David Frisby, Routledge & Kegan Paul (London, England), 1978, second enlarged edition edited by David Frisby, Routledge, 1990.

Die Religion (sociology), Rutten & Loening (Frankfurt), 1906, *Sociology of Religion,* translated by Curt Rosenthal, Arno Press (New York), 1979.

Schopenhauer und Nietzsche: Ein Vortragszyklus (philosophy), Duncker & Humblot, 1907, *Schopenhauer and Nietzsche,* translated by Helmut Loiskandl, Deena Weinstein, and Michael Weinstein, University of Massachusetts Press (Amherst), 1986.

Der Konflikt der modernen Kultur: Ein Vortrag (sociology), 1918, *The Conflict in Modern Culture, and Other Essays,* translated and introduced by K. Peter Etzkorn, Teachers College Press (New York), 1968.

The Sociology of Georg Simmel, translated and edited with an introduction by Kurt H. Wolff, Free Press (Glencoe, IL)/Collier-Macmillan, 1950.

Conflict, translated by Kurt H. Wolff, and *The Web of Group-Affiliations* (sociology), translated by Reinhard Bendix, Free Press/Collier-Macmillan, 1955.

Metropolis and Mental Life (sociology), translated by H. H. Gerth and C. Wright Mills, Syllabus Division, University of Chicago Press, 1961.

On Individuality and Social Forms: Selected Writings (sociology), edited and with an introduction by Donald N. Levine, University of Chicago Press (Chicago, IL), 1971.

Essays on Interpretation in Social Science, translated and edited with an introduction by Guy Oakes, Rowman and Littlefield (Totowa, NJ), 1980.

George Simmel: On Women, Sexuality, and Love (essays), translated and introduced by Guy Oakes, Yale University Press (New Haven, NH), 1984.

Essays on Religion: Georg Simmel, edited and translated by Horst Jurgen Helle with Ludwig Nieder, Yale University Press, 1996.

IN GERMAN

Uber sociale differenzierung. Sociologische und psychologische untersuchungen (sociology), Duncker & Humblot, 1890.

Einleitung in die Moralwissenschaft: eine Kritik der ethischen Grundbegriffe (philosophy), 2 vols., W. Hertz (Berlin), 1892-93, reprint edited by Klaus Christian Kohnke, Suhrkamp (Frankfurt), 1989-1991.

Soziologie: Untersuchenungen uber die formen der vergesellschaftung (sociology), Duncker & Humblot, 1908, reprint edited by Otthein Rammstedt, Suhrkamp, 1992.

Hauptprobleme der philosophie (philosophy), G.J. Goschen (Berlin), 1910.

Deutschlands innere Wandlung (lecture), K.J. Trubner (Strasbourg), 1914.

Grundfragen der Soziologie (Individuum und Gesellschaft) (sociology), G.J. Goschen, 1917.

Rembrandt: ein Kunstphilosophischer versuch (criticism), K. Wolff (Leipzig), 1919.

Zur philosophie der Kunst: Philosophische und kunstphilosophische Aufsatze (philosophy), G. Kiepenheuer (Potsdam), 1922.

Fragmente und Aufsatze aus dem Nachlass und Veroffentlichungen der letzten Jahre (essays), 1923, G. Olms (Hildesheim), 1967.

Goethe (criticism), Klinkhardt & Biermann (Leipzig), 1923.

Philosophische kultur: gesammelte essais (philosophy and sociology), G. Kiepenheuer, 1923.

Kant: Sechzehn Vorlesungen gehalten an der Berliner Universitat (philosophy), Duncker & Humblot, 1924.

Rembrandstudien (criticism), B. Schwabe (Basel, Switzerland), 1953.

Brucke und Tur: Essays des Philosophen zur Geschichte, Religion, Kunst, und Gesellschaft (philosophy), K.F. Koehler (Stuttgart), 1957, reprinted as *Das Individuum und die Greiheit: Essais,* K. Wagenbach (Berlin), 1984.

Vom Wesen der Moderne: Essays zur Philosophie und Asthetik (essays), edited by Werner Jung, Junius (Hamburg, Germany), 1990.

Also author of *Das Wesen der Materie nach Kants physischer Monadologie,* 1881; *Philosophie der Mode,* 1905; *Das Problem der historischen Zeit,* 1916; *Der Krieg und die geistigen Entscheidungen: Reden und Aufsatze,* 1917; *Vom Wesen des historischen Verstehens,* 1918; and *Schulpadogogik,* 1922.

SIDELIGHTS: Georg Simmel is considered one of the founders of the science of sociology. A key aspect of his thought is the view that the very structures which facilitate social interaction significantly conflict with the interests of the individual. Indeed, Simmel's lifelong interest in the individual led him not only to such widely recognized areas of sociological inquiry as competition, domination and subordination, imitation, opposition, and so forth, but gave his work a fragmented, example-driven structure which some faulted as unsystematic. Moreover, his far-reaching interests inpelled him to write on religion, philosophy, psychology, and art, as well as sociology, fueling his critics' belief that Simmel's thought was unfocused. Nevertheless, as the field of sociology became more established, Simmel's influence, particularly on defining this new science as distinct from other social sciences, and his impact on such significant twentieth-century thinkers as Georg Lukacs and Max Weber, have been widely recognized.

The youngest of seven children, Simmel was born in Berlin to a successful businessman who died when Simmel was quite young. A Jew who had converted to Catholicism, Simmel's father was married to a woman whose family had themselves converted from Judaism to Lutheranism, the religion in which Simmel was baptized. Though he eventually abandoned the Lutheran Church, Simmel's lasting interest in religion is demonstrated in several of his writings, as well as in the implications of his theories for such matters as morality and the soul. Simmel's guardian, appointed after the death of his father, owned an international music publishing company, and upon his own death, bequeathed to Simmel his fortune, allowing the young man to pursue his intellectual interests without having to earn a living. Indeed, Simmel was employed in unpaid positions at the University of Berlin from 1885 until 1914, when he was offered a salaried professorship at the University of Strasbourg, just four years before his death. His difficulty in attaining academic recognition is attributed to German anti-Semitism, and the disapproval of his contemporaries over his refusal to focus on a single area of inquiry. "[Jose] Ortega y Gasset compared him to a philosophical squirrel, gracefully leaping from one branch of knowledge to another," noted Franklin Parker in the *McGraw-Hill Encyclopedia of World Biography.*

Though Simmel was recognized as a great thinker and speaker during his lifetime, his contribution to the newly developing field of sociology was hotly contested. Criticism of Simmel's theory and practice of sociology during his lifetime centered on his reliance on individual examples, which at times called forth accusations that he was a psychologist or a social-psychologist rather than a sociologist proper. In addition, his prose style, which was often admired as subtle, was also considered scattered or incomplete, leaving some to assume that the author lacked an overarching system of thought or a systematic approach to his subject.

In 1918, Emile Durkheim, concerned with the formation of this new science, analyzed Simmel's writings along these lines, complaining, in an essay which Lewis A. Coser reprinted in his volume, *Georg Simmel,* "For sociology to merit the name of a science, it must be something quite different from philosophical variations on certain aspects of social life, chosen more or less at random according to the leanings of a single individual. What is needed is the formulation of the problem in a way that permits us to draw a logical solution."

After Simmel's death, however, some of his faults were re-interpreted as assets, evidence of his great yet subtle intellect. Ferdinand Tonnies, in a 1918 essay collected in the Coser volume, recalled, "I said in a discussion of the little volume [*On Social Differentiation*] that there remained in it something at times unsure and perhaps even unfinished. I would not dare to make this criticism of the later sociological works; rather, it seems as if this unfinished quality had here become a special art, characterized by suggestion, shading, halftones, and seemingly magical light effects." By the 1950s, any lingering doubts about whether Simmel's work was sociology or something else had faded away. In 1948, Rudolph Heberle, whose essay "The Sociology of Georg Simmel" was collected by editor Harry Elmer Barnes for his *Introduction to the History of Sociology,* remarked: "Simmel himself admits that he did not develop a system. His sociological work consists of a series of essays on subjects not systematically related but selected because of their importance for the study of forms of social interaction." Finally, even Simmel's formerly troubling diffuse interests could be incorporated into his reputation. Thus, Everett C. Hughes wrote admiringly in a 1965 issue of the journal *Social Problems,* "Simmel was, in the original sense of the word, a dilettante, an *amateur passion.* He appears to have written about human society, art, philosophy, religion and money because he took delight in doing so."

BIOGRAPHICAL/CRITICAL SOURCES:

BOOKS

Georg Simmel, edited by Lewis A. Coser, Prentice-Hall, 1965.
An Introduction to the History of Sociology, edited by Harry Elmer Barnes, University of Chicago Press, 1970.
McGraw-Hill Encyclopedia of World Biography, McGraw-Hill, 1973, p. 69.

PERIODICALS

Social Problems, fall, 1965, pp. 117-18.*

* * *

SIMONS, Margaret A. 1946-

PERSONAL: Born April 4, 1946, in Wyandotte, MI; daughter of John E. and Nina M. (Spencer) Simons; married Mikels Skele (an archaeologist). *Education:* Oakland University, B.A. (cum laude), 1968; Purdue University, M.A., 1972, Ph.D., 1977.

ADDRESSES: Office—Department of Philosophical Studies, Southern Illinois University at Edwardsville, Edwardsville, IL 62026-1433. *E-mail*—msimons@ siue.edu.

CAREER: Southern Illinois University at Edwardsville, instructor, 1976-77, assistant professor, 1977-82, associate professor, 1982-90, professor of philosophical studies, 1990—. Southern Illinois University at Edwardsville, acting director of Women's Studies Program, 1983 and 1985, graduate advisor of Women's Studies specialization, 1987—.

MEMBER: North American Society for Social Philosophy (member of board of directors, 1982-85), Society for the Study of Women Philosophers (member of board of directors, 1985—), Society for Phenomenology and Existential Philosophy (chairperson, Committee on the Status of Women), Midwest Society for Women in Philosophy (executive secretary, 1978-80).

AWARDS, HONORS: French government grant, 1972-73; David Ross Fellowship, Purdue University, 1974-76; Alice Paul Award, Alton-Edwardsville branch, National Organization for Women, 1987; Lover of

Wisdom Award, Southern Illinois University at Edwardsville, 1987, for teaching excellence; grants from National Endowment for the Humanities, 1990 and 1994; grants and fellowships from Southern Illinois University, 1979, 1980, 1984, 1985, 1986, 1988, and 1994.

WRITINGS:

(Editor with Azizah al-Hibri) *Hypatia Reborn: Essays in Feminist Philosophy,* Indiana University Press (Bloomington, IN), 1990.
(Editor) *Feminist Interpretations of Simone de Beauvoir,* Pennsylvania State University Press (University Park, PA), 1995.
(Contributor) Lenore Langsdorf and Stephen Watson, editors, *Selected Studies in Phenomenology and Existential Philosophy,* State University of New York Press (Albany, NY), 1997.

Co-editor, "The Beauvoir Series," University of Chicago Press (Chicago, IL). Contributor of articles and reviews to periodicals, including *Signs, Journal of the History of Ideas, Yale French Studies, Women's Studies International Forum,* and *Feminist Studies.* Editor, *Society for Women in Philosophy Newsletter,* 1979-80; editor, *Hypatia: A Journal of Feminist Philosophy,* 1986-90.

WORK IN PROGRESS: Feminism, Race, and the Origins of Existentialism: Simone de Beauvoir's "The Second Sex."

*   *   *

SMITH, Faye McDonald 1950-

PERSONAL: Born August 26, 1950, in Washington, DC; daughter of W. J. and Lil (Thorpe) McDonald (both retired government workers); married George A. Smith, July 17, 1976; children: Mekka, Midion. *Ethnicity:* "African American." *Education:* Boston University, Massachusetts, B.S., 1972; Columbia University, New York City, M.S., 1973. *Politics:* "Independent." *Religion:* Catholic.

ADDRESSES: Office—P.O. Box 42402, Atlanta, GA 30311. *Agent*—241 Avenue of the Americas, Suite 11H, New York, NY 10014.

CAREER: Journalist and screenwriter.

MEMBER: American Friends Service Committee.

AWARDS, HONORS: Honor Book in African American Fiction, American Library Association, for *Flight of the Blackbird.*

WRITINGS:

Flight of the Blackbird, Scribner (New York), 1996.

WORK IN PROGRESS: "Honey Water and Lemon Tea," a short story; a novel.

SIDELIGHTS: Set in Atlanta, Faye McDonald Smith's first novel, *Flight of the Blackbird,* examines the life of Mel Burke, a successful African American professional whose security is shattered when her job at the Atlanta Chamber of Commerce is eliminated. With her husband's construction company in financial shambles, Mel and her family face an uncertain future. As Merle Rubin of *Christian Science Monitor* summarized, "Smith tells the story of this family's many trials and tribulations in all-too-convincing detail, conveying not only the painful humiliations of their financial straits, but also the devastating toll that these troubles take on what once seemed a secure and happy marriage."

Ultimately, Mel and her husband find they must reevaluate both themselves and their relationship with one another in order to identify the strength and spirit within themselves to persevere and overcome. "Smith's characters are human in their complexity of both their frailty and their courage," commented a *Publishers Weekly* contributor. Trudier Harris of *Emerge* felt differently and wrote, "While these disastrous events should elicit sympathy from readers, they fall short of doing so. The characters are not unlikable, but they fail to engage us thoroughly." However, Rubin's assessment of the book in *Christian Science Monitor* found Smith to be "a sharply observant, sometimes funny, always down-to-earth chronicler of contemporary urban lifestyles and the panic that can lurk beneath glossy surfaces."

Smith told *CA:* "People tell me that the book is very visual, that they see the novel and that they have their own strong images of various scenes. Perhaps because I've produced a lot of audiovisual presentations, certain scriptwriting techniques may have carried over into the book. It's not anything I can definitively point to; I think it's more a matter of interpretation.

"At the core of the novel is the theme of how one's financial stability is often intertwined with self-esteem and self-image. With so many people becoming victims of corporate downsizing, mergers, reorganizations and relocations, job security has become a rare entity. And even for those who aren't directly hit, they most likely have friends, relatives, colleagues or neighbors who have been impacted. I want readers to think of how they might react in a similar situation, when all that's comfortable and familiar starts to slip away. What would it do to their family life? To their marriage? To their own self-worth? These are some of the challenges that Mel and Builder have to confront.

"Through my work as a journalist, I've had the opportunity to write business articles for various publications, profiling large as well as small companies. As a result, I've become very aware of business-related issues involving management, personnel, and office politics. This helped tremendously when I was formulating dialogue about the advantages and pitfalls of working in a major corporation, and it served as a reference to the problems that Builder faced as a struggling entrepreneur."

BIOGRAPHICAL/CRITICAL SOURCES:

PERIODICALS

Booklist, October 15, 1996, pp.405-406.
Christian Science Monitor, January 13, 1997, p.13.
Emerge, November, 1996, pp.104-105.
Publishers Weekly, October 7, 1996, p.60.

*   *   *

SNYDER, John P(arr)   1926-1997

OBITUARY NOTICE—See index for *CA* sketch: Born April 12, 1926, in Indianapolis, IN; died of multiple myeloma, April 28, 1997, in Olney, MD. Chemical engineer, cartographer, and author. Snyder gained prominence in the field of cartography, designing a method of transforming satellite images of the earth into flat maps. In 1956, Snyder began working as a chemical engineer for CIBA-GEIGY Corporation in New Jersey. During his twenty-four-year career at CIBA-GEIGY, Snyder served as a volunteer analyst for the U.S. Geological Survey (USGS). In 1978, he received the USGS's John Wesley Powell Award and began working for the USGS fulltime. Snyder served as president of the American Cartographic Association and as secretary of the Washington Map Society. He became a lecturer at George Mason University

and contributed articles to scientific journals. In addition, Snyder wrote seven books on map projections, including *The Story of New Jersey's Civil Boundaries, 1606-1968, Map Projections Used by the U.S. Geological Survey, Computer-Assisted Maps Projection Research, Space Oblique Mercator Projection—Mathematical Development,* and *Flattening the Earth: Two Thousand Years of Map Projections.*

OBITUARIES AND OTHER SOURCES:

PERIODICALS

New York Times, May 2, 1997, p. A30.
Washington Post, May 1, 1997, p. D5.

*   *   *

SPERRY, Roger W(olcott)   1913-

PERSONAL: Born August 20, 1913, in Hartford, CT; son of Francis Bushnell (a banker) and Florence Kramer Sperry; married Gay Deupree, 1949; children: Glenn Tad, Janet Hope. *Education:* Oberlin College, B.A. in English, 1935, M.A. in psychology, 1937; University of Chicago, Ph.D., 1941. *Avocational interests:* Camping, sculpture, drawing, ceramics, folk dancing, fossil hunting.

CAREER: Psychobiologist. Harvard University, Cambridge, MA, National Research Council postdoctoral fellow, 1941; Yerkes Laboratories of Primate Biology, Orange Park, FL, Harvard biology research fellow, 1942; University of Chicago, IL, assistant professor of anatomy, beginning 1946, associate professor of psychology, 1952-53; Neurological Diseases and Blindness division of the National Institutes of Health, section chief, 1952-53; California Institute of Technology (Caltech), Hixon Professor of Psychobiology, 1954-84. *Military service:* Worked in Office of Scientific Research and Development (OSRD) during World War II.

MEMBER: Pontifical Academy of Sciences, National Academy of Sciences, American Philosophical Society, Psychonomic Society, American Psychological Association (fellow).

AWARDS, HONORS: Ralph Gerard Award, Society for Neuroscience, 1979; Albert Lasker Basic Medical Research Award, 1979; Wolf Prize in Medicine, 1979; Golden Plate Award, American Academy of

Achievement, 1980, Nobel Prize for physiology or medicine (with Torsten N. Wiesel and David H. Hubel), 1981; Mentor Society Award, 1987; National Medal of Science, 1989; recipient of numerous honorary degrees.

WRITINGS:

Problems Outstanding in the Evolution of Brain Function, American Museum of Natural History (New York), 1964.

Science and Moral Priority: Merging Mind, Brain, and Human Values, Columbia University Press (New York), 1983.

Novel Laureate Roger Sperry in Dialogue with Albert Outler (sound recording), Isthmus Institute (Dallas, TX), 1983.

Contributor to journals and periodicals, including *Scientific American* and *Harvey Lectures.*

SIDELIGHTS: Roger W. Sperry, a major contributor to at least three scientific fields—developmental neurobiology, experimental psychobiology, and human split-brain studies—conducted pioneering research in the functions of the left and right hemispheres of the brain. He was awarded the Nobel Prize for physiology or medicine in 1981 for his work. The system of split-brain research that he created has enabled scientists to better understand the workings of the human brain.

Sperry was born on August 20, 1913, in Hartford, Connecticut, to Francis Bushnell Sperry, a banker, and Florence Kramer Sperry. When Sperry was eleven years old, his father died and his mother returned to school and got a job as an assistant to a high school principal. Sperry attended local public schools through high school and then went to Oberlin College in Ohio on a scholarship. There he competed on the track team and was captain of the basketball squad. Although he majored in English, Sperry was especially interested in his undergraduate psychology courses with R. H. Stetson, an expert on the physiology of speech. Sperry earned his B.A. in English in 1935 and then worked as a graduate assistant to Stetson for two years. In 1937 he received an M.A. in psychology.

Thoroughly committed to research in the field of psychobiology by that time, Sperry went to the University of Chicago to conduct research on the organization of the central nervous system under the renowned biologist Paul Weiss. Before Weiss's research, scientists believed that the connections of the nervous system had to be very exact to work properly. Weiss disproved this theory by surgically crossing a subject's nerve connections. After the surgery was performed, the subject's behavior did not change. From this, Weiss concluded that the connections of the central nervous system were not predetermined, so that a nerve need not connect to any particular location to function correctly.

Sperry tested Weiss's research by surgically crossing the nerves that controlled the hind leg muscles of a rat. Under Weiss's theory, each nerve should eventually "learn" to control the leg muscle to which it was now connected. This did not happen. When the left hind foot was stimulated, the right foot responded instead. Sperry's experiments disproved Weiss's research and became the basis of his doctoral dissertation, "Functional results of crossing nerves and transposing muscles in the fore and hind limbs of the rat." He received a Ph.D. in Zoology from the University of Chicago in 1941.

Sperry did other related experiments that confirmed his findings and further contradicted Weiss's theory that "function precedes form" (that is, the brain and nervous system learn, through experience, to function properly). In one experiment, Sperry rotated a frog's eyeball and cut its optic nerve. If Weiss's theory was correct, the frog would reeducate itself, adjust to seeing the world upside down, and change its behavior accordingly. This did not happen. In fact, the nerve fibers became tangled in the scar tissue during healing. When the nerve regenerated, it ignored the repositioning of the eyeball and reattached itself correctly, albeit upside down. From this and other experiments, Sperry deduced that genetic mechanisms determine some basic behavioral patterns. According to his theory, nerves have highly specific functions based on genetically predetermined differences in the concentration of chemicals inside the nerve cells.

In 1941, Sperry moved to the laboratory of the renowned psychologist Karl S. Lashley at Harvard to work as a National Research Council postdoctoral fellow. A year later, Lashley became director of the Yerkes Laboratories of Primate Biology in Orange Park, Florida. Sperry joined him there on a Harvard biology research fellowship. While there, he disproved some Gestalt psychology theories about brain mechanisms, as well as some theories of Lashley's.

During World War II, Sperry fulfilled his military service duty by working for three years in an Office of Scientific Research and Development (OSRD) medical research project run by the University of Chicago and the Yerkes laboratory. His work involved research on repairing nerve injuries by surgery. In 1946, Sperry returned to the University of Chicago to accept a position as assistant professor in the school's anatomy department. He became associate professor of psychology during the 1952-53 school year and also worked during that year as section chief in the Neurological Diseases and Blindness division of the National Institutes of Health.

From there he moved in 1954 to the California Institute of Technology (Caltech) to take a position as the Hixon Professor of Psychobiology. At Caltech, Sperry conducted research on split-brain functions that he had first investigated when he worked at the Yerkes Laboratory. It had long been known that the cerebrum of the brain consists of two hemispheres. In most people the left hemisphere controls the right side of the body and vice versa. The two halves are connected by a bundle of millions of nerve fibers called the corpus callosum, or the great cerebral commissure.

Neurosurgeons had discovered that this connection could be cut into with little or no noticeable change in the patient's mental abilities. After experiments on animals proved the procedure to be harmless, surgeons began cutting completely through the commissure of epileptic patients in an attempt to prevent the spread of epileptic seizures from one hemisphere to the other. The procedure was generally successful, and beginning in the late 1930s, cutting through the forebrain commissure became an accepted treatment method for severe epilepsy. Observations of the split-brain patients indicated no loss of communication between the two hemispheres of the brain.

From these observations, scientists assumed that the corpus callosum had no function other than as a prop to prevent the two hemispheres from sagging. Scientists also believed that the left hemisphere was dominant and performed higher cognitive functions such as speech. This theory developed from observations of patients whose left cerebral hemisphere had been injured; these patients suffered impairment of various cognitive functions, including speech. Since these functions were not transferred over to the uninjured right hemisphere, scientists assumed that the right hemisphere was less developed.

Sperry's work shattered these views. He and his colleagues at Caltech discovered that the corpus callosum

is more than a physical prop; it provides a means of communication between the two halves of the brain and integrates the knowledge acquired by each of them. They also learned that in many ways, the right hemisphere is superior to the left. Although the left half of the brain is superior in analytic, logical thought, the right half excels in intuitive processing of information. The right hemisphere also specializes in non-verbal functions, such as understanding music, interpreting visual patterns (such as recognizing faces), and sorting sizes and shapes.

Sperry discovered these different capacities of the two cerebral hemispheres through a series of experiments performed over a period of several decades. In one such experiment, Sperry and a graduate student, Ronald Myers, cut the nerve connections between the two hemispheres of a cat's brain. They discovered that behavioral responses learned by the left side of the brain were not transferred to the right, and vice versa. In an article published in *Scientific American* in 1964, Sperry observed that "it was as though each hemisphere were a separate mental domain operating with complete disregard—indeed, with a complete lack of awareness—of what went on in the other. The split-brain animal behaved in the test situation as if it had two entirely separate brains." It was evident from this experiment that the severed nerves had been responsible for communication between the two halves of the brain.

In another experiment on a human subject, he showed a commissurotomy patient (one whose corpus callosum had been surgically severed) a picture of a pair of scissors. Only the patient's left visual field, which is governed by the nonverbal right hemisphere, could see the scissors. The patient could not verbally describe what he had seen because the left hemisphere, which controls language functions, had not received the necessary information. However, when the patient reached behind a screen, he sorted through a pile of various items and picked out the scissors. When asked how he knew the correct item, the patient insisted it was purely luck.

Sperry published technical papers on his split-brain findings beginning in the late 1960s. The importance of his research was recognized relatively quickly, and in 1979 he was awarded the prestigious Albert Lasker Basic Medical Research Award, which included a 15,000 dollar grant. The award was given in recognition of the potential medical benefits of Sperry's research, including possible treatments for mental or psychosomatic illnesses.

Two years later, Sperry was honored with the 1981 Nobel Prize in physiology or medicine. He shared it with two other scientists, Torsten N. Wiesel and David H. Hubel, for their research on the central nervous system and the brain. In describing Sperry's work, the Nobel Prize selection committee praised the researcher for demonstrating the difference between the two hemispheres of the brain and for outlining some of the specialized functions of the right brain. The committee, as quoted in the *New York Times,* stated that Sperry's work illuminated the fact that the right brain "is clearly superior to the left in many respects, especially regarding the capacity for concrete thinking, spatial consciousness and comprehension of complex relationships."

In his acceptance speech, as quoted in *Science* in 1982, Sperry talked about the significance of his discovery of the previously unrecognized skills of the nonverbal right half-brain. He commented that an important gain from his work is increased attention to "the important role of the nonverbal components and forms of the intellect." Because split-brain research increased appreciation of the individuality of each brain and its functions, Sperry believed that his work helped to point out the need for educational policies that took into consideration varying types of intelligence and potential.

Sperry rejected conventional scientific thinking that viewed human consciousness solely as a function of physical and chemical activity within the brain. In his view, which he discussed in his Nobel Prize lecture, "cognitive introspective psychology and related cognitive science can no longer be ignored experimentally. . . . The whole world of inner experience (the world of the humanities) long rejected by twentieth-century scientific materialism, thus becomes recognized and included within the domain of science."

Known as a private, reserved person, Sperry was, quite characteristically, camping with his wife in a remote area when the news of his Nobel Prize award was announced. He married Gay Deupree in 1949, and they have two children, Glenn Tad and Janet Hope. In addition to camping, Sperry's avocational interests include sculpture, drawing, ceramics, folk dancing, and fossil hunting.

In addition to the Nobel prize, Sperry has received many awards and honorary doctorates. He has been a member of many scientific societies, including the Pontifical Academy of Sciences and the National Academy of Sciences. Sperry always has been held in high regard by his students. One of them, Michael Gazzaniga, described him in *Science* as "exceedingly generous" to many students at Caltech. Gazzaniga also commented that Sperry "is constitutionally only able to be interested in critical issues and he drove this herd of young scientists to consider nothing but the big questions."

BIOGRAPHICAL/CRITICAL SOURCES:

BOOKS

Brain Circuits and Functions of the Mind: Essays in Honor of Roger W. Sperry, edited by Colwyn Trevarthen, Cambridge University Press (New York), 1990.
Nobel Prize Winners, H. W. Wilson Company, 1987.
Omni Interviews, Ticknor & Fields, pp. 187-191.

PERIODICALS

Newsweek, October 19, 1981, p.110.
New York Times, October 10, 1981, pp. 1, 50-51.
Science, October 30, 1981, pp. 517-18; September 24, 1982.
Scientific American, December, 1981, p. 80.*

*   *   *

SPITZER, Lyman (Jr.) 1914-1997

OBITUARY NOTICE—See index for *CA* sketch: Born June 26, 1914, in Toledo, OH; died of heart disease, March 31, 1997, in Princeton, NJ. Astronomer, physicist, and author. Spitzer was the mind and force behind the Hubble Space Telescope and several other instruments orbiting Earth that have greatly increased our understanding of the universe. Born in Ohio, Spitzer attended Yale University and graduated Phi Beta Kappa in 1935. He received his masters and doctorate degrees in astrophysics from Princeton University. Spitzer helped the United States Navy develop sophisticated sonar during World War II and served as professor at Harvard and Yale. He returned to Princeton after the war, where he would develop the ideas that would shape his career. He first conceived of the Hubble Space Telescope in 1947, developed the project and justified its 2.1 billion dollar price tag until its launch in 1990. Spitzer's work also includes numerous satellites measuring X-ray emissions and other cosmological wonders. His written works include *Physics of Fully Ionized Gases* (1956),

Diffuse Matter in Space (1968), *Physical Processes in the Interstellar Medium* (1978), and *Searching Between the Stars* (1982). In 1946, he edited *Physics of Sound in the Sea.* Spitzer continued working until his death. His later career focused on plasma research and a way to develop nuclear fusion as a source of limitless energy. His early experiments on fusion were promising, but the solution has so far eluded science. Spitzer was awarded a gold medal from the Royal Astronomical Society in 1978 for contributions to astrophysics and in 1980 President Jimmy Carter awarded him the National Medal of Science for his work in the theory of star formation and plasma physics.

OBITUARIES AND OTHER SOURCES:

BOOKS

Who's Who in America, 52nd edition, Marquis, 1997.

PERIODICALS

New York Times, April 2, 1997, p. A19.

* * *

STAMFORD KRAUSE, Shari 1961-

PERSONAL: Born March 16, 1961, in Pittsburgh, PA. *Education:* Metropolitan State College, Denver, CO, B.S. (aviation technology), 1983; Embry-Riddle Aeronautical University, Daytona Beach, FL, M.A.S. (distinguished first graduate), 1990; Pacific Western University, Ph.D. (management), 1991.

ADDRESSES: *Home*—2248 South Sutherland Dr., Montgomery, AL 36116. *E-mail*—SSKrause@aol.com.

CAREER: Martin Marietta Aerospace Co., Denver, CO, engineer, 1984-85; Embry-Riddle Aeronautical University, instructor at satellite campuses on U.S. Air Force bases, 1990-96; writer, 1996—. Federal Aviation Administration, licensed single-engine land pilot, 1980—.

WRITINGS:

Avoiding Mid-Air Collisions, McGraw (New York City), 1994.
Aircraft Safety: Accident Investigation, Analyses, and Applications, McGraw, 1996.

Contributor to periodicals, including *Flight Safety Digest.*

* * *

STEHLING, Kurt R(ichard) 1919-1997

OBITUARY NOTICE—See index for *CA* sketch: Born September 19, 1910, in Giessen, Germany; died of a stroke, March 18, 1997, in MD. Oceanographer and author. Stehling came to North America from Germany and was an early contributor to the United States space program. Born in Germany and raised in Canada, Stehling was a graduate of the University of Toronto, where he also earned his master's degree in astrophysics. He served in the Canadian Army during World War II and studied astrophysics at Princeton University after the war. In 1955, Stehling went to work on the American space program with the group that eventually became NASA. He helped develop the Vanguard space rocket and several satellite projects until 1970. He then became a scientist emeritus at the National Oceanic and Atmospheric Administration and served on a presidential task force on how to expand our food sources from the sea. His writings include *Project Vanguard* (1961), *Skyhooks* (1962), *Lasers and Their Applications* (1966) and *Computers and You* (1972). He also contributed articles to such periodicals as *Smithsonian, Air and Space, Popular Mechanics* and *Scientific American.* Stehling is the featured balloonist in the movie *To Fly,* an attraction at the National Air and Space Museum

OBITUARIES AND OTHER SOURCES:

BOOKS

Who's Who in America, 48th edition, Marquis, 1993.

PERIODICALS

Washington Post, March 22, 1997, p. C4.

* * *

STONE, Jon 1931-1997

OBITUARY NOTICE—See index for *CA* sketch: Born April 13, 1931, in New Haven, CT; died of complications from amyotrophic lateral sclerosis (Lou Gehrig's disease), March 30, 1997, in New York, NY. Children's television script writer and author. Stone was the author of several children's books but was best known for writing, producing and directing the television show *Sesame Street,* for which he also created several characters. Educated at Williams College and Yale University's School of Drama, Stone broke into the television business in 1955 with a CBS training program. He joined the Children's Television workshop, along with Muppets creator Jim Henson and Joe Raposo, in 1968 and wrote the pilot script for *Sesame Street,* which is still broadcast on PBS. He also created (with Henson) the Muppets Big Bird and Cookie Monster. He was one of the show's original producers and was the primary director until 1996. Stone's work earned him eighteen Emmys over his career. Also a children's book author, his titles in that medium include *The Monster at the End of This Book,* (1976) and *Would You Like to Play Hide and Seek in This Book With Loveable, Furry Old Grover?* (1976). Stone also wrote and directed several specials, including *Big Bird in China* (1983), *John Denver and the Muppets* (1976), and wrote the pilot for *The Muppet Show.*

OBITUARIES AND OTHER SOURCES:

BOOKS

Who's Who in Entertainment, Marquis, 1992.

PERIODICALS

New York Times, April 1, 1997, p. B10.

*   *   *

STRAUSS, Botho 1944-

PERSONAL: Born December 2, 1944, in Naumburg, Germany; son of a consultant in the grocery business. *Education:* Attended University of Cologne and University of Munich.

CAREER: Playwright, novelist, and short story writer. *Theater heute* (Theater Today), staff writer, 1967-70; Schaubuhne am Halleschen Ufer, Berlin, Germany, dramaturge, 1970—.

AWARDS, HONORS: Hannover Drama Award, 1974, for *Die Hypochonder;* Play of the Year, German critics, and Forderpreis des Schillerpreises, 1977, for

Trilogie des Wiedersehens; Muhlheim Drama Award, for *Kalldewey, Farce;* Georg Buchner Prize, 1989.

WRITINGS:

IN TRANSLATION

Die Widmung: Eine Erzahlung (novel), Hanser, 1977, translation by Sophie Wilkins published as *Devotion,* Farrar, Straus & Giroux, 1979.
Gross und klein: Szenen (drama), Hanser, 1978, translation by Anne Cattaneo published as *Big and Little: Scenes,* Farrar, Straus, Giroux, 1979.
Rumor (novel), Hanser, 1980, translation by Michael Hulse published as *Tumult,* Carcanet Press (Manchester, U.K.), 1984.
Der Park: Schauspiel (drama), C. Hanser, 1983, translation by Tinch Minter and Anthony Vivis published as *The Park,* Sheffield Academic Press (Sheffield, England), 1988.
Die junge Mann (novel), C. Hanser, 1984, translation by Roslyn Thebold published as *The Young Man,* Northwestern University Press, 1995.

IN GERMAN

Bekannte Gesichter, gemischte Gefuhle: Komodie, Verlag der Autoren (Frankfurt am Main), 1974.
Schutzenehre: Erzahlung, illustrated by Axel Hertenstein, Eremiten-Presse (Dusseldorf, Germany), 1975.
Marlenes Schwester: 2 Erzahlungen, Hanser (Munich, Germany), 1975.
Trilogie des Wiedersehens: Theaterstuck (title means "Trilogy of Reunion"; drama), Hanser, 1976.
Die Hypochonder: Bekannte Gesichter, gemischte Gefuhle. 2 Theaterstucke (title means "The Hypochondriacs"; drama), Hanser, 1979.
Kalldewey, Farce (drama), C. Hanser, 1981.
Paare, Passanten (title means "Couples, Wanderers"), Hanser, 1981.
Diese Erinnerung an einen, der nur einen Tag zu Gast war: Gedicht, Hanser, 1985.
Die Fremdenfuhrerin: Stuck in zwei Akten (title means "The Female Tourist Guide"; drama), Hanser, 1986.
Niemand anderes, C. Hanser, 1987.
Versuch, asthetische und politische Ereignisse zusammenzudenken: Text uber Theater, 1967-1986 (title means "Essay on the Combination of Aesthetic and Political Events"), Verlag der Autoren, 1987.
Besucher: Drei Stucke: Besucher, Die Zeit und das Zimmer, Sieben Turen (title means "Visitors:

Three Plays: Visitors, The Time and the Room, and Seven Doors"), Hanser, 1988.

Kongress: die Kette der Demutigungen, Matthes & Seitz (Munich, Germany), 1989.

Fragmente der Undeutlichkeit, Hanser, 1989.

Angelas Kleider: Nachtstuck in zwei Teilen (title means "Angela's Clothes"), Hanser, 1991.

Schlusschor: drei Akte (title means "Choir Finale"), Hanser, 1991.

Theaterstucke, two volumes, Hanser, 1991.

Beginnlosigkeit: Reflexionen uber Fleck und Linie, C. Hanser, 1992.

Das Gleichgewicht: Stuck in drei Akten, C. Hanser, 1993.

Wohnen, dammern, lugen, C. Hanser, 1994.

Strauss has also translated Eugene Martin Labiche's *Das Sparchwein: Komodie,* Verlag der Autoren, 1981.

SIDELIGHTS: Botho Strauss is a highly regarded German playwright and novelist whose writings in both genres are often considered absurdist. The author's typical subject matter—the inability of human beings to meaningfully connect in the modern world, or as Lore Dickstein put it in a review of *Devotion* in the *Saturday Review,* "the isolation of the self/artist in a world where no one really listens"—is given the grotesquely comical or irrational treatment common in absurdist literature. Though Strauss has also at times evoked the pathos of his characters with a poignancy some critics laud, his generic themes and treatment of them at times draw weary commentary from critics in the United States in particular. Strauss is frequently commended for the precision and subtlety of his language, however, particularly in his dramas, and in Germany and Europe has garnered the highest literary prizes for his fearless depiction of the post-modern human condition.

In Strauss's first novel, *Die Widmung* (translated into English as *Devotion*), Richard Schroubek, a bookseller, fills the days of his lover's unexplained absence with writings that demonstrate his continuing devotion to her. Schroubek stays home from his job and eventually runs out of food while pursuing this goal, but when he presents "H." with his manuscript, she accidentally leaves it in a taxi, and it is returned to him unread. His writings, which move from an examination of his own inner state to what the reviewer for *Publishers Weekly* called "wise speculations on language, eros and love" form the whole of Strauss's novel. Comparing *Devotion* to the classic German novel of a young, brokenhearted artist,

Goethe's *Werther,* Joyce Crick of the *Times Literary Supplement* called Strauss's novel "delicate, intelligent, sometimes even humorous." While Christian Graw complained in a review in *World Literature Today* that "There is too much fashionable suffering in his account of his desperation. It appears exaggerated to me," Dickstein compared *Devotion* to "a sculpture by Giacometti—clean, pared-down, and without a shred of unnecessary flesh."

Like *Devotion,* *Rumor* (translated into English as *Tumult*) is a novel that centers on a character in retreat from modern society. Bekker, the novel's protagonist, has earlier left his job for a company that organizes and disperses information, but at the story's open has returned to work in defeat. In his review in *Times Literary Supplement,* Ray Ockenden briefly summarized, "[*Tumult*] offers a bleak view of the disintegration of a personality, along with a sweeping epitaph on the values and hopes of the 1960s and an exposure of the hollow 'new inwardness' of the 1970s." Peter Carrier of the *New Statesman & Society* praised Strauss's "meticulous observations of daily life, a vividly subjective 'worm's-eye' view of modern West Germany."

Critics noted that Strauss's own experience in the theater as both a playwright and a director provides the most lively insights he offers into the eccentric characters and behind-the-scenes drama featured in *Die junge Mann* (translated as *The Young Man*), a novel about an apprentice theater director. But the tale of Leon Pracht, Strauss's protagonist, merely provides a frame for the center of the novel, which the reviewer for *Publishers Weekly* dubbed a series of "heavier-than-air fantasies that tend to revolve around the usual postmodern problems." Although Bruce Allen, critic for the *New York Times Book Review,* found a few "arresting conceptions" buried among the novel's stories-within-a-story, the majority feature characters who lecture each other on flaws in the German culture, and through these stories Strauss lectures the reader, Allen complained.

Strauss began as a playwright, and his plays may be seen as another venue through which he explores his ideas regarding the radical aloneness of the post-modern individual. "Informed by French structuralist and poststructuralist theories, Strauss casts off the notion of a classical subjectivity in favor of a subject defined by his or her position within ideological, literary, economic, and social structures," according to Peter C. Pfeiffer, who provided a career overview of the influential German playwright for *Dictionary of Liter-*

ary Biography. Strauss's first play, *Die Hypochonder* (The Hypochondriacs), tests both the players' and the audience's notions of reality, as neither can be certain whether the events depicted are real or imagined. In *Trilogie des Wiedersehens* (Trilogy of Reunion), a group of people meet at the opening of an art exhibition, and their conversations reveal their inability to act in accordance with their beliefs or to effect change in their lives. Although *World Literature Today* critic John Hess condemned the play with the response "How tiresome and pointless!" *Trilogie* was a tremendous theatrical success, spawning productions throughout Europe, and garnering literary prizes for the author.

Strauss's most famous play, *Gross und klein: Szenen (Big and Little: Scenes),* follows a woman from her separation from her husband through her initial attempts to connect with others to her eventual disintegration into a homeless person sitting in a doctor's office. According to Pfeiffer, "[Lotte's] ailment is incurable because it is the ailment of the 1970s in Germany: a general sense of loss and helplessness combined with a search for salvation." Franz P. Haberl's review of the play in *World Literature Today* highlights Strauss's precise and subtle use of language, and praises his moving portrait of contemporary loneliness. Haberl concludes: "Strauss's remarkable anti-heroine, his superb use of language, his piercing insights into contemporary society and the ingenious locales of the dramatic action all combine to make *Gross und klein* a first-rate play."

Big and Little established Strauss as a pivotal voice in German theater, though his increased fame made him somewhat reclusive, according to Pfeiffer, and he began refusing all interviews. Strauss's subsequent writings, again according to Pfeiffer, showcase the author's increasingly "obsessive" attitude toward his writing life and this, "combined with a quasi-religious outlook on the function of the writer," has marred the playwright's reception by critics in the United States, who perceive such notions as "notoriously Germanic," in Pfeiffer's words. Subsequent plays include *Der Park (The Park),* a dark version of Shakespeare's *A Midsummer Night's Dream* set in an urban park in Germany, *Besucher* (Visitors), a play within a play that stages the conflict over the use of realism in the theater, *Die Zeit und das Zimmer* (The Time and the Room), which Carrier admiringly described as a "biting parody" of the power of language, and *Angelas Kleider* (Angela's Clothes) and *Schlusschor* (Choir Finale), two plays that deal metaphorically with the reunification of Germany. These plays have failed to garner the kind of accolades showered upon *Gross*

und klein or *Trilogie des Wiedersehens,* however, "which are still his best plays," according to Pfeiffer.

Strauss is an influential German playwright and novelist whose peerless reputation in his homeland and throughout Europe remains to be matched in the United States. Focusing on themes of loneliness, the inefficacy of language to communicate, and the passivity that according to Strauss and other artists of the absurdist school are hallmarks of the post-World War II era, Strauss often writes tales whose realism is bracketed by their relationship to a larger story within which they reside. While some critics find his depressing tales of lonely anomie affected rather than affecting, others remark upon Strauss's fine-tuned sense of language and admire his ability to distill the problems of contemporary life within the confines of the printed or spoken word.

BIOGRAPHICAL/CRITICAL SOURCES:

BOOKS

Contemporary Literary Criticism, Volume 22, Gale, 1982, pp. 407-9.
Dictionary of Literary Biography, Volume 124, Gale, 1992, pp. 380-85.

PERIODICALS

Kirkus Reviews, May 15, 1979, p. 600.
Los Angeles Times Book Review, February 1, 1987, p. 10.
New Statesman & Society, December 1, 1989, pp. 37-38.
New York Times Book Review, February 4, 1996, pp. 16-17.
Publishers Weekly, May 28, 1979, p. 52; October 2, 1995, p. 55.
Saturday Review, July 21, 1979, p. 50.
Times Literary Supplement, May 2, 1980, p. 510; February 2, 1985, p. 210.
World Literature Today, summer, 1977, pp. 436-37; winter, 1977, p. 98; summer, 1979, p. 499; winter, 1979, p. 106.*

* * *

SWINDELLS, Madge

PERSONAL: Born in Dover, England; raised in England and South Africa; daughter of Thomas George (a salvage diver) and Nellie (a homemaker; maiden name, Gilmore) Swindells; married Boris Sokolsky (a coffee planter in the Belgian Congo; marriage ended); married Jacobus Smit (a wheat farmer; marriage ended); married Adolph Ferretti Martola Palma (an artist; marriage ended); married Klaus Arthur Friedland (a chartered accountant; marriage ended); children: Ivan Sokolsky, Geraldine Friedland. *Citizenship:* Great Britain. *Education:* Studied anthropology and archaeology at University of Cape Town, South Africa. *Avocational interests:* Reading, entertaining, theatre, music, travel.

ADDRESSES: Home—Cape Town, South Africa. *Office*—c/o Macdonald and Co. Ltd., Greater London House, Hampstead Rd., London NW1 7QX, England. *Agent*—Denise Marcil, 316 West 82nd St., New York, NY 10024.

CAREER: Writer. Worked as a subeditor with the Daily Mirror Group, London, England, for one year; served as an editor at Thompsons Newspapers, Cape Town, South Africa, for two years; self-employed publisher and managing editor for twenty years for publications including *Business Efficiency, Business Week* (a South African financial newspaper), and *Expansion.*

MEMBER: Authors Guild, Authors League of America, P.E.N.

WRITINGS:

Summer Harvest, Macdonald (London), 1983, Doubleday (Garden City, NY), 1984.
Song of the Wind, Doubleday, 1985.
Shadows on the Snow, Macdonald, 1987.
The Corsican Woman, Warner Books (New York City), 1988.
Edelweiss, Little Brown (London), 1993.
Harvesting the Past, Little Brown, 1995.

Swindells's novels have been translated in Swedish, French, Dutch, Italian, German, and Hebrew.

The author's papers are housed in the Mugar Memorial Library, Boston University.

SIDELIGHTS: Madge Swindells is an English-born romance novelist who lives and works in South Africa. Prior to her success as an author her career was based in journalism for more than two decades, first as a newspaper editor and later as the head of a successful magazine publishing company. During these

years, Swindells's two attempts at a novel each met with rejection. Yet when one of her ventures, a sports trading magazine, became successful enough on its own to allow her to hire her own replacement, she concentrated on writing novels full-time, and this time her efforts yielded success.

Swindells' first book, *Summer Harvest,* was published in 1984 to positive reviews that evoked comparisons to *The Thorn Birds,* Colleen McCullough's epic romance saga of Australia. *Summer Harvest* opens in 1938 in rural South Africa, where heroine Anna van Achtenburgh defies her wealthy family and marries a humble farmer. She eventually triumphs over her reduced circumstances, finding both love and financial success. In a *Twentieth-Century Romance and Historical Writers* essay on Swindells, Ferelith Hordon noted that Swindells's "women, especially the female protagonists, are self-willed, independent, intelligent, assertive, and beautiful, and are seen as succeeding in male-dominated areas of endeavour."

In her second novel, 1985's *Song of the Wind,* Swindells again opens her story just as the events of World War II are underway. Her Czechoslovakian heroine, Marika Magos, has lost her parents in the war and has been adopted by a Jewish couple in South Africa. A few years later, Marika falls in love with a mysterious patient in a hospital; it turns out he is German, though through his false identity Marika believes him to be a Swiss citizen named Gunter. When Marika becomes pregnant with the man's child, a jealous nurse informs the Nazi-hating Marika that her lover's name is not Gunter but the German Hans; devastated, Marika flees to England. Years later, she has become a successful fur designer, and Gunter/Hans becomes the focus of a war-crimes trial. Though they have occasionally reunited—albeit unsuccessfully—the trial brings the couple together in a surprising way.

Marika's desire for avenging her parents' murder in *Song of the Wind* is typical of Swindells's methods, according to Hordon. "It is desire for revenge that directs Swindells's characters and determines their actions and reactions," the critic noted in her *Twentieth-Century Romance and Historical Writers* essay.

Swindells would follow with *Shadows on the Snow* in 1987 and then 1988's *The Corsican Woman.* Sybilia, the heroine of the author's fourth novel, is forced into marriage as a young woman, works as a spy against the Nazis during their occupation of Corsica during World War II, and later bears an illegitimate child after her husband's death; for this she is ostracized by the conservative townspeople of her Mediterranean isle. Again, revenge and courtroom drama bring the narrative to a triumphant conclusion for the heroine, in a "suspenseful tale" that a *Publishers Weekly* reviewer noted contained both "a cinematic urgency and vividness." *The Corsican Woman* was then followed by *Edelweiss* in 1993, and *Harvesting the Past* in 1995.

Swindells told *CA* that although she enjoys writing, her success has made it a "more serious business with deadlines to be met, and responsibilities to publishers, distributors, and readers." She believes that a novel's primary function is to entertain: "It is not simply a soapbox for the author's own personal beliefs and hobbyhorses," Swindells explained. "The story can of course have a message or a moral, but

it must be an integral and natural part of the story and not contrived."

BIOGRAPHICAL/CRITICAL SOURCES:

BOOKS

Twentieth-Century Romance and Historical Writers, third edition, St. James Press (Detroit), 1994, p. 650.

PERIODICALS

Cosmopolitan, May 1986.
Femina, October 1983.
Publishers Weekly, April 12, 1985, p. 99; May 24, 1985, p. 62; March 28, 1986, p. 56; August 19, 1988, p. 57.

T-U

TARSKI, Alfred 1901-1983

PERSONAL: Born Alfred Tajtelbaum, January 14, 1901, in Warsaw, Poland; died of a lung condition from smoking, 1983; son of Ignacy (a shopkeeper) and Rose (Iuussak) Tajtelbaum; married Maria Witkowski, June 23, 1929; children: Jan, Ina. *Education:* University of Warsaw, Ph.D., 1924.

CAREER: Mathematician and logician. University of Warsaw, Warsaw, Poland, docent, 1924-25, adjunct professor of mathematics and logic, 1925-39; Zeromski's Lycee, Warsaw, teacher, 1925-39; Harvard University, Cambridge, MA, research associate in mathematics, 1939-41; City College of New York, New York City, visiting professor, 1940; University of California, Berkeley, lecturer, 1942-45, associate professor, 1945-46, professor, 1946-68, professor emeritus, 1968-73. *Military service:* Polish Army, 1918-20.

AWARDS, HONORS: Elected to National Academy of Sciences and Royal Netherlands Academy of Sciences and Letters; corresponding fellow, British Academy; Alfred Jurzykowski Foundation award, 1966; Berkeley Citation, University of California, 1981; awarded numerous honorary degrees and fellowships.

WRITINGS:

Introduction to Logic and to the Methodology of Deductive Sciences, Oxford University Press (New York, NY), c. 1941.

(With J. C. C. McKinsey) *A Decision Method for Elementary Algebra and Geometry,* University of California Press (Berkeley, CA), 1951.

Ordinal Algebras, North-Holland Publishing (Amsterdam, Netherlands), 1956.

Logic, Semantics, Metamathematics: Papers from 1923 to 1938, Clarendon Press (Oxford), 1956, revised edition, edited by J. Corcoran, Hackett Publishing (Indianapolis, IN), 1983.

(With Angrzej Mostowski and Raphael M. Robinson) *Undecidable Theories,* North-Holland Publishing, 1968.

(With Leon Henkin and J. Donald Monk) *Cylindric Algebras,* North-Holland Publishing, 1971-85.

Alfred Tarski: Collected Papers, four volumes, edited by Steven R. Givant and Ralph N. McKenzie, Birk-heauser (Boston), 1986.

(With Steven R. Givant) *A Formalization of Set Theory without Variables,* American Mathematical Society (Providence, RI), 1987.

Contributor to journals and periodicals, including *Philosophy and Phenomenological Research.*

SIDELIGHTS: Alfred Tarski made considerable contributions to several areas of mathematics, including set theory and algebra, and his work as a logician led to important breakthroughs in semantics—the study of symbols and meaning in written and verbal communication. Tarski's research in this area yielded a mathematical definition of truth in language, and also made him a pioneer in studying models of linguistic communication, a subject that became known as model theory. Tarski's research also proved useful in the development of computer science, and he became an influential mentor to later mathematicians as a professor at the University of California at Berkeley.

Born Alfred Tajtelbaum in Warsaw, Poland (then part of Russian Poland), on January 14, 1901, Tarski was the elder of two sons born to Ignacy Tajtelbaum, a shopkeeper of modest means, and Rose (Iuussak)

Tajtelbaum, who was known to have an exceptional memory. During his teens Tarski helped supplement the family income by tutoring. He attended an excellent secondary school, and although he was an outstanding student, he, surprisingly, did not get his best marks in logic. Biology was his favorite subject in high school, and he intended to major in this discipline when he first attended the University of Warsaw. However, as Steven R. Givant pointed out in *Mathematical Intelligence,* "what derailed him was success." In an early mathematics course at the university, Tarski was able to solve a challenging problem in set theory posed by the professor. The solution led to his first published paper, and Tarski, at the professor's urging, decided to switch his emphasis to mathematics.

Tarski received a Ph.D. from the University of Warsaw in 1924, the same year he met his future wife, Maria Witkowski. They married on June 23, 1929, and later had two children, Jan and Ina. It is believed that the young mathematician was in his early-twenties when he changed his name from Tajtelbaum to Tarski. His son, Jan, told interviewer Jeanne Spriter James that this step was taken because Tarski believed that his new Polish-sounding name would be held in higher regard at the university than his original Jewish moniker. When Tarski was married, he was baptized a Catholic, his wife's religion.

Tarski served in the Polish army for short periods of time in 1918 and 1920. While working on his Ph.D. he was employed as an instructor in logic at the Polish Pedagogical Institute in Warsaw beginning in 1922. After graduating he became a docent and then adjunct professor of mathematics and logic at the University of Warsaw beginning in 1925. That same year he also took a full-time teaching position at Zeromski's Lycee, a high school in Warsaw, since his income from the university was inadequate to support his family. Tarski remained at both jobs until 1939, despite repeated attempts to secure a permanent university professorship. Some have attributed Tarski's employment difficulties to anti-semitism, but whatever the reason, his lack of academic prominence created problems for the young mathematician. Burdened by his teaching load at the high school and college, Tarski was unable to devote as much time to his research as he would have liked. He later said that his creative output was greatly reduced during these years because of his employment situation. The papers he did publish in this period, however, quickly marked Tarski as one of the premiere logicians of the century. His early work was often concentrated in the area of set theory. He also worked in conjunction with Polish mathematician Stefan Banach to produce the Banach-Tarski paradox, which illustrated the limitations of mathematical theories that break a space down into a number of pieces. Other research in the 1920s and 1930s addressed the axiom of choice, large cardinal numbers, the decidability of Euclidean geometry, and Boolean algebra.

Tarski's initial research on semantics took place in the early-1930s. He was concerned here with problems of language and meaning, and his work resulted in a mathematical definition of truth as it is expressed in symbolic languages. He also provided a proof that demonstrated that any such definition of truth in a language results in contradictions. A London *Times* obituary on Tarski noted the groundbreaking nature of his work in this area, proclaiming that the mathematician's findings "set the direction for all modern philosophical discussions of truth." Tarski expanded this early work in semantics over the ensuing years, eventually developing a new field of study—model theory—which would become a major research subject for logicians. This area of study examines the mathematic properties of grammatical sentences and compares them with various models of linguistic communication.

Additionally, Tarski pursued research in many other areas of math and logic during his career, including closure algebras, binary relations and the algebra of relations, cylindrical algebra, and undecidable theories. He also made a lasting contribution to the field of computer science. As early as 1930 he produced an algorithm that was capable of deciding whether any sentence in basic Euclidian geometry is either true or false. This pointed the way toward later machine calculations, and has also had relevance in determining more recent computer applications.

In 1939 Tarski left Poland for a conference and speaking tour in the United States, intending to be gone for only a short time. Shortly after his departure, however, the German Army invaded and conquered Poland, beginning World War II. Unable to return to his homeland, Tarski found himself stranded in the United States without money, without a job, and without his wife and children who had remained in Warsaw. The family would not be reunited until after the war, and in the meantime, Tarski set about finding work in America. He first served as a research associate in mathematics at Harvard University from 1939 to 1941. In 1940 he also taught as a visiting professor at the City College of New York. He had a temporary position at the Institute for Advanced Study at Princeton beginning in 1941, and in 1942 he obtained his first permanent position in the United States when he was hired as a lecturer at the University of California at Berkeley. The university would remain his professional home for the rest of his career.

Tarski became an associate professor at the university in 1945, was appointed to the position of full professor the following year, and was named professor emeritus in 1968. Tarski's contributions to mathematics and science were enhanced by his role as an educator. He established the renowned Group in Logic and the Methodology of Science at Berkeley, and over his long tenure he taught some of the most-influential mathematicians and logicians to emerge after World War II, including Julia Robinson and Robert Montague. His stature was further enhanced through his service as a visiting professor and lecturer at numerous U.S. and international universities. In 1973 Tarski ended his formal teaching duties at Berkeley, but he continued to supervise doctoral students and conduct research during the final decade of his life. He died in 1983 from a lung condition caused by smoking.

Tarski received many awards and honors throughout his career. He was elected to the National Academy of Sciences and the Royal Netherlands Academy of Sciences and Letters, and was also made a corresponding fellow in the British Academy. In 1966 he received the Alfred Jurzykowski Foundation Award, and in 1981 he was presented with the Berkeley Citation, the university's highest faculty honor. He also was awarded numerous fellowships and honorary degrees, and was a member in many professional organizations, including the Polish Logic Society, the American Mathematical Society, and the International Union for the History and Philosophy of Science.

BIOGRAPHICAL/CRITICAL SOURCES:

BOOKS

Dictionary of Scientific Biography, Volume 18, Supplement II, Scribner, 1990, pp. 893-96.
Proceedings of the Tarski Symposium, An International Symposium to Honor Alfred Tarski on the Occasion of His Seventieth Birthday, Volume 25, American Mathematical Society, 1974.
Ulam, Stanislaw M., *Adventures of a Mathematician,* Scribner, 1976, pp. 29, 40, 114, 119, 122.

PERIODICALS

California Monthly, December, 1983.
Chicago Tribune, October 30, 1983.

Mathematical Intelligence, vol. 13, no. 3, 1991, pp. 16-32.
Journal of Symbolic Logic, vol. 51, 1986; vol. 53, 1988.
Times (London), December 6, 1983, p. 16-G.
Washington Post, October 29, 1983.

OTHER

Tarski, Jan, interviews with Jeanne Spriter James conducted November 1, 2, 3, 4, and 21, 1993.*

*   *   *

TAYLOR, Dallas 1948-

PERSONAL: Born in 1948, in Denver, CO; son of a stunt pilot; married Betty Wyman (fourth marriage; a drug treatment coordinator), 1988; children: (first marriage) Dallas III, Sharlotte.

ADDRESSES: Agent—c/o Thunder's Mouth Press, Inc., 632 Broadway, 7th floor, New York, NY 10012.

CAREER: Drummer, bass, keyboard, and guitar player, lecturer and counselor on substance abuse recovery and liver transplantation/donor awareness. Member of Clear Light (music group), 1967-68, and Crosby, Stills, Nash and Young (music group), 1969-70, and has played drums, bass, keyboard, or guitar on numerous rock recordings.

AWARDS, HONORS: Grammy Award, Best Album of the Year, 1969, for *Crosby, Stills, and Nash;* Lifetime Achievement Award, Pearl Drums, 1990.

MEMBER: American Academy of Addiction Specialists, United Liver Association (Board of Directors, 1991-92), and Thunderbird Foundation (Board of Trustees, 1992—).

WRITINGS:

Prisoner of Woodstock (autobiography), Thunder's Mouth Press (New York), 1994.

SIDELIGHTS: Musician Dallas Taylor played drums for many of the biggest rock groups of the late 1960s and early 1970s, including Jimi Hendrix, Van Morrison, Eric Clapton, and the group with which he is most closely identified, Crosby, Stills, Nash and Young. He was reportedly a millionaire by age twenty-one, though not many years later he was a destitute addict contemplating suicide. "I was more famous as a junkie than a drummer," Taylor told *People Weekly* of his early success, and recalled his first experiences with opium at the age of four, administered by his mother to ease the stomach ulcers caused by his parents' divorce. Taylor dropped out of school by age sixteen, married his pregnant girlfriend shortly thereafter, and fathered two children by her.

While still a teenager, Taylor moved to Los Angeles and was hired as a drummer by Stephen Stills of Crosby, Stills and Nash, (later, and Young). After playing on two award-winning albums, Taylor was fired for his excessive drug problems, thus beginning a downward spiral that by 1984 found him in Los Angeles attempting suicide. The attempt brought him to the attention of chemical dependency counselors and started him on the road to sobriety. Taylor's happiness in a fourth marriage and in his work as a counselor at a drug rehabilitation center was marred in 1990 when it was discovered that the musician's extensive use of drugs and alcohol had destroyed his liver. Many of Taylor's old friends in the music business, including David Crosby, Stephen Stills, Graham Nash, Neil Young, Don Henley, and Eddie Van Halen rallied behind him, staging a benefit concert to raise the money to pay for the transplant once a donor became available.

Critics noted that Taylor's life story, as told in his autobiography, *Prisoner of Woodstock,* has two main thrusts: his musical rise and fall, and his struggle with drugs and alcohol. Bill Piekarski of *Library Journal* suggested that the stories of Taylor's drug-induced hijinks with famous people might draw readers, though a *Kirkus Reviews* commentator found this aspect of the autobiography "unsatisfying and not always credible." "A worthy cautionary tale . . . doesn't necessarily make a good book," the *Kirkus* reviewer concluded. However, Piekarski remarked: "Taylor's humor and sometimes painful insights will engage the reader's empathy; his casual prose, while less than substantial, is spirited and lively."

Taylor told *CA:* "I'm resuming my musical career. I published an article in the *Los Angeles Times* regarding Kurt Cobain's death. I continue to consult at treatment centers and do interventions with addicts."

BIOGRAPHICAL/CRITICAL SOURCES:

PERIODICALS

Kirkus Reviews, May 15, 1994, p. 690.

Library Journal, June 1, 1994, pp. 108, 110.
People Weekly, April 2, 1990, pp. 84-86.
Rolling Stone, May 17, 1990, p. 18.

*   *   *

TELLES, Lygia Fagundes 1923-

PERSONAL: Born April 19, 1923 (some sources cite 1924), in Sao Paulo, Brazil; married Gofredo da Silva Telles (divorced, 1961); married Paulo Emilio Salles Gomes (writer and film critic; died, 1977). *Education:* Educated at various institutions; obtained degrees in physical education and law.

ADDRESSES: Office—c/o Livaria Jose Olympio Editora, CP 9018, 22251 Rio de Janeiro RJ, Brazil.

CAREER: Lawyer and author; president of Brazilian Cinematheque.

AWARDS, HONORS: Afonso Arinos prize, 1949; Instituto Nacional do Livro prize, 1958; Boa Leitura Prize, 1961; Cannes Prix International des Femmes, 1969, for "Before the Green Masquerade"; Guimaraes Roas prize, 1972; Coelho Neto prize, Brazilian Academy of Letters, Sao Paulo Association of Art Critics fiction prize, and Jabuti Prize, Association of Brazilian Publishers, all 1973, all for *As Menias;* Pedro Nava award, 1989; elected to Brazilian Academy of Letters.

WRITINGS:

FICTION

Porao e sobrado (short stories), [Sao Paulo], 1938.
Praia viva (short stories; title means "Living Beach"), Martins (Sao Paulo), 1943.
O cacto vermelho (short stories; title means "Red Cactus"), Merito (Rio de Janeiro), 1949.
Ciranda de pedra (novel; title means "Stone Screen"), Nova Fronteira (Rio de Janeiro), 1954, fifth edition, Olympio (Rio de Janeiro), 1976, translation by M. Neves published as *The Marble Dance,* Avon (New York City), 1986.
Historias do desencontro (short stories; title means "Stories of the Conflict"), Olympio, 1958.
Historias escolhidas, Boa Leitura (Sao Paulo), 1961.
Verao no aquario (novel; title means "Summer in the Aquarium"), Martins, 1963, fourth edition, Olympio, 1976.

O jardim selvagem (short stories; title means "Savage Garden"), Martins, 1965.

Antes do baile verde (short stories; title means "Before the Green Dance"), Bloch (Rio de Janeiro), 1970, third edition, Olympio, 1975.

Seleta. Organizaco estudos e notas da professora Nelly Novais Coelho, Olympio, 1971.

As menias (novel), Olympio, 1973, eighth edition, 1976, translation by Margaret A. Neves published as *The Girl in the Photograph,* Avon, 1982.

Seminario dos ratos (title means "Rat Seminar"), Olympio, 1977, translation by M. Neves published as *Tigrela and Other Stories,* Avon, 1986.

Filhos prodigos (short stories; title means "Prodigal Sons"), Cultura (Sao Paulo), 1978.

A disciplina do amor: fragmentos (title means "The Discipline of Love"), Nova Fronteira, 1980.

Misterios: ficcoes, Nova Fronteira, 1981.

Os melhores contos, edited by Eduardo Portella, Global (Sao Paulo), 1984.

Diez contos escolhidos, Horizonte (Brasilia), 1984.

Venha ver o por-do-sol y outros contos, Atica (Sao Paolo), 1988.

As horas nuas, Nova Fronteira, 1989.

Also author of *Os mortos,* 1963, and *A confissao de Leontina,* 1964.

SIDELIGHTS: Writer Lygia Fagundes Telles finished her first fiction in 1938, when she was just fifteen years old; five decades later she was still impressing critics and audiences alike with her sometimes surrealistic examinations of her native Brazil's middle and upper classes. "Her efforts as a writer have brought her to the forefront of contemporary Brazilian fiction," writes Jon M. Tolman of Telles in a *Review* article. "Indeed, she has won virtually every major literary prize in Brazil and her writings have found their way into high school and college curricula around the country."

A consistent best-selling author in Brazil, Telles's best-known translated work is the novel *The Girl in the Photograph,* published in the United States in 1982, nine years after its original Brazilian release. A densely layered tale of three school friends from the 1960s who embody the various roles of women in contemporary Brazil—from Marxist revolutionary to bourgeois idealist—*Photograph* is a work whose plot several critics have likened to Jacqueline Susann's *Valley of the Dolls* as seen through the stream-of-consciousness mind of James Joyce's Molly Bloom.

Indeed, some critics found *Photograph* slow going: The narration, "sometimes buried in subordinate clauses deep within pages-long interior monologues," according to a *Los Angeles Times Book Review* contributor, "is hard for this Philistine mind to follow." William Kennedy, reviewing Telles's novel in the *Washington Post Book World,* elaborates: "The internal monologue is a tool, but only a genius can use it to the degree Fagundes Telles uses it. It becomes repetitive and obvious here, an unpleasant thing to say about a writer of her quality." *Newsweek*'s Jim Miller, comparing Telles's work to those of two other contemporary Brazilian novelists, sees "puzzling, pungent, often starkly political" images in the books. While he found *Photograph* "the most naturalistic and least edgy" of the three Brazilian novels he read, Miller adds that "in all three, there's a sense of fierce urgency, a readiness to try almost anything, as if the raw material of history had sabotaged the comforts of conventional narrative."

BIOGRAPHICAL/CRITICAL SOURCES:

BOOKS

Contemporary World Writers, St. James Press (Detroit, MI), 1993.

Monteiro, Leonardo, editor, *Lygia Fagundes Telles* (selected works and criticism), Abril Educacao (Sao Paulo), 1980.

PERIODICALS

Los Angeles Times Book Review, August 1, 1982, p. 8.

Modern Language Studies, vol. 19, no. 1, 1989.

Newsweek, July 12, 1982, p. 71.

New York Times Book Review, May 4, 1986.

Review, September 1981; vol. 36, 1986.

Washington Post Book World, August 1, 1982, p. 1.

World Literature Today, spring, 1978, p. 276.*

*   *   *

TERVALON, Jervey 1958-

PERSONAL: Born November 23, 1958, in New Orleans, LA; son of Hillary (a postal worker) and Lolita (a retired key-punch operator) Tervalon; married Gina Harris (a retired personal analyst); children: Giselle. *Education:* University of California, Santa Barbara, B.A., 1980; University of California, Irvine, M.F.A. (creative writing).

ADDRESSES: Home—Pasadena, CA. *Office*—1142 Lincoln Ave., Pasadena, CA 91103. *Agent*—Joy Harris, Lance & Harris, Inc., 156 5th Ave., New York, NY 10001.

CAREER: Taught in the Los Angeles public schools during the 1980s; University of California, Santa Barbara, instructor in literature, c. 1992-96; freelance writer, c. 1994—; St. Mary's College, Moraga, CA, instructor, c. 1996—.

AWARDS, HONORS: New Voices Award, Quality Paperback Book Club, 1994; Disney Screenwriters Fellowship; fellowships from University of California, Irvine and Pasadena Arts Commission.

WRITINGS:

Understand This (novel), Morrow (New York, NY), 1994.
(Contributor) *Absolute Disaster: Fiction from Los Angeles,* edited by Lee Montgomery, Santa Monica Review, 1996.

WORK IN PROGRESS: Not Sentimental, a fictional history of black Los Angeles; a third novel.

Contributor of short stories to periodicals, including *Spectrum Magazine, Details,* and *Statement.* Contributor of a nonfiction essay for the *L.A. Weekly.*

SIDELIGHTS: Novelist Jervey Tervalon was born in New Orleans, Louisiana, but moved to Los Angeles, California with his family when he was a young boy. Both parents encouraged him to read and to enter college when the time came. After he obtained his bachelor's degree, he went to teach English at a disadvantaged high school in Los Angeles. The things he saw there touched him deeply, and he was especially affected by the murder of a good student who was in the wrong place at the wrong time. Tervalon left high school teaching to return to college in pursuit of a degree in creative writing. While there he began writing a novel inspired by his experiences and observations as a teacher. The book served as his master's thesis and was published to much acclaim in 1994 under the title *Understand This.*

Understand This begins with a murder. Though the novel is narrated by eight different characters, one of the most important is Francois, a young African-American in his last year of high school. Shortly after he finishes playing football with his friend Doug, Doug is shot and killed by his own drug addict girl-friend, who is pregnant by him. *Understand This* then goes on to present the effects of this killing on Francois, Doug's brother and sister, the killer, and others. Narrators of the story also include Margot, Francois' girlfriend, whose grades and determination will enable her to leave the Los Angeles ghetto through college; Francois' mother, a nurse who is determined to move her family to relative safety in Georgia; and Michaels, a caring high school teacher who is quickly reaching the point of burn-out and leaving the students who desperately need him.

Understand This has met with a great deal of praise from critics. Bob Sipchen in the *Los Angeles Times Book Review* applauded the novel's differences from more typical stories of African-American, urban poor affected by violence. "Shrugging off the *de rigueur* overlay of rage and recrimination, resisting the peer pressure to posture macho, [Tervalon] is freer to flex his wit, work out his fine observational skills, and inject his warmth into the yarn," Sipchen affirmed. He went on to laud the author as "daring," and explained that *Understand This* "explores more difficult landscape—geographic and interior—than many of its angrier and grittier brethren." This comment fits with what Tervalon himself emphasized about his novel to Dennis McLellan in the *Los Angeles Times.* "We rarely talk about the internal psychology of these kids. We kind of ignore it and think only of the external. Sometimes there's fear and depression," he added, "but you don't see it. You just see the veneer of a kid that's unscarred, but inside they're suffering." McLellan approved *Understand This* as "a gritty tale." Alison Baker, discussing the novel in the *Washington Post* commended it as well, judging that "Tervalon succeeds in his larger mission, which is to show us this particular way of American life." She went on to observe that "good literature has no agenda; it's not propaganda. Tervalon offers no 'solutions.' He's given us a portrait of people who live in a certain world at a certain time and do the best they can." Baker concluded: "*Understand This* is perhaps less an order than a plea."

Tervalon told *CA:* "I'm trying to create a body of work focused on black life in south Los Angeles—and in the United States."

BIOGRAPHICAL/CRITICAL SOURCES:

PERIODICALS

Los Angeles Times, April 4, 1994, sec. "View."

Los Angeles Times Book Review, March 20, 1994, pp. 2, 7.
Washington Post, April 7, 1994, p. C2.

*   *   *

TESLA, Nikola 1856-1943

PERSONAL: Born July 10, 1856, in Smiljan, Austro-Hungary (now Yugoslavia); died January 7, 1943, in New York, NY, following coronary thrombosis; son of Milutin (a clergyman) and Djuka (Mandic) Tesla. *Education:* Attended polytechnic institute in Graz, Austria; may have attended University of Prague, c. 1880.

CAREER: Inventor and electrical engineer. Hungarian Government Telegraph Office, inventor 1881; affiliated with Continental Edison, Paris, 1882; Edison Machine Works, New York, designer of direct current dynamos and motors, 1884; Tesla Electric Company, founder, 1887; lecturer.

AWARDS, HONORS: Edison Medal of the American Institute of Electrical Engineers; Honorary Degrees conferred from Columbia University and Yale University, both 1894; John Scott Medal; inducted into National Inventors Hall of Fame, 1975.

WRITINGS:

The Inventions, Researches and Writings of Nikola Tesla, originally published in *The Electrical Engineer,* 1894, reprinted by Barnes & Noble, 1992.
Lectures, Patents, Articles, originally published by the Nikola Tesla Museum, 1956, reprinted by Health Research, 1973.

Contributor to journals and periodicals, including *Scientific American* and *Electrical Experimenter.*

SIDELIGHTS: The first person to prove and perfect the efficient use of alternating-current electricity, Nikola Tesla saw his polyphase system become the standard for power transmission throughout the world. He also pioneered research in such areas as artificial lightning, high-frequency and high-tension currents, and radio telegraphy. Before his death in 1943, Tesla had acquired more than one hundred patents for high-frequency generators, adjustable condensers, thermomagnetic motors, transformers, his famous Tesla coil, and other inventions that were to become integral elements in modern technology.

Tesla was born on July 10, 1856, the son of Serbian parents in the Croatian village of Smiljan. The settlement was located near the town of Gospic, in what was then a part of the Austro-Hungarian empire, an area that later became Yugoslavia. Tesla's father and mother, Milutin Tesla and Djuka Mandic, had expected their son to follow in his father's footsteps as a Greek Orthodox clergyman. But during his early school years in Smiljan and then in nearby Gospic, where his parents moved when he was six or seven years old, he excelled in math and science. Gradually it became clear that the young and independent-minded Tesla was no candidate for the seminary.

In 1871, when Tesla was fifteen, he attended the higher secondary school at Karlovac, Croatia. After four years, Tesla moved to Graz, Austria, to attend the higher technical school or polytechnic institute in 1875. As before, he excelled in math and science, seemed to have a prodigious memory (he was reputed to have memorized Johann Wolfgang von Goethe's epic drama *Faust*), and showed particular interest in electrical engineering. While attending the technical school in Graz, Tesla commented on the unnecessary (and potentially dangerous) sparks that were emitted by a Gramme dynamo, a direct-current induction motor that was being demonstrated in the classroom. The sparks emerged from where the brushes came into contact with the commutator, and Tesla commented that these sparks could be eliminated by creating a motor without a commutator. The professor was skeptical of the young scientist's theory, and at that time nothing came of the idea. Over the coming years, however, Tesla would continue to work to overcome the problems of direct-current motors.

The details of this period of Tesla's life are unclear, but according to one of his biographers, Margaret Cheney in *Tesla: Man Out of Time,* Tesla's education was interrupted during these years by bouts of malaria and cholera. In any event, Tesla may have attempted to continue his university education at the University of Prague in 1880 (although Cheney indicates that there is no record of this). He was said to have gambled frequently in Prague, wagering for pleasure and in the often vain hope of augmenting his meager income. Tesla appears never to have completed his formal education at Prague, however, possibly because the death of his father forced him to become financially independent. As it was, Tesla may have merely audited classes and used the library without actually enrolling in the university.

Tesla's post-Prague years come into sharper focus. In January 1881 he moved to Budapest where he worked in the Hungarian government's new central telegraph office. During his brief tenure here, Tesla invented a telephone amplifier or loudspeaker, yet for reasons unknown he never patented the device. Tesla also continued to ruminate about the sparks created by the Gramme dynamo in the classroom in Graz, and about rotating magnetic fields, which would later become the basis for all polyphase induction motors. The following year, 1882, Tesla took a position with the Continental Edison Company in Paris.

Tesla's job here was to correct problems in the Edison plants in Germany and France. One of his trips took him to Strasbourg, where he earned local gratitude (but not a promised bonus) for having repaired the railroad station's lighting plant. While in Strasbourg, ever mindful of the sparking problem of direct-current motors, Tesla tried to interest the city's mayor and certain of his wealthy colleagues in his design for an alternating-current motor that would eliminate the need for a commutator. In response, the mayor and his friends rewarded Tesla with a few bottles of 1801 St. Estephe wine but gave no financial support.

Tesla decided to try his luck in the United States where there were interesting developments in electrical engineering and presumably greater opportunities for funding. With a reference from the manager of the Edison company in Paris, Tesla secured a position in Thomas Alva Edison's research laboratory in New York. Tesla embarked for the New World in 1884.

Thomas Edison had already made a reputation for himself as an electronics wizard, but he was committed to the use of direct-current electricity. When Tesla explained to Edison his plans for a motor based on alternating current, all he did was create the foundation for a difficult relationship with his unyielding new boss. Edison insisted that Tesla's designs for his new motor were impractical and dangerous. Edison hired Tesla, however, and for a year the new immigrant designed direct-current dynamos and motors for the Edison Machine Works in New York. The experience was limiting and unsatisfying for Tesla, who found that he was unable to overcome the personal and professional differences that separated him from Edison. These factors and a disagreement over compensation that Tesla felt was due to him caused the young Serb to strike out on his own.

In the ensuing year, some entrepreneurs persuaded Tesla to establish an electric company. He established the company's headquarters in Rahway, New Jersey, in 1885. In establishing his own company Tesla saw an opportunity for working out in a practical way his ideas for alternating current. His financial supporters, however, seemed mainly interested in providing arc lighting for streets and factories. Again, Tesla faced disappointment and was forced to work for at least part of 1886 as a common laborer. In his spare time, however, Tesla continued to work on his innovations. During this period he managed to acquire seven patents for his work with arc lighting. Growing interest in electrical innovations gradually worked to Tesla's advantage, and by 1887 he was able to establish the Tesla Electric Company.

Working within his own organization, Tesla was able to create the first efficient polyphase motor. This was achieved by designing a motor that incorporated several wire-taped blocks that surrounded the rotor. When alternating current is supplied to the wires, with the current to each block being slightly out of phase with the others, a rotating magnetic field is created. The movement of the rotor is achieved as it follows this revolving field. The practical effect of Tesla's invention was that it allowed strong electrical currents to be transmitted over long distances. Edison's direct current, on the other hand, was limited to local use and required many electrical relay stations to distribute the current throughout a given area such as a city. Tesla's invention undermined Edison's assertion that alternating current was impractical, and by 1891 Tesla had acquired forty patents having to do with this technology. His inventions attracted attention, and Tesla began giving lectures in the late 1880s. Perhaps the most notable of these lectures was the one he delivered to the American Institute of Electrical Engineers in May 1888, after which his reputation as a preeminent electrical engineer was firmly established.

George Westinghouse, inventor and manufacturer, bought one of Tesla's patents for the polyphase motor and hired the man to work in his Pittsburgh plant. In 1889 Tesla became an American citizen. He was now famous and his future seemed assured. During the ensuing years, Tesla continued to research and lecture to prestigious organizations across the United States and in Europe. In Britain he addressed the Institution of Electrical Engineers and the Royal Society, and in France, the Society of Electrical Engineers and the French Society of Physics. In these lectures Tesla discussed his work in the transmission of electrical power through radio waves. At the Columbian Exposition in Chicago in 1893, the first world's fair to have electricity, Westinghouse provided it using Tesla's system of polyphase alternating current. At the Exposition Tesla also gave lectures and demonstrations of his research.

It was also Tesla's partnership with Westinghouse that allowed Tesla the opportunity to design what may have been the scientist's greatest achievement, the world's first hydroelectric generating plant. The plant, located at Niagara Falls, distributed electrical current to the city of Niagara Falls and to Buffalo, New York, some twenty-three miles away. The Niagara power plant, completed late in 1895, destroyed forever Edison's objections to Tesla's polyphase system of alternating current and established the kind of power system that would eventually be used throughout the United States and the world.

Meanwhile, Tesla had turned his interests to the proposition that radio waves could carry electrical energy and in 1897 demonstrated wireless communication over some twenty-five miles. Tesla also demonstrated the idea of transmitting electrical energy in 1898 with several radio-controlled model boats that he had constructed. The Spanish-American War was underway at this time, however, distracting the public from this new revelation, and it's also possible that this type of remote-control system was too advanced for its usefulness to be fully appreciated. Many of Tesla's other inventions would later prove beneficial in a number of applications. His work with high-frequency currents yielded several generating machines that were forerunners of those used in radio communication, and his Tesla coil, a resonant air-core transformer, proved capable of producing currents at a great number of frequencies and magnitudes. In 1898, Tesla moved to the clear, dry air of Colorado Springs, Colorado, where he continued his experiments on electricity, but this time on a grander scale than model boats. As before, his interests focused on transmission of high energy, sending and receiving wireless messages, and related issues pertaining to high voltage electricity. The two hundred kilowatt transmitting tower that Tesla built in Colorado Springs could produce lightning bolts that were millions of volts in strength, so powerful they could overload the city's electrical generator. Indeed, during one experiment in creating artificial lightning, Tesla did just that, causing the municipal generator to catch fire and plunging the town into darkness.

Tesla's year of experimentation in Colorado Springs produced no immediate practical results. Tesla's work did provide the basis, however, for research by later scientists. Physicist Robert Golka, for example, modeled his research in plasma physics on material he gleaned from Tesla's often cryptic Colorado Springs notes that were housed at the Tesla Museum in Belgrade after World War II. Similarly, Soviet physicist Pyotr Kapitsa, who shared the 1978 Nobel Prize for his research on magnetism, acknowledged Tesla's work as a model for his own research. Richard Dickinson, a researcher at Cal Tech's Jet Propulsion Laboratory, who was involved in research on the transmission of wireless energy, also invoked Tesla's concepts as a guide to further research.

Although Tesla's work had enduring qualities that inspired the research scientists of later generations, Tesla's influence in the scientific community of his contemporaries began to wane after his year in Colorado Springs. Although he had received royalties from his many patents, that income gradually diminished, due in part to a royalty agreement he had renegotiated with Westinghouse before alternating-current electricity attained prominence. As a result, Tesla realized only a fraction of the fortune that alternating current generated, and he was left with scant resources for his later research. In addition, it appeared at least to some minds that Tesla was beginning to lose his grasp on rigorous scientific inquiry. For example, Tesla had received radio signals while at Colorado Springs that he suggested were from intelligent life on Mars or Venus. Although radio signals from space are now a staple of astronomical research, they were not so in the early years of the twentieth century. And to suggest intelligent life as the source of these signals, without the benefit of corroborating evidence, undermined confidence in Tesla's credibility.

During the last four decades of his life Tesla became reclusive and lived alone in a hotel room in New York City. He continued to perform such experiments as he could with his limited resources, but he never recaptured the glory of his earlier years. Those past accomplishments continued to garner attention, however. Late in 1915 the press rumored that the Nobel Prize committee had listed Tesla and Edison as candidates to share the Nobel Prize in physics. Tesla became indignant because he would have to share the prize with his arch-rival, but for reasons never made clear, the Nobel Prize committee gave the award in physics to two other candidates. In 1917, a colleague recommended Tesla for the prestigious Edison Medal of the American Institute of Electrical Engineers. Again, because of the award's association with Edison,

Tesla at first refused the honor. After he was finally induced to receive the medal and attend the banquet in his honor, he soon drifted from the crowd and was found outside feeding the pigeons.

As Tesla grew older his reclusive and eccentric behavior grew more intense. He was reportedly troubled by phobias—an aversion to pearl earrings and billiard balls, for example—and his ideas seemed ever more bizarre. On his seventy-eighth birthday he told an interviewer that he had plans for an invincible death beam with a potential for fifty million volts that could instantly destroy ten thousand airplanes or one million soldiers. He publicly offered to create such a death beam for the U.S. government, which he said he could create in three months for less than two million dollars.

Early in morning of January 8, 1943, the maid at the Hotel New Yorker discovered Tesla's body in his room. He had been ill for the previous two years and had evidently died in his sleep on the evening of January 7 of a coronary thrombosis. He was eighty-six years old. In death he received much of the adulation that he did not receive during his lifetime. Scores of notable people—Franklin and Eleanor Roosevelt, New York mayor Fiorello H. LaGuardia, political figures from Yugoslavia, Nobel Prize winners, leaders in science—lauded Tesla as a visionary who provided the foundations for modern technology. Indeed, within a year of Tesla's death, the United States Supreme Court ruled that Nikola Tesla, and not Guglielmo Marconi, had invented the radio. Yugoslavia made him a national hero and established the Tesla Museum in Belgrade after World War II. In addition to honorary degrees from American and foreign universities (including Columbia and Yale in 1894), and the Edison Medal, Tesla was also recipient during his lifetime of the John Scott Medal. In 1975 Tesla became an inductee into the National Inventors Hall of Fame.

BIOGRAPHICAL/CRITICAL SOURCES:

BOOKS

Cheney, Margaret, *Tesla: Man Out of Time,* Dorset Press, 1981.
Dictionary of Scientific Biography, Scribner (New York), 1980.
Neidle, Cecyle S., *Great Immigrants,* Twayne Publishers (New York), 1973.
Nikola Tesla, Edition de la Societe pour la Foundation de l'Institut Nikola Tesla, 1936.
O'Neill, John J., *Prodigal Genius,* David McKay Co., 1944.

Ratzlaff, John T., and Leland I. Anderson, *Dr. Nikola Tesla Bibliography,* Ragusan Press, 1979.

PERIODICALS

New York Times, Jan. 8, 1943, p. 19.
Omni, March, 1988, pp. 65-66, 68, 116-117.
Science, May 16, 1958, pp. 1147-1159.
Smithsonian, June 19, 1986, pp. 121-134.*

* * *

TING, Samuel C. C. 1936-

PERSONAL: Born January 27, 1936, in Ann Arbor, MI; son of Kuan Hai (an engineering professor) and Tsun-Ying Wang (a psychology professor); married Kay Louise Kune (an architect) in 1960; children: two daughters. *Education:* University of Michigan, B.S., 1959, Ph.D., 1962.

CAREER: Physicist. Columbia University, on faculty, 1965; Massachusetts Institute of Technology (MIT), professor of physics, beginning 1969.

AWARDS, HONORS: Ford Foundation Fellow, 1963; Nobel Prize for Physics, 1976; E. O. Lawrence Award, 1976.

WRITINGS:

(With G. Bellini) *The Search for Charm, Beauty, and Truth at High Energies,* Plenum Press (New York), 1984.
Tsuchi/Shen Chou Hseueh Jen Tsa Chih She Pein, Pei-ching, 1989.

Contributor to journals and periodicals, including *Physical Review Letters.*

SIDELIGHTS: Samuel C. C. Ting is an American physicist who received the 1976 Nobel Prize for his discovery of the J/psi particle, which led to the detection of many new subatomic particles. Ting shared the prize with Burton Richter, who had made the same discovery almost simultaneously, using a different experimental technique. Ting is known as a confident, daring theorist, as well as a precise experimenter. He is a consummate practitioner of physics in the era of "big science," when research is conducted by large international teams using costly, complex experimental apparatus.

Ting was born in Ann Arbor, Michigan, on January 27, 1936, while his father, Kuan Hai Ting, was studying engineering at the University of Michigan. He completed his studies when Ting was two months old, and the family returned to mainland China, where his father became an engineering professor. His mother, Tsun-Ying Wang, was a psychology professor. As a child, Ting was cared for mostly by his maternal grandmother while both his parents worked. Although his grandmother emphasized the strong value of education, Ting was not able to begin school until he was twelve years old, because World War II intervened. After the war, the family moved to Taiwan, where Ting's father taught at the National Taiwan University.

In 1956, Ting enrolled at the University of Michigan, studying both mathematics and physics, and in 1959 he earned bachelor's degrees in both subjects. He married Kay Louise Kune, an architect, in 1960, with whom he would have two daughters. Ting received his Ph.D. in physics in 1962, and the next year he went to the European Center for Nuclear Research (CERN) in Geneva as a Ford Foundation fellow. He worked with Giuseppe Cocconi on the proton synchrotron, a device that accelerates protons (the nucleus of an atom) for analysis and measurement. In 1965 Ting joined the faculty of Columbia University, where he worked with Tsung-dao Lee and Chien-Shiung Wu.

Ting became interested in the production of electron (negatively charged particles of an atom) and positron (positively charged particles of an atom) pairs by photon radiation after experiments conducted at Harvard raised questions regarding some of the predictions of quantum electrodynamic theory (the theory that deals with the interaction of matter with electromagnetic radiation). He took a leave of absence from Columbia and went to Hamburg, Germany, in 1966 to repeat the Harvard experiments at the German synchrotron facility. There his team built a double-arm spectrometer (an instrument used to analyze and measure particle emissions), which enabled them to measure the momentum of two particles simultaneously. It also recorded the angles of their deflection from the radiation beam. The researchers were able to calculate the masses of the particles and their combined energy, making identification of the particles easier and clarifying their interrelationships. Results of these experiments confirmed the accuracy of the quantum electrodynamic description of pair production.

Ting's work at Hamburg led him to ponder the nature of heavy photons (particles of radiation). After his

return from Germany, he moved to the Massachusetts Institute of Technology (MIT), where he became full professor in 1969. In 1971, while still at MIT, Ting began a project to determine the properties of heavy photons at Brookhaven National Laboratory in Long Island, New York. Rather than the usual method of bombarding a beryllium target with photon beams, he used a proton beam of ten trillion protons per second in hopes of creating a heavy particle that would decay into pairs of electrons and positrons.

Because the search for heavy particles requires such high energy levels, Ting's MIT team redesigned the double-arm spectrometer to detect electron-positron pairs between 1.5 and 5.5 giga-electron volts (a giga equals one billion). The spectrometer also had to be capable of adding precise but small amounts of energy incrementally, as well as detecting their effects on the particle pairs. After several months of searching, the Ting team was rewarded in August, 1974 by the appearance of a sharp spike of high-energy electron-positron pairs at 3.1 billion electron volts. This was unexpected. Ting checked his measurements carefully and decided he was looking at evidence of a new particle that had not been predicted, the J/psi particle. It was heavier than known similar particles; it also occupied a very narrow range of energy states, and it lasted a relatively long time.

Ting reported his results to the Frascati Laboratory in Italy, where physicists were able to confirm his observations in only two days. Ting's paper and the results of the Frascati experiment were accepted for publication in *Physical Review Letters*. Just a few days after Ting discussed the paper with the review's editor, he attended a routine scheduling meeting at the Stanford Linear Accelerator Center; here he shared his results with Stanford's Burton Richter. Amazingly, Richter had made the same discovery at virtually the same time by creating collisions between positrons and electrons in an accelerator.

Ting and Richter shared the 1976 Nobel Prize for physics. The two-year period between discovery and award was probably the shortest interval on record and caused considerable comment at the time, because some scientists feared the discovery would not stand the test of time. However, it has since been the basis for a virtual explosion in the detection of many other fundamental particles.

The J/psi particle's lifespan was a thousand times longer than expected for such a heavy particle (three times heavier than a proton). It was believed that most subatomic particles were made up of combinations of even more fundamental particles called quarks, of which only three types were thought to exist before the discovery of the J/psi particle. The peculiarities of the J/psi particle (especially its long life) suggested the existence of a fourth type of quark, called charm. The J/psi particle was interpreted to be composed of a charmed quark and an antiquark, creating a property called "charmonium."

Charm had been predicted in 1970 and its addition to the family of quarks was thought to unify the electromagnetic and weak forces, further encouraging physicists to believe in the possibility of a grand unifying theory in which the fundamental forces of nature would be shown to be equivalent at very high energies.

There are several stories of how the Ting-Richter particle received its name of J/psi, which is a combination of Ting's name for it (J) and Richter's (psi). Classical particles were traditionally assigned Greek letters for names, while newly discovered particles are labeled with capital letters. One story says Ting called his particle J because he had been working with electromagnetic currents carrying a J label.

Another story says the J derives from the physical symbol for angular momentum. A third claims Ting chose the Chinese symbol for his name. In any case, the particle has retained the double label. A similar particle, called the psi-prime, was found by Richter's team within ten days of the first discovery.

Ting is a fellow of the American, European, and Italian physical societies as well as several academies of science, including the Academia Sinica. In addition to the Nobel Prize, Ting received the 1976 E.O. Lawrence Award.

BIOGRAPHICAL/CRITICAL SOURCES:

BOOKS

Close, Frank, et al., *The Particle Explosion,* Oxford University Press, 1987.

PERIODICALS

Science, December 21, 1990, pp. 1648-1650; January 4, 1991, p. 24; November 27, 1992, p. 1441.
Science News, October 23, 1976, p. 260.*

TIPLER, Frank J(ennings III) 1947-

PERSONAL: Born February 1, 1947, in Andalusia, AL; son of Frank Jennings, Jr. (a lawyer) and Anne (a homemaker; maiden name, Kearley) Tipler; married Jolanta Rokicka (a librarian), November 23, 1986; children: Allison Anne, Caroline N. *Education:* Massachusetts Institute of Technology, S.B., 1969; University of Maryland, Ph.D., 1976. *Politics:* Libertarian. *Religion:* Atheist.

ADDRESSES: Home—3915 St. Charles Ave., Apt. 313, New Orleans, LA 70115. *Office*—Departments of Mathematics and Physics, Tulane University, 312 Gibson Hall, 6823 St. Charles Ave., New Orleans, LA 70118.

CAREER: University of California, Berkeley, research mathematician, 1976-79; Oxford University, Oxford, England, research fellow, 1979; University of Texas, Austin, research associate, 1979-81; Tulane University, New Orleans, LA, associate professor of mathematics, 1981—; writer. Visiting fellow at University of Sussex, 1985.

MEMBER: International Society of General Relativity and Gravitation, American Physics Society, Royal Astronomy Society, Sigma Xi.

WRITINGS:

(Editor) *Essays in General Relativity: A Festschrift for Abraham H. Taub,* Academic Press (New York), 1980.
(With John D. Barrow and Marie-Odile Monchicourt) *L'Homme et le cosmos: Le Principe anthropique en astrophysique moderne* (title means "Man and the Cosmos: The Anthropic Principle in Modern Astrophysics"), Imago-Radio France (Paris), 1984.
(With Barrow) *The Anthropic Cosmological Principle,* foreword by John A. Wheeler, Oxford University Press (Oxford, England), 1986.
The Physics of Immortality: Modern Cosmology, God, and the Resurrection of the Dead, Doubleday (New York), 1994.

WORK IN PROGRESS: Work on global general relativity, black-hole physics, cosmology, the quantum theory of measurement, the philosophy of science, and natural theology.

SIDELIGHTS: Frank J. Tipler is a mathematical physicist specializing in both general relativity and cosmology. Among his writings is *The Anthropic*

Cosmological Principle, which he produced with John D. Barrow. In this volume Tipler and Barrow substantiate the anthropic perspective, which maintains that the very existence of human life is a means by which the universe can, to some extent, be understood. Timothy Ferris, writing in the *New York Times Book Review,* noted that the anthropic cosmological principle may be considered "vaguely unsatisfying," but he added that Tipler and Barrow "have written a clear, rigorous and exhaustively researched book." Ferris concluded that *The Anthropic Cosmological Principle* "is a book that impels the reader to think, and it may alter the terms of discourse within which it will be judged." And Martin Gardner, in his appraisal for the *New York Review of Books,* affirmed, "No one can plow through this well-written, painstakingly researched tome without absorbing vast chunks of information about QM (quantum mechanics), the latest cosmic models, and the history of philosophical views that bear on the book's main arguments."

Tipler also collaborated with Barrow, and Marie-Odile Monchicourt, on the French-language volume *L'Homme et le cosmos: Le Principe en astrophysique moderne* (which means "Man and the Cosmos: The Anthropic Principle in Modern Astrophysics"), and he served as editor of *Essays in General Relativity: A Festschrift for Abraham H. Taub.*

BIOGRAPHICAL/CRITICAL SOURCES:

PERIODICALS

New York Review of Books, May 8, 1986, pp. 22-24.
New York Times Book Review, February 16, 1986, p. 20.
Times Literary Supplement, January 2, 1987, p. 5.*

*   *   *

TOMAJCZYK, S. F. 1960-

PERSONAL: Surname is pronounced Toe-*my*-check; born March 30, 1960, in Newport, RI; son of Charles F., Jr. (a naval officer) and Gretchen (Mintz) Tomajczyk; married Joyce J. Welch, June 21, 1991. *Ethnicity:* "White." *Education:* University of Michigan, B.S.N.R., 1982. *Avocational interests:* Archaeology, travel, photography, cooking, antiquing, canoeing.

ADDRESSES: Home—Loudon, NH. *Office*—Turning Point Communications, P.O. Box 7070, Loudon, NH 03301. *E-mail*—stomajczyk@aol.com. *Agent*—Anne Hawkins, John Hawkins and Associates, 71 West 23rd St., New York, NY 10010.

CAREER: CW Communications, Peterborough, NH, new products editor, 1982-83; SoftSide Publications, Amherst, NH, senior editor and associate publisher, 1983-84; Ultimate Press, Nashua, NH, marketing communications director, 1984-88; New Hampshire Division of Public Health Services, Concord, public information officer, 1988-96; Turning Point Communications, Loudon, NH, president, 1996—. Senior lecturer at Franklin Pierce College, 1985-88, and Rivier College, 1988-91; guest on television and radio programs; guest speaker before writer's groups, 1984—. National Public Health Information Coalition, regional representative, 1993-96, vice president, 1994-95, president, 1995-96, founder and managing editor of *American Journal of Health Communications,* 1995—; consultant to Centers for Disease Control and Prevention; also worked with Buckle-Up New Hampshire, Partnership for a Drug Free New Hampshire, Best Friends for Life campaign, and a statewide public information campaign on diabetes.

MEMBER: Author's Guild, American Medical Writers Association, National Writers Union.

AWARDS, HONORS: Numerous advertising awards, including first place, Creative Club of New Hampshire, 1990; second place, New Hampshire Graniteer Awards, 1991; third place, New Hampshire Graniteer Awards, 1991, 1992; first place, New Hampshire Graniteer Awards, 1994, 1996; bronze award, National Public Health Information Coalition Creative Awards, 1992, 1993; silver award, National Public Health Informtion Coalition Creative Awards, 1993, 1995 (two), 1996; gold award, National Public Health Information Creative Awards, 1992, 1993 (two), 1994 (three), 1995, 1996; winner, 14th Annual Telly Awards, 1993; gold award, Golden Mike Awards, 1994; first place, Advertising and Marketing Federation, 1996, for *American Journal of Health Communications.*

WRITINGS:

Eyes on the Gold: An Advanced Training Manual for Running Events, McFarland and Co. (Jefferson, NC), 1986.
The Children's Writers' Marketplace, Running Press (Philadelphia, PA), 1987.
Dictionary of the Modern United States Military, McFarland and Co., 1996.

Elite U.S. Counterterrorist Forces, Motorbooks (Osceola, WI), 1997.

Contributor to health communications manuals. Author of "Running Shorts," a weekly sports column. Contributor of poetry to magazines, including *Suwanee Review, North American Mentor, Odessa Poetry Review,* and *American Poetry Anthology.* Contributor of numerous articles to magazines and newspapers, including *Metropolitan Detroit, Yankee, Lost Treasure, Writer's Digest, Treasure Facts, Commodore, Boston Magazine, 80 Micro, Pico, Telegraph, Transcript* and *Sportscape.*

WORK IN PROGRESS: A novel; two nonfiction books; a screenplay.

SIDELIGHTS: S. F. Tomajczyk told *CA:* "I started my writing career while still attending the University of Michigan. An English professor of mine, Barney Pace, encouraged me to pursue writing. On one of my papers (which I still have) he wrote: 'I accuse you of possessing talent, and I dare you to do something with it.' So I did. I left college with a contract for my first book, *Eyes on the Gold.*

"It was my grandfather who inspired me to write. He adored books and made certain that my bookshelves were always full. During one of our summer trips to New Hampshire, he took my brother and me to Diamond Lake up near the Canadian border. There, one evening, as we sat out on the cabin porch overlooking the lake, admiring the star-littered sky, he told me something that I have never forgotten: 'Steve, whenever you do anything in life, always reach for the stars. If you only reach for the roof, you'll never get off the ground.' So when I dream, I dream big. When I aspire for things, I go for them with all that I have.

"There are many people who want to be professional writers. The only thing that separates them from me is that I actually sit down in front of the computer each day and do it. There is absolutely nothing glorious about writing. It's a tedious and often painful struggle that leaves its tell-tale calluses on your fingertips. I know of several people who are more talented than I am with their writing skills, but since they have never committed themselves to 'the chair,' they are condemned to remain wanna-be authors for life.

"What I truly enjoy about writing is that it presents me with the opportunity to inspire hope, influence decisions, and encourage people to action. I wrote the *Dictionary of the Modern United States Military* because, having been raised as the son of a naval officer, I wanted to give the public a better understanding of what the military is really about. The focus traditionally has been on the technology of war (jets, tanks, weapons) rather than where it belongs: on the individuals. Wars are fought by people, not machines. So I endeavored to portray a slice-of-life of what today's military establishment is like. I delved into social issues (homosexuality, spousal abuse, suicide, rape), diseases common to the battlefield, psychological impacts of combat, battlefield tactics, espionage, electronic warfare, reconnaissance, slang, agencies, installations, chemical and biological warfare, special operations, terrorism, and so on. The book took four years to research and write. I believe it is the most complete and up-to-date reference book of its kind in the world.

"My latest book, *Elite U.S. Counterterrorist Forces,* is the first book of its kind to take an inside look at America's counterterrorism efforts. It is a spin-off from my military book, but was actually spurred into fruition by the World Trade Center bombing in 1993. From my previous research, I sensed that the United States would see more acts of terrorism due to growing anti-government sentiments throughout the country. The Oklahoma City bombing and subsequent thwarted acts of terrorism have convinced me of that. To my knowledge, I was the first civilian allowed an inside look at the system that is in place to protect Americans (as best it can) from acts of terrorism. I spent two years meeting members of elite counterterrorism teams, photographing them in training and learning assault techniques. The book is intended to reassure Americans that a counterterrorism system does indeed exist. Simultaneously, I hope that the book also sends a message to would-be terrorists to forget about taking action because they will be caught. The book was my endeavor to acknowledge the efforts of an elite and highly trained group of individuals who are willing to die to keep the rest of us safe and free."

*　　*　　*

TRACHTENBERG, Alan 1932-

PERSONAL: Born March 22, 1932, in Philadelphia, PA; son of Isadore and Norma Trachtenberg; married Betty Glassman, December 21, 1952; children: Zev, Elissa, Julia. *Education:* Temple University, A.B.

(English), 1954; University of Connecticut, M.A., 1956; University of Minnesota, Ph.D. (American studies), 1962.

ADDRESSES: Office—Department of English, P.O. Box 3545, Yale Station, New Haven, CT 06520.

CAREER: Pennsylvania State University, University Park, faculty member, 1961-69, professor of English, 1969; Yale University, New Haven, CT, visiting professor of English and American studies, 1969-70, faculty member, 1970—, professor, 1972—, director of graduate studies in American studies, 1970-72, 1974-75, chair of American studies, 1971-73.

MEMBER: American Studies Association, Modern Language Association of America.

AWARDS, HONORS: American Council of Learned Societies fellow, 1968-69; Center for Advanced Study in Behavioral Sciences fellow, 1968-69.

WRITINGS:

Brooklyn Bridge: Fact and Symbol, Oxford University Press (New York), 1965.
(Editor) *Man and City in America,* Center for Continuing Liberal Education, Pennsylvania State University (University Park), 1966.
(Editor) *Democratic Vistas, 1860-1880,* Braziller (New York), 1970.
(Editor with Peter Neill and Peter C. Bunnell) *The City: American Experience,* Oxford University Press (New York), 1971.
(Editor) *Critics of Culture: Literature and Society in the Early Twentieth Century,* Wiley (New York), 1976.
(Contributor) Lewis Wickes Hine, *America and Lewis Hine: Photographs, 1904-1940,* Aperture (New York), 1977.
(Editor) *Classic Essays on Photography,* Leete's Island Books, (New Haven, CT), 1980.
(Editor) *Hart Crane: A Collection of Critical Essays,* Prentice-Hall (Englewood Cliffs, NJ), 1982.
(Contributor) Jerome Liebling, *Jerome Liebling Photographs,* University of Massachusetts Press (Amherst), 1982.
The Incorporation of America: Culture and Society in the Gilded Age, Hill and Wang (New York), 1982.
(Contributor) Carl Fleischhauer and Beverly W. Brannan, editors, *Documenting America, 1935-1943,* University of California Press (Berkeley), c. 1988.

(Contributor) Richard S. Field and Robin Jaffee Frank, editors, *American Daguerreotypes: From the Matthew R. Isenburg Collection,* Yale University Art Gallery (New Haven), 1989.
Reading American Photographs: Images as History, Matthew Brady to Walker Evans, Hill and Wang (New York), 1989.
(Contributor) Martha A. Sandweiss, editor, *Photography in Nineteenth-Century America,* Amon Carter Museum (Fort Worth, TX), 1991.

Also author of *American Culture between the Civil War and World War I,* 1985; contributor of articles to periodicals, including *Yale Review.*

SIDELIGHTS: Director of Yale University's department of American Studies, Alan Trachtenberg has written and edited numerous books relating to his field, among them volumes on American writers Hart Crane and Frank Waldo. He has gained the most critical attention, however, for his books *Brooklyn Bridge: Fact and Symbol; The Incorporation of America: Culture and Society in the Gilded Age,* and *Reading American Photographs: Images as History, Matthew Brady to Walker Evans.*

The first of these three, 1965's *Brooklyn Bridge,* is a history of the famous New York suspension bridge, a monument of wire rope, steel, and Gothic towers that spans New York harbor and joins the city to its islands. Built in the nineteenth century, the Brooklyn Bridge was conceived by German immigrant and designer John Roebling, a pioneer in suspension bridge design whose invention of wire rope transformed bridge-building in America. As detailed in Trachtenberg's book, Roebling never lived to see his design erected; while studying the harbor and his design, he was injured by an errant ferry. Roebling later died from lockjaw, and his son, Washington Roebling stepped in to oversee the construction of his father's dream. Unfortunately, the younger Roebling was paralyzed by caisson disease as a result of his work on the bridge's foundations, but he nevertheless continued directing the project.

Trachtenberg relates the Roeblings' dedication to the bridge in his book, but, as the subtitle suggests, also discusses the Brooklyn Bridge as an American symbol. Frequently seen as a background in motion pictures, reproduced as a backdrop in plays, and honored in literature, the bridge represents the transition from Old World ways to a prosperous new way of life in America. Trachtenberg explores the ways various writers and artists have portrayed the bridge, giving particular attention to the writings of poet Hart Crane and the art of painter Joseph Stella.

Reviewers overwhelmingly applauded Trachtenberg's book on the bridge, among them a *Times Literary Supplement* critic who deemed *Brooklyn Bridge* a "brilliant" book, and also opined that "Mr. Trachtenberg is always exciting and illuminating." Writing in the *Yale Review,* A. N. Kaul noted that Trachtenberg is more effective in his historical analysis of the bridge than in his literary analysis, but nevertheless described *Brooklyn Bridge* as "a work of historical synthesis, each of its parts benefits from the whole." Writing in the *New York Review of Books,* Alfred Kazin also praised Trachtenberg's effort: "Alan Trachtenberg has written a good little book about [the Brooklyn Bridge], sensitively intelligent, which in the end reflects the anxious and rhetorical will-to-meaning that is its real subject."

Trachtenberg examines American society during the thirty years after the Civil War in his 1982 book, *The Incorporation of America,* which documents the impact of corporate organization on the traditional values prevalent in that day. Considered a valuable work on the history of corporate organization, *The Incorporation of America,* according to H. L. Horowitz in the *Journal of American History,* "redirects American Studies to fundamental problems and suggests to new social historians the rich possibilities of cultural analysis."

In 1989 Trachtenberg published another well-received book, *Reading American Photographs,* a study of American photography from 1839 to 1938. Trachtenberg focuses on the stories that photographs tell about the society and economics of the era, and examines five phases in the history of photography: the daguerreotype, which produced photographs on silver or silver-covered copper plates; the Civil War portraits captured by Matthew Brady; post-Civil War photographs, typically of Western landscapes; the social commentary photographs from the late-1800s to World War I; and, finally, the work of photographer Walker Evans, whose photographs remain as poignant reminders of the Great Depression. *Reading American Photographs* is illustrated with numerous examples of the photographic work the author covers, and Trachtenberg encourages his audience to *read* the photographs; to apply the rules of literary criticism and interpretation to the illustrations in order to analyze them as one would study literature, seeing beyond the obvious to grasp a deeper understanding of each photograph's meaning.

Reading American Photographs elicited praise from reviewers such as Peter Bacon Hales, who wrote in the *Journal of American History:* "Trachtenberg treats his readers as workers deserving of dignity and reward, and he gives them not simply examples of the interpenetration of photography and American life but something richer and more useful: a model for the way American culture constructed (and constructs) itself, presented through the analysis of one mode of cultural construction—American photography. . . . Trachtenberg's *Reading American Photographs* offers heady rewards indeed." Also expressing his appreciation of Trachtenberg's study, *New York Times Book Review* contributor William S. McFeely remarked: "As Mr. Trachtenberg concludes, 'It is not so much a new but a clarifying light American photographs shed upon American reality.' That light, as he has richly demonstrated, now illuminates our past in inescapable and powerful ways." *Tikkun* contributor Miles Orvell declared: "*Reading American Photographs* combines the virtues of the concentrated subject with that of the broad cultural perspective, and it results in the most sustained and rigorous study of American photography yet produced."

BIOGRAPHICAL/CRITICAL SOURCES:

PERIODICALS

Journal of American History, December, 1982; June, 1990, pp. 268-270.
Los Angeles Times Book Review, September 24, 1989, p. 6.
New York Review of Books, July 15, 1965.
New York Times Book Review, August 20, 1989, p. 15.
Tikkun, November-December, 1990, pp. 88-91.
Times Literary Supplement, November 25, 1965.
Yale Review, October, 1965.*

*   *   *

TUCKER, Lael
See WERTENBAKER, Lael (Tucker)

*   *   *

TUPITSYN, Margarita 1955-

PERSONAL: Born March 23, 1955, in Moscow, U.S.S.R. (now Russia); U.S. citizen; married Victor

Tupitsyn (a professor), June 22, 1973; children: Maria. *Education:* Graduate School of the City University of New York, Ph.D., 1996.

ADDRESSES: Home and office—145 Chambers St., New York, NY 10007; fax 212-233-9867.

CAREER: Sprengel Museum, Hanover, Germany, visiting curator, 1996-98. Rutgers University, visiting professor, 1996—.

MEMBER: College Art Association of America.

WRITINGS:

Margins of Soviet Art, Giancarlo Politi Editore, 1989. *Glaube, Hoffnung, Anpassung,* Plitt Verlag, 1996.

Author of *The Soviet Photograph, 1924-1937,* Yale University Press (New Haven, CT).

WORK IN PROGRESS: El Lissitzky: Beyond the Abstract Cabinet, for Shimler & Mosler (Munich, Germany), completion expected in 1998.

*   *   *

UREY, Harold (Clayton) 1893-1981

PERSONAL: Born April 29, 1893, in Walkerton, IN; died of a heart attack, January 5, 1981, in La Jolla, CA; son of Samuel Clayton (a schoolteacher and lay minister) and Cora (Reinoehl) Urey; married Frieda Daum (a bacteriologist), June 12, 1926; children: Gertrude, Frieda, Mary, John. *Education:* Montana State University, B.S. (zoology), 1917; University of California at Berkeley, Ph.D. (chemistry), 1923; Institute of Theoretical Physics, University of Copenhagen, post-doctoral study under Niels Bohr, c. 1923-24.

CAREER: Chemist and physicist. Indiana, schoolteacher, 1911-12; Montana, schoolteacher, 1912-14; Barrett Chemical Company, Philadelphia, PA, explosives developer, 1917-19; Montana State University, Bozeman, teacher, 1919-21; Johns Hopkins University, Baltimore, MD, associate in chemistry, 1925-29; Columbia University, New York City, associate professor of chemistry, 1929-34, professor, 1934-45; Enrico Fermi Institute of Nuclear Studies, University of Chicago, Chicago, IL, professor, 1945-52, Martin A. Ryerson distinguished service professor, 1952-58;

University of California, La Jolla, professor at large, 1958-81. Uranium Committee, Manhattan Project, member, 1940-42; Substitute Alloys Materials Laboratory, Manhattan Project, director, 1942-45; *Journal of Chemical Physics,* editor, c. 1940s. Committee to Defend America by Aiding the Allies, member, 1930s.

AWARDS, HONORS: Nobel Prize in chemistry, 1934; Ernest Kempton Adams fellow, Columbia University, 1934; Davy medal, Royal Society, 1940; honorary fellow, Chemical Society, 1945; Priestley Medal, American Chemical Society; Johann Kepler medal, American Association for the Advancement of Science, 1973; Exceptional Scientific Achievement Award, National Aeronautics and Space Administration (NASA), 1973; 200th Anniversary plaque, American Chemical Society, 1976; honorary doctorates from numerous universities.

WRITINGS:

(With Arthur Edward Ruark) *Atoms, Molecules, and Quanta,* McGraw-Hill (New York City), 1930.
The Planets: Their Origins and Development, Yale University Press (New Haven, CT), 1952.
Some Cosmochemical Problems, Pennsylvania State University (University Park, PA), 1963.

Contributor to journals and periodicals, including *Physical Review, Angewandte Chemie, Science, Yearbook of the Physical Society,* and *Forbes.*

SIDELIGHTS: In 1934 Harold Urey was awarded the Nobel Prize in chemistry for his discovery of deuterium, an isotope, or species, of hydrogen in which the atoms weigh twice as much as those in ordinary hydrogen. Also known as heavy hydrogen, deuterium became profoundly important to future studies in many scientific fields, including chemistry, physics, and medicine. Urey continued his research on isotopes over the next three decades, and during World War II his experience with deuterium proved invaluable in efforts to separate isotopes of uranium from each other in the development of the first atomic bombs. Later, Urey's research on isotopes also led to a method for determining the earth's atmospheric temperature at various periods in past history. This experimentation has become especially relevant because of concerns about the possibility of global climate change.

Urey was born in Walkerton, Indiana, on April 29, 1893. He was the son of Samuel Clayton Urey, who was a schoolteacher and lay minister in the Church of the Brethren. His mother was Cora Reinoehl Urey. Urey's father died when Harold was only six years old, and his mother later married another Brethren minister. Urey had a sister, Martha, a brother, Clarence, and two half-sisters, Florence and Ina.

After graduating from high school, Urey hoped to attend college but lacked the financial resources to do so. Instead, he accepted teaching jobs in country schools, first in Indiana from 1911 to 1912 and then in Montana from 1912 to 1914 before finally entering Montana State University in September of 1914 at the age of twenty-one. Urey was initially interested in a career in biology, and the first original research he ever conducted involved a study of microorganisms in the Missoula River. In 1917 he was awarded his bachelor of science degree in zoology by Montana State.

The year Urey graduated also marked the entry of the United States into World War I. Although he had strong pacifist beliefs as a result of his early religious training, Urey acknowledged his obligation to participate in the nation's war effort. As a result, he accepted a job at the Barrett Chemical Company in Philadelphia and worked to develop high explosives. In his Nobel Prize acceptance speech, Urey said that this experience was instrumental in his move from industrial chemistry to academic life.

At the end of the war, Urey returned to Montana State University where he began teaching chemistry. In 1921 he decided to resume his college education and enrolled in the doctoral program in physical chemistry at the University of California at Berkeley. His faculty advisor at Berkeley was the great physical chemist Gilbert Newton Lewis. Urey received his doctorate in 1923 for research on the calculation of heat capacities and entropies (the degree of randomness in a system) of gases, based on information obtained through the use of a spectroscope. He then left for a year of postdoctoral study at the Institute for Theoretical Physics at the University of Copenhagen where Niels Bohr, a Danish physicist, was researching the structure of the atom. Urey's interest in Bohr's research had been cultivated while studying with Lewis, who had proposed many early theories on the nature of chemical bonding.

Upon his return to the United States in 1925, Urey accepted an appointment as an associate in chemistry at the Johns Hopkins University in Baltimore, a post he held until 1929. He interrupted his work at Johns Hopkins briefly to marry Frieda Daum in Lawrence,

Kansas, on June 12, 1926. Daum was a bacteriologist and daughter of a prominent Lawrence educator. The Ureys later had four children, Gertrude Elizabeth, Frieda Rebecca, Mary Alice, and John Clayton.

In 1929, Urey left Johns Hopkins to become associate professor of chemistry at Columbia University, and in 1930 he published his first book, *Atoms, Molecules, and Quanta,* written with A. E. Ruark. Writing in the *Dictionary of Scientific Biography,* Joseph N. Tatarewicz called this work "the first comprehensive English language textbook on atomic structure and a major bridge between the new quantum physics and the field of chemistry." At this time he also began his search for an isotope of hydrogen. Since Frederick Soddy, an English chemist, discovered isotopes in 1913, scientists had been looking for isotopes of a number of elements. Urey believed that if an isotope of heavy hydrogen existed, one way to separate it from the ordinary hydrogen isotope would be through the vaporization of liquid hydrogen. Since heavy hydrogen would be more dense than ordinary hydrogen, Urey theorized that the lighter hydrogen atoms would vaporize first, leaving behind a mixture rich in heavy hydrogen. Urey believed that if he could obtain enough of the heavy mixture through a process of slow evaporation, spectroscopic readings would show spectral lines that differed from that of ordinary hydrogen.

With the help of two colleagues, Ferdinand Brickwedde and George M. Murphy, Urey carried out his experiment in 1931. The three researchers began with four liters of liquid hydrogen which they allowed to evaporate very slowly. Eventually, only a single milliliter of liquid hydrogen remained. This sample was then subjected to spectroscopic analysis which showed the presence of lines in exactly the positions predicted for a heavier isotope of hydrogen. This was deuterium.

The discovery of deuterium made Urey famous in the scientific world, and only three years later he was awarded the Nobel Prize in chemistry for his discovery. Since his wife was pregnant at the time, he declined to travel to Stockholm and was allowed to participate in the award ceremonies the following year. Urey's accomplishments were also recognized by Columbia University, and in 1933 he was appointed the Ernest Kempton Adams Fellow. A year later he was promoted to full professor of chemistry. Urey retained his appointment at Columbia until the end of World War II. During this time he also became the first editor of the new *Journal of Chemical Phys-*

ics, which became one of the principal periodicals in the field.

During the latter part of the 1930s, Urey extended his work on isotopes to other elements besides hydrogen. Eventually his research team was able to separate isotopes of carbon, nitrogen, oxygen, and sulfur. One of the intriguing discoveries made during this period was that isotopes may differ from each other chemically in very small ways. Initially, it was assumed that since all isotopes of an element have the same electronic configuration, they would also have identical chemical properties. Urey found, however, that the mass differences in isotopes can result in modest differences in the rate at which they react.

The practical consequences of this discovery became apparent all too soon. In 1939, word reached the United States about the discovery of nuclear fission by the German scientists Otto Hahn and Fritz Strassmann. The military consequences of the Hahn-Strassmann discovery were apparent to many scientists, including Urey. He was one of the first, therefore, to become involved in the U.S. effort to build a nuclear weapon, recognizing the threat posed by such a weapon in the hands of Nazi Germany. However, Urey was deeply concerned about the potential destructiveness of a fission weapon. Actively involved in political topics during the 1930s, Urey was a member of the Committee to Defend America by Aiding the Allies and worked vigorously against the fascist regimes in Germany, Italy, and Spain. He explained the importance of his political activism by saying that "no dictator knows enough to tell scientists what to do. Only in democratic nations can science flourish."

As World War II drew closer, Urey became involved in the Manhattan Project to build the nation's first atomic bomb. In 1940, he became a member of the Uranium Committee of the project, and two years later he was appointed director of the Substitute Alloys Materials Laboratory (SAML) at Columbia. SAML was one of three locations in the United States where research was being conducted on methods to separate two isotopes of uranium. As a leading expert on the separation of isotopes, Urey made critical contributions to the solution of the Manhattan Project's single most difficult problem, the isolation of uranium-235 from its heavier twin.

At the conclusion of World War II, Urey left Columbia to join the Enrico Fermi Institute of Nuclear Studies at the University of Chicago. In 1952 he was named Martin A. Ryerson Distinguished Service Professor there. The postwar period saw the beginning of a flood of awards and honorary degrees that was to continue for more than three decades. He received honorary degrees from more than two dozen universities, including doctorates from Columbia (1946), Oxford (1946), Washington and Lee (1948), the University of Athens (1951), McMaster University (1951), Yale (1951), and Indiana (1953).

The end of the war did not end Urey's concern about nuclear weapons. He now shifted his attention to work for the control of the terrible power he had helped to make a reality. Deeply conscious of a sense of scientific responsibility, Urey was opposed to the dropping of an atomic bomb on Japan. He was also aggressively involved in defeating a bill that would have placed control of nuclear power in the United States in the hands of the Department of Defense. Instead, he helped pass a bill creating a civilian board to control future nuclear development. In later years Urey explored peaceful uses of nuclear energy, and in 1975 he petitioned the White House to reduce production in nuclear power plants. He was also a member of the Union of Concerned Scientists.

Urey continued to work on new applications of his isotope research. In the late 1940s and early 1950s, he explored the relationship between the isotopes of oxygen and past planetary climates. Since isotopes differ in the rate of chemical reactions, Urey said that the amount of each oxygen isotope in an organism is a result of atmospheric temperatures. During periods when the earth was warmer than normal, organisms would take in more of a lighter isotope of oxygen and less of a heavier isotope. During cool periods, the differences among isotopic concentrations would not be as great. Over a period of time, Urey was able to develop a scale, or an "oxygen thermometer," that related the relative concentrations of oxygen isotopes in the shells of sea animals with atmospheric temperatures. Some of those studies continue to be highly relevant in current research on the possibilities of global climate change.

In the early 1950s, Urey became interested in yet another subject: the chemistry of the universe and of the formation of the planets, including the earth. One of his first papers on this topic attempted to provide an estimate of the relative abundance of the elements in the universe. Although these estimates have now been improved, they were remarkably close to the values modern chemists now accept.

Urey also became involved in a study of the origin of the solar system. For well over two hundred years, scientists had been debating the mechanism by which the planets and their satellites were formed. From his own studies, Urey concluded that the creation of the solar system took place at temperatures considerably less than those suggested by most experts at the time. He also proposed a new theory about the origin of the Earth's moon, claiming that it was formed not as a result of being torn from the Earth, but through an independent process of a gradual accumulation of materials.

Urey's last great period of research brought together his interests and experiences in a number of fields of research to which he had devoted his life. The subject of that research was the origin of life on Earth. Urey hypothesized that the Earth's primordial atmosphere consisted of reducing gases such as hydrogen, ammonia, and methane. The energy provided by electrical discharges in the atmosphere, he suggested, was sufficient to initiate chemical reactions among these gases, converting them to the simplest compounds of which living organisms are made, amino acids. In 1951, Urey's graduate student Stanley Lloyd Miller carried out a series of experiments to test this hypothesis. In these experiments, an electrical discharge passed through a glass tube containing only reducing gases resulted in the formation of amino acids.

In 1958 Urey left the University of Chicago to become Professor at Large at the University of California in San Diego at La Jolla. At La Jolla, his interests shifted from original scientific research to national scientific policy. He became extremely involved in the U.S. space program, serving as the first chairman of the Committee on Chemistry of Space and Exploration of the Moon and Planets of the National Academy of Science's Space Sciences Board. Even late in life, Urey continued to receive honors and awards from a grateful nation and admiring colleagues. He was awarded the Johann Kepler Medal of the American Association for the Advancement of Science (1971), the Priestley Medal of the American Chemical Society (1973), National Aeronautics and Space Administration (NASA) Exceptional Scientific Achievement Award (1973), and the 200th Anniversary Plaque of the American Chemical Society (1976). Urey died of a heart attack in La Jolla on January 5, 1981, at the age of eighty-seven.

BIOGRAPHICAL/CRITICAL SOURCES:

BOOKS

Holmes, Frederic L., editor, *Dictionary of Scientific Biography,* Volume 18, Supplement II, Scribner, 1990.
Schoenebaum, Eleanora W., *Political Profiles: The Truman Years,* Facts on File, 1978, pp. 571-72.

PERIODICALS

Current Comments, December 3, 1979, pp. 5-9.
Icarus, vol. 48, 1981, pp. 348-52.
Physics Today, September 1982, pp. 34-39.
Science, vol. 217, 1982, pp. 891-98.*

V

VANCE, Jack
See KUTTNER, Henry

* * *

VAUGHN, Patrika 1933-

PERSONAL: Born October 21, 1933, in Chicago, IL; daughter of Theodore H. (a restaurateur) and Patricia Gizella Szent Miklosy White (a homemaker) Bussmann; married Albert J. Vaughn (divorced); children: Kerry, Elisabeth. *Education:* University of South Florida, B.A., 1987; graduate study at University of Arkansas, 1988-90. *Avocational interests:* Dance, swimming, theater, herb gardening.

ADDRESSES: Home—Sarasota, FL. *Office*—P.O. Box 3691, Sarasota, FL 34230-3691. *E-mail*—acappub@ aol.com.

CAREER: Public relations and marketing consultant. Editorial Associates, Clearwater, FL, past editorial director; Book Wrights, San Diego, CA, past executive director. Ghostwriter.

MEMBER: National Society of Fundraising Executives, Florida Public Relations Association (member of board of directors of Central West Coast chapter, 1996—), Sarasota Literary Society (vice president, 1997—), Author's Guild, Associated Business Writers of America.

WRITINGS:

Siduri Revisioned: A Fictional History of the Future (includes the novel *Eve's Rib*), New College Li-

brary Foundation, University of South Florida (Tampa, FL), 1987.

Riding the Winds of Change, Ican Press Book Publishers (Chula Vista, CA), 1994.

How to Write, Publish, and Market Your Book, A Cappela Publishing (Sarasota, FL), 1997.

Contributor to more than a hundred national journals. Ghostwriter of numerous books for industrialists, psychiatrists, psychotherapists, world travelers, and international executives.

WORK IN PROGRESS: The Clear-Eyed Lover, "a fictional look at the vagaries of love."

SIDELIGHTS: Patrika Vaughn told *CA:* "Books have often been my best friends, loyal and true when everything else in my life was chaotic. After reading and appreciating so many of them, it seemed only natural to write them. I have written in many styles—academic, professional, and trade articles; advertising and public relations copy; biography and fiction. To date, most of my biographical and fictional writings were as a ghostwriter. The titles of these works must remain mysterious, but ghosting has allowed me to span everything from world history, war, and politics to anthropology, psychology, and adolescence—and to keep eating while doing so. It's been a glorious good time.

"The need for income led me to deal with the practical side of books (editing, working as a literary agent, ghostwriting, publishing, copywriting) while struggling to write meaningful prose. The practical side also taught me the importance of clarity and brevity. I passed this knowledge along in my teaching, and my contact with struggling student writers has taught me how to explain the art of writing. *How to Write, Publish, and Market Your Book* has grown out of everything I've learned over a lifetime of loving words, crafting them, and seeing them in print."

* * *

VICUNA, Cecilia 1948-

PERSONAL: Born July 22, 1948, in Santiago, Chile; daughter of Jorge Vicuna Lagarrique (an attorney) and Norma Ramirez Arenas (a tour guide); married Cesar Paternosto (an artist and author), June 12, 1981. *Education:* University of Chile, Santiago, M.F.A., 1971; post-graduate studies at the Slade School of Fine Arts, University College, London, 1972-73.

ADDRESSES: Home—135 Hudson St., New York, NY 10013-2102.

CAREER: Freelance poet, artist, and performance artist. Has conducted workshops and seminars at institutions including Universidad Libre Arke; New York Public Schools; City University of New York; St. Mark's Poetry Project; University of California, Berkeley; Poet's House; State University of New York, Purchase; and Jack Kerouac School of Disembodied Poetics, Naropa Institute.

Artwork shown in solo exhibitions, beginning 1971, at locations including Museo Nacional de Bellas Artes, Santiago, Chile; Institute of Contemporary Arts, London, England; Arts Meeting Place Gallery, London; Galeria La Gruta, Bogota, Colombia; Galeria CAL, Santiago; Exit Art Gallery, New York City; University Art Museum, Berkeley, CA; Center for Contemporary Art, Santa Fe, NM; Kanaal Foundation, Kortrijk, Belgium; and Royal Botanic Garden, Edinburgh, Scotland.

Artwork shown in group exhibitions, beginning 1972, at locations including Museum of Modern Art, New York, 1997; Biennial Exhibition, Whitney Museum of American Art; Institute of Contemporary Arts, Boston; Whitechapel Art Gallery, London; Art Gallery of Western Australia, Perth; Pyramid Gallery, Washington, DC; Royal College of Art, London, England; Stanislaus University, CA; Kunsttamtes Kreuzberg, Berlin, Germany; Havana, Cuba; Greater Lafayette Museum of Art, Lafayette, IN; Archer M. Huntington Gallery, Austin, TX; Galeria Luigi Marrozzini, San Juan, PR; Royal Museum of Art, Antwerp, Belgium; and Henry St. Settlement, Alternative Museum, Center for Interamerican Relations, Franklin Furnace, Art Awareness Gallery, Exit Art Gallery, and New Museum, all New York. Has also given poetry readings, artistic performances, and lectures in locations throughout the United States, South America, and Europe.

MEMBER: American PEN Club, Latin American Writers Institute Steering Committee, 1987-89, New York Foundation for the Arts Poetry Award (juror), 1991.

AWARDS, HONORS: British Council Scholarship from the United Kingdom, 1972-73; Line II Award, for *Precario/Precarious,* 1983; Human Rights Exile Award, Fund for Free Expression, 1985; named Poet in Residence at the Bellagio Study Center in Italy by the Rockefeller Foundation, 1991; Arts International Award, Lila Wallace-Reader's Digest Fund, 1992; Lee Krasner-Jackson Pollock Award, 1995-96; Fund for Poetry Award, 1995-96.

WRITINGS:

POETRY

Sabor a Mi (bilingual edition; title means, "A Taste of Me"), translated by Felipe Ehrenberg and author, Beau Geste Press (Devon, England), 1973.

Siete Poemas (title means, "Seven Poems"), Ediciones Centro Colombo Americano (Bogota, Colombia), 1979.

Luxumei o El Traspie de la Doctrina (title means, "The Luxury of Being Yourself or the Doctrine's Pitfall"), Editorial Oasis (Ciudad de Mexico, Mexico), 1983.

Precario/Precarious (bilingual edition; partially reprinted in *Unravelling Words and the Weaving of Water*), translated by Anne Twitty, Tanam Press (New York), 1983.

PALABRARmas (title means, "The Land is to Work More, to Arm Yourself with the Vision of Words"; partially reprinted in *Unravelling Words and the Weaving of Water*), Ediciones El Imaginero (Buenos Aires, Argentina), 1984.

Samara (title means, "A Seed With Wings"), Ediciones Embalaje (Museo Rayo, Colombia), 1986.

(Editor with Magda Bogin; and author of introduction) *The Selected Poems of Rosario Castellanos,* Graywolf Press (St. Paul, MN), 1988.

La Wik'una (title means, "The Vicuna"; partially reprinted in *Unravelling Words and the Weaving of Water*), edited by Francisco Zegers, (Santiago, Chile), 1990.

Unravelling Words and the Weaving of Water (includes portions of *Precario/Precarious, PALA-BRARmas,* and *La Wik'una*), edited by Eliot Weinberger, translated by Wein-berger and Suzanne Jill Levine, Graywolf Press, 1992.

(Editor) *Wordsoul: The Oral Poetry of the Mbya Guarani,* translated by W. S. Merwin, Graywolf Press.

Word and Thread, translated by Rosa Alcala, Morning Star, (Edinburgh, Scotland) 1996.

The Precarious, The Art and Poetry of Cecilia Vicuna/ Quipoem, edited by M. Catherine de Zegher, translated by Ester Allen, Wesleyan University Press, 1997.

CONTRIBUTOR

Giovani Poeti Sudamericani (poetry), edited by Hugo Garcia Robles and Umberto Bonetti, Giulio Einaudi Editore (Torino, Italy), 1972.

Chile, Poesia de la Resistencia y del Exilio (poetry), edited by Juan Armando Epple and Omar Lara, Ambito Literzrio (Barcelona), 1978.

La Novisima Poesia Latinoamericana (poetry), edited by Jorge Boccanera, Editores Mexicanos Unidos (Ciudad de Mexico, Mexico), 1978.

Palabra de Mujer (poetry), edited by Boccanera, Editores Mexicanos Unidos, 1981.

Chilenas, Drinnen und Draufsen (essays), Kunstamt, Kreuzberg (Berlin, Germany), 1983.

Piesne Pre Chile (poetry), edited by Sergio Macias, Slovensky Spisovatel (Bratislaua, Czechoslovakia), 1984.

Poesia Feminista del Mundo Hispanico (poetry), edited by Angel and Kate Flores, Siglo XXI (Ciudad de Mexico, Mexico), 1984.

Antologia de la Nueva Poesia Femenina Chilena (poetry), edited by Juan Villegas, Editorial la Noria (Santiago, Chile), 1985.

The Defiant Muse (film transcript), edited by Kate and Angel Flores, Feminist Press (New York), 1986.

Fire over Water (poetry), edited by Reese Williams, Tanam Press (New York), 1986.

The Renewal of the Vision (poetry), edited by Marjorie Agosin and Cola Franzen, Espectacular Disease Imprint (London), 1986.

Blasted Allegories: An Anthology of Writings by Contemporary Artists (poetry), edited by Brian Wallis, M.I.T. Press (Cambridge, MA), 1987.

You Can't Drown the Fire: Latin Women Writing in Exile (poetry), edited by Alicia Partnoy, Cleis Press (San Francisco, CA), 1988.

Cartas al Azar: Una Muestra de Poesia Chilena (poetry), edited by Veronica Zondek and Maria Teresa Adriasola, Ediciones Ergo Sum (Santiago, Chile), 1989.

Being America: Essays on Art, Literature, and Identity from Latin America, edited by Rachel Weiss, White Pine Press (New York), 1991.

El Placer de la palabra (poetry), edited by Margarite Fernandez-Olmos and Lizabeth Paravisini, Editorial Planeta (Ciudad de Mexico, Mexico), 1991.

America the Bride of the Sun (exhibition catalogue), Royal Museum of Amberes (Amberes, Belgium), 1992.

Pleasure in the Word: Erotic Writings by Latin American Women, edited by Fernandez-Olmos and Paravisini-Gebert, White Pine Press, 1993.

Voicing Today's Visions (poetry), edited by Mara R. Witzling, Universe Publishing (New York), 1994.

These Are Not Sweet Girls, (poetry by Latin American women), edited by Marjorie Agosin, White Pine Press (Fredonia, New York), 1994.

Veintinco Anos de Poesia Chilean, edited by Teresa Calderon, Lila Caleron and Thoman Haris, Fondo De Cultura Economica, (Santiago, Chile), 1996.

Poems for the Millenium, Vol II, edited by Jerome Rothenberg and Pierre Joris, University of California Press, 1997.

Also author of short films and television series episodes, including *La Puerta Fantastica* (children's television), Santiago, Chile, 1970-71; (and director) *Que es para Ud la Poesia?*, Bogota, Colombia, 1980; (and director) *Tres Trabajos,* New York City, 1981; (and director) *Paracas,* New York City, 1983. Contributor of poetry and essays to periodicals, including *RIF/T* (electronic), *Shambala Sun, The Literary Review, Rolling Stock, Hora de Poesia, Heresies, Quimera, Kritica, Realidad Aparte, El Espiritu del Valle, American Poetry Review, New Observations, The Raddle Moon, Review: Latin American Literature and Arts, City, Latin American Review, Areito, Papeles de Trilce, Palimpsesto, Literatura Chilena, Cuadernos Hispanoamericanos, Araucaria, Sun Dog, Magazin Dominical: El Espectador, Revista Eco, Caballito del Diablo, Acuarimantima, Revista Mexicana de Cultura: El Nacional, Extramuros, Participacion Poesia, Mundo Nuevo, El Corno Emplumado, Isis, Tramemos, Latinoamerica, La Bicicleta, Spare Rib, Sulfur, Mandorla, The Guardian, Chain,* and *Revista Universitaria.*

PALABRARmas has also been published in a bilingual Scottish edition, *PALABRARmas/WURDWAPPINschaw,* translated by Edwin Morgan.

WORK IN PROGRESS: Poetry, *Palabrir;* and essays, *Una Poetica Mestiza, UL, Four Mapuche Poets, A Bilingual Anthology,* edited by Cecilia Vicuna, translated by John Bierhorst, Americas Society (New York City) and *Word Soul, An Anthology of the Oral Poetry of the Mbya-Guarani,* edited by Cecilia Vicuna with versions by Ruben Bareiro Saguier, translated by W. S. Mersin (under review).

SIDELIGHTS: Poet, artist, and performance artist Cecilia Vicuna was born in Santiago, Chile, in 1948. She studied art at University College, London, after obtaining her master's degree; but while she was there, her native country's socialist government was overthrown by a violent military coup, and she has remained in exile ever since. Vicuna settled in New York City in 1980, where she has continued to write poetry and create art. She has had both group and solo exhibitions of her art in galleries in several cities of the world, including Santiago; Kortrijk, Belgium; London, England; Bogota, Colombia; and New York. Volumes of her poetry have been published in many different lands as well; these titles include *Sabor a Mi, Luxumei o El Traspie de la Doctrina,* and *Samara.*

Vicuna's best-known work for readers of English is the 1992 collection *Unravelling Words and the Weaving of Water,* which contains translated portions of three of Vicuna's previous books, *Precario/Precarious* from 1983, *PALABRARmas* from 1984, and *La Wik'una* from 1990. The poet has also made numerous contributions of both poetry and essays to periodicals and anthologies. Among the latter are *The Defiant Muse, You Can't Drown the Fire: Latin American Women Writing in Exile,* and *Pleasure in the Word.* In addition to penning works of poetry, Vicuna has also written the scripts for short films and for the Chilean children's television series, *La Puerta Fantastica.*

Unravelling Words and the Weaving of Water is divided into three sections, each made up of a portion of the aforementioned books by Vicuna. This structure illustrates the author's poetic growth. As Hugo Mendez-Ramirez explained in *Review: Latin American Literature and Arts,* "the first book was the discovery of the secret forces contained in (in)significant objects, the second explores the linguistic and philosophical foundations of her poetic vision, and this last

book is the actual performing of poetry." He noted further: "It centers on the process and the elements of the ritual."

Mendez-Ramirez also discussed Vicuna's career-long concern with reconciling the two cultures and language sources of her heritage—the Spanish and the Native South Americans, particularly the ancient Incans. "Vicuna is one of the few," he declared, "who have found a harmonious balance between new and ancient forms, between European and American origins, between indigenous language schemes and modern developments in linguistics."

The critic praised the contents of *Unravelling Words and the Weaving of Water* as displaying Vicuna's "genuine voice and artistic maturity." In addition to poetry, *Unravelling Words and the Weaving of Water* also includes pieces of Vicuna's artistic expression in other forms. For instance, there are photographs of performance art, and even what Mendez-Ramirez described as "collages made up of natural rubbish." Rachel Blau DuPlessis, reviewing the book in *Sulfur,* gave it high marks for this multiplicitous quality. Within its pages, according to DuPlessis, "the spiritual and earthbound forces join and mingle in an art work at once visual, performative, poetic, and ethical." She concluded that "this is serious, nourishing work."

Vicuna told *CA:* "By age nine, I knew I was a writer. It was the need to write a dream that got me started. Later, the signs on the page became a necessary reflection of all other aspects of life.

"I lived at the foot of the Andes Mountains, in Santiago, Chile, a place where many ancient cultures met with the European invaders. My family spoke a brand of Spanish entirely transformed by the music of the old languages which had been erased. As I grew older, my ear for those particular intonations became my guide. Through listening, I found a way of discovering new and ancient thought forms.

"Writing is a form of seeing and listening at once."

BIOGRAPHICAL/CRITICAL SOURCES:

PERIODICALS

Review: Latin American Literature and Arts, spring, 1994, pp. 96-98.
Sulfur, No. 34, 1994, pp. 192-93.

VIGEE, Claude (Andre Strauss) 1921-

PERSONAL: Born January 3, 1921, in Bischwiller, France; son of Robert (in business) and Germaine (a homemaker; maiden name, Meyer) Strauss; married Evelyne Meyer (a homemaker), November 29, 1947; children: Claudine, Daniel-Francois. *Education:* University of Strasbourg, France, B.A. 1938; Ohio State University, M.A., 1945, Ph.D. (Romance languages), 1947. *Religion:* Jewish. *Avocational interests:* Classical music, sculpture, archaeology.

ADDRESSES: Home—21 Radak St., Jerusalem 92187, Israel; and 12 bis, rue des Marronniers, Paris 75016, France.

CAREER: Poet, essayist, translator. Professor of French and comparative literature, Ohio State University, Columbus, OH, 1947-49, Wellesley College, Wellesley, MA, 1949-50, Brandeis University, Waltham, MA, 1949-60, and The Hebrew University, Jerusalem, Israel, 1960-84.

MEMBER: Writers' Union (Israel), Societe des Gens de Lettres, Academie Mallarme, Academie d'Alsace, Societe des Ecrivains d'Alsace et de Lorraine, Deutsche, Akadamie fur Sprache und Dichtung.

AWARDS, HONORS: Pierre de Regnier prize, Academie Francaise, 1972, for Vigee's body of work; Jacob-Burckhardt prize, University of Bale (Switzerland), 1977, for Vigee's body of work; Femina-Vacaresco prize for criticism (Paris), 1979; Johann-Peter Hebel prize, 1984, for Vigee's body of work; Rockefeller Foundation scholar, 1986; Grand Prix de la poesie de la Societe des Gens de Lettres, Paris 1987; Chevalier de la Legion d'honneur, Palmes academiques.

WRITINGS:

La Lutte avec l'ange (poems), Les Lettres (Paris), 1950.
L'Aurore souterraine, Pierre Seghers (Paris), 1952.
La Come du Grand Pardon, Pierre Seghers (Paris), 1954.
L'Ete indien (poems and journal), Gallimard (Paris), 1957.
Les Artistes de la faim (criticism), Calmann-Levy (Paris), 1960.
Revolte et louanges (criticism), Jose Corti (Paris), 1962.
Moisson de Canaan, Flammarion (Paris), 1967.
La Lune d'hiver, Flammarion, 1970.

Le Soleil sous la mer (poems), Flammarion, 1972.
Delivrance du souffle Flammarion, 1977.
Du bec a l'oreille, Editions de la Nuee-Bleue (Strasbourg), 1977.
L'Art et le demonique (essays), Flammarion, 1978.
L'Extase et l'errance (essay), Grasset (Paris), 1982.
Paque de la parole, Flammarion, 1983.
Le Parfum et la cendre (autobiography), Grasset, 1984.
Les Orties noires (poems and prose), Flammarion, 1984.
Heimat des Hauches, Elster Verlag (Baden-Baden, Germany), 1985.
(With Luc Balbont) *Une Voix dans le defile* (autobiography), Nouvelle Cite (Paris), 1985.
La Manne et la Rosee (essay), Descelee de Brouwer (Paris), 1986.
La Faille du regard (essays and interviews), Flammarion, 1987.
Wenderowefir, Association Jean-Baptiste Weckerlin (Strasbourg), 1988.
La Manna e la rugiada, Editiones Borla (Rome, Italy), 1988.
Aux Sources de la litterature moderne I, (essays), Entailles-Philippe Nadal (Bourg-en-Bresse, France), 1989.
Le Feu d'une nuit d'hiver (poems), Flammarion, 1989.
Leben in Jerusalem, Elster Verlag, 1990.
Apprendre la nuit (poems), Arfuyen (Paris), 1991.
La Terre el le Souffle, Claude Vigee, Albin Michel (Paris), 1992.
Dans le silence de l'Aleph (essays), Albin Michel, 1992.
Flow Tide: Selected Poetry and Prose, edited and translated by Anthony Rudolf, Menard-King's College Press (London), 1992.
L'Heritage du feu (essays, poems, and interviews), Mame (Paris), 1992.
Les Cinq rouleaux (Bible studies), Albin Michel, 1993.
Un Panier de Houblon (memoirs), Albin Michel, volume one, 1994, volume two, 1995.
Treize inconnus de la Bible, Albin Michel, 1996.
La Maison des Vivants, La Nuee Bleue (Strasbourg), 1996.
Aux portes du labyrinthe (poems), Flammarion, 1996.
Demain la seule demeure (essays), L'Harmattan (Paris), 1997.
La lucarne aux etoiles (notebooks), Editions du Cerf (Paris), in press.

Contributor of poems and essays to journals, including *PMLA, Partisan Review, Comparative Literature,*

Webster Review, Southern Review, Poesie 42, Steering Committee and *Chelsea Review.* Contributor of poetry to anthologies, including *Modern European Poetry,* Bantam Classics, 1966; *Jewish Frontier Anthology,* 1967; and *Voices within the Ark,* Avon Books, 1978. Translator into French of poems by R. M. Rilke, D. Seter, David Rokeah, Yvan Goll, and T. S. Eliot.

SIDELIGHTS: A poet, essayist, and professor, Claude Vigee was born into a Jewish family in the Alsace region of France along the Rhine River. In 1939, Vigee and his family were expelled from the area by the Nazis, and they took up residence in southern France. While studying medicine in Toulouse, from 1940 to 1942 Vigee helped organize the Jewish resistance against the German occupiers and the collaborating Vichy government of France. Because his family had been residents of the Alsace region for ten generations, Vigee, though a Jew, was allowed to travel freely, and he used this freedom to recruit others into the resistance movement. Vigee's first poems were published in *Poesie 42,* a resistance magazine. During this time he met the poet and novelist Louis Aragon, as well as poet Pierre Emmanuel, who became his lifelong friend.

When his life was endangered by his resistance activities, Vigee and his mother used forged travel papers to escape to Spain and eventually to emigrate to the United States in 1943. He earned a doctorate degree in Romance languages and literatures from Ohio State University and married his longtime sweetheart, his cousin Evelyne. An illustrious teaching and writing career followed, in the United States and later in Israel, to which Vigee and his family emigrated in 1960. Since the publication of his first collection of poetry *La Lutte avec l'ange,* in 1950, Vigee has published a steady stream of poetry, narratives, journal entries, essays, and translations. He has known and corresponded with many famous literary contemporaries, including Andre Gide, Albert Camus, Saint-Jean Perse, and T. S. Eliot, whose *Four Quartets* Vigee translated.

While his writings are varied, Vigee prefers to be described as a poet, "because narratives and essays constitute attempts at elaboration of the thematic cores of my poems," he wrote in *Le Parfum et la cendre.* "These throbbing cores are the primary elements of my sensibility. I am a storyteller but in no way a novelist. I am not gifted with the ability to invent characters or situations. But those that I live, those that I note around me, I seize them with my gaze, I garner them, I make them my own, and I know how to make them live in the eyes of others because I love to recount them. From mouth to ear first of all; in the secret of the thing written down, finally."

According to Freema Gottlieb in an article published in *Flow Tide: Selected Poetry and Prose,* it was in the United States that Vigee "first tasted true exile which, together with the longing for 'origins,' was to be the driving force in his writing." In the United States, Vigee felt deprived of a native land, a family, and a personal landscape. "In a sense, Vigee's whole oeuvre amounts to a yearning for lost origins, a perennial nostalgia transcended through return to Jerusalem, the 'origin of origins.' And yet, there remains the ache of betrayal that he tried to overcome," Gottlieb remarked.

Since retiring from teaching in 1984, Vigee has divided his time between France and Jerusalem, visiting Germany, Italy, and Greece.

BIOGRAPHICAL/CRITICAL SOURCES:

BOOKS

Lartichaux, Jean-Yves, *Claude Vigee,* Seghers (Paris), 1978.
Vigee, Claude, *Flow Tide: Selected Poetry and Prose,* edited and translated by Anthony Rudolf, Menard-King's College Press (London), 1992.

*   *   *

VOLKOGONOV, Dmitri (A.) 1928-1995

PERSONAL: Born March 22, 1928, in Chita, U.S.S.R. (now Russia); died from stomach cancer, December 6, 1995, in Moscow, Russia; married; children: two daughters. *Education:* Graduated from the Orel Tank School and the Lenin Military-Political Academy; earned degree as a doctor of philosophy.

CAREER: Soviet soldier and historian; became colonel general. Lenin Military-Political Academy, lecturer, 1964-70; Soviet Army and Navy, deputy head of the Chief Political Administration, beginning in 1970; chief of Russian military's Psychological Warfare department, 1980s; deputy and member of Russian Federation Supreme Soviet, beginning in 1990; Russian Supreme Soviet Council of Nationalities, vice chair, 1990; security and defense advisor to the Russian Federation Supreme Soviet chair, 1991; Russian State Counsellor for Defense, 1991; Russian chair of United States-Russia Joint Commission on Prisoners of Wars and Missing in Action, 1992. Soviet Institute of Military History, director; people's deputy; coordinator of the Left-Center Parliamentary Faction; council member of the Socio-Political Studies Foundation; adviser to Russian president Boris Yeltsin; writer.

WRITINGS:

Stalin: Triumph and Tragedy, edited and translated by Harold Shukman, Grove Weidenfeld, 1992.
Lenin: Life and Legacy (also published as *Lenin: A New Biography*), edited and translated by Shukman, Free Press, 1994.

Also author of *Seven Portraits,* a biography of the seven leaders who ran the Soviet Union; a history of Russia's involvement in World War II; and a biography of Leon Trotsky.

SIDELIGHTS: Dmitri Volkogonov was a former Soviet general who became known, at least to English-language readers, for his biographies of Russian leaders Josef Stalin and Vladimir Lenin. Volkogonov grew up in a poor family. His father eventually fell victim to one of dictator Stalin's purges and was executed. Volkogonov later entered the military, where he proved quite proficient. During the course of his long career—approximately forty years—he rose to the rank of colonel general.

Throughout much of his military career Volkogonov was a staunch Communist. But as he gained access to secret documents and banned books, his perception of Stalin changed, and he eventually came to believe that the dictator's grim reign, which left millions of Soviets dead from a series of murderous purges, was counter-productive to Soviet improvements and was, furthermore, inconsistent with the very tenets, socialist and communist, that Stalin espoused.

Volkogonov commenced writing a biography of Stalin as part of a ten-volume history chronicling Russia's involvement in World War II. His research revealed horrifying truths about the Russian dictator that had previously only been suspected—including Stalin personally signing death warrants for three thousand victims in a single day. Despite numerous documents corroborating this information, Volkogonov's presentation of these facts in 1983 caused a tremendous furor and the book was eventually banned. Hardline Communists were horrified that a general in the So-

viet military would write such things about Stalin, who, at the time was still considered above reproach for his leadership practices. Soviet leader Mikhail Gorbachev's late 1980s policy of *perestroika* or "openness" allowed for greater artistic and journalistic freedom in Russia. These policies led to the Soviet publication of the general's book in 1988.

Volkogonov's revelatory work was published in English as *Stalin: Triumph and Tragedy,* and it was generally hailed as an incisive and provocative volume. W. Bruce Lincoln, writing in *Chicago Tribune Books,* declared that the publication of *Stalin* "is a major event" and he affirmed that the book "serves . . . as a verification and elaboration of what has been written recently in the West about Stalin and Stalinism." *New Republic* reviewer Terence Emmons, meanwhile, called *Stalin* "a kind of triumph" and acknowledged it as "a monumental research effort performed in a historiographical wasteland. . . , and a bold confrontation with what could only have been unpleasant truths about Soviet history for a Soviet patriot and an avowed Marxist-Leninist." And David Remnick, in his appraisal for the *New York Review of Books,* observed that Volkogonov's work "gives us a new texture, at once horrifying and bland, to our knowledge of one of the worst passages in human history."

Volkogonov followed *Stalin* with *Lenin: Life and Legacy,* a biography of the Russian revolutionary who established the country's Communist Party and its subsequent dictatorial rule. According to Volkogonov, Stalin's murderous political practices were an extension of Lenin's own actions: In *Lenin,* Volkogonov reveals that Lenin intended to eliminate his enemies much as Stalin later tried to destroy his opponents, both real and imagined. William Taubman, writing in the *New York Times Book Review,* distinguished *Lenin* as "not so much a 'new biography' as an old polemic," and added, "The sermon is familiar, but it is preached with special fervor by a recent convert, and buttressed by a stunning barrage of new evidence from archives to which few besides Mr. Volkogonov have had . . . access." Vassily Aksyonov, meanwhile wrote in the *Los Angeles Times Book Review:* "[Volkogonov] must be given great credit for writing [*Lenin*]," and he deemed the biography "extraordinary." And *Times Literary Supplement* reviewer Robert Service, who claimed that Lenin emphasizes the revolutionary's character at the expense of his ideas, conceded that "Volkogonov writes attractively" and that Volkogonov's inclusion of autobiographical material in *Lenin* is "exciting for countless Russians left cold by academic historiography."

Upon leaving the military, Volkogonov remained active in Russian affairs, serving as an adviser to President Boris Yeltsin as well as several post-Communist political organizations. He was diagnosed with stomach cancer in the mid-1990s, though he continued to work to expose the myths of the Soviet leadership. His last work, which he finished just prior to his death, is titled *Seven Portraits*. It provides biographies on the seven leaders who held power in the Communist era of Russia. Volkogonov died in 1995.

BIOGRAPHICAL/CRITICAL SOURCES:

PERIODICALS

Chicago Tribune Books, January 12, 1992, pp. 6, 9.
Christian Science Monitor, May 5, 1992, p. 12.
Los Angeles Times, October 25, 1989, p. A6.
Los Angeles Times Book Review, October 16, 1994, pp. 1, 8, 14.
New Republic, March 9, 1992, pp. 33-41.
New Statesman and Society, March 1, 1991, pp. 33-34.
New York Review of Books, November 5, 1992, pp. 12, 14-17.
New York Times, January 30, 1992, p. A8; December 17, 1992, p. A17; April 22, 1993, p. A3.

New York Times Book Review, September 29, 1991, p. 9; November 5, 1992; November 13, 1994, pp. 11-12.
Times Literary Supplement, January 6, 1995, p. 9.
USA Today, June 29, 1992, p. A5.
Washington Post, November 4, 1992, p. A19.

OBITUARIES:

BOOKS

Who's Who in Russia and the CIS Republics, Holt, 1995, p. 264.

PERIODICALS

Economist, December 16, 1995, p. 85.
New York Times Biographical Service, December, 1995, p. 1809.*

*   *   *

von WRIGHT, G(eorg) H(enrik)
See WRIGHT, G(eorg) H(enrik) von

W

WALDBAUER, Gilbert (P.) 1928-

PERSONAL: Born April 18, 1928, in Bridgeport, CT; son of George Henry and Hedwig Martha Waldbauer; married Stephanie Stiefel, January 2, 1955; children: Gwen Ruth Waldbauer Rose, Susan Martha Waldbauer Yates. *Ethnicity:* "German." *Education:* University of Massachusetts at Amherst, B.S., 1953; University of Illinois at Urbana-Champaign, M.S., 1956, Ph.D., 1960. *Politics:* Democrat. *Religion:* "None." *Avocational interests:* Birding.

ADDRESSES: Home—807A Ramblewood Ct., Savoy, IL 61874. *Office*—c/o Department of Entomology, 320 Morrill Hall, University of Illinois at Urbana-Champaign, 505 South Goodwin, Urbana, IL 61801; fax: 217-244-3499.

CAREER: University of Illinois at Urbana-Champaign, began as instructor, became professor of entomology, 1953-95; writer, 1995—. *Military service:* U.S. Army, 1946-47.

MEMBER: American Birding Association.

WRITINGS:

Insects through the Seasons, Harvard University Press (Cambridge, MA), 1996.

WORK IN PROGRESS: The Birder's Bug Book, publication by Harvard University Press expected in 1998.

SIDELIGHTS: Gilbert Waldbauer told *CA:* "Almost as long as I can remember, I have had a consuming interest in natural history. Life has been kind to me, allowing me to indulge that interest as I pursued an academic career as an entomologist in an outstanding department in one of the country's great universities. Since my retirement from teaching and research in 1995, I have been writing full-time, inspired by the awesome beauty of nature and by the work of the many entomologists and other biologists I have known and by the work of those who came before me.

"I write because I love doing it, and because I want to open the eyes of others to the wonder of nature and communicate to them my own enthusiasm for the study of biology. I try to be scientifically accurate and to explain significant biological concepts while using language that can be understood by non-biologists. At first it wasn't easy to write without using the jargon of the field, but I think that I have now mastered that art."

*   *   *

WARD, Maurine Carr 1939-

PERSONAL: Born January 29, 1939, in Salt Lake City, UT; daughter of Cecil Alma (a printer) and Ivy (a printer, bookkeeper, and homemaker; maiden name, Streeper) Carr; married Gary A. Ward (a sales representative in marketing), September 21, 1960; children: Lyle, Betsy, Adam. *Ethnicity:* "Caucasian." *Education:* Attended University of Utah, 1957-59; Utah State University, B.A. (magna cum laude), 1978. *Politics:* "Mostly Republican." *Religion:* Church of Jesus Christ of Latter-day Saints (Mormons).

ADDRESSES: Home and office—433 East 300 S., Hyrum, UT 84319-1728. *E-mail*—mcward@n1.net.

CAREER: Self-employed historical researcher and publisher of family histories. Piano instructor, 1960-96; Utah State University, adjunct instructor in piano and instructor with Youth Conservatory; piano and organ accompanist. Cache Pioneer Museum, volunteer curator of photograph collection.

MEMBER: Mormon History Association, National Piano Teachers Association, Daughters of the American Revolution, Iowa Mormon Trails Association, Utah State Historical Society, Utah Piano Teachers Association, Daughters of the Utah Pioneers, Phi Kappa Phi.

AWARDS, HONORS: Evans Handcart Award, 1997.

WRITINGS:

(Editor) *Winter Quarters: The 1846-1848 Life Writings of Mary Haskin Parker Richards,* Utah State University Press (Logan, UT), 1996.

Editor, *Nauvoo Journal,* 1991—.

WORK IN PROGRESS: A history of Centerville, Utah.

SIDELIGHTS: Maurine Carr Ward told *CA:* "I love historical research, primarily in the early Latter-day Saints period. The magazine that I edit publishes many previously unpublished letters, journals, and stories. Each story I read or research for myself, my magazine, or my clients suggests ideas for further writing. I especially am drawn to the stories of Mormon women and their lives. Many of their stories have never been told."

*   *   *

WARTOFSKY, Marx W(illiam)   1928-1997

OBITUARY NOTICE—See index for *CA* sketch: Born August 5, 1928, in Brooklyn, NY; died of a heart attack, March 4, 1997, in New York, NY. Philosophy professor and author. As a philosophy professor and writer, Wartofsky's interest was in the ways social customs influence a society's philosophical themes. He received his bachelor's, master's and doctorate degrees from Columbia University and taught for

twenty-six years at Boston University. In 1967, he was named the philosophy department chair at the university. Wartofsky was a contributor to *Diderot Studies II* (1953), *Marx and the Western World* (1967), *Planning for Diversity and Choice* (1968), *Human Dignity: This Century and Next* (1970), and *Logic and Art: Essays in Honor of Nelson Goodman* (1972). His writings include *Conceptual Foundations of Scientific Thought* (1968), *Feuerbach* (1977), and *Models: Representation and Scientific Understanding* (1979). With his wife, Carol C. Gould, he co-edited *Women and Philosophy* (1976). In 1970, Wartofsky also founded and edited *The Philosophical Forum,* a quarterly publication. He was named Distinguished Professor of Philosophy at Baruch College and the Graduate Center of the City University of New York in 1983.

OBITUARIES AND OTHER SOURCES:

BOOKS

Directory of American Scholars, Volume 4: *Philosophy, Religion, and Law,* eighth edition, Bowker (New Providence, NJ), 1982.

PERIODICALS

New York Times, March 10, 1997, p. B9.

*   *   *

WEBER, Katharine   1955-

PERSONAL: Born November 12, 1955, in New York, NY; daughter of Sidney (a film producer) and Andrea (a photographer/birdwatcher; maiden name, Warburg) Kaufman; married Nicholas Fox Weber, September 19, 1976; children: Lucy Swift, Charlotte Fox. *Education:* Attended New School for Social Research, 1972-76; attended Yale University, 1982-84. *Politics:* "Quite left—a red diaper baby." *Religion:* "Cultural identity, mostly Jewish—religious beliefs, mostly absent."

ADDRESSES: Home—108 Beacon Rd., Bethany, CT 06524. *Office*—210 Prospect St., New Haven, CT 06510. *Agent*—Watkins/Loomis, 133 East 35th St., New York, NY 10016.

CAREER: Harper & Row, New York City, editorial assistant, 1975; Richard Meier and Partners Architects, New York City, in-house editor, 1975; American Institute of Graphic Arts, New York City, assistant to director, 1976; Josef Albers Foundation, Orange, CT, archivist, 1976-81; *Sunday New Haven Register,* New Haven, CT, weekly columnist, 1985-87; *Publishers Weekly,* weekly fiction reviewer, 1988-92. Residents for Rural Roads, founding member, 1980-84; Fairfield University, guest speaker, 1988-90; One Day Writer's Conference, Mattatuck Community College, teacher, 1992; archival research in Warburg family papers in conjunction with Ron Chernow's work for *The Warburgs;* administrator, estate of Kay Swift, 1990-94; trustee, Kay Swift Memorial Trust, 1995—. Visiting writer in residence, Connecticut College, 1996-97. Visiting lecturer, Yale University, 1997.

MEMBER: National Book Critics Circle, Authors Guild, PEN.

AWARDS, HONORS: Best Columnist of the Year, New England Women's Press Association, 1986; Discovery Award, New England Booksellers Association, 1995; "Discover Great New Writers" designation, Barnes and Noble, 1995; "New Voices" designation, Borders Books, 1995; included among *Granta*'s Best Young American Novelists, 1996.

WRITINGS:

Objects in Mirror Are Closer than They Appear, Crown Publishers (New York), 1995, Picador, 1996.

Author of numerous articles, stories, and reviews in a variety of publications, including *Publishers Weekly, New York Times Book Review, New Yorker, Boston Sunday Globe, New Haven Register, Connecticut Magazine, Story, Redbook, Journal-Courier,* and *Architectural Digest.*

WORK IN PROGRESS: The Music Lesson, a novel, in press; short stories.

SIDELIGHTS: Katharine Weber's first novel, *Objects in Mirror Are Closer than They Appear,* has been greeted enthusiastically by critics. "Tender and funny and sometimes remarkably jolting, this is a first novel of remarkable accomplishment," said a contributor to *Publishers Weekly.* Set in Geneva, Switzerland, the story traces the experiences and thoughts of Harriet Rose, a young American photographer, through a combination journal/letter she sends to her boyfriend, Benedict.

In the novel, events from both the past and present serve to expose the darkness underlying each character's life. Harriet observes Anne Gordon—the friend she is visiting—embark on a self-destructive affair with Victor, her father's friend and fellow Auschwitz survivor, and the relationship causes much concern for Harriet. While wandering the streets of Geneva so that Anne and Victor can continue their daily lunch-time trysts in privacy, Harriet ponders her friend's happiness and gradually succumbs to memories of her own past.

Written in a style that critics found both witty and humorous, as well as dramatic, *Objects in Mirror Are Closer than They Appear* reminds the reader that the past has a constant influence over the present. Truth can be interpreted on many levels, according to Weber. Harriet's letters and journals may record the events experienced inside a day and interpret her feelings; however, she can never precisely capture the day as it happened—written words can only be impressions and fragments of the complete truth, which is acted on by outside forces and events from the distant past. "Life is nothing but images transformed by reflection, and we rarely understand what we think we see," summarized Sally Eckhoff in the *Voice Literary Supplement.* Harriet's experiences reflect these limits of perception and fragmentation of memory. Elizabeth Benedict wrote in the *New York Times Book Review,* "As her title suggests, Katharine Weber is wise to these issues of artifice, distance and what seems like candor." Despite such weighty thoughts woven through the novel's plot, Weber's novel is never heavy-handed. As Eckhoff observed in the *Voice Literary Supplement,* Harriet's buoyant character keeps the darkness and danger from oppressing the reader. "Her jokey patter and enthusiastic innocence—that's the book's brightest idea."

Weber told *CA:* "I have rarely done things in the usual order. I have no high school diploma, having left after eleventh grade to attend The New School, when I was sixteen, and I have no college degree, though several years of part-time college at The New School and Yale. One way of thinking about this as an asset rather than a liability is to consider my education as being an ongoing activity rather than something that has been completed.

"Though I worked as a journalist and critic for several years, my fiction was never published anywhere until a story of mine was selected off the slush pile for publication in *New Yorker* in January of 1993. That story was to form part of my first novel.

"I tell this story to encourage all unpublished fiction writers. It can happen."

BIOGRAPHICAL/CRITICAL SOURCES:

PERIODICALS

New York Times Book Review, April 30, 1995, p. 20.
Publishers Weekly, February 13, 1995, pp. 62-63.
Voice Literary Supplement, May, 1995, p.10.

*   *   *

WEDGWOOD, C(icely) V(eronica)   1910-1997

OBITUARY NOTICE—See index for *CA* sketch: Born July 20, 1910, in Stocksfield, Northumberland, England; died March 9, 1997, in London, England. Historian and author. Wedgwood's narrative style in writing historical tomes made her work appeal to the layman yet was so accurately researched and detailed that some of her books, especially ones on the English Civil War and Thirty Years War, became standard texts for history classes. Educated at Bonn University in Germany, the Sorbonne in Paris and later at Oxford University, Wedgwood published her first historical work, *Strafford,* the biography of an advisor to King Charles I, in 1935. Her two most important works were considered to be *The Thirty Years War* (1938) and *The Great Rebellion* trilogy—*The King's Peace: 1637-1641* (1955), *The King's War: 1641-1647* (1958), and *A Coffin for King Charles: The Trial and Execution of Charles I* (1964). Her study of the Thirty Years War became recognized as the standard book on the time. Wedgwood looked at the personalities of history but was also so meticulous in her detail that she would often spend hours diagramming a battlefield on paper then visit the sight to gain perspective. Her other works include *Oliver Cromwell* (1939), *William the Silent: William of Nassau, Prince of Orange, 1533-1584* (1944), *Richelieu and the French Monarchy* (1949), *Seventeenth-Century English Literature* (1950), *Montrose* (1952), *The Common Man in the Great Civil War* (1957), *Poetry and Politics under the Stuarts* (1964), *Milton and His World* (1969), *The Political Career of Peter Paul Rubens* (1975), and *The Spoils of Time: A Short History of the World* (1984). In 1944 she won the James Tait Black Memorial Prize for *William the Silent* and was made an Officer of the Order of Orange-Nassau in 1946. Wedgwood became a Member of the Order of the British Empire in 1956 and in 1968 was made a Dame

of the Empire. In 1969, she received the Order of Merit, Britain's highest civilian honor.

OBITUARIES AND OTHER SOURCES:

BOOKS

The Writers Directory: 1996-1998, St. James Press, 1995.

PERIODICALS

New York Times, March 11, 1997, p. D23.
Times (London), March 11, 1997, p. 23.
Washington Post, March 11, 1997, p. E4.

*   *   *

WEENOLSEN, Patricia   1930-
(Patricia Otway-Ward, a pseudonym)

PERSONAL: Born June 12, 1930, in Paris, France; divorced; children: Anne Olson Gray, Pamela Marott Wellman, Valerie Marott, Melissa Marott Sirovina, Jennifer Marott. *Education:* Barnard College, Columbia University, B.A., 1952; California State University, Long Beach, M.A., 1975; University of Chicago, M.A., 1977; University of California, Santa Cruz, Ph.D, 1982. *Politics:* "Bleeding heart liberal." *Religion:* Episcopalian. *Avocational interests:* "Travel, American history and culture, walking, nature, caves, and of course, reading."

ADDRESSES: Office—403 14th Ave. E., #22, Seattle, WA 98112.

CAREER: Writer, psychologist, public speaker, and consultant. Worked as research associate, assistant professor of psychology, instructor, and teaching fellow.

MEMBER: Association for Death Education and Counseling.

WRITINGS:

Transcendence of Loss Over the Life Span, Hemisphere (Bristol, PA), 1988.
The Art of Dying: How to Leave This World with Dignity and Grace, at Peace with Yourself and Your Loved Ones, St. Martin's Press (New York), 1996.

Contributor of stories under the pseudonym Patricia Otway-Ward to periodicals and journals, including *Triquarterly, Southern Humanities Review, Confrontation, Pulpsmith, Aberrations, Standard,* and *Dreams and Visions;* contributor of articles to professional publications.

WORK IN PROGRESS: Soul Travel: A Memoir of Healing and Transformation Across America, short stories, articles, a novel, and two other nonfiction books.

SIDELIGHTS: With regard to *The Art of Dying: How to Leave This World with Dignity and Grace, at Peace with Yourself and Your Loved Ones,* Patricia Weenolsen explained to *CA,* "After many years of teaching, counseling, and research in the death and dying field, I was suddenly asking, 'Why have so many thousands of books been written for the bereaved and for the caregivers, but almost nothing for those facing their own death? Why are there no handbooks to help us deal with the physical, emotional, social, and spiritual issues of our end time? Might not such a guide relieve the intensity of suffering that currently surrounds the process of dying in our culture?'" Weenolsen's book is a response to this lack of guidance. As she related, "It is a manual that aids those facing death, whether they have just received a terrifying diagnosis, or are farther along in the process. It offers a variety of options for resolving issues. These range from early physical concerns about pain and changes in appearance; to emotional concerns over relatives, reconciliation, and our own daily roller coaster of highs and lows; to psychological concerns over loss of control and loss of identity; to spiritual concerns about our need to feel that our life has had meaning, about what dying is like, and what happens next."

The Art of Dying addresses a variety of options with a reassuring voice, ranging from physical and emotional concerns, such as coping with fear, pain, and grief, to spiritual concerns. "While the topic may be morbid, Weenolsen's writing style is not. Her touch is light and informative, never depressing," said Tom Depoto of the *Newark Star-Ledger.* A contributor to *Publishers Weekly* commented that *The Art of Dying* "speaks to modern readers with refreshing frankness and wit."

Critics noted that the strength of *The Art of Dying* is that it speaks to all humans, not just those who are terminally ill. Barbara Lloyd McMichael of the *Olympian* advised, "Weenolsen's sage counsel pertains to

intentional living, no matter where you are in your lifespan, as well as making a graceful exit. . . . no matter how much time we have left to live, there are almost always opportunities to make life more meaningful and loving." Patricia Holt in the *San Francisco Chronicle* called *The Art of Dying* "a no-nonsense compassionate guide. . . . Weenolsen takes the panic and paralysis out of such news through wise, aggressive, no-holds-barred approaches."

Transcendence of Loss Over the Life Span, an earlier book by Weenolsen, touches similar themes in its examination of how people create meaning in life by transcending loss. Using excerpts from the life histories of forty-eight women interviewed, Weenolsen offers the reader a model, the loss/transcendence paradigm.

Weenolsen told *CA:* "My life has been a series of seminal experiences with death, all leading me to where I am now.

"Lingering screams followed me down the halls of a hospital where I worked after college. For weeks, the nursing supervisor assured me that this lady, who was dying of cancer, 'didn't feel a thing.' Not the nurse's fault—she had been trained to believe this. Years later, I gave birth among mothers who also screamed, but, as I was assured, 'didn't feel a thing.' When my own screams joined theirs, I knew they felt 'a thing,' and that the dying lady had as well."

As to the writing process, Weenolsen said, "For me, an idea begins as a physical experience. *The Art of Dying* came to me as I was walking down a Seattle street. I felt as though I'd been hit on the side of the head, in fact, I'm sure I ducked.

"*The Art of Dying* now comforts and guides many patients who use it as a handbook, relatives who rely on it as a resource to help their dying loved ones, and hospices that employ it in their training of both volunteer and professional staffs. For this I am profoundly grateful.

"Ideas for short stories come to me in a different way from those for nonfiction books, although they are still physical. An image catches me in the chest, I gasp, and I know that this is a great idea, even though I don't yet know what it is. Early in life, I discovered that the everyday experiences of women were not given voice and honored, as were those of men. There were hundreds of fine books on war, for example, but much less on the daily lives of women, giving birth and raising children, as well as the losses they must typically transcend. My stories are devoted to articulating those experiences. Some of the fiction writers I most admire are Amy Bloom, Tim O'Brien, Margaret Atwood, Jane Smiley, Robert Olen Butler, and Ruth Rendell.

"I have always wanted the life of a full-time writer. The conventional wisdom is, 'don't quit your day job.' But my day job quit me, when state funding for a teaching position I'd been offered disappeared. As I stood in front of my computer—the only thing I had not packed—a voice said, 'If not now, when?' I took the vow of poverty and have never regretted it."

BIOGRAPHICAL/CRITICAL SOURCES:

PERIODICALS

Choice, March, 1989, p.1256.
Contemporary Psychology, July, 1990, pp.691-692.
Humanistic Psychologist, 1988, p.328.
Library Journal, June 6, 1996.
Newark Star-Ledger, July 28, 1996.
Olympian, June 23, 1996.
Press Enterprise, August 25, 1996.
Publishers Weekly, April 15, 1996, pp. 59-60.
San Francisco Chronicle, June 2, 1996.

*   *   *

WERTENBAKER, Lael (Tucker)   1909-1997
(Lael Tucker)

OBITUARY NOTICE—See index for *CA* sketch: Born March 28, 1909, in Bradford, PA; died of lung cancer, March 24, 1997, in Keene, NH. Author and journalist. Labeled a "dangerous woman" by a Nazi propaganda official for her reporting from Germany for *Time* magazine, Wertenbaker went on to have a successful career both as a journalist and novelist. She joined the *Time* staff in 1938 and from 1940 to 1941 covered the Nazi government in Germany. During the war, she covered governments in exile in London and later reported from Paris. Her breakthrough book, *Death of a Man,* was published in 1957 under the name Lael Tucker and was a memoir of her husband's death from colon cancer. Wertenbaker's other books include *Lament for Four Virgins* (1952— also as Lael Tucker), *Festival* (1954), *Mister Junior* (1958), *A Portrait of Hotchkiss* (1965), *The Eye of the Lion* (1965), *The Afternoon Women* (1966), *Unbidden*

Guests (1970), *Perilous Voyage* (1975), and *To Mend the Heart* (1980). She mixed novel writing and journalism throughout her career and was a regular contributor to *Fortune, Life,* and *U.S. News and World Report.* Wertenbaker also wrote television scripts for the *20th Century* series for CBS.

OBITUARIES AND OTHER SOURCES:

BOOKS

The Writers Directory: 1996-1998, St. James Press, 1995.

PERIODICALS

New York Times, March 29, 1997, p. 20.
Washington Post, April 3, 1997, p. D5.

*   *   *

WEYL, (Claus Hugo) Hermann   1885-1955

PERSONAL: Born November 9, 1885, in Elmshorn, Germany; died December 8, 1955, in Zurich, Switzerland, following a heart attack; son of Ludwig (a bank clerk) and Anna (Dieck) Weyl; married Helene (Hella) Joseph (deceased 1948) in 1913, married Ellen Bair in 1950; children: (first marriage) Fritz Joachim, Michael. *Education:* University of Gottingen, Ph.D., 1908; studied at University of Munich. *Avocational interests:* Reading literature and poetry.

CAREER: Mathematician and educator. National Technical University (ETH), Zurich, Switzerland, professor, 1913; Gottingen University, Gottingen, Germany, professor and chair of the mathematics department, 1930-33; affiliated with Institute for Advanced Study, Princeton, NJ, beginning 1933. *Military service:* Served with the German Army during World War I.

WRITINGS:

Die Idee der Riemannschen Fleache, Teubner, 1913.
Raum, Zeit, Materie, 1918, translated by Henry L. Brose as *Space-Time-Matter,* Metheun (London), 1922.
Philosophie der Mathematik und Naturwissenschaft, (title means "Philosophy of Mathematics and Natural Science"), R. Oldenbourg, 1926.

Der Epileptiker: Erzeahlung, Verlag Kirchberger, 1927.

Gruppentheorie und Quantenmechanik, (title means "The Theory of Groups and Quantum Mechanics") Metheun, 1931.

The Classical Groups, Their Invariants and Representations, Princeton University Press (Princeton, NJ), 1946.

Symmetry, Princeton University Press, 1952.

Selecta Hermann Weyl, Birkeauser (Basel, Switzerland), 1956.

Gesammelte Abhandlungen, four volumes, Springer-Verlag (Berlin, New York), 1968.

Centenary Lectures Delivered by C. N. Yang, R. Penrose, A. Borel at the ETH Zurich, Springer-Verlag (New York), c. 1986.

Kontinuum (title means "The Continuum: A Critical Examination of the Foundation of Analysis") translated by Stephen Pollard and Thomas Bole, Thomas Jefferson University Press (Kirksville, MO), c. 1987.

Riemanns Geometrische Ideen, Ihre Auswirkung und Ihre Verkneupfung mit der Gruppentheorie, Springer-Verlag (New York), c. 1988.

The Open World: Three Lectures on the Metaphysical Implications of Science, Ox Box Press (Woodbridge, CT), 1989.

SIDELIGHTS: Hermann Weyl was one of the most wide-ranging mathematicians of his generation, following in the footsteps of his teacher David Hilbert. Weyl's interests in mathematics ran the gamut from foundations to physics, two areas in which he made profound contributions. He combined great technical virtuosity with imagination, and devoted attention to the explanation of mathematics to the general public. He managed to take a segment of mathematics developed in an abstract setting and apply it to certain branches of physics, such as relativity theory—a theory that holds that the velocity of light is the same for all observers, no matter how they are moving, that the laws of physics are the same in all inertial frames, and that all such frames are equivalent—and quantum mechanics—a theory that allows mathematical interpretation of elementary particles through wave properties. His distinctive ability was integrating nature and theory.

Claus Hugo Hermann Weyl was born on November 9, 1885, in Elmshorn, near Hamburg, Germany. The financial standing of his parents (his father, Ludwig, was a clerk in a bank and his mother, Anna Dieck, came from a wealthy family) enabled him to receive a quality education. From 1895 to 1904 he attended

the Gymnasium at Altona, where his performance attracted the attention of his headmaster, a relative of an eminent mathematician of that time, David Hilbert. Weyl soon found himself at the University of Gottingen where Hilbert was an instructor. He remained there for the rest of his student days, with the exception of a semester at the University of Munich. He received his degree under Hilbert in 1908 and advanced to the ranks of privatdocent (unpaid but licensed instructor) in 1910.

Weyl married Helene Joseph (known as Hella to the family) in 1913 and in the same year accepted a position as professor at the National Technical University (ETH) in Zurich, Switzerland. He declined the offer to be Felix Klein's successor at Gottingen, despite the university's central role in the mathematical world. It has been suggested that he wanted to free himself, somewhat, of the influence of Hilbert, especially in light of the fact that he had accepted an invitation to take a chair at Gottingen when Hilbert retired. In any case, he brought a great deal of mathematical distinction to the ETH in Zurich, where his sons Fritz Joachim and Michael grew up.

It is not surprising that Weyl's early work dealt with topics in which Hilbert held an interest. His *Habilitationsschrift* was devoted to boundary conditions of second-order linear differential equations. (The way the German educational system worked, it was necessary to do a substantial piece of original research beyond the doctoral dissertation in order to qualify to teach in the university. This "entitling document" was frequently the launching point of the mathematical career of its author.) In other words, he was looking into the way functions behaved on a given region when the behavior at the boundary was specified. His results were sufficient for the purpose of enabling him to earn a living, but he rapidly moved on to areas where his contributions were more innovative and have had a more lasting effect.

One of the principal areas of Weyl's research was the topic of Hilbert spaces. The problem was to understand something about the functions that operated on the points of Hilbert space in a way useful for analyzing the result of applying the functions. In particular, Weyl wanted to know where the functions behaved more simply than on the space as a whole, since the behavior of the function on the rest of the space could be represented in terms of its behavior on the simpler regions. Different kinds of functions behaved in radically different ways on a Hilbert space, so Weyl had to restrict his attention to a subclass of functions small enough to be tractable (for example, the functions could not "blow up") but large enough to be useful. His choice of self-adjoint, compact operators was justified by their subsequent importance in the field of functional analysis.

Among the areas he brought together were geometry and analysis from the nineteenth century and topology, which was largely a creation of the twentieth century. Topology sought to understand the behavior of space in ways that require a less-detailed understanding of how the elements of a structure fit together than geometry demanded. One of the basic ideas of topology is that of a "manifold," first introduced by G. F. B. Riemann in his *Habilitationsschrift* as a student of Gauss. Riemann had little material with which to work, while Weyl was able to take advantage of the work of Hilbert and the Dutch mathematician Luitzen Egbertus Jan Brouwer. This effort culminated in his 1913 book on Riemann surfaces, an excellent exposition on how complex analysis and topology could be used together to analyze the behavior of complex functions.

Weyl served briefly in the German army at the outbreak of World War I, but before this military interlude, he did research that led to one of his most important papers. He looked at the way irrational numbers (those that cannot be expressed as a ratio of two whole numbers) were distributed. What he noticed was that the *fractional* parts of an irrational number and its integral multiples seemed to be evenly distributed in the interval between O and 1. He succeeded in proving this result, and it is known as the Kronecker-Weyl theorem, owing half of its name to an influential number theorist who had an effect on Hilbert. Although the result may seem rather narrow, Weyl was able to generalize it to sequences of much broader application.

During his time in Zurich, Weyl spent a year in collaboration with Albert Einstein and picked up a dose of enthusiasm for the relativity theory. Among the other results of this collaboration was Weyl's popular account of relativity theory, *Space, Time, Matter* (the original German edition appeared in 1918). In those early days of general relativity, which describes gravity in terms of how mass distorts space-time, the correct mathematical formulation of some of Einstein's ideas was not clear. He had been able to use ideas developed by differential geometers at the end of the nineteenth century that involved the notion of a tensor. A tensor can be thought of as a function on a number of vectors that takes a number as its value.

Weyl used the tensor calculus that had been developed by the geometers to come up with neater formulations of general relativity than the original version proposed by Einstein. In later years, he took the evolution of tensors one step further while maintaining a strict mathematical level of rigor.

One of the most visible areas in which Weyl worked after World War I was in the foundations of mathematics. He had used some of the topological results of the Dutch mathematician Brouwer in working on Riemann surfaces. In addition, he had looked at some of Brouwer's ideas about the philosophy of mathematics and was convinced that they had to be taken seriously. Although it was not always easy to understand what Brouwer was trying to say, it was clear that he was criticizing "classical" mathematics, that is, the mathematics that had prevailed at least since Euclid. One of the standard methods of proof in classical mathematics was the reductio ad absurdum, or proof by contradiction. If one wished to prove that P was true, one could assume that not-P was true and see if that led to a contradiction. If it did, then not-P must not be true, and P must be true instead. This method of proof depended on the principle that either P was true or not-P was true, which had seemed convincing to generations of mathematicians.

Brouwer, however, found this style of argument unacceptable. For reasons having to do with his understanding of mathematics as the creation of the human mind, he wanted to introduce a third category besides truth and falsity, a category we could call "unproven." In other words, there was more to truth than just the negation of falsity—to claim P or not-P, something had to be proven. This argument of Brouwer was especially directed against so-called nonconstructive existence proofs. These were proofs in which something was shown to exist, not by being constructed, but by arguing that if it didn't exist, a contradiction arose. For ordinary, finite mathematics it was usually easy to come up with a constructive proof, but for claims about infinite sets nonconstructive arguments were popular. If Brouwer's objections were to be sustained, a good part of mathematics even at the level of elementary calculus would have to be rewritten and some perhaps have to be abandoned.

This attitude aroused the ire of David Hilbert. He valued the progress that had been made in mathematics too highly to sacrifice it lightly for philosophical reasons. Although Hilbert had earlier expressed admiration for Brouwer's work, he felt obliged to negate Brouwer's philosophy of mathematics known as intuitionism. What especially disturbed Hilbert was Weyl's support of Brouwer's concepts, since Hilbert knew the mathematical strength of his former student. In the 1920s, while the argument was being considered, Hilbert was discouraged about the future of mathematics in the hands of the intuitionists.

Although Weyl never entirely abandoned his allegiance to Brouwer, he also recognized that Hilbert's program in the philosophy of mathematics was bound to appeal to the practicing mathematician, more than Brouwer's speculations. In 1927, responding to one of Hilbert's lectures concerned with the foundations of mathematics, Weyl commented on the extent to which Hilbert had been led to a reinterpretation of mathematics by the need to fight off Brouwer's criticisms. The tone of Weyl's remarks suggested that he would not have been unhappy if Hilbert's point of view was to prevail. This flexibility with regard to the foundations of mathematics indicates that Weyl was sensitive to the changes in attitude that others ignored, but also may explain why Weyl never founded a philosophical school: he was too ready to recognize the justice of others' points of view.

In general, Weyl took questions of literature and style seriously, which goes far to explain the success of his expository writings. His son recalls that when Weyl would read poetry aloud to the family, the intensity and volume of his voice would make the walls shake. He kept in touch with modern literature as well as the classics of his childhood. While he continued to enjoy the poetry of Friedrich Holderlin and Johann Wolfgang von Goethe, he also read Friedrich Nietzsche's *Also Sprach Zarathustra* and Thomas Mann's *The Magic Mountain*. He could cite quotations from German poetry whenever he needed them. For those of a psychologizing bent, it has even been argued that his fondness for poetry may be in line with his preference for intuitionism as a philosophy of mathematics. The kind of poetry he preferred spoke to the heart, and he used quotations to add a human dimension to otherwise cold mathematical writing.

After he accepted a chair at Gottingen in 1930, Weyl did not have long to enjoy his return to familiar surroundings. In 1933 he decided that he could no longer remain in Nazi Germany, and he took up a permanent position at the Institute for Advanced Study, newly founded in Princeton, New Jersey. Although Weyl himself was of irreproachably Aryan ancestry, his wife was partly Jewish, and that would have been enough to attract the attention of the authorities. There may have been the additional attraction of the

wealth of intellectual company available at the institute, between its visitors from all over the globe and permanent residents such as Einstein. Weyl took his official duties as a faculty member seriously, although his reputation could be terrifying to younger mathematicians unaware of the poet within.

Weyl's work continued to bridge the gap between physics and mathematics. As long ago as 1929, he developed a mathematical theory for the subatomic particle the neutrino. The theory was internally consistent but failed to preserve left-right symmetry and so was abandoned. Subsequent experimentation revealed that symmetry need not be conserved, with the result that Weyl's theory reentered the mathematical physics mainstream all the more forcefully. Another area for the interaction of mathematics and physics was the study of spinors, a kind of tensor that has proven to be of immense use in quantum mechanics. Although spinors had been known before Weyl, he was the first to give a full treatment of them. Perhaps it was this work that led Roger Penrose, one of the most insightful mathematical physicists of the second half of the twentieth century, to label Weyl "the greatest mathematician of this century."

One of the challenges of physical theories is to find quantities that do not change (are conserved) during other changes. Felix Klein in the nineteenth century had stressed the importance of group theory, then a new branch of mathematics, in describing what changed and what remained the same during processes. Weyl adapted Klein's ideas to the physics of the twentieth century by characterizing invariant quantities for relativity theory and for quantum mechanics. In a 1923 paper Weyl had come up with a suitable definition for congruence in relativistic space-time. Even more influential was his book on group theory and quantum mechanics, which imposed a model that would have been welcome to Klein due to the previously rather disjointed results assembled by quantum physicists. Weyl was an artist in the use of group theory and could accomplish wonders with modest mathematical structure.

After the end of World War II, Weyl divided his time between Zurich and Princeton. His first wife died in 1948, and two years later he married Ellen Bair. He took a serious view of the history of mathematics and arranged with Princeton to give a course on the subject. One of his magisterial works was a survey of the previous half-century of mathematics that appeared in the *American Mathematical Monthly* in 1951. Although he never became as fluent in English as he had in German, he retained a strong commitment to the public's right to be informed about scientific developments.

John Archibald Wheeler, an American physicist, called attention to Weyl's anticipation of the anthropic principle in cosmology. In a 1919 paper Weyl had speculated on the coincidence of the agreement of two enormous numbers of very different origin. In the 1930s this speculation had been given with the title "Weyl's hypothesis," although later authors referred more to its presence elsewhere. What cannot be denied is that the recent discussion of the anthropic principle concerning features necessary for human existence in the universe has, as Wheeler noted, taken up Weyl's point once again.

Weyl was unaware of the rules governing the length of time that a naturalized citizen could spend abroad at one time without losing citizenship. By inadvertence he exceeded the time limit and lost his American citizenship in the mid-1950s. To remedy the situation required an act of Congress, but there was no lack of help in securing it. In the meantime, Weyl celebrated his seventieth birthday in Zurich amid a flurry of congratulations. On December 8, 1955, as he was mailing some letters of thanks to well-wishers, he died of a heart attack. With his death passed one of the links with the great era of Gottingen as a mathematical center and one of the founders of contemporary mathematical physics, but even more, a mathematician who could convey the poetry in his discipline.

BIOGRAPHICAL/CRITICAL SOURCES:

BOOKS

Chandrasekharan, K., editor, *Hermann Weyl: Centenary Lectures,* Springer, 1986.
Deppert, Wolfgang, and others, editors, *Exact Sciences and Their Philosophical Foundations,* Peter Lang, 1988.
Dictionary of Scientific Biography, Volume 14, Scribner, pp. 281-285.*

*   *   *

WIENER, Norbert   1894-1964

PERSONAL: Born November 26, 1894, in Columbia, MO; died March 18, 1964, in Stockholm, Sweden; son of Leo (a linguist and professor of Slavic languages) and Bertha (Kahn) Wiener; married Margaret Engemann (a professor of modern languages), 1926; children: Barbara, Peggy. *Education:* Tufts University, B.A., 1910; Harvard University, Ph.D.; studied at Cornell University, Columbia University, and Gottingen University, Germany.

CAREER: Mathematician. Massachusetts Institute of Technology (MIT), Cambridge, MA, instructor of mathematics, 1919, assistant professor of mathematics, 1924, associate professor 1929, full professor, 1932.

AWARDS, HONORS: Guggenheim fellowship, 1926; Bocher Prize, American Mathematical Society, 1933; National Medal of Science, 1964; elected to the National Academy of Sciences; received honorary degree from Tufts University, 1966.

WRITINGS:

The Fourier Integral and Certain of its Applications, Cambridge University Press (London), 1933.
Cybernetics, or, Control and Communication in the Animal and the Machine, Massachusetts Institute of Technology Press (Cambridge, MA), 1948.
The Human Use of Human Beings, Houghton (Boston, MA), 1950.
Ex-Prodigy (autobiography), Simon & Schuster (New York), 1953.
Time and Organization, University of Southampton (Southhampton, England), 1955.
I Am a Mathematician, Doubleday (Garden City, NY), 1956.
Nonlinear Problems in Random Theory, Technology Press of Massachusetts Institute of Technology (Cambridge, MA), 1958.
Selected Papers of Norbert Wiener, Including Generalized Harmonic Analysis and Tauberian Theorems, M.I.T. Press, c. 1964.
God and Golem, Inc.: A Comment on Certain Points Where Cybernetics Impinges on Religion, M.I.T. Press, 1964.
Differential Space, Quantum Systems and Prediction, M.I.T. Press, 1966.
Invention: The Care and Feeding of Ideas, M.I.T. Press, 1993.

Contributor to journals and periodicals, including *Atlantic, Nation, New Republic,* and *Colliers.*

SIDELIGHTS: Norbert Wiener was one of the most original mathematicians of his time. The field concerning the study of automatic control systems, called cybernetics, owes a great deal not only to his researches, but to his continuing efforts at publicity. He wrote for a variety of popular journals as well as for technical publications and was not reluctant to express political views even when they might be unpopular. Perhaps the most distinctive feature of Wiener's life as a student and a mathematician is how well documented it is, thanks to two volumes of autobiography published during his lifetime. They reveal some of the complexity of a man whose aspirations went well beyond the domain of mathematics.

Wiener was born in Columbia, Missouri, on November 26, 1894. His father, Leo Wiener, had been born in Bialystok, Poland (then Russia), and was an accomplished linguist; he arrived in New Orleans in 1880 with very little money but a great deal of determination, some of it visible in his relations with his son. Leo met his wife, Bertha Kahn, at a meeting of a Browning Club. As a result, when his son was born, he was given the name Norbert, from one of Browning's verse dramas. Despite the absence of Judaism from the Wiener home (Norbert was fifteen before he learned that he was Jewish), one of Leo Wiener's best-known works was a history of Yiddish literature.

As the title of the first volume of his autobiography *Ex-Prodigy* suggests, Wiener was a child prodigy. Whatever his natural talents, this was partly due to the efforts of his father. Leo Wiener was proud of his educational theories and pointed to the academic success of his son as evidence. Norbert was less enthusiastic and in his memoirs describes his recollections of his father's harsh disciplinary methods. He entered high school at the age of nine and graduated two years later. In 1906 he entered Tufts University, as the family had moved to the Boston area, and he graduated four years later.

Up until that point Wiener's education had clearly outrun that of most of his contemporaries, but he was now faced with the challenge of deciding what to do with his education. He enrolled at Harvard to study zoology, but the subject did not suit him. He tried studying philosophy at Cornell, but that was equally unavailing. Finally, Wiener came back to Harvard to work on philosophy and mathematics. The subject of his dissertation was a comparison of the system of logic developed by Bertrand Russell and Alfred North Whitehead in their *Principia Mathematica* with the earlier algebraic system created by Ernst Schroder. The relatively recent advances in mathematical research in the United States had partly occurred in the

area of algebraic logic, so the topic was a reasonable one for a student hoping to bridge the still-existent gap between the European and American mathematical communities.

Although Wiener earned a Harvard travelling fellowship to enable him to study in Europe after taking his degree, his father still supervised his career by writing to Bertrand Russell on Norbert's behalf. Wiener was in England from June 1913 to April 1914 and attended two courses given by Russell, including a reading course on *Principia Mathematica*. Perhaps more influential in the long run for Wiener's mathematical development was a course he took from the British analyst G. H. Hardy, whose lectures he greatly admired. In the same way, Wiener studied with some of the most eminent names in Gottingen, Germany, then the center of the international mathematical community.

Wiener returned to the United States in 1915, still unsure, despite his foreign travels, of the mathematical direction he wanted to pursue. He wrote articles for the *Encyclopedia Americana* and took a variety of teaching jobs until the entry of the United States into World War I. Wiener was a fervent patriot, and his enthusiasm led him to join the group of scientists and engineers at the Aberdeen Proving Ground in Maryland, where he encountered Oswald Veblen, already one of the leading mathematicians in the country. Although Wiener did not pursue Veblen's lines of research, Veblen's success in producing results useful to the military impressed Wiener more than mere academic success.

After the war two events decisively shaped Wiener's mathematical future. He obtained a position as instructor at the Massachusetts Institute of Technology (MIT) in mathematics, where he was to remain until his retirement. At that time mathematics was not particularly strong at MIT, but his position there assured him of continued contact with engineers and physicists. As a result, he displayed an ongoing concern for the applications of mathematics to problems that could be stated in physical terms. The question of which tools he would bring to bear on those problems was answered by the death of his sister's fiance. That promising young mathematician left his collection of books to Wiener, who began to read avidly the standard texts in a way that he had not in his earlier studies.

The first problem Wiener addressed had to do with Brownian motion, the apparently random motion of particles in substances at rest. The phenomenon had earlier excited Albert Einstein's interest, and he had dealt with it in one of his 1905 papers. Wiener took the existence of Brownian motion as a sign of randomness at the heart of nature. By idealizing the physical phenomenon, Wiener was able to produce a mathematical theory of Brownian motion that had wide influence among students of probability. It is possible to see in his work on Brownian motion, steps in the direction of the study of fractals (shapes whose detail repeats itself on any scale), although Wiener did not go far along that path.

The next subject Wiener addressed was the Dirichlet problem, which had been reintroduced into the mathematical mainstream by German David Hilbert. Much of the earliest work on the Dirichlet problem had been discredited as not being sufficiently rigorous for the standards of the late nineteenth century. Wiener's work on the Dirichlet problem produced interesting results, some of which he delayed publishing for the sake of a couple of students finishing their theses at Harvard. Wiener felt subsequently that his forbearance was not recognized adequately. In particular, although Wiener progressed through the academic ranks at MIT from assistant professor in 1924 to associate professor in 1929 to full professor in 1932, he believed that more support from Harvard would have enabled him to advance more quickly.

Wiener had a high opinion of his own abilities, something of a change from colleagues whose public expressions of modesty were at odds with a deep-seated conviction of their own merits. Whatever his talents as a mathematician, Wiener had expository standards that were at odds with those of most mathematicians of his time. While he was always exuberant, this was often at the cost of accuracy of detail. One of his main theorems depended on a series of lemmas, or auxiliary propositions, one of which was proven by assuming the truth of the main theorem. Students trying to learn from Wiener's papers and finding their efforts unrewarding discovered that this reaction was almost universal. As Hans Freudenthal remarked in the *Dictionary of Scientific Biography,* "After proving at length a fact that would be too easy if set as an exercise for an intelligent sophomore, he would assume without proof a profound theorem that was seemingly unrelated to the preceding text, then continue with a proof containing puzzling but irrelevant terms, next interrupt it with a totally unrelated historical exposition, meanwhile quote something from the 'last chapter' of the book that had actually been in the first, and so on."

In 1926 Wiener married Margaret Engemann, an assistant professor of modern languages at Juniata College. They had two daughters, Barbara (born 1928) and Peggy (born 1929). Wiener enjoyed his family's company and found there a relaxation from a mathematical community that did not always share his opinion of the merits of his work.

During the decade after his marriage, Wiener worked in a number of fields and wrote some of the papers with which he is most associated. In the field of harmonic analysis, he did a great deal with the decomposition of functions into series. Just as a polynomial is made up of terms like x, x2, x3, and so forth, so functions in general could be broken up in various ways, depending on the questions to be answered. Somewhat surprisingly, Wiener also undertook putting the operational calculus, earlier developed by Oliver Heaviside, on a rigorous basis. There is even a hint in Wiener's work of the notion of a distribution, a kind of generalized function. It is not surprising that Wiener might start to move away from the kind of functions that had been most studied in mathematics toward those that could be useful in physics and engineering.

In 1926 Wiener returned to Europe, this time on a Guggenheim fellowship. He spent little time at Gottingen, due to disagreements with Richard Courant, perhaps the most active student of David Hilbert in mathematical organization. Courant's disparaging comments about Wiener cannot have helped the latter's standing in the mathematical community, but Wiener's brief visit introduced him to Tauberian theory, a fashionable area of analysis. Wiener came up with an imaginative new approach to Tauberian theorems and, perhaps more fortunately, with a coauthor for his longest paper on the subject. The quality of the exposition in the paper, combined with the originality of the results, make it Wiener's best exercise in communicating technical mathematics, although he did not pursue the subject as energetically as he did some of his other works.

In 1931 and 1932 Wiener gave lectures on analysis in Cambridge as a deputy for G. H. Hardy. While there, he made the acquaintance of a young British mathematician, R. E. A. C. Paley, with whom a collaboration soon flourished. He brought Paley to MIT the next academic year and their work progressed rapidly. Paley's death at the age of twenty-six in a skiing accident early in 1933 was a blow to Wiener, who received the Bocher Prize of the American Mathematical Society the same year and was named a fellow of the National Academy of Sciences the next. Among the other areas in which Wiener worked at MIT or Harvard were quantum mechanics, differential geometry, and statistical physics. His investigations in the last of these were wide-ranging, but amounted more to the creation of a research program than a body of results.

The arrival of World War II occupied Wiener's attention in a number of ways. He was active on the Emergency Committee in Aid of Displaced German Scholars, which began operations well before the outbreak of fighting. He made proposals concerning the development of computers, although these were largely ignored. One of the problems to which he devoted time was antiaircraft fire, and his results were of great importance for engineering applications regarding filtering. Unfortunately, they were not of much use in the field because of the amount of time required for the calculations.

Weiner devoted the last decades of his life to the study of statistics, engineering, and biology. He had already worked on the general idea of information theory, which arose out of statistical mechanics. The idea of entropy had been around since the nineteenth century and enters into the second law of thermodynamics. It could be defined as an integral, but it was less clear what sort of quantity it was. Work of Ludwig Boltzmann suggested that entropy could be understood as a measure of the disorder of a system. Wiener pursued this notion and used it to get a physical definition of information related to entropy. Although information theory has not always followed the path laid down by Wiener, his work gave the subject a mathematical legitimacy.

An interdisciplinary seminar at the Harvard Medical School provided a push for Wiener in the direction of the interplay between biology and physics. He learned about the complexity of feedback in animals and studied current ideas about neurophysiology from a mathematical point of view. (Wiener left out the names of those who had most influenced him in this area in his autobiography as a result of an argument.) One area of particular interest was prosthetic limbs, perhaps as a result of breaking his arm in a fall. Wiener soon had the picture of a computer as a prosthesis for the brain. In 1947 he agreed to write a book on communication and control and was looking for a term for the theory of messages. The Greek word for messenger, *angelos,* had too many connections with angels to be useful, so he took the word for helmsman, *kubernes,* instead and came up with *cybernetics.*

It turned out that the word had been used in the previous century, but Wiener gave it a new range of meaning and currency.

Cybernetics was treated by Wiener as a branch of mathematics with its own terms, like signal, noise, and information. One of his collaborators in this area was John von Neumann, whose work on computers had been followed up much more enthusiastically than Wiener's. The difference in reception could be explained by the difference in mathematical styles: von Neumann was meticulous, while Wiener tended to be less so. The new field of cybernetics prospered with two such distinct talents working in it. Von Neumann's major contribution to the field was only realized after his death. Wiener devoted most of his later years to the area. Among his more popular books were *The Human Use of Human Beings* in 1950 and *God and Golem, Inc.: A Comment on Certain Points Where Cybernetics Impinges on Religion* in 1964.

In general, Wiener was happy writing for a wide variety of journals and audiences. He contributed to the *Atlantic, Nation,* the *New Republic,* and *Collier's,* among others. His two volumes of autobiography, *Ex-Prodigy* and *I Am a Mathematician,* came out in 1953 and 1956, respectively. Reviews pointed out the extent to which Wiener's memory operated selectively, but also admitted that he did bring the mathematical community to life in a way seldom seen. Although Wiener remarked that mathematics was a young man's game, he also indicated that he felt himself lucky in having selected subjects for investigation that he could pursue later in life. He received an honorary degree from Tufts in 1946 and in 1949 was Gibbs lecturer to the American Mathematical Society.

In 1964 Wiener received the National Medal of Science. On March 18, while travelling through Stockholm, he collapsed and died. A memorial service was held at MIT on the June 2, led by Swami Sarvagatananda of the Vedanta Society of Boston, along with Christian and Jewish clergy. This mixture of faiths was expressive of Wiener's lifelong unwillingness to be fit into a stereotype. He was a mathematician who talked about the theology of the Fall (the Judeo-Christian story of Adam and Eve and their expulsion from the Garden of Eden). He did not discover that he was Jewish until he was in graduate school but found great support in the poems of Heinrich Heine. Nevertheless, his intellectual originality led him down paths subsequent generations have come to follow.

BIOGRAPHICAL/CRITICAL SOURCES:

BOOKS

Dictionary of Scientific Biography, Volume 14, *1970-1978,* Scribner (Old Tappan, NJ), 1978, pp. 344-347.

Heims, Steve J., *John von Neumann and Norbert Wiener,* MIT Press, 1980.

Masani, P. R., *Norbert Wiener,* Birkhauser, 1990.*

* * *

WIGGLESWORTH, Vincent B(rian) 1899-1994

PERSONAL: Born April 17, 1899, in Kirkham, Lancashire, England; died February 12, 1994; son of Sidney (a doctor); married Mabel Katherine Semple, 1928 (died 1986); children: three sons and a daughter. *Education:* Attended Gonville and Caius College; Cambridge University, M.A.; St. Thomas's Hospital, London, M.D.; University of Kent, Canterbury, B.Ch.

CAREER: Entomologist. Caius College, Cambridge, Frank Smart Student, 1922-24; London School of Hygiene and Tropical Medicine, England, lecturer in medical entomology, 1926-36; University of London, England, reader in entomology, 1936-44; Cambridge University, England, reader in entomology, 1945-52, Quick Professor of Biology, 1952-66. Unit of Insect Physiology, Agricultural Research Council, director, 1943-67. *Military Career:* Royal Field Artillery, 1917-18, became second lieutenant; served in France.

AWARDS, HONORS: Companion of the Order of the British Empire; Fellow of the Royal Entomological Society; Fellow of the Royal Society, 1939; Royal medal, Royal Medal Society, 1955; knighted, 1964; Swammerdam medal, Amsterdam, 1966; Gregor Mendel Gold Medal, Czechoslovak Academy of Science, 1967; Frink medal, Zoological Society, 1979; Wigglesworth medal, Royal Entomological Society, 1981; Honorary Fellow of the Royal College of Physicians, 1989; recipient of numerous honorary degrees, including doctor of philosophy, University of Bern, and doctor of sciences from University of Paris, University of Newcastle upon Tyne, and Cambridge University.

WRITINGS:

Insect Physiology, Methuen and Co. (London), 1934, Wiley (New York City), 1956.

The Principles of Insect Physiology, Methuen and Co., 1939, E.P. Dutton (New York City), 1950.

Physiology of Insect Metamorphosis, Cambridge University Press (Cambridge, England), 1954.

The Control of Growth and Form: A Study of the Epidermal Cell in an Insect, Cornell University Press (Ithaca, NY), 1959.

The Life of Insects, World Publishing Co. (Cleveland, OH), 1964.

Insect Hormones, W.H. Freeman (San Francisco, CA), 1970.

Insects and the Life of Man: Collected Essays on Pure Science and Applied Biology, Wiley/Halstead Press (New York City), 1976.

EDITOR

(With James Arthur Ramsay) *The Cell and the Organism: Essays Presented to Sir James Gray,* University Press (Cambridge, England), 1961.

(With M J. Berridge and J. E. Treherne) *Advances in Insect Physiology,* Volume 17, Academic Press (New York City), 1984.

(With P. D. Evans) *Advances in Insect Physiology,* Academic Press, Volume 20, 1988, Volume 21, 1989, Volume 22, 1990.

Author of numerous papers on comparative physiology.

SIDELIGHTS: Vincent B. Wigglesworth was a British entomologist who took the study of entomology from the mere collection and classification of insects to a field of knowledge with significant scientific applications. He specialized in insect physiology, conducting studies to determine how brain hormones trigger molting, metamorphosis, and reproduction in insects. As Antony Tucker writes in an obituary in the *Guardian,* Wigglesworth's most important contribution may have been his recognition "that insects could be used—instead of mice or other laboratory animals—for the fundamental investigation of animal physiology and function."

Wigglesworth was born on April 17, 1899, in Kirkham, Lancashire, England. His father, Sidney Wigglesworth, was a medical doctor in general practice. Wigglesworth attended Repton School and then Gonville and Caius College at Cambridge. He entered the army during World War I, and he served in the field artillery in France from 1917 to 1918. Upon his return, he completed his graduate work in physiology and biochemistry at Cambridge, including two years as a researcher under John Burdon Sanderson Haldane and Frederick Gowland Hopkins. Wigglesworth demonstrated an aptitude for and a deep interest in basic research. He decided to take up the challenge, issued by Patrick Buxton, to improve the practical application of entomology by increasing the scientific knowledge of insect physiology. Most of Wigglesworth's research at the time was on the role of insects in the transmission of human diseases; diseases such as malaria and Chagas' disease made this issue of immediate importance but it was poorly understood.

In order to further his understanding of human diseases, Wigglesworth completed a medical degree at St. Thomas's Hospital in London. In 1926, he became a lecturer at the London School of Hygiene and Tropical Medicine, where he began his famous studies with *rhodnius prolixus,* a South American blood-sucking insect known to be a carrier of Chagas' disease. The insect was thereafter known among entomologists as "Wigglesworth's bug." Wigglesworth was appointed reader in entomology at London University in 1936. He returned to Cambridge in 1945 and in 1952 was named Quick Professor of Biology at Cambridge. He served as director of the Agricultural Research Council's entomological unit from 1943 to 1967.

Wigglesworth's research concentrated on insect hormones and how they affected physiological processes. It was known that brain secretions initiated certain physiological processes; for example, a decapitated insect would live but it would not molt. Wigglesworth implanted different sections of the brain into the bodies of decapitated insects, and he was thus able to identify the particular areas of the brain where neurosecretory cells were located. He also proved that the brain was the only place in the body of these insects that produced the triggering hormones. This was the first time the role of neurosecretory brain cells in animal development was established experimentally.

Wigglesworth's further studies of insect hormones showed that brain secretions controlled not only molting but also how and when insect larvae would metamorphose into adult forms. He established that it was a hormone, identified as the juvenile hormone, which prevented larvae from developing adult characteristics until they were fully grown. He conducted an experiment in which larvae were continually exposed to the juvenile hormone; as a result of this exposure, larvae maintained their immature form but continued to grow in size. The study of this and other phenomena associated with insect hormones led Wigglesworth to develop a theory of metamorphosis which proposes that the genetic factors necessary for larval development are regulated by the juvenile hormone.

Wigglesworth's research did not concentrate solely on neurological issues but ranged over a wide array of physiological phenomena. He determined how insects are able to make their feet adhere to walking surfaces, how insect eggs breathe, and how symbiotic microorganisms provide vitamins to insects which live solely on blood. The comprehensive nature of his curiosity and understanding enabled him to write books integrating the complete scope of knowledge about insect physiology. His book, *Principles of Insect Physiology,* first published in 1939, became a standard international text. His work has become so basic to entomology that most of it has been incorporated into the standard body of educational material.

Tucker writes of Wigglesworth: "His manner always remained that of a very senior medical consultant; the careful form of question, the cautious, almost shy, analytical progression of thought, and the decisive separation of important and trivial evidence." Wigglesworth continued to work full time until shortly before his death. Known for his strong scientific judgment, care in formulating hypotheses, and precision in discussing scientific ideas, Wigglesworth also advocated caution in using sweeping measures to control insects. He warned against heavy use of pesticides and supported the study of species-specific pheromones to affect insect populations.

Wigglesworth was a member of scientific societies around the world, and he lectured at many universities in the United States and Europe. He was a member of the Royal Entomological Society and the U.S. National Academy of Sciences, and he received several honorary degrees. He was awarded the Gregor Mendel Gold Medal in 1967 from the Czechoslovak Academy of Science. He was knighted in 1964, and the British Royal Entomological Society awards a Wigglesworth Medal in his name.

Wigglesworth married Mabel Katherine Semple in 1928. They had three sons and a daughter. His wife died in 1986. One of their sons, William R. B. Wigglesworth, became England's Deputy Director General of Telecommunications. Wigglesworth died on February 12, 1994.

BIOGRAPHICAL/CRITICAL SOURCES:

BOOKS

McGraw-Hill Modern Scientists and Engineers, Volume 3, McGraw-Hill (New York), 1980, pp. 316-17.

PERIODICALS

Guardian, February 14, 1994, p. 12.

*   *   *

WILKINS, Arnold J(onathan) 1946-

PERSONAL: Born January 25, 1946, in London, England; son of Leslie Thomas (a statistician) and Barbara Lucy (Swinstead) Wilkins; married Elizabeth Jacob (an educational psychologist), 1975; children: Martha, Jonathan. *Education:* Exeter University, B.Sc., 1968; Sussex University, D.Phil., 1973. *Politics:* "Humanitarian!" *Religion:* "None." *Avocational interests:* Sailing, playing the flute, making things and making things work.

ADDRESSES: Home—Cambridge, England. *Office*—Medical Research Council, Applied Psychology Unit, 15 Chaucer Rd., Cambridge CB2 2EF England; fax 44 1223 359062. *E-mail*—arnold.wilkins@MRC-APU. CAM.AC.UK.

CAREER: Montreal Neurological Institute, Montreal, Quebec, Canada, research fellow, 1972-74; Medical Research Council, Applied Psychology Unit, Cambridge, England, scientist, 1974-78, grade 1 scientist, 1978-84, senior scientist, 1984-91, special appointment, 1991—. Holds several patents and has been important in the development of many devices related to the field of visual science, including a reading mask and tinted lenses; has taught courses at Cambridge University; has served as a consultant to various ophthalmic concerns. Has appeared on radio and television programs in Great Britain, the United States, Canada, and Australia, including *Today, Science Now, You and Yours, British Broadcasting Corporation (BBC) World Service, Quarks and Quasars, Tomorrow's World, Horizon, Nova, News at Ten, Anglia News, GMTV, Beyond 2000, National Broadcasting Corporation (NBC) News,* and *Open University.*

MEMBER: International League against Epilepsy; British Psychology Society; Experimental Psychology Society; Electroencephalographic Society; Association for Research in Vision and Ophthalmology; Applied Vision Association; Color Group.

AWARDS, HONORS: Recipient of several research grants, including Health and Safety Executive, 1986-89, Paul Hamblyn Foundation, 1990, and Node on Biomed, 1994; fellowship from the British Psychological Society, 1990; named Chartered Psychologist, 1990; Leon Gascer Medal, Chartered Institution of Building Services Engineers (CIBSE), 1990; Bronze Medal, CIBSE, 1991.

WRITINGS:

Visual Stress (nonfiction), Oxford University Press (Oxford, England), 1995.

Also contributor of chapters to books and articles to scientific journals and periodicals.

WORK IN PROGRESS: Helping Reading with Color; research on visual deficits in children with reading difficulties.

SIDELIGHTS: British neuropsychologist Arnold J. Wilkins has had a long and fruitful career with his native country's Medical Research Council in Cambridge. Prior to that, he spent two years as a research fellow at the Montreal Neurological Institute in Quebec, Canada. He has been instrumental in the development of many breakthroughs in the areas of epilepsy, migraine, and vision, including a reading mask, tinted lenses, reading tests, and color filters for classroom use.

A recognized expert in his several fields, Wilkins has discussed his findings on many radio and television programs in Great Britain, Canada, Australia, and the United States, including *Beyond 2000, NBC News,* and *Nova.* He has written numerous articles on the subjects of headaches, epilepsy, reading, typography, and vision for scientific journals and has contributed chapters on these and similar topics to many books edited by others. Wilkins's own first book, *Visual Stress,* was published by Oxford University Press in 1995.

In *Visual Stress,* Wilkins proposes the first general unified theory of visual stress. The book examines and discusses the ways in which our workplaces, and other public environments such as malls and superstores, are damaging to our visual, mental, and physical health. People who are light-sensitive, for instance, find the lighted, shiny striped metal of the escalator steps in the London subway stations extremely disorienting and even nauseating. Epileptic fits and migraine headaches can be brought on by certain patterns of light, and the fluorescent lighting used in many offices are bad for workers' health. Also potentially visually disturbing are herringbone patterns in brick walkways used as ornamentation by modern urban planners.

As Jonathan Glancey, reviewing *Visual Stress* in the *Independent,* observed: "An increasing number of office workers are opting to work at home whenever possible. This is not simply because they want to sit with the dog under their bare feet," he explained, "but because, as *Visual Stress* discloses, they feel wobbly and uncomfortable at work. This is not," Glancey added, "a reflection on their colleagues, but on the design of their offices." Glancey went on to provide his readers with Wilkins's prescription for a more healthful office environment, which includes a measure of privacy, both light and shade, and very few patterns with stripes.

Wilkins also provides a way for the light-sensitive to ease their discomforts while using the offending escalators—one may simply cover one eye while going down them. Other highlights of *Visual Stress* include the author's citation of a 1971 art exhibit by an artist whose paintings included several strong, striped patterns. Several curators of the exhibit reported an unusual number of headaches and symptoms of dizziness. Glancey praised *Visual Stress*. After citing the volume's "graphs, charts, diagrams and the minutiae of academic research," he declared: "Here is one of those books that you read in the bath and feel like jumping out and exclaiming 'Eureka!'"

Wilkins told *CA:* "Writing about how one writes is disturbingly recursive. The task engenders an introspection which prejudices the whole enterprise! For me, the process of writing is more a process of reading. I write and read, write and read, over and over again. With each reading I attempt to purge the draft of unnecessary verbiage without compromising clarity: a reflection of the obsessional nature of a scientist. To do this effectively requires a long enough period between each reading for my memory of the previous readings to have evaporated. The process is time-consuming and it is for this reason, amongst many others, that my book took ten years to write, and why I have only written one. Clearly, obsessionality of this kind is not a good model for an aspiring writer!

"As one ages, the memory declines, and one comes afresh to something one has written only days before. As a consequence, the process of revision is speeded. Aging has another beneficial effect. One becomes less and less concerned about making a fool of oneself in print, as it dawns on one that all fools are in good

company. Therefore, I look forward to writing many books to come, produced at an ever-increasing rate, but perhaps ultimately with fewer and fewer people willing to read them!"

BIOGRAPHICAL/CRITICAL SOURCES:

PERIODICALS

Independent, September 10, 1996, sec. 2, p. 16.

* * *

WILLIAMS, Glanville Llewelyn 1911-1997

OBITUARY NOTICE—See index for *CA* sketch: Born February 15, 1911, in Bridgend, Wales; died April 10, 1997. Educator and author. Williams was a noted expert in matters concerning British civil and criminal law. In addition to studying legal issues, he devoted his career to teaching, first at Cambridge University beginning in 1936, then at the University of London starting in 1945. He rejoined Cambridge in 1957 as a reader, then became professor of law in 1966. Named a fellow of the school's Jesus College in 1955, he also became Rouse Ball Professor of English Law in 1968. His other teaching stints included Hebrew University of Jerusalem, University of Colorado, New York University, and University of Washington.

Williams served about twenty-one years as a member of the Standing Committee on Criminal Law Revision. He was a one-time president of the Abortion Law Reform Association and served as vice president of Voluntary Euthanasia. He was well-regarded for his books of law, including *The Sanctity of Life and the Criminal Law, Criminal Law: The General Part, Learning the Law, Joint Torts and Contributory Negligence,* and *Liability for Animals.*

OBITUARIES AND OTHER SOURCES:

BOOKS

Who's Who, 149th edition, St. Martin's (New York), 1997.

PERIODICALS

New York Times, April 21, 1997, p. B10.
Times (London; electronic), April 14, 1997.

WILLIAMSON, Philip G. 1955-
(Philip First, Joe Fish)

PERSONAL: Born November 6, 1955, in Worcestershire, England; son of George (a farmer, postmaster and shopkeeper) and Patricia (a postmistress and shopkeeper). *Education:* Goldsmith's College, London, graduate degree. *Politics:* "Left, into Green." *Religion:* "No formal religion." *Avocational interests:* Art, music, film, stage, science, and theory thereof; education, nature, spirituality, computers, mystery, history, culture, life.

ADDRESSES: Home—London, England. *Agent*—Charles Walker, Peters Fraser & Dunlop, 503/4 The Chambers, Chelseaharbour, London, SW10 0XF, England.

CAREER: British fantasy novelist, formerly in the music business, member of several rock bands, travelled Europe for some years working at beaches, ski resorts, farms, vineyards, boatyards and bars.

WRITINGS:

AS PHILIP FIRST

The Great Pervader (novel), Paladin (Lake Geneva, WI), 1983.
Paper Thin and Other Stories, Paladin, 1986.
Dark Night (novel), Paladin, 1986.

AS PHILIP G. WILLIAMSON

Dinbig of Khimmur (first volume of "Firstworld Chronicles"), Grafton (London), 1991.
The Legend of Shadd's Torment (second volume of "Firstworld Chronicles"), Grafton, 1993.
Moonblood (fantasy), Legend (London), 1993.
From Enchantery (third volume of "Firstworld Chronicles"), HarperCollins UK, 1993.
Heart of Shadows, Legend, 1994.
Citadel, Legend, 1995.
Enchantment's Edge Volume 1, Hodder & Stoughton (London), 1996, New English Library, 1996.
Enchantment's Edge II: Orbus's World, Hodder & Stoughton, 1997.
Enchantment's Edge Volume 3: The Soul of the Orb, Hodder & Stoughton, 1998.

Also writes under the pseudonym Joe Fish.

WORK IN PROGRESS: A light-hearted space fantasy for children; several planned novels with near future or contemporary settings and some 'mainstream' fiction.

SIDELIGHTS: Philip G. Williamson plunged into the fantasy novel genre full-steam in the 1990s, publishing eight novels between 1991 and 1997. His accustomed turf was Firstworld, a land of magic containing a hero named Dinbig of Khimmur, who was the title character of Williamson's first book in 1991. Dinbig died at the end of that book, but reappeared as the narrator of the second volume, the 1993's *The Legend of Shadd's Torment.* The secret of his reappearance was his reincarnation as a wolflike creature called a *vhazz,* which, in addition to canine attributes, can assume a bipedal posture and fight with a sword. As the novel's title suggests, the protagonist is Shadd, a hero who is accompanied by a sentient rock and a small elfin helper. Reviewer Wendy Bradley, in *Locus,* found the layers of narrative hard to grasp and the novel itself slow; however, she much enjoyed the third volume of Williamson's "Firstworld Chronicles," *From Enchantery,* which also appeared in 1993. Dinbig was once again the narrator, but in this volume he was his old self rather than an animal. Bradley especially appreciated the novel's "cracking climax," and looked forward to further volumes about Firstworld.

Such a volume did appear in 1994: *Heart of Shadows* was set on Firstworld, though it did not center on Dinbig but instead a merchant who discovers a mysterious jewel, triggering a plot in which the merchant's son and daughter must evade the snares of a shape-changing sorcerer. The novel has a feminist element, holding up for implicit criticism a society in which women are not allowed to speak. In this connection, Bradley commented, "Williamson's female characters are good and he is sound on the perils of solo female travelling." Once again, Bradley pointed out the ending as especially powerful; she cautioned against reading it ahead of time, because it "will both surprise you and chill you to the bone if you can bring yourself to wait."

Williamson told *CA:* "All my fiction tends to in someway or other be a form of speculative enquire into the strange nature of our existence. Fantasy can be a perfect vehicle for this. It is perhaps the nearest thing we have to a literature of the subconscious, permitting access to and exploration of the deepest levels of the human psyche like no other fictional form. It is replete with subconscious imagery, a universe of symbol and semiotic . . . so much there beneath the surface.

"I am attracted to and inspired by anything that helps us to build an understanding of what we are, what this universe is, in all its aspects, how and why we exist as spiritual beings, conscious souls in a world of matter and perplexity. To this end I immerse myself in a broad range of studies, including philosophy, psychology, parapsychology, anthropology, science (particularly theoretical physics, which fascinates and thoroughly baffles me), cosmology, sacred literature, certain forms of Mysticism, myth and legend, archaeology, history, music, art, nature, etc. I'm burning to know as much as I possibly can. Anything learned becomes condensed in some way and reflected in Story.

"Like many others I have a profound sense of passing through, that this is not the first time I have walked upon this Earth, and may be far from the last. We all stand here on the edge of the ungraspable, and it's impossible not to be filled with wonder.

"Literary influences are too many and diverse to list. Nevertheless, a few that spring immediately to mind are Kurt Vonnegut, Harold Pinter, David Bowie (yes, *very* much so!), Lewis Carroll, Borges, Kafka, Mervyn Peake, Arthur C. Clarke, Fyodor Dostoyevsky, Jane Siberry, Alexandre Dumas, Jean Rhys, Joseph Conrad, The Beatles, F. Scott Fitzgerald, George Orwell, the Brontes, T.S. Eliot and, oh, the list just goes on and on. It's hopeless. I've missed so many, and I could be here till the middle of next week. I think I'll just stop now."

BIOGRAPHICAL/CRITICAL SOURCES:

PERIODICALS

Locus, April, 1994, p. 27; July, 1994, p. 66.

*   *   *

WILLMOTT, H(edley) P(aul) 1945-

PERSONAL: Born December 26, 1945, in Bristol, England; son of Donald Arthur Frederick and Olive Edna (Reed) Willmott; married Pauline Anne Burton, December 9, 1978; children: Gaynor Marie, Stephen James Tuite. *Education:* University of Liverpool, England, B.A. with honors, 1967, M.A., 1971; London University, Ph.D., 1991.

ADDRESSES: Home—907 Sixth Street SW, Apt. 902C, Washington, DC 20024. *Office*—National War

College, Fort Leslie J. McNair, Washington, DC 20319.

CAREER: Military writer and lecturer. Royal Military Academy, Sandhurst, England, lecturer, 1969—. Temple University, Philadelphia, PA, visiting lecturer, 1989; Memphis State University, visiting lecturer, 1989-90; National War College, Department of Defense, Washington, DC, visiting lecturer, 1992—.

AWARDS, HONORS: Leman Award, 1984, for *The Barrier and the Javelin: Japanese and Allied Pacific Strategies, February to June 1942.*

WRITINGS:

Warships, with an introduction by Aram Bakshian, Jr., Octopus Books (London), 1975.
B-17 Flying Fortress, Arms and Armour Press (London), 1980, Prentice-Hall (Englewood Cliffs, NJ), 1983.
Sea Warfare: Weapons, Tactics and Strategy, with an epilogue by Lord Hill-Norton, A. Bird (Strettington, Chichester, England), 1981, Hippocrene Books (New York), 1982.
Empires in the Balance: Japanese and Allied Pacific Strategies to April 1942, Naval Institute Press (Annapolis, MD), 1982.
The Barrier and the Javelin: Japanese and Allied Pacific Strategies, February to June 1942, Naval Institute Press, 1983.
Pearl Harbor, Prentice-Hall, 1983.
Zero A6M, Prentice-Hall, 1983.
June 1944, Blandford Press (Poole, Dorset, England), 1984.
The Great Crusade: A New Complete History of the Second World War, Michael Joseph (London), 1989, Free Press (New York), 1990.
Grave of a Dozen Schemes: British Naval Planning and the War against Japan, 1943-1945, Naval Institute Press, 1996.

OTHER

British Broadcasting Corporation (BBC) World Service, program writer, 1986-92.

SIDELIGHTS: Trained in history, politics and war studies at British universities, naval war historian H. P. Willmott has authored several works on World War II military operations, from popular studies of a single Allied bomber (*B-17 Flying Fortress,* 1980) and a specific Japanese fighter plane (*Zero A6M,* 1983), to a comprehensive history of the war, *The Great*

Crusade: A New Complete History of the Second World War, published in 1989.

Following Willmott's debut work, *Warships,* which was published in 1975, his 1981 study *Sea Warfare: Weapons, Tactics, and Strategy* offered a survey of naval warfare. The latter book was criticized by a reviewer in *Choice* as lacking citations and source notes, although that commentator did call it "a readable . . . collateral source for the upper-division undergraduate." Far more distinguished was the reception for Willmott's major book of 1982, *Empires in the Balance: Japanese and Allied Pacific Strategies to April 1942.* This, the first volume in a series on the subject of the Pacific naval war, deals with the period of initial, whirlwind victories by the Japanese fleet over the Americans, British, and Dutch during late 1941 and early 1942—a period when Japan captured the sphere of influence that had been its intended object since before the war began. Willmott describes the economic and historical background of Japanese expansionism, and in addition, speculates on what might have happened had Japan tried to invade as far westward as India. (He hypothesizes a possibly improved outcome for Japan.)

New York Review of Books critic and war historian John Keegan called *Empires in the Balance* "a major chronicle" of Japan's rise to power. Keegan noted the value of Willmott's approach to the subject as the realistic merit of taking "for granted that the world is one of hierarchies, moral or economic or both," and of being "concerned chiefly to demonstrate such hierarchies at work." The *Choice* reviewer complained of some missing sources and surmising a lack of familiarity with "Orientalia." A reviewer for the *Economist,* however, was especially laudatory, calling *Empires in the Balance* "a brilliant book which holds the reader from title pages to index." The reviewer stated, "Each paragraph, indeed each phrase, is constructed with care, making the whole a delight to read," adding that "a wry thread of tragedy"—the tragedy of the nation of Japan—runs through the work.

Empires in the Balance was followed in 1983 by a second volume, *The Barrier and the Javelin: Japanese and Allied Pacific Strategies, February to June 1942,* which received the Leman Award. This volume covers a mere five months of battle, but they were months that culminated in a major turning point of the Pacific war, for in early June, 1942, the Allied victory at the Battle of Midway stopped the Japanese advance toward Hawaii and devastated the Japanese fleet.

In a later book, Willmott jumped ahead a couple of years and treated the subject of *June 1944,* one of the truly momentous months in the history of the world. The popular imagination associates that month with D-Day, but Willmott, while giving full justice to the Normandy invasion, also discusses other aspects of the war that helped turn the tide during that month: Rome was captured, the Russian Army won a victory in Belorussia, the Japanese were defeated in Burma, the Americans landed on Saipan and were victorious in the Philippine Sea, and the first B-29 raids against the Japanese mainland took place.

According to a *Publishers Weekly* reviewer, *June 1944* is strong in its appraisal of the weakness of the Anglo-American alliance and its criticisms of Churchill as a military leader. Philip Warner, writing in the *Spectator,* commented: "As an unemotional exposition of military events this book is excellent." With a forty thousand-copy first printing and a sale to the Military Book Club, *June 1944* was a success.

Five years were to pass between that study and Willmott's massive work *The Great Crusade: A New Complete History of the Second World War,* five hundred pages long, with twenty-nine maps and thirty-five illustrations. A reviewer for *Encounter,* appraising it along with eight other World War II books in a single critique, called *The Great Crusade* "the one to give to a military professional keen on war games." Meanwhile, Michael Carver, in another group book review in the *Times Literary Supplement,* singled out *The Great Crusade* for "offering a critique both of the conduct of the war and of how it has been historically represented." Willmott's book, wrote Carver, "sets out to challenge accepted views, particularly that the Germans were expert at war."

In 1996, Willmott published another detailed study of a specific period of time during the Pacific war, *Grave of a Dozen Schemes: British Naval Planning and the War against Japan, 1943-1945.*

BIOGRAPHICAL/CRITICAL SOURCES:

PERIODICALS

Choice, December, 1982, p. 629; June, 1983, p. 1514.
Economist, June 11, 1983, p. 104.
Encounter, December, 1989, p. 26.
New York Review of Books, September 23, 1982, pp. 27-29.
Publishers Weekly, May 11, 1984, p. 266.

Spectator, June 9, 1984, pp. 22-23.
Times Literary Supplement, September 1-7, 1989.*

*   *   *

WINCH, Peter G(uy) 1926-1997

OBITUARY NOTICE—See index for *CA* sketch: Born January 14, 1926, in London, England; died April 27, 1997. Educator, philosopher, and author. Winch is remembered for his contributions to the field and study of philosophy. He began more than forty years as an educator at University College of Swansea at the University of Wales in 1951. When he left the Swansea faculty in 1964, he was senior lecturer in philosophy. His next post was at the University of London as a reader in philosophy at Birkbeck College. He remained there until 1967 when he became a professor of philosophy at King's College, where he stayed until 1984. He then began a stint at the University of Illinois at Urbana. He also taught briefly at the University of Rochester, University of Arizona, University of Konstanz, City University of New York, the Academy of Finland, and the University of Tubingen. In addition, he edited the periodical *Analysis* from 1965 to 1971. Winch was the author and editor of numerous books, especially on philosopher Wittgenstein. Among Winch's books were *The Idea of a Social Science and Its Relation to Philosophy, Wittgenstein: Attention to Particulars, The Just Balance, Understanding a Primitive Society, Studies in the Philosophy of Wittgenstein, Ethics and Action,* and *The Political Responsibility of Intellectuals.* He also served as president of the Aristotelian Society and was a member of the American Philosophy Association.

OBITUARIES AND OTHER SOURCES:

BOOKS

Who's Who in America, 47th edition, Marquis, 1992.

PERIODICALS

Times (London; electronic), May 19, 1997.

*   *   *

WINTERGREEN, Jane
See DUNCAN, Sara Jeannette

WORCESTER, Kent 1959-

PERSONAL: Born September 13, 1959, in Omaha, NE; son of Robert and Joann (Ransdell) Worcester; married Jennifer Scarlott, October 8, 1987; children: Julia Corsaut Scarlott Worcester. *Education:* Columbia University, Ph.D., 1990. *Avocational interests:* Writing, reading.

ADDRESSES: Home—New York, NY. *Office*—Social Science Research Council, 810 Seventh Ave, New York, NY 10019. *E-mail*—Worceste@ssrc.org.

CAREER: Columbia University, New York City, Department of Political Science, instructor, 1986-91; Social Science Research Council, New York City, program director, 1991—. Member of the editorial boards of *New Politics* and *New Political Science;* member of the board of directors of the Campaign for Peace and Democracy.

MEMBER: American Political Science Association, Council for European Studies, Caribbean Studies Association.

WRITINGS:

(Coeditor, with Glenn Perusek) *Trade Union Politics: American Unions and Economic Change, 1960s-1990s* (nonfiction), Humanities Press (Atlantic Highlands, NJ), 1995.
C. L. R. James: A Political Biography, SUNY Press (Albany, NY), 1996.

Also editor, with Chris Toulouse, of *After Thatcher,* a special double issue of *New Political Science,* 1995.

SIDELIGHTS: Kent Worcester is a political scientist and author whose works include *Trade Union Politics: American Unions and Economic Change, 1960s-1990s* and *C. L. R. James: A Political Biography,* an examination of the twentieth-century radical intellectual best known for his numerous writings on Caribbean history, Marxist theory, and Hegelian philosophy. Paul Berman, writing in the *New Yorker,* called *C. L. R. James* a "scrupulous" study, and a commentator in *Kirkus Reviews* found the work "well-crafted" and "engaging," noting that "Worcester's biography should do much to bring James his proper due." Michael Hanchard in the *Nation* praised the book as "a careful, thorough piece of scholarship," and added, "Though Worcester clearly admires his subject, he maintains a critical distance that allows him to dissect James' evolution as a thinker and strategist."

BIOGRAPHICAL/CRITICAL SOURCES:

PERIODICALS

Kirkus Reviews, October 15, 1995, p. 1481.
Nation, May 27, 1996.
New Yorker, July 29, 1996.

*   *   *

WRIGHT, Daphne 1951-
(Kate Hatfield)

PERSONAL: Born in May, 1951, in London, England; daughter of Claud William and Alison Violet (Readman) Wright. *Ethnicity:* "English."

ADDRESSES: Agent—c/o A.M. Heath & Company Limited, 79 St. Martin's Lane, London WC2N 4AA, England.

CAREER: Novelist.

MEMBER: Society of Authors, Crime Writers' Association, Romantic Novelists' Association.

AWARDS, HONORS: Tony Godwin Memorial Trust Award.

WRITINGS:

The Distant Kingdom (novel), Michael Joseph (London), 1987, Delacorte (New York), 1987.
The Longest Winter (novel), Michael Joseph, 1989.
The Parrot Cage (novel), Michael Joseph, 1990.
Never Such Innocence (novel), Michael Joseph, 1991.
Dreams of Another Day (novel), Little, Brown (Boston), 1992, Warner (London), 1992.
The Tightrope Walkers (novel), Little, Brown, 1993, Warner, 1994.
(As Kate Hatfield) *Drowning in Honey* (novel), St. Martin's Press, 1996.

SIDELIGHTS: Daphne Wright is an English novelist whose works combine romance with historical settings that depict such events as the London Blitz and colonial warfare in Afghanistan. Wright's first novel, *The Distant Kingdom,* was published in 1987. At the time, *Books* reviewer Emma Dally termed it "very entertaining," and called attention to "interesting characters and masterly command of a well-integrated setting [which] make this superior saga a good read."

The Distant Kingdom is set during the British Raj in the year 1836. Following the death of her mother, the heroine, Perdita Whitney, flees the household of her unpleasant uncle and travels to India to be reunited with her father, whom she has not seen in many years. As she gradually sheds her inhibitions and blossoms in Anglo-Indian society, she becomes the wife of an earl—and a tool by which her husband keeps a deep personal secret. Experiencing the new pressures of adulthood and the sometimes difficult conditions of colonial life, Perdita ultimately achieves true love.

A reviewer for *Library Journal,* Judith A. Gifford, called *The Distant Kingdom* a "realistic portrait of a not-altogether admirable period of British colonial history." A commentator in *Publishers Weekly* praised the novel's historical atmosphere and opined, "the historical background of the unsuccessful British attempt on Afghanistan propels the story forward."

Wright's second novel, 1989's *The Longest Winter,* is set in Russia during World War I. The heroine, an English woman whom *Books* reviewer Henrietta Scott Fordham described as "proud and icy" and "formidable," visits cousins in Russia in an attempt to forget her great love, an Englishman missing in action. Amid a background of world war, civil war, and revolution, Evelyn finds romance at last. Fordham judged the novel "a well-crafted story."

In 1990 Wright issued *The Parrot Cage,* which takes place in London during the Blitz. The story centers on three sisters, each of whom is separately involved with, and used by, the head of a British intelligence department whose work concerns the French resistance. Commenting on the multiplicity of romantic heroines in this "nice tapestry of . . . wartime emotions," a *Books* reviewer said, "Since three is no mean score, the success of the writing is in managing to remain believable." Following the favorable reception of those first three novels, Wright published several more during the early 1990s, including *Drowning in Honey* under the pseudonym Kate Hatfield.

Wright told *CA:* "I have always been interested in the way that war (terrible though it is) has had a liberating effect on women. When lives are at risk the customs and rules that have restricted women to subordinate (and domestic) roles can no longer be enforced and can be seen for the absurdities they always were."

BIOGRAPHICAL/CRITICAL SOURCES:

PERIODICALS

Books, July, 1987, p. 23; March, 1989, p. 25; February, 1990, p. 16.
Library Journal, January, 1988, pp. 101-02.
Publishers Weekly, December 4, 1987, p. 63.

*   *   *

WRIGHT, G(eorg) H(enrik) von 1916-

PERSONAL: Born June 14, 1916, in Helsinki, Finland; son of Tor and Ragni Elisabeth (Alfthan) von Wright; married Baroness Marie Elisabeth von Troil, May 31, 1941; children: one son, one daughter. *Ethnicity:* Finnish. *Education:* Received degree from University of Helsinki.

ADDRESSES: Home—4 Skepparegatan, Helsinki, Finland.

CAREER: University of Helsinki, Helsinki, Finland, lecturer and acting professor of philosophy, 1943-46, professor of philosophy, 1946-61; Cambridge University, professor of philosophy, 1948-51; Academy of Finland, research fellow, 1961-86; Cornell University, Ithaca, NY, Andrew D. White professor-at-large, 1965-77; Abo Academy, chancellor, 1968-77.

Wright has held visiting professorships at Cornell University, 1954, 1958; University of St. Andrews, 1959-60; University of California at Los Angeles, 1963; University of Pittsburgh, 1966; Columbia University, 1972; University of Karlsruhe, 1975; and Leipzig University, 1994-95.

MEMBER: International Union of History and Philosophy of Science, (president, 1963-65), Institut Internationale de Philosophie Paris (president, 1975-78), European Academy of Arts, Science, and Humanities, Philosophical Society of Finland (president, 1962-73), Finnish Society of Science (president, 1966-67; honorary fellow, 1978), Finnish Academy of Sciences, New Society of Letters (Lund), British Academy, Royal Danish Academy of Science, Royal Academy of Arts and Sciences (Uppsala, Sweden), Norwegian Academy of Science and Letters, Royal Academy of Science (Trondheim, Norway), and honorary foreign member of the American Academy of Arts and Sciences.

AWARDS, HONORS: Wihuri International Prize, Wihuri Foundation for International Prizes (Finland), 1976, in philosophy; Alexander von Humboldt-Strif-tring Research Award, Swedish Academy, 1986; honorary degrees from University of Helsinki, University of Liverpool, University of Lund, Turku University, Abo Academy, Tampere University, University of Buenos Aires, University of Salta, Stockholm University, Leipzig University, St. Olav College, and Northfield.

WRITINGS:

The Logical Problem of Induction, University of Helsinki (Helsinki, Finland), 1941, Macmillan (New York), 1957.
A Treatise on Induction and Probability, Harcourt, Brace (New York), 1951.
Logical Studies, Humanities Press (New York), 1957.
The Logic of Preference: An Essay, University Press (Edinburgh), 1963.
Norm and Action: A Logical Enquiry, Humanities Press, 1963.
The Varieties of Goodness, Humanities Press, 1963.
Explanation and Understanding, Cornell University Press (Ithaca, NY), 1971.
Causality and Determinism, Columbia University Press (New York), 1974.
What Is Humanism? University of Kansas (Lawrence), 1977.
Wittgenstein, Blackwell (Oxford, England), 1982.
Philosophical Logic, Blackwell, 1983.
Practical Reason, Blackwell, 1983, Cornell University Press (Ithaca, NY), 1984.
Truth, Logic, and Modality, Blackwell, 1983.
The Tree of Knowledge and Other Essays, E. J. Brill (New York), 1993.
Six Essays in Philosophical Logic, [Helsinki, Finland], 1996.

EDITOR

(With R. Rhees and G. E. M. Anscombe) *Remarks on the Foundations of Mathematics,* by Ludwig Wittgenstein, translation by Anscombe, M.I.T. Press (Cambridge, MA), 1967.
(With Anscombe) *Zettel,* University of California Press (Berkeley), 1967.
(With Anscombe) *On Certainty,* translation by Denis Paul and Anscombe, Harper (New York), 1969.
(With Anscombe; also author of introduction) *Notebooks, 1914-1916,* by Ludwig Wittgenstein, translation by Anscombe, Harper Torchbooks (New York), 1969.

(With B. F. McGuinness and T. Nyberg) *Prototractatus: An Early Version of Tractatus Logicophilosophicus,* translation by D. F. Pears and McGuinness, Cornell University Press (Ithaca, NY), 1971.

(And author of introduction) *Letters to C. K. Ogden with Comments on the English Translation,* by Ludwig Wittgenstein, Routledge & Kegan Paul (Boston, MA), 1973.

(With Brian McGuinness) *Cambridge Letters: Correspondence with Russell, Keynes, Moore, Ramsey, and Sraffa,* by Ludwig Wittgenstein, Blackwell, 1995.

(With Heikki Nyman) *Culture and Value,* by Ludwig Wittgenstein, translation by Peter Winch, University of Chicago Press (Chicago IL), 1980.

(With Anscombe) *Remarks on the Philosophy of Psychology,* by Ludwig Wittgenstein, translation by Anscombe, University of Chicago Press, 1980.

(With Nyman) *Last Writings on the Philosophy of Psychology,* by Ludwig Wittgenstein, Blackwell, 1982.

Wittgensteinian Themes: Essays, 1978-1989, by Norman Malcolm, Cornell University Press, 1995.

SIDELIGHTS: G. H. von Wright enjoys a reputation as one of the modern era's foremost scholars in the discipline of philosophy. The Finnish-born academic, who wrote or edited numerous works in the field, began his career in 1943 as a professor at his alma mater, the University of Helsinki; he also taught at Cambridge University. Since 1961 Wright has been a research professor with the Academy of Finland but has also served as chancellor of Abo Academy and professor-at-large at Cornell University. Wright has devoted much of his career to advancing the works of Ludwig Wittgenstein, an Austrian philosopher who died in 1951. Wittgenstein made significant contributions to the branch of philosophy known as logical positivism, which attempts to use the precision of mathematics to clarify abstract ideas. In addition to his own writing, Wright has edited numerous volumes of Wittgenstein's writings, including the 1967 tome *Zettel.* Among numerous other volumes, Wright has also served as the editor of one of Wittgenstein's first major works, *Prototractatus: An Early Version of Tractatus Logico-philosophicus.* He shares credit for the editorship of the 1971 volume with B. F. McGuinness and T. Nyberg.

In his own research and writing, Wright has published several works in English. Much of it is concerned with deontic logic, or the study of moral and legal obligations. He has also explored the field of induc-tion, which entails making generalizations about a group based on the study of a representative sampling; it is the opposite of "deductive" reasoning. A representative sampling of Wright's own scholarship can be found in the volumes *Logical Studies* and *Philosophical Logic.* Many of the studies are concerned with various paradoxes, or riddles that philosophers use to discuss concepts. Other essays look at modal logic (the use of such modifying language elements as "possibly" and "necessary"), and perceptions of time and space. In the academic journal *Philosophical Review,* a contributor critiqued his work and found it weak in some areas, according to writer Steven J. Wagner. Yet the critic conceded that *Philosophical Logic* "offers clear, accessible samples of a significant body of work."

BIOGRAPHICAL/CRITICAL SOURCES:

BOOKS

Dictionary of Philosophy and Religion, Humanities Press, 1980, pp. 616-17.

The Library of Living Philosophers, Volume 19: *The Philosophy of Georg Henrik von Wright,* edited by P. A. Schilpp and L. E. Hahn, Open Court (La Salle, IL), 1989.

PERIODICALS

Listener, July 13, 1967.
Philosophical Review, July, 1986, pp. 427-29.

*   *   *

WRIGLEY, Elizabeth S(pringer) 1915-1997

OBITUARY NOTICE—See index for *CA* sketch: Born October 4, 1915, in Pittsburgh, PA; died April 26, 1997, in Temple City, CA. Librarian, executive, and author. Wrigley is best remembered for her work concerning seventeenth-century lawyer and statesman Francis Bacon. Wrigley earned degrees from the University of Pittsburgh and the Carnegie Institute of Technology. During World War II, she worked as a procedure analyst at the U.S. Steel Corporation. In 1944, she joined the staff of the Francis Bacon Foundation of Los Angeles as a research assistant. She served the organization as an executive, trustee, director of research, president, and director of its library during a lengthy career there. She prepared a number of books published by the Foundation, including *The Skeleton Text of the Shakespeare Folio, A Concordance to the Essays of Francis Bacon,* and *Wing Numbers in the Library of the Francis Bacon Foundation.*

OBITUARIES AND OTHER SOURCES:

BOOKS

Who's Who in America, 50th edition, Marquis, 1995.

PERIODICALS

Los Angeles Times, May 21, 1997, p. A20.

* * *

WURTS, Janny 1953-

PERSONAL: Born December 10, 1953, in Bryn Mawr, PA. *Education:* Hampshire College, B.A. in creative writing and illustration, 1975; Moore College of Art, one semester of graduate study.

ADDRESSES: Office—Frazer, PA. *Agent*—c/o HarperCollins, Inc., 1000 Keystone Industrial Park, Scranton, PA 18512.

CAREER: Fantasy and science-fiction writer and illustrator. Worked as a laboratory assistant in the Astronomy College of Hampshire College.

WRITINGS:

NOVELS

Sorcerer's Legacy (illustrated by Wurts), Ace (New York), 1982.
Stormwarden (first volume in "Cycle of Fire" series), Ace, 1984.
(With Raymond E. Feist) *Daughter of the Empire* (first volume in "Empire" series), Doubleday (Garden City, NY), 1987.
Keeper of the Keys (second volume in "Cycle of Fire" series), Ace, 1988.
Shadowfane (third volume in "Cycle of Fire" series), Ace, 1988.
(With Feist) *Servant of the Empire* (second volume in "Empire" series), Doubleday, 1990.
(With Feist) *Mistress of the Empire* (third volume in "Empire" series), Doubleday, 1992.
The Master of White Storm, Penguin/ROC, 1992.

The Curse of the Mistwraith (first volume in "The Wars of Light and Shadow" series), HarperCollins (London), 1993.
Ships of Merior (second volume of "The Wars of Light and Shadow"), HarperCollins, 1995.

SHORT STORIES

That Way Lies Camelot, HarperPrism (New York), 1996.

SIDELIGHTS: Janny Wurts is a science fiction illustrator and author whose dual career originated in her lifelong interest in space and the fantastic. As an illustrator she has created book covers for James Blish's *A Case of Conscience,* for *Best SF of the Year 13* (1984), and for her own books, the first of which—*Sorcerer's Legacy*—was published in 1982. A tale of wizardry, court intrigue, and escapades in another world, the book was recommended for older readers of young-adult fantasy by Peggy Murray in *VOYA* (*Voice of Youth Advocates*), the young adult literature review.

Next, in 1984, came *Stormwarden,* the well-regarded first volume in Wurts's "Cycle of Fire" series. The novel, which combines elements of fantasy with those of science fiction, takes place in a distant world dominated by demons, where the survivors of humanity, guarded by their spaceship's computer, try to thwart the demons' plans for hegemony. The plot follows three young humans who take different, though intertwined, paths to maturity. Reviewer Peter Kobel, in *Booklist,* found the work an "engrossing fantasy. . . . [which is] fast paced and intelligently written." Two separate reviewers for *Fantasy Review*—Fred Runk and Diana Waggoner—found the novel's ambitions to outrun its achievements; but Hal Hoover, a reviewer for *VOYA,* was of the opinion that the novel's various story threads were "masterfully woven to a final conclusion."

"The Cycle of Fire" series continued with two volumes published in 1988: *Keeper of the Keys* and *Shadowfane.* Discussing *Shadowfane, Booklist*'s Roland Green called Wurts "excellent at world building and characterization" and noted improvements, too, in narrative technique. *VOYA*'s Deborah L. Dubois called the book a "well-written fantasy," but suggested that its violence detracted from it as a young adult library purchase.

Wurts, meanwhile, was writing another series of fantasy novels, the "Empire" series, in collaboration with Raymond E. Feist, while continuing with solo projects as well. *The Master of White Storm,* published in 1992, is set in the mythical Eleven Kingdoms and centers on two galley slaves who lead a rebellion against wizard masters. *Booklist*'s Green found the novel's opening section, the slave revolt, "gripping, [and] superlatively well realized." Although finding the continuity between scenes less effective than the scenes themselves, Green said, "The book still manages to uphold Wurts's reputation for fantasy more unconventional and intelligent than not." A *Publishers Weekly* reviewer was less enthusiastic but noted the thickness of the book's action.

In 1993 Wurts instituted a new series, "The Wars of Light and Shadow," with the novel *The Curse of the Mistwraith.* The plot follows the adventures of two half-brothers, one the master of light and the other the master of shadows, as they attempt to overcome their suspicions of each other in order to unite against the Mistwraith, a force that has kept the world of Athera in its thrall. A commentator in *Publishers Weekly* found the book "entertaining and readable" but suggested that the plot was made to bear the weight of too much foreshadowing of sequel volumes. More than one critic admired the novel's characterizations and setting: *Library Journal*'s Jackie Cassada called attention to "elaborate and vivid world-building and complex protagonists," while *Booklist*'s Candace Smith noted "strongly sympathetic characters and a well-conceived setting." The novel, Smith predicted, would "hook readers of epic fantasy."

The second volume in the cycle, *Ships of Merior* (1995) was published in hardcover by HarperCollins. Weighing in at 928 pages compared to *The Curse of the Mistwraith*'s 688, *Ships of Merior* finds the half-brothers deadly enemies after their defeat of the Mistwraith. "Wurts," wrote a reviewer for *Publishers Weekly,* "creates a complex, beautiful world."

Wurts herself has remained true to the genres of fantasy and science fiction for many years. One critic hinted that Wurts might have greater success with the latter genre than with the former: when Wurts's 1996 collection of short stories, *That Way Lies Camelot,* was reviewed by *Kirkus Reviews,* the contributor praised the stories that were pure fantasy, professed ambivalence about those that mixed fantasy with realism—and judged the hard science fiction stories in the group "reminiscent of the original *Star Trek* and Robert Heinlein's juveniles—and better than either." Calling the compilation a "compassionate, cynical, smart" collection, the *Kirkus* contributor particularly praised the story "No Quarter," in which a space commander destroys his ship in order to cover up his errors in letting it be ambushed—and is rewarded for his ruthlessness by Headquarters.

BIOGRAPHICAL/CRITICAL SOURCES:

BOOKS

Weinberg, Robert, *Biographical Dictionary of Science Fiction and Fantasy Artists,* Greenwood Press (Westport, CT), 1988, pp. 299-300.

PERIODICALS

Booklist, December 1, 1984, p. 484; November 1, 1988, p. 452; March 15, 1992, p. 1344; February 1, 1994, p. 997.
Fantasy Review, February, 1985, p. 28.
Kirkus Reviews, December 15, 1995, p. 1738.
Library Journal, February 15, 1994, p. 188.
Publishers Weekly, January 27, 1992, p. 94; December 6, 1993, p. 60; January 30, 1995, p. 89.
VOYA, June, 1983, p. 101; June, 1985, p. 141; April, 1989, p. 48.*

* * *

WYCLIFFE, John
   See BEDFORD-JONES, H(enry James O'Brien)

Y-Z

YALOW, Rosalyn Sussman 1921-

PERSONAL: Born July 19, 1921, in Bronx, NY; daughter of Simon (in business) and Clara (Zipper) Sussman; married Aaron Yalow, June 6, 1943; children: Benjamin, Elanna. *Education:* Hunter College, A.B., 1941; attended New York University, 1941; University of Illinois, M.S., 1942, Ph.D. (physics), 1945.

ADDRESSES: Office—Veteran Affairs Medical Center, 130 West Kingsbridge Rd., Bronx, NY 10468-3904.

CAREER: Medical physicist. Federal Telecommunications Laboratory, New York City, assistant electrical engineer, 1945-46; Hunter College, New York City, lecturer and temporary assistant professor of physics, 1946-50; Radioisotope Services, Veterans Administration hospital, Bronx, physicist and assistant chief, 1950-70, acting chief, 1968-70, chief of nuclear medicine, 1970-80; Department of medicine, Mt. Sinai School of Medicine, City University of New York, research professor, 1968-74, distinguished service professor, 1974-79; Veterans Administration Hospital, Bronx, senior medical investigator, 1972-92, emeritus senior medical investigator, 1992—. Radioisotope unit, Veterans Administration Hospital, consultant, 1947-50; Lenox Hill hospital, consultant, 1952-62; U.S. National Committee on Medical Physics, secretary, 1963-67; Medical advisory board, National Pituitary Agency, member, 1968-71; Radioimmunassay Reference Lab, Veterans Administration medical center, chief, 1969—; Endocrinology Study Section, National Institutes of Health, member, 1969-72; Institute on Atomic Energy, agency expert, 1970; Nuclear Medical Services, member, 1970-80, senior medical investigator, 1972—; Task Force on immunology disorders, National Institute on Allergy and Infectious Disease, member, 1972-73; New York City Department of Health, consultant, 1972—; Solomon A. Berson Research Laboratory, Veterans Administration hospital, director, 1973—; Albert Einstein College of Medicine, Yeshiva University, New York City, Distinguished Professor-at-Large, 1979-85, emeritus professor, 1985—; Montefiore Medical Center, department of clinical sciences, chair, 1980-85; Mt. Sinai School of Medicine, Solomon A. Berson distinguished professor-at-large, 1986—. President's Study Group on Careers for Women, member, 1966-72.

MEMBER: National Academy of Sciences, American Academy of Arts and Sciences, American Physics Society, Endocrine Society (president, 1978-79), New York Academy of Sciences (fellow), American Association of Physicists in Medicine, American College of Radiology, Biophysics Society, American Diabetes Association, Society of Nuclear Medicine, American Physiology Society, Radiation Research Society, French Academy of Medicine, Phi Betta Kappa.

AWARDS, HONORS: William S. Middleton Research Award, Veterans Administration, 1960; Eli Lilly Award, American Diabetes Association, 1961; Federal Woman's Award, 1961; Van Slyke Award, American Association of Clinical Chemists, 1968; Gairdner Foundation International Award, 1971; American College of Physicians Award, 1971; Koch Award, Endocrine Society, 1972; A. Cressy Morrison Award in natural sciences, New York Academy of Sciences, 1975; exceptional service award, Veterans Administration, 1975; Boehringer-Mannheim Award, American Association of Clinical Chemists, 1975; scientific achievement award, American Medical Association, 1975; Albert Lasker Basic Medical Research Award, 1976; Nobel Prize for Physiology/ Medicine, 1977; Banting Medal, 1978; Gratum Genus Humanum Gold Medal, World Federation of Nuclear Medicine and Biology, 1978; G. von Hevesy Medal, 1978; Theobold Smith Award, 1982; Georg Charles de Henesy Nuclear Medicine Pioneer Award, 1986; National Medal of Science, 1988. Recipient of numerous honorary degrees.

WRITINGS:

(Editor with Solomon A. Berson) *Peptide Hormones,* American Elsevier Publishing Co. (New York City), 1973.

(Editor with R. Luft) *Radioimmunoassay: Methodology and Applications in Physiology and in Clinical Studies,* Publishing Sciences Group (Acton, MA), 1974.

(Editor with S. Philip Bralow, and others) *Basic Research and Clinical Medicine,* McGraw-Hill (New York City), c. 1981.

(Editor with J. P. Young) *Radiation and Public Perception: Benefits and Risks,* American Chemical Society (Washington, DC), 1995.

Contributor to journals and periodicals, including *Journal of Clinical Investigation* and *Nature. Hormone and Metabolic Research,* co-editor, 1973-79; *Acta Diabetologica Latina,* editorial advisory board, 1975-77; *Encycolopedia Universalis,* editorial advisory board, 1978—; member of editorial board of *Endocrinology,* 1967-72, *Diabetes,* 1976, and *Mt. Sinai Journal of Medicine,* 1976-79.

SIDELIGHTS: Rosalyn Sussman Yalow was co-developer of radioimmunoassay (RIA), a technique that uses radioactive isotopes to measure small amounts of biological substances. In widespread use, the RIA helps scientists and medical professionals measure the concentrations of hormones, vitamins, viruses, enzymes, and drugs, among other substances. Yalow's work concerning RIA earned her a share of the Nobel Prize in physiology or medicine in the late 1970s. At that time, she was only the second woman to receive the Nobel in medicine. During her career, Yalow also received acclaim for being the first woman to attain a number of other scientific achievements.

Yalow was born on July 19, 1921, in the Bronx, New York, to Simon Sussman and Clara Zipper Sussman. Her father, owner of a small business, had been born on the Lower East Side of New York City to Russian

immigrant parents. At the age of four, Yalow's mother had journeyed to the United States from Germany. Although neither parent had attended high school, they instilled a great enthusiasm for and respect of education in their daughter. Yalow also credits her father with helping her find the confidence to succeed in school, teaching her that girls could do just as much as boys. Yalow learned to read before she entered kindergarten, although her family did not own any books. Instead, Yalow and her older brother, Alexander, made frequent visits to the public library.

During her youth, Yalow became interested in mathematics. At Walton High School in the Bronx, her interest turned to science, especially chemistry. After graduation, Yalow attended Hunter College, a women's school in New York that eventually became part of the City University of New York. She credits two physics professors, Dr. Herbert Otis and Dr. Duane Roller, for igniting her penchant for physics. This occurred in the latter part of the 1930s, a time when many new discoveries were made in nuclear physics. It was this field that Yalow ultimately chose for her major. In 1939 she was further inspired after hearing American physicist Enrico Fermi lecture about the discovery of nuclear fission, which had earned him the Nobel Prize the previous year.

As Yalow prepared for her graduation from Hunter College, she found that some practical considerations intruded on her passion for physics. At the time, most of American society expected young women to become secretaries or teachers. In fact, Yalow's parents urged her to pursue a career as an elementary school teacher. Yalow herself also thought it unrealistic to expect any of the top graduate schools in the country to accept her into a doctoral program or offer her the financial support that men received. "However, my physics professors encouraged me and I persisted," she explained in *Les Prix Nobel 1977.*

Yalow made plans to enter graduate school via other means. One of her earlier college physics professors, who had left Hunter to join the faculty at the Massachusetts Institute of Technology, arranged for Yalow to work as secretary to Dr. Rudolf Schoenheimer, a biochemist at Columbia University in New York. According to the plan, this position would give Yalow an opportunity to take some graduate courses in physics, and eventually provide a way for her to enter a graduate school and pursue a degree. But Yalow never needed her plan. The month after graduating from Hunter College in January, 1941, she was offered a teaching assistantship in the physics department of the University of Illinois at Champaign-Urbana.

Gaining acceptance to the physics graduate program in the College of Engineering at the University of Illinois was one of many hurdles that Yalow had to cross as a woman in the field of science. For example, when she entered the University in September, 1941, she was the only woman in the College of Engineering's faculty, which included four hundred professors and teaching assistants. She was the first woman in more than two decades to attend the engineering college. Yalow realized that she had been given a space at the prestigious graduate school because of the shortage of male candidates, who were being drafted into the armed services in increasing numbers as America prepared to enter World War II.

Yalow's strong work orientation aided her greatly in her first year in graduate school. In addition to her regular course load and teaching duties, she took some extra undergraduate courses to increase her knowledge. Despite a hectic schedule, Yalow earned A's in her classes, except for an A- in an optics laboratory course. While in graduate school she also met Aaron Yalow, a fellow student and the man she would eventually marry. The pair met the first day of school and wed about two years later on June 6, 1943. Yalow received her master's degree in 1942 and her doctorate in 1945. She was the second woman to obtain a Ph.D. in physics at the university.

After graduation the Yalows moved to New York City, where they worked and eventually raised two children, Benjamin and Elanna. Yalow's first job after graduate school was as an assistant electrical engineer at Federal Telecommunications Laboratory, a private research lab. Once again, she found herself the sole woman there. In 1946 she began teaching physics at Hunter College. She remained a physics lecturer from 1946 to 1950, although by 1947 she began her long association with the Veterans Administration by becoming a consultant to Bronx VA Hospital. The VA wanted to establish some research programs to explore medical uses of radioactive substances. By 1950, Yalow had equipped a radioisotope laboratory at the Bronx VA Hospital and decided to leave teaching to devote her attention to full-time research.

That same year Yalow met Solomon A. Berson, a physician who had just finished his residency in internal medicine at the hospital. The two would work together until Berson's death in 1972. According to Yalow, the collaboration was a complementary one.

In Olga Opfell's *Lady Laureates: Women Who Have Won the Nobel Prize,* Yalow is quoted as saying, "[Berson] wanted to be a physicist, and I wanted to be a medical doctor." While her partner had accumulated clinical expertise, Yalow maintained strengths in physics, math, and chemistry. Working together, Yalow and Berson discovered new ways to use radioactive isotopes in the measurement of blood volume, the study of iodine metabolism, and the diagnosis of thyroid diseases. Within a few years, the pair began to investigate adult-onset diabetes using radioisotopes. This project eventually led them to develop the groundbreaking radioimmunoassay technique.

In the 1950s some scientists hypothesized that in adult-onset diabetes, insulin production remained normal, but a liver enzyme rapidly destroyed the peptide hormone, thereby preventing normal glucose metabolism. This contrasted with the situation in juvenile diabetes, where insulin production by the pancreas was too low to allow proper metabolism of glucose. Yalow and Berson wanted to test the hypothesis about adult-onset diabetes. They used insulin "labeled" with iodine-131. (That is, they attached, by a chemical reaction, the radioactive isotope of iodine to otherwise normal insulin molecules.) Yalow and Berson injected labeled insulin into diabetic and non-diabetic individuals and measured the rate at which the insulin disappeared.

To their surprise and in contradiction to the liver enzyme hypothesis, they found that the amount of radioactively labeled insulin in the blood of diabetics was higher than that found in the control subjects who had never received insulin injections before. As Yalow and Berson looked into this finding further, they deduced that diabetics were forming antibodies to the animal insulin used to control their disease. These antibodies were binding to radiolabeled insulin, preventing it from entering cells where it was used in sugar metabolism. Individuals who had never taken insulin before did not have these antibodies and so the radiolabeled insulin was consumed more quickly.

Yalow's and Berson's proposal that animal insulin could spur antibody formation was not readily accepted by immunologists in the mid-1950s. At the time, most immunologists did not believe that antibodies would form to molecules as small as the insulin peptide. Also, the amount of insulin antibodies was too low to be detected by conventional immunological techniques. So Yalow and Berson set out to verify these minute levels of insulin antibodies using radiolabeled insulin as their marker. Their original report about insulin antibodies, however, was rejected initially by two journals. Finally, a compromise version was published that omitted "insulin antibody" from the paper's title and included some additional data indicating that an antibody was involved.

The need to detect insulin antibodies at low concentrations led to the development of the radioimmunoassay. The principle behind RIA is that a radiolabeled antigen, such as insulin, will compete with unlabeled antigen for the available binding sites on its specific antibody. As a standard, various mixtures of known amounts of labeled and unlabeled antigen are mixed with antibody. The amounts of radiation detected in each sample correspond to the amount of unlabeled antigen taking up antibody binding sites. In the unknown sample, a known amount of radiolabeled antigen is added and the amount of radioactivity is measured again. The radiation level in the unknown sample is compared to the standard samples; the amount of unlabeled antigen in the unknown sample will be the same as the amount of unlabeled antigen found in the standard sample that yields the same amount of radioactivity. RIA has turned out to be so useful because it can quickly and precisely detect very low concentrations of hormones and other substances in blood or other biological fluids. The principle can also be applied to binding interactions other than that between antigen and antibody, such as between a binding protein or tissue receptor site and an enzyme. In Yalow's Nobel lecture, recorded in *Les Prix Nobel 1977,* she listed more than one hundred biological substances—hormones, drugs, vitamins, enzymes, viruses, non-hormonal proteins, and more—that were being measured using RIA.

In 1968 she became a research professor at the Mt. Sinai School of Medicine, and in 1970, she was made chief of the Nuclear Medicine Service at the VA Hospital. Yalow also began to receive a number of prestigious awards in recognition of her role in the development of RIA. In 1976, she was awarded the Albert Lasker Basic Medical Research Prize. She was the first woman to be honored this laurel—an award that often leads to a Nobel Prize. In Yalow's case, this was true, for the very next year, she shared the Nobel Prize in physiology or medicine with Andrew V. Schally and Roger Guillemin for their work on radioimmunoassay. Schally and Guillemin were recognized for their use of RIA to make important discoveries about brain hormones.

Berson had died in 1972, and so did not share in these awards. Ecstatic to receive such prizes, Yalow was also saddened that her longtime partner had been excluded. According to an essay in *The Lady Laureates,* she remarked that the "tragedy" of winning the Nobel Prize "is that Dr. Berson did not live to share it." Earlier Yalow had paid tribute to her collaborator by asking the VA to name the laboratory, in which the two had worked, the Solomon A. Berson Research Laboratory. She made the request, as quoted in *Les Prix Nobel 1977,* "so that his name will continue to be on my papers as long as I publish and so that his contributions to our Service will be memorialized."

Yalow has received many other awards, honorary degrees, and lectureships, including the Georg Charles de Henesy Nuclear Medicine Pioneer Award in 1986 and the Scientific Achievement Award of the American Medical Society. In 1978, she hosted a five-part dramatic series on the life of French physical chemist Marie Curie, aired by the Public Broadcasting Service (PBS). In 1979 she became a distinguished professor at the Albert Einstein College of Medicine at Yeshiva University, leaving to become the Solomon A. Berson Distinguished Professor at Large at Mt. Sinai in 1986. She also chaired the Department of Clinical Science at Montefiore Hospital and Medical Center in the early- to mid-1980s.

By all accounts, Yalow was an industrious researcher, rarely taking time off. For example, some reports claim that she only took a few days off of work following the birth of her two children. In *The Lady Laureates,* Opfell reported that when the VA Hospital put on a party in honor of Yalow's selection for the Lasker Prize, Yalow herself "brought roast turkeys from home and stood in the middle of a meeting peeling potatoes and making potato salad while fellows reported to her."

The fact that Yalow was a trailblazer for women scientists was not lost on her, however. At a lecture before the Association of American Medical Colleges, as quoted in *Lady Laureates,* Yalow opined: "We cannot expect that in the foreseeable future women will achieve status in academic medicine in proportion to their numbers. But if we are to start working towards that goal we must believe in ourselves or no one else will believe in us; we must match our aspirations with the guts and determination to succeed; and for those of us who have had the good fortune to move upward, we must feel a personal responsibility to serve as role models and advisors to ease the path for those who come afterwards."

BIOGRAPHICAL/CRITICAL SOURCES:

BOOKS

Les Prix Nobel 1977, Almquist & Wiskell International, Stockholm, 1978, pp. 237-64.
Opfell, Olga, *The Lady Laureates: Women Who Have Won the Nobel Prize,* Scarecrow Press, Inc., 1978.*

* * *

YANG, Chen Ning 1922-

PERSONAL: Born September 22, 1922, in Hofei, Anhwei, China; son of Ke Chuan (a professor of mathematics) and Meng Hwa (Loh) Yang; married Chih Li Tu, 1950; children: Franklin, Gilbert, Eulee. *Education:* National Southwest Associated University, K'un-ming, China, B.S. (physics), 1942; Tsinghua University, China, M.S., 1944; University of Chicago, Ph.D. (physics), 1948.

ADDRESSES: Office—State University of New York at Stony Brook, Institute of Theoretical Physics, Stony Brook, NY 11794-3840. *E-mail*—Chen.Yang@sunysb.edu.

CAREER: Physicist and educator. University of Chicago, IL, instructor of physics, 1948-49; Institute for Advanced Study, Princeton, NJ, member, 1949-66, professor, 1955-66; State University of New York, Stony Brook, Albert Einstein Professor of Physics, 1966—, Institute for Theoretical Physics, director, 1966—. Member of board of trustees at Woods Hole Oceanographic Institute, 1962-78; Rockefeller University, 1970-76; Salk Institute, 1978-79; and Ben Gurion University, 1980—. Member of Governing Council, Courant Institute of Math and Science, 1963—, and Science Advisory Committee, International Business Machines (IBM), 1966-71. Chair of Panel of Theoretical Physics and Physics Survey Committee, National Academy of Sciences, 1965; Division of Particles and Fields, International Union of Pure and Applied Physics, 1972-76; and fachbeirat Max Planck Institute for Physics, 1980-83. Member of board of directors American Association for the Advancement of Science, 1975-79; Neuroscience Institute, 1983-88; and Scientific American, Inc., 1983-90.

MEMBER: National Academy of Sciences, American Philosophical Society, Royal Spanish Academy of Sciences, Polish Academy of Sciences, Royal Society, London.

AWARDS, HONORS: Bower Achievement in Science Award, Franklin Institute; joint Nobel Prize in Physics, 1957; Albert Einstein Commemorative Award, 1957; Rumford Medal, American Academy of Arts and Sciences, 1980; National Medal for Science, 1986; Liberty Award, 1986; Benjamin Franklin Medal, 1993; honorary doctorates of science from Princeton University, Polytechnic Institute, University of Wroclaw, Gustavus Adolphus College, University of Maryland, University of Durham, Fundan University, Eidg Technische Hochschule, and Moscow State University.

WRITINGS:

Elementary Particles: A Short History of Some Discoveries in Atomic Physics, Princeton University Press (Princeton, NJ), 1961.
Selected Papers, 1945-80, with Commentary, W. H. Freeman (San Francisco, CA), 1983.
(Editor with M.L. Ge and X.W. Zhou) *International Conference on Differential Geometric Methods in Theoretical Physics,* World Scientific (River Edge, NJ), c. 1993.
(Editor with M.L. Ge) *Braid Group, Knot Theory, and Statistical Mechanics II,* World Scientific, c. 1994.

Contributor to journals and periodicals, including *Physical Review.*

SIDELIGHTS: In 1945, Chen Ning Yang came to the United States, where he studied physics at the University of Chicago under Enrico Fermi. At Chicago, Yang struck up a friendship with another graduate student from China, Tsung-Dao Lee, with whom he would have a long and productive professional relationship. In 1956 Yang and Lee developed a hypothesis that one of the fundamental laws of physics, the conservation of parity, might not in fact be valid. As a result of experiments conducted by Chien-Shiung Wu along lines suggested by Yang and Lee, that hypothesis was confirmed. The discovery was momentous because it called into question the validity of all conservation laws—laws that support a major part of modern physical theory. For the discovery of the violation of parity conservation, Yang and Lee were jointly awarded the 1957 Nobel Prize in Physics.

Yang was born in the city of Hofei, in the Anhwei province of China, on September 22, 1922, the son of

Ke Chuan Yang, a professor of mathematics, and the former Meng Hwa Loh. The Yang family moved in 1929 from Hofei to Peking, where Professor Yang took a job with Tsinghua University. In Peking, Yang attended the Chung Te Middle School. The family moved once more eight years later to escape the invading Japanese army. At that time, Tsinghua University was moved to K'un-ming, where it was consolidated with National Southwest Associated University. When Yang finished high school, he entered the National Southwest Associated University, where he majored in physics and earned his B.S. degree in 1942. He then continued his studies at Tsinghua University, where his father was still professor of mathematics. Yang earned his M.S. at Tsinghua in 1944. He then taught high school for one year before deciding to begin work on a Ph.D. in physics. Because doctoral programs in physics were not then available in China, Yang decided to come to the United States, where he particularly wanted to study with physicist Enrico Fermi. According to an article by Jeremy Bernstein in the *New Yorker,* Yang traveled to New York City (by way of India, the Suez Canal, and Europe) under the impression that Fermi was still at Columbia, where he had come upon his arrival in the United States in 1938. When Yang heard that Fermi had only recently left for a new post at the University of Chicago, he followed Fermi and enrolled in the doctoral program at Chicago.

One of the many benefits of Yang's tenure at Chicago was the association he developed with fellow student Tsung-Dao Lee. Yang and Lee had attended National Southwest Associated University in China at the same time, but Yang was a year ahead of Lee, and the two were not particularly close. The situation at Chicago was very different. The two compatriots shared housing at the university's international house and soon became close friends. They began to spend time together, talking almost every day about issues in physics. When Yang received his doctorate in 1948, he remained at Chicago as an instructor for one year and then took a job at the Institute for Advanced Study in Princeton, New Jersey. As Lee was not to complete his own degree for two more years, it appeared that their close association was to end; however, in 1951 Lee joined Yang at Princeton for a period of two years. When Lee then took a job at Columbia University in 1953, the two agreed to continue meeting once each week, alternating between New York and Princeton. By the spring of 1956 they had settled on a problem of particular interest to both of them, the decay of the K-meson (a subatomic particle) and the question of parity conservation.

Conservation laws lie at the heart of physics, and they are familiar to most students of high school physics. Such laws say that a particular property—mass, energy, momentum, or electrical charge, for instance—is conserved during any change. As an example, when two moving objects strike each other, their total momentum after the collision must be the same as their total momentum before the collision.

The law of parity conservation, first proposed in 1925, defines the basic symmetry of nature, referring to the theory that the laws of nature are not biased in any particular direction. Consequently, nature is unable to distinguish between right- and left-handedness in particles—the smallest building blocks of energy and matter. Any reaction that involves a right-handed particle would be the same for a left-handed particle. By the 1950s, however, one particular kind of nuclear reaction had raised some questions about the validity of that law. That reaction involved the decay of an elementary particle called the K-meson.

Experiments appear to have shown that K-mesons can decay in one of two ways. The explanation that had been postulated for this observation was that two kinds of K-mesons exist; Yang and Lee suggested another possibility. Perhaps only one form of the K-meson exists, they said, and it sometimes decays in such a way that parity is conserved and sometimes in such a way that parity is not conserved. In June of 1956 Yang and Lee formulated their thoughts on the K-meson puzzle in a now-classic paper titled "Question of Parity Conservation in Weak Interactions." They not only explained why they thought that parity conservation might not occur, but they also outlined experimental tests by which their hypothesis could be evaluated.

Within a matter of months, the proposed experiments were under way. They were carried out by a group of researchers under the direction of Chien-Shiung Wu, a compatriot of Yang and Lee at Columbia University. Wu assembled a team of colleagues at Columbia and at the National Bureau of Standards to study K-meson decay along the lines suggested by Yang and Lee. By January of 1957, the preliminary results were in. The evidence confirmed that Yang and Lee were correct: parity was not conserved in the decay of K-mesons. For their work on this problem, Yang and Lee were awarded the Nobel Prize in Physics only ten months after Wu's experiments had been completed—almost record time for recognition by a Nobel Prize committee.

In the mid-1960s, Yang ended his long affiliation with the Institute for Advanced Study to accept an appointment as Albert Einstein Professor of Physics and Director of the Institute of Theoretical Physics at the State University of New York at Stony Brook. In 1950 he had married Chih Li Tu, a former high school student of his in China. They have two sons, Franklin and Gilbert, and a daughter, Eulee. In addition to the Nobel Prize, Yang has been awarded the 1957 Albert Einstein Commemorative Award and the 1980 Rumford Medal of the American Academy of Arts and Sciences.

BIOGRAPHICAL/CRITICAL SOURCES:

BOOKS

Magill, Frank N., editor, *The Nobel Prize Winners—Physics,* Volume 2, Salem Press, 1989, pp. 707-13.

McGraw-Hill Modern Men of Science, Volume 1, McGraw-Hill, 1984, pp. 545-46.

Wasson, Tyler, editor, *Nobel Prize Winners,* H. W. Wilson, 1987, pp. 1150-1152.

PERIODICALS

New Yorker, May 12, 1962, pp. 49-104.*

*   *   *

YICK, Joseph K(ong) S(ang) 1953-

PERSONAL: Born January 2, 1953, in Hong Kong; immigrated to the United States, 1987; naturalized U.S. citizen, 1993; son of Fun Nam Yik (in business) and Sin Kai Lau (a homemaker); married Hideko Ishida (an auditor), 1978. *Ethnicity:* "Chinese." *Education:* Attended Belmont College, 1973-74; University of Texas at Austin, B.A., 1976; University of California at Santa Barbara, M.A., 1978, Ph.D., 1988.

ADDRESSES: Office—Department of History, Southwest Texas State University, San Marcos, TX 78666; fax (512) 245-3043. *E-mail*—jy02@swt.edu.

CAREER: Hong Kong Baptist College, Hong Kong, lecturer in history, 1979-83; Hong Kong Government, Examinations Authority, Hong Kong, center supervisor and history marker, 1981-82; University of Hong Kong, Hong Kong, lecturer in history, 1981-83; Santa Barbara City College, Santa Barbara, CA, instructor of history, 1984-87, and consultant, 1985-87; Auburn University at Montgomery, Montgomery, AL, assistant professor of history, 1988-89; Southwest Texas State University, San Marcos, TX, assistant professor, 1989-95, associate professor of history, 1995—. Visiting lecturer at the University of California at Santa Barbara, 1984; associate in research at the John King Fairbank Center for East Asian Research at Harvard University, 1991, 1996. Has served on many academic committees at Auburn University and Southwest Texas State University. Has given lectures and/or papers on Asian history in Hong Kong, Mexico City, and in many locations in the United States.

MEMBER: Phi Alpha Theta, Pi Sigma Alpha, Sigma Iota Rho, American Association for Chinese Studies, American Historical Association, Association for Asian Studies.

AWARDS, HONORS: Has received many academic grants and fellowships; Presidential Award for Excellence in Scholarly/Creative Activities at the Rank of Assistant Professor, Southwest Texas State University, 1994-95; Joseph Levenson Prize nomination, Association for Asian Studies, 1996, for *Making Urban Revolution in China: The CCP-GMD Struggle for Beiping-Tianjin, 1945-1949.*

WRITINGS:

Making Urban Revolution in China: The CCP-GMD Struggle for Beiping-Tianjin, 1945-1949, M.E. Sharpe (Armonk, NY), 1995.

Contributor to books, including *Historical Dictionary of Revolutionary China, 1839-1976,* edited by Edwin Pak-wah Leung, Greenwood Press (Westport, CT), 1992; *Modern China in Transition: Studies in Honor of Immanuel C. Y. Hsu,* edited by Philip Yuen-sang Leung and E. P. Leung, Regina Books (Claremont, CA), 1995; and *East Asian Nationalism: An Encyclopedia of Modern History and Culture in China and Japan,* edited by Ke-wan Wang and James L. Huffman, Garland (New York, NY), 1997.

Also contributor of articles to periodicals, including *Modern China, Methodist History, Asian Studies in the Southwest, Modern Chinese History Society of Hong Kong Bulletin,* and *Hong Kong Baptist College Academic Journal.*

WORK IN PROGRESS: Further work on modern Chinese history and on China's communist revolution.

SIDELIGHTS: Hong Kong-born scholar Joseph K. S. Yick is an expert on modern Chinese history, particularly on the subject of China's communist revolution. A naturalized citizen of the United States since 1993, he has taught history classes and given lectures at institutions ranging from Hong Kong Baptist College to Southwest Texas State University. Yick has penned articles for academic journals, contributed chapters to books, and is the author of his own volume about China's route to communism, *Making Urban Revolution in China: The CCP-GMD Struggle for Beiping-Tianjin, 1945-1949.*

Unlike most other works about the Chinese Revolution, which emphasize the rural nature of many of the political and fighting movements that were a part of the struggle, *Making Urban Revolution in China*—as its title indicates—focuses on revolutionary events that took place within the cities, especially Beijing and Tianjin. Reviewers of *Making Urban Revolution in China* have noted and appreciated this difference. Gregor Benton wrote in *American Historical Review,* "Yick's study adds to and radically revises our understanding of the causes of Communist success in the civil war." Hailing it as "the first case study of the civil war in two of China's largest cities," Patricia Stranahan in *China Quarterly* went on to assert that "in his discussion of the political model . . . Yick makes his most significant contribution to understanding the urban revolution." She further applauded Yick's study for the way it investigates the Communist Party's efforts to organize "disillusioned urban social forces." According to Stranahan, Yick finds "students and intellectuals composed the underground party, not proletariat."

This last fact was the source of one of the few criticisms of Yick's book from Hung-yok Ip in *China Information,* who expressed the wish for "a more substantive treatment of a few related issues, for example why young men and women from elite families were willing to join the Communist revolution." Ip praised many other aspects of *Making Urban Revolution in China,* however, including Yick's discussion of the vigorous and active communist student movement. This group produced as one of their offshoots an anti-examination movement in order to attract more beleaguered college students to the communist cause. They also played on anti-American and anti-imperialist sentiment by organizing demonstrations against the United States and other similarly resented nations. In this manner, they associated Chinese patriotism with their own communist philosophy, while painting their opposition as being weak puppets under the protection of foreigners. Yick also reviews the underground activities of the urban communist groups, which had methods of recruitment, communication and training that Ip described as "sophisticated." As Ip pointed out, part of Yick's effectiveness in the treatment of his subject is that he had access to a large number of new sources and information that has only become available since the 1970s. Ip summed up *Making Urban Revolution in China* as "a significant contribution to our understanding of the Communist victory in 1949." Said Benton in *American Historical Review,* "Its impact will extend beyond Chinese Communist studies to the growing literature on Chinese urban sociology and the broader field of labor history."

Yick told *CA:* "I published my first scholarly article in 1982. My serious writing career emerged, however, during my doctoral studies from 1983 to 1988. Influenced by numerous Western and Chinese scholars who published on the Chinese Communist movement (1919 to the present), I was determined to make a contribution to the study of Chinese Communism. Five years of painstaking research and writing ended in a dissertation which turned into a monograph titled *Making Urban Revolution in China: The CCP-GMD Struggle for Beiping-Tianjin, 1945-1949.* It details the political struggle between the Chinese Communist Party (CCP) and the Guomindang (GMD, or the Nationalist Party) during the period of the Chinese Civil War.

"The primary motivation for writing this monograph was the fact that as compared with the rural dimension of the Chinese Communist movement, their urban activities were little-studied. It is an odd situation, because in Communist theory the city, not the countryside, should always be the focus of the revolution and development. In order to modify the dominant 'peasant revolution' thesis in the study of the Chinese Communist Revolution (1919-1949), I have focused on the political and non-military struggle between the Communists and the Nationalists in Beiping (Beijing) and Tianjin, two of China's largest cities during the late 1940s.

"I expect that other scholars will undertake serious studies on the strategy, tactics, and activities of the underground CCP in other urban areas of China. After all, the urban dimension of the Communist revolution and development should be a very important subject of inquiry not only in the field of Chinese Communism but also in modern Chinese history. I encourage aspiring writers to make contributions to such a vital subject.

"Last but not least, in this post-Cold War era and the age of collapsing Communism around the globe, the study of both the urban and rural aspects of the Chinese Party-State (which rules 1.2 billion people) should help us better understand the course of the tremendous transformations of Communist China. It is imperative for us to understand China—whether it soon becomes a Western-style democracy or not."

BIOGRAPHICAL/CRITICAL SOURCES:

PERIODICALS

American Historical Review, April, 1997, pp. 500-501.
China Information, winter/spring 1995-96, pp. 211-13.
China Quarterly, June 1996, pp. 617-18.

*   *   *

YOUNG, J(ack) P. 1929-

PERSONAL: Born October 28, 1929, in Huntington, IN; son of Jacob P. and Marie (Scully) Young; married Jean Kennedy, June 18, 1955; children: James P., Mark K., David V., Timothy S., Karen E. *Ethnicity:* "Caucasian." *Education:* Attended Huntington College, 1946-48; Ball State University, B.S., 1950; attended University of Notre Dame, 1950-51; Indiana University, Ph.D., 1955. *Religion:* Roman Catholic. *Avocational interests:* Travel, gardening.

ADDRESSES: Home—100 Westlook Circle, Oak Ridge, TN 37830. *Office*—Oak Ridge National Laboratory, Box 2008, MS-6142, Oak Ridge, TN 37831-6142; fax 423-574-8363. *E-mail*—qyp@ornl.gov.

CAREER: Oak Ridge National Laboratory, Oak Ridge, TN, member of senior research staff, 1955—. Oak Ridge Children's Museum, member of board of directors, 1978-84, president, 1982-84; Oak Ridge Arts Council, 1982-86; Oak Ridge Music Association, 1994—.

MEMBER: American Chemical Society (local section chairperson, 1993), American Association for the Advancement of Science (fellow, 1983), Society for Applied Spectroscopy, Sigma Xi.

AWARDS, HONORS: IR-100 Award, for the development of a single-atom detector.

WRITINGS:

(Editor with Rosalyn Sussman Yalow) *Radiation and Public Perception: Benefits and Risks,* American Chemical Society (Washington, DC), 1995.

Contributor of more than one hundred and fifty articles to scientific journals.

WORK IN PROGRESS: Research on actinides, transuranium element chemistry, molten salts, laser spectroscopy, fiber optics, analytical chemistry, and paleontology.

SIDELIGHTS: Young told *CA:* "My area of interest is chemical research. In my research I am relatively well versed in basic nuclear research areas with a strong interest in nuclear energy. At a certain stage in my career (1992) I felt it was time to organize a symposium relating scientifically-based studies to the public perception of nuclear radiation.

"Apparently others in this area of the scientific community thought the time was ripe also. With the help of my co-editor, Nobel Laureate Dr. Rosalyn Sussman Yalow, such a symposium was organized at a national meeting of the American Chemical Society. Later that society chose to publish the proceedings of this symposium, with chapters written by the speakers, as the book *Radiation and Public Perception: Benefits and Risks.* It was published in their prestigious *Advances in Chemistry* series.

"The story of the development of this book may be a bit unusual, but it points to an opportunity that timeliness lends to the creation of a publication."

*   *   *

ZAMPA, Luigi 1905-1991

PERSONAL: Born January 2, 1905, in Rome, Italy; died of complications following surgery, August 15, 1991, in Rome; children: two sons, one daughter. *Education:* Attended Experimental Film Center (Rome), 1935-38.

CAREER: Screenwriter, director, and author.

AWARDS, HONORS: Award for best foreign film, New York Film Critics, 1947, for *To Live in Peace.*

WRITINGS:

Il primo giro di moanovella: Il romanzo sull'ambiente del cinema, Trevi (Rome), 1980.

Also author of the novel *Il succeso,* 1948, and other novels and plays.

SCREENPLAYS

Author of *Il capiano degli ussari, La danza dei milioni, Un mare di guai, Tutta per la donna, Manovre d'amore,* and *Dora Nelson,* all 1939.

COLLABORATOR ON SCREENPLAYS, AND DIRECTOR

L'attore Scomparso, 1941.
Fra' Diavolo, 1941.
Signorinette, 1942.
C'e sempre un ma . . . , 1942.
L'abito Nero da sposa, 1943.
Un Americano in vacanza, 1945, released in the United States as *A Yank in Rome.*
Vivere in pace, 1946, released in the United States as *To Live in Peace.*
L'onorevole Angelina, 1947, released in the United States as *Angelina.*
(With Vitaliano Brancati) *Anni difficili* (adapted from Brancati's story), 1948, released in the United States as *Difficult Years.*
Campane a Martello, 1949, released in the United States as *Children of Change.*
Cuori senza frontiere, 1950, released in the United States as *The White Line.*
E piu facile che un cammello, 1950, released in the United States as *His Last Twelve Hours.*
Signori in carrozza, 1951.
Processo all citta, 1952, released in the United States as *City on Trial.*
"Isa Miranda" in *Siamo donne,* 1952, released in the United States as *We, the Women.*
Anni facili, 1953, released in the United States as *Easy Years.*
"La Patente" in *Questa e la vita,* 1954.
La Romana, 1954, released in the United States as *Woman of Rome.*
L'arte di arrangiarsi, 1954.
Ragazze d'oggi, 1955.
La ragazza del Palio, 1957, released in the United States as *The Love Specialist.*
Ladro lui, ladro lei, 1958.
Il magistrato, 1959, released in the United States as *The Magistrate.*
Il vigile, 1960.

Gli anni rugenti (adapted from Nikolai Gogol's *The Inspector General*), 1962, released in the United States as *Roaring Years.*
Frenesia dell'state, 1963.
Una questione d'onore, 1965, released in the United States as *A Question of Honor.*
"Il marito de Olga" in *I nostri mariti,* 1966.
Le dolci signori, 1967, released in the United States as *Anyone Can Play.*
Il medico della Mutua, 1968.
Bello onesto emigrato Australia sposerebbe compaesana illibata, 1971, released in the United States as *A Girl in Australia.*
Bisturi: La mafia bianca, 1973, released in the United States as *Hospitals: The White Mafia.*
Gente di rispetto, 1975.
Il mostro, 1977.
Letti selvaggi, 1979, released in the United States as *Tigers in Lipstick.*

SIDELIGHTS: Luigi Zampa was a prolific Italian filmmaker. His status probably reached its peak among American filmgoers with *To Live in Peace,* a neorealist drama about an Italian family sheltering two prisoners during World War II. *To Live in Peace* was named best foreign film by the New York Film Critics in 1947. Another of Zampa's better-known works in the United States is *Angelina,* which featured actress Anna Magnani as a woman beset with personal and political issues while living in a Roman slum.

Although Zampa is probably best known outside Italy for his neorealist dramas, he was also an accomplished comic filmmaker. Among his many works in the comedy genre is *A Girl in Australia,* in which an Italian immigrant in Australia becomes involved with a prostitute who presents herself to him as a virgin. In addition to his film work, Zampa published novels, including *Il succeso,* and wrote productions for the stage. After a long career, the filmmaker died in Rome in 1991.

BIOGRAPHICAL/CRITICAL SOURCES:

PERIODICALS

Variety, February 20, 1985, p. 27.

OBITUARIES:

PERIODICALS

Boston Globe, August 17, 1991, p. 31.
Detroit Free Press, August 19, 1991, p. 2B.

New York Times, August 17, 1991.
Variety, August 26, 1991.*

*   *   *

ZINGG, Paul J(oseph) 1945-

PERSONAL: Born July 22, 1945, in Newark, NJ; son of Carl William and Dolores (Lucking) Zingg; married Candace A. Slater (a professor), August 9, 1980. *Education:* Belmont Abbey College, Belmont, NC, B.A., 1968; University of Richmond, M.A., 1969; University of Georgia, Athens, Ph.D., 1974. *Politics:* Independent. *Religion:* Roman Catholic.

ADDRESSES: Home—1563 Corbett Canyon Rd., Arroyo Grande, CA 93420; and 47 Northampton Ave., Berkeley, CA 94707. *Office*—Provost's Office, California Polytechnic State University, San Luis Obispo, CA 93407. *E-Mail*—pzingg@oboe.aix.calpoly.edu.

CAREER: Southern Benedictine College, Cullman, AL, assistant professor of history, 1975-77; Williams University, Chicago, IL, executive dean for academic affairs, 1977-78; University of Pennsylvania, Philadelphia, adjunct assistant professor, 1978—, adjunct associate professor of history, 1986, vice-dean for College of Arts and Sciences' undergraduate studies and admissions, 1979-81, and College of Arts and Sciences, 1981-83, assistant to the president, 1983-86; Saint Mary's College of California, Moraga, professor of history and dean of liberal arts school, 1986-93; California Polytechnic State University, San Luis Obispo, CA, professor of history and dean of liberal arts college, 1993-95, provost and vice president for academic affairs, 1995—; writer. Member of board of directors for Hearst Art Gallery, 1988-90; member of executive committee of American Council on Education, 1988-94; chairman of Cal Poly Arts, 1993-95; member of the Central Coast Performing Arts Center Commission, 1993—; charter member, California Council of the Oakland Museum, 1995—. Consultant to various institutions, organizations, and businesses.

MEMBER: Organization of American Historians, Society for History Education, American Studies Association, Society for American Baseball Research, American Council on Education, Association of American Colleges, North American Society for the Study of Sport, Phi Alpha Theta, Phi Beta Delta.

AWARDS, HONORS: Fellowships from National En-

dowment for the Humanities, 1975, Center for International Study and Research, 1980-82, and American Council on Education, 1983-84; named University of Pennsylvania's faculty member of the year by Friar's Senior Society, 1983-84; Research Foundation Awards from University of Pennsylvania, 1983-84 and 1984-85; grants from National Endowment for the Humanities, 1989, and Saint Mary's College, 1987, 1990, 1991, and 1993; Alumni Faculty Scholarship from Saint Mary's College of California, 1992.

WRITINGS:

SPORTS HISTORY

The Sporting Image: Readings in American Sport History, University Press of America, 1987.
Pride of the Palestra, Colonial Press, 1987.
Harry Hooper, 1887-1974: An American Baseball Life, University of Illinois Press, 1993.
(With Mark D. Medeiros) *Runs, Hits, and an Era: The Pacific Coast League, 1903-1958,* University of Illinois Press, 1994.

Contributor to periodicals, including *Journal of American Culture, Historian, History Teacher, NCAA News, Journal of Sport History,* and *Nine: A Journal of Baseball History and Social Policy Perspectives.*

OTHER

(With James J. Cooke and Aurie H. Miller) *Through Foreign Eyes: Western Attitudes Toward North Africa,* University Press of America, 1982.
(Editor) *In Search of the American National Character,* 1984.
(Editor with Thomas Purdom) *The Academic Penn,* illustrations by Seymour Chwast, University of Pennsylvania, 1986.

Contributor to periodicals, including *African Studies Review, Educational Perspectives, Educational Record, International Journal of Middle East Studies, Journal of General Education, Liberal Education, Pennsylvania Gazette,* and *South Atlantic Quarterly.*

WORK IN PROGRESS: A Good Round: A Journey through the Landscapes and Memory of Golf, an examination of golf in various cultural and contextual settings, e.g., in the U.S. and Scotland and in the imagination; research on morale issues in higher education and on building academic communities of civility and respect.

SIDELIGHTS: Paul J. Zingg is a university administrator and a historian specializing in sports. Notable among his sports books is *Harry Hooper 1887-1974: An American Baseball Life,* a 1993 publication which recounts the exploits of the Hall-of-Fame outfielder who played for the Boston Red Sox and the Chicago White Sox from 1909 to 1925. Zingg notes that although Hooper's lifetime batting average falls under .300, the player rates as one of the most successful leadoff batters of his era, for he held an impressive on-base percentage and showed considerable prowess as a base stealer. In addition, Hooper is credited as the player responsible for convincing Red Sox manager Ed Barrow that team pitcher Babe Ruth might be used to greater advantage by playing everyday as an outfielder. Ruth, who then ranked among the American League's better pitchers, made the switch and became a legendary slugger.

George W. Hunt, writing in *America,* described *Harry Hooper* as "a coming-of-age tale of a California farm boy who becomes an idol in faraway Boston and whose integrity and gentlemanliness gentrify a national game." Jules Tygiel, writing in the *American Historical Review,* proclaims the book "really distinguishes itself when Zingg takes his eye off the ball. Interwoven through *Hooper* are outstanding sections on growing up in turn-of-the-century California, the evolution of colleges and collegiate sports, and the life of the ball player off the field."

In 1994 Zingg followed *Harry Hooper* with *Runs, Hits, and an Era: The Pacific Coast League, 1903-1958,* a chronicle of the minor league that spawned such major-league greats as Ted Williams, Joe DiMaggio, and Harry Heilman. This volume, which Zingg wrote in collaboration with Mark D. Medeiros, also relates the achievements of such colorful players as Ox Eckhardt, Smeed Jolley, slugger Steve Bilko, and Buzz Arlett, whose Pacific Coast accomplishments have significantly contributed to his status as a particularly legendary minor-league player. John Schulian wrote in the *Los Angeles Times Book Review* that *Runs, Hits, and an Era* "commemorates" the Pacific Coast League. In addition to writing sports histories, Zingg has published works on such subjects as race and education.

Zingg told *CA:* "The questions that anyone who considers writing a biography must ask are: is this a life worth telling? does it interest me? do the sources exist to tell it accurately? can I tell it well? The latter, of course, will largely be answered in the reviews and reactions of others. But the other questions must be answered affirmatively if the project is to muster both enthusiasm and the prospect of success. My work in sports history now includes four books and a score of articles. But this was hardly the direction towards which my graduate studies in diplomatic history initially pointed me. Although both at the University of Richmond and the University of Georgia I expressed interested in sports-related topics, (in particular, sports competitions and their bearing on international relations), my professors discouraged me, dismissing sports history as not particularly compelling or legitimate. It was not until I settled in as a dean at the University of Pennsylvania, five years after earning my doctorate, that I began to write about the student-athlete and other aspects of intercollegiate athletics. The books and articles which have followed confirmed the importance of the subject matter, brought me 'out of the closet' as an unapologetic sports historian, and underscored the value and satisfaction in writing about something I find truly interesting and meaningful.

"The same can be said about my writing on various aspects of American higher education, especially curricular issues, multi-culturalism, and matters of institutional morale. Like sports history, a convergence of personal interests and engagements have provided the context and enthusiasm for my writing. I cannot imagine approaching writing in any other way."

BIOGRAPHICAL/CRITICAL SOURCES:

PERIODICALS

America, February 26, 1994, p. 2.
American Historical Review, April, 1995, p. 599.
Christian Science Monitor, April 29, 1994.
Journal of American Studies, fall, 1994.
Journal of Sport History, spring, 1995.
Los Angeles Times Book Review, April 24, 1994, p. 6.
New England Quarterly, September, 1994.
San Francisco Chronicle, July 24, 1994.
Washington Post Book World, April 17, 1994, pp. 8-9.

*   *   *

ZWORYKIN, Vladimir Kosma 1889-1982

PERSONAL: Born July 30, 1889 in Mourom, Russia; immigrated to the United States, 1919; became U.S.

citizen, 1924; died July 29, 1982, in the United States; son of Vladimir Kosma (a river boat owner and operator) and Elaine Zworykin; married Tatiana Vasilieff, c. 1914 (later divorced); married Katherine Polevitsky, 1951; children: (from first marriage) two. *Education:* Degree in electrical engineering from St. Petersburg Institute of Technology, 1912; attended College de France, Paris, France, c. 1912-14; University of Pittsburgh, Ph.D. (physics), c. 1920.

CAREER: Physicist and engineer. Bookkeeper for Russian Embassy in the United States, c. 1919-29; researcher at Westinghouse Laboratories, 1920-29; associate research director at Radio Corporation of America (RCA), Camden, NJ, beginning 1929, became director of electronic research, 1946, then vice president of laboratories division, 1947-54, honorary vice president and technical consultant, 1954-82. Appointed director of the Medical Electronics Center at the Rockefeller Institute for Medical Research (now Rockefeller University). *Military service:* Served as a radio officer in the Russian signal corps during World War I; served on Scientific Advisory Board to U.S. Air Force and committees of the National Defense Research Council during World War II.

MEMBER: National Academy of Sciences, National Academy of Engineering.

AWARDS, HONORS: Morris Liebmann Memorial Prize from the Institute of Radio Engineers, 1934; Edison Medal from the American Institute of Electrical Engineers, 1952; National Medal of Science from the National Academy of Sciences, 1967; honored by the French Legion of Honor.

WRITINGS:

Television: The Electronics of Image Transmission, Wiley, 1940.
Electron Optics and the Electron Microscope, Wiley, 1946.
Photoelectricity and Its Applications, Wiley, 1949.
Television in Science and Industry, Wiley, 1958.

Contributor to periodicals and journals, including *American Magazine.*

SIDELIGHTS: Vladimir Kosma Zworykin is best remembered for developing the iconoscope and the kinescope, two inventions for which he became known as "the father of television." During his lifetime he

obtained more than 120 patents on a wide variety of electronic devices and applied many of the principles from his work with television to microscopy, leading to the development of the electron microscope.

Zworykin was born to Vladimir Kosma and Elaine Zworykin on July 30, 1889, in Mourom, Russia. His early years were spent in Mourom, where his father owned and operated a fleet of river boats on the Oka River. He was educated locally before studying electrical engineering at the St. Petersburg Institute of Technology (also known as Petrograd Institute of Technology). In St. Petersburg, he studied with professor Boris Rosing, who maintained that cathode ray tubes, with their ability to shoot a stream of charged particles, would be useful in the development of television. This belief contrasted with efforts at the time to use mechanical systems based on a variety of synchronized moving parts. Although Rosing's ideas could only be demonstrated by transmission of crude geometric images in his laboratory in St. Petersburg, these early experiments inspired much of Zworykin's later successful work on the television.

After receiving his degree from St. Petersburg in 1912, Zworykin entered the prestigious College de France in Paris, where he studied x-ray technology under the well-known French physicist Paul Langevin. With the outbreak of World War I in 1914 in Europe, he returned to Russia and spent the war years as a radio officer in the Russian signal corps. During the war Zworykin married Tatiana Vasilieff, a union that produced two children. At the war's end in 1918, he left Russia and traveled widely before emigrating with his family to the United States in 1919. When he arrived in the United States, Zworykin obtained a position as a bookkeeper for the financial agent of the Russian embassy.

In 1920 Zworykin was invited to join the research laboratories at Westinghouse to work on the development of radio tubes and photoelectric cells (small devices whose electrical properties are modified by the action of light). While at Westinghouse, Zworykin earned his Ph.D. in physics at the University of Pittsburgh, writing his dissertation on the improvement of photoelectric cells. It was the concept of television, however, that most excited him, and in December 1923 he filed a patent application for his iconoscope, an invention that would revolutionize the development of television (although the actual patent was not granted until 1938). Until this time most television research involved mechanical systems. These relied on a rapidly rotating, perforated disk. The perforations were arranged in a spiral which could be quickly rotated. Light was transmitted from a photoelectric device behind the disk through the holes to form a series of successive parallel lines on a viewing screen. Unfortunately, the amount of light transmitted for each picture was very small, making the pictures quite dim and lacking in detail.

Zworykin's landmark iconoscope was an attempt to reproduce the human eye electronically. In human vision, light enters the eye through the iris, passes through a lens, and focuses an image on the retina, which registers colors via photosensitive receptor cells known as cones and light intensities via cells called rods. The optic nerves of the eye transmit this information to the brain in the form of electrical impulses which register as an image for the viewer. The iconoscope, like the eye, used a lens to focus an image on a signal plate of mica, covered with tiny dots of photoelectric cells (corresponding to and simulating the rods and cones of the retina). An electron beam (corresponding to and simulating the optic nerves) scanned the signal plate from top to bottom in parallel lines detecting the electrical emissions. This formed the picture. This system was more sensitive than any mechanical system then being explored and greatly reduced the amount of light necessary to produce a clear picture.

To reconstruct the transmitted image, Zworykin needed a special kind of cathode-ray tube which could send a steady stream of electrons to the signal plate. The kinescope was his ingenious solution, an idea whose essential elements were suggested by Scottish physicist A. A. Campbell Swinton in 1908 and amplified in an address to the Roentgen Society of London in 1911. Until Zworykin's efforts, however, a series of technical barriers had prevented a practical demonstration of Swinton's ideas. The kinescope, or picture tube, corresponded to the brain in human vision. An electron beam is applied to an electrode grid (invented in 1906 by the American Lee DeForest) with modulation occurring through the use of electromagnetic fields. With the addition of the kinescope, for which Zworykin filed a patent in 1924, television as we know it was now feasible.

In 1924, the year Zworykin gained American citizenship, he demonstrated his new system to Westinghouse executives. As he later wrote in an article in *American Magazine,* "I was terribly excited and proud. After a few days I was informed, very politely, that my demonstration had been extremely interesting, but that it might be better if I were to spend my time on something 'a little more useful.'" Apparently, Zworykin was too forthcoming about the technological problems still to be surmounted even as he persisted in pleading his cause with management. Westinghouse decided not to pursue Zworykin's research, which kept the company from reaping the profits in subsequent years of the major industry that developed around the new communications medium.

In 1929 Zworykin, still determined to prove the worth of his ideas, found a receptive audience at Radio Corporation of America (RCA) and was hired away from Westinghouse as associate research director of the RCA electronic research laboratory in Camden, New Jersey. The story is told that when RCA's president, the famous scientist-administrator David Sarnoff, asked Zworykin how much it would cost to perfect his system, he replied, "About $100,000." Sarnoff later said, as quoted in the *New York Times Biographical Service,* "RCA spent $50 million before we ever got a penny back from TV." The same year that Zworykin moved to RCA, he filed his first patent for color television. It took the end of World War II, however, with the lifting of restrictions on manufacturing of receivers to fuel explosive growth in television communications. As a result of the quality of his efforts at RCA, Zworykin was elevated to director of electronic research in 1946 and to vice president of the laboratories division in 1947, a position he held, later in an emeritus capacity, until his death in 1982.

A man of many interests, Zworykin began work with G. A. Morton in 1930 on the infrared (electron) image tube, which converted infrared rays into visible light. This device enabled humans to see in the dark and became the basis for the Sniperscope and Snooperscope used during World War II and all subsequent night sighting instruments.

Believing that the refinement of television could be left to fellow engineers, Zworykin then sought to apply television technology to microscopy. Under his leadership the electron microscope was developed by James Hillier and others at the RCA labs. This device enabled researchers to see objects much smaller than was possible with a conventional microscope and revolutionized scientific understanding of the fine structure of matter, especially in the fields of molecular and cell biology. The number of scientific applications for this technology continue to multiply. Zworykin's remaining patents consisted of such inventions as the electric eye used in security systems and automatic door openers, electronically controlled missiles and automobiles, a clock which operated without moving parts, and a device which enabled the blind to read print—a very early precursor to textual recognition systems which combine light-based technologies with electronics and microprocessors.

During World War II, Zworykin served on the Scientific Advisory Board to the U.S. Air Force and on a number of committees of the National Defense Research Council which advised the U.S. government on scientific contributions to the war effort. In the early years of the Cold War, Zworykin collaborated with John von Neumann of the Institute for Advanced Study at Princeton University to lay the conceptual groundwork for a computer sophisticated enough to open the possibility of accurate weather forecasting—an application whose possibilities were not lost on the American military command.

Zworykin was honored with numerous awards during his lifetime. The first major award he received was the Morris Liebmann Memorial Prize given him in 1934 for his television contributions by the Institute of Radio Engineers. The American Institute of Electrical Engineers bestowed its highest honor, the Edison Medal, on Zworykin in 1952 citing his "outstanding contributions to the concept and development of electronic components and systems." In 1967 he was awarded the National Medal of Science by the National Academy of Sciences for his work in television, science, and engineering and the application of science to medicine. Among other tributes, he was elected to the National Academy of Sciences in 1943,

was one of the earliest inductees into the newly founded National Academy of Engineering in 1965, and was honored by the French Legion of Honor.

After his first marriage ended in divorce, Zworykin married Katherine Polevitsky in 1951. He retired from RCA in 1954 at which time he was named an honorary vice president and technical consultant for the company. He was appointed director of the Medical Electronics Center at the Rockefeller Institute for Medical Research (now Rockefeller University), where he worked for a number of years in an attempt to broaden the range of electronically based applications in medicine.

Zworykin died July 29, 1982, one day before his ninety-third birthday. He is best remembered for his pioneering work in the development of television, a technology which has evolved into a major shaper of cultures and events around the world. Ironically, as quoted in his *New York Times* obituary, when asked to comment on the content of American television in an interview in 1981, Zworykin replied, "Awful."

BIOGRAPHICAL/CRITICAL SOURCES:

PERIODICALS

Journal of the Society of Motion Picture and Television Engineers, July, 1981, pp. 579-90.
New York Times Biographical Service, August, 1982, p. 1119.*